endorsed for
edexcel

Edexcel AS/A level
BUSINESS

T0313678

Dave Hall

Rob Jones

Carlo Raffo

Alain Anderton

Jennifer Lee

Keith Hirst

Andrew Redfern

Edited by Dave Gray

5th EDITION

PEARSON

Published by Pearson Education Limited, 80 Strand, London, WC2R 0RL.

www.pearsonschoolsandfecolleges.co.uk

Copies of official specifications for all Edexcel qualifications may be found on the website: www.edexcel.com

Text © Dave Hall, Rob Jones, Carlo Raffo, Alain Anderton, Jennifer Lee, Keith Hirst, Andrew Redfern and Dave Gray 2015
Edited by Julia Bruce
Designed by Pearson Education
Typeset by Tech-Art
Original illustrations © Pearson Education 2015
Illustrated by Tech-Art
Cover design by Elizabeth Arnoux for Pearson Education
Picture research by Rebecca Sodergren
Cover photo/illustration © Fancy Images (George Hammerstein) / Plainpicture Ltd
The rights of Dave Hall, Rob Jones, Carlo Raffo, Alain Anderton, Jennifer Lee, Keith Hirst, Andrew Redfern and Dave Gray
to be identified as authors of this work have been asserted by them in accordance with the Copyright, Designs and Patents Act 1988.

First published 2015

24

15

British Library Cataloguing in Publication Data
A catalogue record for this book is available from the British Library

ISBN (Student Book bundle) 978 1 447 98354 5

ISBN (ActiveBook) 978 1 447 98350 7

ISBN (Kindle edition) 978 1 447 98351 4

Some of the examples in this book are fictionalised accounts based upon real-life events. All brand names and sensitive
business data have been changed.

Printed and bound in Great Britain by Bell and Bain Ltd, Glasgow

Websites
Pearson Education Limited is not responsible for the content of any external internet sites. It is essential for tutors to preview
each website before using it in class so as to ensure that the URL is still accurate, relevant and appropriate. We suggest that
tutors bookmark useful websites and consider enabling students to access them through the school/college intranet.

A note from the publisher
In order to ensure that this resource offers high-quality support for the associated Pearson qualification, it has been through
a review process by the awarding body. This process confirms that this resource fully covers the teaching and learning content
of the specification or part of a specification at which it is aimed. It also confirms that it demonstrates an appropriate balance
between the development of subject skills, knowledge and understanding, in addition to preparation for assessment.

Endorsement does not cover any guidance on assessment activities or processes (e.g. practice questions or advice on how to
answer assessment questions), included in the resource nor does it prescribe any particular approach to the teaching or delivery
of a related course.

While the publishers have made every attempt to ensure that advice on the qualification and its assessment is accurate, the
official specification and associated assessment guidance materials are the only authoritative source of information and should
always be referred to for definitive guidance.

Pearson examiners have not contributed to any sections in this resource relevant to examination papers for which they
have responsibility.

Examiners will not use endorsed resources as a source of material for any assessment set by Pearson.

Endorsement of a resource does not mean that the resource is required to achieve this Pearson qualification, nor does it mean
that it is the only suitable material available to support the qualification, and any resource lists produced by the awarding body
shall include this and other appropriate resources.

Contents

About this book

This Student Book contains a wealth of features that will help you to access the course content, prepare for your exams, and take your knowledge and understanding further. The pages below show some of the key features and explain how they will support you in developing the skills needed to succeed on your A level Business course.

Features

'Key points' These provide a clear overview of the content covered in the topic, clearly matched to the specification.

> **Key points**
> 1. Calculation of price elasticity of demand.
> 2. Interpretation of numerical values of price elasticity of demand.
> 3. The factors influencing price elasticity of demand.
> 4. The significance of price elasticity of demand to businesses in terms of implications for pricing.
> 5. Calculation and interpretation of the relationship between price elasticity of demand and total revenue.

'Getting started' These activities are designed to help you start thinking about the topics and issues you will be covering in the unit.

> **Getting started**
>
> Albert Rogers owns a milk round in Dorset. He delivers milk to over 300 homes in the town. However, 30 years ago his business used to deliver to over 1,000 homes. The business has been hit hard by competition from retailers, particularly supermarkets, selling cheap milk. In 2013 he decided that he would need to generate more revenue. He raised the price of a pint of fresh milk (delivered to the doorstep) from 50p to 60p. As a result sales fell from 16,000 bottles to 12,000 bottles a month.
>
> Calculate the total revenue the business earned (price x quantity sold) before the increase in price. Now calculate the revenue it earned after it increased price. Was the price increase a wise move for the business? Do you think the same would happen to any business that raised its price by 20 per cent?

'Questions' Throughout each unit you will find questions that will test your understanding of topics and help you to build your analytical and critical thinking skills.

> **Question 1**
>
> Coolpop Ltd sells fizzy citrus drinks in the very competitive soft drinks market. In 2013, the company sold 2,000,000 cans of Lemon Coolpop at a price of 50p. In 2014, the company decided to reduce the price of Lemon Coolpop to try and win a bigger market share. The price was reduced to 40p and sales rose to 2,600,000.
>
> (a) Calculate the price elasticity of demand for Coolpop.
> (b) State whether demand is price elastic or price inelastic.

'Thinking bigger' These features provide opportunities for you to explore an aspect of business studies in more detail. The information in these features goes beyond the specification and will help you to deepen your understanding and think like a business person.

> **Thinking bigger**
>
> When using price elasticity of demand to help make pricing decisions, businesses need to be aware of some possible drawbacks with the concept. The main problem is the origin of elasticity values. A business might estimate the value of price elasticity by measuring the effect on sales of previous price changes. For example, if a business cut the price by 12 per cent four years ago and demand rose by 18 per cent, price elasticity would be −1.5. However, this data is historic; what happened four years ago may not happen again in the future.
>
> Another way of estimating elasticity values is to carry out market research to find out how consumers will react to price changes in the future. This would give more up-to-date values, but there could be problems with the accuracy of the data collected by market researchers. For example, the sample may not be representative or consumers might not behave in the way they said they would. Consequently the data would be flawed. Businesses need to be aware, therefore, that elasticity values may not be entirely accurate.

'Worked examples' and 'Maths tips' Practical worked examples will help you apply new methods or formulae to your own work. Maths tips will help you to simplify complex calculations. A 'calculator' icon on any question identifies opportunities for you to practise your maths skills and signposts topics where calculations and formulae are found.

Maths tip

There is a minus number in the calculation below because the price fell by 40 per cent (from £10 to £6). Since the price change was negative a minus sign must be shown. Whenever price or demand falls in the calculation, it is proper, and may be helpful, to show the minus sign.

Worked example

For product A in Figure 1, the price elasticity of demand would be:

$$= \frac{20\%}{-40\%} = -0.5$$

For product B in Figure 1, the price elasticity of demand would be:

$$= \frac{100\%}{-40\%} = -2.5$$

'Key terms' These are highlighted in the text and complex terminology or specialist business terms are clearly defined in a handy box at the end of each unit.

Key terms

Price elastic demand – a change in price results in a greater change in demand.
Price elasticity of demand – the responsiveness of demand to a change in price.
Price inelastic demand – a change in price results in a proportionately smaller change in demand.

'Exam tips' Within units you will find tips that give practical advice and guidance to ensure you're well prepared for your exams.

Exam tip

A common mistake made by students in examinations relates to products with inelastic demand. Sometimes students say 'demand for product x is inelastic. This means that a business can raise the price and there will be no change in demand'. This is not the case. Even when demand is price inelastic, a price change will still cause a change in demand. It is just that the percentage change in demand is smaller than the percentage change in price.

'Knowledge check' Questions at the end of each unit provide a quick test of your understanding of the unit content.

Knowledge check

1. What is meant by price elasticity of demand?

2. Give two examples of products that might have inelastic demand.

3. What is the formula for calculating price elasticity of demand?

4. The price of a product is increased by 8 per cent; as a result demand falls by 12 per cent. Calculate price elasticity of demand.

5. The price elasticity of demand for a product is −0.67. What will happen to total revenue if price is reduced?

6. The price elasticity of demand for a product is −2.7. What will happen to total revenue if price is raised?

7. State two factors that affect the price elasticity of demand for a product.

'Links' This feature in Themes 3 and 4 helps you to develop the synoptic skills required in your exam for Paper 4 by suggesting ways that the topics in one unit link to others. The links feature helps you to understand how to demonstrate your accumulated knowledge and understanding of a topic or subject area.

Links 🔗

Information in this unit could be used in a range of answers. For example, if you are discussing sources of finance for a business you could explain how the capital structure of the business might influence the decision. Businesses that already have a large quantity of borrowings might be better to raise fresh capital, for example. This unit could also be linked with Internal finance (Unit 26), External finance (Unit 27), Planning (Unit 29), Break-even (Unit 32), Profit (Unit 34), Liquidity (Unit 35), SWOT analysis (Unit 46), Decision trees (Unit 54), Ratio analysis (Unit 61) and Global competitiveness (Unit 75).

'Case study' These exam-style, data response questions contain an authentic piece of writing that provides you with an opportunity to practise your own extended writing and to develop your ability to combine your knowledge, skills and understanding with the breadth and depth of the subject of business studies.

Case study

THOMPSON ENGINEERING LTD

Thompson Engineering Ltd is a family business based in Chesterfield. The company makes three components for the engines that power microlights. The work undertaken by the company is quite specialised and it was thought that few rivals operated in the same market. At the end of 2013 the company had to make some modifications to two of the components, A and C. This was to comply with some new health and safety specifications. As a result the directors decided to raise the price of these two components by 20 per cent in 2014. Some financial information for the three components is shown in Table 2.

Table 2 Financial information and price elasticity of demand (PED) for three products (2013)

	Price	Sales	PED
Component A	£10	100,000	−0.8
Component B	£7	150,000	−1.1
Component C	£5	300,000	−1.2

Q

(a) What is meant by the term 'price elastic demand'? (2 marks)

(b) Explain one factor that might affect the price elasticity of demand. (4 marks)

(c) Calculate the expected change in revenue generated by product A in 2014 if the price is increased by 20 per cent. (4 marks)

(d) Calculate the expected change in revenue generated by product C in 2014 if the price is increased by 20 per cent. (4 marks)

(e) Assess the possible impact on Thompson Engineering Ltd of the price changes. (12 marks)

'Preparing for your exams' At the end of Themes 1 and 4 you'll find detailed exam preparation sections to help consolidate your learning. Exam-style questions, mark schemes and answers, together with useful tips for how to approach the exams, will give you extra confidence in your performance.

Extract D

The global hotel market

Following a dip in 2009, possibly the result of a global downturn in demand, revenue in the global hotel market has shown consistent growth. It was expected to generate around $550 billion in 2016.

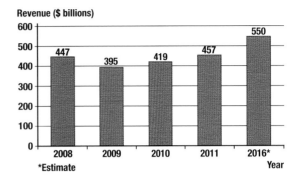

Global hotel industry revenue from 2008 to 2016

Source: adapted from www.statista.com

Question 2 (b), Student answer

Since 2008 revenue in the global hotel industry has grown significantly. By 2016 it is expected to have grown by 23 per cent from $447 billion to $550 billion. One possible reason for this pattern of spending on hotel accommodation could be the growth in global incomes. There is usually a strong link between consumer incomes and the demand for products. In recent years the BRIC countries of Brazil, Russia, India and China, have enjoyed relatively high levels of economic growth. This has resulted in people earning more money and having extra to spend on non-essentials, such as hotel accommodation. The expansion in India planned by InterContinental Hotels (IHG) supports this view. IHG currently operates 19 hotels across 10 cities in India. It also expects to open another 45 hotels in the country over the next few years. The company is likely to be responding to rising demand for hotel accommodation in India resulting from growth in incomes. The hotels are likely to serve both Indians and overseas tourists visiting the country.

Comment, Question 2 (b)

Questions like this require you to demonstrate knowledge, application and possibly analysis. One or two marks might be awarded for identifying one factor that might have led to more spending on hotel accommodation over the time period, i.e. growing incomes. Up to two application marks might be awarded for keeping the answer in context. This answer focuses on the hotel industry. Finally, credit may be given for analysis. In this case, explaining how economic growth in developing nations has resulted in higher spending on hotel accommodation.

Getting the most from your online ActiveBook

This book comes with 3 years' access to ActiveBook* – an online, digital version of your textbook. Follow the instructions printed on the inside front cover to start using your ActiveBook.

Your ActiveBook is the perfect way to personalise your learning as you progress through your A level Business course. You can:

- access your content online, anytime, anywhere.
- use the inbuilt highlighting and annotation tools to personalise the content and make it really relevant to you.

Highlight tool

Use this to pick out key terms or topics so you are ready and prepared for revision.

Annotations tool

Use this to add your own notes; for example, links to your wider reading, such as websites or other files. Or make a note to remind yourself about work that you need to do.

*for new purchases only. If this access code has already been revealed, it may no longer be valid. If you have bought this textbook secondhand, the code may already have been used by the first owner of the book.

Introduction

The 5th edition of **Edexcel AS/A level Business** is designed to develop the skills and approaches you may need, in a variety of contexts, when making business decisions. It develops an analytical, rigorous and critical approach to the decision-making process and to your studies of business. It does not provide a step-by-step guide to how to be 'good at business' as there is no simple set of rules that can be applied in all contexts that will always be successful. It is possible that different approaches may be used by different people in business and there may be disagreement about which approach to take.

Business is integrated and different areas of business are interdependent. There are links, for example, between:

- what is being produced and the funds available to pay for it (production and finance)
- the selling of the product and ethical considerations (marketing and ethics)
- the type of business and many aspects of its operation.

Being aware of these aspects of business will help you to understand how and why business decisions are made, and how they affect a variety of people, both within and outside the business. The aim of the 5th edition of Business is to help you as you study Edexcel AS level and A level Business to understand business decisions and to be analytical, rigorous and critical in your business thinking. A number of features are included in the book to develop and extend your skills and approaches – see About this book, page iv.

Comprehensive course coverage

This book covers the material found in all four themes of the Edexcel A level Business specification:

- **Theme 1** Marketing and people
- **Theme 2** Managing business activities
- **Theme 3** Business decisions and strategy
- **Theme 4** Global business

By covering all four themes of the specification in detail, this book takes you through the course, ensuring your skills and understanding are developed, so that you can have confidence when approaching your exams. Units in Theme 1 and Theme 2 allow you to gain an in-depth understanding of core business concepts, with the content in Theme 3 and Theme 4 building on these topics. Theme 3 and Theme 4 extend breadth and depth of knowledge through focusing on business strategy and decisions, and exploring the global context in which modern businesses operate. This focus on developing a breadth and depth of knowledge across the course will allow you to develop the synopticity needed for your final paper.

1 The market

Key points

1. Mass markets and niche markets:
   - characteristics
   - market size and market share
   - brands.
2. Dynamic markets:
   - online retailing
   - how markets change
   - innovation and market growth
   - adapting to change.
3. How competition affects the market.
4. The difference between risk and uncertainty.

Getting started

The market for holidays has changed dramatically over time. In the 1960s a typical holiday for a UK person might have been an annual two-week family trip to the seaside at Blackpool, Scarborough or Brighton, staying in a caravan, a holiday camp or small hotel. Today people might take several holidays a year and the choice of destination, duration and style is enormous. Holidays can range from a weekend break with friends in an Eastern European city, such as Prague, or a romantic mini-break for two in Paris, to a fortnight in the sun in the Caribbean, or a camping expedition in the Lake District. There are specialist holidays, such as trekking in the Atlas Mountains, golfing trips in Dubai or white-water rafting down the River Wye, and theme-park holidays, such as Disneyland®. Increasingly people are going to long-haul destinations, such as Australia, China and South Africa.

How has the market for holidays changed over time? What might have caused these market changes? How do people choose their holiday destinations? What role does the internet play in the sale of holidays by businesses?

Markets and marketing

Businesses make money by selling their goods and services in markets. Historically, markets were places where buyers and sellers would meet to exchange goods. However, today it is possible to trade goods and services without buyers and sellers meeting up. For example, trading can be done over the telephone, using newspapers, through mail order or on the internet. Some examples of markets are given below.

- Consumer goods markets – where products such as food, cosmetics and magazines are sold.
- Markets for services – this can include services for individuals, such as hairdressing, or business services, such as auditing.
- The housing market – where people buy, sell and let property.
- Commodity markets – where raw materials such as oil copper, wheat and coffee are traded.
- Financial markets – where currencies and financial products are traded.

Marketing involves a range of activities that help a business sell its products. However, marketing is not just about selling, it involves:

- identifying the needs and wants of consumers
- designing products that meet these needs
- understanding the threats from competitors
- telling customers about products
- charging the right price
- persuading customers to buy products
- making products available in convenient locations.

According to the Chartered Institute of Marketing, 'Marketing is the management process responsible for identifying, anticipating and satisfying customer requirements profitably'.

The characteristics of mass markets and niche markets

Some businesses sell their products to **mass markets**. This is when a business sells the same products to all consumers and markets them in the same way. Fast-moving consumer goods, such as crisps, breakfast cereals, computer software and Coca-Cola®, are sold in mass markets. The number of customers in these markets is huge – possibly billions if products are sold globally. This means that businesses can produce large quantities at a lower unit cost by exploiting economies of scale. This might result in higher sales and higher profits. However, there is often a lot of competition in mass markets and therefore businesses may spend a lot of money on marketing. For example, *Advertising Age* reported that the Coca-Cola Company spent around $3.3 billion on global advertising in 2013.

A **niche market** is a small market segment – a segment that has sometimes gone 'untouched' by larger businesses. Niche marketing is the complete opposite of mass marketing. It involves selling to a small customer group, sometimes with specific needs. Small firms can often survive by supplying niche markets. They may also avoid competition. It is a lot easier to focus on the needs of the customer in a niche market. Also, if there is no competition it may also be possible to charge premium prices. An example of a business that targets niche markets is Zumiez, which sells products related to surfing, skateboarding and snowboarding.

However, if a business successfully exploits a niche market it still may attract competition. Niche markets, by their nature, are very small and unable to support many competing firms. As a result, if a large business decides to enter a niche market they may find it easy to overrun a smaller rival. Also, businesses that rely on a single niche market may be vulnerable because they are not spreading their risk. If they lose a grip in their chosen market, they may collapse because they do not have other products or markets as a back-up.

> **Exam tip**
> In examinations it is helpful to give examples when explaining the meaning of business terms and concepts. Relevant examples support your answer and show that you understand the meaning of the term or concept. It is also important to use information in the case material in the question to support your answer. This approach will show your skills in 'application' in your answer.

Question 1

David Algunik, a Canadian Emergency Room doctor, designed Banana Guards. He wanted to prevent bananas from being bruised and squashed during his journey from home to work, so designed Banana Guards from lightweight plastic. Once shut inside a Banana Guard, a banana of almost any shape or size can be transported completely undamaged inside a lunchbox, bag or backpack – even when travelling on a packed tube. The contents are kept fresh by ventilation holes in the side of the bright yellow Banana Guard, which also prevent the banana from ripening prematurely until ready for consumption. The Banana Guard is also safe for the dishwasher.

Sources: adapted from www.bananaguard.com and www.johnlewis.com

(a) Explain what type of market the Banana Guard is aimed at.

(b) Explain one possible disadvantage of targeting a niche market for a business selling a product like Banana Guard.

Market size

The size of a market can be estimated or calculated by the total sales of all businesses in the market. Market size is usually estimated in a number of ways.

Value: This is the total amount spent by customers buying products. For example, it was estimated that the value of the fast-food market in 2014 was just over £29.4 billion. This included branded fast-food chains and independent outlets selling hot or cold eat-in food without table service, or takeaway food.

Volume: This is the physical quantity of products which are produced and sold. For example, the global crude steel production in 2014 was 1,661 million tonnes (worldsteel.org). Some estimates of volume are based on the number or percentage of users, subscribers or viewers. This is often the case in markets for services, such as the number of mobile phone users, the number of television viewers or the percentage of households with digital television.

Different markets are likely to differ in size. For example, the sale of savory snacks in one year is likely to be much smaller than the sales of footwear in the same year in the UK.

Market share

Market share or market penetration is the term used to describe the proportion of a particular market that is held by a business, a product, a brand or a number of businesses or products. Market share is shown as a percentage. The market share of a business can be calculated as:

$$\frac{\text{Sales of a business}}{\text{Total sales in the market}} \times 100\%$$

Why might the measurement of market share be important? It might indicate a business that is a market leader. This could influence other companies to follow the leader or influence the leader to maintain its position. It might influence the strategy or objectives of a business. A business that has a small market share may set a target of increasing its share by 5 per cent over a period of time. It may also be an indication of the success or failure of a business or its strategy.

Figure 1 shows the market shares of supermarkets in the UK in 2013. It shows, for example, that Tesco was the market leader with nearly one-third of the total market. It also shows that the top four supermarkets share 75.3 per cent of the total market, i.e. the market is dominated by just four firms.

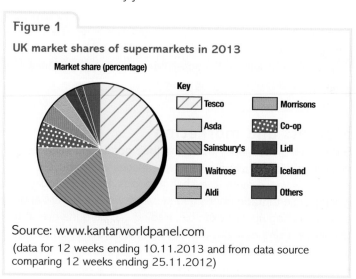

Figure 1

UK market shares of supermarkets in 2013

Market share (percentage)

Key: Tesco, Asda, Sainsbury's, Waitrose, Aldi, Morrisons, Co-op, Lidl, Iceland, Others

Source: www.kantarworldpanel.com
(data for 12 weeks ending 10.11.2013 and from data source comparing 12 weeks ending 25.11.2012)

Brands

Many businesses try to establish themselves in markets by giving their products a **brand name**. Products are given brand names to distinguish them from other products in the market. Branding is particularly important in mass markets where lots of products are competing for a share of the market. Examples of common brand names include Google, BBC, Toyota, Nike and

Apple. Branding might be used to:
- differentiate the product from those of rivals
- create customer loyalty
- help product recognition
- develop an image
- charge a premium price when the brand becomes strong.

Branding is discussed in more detail in Unit 10.

Dynamic markets

Most markets do not remain the same over time – they tend to be dynamic, which means they are likely to change. They may grow, shrink, fragment, emerge or completely disappear. For example, there is no longer a market in the UK for cassettes. Most people buy DVDs or download music from the internet.

Dynamic markets can have a huge impact on businesses. A failure to adapt in a dynamic market can lead to the collapse of a business. For example, when digital photography emerged in the 1980s, Kodak (the camera company) continued to rely on sales of film cameras. Eventually, the market for these types of cameras collapsed and Kodak went into liquidation. Those businesses that can adapt to changes in dynamic markets are more likely to survive in the long term. The changing nature of markets is discussed in more detail later.

Online retailing

One of the biggest changes to occur in the marketing of products has been the development of online retailing or e-tailing. This is a popular branch of e-commerce that has emerged along with the development of the internet. It involves shoppers ordering goods online and taking delivery at home. There are specialist e-tailers such as Amazon and Alibaba – retail 'giants' that sell a huge range of goods online. However, many retailers, both large and small, now have online services. Growth in online retailing is rapid and expected to continue into the future.

Businesses may enjoy a number of benefits from offering online retail services.
- Retailers can market their goods to people who prefer to shop from home or who find it difficult to get to traditional shops. For example, people who do not enjoy the physical shopping experience, people too busy to go shopping and people with conditions or disabilities that make physical shopping difficult.
- It is easier to gather personal information from customers so that they can be targeted with other products and offers in the future.
- Selling costs such as sales staff, rent and other store overheads can be avoided. The savings might be enormous and allow online retailers to charge lower prices.
- Marketing costs will also be lower. It is much cheaper, for example, to send a marketing message by e-mail to 1,000 customers than it is to send 1,000 newsletters by post.
- Online retailers can reach more customers. A single store in a high street can only attract a limited number of customers. However, a website advertising a 15,000-item product range can have a global reach.
- An online retailer is open 24/7. There are not many stores that can match this level of service.

- Online retailing affords greater flexibility. An online store can be updated instantly and as frequently as is necessary. For example, it is possible to promote a 'deal of the day' on the home page, without the need for expensive printed display material.
- Distance is no object with online retailing. Customers can buy products from anywhere in the world.

Question 2

Online grocery retailing has not quite taken off in the same way that other forms of online retailing have.

However, reports estimate that online grocery sales may rise from 4.4 per cent to 8.3 per cent in the period 2014–2019. This may be due to busier lifestyles and the further integration of mobile technology into daily life as people increasingly become on-the-go consumers. Online shopping is convenient and saves time and fuel. Research shows that 27 per cent of people shopped online for groceries in 2014, with 10 per cent buying the majority of their groceries via the internet.

It was reported in 2014 that click & collect was also being used by around a quarter of online shoppers and this figure was growing as more services were made available.

Click & collect is a good example of a trend that took off. Major retailers, including Tesco and ASDA, invested heavily to roll out the service to the majority of their stores, as well as convenient locations such as London travel hubs. Click & collect became available at some London tube stations, with plans to include travel hubs and workplaces as future locations, as retailers continue to experiment and innovate.

Source: adapted from www.essentialretail.com

(a) Explain one reason why online grocery retailing is likely to grow in the future.
(b) Assess the benefits and drawbacks to supermarkets of online retailing.

How markets change

The size of markets: The size of some markets can remain quite stable over a period of time. For example, the size of the milk market in the UK probably hasn't changed much for many years. This is because consumption of milk is fairly constant.

However, the majority of markets are likely to grow. For example, *The Future of Global Packaging to 2018* reports that the global packaging market stood at $799 billion in 2012, increasing by 1 per cent over 2011 with sales projected to increase by 3 per cent. Some forecasters reckoned growth to 2018 would reach 4 per cent per year, with sales reaching over 1 trillion US dollars. Factors for growth in packaging include increasing urbanisation, investment in construction and housing, development of retail chains, and the expanding cosmetics and healthcare sectors in the emerging economies.

Some markets are in decline. For example, the market for coal in the UK has fallen sharply since 1970. Markets often decline because the need for a product ceases to exist. In the case of coal, other fuels, such as oil, gas, nuclear and renewable sources are now preferred by households and industry.

The nature of markets: Many markets are in a state of flux. This means that the structure and nature of the market is subject to constant change. For example, in many markets products are constantly updated, modified and re-launched – the choice available increasing enormously over time. This is the result of new entrants into the market and existing firms widening their ranges and extending their lines. For example, the restaurant market in the UK, worth around £40 billion in 2014, has seen many changes. In the 1960s, the industry was dominated by fish and chip shops, the occasional Chinese restaurant, cafés, independents and hotel restaurants. Today the sector is large and diverse. Restaurants range from top-end fine-dining establishments to quick service takeaway outlets. UK high streets tend to be dominated by chains, such as Nando's, Prezzo and Domino's Pizza, and café chains, such as Costa Coffee and Caffè Nero. There has been a significant development of 'upmarket' restaurants, some of which evolved around famous chefs, for example Jamie Oliver, Marcus Wareing and Gordon Ramsay. Add to this the huge range of ethnic restaurants selling, among others, Indian, Thai, Chinese, Vietnamese, Malaysian and Japanese cuisines.

New markets: While it is possible for some markets to completely disappear, new markets are always developing. One big source of new markets is from the development of 'emerging economies'. These include the BRIC (Brazil, Russia, India and China) countries and other developing nations, such as Mexico, Thailand, Indonesia and some South American countries. New markets also appear when completely new products are launched. In the 1970s no one had a mobile phone. In the 1980s no one had a smartphone. In the 1990s no one had a flat-screen television. In the 2000s few people had e-books. These are all examples of brand-new markets.

Innovation and market growth

Markets can grow over time – some rapidly, some more slowly. Growth in existing markets and new markets may occur for the following reasons.

- **Economic growth.** Global living standards tend to rise over time. This means that the world's population has more money to spend. As a result businesses can supply more of their output to growing global markets. Also, as people get wealthier they are likely to demand different types of goods. For example, the markets for holidays, electronic goods, cars, air travel, cosmetics, furniture and luxury goods will grow.

- **Innovation.** Businesses can grow their markets through the process of innovation. They can create new wants and needs and meet them with new products. A lot of innovation emerges through technological research and development. The arrival of smartphones, tablets, the internet, 3D printing, driverless cars, wearable technology and space travel have all created brand-new markets that did not exist before the technological breakthroughs. However, innovation can take other forms. Businesses can use clever marketing techniques to develop new wants. They can supply their products in new locations – for instance supermarkets offering a click & collect service at London tube stations. New businesses can cash in on the inadequacies of others. For example, since the 'credit crunch' in 2008, new businesses have been set up to compete with banks. Crowd funding and peer-to-peer websites have started to provide unsecured loans. At the moment their market shares are relatively small. But if they prove successful the established banks will have to match these new innovations.

- **Social changes.** Changes in society can have a big impact on markets. For example, the decline in the number of marriages, an increase in the proportion of working women and the growth in the number of one-parent families have increased the market size for childcare and housing.

- **Changes in legislation.** New laws can affect markets. For example, environmental legislation has helped to foster growth in renewable energies and 'green goods'. Tighter laws relating to payday lending has resulted in many firms leaving the market. A ban on tobacco advertising in the UK might have reduced the market size for cigarettes.

- **Demographic changes.** Changes in the structure of the population can affect the size of markets. In most countries the population is aging. This will help a lot of markets to grow because populations get bigger. But there will also be an increase in the markets for specialist holidays for the elderly, healthcare, care homes and mobility aids.

Adapting to change

If businesses do not adapt to market changes, they are likely to lose market share. At worst they could collapse. In 2014, it was reported that Tesco was losing market share to other supermarkets. There were a number of reasons for this, but several reports suggested that they were failing to meet customer needs. They were losing market share to the big discounters such as Aldi and Lidl. There was a need for Tesco to adapt quickly, or risk losing more of their market share. What might help businesses adapt to market changes?

Flexibility: Businesses need to be prepared for change. One way is to develop a culture of flexibility within an organisation. A business might need flexible working practices, machinery and equipment, pricing and staff. This could mean that staff have to be trained in a variety of skills and be prepared to change the tasks they undertake in the workplace. This might help businesses to serve customers more effectively when changes occur. For example, if customers want access to the business during the evening, then staff might have to work shifts. If businesses have flexible operations it will be a lot easier for them to adapt to market changes.

Market research: Businesses must keep in touch with developments in the market. One way to do this is to undertake regular market research. This might be aimed at current customers or potential customers. Firms need to be aware of any changes in customer needs or tastes. Communication with customers and potential customers should be an ongoing process if firms want to keep completely up to date. Market research is discussed in Unit 2.

Investment: Those businesses that invest in new product development are likely to survive for longer in the market. Although expenditure on research and development is expensive, a failure to innovate could be costly. A unique new version of a product or a brand-new model could rejuvenate sales and help win a larger share of the market. In the car industry, firms spend very large sums of money in product development. BMW has enjoyed a larger slice of the small car market by extending the range of its Minis. Investment might also be needed in training and use of flexible machinery.

Continuous improvement in the increasingly competitive environment: Businesses need to make continual improvements in all aspects of their operations. For example, if they can improve efficiency, costs will be lower and prices can be held or reduced. If customer service is flawless, customers are more likely to return. If new product ideas are encouraged, they may gain a competitive edge. A culture of continuous improvement can help businesses be more adaptable in the market.

Develop a niche: If a market is in decline and a business is unable to diversify, it may survive by serving a niche. A niche strategy is appropriate if groups of loyal customers can be served profitably. For example, Harley-Davidson survived by leaving most of the motorcycle market to the Japanese. They sold high-horsepower 'hogs' to a small segment of motorcycle enthusiasts. As a result they became quite profitable and survived. Generally, if firms cannot adapt quickly to the changing needs of customers, they will lose out to rivals that do adapt.

How competition affects the market

Competition is the rivalry that exists between businesses in a market. It would be rare for a business to operate in a market where there was absolutely no competition. The existence of competition will have an impact on both businesses and consumers in the market.

Businesses: Competition puts businesses under some pressure. It means that they have to encourage customers to buy their products in preference to those of rivals. They will use a range of methods to attract customers. These methods include:
- lowering prices
- making their products appear different to those of rivals
- offering better quality products
- using more powerful or attractive advertising or promotions
- offering 'extras' such as high-quality customer service.

All of these methods cost money and generally reduce the amount of profit a business can make. However, businesses have to use such methods in order to survive in the market.

Because competition makes running a business more challenging and reduces the profit potential, owners and managers might try to reduce competition in the market. One way of doing this is to take over their rivals. This might be achieved by purchasing a rival in the market. Alternatively, they might try to create obstacles that make it difficult for others to enter the market. For example, they may spend huge amounts of money on advertising, which potential entrants might struggle to match. It is generally the larger businesses in the market which are able to reduce competition in this way. However, there is a range of legislation which prevents businesses restricting competition using practices that are considered unfair.

Consumers: Consumers will generally benefit from competition in markets. In markets where there are lots of businesses competing with each other, there will be more choice. Most people enjoy having lots of choice because it makes their life more interesting. For example, when people buy a car they can choose from a huge range of different models, styles, colours and endless variations in specifications. Consumers may also enjoy better quality products and lower prices.

In the absence of competition consumers might be exploited. A business with little or no competition might raise prices and restrict choice. They will lack the incentive to innovate. For example, they are unlikely to invest money to develop new products. Consequently, one of the roles of a government is to ensure that competition exists in markets.

The difference between risk and uncertainty

One of the challenges when running a business is dealing with risk and uncertainty. Although both risk and uncertainty are likely to pose threats to a business, they are not the same.

Risk: Owners take risks when running a business. This means they take actions where the outcomes are unknown. More specifically, they commit resources that could be lost. Initially, they take a risk when setting up a business. This is because they invest their own money to get the business 'up and running' and there is a chance that the business will not succeed. If the worst happens and the business collapses it is possible that all the money invested by the owner is lost.

In the UK, around 23,000 businesses each year are expected to fail. It is also reckoned that about 90 per cent of all new businesses do not survive beyond five years.

Even when businesses are established, they may continue to take risks. This is because they often spend money on ventures that may not yield positive results. For example, they may invest in a new product which subsequently fails in the market. If the product is withdrawn, most of the money spent on development and launch will be lost.

In 2014, Amazon, the online retailer, launched a mobile phone called the Amazon Fire Phone. It failed in the market and the price was reduced very quickly from $199 to just 99 cents. It was reported that Amazon lost $170 million as a result.

Uncertainty: The markets in which businesses operate are often subject to external influences. This means that events which are completely beyond the control of businesses can have an impact in the market, which can have financial consequences. For example:

- a new competitor might enter the market with a superior product

- consumer tastes might change as a result of a new social trend
- the government might introduce a new policy or piece of legislation
- some new technology might be invented
- there may be a natural disaster such as a flood
- the economy might go into recession.

Unfortunately, such influences are very difficult to predict. This means that businesses have to operate all of the time in an environment of uncertainty.

However, the consequences of uncertainty are not always negative. For example, new technologies can provide new opportunities. The introduction of the internet has resulted in an enormous range of new business opportunities. Generally though, businesses do not like uncertainty. It makes decision making more difficult – particularly when making investments for the future.

Key terms

Brand name – a name, term, sign, symbol, design or any other feature that allows consumers to identify the goods and services of a business and to differentiate them from those of competitors.

E-commerce – conducting business transactions online.

Online retailing or **e-tailing** – the retailing of goods online.

Market – a set of arrangements that allows buyers and sellers to communicate and trade in a particular range of goods and services.

Marketing – a management process involved in identifying, anticipating and satisfying consumer requirements profitably.

Market share – the proportion of total sales in a particular market for which one or more businesses or brands are responsible. It is expressed as a percentage and can be calculated by value or volume.

Mass market – a very large market in which products with mass appeal are targeted.

Niche market – a smaller market, usually within a large market or industry.

Knowledge check

1. What is the difference between a mass market and a niche market?

2. What is a key advantage of selling in a mass market?

3. State two disadvantages of selling in a niche market.

4. How is market share calculated?

5. State three advantages of giving products brand names.

6. State two advantages to customers of online retailing.

7. What is meant by a dynamic market?

8. How might the nature of a market change over time?

9. State three reasons why a market might grow.

10. Describe two ways a business might adapt to changes in markets.

Case study

HYBRID AND ELECTRIC CARS

Growing concerns about the environment, and agreements by many countries in the world to cut carbon emissions, have helped to encourage sales of hybrid vehicles, electric cars and other alternatively fuelled vehicles (AFVs). A hybrid vehicle is one that uses two or more power sources. Hybrid electrical vehicles (HEVs) combine an internal combustion engine and an electric motor. These vehicles are now beginning to grab market share from traditional petrol and diesel models.

It was reported by the Society of Motor Manufacturers and Traders (SMMT) that 9,955 AFVs were registered in September 2014, a 56 per cent rise on the same time in 2013. This accounted for 2.3 per cent of the total market – a 44 per cent year-on-year rise.

An SMMT spokesman said the AFV market is seeing the benefit of more models coming on to the market – in 2014 there were more than 20 plug-in vehicles available compared to six in 2011, ranging from hatchbacks and saloons to sports utility vehicles (SUVs) and sports cars.

Of the 9,955 AFVs registered in September 2014, 3,090 were eligible for the government's plug-in grant that offered up to £5,000 off the cost of a pure-electric or plug-in hybrid vehicle. The volumes started off small, but with the government investing £500 million in supporting the market and car makers unveiling an even wider range of models, the direction of travel is increasingly clear.

One of the barriers to rapid growth in the market is uncertainty about supporting infrastructure – stations that provide facilities

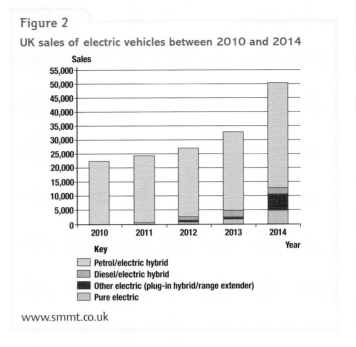

Figure 2

UK sales of electric vehicles between 2010 and 2014

Key
- Petrol/electric hybrid
- Diesel/electric hybrid
- Other electric (plug-in hybrid/range extender)
- Pure electric

www.smmt.co.uk

for recharging batteries. In 2014 awareness about the locations of recharging facilities was not yet widespread. Figure 2 shows UK sales of electric vehicles between 2010 and 2014. Figure 3 shows oil prices from 2000 to 2014.

Sources: adapted from www.smmt.co.uk and www.blueandgreentomorrow.com

Q

(a) What is meant by market share? (2 marks)

(b) Explain one reason why the global car market is likely to grow in the next five years. (4 marks)

(c) Assess how a car manufacturer might adapt to changes in the market. (8 marks)

(d) Assess the factors that might affect the growth of the hybrid and electrical vehicles markets in the future. (12 marks)

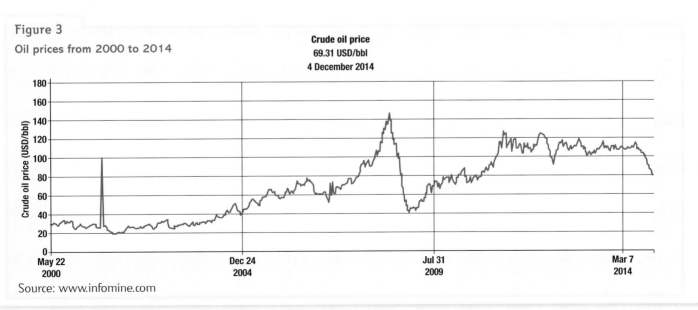

Figure 3

Oil prices from 2000 to 2014

Crude oil price
69.31 USD/bbl
4 December 2014

Source: www.infomine.com

2 Market research

Key points

1. Product and market orientation.
2. Primary and secondary market research data (qualitative and quantitative) used to identify and anticipate customer needs and wants, quantify likely demand and gain insight into consumer behaviour.
3. Limitations of market research, sample size and bias.
4. Use of ICT to support market research: websites, social networking and databases.
5. Market segmentation.

Getting started

In 2014, Alok Hossain decided to set up a Bangladeshi takeaway food service in Great Harwood, Lancashire. Before he started trading he gathered information about the market for takeaway food in the town. He spent a lot of time finding out about competitors. He found out about the:

* number and location of takeaway restaurants in Great Harwood
* menus and prices charged
* opening times
* advertising and promotions used
* additional services offered such as delivery
* speed of service
* types of customers who bought Bangladeshi cuisine.

The information gathered by Alok was very helpful. For example, he found that one of the main criticisms of current takeaways was the slow speed of service. When Alok opened Chittagong Paradise his speed of service was a unique selling point.

Why would it have been a mistake for Alok not to carry out research? Alok used primary or field research. What does this mean? Is market research expensive? What might be the limitations of Alok's research?

Product and market orientation

Some businesses are said to be relatively **product orientated** or **market orientated**.

Product orientation: Many businesses in the past, and some today, could be described as product orientated. This means that the business focuses on the production process and the product itself. It puts most of its efforts into developing and making products which it believes consumers want and which will sell well.

In the past, businesses producing radios and televisions could be said to have been relatively product orientated. It was their novelty and the technical 'wonder' of the product that sold them. There were few companies to compete against each other, and there was a growing domestic market. There were also few overseas competitors. The product sold itself.

Some industries today are still said to be product orientated. The machine-tool industry, which produces machines used in the production of other goods, has to produce a final product which exactly matches a technical specification. However, because of increased competition, such firms are being forced to take consumers' needs into account. The technical specification to which a machine-tool business produces might be influenced by what customers want, for example.

Product-orientated businesses thus place their emphasis on developing a technically sound product, producing that product and then selling it. Contact with the consumer comes largely at this final stage. There will always be a place for product orientation. A great deal of pure research, for example, with no regard to consumers' needs, still takes place in industry, as it does in the development of pharmaceuticals.

Market orientation: A business that is market orientated is one which continually identifies, reviews and analyses consumers' needs. It is led by the market. A market orientated business is much more likely to be engaged in effective marketing if it is market orientated. Henry Ford was one of the first industrialists to adopt a market orientated approach. When the Ford Motor Company produced the Model T, it did not just design a car, produce it as cheaply as possible, and then try to sell it to the public. Instead, in advance of production, Ford identified the price at which he believed he could sell large numbers of Model Ts. His starting point was the market and the Model T became one of the first 'mass-market' products. This illustrates the market orientated approach – consumers are central to a firm's decision making. Sony is one of many modern businesses that has taken a market orientated approach. The iPhone® 6 by Apple is an example of a product being developed in response to the wishes of consumers.

A more market orientated business may have several advantages over one which is more product orientated.

* It can respond more quickly to changes in the market because of its use of market information.
* It will be in a stronger position to meet the challenge of new competition entering the market.
* It will be more able to anticipate market changes.
* It will be more confident that the launch of a new product will be a success.

What effect will taking a market orientated approach have on a business? It must:

* consult the consumer continuously (market research)

- design the product according to the wishes of the consumer
- produce the product in the quantities that consumers want to buy
- distribute the product according to the buying habits and delivery requirements of the consumer
- set the price of the product at a level that the consumer is prepared to pay.

The business must produce the right product at the right price and in the right place, and it must let the consumer know that it is available. This is known as the marketing mix.

The adoption of a market orientated approach will not always guarantee success. Many well-researched products have been failures. Coloroll was a business which started in the wallpaper market and expanded into home textiles and soft furnishings. Its attempt to enter the DIY burglar alarm market, however, was a failure. The company's reputation and design skills had little value in that section of the DIY market compared with other companies, whose reputations were based on home security or electronics. Whether a business places a greater emphasis on the product or on the market will depend on a number of factors.

The nature of the product: Where a firm operates in an industry at the edge of new innovation, such as bio-technology, pharmaceuticals or electronics, it must innovate to survive. Although a firm may try to anticipate consumer demand, research is often 'pure' research, i.e. the researcher does not have a specific end product in mind.

Policy decisions: A business will have certain objectives. Where these are set in terms of technical quality or safety, the emphasis is likely to be on production. Where objectives are in terms of market share or turnover, the emphasis is likely to be on marketing.

The views of those in control: An accountant or a managing director may place emphasis on factors such as cash flow and profit forecasts, a production engineer may give technical quality control and research a high priority and a marketing person may be particularly concerned with market research and consumer relations.

The nature and size of the market: If production costs are very high, then a company is likely to be market orientated. Only by being so can a company ensure it meets consumers' needs and avoid unsold goods and possible losses.

The degree of competition: A company faced with a lack of competition may devote resources to research with little concern about a loss of market share. Businesses in competitive markets are likely to spend more on marketing for fear of losing their share of the market.

The distinction between product and market orientation can be seen as a spectrum, as in Figure 1. Most business are somewhere along the spectrum. For example, supermarkets may be more market orientated and a copper mining company more product orientated.

Figure 1

Product vs market orientation

Examples	Examples
Coal mining business	Clothing retailer
Wheat farmer	Soap powder manufacturer
Water supply business	Supermarket chain

Question 1

AstraZeneca is a large British-Swedish pharmaceuticals company, which serves the global market. It focuses on particular areas of healthcare, including treatments for cancer and heart diseases. The company has around 57,500 employees globally and has manufacturing sites in 16 different countries. In 2014, its total sales revenue was just over $26 billion.

The UK is the major location for AstraZeneca's research and development of new medicines. One research and development (R&D) centre in Alderley Park plays a vital role in their strategy as the lead centre for cancer research. The site houses the Advanced Lead Discovery Centre, which has innovative compound management and high throughput screening facilities to assist with the drug discovery process. AstraZeneca is one of the world's largest spenders in R&D. Figure 2 shows the amount spent on R&D between 2006 and 2013.

Figure 2
AstraZeneca R&D expenditure 2006–2013

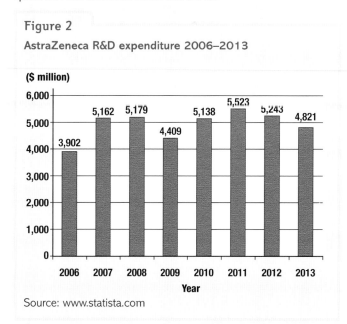

Source: www.statista.com

(a) Comment on the pattern of R&D expenditure shown in Figure 2.

(b) Explain one benefit to AstraZeneca of being product orientated.

(c) Assess to what extent AstraZeneca is product orientated.

Market research

Market research involves gathering, presenting and analysing information about the marketing and consumption of goods and services. Businesses spend money on market research because it helps to reduce the risk of failure. Products that are well researched are more likely to be successful. Market research data can be used for the following specific purposes.

Identify and anticipate customer needs and wants:

Businesses will benefit if they can clarify the specific needs and wants of consumers. In order to design products that are likely to sell, they need to identify as precisely as possible the product features that people desire. For example, a car manufacturer will need to find out which product features are important to potential customers. Examples include:

- body design and style
- colour
- interior design and style
- economy
- ease of maintenance
- durability
- performance (e.g. acceleration and top speed).

The data that market researchers gather need to be as comprehensive as possible so that all the needs and wants are identified. This data will be **qualitative**. This is explained later in the unit.

Quantify the likely demand for a product: It is important

to find out how much of a product a business might expect to sell in a market. This data will be **quantitative**. This is discussed in detail later in the unit. One reason for this is to help determine whether or not a particular product is going to be commercially viable. If market research finds that demand is inadequate, a business might cancel the launch of a product. This could save the business a lot of money. This is one of the reasons why businesses carry out research.

Assuming that demand is adequate, a business will need to know how much it should produce. Once demand has been quantified a business can plan production of the product. This means that it can start to organise the resources that will be needed for production and draw up production schedules. For example, it might need to recruit more staff to work in the factory and co-ordinate with different departments to ensure that the necessary resources can be acquired.

Provide an insight into consumer behaviour: Some

market research is aimed at analysing consumer behaviour. Businesses might be more successful if they can identify and understand patterns of consumer behaviour. For example, a holiday company selling package holidays abroad might use market research to find out:

- when consumers book their holidays
- when consumers are most likely to go on holiday
- the number of holidays people take each year
- which methods consumers use to book their holidays, e.g. online or travel agent
- how much money people spend on holiday

- whether customers take out holiday insurance
- how people travel to the airport.

Getting an insight into how people behave will help a business to meet customer needs more effectively. This is qualitative data and might also help them to identify new opportunities. Businesses can use a number of different methods to gather market research data. Some of these methods are explained in detail below.

Primary research

Primary research or **field research** involves collecting primary data. This is information which did not exist before the research began. In other words, it has to be collected by the researcher. It can either be carried out by a business itself or by a market research agency. Because of the high costs of using the services of a market research agency, many small businesses choose to conduct market research themselves.

Most primary information is gathered by asking consumers questions or by monitoring their behaviour. The most accurate way to do this would be to question or observe all consumers of a particular product (known as the **population**). However, in all but a few instances this would be either impractical to carry out or expensive. It is usual to carry out a survey of a **sample** of people who are thought to be representative of the total market.

Methods of primary research

Some of the main methods of gathering data are discussed briefly below.

Questionnaires: A questionnaire is a list of written questions. They are very common in market research and are used to record the views and opinions of **respondents**. A good questionnaire will display the following qualities.

- Have a balance of *open* and *closed* questions.
  - Closed questions allow respondents a limited range of responses. An example would be 'How many times have you flown with Emirates this year?' The answers to closed questions are easier to analyse and represent numerically.
  - Open questions let people say whatever they want. They do not have to choose from a list of responses. Open questions are best used if there are a large number of possible responses. An example would be 'How would you improve the quality of service provided by Emirates?'
- Contain clear and simple questions. Questions must be clear, avoiding the use of jargon, poor grammar and bad spelling.
- Not contain leading questions. Leading questions are those that 'suggest' a certain answer. They should be avoided because otherwise the results will be biased.
- Not be too long. If questionnaires are too long people will not give up their time to answer them.

Questionnaires can be used in different situations.

- **Postal surveys.** Questionnaires are sent out to people and they are asked to complete them in their own time. They may be more convenient for people but the vast majority of questionnaires are never returned. This means that resources are wasted.

- **Telephone interviews.** The main advantage of interviewing people over the telephone is that it is cheaper. People from a wide geographical area can be covered. However, some people do not like being telephoned by businesses.
- **Personal interviews.** These are often carried out in the street and the interviewer fills in the answers. The advantage is that questions can be explained if a respondent is confused. It may be possible to collect more detailed information. However, many people do not like being approached in the street.
- **Focus groups or consumer panels.** If a business wants very detailed information from customers it might use **focus groups** or **consumer panels**. A focus group is where a number of customers are invited to attend a discussion led by market researchers. The group must be representative of the whole population and be prepared to answer detailed questions. This is a relatively cost-effective method of collecting information but the group may be a little small. Consumer panels are similar to focus groups except that groups of customers are asked for feedback over a period of time. This approach allows businesses to see how consumers react to changes in their products.
- **Observation.** This is where market researchers 'watch' the behaviour of customers. This approach might be used in retail outlets. Observers might record the amount of time customers spend looking at particular products and displays in the store. However, because there is no feedback when using this method a lot of questions go unanswered.
- **Test marketing.** This involves selling a new product in a restricted geographical area to test it before a national launch. After a period of time feedback is gathered from customers. The feedback is used to make modifications to the product before the final launch. This reduces the risk of failure.

Secondary research

Secondary research or **desk research** involves the collection of secondary data. This is information which already exists in some form. It can be internal data, from records within the business, or external data, from sources outside the business.

Internal data: This may be collected from existing business documents or other publications, including the following.
- Existing market research reports.
- Sales figures. The more sophisticated these are the better. For example, sales figures which have been broken down according to market segments can be particularly useful.
- Reports from members of the sales force resulting from direct contact with customers.
- Annual report and accounts published by businesses.
- Businesses increasingly make use of company intranets to provide up-to-date information. These are restricted to company employees. But some information may be available on the internet on company websites.
- Stock movements. These can often provide the most up-to-date information on patterns of demand in the market. This is because they are often recorded instantly, as opposed to sales figures, which tend to be collected at a later date.

External data: Secondary data will also be available from sources outside the business. Individuals or other organisations will have collected data for their own reasons. A business might be able to use this for its own market research. Examples are given below.
- Information from competitors. This may be, for example, in the form of promotional materials, product specifications or price lists.
- Government publications. There are many government publications that businesses can use. These include general statistical publications such as *Social Trends*, the *Census of Population* and the *Annual Abstract of Statistics*. Many are now online.
- Data from customer services on complaints which have been received about a product.
- The European Union. The EU now provides a wide range of secondary data which can be highly valuable to businesses operating within EU countries. Such publications include *Eurostatistics*, which is published by Eurostat (the Statistical Office of the European Union).
- International publications. There is a huge amount of information about overseas marketing published each year by organisations such as the World Bank and the International Monetary Fund.
- Commercial publications. A number of organisations exist to gather data about particular markets. This information is often highly detailed and specialised. Mintel, Dun & Bradstreet and Verdict are examples of such organisations.
- Retail audits. The widespread use of EPoS (electronic point of sale) has meant that it is now much easier to collect detailed and up-to-the-minute data on sales in retail outlets such as supermarkets and other retail chains. Retail audits provide manageable data by monitoring and recording sales in a sample of retail outlets. Businesses find these audits especially helpful because of the way in which they provide a continuous monitoring of their performance in the market. A well-known example is data on the best-selling CDs which make up weekly music charts. The data to compile the official charts is drawn from a highly complex tracking service representing one of the most sophisticated ongoing market research programmes anywhere in the world. Traditionally, this data has been limited to sales of vinyl and CDs – but this has been enhanced with the addition of digital download sales (of singles and albums) and also streaming information – which was added to the singles chart in July 2014 and the official albums chart in February 2015.
- General publications. A business may use a range of publications widely available to members of the public for its market research. These include newspaper and magazine articles.
- Internet website pages. Increasingly businesses make use of the internet to search for secondary data outside of their own organisations. Many of the sources of secondary information above (including, for example, government publications) can now be found on the internet.

Quantitative and qualitative research

Data collected through desk and field research can be either quantitative or qualitative in nature. **Qualitative research** involves the collection of data about attitudes, beliefs and intentions. Focus groups and interviews are common methods used to collect qualitative data. An example of qualitative research could be face-to-face interviews with 100 purchasers of new Land Rover Discoveries to find out why they prefer this product to similar four-wheel drives sold by other car manufacturers. The information collected through qualitative research is usually regarded as being open to a high degree of interpretation. This means that there are often disagreements within businesses about the significance and importance of qualitative research data.

Quantitative research involves the collection of data that can be measured. In practice this usually means the collection of statistical data such as sales figures and market share. Surveys and the use of government publications are common methods of collecting quantitative research data. An example of quantitative research would be a survey of four-wheel drive owners in West Derbyshire to establish their places of residence, ages, occupations, incomes and gender. The information collected through quantitative research is usually regarded as being open to less interpretation than that collected through qualitative research.

Limitations of market research

If market research was totally dependable, businesses could use it when introducing or changing products and be completely confident about how consumers would respond to them. This would mean that all new products launched onto the market, which had been researched in advance, would be a success. Similarly, no products would flop because businesses would receive advance warning from their research and take any necessary measures.

In reality, things can be different. It has been estimated that 90 per cent of all products fail after they have been initially launched. Some of this may be put down to a lack of, or inadequate, market research. However, a number of businesses that have conducted extensive research among consumers before committing a product to the market place have launched products which have failed. Given estimates which suggest that the minimum cost of launching a new product nationally is £1 million, this is a risky business. Famous examples of thoroughly researched products which have turned out to be flops include the Sinclair C5, a cheap vehicle with more stability than a moped and lower costs than a car. In research, consumers enthused over this vehicle. In reality, it was almost impossible to sell. Similarly, when the Coca-Cola Company launched 'New Coke' with a new formula flavour onto the market, research suggested it would be a huge success. In practice, 'New Coke' was quickly withdrawn from the shops.

Businesses want to be sure that the data they collect is reliable. One way of checking the reliability of data is to pose the question, 'If this information was collected again would the same or broadly similar results be obtained?' Businesses acting upon research data need to be sure that they can depend upon it. There is a great deal of debate among researchers about the reliability of different research methods. There are a number of reasons why primary research does not always provide reliable information for businesses.

- **Human behaviour.** Much marketing research depends upon the responses of consumers who participate in the collection of primary data. While the responses of consumers may be honest and truthful at the time, it does not mean that they will necessarily respond in the same manner in future. This is because all human behaviour, including the act of consuming and purchasing goods, is to some extent unpredictable.
- **Sampling and bias.** When carrying out market research, it is usual to base the research upon a sample of the total population. This is because it would be impossible and costly to include every person when dealing with a large population. It is possible, however, that results from the sample may be different from those that would have been obtained if the whole population had been questioned. This is known as a sampling discrepancy. The greater the sampling discrepancy, the less reliable the data obtained.
- As mentioned earlier, questionnaires need to be carefully constructed to avoid the problem of encouraging particular responses from consumers through the use of leading questions. Similarly, the behaviour of interviewers can affect the outcome of interviews.

Businesses must also be careful when using secondary data. For example, businesses may use a government publication to estimate the size of markets in which they might wish to operate. However, these market sizes may not always accurately match the product market being researched.

Use of ICT to support market research

Developments in information and communications technology (ICT) have had an impact on the way businesses carry out market research. ICT can provide support in a number of ways.

Company websites: These can be used to provide access to online surveys. These are similar to postal surveys except respondents may be directed to a questionnaire after receiving an email confirming an online transaction, for example. Online surveys may be more sophisticated because they are flexible and can be tailored to the responses of individuals – for instance if someone responds 'yes' to a particular question the survey can then take them to a further set of questions, and if 'no' it takes them to a different set of questions. They are cheap to administer and can be made available to respondents 24/7. However, many people still ignore them.

Some businesses have review systems on their websites. These allow customers to write accounts of their experiences after buying or consuming a product or service. TripAdvisor, the online hotel booking site, offers such a facility. Not only can a business collect information from their own customers, but they can also look at the reviews of rivals' customers.

A business can also carry out secondary research by gathering data from the websites of rivals. By analysing the websites of competitors a wide range of information can be gathered very easily and cheaply. For example, information about prices charged, product ranges, delivery terms, payment terms, store locations, details of special offers and useful links that might provide even more information. A business might also use comparison websites to identify the cheapest suppliers in the market.

Social networking: Few businesses can afford to neglect the role social media can play in marketing. A very fast growing number of businesses make use of social media platforms such as Facebook, Twitter, YouTube, blogs and coupon sites. Social media can provide a cost-effective and in-depth tool for gaining insights into a firm's customers, market, brand appearance and other important market research aspects.

For example, most social media platforms offer numerous ways to analyse trends and conduct market research. By simply searching the latest posts and popular terms, it is possible to gain insight into emerging trends and see what customers are talking about in real-time. One example of this is conducting hashtag searches on Twitter. By setting up a few searches with hashtags related to a specific brand, industry or product, instant notifications can be received when customers, clients or competitors use key terms.

One of the biggest weaknesses to most marketing research methods is that they are driven by questions. To obtain the proper information, you must first know what to ask. At the same time, simply rewording a question can result in drastically different answers. This means that market research is only as good as the questions used. With the broad scope and interactive nature of social media, information is gained through interaction and observation. Instead of leading the discussions, businesses can simply observe or join in as an equal. This can result in a variety of answers and discoveries that might have remained hidden using other research methods.

Table 1 summarises the advantages of using social media for market research.

Table 1 The advantages of using social media for market research

Broad reach	It can reach millions of people all around the world.
Ability to target	Social media allows specific groups of people to be targeted.
Free or low cost	The use of social media may be free for businesses and paid options are usually cheap.
Personal	It allows communication on a personal basis with individual customers and groups.
Fast	Information can be collected very quickly from large numbers of people.
Easy	High level IT skills and complex equipment are not needed.

Databases

A **database** is really an electronic filing system. It allows a great deal of data to be stored. Every business which uses computers will compile and use databases. The information is set up so that it can be updated and recalled when needed. Table 2 shows part of a database of a finance company which gives details about their clients. The collection of common data is called a file. A file consists of a set of related records. In Table 2 all the information on Jane Brown, for example, is a record. The information on each record is listed under headings known as fields, e.g. name, address, age, occupation, income each year. A good database will have the following facilities.

- User-definable record format, allowing the user to enter any chosen field on the record.
- File-searching facility for finding specified information from a file, e.g. identifying all clients with an income over £33,000. It is usually possible to search on more than one criterion, e.g. all females with an income over £33,000.
- File sorting facility for rearranging data in another order, e.g. arranging the file in Table 2 in ascending order of income.
- Calculations on fields within records for inclusion in reports.

In the world of business and commerce there is actually a market for information held on databases. It is possible to buy banks of information from market researchers who have compiled databases over the years. Names and addresses of potential customers would be information well worth purchasing if it were legally available. The storage of personal data on a computer is subject to the Data Protection Act. Any company or institution wishing to store personal data on a computer system must register with the Data Protection Office. Individuals have a right under the Act to request details of information held on them.

Table 2 An extract from a simple database

Surname	First name	Address	Town	Age	Occupation	Income p.a.
Adams	John	14 Stanley St	Bristol	39	Bricklayer	£32,000
Appaswamy	Krishen	2 Virginia St	Cardiff	23	Welder	£26,000
Atkins	Robert	25 Liverpool Rd	Cardiff	42	Teacher	£32,000
Biddle	Ron	34 Bedford Rd	Bath	58	Civil servant	£35,000
Brown	Jane	111 Bold St	Newport	25	Solicitor	£41,000

Question 2

Some businesses use online surveys to gather data. This involves providing a link to a questionnaire on a company website and inviting people to complete it. An online questionnaire can be completed quickly and responses can often be analysed immediately. Survey costs are low because there are no printing and postage charges. Online surveys can be interactive and may be fun to complete. They can also be accessed 24/7 and be completed when it is convenient. However, there are problems.

The sample of respondents may not be representative. This is because online surveys are only presented to internet users. The views of others may not be taken into account even though they may be potential customers.

Some businesses are keen to find out what customers think of their websites. They might use an online survey similar to the one shown in Figure 3.

Figure 3
An example of a website survey

Website survey

Thank you for using our website. We'd like to ask you some questions about your experience so that we can improve.

We would like your feeeddback about the content on our site. How satisfied are you with the content?

○ Very dissatisfied   ○ Dissatisfied   ○ Neutral   ○ Satisfied
○ Very satisfied

Please tell us how our site compares with similar sites for each of the items below If you did not experience an item, please select "N/A".

	Much worse	Worse	About the same	Better	Much better	N/A
Overall organisation/ navigation	○ 1	○ 2	○ 3	○ 4	○ 5	○ -
Home page content	○ 1	○ 2	○ 3	○ 4	○ 5	○ -
Product information	○ 1	○ 2	○ 3	○ 4	○ 5	○ -
Ease of finding how to contact us	○ 1	○ 2	○ 3	○ 4	○ 5	○ -
Downloading information	○ 1	○ 2	○ 3	○ 4	○ 5	○ -

How likely are you to recommend our site to others?

○ Definitely not   ○ Unlikely   ○ Neutral   ○ May be likely
○ Very likely

What prompted you to visit our site today? Please select all that apply.

☐ Comparison shopping
☐ Interested in purchasing products/services
☐ Looking for contact information
☐ Looking for technical support
☐ Other, please specify

How did you find our site? Please select all that apply.

☐ Recommended by others
☐ Link from email our site sent you
☐ Link from another website
☐ Link from marketing leaflet
☐ Search engine results
☐ Other, please specify

How frequently do you visit our site?

○ First choice   ○ Daily   ○ A few times per week
○ A few times per month ○ Once per month ○ Less frequently than once per month

The next questions will only be used to group your answers with others like yourself.

Please tell us how you access the internet. Check all that apply.

☐ Home   ☐ Cafe
☐ Work   ☐ Mobile phone
☐ College   ☐ Computer tablet (eg iPad)
☐ Library   ☐ Other, please specify

How long do you spend on the internet each day? Select a choice.

○ 1–2 hours   ○ 3–4 hours   ○ More than 8 hours

Please indicate your gender

○ Male   ○ Female

Please select the category that includes your age.

○ 18–30   ○ 31–55   ○ 56 or older

Which one of the following ranges includes your total yearly household income before taxes?

○ up to £28,000   ○ over £28,000
○ Prefer not to answer

(Submit)   Back

(a) Give one reason why it might be important to find out what people think of a business website.

(b) Explain whether an online survey would benefit a company selling to: (i) customers in isolated areas (ii) less developed countries, such as Ethiopia, Bhutan and Haiti.

(c) Discuss the advantages and disadvantages of online surveys.

Market segmentation

Markets can be divided into different sections or market segments. Each segment is made up of consumers that have similar needs. Businesses recognise this and target particular market segments with their products.

- Some businesses concentrate on producing one product for one particular segment, for example luxury cars targeted at a very wealthy market segment in the car market.
- Some businesses produce a range of different products and target them at several different segments.
- Some businesses aim their products at nearly all consumers. For example, large food manufacturers are likely to target their brands at everyone.

However, by dividing markets into segments businesses can more easily supply products that meet customers' needs.

Geographic and demographic segmentation

Geographic segmentation: Different customer groups are likely to have different needs depending on where they live. For example, groups living in hot climates, such as Australia or South Africa, will have different needs to groups living in temperate climates such as the UK. There might also be differences between groups living in different parts of the same country. For example, in India different regions have slightly different tastes in cuisine.

Demographic segmentation: It is common for businesses to divide markets according to age, gender, income, social class, ethnicity or religion of the population.

- **Age.** Infants, teenagers, young adults and the over 65s are all likely to have different needs because of their different ages. Many products are targeted to different consumer groups on the grounds of age. For example, clothes are produced in different styles for people in different age groups.
- **Gender.** Men and women are likely to be targeted by businesses with different products. For example, producers of clothes, cars, magazines, toiletries and drinks target different products to different genders.
- **Income.** Incomes in most countries vary considerably. As a result businesses target products at certain income groups. For example, luxury watchmakers target products at very high-income groups. In contrast, low-cost supermarket chains target lower income groups.
- **Social class.** Businesses pay a lot of attention to different socio-economic groups. Such groups are usually based on occupations. An example of a commonly used measure of social class is shown in Table 3. It is compiled by the Institute of Practitioners in Advertising (IPA) and divides social class into six categories. These can be used by businesses to target products.
- **Ethnicity.** Many countries in the world are becoming more cosmopolitan. This means that people from different ethnic groups are likely to live in the same country. This is important for businesses because different ethnic groups are likely to have different needs and tastes due to their different cultures. For example, in Canada, where there are over 200 different ethnic groups, Chinese consumers are likely to spend

more than other ethnic groups on leather goods, furniture, appliances and electronic equipment.

- **Religion.** Different religious groups can display different tastes. For example, Muslims do not eat pork or drink alcohol. In the US the market for kosher (Jewish) food is thought to be worth $100 billion.

Table 3 Socio-economic groups

Social grade	Social status	Head of household occupation	% of UK population (approx)
A	Upper middle	Higher managerial, administrative or professional – doctors, lawyers and company directors	4%
B	Middle class	Intermediate managerial, administrative or professional – teachers, nurses and managers	12%
C1	Lower middle class	Supervisory or clerical and junior managerial, administrative or professional – shop assistants, clerks and police constables	22%
C2	Skilled working class	Skilled manual workers – carpenters, plumbers, cooks and train drivers	33%
D	Working class	Semi-skilled and unskilled manual workers – fitters, window cleaners and storekeepers	19%
E	The poor	State pensioners or widows, casual or lower grade workers, or long term unemployed	10%

Psychographic segmentation

Geographic and demographic segmentation have limitations. For example, there is a wide variety of spending patterns among females aged 16–18 living in Manchester. Yet people in this consumer group share the same gender, age and location. An alternative way of grouping customers is through psychographic segmentation. This groups customers according to their attitudes, opinions and lifestyles.

- Sports products may be aimed at those who are interested in 'extreme' sports such as skiboarding.
- Chocolate manufacturers have identified two categories of chocolate eaters. 'Depressive' chocolate lovers eat chocolate to unwind, predominantly during the evening. 'Energetic' chocolate eaters eat chocolate as a fast food and live life at a fast pace.
- People's attitudes to life may also be used to segment the market. Some pension funds are geared towards those who only want investments in 'ethical' businesses.
- Clothes may be geared at those who are interested in 'retro' fashions from earlier decades.
- Travel companies target holidays at families with younger children.
- Certain newspapers are geared towards Labour voters, while others are geared towards Conservative voters.

One of the drawbacks of psychographic segmentation is that it can be difficult for businesses to collect data about the beliefs, attitudes and lifestyles of consumers. In order to do this they may require the help of specialist businesses.

Behavioural segmentation

Behavioural segmentation attempts to segment markets according to how consumers relate to a product. There are a number of different methods of behavioural segmentation.

Usage rate: This is when consumers are categorised according to the quantity and frequency of their purchases. One example of this is British Airways, which established an 'Executive Club' to encourage and develop the custom of regular business travellers.

Loyalty: Consumers can be categorised according to their product loyalty. The Tesco Clubcard, for example, which offers discounts to regular customers of Tesco supermarkets, seeks to reward and encourage loyalty to Tesco and its products.

Time and date of consumption: Consumers often consume particular products at particular times and dates. Businesses can take advantage of this in order to improve their marketing. So, for example, manufacturers of breakfast cereals, while recognising that their product will be primarily consumed in the morning, encourage consumers also to consume their products in the evening. Similarly, many bars and clubs seek to encourage different groups of consumers according to the night of the week. For example, Thursday nights are often for older singles and Friday nights for younger consumers.

Like other segmentation methods, a drawback of behavioural segmentation is that on its own it may fail to adequately capture a target market for a business. For this reason, in many cases a business might employ a variety of the segmentation methods explained above. So, for example, a manufacturer of luxury apartments may be interested in segments that included single men or women with no children, in the 30–40 age range, with high incomes that fall into social class AB. Because of the likely one-off nature of such a purchase, behavioural segmentation would be less important in this instance.

Benefits of market segmentation

Generally a business is more able to meet the needs of different customer groups if the market is segmented. Some specific advantages include the following.

- Businesses that produce different products for different market segments can increase revenue. For example, airlines charge first class passengers many times more than they charge economy passengers for the same flight. This helps to increase revenue from the flight.
- Customers may be more loyal to a business that provides products that are tailored specifically to them.
- Businesses can avoid wasting promotional resources by not targeting products at customers that do not want them.
- Some businesses can market a wider range of goods to different customer groups. For example, many car manufacturers have several different models, each of which is targeted at a different segment.

Question 3

In common with many airlines, Emirates offers three distinct services on most of their flights. For example, on 22nd June 2015, a flight from Manchester to Dubai was showing the following services.

Economy class	Price = £432.60
Business class	Price = £2,349.60
First class	Price = £3,237.60

(a) Describe the different customer groups targeted by Emirates in this example.

(b) Discuss how Emirates might benefit from this method of market segmentation.

Key terms

Consumer panels – groups of customers are asked for feedback about products over a period of time.
Database – an organised collection of data stored electronically with instant access, searching and sorting facilities.
Focus groups – where a number of customers are invited to attend a discussion about a product led by market researchers.
Market orientation – an approach to business which places the needs of consumers at the centre of the decision-making process.
Market research – the collection, presentation and analysis of information relating to the marketing and consumption of goods and services.
Market segment – part of a whole market where a particular customer group has similar characteristics.
Primary research or field research – the gathering of 'new' information which does not already exist.
Product orientation – an approach to business which places the emphasis upon the production process and the product itself.
Qualitative research – the collection of data about attitudes, beliefs and intentions.
Quantitative research – the collection of data that can be quantified.
Respondent – a person or organisation that answers questions in a survey.
Sample – a small group of people who must represent a proportion of a total market when carrying out market research.
Secondary research or desk research – the collection of data that is already in existence.
Socio-economic groups – division of people according to social class.

Case study

MARKET RESEARCH ON 'CLICK & COLLECT' ORDERS

Mintel is the world's leading market intelligence agency. It provides a wide range of services in the field of market research. For example, it carries out primary research, analyses market data and market trends, and produces specialist market research reports for its clients. Some of Mintel's reports can be purchased online and can cost up to £2,500. The research data below about click & collect orders was gathered by Mintel in 2014.

- Click & collect orders made up 15 per cent of all internet retail sales of goods in 2014. The collection rate was much higher for non-grocery orders than in groceries.

- In 2014, online retail sales were expected to contribute to 11.6 per cent of all retail sales. This means, in turn, that click & collect orders would make up 1.7 per cent of all retail sales in 2014.

- The survey estimated that in 2015, 17 per cent of all internet retail sales (or 2.2 per cent of all retail sales) would be collected by customers. In September 2014, Transport for London reported that it had processed 10,000 orders at its click & collect stations in the first 10 months of operation.

- 35 per cent of UK consumers had used click & collect services in the previous year and 64 per cent said that they shopped online more now because retailers offer click & collect services. Furthermore, 58 per cent said that click & collect encouraged them to visit stores more frequently.

- 60 per cent of UK consumers only used click & collect for smaller items that were easy to carry, but 53 per cent said they would like drive-through points that offered click & collect for a number of retailers — suggesting opportunities to extend click & collect to heavier or bulkier items.

- New click-and-collect fashion hubs are likely to drive up online sales. In the survey, 80 per cent of consumers agreed that when shopping online it is difficult to tell if clothes will fit — consumers aged under 35 see this as the main issue.

- 50 per cent of consumers (rising to 57 per cent of women) said the hassle of returning goods through the post was one of the main barriers to buying clothes online. 31 per cent of consumers preferred to be able to return their online order to an actual store — and 23 per cent of UK consumers said that an option to deliver to a store to try on before purchasing would encourage them to buy from one online retailer over another.

Source: adapted from www.mintel.com

(a) What is meant by primary research? (2 marks)

(b) Explain one benefit of using qualitative market research. (4 marks)

(c) Explain one way in which the data in the Mintel report might be used by retailers. (4 marks)

(d) Assess the usefulness of market research data, like the above information, to retailers. (12 marks)

Knowledge check

1. How might market research reduce the risk in business?

2. State two benefits that a market orientated business might enjoy.

3. State three advantages of primary research.

4. What is meant by desk research?

5. State four sources of data for secondary research.

6. What is meant by quantitative market research?

7. Why might qualitative data be open to different interpretations?

8. How might a business use social media to conduct market research?

9. Give three advantages of using online surveys.

10. How might a business use databases for market research?

11. What is meant by behavioural segmentation?

12. State two benefits of market segmentation.

Key points

1. Market mapping.
2. Competitive advantage of a product or service.
3. The purpose of product differentiation.
4. Adding value to products and services.

Getting started

The market for automobiles is very competitive. Consider the market for the cars below.

To what extent are the two cars the same or different? What might be the target markets for these two products? How might the manufacturers differentiate two products? How might one of the manufacturers try to gain a competitive edge over their rival?

Market positioning

Market positioning is concerned with the perceptions consumers have about products. To simplify the choice from a vast array of products, consumers categorise them according to a range of factors. Such factors include the quality, status and value for money of products. It is the categories into which consumers place products that define their 'position'.

Consumers often position a business's products in relation to those of its competitors. This can be in the form of 'pecking order' or product ladder. Firms will plan marketing activities to shape consumer perceptions and therefore achieve a desired position. Some approaches that a business might use to position its products are outlined below.

- **The benefits offered by the product.** For example, in the automobile market, some manufacturers emphasise safety, others the quality of work and style, and yet more value for money.
- **The unique selling point.** The unique selling point or unique selling proposition (USP) of the product. This is the key aspect of the product or service that sets it apart from those of competitors. For example, some shampoos claim to remove dandruff.
- **The attributes of the product.** This is a common method used to position products. For example, the slogan 'M&Ms melt in your mouth, not in your hand' emphasises clearly an attribute of this confectionery.
- **The origin of the product.** In the market for cheese, the names of many products are derived from where they were originally manufactured. Examples might be Lancashire, Munster, Gloucester, Wensleydale and Cheshire.
- **The classification of the product.** The product name, I Can't Believe It's Not Butter® may be a claim to position margarine against butter, despite the fact that it is not butter.

As markets change in response to shifting consumer demand, some businesses find they need to reposition their products. This usually involves changing their target market, the features of the product or the image of the product that distinguishes it from those of rivals. For example, detergents originally designed for washing babies' nappies faced a sharp fall in demand when disposable nappies were introduced. However, some companies successfully repositioned their brand for a new use – being an ideal laundry detergent for tough stains.

Market mapping

The positioning of a brand is influenced by customer perception rather than by those of businesses. For example, a business may feel its brand is a high-quality, up-market product. But if customers see it as low quality and down-market, it is their views that will influence sales.

So, if a business wants to find out where its brand is positioned in the market, it might carry out market research. This will help it to understand how customers see the brand in relation to others in the market.

A business may also wish to launch a new brand. Having decided the target market, market research might show what characteristics the brand must have to succeed in that market. It could reveal the price that customers are prepared to pay. It could also suggest what sort of promotional support will be needed. For example, will a national television advertising campaign be used? Will promotion to retailers be a better strategy?

The results of market research can be displayed on perceptual maps (sometimes also called market maps or positioning maps). An example is shown in Figure 1. This illustrates a perceptual map for a sample of motor cars.

Figure 1

A perceptual map for cars

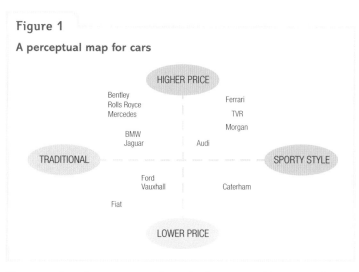

The use of market maps can have its limitations. For example, perceptual maps are two dimensional, which means that only two product attributes can be analysed on the same map. They can also be more relevant for individual brands, and less helpful for a corporate brand image. The information needed to plot the maps can be expensive to obtain, requiring the use of primary market research. There may also be a difference between consumers' perception of the brand's benefits and the actual benefits.

Finally, perceptual maps need not come from a detailed study. There are also intuitive maps (also called judgemental maps or consensus maps) that are created by marketers based on their understanding of their industry. Management uses its best judgement. It is questionable how valuable this type of map is. Often they just give the appearance of credibility to management's preconceptions.

Question 1

Figure 2 shows a perceptual map for supermarket brands.

(a) Explain how a French supermarket chain might use the map in Figure 2 if it was considering an entry into the UK market.

(b) Explain one drawback to the French supermarket chain of using the perceptual map in Figure 2.

(c) Assess the position of Tesco compared to that of Aldi using the perceptual map in Figure 2.

Figure 2

A perceptual map for supermarket brands (as perceived by the author)

High price — Marks & Spencer, Waitrose, Spar, Sainsbury's, Quality −ve, Tesco, Quality +ve, Morrisons, Asda, Aldi, Lidl, Low price

Thinking bigger

From time to time there may be a need to reposition an entire company, rather than just a product line. Reasons for repositioning an entire company might be to deal with a tarnished image, to differentiate the company from rivals, to clarify the company's position, to create more business opportunities or to increase the value of the company. In 2014, many felt that Tesco would need to reposition itself in the market. This followed a major corporate accounting issue when a whistle-blower revealed that Tesco's finance department had overstated the first half year's profits by £250 million, a figure later adjusted to £263 million. Figure 2 also shows that Tesco may be perceived as a supermarket without a well-defined position. It may be perceived as neither very cheap nor very expensive, and neither high quality nor low quality.

Repositioning a company is an enormous task. It involves more than a marketing challenge. It requires making hard decisions about how a market is shifting and how a firm's competitors will react. Often these decisions must be made without the benefit of sufficient information. Positioning is also difficult to measure because customer perception of a product may not have been tested using quantitative techniques.

Source: adapted from the *Financial Times*, all rights reserved.

Competitive advantage of a product or service

A business is likely to be more successful if it can gain a competitive advantage in the market place. Competitive advantage is a set of unique features of a company and its products that are perceived by customers as significant and superior to the competition. For example, a product may save time, save money, make money, improve health, taste better, be more convenient or offer more comfort. A business can develop a competitive advantage in a number of ways.

- **Product design.** If a firm can develop a product that has superior design, this might appeal to a significant proportion of a market. A business may emphasise a specific design feature to differentiate its product from those of its rivals and gain a competitive advantage. It could stress the superior functionality of the product – it might be ergonomically designed for example. Alternatively a design might focus on the aesthetics of a product. This approach may be used by jewellery producers. Product design is discussed in Unit 9.

- **Product quality.** Offering high-quality products is a common way of gaining a competitive edge in a market. The main advantage of this approach is that a premium price can be charged. However, costs may be higher if superior raw materials are required along with higher standards of quality. Savile Row tailors in London, for instance, have a reputation for high-quality hand-made suits.

- **Promotion.** Effective promotion using creative advertising, for example, might give a firm a competitive edge. The use of persuasive advertising may be capable of changing consumer perceptions so that they are more inclined to buy the product. For example, the use of TV adverts for products that claim to reduce pain may be perceived as persuasive.

- **Customer service.** Some businesses pay less attention to the product itself and rely on high-quality customer service to gain a competitive edge. For example, Enterprise, the car hire firm, delivers and collects cars from a chosen customer location (e.g. at home) to encourage sales.

19

- **Delivery times.** Some customers demand fast delivery of products. Where speed of delivery is important, a prompt service will be a way of gaining an advantage. An example might be a components supplier in the car industry that can guarantee to deliver just-in-time (see Unit 39).
- **Economies of scale.** Firms that can produce efficiently at low cost can afford to charge a lower price and therefore gain a competitive advantage by being a cost leader in their market. Larger firms are likely to be better placed to exploit this advantage.
- **Flexibility.** Some customers appreciate a flexible service. For example, firms that supply other businesses may win a bigger market share if they can change designs or specifications while production is in progress. Or if they can speed up production to meet a more urgent delivery time.
- **Ethical stance.** It might be possible to gain a competitive edge by adopting a particular ethical stance. For example, Fairtrade aims to deal ethically and fairly with the producers of the commodity being sold. A furniture-maker might attract environmentally aware consumers if it ethically sources its raw materials. It could do this by avoiding the use of wood from trees that are threatened with extinction.
- **Focusing on a particular market segment.** For example, a gym could gain a competitive advantage by focusing on an audience not typically catered for by gyms and fitness clubs such as the over-60s or parents with young children.

The purpose of product differentiation

Product differentiation is used by businesses to gain a competitive edge over their rivals. In highly competitive markets, where lots of firms produce similar products, firms will try to make their product unique in some way so that it stands out from the pack. This involves supplying goods and services that have different features or physical attributes. The differences in products may be real – the products look different, or have different technical specifications or have different capabilities or performance levels. Energizer, for example, claims that its AA lithium batteries have a longer life than any other AA batteries. Or in contrast the differences may be perceived – consumers believe there is a difference even if there is not one, or it is not a significant one. Consumers attach a value to products in their own minds based on information that they receive – an elaborate persuasive advertising campaign, for example. Attractive packaging might also be used to create a perceived difference.

The purpose of product differentiation may include the following.

Flexible pricing: If a business can demonstrate clear physical differences between their products and those of rivals, it may be able to charge higher prices. In the case of perceived differences, consumers sometimes attach a value to a product that may be priced well above the costs of production. For example, perceived value is often used with perfumes. Perfumes are frequently associated with a glamorous celebrity in order to create a mystique and perception of luxury. Or, they may be the subject of elaborate and expensive advertising campaigns to create a strong image for the perfume. Consumers may not realise that production costs for perfumes are relatively low. As a result, perfume manufacturers can often charge high prices.

Recognition: One of the main purposes for product differentiation is to gain recognition in the market place. Consumers often find products more appealing if they stand out from the pack. Confectionery products tend to be packaged in attractive and colourful wrappings so that consumers are drawn to them. Also, some consumers 'like to be different' and will naturally be drawn to products that are explicitly different from those of rivals.

Extend product range: If businesses can differentiate products they may be able to serve more than one market segment in the same industry. For example, cruise ships offer different standards of cabin accommodation to consumers with different levels of spending power. They also offer different destinations, different length cruises and different on-board facilities. In the biscuits market, producers supply a very wide range of different products in an effort to appeal to different tastes and to compete aggressively with rivals.

Brand development: A business that can differentiate its product successfully for a sustained period of time can develop a strong brand. The Coca-Cola Company, with its distinctive formula, has built one of the strongest brands in the world as a result of initial product differentiation. Over the years the brand has been supported by constant advertising and other forms of promotion to stay at the top. But it all started with successful product differentiation.

Overcome competition: Generally, a business will differentiate its products to try and outcompete rivals. By creating real or perceived differences businesses can attract new customers and win larger market shares. With an increase in scale a business might also be able to lower costs and raise profits.

Adding value to products and services

In highly competitive markets a business may try to **add value** to its product. This means that the business provides 'extra' features for the customer that go beyond their standard expectations. For example, a car MOT centre may valet a customer's car as part of a £50 MOT inspection. It normally costs £50 to have an MOT inspection, so the car valet is adding value for the customer. Businesses can add value to their products and services in a number of ways. Some examples are outlined below.

Bundling: A business might be able to add value by putting together a 'package' of benefits or services that make up the whole product. For example, in the holiday industry tour operators may offer flights, accommodation, transfers, insurance, childcare facilities and excursions all for one price. The product may also be presented in such a way that suggests that some of the services, such as insurance and excursions, are free in the package. This will help to add value for consumers.

Customer service: Staff that come into direct contact with customers can play a very big role in adding value. Well-groomed, friendly, attentive and professional staff create a good image and make customers feel at ease. Staff with a sound knowledge of the products that they are selling, coupled with the willingness to 'go out of their way' to help customers are likely to be a source of added value. After-sales service can also be an important feature of added value. Customers may be happier buying from a business that operates a helpdesk, makes follow-up calls or offers a free maintenance service.

Speed of response to customers: This is linked to customer service. A lot of people do not like waiting – this might include queuing at checkouts, waiting for appointments and waiting for deliveries. A business can add value by reducing waiting times or eliminating them completely. For example, airlines allow first class passengers to disembark first. A customer might choose a particular dry-cleaning service because it can return garments within four hours.

Packaging: The packaging of products can add value. Many businesses make an effort to present products in attractive wrappings. For some products, such as jewellery for example, a business might offer to gift-wrap a product. In agriculture many farms add value by packing produce, such as vegetables, in customised bags for supermarkets.

Frequent buyer offers: It might be possible to add value by rewarding customers for repeated purchases. Regular customers are offered benefits such as a more valuable service, preferential pricing and free products. For example, many regular travellers collect air miles, which can be accumulated and used to get free flights.

Customisation: Customising products might involve embedding a customer's logo or brand in the product, or simply using customised wrapping to distinguish a product from those of competitors. It could also involve changing or adapting product designs to suit the needs of individual customers.

Adding value can generate a number of benefits for a business.

- It may be possible for a business to charge a higher price. However, businesses may want to disguise higher prices so that the value-added element appears to be free. Some tour operators do this by giving free holiday insurance when a package is purchased.

Question 2

In common with most commercial banks, Lloyds Bank offers free banking to customers. For example, customers can open a current account and enjoy free cash withdrawals and access to account information from ATMs, free direct debits and free cheque books. However, in 2014 Lloyds Bank offered two other 'added value' current accounts.

Silver account – £9.95 a month fee

- European and UK travel insurance for customers and their partners.
- Motor vehicle breakdown insurance with roadside assistance.
- Mobile phone insurance.
- £50 interest and fee-free planned overdraft, subject to application and approval.

Platinum account – £17 a month fee

- Worldwide and UK travel insurance with either family or winter sports cover.
- Motor vehicle breakdown insurance with roadside assistance, relay and home start.
- Mobile phone insurance.
- £300 interest and fee-free planned overdraft, subject to application and approval.

Source: adapted from www.lloydsbank.com

(a) Explain how Lloyds Bank has added value in this case.
(b) Explain one benefit to Lloyds Bank of adding value to its products.

> **Exam tip**
>
> When discussing a concept, such as added value in this unit, it is not necessary to remember all of the different methods. You only need to remember one or two. However, you must be able to explain them in detail and perhaps give an example.

- Adding value can be used to differentiate a product and gain a competitive edge. For example, some customers may prefer to shop with retailers that offer high-quality customer service.
- Adding value may help a business protect itself from competitors charging lower prices in a bid to steal customers.
- A business might focus more closely on its target market segment by adding value, for example by meeting the needs of customers more effectively.

Case study

BEST WESTERN HOTELS

A few years ago the Best Western hotel chain felt that it had lost its identity in the market and was not effectively differentiating itself. The rise of independent boutique hotels in the UK suggested that customers prefer hotels with character. As a result the chain organised a re-launch campaign with the message 'Hotels with personality'. The campaign emphasised the individuality of each member hotel and targeted 'independently minded' people in the market.

The structure of the hotel chain meant that Best Western could do this because each hotel in the group is independently owned. Hotels range from 12th-century castles to modern, purpose-built venues; establishments that grow their own produce to those with deer parks and golf courses. This enabled them to emphasise the independence and variety of hotels within the group with a new market position and strapline. Tim Wade, head of marketing, said, 'Because every hotel is independent, every hotel has its own personality, and we had a real opportunity to stand out against the formulaic hotel chains and say something very different about ourselves.' Rather than going for traditional demographic segmentation, the new position targeted 'independent-minded people, who don't want the same experience everywhere . . . We already had the product; it was really about getting people to take notice or look at it from a different perspective.'

Tim Wade said that brand repositioning was a 'huge project', which should not be undertaken without thorough planning and research: 'You've got to make sure your positioning is right and really get the people in the business behind what you're doing. Once the repositioning strategy was devised, it was tested with consumers at focus groups to establish whether the new position was really relevant and appealing to customers.'

David Clarke, CEO of Best Western, said 'It has been a highly successful campaign and ensured that Best Western is a group that stands apart from our competitors.' Sales have increased by nearly 30 per cent year-on-year, the most in the chain's history, with corporate sales also up significantly. According to Tim Wade the repositioning campaign has been a resounding success with expectations being surpassed on several levels. Growth in the business can be traced back to the first TV advert that launched the campaign.

Source: adapted from www.startups.co.uk

 ━━━━━━━━━━━━━━━━━━━━━━━━━━━━━

(a) What is meant by market positioning? (2 marks)

(b) Explain one reason why Best Western felt the need to reposition its hotel chain. (4 marks)

(c) Explain one way in which Best Western has developed a competitive edge. (4 marks)

(d) Assess the importance to Best Western of product differentiation in this case. (12 marks)

Key terms

Added value – the extra features that may be offered by a business when selling a product, such as high quality customer service, which helps to exceed customer expectations.

Competitive advantage – an advantage that enables a business to perform better than its rivals in the market.

Market maps or **perceptual maps** – typically a two-dimensional diagram that shows two of the attributes or characteristics of a brand and those of rival brands in the market.

Market positioning – the view consumers have about the quality, value for money and image of a product in relation to those of competitors.

Product differentiation – an attempt by a business to distinguish its product from those of competitors.

Reposition – change the view consumers have about a product by altering some of its characteristics.

Unique selling point (or proposition) – the aspect or feature of a product that clearly distinguishes it from its rivals.

Knowledge check

1. State three ways a business might position its products.

2. Perceptual maps are two dimensional. What does this mean?

3. State two benefits of using perceptual maps.

4. State one key disadvantage of using perceptual maps.

5. Why might a business choose to reposition the whole corporation?

6. State three ways a business might try to gain a competitive advantage in the market.

7. What is a USP?

8. State two reasons why a business should differentiate its product.

9. What is meant by adding value?

10. State three ways a business might add value to products.

4 Demand

Key points

1. Factors leading to a change in demand:
   - changes in the prices of substitutes and complementary goods
   - changes in consumer incomes
   - fashions, tastes and preferences
   - advertising and branding
   - demographics
   - external shocks
   - seasonality.

Getting started

What might happen to sales of these products if there was a recession in the economy? What might happen to sales of these products if free Wi-Fi was introduced? What other factors might encourage more people to buy these products?

Demand

Demand is the amount of a product that consumers are willing and able to purchase at any given price. Demand is concerned with what consumers are actually able to buy (what they can afford to and would buy), rather than what they would like to buy. So, for example, we could say that the demand for cars in the UK market at an average price of £9,000 might be 130,000 a year.

Table 1 shows a demand schedule for button mushrooms. These figures can be used to draw a **demand curve** as in Figure 1. In practice, demand curves are not a straight line, but are usually drawn in this way for simplicity.

The curve shows the quantity of a good or service that will be demanded at any given price. As with nearly all such curves, it slopes downwards from left to right. This is because the quantity demanded is likely to be higher at lower prices and lower at higher prices – ceteris paribus (assuming no other things change). In Table 1 more button mushrooms are bought at a price of £0.50 than at a price of £2.50.

A change in the price of a good or service will lead to a change in the quantity demanded. This is shown on the demand

curve as a movement along (up or down) the curve. In Figure 1, a fall in price from £1.50 to £1, for example, will result in a movement along the curve from point X to point Y.

This will result in a rise in the quantity demanded from 60,000 to 80,000 kilos. The demand curve itself has not moved from its original position. Price changes only lead to an extension (rise) or contraction (fall) in the quantity demanded.

Table 1 The demand schedule for button mushrooms

Price per kilo (£)	Quantity demanded (000 kilos)
0.50	100
1.00	80
1.50	60
2.00	40
2.50	20

Figure 1

The demand curve for button mushrooms

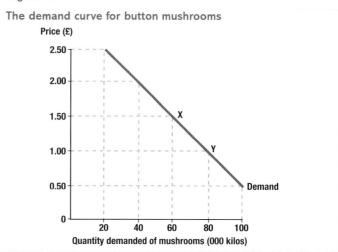

Maths tip

When a demand curve slopes down from left to right, this reflects the **inverse** relationship between price and quantity demanded. When the price goes up, the quantity demanded goes down. When the price goes down, the quantity demanded goes up.

Factors leading to a change in demand

The price of a product has a significant influence on its demand. For most goods and services higher prices will tend to reduce demand and lower prices will tend to raise demand. However, there are several other factors that can lead to a change in demand. Changes in these factors, which are outlined below, will actually shift the demand curve. This is different from a price change, which results in a movement along the demand curve.

Prices of substitutes: Many goods sold by businesses have **substitutes**. For example, a consumer buying a can of Coca-Cola might have considered other brands such as Pepsi-Cola® or a supermarket 'own label'. Most consumers would consider these as good substitutes. The price of substitutes will affect demand. If the price of a substitute product falls, the quantity demanded of the substitute rises. As a result the demand for the product would fall. If a good has a lot of close substitutes then the prices of these will affect demand significantly. In Figure 2, the line labelled D represents the demand for skiing holidays in the UK. A decrease in the price of a substitute, such as 'winter sun holidays', may reduce the demand for skiing holidays. This would result in a shift from D to D_2 in Figure 2.

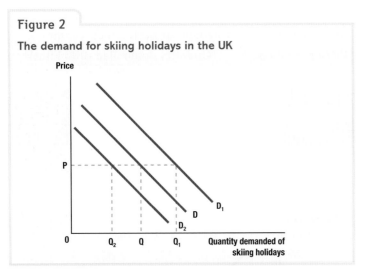

Figure 2

The demand for skiing holidays in the UK

Prices of complements: Consumers sometimes purchase certain goods together. This is because the two goods are used together. For example, consumers of cornflakes will also buy milk and people who buy cars will also buy car insurance. In these examples milk and cornflakes and cars and car insurance are **complementary goods**. Demand for such products is likely to be affected by the price of complementary goods. For example, a reduction in the price of skiing accessories may encourage more people to try skiing. This would be shown by a shift from D to D_1 in Figure 2.

Changes in consumer incomes: The amount of money that people earn will influence the amount and types of goods that they buy. Generally, when income rises, demand for goods will also rise. For example, if wages and salaries go up people may decide to spend more money going out to restaurants, they may take an extra holiday or they may buy a new car. These are all **normal goods** – goods for which demand will

rise when income rises. Most goods in the economy are normal goods; however, a minority are **inferior goods**. This means that demand for them will actually fall when incomes rise. Supermarket 'own-label' brands or public transport can be examples of inferior goods. For example, consumers who generally buy Morrisons' own-label canned beans may switch to a more expensive brand, such as Heinz, when their incomes rise. Therefore demand for the Morrisons' own-label brand will fall.

In Figure 2, if consumer incomes rise, the demand for skiing holidays would also probably rise causing a shift in the demand curve from D to D1.

Question 1

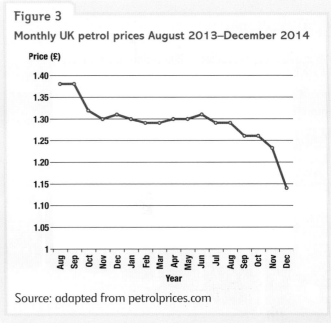

Figure 3

Monthly UK petrol prices August 2013–December 2014

Source: adapted from petrolprices.com

(a) What is meant by the term complementary goods?

(b) Explain how the pattern of prices shown in Figure 3 might influence the demand for (i) cars (ii) public transport.

Fashions, tastes and preferences: Over a period of time, demand patterns change because of changes in consumer tastes and fashion. For example, the growth in demand for 4 wheel drive cars in the UK, not because an increasing number of people need to drive off-road but because increasing numbers of drivers find them appealing. The clothes industry in particular is influenced strongly by changes in fashion. In many countries there are buying seasons for clothes – many clothes items bought in one season would not be in demand in later seasons because they will have gone out of fashion.

Since 2005 there has been a significant increase in the demand for bicycles in the UK. This demand has been led by Bradley Wiggins' road cycling success in the Tour de France and Olympic Games, and the success of the British Olympic track cyclists. There has also been an improvement in the UK cycling infrastructure, such as more bicycle-only lanes, to get people back on their bikes. In 2013, 50 million journeys were made by bicycle, up 7 per cent on the previous year.

Advertising and branding: Businesses try to influence demand for their products through advertising and other forms of promotion. If goods are heavily advertised demand for them is likely to increase. This helps to explain the huge amounts of money that some businesses are prepared to spend on advertising. For example, from figures widely available it was possible to identify that Sky spent more on advertising than any other company in the UK in 2013, with expenditure of over £264 million. This was £87 million more than Proctor & Gamble, reported as the second biggest UK advertiser. The range of expenditure of the top 10 advertisers in the UK in 2013 was widely reported from DFS at number 10 with over £75 million to Sky at number one with over £264 million.

Businesses also use branding to influence demand. By giving products a name, term, symbol or any other sign, to distinguish them from those of competitors, businesses can develop brand recognition and increase sales. They do this by investing heavily in positioning, promoting and advertising to make the brand strong. Branding is discussed in Unit 10. In Figure 2, if businesses selling skiing holidays increase spending on advertising and branding, demand will probably increase from D to D_1.

Demographics: As population grows there will be an increase in demand for nearly all goods and services. However, demand is also affected by the structure of the population as well as its size.

- The **age distribution** of a population is the numbers of people that fall into different age groups. For example, in many countries there has been growth in the number of people aged over 60. This will have an effect on demand patterns. For example, as the population ages there will be more demand for goods such as retirement homes, specialist holidays for the elderly and healthcare. In Figure 2, if there was an increase in the 18 to 40 age group, there might be an increase in the demand for skiing holidays. This would shift the demand curve from D to D_1.
- There are slightly more women than men overall in the UK population. In the older age groups the number of women compared to men increases. Consequently, the **gender distribution** of the population is likely to affect demand patterns. For example, there will be a greater demand for women's clothes than men's clothes.
- **Geographical distribution** can also affect demand. Increasingly, in most developed and developing countries more and more people live in urban areas. As a result demand for schools and hospitals in these areas, for example, will be higher than in rural areas.
- Other factors can affect the structure of the population, such as the nature of households. For example, in some parts of the world there has been a growth in the number of one-person households. This trend increases the demand for single accommodation. Many countries have **ethnic groups** in their population structure. If these ethnic groups grow in size there is also likely to be an increase in demand for products associated with their culture.

Also, there are likely to be changes in the size and structure of populations over time. For example, if the birth rate or immigration rises they will increase the size and structure of the population. Since 2005 there has been growth in the number of Eastern Europeans moving into the UK as more countries join the EU. As a consequence many specialist retail outlets have been established to serve this population, such as Polish food shops.

External shocks: Factors beyond the control of businesses can have an impact on the demand for products. Some key examples are outlined below.

- **Competition.** If a strong new competitor enters the market for the first time, demand is likely to fall for the original firm's product. For example, it is possible that Sky may be adversely affected following BT winning the right to broadcast Barclays Premier League football for the first time in 2014.
- **Government.** A government can influence demand in a number of ways. Raising taxes, for instance, could dampen demand for many products because spending power would be curbed. New laws can affect demand. For example, legal measures designed to increase competition in the market for gas and electricity might result in a fall in demand for the existing operators in the market.
- **Economic climate.** If the economy is growing, demand for most goods and services will tend to rise. In contrast, during a recession, demand for non-essential goods such as skiing holidays is likely to fall. This would be represented by a shift from D to D_2 in Figure 2.
- **Social and environmental factors.** Demand for some goods might be affected by changes in society. For example, there has been a huge increase in demand for social media. New social websites have emerged as a major means of communication. This has helped to increase the demand for mobile phones, apps, tablets, smartphones and related services. Concerns about global warming have changed consumers' attitudes towards goods and services that raise carbon emissions. For example, there has been a significant increase in demand for electric cars and hybrids (cars which run on both petrol and electricity).

Seasonality: Some goods and services have seasonal demand. This means that demand rises at particular times of the year. For example, in the UK, demand for garden furniture rises in late spring when the weather starts to improve. Similarly, demand for warm clothing, such as overcoats and woolly jumpers, rises in the late autumn when the weather turns colder. Demand is also influenced by calendar events, such as Christmas, Easter, Mother's Day, St Valentine's Day and Halloween.

Exam tip

When drawing demand curves to help illustrate answers in examinations, it is acceptable to draw straight lines. Remember the price is always on the vertical axis and quantity on the horizontal axis.

Case study

BARCHESTER HEALTHCARE LTD

Barchester Healthcare Ltd is one of the UK's largest providers of care homes. It employs over 17,000 staff providing care for over 11,000 residents in over 200 locations. The profit-making company is currently constructing a high-quality, purpose-built care home at a picturesque site by a marina in Burton Waters, Lincolnshire. The home will provide residential and nursing care, including dementia care, to the elderly.

The home's publicity states it will employ highly trained staff and provide facilities specifically designed to help people with dementia, including memory boxes for each person containing mementoes to help them to remember. Initiatives to help residents to partake in everyday activities include adapted kitchen equipment and sensory gardens.

Sources: adapted from www.barchester.com and www.carehome.co.uk

Q

(a) Draw a diagram showing the likely effect on the demand for Barchester Healthcare's services in the future. (4 marks)

(b) Assess how the information shown in Figures 4 and 5 might affect demand patterns in the UK. (8 marks)

(c) Assess the impact that external factors might have on the demand for services supplied by companies like Barchester Healthcare. (12 marks)

Figure 4

UK population 1971 to 2031 (millions)

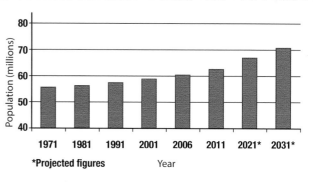

*Projected figures   Year

Source: adapted from Office for National Statistics, www.ons.gov.uk

Figure 5

UK population (male and female over 75s) 1971 to 2016 (000s)

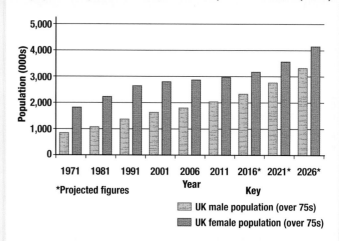

*Projected figures   Year   Key

☐ UK male population (over 75s)
■ UK female population (over 75s)

Source: adapted from Office for National Statistics, www.ons.gov.uk

Key Terms

Complementary goods – goods that are purchased together because they are consumed together.
Demand – the quantity of a product bought at a given price over a given period of time.
Demand curve – a line drawn on a graph that shows how much of a good will be bought at different prices.
Inferior goods – goods for which demand will fall if income rises *or* rise if income falls.
Normal goods – goods for which demand will rise if income rises *or* fall if income falls.
Substitute goods – goods that can be bought as an alternative to others, but perform the same function.

Knowledge check

1. What is the relationship between price and the quantity demanded?

2. Give two examples of goods that are close substitutes.

3. If the price of a good rises what will happen to demand for a complementary good?

4. What might happen to the demand for furniture if incomes fall?

5. If a business increases its spending on advertising, how will this affect the position of the demand curve?

6. How might demand be affected by a change in the structure of the population caused by an increase in immigration?

7. Give three examples of external shocks that might affect demand.

8. What might affect the demand for ice cream?

5 Supply

Key points

1. Factors leading to a change in supply:
   - changes in the costs of production
   - introduction of new technology
   - indirect taxes
   - government subsidies
   - external shocks.

Getting started

In 2014 it was widely reported that supplies of electricity might be threatened during the winter in the UK. National Grid offered to pay businesses to reduce or shut down their energy use during peak hours. The threat to supplies came about from lack of investment in power generation this century and from the loss of capacity due to breakdowns. National Grid, which manages the UK's energy infrastructure, also announced plans to contract additional UK power stations to be on standby, in preparation for high winter demand for lights and heating.

What might happen to future supplies of electricity if the price of oil and gas continues to fall? How might the government affect the future supply of electricity? Will plans to construct some new nuclear power stations avoid winter electricity shortages? What other factors influence the supply of electricity in the UK?

Figure 1

The supply curve for button mushrooms

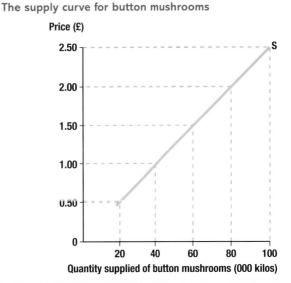

Supply

Supply is the amount of a product which suppliers will offer to the market at a given price. The higher the price of a particular good or service, the more that will be offered to the market. For example, the amount of button mushrooms supplied to a market in any given week may be as shown in Table 1.

These figures have been plotted onto a graph in Figure 1, which shows the **supply curve** for button mushrooms. The supply curve slopes up from left to right. This is because at higher prices a greater quantity will be supplied to the market and at lower prices less will be supplied.

A change in price will cause a movement either up or down the supply curve. The curve will not change its position assuming that all other factors remain the same. There are a number of other factors that may affect supply other than price. Changes in these factors will cause the whole supply curve to shift.

Table 1 The supply schedule for button mushrooms

Price per kilo (£)	Quantity supplied (000 kilos)
0.50	20
1.00	40
1.50	60
2.00	80
2.50	100

Maths tip

Most supply curves slope up from left to right, like the one in Figure 1. This reflects the **direct** relationship that exists between the price of the product and the quantity supplied. It shows that when price goes up, the quantity supplied also goes up. When the price goes down, the quantity supplied goes down.

Thinking bigger

In some circumstances the supply of a product or service may be fixed. If this is the case the supply curve will be vertical. Supply will be fixed if it is impossible for sellers to increase supply even when prices rise. The supply at venues such as cinemas, theatres and sports stadiums may be fixed. For example, the Royal Albert Hall, a major music venue, can accommodate around 6,000 people for the Proms. Even if the price of tickets were to rise, say, from £100 to £300 for a concert, no more seats could be supplied (see Figure 2).

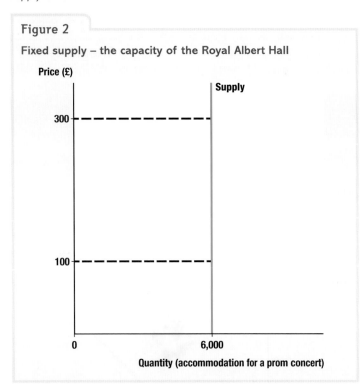

Figure 2

Fixed supply – the capacity of the Royal Albert Hall

Factors leading to a change in supply

The main determinant of supply is price. For most goods and services, when the market price rises suppliers are willing to supply more. This is because they are likely to make more profit at higher prices. However, a number of other factors can lead to a change in supply. Changes in these factors, which are outlined below, will actually shift the supply curve. This is different from a price change, which results in a movement along the supply curve.

Changes in the costs of production: The supply of any product is influenced by the costs of production, such as wages, raw materials, energy, rent and machinery. If production costs rise, sellers are likely to reduce supply. This is because their profits will be reduced. For example, in 2013, Tata Chemicals shut its soda ash factory at Winnington in Northwich. This factory had supplied soda ash for industries such as glass and soap-making since 1874. The factory closed because it was being squeezed by rising gas prices.

A rise in costs will cause the supply curve to shift to the left. This is shown in Figure 3. When costs rise, the whole supply curve will shift to the left, from S to S_2. At a price of P the quantity supplied in the market falls from Q to Q_2. If costs fall, supply will increase because production becomes more profitable. As a result the supply curve will shift to the right. This shows that more is supplied at every price. In Figure 3 the new supply curve would be S_1 and the amount supplied at P will rise from Q to Q_1.

The availability of resources will also affect supply. If there is a shortage in some of the factors of production, such as land, labour, raw materials or capital, it will make it difficult for producers to supply the market. For example, in the UK in 2013 and 2014, it was widely reported that there were labour shortages. Kevin Green, chief executive of the Recruitment & Employment Confederation (REC), suggested that there were around 40 areas of skills shortage, compared to previous years when it was reported as fewer than 10 areas. Engineering skills were reported to be in short supply, including electrical, civil, software and mechanical. IT skills were also reported to be in short supply, including programmers, developers and coders. A shortage of National Health Service nurses and doctors was also reported, along with a need for around 20,000 further teachers in the UK. It was reckoned by many that economic growth would be hampered by the shortages of skilled labour in the UK.

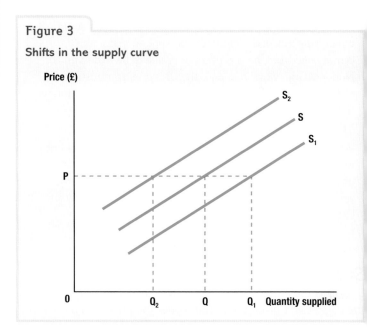

Figure 3

Shifts in the supply curve

Introduction of new technology: As new technology becomes available many businesses will start to use it in their production processes. New technology is usually more efficient than older technology and will help to lower production costs, encouraging firms to offer more for sale. For example, Britain's manufacturers are using cutting-edge technology to improve products and processes in car manufacturing and the aerospace industry. The strength of these two industries since 2008 has helped the revival in manufacturing – a sector of the UK economy that had been declining in the previous 30 years.

The introduction of new technology will shift the supply curve to the right, from S to S_1 in Figure 3. The amount supplied in the market at price P will rise from Q to Q_1.

Question 1

According to farmers and the government, farming might be changed by the increasing number of 'farmbots' used in agriculture. The development of the machines aims to raise efficiency and complete complex tasks that have not been possible with the large-scale agricultural machinery of the past. For example, a 'lettuce bot' can hoe weeds away from the base of young lettuce plants. A 'wine bot' (shown in the photograph) can prune vines, moving through the vineyards. Other bots are under development to remotely check crops for their growth, moisture and signs of disease. Drone technology (use of remotely controlled aircraft) is also being adapted for use on farms. For example, in South America, drones are being used for the surveillance of herds and to monitor crops, and in Japan smaller models are programmed to spray pesticide on crops.

However, there are doubts about how likely it is that new robot technology will take off. Emma Hockridge, head of policy at the Soil Association, has said that: 'The potential use of robots on farms has been discussed for years, but we haven't yet seen anything practical close to reaching the market.'

While the prospect of replacing seasonal workers with robots may be attractive for farm bosses looking to consolidate into bigger units, farm workers may be less keen. Even enthusiasts for the technology think that it will probably be decades before farmbots are used commercially. The head of engineering at Harper Adams University, Professor Simon Blackmore, said that his vision was for "farming with robots in 2050", by which time he believes this should be practical.

Source: adapted from www.theguardian.com

(a) Explain one impact that the introduction of farmbots might have on agriculture.

(b) Draw a diagram and analyse the effect that the introduction of farmbots might have on the supply of food in the UK.

Indirect taxes: Indirect taxes are taxes imposed by the government on spending. VAT and excise duties, such as those levied on petrol and tobacco, are examples of indirect taxes. Such taxes have an effect on supply. When they are imposed or increased, the supply curve will shift to the left, from S to S_2 in Figure 3. This is because indirect taxes represent a cost to firms. If indirect taxes are reduced, the supply curve will shift to the

right, from S to S_1 in Figure 3. This is because costs are lower and firms will be encouraged to supply more in the market.

Following the imposition of an indirect tax, the burden is likely to be shared between the consumer and the producer. The size of the price increase faced by consumers will depend largely on the price elasticity of demand (this is discussed in Unit 7). If an indirect tax is imposed and demand is relatively inelastic, the consumer will bear a greater burden of the tax.

In January 2011 the UK government raised the rate of VAT from 17.5 per cent to 20 per cent. Many argued that this measure would prolong the recession as it acts as a disincentive to producers.

Government subsidies: Sometimes the government may give money to businesses in the form of a grant. This is called a **subsidy**. Subsidies may be given to firms to try and encourage them to produce a particular product. For example, in 2014 the UK government announced that it would give £300 million subsidies to the renewable energies industry to encourage further developments in power generation using renewable power sources. This was part of Britain's plans to cut greenhouse gas emissions by 80 per cent from 1990s levels by 2050. The extra subsidies will be awarded to low-carbon electricity projects, bid for at auctions and distributed on 15-year contracts.

If the government grants a subsidy on a good the effect is to increase its supply. This is because subsidies help to reduce production costs. As a result the supply curve will shift to the right, from S to S_1 in Figure 3.

External shocks: Factors beyond the control of businesses can have an impact on the supply of products. Some examples are outlined below.

- **World events.** Global events can have an impact on the supply of some products. For example, in recent years the political situation in the Middle East has been quite volatile. Consequently, when the situation becomes hostile, supplies of oil are threatened and the price rises. This is because a significant proportion of the global oil supply comes from this region.

  In 2008, the global financial crisis led to a 'credit crunch'. This meant that many firms were unable to borrow the money they needed to trade and invest for the future. As a result some businesses collapsed and others were unable to grow.
- **Weather.** The supply of agricultural products in particular can be affected by the weather. Good growing conditions will result in high crop yields and increased supply. Conversely, bad weather, such as a drought, can reduce crop yields severely and cause shortages. In 2014, there were bumper crops of wheat in Europe and the Black Sea region due to favourable growing conditions. The increase in the global supply of wheat helped to reduce prices.

  Bad weather, such as snow storms, can disrupt the supply of many goods in the short term, for instance by hampering the distribution of goods due to closed roads, railway lines and airports.
- **Government.** Government economic policies can have an impact on supply. For example, if the Bank of England increased interest rates (in order to meet a government

inflation target), this could increase business costs for firms with debt. Borrowing to invest might also be discouraged.

Government legislation can have an impact on supply. For example, if the government passes laws to make a particular market more competitive, then supply in that market is likely to increase as new entrants join the market.

- **Price of related goods.** In some markets supply can be affected by price changes of related goods. For example, if an arable farmer producing mainly potatoes sees that the price of carrots and parsnips are rising in the market place, their response might be to grow more carrots and parsnips next season instead of potatoes. As a consequence the supply of potatoes could fall.

Case study

THE SUPPLY OF NEW HOUSES IN THE UK

In 2007 house prices peaked in the UK. The average price was over £180,000. Then the financial crisis of 2008 caused prices to fall sharply back down to around an average of £150,000 in 2009. However, since then house prices have risen again. As the population in the UK rises, demand for housing increases. Unfortunately this has not been matched by an equivalent increase in the supply. Figure 4 shows the number of new houses built by the private sector over the last 10 years. Some new houses have been built by the public sector but the numbers are very small in comparison.

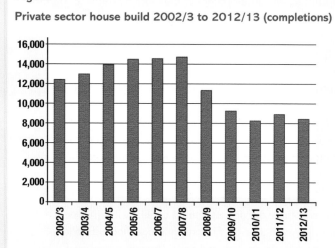

Figure 4

Private sector house build 2002/3 to 2012/13 (completions)

Source: adapted from www.shelter.org.uk

(c) Explain the impact that higher land prices would have on the supply of houses. (4 marks)

(d) Assess the possible factors that have reduced the supply of new houses in the private sector in recent years. (12 marks)

Q

(a) What is meant by supply? (2 marks)

(b) Explain one effect on the supply of housing if construction companies were given a government subsidy. (4 marks)

Knowledge check

1. Describe the relationship between price and the quantity supplied in a market.
2. What is meant by fixed supply?
3. What might happen to the supply of laptop computers if wages of assembly workers rose significantly?
4. How might a fall in gold prices affect the supply of gold wedding rings?
5. What impact does the introduction of new technology have on the supply of goods and services?
6. What would happen to the supply curve for gardening services if VAT was increased?
7. Why is the supply of a good or service likely to increase if the government grants producers a subsidy?
8. How can government legislation affect supply?
9. State two external shocks that might affect the global supply of oil.

Key terms

Subsidy – a grant given to producers, usually to encourage production of a certain good.
Supply – the amount of a product that suppliers make available to the market at any given price in a given period of time.
Supply curve – a line drawn on a graph that shows how much of a good sellers are willing to supply at different prices.

6 Markets

Key points

1. The interaction of supply and demand.
2. The drawing and interpretation of supply and demand diagrams to show the causes and consequences of price changes.

Getting started

The prices of some goods change slowly over time; others are more volatile. For example, it was widely reported that the global price of oil was around $90 per barrel in October 2014. By the end of December the price had fallen to around $55. The price of flowers can increase greatly in the few days leading up to Mother's Day. On Christmas Day and New Year's Eve it is common for taxi drivers to double their prices. In general, prices are determined by the interaction of supply and demand.

What market factor do you think has the most influence on the price of oil? Why does the price of flowers rise by so much in the run up to Mother's Day? Why can't taxi drivers double their prices all year round?

The interaction of supply and demand

In any market the price is set where the wishes of consumers are matched exactly with those of producers. This price, called the equilibrium price, is where supply and demand are equal. The way in which the forces of supply and demand determine prices in a market can be shown graphically. Figure 1 shows the supply and demand curves for button mushrooms. Here the equilibrium price is £1.50. At this price consumers want to buy 60,000 kilos and producers want to sell 60,000 kilos. There is no other price where this happens. For example, if the price were £2, sellers would want to supply 80,000 kilos. However, at this price, buyers only demand 40,000 kilos because the price is too high.

The equilibrium price is also known as the market clearing price. This is because the amount supplied in the market is completely bought up by consumers. There are no buyers left without goods and there are no sellers left with unsold stock. The market is cleared.

Figure 1 also shows the total revenue or total expenditure at the equilibrium price. Total revenue is the amount of money generated from the sale of output. It is calculated by multiplying price and quantity.

Total revenue (TR) = Price (P) × Quantity (Q)

In Figure 1, total revenue at the equilibrium price of £1.50 is:

TR = P × Q = £1.50 × 60,000 = £90,000

There are many different factors that can cause a change in supply or demand. When such changes occur the supply and demand curves will shift. As a result there will be a change in the equilibrium price.

Figure 1

The demand for and supply of button mushrooms

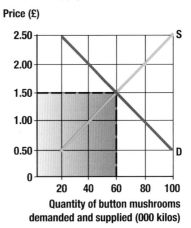

Question 1

During the summer months, livestock, such as cows and horses, are left to roam in fields and eat grass. However, in the winter many of them are housed under cover and need to be fed on hay. The market for large, round hay bales is represented by the supply and demand curves shown in Figure 2.

Figure 2

The market for large, round hay bales

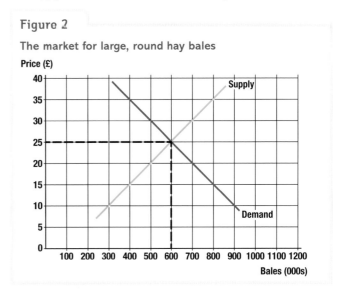

(a) State the equilibrium price and quantity.

(b) Using this diagram, explain what is meant by equilibrium price.

(c) What is the value of total revenue at the equilibrium price?

Changes in demand

If demand increases, price will rise. This is because producers react to rising consumer demand by putting up their prices. They can do this because customers are wanting the product in higher numbers. In Figure 3(a), an increase in demand for a product is shown by a shift in the demand curve to the right, from D to D_1. This changes the equilibrium price because supply and demand are now equal at a different point. The price is forced up from P to P_1 and the amount sold in the market has gone up from Q to Q_1.

If demand were to fall, the opposite would happen. This is because producers are forced to lower their prices. Otherwise they would be left with too much unsold stock. They are forced to do this because customers are wanting much less of the product. The demand curve would shift to the left from D to D_2 and the price would fall to P_2. The amount traded in the market would fall from Q to Q_2.

Figure 3

The effect on equilibrium price of a change in demand and supply

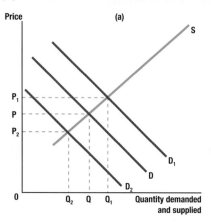

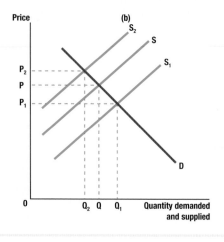

Question 2

In 2014, the UK enjoyed one of the warmest and sunniest summers on record. Demand for a number of summer-related products soared. One example was gas-fired BBQs. Figure 4 shows the market for such a product.

Figure 4

The market for gas-fired BBQs

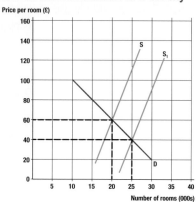

(a) Explain one reason for the shift in the demand curve from D to D_1.

(b) What has happened to the equilibrium price and quantity as a result of the shift in demand?

Changes in supply

A change in supply will also affect equilibrium price. For example, if supply increases the price will fall. In Figure 3(b), an increase in supply for the product is shown by a shift in the

Worked example

Figure 5 shows the market for accommodation in a UK city. The equilibrium price per room is currently £60. What might happen to the price of rooms if some new hotels open up?

The arrival of new hotels in the city would increase the supply of rooms available. This would shift the supply curve to the right from S to S_1. As a result the equilibrium price per room is forced down from £60 to £40. The equilibrium number of rooms let rises from 20,000 to 25,000.

Figure 5

The market for accommodation in a UK city

supply curve to the right, from S to S₁. This changes equilibrium price because supply and demand are now equal at a different point. The price is forced down from P to P₁ and the amount sold on the market has gone up from Q to Q₁. If supply were to fall, the opposite would happen. The supply curve would shift to the left from S to S₂, price would rise from P to P₂ and the amount traded in the market would fall from Q to Q₂.

Changes in supply and demand together

It is possible for both supply and demand to change at the same time in a market. For example, demand might increase and supply decrease at the same time. This is shown in Figure 6. The original equilibrium price is P where S = D. The increase in demand is represented by a shift to the right from D to D₁. The decrease in supply is represented by a shift to the left from S to S₁. The new equilibrium price, where D₁ = S₁, is P₁. The price is higher and the amount sold in the market has fallen from Q to Q₁.

Figure 6

A change in supply and demand

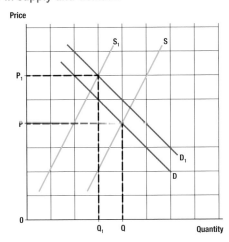

Note that it would be possible to redraw the diagram to show that, although the price will be higher, the quantity sold could also be higher. To do this it would be necessary to make the increase in demand greater than the decrease in supply. When there is a change in both supply and demand, it is not possible to show exactly what will happen to price and quantity unless it is known precisely by how much supply and demand shift.

Disequilibrium in the market

If the price in a particular market is not set at the point where supply and demand are equal, there will be **disequilibrium** in the market. Two situations might occur.

Excess demand: If the price charged in a market is below the equilibrium price, supply and demand will not be equal. In Figure 7 the equilibrium price for button mushrooms is £1.50. At this price, supply and demand are both 60,000 kilos. However, if the price is set lower, say at 50p a kilo, the market is not in equilibrium. At this lower price demand is 100,000 kilos and supply is only 20,000 kilos. There is **excess demand**, which means there is a shortage of goods in the market. In this case there is a shortage of 80,000 kilos (100,000–20,000).

Figure 7

The excess demand for and excess supply of button mushrooms

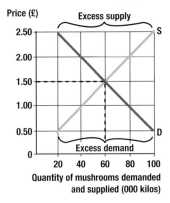

Excess supply: If the price charged is set above the equilibrium price, again, supply and demand are not equal. In Figure 7, if the price is set higher, say at £2.50, demand is only 20,000 kilos while supply is 100,000 kilos. This time there is **excess supply**, which means that goods would remain unsold. In this case, the quantity of unsold goods is 80,000 kilos (100,000–20,000).

Thinking bigger

Every year the FA Cup Final is played at Wembley Stadium. Unfortunately, there are never enough tickets for all the supporters that would like to go; there is always a shortage. The English FA are aware of this, but don't set the price very high as they say that they would prefer to keep the tickets 'reasonably priced' so that genuine football supporters can afford to go to the match. Evidence of ticket shortages is shown by the price of tickets on the 'black market' (an illegal market where touts sell tickets above face value). In some years a ticket with a face value of £60 might be sold for £500 or more. Figure 8 is an illustration of what is happening in the market. Note that the supply curve is vertical because supply is fixed. The capacity of Wembley Stadium is 90,000.

Figure 8

The market for FA Cup Final tickets

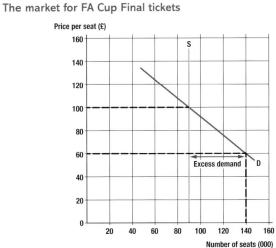

In Figure 8, the average price of tickets is set at £60 per ticket. At this price there is excess demand of 50,000. This is because the price is set below the equilibrium, which in this example is £100 per ticket.

Case study

THE MARKET FOR READY MIXED CONCRETE

The construction industry has suffered badly since the financial crisis of 2008 and the subsequent recession. Output in the construction sector fell faster than the economy as a whole in 2008. 2009 saw the sector recover faster than the economy as a whole, but during 2010 and 2011 growth was flat. There was another contraction in 2012 but the sector grew through 2013. In 2014 the industry was still 11.6 per cent down on the 2007 level.

Many of the companies operating in the sector have struggled to remain profitable. Some of the marginal operators have left the market. One important part of the supply chain in the construction industry is the contribution made by suppliers of ready mixed concrete. This is concrete that can be transported to building sites and pumped directly to where it is needed. When the construction industry declined, demand for ready mixed concrete naturally fell. The price of ready mixed concrete can vary depending on how much is purchased, but a builder can expect to pay around £100 per cubic metre.

Sources: adapted from Parliament briefing papers: *The construction industry: statistics and policy, House of Commons* and www.singletrackworld.com

Q

(a) Explain one factor that might cause excess supply of ready mixed cement. (4 marks)

(b) Using a supply and demand diagram, illustrate the impact on the market for ready mixed concrete of the decline in the construction industry. (4 marks)

(c) Using a supply and demand diagram, illustrate the impact on the market for ready mixed concrete if a number of suppliers are forced out of business. (4 marks)

(d) Assess the impact on the price of ready mixed concrete of both a decline in the construction industry and the collapse of several suppliers. (8 marks)

Key terms

Equilibrium price or market clearing price – the price where supply and demand are equal.
Excess demand – the position where demand is greater than supply at a given price and there are shortages in the market.
Excess supply – the position where supply is greater than demand at a given price and there are unsold goods in the market.
Total revenue or total expenditure – the amount of revenue generated from the sale of goods calculated by multiplying price by quantity in a given period of time.

Knowledge check

1. Explain how the prices of goods and services are determined.
2. What is meant by the equilibrium price?
3. What will happen to the equilibrium price if there is a fall in demand?
4. What will happen to the equilibrium price if there is a fall in supply?
5. What is meant by fixed supply?
6. What would cause excess demand in a market?
7. What will happen to the equilibrium price if there is both an increase in demand and a fall in supply?

Exam tip

When drawing supply and demand curves you need to remember that demand curves always slope down from left to right and supply curves slope up from left to right (unless supply is fixed). You also need to remember to label the axes correctly. Marks may be awarded in examinations for labelling axes correctly and showing clearly the units measured.

7 Price elasticity of demand

Key points

1. Calculation of price elasticity of demand.
2. Interpretation of numerical values of price elasticity of demand.
3. The factors influencing price elasticity of demand.
4. The significance of price elasticity of demand to businesses in terms of implications for pricing.
5. Calculation and interpretation of the relationship between price elasticity of demand and total revenue.

Getting started

Albert Rogers owns a milk round in Dorset. He delivers milk to over 300 homes in the town. However, 30 years ago his business used to deliver to over 1,000 homes. The business has been hit hard by competition from retailers, particularly supermarkets, selling cheap milk. In 2013 he decided that he would need to generate more revenue. He raised the price of a pint of fresh milk (delivered to the doorstep) from 50p to 60p. As a result sales fell from 16,000 bottles to 12,000 bottles a month.

Calculate the total revenue the business earned (price x quantity sold) before the increase in price. Now calculate the revenue it earned after it increased price. Was the price increase a wise move for the business? Do you think the same would happen to any business that raised its price by 20 per cent?

Figure 1

The effect of a price change on the demand for products A and B

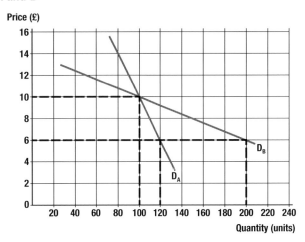

What is price elasticity of demand?

For some goods a price change will result in a large change in demand and for others a smaller change. Figure 1 helps to illustrate this. Two demand curves (D_A and D_B) are shown with different slopes representing two different products: A and B. The demand curve for product A is steep and the demand curve for product B is flatter. At a price of £10, demand for both products is 100 units. However, when the price falls to £6 demand increases by different amounts for each product. Demand for product A only increases slightly to 120 units. But for product B demand increases a lot more to 200 units. Demand for product B is more **responsive** to the price change. This relationship that exists between the responsiveness of demand and a change in price is called price elastic demand.

Price inelastic demand

In Figure 1, for product A, the price change resulted in a less than proportionate change in demand. This means that the change in demand was not as big as the change in price. Price fell by 40 per cent (from £10 to £6) but demand only increased by 20 per cent (from 100 units to 120 units). When this happens economists say that the good has price inelastic demand or that demand is price inelastic. A minority of goods, such as petrol, have price inelastic demand.

Price elastic demand

In Figure 1, for product B, the price change resulted in a more than proportionate change in demand. This means that the change in demand was greater than the change in price. Price fell by 40 per cent (from £10 to £6) while demand increased by 100 per cent (from 100 units to 200 units). When this happens economists say that the good has price elastic demand or that demand is price elastic. Goods with elastic demand are more responsive to price changes. Most goods have price elastic demand.

Calculation of price elasticity of demand

It is possible to calculate the price elasticity of demand of a good using the formula shown below.

$$\text{Price elasticity of demand} = \frac{\text{Percentage change in quantity demanded}}{\text{Percentage change in price}}$$

Maths tip

In the formula for elasticity calculation you need to work out percentage changes. The method below can be used.

$$\text{Percentage change} = \frac{\text{Difference between the two numbers}}{\text{Original number}} \times 100$$

The percentage change in the quantity demanded for product A is:

$$\text{Percentage change} = \frac{(120 - 100) \times 100}{100} = \frac{20 \times 100}{100} = 20\%$$

Worked example

For product A in Figure 1, the price elasticity of demand would be:

$$= \frac{20\%}{-40\%} = -0.5$$

For product B in Figure 1, the price elasticity of demand would be:

$$= \frac{100\%}{-40\%} = -2.5$$

Maths tip

There is a minus number in the calculation above because the price fell by 40 per cent (from £10 to £6). Since the price change was negative a minus sign must be shown. Whenever price or demand falls in the calculation, it is proper, and may be helpful, to show the minus sign.

Interpretation of numerical values of price elasticity of demand

The values calculated above show whether demand is price elastic or price inelastic.

- If the value of price elasticity is **less than 1** (i.e. a fraction or a decimal), demand is said to be **price inelastic**. Demand for product A in Figure 1 is price inelastic because price elasticity is – 0.5.
- If the value of price elasticity is **greater than 1**, demand is said to be **price elastic.** Demand for product B in Figure 1 is price elastic because price elasticity is – 2.5.
- Note that the minus sign is not used to determine whether goods are price elastic or price inelastic. It is enough to focus on the numerical value.

Question 1

Coolpop Ltd sells fizzy citrus drinks in the very competitive soft drinks market. In 2013, the company sold 2,000,000 cans of Lemon Coolpop at a price of 50p. In 2014, the company decided to reduce the price of Lemon Coolpop to try and win a bigger market share. The price was reduced to 40p and sales rose to 2,600,000.

(a) Calculate the price elasticity of demand for Coolpop.

(b) State whether demand is price elastic or price inelastic.

The factors influencing price elasticity of demand

The value of price elasticity of demand for a product is mainly determined by the ease with which customers can switch to other similar substitute products. A number of factors is likely to determine this.

- **Time.** Price elasticity of demand tends to fall the longer the time period. This is mainly because consumers and businesses are more likely to turn to substitutes in the long term. For example, the demand for fuel oil is highly price inelastic in the short term. If the price of petrol goes up 20 per cent in a week, the fall in quantity demanded is likely to be only a few per cent. This is because car owners have to use their cars to get to work or to go shopping. But over a ten-year period, car owners will tend to buy more fuel-efficient cars. Businesses with boilers using oil may replace these with gas boilers. Homeowners with oil-fired central heating systems might install more insulation in their houses to cut running costs or change to gas boilers. As a result, demand for oil in the long run is likely to be price elastic.
- **Competition for the same product.** Some businesses face highly price elastic demand for their products. This is because they are in very competitive markets, where their product is either identical (i.e. are perfect substitutes) or little different from those produced by other businesses. Farmers, for example, when selling wheat or potatoes are in this position. If they push their prices above the market price, they won't be able to sell their crop. Customers will simply buy elsewhere at the lower market price.
- **Branding.** Some products are branded. The stronger the branding, the less substitutes are acceptable to customers. For example, many buyers of Kellogg's corn flakes do not see own-label brands, such as Tesco or Asda cornflakes, as good substitutes for Kellogg's. They will often pay 50 per cent more to buy Kellogg's rather than another brand. Successful branding therefore reduces the price elasticity of demand for the product.
- **The proportion of income spent on a product.** For inexpensive products, where the proportion of a consumer's income spent on the transaction is very small, demand is likely to be price inelastic. For example, if the price of a box of matches rises by 20 per cent from 10p to 12p, the fall in demand is likely to be a lot less than 20 per cent because the amounts of money involved are 'trivial'. In contrast, the demand for products where the proportion of a consumer's income spent on the transaction is much larger is likely to be price elastic. For example, if the price of a car rises by 20 per cent from £20,000 to £24,000, there is likely to be a more than proportionate fall in demand (i.e. greater than 20 per cent). This is because the increase in price of £4,000 is likely to deter a significant number of consumers from purchasing the product. £4,000 will represent a sizable proportion of many consumer's incomes.

- **Product types vs the product of an individual business.** Most products are made and sold by a number of different businesses. Petrol, for example, is processed and sold by companies such as Shell, Esso and Total. The major supermarkets also sell petrol which they have bought from independent refiners. The demand for petrol is price inelastic in the short term. But the demand for Shell petrol or Esso petrol is price elastic. This is because petrol has no real substitutes in the short term. But Esso petrol is a very good substitute for Shell petrol. In general, a product category like petrol, carpets or haircuts has a much lower price elasticity of demand than products within that category made by individual businesses.

However strong the branding and however little the competition that an individual product faces, it is still likely that a business will sell at a price where demand is price elastic. To understand why, consider a product which has price inelastic demand. As explained above, raising the price of the product would increase sales revenue. It would also reduce sales and costs of production would fall. So profits would rise. A profit-maximising firm should therefore continue raising price until demand is price elastic.

If demand is price elastic, raising price leads to a fall in sales revenue, but also a fall in costs because less is sold. At the profit-maximising point, any further increase in price would see the fall in sales revenue being greater than the fall in costs.

This would suggest that even strongly branded goods, such as Coca-Cola or McDonald's meals, have a price elasticity of demand greater than one at the price at which they are sold. It also suggests that luxury brands, such as Chanel or Gucci, also have price elastic demand at their current price.

Price elasticity of demand and pricing

A business may consider price elasticity of demand when setting the prices of its products. For a minority of products demand is price inelastic. This means that if a business raises its price there will be a less than proportionate fall in demand. For example, if a business (selling a product that is price inelastic) raises price by 10 per cent, demand might fall by, say, 7 per cent. This suggests that raising price when selling products with inelastic demand would be a good strategy.

Since 2007 in the UK, energy companies selling gas and electricity have increased their prices substantially. Figure 2 shows that the price of gas, for example, has almost doubled between 2007 and 2013. However, there is no evidence that demand has fallen by any significant amount (if at all). This suggests that demand for gas and electricity is price inelastic and energy companies can increase price without suffering any significant fall in demand.

If goods have price elastic demand, a price change will result in a more than proportionate change in demand. For example, if a business selling a product that is price elastic raises the price by 10 per cent, demand might fall by, say, 18 per cent. This suggests that raising the price when selling products with price elastic demand would **not** be a good strategy. However, if the business lowers the price, demand

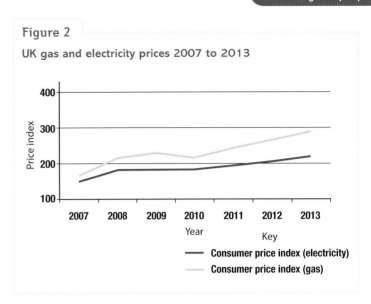

Figure 2

UK gas and electricity prices 2007 to 2013

Key
— Consumer price index (electricity)
···· Consumer price index (gas)

will rise by a larger proportion than the price cut. This might help to explain the success of low-cost supermarkets, such as Aldi and Lidl. Their sales have risen significantly, probably due to charging lower prices in a highly competitive market.

Price elasticity of demand and total revenue

When a business changes its price there will be a change in demand and therefore a change in total revenue. It would be useful for a business to know what effect a particular price change might have on total revenue. The value of price elasticity can help here. In Figure 1, the demand for product A is price inelastic and the demand for product B is price elastic. At the price of £10 the demand for both products is 100 units. However, when the price falls demand for product A rises to 120 units while the demand for B rises to 200 units. The different effects on total revenue for each product are outlined below.

For product A: When the price falls from £10 to £6 there is an increase in demand from 100 units to 120 units. This means that total revenue will change. This is shown by the following calculations.

When P = £10 TR = £10 × 100 = £1,000
When P = £6 TR = £6 × 120 = £720

The price reduction from £10 to £6 has resulted in a £280 fall in total revenue (£1,000 – £720). This shows that when demand is inelastic, a price cut will cause total revenue to fall. The opposite will happen if the price is increased. If demand is inelastic, a price increase will cause total revenue to rise.

For product B: When the price falls from £10 to £6, demand rises from 100 units to 200 units. The effect on total revenue is calculated below.

When P = £10 TR = £10 × 100 = £1,000
When P = £6 TR = £6 × 200 = £1,200

This time, for product B, the price reduction has resulted in a £200 increase in revenue from £1,000 to £1,200. This shows that when demand is price elastic, a price cut will result in an increase in total revenue. The opposite will happen if the price is increased. If demand is price elastic, a price increase will cause total revenue to fall. The effect of price changes on total revenue for different price elasticities is summarised in Table 1.

Table 1 The effect of price changes on total revenue when demand is elastic and inelastic

Price elasticity	Value of elasticity	Price change	Effect on TR
Inelastic	< 1	Decrease	Fall
Inelastic	< 1	Increase	Rise
Elastic	> 1	Decrease	Rise
Elastic	> 1	Increase	Fall

To conclude, if businesses know the value of price elasticity for their products, they can predict the effect on total revenue of any price changes they make. They will know, for example, that if demand for their product is elastic, a price reduction will increase total revenue. This might help to explain why many rail companies charge lower prices for off-peak rail travel. By lowering the price more travellers are attracted and revenue rises. Demand during the off-peak period must be price elastic.

Question 2

Cheryl Newman runs a pizza takeaway restaurant called GrandPizza in a large town in Cornwall. The market for pizzas is competitive and she faces very stiff competition from Domino's Pizza in particular. However, she has traded profitably for nearly five years. She provides excellent customer service and uses a combination of flour and semolina to make the pizza bases, which gives them a distinctive taste.

In 2013, she wondered if she could increase her sales by undercutting her rivals. For example, a large cheese and tomato pizza from Domino's Pizza costs just under £12. Cheryl currently charges £10 for an equivalent product. She is considering a price cut to £8 to make the price difference more significant. Cheryl has done some research and reckons that the price elasticity of demand for her pizzas is about −2. In 2013 Cheryl sold 10,000 cheese and tomato pizzas.

(a) Calculate the number of pizzas Cheryl would expect to sell in 2014 if she cut the price to £8.

(b) Calculate the change in total revenue resulting from the price change above.

(c) Assess whether Cheryl's decision to cut the price might be successful.

Exam tip

A common mistake made by students in examinations relates to products with inelastic demand. Sometimes students say 'demand for product x is inelastic. This means that a business can raise the price and there will be no change in demand'. This is not the case. Even when demand is price inelastic, a price change will still cause a change in demand. It is just that the percentage change in demand is smaller than the percentage change in price.

Thinking bigger

When using price elasticity of demand to help make pricing decisions, businesses need to be aware of some possible drawbacks with the concept. The main problem is the origin of elasticity values. A business might estimate the value of price elasticity by measuring the effect on sales of previous price changes. For example, if a business cut the price by 12 per cent four years ago and demand rose by 18 per cent, price elasticity would be −1.5. However, this data is historic; what happened four years ago may not happen again in the future.

Another way of estimating elasticity values is to carry out market research to find out how consumers will react to price changes in the future. This would give more up-to-date values, but there could be problems with the accuracy of the data collected by market researchers. For example, the sample may not be representative or consumers might not behave in the way they said they would. Consequently the data would be flawed. Businesses need to be aware, therefore, that elasticity values may not be entirely accurate.

Knowledge check

1. What is meant by price elasticity of demand?

2. Give two examples of products that might have inelastic demand.

3. What is the formula for calculating price elasticity of demand?

4. The price of a product is increased by 8 per cent; as a result demand falls by 12 per cent. Calculate price elasticity of demand.

5. The price elasticity of demand for a product is −0.67. What will happen to total revenue if price is reduced?

6. The price elasticity of demand for a product is −2.7. What will happen to total revenue if price is raised?

7. State two factors that affect the price elasticity of demand for a product.

Key terms

Price elastic demand – a change in price results in a greater change in demand.
Price elasticity of demand – the responsiveness of demand to a change in price.
Price inelastic demand – a change in price results in a proportionately smaller change in demand.

Case study

THOMPSON ENGINEERING LTD

Thompson Engineering Ltd is a family business based in Chesterfield. The company makes three components for the engines that power microlights. The work undertaken by the company is quite specialised and it was thought that few rivals operated in the same market. At the end of 2013 the company had to make some modifications to two of the components, A and C. This was to comply with some new health and safety specifications. As a result the directors decided to raise the price of these two components by 20 per cent in 2014. Some financial information for the three components is shown in Table 2.

Table 2 Financial information and price elasticity of demand (PED) for three products (2013)

	Price	Sales	PED
Component A	£10	100,000	−0.8
Component B	£7	150,000	−1.1
Component C	£5	300,000	−1.2

(a) What is meant by the term 'price elastic demand'? (2 marks)

(b) Explain one factor that might affect the price elasticity of demand. (4 marks)

(c) Calculate the expected change in revenue generated by product A in 2014 if the price is increased by 20 per cent. (4 marks)

(d) Calculate the expected change in revenue generated by product C in 2014 if the price is increased by 20 per cent. (4 marks)

(e) Assess the possible impact on Thompson Engineering Ltd of the price changes. (12 marks)

8 Income elasticity of demand

Getting started

The demand for some products can be affected by changes in income. However, for some other products changes in income will have very little impact on demand.
Look at the two photographs below.

How do you think changes in income will affect demand for the two products? What would you expect to happen to the demand for luxury goods in the next 20 years? Can you think of any goods for which demand might actually fall if incomes rose? What might account for this fall in demand?

What is income elasticity of demand?

One of the main factors that can change the demand for products is the amount of income consumers have to spend. **Income elasticity of demand** measures the responsiveness of demand to a change in income.

Consider two products: A and B. If incomes rise by 10 per cent and demand for product A rises by 25 per cent, the change in demand is proportionately greater than the change in income. Economists would say that demand for product A is **income elastic**. Demand for many goods and services is income elastic. Examples might include cars, fashion accessories, entertainment, holidays and a wide range of luxury goods.

In contrast, if demand for product B only rose by 5 per cent, economists would say that demand for product B is **income inelastic**. This is because the percentage increase (or change) in demand is proportionately less than the percentage increase (or change) in income. Demand for some goods and services may be income inelastic. Examples are likely to be essential goods, such as milk, food in general and heating fuel.

Calculation of income elasticity of demand

It is possible to calculate the income elasticity of demand for a good using the formula:

$$\text{Income elasticity of demand} = \frac{\text{Percentage change in quantity demanded}}{\text{Percentage change in income}}$$

Worked example

For product A in the earlier example, income elasticity of demand would be:

$$\frac{25\%}{10\%} = \mathbf{2.5}$$

For product B in the earlier example, income elasticity of demand would be:

$$\frac{5\%}{10\%} = \mathbf{0.5}$$

Interpretation of the numerical values of income elasticity of demand

The values calculated above show whether demand is income elastic or income inelastic.

- If the value of income elasticity is **greater than 1**, demand is said to be **income elastic**. Demand for product A is income elastic because income elasticity is 2.5. This means that the change in demand is proportionately greater than the change in income.

- If the value of income elasticity of demand is **less than 1**, demand is said to be **income inelastic**. Demand for product B is income inelastic because income elasticity is 0.5. This means that the change in demand is proportionately less than the change in income.

The value of income elasticity can also show whether goods are **normal goods** or **inferior goods**. For normal goods, where an increase in income results in an increase in demand, the value of income elasticity will be **positive (+)**. Products A and B above are both normal goods because income elasticity is positive in both cases. For inferior goods, where, for example, an increase in income results in a decrease in demand, the value of income elasticity will be **negative (−)**. Some examples are shown in Table 1.

Table 1 Some examples of goods with different income elasticities of demand

Good	Income elasticity	Elastic or inelastic	Type of good	The effect of a 10% increase in income
Product W	0.6	Inelastic	Normal	Demand would increase by 6%
Product X	−2.4	Elastic	Inferior	Demand would fall by 24%
Product Y	1.9	Elastic	Normal	Demand would rise by 19%
Product Z	−0.8	Inelastic	Inferior	Demand would fall by 8%

Maths tip

Always show the positive (+) and negative (−) signs when performing elasticity calculations. If you leave a negative sign out, you could end up getting a wrong answer. The signs also tell you whether the good is normal or inferior.

Question 1

Healy Ltd is a paper merchant. The company sells standard A4 paper to a wide variety of stationers, other retailers and office equipment suppliers. In 2014, incomes rose by two per cent; as a result, demand for paper rose from 2,000,000 reams to 2,030,000 reams.

(a) Calculate the income elasticity of demand for paper in this case.
(b) Explain whether (i) demand for paper in this case is income elastic or income inelastic and (ii) whether paper is a normal good or an inferior good.

The factors influencing income elasticity of demand

The main factor affecting income elasticity of demand is whether or not goods are **necessities** or **luxuries**.

- **Necessities** are basic goods that consumers need to buy. Examples include food in general, electricity and water. Demand for these types of goods will be income inelastic. Another example of a good which has income inelastic demand is cigarettes. A study in Ukraine a number of years ago found that the income elasticity of demand for cigarettes was 0.06. It could be argued that cigarettes are a necessity once people become addicted to them.
- **Luxuries** are goods that consumers like to buy if they can afford them. Spending on these types of goods is **discretionary**, which means that it does not have to be undertaken. Demand for these goods is income elastic. Examples include air travel, satellite television, fashion accessories, and many goods and services in the leisure and tourism industry. It is also argued that the demand for imported goods is income elastic. It has been found that as developing nations become better off, their demand for imports rises significantly.
- The price of a product relative to incomes can also influence income elasticity. Demand for products that are relatively cheap, such as pencils, will tend to be income inelastic. However, demand for expensive items, such as houses, will be income elastic.

The significance of income elasticity of demand to businesses

Businesses may be interested in income elasticity of demand because changes in income in the economy can affect the demand for their products.

Businesses selling goods with high income elasticity: The demand for goods that are very sensitive to changes in income (i.e. highly income elastic) is often cyclical. This means that when the economy is growing, demand for these types of goods, such as air travel, restaurants and luxury goods, is also growing. But when the economy falls into recession, demand also falls. This can cause difficulties for such businesses. During a recession they may lay off workers and postpone or cancel investment projects. Forecasting demand for goods that are influenced by the business cycle can be quite difficult. The business cycle is discussed in Unit 41.

Businesses selling goods with low income elasticity: Demand for goods that are income inelastic tends to be more stable during the different phases in the business cycle. For example, farmers are much less affected by income changes because demand for many food products is fairly stable. This makes production planning and investment decisions a little easier. In countries where economic growth is steady, over a period of time the demand for inferior goods and normal necessities tends to decline. It could be argued that businesses operating in these sectors should attempt to diversify into goods with higher income elasticity of demand in the long run.

Production planning: If businesses know the income elasticity of demand for their products they can respond to predicted changes in incomes. Businesses that produce goods that have income elastic demand will expect changes in income to affect demand. So if incomes are expected to rise in the future they can plan ahead, making sure they have enough capacity, for example. On the other hand, if a recession is expected, these businesses would plan to cut output. This is because incomes are likely to fall during a recession. In 2008, as a result of the global recession, car manufacturers started to cut their output. For example, it was widely reported that Honda, the Japanese car manufacturer, halted production at their UK Swindon factory for four months between February and March 2009. On the other hand, producers of inferior goods might start to build capacity if they believed a recession was coming. When incomes fall, demand for inferior goods, such as those sold by low-cost 'no-frills' supermarkets, starts to rise.

Product switching: Some manufacturers have flexible resources and can switch from the production of one good to another. For example, a manufacturer of plastic moulded products may be able to switch from the production of plastic household goods to plastic toys. A predicted rise in incomes may encourage such a business to make more plastic toys if demand for them was income elastic.

Case study

FRESHBAKE LTD

Figure 1

UK gross domestic product (GDP) per capita (average individual income) between 2004 and 2014

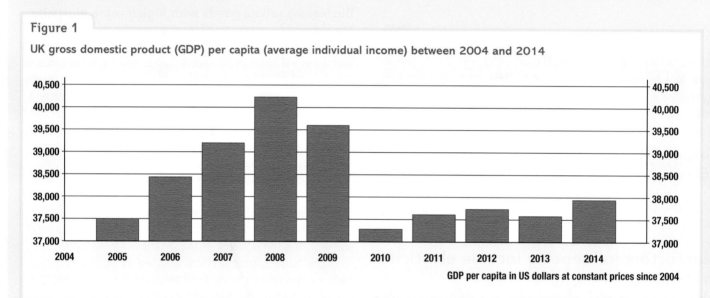

GDP per capita in US dollars at constant prices since 2004

Source: adapted from www.tradingeconomics.com

Freshbake Ltd is a large baker in the West Midlands. It delivers to independent retailers and small supermarkets in the region. Up until 2003, 80 per cent of its sales were bread, bread rolls and other bread-related products.

In 2003 it started to focus more on the market for cakes – fresh cream cakes in particular. The switch in emphasis paid off. By 2008, slightly more than 40 per cent of Freshbake's revenue was from the sale of cakes – while sales of bread products remained stable.

Unfortunately, between 2008 and 2010, sales of cakes fell sharply. This caused the business difficulties. It had built up cake-baking capacity since 2003 and the fall in demand from 2008 meant that staff had to be laid off and some investment in new machinery cancelled. It was estimated by the business that income elasticity of demand for bread and cakes was 0.6 and 3.9 respectively. Figure 1 shows UK GDP per capita (average individual income) between 2004 and 2014.

Q

(a) What is meant by the term income inelastic demand? (2 marks)

(b) Assuming average income fell by 7 per cent, calculate the percentage change in demand for Freshbake's cakes between 2008 and 2010. (4 marks)

(c) Explain one reason why demand for Freshbake's cakes changed between 2008 and 2010. (4 marks)

(d) Assess how useful income elasticity is for a business like Freshbake Ltd. (12 marks)

Key terms

Discretionary expenditure – non-essential spending or spending that is not automatic.

Income elastic demand – the percentage change in demand for a product is proportionately greater than the percentage change in income.

Income elasticity of demand – the responsiveness of demand to a change in income.

Income inelastic demand – where the percentage change in demand is proportionately less than the percentage change in income.

Knowledge check

1. What does it mean when it is said that a good is 'income elastic'?

2. Give two examples of goods that might be income inelastic.

3. What is the formula for calculating income elasticity of demand?

4. If incomes rise by 12 per cent and demand rises by 20 per cent, what is income elasticity of demand?

5. A good has income elasticity of −0.9. Is this good normal or inferior?

6. State two factors that might affect income elasticity of demand.

7. Why are imports believed to be income elastic?

8. State two implications of income elasticity for businesses.

Product/service design

Key points

1. Design mix: function, aesthetics and cost.
2. Changes in elements of the design mix to reflect social trends, such as:
   - concern over resource depletion
   - designing for waste minimisation, re-use and recycling
   - ethical sourcing.

Getting started

Look at the product in the image. Do you like the design? Explain your reasons. State three factors that might be important when designing a product like this. How might the design be affected by changes in social trends, such as health and safety issues, resource depletion and waste minimisation?

Design mix

When designing any product or service a number of key features have to be considered. These features may be referred to as the **design mix** and are summarised in Figure 1.

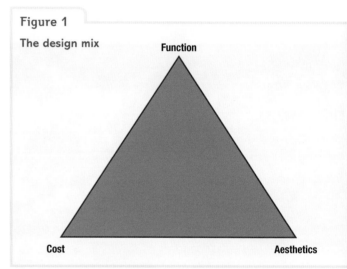

Figure 1

The design mix

Function

Cost

Aesthetics

Product/service design

Many businesses are keen to bring new products and services to the market. New products and services help to generate more revenue and ensure that businesses remain competitive. The process of creating a new product or service is called **product design**. It involves the generation and development of ideas through a process that leads to new products/services.

Once a business has identified a need for a product, a design brief can be written. This will contain features about a product that the designers can use. For example, a business aiming to produce a new travel iron may write a design brief such as 'a new travel iron that is compact and possesses all the features of a full-sized model'. Designers can work from this design brief. When designing the new travel iron they may take into account:

- the shape and appearance of the iron
- whether it fits the intended need
- how easily and cost-effectively it can be produced from the design
- the dimensions and preferred materials to be used
- the image it gives when displayed
- whether the design should create a 'corporate identity', saying something about the image of the company.

Function: A product or service must be fit for purpose, which means that it must be capable of doing the job that it is sold to do. For example, a waterproof jacket must not let in rain. It must also be reliable and work every time the customer uses it. For example, an internet service provider must provide a reliable and safe connection. The manufacturers of many **consumer durables** offer long warranties to show that they have confidence in the reliability and durability of their products. Products that are not fit for purpose are also likely to be returned, which will add to business costs.

Products and services should also be convenient and easy for the customer to use. People will get frustrated if they cannot download an app quickly or understand how to assemble flat-pack furniture from a set of instructions. Technical products and machinery often need maintenance, so these products should be designed so that maintenance can be carried out easily. However, if there is adequate competition in the market this might not be an issue. Consumers can find another supplier if they are unhappy with the level of convenience offered by a particular business.

Some products are **ergonomically** designed. This means that they are designed so that people can interact with them safely and without using unnecessary effort. Figure 2 shows how a workstation might be ergonomically designed to ensure that a person at work is entirely comfortable.

If a business can design a product or service with superior functionality, it may be used as a unique selling point, or USP. Most people recognise that Volvo emphasise the safety of their cars. This is their USP.

Designers must also ensure that new products or services are safe. Safety is particularly important if children, the elderly or pregnant women use the products. Safety issues could include ensuring that products do not contain poisons or dangerous materials, such as toxic paint. If potentially dangerous features are necessary, such as a sharp edge on a power tool, then it is important to design the product to provide adequate protection.

Question 1

An office supplies company has produced a new ergonomically designed computer workstation. Figure 2 shows how it has taken into account the needs of users.

Figure 2
An ergonomically designed computer workstation

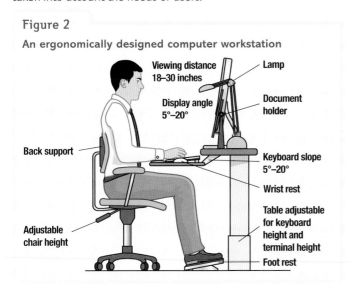

(a) Explain what is meant by an ergonomically designed product.

(b) Explain the possible benefits to a business of using ergonomically designed workstations.

Aesthetics: Products and services should provide a sensory stimulation in addition to performing a function. This is the product or service's aesthetic appeal. Designers must consider elements of a product, such as its size, appearance, shape, smell or taste, or the presentation of a service, because it has an impact on the choices that consumers make. For example, some companies choose designs that use more expensive materials to add to the aesthetic appeal of a product, because a product that appeals to the senses may sell better. Someone may buy a luxury car because they like the smell of leather seats or the appearance of wooden panelling, and the atmosphere that these features create, rather than because of its fuel economy or speed.

As the cost of resources and manufacturing comes down over time, aesthetics is likely to become more important in

the design mix. Product and service design has changed dramatically in recent years, as computers, vehicles, mobile phones and music players have become more compact and more powerful. Many consumers prefer smaller and more portable products that are more user-friendly.

Cost: A well-designed product or service is more likely to be economically viable. This means that a business should be able to produce and sell the product or service at a profit. Therefore designers will need to select materials and processes that minimise costs. For example, it was reported that Apple wanted to use curved glass for early iPhones. However, the prototypes were too expensive to manufacture, so they were shelved. In the airline industry, new routes must be cost-effective if they are to be introduced. Businesses often have to reach a compromise between design and cost. If costs are high, products or services may be dropped altogether.

Question 2

Figure 3
The design mix – positions 1 to 5 represent different products

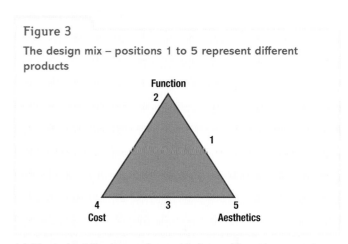

(a) Match the following products with the positions shown on the triangle which best represent the design mix in Figure 3. Each of the positions suggests which aspect of the mix may be relatively more important for particular products. (i) designer high heeled shoes, (ii) a sports car, (iii) a life assurance policy, (iv) a dining room table, (v) a smartphone.

(b) Explain how cost might affect the design of a package holiday.

Exam tip
The design of individual products may require emphasis on a particular element in the design mix. When answering questions, it will be helpful to give examples of products where a particular element is important. Functionality is important for products like hiking boots, tools, central heating systems and exercise bikes. Aesthetic appeal is important for products like fashion accessories, sunglasses, carpets and luxury goods. Cost is important for consumer durables, public transport and financial services such as house and car insurance. This may help you to demonstrate that you understand the nature of the design mix and can apply your knowledge.

The design mix and social trends

People have become increasingly aware about the effects their lifestyles have on the environment. Worries about global warming, **resource depletion** and pollution have encouraged many to adopt more environmentally friendly lifestyles. Businesses have also responded to pressure from the government, media and consumer groups by taking into account environmental issues in the design of their products. For example, their designs may now attempt to reduce waste and facilitate the re-use and **recycling** of products and packaging.

Design for waste minimisation: Firms are under increasing pressure to design products that minimise waste. **Waste minimisation** can take place in a number of ways.

- Products that use a lot of energy and other resources in manufacturing should be designed to be more durable by designing products that might last a lifetime. This could be achieved by including components in a design that can be replaced, or better still, repaired. For example, the Apple iPhone 6 included new design features that enabled the handset to be opened and repaired more easily than earlier models.
- Products could be designed to be smaller and lighter. This will help to save the amount of material used in production. Resources used in handling, packaging and transport will also be reduced. Examples of this include laptops, tablet computers, smartphones, digital cameras, music systems and flat-screen televisions.
- Designers could be discouraged from designing disposable products. Products such as disposable razors, plastic cutlery, cardboard plates and paper cups can be replaced with durable equivalents. There is probably a lot more scope here for businesses to make improvements. At the moment, the amount of packaging used by businesses and discarded by customers is considerable.
- In the restaurant industry, dishes and menus could be designed to reduce food waste, such as meat off-cuts.

Although there are clear benefits of designing products that reduce waste, many businesses have not embraced the idea. For example, many products are discarded because they are considered 'out of date'. In the fashion industry, for example, clothes and accessories are often worn for a limited period of time only. They are discarded even though they are still functional. This is because fashions change and businesses can make money by selling consumers 'new season' collections. At the moment this is unlikely to change. There would need to be a radical change in social trends for people to change their behaviour.

Design for re-use: Resources can be saved if products are designed so that they can be re-used. For example, mobile phones are designed to last for years but are thought to have an average first use of around 18 months, so it is important that their component parts can be re-used to prevent waste.

- Businesses could be encouraged to design packaging which can be re-used. In the past, fizzy drinks and beer were sold in returnable bottles. Customers would return their 'empties' and get a refund. The empty bottles would then be returned to the supplier, washed and re-used. Many countries around the world, such as Holland and Germany, still give customers money for returning their empty bottles.
- Another approach is to design products so that components can be easily re-used. For example, Philips designed a new light bulb that was easier to dismantle than previous light bulbs, so that the component parts could be re-used.
- In the theatre industry, sets and props could be designed so that they could be adapted and re-used for different plays.

Design for recycling: Businesses are making increasing use of recycled materials in their designs.

- Some businesses are adapting their production methods so that newly designed products can be produced using recycled materials. For example, carpet manufacturers are developing ways of using their old carpets in the production of new ones. Glass manufacturers have long used recycled glass in the production of new glass.
- Some businesses specialise in the sole use of recycled materials in their manufacture. For example, the Reefer Sail Company makes its products from recycled materials, including boat and windsurf sails and kites, as well as from sail-makers' roll ends and offcuts. Its product range includes deck chairs, cushions, buckets, bags and children's toys.
- Some firms make use of waste discarded by other businesses in their designs. For example, Yübe is a modular storage system built with reconstituted sugar cane waste fibre panels. The Yübe frames, which allow for multiple stacking configurations, are made of a combination of sugar cane fibre, recycled plastic and bamboo.
- In the media, it may be possible to recycle material to save time and effort. For example, the same news stories might be adapted and used in several different formats. They might appear in print, online, as television broadcasts, as radio broadcasts and as podcasts.

Question 3

Jaguar Land Rover is developing a recycling process to increase the use of recycled aluminium in their vehicles. Working with the REAL CAR initiative, they have developed a technique to produce a sheet metal alloy using scrap aluminium. They have also developed a recycling system at their production centre, reducing transport emissions by using materials recycled in the UK instead of importing them from overseas suppliers. Jaguar Land Rover aim to reduce aluminium waste by increasing the amount of recycled aluminium used in vehicle manufacturing to up to 75 per cent where possible.

(a) Explain how Jaguar is designing a method to reduce waste.

(b) Explain how Jaguar's approach reflects social trends.

Ethical sourcing: In order to reflect social trends, some businesses use ethically sourced resources in their designs. Ethical sourcing means that businesses only use materials, components and services from suppliers that respect the environment, treat their workforce well by paying them a fair wage and providing a safe working environment, and generally trade with integrity. For example, a clothes designer might insist that their collections are not manufactured by overseas businesses that use child labour in their factories.

In 2007, British supermarket Sainsbury's made the decision to sell only Fairtrade bananas. Fairtrade banana growers get a fair price for their crop, as well as a premium that is used to fund projects in their local communities. In addition, Fairtrade growers are required to use environmentally friendly techniques, so this decision also has a positive environmental impact.

Although some businesses try to adopt an ethical stance when supplying products, it could be argued that the majority are still focused on lowering costs. For example, the cheap 'value brands' in supermarkets are still very popular. Perhaps this is because people are more concerned with getting products for the lowest possible price. They may have little regard for ethically sourced products.

Benefits of adapting product designs to changes in social trends

Although businesses may have to make an effort to reflect social trends in their designs, which could possibly increase costs, there are likely to be some lucrative benefits.

- If businesses can reduce waste they will use fewer resources. This will result in lower costs and higher profits.
- If designs reflect social trends, products are likely to be more popular and sell in larger quantities. This will raise revenue and improve profits.

- Some businesses use their design features as a USP. This will help to market their products more effectively. For example, Ecover produces household cleaners made from plant and mineral materials. Avoiding the use of chemicals is environmentally friendly, and it is also their USP.
- Businesses that adopt some of the emerging design features relating to social trends are more likely to be viewed as good corporate citizens. Many businesses attempt to emphasise corporate social responsibility in their marketing strategy. By doing this they aim to raise sales revenue and profit. They may also avoid criticism for trading unethically.

Key terms

Consumer durables – goods that can be used repeatedly over a period of time, such as cars and household appliances.
Design mix – the range of features that are important when designing a product.
Ergonomics – the study of how people interact with their environment and the equipment they use – often in the workplace.
Ethical sourcing – using materials, components and services from suppliers that respect the environment, treat their workforce well and generally trade with integrity.
Product design – the process of creating a new product or service.
Recycling – making use of materials that have been discarded as waste.
Resource depletion – the using up of natural resources.
Waste minimisation – reducing the quantity of resources that are discarded in the production process.

Knowledge check

1. State two examples of products where aesthetics is particularly important in the design mix.

2. State two examples of products where functionality is of prime importance in the design mix.

3. Explain one way in which the government might affect the design of products.

4. State three examples of products that are likely to be ergonomically designed.

5. State two benefits to consumers of designs that reflect changes in social trends.

6. State two benefits to businesses of designs that reflect changes in social trends.

7. How might ethical sourcing affect the design of clothing?

Case study

STANLEY MODULAR

The construction sector generates millions of tonnes of waste every year in the UK. This includes building materials, such as insulation, nails, electrical wiring, steel reinforcement and waste from site preparation such as dredging materials, tree stumps and rubble. Some construction waste can be dangerous, as it can contain lead, asbestos or other hazardous substances, and this sort of waste needs to be disposed of carefully.

Construction companies have come under increasing pressure to reduce this waste. A construction firm in New Zealand, Stanley Modular, is committed to reducing waste and has come up with some effective designs. Stanley constructs modular buildings supplied as prefinished panels for schools and homes in New Zealand. Wall, ceiling and floor panels are constructed in a factory and then transported to the building site. Almost all of the work is done in the factory, with just a small proportion done on site.

Constructing the panels in a factory cuts down the amount of waste on site, and the management of waste and materials becomes easier as they are all in one place, making it easier to collect and sort the waste.

Almost all the materials used by Stanley Modular end up in their completed buildings, because the parts of each building are created to fit the exact size of the finished structure. The small amount of excess is mostly recycled, with a tiny proportion sent to landfill. Keeping the amount of waste to these levels requires more employees to actively work on waste management, as the factory environment has to be strictly controlled to ensure that waste is kept to a minimum.

Waste is minimised in a wide range of areas.

- **Transportation.** A Stanley Modular house can be transported to site on a single truck, with flat-pack panels on the front, roofing on the back and a 4-metre trailer containing the bathroom modules. More complex parts of the building process require more trips, but far fewer than would be required on a traditional building site.

- **Materials.** In a typical build, 1,200 kg of timber is wasted – Stanley Modular only waste around 10 per cent of this. Reductions in waste have been found when all gun nails use galvanised nail strips, which prevents operators from mixing up nail types, resulting in rework. The use of computer numerical control (CNC) machinery maximises the usable material from sheets and planks.

- **Time wastage.** Stanley Modular save a lot of time in their operations. They estimate that modular building is up to a third faster than traditional construction. The use of CNC machinery is also 50 per cent faster than manually controlled machinery.

Stanley Modular continually explore ways to decrease the impact of construction on the environment. Their projects show how a well-designed prefabricated building system can minimise waste, improve productivity and speed up construction projects.

Source: adapted from www.branz.co.nz/REBRI

Q

(a) Explain how designs that reduce waste benefit Stanley Modular. (4 marks)

(b) Explain the aspects of the traditional design mix that might be important to Stanley Modular. (8 marks)

(c) Evaluate the benefits to Stanley Modular of adapting its designs to reflect changes in social trends. (12 marks)

Branding and promotion

Key points

1. Types of promotion.
2. Types of branding.
3. The benefits of strong branding: added value, ability to charge premium prices and reduced price elasticity of demand.
4. Ways to build a brand: unique selling points (USPs)/differentiation, advertising, sponsorship and the use of social media.
5. Changes in branding and promotion to reflect social trends: viral marketing, social media and emotional branding.

Getting started

In 2014 the total amount of money spent by businesses worldwide on advertising was around $537 billion. Internet advertising accounted for nearly one-quarter of that, at around $121 billion, according to forecasts by ZenithOptimedia, an industry specialist. Figure 1 shows the share of global advertising by medium in 2013 and 2016*.

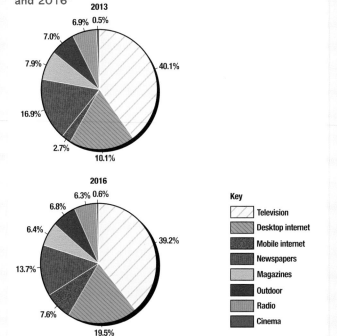

Figure 1

The share of global advertising by medium in 2013 and 2016*

2013

6.9% 0.5%
7.0%
7.9%
16.9%
2.7%
10.1%
40.1%

2016

6.3% 0.6%
6.8%
6.4%
13.7%
7.6%
19.5%
39.2%

Key

- Television
- Desktop internet
- Mobile internet
- Newspapers
- Magazines
- Outdoor
- Radio
- Cinema

*Predicted

Source: adapted from: www.zenithoptimedia.com

Why do businesses spend so much on advertising? What might account for the changes in spending by businesses on newspaper and mobile internet advertising between 2013 and 2016* as shown in Figure 1? What other methods might a business use to promote its products?

What is promotion?

An important element in the **marketing mix** is **promotion**. This involves businesses drawing attention to their products, services or companies. Generally, businesses use promotion to obtain and retain customers. However, promotion is also likely to be used to achieve some specific aims.

- Tell consumers about a new product.
- Remind customers about an existing product.
- Reach a widely dispersed target audience.
- Reassure customers about products.
- Show consumers that rival products are not as good.
- Improve or develop the image of the business.

Above-the-line promotion

Above-the-line promotion involves **advertising** in the media. Businesses pay television companies or newspapers, for example, to have their adverts broadcast or printed. Advertising may be placed into different categories.

- **Informative advertising.** This means that the adverts are designed to increase consumer awareness of products. They may give clear information about the features of a product, for example. The classified advertisements in newspapers are examples of informative advertising.
- **Persuasive advertising.** Some advertising is designed to put pressure on consumers to buy a product. Persuasive advertisements often try to convince consumers to buy a particular brand rather than that of a competitor. They are often designed to appeal to people's emotions, such as fear and pity. Persuasive adverts may also appeal to people's respect for authority and fascination with celebrity. A lot of television and cinema adverts are persuasive.
- **Reassuring advertising.** This advertising is aimed at existing customers. It is designed to be comforting and suggest to consumers that they were 'right' to buy a particular product and that they should continue to do so. Businesses selling financial services may use this approach to reassure people that their money is 'safe'.

Table 1 shows the advantages and disadvantages of the main media.

Table 1 The advantages and disadvantages of selected advertising media

Media	Advantages	Disadvantages
Television	Huge audiences can be reached The use of products can be demonstrated Sound and movement can be used Scope for targeting groups with digital TV	Very expensive Message may be short-lived Some viewers avoid TV ads Delay between seeing ads and shopping
Newspapers and magazines	National and local coverage Reader can refer back Ads can be linked to articles and features Vouchers and coupons can be used Scope for targeting with specialist magazines Relatively cheap	No movement or sound Individual ads may be lost in a 'sea of ads'
Cinema	Big impact with a big screen Can be used for local and national advertising Specific age groups can be targeted Sound and movement can be used	Limited audience Message may only be seen once Message is short-lived
Radio	Sound can be used Minority audiences allow targeting Cheap production Can target youngsters	Not visual May be ignored May lack impact Can be intrusive when listening
Posters and billboards	Can produce national campaigns Seen repeatedly Good for short sharp messages Large posters can have big impact	Posters can get damaged by vandals Only limited information can be shown Difficult to evaluate effectiveness
Internet	Can be updated regularly Can be targeted Hits and response can be measured Can be sent to mobile devices For goods available online, there is no delay between seeing ads and shopping for the product online	Some ads such as pop-up ads are irritating Possible technical problems

Question 1

This advertisement has been used by the RSPCA as part of a poster campaign to raise money for the charity.

(a) What is meant by above-the-line promotion?

(b) Explain one advantage of using posters as an advertising media.

(c) Assess to what extent this advert is meant to be persuasive.

Below-the-line promotion

Below-the-line promotion refers to any form of promotion that does not involve advertising. It can take many forms.

Sales promotions: Incentives used to encourage people to buy products are called **sales promotions**. They are used to boost sales in the hope that if new customers are attracted they will continue to buy the product. They might be used to break into a new market. They may also be used to reward loyal customers and allow businesses to measure the impact of promotion, by counting the number of returned coupons, for example.

- **Free gifts.** Businesses might give free gifts to customers when they buy the product; for example, computer companies often give away free software.
- **Coupons.** Money-off vouchers can be used by businesses to attract customers. They may be attached to products, appear in newspaper adverts, or pushed through letterboxes.
- **Loyalty cards.** Some businesses reward customers according to how much they spend. Points are collected and then exchanged for cash, vouchers or free goods. Loyalty cards are popular with supermarkets, credit card companies and stores.
- **Competitions.** People may be allowed free entry into a competition when they buy a particular product. An attractive prize is offered to the winners.
- **BOGOF offers.** BOGOF stands for 'Buy One, Get One Free'. These offers are popular with many businesses, such as supermarkets, transport services and restaurants.
- **Money-off deals.** Businesses may offer customers discounts such as '30 per cent off' or 'an extra 20 per cent free'. These are similar to BOGOF deals and are used by a range of suppliers.

Public relations: Some businesses communicate with stakeholders using **public relations** (PR). The main purpose of PR is to increase sales by improving the image of the business. A number of approaches might be used by businesses to attract publicity.

- **Press releases.** Some information about the business may be presented to the media. This might be used to write an article or feature in a television programme. For example, a business might announce that it is to create 2,000 new jobs. Such positive news would be of interest to the media and they might want full details.
- **Press conferences.** This is where representatives meet with the media and present information verbally. This allows for questioning and other feedback. The press might be invited to a product launch, for example.
- **Sponsorship.** Sponsorship is when businesses attract publicity by linking their brands with events, particularly sporting events, TV programmes and films. For example, Pepsi, Vodafone and Yes Bank were some of the companies making financial contributions to the Indian Premier League in return for publicity at events in 2014. They were the sponsors. The sponsoring of TV programmes is also popular. For example, in 2015, ITV's *Coronation Street* was sponsored by comparethemarket.com and Sky's *Goals on Sunday*

was sponsored by Ford. The main advantage of sports sponsorship is that brand names are projected globally on the television without having to pay the owners of television companies.

- **Donations.** Donations to charities and the local community might be used by businesses to improve their image. A large donation from a business is likely to be reported in the media, which is good publicity.

The main advantage of PR to businesses is that it is often a cheap method of promotion. Some businesses have been known to deliberately seek bad publicity by being controversial. This can raise the profile of a business very quickly, sometimes at no cost.

Question 2

Sport has attracted funding from sponsors for many years. High-profile sporting events, such as the FIFA World Cup, the Wimbledon Tennis Championships, the Open Golf Championship and many others, raise considerable sums from a wide variety of different sponsors. In 2013, around $50 billion was reported to have been spent on sponsorship worldwide, most of which went on sport.

Rolex, the luxury watchmaker, spends a lot of money on promoting its products. In 2013, it was reported to have spent $61.48 million on advertising. It is also reported to be the most active sports sponsor. Sponsors like Rolex benefit from having their name and logo 'splashed' everywhere at an event. For example, Rolex were one of the official partners of the US Open Golf Championship, which was broadcast around the world – this represents a massive potential audience.

Source: www.statista.com

(a) What is meant by sponsorship?

(b) Explain the advantages of sponsorship to a company like Rolex.

Merchandising and packaging: Some businesses may arrange the point of sale so that it is interesting and eye catching, and likely to encourage sales. This is called merchandising. Some examples are outlined below.

- **Product layout.** The layout of products in a store is often planned very carefully to encourage shoppers to follow particular routes and look at certain products. Products that stores want you to buy are placed at prominent locations, such as at the end of aisles and at eye level.
- **Display material.** Posters, leaflets and other materials may be used to display certain products with the aim of persuading customers to buy. Lighting and other special effects can improve the shopping environment. Window displays are considered important by retailers as they can draw in customers.
- **Stock.** Businesses must keep shelves well stocked because empty shelves create a bad impression. Also, if items are out of stock customers may shop elsewhere.

Direct mailing: This is where businesses mail out leaflets or letters to households. Sometimes personal letters are used. They may contain information about new products or details of price changes, for example. Increasingly, email and text messages (often called spam) are being used to contact consumers rather than the postal system. The development of ICT and use of customer databases has resulted in more use of personalised marketing.

Direct selling or personal selling: This might involve a 'sales rep' calling at households or businesses hoping to sell products. It could also be a telephone call from a call centre where a battery of sales staff is employed to sell over the telephone. One advantage of this approach is that the features of the product can be discussed. However, people are often irritated by this approach because the callers have not been invited.

Exhibitions and trade fairs: Some businesses attend trade fairs or exhibitions to promote their products. Businesses set up a stand and promote their products face-to-face. Trade fairs can be attended by commercial buyers or consumers, or both. In the UK some popular exhibitions are the Motor Show, the Ideal Homes Exhibition and the Boat Show. There are certain advantages of this method of promotion.

- Products can be tested out on consumers before a full launch.
- Some exhibitions are overseas and can be used to break into foreign markets.
- Products can be physically demonstrated and questions answered.
- Exhibitions often attract the media.
- Customers can speak to business owners or senior personnel face-to-face.

Choosing methods of promotion

Many businesses use a range of different promotional methods. However, these must be co-ordinated so that they support each other. Small businesses often have limited budgets so careful consideration is needed when choosing a method of promotion.

What affects the choice of promotion?
- **Cost.** Not all businesses can afford to advertise on television and in national newspapers so they have to find other more cost-effective, and often more appropriate, means.
- **Market type.** Local businesses often rely on adverts in local newspapers and the *Yellow Pages.* In contrast, businesses aiming their products at mass markets are more likely to use television and national newspapers, or specialist magazines.
- **Product type.** Certain products are better suited to certain methods of promotion. For example, a car manufacturer is not likely to use sales promotions such as coupons, BOGOF deals or loyalty cards, preferring TV and cinema advertising, and billboards. Similarly, supermarkets are unlikely to use personal selling.
- **Stage in the product life cycle.** It is common for promotional methods to change as a product gets older. For example, PR is often used at the launch of a product, but when the product matures other methods will be used.
- **Competitors' promotions.** It is common for businesses to copy successful methods of promotion used by rivals. Once one business comes up with a successful promotion, others soon bring out their own versions.

- **Legal factors.** In many countries legislation designed to protect consumers can affect the method and style of promotion. For example, in the EU tobacco products cannot be advertised on television.

Types of branding

The aim of many businesses is to build a powerful brand. Branding involves giving a product a name, sign, symbol or logo, design or any feature that allows consumers to instantly recognise the product and differentiate it from those of competitors.

Brands can come in a number of forms.
- **Manufacturer brands. Manufacturer brands** are brands created by the producers of goods and services. The goods or services bear the producer's name. Examples might be Kellogg's Corn Flakes®, Gillette razors or Dell computers. The manufacturers are involved in the production, distribution, promotion and pricing decisions of these products.
- **Own-label brands. Own-label brands** (also known as **distributor** or **private brands**) are products which are manufactured for wholesalers or retailers by other businesses. But the wholesalers and retailers sell the products under their own name. One example of a product containing the retailer's name is Tesco® Baked Beans. Sometimes the retailer will create its own brand name, for example F&F clothes sold at Tesco. These products allow a retailer to buy from the cheapest manufacturer, reducing its cost. It will hope to promote its own products effectively to shoppers in its outlets.
- **Generic brands.** Some **generic brands** are products that only contain the name of the actual product category rather than the company or product name. Examples are aluminium foil, carrots or aspirin. These products are usually sold at lower prices than branded products. They tend to account for a small percentage of all sales.

The benefits of strong branding

If a business can establish a strong brand it will enjoy a number of benefits.

Added value: A strong brand may add value to a product in the eyes of customers. For example, if a business can capture a desirable image that is reflected in the brand, it is likely to have a competitive edge. It could be argued that perfume manufacturers are able to do this. They may use powerful television adverts that feature celebrities using the product. Some adverts suggest that if you buy a particular brand you will belong to a group of elegant and sophisticated consumers, similar to those featured in adverts. Such adverts may offer consumers glamour, confidence and style. This approach can add value for some consumers.

Ability to charge premium prices: Products with strong brands can be priced higher than those of competitors. This is because of the customer loyalty that has been built up over a period of time. People are less likely to switch to cheaper brands if they have developed the habit of buying a 'favourite' brand. Heinz, the food processing company, generally charges higher prices for its canned and bottled products because they are perceived to be 'superior' to those of rival brands.

Reduced price elasticity of demand: The strength of a brand may be reflected in the price elasticity of demand for a product (price elasticity of demand is explained in Unit 7).

Firms would prefer their brands to have a lower price elasticity of demand. This means that a price increase will have less impact on demand. For example, if a product has price elasticity of demand of −1.5, a 10 per cent increase in price will result in a 15 per cent decrease in demand. However, if price elasticity is lower at −0.9, a 10 per cent increase in price will reduce demand by just 9 per cent. Consequently, with a strong brand and lower price elasticity, price increases are more viable.

Ways to build a brand

Different companies may use different methods in an effort to build a brand.

Exploiting a unique selling point: One of the best ways to build a brand is to develop a **unique selling point (USP)** for a product. If a product has a USP it is much easier to differentiate the brand and make it 'stand out from the pack'. Some companies develop USPs by incorporating special features in their designs. Another approach is to make promises to customers. For example, some companies offer to give customers their money back if they are not satisfied. Producers of luxury goods, such as Prada or Gucci, use exclusivity as their USP.

Advertising: Advertising may be used in different ways. A business might use advertising to introduce a new brand. If the brand becomes popular and established, advertising is likely to continue in order to remind consumers that 'it is still out there'. Advertising spreads the word about a brand, and the more people who are familiar with the brand the greater the firm's market power. Advertising also reassures customers. An important element of advertising is pride. Advertising may be a source of pride for customers who have chosen the brand. The importance of advertising to help build brands is reflected in the amount of money spent by businesses on advertising. In 2013, over $500 billion was spent worldwide. Table 2 shows the top 10 global advertisers in 2013.

Table 2 Top 10 global advertisers in (2013)

	Company	Ad spend ($ billion)
1	Procter & Gamble	11.47
2	Unilever	7.91
3	L'Oréal	5.93
4	Toyota	3.44
5	General Motors	3.35
6	Volkswagen	3.23
7	Nestlé	3.12
8	Coca-Cola	2.9
9	McDonald's	2.86
10	Pepsi	2.74

Source: adapted from www.statista.com

Sponsorship: Some companies favour the use of sponsorship to help build their brands. Many argue that sponsorship is a cheaper method of promotion than advertising – although many companies use both. The majority of sponsorship spending is in sport. Companies sponsor both national and international sporting events. For example, Barclays Bank sponsors the English Premier League. Sponsorship helps to:

- raise brand awareness, create preference and develop brand loyalty
- create positive PR and raise corporate awareness
- build brand positioning by linking the product to attractive images at events
- support other promotional campaigns
- create emotional commitment to the brand
- promote good relations with customers because sponsors often provide corporate hospitality at events.

Using social media: An increasing number of businesses are switching marketing resources into social media. Social media can be used in more than one way. For example, a business can place its adverts in strategic places on sites such as Facebook, Twitter, Instagram and Google+. The use of social media often allows businesses to focus more easily on particular customer groups. Social media also helps businesses to get to know their customers better and enables them to communicate with them more effectively. Social media may help to increase trust in a business or brand. Seeing that a particular business is active on social media helps customers to develop trust. A social media presence may suggest that a business cares about its customers. For example, if anything goes wrong customers will feel more secure if they know that it is easy for them to make contact and raise their issues.

A large and increasing number of businesses use social media to help build their brands. For example, Kentucky Fried Chicken (KFC) used a social media campaign to attract more young female customers. It used a viral ad featuring the comedian Jenny Bede suggesting reasons for eating unhealthy food.

Building a brand is an ongoing process. Even companies with extremely strong brands, continually invest in advertising and promotional campaigns to support and reinforce their brands.

Changes in branding and promotion to reflect social trends

Businesses are under constant pressure to keep up to date with trends, patterns, fashions and new technology. This pressure extends to the methods they use to promote and brand their products. For example, since the rise of the internet, most firms have set up their own business websites. These are used to provide information, promote products and in some cases to sell goods directly to customers. Some other very recent developments are outlined below.

Viral marketing: Communication using the internet has provided the opportunity for **viral marketing**. This involves any strategy that encourages people to pass on messages to others about a product or a business electronically. It creates the potential for exponential growth in the exposure of a message. Like a virus, these strategies exploit the process of rapid multiplication that results from people sending messages to family, friends and colleagues, who then send them on again. Not only can people send text relating to a marketing message, but they also can send images, such as photographs and video clips. One example of a successful viral marketing campaign was produced by Volvo. It featured a video clip of Jean-Claude Van Damme doing the splits between two Volvo trucks as they were being driven along a road. The clip was used to demonstrate the stability and precision of Volvo's steering system. The video had been viewed over 76 million times at the time of writing.

Social media: A survey of marketing leaders in 2013 showed they devoted around 9.4 per cent of their marketing budgets to social media – a figure that continues to rise (see Figure 2).

Using social media, such as Facebook and Twitter, to help build a brand is important but many businesses go further. An increasing number are developing their own social networks, which are linked to the main platforms. Some analysts suggest that, while Facebook is a good platform to use to find customers and raise brand awareness, most people who 'like' a brand page on Facebook never visit it again. In comparison, some companies create their own social networks. Virgin Atlantic is one example of a business that has developed its own social hub. This is discussed in Question 3 on the next page.

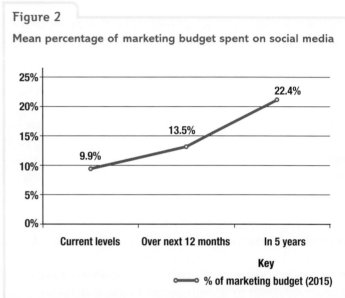

Figure 2

Mean percentage of marketing budget spent on social media

Current levels: 9.9%
Over next 12 months: 13.5%
In 5 years: 22.4%

Key
⊶ % of marketing budget (2015)

Source: *The CMO Survey – Highlights and Insights Report*, Figure 5.1, February 2015

Emotional branding: Emotional branding refers to the practice of using the emotions of a consumer to build a brand. It is designed to appeal to a customer's emotion, human need, or a perceived aspiration. The aim of emotional marketing is to develop a love affair between a consumer and a brand. Businesses try to instil in their customers the emotional attachment that football supporters have with their chosen clubs. The overwhelming majority of football supporters all over the world could not switch their support to another club even when theirs is performing badly – the bond is just too strong. Emotional branding is also based on the idea that people's actions are driven more by emotion than reason.

One example of a business that has used emotional branding effectively is Apple. Apple has found a way to connect with its customers and create with them a powerful bond. They achieved this by connecting with younger people in particular and creating a 'cool' product image. The Apple brand has aligned itself with design innovation; the release of a new Apple product is an event and people will queue for hours. They have created an emotional attachment with their customers, one which is not defined by commerce.

Question 3

Virgin Atlantic,
the London-based airline, has used social media to help promote its business for several years. In 2010, Virgin Atlantic had over 200,000 Facebook fans, 115,000 Twitter followers and 1.2 million followers on its Virgin Google+ page. However, the amount of traffic driven from these to where bookings are made was considered inadequate. Virgin realised that it needed its own social platform so it created the Virgin Atlantic Blog. When the blog was launched it had four specific aims.

1   To become an authority on travel. They did this by employing writers to provide useful 'insider' information about different destinations – some of which coincided with Virgin Atlantic routes.

2   Create a central hub for their social media outreach. This had links to Facebook, Twitter, Instagram and Pinterest, which meant that people could be directed from these platforms to Virgin's own hub where blogs were posted.

3   Add reach, depth and longevity to their marketing campaigns. Major ad and marketing campaigns are, by necessity, short, but the blog gives Virgin a more in-depth opportunity to tell a campaign's story, whether it's interviewing the chefs behind a new meal programme or getting to know the pilots, flight attendants and other staff who make the airline run.

4   Boost sales. The best way to encourage customers to shop is to provide relevant links in the right places. For example, creating interest in a Virgin holiday or a new service, then providing the chance to click through and book.

As a result of creating their own social hub, Virgin Atlantic enjoyed three key benefits:

- a 12 per cent increase in search traffic after six months
- customers referred from their blog spent an extra 20 per cent.
- first-time buyers referred from the blog rose by 40 per cent.

Source: Copyright © 2013 Lithium Technologies, Inc. All rights reserved.

(a) Explain one way in which Virgin Atlantic is responding to social changes with its promotion.

(b) Explain one aim of Virgin's social media hub.

(c) Assess the benefits to Virgin Atlantic of setting up its own social media hub.

Key terms

Above-the-line promotion – placing adverts using the media.

Advertising – communication between a business and its customers where images are placed in the media to encourage the purchase of products.

Below-the-line promotion – any promotion that does not involve using the media.

Emotional branding – the practice of using the emotions of a consumer to build a brand.

Generic brands – products that only contain the name of the product category rather than the company or product name.

Manufacturer brands – brands created by the producers of goods or services.

Marketing mix – the elements of a business's marketing that are designed to meet the needs of customers. The four elements are often called the '4Ps' – product, price, promotion and place.

Merchandising – a promotion specifically at the point of sale of a product.

Own-label, distributor or private brands – products that are manufactured for wholesalers or retailers by other businesses.

Point of sale – any point where a consumer buys a product.

Promotion – an attempt to obtain and retain customers by drawing their attention to a firm or its products.

Public relations – an organisation's attempt to communicate with interested parties.

Sales promotions – methods of promoting products in the short term to boost sales.

Sponsorship – making a financial contribution to an event in return for publicity.

Viral marketing – any strategy that encourages people to pass on messages to others about a product or a business electronically.

Knowledge check

1. State six examples of advertising media.

2. What is meant by below-the-line media?

3. What is direct mailing?

4. State four aims of promotion.

5. Identify four different methods of sales promotion.

6. State three different types of branding.

7. State two benefits of sponsorship.

8. Why can strong brands charge premium prices?

9. How might a business use social media as a promotional aid?

10. Why are businesses spending more money on social media to promote products?

11. What is meant by emotional branding?

12. Why might viral marketing benefit a business?

Case study

PREMIER INN

Premier Inn is the UK's largest budget hotel chain with over 600 hotels in 2015. It plans to increase its number of rooms to over 85,000 (from 59,138). Premier Inn saw total sales grow by 4 per cent to £531 million in 2014, with room occupancy at 78.8%. per cent.

The company operates a guarantee system to help differentiate its service from those of competitors. Premier Inn claims to have thought of everything that is needed to have a great night's sleep. They provide guests with super comfy, king size Hypnos beds with a choice of firm or soft pillows. The company is so confident that guests will have a great night's sleep that they will return their money if they do not. This is called their Good Night Guarantee.

To help the company grow and develop its brand, Premier Inn is committed to advertising. In 2014 it launched its biggest to date advertising campaign – starring comedian Lenny Henry who has featured in Premier Inn ads since 2008. The aim of the campaign is to encourage potential customers to consider the various reasons for staying at a Premier Inn. In the television advert, Henry is shown sleeping in a Premier Inn bed in a range of places, including a beach, a railway station and a wedding reception.

Finally, a poster ad featuring Lenny Henry went viral in April 2014. The billboard showing Lenny Henry in a Premier Inn bed appeared just after William Henwood, a UK Independence Party (UKIP) candidate, suggested that Lenny Henry should emigrate to a 'black country' after the comedian's comment about the lack of black and ethnic minority people working in the creative industries. However, it was revealed that Premier Inn did not produce the image. This was a great example of 'real-time marketing'. Even though the ad was a spoof, Premier Inn benefited from a great deal of free exposure as the image was sent repeatedly around the world.

Q

(a) What is meant by viral marketing? (2 marks)

(b) Explain one way in which Premier Inn might have benefited from the spoof poster ad. (4 marks)

(c) Explain one way in which Premier Inn has differentiated its brand. (4 marks)

(d) Assess the benefits to Premier Inn of having a strong brand. (12 marks)

11 Pricing strategies

Key points

1. Types of pricing strategy: cost plus (calculating mark-up on unit costs), price skimming, penetration, predatory, competitive and psychological.
2. Factors that determine the most appropriate pricing strategy for a particular situation: number of USPs/ amount of differentiation, price elasticity of demand, level of competition in the business environment, strength of brand, stage in the product life cycle, costs and the need to make a profit.
3. Changes in pricing to reflect social trends: online sales and price comparison sites.

Getting started

Hambleton Farm

Ruth and Carl Fletcher run Hambleton Farm, a dairy farm in Warwickshire. In most of 2014 they sold their milk to a wholesaler for around 32p per litre. Ruth and Carl are 'price takers', they have no control over the price of their output. During the year Hambleton Farm made a very small profit – total costs were £1,560,500 and total revenue was £1,561,000.

Virgin Media

In 2014 Virgin Media launched a new TV, home phone and broadband bundle, the 'Essential Family Sports Collection'. This allowed subscribers access to some sports channels so they could watch all 154 Barclays Premier League games shown live on TV. New customers were offered the package for just £46.75 per month plus line rental. After six months, the price rose to £66.25 per month.

What would happen if Ruth and Carl tried to increase the price of their output to 35p per litre? Why is Virgin Media offering its new package £19.50 cheaper than the long-term price? How might price elasticity of demand influence the price set by a business?

Pricing strategies

A strategy is a set of plans designed to meet objectives. **Pricing strategy** is part of the marketing strategy of the business. Other strategies such as product and distribution strategy also make up a marketing strategy. Marketing strategy is then part of the corporate strategy of the business. Other strategies include production and financial strategy.

Pricing strategy is therefore a set of plans about pricing which help a business to achieve its marketing and corporate objectives. For example, a corporate objective might be to double in size over the next five years. A marketing objective to achieve this might be to take the products of the business 'up-market'. The pricing strategy developed from this could be to increase the average price of the products made by the business.

- Some pricing strategies can be used for new products, such as market skimming or penetration pricing (these strategies will be discussed on the next page).

- Some strategies may be more suitable for existing products.

Cost plus pricing

Businesses have to set prices that generate a profit. One method that ensures that all costs are covered is **cost plus pricing**. It involves adding a **mark-up** to **unit costs**. The mark-up is usually a percentage of the unit cost. This method is common with retailers. However, one of the drawbacks of this method is that it ignores market conditions. For example, the mark-up used by a business may be far too high in relation to the prices of rival products. This might result in low sales. Another problem is that it may be difficult to identify precisely all the costs associated with the production of a particular product – particularly for multi-product businesses.

Worked example

The unit cost to a manufacturer of making a fibreglass canoe is £80. The manufacturer adds a mark-up of 25 per cent to get the price. Therefore the price of the canoe is:

Price = unit cost + (mark-up x unit cost)

£80 + (25% x £80) = £80 + £20 – **£100**

Question 1

Harvey Milton Ltd is a family butcher with a busy shop in Harrogate. The shop sells a wide variety of game, poultry and meat, and a number of homemade pies. His three best-selling pies and their unit production costs are:

- game pie – £3.80
- chicken and leek pie – £2.90
- steak and kidney pie – £3.20.

Harvey uses cost plus pricing to set the price of his pies. He adds a 50 per cent mark-up. Harvey believes that this gives him a satisfactory profit margin on the pies.

(a) Calculate the price of the three best-selling pies.

(b) Explain one disadvantage of using cost plus pricing to a business such as Harvey Milton Ltd.

Price skimming

Some businesses may launch a product into a market charging a high price for a limited time period. This is called **skimming** or **creaming**. The aim of this strategy is to generate high levels of revenue with a new product before competitors arrive, and exploit the popularity of a new product while it is unique.

This method is common with technical products. For example, when laptop computers were first introduced into the UK market they were over £1,000. However, they can now be purchased for less than £200. Pharmaceutical companies also use this method. They sell new drugs for high prices when they are first launched. However, when a patent (a licence that prevents competition for a number of years) runs out, competition emerges and prices fall. Charging a high price initially helps such companies recover high development costs.

An advantage of skimming is that high prices are charged in a market where there are people who are prepared to pay them. This helps to maximise revenue. As the price is lowered, other customer groups are drawn into the market. The higher, initial revenues help a business to recover the cost of research and development. The higher price also helps to elevate the image of a product. However, skimming can only be used if demand is price inelastic. Skimming might also attract competitors into the market.

Penetration pricing

Sometimes a business will introduce a new product and charge a low price for a limited period. This is called **penetration pricing**. The aim of this strategy is to get a foothold in the market. Businesses using this strategy hope that customers are attracted by the low price, and then carry on buying it when the price rises. One approach is to offer products at a very cheap rate for a trial period – sometimes as low as half price or even free. Another is to offer the first one or few items free, or at a low price, such as driving lessons. Such a strategy is sometimes called an introductory offer. Penetration pricing has a number of benefits.

- It is particularly beneficial when products are targeted at middle- or low-income consumer groups. This is because such groups are more likely to be responsive to low-price introductory offers.
- It can grow sales of new product lines very quickly. Usually, the lower the introductory offer the faster the growth in sales.
- Fast growth in sales may allow a business to lower production costs by exploiting economies of scale.
- This strategy can put pressure on rivals. They may have to lower their prices or make an effort to differentiate their products. Either way financial pressure is applied.

Businesses using this strategy are better placed if they have a relatively low cost base. They must also resist the temptation of extending such offers for too long. If consumers become accustomed to low prices they may be lost when the introductory offer expires as they are not prepared to pay the higher price.

Penetration pricing is used by a variety of industries. For example, sports clubs to attract members, online gaming sites to attract customers, satellite broadcasters to attract subscribers and driving schools to attract learners.

Predatory pricing

Predatory pricing or **destroyer pricing** aims to eliminate competitors from the market. It involves charging a very low price for a period of time until one or more rivals leave the market. Some forms of predatory pricing are illegal in the UK and the EU. This is when a business is selling a product below the cost of production with the deliberate aim of forcing a competitor out of the market. This practice is outlawed because in the long term it can lead to a lack of competition in a market. As a result, if all firms have left the market except for the predator, the price is likely to be raised beyond the initial level.

Such low-price strategies are allowed if low-cost businesses are prepared to endure low profit margins for extended periods of time. They can also be used to sell stocks that would otherwise remain unsold or as a means of breaking into a new market.

In 2013, Esso and Shell were accused of localised predatory pricing. The RMI Petroleum Retailers Association (PRA) made a submission to the Office of Fair Trading. According to the *Sunday Telegraph*, this said: 'From evidence submitted, certain oil companies, notably Esso and Shell, appear to indulge in localised predatory pricing whereby franchised dealers have to buy their branded fuels at wholesale prices higher than the retail prices on sites owned and operated by the same oil company.'

Competitive pricing

Some businesses take a very close look at what their rivals are charging when setting their prices. This approach is called **competitive pricing** and is likely to be used by businesses operating in a fiercely competitive market. One approach is to charge the same price as competitors. The advantage of this strategy is that a price war is likely to be avoided. It is considered to be a safe pricing strategy. Another approach is for the market leader to set the price and all others follow. This is called **price leadership**. Price leaders are usually the dominant firms in the market. They may have developed their dominance through being a low-cost operator or perhaps by building a strong brand over a period of time.

Psychological pricing

One common pricing strategy is to set the price slightly below a round figure – charging £99.99 instead of £100. This is called **psychological pricing**. Consumers are 'tricked' into thinking that £99.99 is significantly cheaper than £100. Of course it is not but this psychological effect often works for businesses. This approach targets consumers who are looking for bargains. It is not likely to be used by businesses selling 'up-market' products.

Question 3

(a) Explain the pricing strategy used in this case.

(b) Explain one reason why such a pricing strategy might be so popular with businesses such as petrol stations.

Exam tip

You should avoid confusing penetration pricing with predatory pricing. Both of these pricing strategies involve charging a low price. However, penetration pricing involves charging a low price for a short time in order to break into a new market. Predatory pricing involves trying to eliminate rivals in the market. Penetration pricing is legal, but predatory pricing may be illegal. This is likely to be the case if a business is selling a product below cost price for a period of time with the deliberate aim of driving out a rival.

Factors that determine the most appropriate pricing strategy for a particular situation

Setting the right price is an important marketing decision for businesses. A number of factors have to be taken into account before the price is set.

Differentiation and USP: A business can generally charge a higher price if its product has a USP or is sufficiently differentiated from those of its rivals. This is because many consumers are prepared to pay more for products with some individuality or additional features. For example, restaurants can differentiate their service if they offer innovative dishes, in a uniquely interesting and comfortable environment with warm and friendly customer service. As a result they may be able to charge higher prices.

Price elasticity of demand: If the demand for a firm's products is price inelastic, there will be scope for price increases. For example, if price elasticity was −0.8, a business could raise its price by 10 per cent and demand would only fall by 8 per cent. As a result, total revenue would rise. Some utility companies, such as those supplying gas, electricity and water, have been able to raise prices quite significantly in recent years without any serious negative impact on demand. This is because demand for these services is price inelastic. In contrast, if a firm's product is price elastic, it may benefit from price cuts. For example, if price elasticity was −2.7, a 10 per cent reduction in price would result in a 27 per cent increase in demand. This would increase total revenue. Some of the low-cost supermarkets in the UK have benefited from this strategy. See Unit 7 for detailed information about price elasticity of demand.

Amount of competition: The amount of competition in a market will have a big influence on pricing. If there is very little competition in the market, a business can charge much higher prices because consumers cannot switch to a rival. For example, a grocery shop in an isolated village in the Scottish Highlands may be able to charge much higher prices because there is no other shop in the vicinity. In contrast, in highly competitive markets, firms are not generally able to charge higher prices. In some cases, firms might be price takers. This means they have to charge the market price. This is often the case for farmers who sell their produce in national or international commodity markets.

In competitive markets, businesses are likely to use competition-based pricing strategies. Many will prefer to charge the 'going rate' price, i.e. the same or very similar price to those of competitors. This will help to avoid price wars. If a firm has some power in a competitive market it may become the price leader. In this situation all other firms are likely to be content just copying or following the leader.

Strength of the brand: A business with a strong brand can generally charge a higher price than those with weaker brands. One of the reasons why companies like Coca Cola and Unilever spend so much money on supporting their brands, with advertising for example, is so they are able to charge higher prices. Companies with strong brands are in a better position to use price skimming when introducing new products. They might also consider predatory pricing to deter entry into the market.

Stage in the product life cycle: Products pass through a number of stages over their lifetime. Life for a product begins with their development and, for many products, ends when they are withdrawn from the market. The level of sales that can be expected in each stage over this time period is called the **product life cycle**. This is discussed in detail in Unit 13.

As a product passes through the different stages of this cycle, a business may adjust the price charged. For example, when a product is first launched a business might use penetration pricing to try and get established in the market. Later, when sales start to grow, the price can be increased. As the product matures, prices might be reduced a little in order to remain competitive. Alternatively, a business may use price skimming when the product is launched. This approach might be used if the product is new and has few, if any, rivals. Later, when rivals copy the product or bring out versions of their own, prices are likely to gradually decrease.

Costs and the need to make a profit: In the long term, price must cover all the costs of production and generate a profit. This might explain why many businesses use cost plus pricing. Once the unit cost of a product has been calculated, a business knows that if it adds mark-up a profit will be made. However, customers do not care about costs, they care about value for money. It is possible to under-price a product and not maximise potential revenue using this approach. Businesses need to consider the value of their products in addition to costs if they are to extract the most from consumers.

Changes in pricing to reflect social trends

It is possible for social trends to have an impact on pricing strategies. For example, it could be argued that today's consumers are more aware and better informed than ever before. As a result they may challenge the prices charged by businesses. They may haggle or spend more time searching for bargains. They may also be less tied to particular brands and consider instead the views and experiences of friends and colleagues posted on social media sites.

Online sales: Businesses are having to adapt to selling goods online. Many businesses use traditional pricing strategies, such as cost plus pricing. However, for others, selling goods online has provided opportunities for new pricing strategies.

- **Dynamic pricing.** Often used in the travel industry. For example, in the airline industry prices are flexible and different passengers can pay different fares depending on the day of the week, time of day, and number of days before the flight. For airlines, there are dynamic pricing factors in different components, such as how many seats a flight has, departure time, and average cancellations on similar flights. Dynamic pricing is also used in the hotel industry, entertainment and retail. The aim of dynamic pricing is to maximise revenue and profits by filling capacity such as stadiums, flights or sales quotas.

- **Auction sites.** Gumtree, Avabid and eBay, for instance, sell goods to the highest bidder. This allows sellers to get the best possible price for goods. However, the seller has to pay a fee for the use of the site. One other advantage of this method of pricing is that online auction platforms create a sense of urgency. Consumers fear losing out on a bargain if they wait too long. This helps to induce more sales.

- **Personalised pricing.** Involves the use of data relating to a specific online shopper, such as purchase history, browsing history, demographic data, hardware and operating system used, to set a unique price for that shopper. This data could come from a retailer's own database, be enhanced by a third party or be offered up by the user's own computer, tablet or mobile phone. The advantage of this method to businesses is that they can charge higher prices to those customers who are prepared to pay more. It has been reported that Amazon has tried this method of pricing.

- **Subscription pricing.** Usually involves charging customers a regular monthly fee for the use of a service or access to a specific product range. This is not a new concept, but it lends itself well to online shopping. Online magazines and newspapers; software providers, such as Adobe Systems; audio streaming services such as Spotify; gaming sites, such as PlayStation Plus; fashion retailers, such as ASOS Premier; and TV and film providers, such as Netflix, are examples of businesses that use subscription pricing. The main advantage is that customers are tied into long-term agreements with businesses. Although customers have the right to cancel subscriptions, many do not. This is an attractive proposition. It helps to improve cash flow and removes some of the uncertainty about future sales levels.

Price comparison sites: Many online shoppers make use of comparison websites. The sites simply compare the prices of goods and services from a range of suppliers. Some sites are general, but an increasing number are specialists. For example, trivago provides a comparison of hotel prices, KAYAK the prices of flights, Carrentals the prices of car hire, uSwitch energy prices and Mobile Checker for mobile phone prices. Comparison sites are useful for consumers because they may be able to identify the cheapest deals available. These sites might also be used by people who prefer not to shop online. They may check out prices online and then go to the store that is offering the best deal.

Consumers should understand that no two price-comparison websites are likely to yield exactly the same results – even if you provide them with identical information. This is because they may provide quotations from different providers, depending on which companies they have access to.

Case study

ADOBE

Adobe Systems is a multinational software provider based in California, USA, and is probably best known for creating Photoshop®, Acrobat®, InDesign® and Dreamweaver®. In 2013, Adobe announced that subscription pricing would be introduced. Before the new pricing system, customers paid a single fee for Adobe's Creative Suite® (many of its applications integrated to one product) and had perpetual access. However, from June 2013, a monthly fee was required to continue to access programs individually or as a suite of programs through Adobe's Creative Cloud®. Although Creative Suite standalone products were still available, there were no further upgrades. outside Creative Cloud.

The announcements from Adobe stated that improvements to Creative Cloud from June 2013 would be released on a regular basis as features rolled out. The subscription system would no longer be constrained by a traditional upgrade cycle that meant that customers waited for new features. Development of Creative Suite was frozen at version 6, with no new enhancements or features, though bug fixes were available. Before June 2013, it cost over £1500 for the standalone version of Creative Suite 6, where 16 programs including Dreamweaver, Photoshop, Illustrator®, Adobe Premiere® and Adobe Audition® were bundled together.

Customers were only able to access updates and changes to Creative Suite applications by subscription to Adobe's Creative Cloud®, a web-based system that gave access to all

of Adobe's software. It also provided an online storage system and project management tools. The cost for UK customers to access all programs in the Creative Cloud was £47 a month, if they agreed this payment for at least a year.

Some Adobe customers preferred the company's traditional sales approach. However, it was widely reported that by the end of 2014 there were over 3 million subscribers to Creative Cloud, and feedback that the satisfaction level was high.

In 2011, Microsoft introduced Office 365, a subscription version of Office applications plus other productivity programs. Adobe's introduction of a subscription pricing strategy in 2013 reflected a growing trend for large software firms to adopt a subscription pricing strategy. Feedback on customer satisfaction indicated that more customers were comfortable, as part of this trend, in paying for an online service.

(a) What is meant by subscription pricing? (2 marks)

(b) Explain one reason why Adobe switched to subscription pricing. (4 marks)

(c) Assess the success of Adobe's subscription pricing strategy. (8 marks)

(d) Evaluate the factors that might influence the prices set by a business like Adobe. (20 marks)

Knowledge check

1. In competitive markets some firms are price takers. What does this mean?

2. What is the main disadvantage of cost plus pricing?

3. If a product costs £500 and sells for £600, what is the percentage mark-up?

4. When is a business likely to use penetration pricing?

5. What is likely to happen to price as a product nears the end of its life in the product life cycle?

6. State two advantages of skimming.

7. How can firms avoid a price war in a highly competitive market?

8. What is the aim of predatory pricing?

9. How might price comparison sites benefit consumers?

10. What is meant by dynamic pricing?

Key terms

Competitive pricing – pricing strategies based on the prices charged by rivals.

Cost plus pricing – adding a percentage (the mark-up) to the costs of producing a product to get the price.

Mark-up – the percentage added to unit cost that makes a profit for a business when setting the price.

Penetration pricing – setting a low price when launching a new product in order to get established in the market.

Predatory or **destroyer pricing** – setting a low price forcing rivals out of business.

Pricing strategy – the pricing policies or methods used by a business when deciding what to charge for its products.

Product life cycle – shows the different stages in the life of a product and the sales that can be expected at each stage.

Psychological pricing – setting the price slightly below a round figure.

Skimming or **creaming** – setting a high price initially and then lowering it later.

Unit costs – the same as average cost (total cost divided by output).

12 Distribution

Key points

1. Distribution channels.
2. Changes in distribution to reflect social trends – online distribution and changing from product to service.

Getting started

Cadbury is a well-known confectionery manufacturer. It is owned by Mondelēz International and is famous for its brands, including the Cadbury's Creme Egg®, Cadbury's Roses®, Cadbury's Flake® and Cadbury Dairy Milk®. Cadbury sells its products in as many outlets as possible, for instance newsagents, sweet shops, supermarkets, petrol stations, bars, cinemas, sports venues and vending machines.

Love4Bags is a family-owned business selling handbags, purses, accessories and jewellery. It is based in Yorkshire, with a shop in Otley. It also has a website, which can be used by online shoppers. However, Love4Bags specialises in shopping parties as a way to generate sales. This is where a person invites friends and family to a party, usually at a home location, and Love4Bags supplies a small range of stock for display, which partygoers are encouraged to buy. The party host receives a generous discount or free gift.

In what ways do these businesses sell their products to customers? Do you think Cadbury sells to online shoppers via a website? Give a reason for your answer. What are the advantages to Love4Bags of using shopping parties to sell goods?

Distribution

One important marketing activity is the distribution of products, which refers to the location where consumers can buy products from. If businesses cannot get products in the right place at the right time they are not likely to be successful. If products are not available in convenient locations consumers may not have the time to search for them. For example, if motorway service stations were located two or three miles from the motorway, they might struggle to survive. Food producers in the UK would have limited sales if they did not make groceries available in supermarkets.

Distribution channels

The route taken by a product from the producer to the customer is called a distribution channel. Businesses can choose from a number of different distribution channels. Some of the main channels used for consumer goods are shown in Figure 1. One approach is to sell goods directly to consumers, but others involve using intermediaries, such as retailers and wholesalers. These are businesses that provide links between producers and consumers. The diagram shows that some producers may use more than one channel of distribution.

Figure 1

Distribution channels for consumer goods

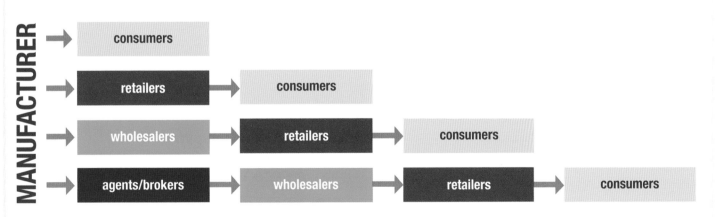

Direct selling

Some producers market their products directly to consumers. For example, many services are sold directly – banks, solicitors, hairdressers, dentists, plumbers, restaurants and taxis, for instance, do not normally use intermediaries. Some manufacturers may use **direct selling** as well. This can take a number of forms; for example, Avon uses door-to-door agents to sell its cosmetic products. Other methods include the following.

- **The internet.** A rapidly growing number of retailers sell their products online. Some manufacturers also have their own websites. Online distribution is discussed in more detail later in the unit.
- **Direct mail.** This is where suppliers send promotions through the post direct to customers inviting them to buy products. The utilities industry, for example, spent £11.9 million on direct mail in 2010, while almost 25 per cent of all direct mail is sent by financial services companies.
- **Door-to-door selling.** This is where salespeople visit households directly on spec, inviting people to buy products or services. Energy providers have used this method to try and persuade customers to change their supplier. However, after complaints about the tactics used by some of the door-to-door sellers, and the growth of comparison websites, the practice has been stopped by most energy providers. Arguably, this method of distribution is in decline.
- **Mail order catalogues.** This is where catalogues are distributed to customers who may buy the products illustrated – sometimes on credit. Traditionally people would fill in an order form and post it back to the company. However, most businesses using this method, such as Next, Littlewoods and Freemans, now also offer online ordering.
- **Direct response adverts.** Some businesses place adverts in newspapers, magazines or on television inviting people to buy goods and services. For example, local service providers, such as cleaners, gardeners, tutors, builders, childminders and many other traders offer their services in this way.
- **Shopping parties.** Representatives organise parties and invite people to attend for an enjoyable social occasion while having the opportunity to buy products such as jewellery, cosmetics, Tupperware, fashion accessories and lingerie.
- **Telephone selling.** Although many people do not welcome telephone calls from businesses trying to sell them goods and services, the practice is still widespread. Suppliers of insurance, home improvements, legal services (to help you make claims from the mis-selling of financial products, for example), energy-saving improvements and energy providers are often associated with this method of distribution. A development in telephone selling (sometimes called telemarketing) is the use of 'robocalls'. This is where an automated telephone call produced by a computerised autodialer delivers a message. The message usually invites people to press a number on the phone to continue the conversation.

The main advantage of direct selling is that intermediaries are not required, so producers are able to make more profit. Producers can also reach customers who do not like going to shops. The main drawback is that with some methods people cannot physically see the products until they have been purchased. Also, some people object to direct mail, door-to-door salespeople and unwanted telephone calls.

Retailing

Figure 1 showed that most distribution channels use **retailers**. These are businesses that buy goods and sell them straight to consumers. They provide a number of services.

- They buy large quantities from manufacturers and wholesalers, and sell small quantities to customers. This is called **breaking-bulk**.
- They sell in locations that are convenient to consumers. Most supermarkets, for example, are conveniently located and have ample parking space.
- They may add value to products by providing other services. These might include help with packing or delivery, repair services, information about products, warranties and gift-wrapping. Table 1 summarises the main forms of retail outlet used in the UK.

Table 1 Common types of retail outlet in the UK

Retailer	Description
Independents	Mainly small shops, though some can be quite large, such as newsagents, grocers and specialists (e.g. jewellers).
Supermarkets	Large chain stores selling up to 20,000 lines, including food and non-food products.
Department stores	Large stores divided into separate departments, such as menswear, lingerie, electricals and cosmetics.
Multiples	Chains of stores selling common goods, e.g. Next, WHSmith, Boots, H.Samuel and Jaeger.
Online retailers	Wide-ranging, from giants such as Amazon selling many goods, to small independents.
Superstores	Sometimes called hypermarkets – very large stores selling a wide variety of goods, often very cheaply.
Kiosks/street vendors	Small outlets, usually specialists, selling limited ranges in airports, stations, malls, etc.
Market traders	Usually sole traders selling from market stalls in streets, squares and market halls – can be temporary or permanent.

The UK grocery market was worth £174.5 billion in 2014, with around 55p in every £1 being spent on groceries. By 2019 it is expected to have grown to £203 billion. Figure 2 shows the distribution methods used in the grocery industry in the UK in 2014.

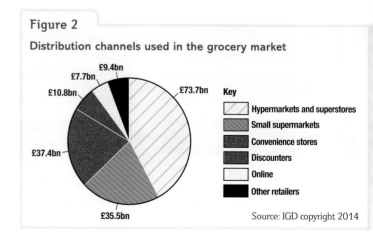

Figure 2

Distribution channels used in the grocery market

£9.4bn
£7.7bn
£10.8bn
£73.7bn
£37.4bn
£35.5bn

Key
- Hypermarkets and superstores
- Small supermarkets
- Convenience stores
- Discounters
- Online
- Other retailers

Source: IGD copyright 2014

Question 1

Shetland Blankets Ltd manufactures blankets made from Shetland wool. The company has a limited product line, but has been trading for 80 years. The company is profitable, but a new managing director wants to grow the business. Most of the blankets are distributed to independent retailers in Scotland. However, the company has a contract to supply a small multiple in the north of England. The new managing director wants to widen the distribution network. She thinks that contracts with department stores and one or two larger multiples would be a good short-term target. In the future the company could look into online selling, but at the moment the product line is too small to justify the investment needed to set up an online selling operation.

(a) What is the difference between a department store and a multiple?

(b) Explain one reason why distribution through multiples might be more profitable than independent retailers.

Wholesaling

Some producers use **wholesalers** to help distribute goods. Wholesalers usually buy from manufacturers and sell to retailers. Wholesalers may break bulk, repack goods, redistribute smaller quantities, store goods and provide delivery services. A wholesaler stocks goods produced by many manufacturers. Therefore retailers get to select from a wide range of merchandise.

Agents or brokers

The role of **agents** or **brokers** is to link buyers and sellers. They are used in a variety of markets. For example, travel agents sell holidays and flights for holiday companies, airlines and tour operators. Estate agents sell properties on behalf of vendors. Agents are also used to sell insurance, life insurance and other financial products. Manufacturers may also use agents when exporting. Agents can reduce the risk of selling overseas because they have knowledge of the country and the market.

Question 2

The use of agents when selling goods overseas is common. Agents are people who know the foreign market and can introduce a business to overseas customers. They are paid a commission for any sales made, ranging between 2.5 per cent and 15 per cent. When a business exports for the first time it may lack the experience and confidence to 'go it alone'. For example, a UK company trying to penetrate the Chinese market is likely to face a number of obstacles. The use of an agent may reduce the risk of exporting and provide a number of specific advantages.

* The costs of recruiting, training and paying specialist staff for sales overseas are avoided.

* An agent is likely to have a network of contacts that can be exploited immediately. Such contacts would take time to develop when 'going it alone'.

* Agents may be preferred to distributors because the seller then has more control over matters such as prices, display and brand image.

* Agents have the experience and knowledge needed to sell in places where culture, trading practices, commercial laws and other customs are different from the UK.

Despite the advantages of using agents when selling overseas there may be some drawbacks. For example, shipping and other related costs may not be met by an agent. After-sales service may be difficult to provide and the amount of control over marketing and brand image will be less than it would be if selling abroad independently.

Source: adapted from www.nibusinessinfo.co.uk

(a) Explain one motive for using an agent when selling overseas.

(b) Assess the advantages of using agents when trying to penetrate overseas markets.

Choosing the appropriate distribution channel

The channels of distribution chosen by a business will depend on a number of factors. It should also be noted that many businesses use a combination of different channels. This will help to widen the distribution network and reach a larger number of potential customers.

The nature of the product: Different types of products may require different distribution channels. Some examples are given below.

* Most **services** are sold directly to consumers. It might not be appropriate for window cleaners, gardeners and hairdressers, for example, to use intermediaries. This is because unlike goods, services cannot be held in stock.

* **Fast-moving consumer goods** like breakfast cereals, confectionery, crisps and toilet paper cannot be sold directly

by manufacturers to consumers. This is because such goods could not be sold effectively by manufacturers in single units. Wholesalers and retailers are used because they break bulk.

- Businesses producing **high-quality 'exclusive' products**, such as perfume and designer clothes, will choose their outlets very carefully. The image of their products is important, so they are not likely to use supermarkets, for example.
- **Products that need explanation or demonstration**, such as technical products or complex financial products might need to be sold by expert salespeople or specialists.

Cost: Businesses will normally choose the cheapest distribution channels. They also prefer direct channels. This is because if intermediaries are used they will take a share of the profit. Large supermarkets will try to buy direct from manufacturers as they can bulk buy and get lower prices. Independents are more likely to buy from wholesalers and will have to charge higher prices as a result. Many producers now sell direct to consumers from their websites. This helps to keep costs down.

The market: Producers selling to mass markets are likely to use intermediaries. In contrast, businesses targeting smaller markets are more likely to target customers directly. For example, a building contractor in a small town will deal directly with customers. Producers selling in overseas markets are likely to use agents because they know the market better. Businesses selling goods to other businesses are likely to use more direct channels.

Control: For some producers it is important to have complete control over distribution. For example, producers of exclusive products do not want to see them being sold in 'downmarket' outlets as this might damage their image. Some products, such as heating systems, require expert installation and need to comply with health and safety legislation. Producers of such products might prefer to handle installation themselves and deal directly with customers. They can then ensure safe installation more easily.

Changes in distribution to reflect social trends

The way in which goods and services are sold is subject to change. Many of these changes reflect social trends. Here are some examples.

- A huge growth in online shopping (this is discussed below).
- Building of large US-style shopping malls.
- Sellers using call centres to sell products, such as financial services.
- Supermarkets extending their product ranges and opening hours.
- Shopping becoming more of a leisure activity for many people.
- A growth in the use of TV shopping channels.
- The flourishing of charity shops on the high street.

Online distribution: The most important new trend is probably the development of online distribution. It is often called **e-commerce** because it involves the use of electronic systems to sell goods and services. There are two main types.

- **Business to consumers (B2C).** This is the selling of goods and services by businesses directly to consumers. Most e-tailing involves ordering goods online and taking delivery at home or work. However, new 'click & collect' services are being developed where people order goods online and then pick them up from a store or a central hub. In London, tube stations are being used as sites for hubs. Amazon has a well-developed network of pick-up points in the UK where they utilise lockers and post offices. Most large retailers now have online services. Other examples of B2C e-commerce include:
  - o tickets for air, rail and coach travel
  - o tickets for sports fixtures, cinemas, theatres and attractions
  - o holidays, weekend breaks and hotel rooms
  - o access to online audio and film broadcasts
  - o a wide range of goods on eBay and other auction sites.
- **Business to business (B2B).** This involves businesses selling to other businesses online. Businesses can also use specialist software to purchase resources. The software helps to find the cheapest supplier and carries out all the paperwork. The benefits to consumers and businesses of online distribution are summarised in Tables 2 and 3 respectively.

Table 2 Benefits to consumers of online distribution

• It is cheaper because online retailers often have lower costs
• Consumers can shop 24/7
• There is generally a huge amount of choice
• People can shop from anywhere if they have access to the internet

Table 3 Benefits to businesses of online distribution

• E-tailers may not have to meet the costs of operating stores
• Lower start-up costs – both fixed and variable costs are lower
• Lower costs when processing transactions – many systems are automated
• Less paper is needed for documents, such as invoices and receipts
• Payments can be made and received online using credit cards or PayPal
• B2C businesses can offer goods to a much wider market – e.g. global
• Businesses can serve their customers 24/7
• Businesses have more choice of where to locate their operations

Despite the advantages to both consumers and businesses of online distribution, there are some drawbacks for businesses. They face increasing competition, since selling online is a relatively cheap method of distribution. As it can be organised from any location in the world, at any time of the day, businesses will face more competition from overseas. There is also a lack of human contact, which might not suit some customers, and there is heavy reliance on delivery services where e-tailers often lack control on the quality of delivery. There may also be technical problems online. For example, websites can crash or be attacked by viruses, and internet connections can be unreliable. Finally, there is also a security risk as computer hackers might gain access to sensitive information.

Additional drawbacks for consumers include not being able to physically inspect goods before purchase, the risk of a poor after-sales service, and the exclusion of customers without internet access or credit cards. In addition, bogus traders may be more difficult to identify online and people may have problems taking delivery of goods, for instance if they are at work all day.

Question 3

Figure 3

UK online spending 2011–2014

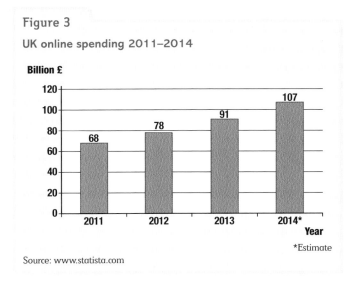

Source: www.statista.com

(a) Calculate the percentage change in online retail spending between 2011 and 2014.

(b) Explain the advantages to businesses of online distribution.

(c) Assess what might account for the change in online spending.

Changing from product to service: In most Western economies the size of the tertiary (service) sector has grown at the expense of the primary (agriculture and mining) and secondary (manufacturing and construction) sectors. Consequently, businesses have had to focus more on the distribution of services. Most services are sold directly to consumers, so businesses have to consider more carefully the range of direct distribution channels that are available.

In some cases businesses that once sold products (goods) are now selling services and have to consider how this impacts on their distribution. Businesses have had to adapt to changes in technology and consumer buying habits. Here are some examples.

- People used to buy music on CDs, which may have been sold by a retailer or wholesaler. However, people now listen to music by streaming or downloading via the internet direct to computers, tablets and mobile phones. Consumers are able to access vast databases of music from a variety of different locations.

- To watch a film, people could buy a DVD sold in a retail outlet. Now there are film channels that stream films that can be viewed on a computer, mobile phone or television via the internet.

- Instead of buying a newspaper from a local shop, some businesses provide a subscription service which allows consumers to view news online.

Case study

UNILEVER

Unilever is an Anglo-Dutch multinational company selling a huge range of fast-moving consumer goods. Examples include food, beverages, cleaning agents and personal care products. Its 400 or more brands include well-known names such as Knorr®, Hellmann's®, PG Tips® and Surf®. Unilever distributes its products to over 190 countries using a network of outlets, from multinational retailers, wholesalers and distributors to small independent shops. Large national and international retailers, including Metro, Walmart, Carrefour and Tesco, play an important role in developed markets, such as the US and Europe.

Unilever also sells products through a diverse group of distributors, wholesalers and millions of small independent outlets and kiosks, particularly in developing countries. This diversified distribution network supports the incomes of millions of small-scale businesses and individual sellers around the world.

Isolated or remote areas without the infrastructure of more developed regions are difficult to penetrate. Unilever is therefore encouraging small retailers in such areas to undertake door-to-door selling. People receive practical help in the form of marketing, accounting and sales training, access to credit and even the provision of bicycles to help them get around. This initiative provides employment and the opportunity for people to become part of Unilever's large sales network in countries such as Sri Lanka, Pakistan and Bangladesh. In India, for instance, Unilever's door-to-door selling operation is called Shakti and it employs 65,000 women in some of the country's poorest rural areas.

(a) What is meant by wholesaling? (2 marks)

(b) Explain one reason why Unilever uses door-to-door selling in emerging economies, such as India. (4 marks)

(c) Explain one reason why online selling might be an unsuitable distribution channel for Unilever. (4 marks)

(d) Assess the factors that might influence a business like Unilever when choosing distribution channels. (12 marks)

Key terms

Agent or **broker** – an intermediary that brings together buyers and sellers.

Breaking-bulk – dividing a large quantity of goods received from a supplier before selling them on in smaller quantities to customers.

Direct selling – producers selling their products directly to consumers.

Distribution – the delivery of goods from the producer to the consumer.

Distribution channel – the route taken by a product from the producer to the customer.

E-commerce – the use of electronic systems to sell goods and services.

Intermediaries – links between the producer and the consumer.

Retailer – a business that buys goods from manufacturers and wholesalers, and sells them in small quantities to consumers.

Wholesaler – a business that buys goods from manufacturers and sells them in smaller quantities to retailers.

Knowledge check

1. Explain why it is important for a business to have goods available for sale (a) at the right place (b) at the right time.

2. Give three examples of direct selling.

3. What is one main disadvantage of telephone selling?

4. State three functions undertaken by retailers.

5. Explain the difference between a supermarket and a department store.

6. State two types of business that might use an agent to distribute goods.

7. Explain why a cereal farmer is unlikely to use retailers to distribute goods.

8. What are three advantages to consumers of online distribution?

9. Give three examples of recent developments in distribution.

10. How is car insurance most likely to be distributed?

13 Marketing strategy

Key points

1. The product life cycle.
2. Extension strategies: product and promotion.
3. Boston Matrix and the product portfolio.
4. Marketing strategies for different types of market: mass markets, niche markets, business to business (B2B) and business to consumer (B2C) marketing.
5. Consumer behaviour – how businesses develop customer loyalty.

Getting started

Some products have long product life cycles. This means that they are on the market for many years. One example is Bisto gravy powder, which was first introduced in 1908. It can still be bought in shops today. Other products have shorter life cycles. They are introduced and marketed for a while, but then withdrawn. For example, the Sony Walkman® (a portable compact cassette player) was on the market for about 30 years before being withdrawn in 2009. Some products have very short lives indeed. They are sometimes called 'fads'. Certain children's toys are a good example.

Describe some possible marketing activities that Bisto's manufacturer might have used to keep the product 'alive' in the market. Why did the Sony Walkman disappear from the market in 2009? How might the marketing of a product or service change over its lifespan?

The product life cycle

Product is one part of the marketing mix. For marketing to be effective, a business must be aware of its product life cycle. The product life cycle shows the different stages that a product passes through over time and the sales that can be expected at each stage. By considering product life cycles, businesses can plan for the future. Most products pass through six stages – development, introduction, growth, maturity/saturation and decline. These are illustrated in Figure 1.

Figure 1

The product life cycle

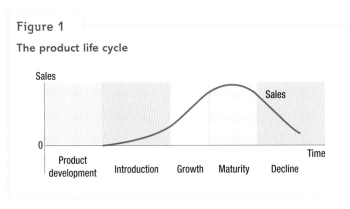

Development: During the development stage the product is being **researched** and **designed**. Suitable ideas must be investigated, developed and tested. If an idea is considered worth pursuing then a prototype or model of the product might be produced. A decision will then be made about whether or not to launch the product. A large number of new products never progress beyond this stage and will **fail**. This is because businesses are often reluctant to take risks associated with new products. During the development stage it is likely that the business will spend to develop the product and **costs** will be high. As there will be no sales at this stage, the business will initially be spending but receiving no revenue.

Introduction: At the start of this stage the product will be **launched**. As the product is new to the market, sales initially are often slow. Costs are incurred when the product is launched. It may be necessary to build a new production line or plant, and the firm will have to meet promotion and distribution costs. A business is also likely to spend on **promotion** to make consumers aware of the new product. Therefore, it is likely that the product will still not be profitable. **Prices** may be set high to cover promotion costs. But they may also be set low in order to break into the market. Few outlets may stock products at this stage. The length of this stage will vary according to the product. With brand-new technical products, for example, the introduction stage can be quite long. It takes time for consumers to become confident that such products 'work'. At first the price of such products may be quite high. On the other hand, a product can be an instant hit resulting in very rapid sales growth. Fashion products and some **fast-moving consumer goods** may enjoy this type of start to their life.

Growth: Once the product is established and consumers are aware of it, sales may begin to grow rapidly, new customers buy the product and there are repeat purchases. Unit costs may fall as production increases. The product then becomes **profitable**. If it is a new product and there is a rapid growth in sales, **competitors** may launch their own versions. This can lead to a slowdown of the rise in sales. Businesses may need to consider their **prices and promotion**. For example, a high price charged initially may need to be lowered, or promotion may need to increase to encourage brand loyalty.

Maturity and saturation: At some stage the growth in sales will level off. The product has become established with a stable market share at this point. Sales will have peaked and competitors will have entered the market to take advantage of profits. As more firms enter the market, it will become saturated. Some businesses will be forced out of the market, as there are too many firms competing for consumers. During the maturity and saturation stages of the product life cycle, many businesses use extension strategies to extend the life of their products. These are discussed below.

Decline: For the majority of products, sales will eventually decline. This is usually due to changing consumer tastes, new technology or the introduction of new products. The product will lose its appeal to customers. At some stage it will be withdrawn or sold to another business. It may still be possible to make a profit if a high price can be charged and little is spent on promotion or other costs.

Extension strategies

Extension strategies, ways to prolong the life of a product before it starts to decline, are popular with businesses. This is because the costs of product development are high and extension strategies help a product to generate more cash. Two general approaches are often used. One is to make some adjustments to the product; the second is to invest in promotion.

Product adjustments: Many companies try to prolong the life of the product by 'freshening' it up. This might involve making improvements, updating the product, repackaging the product or extending the range.

- Updating is quite a common approach for technical products and certain types of consumer durables. For example, in the car industry firms are keen to bring out updated versions of their successful models. An example is shown in Question 1 on the next page.
- Some businesses add value to their products by making improvements. For example, computer manufacturers bring out new machines that are faster, have more memory, look more stylish and have more functions than previous versions. In the service industry, banks offer new accounts with extra services, such as travel insurance, breakdown cover and mobile phone insurance.
- Another common approach is to extend the product range. Crisp manufacturers have used this method in the past by bringing out new flavours. In 2014, Walkers launched 'pulled pork in a sticky BBQ sauce' flavoured crisps after inviting consumers to vote for their favourite from a list of proposed new flavours submitted by members of the public.
- Some businesses give the impression that the product has been modified by changing the packaging. For example, many soft drinks manufacturers sell their brands in cans, glass bottles and different-sized plastic bottles. In the music industry, record companies often release compilations of hits from a number of previously released albums. The new compilation is supported with a new cover.

Promotion: Some businesses prefer to leave the product unchanged but give a boost to flagging sales by investing in promotion campaigns.

- One approach is to find new uses for a product. For example, WD-40 was first developed in 1953 to repel water and prevent corrosion. Today it has multiple advertised uses, such as removing dirt and residue, loosening screws and displacing moisture in car engines.
- Some businesses try to find new markets for their products. For example, a local business might start to serve a larger region. A regional business might try to market its products nationally. A business with a national market might begin to export its products. Some UK retailers, such as Tesco and Marks & Spencer, have tried this approach with mixed success.
- Investment in a sizeable advertising campaign can sometimes rejuvenate sales. A big advertising campaign on television, for example, can get people interested in a product again.
- Another approach is to encourage more frequent use of the product. An example of this might be cereal manufacturers persuading people to eat cereals for supper as well as for breakfast.

The effect that an extension strategy can have on a product life cycle is shown in Figure 2. As the market becomes saturated and sales begin to fall, the decline in sales is delayed by the use of an extension strategy. It would be sensible for a business to extend the life of a mature product before sales start to decline. Firms that can predict falling sales from market forecasts may attempt to use extension strategies before the decline takes place – that is at the maturity stage.

Figure 2

Extension strategies

Question 1

The Golf GTI is produced by Volkswagen (VW), the German-based multinational car manufacturer. The Mk I GTI was unveiled at the Frankfurt Motor Show in 1975. The powerful hatchback could reach 60 mph in nine seconds. Designed with the emphasis on fun, it had a tartan trim and an iconic golf ball gearshift. To extend the life of the model a further six versions were introduced, as outlined below.

- **1984** The Mk II GTI was launched with a new chassis structure, a 1,781 cc engine and new styling to appeal to a new generation of drivers.
- **1987** The Mk III GTI had a new 2.0-litre eight-valve engine and improved aerodynamics. This reduced the 0–60 mph time to 8.3 seconds.
- **1998** The Mk IV GTI had improved refinement and safety. In 2002 the fastest and most powerful GTI produced to date was released for the 25th Anniversary Edition.
- **2004** Launched at the Paris Motor Show, the Mk V GTI was the most powerful GTI yet produced. The vehicle had new springs, dampers and anti-roll bars.
- **2009** Mk VI GTI won the 'Best Hot Hatch' award at the Auto Express Awards. Testers complimented the sharp handling, impressive refinement and excellent comfort, and called it the best Golf to date.
- **2012** The Golf GTI Mk VII was launched with a lighter but stronger platform. This was the most fuel-efficient GTI to date, and was capable of 0–62mph in 6.5 seconds.

Source: adapted from www.volkswagen.co.uk

(a) What is meant by an extension strategy?

(b) Explain one way in which VW extended the life of the Golf GTI.

(c) Explain one advantage to VW of using an extension strategy.

Boston Matrix and the product portfolio

Product life cycle analysis shows businesses that sales of products eventually decline. A well-organised business with one or more products will attempt to phase out old products and introduce new ones. This is known as managing the **product portfolio** or product mix.

The product portfolio: The product portfolio will be made up of **product lines**. A product line is a group of products which are similar. For example, televisions are a product line including flat screen, HD widescreen and portable televisions. With a constant launch of new products, a business can make sure a 'vacuum' is not created as products reach the end of their life.

Figure 3 shows how a business can manage its product portfolio. Say that a business over a particular time period aims to launch three products. By organising their launch at regular intervals, there is never a gap in the market. As one product is declining, another is growing and further launches are planned. At point (i), as sales of product X are growing, product Y has just been launched. This means that at point (ii), when sales of product X have started to decline, sales of product Y are growing and product Z has just been launched.

This simple example shows a 'snapshot' of three products only. In practice, a business may have many products. It would hope that existing products remain in 'maturity' for a long period. The profit from these mature products would be used to 'subsidise' the launch of new products. New products would be costly at first, and would make no profit for the business.

Examples of businesses that have successfully managed their product portfolios are sweet manufacturers. Companies such as Nestlé produce a wide range of products, including KitKat, Milkybar and Yorkie, and constantly look to launch new products.

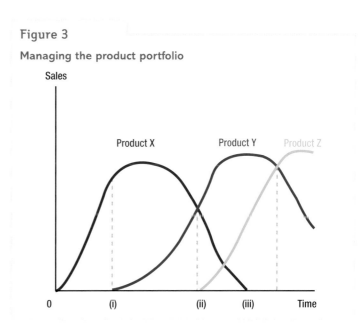

Figure 3

Managing the product portfolio

The Boston Matrix: One problem for firms when planning their product portfolios is that it is very difficult in practice to tell what stage of the life cycle a product is at. Also, there is no standard lifetime for products. For example, young people's fashion clothing has life cycles which can be predicted with some certainty. Other products are less reliable. Who, for example, could have predicted the lengthy life cycles of products such as Heinz baked beans and the VW Beetle, or the short life cycle of products such as the Sinclair C5 – a sort of 'mini-car' introduced in the 1980s?

A useful technique for allowing firms to analyse their product portfolios is the Product Portfolio Matrix developed by the Boston Consulting Group. It is sometimes called the **Boston Matrix** or the Growth Share Matrix. This is shown in Figure 4 on the next page. Products are categorized according to two criteria.

- **Market growth.** How fast is the market for the product growing? The market may be declining or it may be expanding. Sales of a product in a fast expanding market have a better chance of growing than a product in a stagnant or declining market.

- **Relative market share.** How strong is the product within its market? Is it a market leader that other products follow? Is it a product that is twelfth in terms of sales? To measure this the market share of a product is compared with the strongest rival product. For example, if Product X had a market share of 10 per cent and the market leader had 40 per cent, then the relative market share of Product X is 0.25 (10 per cent ÷ 40 per cent). If Product Y is a market leader with 50 per cent market share and the next most important product had a market share of 25 per cent, the relative market share of product Y is 2.0 (50 per cent ÷ 25 per cent).

Using these criteria the products of a business can be placed into one of four categories on the Boston Matrix.

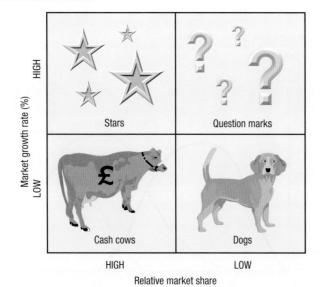

Figure 4

The Boston Matrix

Market growth rate (%) — HIGH / LOW

Stars | Question marks
Cash cows | Dogs

HIGH — LOW

Relative market share

Source: adapted from The BCG Portfolio Matrix from the Product Portfolio Matrix, © 1970, The Boston Consulting Group (BCG)

Stars: A star is a product with a high market growth and a relatively high market share. Stars are valuable to businesses. The product will be in a strong position in its market as it has a high market share and the business can take advantage of a fast-growing market. A star is already likely to be **profitable** as it has a relatively high market share. But a business will need to **invest** in the product to cope with a growing market and growing sales. This could mean investing in new production facilities or promotion to fend off competition. **Net cash flow** may be nearly zero. This is because although profits will be high, bringing money in, investment spending will also be high, leading to outflows.

Cash cows: A cash cow is a product with a relatively high market share. It is therefore well positioned in the market and likely to be **profitable**. But the market it is in will have weak growth. So there will be little chance of increasing sales and profits in future. There will be little need for **investment**. With slow growth in sales there should be little need for new premises, for example. Cash cows have strong positive **net cash**

flow. Money coming into the business from profits will not be taken out via investment.

Question marks: Question marks, sometimes known as problem children or wildcats, are products with a relatively low market share in a fast-growing market. This can be a problem for a business because it is unclear what should be done with these products. If a product is performing weakly it is unlikely to be **profitable**. But as it is in a fast-growing market, there is potential to turn it into a star. **Net cash flow** is likely to be zero or negative. Weak relative market share means that it will not be profitable. But **investment** will be needed to cope with expanding sales in a fast-growing market.

Dogs: These are products with a relatively low market share in a market with low growth. Dogs have poor prospects for future sales and **profits**. They may generate some **positive net cash flow** because they will need little **investment** but may earn some profit. But if they make little or no profit, net cash flow may be zero or even negative.

Businesses can make use of the Boston Matrix to manage their product portfolios.

Balancing product lines: Businesses must ensure that their product portfolios do not contain too many items within each category. Naturally, they do not want lots of 'Dogs', but they should also avoid having too many 'Stars' and 'Question marks'. Products on the top of the Boston Matrix are in the early stages of the product life cycle and are in growing markets. But the cost of developing and promoting them will not yet have been recovered. This will drain resources. Balancing these with 'Cash cows' will mean that the positive net cash flow from the 'Cash cows' can be used to support products in a growing market. The development cost of 'Cash cows' is likely to have already been recovered and promotional costs should be low relative to sales. This does not mean though that a business would want lots of 'Cash cows' and few 'Question marks' and 'Stars'. This is because many of the 'Stars' and perhaps some 'Question marks' might become the 'Cash cows' of the future.

Taking appropriate decisions: Products in different categories in the Matrix may require different approaches.
- Stars have great future potential. They are future cash cows. A business will need to **build** the brand of these products so that sales increase and competition is fought off successfully.
- Cash cows might be **milked** for cash, which can then be used to develop other products. Or the business may decide to spend just enough on promotion and development to maintain sales and market share, known as **holding**.
- For question marks a business has choices. It can **build** the brand, hoping to turn it into a star, **harvest** the product by raising price and cutting promotion so that profits are increased, or **divest** itself of the product, withdrawing it or selling it because it is not making a profit.
- Dogs may be divested if they are not making a profit or in some cases harvested.

Question 2

CheezyBix Ltd manufactures a range of cheesy snacks. The business currently has four products in its portfolio. They are shown in Figure 5. CheezyBix, a product first launched in 1987, earns about 65 per cent of the company's revenue. It has a high market share and it is still growing.

Figure 5

CheezyBix Ltd product portfolio

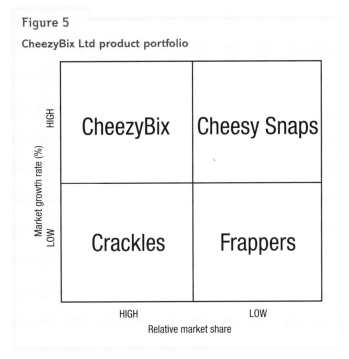

(a) Explain how you would categorise the position of Crackles in the Boston Matrix using Figure 5.

(b) Explain one way in which CheezyBix Ltd might use the information in Figure 5.

Marketing strategies

A marketing strategy is a set of plans that aim to achieve a specific marketing objective. For example, a local car rental company might aim to become the market leader in the region. Its strategy to achieve this objective might be to:

- improve the quality of customer service by delivering cars to people's homes
- contact all previous customers offering them a half-price deal
- offer a three-day weekend rental for the price of two days
- invest £500 in a local newspaper advert
- donate a vehicle to a local community group to get some PR
- set up a website to promote the business and take online bookings.

This strategy involves all aspects of the marketing mix and a number of different promotional methods.

Strategies for mass markets: Some businesses sell products into mass markets. Such markets are huge, often global, and can have millions of potential customers. Procter & Gamble, Heinz, Kellogg's, Coca-Cola and General Motors are examples of businesses that sell into mass markets. Mass markets are usually very competitive because the rewards for success can be significant. A wide range of different marketing strategies can be used in a mass market, but some general similarities are as follows.

- **Product.** In a mass market there will be many products vying for customer attention. Most of these products will be very close substitutes for each other. The most successful businesses are likely to be those that can differentiate their product in some way. Developing a USP will help a business's product 'stand out from the pack'. If a business is unable to differentiate its product it will have to rely on other elements in the marketing mix to compensate.
- **Price.** The prices charged by businesses in a mass market are likely to be very similar. All businesses in the market are likely to fear a price war because they usually reduce revenue for every competitor. This helps to explain why businesses are happy to charge the 'going rate' in the market. Price leadership is common in mass markets where the dominant business, perhaps the one with the lowest unit costs, sets the price and everyone else follows.
- **Promotion.** In the absence of price competition, firms look to non-price competition to help gain an edge. This means they are prepared to invest heavily in advertising and promotion because it is such an important part of the marketing mix in mass markets. An overwhelming majority of TV adverts are placed by businesses selling into mass markets. Perhaps less than five per cent of those that see the adverts will buy the product. However, five per cent of several million is a significant number.
- **Place.** Businesses serving mass markets will often use multiple channels to distribute their goods. Businesses selling fast-moving consumer goods will target supermarkets, wholesalers, independents and any other outlet that is suited to their particular product. Some manufacturers pay supermarkets to display their goods in prominent places – at eye level or at the end of aisles, for example. The internet is used increasingly by businesses to sell goods and services in mass markets. All banks, for instance, offer online bank accounts and an increasing number of supermarkets offer online shopping and delivery or 'click & collect' services. The internet has allowed small businesses and other independents to have access to mass markets. For example, a small glove manufacturer based in, say, Dumbarton in Scotland, could distribute its products to individual customers anywhere in the world.

Strategies for niche markets: Customers in niche markets have very particular needs, which are sometimes neglected by larger firms. Consequently, there is a gap in the market for a business that is prepared to tailor goods or services to this small customer group. Businesses selling to niche markets will use different marketing strategies from those selling into mass markets.

- **Product.** In a niche market the product is likely to have quite significant differences from its rivals. For example, in the dining out market there are around 420,000 restaurants in the UK. However, only four of these have been awarded three

Michelin stars (the highest award possible for food quality and service). These four restaurants serve stunning food of the highest possible quality – very different from that served in the overwhelming majority of other restaurants. They cater for a particular niche – people who want to experience the very best dining, perhaps just as a one-off, and are prepared to pay for it. In niche markets products will be designed carefully in order to meet the very specific needs of the customer group. Product will be a key element in the marketing mix.

- **Price.** Businesses selling in niche markets have more flexibility in their pricing. There is less competition in niche markets so higher prices can be charged without losing significant market share to rivals. Also, customers may be prepared to pay higher prices if their specific needs are being met effectively. For example, the prices charged by restaurants with three Michelin stars can be over £100 per person (without wine).
- **Promotion.** In niche markets promotion and advertising will tend to be more targeted. Since niche markets are smaller there is less need to use national media when advertising. Businesses need to identify their customer profile very accurately to ensure that advertising and promotion expenditure is not wasted. Adverts are likely to be placed in specialised publications. For example, yachts and chandlery (boat equipment and accessories) are likely to be advertised in magazines such as *Yachting Monthly* and *Boating World*. Some manufacturers of golf clubs and golf accessories advertise on TV, but only use specialised channels, such as Sky Sports.
- **Place.** Businesses selling into niche markets are often more selective when choosing distribution channels. They are more likely to use exclusive distributors or to handle distribution privately. They will also use the internet if it is practical. One example is Blue Mountain coffee. This is a high-quality coffee grown mainly in Jamaica, which can only be purchased from selected stores in the UK, and online. It is marketed at around £24 for 227g compared to around £3.50 for rival beans, which might be sold in supermarkets, for example.

Strategies for business-to-business (B2B) and business-to-consumer (B2C) markets

Many businesses supply goods and services to other businesses. For example, JCB produces a wide range of machinery for use in the construction industry. It sells most of its products to construction companies and plant hire companies all over the world. The marketing strategies used by companies that sell to other businesses (B2B) are likely to be different from those discussed above, that sell to consumers (B2C). In B2B marketing, one approach is to distinguish between outbound and inbound marketing strategies.

Outbound marketing strategies: This involves directing marketing material at potential customers whether they are expecting it or not. This could include sending direct mail, email, telemarketing, sponsorship, targeted adverts in specialist publications or trade shows. However, there are some drawbacks using this approach. People are increasingly ignoring adverts. How many do people remember? Also, many people object to cold calling and other intrusive methods. Persistence in the use of these could damage a brand's reputation. Many of the leads obtained using these methods are poor quality, 'fizzling out' and wasting resources. It has also been reported that outbound leads cost significantly more to acquire than inbound leads.

Inbound marketing strategies: This involves attracting potential customers to websites when they are looking for suppliers or solutions to problems. Some of the common inbound marketing techniques are summarised in Table 1.

Table 1 Common inbound marketing techniques

Method	Description
Blogging	Provide content on company blogs to help draw in potential customers
Social media marketing	Develop a following on social media, such as Twitter, LinkedIn and Facebook
Search engine optimisation	Increase website traffic by getting a high-ranking placement in searches
Free e-books	Offer useful, in-depth information for website visitors to download
Video marketing	Produce short and informative video clips for website visitors
Targeted email marketing	Send personalised emails targeted to people – for example, those who who have downloaded a free e-book

The use of inbound methods also has challenges. For example, it requires effort and resources to build up enough useful content on websites to change visitors into leads. Recruitment of experienced inbound marketers can be difficult, and it can be tricky to keep the strategy up-to-date with rapidly emerging trends.

Hybrid strategies: This involves a combination of both outbound and inbound methods. It is reckoned that inbound strategies take at least six months to generate results, so some outbound methods can be employed in the short term. Once inbound methods start to generate meaningful leads some of the less effective outbound methods can be dropped. This will help to reduce costs and create sustainable growth in market share.

Exam tip
You need to understand that marketing strategies can vary hugely. They depend on a wide range of factors, such as the nature of the product, the resources available to a company, the aim of the strategy, the size and nature of the market, corporate strategy and the creativity of employees. You would expect very different products to be marketed differently; for instance, the way healthcare and confectionery are marketed is likely to be very different. However, businesses in the same industry can also have different marketing strategies. Small businesses will use different approaches to multinationals because they have fewer resources. Some businesses may have similarities in their marketing strategies, but rarely will they be identical.

Developing customer loyalty

A business is likely to be more successful if it can persuade customers to keep returning. How can businesses develop customer loyalty?

- **Communication.** A business must keep customers informed. In a mass market this might involve using national advertising campaigns to tell customers about new products. Some businesses may use reassuring adverts. These help to convince customers that they have made the right purchase. Some firms send out regular newsletters, usually by email, to keep customers up to date with company events. Regular communication helps to build a relationship between a business and a customer. If a bond can be formed customers are more likely to return.

- **Customer service.** Customers are more likely to return to a business if they receive high-quality customer service. Employees who come into contact with customers must be professional, consistent and conduct themselves with integrity. Customer service can often be improved by dealing with matters more promptly, providing a more effective after-sales service or making the 'purchasing experience' a pleasant one. Some businesses provide customers with refreshments while they are conducting a transaction.

- **Customer incentives.** Many businesses reward their customers if they keep returning. Some supermarkets use loyalty cards. In 2014, Morrisons launched its Match & More loyalty card. Under the scheme, Morrisons' prices are checked against a database of thousands of products at other retailers. Consumers are awarded points if a product they have bought from Morrisons is sold more cheaply by a rival. For example, if a rival's product is 50 pence cheaper than Morrisons, then 500 points are added to a customer's Match & More account. Points are also awarded on hundreds of the store's products. Customers are rewarded with a £5 voucher for every 5,000 points they collect. Such schemes encourage people to keep returning to the same provider in order to accumulate enough points for the reward.

- **Personalisation.** Some businesses try to deal with customers on a personal level. They may address individual customers by their name – perhaps in person or in mail shots. Some firms send customers birthday cards and Christmas cards to help build relationships. However, dealing with a customer at a personal level is a lot easier for a smaller business than, say, a multinational.

- **Preferential treatment.** Many people like the idea of receiving preferential treatment from a business. For example, some nightclubs offer VIP areas reserved exclusively for selected customers – this treatment is usually for customers that spend a lot of money. Many airlines have VIP lounges at airports where first class, business class, or other select passengers can relax away from the 'hustle and bustle' of normal airport business. The lounges usually offer free refreshments, free access to Wi-Fi, satellite television, comfortable seating and showers. The principle behind all this is that if a business can provide customers with preferential treatment they may return for more.

Question 3

A number of banks offer their customers 'cashback deals' when using credit cards. This means that a credit card user can receive an amount of cash depending on how much is spent on the card. For example, American Express offered customers 5 per cent cashback if they spent up to £2,000 in the first three months of a platinum card membership. After the initial three months customers could earn up to 1.25 per cent cashback, depending on how much they spent each month. If customers spent:

- between £0 and £3,500, they got 0.5 per cent cashback

- between £3,500 and £7,500, they got 1 per cent cashback

- over £7,501, they got 1.25 per cent cashback.

Provided customers spent a minimum of £3,000 in a year, almost every pound spent using the card qualified for cashback. There was no annual fee charged on this level of membership (the Platinum Cashback Everyday Credit Card).

(a) Calculate the amount of cashback a customer would be entitled to if £5,000 is spent on the card in the ninth month of ownership.

(b) Explain one way in which cashback cards might help to develop customer loyalty.

Case study

WATER FUSION

In 2012 Water-First launched Water Fusion, a brand extension of its best-selling soft drink. It contained less sugar and fewer calories than most leading brands of soft drinks. It was launched as part of a summer promotion, associated with government and industry efforts to tackle obesity. The mass appeal marketing campaign targeted young professionals, emphasising the lower sugar content and lower calories. It highlighted the blend of water and natural fruit juices, and used attractive yellow packaging.

The launch of Water Fusion was supported by a multi-million-pound media campaign. Features of the marketing strategy included the following.

- Raising awareness of the new yellow packaging, using print and digital methods to encourage consumers to try the drink at a special summer discount price.
- Driving awareness through shopper marketing activity and a presence at key summer events in major cities.
- Product sampling in major retailers.
- Advertising on public transport using outdoor posters, alongside digital screens, Facebook and Twitter. Water Fusion used over 4,000 sites, including significant locations on major routes for rail, underground, bus and commuter traffic.

The whole marketing strategy was designed to establish the product features, raise awareness of the benefits of lower calories with natural sweetness, and encourage people to

try the product. It was reported that television advertising involving celebrities would be used at a later date. The retail price of Water Fusion was set at the same level as other leading brands.

Figure 6 shows the amount of money Water-First spent on advertising between 2009 and 2013.

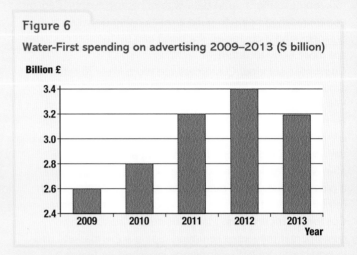

Figure 6

Water-First spending on advertising 2009–2013 ($ billion)

Q

(a) Explain Water-First's distribution policy in this case. (4 marks)

(b) Explain how Water-First is using an extension strategy in this case. (4 marks)

(c) Evaluate the importance of marketing to Water-First. (20 marks)

Key terms

Boston Matrix – a 2x2 matrix model that analyses a product portfolio according to the growth rate of the market and the relative market share of products within the market.
Extension strategies – methods used to prolong the life of a product.
Marketing strategy – a set of plans that aim to achieve a specific marketing objective.
Product lines – a group of products that are very similar.
Product portfolio – the collection of products a business is currently marketing.

Knowledge check

1. Explain the first stage in the product life cycle.
2. What pricing strategy might be used in the launch stage of the product life cycle?
3. What happens to sales in the maturity stage of the product life cycle?
4. Why might some products decline very quickly?
5. Give three examples of possible extension strategies.
6. What is the difference between a product portfolio and a product line?
7. What is meant by a 'Question mark' in the Boston Matrix?
8. How might businesses distribute their products in a mass market?
9. Why are prices likely to be higher in niche markets?
10. What is the difference between outbound and inbound B2B marketing?
11. Give three examples of inbound B2B marketing.
12. State three ways in which a business might develop customer loyalty.

14 Approaches to staffing

Key points

1. Staff as an asset and staff as a cost.
2. Flexible workforce: multi-skilling, part-time and temporary, flexible hours and home working, outsourcing.
3. Distinction between dismissal and redundancy.
4. Employer/employee relationships: individual approach and collective bargaining.

Getting started

Agueda Bega runs a gym in Brighton. She employs nine staff, six of whom are part-time. Most of the part-time staff work evenings and weekends when the gym is busy. Agueda has a very good relationship with her employees. Every month she takes all of her staff out for a meal. She encourages her employees to work as a team and sees the monthly meal out as an opportunity to bond team members and discuss work issues. She also encourages staff to come up with new ideas for the business in the future.

What is an advantage to Agueda of employing part-time staff? What might be the benefits to the business of having a good relationship with employees? Agueda thinks she treats staff as an asset. What does this mean? What are the advantages of organising staff as a team?

Approaches to staffing

In some businesses the owner is the only person working in the organisation. However, as a business grows there is usually a need to employ people to share the workload. Businesses can be defined according to the number of people they employ. For example, using the definition of size of a business in the UK:

- small businesses employ between 1 and 49 people
- medium-sized businesses employ between 50 and 249 people
- large businesses employ 250 people or more.

Tesco was one of the largest business employers in the UK in 2015, with its website referring to around 310,000 staff.

Different businesses have different approaches to their staff. Some view staff as assets, while others view them as costs. These approaches might have implications for levels of productivity.

Staff as an asset: Employers who view their staff as assets will value their employees and have concern for their welfare. Staff will be valued because employers recognise that their efforts will help the business to perform more effectively. Such employers will therefore try to meet the needs of employees. This might involve providing:

- acceptable remuneration
- reasonable holidays, sick leave, maternity/paternity leave and pensions

- a safe and comfortable working environment
- training, so that staff can develop skills and carry out work tasks competently and safely
- job security and opportunities to interact with colleagues
- recognition and professional relationships
- clear and effective leadership
- chances for promotion
- opportunities to solve problems, work in teams and be creative.

If employers treat staff as assets, they will also make an effort to retain them. They know employees want to be challenged, acknowledged and rewarded. These employers know that while money may not be the motivator for all employees, it is still important and they may well provide above-average wages. This approach is likely to help recruit, retain and motivate high-quality staff.

In 1991 the UK government set up an organisation, Investors in People (IIP). Its purpose was to help employers to maximise the potential of employees. IIP encourages businesses and other organisations to improve the management and development of their employees. It does this by giving accreditation to businesses that can demonstrate very high standards of practice in people management and development. IIP uses ten performance indicators, such as empowerment, continuous improvement and leadership, when assessing an organisation's commitment to its people. Businesses also have to meet 39 accreditation requirements to gain the IIP award.

Staff as a cost: If employers view their staff as a cost, their focus is likely to be different. Like any other cost, they will try to minimise it wherever possible. This might involve:

- paying just the legal national minimum wage
- using **zero-hours contracts**
- neglecting investment in training
- using financial incentives to raise productivity
- providing the minimum legal 'employee rights' in relation to sick leave, holiday pay and working conditions
- having penalties for employees who are late, break rules, etc. that incur costs for the business
- using cheap and inferior recruitment methods.

This approach might lower employment costs, but it may also be a 'false economy'. This is because productivity might be lower due to poor motivation. Staff turnover and absenteeism may also be higher and there may be more conflict between staff and management. Treating staff as costs may leave workers feeling exploited, neglected, stressed and unhappy in their work.

Question 1

W. L.Gore & Associates is an innovative, technology-driven business that makes medical devices and Gore-Tex fabrics. It is a privately owned company, with sales of more than $3 billion. Its UK operations are run from Scotland where around 400 of the company's total 10,000 workforce are employed.

In 2014, Gore earned a spot on the World's Best Multinational Workplaces list by the Great Place to Work® Institute. The ranking is the world's largest annual study of workplace excellence and identifies the top 25 best multinational companies in terms of workplace culture. For the 18th consecutive year, Gore also earned a position on the FORTUNE 100 Best Companies to Work For®, ranking 17th overall in 2015. In relationship to the 2014 awards, the following factors were considered of high value by employees. Gore calls its staff 'associates' and more than 80 per cent of employees have been with the business for at least five years. This includes 167 people who have been with the company for over 15 years. Voluntary staff turnover is around 3 per cent (the national average for staff turnover is around 15 per cent) with less than 20 per cent saying they would consider leaving if offered a job elsewhere.

Gore organises its workers into teams, but still encourages personal initiative. Although clearly operating as a business, associates in 2014 valued the following factors. There are no job titles and pay is negotiated on an individual level. Provided that associates fulfil their work commitments there are no set hours of work. Employees are in complete control of their own working day and week (apart from a small number who are required for specific time-dependent tasks).

Further factors valued by associates in the context of the 2014 awards included receiving profit-related pay, free private healthcare and a contributory pension into which the business puts 15 per cent of employees' pay. In a survey 84 per cent of staff found their job good for personal development, 81 per cent said they have no time to be bored, 75 per cent said that company deadlines were realistic and 83 per cent said that their health was not adversely affected by their work.

Sources: adapted from www.gore.com and www.b.co.uk

(a) Describe one piece of evidence that could suggest that W. L.Gore & Associates treats its staff as assets.

(b) Explain one advantage to W. L.Gore & Associates of treating their staff in this way.

Flexible workforce

Most businesses prefer to employ a flexible workforce. This helps a business to adapt to change more easily. For example, if output needs to be increased quickly a business with a

Exam tip

The word 'asset' is perhaps more commonly used in finance. In finance it is used to describe a tangible resource that is used repeatedly over a period of time, such as a machine, computer, vehicle or item of equipment. These are all assets that belong to a business. However, the word asset can also relate to people and the qualities they have and can impart to the business. The word is used in a very positive and complimentary sense. If people are assets they are valued.

flexible workforce might be able to make more use of temporary workers. Businesses can increase the flexibility of their workforce using a number of methods.

Multi-skilling: Multi-skilling is a term used to describe the process of enhancing the skills of employees. It is argued that giving individuals the skills and responsibilities to deal with a greater variety of issues will allow a business to respond more quickly and effectively to problems. So for example, a receptionist might have been trained to pass on calls to other people in a business. Multi-skilling this job could mean that the receptionist now deals with more straightforward enquiries him/herself. This would result in a quicker response to the customer's enquiry. It would also free up time for other people to work on more demanding activities.

Certain motivation theories suggest that giving individuals more skills and responsibilities can improve their work performance. A criticism of multi-skilling is that individuals are only given more skills so that they are expected to work harder without any extra pay. Problems may also result if workers are not trained adequately for their new roles.

Part-time and temporary staff: Part-time workers are defined in the *Economic and Labour Market Review* as people who normally work for not more than around 30 hours a week except where it's stated otherwise. Some people prefer to work part-time because it suits their lifestyle. For example, many students take part-time jobs to help support themselves while at college. However, in 2014, it was widely reported that over one million of the UK's part-time employees would prefer full-time employment. The use of part-time staff provides flexibility for businesses. Part-time staff can be employed during weekend peak hours in restaurants, for example.

Temporary workers are those employed for a limited period only. For example, during the 2012 London Olympics it was reported that more than 100,000 temporary jobs were created. Many businesses need temporary workers from time to time. For example, farmers need workers to help out during the busy harvest period and the Royal Mail takes on temporary staff to help deal with a greater volume of post at Christmas.

The use of part-time and temporary workers has grown significantly. In the UK the working population is over 30 million people, but it has been reported that nearly half of these do not work full-time. Those not engaged in full-time employment were widely reported in 2014 to include around 4.1 million people who are self-employed, 1.6 million temporary workers, 6.7 million part-time workers, 1 million unpaid people on apprenticeships or work schemes, the 1.5 million people acting as unpaid carers and 1.1 million workers with second jobs.

Flexible hours and home working: The workforce is more flexible if staff work flexible hours. However, there are different ways of arranging this. For example, staff might have to work a number of hours in a particular time period, say one week, but have the choice as to when they work during that week. Or they might work a reduced number of days, but longer hours each day. Some people might be asked to undertake shift work. For example, a factory that wants to operate 24 hours a day is likely to operate three eight-hour shifts. One of the main advantages to businesses of flexible hours is that they can often remain open for longer.

One example of a business that offers their employees flexible working hours is BMW. A range of options for full-time employees is available. For example, workers can take days off using a flexitime system. They can also take sabbaticals of between one and six months. Another scheme offers full-time employees the chance to take up to 20 extra days of unpaid holiday each year (subject to conditions). There are also schemes for part-time workers that help staff when planning their childcare arrangements.

Some businesses in the UK have started to offer their workers zero-hours contracts. This means that workers are only employed when employers need them and often at short notice. This arrangement provides businesses with a great deal of flexibility. However, such contracts are unpopular with many employees. This is because they do not offer enough financial security. Figures from the Office for National Statistics (ONS), based on a survey of workers, found 700,000 people were on zero-hours contracts. That represents about 2.3 per cent of the UK workforce. Examples of businesses that employ a high proportion of its workforce using zero-hours contracts include Sports Direct and pub chain JD Wetherspoon.

A wide range of people working in the UK might be classified as home workers. They include farmers, shop owners, writers, musicians, telesales people, hotel owners and software designers. They may be full-time or part-time and may also be self-employed. Some people prefer to work at home because it suits their lifestyle. It also reduces travelling time to and from work. Businesses benefit from home working because certain costs, such as office space, equipment, heating and lighting might be reduced. There will also be fewer problems with absenteeism and less disruption due to bad weather and transport delays. However, there may be communication problems if staff cannot be contacted and it is more difficult to monitor the quality and quantity of work undertaken. Figures from the ONS state that of the 30.2 million people in work in January to March 2014, 4.2 million were home workers.

Outsourcing: Another way of introducing flexibility into an organisation is to outsource work. This involves getting other people or businesses to carry out tasks that were originally carried out by people employed by the business. Outsourcing allows a business to focus on its core capabilities and lets others carry out peripheral work. For example, a business manufacturing aircraft components may outsource payroll, marketing or IT work. The key advantages of outsourcing are that costs are lower and capacity can be increased. The work outsourced may also be undertaken more effectively

– especially if specialists are employed. However, major drawbacks are the loss of control and the reliance that businesses place on suppliers. For example, if suppliers fail to deliver on time the whole production process can be held up. Employees may also resent outsourcing because their jobs might be threatened.

Both large and small businesses are happy to outsource work. It was widely reported in 2014 that companies were increasingly outsourcing work to the developing world, with a growth in the number of businesses using offshore services. It was thought that the trend would continue. Computer programming, other IT services and marketing were popular targets for outsourcing.

The advantages and disadvantages of a flexible workforce

There are a number of advantages of a flexible workforce for a business.

- A flexible workforce allows a business to expand and contract quickly in response to changes in demand for its products. In contrast, a workforce made up of permanent staff is difficult to slim down quickly because of the cost and because of the time it takes to fulfil legal requirements. Businesses may also be reluctant to take on new permanent staff in case demand falls again and they are left with too many staff.

- Some specialist jobs need to be done but it would be wasteful to employ a permanent worker to do them. For example, most small businesses employ external accountants to manage their accounts. It is far cheaper to do this than to employ an accountant within the business because the amount of work needed is relatively small.

- In some cases, temporary staff or subcontractors are cheaper to employ than permanent staff. For example, a business may not offer certain benefits to certain staff, although it must be careful not to infringe legislation. If the temporary staff are treated as self-employed or subcontractors, the business may also be able to save on National Insurance contributions. It isn't always cheaper to employ temporary staff and in some cases it may be more expensive because temporary staff or their agencies are able to secure higher pay. But temporary staff can be laid off almost immediately when they are not needed, with little cost, which is not the case for permanent staff.

- Employers are responsible for training their permanent workers. By outsourcing work or employing temporary workers, businesses may be able to pass that cost onto subcontractors or whoever has paid for the training of a temporary worker.

- Employing workers who can job share or work flexible hours may allow a business to operate more efficiently. For example, a business may be able to employ an employee in the day and another in the evening to respond to clients' needs over a longer period. A restaurant may be able to react to increased orders by asking staff to work longer hours at certain times of the week than others.

However, using peripheral workers has its disadvantages.

- Peripheral workers may have less loyalty to the business where they work temporarily. They may be motivated mainly by financial gain.
- Some businesses have found that their outsourced work has been of poor quality, damaging their reputation with customers. The peripheral workers move on and don't have to take responsibility for the poor work. But the business may have lost customers as a result.
- Communication can be a problem. Peripheral workers are not necessarily available when the business would like to communicate with them, although IT and the mobile phone has to some extent solved this problem.
- Employing peripheral workers can be a costly process. For example, a business may put a piece of work out to tender to a subcontractor. It might get the lowest price as a result, but the efficiency gains from putting it out to tender rather than hiring core permanent staff to do the job might be more than outweighed by the costs of the tender process itself.
- Temporary staff can be excellent, well qualified and highly motivated. But equally, some temporary staff are simply workers who have found it difficult to hold down a permanent job. When employing temporary staff, there is no guarantee that they will perform their job as well as a permanent member of staff.
- Too many peripheral workers employed alongside core workers can cause demotivation amongst the core workers. Core workers may want to be part of a stable team to form relationships and fulfil some of their higher order needs. Constant turnover of peripheral workers may lead to core workers feeling disorientated.

Distinction between dismissal and redundancy

Most people leave a job because they are moving on to another job or because they are retiring. However, some people are forced out of work. They may be dismissed or made redundant.

Dismissal: Employees may be dismissed for a number of reasons. These may be for unfair reasons, such as joining a trade union. If an employment tribunal finds that a person has been dismissed unfairly, it has the power to reinstate the employee. There are lawful reasons, however, for dismissing an employee. These may include misconduct or because an employee is incapable of doing a job. A period of notice is required, but the length will vary depending on how long the employee has worked for the business.

Redundancy: Another lawful method of dismissing an employee is on grounds of redundancy. This is where there is no work or insufficient work for the employee to do. Employees are entitled to redundancy or severance payments by law. They also need to meet other criteria. For example, they must have a contract of employment (i.e. not be self-employed). Some people, such as members of the armed forces, The House of Commons and the House of Lords are not covered by the Act. Neither are people who are retiring over the age of 60/65 or who are coming to the end of a contract or an apprenticeship.

Workers are most likely to be made redundant during a recession or when a business is struggling due to external factors. For example, in 2014 BP announced that it would spend

Question 2

Many large multi-national businesses use zero-hours contracts. It has been argued that these work arrangements have created a more flexible workforce and helped to keep unemployment down in the UK. They also allow individuals more say over when, where and how much they work.

Some employers like zero-hour contracts because they help provide a flexible workforce and are a cheaper alternative to employing agency staff. For example, a pub landlord may need extra workers to help out at busy weekends. Other businesses use zero-contract workers to cover temporary staff shortages. The main advantage to workers is the opportunity to gain work experience and skills without the requirement to accept full-time contracts. An ONS survey of people on zero-hour contracts found that around 66 per cent did not want more hours of work.

In contrast, a recent Trades Union Congress (TUC) report said zero-hours workers:

- on average, earn nearly £300 a week less than permanent employees
- get weekly average earnings of just £188, compared to £479 for permanent workers
- are five times more likely not to qualify for statutory sick pay than permanent workers.

In addition:

- 39 per cent of zero-hours workers earn less than the qualifying threshold for statutory sick pay (£111 a week) compared to 8 per cent of permanent employees
- only 25 per cent of zero-hours workers work a full week compared to 66 per cent of other employees
- a third of zero-hours workers report having no regular amount of income
- on average, women on zero-hours contracts earn £32 a week less than men on zero-hours contracts.

TUC General Secretary Frances O'Grady suggested that the growth of zero-hours contracts is one of the main reasons why working people have seen living standards worsen significantly in recent years, along with other precarious forms of employment.

Sources: adapted from www.ons.gov.uk and www.tuc.org.uk

(a) What are zero-hours contracts?

(b) Explain one reason why zero-hours contracts provide businesses with flexibility.

(c) Explain one reason why zero-hours contracts might be unpopular with employees.

about $1 billion laying off hundreds of workers as a result of falling oil prices. It was reported that a number of back-office jobs were no longer needed because BP had 50 per cent fewer offshore fields and pipelines and 30 per cent fewer wells. This was as a result of paying costs resulting from the Deepwater Horizon rig explosion in the Gulf of Mexico.

Employer/employee relationships

When someone gets a job a relationship begins between the employee and the employer. The quality of this relationship is important because it has an impact on the welfare of the employee and the performance of a business. If the relationship flourishes employees will be relatively happy in their work, motivated and productive. As a result the business should enjoy an adaptable and co-operative workforce, and high levels of skill and output. However, relationships between employees and employers can be difficult. This is because the objectives of the two groups are sometimes in conflict, for instance over the following.

- **Rates of pay.** Employers often attempt to keep wages suppressed to help control their costs and remain competitive. In contrast, employees want higher wages to keep up with rises in the cost of living and hopefully raise their living standards.
- **The introduction of technology.** Employers are often keen to use new technology because it helps to increase efficiency in the business. However, employees may resist the introduction of technology because they are anxious about learning new production techniques or may fear losing their jobs as work processes are taken over by machines.
- **Flexible working.** Employers prefer to employ a flexible workforce because it helps to manage production more effectively and keeps costs down. However, some of the methods used to develop more flexibility, such as zero-hours contracts, can be unpopular with employees.
- **Work conditions.** Employees may want better conditions or facilities from employers, such as the provision of a crèche for workers' children. However, employers may consider such things inappropriate or too expensive.

The relationship that exists between employers and employees can be shaped using two approaches. They are both often concerned with finding resolutions to the areas of conflict outlined above.

Individual approach: An increasing number of employers develop relationships with employees at an individual level. This means that terms of employment and disagreements are settled through negotiation between an individual employee and a representative of the employer. In a small business the employer representative is likely to be the owner. In a large business it could be a manager – perhaps from the human resources department.

This approach means that individuals will negotiate wages, holiday and other entitlements, hours of work and other terms of employment, directly with the employer. If an employee has a work-related grievance, it also has to be raised and discussed with their employer. For example, if an employee feels that more training is required, they would have to make a case and present it individually.

With an individual approach, pay and other conditions may vary between employees. Those individuals with good bargaining skills may get a 'better deal'. This might be a source of conflict in itself. Many would argue that individual bargaining in this way favours the employer. In a large firm the bargaining skills of most individuals would not be much of a match when pitched against those of an experienced and trained human resources manager. Many employees would prefer to be represented by an equally skilled and trained body – perhaps collectively.

Collective bargaining: The alternative to individual bargaining is **collective bargaining**. This involves determining wages, conditions of work and other terms of employment through a negotiation process between employers and employee representatives, such as **trade unions** representatives. Trade unions represent the views of their members and try to negotiate in their interests. One individual in a large company employing, say, 10,000 staff, would have little or no influence in determining wages and conditions. A representative body, such as a trade union, however, would have more strength and influence to negotiate for its membership. Without such a bargaining process, employers and managers would be able to set wages and conditions without taking into account the interests of employees.

For collective bargaining to take place:

- employees must be free to join representative bodies, such as trade unions
- employers must recognise such bodies as the legal representatives of workers and agree to negotiate with them
- such bodies must be independent of employers and the state
- bodies should negotiate in good faith, in their members' interests
- employers and employees should accept negotiated agreements without having to use the law to enforce them.

Bargaining between employers and employee representatives has often led to conflict in the past. A failure to reach agreement may result in **industrial action**. The worst that can happen is that workers go on strike. In April 2014, strikes disrupted London Underground services. The RMT, Britain's largest transport union, was in dispute with Transport for London, the tube operator, over job losses caused largely by the closure of ticket offices in tube stations. Strikes can damage both employers and employees. In this case, Transport for London lost revenue because trains were cancelled, and striking employees lost wages because they do not get paid when they withdraw their labour. Table 1 on the next page summarises the possible advantages and disadvantages of collective bargaining.

Table 1 The possible advantages and disadvantages of collective bargaining

Advantages

- Agreements are transparent and binding
- May be more cost-effective to have just one set of negotiations
- Rules and terms are more likely to be respected by both parties
- More equitable because power between both sides is equalised
- Favouritism and victimisation might be reduced at work
- Employee representatives are democratically elected

Disadvantages

- Negotiations can result in more bureaucracy and take longer
- The views of individuals are not always reflected by unions
- Negotiation costs can be high and are usually met by businesses
- A failure to agree can have serious consequences, e.g. strike action
- Owners may feel their freedom to manage is compromised

Thinking bigger

Trade unions are organisations of workers who join together to further their own interests in the workplace. There are over 150 trade unions in the UK. They tend to represent groups of workers with different skills and needs. It is important for employees to have their voice heard at work – they need representation – because individual workers find it difficult to stand up for themselves. When trying to exert their rights against a large multinational, for example, they need a more powerful authority to represent them. Trade unions can provide this authority.

If workers join a trade union they will have to pay an annual membership fee. In return they get a number of benefits. Trade unions:

- represent workers by negotiating with employers on their behalf. They employ skilled negotiators to get the best possible deal for workers. They press for higher pay, better working conditions, improved health and safety, and they fight against redundancies

- have a legal network that will represent individual members in cases such as discrimination and unfair dismissal. The cost to workers of legal representation would be huge without their support

- act as a pressure group to influence business decision-making in general

- provide other benefits such as access to cheap insurance, discounts on mortgages and travel, social facilities and support when times are hard

- play a key role in industrial relations at work. For example, they communicate the views of workers when big changes are about to take place, such as the introduction of new technology.

Question 3

In October 2013, workers at the Grangemouth oil refinery and petrochemical plant in Scotland threatened to go on a 48-hour strike. The Unite union, which represented Grangemouth's workers, said that a walkout would be organised for 20 October beginning at 7.00 a.m. The union was in dispute with Ineos, the owners of the plant, over the company's investigation into the alleged misconduct of a trade union official. It also accused the company of planning job losses, an end to the final salary pension scheme and the withdrawal of collective bargaining.

As the dispute escalated, Ineos threatened to shut the Grangemouth plant with the loss of 800 jobs. In the end talks succeeded and a rescue deal was agreed. It was reported that the dispute cost the Scottish economy around £65 million in lost output.

(a) Explain one factor that led to the breakdown in the employer/employee relationship in this case.

(b) Discuss the possible disadvantages to Ineos of collective bargaining.

Key terms

Collective bargaining – a method of determining conditions of work and terms of employment through negotiations between employers and employee representatives.
Flexible workforce – a workforce that can respond, in quantity and type, to changes in market demand.
Home workers – people who undertake their regular work from home.
Industrial action – disruptive measures taken by workers to apply pressure on employers when disagreements cannot be resolved.
Outsourcing – getting other people or businesses to undertake work that was originally done in-house.
Multi-skilling – the process of increasing the skills of employees.
Trade unions – organisations of workers that exist to promote the interests of their members.
Zero-hours contract – a contract that does not guarantee any particular number of hours' work.

Case study

BLACKBIRD POWER TOOLS LTD

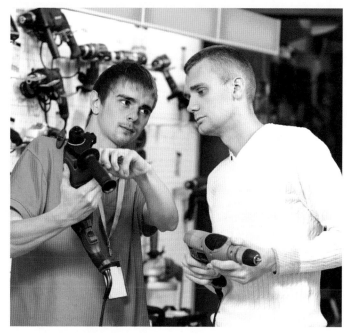

Blackbird Power Tools Ltd makes a range of power tools for the construction industry and DIY enthusiasts. It has a reputation for high-quality durable products and good after-sales service. Its products are distributed from large DIY stores, independents and, increasingly, online. In 2009, Blackbird Power Tools Ltd was hit hard by the recession. Demand for its products fell sharply as the construction industry went into decline and people spent less on DIY. As a result the business had to make 20 of its production and back room office staff redundant.

After making small losses for three years between 2009 and 2012, the directors decided that some changes were needed to make the business more competitive. It was felt that the workforce needed to be more flexible. The proposals included the following.

- Training production staff in all aspects of production so that they could be moved from one workstation to another easily.
- Introducing flexible working hours in the office so that the business could answer customer calls from 7.00 a.m. to 8.00 p.m.
- Employing more temporary staff to help deal with high levels of demand in the spring and summer months. Temporary staff also give more flexibility if there is another downturn in demand.
- Outsourcing the production of some components to a Chinese supplier to save £1.3 million per year. This would result in the loss of 12 more jobs.

The directors expected a negative reaction from the workforce when the proposals were announced. Therefore it was agreed that wages would have to be increased by the CPI (cost of living) plus 1 per cent for the next three years.

(a) What is meant by redundancy? (2 marks)

(b) Explain one advantage to workers at Blackbird Power Tools Ltd of multi-skilling. (4 marks)

(c) Explain one possible drawback to Blackbird Power Tools Ltd of outsourcing the production of some components. (4 marks)

(d) Evaluate the impact on Blackbird Power Tools Ltd of introducing more flexibility in the workforce. (20 marks)

Knowledge check

1. State three employee needs.
2. What is the main disadvantage of treating staff like costs?
3. State two advantages of multi-skilling to a business.
4. What is the difference between part-time and temporary staff?
5. What are the advantages to a business of using more home workers?

6. Explain one motive for outsourcing jobs.
7. What is the difference between dismissal and redundancy?
8. State two advantages of collective bargaining to a business.
9. Why might employees prefer not to negotiate their pay and conditions individually?
10. What are the benefits of a positive relationship between employees and employers?

15 Recruitment, selection and training

Key points

1. Recruitment and selection process: internal versus external recruitment.
2. Costs of recruitment, selection and training.
3. Types of training: induction, on-the-job and off-the-job.

Getting started

Stella Hammond has just landed a £45,000 a year job at a major marketing agency in London. Her job title will be Head of Creative Design. She saw the job advertised online and was invited to an interview within two weeks. Part of her job when she starts is to recruit three up-and-coming creative designers. She will also be responsible for providing them with on-the-job training.

Why might the marketing agency use the internet to recruit staff like Stella? What costs might the business have incurred when recruiting Stella? Explain how Stella might recruit three new creative designers. What do you think is meant by on-the-job training?

Recruitment

When businesses hire new employees they need to attract and appoint the best people – those with the right skills and appropriate experience. This is called recruitment and selection. In a very small business recruitment might be undertaken informally – a chat between a business owner and someone who is searching for a job. In a large business, the human resources department is likely to be responsible for employing staff, following a lengthy, formal recruitment process, as explained below.

A business may need new staff because:

- the business is expanding and more labour is needed
- people are leaving and they need to be replaced
- positions have become vacant due to promotion
- people are required for a given period to cover temporary staff absence, due to maternity or paternity leave, for example.

Stages in the recruitment and selection process

The recruitment process may be broken down into a number of stages, as shown in Figure 1.

- The first stage is to identify the number and type of staff that need to be recruited. The overall business plan will help provide this information. For example, if the business is planning to expand, larger numbers of applicants will need to be attracted. A business may also need to choose between full-time, part-time, temporary and permanent workers.

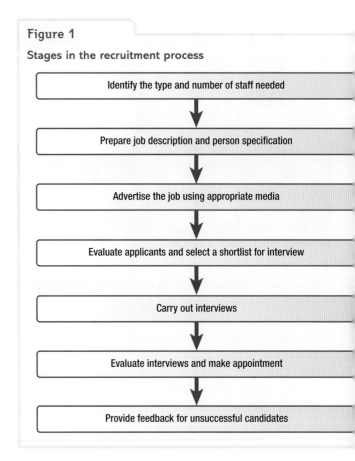

Figure 1

Stages in the recruitment process

Identify the type and number of staff needed

↓

Prepare job description and person specification

↓

Advertise the job using appropriate media

↓

Evaluate applicants and select a shortlist for interview

↓

Carry out interviews

↓

Evaluate interviews and make appointment

↓

Provide feedback for unsuccessful candidates

- The right people are more likely to be selected if a **job description** and **person specification** are drawn up. These are explained on the next page.
- Advertising costs money, so businesses must place job advertisements in media where they are likely to attract sufficient interest from the 'right' sort of applicants. For example, a hospital would not use a national newspaper to advertise jobs for porters; a local newspaper or a jobcentre would be more suitable. On the other hand, a vacancy for a senior manager is an important position and a business would want to attract interest from a wide area. Therefore a national newspaper would be appropriate.
- Job applications can be made on standard forms sent out to applicants who respond to an advert. Some applicants might write letters and include a **curriculum vitae (CV)**. This is a document that contains personal details, qualifications, experience, names of referees, hobbies and reasons why the person is suitable for the job. A business must sort

through all the applications and might draw up a longlist and a shortlist. This is because it is not normally possible to interview every single applicant. Also, some applicants will be unsuitable.

- Shortlisted applicants may then be invited for an interview. This is where interviewers can find out more about the applicants by asking questions. It also gives candidates the opportunity to provide more detailed information and ask questions about the job and the business. Interviewing is often best done by people who are experienced or have been trained in interviewing. For many jobs interviews are carried out by more than one person. This provides an opportunity for a discussion about the performance of candidates in their interviews.
- After the interviews the interviewers must decide who to appoint. In many cases, interviewees are told the outcome of the interview by post at a later date. This gives the business more time to evaluate the performance of the candidates. A business might also check references before making a final decision.
- The recruitment process ends when a job offer has been made and accepted. It is also courteous to provide feedback to the unsuccessful candidates.

An increasing number of businesses are using online recruitment methods. People can submit application forms online and in some cases might be asked to complete an online test. For example, the retailer Next uses online testing (a focus in the case study at the end of this unit). The main advantage of online recruitment is that people can apply for jobs at any time and their application details can be stored by a business until they are needed. Online recruitment is also a cheap alternative to traditional methods.

Job description

A job description states the title of a job and outlines the tasks, duties and responsibilities associated with that job. If a new job is created, a new job description may have to be prepared. If a business is replacing someone who is leaving, the job description may be the same. However, when someone leaves a post the job description may be updated.

The main purpose of a job description is to show clearly what is expected of an employee. Extracts from it are likely to be used in a job advert. It might also be used during appraisal to see how well an employee has performed in relation to what was expected of them. Figure 2 shows an example of a job description.

Person specification

A person specification provides details of the qualifications, experience, skills, attitudes and any other characteristics that would be expected of a person appointed to do a particular job. It is used to 'screen' applicants when sorting through the applications. Applications that do not match the person specification can be ignored. It is common to state on the specification whether a particular requirement is 'essential' or 'desirable'. An example of a person specification is shown in Figure 3. The style of both job descriptions and person specifications is likely to vary between different businesses according to their specific needs.

Figure 2

A job description for a cabin crew assistant for an airline

Job title
Cabin crew member.

Function
Perform ground and air duties that the company may reasonably require. Ground duties apply to any area of work connected to aircraft operational requirements.
Other duties, including boardroom functions and publicity, are voluntary.

Cabin crew must also:
- be familiar and comply with company policy and procedures
- provide a high standard of cabin service and perform their duties conscientiously at all times
- not behave in any way that reflects badly upon the company or harms its reputation.

Pay and expenses
Salary will be £17,000 per annum.
Payment will be one month in arrears, paid directly into the employee's bank account.
Expenses will be paid as set out in the current contract.
If flights are cancelled, you will be entitled to a reporting allowance as set out in the current contract.

Work time
You are required to work 20 days in every 28-day roster period.
Days and hours will vary according to the company's requirements.
Details of rest periods and flight time limitations are set out in the staff manual.

Figure 3

A person specification for an administrative assistant in an engineering plant

	Essential/Desirable
Aptitudes/skills/abilities	
Able to take a flexible approach to working conditions and a changing working environment	E
Self-motivated and enthusiastic	E
Ability to work on own initiative	D
Work effectively as part of a team	D
Qualifications/knowledge and experience	
4 GCSEs grade 4 or above	E
Computer literate in Word and Excel	E
Good written and verbal communication skills	E
Able to solve problems effectively	E
Planning and organisational skills	D
Experience of working in a manufacturing environment	D

Question 1

Figure 4

Job description for an accounts clerk

Job title
Accounts Assistant
Grade 1

General role
To join the accounting team in the recording of financial
transactions and the generation of financial information.

Responsibilities
- Matching, batching and coding of invoices.
- Investigating aged debtor services.
- Allocating cost codes.
- Matching invoices to purchase orders.
- Arranging payments through cheque runs, BACS or CHAPs.
- Allocating items of expenditure to cost centres.
- Potentially dealing with internal expenses.

Salary
£14,500-£19,000 p.a. depending on experience.

Hours and conditions of work
- 35 hours per week
- 8.30 a.m.–4.30 p.m.
- 21 days annual holiday

(a) Explain what is meant by a job description, illustrating your
answer with examples from Figure 4.

Internal and external recruitment

Internal recruitment is recruitment from within the business.
An employee may be chosen to be offered a post. Or the
business may advertise internally, asking employees to apply for
the vacancy. The advertisement may be sent round via email and
posted on a noticeboard. Larger organisations may have regular
newsletters devoted to internal vacancies, or notices may be put
in the company magazine or on the company website. Internal
recruitment has a number of advantages compared to external
recruitment.

- It is often cheaper because no adverts have to be placed and
  paid for at commercial rates.
- Internal recruits might already be familiar with the
  procedures and working environment of the business. They
  may, therefore, need less induction training and be more
  productive in their first year of employment.
- The qualities, abilities and potential of the candidates should
  be better known to the employer. It is often difficult to foresee
  exactly how an external recruit will perform in a particular
  work environment.
- Regular internal recruiting can motivate staff. They might see
  a career progression with their employer. Even for those who

aren't seeking promotion, internal recruitment suggests
that the employer is looking after existing staff.

External recruitment is when someone is appointed from
outside the business. External recruitment has two main
advantages over internal recruitment.

- The employer may want someone with new and different
  ideas to those already working in the business. Bringing in
  experience of working in different organisations can often
  be helpful in keeping a business competitive.
- External recruitment might attract a larger number of
  applicants than internal recruitment. The employer then
  has more choice of whom to appoint.

External recruitment requires the employer to communicate
with potential employees. Ideally, every person who is
suitable and who might consider the job should apply.
That way, the employer will have the maximum number of
candidates from which to choose. There are a number of
ways in which an employer can do this.

Word of mouth: A common method of hearing about a
job is through word of mouth. This means a person hearing
about a job from someone else, often someone who works in
the place of employment. For example, a person might hear
about a vacancy for a hospital porter from their next-door
neighbour who works as a nurse in a local hospital.

Direct application: Many jobseekers send their details
to employers for whom they would like to work on the off-
chance that they have a vacancy. An employer might then use
these to recruit if a vacancy arises.

Advertising: The employer may place advertisements
in local or national newspapers, and specialist magazines
and journals. The internet is another medium for job
advertisements. Advertisements may appear on a company
website. The largest sector covered by internet advertising
is jobs in IT. Advertisements on a board or window on the
employer's premises can also be successful. Advertisements
are sometimes costly. But they can reach a wide number of
potential applicants. People wanting to change their job are
likely to seek out advertisements.

Private employment agencies: The business may employ
a private employment agency to find candidates. Private
employment agencies are probably best known for finding
temporary workers (temps). However, many also specialise in
finding permanent staff. At the top end of the range, private
employment agencies tend to call themselves executive
agencies. They specialise in recruiting company executives
and finding jobs for executives seeking a change or who have
been made redundant. Using an employment agency should
take much of the work out of the recruitment process for
the employer. But it can be costly because the employment
agency charges a fee. Private employment agencies have
a website where specialist workers can look for jobs or
advertise their services.

Headhunting: For some posts, such as chief executive of a company, it may be possible to headhunt a candidate. This is where the agency draws up a list of people they think would be suitable for a job. Having cleared the list with the organisation making the appointment, the agency will approach those on the list and discuss the possibility of them taking the job. Some will say no. Others will indicate that, if the terms were right, they might take the job. A final selection is then made and one person is offered the job. Nobody has formally applied or been interviewed. Headhunting works best where there is only a limited number of people who potentially could take on the post and where the agency knows about most of those people.

Jobcentres: Businesses can advertise vacancies through jobcentres run by the government. Jobcentres are often used by the unemployed and vacancies tend to pay less than the average wage. So a cleaner's post is more likely to be advertised in a jobcentre than a chief executive's post. For a business, this is a relatively cheap way of advertising, but it is not suitable for many vacancies.

Government funded training schemes: Some businesses take on trainees from government funded training schemes. For example, for the period 2015–2016, an apprenticeship grant was made available to employers through the Skills Funding Agency, sponsored by the Department for Business, Innovation and Skills. This grant was set up to fund businesses that could not otherwise afford to employ apprentices, targeting those aged 16–24.

Thinking bigger

Both large and small businesses make use of online recruitment. A number of online tools can be used by businesses, such as internet job boards, applicant tracking systems, CV databases, and online testing and assessments. Such tools can be used to identify and filter applicants, assess personalities and screen applicants to see if qualified candidates match the company's values and culture. Some recruitment software providers combine all of these technologies into a simple-to-use package. Software can also be adapted to meet the needs of individual businesses.

One of the main advantages of online recruitment is that applicants can be drawn from a much wider area – global if necessary, twenty-four hours a day. Specialists may be attracted by positions with niche industries that are targeted by some online job boards. Employers may also post job advertisements on the websites of many professional associations. This can attract candidates who may not actively be looking for employment, as well as attracting candidates with specific skills.

The cost of using the internet to recruit staff is very low compared with other methods. It has been reported that the costs of posting jobs and/or searching for candidates online can be up to 90 per cent lower than the costs of using conventional methods. Recruiting online reaches a broad audience with reduced human interaction. It also reduces cost and time through the use of automated selection tools, electronic recording of files, and less demand on storage. The pressure on employee time for maintaining and administering selection procedures is also reduced.

Question 2

The advertisement below is an example of external recruitment that might appear in a local newspaper.

Figure 5

Recruitment advertisement from a local newspaper

EMPLOYMENT OPPORTUNITY

The Ferns exclusive fitness facility is looking for:

FULL-TIME AND PART-TIME FITNESS COACHES

Applicants must have:

- A recognised qualification for fitness instruction
- A desire to help others achieve their goals
- A passion for fitness

Excellent benefits are included with this opportunity.

Please send in CV and cover letter to:

The Manager
The Ferns Health Club
Eastern Close
Upgard
Hallshire
HL1 1RJ

(a) Explain one benefit of using external recruitment for The Ferns Health Club.

(b) Discuss the suitability of using a local newspaper to advertise the job shown above.

Costs of recruitment, selection and training

At each stage in the recruitment process shown in Figure 1, a business will incur costs. These costs can be significant and underline the importance of employing an effective recruitment process to attract and retain high-quality staff. According to a report carried out by *Oxford Economics*, the cost of replacing a single member of staff can be as much as £30,614. There are two elements to this cost – lost output while a replacement is found and inducted, and the process costs of recruiting and selecting a new worker. Generally, recruitment costs will tend to rise directly in relation to the seniority of the post. Some of the main costs incurred are outlined below.

Recruitment and selection costs: Costs are incurred throughout the whole recruitment and selection process.

- The human resources department will incur costs when identifying the number and type of staff required. For a single post the cost might be quite small, but if, for example, a chain store is opening a new branch, and requires, say, 80 new recruits, the task is significant and will require more time and planning. If a manufacturer is expanding production in a new plant and requires 1,500 new staff, then the task is even more burdensome, financially and logistically.

- Some administrative costs will be incurred when checking and updating job descriptions and person specifications. These costs will be higher if the nature of the jobs have changed or if the jobs are freshly created.
- Jobs will have to be advertised. If internal recruitment is being used, such costs will be quite modest since internal communication systems will be used. However, if external recruitment is being used there will be a cost.
- Time will be spent handling and sorting applications. Some adverts can attract thousands of applications – particularly when unemployment is high. This cost can be miminised by designing a job advert that attracts a small number of perfectly suitable candidates and actively discourages unsuitable ones. However, this can be a challenging task. The aim of this sorting process is to compile a shortlist of candidates to interview. Further costs are incurred if interviewees are contacted by post or phone.
- The interviewing process can also be expensive for a business. It is likely to involve some highly paid senior staff. While these people are involved in the interview process, they are not undertaking their normal tasks; this can have a financial impact. Some businesses use two or even three rounds of interviews when selecting staff. Interviews can require candidates to sit tests or undertake personality profiling – these activities will also incur costs. Documents need to be photocopied and circulated, rooms booked, interviewees welcomed and briefed, refreshments provided and interview staff co-ordinated.
- After the interviews have taken place the performance of interviewees will have to be evaluated. The more people involved in the interview process, the higher the cost. Finally, the selection is made, unsuccessful candidates are given feedback and the successful candidate receives a formal job offer. There may be some legal formalities to complete, which might also add to the cost.
- Sometimes the new person recruited will negotiate a higher salary or better benefits than the outgoing person they are replacing, again adding to the business's costs.

Training costs: Costs can be so high that businesses can be reluctant to invest heavily in training. Some training costs are essential and have to be met by a business. For example, employees often have to be trained in health and safety by law. Examples of training costs are outlined below.

- **Training courses and other resources.** Businesses will have to pay training providers if they use external training. Even internal training can be expensive if specialist training staff and equipment is needed.

- **Loss of output.** If workers are involved in off-the-job training they will not be producing anything. This will result in lower output levels. Even if workers are trained on the job, there may be a loss of output due to mistakes and slow work associated with the fact people are learning.
- **Employees leaving.** Businesses are likely to get very frustrated if employees leave and join a rival company after they have invested in training them. Some businesses actually prefer to recruit workers that have already been trained by others to avoid such losses.

Training

Training is the process of increasing the knowledge and skills of workers so that they are better able to perform their jobs. The objectives of training differ from business to business but they include:

- making workers more productive by teaching them more effective ways of working
- familiarising workers with new equipment or technology being introduced
- educating workers in new methods of working, such as shifting from production line methods to cell methods
- making workers more flexible so that they are able to do more than one job
- preparing workers to move into a different job within the business, which could be a new job at a similar level or a promotion
- improving standards of work in order to improve quality
- implementing health and safety at work policies
- increasing job satisfaction and motivation, because training should help workers feel more confident in what they are doing and they should gain self-esteem
- assisting in recruiting and retaining high-quality staff, attracted by the quality of training offered.

Sometimes, individual employees request training or undertake training without the financial or time support of their employers. For example, a manager may take an MBA (Masters of Business Administration) university course in her own time. More frequently, training is provided by the employer. The need for training is sometimes identified in the appraisal process.

Induction training

Many businesses put on training for people starting a job. This is known as **induction training**. It is designed to help new employees settle quickly into the business and their jobs. Exactly what is offered differs from business to business and job to job. For example, a small business might simply allocate another worker to look after the new employee for a day to 'show them the ropes'. A young person just out of university might have a year-long induction programme to a large company. They might spend time in a number of departments, as well as being given more general training about the business. But most induction training attempts to introduce workers to the nature of the business and work practices, including health and safety issues.

On-the-job training

On-the-job training is training given in the workplace by the employer. There are many ways in which this could happen.

Learning from other workers: An employee might simply work next to another worker, watch that worker do a task and with their help repeat it.

Mentoring: This is where a more experienced employee is asked to provide advice and help to a less experienced worker. The less experienced worker can turn for help and advice to another more experienced worker at any time.

Job rotation: This is where a worker spends a period of time doing one job, then another period of time doing another job, and so on. Eventually they have received the broad experience needed to do a more specialist job.

Traditional apprenticeships: In the past, workers in traditional skilled trades, such as carpentry or engineering, would undertake training over, say, three–five years in an apprenticeship. This would involve a mix of training methods. When the business decided they had 'qualified' they would be employed as a full-time worker. Many of these schemes died out due to the cost for the business, the decline in traditional trades, mechanisation and the need for more flexible work practices.

Graduate training: Medium- to large-sized businesses may offer graduate training programmes. They are typically designed to offer those with university degrees either professional training, such as in accountancy or law, or managerial training.

Table 1 Advantages and disadvantages of on-the-job training

Advantages
• Output is being produced
• Relevant because trainees learn by actually doing the job
• Cheaper than other forms of training
• Can be easy to organise
Disadvantages
• Output may be lost if workers make mistakes
• May be stressful for the worker – particularly if working with others
• Trainers may get frustrated if they are 'unpaid' trainers
• Could be a danger to others, e.g. surgeon or train driver

Off-the-job training

Off-the-job training is training which takes place outside the business by an external training provider like a local college or university. For example, 16–25 year olds might go to college one day a week to do a catering course or an engineering course. A trainee accountant might have an intensive course at an accountancy college or attend night classes before taking professional exams. A graduate manager might do an MBA course at a business school in the evenings and at weekends.

Off-the-job training can provide courses which a business internally would be unable to provide. But it can be expensive, particularly if the business is paying not just for the course but also a salary for the time the employee is attending the course.

Table 2 Advantages and disadvantages of off-the-job training

Advantages
• Output is not affected if mistakes are made
• Workers' learning cannot be distracted by work
• Training could take place outside work hours if necessary
• Customers and others are not put at risk
Disadvantages
• No output because employees do not contribute to work
• Some off-the-job training is expensive if provided by specialists
• Some aspects of work cannot be taught off the job
• Trainees may feel that some of the training is not relevant to them
• It may take time to organise

Benefits of training

Although it is expensive, a number of stakeholders will benefit from training.

- **Managers.** Managers will benefit because workers may be better motivated and more satisfied. This makes them more co-operative and easier to work with. They will be better at doing their job. Workers may also be more flexible which will help managers in their organisation. Providing training may also improve the image of the business and make it easier to attract and retain high-quality staff.
- **Owners.** Businesses will benefit from training if productivity is higher. This means that costs will be lower and the business might gain a competitive edge in the market. This should improve the financial performance of the business, with higher profits and higher rewards for the owners.
- **Employees.** If workers have been trained they will be able to do their jobs more effectively. This should reduce anxieties about their work and provide more job satisfaction. Employees will feel valued if their employer is paying for their training. They may also feel better motivated, less stressed out and enjoy more job satisfaction. They are likely to develop a range of skills that they can use in the future – to gain promotion or get a better job.
- **Customers.** If training improves quality and skills, then customers will benefit from better quality products. Customers will benefit from improvements in customer service following training, such as a better outcome when making complaints.

One example of a business that recognises the benefits of training is the retailer and owner of Waitrose, John Lewis Partnership (JLP). It offers their employees, who are addressed as partners, a wide range of training opportunities. For example, JLP have two apprentice training programmes – Retail Apprentice Scheme (Level 2) and Advanced Retail Apprentice Scheme (Level 3). Both schemes use a combination of on-the-job and off-the-job training methods. JLP also use online recruitment methods to help in their selection process.

Question 3

GymTec makes workout machines and apparatus for gyms. It has some high-profile customers and is benefiting from an export drive that was launched in 2013. To keep up with fast-moving technology it has recently invested in some new computerised shaping machinery. However, the introduction of the new technology has not been without problems. The conversation below took place between the production manager (PM) and the managing director (MD) of GymTec.

MD: *Another £100,000 on training is too much. It is double the annual training budget.*

PM: *But without the training it will take at least another six months before the new system is up and running.*

MD: *I know that training is necessary but it's so expensive. Plus, what happens when the trained workers leave, and go and work for someone else?*

PM: *I appreciate that, but* **we** *often get workers that have been trained elsewhere.*

MD: *How many need to be trained?*

PM: *About 15 – but if we trained all 30 staff we get more flexibility and won't have to spend on training again for quite a while.*

MD: *Look – here's the deal. You can have £60,000 for on-the-job training. I don't want workers going off on one of these 'training holidays' for two weeks. We lose too much production and I would rather staff were trained on our system – not some simulator.*

(a) Explain one reason why training is needed at GymTec.

(b) Explain one reason why GymTec might be reluctant to spend on training.

(c) Assess the advantages and disadvantages of on-the-job training to GymTec.

Key terms

Curriculum vitae – a document that lists personal details, qualifications, work experience, referees and other information about the jobseeker.
External recruitment – appointing workers from outside the business.
Induction training – training given to new employees when they first start a job.
Internal recruitment – appointing workers from inside the business.
Job description – a document that shows clearly the tasks, duties and responsibilities expected of a worker for a particular job.
Off-the-job training – training that takes place away from the work area.
On-the-job training – training that takes place while doing the job.
Person specification – a personal profile of the type of person needed to do a particular job.
Training – a process that involves increasing the knowledge and skills of a worker to enable them to do their jobs more effectively.

Knowledge check

1. State three reasons why a business might need to recruit new staff.
2. Outline the different stages in the recruitment process.
3. What is the difference between internal and external recruitment?
4. Explain one advantage of internal recruitment.
5. Explain one drawback of external recruitment.
6. Give three examples of external recruitment.
7. State three specific costs of recruitment and selection.
8. What is the purpose of induction training?
9. State two disadvantages of on-the-job training.
10. Explain the possible benefits of training employees to be shareholders in a plc.

Case study

AMY'S WARDROBE

Amy's Wardrobe is a large multinational retailer selling clothing and footwear. It has more than 200 stores worldwide with around 100 in the UK. In 2014 the business generated a turnover of £1.54 billion and made a profit after tax of £204.3 million. The company employs over 20,000 people worldwide and uses online recruitment to attract some of its staff. Graduates can apply online for jobs in buying, merchandising and design.

The online recruitment process used by Amy's Wardrobe can be rigorous, and can take several months to complete. There are usually three key stages, beginning with an online application.

1. Candidates have to complete an application form online. These are then reviewed and successful candidates are invited to complete a short test, which is also online.
2. If candidates do well on the test they are then invited to participate in a video interview, normally held via Skype. These consist of a set of questions that all applicants are asked and often are competency-based questions. So, candidates might be asked to describe a time when they dealt with a difficult customer, for example. These interviews last around an hour and are conducted by a Manager.
3. Once the interviews are over, candidates are then moved to the 'offline' stage of the process. Candidates will be invited to group interviews at local stores where they will be assessed by at least two people. Activities such as role plays are used to assess suitability.

Many companies have their own training programme for graduates. The training and development provided is revered across the industry and is often tailored to the company's needs. Training at Amy's Wardrobe starts with an introduction to the whole of the business, so that recruits understand the overall objective of the business before delving into the detail of their specific business area. Recruits are paired up with more experienced staff members so that they have all the support they need. By offering numerous training opportunities and encouraging their recruits to learn from colleagues, Amy's Wardrobe encourages promotion in less than two years.

Q

(a) Explain one reason why recruitment is such an important activity for Amy's Wardrobe. (4 marks)

(b) Explain how Amy's Wardrobe attempts to overcome the problem of recruiting sufficiently high-quality staff. (4 marks)

(c) Assess the benefits of online recruitment to Amy's Wardrobe. (8 marks)

(d) Evaluate the importance of training to a business like Amy's Wardrobe. (20 marks)

16 Organisational design

Theme 1

Key points

1. Structure: hierarchy, chain of command, span of control, and centralised and decentralised control.
2. Types of structure: tall, flat, matrix.
3. Impact of different structures on business efficiency and motivation.

Getting started

The Theatre Grand is a large theatre in Northern Ireland owned by a private consortium. It employees 26 staff and is divided into four departments organised as follows (the figures in brackets represent the number of additional staff in each department).

General manager (2) Emma is in charge of the whole operation. She meets every day with the departmental heads and is the figurehead of the organisation. She spends a lot of her time trying to raise funds – from the Arts Council, for example.

Booking and administration (5) Adnan is head of this department, which handles all the ticketing and booking arrangements. It also keeps financial records and works closely with the external accountant.

Theatre maintenance (8) Francesca is responsible for ensuring that the theatre is cleaned after every performance and maintaining what is an old building requiring significant repair and refurbishment.

Production liaison (4) Leroy and his small team are responsible for working with the groups of actors and production teams that put on plays and other events.

Marketing (2) Carl is in charge of promoting the theatre and its productions.

Figure 1

Organisational chart for the Theatre Grand

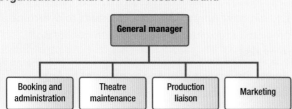

Who is control of the Theatre Grand? Describe briefly how staff are organised at the theatre. What is Celia's role in the organisation? To whom is Leroy accountable? What might be an advantage of drawing a chart to represent people in an organisation?

Organisational structures

Each business has its own organisational structure or business structure. The structure is the way in which positions within the business are arranged. It is often know as the **internal structure** or **formal organisation** of the business.

The organisational structure of the business defines
- the workforce roles of employees and their job titles
- the route through which decisions are made
- who is responsible and who is accountable to whom, and f what activities
- the relationship between positions in a business
- how employees communicate with each other and how information is passed on.

Different businesses tend to have different objectives, relationships and ways in which decisions are made. So they may have different structures. But there may also be some similarities. For example, small businesses are likely to have simple structures. Larger businesses are often divided into departments with managers.

Structure is important to all businesses. It helps them to divic work and co-ordinate activities to achieve objectives. But it may more important for larger businesses. For example, a two-perso plumbing business is likely to have fewer problems deciding 'wh does what' than a business operating in many countries.

One method of organising a business is where managers put people together to work effectively based on their skills ar abilities. The structure is 'built up' or it 'develops' as a result o the employees of the business. In contrast a structure could be created first, with all appropriate workforce roles outlined, and then people employed to fill them. It has been suggested that the entrepreneur Richard Branson worked out a complete organisation structure for his Virgin Atlantic airline before setti up the company, and then recruited the 102 people needed tc fill all the positions.

Hierarchy

Some businesses produce **organisational charts**. These illustrate the structure of the business and the workforce roles people employed in the business. Organisational charts show:
- how the business is split into divisions or departments
- the roles of employees and their job titles
- who has responsibility
- to whom people are accountable
- communication channels
- the relationships between different positions in the busines

Figure 2

A formal organisational chart for Able Engineering

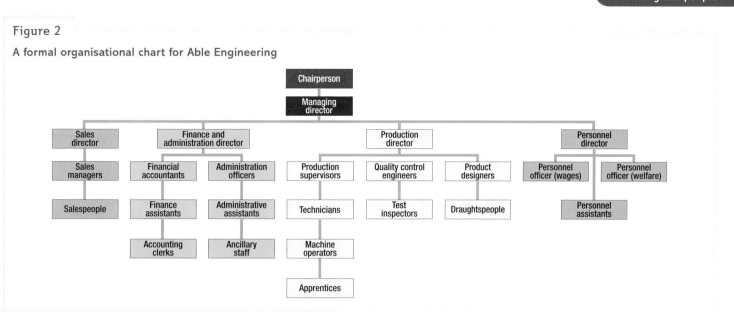

An organisation chart for Able Engineering, an engineering company, is shown in Figure 2. It is a traditional organisational chart and the person in charge, at the top of the hierarchy, is the chairperson, accountable to the shareholders. The hierarchical nature of the structure shows that employees have different levels of **authority** and **responsibility**. The chairperson at the top of the hierarchy has the most, while the apprentices, at the very bottom, have the least. The roles played by the different employees in an organisation are outlined below.

> **Exam tip**
> Remember not to get authority and responsibility mixed up. They do not mean the same thing. Someone with responsibility is accountable for the work of others. A person with authority has the right to carry out a particular task or duties.

Employee roles in the organisational hierarchy

The positions in an organisation will have particular workloads and jobs allocated to them.

Directors: Directors are appointed to run the business in the interest of its owners. In smaller businesses, owners may also be directors. But in larger businesses owned by shareholders, for example, they may be different. Directors are in overall charge of activities in an organisation. They meet, as the **board of directors**, to make major decisions that will affect the owners. Some directors, known as executive directors, will be involved in the running of a business. Non-executive directors may play little part in its running. The **managing director** (MD) will have overall responsibility for the organisation and have authority over specific directors, such as the **finance** or **marketing director**.

Managers: Managers are responsible for controlling or organising within the business. They often make day-to-day decisions about the running of the business. The sales manager, for example, would have responsibility for sales in the business and be responsible to the marketing director. Businesses often have **departmental** managers, such as the marketing, human resources, finance and production manager. There may also be **regional** managers, organising the business in areas of a country, or **branch** managers, organising particular branches or stores.

Team leaders: Team leaders are members of a team whose role is to resolve issues between team members and co-ordinate team efforts so that the team works effectively. A team leader may be part of a permanent cell production team or a team set up for a particular job, such as investigating staff morale. A team leader may also take responsibility for representing the views of a team to the next higher reporting level, for example to report the findings of a market research team.

Supervisors: Supervisors monitor and regulate the work in their assigned or delegated area, for example stock supervisor or payroll supervisor. Supervisors may be given some of the roles of managers, but at a lower level. Their roles in this case may be to hire, discipline, promote, punish or reward.

Professionals: These are positions for staff with high levels of qualifications and experience. The job roles are likely to involve a degree of decision making and responsibility for ensuring that tasks are carried out effectively to a high standard. Examples might include doctors, architects, stockbrokers, product designers, chefs and accountants.

Operatives: These are positions for skilled workers who are involved in the production process or service provision. They carry out the instructions of managers or supervisors. In their own area of activity they may have to ensure targets are met and tasks are carried out effectively. Examples of operatives in business might include staff in:
- production, for example assembling a car or manufacturing furniture
- warehousing, for example checking invoices against goods and ensuring effective deliveries
- IT, for example giving technical support for machinery.

General staff: There are a variety of positions in business which are carried out by staff with non-specific skills. They follow instructions given by superiors to carry out particular tasks and are an essential part of the production process or service provision. Examples might include checkout staff and shelf stackers in supermarkets, cleaners and receptionists in offices. They might also include general jobs on a farm or building site, such as cleaning out.

Although there may be similar generic job roles, there will be differences between organisations in the precise nature of these roles, relationships between various job roles, how they are managed and how decisions are made.

Chain of command

The hierarchy in a business is the levels of management in a business, from the lowest to the highest rank. It shows the chain of command within the organisation – the way authority is organised. Orders pass down the levels and information passes up. Businesses must also consider the number of links or levels in the chain of command. R. Townsend, in his book *Up the Organisation*, estimated that each extra level of management in the hierarchy reduced the effectiveness of communication by about 25 per cent. No rules are laid down on the most effective number of links in the chain. However, businesses generally try to keep chains as short as possible.

Span of control

The number of people, or subordinates, a person directly controls in a business is called the span of control. For example, if a production manager has ten subordinates, their span of control is ten. If a business has a *wide* span of control it means that a person controls relatively more subordinates. Someone with a *narrow* span of control controls fewer subordinates. If the span of control is greater than six, difficulties may arise. Henri Fayol, who developed a general theory of business administration in his 2001 work *Critical Evaluations in Business Management*, argued that the span of control should be between three and six because:
- there should be tight managerial control from the top of the business
- there are physical and mental limitations to any single manager's ability to control people and activities.

The implications of wide and narrow spans of control are discussed in more detail below.

Authority and responsibility

Employees in the hierarchy will have responsibility and authority. However, as we mentioned earlier these terms do not mean the same thing. Responsibility involves being accountable or being required to justify an action. So, for example, managers who are responsible for a department may be asked to justify poor performance to the board of directors. The human resources department may be responsible for employing workers. If a new worker was unable to do a particular job, they would be asked to explain why.

Authority, on the other hand, is the ability to carry out the task. For example, it would make no sense asking an office worker to pay company debts if she did not have the authority to sign cheques. Employees at lower levels of the hierarchy have less responsibility and authority than those further up. However, it may be possible for a superior to delegate (pass down) authority to a subordinate, e.g. a manager to an office worker, but retain responsibility. Increasingly, businesses are realising the benefits of delegating both authority and responsibility.

Question 1

Idris Textiles Ltd produces a range of clothing. Its factory has three production lines, where machinists are employed to make the clothes. Figure 3 shows part of the organisational chart.

Figure 3

Extract from the organisational chart of Idris Textiles Ltd

Chairperson

Managing director

Production manager

Line A manager	Line B manager	Line C manager
Line A supervisors (2)	Line B supervisors (3)	Line C supervisors (1)
Machinists (12)	Machinists (15)	Machinists (4)

(a) What is the span of control for the manager of Line B?

(b) Using Figure 3, describe the chain of command at Idris Textiles, from the chairperson to the machinists working on all lines.

(c) Explain one reason why the business might produce an organisational chart.

Centralisation and decentralisation

Centralisation and decentralisation refer to the extent to which authority is delegated in a business. If there was complete centralisation, subordinates would have no authority at all. Complete decentralisation would mean subordinates would have all the authority to take decisions. Some delegation may always be necessary in all firms because of the limits to the amount of work senior managers can carry out. Tasks that might be delegated include staff selection, quality control, customer relations, and purchasing and stock control. Even if authority is delegated to a subordinate, it is usual for the manager to retain responsibility.

In pyramid structures, subordinates often have little authority, with most decisions being taken at the top of the organisation. Open systems thinking would suggest that this form of organisation may not suit the various markets that a growing and competitive business could face. Individuals close to consumers might be better placed to make decisions. Hence regional, divisional, or in some cases for multinational companies, national operations may become a 'business unit' with its own cost and profit centre. However, it would still remain accountable to the head office. The advantages of centralisation and decentralisation are shown in Table 1.

Table 1 Advantages of centralisation and decentralisation

Advantages of centralisation

- Senior management has more control of the business, e.g. budgets.
- Procedures, such as ordering and purchasing, can be standardised throughout the organisation, leading to economies of scale and lower costs.
- Senior managers can make decisions from the point of view of the business as a whole. Subordinates would tend to make decisions from the point of view of their department or section. This allows senior managers to maintain a balance between departments or sections. For example, if a company has only a limited amount of funds available to spend over the next few years, centralised management would be able to share the funds out between production, marketing, research and development, and fixed asset purchases in different departments, etc.
- Senior managers should be more experienced and skilful in making decisions. In theory, centralised decisions by senior people should be of better quality than decentralised decisions made by others less experienced.
- In times of crisis, a business may need strong leadership by a central group of senior managers.
- Communication may improve if there are fewer decision makers.

Advantages of decentralisation

- It empowers and motivates workers.
- It reduces the stress and burdens of senior management. It also frees time for managers to concentrate on more important tasks.
- It provides subordinates with greater job satisfaction by giving them more say in decision making, which affects their work, as explained by McGregor's Theory Y.
- Subordinates may have a better knowledge of 'local' conditions affecting their area of work. This should allow them to make more informed, well-judged choices. For example, salespeople may have more detailed knowledge of their customers and be able to advise them on purchases.
- Delegation should allow greater flexibility and a quicker response to changes. If problems do not have to be referred to senior managers, decision making will be quicker. Since decisions are quicker, they are easier to change in the light of unforeseen circumstances which may arise.
- By allowing delegated authority, management at middle and junior levels are groomed to take over higher positions. They are given the experience of decision making when carrying out delegated tasks. Delegation is therefore important for management development.

Question 2

In 2006, Dewhurst, the chain of butchers, went into administration. High street butchers had lost out to supermarkets and there was a lack of trust in the meat trade. Consumers went to supermarkets because they trusted their brands. However, a revival for high street butchers began in the early 2000s, when celebrity chefs such as Jamie Oliver and Nigella Lawson started to influence consumers. Lawson suggested, following the crisis of confidence from the BSE scare, that it was essential to go to a trusted butcher for good meat, as with the butcher she used who sourced beef from organic herds.

Harry Enkleman, the owner of Enkleman's Butchers, a chain based in Nottingham, decided that he must make some changes in his organisation. Purchase of all meat for his shops had been made by the head office in Nottingham. Centralised purchasing ensured standard quality and discounts for bulk-buying. About 40 per cent of the meat purchased for his 36 shops was imported from Poland. He decided that meat should in future be purchased from local suppliers by the shop managers. He thought that it was important to meet the expectations of local customers and 'cash in' on the revival of high street butchers.

Source: adapted from the *Financial Times*, 04.04.2014. All rights reserved.

(a) Assess the possible impact on Enkleman's Butchers of the switch to decentralised purchasing.

Types of organisational structure

Organisational structures can vary between different businesses. This is because different businesses have different needs and possibly have different views about the way staff should be organised and controlled. Organisational structures may be flat, tall or matrix. Examples are shown in Figure 4 on the next page.

Tall structures: Figure 4a shows a tall structure. Here there is a long chain of command, but a narrow span of control. In this chart there are five levels in the hierarchy. Some advise that the number of levels should not exceed eight, the point at which the disadvantages of tall structures begin to outweigh the advantages.

Flat structures: A flat structure means there are fewer layers in the hierarchy. In Figure 4b the flat structure only has three layers in the hierarchy. The chain of command is short but the span of control is wide. This type of structure means that employees are free from strict, close control in the workplace. They have more freedom and responsibility.

Matrix structures: Matrix structures allow businesses to connect people with particular specialist skills, as shown in Figure 4c. They involve getting people together from different areas in the business to form a project team. Individuals within the team each have their own responsibility. Teams are fluid, and can be made, altered or dissolved to suit the business need at the time. Matrix structures are often used to solve problems in a business – particularly problems which require multi-disciplinary solutions.

Figure 4

Tall, flat and matrix organisational structures

(a) Tall structure

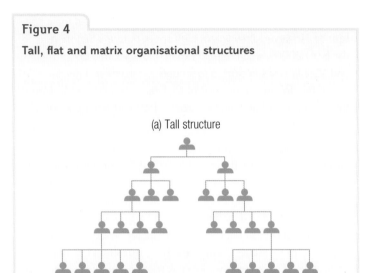

A long chain of command and a narrow span of control. A production department may look like this. One manager is helped by a few assistant managers, each responsible for supervisors. These supervisors are responsible for skilled workers, who are in charge of a group of semi-skilled workers. Close supervision is needed to make sure quality is maintained. This is sometimes referred to as a tall organisational structure.

(b) Flat structure

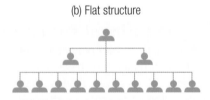

A short chain of command and a wide span of control. A higher or further education department may look like this, with a 'head' of department, a few senior staff and many lecturing staff. Staff will want a degree of independence. This is sometimes referred to as a flat organisational structure.

(c) Matrix structure

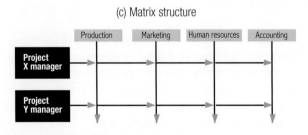

The matrix structure here shows two specific business projects, X and Y, drawing people from four different departments – production, marketing, human resources and accounting.

Implications of different organisational structures

The different structures used by businesses to organise their workforces have advantages and disadvantages. The implications of each type are outlined below.

Tall structures: With tall structures the span of control can be small. This means that managers have a tighter control over their subordinates. As a result employees can be more closely supervised. There is a clear management structure and a clear route for promotion. This might help to motivate staff. However, management costs will be higher since there are more managers. Communication through the whole structure can be poor because there is a long chain of command. Messages may get distorted as they get passed down through the different layers in the hierarchy. It might also slow down the decision-making process as approval may be needed at each level of management. Finally, close-quarters control may be resented by some staff and they could become demotivated.

Flat structures: With flat structures, communication is better because the chain of command is generally shorter. Communication can be quicker and there is less scope for message distortion. Management costs are lower because there are fewer layers of management. Decision making may be quicker because approval from several managerial layers is not required. Also, employees may be better motivated because they are less closely controlled. Indeed, in many flat structures employees are empowered. They have more responsibility for organising their work and may be allowed to solve their own problems. This can help to make their work more interesting. However, managers may lose control of the workforce because the span of control is too wide. As a result discipline may be lacking, which could have a negative impact on productivity. There could also be co-ordination problems if managers are responsible for too many subordinates. As a result they may become over-burdened.

Matrix structures: Managers often argue that this is the best way of organising people. This is because it is based on the expertise and skills of employees, and gives scope for people lower down the organisation to use their talents effectively. For example, a product manager looking into the possibility of developing a new product may draw on the expertise of employees with skills in design, research and development, marketing, costing, etc. In this way, a matrix structure can also operate within a business that has a bureaucratic structure.

The matrix model fits with some of the motivational theories discussed in Unit 17, which view employees in a very positive light. It is suggested that this structure improves flexibility and the motivation of employees. However, the method often needs expensive support systems, such as extra secretarial and office staff. There may also be problems with co-ordinating a team drawn from different departments and with the speed of decision making.

Thinking bigger

Delayering also involves a business reducing its staff. The cuts are directed at particular levels of a business, such as managerial posts. Many traditional organisational charts are hierarchical, with many layers of management. Delayering involves removing some of these layers. This gives a flatter structure. In the late 1980s, the average number of layers in a typical organisational structure was 7, although some were as high as 14. By the early 2000s this was reduced to less than five. The main advantage of delayering is the savings made from laying off expensive managers. It may also lead to better communication and a better motivated staff if they are **empowered** and allowed to make their own decisions.

However, remaining managers may become demoralised after delayering. Also staff may become over-burdened as they have to do more work. Fewer layers may also mean less chance of promotion.

Key terms

Authority – the right to command and make decisions.

Centralisation – a type of business organisation where major decisions are made at the centre or core of the organisation and then passed down the chain of command.

Chain of command – the way authority and power is organised in an organisation.

Decentralisation – a type of business organisation where decision making is pushed down the chain of command and away from the centre of the organisation.

Delayering – removing layers of management from the hierarchy of an organisation.

Delegation – authority to pass down from superior to subordinate.

Formal organisation – the internal structure of a business as shown by an organisational chart.

Hierarchy – the order or levels of responsibility in an organisation, from the lowest to the highest.

Organisational chart – a diagram that shows the different job roles in a business and how they relate to each other.

Responsibility – the duty to complete a task.

Span of control – the number of people a person is directly responsible for in a business.

Subordinates – people in the hierarchy who work under the control of a senior worker.

Knowledge check

1. Why do some businesses need a formal organisation?
2. State three benefits of drawing an organisational chart.
3. What is the advantage of a short chain of command?
4. What is the advantage of having a small span of control?
5. State two advantages of a centralised organisation.
6. State two benefits of decentralisation.
7. Explain one disadvantage of a tall organisational structure.
8. Explain the benefits of using a matrix organisational structure.
9. How might motivation be affected by employing a flatter organisational structure?
10. How might communication be less effective in a tall organisational structure?

Case study

MORRISONS

Morrisons is a national supermarket chain with headquarters in Bradford. It operates more than 600 stores and employs over 120,000 people. Like other big supermarket chains in the UK, the business has been feeling the effects of stiff competition from low-price supermarkets such as Aldi and Lidl, and the 'up-market chain' Waitrose.

In 2014, it was reported that Morrisons was going to cut 2,600 jobs as a result of changing its management structure. The plan was to remove layers of management in stores, leading to a flatter organisational structure. Some stores had as many as seven layers between the shop floor and the store manager. Dalton Philips, Morrisons' chief executive at the time of the restructure, suggested that it was the right time to modernise the management of the stores, and that changes would improve the focus on customers and lead to smarter and simpler ways of working.

Morrisons planned to increase the responsibility of duty managers in the stores. The new structure would merge department managers and supervisors into a single and smaller tier of team managers. The new arrangement would promote 1,000 from this group into new duty manager roles. This was designed to strengthen the senior management team in each store. Morrisons also planned to provide more resources for customer-facing jobs on the shop floor. The new system was trialled and found to improve performance and also led to clearer lines of responsibility.

Morrisons also pledged to create 1,000 new jobs in its M Local convenience stores and a further 3,000 positions in its supermarkets, looking to offer displaced colleagues an opportunity to work in the growing businesses. An official from the union representing the workers, Usdaw, reported that they would do all they could to support those members affected by the restructure. They planned to look in detail at the company's business case during the consultation period and safeguard as many jobs as possible.

Figures 5 and 6 show Morrisons' turnover and profit after tax.

Figure 5

Morrisons' turnover 2010–2014 (£ million)

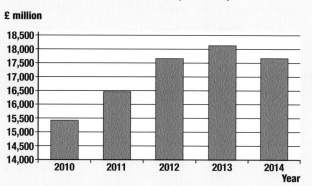

Figure 6

Morrisons' profit 2010–2014 (£ million)

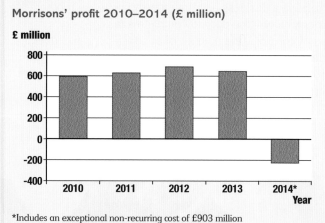

*Includes an exceptional non-recurring cost of £903 million

Source: adapted from the *Financial Times*, 23.06.2015. All rights reserved.

Q

(a) What is meant by a flat organisational structure? (2 marks)

(b) Evaluate the possible impact on Morrisons of using a flatter organisational structure. (20 marks)

Motivation in theory and practice

Key points

1. The importance of employee motivation to a business.
2. Motivation theories: Taylor (scientific management), Mayo (human relations theory), Maslow (hierarchy of needs), Herzberg (two-factor theory).
3. Financial incentives to improve employee performance: piecework, commission, bonus, profit sharing, performance-related pay.
4. Non-financial techniques to improve employee performance: delegation, consultation, empowerment, teamworking, flexible working, job enrichment, job rotation, job enlargement.

Getting started

Panna Alam works for a financial services business selling private pensions. She is in charge of a small team of six sales staff. She receives a basic pay of £12,000 a year, but gets 2 per cent per month commission based on the team's monthly sales. Last month the team sold £120,000 worth of policies. Panna enjoys her job and is well motivated. She can choose her hours of work and gets up to eight weeks holiday a year.

Calculate the amount of money that Panna earned last month. How do you think her employer motivates sales staff in this case? What do you think would motivate you? What are the advantages to a business of teamworking?

The importance of motivation

Why is it important for a business to find out what satisfies the needs of its employees? It is argued that if an individual's needs are not satisfied, then that worker will not be motivated to work. Businesses have found that even if employees are satisfied with pay and conditions at work, they complain that their employer does not do a good job in motivating them. This applies to all levels, from the shop floor to the boardroom. It appears in many companies that employers are not getting the full potential from their employees because they are not satisfying all of their employees' needs.

It is important for a business to motivate its employees. In the short run a lack of motivation may lead to reduced effort and lack of commitment. If employees are watched closely, fear of wage cuts or redundancy may force them to maintain their effort even though they are not motivated. This is negative motivation.

In the long term, a lack of motivation may result in high levels of absenteeism, industrial disputes, and falling productivity and profit for a business. So it is argued that well-motivated employees will be productive, which should lead to greater efficiency and profits.

There are a number of motivational theories used in business.

Taylor's theory of scientific management

Frederick W. Taylor set out a theory of scientific management in his book *The Principles of Scientific Management* in 1911. Many of the ideas of today's 'scientific management school' come from the work of Taylor.

The turn of the 20th century in the USA was a time of rapid expansion. Compared to today, the organisation of work on the shop floor was left much more in the hands of workers and foremen. Workers often brought their own tools and decisions about the speed of machines were left to operators. There were few training programmes to teach workers their jobs, and skills were gained simply by watching more experienced colleagues. Decisions about selection, rest periods and layoffs were frequently made by foremen.

Taylor suggested that such arrangements were haphazard and inefficient. Management did not understand the shop floor and allowed wasteful work practices to continue. Workers, on the other hand, left to their own devices, would do as little as possible. 'Soldiering' would also take place (working more slowly together so that management did not realise workers' potential) and workers would carry out tasks in ways they were used to rather than the most efficient way.

Taylor's scientific principles were designed to reduce inefficiency of workers and managers. This was to be achieved by 'objective laws' that management and workers could agree on, reducing conflict between them. Neither party could argue against a system of work that was based on 'science'. Taylor believed his principles would create a partnership between manager and worker, based on an understanding of how jobs should be done and how workers are motivated.

Taylor's approach: How did Taylor discover what the 'best way' was of carrying out a task? Table 1 on the next page shows an illustration of Taylor's method. Taylor had a very simple view of what motivated people at work – money. He felt that workers should receive a 'fair day's pay for a fair day's work', and pay should be linked to output through piece rates. A worker who did not produce a 'fair day's work' would face a loss of earnings; exceeding the target would lead to a bonus.

In 1899 Taylor's methods were used at the Bethlehem Steel Works in the USA, where they were responsible for raising pig iron production by almost 400 per cent per man per day. Taylor found the 'best way to do each job' and designed incentives to motivate workers.

Taylor's message for business is simple – allow workers to work and managers to manage based on scientific principles of work study. Many firms today still attempt to use Taylor's principles. In the 1990s, for example, some businesses introduced **business process reengineering (BPR)**. This is a management approach where organisations look at their business processes from a 'clean slate' perspective and determine how they can best construct these processes to improve how they conduct business. Taylor's approach is similar in that it advocates businesses finding the best way of doing something to add value to the business.

Table 1 Taylor's method, designed to find out the 'best way' to carry out a task at work

- Pick a dozen skilled workers.
- Observe them at work and note down the elements and sequences adopted in their tasks.
- Time each element with a stop watch.
- Eliminate any factors which appear to add nothing to the completion of the task.
- Choose the quickest method discovered and fit them in their sequence.
- Teach the worker this sequence; do not allow any change from the set procedure.
- Include time for rest and the result will be the 'quickest and best' method for the task. Because it is the best way, all workers selected to perform the task must adopt it and meet the time allowed.
- Supervise workers to ensure that these methods are carried out during the working day.

Problems with Taylor's approach: There are a number of problems with Taylor's ideas. The notion of a 'quickest and best way' for all workers does not take into account individual differences. There is no guarantee that the 'best way' will suit everyone.

Taylor also viewed people at work more as machines, with financial needs, than as humans in a social setting. There is no doubt that money is an important motivator. Taylor overlooked that people also work for reasons other than money. A survey in America by Robb and Myatt in 2004, for example, found that of the top ten factors motivating workers, the first three categories were a sense of achievement, having that achievement recognised, and positive working relationships. This suggests there may be needs that must be met at work, which Taylor ignored, but were recognised in Maslow's ideas which came later.

Mayo's theory of human relations

Taylor's scientific management ideas may have seemed appealing at first glance to business. Some tried to introduce his ideas in the 1920s and 1930s, which led to industrial unrest. Others found that financial incentives did motivate workers, and still do today. However, what was becoming clear was that there were other factors which may affect workers' motivation.

The Hawthorne studies: Many of the ideas which are today known as the 'human relations school' grew out of experiments between 1927 and 1932 at the Hawthorne Plant of the Western Electric company in Chicago. Initially these were based on 'scientific management' – the belief that workers' productivity was affected by work conditions, the skills of workers and financial incentives. Over the five-year period, changes were made in incentive schemes, rest periods, hours of work, lighting and heating, and the effect on workers' productivity was measured. One example was a group of six women assembling telephone relays. It was found that whatever changes were made, including a return to the original conditions, output rose. This came to be known as the **Hawthorne effect**.

The study concluded that changes in conditions and financial rewards had little or no effect on productivity. Increases in output were mainly due to the greater cohesion and communication which workers in groups developed as they interacted and were motivated to work together. Workers were also motivated by the interest shown in their work by the researchers. This result was confirmed by further investigations in the Bank Wiring Observation where 14 men with different tasks were studied.

The work of **Elton Mayo** (and Roethlisberger and Dickson) in the 1930s, who reported on the Hawthorne Studies, has led to what is known today as the human relations school. A business aiming to maximise productivity must make sure that the 'personal satisfactions' of workers are met for workers to be motivated. Management must also work and communicate with informal work groups, making sure that their goals fit in with the goals of the business. One way to do this is to allow such groups to be part of decision making. Workers are likely to be more committed to tasks that they have had some say in.

There are examples of these ideas being used in business. The Volvo plant in Uddevalla, opened in 1989, was designed to allow workers to work in teams of eight to ten. Each team built a complete car and made decisions about production. Volvo found that absenteeism rates at Uddevalla averaged 8 per cent, compared to 25 per cent in their Gothenburg plant which used a production line system. Other examples have been:

- Honda's plant in Swindon where 'teamwork' has been emphasised – there were no workers or directors, only 'associates'
- McDonald's picnics, parties and McBingo for their employees where they were made to feel part of the company
- Mary Kay's seminars in the USA, which were presented like the American Academy awards for company employees.

Problems: There are a number of criticisms of the human relations school.

- It assumes workers and management share the same goals. This idea of workplace 'consensus' may not always exist. For example, in the 1980s Rover tried to introduce a programme called 'Working with Pride'. It was an attempt to raise quality by gaining employee commitment. This would be achieved by greater communication with employees. The programme was not accepted throughout the company. As one manager stated: 'We've tried the face-to-face communications approach. It works to a degree, but we are not too good at the supervisory level ... enthusiasm for the Working with Pride programme is proportionate to the level in the hierarchy. For supervisors it's often just seen as a gimmick ...'

- It is assumed that communication between workers and management will break down 'barriers'. It could be argued, however, that the knowledge of directors' salaries or redundancies may lead to even more 'barriers' and unrest.
- It is biased towards management. Workers are manipulated into being productive by managers. It may also be seen as a way of reducing trade union power.

Maslow's hierarchy of needs

The first comprehensive attempt to classify needs was by Abraham Maslow in his book *Motivation and Personality*, published in 1954. Maslow's hierarchy of needs theory consisted of two parts. The first concerned classification of needs. The second concerned how these classes are related to each other. Maslow suggested that 'classes' of needs could be placed into a hierarchy. The hierarchy is normally presented as a 'pyramid', with each level consisting of a certain class of needs. This is shown in Figure 1. The classes of needs were:

- physiological needs, e.g. wages high enough to meet weekly bills, good working conditions
- safety needs, e.g. job security, safe working conditions
- love and belonging, e.g. working with colleagues that support you at work, teamwork, communicating
- esteem needs, e.g. being given recognition for doing a job well
- self-actualisation, e.g. being promoted and given more responsibility, scope to develop and introduce new ideas, and take on challenging new job assignments.

Figure 1 can also be used to show the relationship between the different classes. Maslow argued that needs at the bottom of the pyramid are basic needs. They are concerned with survival. These needs must be satisfied before a person can move to the next level. For example, people are likely to be more concerned with basic needs, such as food, than anything else. At work an employee is unlikely to be concerned about acceptance from colleagues if he has not eaten for six hours. Once each level is satisfied, the needs at this level become less important. The exception is the top level of **self-actualisation**. This is the need to fulfil your potential. Maslow argued that although everyone is capable of this, in practice very few reach this level.

Each level of needs is dependent on the levels below. Say an employee has been motivated at work by the opportunity to take responsibility, but finds he may lose his job. The whole system collapses, as the need to feed and provide for himself and his dependants again becomes the most important need.

Maslow's ideas have great appeal for business. The message is clear – find out which level each individual is at and decide on suitable rewards. Unfortunately the theory has problems when used in practice. Some levels do not appear to exist for certain individuals, while some rewards appear to fit into more than one class. Money, for example, needs to be used to purchase 'essentials' such as food, but it can also be seen as a status symbol or an indicator of personal worth. There is also a problem in deciding when a level has actually been 'satisfied'. There will always be exceptions to the rules Maslow outlined. A well-motivated designer may spend many hours on a creative design despite lack of sleep or food.

Herzberg's two-factor theory

In 1966 Fredrick Herzberg attempted to find out what motivated people at work. He asked a group of professional engineers and accountants to describe incidents in their jobs which gave them strong feelings of satisfaction or dissatisfaction. He then asked them to describe the causes in each case.

Results: Herzberg divided the causes into two categories or factors. These are shown in Figure 2 on the next page.

- Motivators. These are the factors which give workers **job satisfaction**, such as recognition for their effort. Increasing these motivators is needed to give job satisfaction. This, it could be argued, will make workers more productive. A business that rewards its workforce for, say, achieving a target is likely to motivate them to be more productive. However, this is not guaranteed, as other factors can also affect productivity.
- Hygiene or maintenance factors. These are factors that can lead to workers being **dissatisfied**, such as pay or conditions. Improving hygiene factors should remove dissatisfaction. For example, better canteen facilities may make workers less dissatisfied about their environment. An improvement in hygiene factors alone is not likely to motivate an individual. But if they are not met, there could be a fall in productivity.

There is some similarity between Herzberg's and Maslow's ideas. They both point to needs that have to be satisfied for the employee to be motivated. Herzberg argues that only the higher levels of Maslow's hierarchy motivate workers.

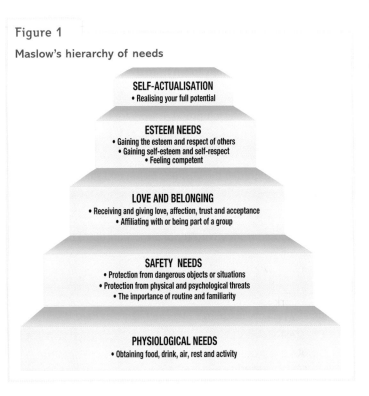

Figure 1

Maslow's hierarchy of needs

SELF-ACTUALISATION
- Realising your full potential

ESTEEM NEEDS
- Gaining the esteem and respect of others
- Gaining self-esteem and self-respect
- Feeling competent

LOVE AND BELONGING
- Receiving and giving love, affection, trust and acceptance
- Affiliating with or being part of a group

SAFETY NEEDS
- Protection from dangerous objects or situations
- Protection from physical and psychological threats
- The importance of routine and familiarity

PHYSIOLOGICAL NEEDS
- Obtaining food, drink, air, rest and activity

Figure 2

Herzberg's two-factor theory

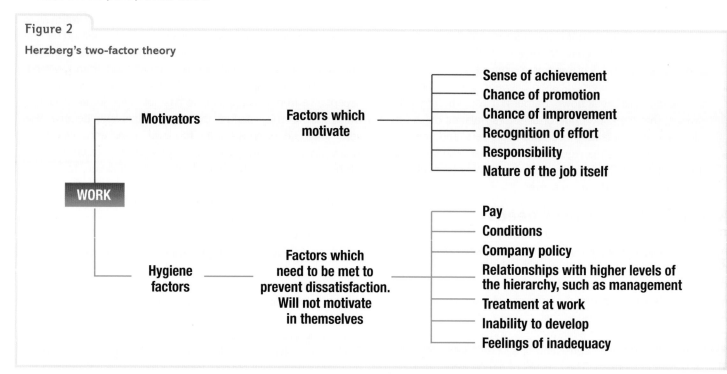

Herzberg's ideas are often linked with **job enrichment**. This is where workers have their jobs 'expanded', so that they can experience more of the production process. This allows the workers to be more involved and motivated, and have a greater sense of achievement. Herzberg used his ideas in the development of clerical work. He selected a group of workers in a large corporation. Performance and job attitudes were low. Herzberg redesigned these jobs so that they were given more responsibility and recognition.

Problems: Herzberg's theory does seem to have some merits. Improving pay or conditions, for example, may remove dissatisfaction at first. Often, however, these things become taken for granted. It is likely that better conditions will be asked for in following years. Evidence of this can be seen in wage claims which aim to be above the rate of inflation in some businesses every year. Job enrichment may also be expensive for many firms. In addition, it is likely that any benefits from job improvements will not be seen for a long time and that businesses will not be able to continue with such a policy in periods of recession.

Surveys that have tried to reproduce Herzberg's results have often failed. This may have been because different groups of workers have been examined and different techniques used. Also, there is a problem in relying too much on what people say they find satisfying or dissatisfying at work, as this is subjective. For example, if things go wrong at work individuals have a tendency to blame it on others or factors outside of their control. On the other hand, if individuals feel happy and satisfied when they are at work then they tend to see it as their own doing.

Question 1

Cambridge-based Bard is a pharmaceuticals company that employs over 400 people. In 2014 the company came nineteenth in a national survey carried out by the *Sunday Times* to find the best employers in the UK. The survey showed that the majority of staff were happy working for Bard. Indeed, the staff turnover rate was only 4 per cent (the national average is around 15 per cent).

Colm Moody, director of production and supply chain, says the leadership style is all about trusting employees. 'I tell people what I expect,' he says, 'and I do not need to hear from them again unless something goes wrong. I also insist my managers know their team members as individuals. Do they know who might need an arm around the shoulder to perform better?'

Some of the notable results taken from the survey included:

- 78 per cent said they loved what they did
- 84 per cent said they felt proud to work for the organisation
- 82 per cent said they believed they could make a valuable contribution to the success of the organisation
- 80 per cent regarded the business as fun and said that colleagues went out of their way to help one another
- 83 per cent were happy with the pay and benefits they receive.

Sources: adapted from www.bardpharmaceuticals.co.uk and www.b.co.uk

(a) Explain one reason why motivation is important to a business like Bard Pharmaceuticals.

(b) Identify two of Herzberg's hygiene factors at Bard Pharmaceuticals.

(c) Explain one factor that will help to motivate staff at Bard Pharmaceuticals, according to Herzberg.

Financial incentives to improve staff performance

A number of theories have tried to explain the factors that motivate people at work. Some of these theories stress that money is the most important factor. The scientific approach, in particular, argues that workers respond to financial rewards. It is argued that such rewards are necessary to motivate a reluctant workforce. Employees see work as a means to an end. As a result they are far more likely to be interested in **financial rewards**. In contrast, the human relations view argues that workers are motivated by a variety of factors. An employee working in a car assembly plant, for example, may be highly motivated by working as part of a team.

Piecework: Piece rates are payments for each unit produced. They are an example of **payment by results**. For example, a worker might be paid £0.50 per parcel delivered or £1.00 per kilo of strawberries picked. **Piece rates** were recommended by Frederick Taylor, founder of the scientific management school. He thought they were an ideal way to motivate workers. Workers who produced more were more highly paid. However, piece rates are only suitable for jobs where it is easy to identify the contribution of an individual worker. It would be difficult to devise a piece rate system for, say, secretaries or managers. Piece rates have been criticised on health and safety grounds. They might encourage workers to take dangerous short cuts in a bid to reduce the amount of time taken for each item. Rushing production might also affect the quality of the product.

Question 2

Paying workers according to what they produce is common in a number of industries. One such industry is textiles. For example, people employed on machines to make garments are likely to be paid according to how many units they produce in a shift.

(a) Explain the payment system used in this case.

(b) Explain which motivational theory this payment system might be based on.

(c) Explain one possible disadvantage of this method as a means of motivating machinists.

Commission: Commission is a payment system mainly used with white collar workers. Commission, like piece rates, is a payment for achieving a target. For example, car salespeople may get a commission of £100 for each car they sell. Some white collar workers are paid entirely on commission. A salesperson, for example, may be paid entirely on the basis of their sales record. Alternatively, a worker may be paid a basic salary and then receive commission on top. Commission-based pay systems are intended to 'incentivise' workers by tying in pay with output.

Bonus: Some firms make bonus payments to workers. Bonuses are paid in addition to the basic wage or salary. They are usually paid if targets are met. For example, machinists may be paid a bonus if they reach a weekly production target. Bonuses can also be paid to groups of workers. For example, a sales team may get a bonus if the whole team meets a sales target.

The main advantage to businesses of bonus payments is that they are only paid if targets are met. This means that money is only paid if it has been earned. Bonus payments may help to motivate workers as they strive to reach a target to earn their bonus. Finally, some businesses pay their staff **loyalty bonuses**. These are usually paid annually, often at Christmas. Such bonuses are not necessarily linked to productivity. They are designed to reward workers for staying with the company.

Profit sharing: Some businesses have profit sharing schemes. In a company, profits would normally be distributed to shareholders. Profit sharing occurs when some of the profits made are distributed to workers as well as shareholders.

Profit sharing can motivate workers to achieve the objectives of the business. Shareholders want higher profits. So too do workers if they are to receive a share of them. Profit sharing therefore unites the goals of both owners and workers for extra money. Profit sharing can also be a way of showing staff that they are appreciated. In Maslow's hierarchy of needs, it may help satisfy the need for love and belonging.

However, most individual workers will have little or no control over how much profit their company makes. If they make extra effort to raise sales or reduce costs, the benefit of that extra effort will be shared between all the other workers. There is no link between individual effort and individual reward in profit sharing. Profit sharing is also unlikely to motivate financially if the amount received is fairly small.

A UK business which uses profit sharing is the John Lewis Partnership, which owns the John Lewis department stores and the supermarket chain Waitrose. The John Lewis Partnership is owned in trust for its workers. So all the profits after tax and retentions are distributed to its workers. The amount given varies according to the salary of the worker. In a good year, Waitrose workers will receive a profit share handout of more than 20 per cent of their salary. This is a substantial sum. Whether it motivates John Lewis Partnership workers to work harder is debatable.

Performance-related pay: Performance-related pay (PRP) is a pay system designed specifically to motivate staff. Introduced in the 1980s and 1990s, it is now used widely in the UK among white collar workers, especially in the financial services industry, such as banking, and in the public sector.

PRP gives workers extra pay for achieving targets. The extra pay may be a lump sum such as £1,000 or it could be a percentage of salary. Some PRP systems make distinctions between levels of achievement. For example, one worker may be rated 'excellent' and receive a 10 per cent bonus, another 'good' and receive a 5 per cent bonus, another 'satisfactory' and receive no bonus.

The targets are likely to be set through a system of **appraisal**. This is where the performance of individual staff is reviewed against a set of criteria. These criteria could include factors such as arriving for work on time, ability to get on with other workers, improving skills through training or achieving a particular task within the job. Staff are likely to have a performance appraisal interview where someone more senior, such as their line manager, conducts the appraisal.

PRP is widely used because it directly links performance with pay. According to the scientific management school, it should motivate workers to achieve the goals set for them by the organisation.

However, PRP and performance appraisal have been widely criticised for a number of reasons.

- The bonus may be too low to give workers an incentive to achieve their targets.
- Achieving the targets may have far more to do with the smooth running of machinery or technological systems, or how a group of workers perform than the performance of an individual. For example, a worker may set a goal of increasing forms processed by 5 per cent. But the number of forms she receives may depend on how many are processed by other members of her team or whether the printing machines are working smoothly. Where teamworking is an important management tool, it is likely to be better to give bonuses based on the output of a team rather than an individual.
- Targets may be difficult or even impossible to achieve in the eyes of workers. If this is the case, then they are unlikely to make any effort to achieve them.
- Few staff see appraisal as an independent objective procedure. Staff are quite likely to put their failure to achieve a grade in an appraisal interview down to the unfairness of the interviewer. This is particularly true when there are already problems in the relationship between, say, a worker and his or her boss. Staff who do achieve highly in appraisal interviews may be seen by others as 'favourites' of the interviewer.

Failure to receive a high enough grade in the appraisal process may act as a demotivator of staff. Instead of staff wanting to improve their performance, they may simply give up attempting to change their behaviour and attitudes. Failure to receive a PRP bonus could challenge the physiological needs of staff in Maslow's hierarchy of needs because it deprives them of money. It could also make them feel less 'loved' by the organisation, challenging their need for love and belonging. It will almost certainly knock their self-esteem.

Non-financial techniques to improve staff performance

Financial rewards have often been used in the past by firms in an attempt to motivate employees to improve productivity. However, increasingly businesses have realised that:

- the chance to earn more money may not be an effective motivator
- financial incentive schemes are difficult to operate
- individual reward schemes may no longer be effective as production has become organised into group tasks
- other factors may be more important in motivating employees.

If other factors are more important than pay in motivating workers, it is important for firms to identify them. Only then can a business make sure its workforce is motivated.

Delegation: In some situations a manager may hand a more complex task to a subordinate. This is called **delegation**. The manager will still have responsibility, but authority is passed down the hierarchy. However, time can be saved if a subordinate completes the task. Sometimes delegation can motivate workers. This is because they feel they are being trusted to carry out more difficult work. Delegation is most likely to improve motivation if managers:

- only delegate when they are overloaded, otherwise subordinates may feel resentful
- take time to explain the tasks carefully and be sure subordinates have the skills to complete them
- give subordinates complete authority to carry out the task and that colleagues are aware of the delegation
- do not interfere with delegated tasks
- provide the support and resources that are needed to carry out the delegated task.

Consultation: Staff often complain when changes are made and they are not consulted. For example, if a business introduced flexible working hours so that it could remain open seven days a week without consulting staff, it is likely that the workforce would feel resentful. If staff are consulted by employers when changes are proposed they are more likely to feel that their views are valued. This can improve motivation. **Consultation** has other advantages. Changes are less likely to be resisted if staff are consulted. It is also possible that employees may have ideas of their own that could benefit the business. Such ideas can only be expressed if there is a proper consultation process. However, some might argue that consultation takes too long and slows down the process of change. Also, some see consultation as a 'cosmetic' process where the views of workers are heard but then ignored.

Empowerment: Delegated decision-making can be more successful if employees are empowered. **Empowerment** of employees involves a number of aspects.

- Recognising that employees are capable of doing more than they have in the past.
- Making employees feel trusted, so that they can carry out their jobs without constant checking.

- Giving employees control of decision making.
- Giving employees self-confidence.
- Recognising employees' achievements.
- Developing a work environment where employees are motivated and interested in their work.

Many businesses now recognise the need to empower employees. There are a number of advantages of this for a business and for employees.

- Employees may feel more motivated. They feel trusted and feel that businesses recognise their talents. This should improve productivity and benefit the business in the long term, for example by reducing absenteeism.
- Employees may find less stress in their work as they have greater control over their working lives. This could reduce illness and absenteeism.
- Decisions may be made by those most suited to make them. Also, employees may feel less frustrated that senior staff who are less equipped to make decisions are making them.
- There may be greater employee skills and personal development.
- Businesses may be able to streamline their organisations and delegate decision making.
- Workers may feel less frustrated by more senior staff making decisions which they feel may be incorrect.

However, empowerment is sometimes criticised as simply a means of cutting costs and removing layers from the business. Passing decision making down the hierarchy might allow a company to make managers redundant. Employees are given more work to do, but for the same pay. Some businesses argue that they want to empower workers, but in practice they are unable or unwilling to do this. For example, a manager may feel insecure about subordinates making decisions that might affect his position in the business. Feeling that they may 'make the wrong decision' might lead to constant interruptions which are counter-productive. A further problem is the cost involved to the business, such as the cost of training employees or changing the workplace.

Teamworking: The Swedish car firm Volvo is a well-quoted example of a company that has effectively introduced 'teamwork'. In both its plants at Kalmar and Uddevalla, it set up production in teams of eight to ten highly skilled workers. The teams decided between themselves how work was to be distributed and how to solve problems that arise. It is arguable whether these practices led to an increase in productivity, but the company firmly believed that this method of organisation was better than an assembly line system. A similar system has been used at Honda UK. Teamworking has a number of benefits.

- Productivity may be greater because of pooled talents.
- People can specialise and draw on the skills and knowledge of others in the team.
- Increasingly businesses are finding that the abilities of teams are needed to solve difficult business problems.
- Responsibility is shared. People may be more prepared to take risks.
- Ideas may be created by brainstorming.
- It allows flexible working.

However, in practice teamwork does not always produce the desired results. Part of the problem may lie in the way teams are organised. Members may fail to work well together for several reasons, from lack of a sense of humour to clashing goals. Studies of teams in the US have shown a number of problems with teamwork.

- Too much emphasis on harmony. Teams probably work best when there is room for disagreement. Papering over differences sometimes leads to vague or bland recommendations.
- Too much discord. Tension can destroy team effectiveness.
- Poor preparation. It is important that team members prepare for meetings by focusing on the facts. Members should have a detailed knowledge of the issues at hand and all work with the same information.
- Too much emphasis on individualism. For example, teams may fail to deliver results if the emphasis of the company is placed on individualism.
- A feeling of powerlessness. To work well, teams must be able to influence decisions.
- The failure of senior management to work well together. This creates problems because team members may walk into meetings with different priorities.
- Meeting-itis. Teams should not try to do everything together. Too many meetings waste the team's time.
- Seeing teams as the solution for all problems. Some tasks are better accomplished by individuals, rather than groups.

Flexible working: Employing a flexible workforce has a number of benefits for a business. For example, it can cope with fluctuations in demand more easily and extend opening hours. However, flexible working may also help to motivate workers. This is most likely if staff can choose their hours of work, work from home or take lengthy periods of leave, for example. Flexible working is discussed in detail in Unit 14.

Job enrichment: The idea of job enrichment came from Herzberg's two-factor theory. Job enrichment attempts to give employees greater responsibility by 'vertically' extending their role in the production process. An employee, for example, may be given responsibility for planning a task, quality control, work supervision, ordering materials and maintenance.

Job enrichment gives employees a 'challenge', which will develop their 'unused' skills and encourage them to be more productive. The aim is to make workers feel they have been rewarded for their contribution to the company. Employees will also be provided with varied tasks, which may possibly lead to future promotion. It is not, however, without problems. Workers who feel that they are unable to carry out the 'extra work', or who consider that they are forced into it, may not respond to incentives. In addition, it is unlikely that all workers will react the same to job enrichment. Trade unions sometimes argue that such practices are an attempt to reduce the labour force, and disputes about the payment for extra responsibilities may arise. In practice, job enrichment has been found to be most successful in administrative and technical positions.

Question 3

Kwik Fit Insurance Services (KFIS), owned by Ageas, provides general insurance services from its call centre near Glasgow. In 2014, the company employed around 950 people. When the company was Kwik Fit Financial Services (KFFS) in around 2010, it decided to make some key changes in its organisation. KFFS wanted to create a working environment that empowered and involved people. It wanted to reduce levels of staff turnover, raise morale, attract and recruit employees and increase financial performance.

Kwik Fit began by consulting the workforce. It invited all 650 workers (at the time) to attend a one-day workshop. The event was designed to generate ideas for improvements to the working environment. The outcome of the day was a total of 6,500 proposals. Some of the important ones were as follows.

- A flexible benefits scheme for staff. This was developed by an empowered and autonomous staff project team.

- The provision of proper career paths to dismiss the view that you could not develop a career in a call centre. KFFS produced coaching programmes for managers to help them advise and guide staff along their career paths.

- A culture of employee recognition, with internal call quality competitions and 'Going the Extra Mile' awards.

- The appointment of a 'Ministry of Fun' to help staff engage in social networking.

- Community involvement schemes, with purpose and meaning for staff.

By fostering an involvement culture, KFFS reduced staff turnover to 34 per cent, increased sales per hour in the next two years by 15 per cent and 23 per cent respectively, and reduced customer complaints by a half. Customer retention rates were also the highest for four years.

Sources: adapted from www.theworkfoundation.com and www.xperthr.co.uk

(a) Explain one reason why consultation was important in the process used by KFFS.

(b) Explain how staff were empowered at KFFS.

(c) Assess the benefits to a business like KFFS of empowerment.

Job rotation: Job rotation involves an employee changing jobs or tasks from time to time. This could mean, for example, a move to a different part of the production line to carry out a different task. Alternatively, an employee may be moved from the human resources to the marketing department where they have skills which are common to both. From an employee's point of view this should reduce boredom and enable a variety of skills and experience to be gained. An employer might also benefit from a more widely trained workforce.

Although job rotation may motivate a worker, it is possible that any gains in productivity may be offset by a fall in output as workers learn new jobs and take time to 'settle in'. Worker motivation is not guaranteed if the employee is simply switched from one boring job to another. In fact some workers do not like the uncertainty that job changes lead to and may become dissatisfied. Although used by firms such as Volkswagen in the past, where employees carried out a variety of production tasks, job rotation has declined in popularity.

Job enlargement: Job enlargement involves giving an employee more work to do of a similar nature. For example, instead of an employee putting wheels onto a bicycle he could be allowed to put the entire product together. It is argued that this variety prevents boredom with one repetitive task and encourages employees' satisfaction in their work, as they are completing the entire process. Job enlargement is more efficient if workers are organised in groups. Each worker can be trained to do all jobs in the group and job rotation can take place. Other forms of job enlargement include job rotation and job loading.

Critics of this method argue that it is simply giving a worker 'more of the same'. It is often called the problem of **horizontal loading** – instead of turning five screws the worker turns ten. In many businesses today such tasks are carried out more effectively by machines, where repetitive tasks can be completed quickly and efficiently without strain, boredom or dissatisfaction. It could even be argued that allowing employees to complete the entire process will reduce efficiency. This is because the fall in productivity from carrying out many tasks more than offsets any productivity gains from increased worker satisfaction.

> **Exam tip**
> Do not confuse job enlargement with job enrichment. They are similar, but not the same. Remember that job enrichment 'vertically' extends the job by giving an employee greater responsibility. Job enlargement expands the job 'horizontally' by giving an employee 'more of the same'.

Case study

PENINSULA BUSINESS SERVICES

Peninsula Business Services provides employment law and health and safety services for businesses. Based in Manchester, the company employs around 1,000 people in the UK, Ireland and Australia. It was established in 1983 and since then has worked with over 28,000 businesses. In 2014 the business generated around £65 million in revenue and made a profit of around £14.5 million. It also came third in a national survey carried out by the *Sunday Times* to find the best employers in the UK for 2014.

The survey revealed a number of good employment practices used by the business. Every Monday morning staff get a free breakfast, which is popular and very much appreciated. Also, the survey found that most people in the organisation were paid between £15,000 and £35,000 a year and that 77 per cent of staff were happy with their remuneration and benefits, despite a pay freeze. Employees receive incentives, such as trips abroad and bonuses for attracting new clients. They also get some profit-related earnings. The company pays for monthly social events and a weekly keep-fit session for staff.

Peninsula Business Services makes use of flexible working in its organisation. For example, it offers term-time only contracts, compressed hours contracts and sabbaticals. It has also shortened the hours of its telemarketers and human resource advisers.

The survey found that:

- 91 per cent of staff said that their job did not adversely affect their health

- 86 per cent said that their jobs did not interfere with their home responsibilities

- 86 per cent said that they loved their jobs and that their jobs were fun.

Peninsula is also committed to the personal development of staff. Mentoring and knowledge sharing are emphasised. Staff have the opportunity to attend the company's leadership and development course in the Lake District. Their career prospects are good, with a high percentage of internal promotions to senior managers. Some 87 per cent of employees said that the experience and training they are gaining will help to develop their future careers.

Sources: adapted from www.peninsulagrouplimited.com and www.b.co.uk

(a) What is meant by profit-related pay? (2 marks)

(b) Explain one possible drawback of profit-related pay. (4 marks)

(c) Explain one way in which the use of flexible working at Peninsula Business Services helps to motivate staff. (4 marks)

(d) Evaluate the extent to which Peninsula Business Services meets the needs of employees, as identified by Maslow. (20 marks)

Key terms

Bonus – a payment in addition to the basic wage for reaching targets or in recognition for service.

Commission – percentage payment on a sale made to the salesperson.

Consultation – listening to the views of employees before making key decisions that affect them.

Delegation – the passing of authority further down the managerial hierarchy.

Empowerment – giving official authority to employees to make decisions and control their own work activities.

Hawthorne effect – the idea that workers are motivated by recognition given to them as a group.

Hygiene or **maintenance factors (Herzberg's)** – things at work that result in dissatisfaction.

Job enlargement – giving an employee more work to do of a similar nature; 'horizontally' extending their work role.

Job enrichment – giving employees greater responsibility and recognition by 'vertically' extending their work role.

Job rotation – the periodic changing of jobs or tasks.

Maslow's hierarchy of needs – the order of people's needs starting with basic human requirements.

Motivated – the desire to take action to achieve a goal.

Motivators (Herzberg's) – things at work that result in satisfaction.

Payment by results – payment methods that reward workers for the quantity and quality of work they produce.

Performance-related pay (PRP) – a payment system designed for non-manual workers where pay increases are given if performance targets are met.

Piece rates – a payment system where employees are paid an agreed rate for every item produced.

Profit sharing – where workers are given a share of the profits, usually as part of their pay.

Scientific management – a theory that suggests there is a 'best way' to perform work tasks.

Self-actualisation – a level in Maslow's hierarchy where people realise their full potential.

Teamworking – organising people into working groups that have a common aim.

Knowledge check

1. State three reasons why it is important for a business to motivate staff.
2. What method of pay might Taylor recommend to help motivate staff?
3. What helps to motivate people at work according to Mayo?
4. What is meant by self-actualisation needs in Maslow's hierarchy of needs?
5. How might a business meet its workers' esteem needs?
6. What is the difference between piece rates and performance-related pay?
7. How might profit sharing motivate workers?
8. State two advantages of flexible working to employees.
9. Give two advantages of delegation as a means of motivating staff.
10. What is the difference between job enrichment and job enlargement?
11. How might job rotation help to motivate staff?
12. State two advantages of job enrichment to a business.

18 Leadership

Key points

1. The distinction between management and leadership.
2. Types of leadership style: autocratic, paternalistic, democratic and laissez-faire.

Getting started

Pauline Allen worked for a toy manufacturer helping to make teddy bears and other soft toys. She disliked her job and spent at least ten hours every week searching for another. The main problem was her boss. The managing director of the company was unpopular with everyone. He was rarely to be seen and did not know the names of the 21 staff that worked for him. In the last 15 weeks Pauline had spoken to him twice. On both occasions he called her Paula and failed to listen to her answer after asking a question. All decisions were made by the managing director without consultation. Staff turnover at the company was 86 per cent and the working atmosphere was oppressive and negative.

Describe the approach to leadership used by the managing director in this case. Explain why this approach may not be working. What characteristics might it be useful for leaders to have? Does every person have the potential to lead?

The distinction between management and leadership

Management has a number of functions. For example, managers, according to the management theorist Henri Fayol, should predict what will happen in the future, plan to achieve their objectives, organise resources, exercise command over staff lower down the hierarchy, co-ordinate day-to-day tasks and monitor how well objectives are being achieved. Peter Drucker, writing 40 years later, *The Practice of Management* added to this list motivating and communicating with staff, and giving them training opportunities.

Some writers make no distinction between management and leadership in an organisation. Managers are leaders because of the roles they play. Others, however, suggest that leaders are not necessarily the same as managers. Leaders may perform the same functions as managers. But in addition, they may do some or all of the following.

- Leaders can be **visionaries**, understanding where an organisation is at today and seeing the direction in which an organisation has to change to survive and flourish.
- Leaders tend to be good at carrying through the **process of change**. Because they understand the starting point and the end point, they can chart a route from one to the other. Where others may see only chaos and think the organisation is taking the wrong road, the leader has the ability to see through the details and small setbacks which are a part of any change.

- Leaders are often excellent at **motivating** those around them, allowing them to perform at their best. They are particularly good at motivating others to change both themselves and the organisation.

It could be argued that, in large businesses, leaders devise **strategies** whilst managers are responsible for implementing them. However, sometimes leaders do get involved in implementation because they appreciate that it is just as important to implement change as it is to devise strategies. In small businesses, leaders often have the skills to both devise and carry out a strategy.

The characteristics of leaders

One approach to finding out what makes good leaders is to identify the **qualities**, **characteristics** or **traits** that they should have (see Figure 1). A number of characteristics have been suggested.

- Effective leaders have a positive self-image, backed up with a genuine ability and realistic aspirations. This is shown in the confidence they have. An example in UK industry might be Richard Branson, in his various pioneering business activities. Leaders also appreciate their own strengths and weaknesses. It is argued that many managers fail to lead because they often get bogged down in short-term activity.
- Leaders need to be able to get to the 'core' of a problem and have the vision and commitment to suggest radical solutions. For example, after working at Apple for a period of time, Steve Jobs left in 1985. However, he returned in 1996 to help recover the company's successful position. Steve Jobs cut the number of Apple development projects from 350 to 10. He was then responsible for launching the iMac, the iPod, iTunes and the iPhone. Jobs helped Apple's shares to rise by 9,000 per cent.

Figure 1

Leadership traits

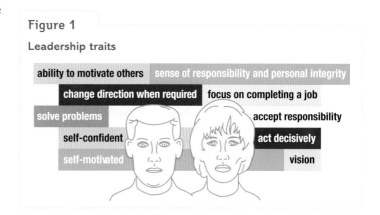

ability to motivate others — sense of responsibility and personal integrity

change direction when required — focus on completing a job

solve problems

self-confident — accept responsibility

self-motivated — act decisively

vision

- Studies of leaders in business suggest that they are experts in particular fields and well read in everything else. They tend to be 'out of the ordinary', intelligent and articulate. Examples might be Anita Roddick, the founder of Body Shop, or Bill Gates, the founder of Microsoft.
- Leaders are often creative and innovative. They tend to seek new solutions to problems, make sure that important things are done and try to improve standards.
- Leaders often have the ability to sense change and can respond to it. This is dealt with later in this unit.

Leadership styles

Successful businesses often have very good leaders. However, the style of leadership adopted by individual leaders may be very different. Some of the most common leadership styles are outlined below.

Autocratic leadership: An autocratic leadership style is one where the manager sets objectives, allocates tasks and insists on obedience. Therefore the group become dependent on him or her. The result of this style is that members of the group are often dissatisfied with the leader. This results in little cohesion, the need for high levels of supervision, and poor levels of motivation amongst employees.

Autocratic leadership may be needed in certain circumstances. For example, in the armed forces there may be a need to move troops quickly and for orders to be obeyed instantly.

Paternalistic leadership: Paternalistic leaders are similar to autocratic leaders. They make all the decisions and expect subordinates to obey these decisions. However, whereas an autocratic leader may be uninterested in the well-being of subordinates, a paternalistic leader places a great deal of importance on their welfare. In the past there have been a number of paternalistic leaders, such as Joseph Rowntree and George Cadbury. Examples of their concern for employees included the building of new houses which they could rent at low rates. As with autocratic leaders, paternalistic leaders do not give subordinates control over decision making.

Democratic leadership: A democratic leadership style encourages participation in decision making. Democratic leadership styles can be persuasive or consultative.
- **Persuasive.** This is where a leader has already made a decision, but takes the time to persuade others that it is a good idea. For example, the owner of a business may

Question 1

Helen Beaumont was appointed CEO of Keymex airlines in 2008. The airline company was suffering difficulties given the success of competitors who were quicker at adapting to market trends. When Helen Beaumont was appointed she identified that slow decision-making was a key reason why this problem kept occurring. She felt that there were too many levels of management and too many people had to discuss and approve decisions before change could happen. To stop this being an issue, Beaumont took swift action and made 50 people redundant, removing an entire management layer and placing herself closer to key people in the organisation's structure.

Beaumont could be described as an autocratic leader. She makes all the key decisions and when she passes these down to her management team, she expects them to be implemented without any question. Beaumont has many of the traits of a successful leader — she is ambitious and assertive, and decisive and dominant. Furthermore, she is a dynamic leader and is popular with her shareholders, if not always with the staff members below her. Her popularity with shareholders might be due to how her decisiveness affects the revenue of the company. Figure 2 shows the substantial increase in revenue growth trends under Beaumont's leadership.

In 2011 a cloud of volcanic ash from an erupting volcano was heading towards the airline flightpaths. Following

guidelines regarding air safety the government grounded all flights. Beaumont felt that the closure was maintained for too long and started flying planes before the ban had been fully lifted, with no problems. The ban was lifted after this and Beaumont proved herself a strong leader, willing to risk her personal reputation.

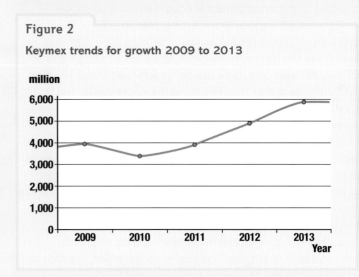

Figure 2

Keymex trends for growth 2009 to 2013

(a) Assess the advantages and disadvantages to Keymex of employing an autocratic leader.

decide to employ outside staff for certain jobs and persuade existing staff that this may ease their work load.

- **Consultative.** This is where a leader consults others about their views before making a decision. The decision will take into account these views. For example, the views of the marketing department about whether to launch a new range of products may be considered.

Democratic leadership styles need good communication skills. The leaders must be able to explain ideas clearly to employees and understand any feedback they receive. It may mean, however, that decisions take a long time to be reached as lengthy consultation can take place.

It has been suggested that a democratic style of leadership can be more effective in business for a number of reasons.

- There has been increased public participation in social and political life. Democratic management reflects this trend.
- Increasing income and educational standards means that people now expect greater freedom and a better quality of working life.
- Research suggests that this style is generally more effective. Managers are able to 'tap into' the ideas of people with knowledge and experience. This can lead to better decisions being made.
- People involved in the decision-making process are likely to be more committed and motivated, to accept decisions reached with their help, to trust managers who make the decisions, and to volunteer new and creative ideas.

Laissez-faire leadership: A laissez-faire leadership style is more of a 'hands-off' approach to leadership. A laissez-faire leader provides others with the proper tools and resources needed, and then backs off. The leader gives little guidance and direction, and allows others the freedom to make decisions. This leadership style can be effective when the group members are highly skilled, experienced, motivated and capable of working on their own. However, it is not ideal in many situations. This is particularly the case if others lack the experience or knowledge needed to complete the tasks or make decisions. Also, some people are not capable at setting their own deadlines or managing their own projects. Some people in the group may also lack the motivation needed to get certain tasks done on time. Such people usually need an 'extra push' from the leader. As a result deadlines may be missed, which could cost a business money.

Exam tip

You need to show that you appreciate that business leaders may not necessarily adopt just one of the particular leadership styles described. Some leaders may have styles that are a mixture or combination of two or more of the styles. For example, it was often argued that Sir Alex Ferguson (ex Manchester United manager) was an autocratic leader. However, he demonstrated paternalistic tendencies when protecting some of his younger players from the press, for example.

Question 2

Warren Buffett is one of the wealthiest individuals in the world. In 1964 he was appointed CEO of Berkshire Hathaway, now a US multinational holding company. The company owns businesses in a wide range of industrial sectors, such as confectionery, retail, railways, home furnishings, vacuum cleaners, jewellery and newspaper publishing, as well as several regional electric and gas utilities. In 2014, the business was worth around $350 billion with the share price reaching $200,000 for the first time in August 2014.

Warren Buffett is known internationally as an investment guru as a result of his success in buying businesses and watching them grow. His leadership style is widely reported as laissez-faire. He allows subsidiary heads lots of freedom. In his 2009 letter to shareholders he said, 'We tend to let our many subsidiaries operate on their own, without our supervising and monitoring them to any degree', and that most managers 'use the independence we grant them magnificently, rewarding our confidence by maintaining an owner-oriented attitude that is seldom found in huge organisations.'

Some people argue that a laissez-faire style of leadership results in low levels of productivity. However, in the case of Berkshire Hathaway it was widely reported to have worked well. This might be because Warren Buffett was effective in hiring talented and well-motivated people to run the various businesses. He also gave them complete autonomy and enough resources to enable them to meet company objectives. However, if these employees needed guidance or support, Warren was available for consultation. It was also widely reported that laissez-faire leadership worked well because each business had its own culture, and each person appointed by Warren understood the way that each particular business worked.

Source: adapted from www.berkshirehathaway.com

(a) Explain the style of leadership used by Warren Buffett.

(b) Explain one reason why this style of leadership has been successful at Berkshire Hathaway.

(c) Assess the possible benefits to Berkshire Hathaway of this style of leadership.

Thinking bigger

The media often suggests that 'heroic' leaders are vital to making a successful business. Such leaders make things happen. They are heroes because they alone have the vision, personality and capability to bring things about in the business, either by themselves or through others. Although not denying that leaders have special qualities, it could be argued that focusing too much on leadership can create problems. For example, this approach may lead to the conclusion that a business without a heroic leader may not be able to function properly. Or it might suggest that the heroic leader is the most important thing to organisational effectiveness. It also perhaps devalues the role and importance of other employees.

There is evidence to suggest that effective businesses are those which are more concerned with the creativity of their products and organisational structures that enable those products to be produced and sold than those that rely heavily on leadership. It could be argued that the ability to teamwork, delegate and manage others effectively is more important in the daily workings of creative organisations than the attributes of heroic leadership, such as vision, command and personality.

Mainstream approaches to leadership also take consensus in organisations for granted, i.e. that employees are generally happy to be at work and that leadership is about providing them with the direction to get the most out of them. Where there is conflict, this is often seen as being related to problems with an individual or about resistance to change. The possibility that there might be underlying conflicts associated with inequalities of wealth, status or power between leaders and subordinates is not considered. Critics argue that although businesses may appear to be consensual, this is because leaders occupy positions in the hierarchy that enable them to suppress conflict or because subordinates have an understanding that compliance or consent is in their own 'best' interests. In other words, the absence of conflict is a consequence of dependence – subordinates depend on managers for terms and conditions, including retaining their jobs, promotion, future employment and references.

Key terms

Autocratic leadership – a leadership style where a manager makes all the decisions without consultation.
Democratic leadership – a leadership style where managers allow others to participate in decision making.
Laissez-faire leadership – a leadership style where employees are encouraged to make their own decisions, within certain limits.
Paternalistic leadership – a leadership style where the leader makes decisions but takes into account the welfare of employees.

Knowledge check

1. What are the main differences between a leader and a manager?
2. State three different leadership traits.
3. Under what circumstances might an autocratic leadership style be particularly appropriate?
4. Some people argue that Sir Alex Ferguson (ex-manager of Manchester United) had an autocratic leadership style. To what extent do you agree with this?
5. State two disadvantages for a business of an autocratic leadership style.
6. What is the difference between an autocratic leader and a paternalistic leader?
7. What is the difference between persuasive and consultative democratic leadership?
8. State two disadvantages of democratic leadership.
9. State the main advantage of laissez-faire leadership.

Case study

ISLIP TRAVEL

Islip Travel organises specialist holidays for the 55+ age group. The company was the subject of a management buy-out in 2009 after the previous owners decided to 'ditch' the business because of poor financial performance. The management team, led by Ellen Bridges, bought the indebted company for £1. It had debts of £1.2 million and was struggling due to the economic recession. The previous owners had run the business very badly. However, the new management team believed that they could manage the company much better. They aimed to counter earlier poor marketing decisions, weak leadership and to raise workforce motivation levels.

The management team raised £500,000 privately and persuaded a venture capitalist to invest a further £1.5 million for 49 per cent of the company. Ellen Bridges was appointed CEO and some key changes were made. The company:

- redesigned its website. It was made more attractive and easier to navigate. The site also introduced a review system so that clients could describe their experiences and rate the company's performance

- carried out some market research to find out which types of holiday were most popular with the 55+ age group and which particular features were most important to them

- outsourced marketing to an agency with particular experience in the holiday industry

- introduced a new pay system to help motivate sales staff. The system organised sales people into three teams of eight and awarded a monthly team bonus linked to monthly sales. If teams performed well, each team member could earn up to an extra £1,000 per month on top of their basic pay of £15,000 per annum.

- introduced an annual profit-related bonus for all staff, which was paid just before Christmas. In 2014 this

amounted to £3,300 each for the 50 staff employed by the company.

After a slow start the fortunes of the company started to change. Figure 3 shows the profit made from 2007 to 2014. Ellen led the company with confidence and verve. She had charm, was well liked by staff and led by example. All key decisions made by the business were 'thrashed out' at management meetings. In the early days of the 'buy-out' some of these meetings were hard work and lasted for several hours – sometimes a whole day. At the end of the meetings the four senior managers and Ellen would vote on new company policies. Most of the votes were carried unanimously. Ellen also consulted staff and held voluntary meetings in work time to get their views and ideas. The new pay system introduced for sales staff was the idea of a sales assistant.

In 2014 the company made a record profit. The new website was starting to attract an increasing amount of traffic and bookings made via the website doubled in two years. The marketing agency was also producing good results – it was expert at placing ads that the target market would see. Finally, as the economy started to grow in 2014, consumer confidence improved and the holiday industry in general picked up. Demographics were also working in the company's favour. The proportion of people aged over 55 in the UK is a fast-growing sector.

Figure 3

Islip Travel profit after tax 2007 to 2014

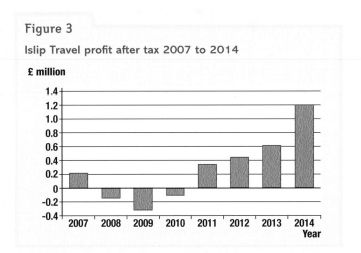

Q

(a) Explain the style of leadership used by Ellen Bridges. (4 marks)

(b) Explain one benefit to Islip Travel of this style of leadership. (4 marks)

(c) Assess the extent to which Ellen's leadership style contributed to the recovery of Islip Travel. (12 marks)

Key points

1. Creating and setting up a business.
2. Running and expanding/developing a business.
3. Innovation within a business (intrapreneurship).
4. Barriers to entrepreneurship.
5. Anticipating risk and uncertainty in the business environment.

Getting started

Sophie Helston worked for a large US film producer for ten years as a make-up artist. In 2011 she moved to England and immediately wanted to set up her own business. She considered starting a health farm, but thought that such an enterprise would cost too much to set up. After doing some market research, talking to a number of business people, and undertaking a great deal of planning, Sophie opened an 'up-market' beauty parlour in Manchester. She invested £20,000 of her own money and provided services such as facials, waxing, skin treatments, hair-styling, make-up and pedicures. The business was a success and by 2014 she employed 16 staff. The business was turning over £1.8 million per annum. Sophie now plans to develop a chain of beauty parlours in the north west of England.

State four tasks that Sophie might have carried out before setting up her business. What resources might Sophie have needed before setting up her business? What role do entrepreneurs like Sophie play in their businesses? How might Sophie's role change if she starts to develop a chain of parlours?

Creating and setting up a business

The role of entrepreneurs: Entrepreneurs are people who have a business idea and want to make money working for themselves. They are the owners of a business and without them the business would not exist. The roles played by entrepreneurs in business are summarised below.

- Entrepreneurs are **innovators** because they try to make money out of a business idea. Such ideas might come from spotting a gap in the market, a new invention or market research. However, many people set up a business by copying or adapting what another business does. Business ideas are discussed below.
- Entrepreneurs are responsible for **organising** other factors of production. They buy or hire resources, such as materials, labour and equipment. These resources are used to make or deliver products. Organising involves giving instructions, making arrangements and setting up systems.
- Since entrepreneurs are the owners they have to make all the key **decisions**. They may make decisions on how to raise finance, product design, choice of production method, prices, recruitment and wages.

- Entrepreneurs are **risk takers**. This is because they risk losing any money they put into the business if it fails. However, if the business is successful they will be rewarded with profit. The risks faced by entrepreneurs are discussed below.

Risks and rewards for entrepreneurs: In 2013 over 500,000 businesses were set up. However, less than half of these were predicted to survive beyond five years. Starting up a new business offers the potential for high rewards. Some entrepreneurs, like Richard Branson, have become rich through developing their own businesses. Starting a new business also offers a chance for many people to do something different. If nothing else, it means working for yourself rather than for someone else.

However, being an entrepreneur is risky. The downside of success is business failure. If the business fails, it may leave debts to be paid off. The entrepreneur might have borrowed money to start the business or to finance growth. Getting back into a normal job may also be difficult, especially if the entrepreneur left a well-paid job in the first place. The risk of failure is a major motivator for entrepreneurs to carry on and make a success of their enterprise even when the going is tough.

Success and failure have an opportunity cost. The opportunity cost of an activity is the benefits lost from the next best alternative. For example, an entrepreneur who has just started up a business might have left a job earning £40,000 a year. Part of the opportunity cost of setting up the business would then be the benefits gained from earning £40,000 a year. They would only be part of the opportunity cost because the job would probably have had other benefits too, including the satisfaction from doing the job. For a successful entrepreneur, the opportunity cost of being an entrepreneur is likely to be lower than the benefits of owning a business. For an unsuccessful entrepreneur, the opportunity cost is likely to be higher. This is why the unsuccessful entrepreneur is likely to close the business and move on to something else.

Entrepreneurs and business ideas: Each year, hundreds of thousands of people set themselves up in business. Instead of working for someone else, they become the owner. Or, they move from owning one business to owning another business. If they are successful, they may start to own and set up a string of businesses. But how do most would-be **entrepreneurs** (those who risk their own capital in setting up and running a business) find a business idea? There are a number of ways.

Business experience. For most people starting a small business, the business idea comes from their existing job. A plumber might work for a plumbing company and decide to set up on her own. A marketing consultant working for an advertising agency sets up his own marketing agency. This is likely to be the most risk-free way of setting up a business because the would-be entrepreneur already has knowledge of the market.

Personal experience. Some people draw on their personal experience outside of work to find a business idea. Some turn a hobby into a job. An amateur cyclist might buy a cycle shop. A keen gardener might set up a nursery. Some use their customer experience to spot a gap in the market. A mother might find it difficult to find a baby product and so set up a business to provide it.

Skills. Some entrepreneurs draw on their broad skills base to start a business. A person with an administration job might judge that they have good 'people skills' and decide to set up a business in selling. A plumber might judge that in his area electricians can charge more for their work. So he gets training as an electrician and sets himself up as a self-employed electrician.

Lifestyle choices. Some business areas attract people who want to make a lifestyle change. They might want to move to the country and invest in a small holding. They might always have wanted to run a pub and so buy a pub. Or they might be retiring from a full-time job but still want to carry on working on their own. So they invest in a seasonal bed and breakfast (B&B) business.

Stages in setting up a business: The way an entrepreneur goes about setting up a business is important. It needs to be carried out in a methodical way and carefully planned. The future success of a business might depend on the quality of work undertaken during the setting-up process. One approach to setting up a business is summarised in Figure 1.

- **Idea.** A business cannot start without an entrepreneur having a business idea. The sources of ideas are discussed above.
- **Research.** The viability of a business idea has to be researched. This might involve carrying out market research and analysing the competition to decide whether the idea is likely to work. Other research might involve meeting people, such as bankers and business people, to get advice on setting up and running a business. It may also be possible to attend a course designed for new entrepreneurs.
- **Planning.** Planning is a very important stage in setting up a business. Business planning is discussed in Unit 29.
- **Financing.** Entrepreneurs will provide some of the money needed to set up a business. Finance may also be needed when the business is 'up and running'. Entrepreneurs have to decide how much finance they will need and which sources they will use to obtain this. Sources of finance are discussed in Units 26 and 27.

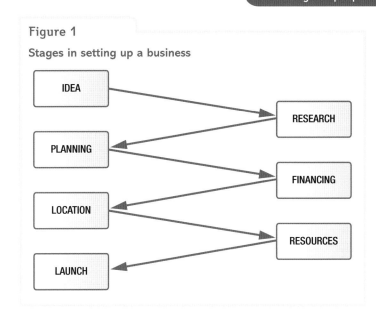

Figure 1

Stages in setting up a business

- **Location.** The location an entrepreneur chooses will depend on the nature of the business. Some people, such as tradespeople or tutors, offer services to the local area. Others work from home and yet offer services nationally, such as website designers. Restaurants and shops may be located close to their target-market customers. Manufacturers will have to decide whether their factories will be close to business customers and suppliers, or whether they will transport their products. Certain types of business activity may need planning permission. For example, to change the use of a building from a computer repair shop to a fast-food takeaway is likely to need planning permission. This could take many months to obtain.
- **Resources.** The business plan will contain a list of the resources needed to set up and run the business. For example, a dentist will need suitable premises, furniture, specialist dental equipment, a computer, uniforms, protective gear, and so on. Adverts might have to be placed to attract workers. Entrepreneurs will also have to find suppliers of materials, utilities and other day-to-day resources.
- **Launch.** This is an exciting time for an entrepreneur. It is when the business first starts trading. Some entrepreneurs organise an opening event. For example, a new restaurant might have a special opening night where guests are invited for a free meal. Special launches like this are designed to create good public relations (PR) with customers, so that people become aware of the new enterprise. Some entrepreneurs 'ease' themselves into their new business life by retaining their jobs for a while until the business gets established.

Although the information above suggests that setting up a business in an organised and methodical way will help to reduce the risk of failure, some entrepreneurs may bypass many of these stages and set up anyway. Such people, driven by an entrepreneurial spirit, just cannot wait to try out their business idea. They run their businesses in an instinctive and responsive way, some may say by 'flying by the seat of their pants'. It is possible that they might succeed – and many do. However, others would argue that 'failing to plan is planning to fail'.

Running and expanding/developing a business

After the launch, entrepreneurs become immersed in the day-to-day running of the business. For many this involves working in production or delivering a particular service. For example, someone opening a hair salon will be cutting customers' hair, and someone setting up a microbrewery will be busy brewing beer. However, running a business requires owners to undertake a range of other tasks that are crucial to the success of the business. As the business expands and develops, more and more time will be spent attending to these 'functional' business activities.

- **Financial management.** The business needs enough money to fund its operations. This might require producing cash-flow forecasts, arranging loans and overdrafts, making payments, chasing debts and monitoring cash movements into and out of the business.

- **Administration.** This usually involves accurate record keeping. For example, a business must record all of its transactions so that profit and tax liabilities can be calculated. It may be necessary to send out invoices, keep stock records, process wage slips, deal with the tax authorities and comply with legislation. If an entrepreneur sets up a limited company there will be other administrative duties to perform.

- **Marketing.** Initially, depending on the nature of the business, marketing might involve obtaining a *Yellow Pages* or online business listing, developing an attractive website, using an email campaign, distributing leaflets, placing advertisements in a newspaper, organising promotions or giving special offers. It will also involve developing relationships with customers. However, as the business develops there may be a need to carry out more market research, investigate new distribution channels, raise the profile of the business by using social media and invest in some sophisticated promotions. Investment in marketing may be necessary to retain market share, launch new products and penetrate new markets.

- **Purchasing.** Businesses will have to buy resources all the time. They may also have to buy in commercial services, such as cleaning, printing and accountancy. Entrepreneurs need to get the best quality resources at the lowest possible price. Many business owners will develop relationships with their suppliers. However, it will also be important to explore new opportunities in the supply chain. Purchasing may require entrepreneurs to develop negotiating skills so that they can reduce their costs.

- **Managing people.** Some entrepreneurs run their businesses independently without the help of others. However, if a business is successful it will probably need staff to help out. This will involve spending time on recruitment, selection and training. Entrepreneurs may need to develop skills in managing people and motivating staff.

- **Production.** In manufacturing and construction, the production process is an important business function. For example, an entrepreneur setting up a small factory to make soft drinks will need to organise the various manufacturing processes, from mixing raw materials to bottling and packaging products for distribution. The entrepreneur will need to monitor product quality and consistency, consider health and safety issues in the factory, and ensure that production levels match orders.

It is clear that once the hard work of setting up a business has been done, it does not get any easier. The pressure on entrepreneurs can be considerable, and because their livelihoods depend on its success, running a business can be stressful. It is reckoned that more than half of new businesses fail within five years. However, some businesses survive and become established. If entrepreneurs develop and expand their businesses, their role is likely to change. They are less likely to be involved in production and spend more of their time addressing issues related to marketing, finance, administration, and so on. Eventually, when it becomes cost-effective, an entrepreneur is likely to organise the business into departments and employ specialists to handle marketing, finance, human resources, etc. The business owner will probably take on the role of leader in the organisation. This change in role from entrepreneur to leader is discussed in Unit 25.

One example of a new business that expanded and developed successfully is OneMinuteLondon.com. This business was launched in 2013 by Nelson Sivalingam, a film and video production specialist. It provides an online guide to eating and drinking in London. Before making a booking, or prior to turning up at a venue, people can watch a one-minute video clip of places under their consideration using their mobile phones or other internet devices. Some high-profile venues, such as Buddha Bar, Hix, Hyatt Group and Be At One, signed up to the platform and saw it as a way of converting visitors into bookings. The site was generating over 1,500 bookings a month in 2013/14. OneMinuteLondon.com attracted attention from *The Guardian* and the *Evening Standard* which generated some positive publicity. The business planned to raise more finance, diversify into hotels and experiences, and expand into two other major cities.

Question 1

Right Formula is a London-based sports marketing agency. It deals with clients who want their businesses and products associated with Formula One racing. They organise promotions, hospitality and events, and business-to-business opportunities for customers who have included Hilton, BlackBerry and Sky Sports. For example, Right Formula might organise an exclusive, intimate VIP hospitality event as part of a grandstand programme for a client. A package might include catering, grandstand seating, VIP transportation, arranging driver appearances, access to show-cars and simulators, driving experiences and the organisation of merchandise and gifts.

The business was set up in 2009 by Robin Fenwick. Since then Right Formula has grown quickly and in 2013 turnover was £5.7 million with 20 staff employed. In 2014 the business featured in the *Sunday Times Virgin Fast Track 100* companies as the sixth fastest-growing company in the UK. Before setting up Right Formula, Fenwick was employed by Sky Sports, marketing agency Octagon, McLaren and then Hilton Hotels, where he was in charge of sports marketing. A few years later Hilton was bought out and Fenwick decided to set up his own business, with Hilton immediately prepared to become his first client.

The business went from strength to strength. In an interview in 2013 Fenwick reported a really busy year where they had to increase the number of staff quite quickly but still maintain quality. Fenwick suggested it was a challenge that a lot of small businesses go through when they grow quite quickly. They need to manage the growth effectively, especially in an industry like Formula One where reputation is everything. He couldn't take on too much and then let down the clients already on their books. Despite the glamorous image of Formula 1, Fenwick acknowledged that long working hours were required to be successful in business.

Source: adapted from www.rightformula.com

(a) Explain the role of an entrepreneur using examples from this case.

(b) Explain one way in which Robin's role might have changed between 2009 and 2014.

Exam tip

Becoming an entrepreneur is very challenging. It requires a person to take a financial risk and the chances of success may not be good. Entrepreneurs also have to be multi-talented and work very hard indeed. The majority of people may not be 'cut out' to set up and run businesses. However, entrepreneurs perform a very important role in the economy and consequently should be encouraged. These are important factors to consider when evaluating the impact on entrepreneurs of running their own business, for example.

Intrapreneurship

Entrepreneurs are business owners and risk their own personal finances when developing a business idea. **Intrapreneurs** are employees, usually in large businesses, who use entrepreneurial skills to find and develop initiatives that will have financial benefits for their companies. These might be new products, services or systems. However, unlike entrepreneurs, intrapreneurs carry no financial risk. If their initiatives fail, the employer shoulders the financial burden.

Some businesses encourage the spirit of entrepreneurship through the whole of the organisation. It is embedded in their culture. Examples of businesses that adopt this approach include Google, Apple and Zappos. Such companies believe that entrepreneurial spirit helps a company to grow and evolve rather than become stale and stagnate.

Intrapreneurs are usually employed in product development. The advantages of employing intrapreneurial staff include the following.

- Intrapreneurs can drive innovation in a business and uncover new commercial opportunities. This can help a business gain a competitive edge and increase profits significantly. In some cases the discoveries and inventions made by intrapreneurs can have a huge positive impact on a business.
- It is a means of satisfying the self-actualisation needs of employees. Self-actualisation is the highest level of need, according to Maslow's hierarchy of needs. If staff adopt this role they are being given the opportunity to be creative and reach their full potential. This will help to motivate staff and hopefully raise their productivity.
- A number of awards can be won by businesses if they develop unique or ground-breaking products. For example, the Queen's Award for Enterprise, which has three categories, including one for innovation, is awarded each year for outstanding achievements by UK businesses. These awards are prestigious and can help to enhance the image of a business. Receiving one of these awards can also attract free PR which will help to promote the business.
- Individuals benefit by getting the opportunity to experiment and be creative without having to meet the cost of failure. This should improve their job satisfaction and help them develop entrepreneurial skills which they might use in the future – perhaps by setting up their own business.

Barriers to entrepreneurship

Many would argue that it is important for an economy to encourage entrepreneurship. This is because businesses are the main source of income, employment and wealth for a country. However, despite this, a number of barriers exist that discourage many would-be-entrepreneurs from getting started.

Question 2

Richard Branson's business, Virgin, is an example of a business that employs intrapreneurs. Branson suggests that the growth of a business requires a number of intrapreneurs who drive new projects and explore new and unexpected directions for business development. Virgin would never have grown into a diverse group of over 200 companies without employing intrapreneurs. For example, Branson reports that when Virgin Atlantic could not find a supplier able to meet the design specifications for a seat in its upper class cabins, a young in-house designer, Joe Ferry, volunteered to take on the project. He came up with the designs for the herringbone-configured private sleeper suites. This inspired piece of creativity gave Virgin a competitive advantage in the market and improved the comfort of millions of passengers.

When Virgin ventures into new markets, it has a policy of recruiting the best managers possible and giving them the freedom to set up their own ventures within the Virgin Group. Examples include Tom Alexander in the UK and Andrew Black in Canada. Their appointment and subsequent freedom of operation has led Virgin companies in new and unexpected directions. Branson suggests that the greatest thing about this form of enabled intrapreneurship is that everyone can become so immersed in what they're doing that they don't feel like they are working for someone else as employees. They feel like they own their companies.

(a) What is the difference between an entrepreneur and an intrapreneur?

(b) Explain one advantage to a company like Virgin of employing intrapreneurs.

Lack of finance: Some people with a good business idea do not start trading because they cannot attract the necessary finance. The main problem is that the providers of capital and loans may be reluctant to lend money to entrepreneurs. This is because the failure rate can be high for new businesses and financial institutions cannot afford to lose money. In 2012 around 400,000 new businesses were set up but 20 per cent failed in the first year. A further 50 per cent were not expected to survive for three years. The inability to get finance is one of the main barriers to entrepreneurship.

Lack of entrepreneurial capacity: To be successful in business people have to be equipped with the necessary entrepreneurial skills and characteristics. Running a business requires a multitude of talents and skills, and needs considerable energy and commitment. These are discussed in Unit 20. Many people lack the entrepreneurial capacity needed and therefore fewer businesses are set up. However, this may not prevent some people trying. Although some make a success of it, perhaps by learning from their mistakes, they may be a very small minority.

Becoming an employer: Employing a person for the first time is quite a big step in the development of a business. Employers have responsibilities to their employees. For example:
- employees have to be paid a regular wage
- employees may be entitled to sick pay and other benefits
- health and safety issues have to be considered
- employers have to pay National Insurance contributions
- new employees may have to be trained, which is expensive.

It is these responsibilities that often discourage employment and therefore prevent business development. Employees may also turn out to be unreliable and possibly damage the reputation of the business. Becoming an employer may be an unattractive proposition for some entrepreneurs.

Legal barriers (red tape): Bureaucratic 'red tape' can discourage potential entrepreneurs. Legislation and other regulations can be demanding – complying with legislation relating to employment, the environment, consumers, corporate governance, health and safety, taxation, property rights and competition costs money and diverts an entrepreneur's focus away from what is important to them – i.e. running the business and 'making money'. This can be a big barrier to entrepreneurship.

Lack of ideas: Some people would like to run their own business, but do not have any original ideas. A lot of markets are saturated or so competitive that the potential for profit is limited. It is possible to take out a franchise or reflect the ideas of others. However, for many people this does not reflect the 'spirit' of enterprise.

Fear of failure: The failure rate for business start-ups can be high. Many new entrepreneurs may not realise that statistically their chances of success may be quite low. However, many do recognise that failure is a possibility and a fear of failure stops them from starting an enterprise. In many cultures failure has very negative associations and is best avoided if possible.

Aversion to risk: Entrepreneurs have to take risk. But many people are risk averse and are not inclined to undertake activities where the outcome is uncertain. This is a psychological barrier to enterprise and one that is difficult to overcome. It is hard to encourage a person to 'take a gamble' if they are not that way inclined.

Corrupt and unsupportive environment: Some countries may have an unsupportive business environment. This might be because they are politically unstable, have contract and property laws that may be unclear, enforce regulations inconsistently or may be impacted by corruption and bribery. In these countries, some regulators and inspectors might act as predators. This means that entrepreneurs might have to develop friendly ties with government officials and bureaucrats to 'smooth the way' for their businesses to operate.

Anticipating risk and uncertainty in the business environment

In Unit 1 it was explained that businesses have to deal with both risk and uncertainty. The key difference between the two is that entrepreneurs have some control over risk. They make a conscious decision to take a risk and to a certain extent they can choose the levels of risk they take. In contract, although it is known that uncertain events might occur, their timing is often impossible to predict. For example, no one can predict when an earthquake might occur. Also, the impact on businesses of some uncertain events can be devastating. Arguably, dealing with uncertainty is more challenging than dealing with risk.

Anticipating risk: Entrepreneurs understand the nature of risk right from the point when they first set up a business. For example, a significant number of entrepreneurs have probably sacrificed secure employment with a regular income to start their businesses. Also, most of them will have used some of their own money for start-up capital. Entrepreneurs know that if their business fails, they could lose their investment and they may not find another job easily. Even if entrepreneurs are successful, they are likely to take further risks in the future. For example, a business may grant trade credit to a new customer for a highly lucrative order. However, there is a risk that the customer might not pay once the order has been delivered.

Entrepreneurs can take measures to reduce the amount of risk they take. For example, before launching a brand new product nationally, they could test it out in a smaller market. In the above example, before granting trade credit a business can undertake a credit search to check the creditworthiness of a new customer. Entrepreneurs can also deal with risk by using quantitative techniques, such as decision trees, when making important decisions. Using quantitative techniques often helps to quantify the possible outcomes of actions, which makes them easier to evaluate.

Finally, entrepreneurs usually know that if they take more risk, the rewards could be greater – however, so could the losses. For example, a business might decide to export products. In overseas markets where these products might be completely new, sales, revenues and profits could be very high. However, different countries have different cultures, tastes and preferences. As a result, a product that was successful in the domestic market may be a 'flop' overseas. Such a failed venture could be very expensive.

Anticipating uncertainty: Dealing with uncertainty is more of a problem for entrepreneurs as they have no control over the nature or timing of some events. For example, the outcome of an election might lead to uncertainty about future policies, such as the status of the UK's membership of the EU. Many businesses feel that not belonging to the EU could be a disaster, and that any uncertainty of status with the EU could cause businesses to postpone investment in projects.

There is nothing that businesses can do to prevent uncertain events from happening, but they may be able to make some preparations to deal with their consequences, should they occur. For example, they may set aside contingency funds to deal with unexpected events. Entrepreneurs might also use methods such as PESTLE analysis, SWOT analysis, risk assessment and scenario planning to help reduce uncertainty, prepare for unexpected events and improve the quality of decision making.

Key terms

Entrepreneurs – individuals who, typically, set up and run a business and take the risks associated with this.
Intrapreneurs – employees who use entrepreneurial skills, without having to risk their own money, to find and develop initiatives that will have financial benefits for their employer.

Knowledge check

1. Entrepreneurs are innovators. What does this mean?
2. What risks might an entrepreneur take in addition to putting personal money into a business start-up?
3. Describe the possible stages that need to be completed when setting up a business.
4. How important is the planning stage when starting a new business?
5. What is meant by financial management?
6. State three benefits to a business of employing intrapreneurs.
7. What is meant by risk aversion?
8. State three other possible barriers to entrepreneurship.

Case study

Piotr Santos

Piotr Santos came to the UK from Poland in 2006. He was a qualified chef and wanted to open his own Polish restaurant in Liverpool city centre. He had recently spent four months in his spare time researching the business idea. Two important pieces of information had come to light. There were around 10,000 Poles living in Merseyside and there was no uniquely Polish restaurant currently operating in Liverpool. This suggested that there was a chance his business idea was viable. After collecting questionnaires from 250 people the results were encouraging. However, there was a snag. The cost of setting up the restaurant was going to be far more than he had imagined. Piotr had saved up £12,000 but needed a total of £20,000 to fund the start-up.

Piotr was not discouraged. He wrote a detailed business plan, attended a local business course funded by the Liverpool and Sefton Chambers of Commerce and made appointments with four different banks to discuss funding. Unfortunately his meetings with banks were fruitless. None of them was interested in lending him the £8,000 he needed to start a business. He approached the Polish community to see if anyone would be interested in making a private loan. He had one offer of £5,000 but the person wanted a 50 per cent share of the business and also insisted that Piotr employed two of his daughters in the restaurant. Piotr could not accept these terms and was on the verge of 'throwing in the towel' when a friend mentioned peer-to-peer funding. This involves getting a loan from unrelated individuals online via a specialist website. If people are interested they can lend money in return for interest. Within two months of making the application Piotr had raised the money needed.

Piotr spent a lot of time finding a suitable location for the restaurant. He felt it was vital to find exactly the right place. He contacted 12 estate agents and got them to help with

the searching. Eventually he found some suitable premises in a part of the city popular with the Polish community. It was also on a bus route popular with Polish people going into town. He left his full-time job and spent two months preparing for his restaurant launch. He employed an assistant chef to help him out in the kitchen, a general kitchen assistant and two waiting staff. On the opening night he invited 100 people who paid £5 each for a five-course meal (drinks not included). It was a resounding success. After 12 months of trading Piotr had made £48,000 profit. What surprised Piotr most of all was the number of non-Polish customers that used the restaurant regularly.

In 2013 he opened a second restaurant in Manchester and started to dream of a restaurant chain – 'PIOTR'. This was also a success and in 2014 he opened two more restaurants, another in Manchester and one in Leeds. By the end of 2014 Piotr was spending most of his time on financial management, marketing and business development. Each of his four restaurants had their own manager and three more openings were in the 'pipeline'.

(a) Explain one risk that Piotr has taken in this case. (4 marks)

(b) Explain one factor that could have affected where Piotr decided to locate the restaurant when setting up his business. (4 marks)

(c) Explain one barrier to entrepreneurship that almost prevented Piotr from setting up his business. (4 marks)

(d) Assess the impact on Piotr's role in the business as it started to expand. (12 marks)

20 Entrepreneurial motives and characteristics

Key points

1. Characteristics and skills required.
2. Reasons why people set up in businesses: financial motives like profit maximisation and profit satisficing.
3. Reasons why people set up in businesses: non-financial motives like ethical stance, social entrepreneurship, independence and home working.

Getting started

Suzi Trebowic left the hospital where she worked because she felt overworked and unappreciated. She was employed as a radiographer for 22 years. She now wants a complete change and plans to start her own business. Her passion is health food. She enjoys cooking exciting meals on a very small budget. She plans to set up a website showing how people can eat well and lose weight on a very small budget. She believes that if she can generate enough website traffic she can earn revenue from selling advertising space. At work Suzi was quiet, conscientious, and good at following instructions. However, although she was a proficient radiographer, she lacked drive and self-confidence, and did not seek promotion like most of her colleagues.

State three skills that might be needed to run an online business. State three characteristics that might be needed to be a successful entrepreneur. Do you think Suzi might be a successful entrepreneur? What might be Suzi's motive for setting up a business?

Characteristics of entrepreneurs

Starting your own business is very common. Hundreds of thousands of small businesses are started each year. People give up their jobs to work for themselves or they start a new business alongside a normal full-time job. Not everyone is suited to becoming an entrepreneur, either because they lack the skills needed or because they don't want to cope with the risk involved in setting up a business. Business Link, a government agency that encouraged business start-ups, identified seven characteristics of successful entrepreneurs.

Self-confidence: Successful entrepreneurs are people who believe that they are going to succeed. They think they have a winning formula for their business. They can persuade other people, for example, to buy the product or help finance the business.

Self-determination: Successful entrepreneurs are ones who think they can take control of events going on around them.

They can influence those events and turn them into something which will benefit their business.

Being a self-starter: Many people work best when being told what to do. But to be a successful entrepreneur, you have to be a self-starter. Entrepreneurs are able to work independently and can take decisions. They have their own ideas about how things should be done and they are able to develop those ideas.

Judgement: The business environment is changing all the time. A successful entrepreneur is one who is taking in information and listening to advice. At the same time, they are able to see where the business might go in the future and what they want out of the business. This helps them to make judgements and decisions.

Commitment: Many people think when starting up a business that it is going to be easier than working for someone else. All the evidence shows that entrepreneurs work longer hours than those with a normal job. Running your own business can sometimes be more stressful because of the risks that are always present. So successful entrepreneurs are ones who are committed to what they do.

Perseverance: All businesses have successes and failures. There is always an element of risk that their business could perform poorly or even fail. Therefore, successful entrepreneurs have to show perseverance. They have to be able to get through the bad times and the setbacks.

Initiative: Successful entrepreneurs are able to take the initiative in situations. They don't allow events to overwhelm them by doing nothing. They are able to change and be proactive.

Not every successful entrepreneur has all of these characteristics. Few entrepreneurs are strong in every area. But people who run their own businesses tend to show different characteristics from people who work for someone else.

One example of an entrepreneur is 26-year-old Pippa Murray. In 2014, she set up a business called Pip & Nut, which produces a range of nut butters that are sold in capsules. Flavours include peanut, almond, and almond and coconut. The idea came to her as a result of her interest in running. She saw the potential of products which were high in protein.

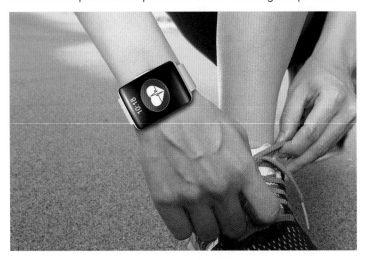

She started out in her kitchen and spent the whole of 2013 experimenting with different flavours and testing them at Maltby Market in London. Pippa then started production in a commercial kitchen in London's Royal Park, which provides facilities for new businesses in the food industry. Most of her start-up capital came from small loans from family and friends, with a further contribution from a government-backed scheme for business start-ups.

Like many entrepreneurs, Pippa took a risk by leaving paid employment to start the business. She worked as a producer at the Science Museum. However, she won a competition called 'Escape The City', which helped people to leave jobs they found unfulfilling. To help save money for the business she moved into a shed. This was to be her home for a few months while she launched Pip & Nut. Pippa said in a report in *The Telegraph*, 'Escape The City enabled me to quit my day job… I needed it to pay my rent but I really wanted to give the business more time. Now, I sleep in the shed and there's a desk space in their Battersea headquarters.' Pippa's products went on sale in Selfridges.

Skills required by entrepreneurs

Not only do entrepreneurs need to possess a number of important characteristics to be successful, they also need to use a wide range of different skills. To begin with it helps if entrepreneurs are capable to some extent in their chosen line of business. For example, an entrepreneur setting up a flying school will need aviation experience and an instructor's certificate. Someone starting a commercial radio station may need some broadcasting, transmitting and programming experience.

However, it is possible to set up a business in unfamiliar fields. For example, the skills needed in retailing, window cleaning and running an online sales operation can be learnt fairly quickly. There are also examples of entrepreneurs entering quite diversified lines of business without any relevant

Question 1

Grant Travers left school at the age of 16. He obtained C grades in 3 GCSEs – Maths, English and French. However, he did not really enjoy school because the education system, he felt, did not meet his needs and he was never really interested in schoolwork. Grant was very sporty, creative and enjoyed organising events, such as discos and sports tournaments. When he turned 16 he started organising transport from Plymouth, his home town, to Plymouth Argyle away football fixtures. He booked a coach with a local coach company and sold tickets to friends at school and others near where he lived. He organised 11 trips between December and May. His main motive for this venture was to provide affordable transport to away matches for him and his friends. However, he made an average profit of £100 per trip. Grant is now in the process of setting up his own travel company. His final school reference, written by the Head of Year, is shown in Figure 1 (written in May before exam results were published in August).

Figure 1

Grant Travers – school reference

Grant Travers

Grant is a charming young man. He is loyal, honest, open and friendly. However, his five years spent at The Plymouth Academy have been somewhat wasted – although he will probably 'scrape through' with C grades in Maths and English. Grant had plenty of ability but was not motivated to reach his full academic potential. It is regretful that he has chosen to leave and not enrol on one of the academy's vocational courses, to which he might be better suited.

To his credit, outside the classroom Grant excelled. He was the captain of the school football team for five consecutive years and led his team to win the South West Schools Cup in his final year. He also organised discos and other events, working alongside academy staff. He was well liked by everyone. He is full of self-confidence, shows initiative and when interested can be extremely determined.

I'm not sure what will become of Grant. He says that he is going to start his own business. A little ambitious perhaps for a sixteen-year-old – but it wouldn't surprise me at all if he made a great success of it.

Good luck, Grant!

Liz Welland

Elizabeth Welland (Head of Year)

(a) Discuss whether Grant has the characteristics to become an entrepreneur.

experience. For example, Sir Stelios Haji-Ioannou set up easyJet after being involved in his father's shipping business. It is possible to do this by employing experts in the chosen field right from the start. Other important entrepreneurial skills are outlined on the next page.

Organising: Entrepreneurs play an important organisational role. They have to project manage the setting up and running of their business ventures. This involves organising and co-ordinating a wide range of resources in order to get the business up and running. In this organisational role, entrepreneurs will be planning, scheduling, giving instructions, prioritising, setting up systems, monitoring, time managing and meeting deadlines. If things go wrong, entrepreneurs will sometimes be 'fire-fighting', that is resolving conflict, dealing with business issues and sorting out problems.

Financial management: This is a very important skill and if it is neglected can lead to the demise of the business. The main aim of financial management is to make sure that the business has enough money whenever it is needed. This might involve budgeting, cash-flow forecasting, chasing debts, keeping up-to-date financial records, arranging loans and overdrafts, and analysing financial information (in business accounts, for example).

Communication: Entrepreneurs will need to interact with a wide range of different stakeholders. These might include customers, employees, suppliers, the local community and the authorities. Entrepreneurs will need to develop effective face-to-face communication skills to deal directly with people. Charm, courtesy, assertiveness, professionalism and a convincing manner are all useful entrepreneurial attributes. Entrepreneurs might also be required to write letters, memos and reports, fill in forms and design documents for both internal and external use. Presentational skills might also be needed – when making a sales pitch, for example. If entrepreneurs have good communication skills, their businesses are likely to perform better.

Managing people: As a business grows there will be a need to take on more staff. It is often said that managing people is one of the most difficult tasks when running a business. Individuals are all different and may require different approaches to motivation. Entrepreneurs need to recruit the 'right people' in the first place and then show clear leadership and direction. People should be easier to manage if their needs are met, and if they are treated with respect and valued.

Decision making: Running a business will require a lot of decision making. The level of decisions however will differ. Most decisions are about low-level, day-to-day issues such as what materials or stock to order, which tools to use and where to advertise for a new operative. In contrast, a small number of decisions are strategic. These are important and can have long-term effects on the business. An example might be whether to move premises to a new location. Entrepreneurs will also have to solve problems when they occur. Decision making and problem solving require entrepreneurs to process, analyse and evaluate information.

Negotiating: Inevitably entrepreneurs will spend some of their time negotiating. This often means agreeing the terms of a contract, such as agreeing a price for undertaking some work or completing an order for a customer. However, negotiation might also be needed when dealing with suppliers and employees. Entrepreneurs need to be able to get their points across in a calm and assertive manner, develop arguments with reasoning, know when to compromise, and try to arrive at a settlement that is agreeable to both parties.

IT skills: Entrepreneurs will be able to run their business more efficiently if they have good IT skills. For example, they might need to:
- set up filing systems for business documents and other information
- communicate with stakeholders using email or conference calling
- use spreadsheets to prepare budgets and cash-flow forecasts
- design documents, such as invoices, order forms, job descriptions, expense claim forms, flyers and newsletters
- set up a business website and provide a system for online purchases
- use social media to help raise the profile of the business and direct potential customers to the business website
- use computer software to give presentations
- use specialist software, for designing products, for example.

Exam tip

Be careful not to confuse the characteristics of an entrepreneur with the skills required to be an entrepreneur. Most of the characteristics may be inherent – 'you either have them or you don't', although some might argue that they could be acquired over time. In contrast, most of the skills needed can be learned either by experience – 'learning by doing' – or through education and training. It is possible, for instance, to attend specialist training courses where many skills required by entrepreneurs can be learned and practised. For example, most local councils provide courses for people who want to set up and run a business.

Reasons why people set up businesses

People set up businesses for a wide range of reasons. For example, they may not want to work for an employer any more, they may want to develop a personal interest into a business or they may have been made redundant and want to start afresh. These motives, and others, fall into one of two different categories: financial and non-financial.

Financial motives: Many people set up a business because they want to make money. They often think that they could earn far more if they worked for themselves. Profit is the driving force behind many entrepreneurs and most businesses would not exist if it wasn't for the likelihood of making a profit.

Two approaches to the pursuit of profit can be identified.

- **Profit maximisation.** Some entrepreneurs try to make as much profit as they possibly can in a given time period. This is called **profit maximisation**. These entrepreneurs are motivated by money and their key focus is the financial return on their efforts. It might be argued that entrepreneurs that try to maximise profits are likely to take bigger risks. This is because there is usually a direct relationship between risk and reward. For example, a small manufacturer might decide to replace some workers with a computer numerically controlled (CNC) machine costing £250,000. However, if production levels cannot be raised sufficiently to cover the cost of the machine, the financial burden might cause extreme cash-flow difficulties. It might also be argued that entrepreneurs that aim to maximise profits are more likely to marginalise the needs of other stakeholders. For example, an entrepreneur might enforce zero hours contracts and only pay the legal minimum wage.

- **Profit satisficing.** Some entrepreneurs might take a different approach to profit. For example, they may aim to make enough profit to maintain their interest in the business. This is called **profit satisficing**. One reason why some entrepreneurs do not seek to maximise profits is because they do not want to take on the extra responsibility of expanding their business – which is often required to make more profit. Also, some entrepreneurs run 'lifestyle' businesses. This means a business that generates enough profit to provide the flexibility needed to sustain a particular lifestyle. This type of business allows owners to spend more time pursuing other interests or with family. For example, a couple running a bed and breakfast business might shut down for four months in the winter so that they can visit family in Australia.

Non-financial motives: For some people, other motives for setting up a business might be as important or more important than making money. They will obviously need to make enough profit in order for the business to continue in operation, but the main driving force is non-financial. A number of non-financial motives exist.

- **Ethical stance.** A minority of people set up a business in support of a moral belief they possess. For example, a vegetarian who believes that it is wrong to kill animals for meat may open up a vegetarian restaurant. By encouraging more people to use the restaurant, particularly if non-vegetarians can be attracted, fewer animals would be slaughtered. Another example might be setting up a business to generate 'clean' electricity. A keen environmentalist might feel that setting up a solar farm could contribute towards the reduction of carbon emissions.

- **Social enterprise.** These are organisations that trade with the aim of improving human and environmental well-being. They are sometimes referred to as not-for-profit organisations. Generally, social enterprises have a clear social and/or environmental mission and generate most of their income through trade or donations. Fairtrade is an example of a social enterprise. It markets products produced by small-scale farmers and workers who are marginalised from trade in a variety of ways. Fairtrade ensures that these people get a better price for their produce, such as coffee. Social enterprises are discussed in Unit 22.

- **Independence.** A lot of people want to be 'their own boss'. This is an important non-financial motive for setting up a business. These entrepreneurs are driven by the desire to be independent. The freedom to make all the decisions when running a business is very appealing. Some people often resent being told what to do at work. Being able to make your own decisions is often regarded as the main key benefit of being an entrepreneur. Nearly 90 per cent of respondents to a poll by Startups.co.uk said this was very important. However, in practice this independence may be limited. Work has to be done. Taxes have to be paid. Those financing the business, like a bank giving a loan, have to be kept satisfied that the business is doing OK. But those who own their own business, in general, do have more independence than those who work for an employer.

- **Home working.** Quite a number of entrepreneurs set up their businesses from home. They may be tradespeople such as plumbers, decorators or electricians that use their home as a base for their business. Or, increasingly, they may work from a room or an office at home. Examples include writers, accountants, software designers, app developers, artists, tutors and financial analysts. There are two key benefits for home workers. The time and expense spent travelling to and from work is eliminated. They also enjoy more flexibility. For example, they can take meals and breaks whenever they want and a parent may be able to fit work around the needs of their children.

Key terms

Profit maximisation – an attempt to make as much profit as possible in a given time period.
Profit satisficing – making enough profit to satisfy the needs of the business owner(s).

Knowledge check

1. State three characteristics of an entrepreneur.
2. What is meant by financial management?
3. State two communication skills that an entrepreneur might need.
4. Why will an entrepreneur need negotiating skills?
5. What IT skills might an entrepreneur need?
6. What is meant by profit satisficing?
7. State two non-financial motives for becoming an entrepreneur.

Case study

PICALOULOU

Shireen Cunliffe is an entrepreneur who set up Picaloulou, an online retailer of natural and sustainable children's knitwear, in 2011. Its target market is an affluent, eco-aware internet customer base. Shireen set up the business when she was unable to find quality British-made children's knitwear that was stylish and used natural fibres. She began by designing a hand-knitted range using naturally dyed British wools. She then found a team of home working knitters to make them.

As a mum, Shireen needed a flexible business arrangement. She combined working on Picaloulou with looking after her young children and helping on the administrative side of her husband's business. This often meant burning the midnight oil on her Picaloulou work. The business used a spare bedroom in the family home in Cornwall. This served as a storeroom, packaging and distribution centre, show room and studio.

Shireen used high speed internet, email, social networking and hosting services to keep in touch with her freelancers and home working knitters across the country.

Shireen does not believe in throwaway fashion. Picaloulou's knitwear is all designed and made in Britain using 100 per cent natural yarns such as Merino wool, cotton and cashmere. Picaloulou develops a small collection each autumn and has started to expand beyond children's styles into teenage and adult fashion. Shireen does not appear to be driven by profit, loving the fact that Picaloulou supports British wool growers and mills, and is helping to keep the craft of hand knitting alive.

Sources: adapted from www.picaloulou.com

(a) Explain why Shireen might be profit satisficing in this case. (4 marks)

(b) Explain one benefit to Picaloulou from being a home-based business. (4 marks)

(c) Explain two entrepreneurial skills that Shireen has used to help make Picaloulou successful. (4 marks)

(d) Assess whether Shireen's motives for setting up Picaloulou were mainly financial or non-financial. (10 marks)

21 Business objectives

Key points

1. Survival.
2. Profit maximisation.
3. Other objectives: sales maximisation, market share, cost efficiency, employee welfare, customer satisfaction, social objectives.

Getting started

Solomon Cohen is a social media enthusiast. He wanted to set up an organisation advising small businesses on how to raise their profile and generate sales using social media. He wrote a comprehensive business plan, invested £50,000 of his own money in the start-up and began designing his own website. The plan detailed three important business objectives.

- Break-even by the end of the first year.
- Generate £100,000 sales by the end of the second year.
- Make customer satisfaction a business priority.

State two advantages of setting business objectives. Do you think Solomon's business objectives are realistic? What other business objectives might you have if you set up in business?

Business objectives

The **aims** of a business are what the business wants to achieve in the long term. Aims tend to be general and examples might be to be the 'best' in the market or the 'market leader'. The **objectives** of a business are the goals or targets that need to be met in order to achieve an aim. For example, a business might aim to grow and set annual sales targets as objectives to help achieve it. Businesses are more likely to be successful if they set clear objectives. Businesses need to have objectives for the following reasons.

- Employees need something to work towards. Objectives help to motivate people. For example, sales staff might get bonuses if they reach certain sales targets.
- Without objectives owners might not have the motivation needed to keep the business going. Owners might lose grip and allow their business to 'drift'. This could result in business failure.
- Objectives help owners decide where to take a business and what steps are necessary to get there. For example, if a business aims to grow by 10 per cent, it might decide that launching products overseas would be the best way to achieve this.

It is easier to assess the performance of a business if the objectives set are SMART. This means that they should be

- **S**pecific – stating clearly what is trying to be achieved
- **M**easurable – capable of numeric measurement
- **A**greed – have the approval of everyone involved
- **R**ealistic – able to be achieved given the resources availabl
- **T**ime-specific – have a stated time by which they should be achieved.

An example of a SMART objective might be for a business to increase turnover by 8 per cent in the next 12 months. If the objectives are achieved it could be argued that the business h performed well.

Survival

All businesses will consider survival to be important. However, from time to time survival can become the most important objective. For example, when a business first starts trading it may be vulnerable. It often takes time for people to recognise the existence of a new business. Entrepreneurs may lack experience and there may be a shortage of resources. Therefore, a target for a new business may be simply to surviv in the first 12 months. A business might also struggle to survive if new competitors enter the market. If the new entrant have better or cheaper products, or more financial resources, entrepreneurs may need to focus on survival in the changed business environment at the expense of other objectives.

The survival of a business might also be threatened when trading conditions become difficult. During the recession in the between 2008 and 2013, a large number of businesses started to struggle for survival. One such business was the British airline carrier British Airways (BA). In 2009, it was widely reported that BA's 40,000 staff were told that the business was struggling as the whole industry was trying to come to terms with the global downturn. BA had lost £401 million in the previous year. It was reported that Willie Walsh, BA's CEO, told his employees that he would work for nothing in the month of July. Walsh, who went without £61,000 as a result, wrote to the airline's employees asking them to volunteer for either unpaid leave or even to work for nothing for up to a month. Walsh suggested that the trading environment was the toughest it had ever been with no evidenc of improvement, and that it was probably the most difficult perio in the history of the industry. BA did survive and returned to pro It was reported as making £631 million in 2013.

Question 1

Sears, one of North America's highest profile retailers, announced in 2014 that it would be closing a number of stores and taking out loans from the billionaire chairman and CEO, Eddie Lampert. Sears had seen its revenue fall for eight consecutive years. It had made losses for the last four of those years. The struggling superstore, which also owns Kmart, lost $548 million in the quarter up to November 2014. The reasons for the decline of Sears were reported as two-fold. The slow economic recovery from a deep recession hit the store hard because its target market was middle- and low-income consumers, who may have been most affected by the recession. Also, stiff competition was reported from 'leaner' operators such as Walmart, Home Depot and Amazon. It was reported that Eddie Lampert thought that many of the Sears stores were too large and in the wrong locations.

In an effort to revive the company the following measures were announced.

- More stores would be closed. Sears once owned 3,523 stores. This figure reduced to fewer than 2,000 by 2015.

- $400 million would be borrowed from a hedge fund owned by Eddie Lampert.

- Between 200 and 300 buildings would be sold and leased back to improve liquidity.

(a) Using an example from this case, explain one reason why Sears might have pursued survival as a business objective.

(b) Discuss whether the measures Sears has taken to survive are likely to be successful.

Profit maximisation

Without profit most businesses would not exist. However, some businesses focus on profit more aggressively, usually because the owners want to make as much profit as they possibly can. This is called profit maximisation. This might be more likely if businesses are owned by institutional shareholders, such as pension funds and investment funds. These owners need to maximise the returns on their investments to meet the needs of their clients. Many entrepreneurs are unlikely to pursue profit maximisation, they are more likely to pursue profit satisficing. This is discussed in Unit 20.

If entrepreneurs want to maximise profit, they will focus on keeping costs as low as possible while raising prices as high as they can before customer loyalty is damaged. Skim pricing is often used by profit maximisers. This strategy is usually used in the luxury goods market, for instance jewellery and designer clothes. The prices are set unnaturally high, as customers for these goods are wealthy and not price sensitive so don't object to such inflated values.

One criticism of this approach is that it is too short-termist. By focusing aggressively on maximising short-term profits, it is possible that more lucrative long-term opportunities are overlooked. Profit maximisation as an objective might also alienate other stakeholders, such as employees and customers. Higher profits often mean lower wages for employees and higher prices for customers.

Other objectives

Although survival and profit maximisation are two important business objectives, there are others.

Sales maximisation: Some entrepreneurs might try to increase sales as an objective. This is called sales maximisation. It involves a business selling as much as it possibly can in a particular period of time. Sales levels are an important performance indicator and generally growing sales is a healthy sign for a business. Most businesses can raise profits by selling more output.

Sales maximisation might be used by an entrepreneur to win a larger market share. This could be important when trading first begins. Also, as a business grows, specialist sales staff might be employed. If the pay of sales staff is linked to physical sales levels, a business is likely to pursue sales maximisation as sales staff try to maximise their earnings.

> ## Thinking bigger
>
> There is a difference between physical sales levels and sales revenue. Maximising physical sales levels is likely to benefit a business. However, it might be more appropriate to focus on sales *revenue* as an objective, i.e. the money generated by physical sales. It may be possible to sell more units by lowering the price. However, this might actually reduce sales revenue. The impact on revenue of reducing price to increase sales depends on price elasticity of demand. This is discussed in Unit 7.
>
> Consider this example. An entrepreneur currently sells 6,000 units a month at £5 per unit. This generates sales revenue of £30,000. In an effort to sell more, the entrepreneur lowers price to £4. As a result sales rise to 7,000. However, sales revenue drops to £28,000. This is likely to have a negative impact on profit. This example shows that an effort to maximise physical sales levels has actually resulted in lower levels of sales revenue.

Market share: Most businesses would prefer a large market share than a small one. Consequently, trying to increase market share is a common business objective. If a business can get a larger market share this should help to increase revenue and raise the profile of the business in the market. If a business can build a bigger market share than its rivals, it may be able to dominate the market. This might mean that it has more control over price. A larger market share also means that output levels will be higher so a business might be able to lower its costs. This will increase profit margins and generate more profit for the owners.

Cost efficiency: From time to time businesses may consider how to reduce their costs. It is an objective that might be pursued when trading conditions become difficult due to more competition or an economic downturn. However, some businesses look to cut costs all of the time. If costs are lower, profit margins will be higher. Businesses with lower costs might also gain a competitive edge in the market.

A business can use a variety of methods to cut costs. It might:
- lay off staff to cut labour costs
- find new suppliers to get cheaper resources
- increase the usage of recycled materials
- develop new working practices that use fewer resources
- develop ways of saving energy.

One of the drawbacks of cutting costs is that product quality or customer service might suffer. For example, if a pub cuts down on bar staff to reduce costs, customers might get fed up waiting to get served and go somewhere else.

Employee welfare: In recent years a number of businesses have realised the benefits of meeting the needs of employees more effectively. If employee welfare is improved workers will be happier, better motivated, more productive, more co-operative, more flexible and less likely to leave. Therefore another objective might be to improve employee welfare. A number of measures can be taken to achieve this, including:
- improving the working environment by making it cleaner, less noisy and less crowded
- ensuring that staff are given proper breaks and somewhere comfortable to interact with colleagues during those breaks
- ensuring that staff are equipped with the necessary tools and equipment, providing ergonomically designed chairs for call centre workers, for example
- maintaining high standards of courtesy between all staff members
- encouraging regular exercise by organising fitness sessions or providing a staff gym, for example.

Improving employee welfare is also likely to reduce staff absenteeism through sickness, enhance the image of the business, help to comply with health and safety legislation, and make it easier to recruit and retain good quality people.

Customer satisfaction: Most businesses will try to meet the needs of customers. The benefits are clear. If customers are satisfied they are more likely to return. Loyal customers are valuable to a business. In order to win their loyalty, some businesses aim to exceed customer expectations. How might they do this?
- Ensure that all customer-facing staff are trained to a very high level in communication. Their conduct must be courteous, professional and friendly 100 per cent of the time.
- Provide a platform for customer feedback – an online review system, for example.
- Interact with customers using social media – encourage a two-way flow of information.
- Deal with customer complaints promptly and effectively – to the evident satisfaction of the customer.
- Monitor customer service regularly – using mystery shoppers, for example.

In order to have effective customer service, businesses must know what customers want, provide them with it on a consistent basis and receive feedback on how the business is doing.

Social objectives: A business that sets social objectives is one that shows concern for the local area. A business should aim to promote prosperity and develop a strong relationship with the local community so it can co-exist harmoniously. This might involve:
- keeping noise levels down
- maintaining sensible opening hours

Question 2

Brad Jones runs FancyThat, a manufacturing company based in Bradford that makes fancy dress costumes and accessories for shops and other outlets around the country. After a quiet start in 2010 the business is now booming. Interest in fancy dress costumes has escalated in recent years. Brad got the idea after going to sporting and social events, and talking to some people who had dressed up for the day. Brad could not believe what people were prepared to pay for fancy dress costumes. Also, there were whole groups of people in the crowd dressed in identical costumes. Brad saw a business opportunity.

When Brad first started he just wanted to survive in the first year. However, he was ambitious and by 2013 he was still in business and wanted to grow turnover to £200,000. He succeeded; however he has noticed recently that costs are rising sharply. His objective now is to cut fixed costs by 20 per cent and variable costs by 25 per cent, both by the end of the year.

(a) Explain what is meant by a SMART objective.

(b) Explain how Brad might cut costs in his business.

- demonstrating responsibility to the environment by minimising pollution
- providing employment for local people
- maintaining open channels of communication between the business and the local community so that issues can be raised and discussed
- making contributions to community life, such as visiting local schools, sponsoring local events or making donations to local charities.

It is not in the interests of a business to upset the local community. This is because collectively, the local population may be a formidable force should they lodge any form of objection. A business has a duty to be considerate and respectful when operating in a residential area, for example.

Exam tip
You need to appreciate that a business may pursue more than one business objective. For example, an established business might be trying to increase its market share, cut costs and improve employee welfare all at the same time. Also, the objectives of a business are likely to change over time. For example, when a business is first set up the main objective might be to survive the first two years. The next objective might be to build market share, and then further on in time, to maximise profits.

Case study

THE HAWKSHEAD RELISH COMPANY

Maria and Mark Whitehead run the Hawkshead Relish Company based in the Lake District. It makes handmade relishes, pickles and preserves in small batches using locally sourced ingredients. The company started to take off in 2001. Prior to that, the couple's café business was devastated by the outbreak of Foot and Mouth where Mark and Maria nearly lost everything. However, they then started to manufacture the relishes, pickles and preserves they had made at home for the café, on a larger scale. The business developed when local retailers agreed to stock their products, and it has been growing ever since.

All the products are handmade in small batches with no colourings, preservatives, artificial flavourings or padding out. According to Mark, who is the creative influence in the partnership, 'If it doesn't add flavour it doesn't get added … Allowing the great quality of the ingredients to speak for themselves is the key to creating a product that bursts with flavour.'

Hawkshead Relish is all about preserving in the traditional way and using locally sourced products and local people to make everything by hand without any artificial ingredients.

In 2005 they received the Speciality Producer of the Year award from the Guild of Fine Food, and have since gone on to win over 50 Great Taste awards for the products. Things got even better in 2011 when Mark and Maria received joint MBEs from Her Majesty the Queen for services to the food industry in South Lakeland.

In 2007 the business moved production a short distance into a sixteenth-century restored barn. This has helped to ensure long-term employment for the small but dedicated workforce. Supporting the local economy and community is very high on the company's list of priorities. It employs between 18 to 24 local and highly valued staff.

Hawkshead Relish now supplies around 500 stores in the UK and exports to over 30 countries. Over the next five years Mark and Maria aim to build Hawkshead Relish so that it is widely recognised around the UK as a high-quality handmade brand. The company will continue to grow its sales and look at new markets, while retaining its base in South Lakeland, 'where our hearts belong,' said Mark.

Sources: adapted from www.hawksheadrelish.com, www.countrylife.co.uk and *Invest in South Lakeland*

(a) Explain one reason why survival may have been an objective for the Hawkshead Relish Company when it was set up in 2001. (4 marks)

(b) Explain one benefit to a business like the Hawkshead Relish Company of pursuing social objectives. (4 marks)

(c) Assess the importance of sales maximisation in helping the Hawkshead Relish Company achieve its aim of establishing the brand over the next five years. (12 marks)

Key terms

Aims – what a business tries to achieve in the long term.
Objectives – the goals or targets set by a business to help achieve its long-term purpose.
Sales maximisation – an attempt to sell as much as possible in a given time period (or an attempt to generate as much sales revenue as possible in a given time period).

Knowledge check

1. State two situations where survival is likely to be an important business objective.
2. What is meant by profit maximisation?
3. Explain one benefit of increasing market share as a business objective.
4. State three ways a business can cut costs.
5. Why might a business aim to improve employee welfare?
6. State three ways a business can improve employee welfare.
7. How important is customer satisfaction as a business objective?
8. What is meant by the social objectives of a business?

Key points

1. Sole trader, partnership and private limited company.
2. Franchising, social enterprise, lifestyle businesses and online businesses.

Getting started

There are many kinds of business organisation. Some examples include your local hairdresser, Amazon, EasyJet, a window cleaner, Nissan and Oxfam.

Who might own these businesses? How are these businesses different? What might be the advantages to a business like Amazon of operating an online business? Do all of these businesses aim to make a profit?

Sole traders

In January 2014, there were around 5 million businesses in the UK. They vary in their size, ownership and legal structure.
A **sole trader** or **sole proprietor** is the simplest form of business organisation. It has one owner, but can employ any number of people. Sole traders can be involved in a wide range of business activity. In the **primary sector**, they may be farmers or fishermen. In the **secondary sector**, they may be small building or manufacturing businesses. However, most sole traders will be found in the **tertiary sector**. Many of these are retailers running small shops. Others may offer services such as web design, tutoring, hairdressing, taxi driving and garden maintenance. Setting up as a sole trader is easy, as there are no legal formalities. However, sole traders do have some legal responsibilities.

- They may have to pay income tax and National Insurance contributions.
- Once their turnover reaches a certain level, they must register for value added tax (VAT). However, some sole traders choose to register because they can claim back VAT that they have paid, even though they do not charge VAT.
- They may need a licence to trade if they are involved in activities such as selling alcohol or supplying a taxi service or public transport.
- They may need planning permission – for example, a person may have to apply to the local authority for planning permission to convert a warehouse into a nightclub.
- They must comply with legislation aimed at business practice – for example, they are legally required to provide safe working conditions for their employees.

All sole traders have **unlimited liability**. This means that if the business fails, a sole trader can lose more money than was originally invested. This is because a sole trader can be forced to use personal wealth to pay off business debts. The advantages and disadvantages of operating as a sole trader are summarised in Table 1.

Table 1 Advantages and disadvantages of sole traders

Advantages	Disadvantages
The owner keeps all the profit.	The owner has unlimited liability.
The business is independent and the owner has complete control.	The owner may struggle to raise financ as lenders may consider them too risky to offer credit.
The business is simple to set up, with no legal requirements.	Independence may be a burden, for example if an owner is ill.
The business can be flexible and can adapt to change quickly.	The owner and any employees are likel to work very hard, with long hours.
The business can offer a personal service because it is small.	The business is usually too small to exploit economies of scale.
The business may qualify for government help.	The business will have no continuity if owner passes away.

Partnerships

A **partnership** is defined in The Partnership Act, 1890 as the 'relation which subsists between persons carrying on busines with common view to profit'. Put simply, a partnership has mo than one owner. The 'joint' owners will share responsibility for running the business and also share the profits. Partnerships are often found in professions such as accountants, doctors, estate agents, solicitors and veterinary surgeons. After sole traders, partnerships are the most common type of business organisation. It is usual for partners to specialise. A firm of chartered accountants with five partners might be organised s that each partner specialises in one aspect of finance, such as tax law, investments or VAT returns.

There are no legal formalities to complete when a partnership is formed. However, partners may draw up a **Dee of Partnership**. This is a legal document which states partner rights in the event of a dispute. It covers issues such as:

- how much capital each partner will contribute
- how profits (and losses) will be shared amongst the partne
- the procedure for ending the partnership
- how much control each partner has
- rules for taking on new partners.

If no Deed of Partnership is drawn up the arrangements between partners will be subject to the Partnership Act. For example, if there is a dispute regarding the share of profits, th Act states that profits are shared equally among the partners.

The advantages and disadvantages of partnerships are shown in Table 2 on the next page.

Table 2 Advantages and disadvantages of partnerships

Advantages	Disadvantages
The partnership is easy to set up and run, with no legal formalities.	Partners have unlimited liability.
Partners can specialise in their area of expertise.	Partners have to share the profit.
Partners share the burden of running the business.	Partners may disagree and fall out with one another.
More owners can raise more capital.	One partner's decision is legally binding on all other partners.
The partnership does not have to publish financial information.	Partnerships have limited growth potential.

Limited partnerships

The Limited Partnerships Act 1907 allows a business to become a limited partnership, although this is rare. This is where some partners provide capital but take no part in the management of the business. Such a partner will have limited liability – the partner can only lose the original amount of money invested. A partner with limited liability cannot be made to sell personal possessions to meet any other business debts. This type of partner is called a sleeping partner. Even with a limited partnership there must always be at least one partner with unlimited liability. The Act also allows this type of partnership to have more than 20 partners.

The Limited Liability Partnership Act, 2000 allows the setting up of a limited liability partnership. All partners in this type of partnership have limited liability. To set up as a limited liability partnership, the business has to agree to comply with a number of regulations, such as filing annual reports with the Registrar of Companies.

Limited companies

A limited company has a separate legal identity from its owners. The company can own assets, form contracts, employ people, sue people and be sued.

Certain features are common to limited companies.

- Capital is raised by selling shares. Each shareholder owns a number of these shares and is a joint owner of the company. They are entitled to vote on important business decisions, such as a choice of who should run the company. They also get dividends paid from profits. Shareholders with more shares will have more control and get more dividends.
- Unlike sole traders or partnerships, the owners (shareholders) have limited liability. If a limited company has debts, the owners can only lose the money they originally invested. They cannot be forced to use their own money to pay any debts that have been run up by the business.
- Limited companies are run by directors who are elected by the shareholders. The board of directors, headed by a chairperson, is accountable to shareholders. The board runs the company as the shareholders wish. If the company performs badly, directors can be voted out at an annual general meeting (AGM).
- Unlike sole traders and partnerships, who pay income tax on profits, limited companies pay corporation tax.

Forming a limited company: To form a limited company, it is necessary to follow a legal procedure. This involves sending some important documents to the Registrar of Companies: these are the Memorandum of Association and the Articles of Association. These are shown in Figures 1 (below) and 2 (on the next page).

Question 1

Jones, Thomas and Wilson is a firm of chartered accountants based in Aylesbury. The partnership was formed in 2009 when each of the partners contributed £50,000 in capital. A Deed of Partnership was drawn up and it was agreed that the profits from the business would be shared 40 per cent, 40 per cent and 20 per cent between Jones, Thomas and Wilson respectively. Wilson's share was lower because he was a newly qualified accountant and therefore had less experience than the others.

One of the business's strengths is that each partner is a specialist in a particular field of accountancy. Jones is a tax specialist, Thomas is an investment analyst and Wilson is in charge of external audits. This helped the business to serve a range of customers with different financial needs.

In 2011, the partners decided to expand. They needed to raise £100,000 to obtain more office space and upgrade their computer systems. The partners considered inviting a sleeping partner to contribute some capital. However, in the end, they borrowed the money from a bank.

(a) (i) Why do you think Jones, Thomas and Wilson drew up a Deed of Partnership?

(ii) In 2013, the partnership made a profit of £240,000. In the absence of a Deed of Partnership, how much profit would Wilson be entitled to?

(b) Explain two advantages of a partnership illustrated by this case.

(c) Discuss two possible reasons why Jones, Thomas and Wilson decided against inviting a sleeping partner into the business.

Figure 1

Memorandum of Association

The Memorandum of Association sets out the constitution and gives details about the company. The following details must be included:
- name of the company
- name and address of the company's registered office
- objectives of the company and the nature of its activities
- amount of capital to be raised and the number of shares to be issued.

Figure 2

Articles of Association

This document deals with the internal running of the company. The Articles of Association include details such as:
- rights of shareholders depending on the type of share they hold
- procedures for appointing directors
- length of time directors should serve before re-election
- timing and frequency of company meetings
- arrangements for auditing company accounts.

If the documents in Figures 1 and 2 are acceptable, the company gets a **Certificate of Incorporation**. This allows it to trade as a limited company. The shareholders have a legal right to attend the AGM and must be told of the date and venue in writing.

A limited company can be set up online, and a number of websites offer such services. Such websites provide templates for the Memorandum of Association and the Articles of Association, which makes the whole process easier.

Private limited companies

Most private limited companies are small or medium-sized businesses, though some are large businesses, similar in size to public limited companies. Private limited companies share the following features.
- Their business name ends in Limited or Ltd.
- Shares can only be transferred privately, from one individual to another. All shareholders must agree on the transfer and they cannot be advertised for sale.
- They are often family businesses owned by family members or close friends.
- The directors of private limited companies tend to be shareholders and are involved in running the business.

The advantage and disadvantages of private limited companies are outlined in Table 3.

Table 3 Advantages and disadvantages of private limited companies

Advantages	Disadvantages
Shareholders have limited liability.	Private limited companies have to publish their financial information.
More capital can be raised by issuing shares.	Setting-up costs have to be met.
Control over the business cannot be lost to outsiders.	Profits are shared between more members.
The owners have tax advantages. Owners may pay less tax, for example.	It takes time to transfer shares to new owners.
Private limited companies are considered to have a higher status than some other types of business organisations, such as a sole trader.	Private limited companies cannot raise large amounts of money like public limited companies.

Question 2

Ilene Bracken owns VegPack, a food processing business in Wigan. The business supplies small retail outlets in the north-west region of the UK with pre-packed vegetables. She buys vegetables in bulk from local farmers and then washes, trims and packs them attractively before dispatching them to customers. She set up as a sole trader in 2006, but the growth of the business has taken her by surprise. The success is down to a 'sale-or-return' policy that customers like. This results in some waste, but her premium pricing helps to compensate for any losses.

In order to meet the demands of rapid growth and to help expand into new markets, Ilene needs to raise £400,000. She has approached a number of banks, but has found that they are reluctant to lend to her. Her accountant has suggested forming a private limited company to raise money by issuing some shares to members of her family and two key employees of the business.

(a) Explain two advantages of becoming a shareholder in VegPack.

(b) Explain who runs a private limited company.

(c) Assess the likely impact on Ilene of VegPack becoming a private limited company.

Franchising

Starting up your own business carries a lot of risk. Most new start-ups have ceased to exist after five years of trading. One way of possibly reducing this risk is to buy a **franchise**. The **franchisor** is a company which owns the franchise. It has a track record of running a successful business operation. It allows another business, the **franchisee**, to use its business ideas and methods in return for a variety of fees. In the UK, there are a large number of franchise operations including Dairy Crest, Domino's Pizza, Dyno-Rod, McDonald's, SUBWAY and Tumble Tots.

The franchisor provides a variety of services to its franchisees.
- It gives the franchisee a licence to make a product which is already tried and tested in the market place. This could be a physical product but is far more likely to be a service.
- The franchisor provides a recognised brand name which customers should recognise and trust. This helps generate sales from the moment the franchise starts trading.
- The franchisor will provide a start-up package. This will include help and advice about setting up the business. The franchisor might provide the equipment to start the business. It might help find a bank which will lend money. It will provide training for the new franchisee.
- Many franchises provide materials to use to make the product. A company like McDonald's, for example, sells food ingredients to its franchisees. If the franchisor doesn't directly sell to the franchisee, it might organise bulk-buy deals with suppliers to cut costs for all its franchise operation.
- It is likely to provide marketing support. For example, it might have national advertising campaigns. It may provide marketing materials like posters to place in business premises, or leaflets to circulate to customers.

- There should be ongoing training. This will be linked to issues such as maintaining standards, sales and new products.
- There is likely to be a range of business services available at competitive prices. For example, the franchisor might negotiate good deals on business insurance or vehicle leasing with suppliers.
- Many franchises operate exclusive area contracts. This is where one franchisee is guaranteed that no franchise deal will be signed with another franchisee to operate in a particular geographical area. This prevents competition between franchisees and so helps sales.
- Over time, the brand should be developed by the franchisor. For example, new products should be developed to appeal to customers.

In return for these services, the franchisee has to pay a variety of fees.

- There will be an initial start-up fee. Part of this will cover the costs of the franchisor in giving advice or perhaps providing equipment. Part of it will be a payment to use the franchise name.
- Most franchisors charge a percentage of sales for ongoing management services and the ongoing right to use the brand name.
- Franchisors will also make profit on the supplies they sell directly to their franchisors.
- There may also be one-off fees charged for management services such as training.

There are advantages and disadvantages of franchising. Table 4 shows some general advantages and disadvantages for the franchisee. Although one of the advantages is that the franchisor provides national advertising, some of it can be quite poor. Also, like any other business enterprise they can prosper or they can fail. For example, when buying a franchise, it is important for the franchisee to be vigilant when assessing the opportunities that the franchisor is offering. It is worth remembering that often 'you get what you pay for'. If someone who is not suited to running a business buys a franchise, the prospect of failure is still relatively high. Some of the advantages and disadvantages to franchisors of franchising are summarised in Table 5.

Table 4 Advantages and disadvantages to franchisees of franchising

Advantages to the franchisee	Disadvantages to the franchisee
Franchises are lower risk, as they use an idea that has already been tried and tested.	A franchisee's profit is shared with the franchisor.
Franchisees get support from the franchisor.	Franchisees have to sign contracts with franchisors, which can reduce independence.
The set-up costs of a franchise are predictable.	Setting up a franchise can be an expensive way to start a business.
Franchisees can benefit from national marketing campaigns organised by the franchisor.	Franchisees lack independence and must abide by strict operating rules.

Table 5 Advantages and disadvantages to franchisors of franchising

Advantages to the franchisor	Disadvantages to the franchisor
Franchising is a fast method of growth.	Potential profit is shared with franchisees.
Franchising is a cheaper method of growth because franchisees take some of the financial risk.	Poor franchisees may damage the brand's reputation.
Franchisees take some of the risk on behalf of the franchisor.	Franchisees may get their merchandise from elsewhere.
Franchisees are more motivated than employees.	The cost of supporting franchisees may be high.

Question 3

The Soya Bean is an international franchise operation selling vegetarian snacks. Their outlets offer a fresh, healthy alternative to fast-food restaurants. The success of the UK-based franchise is due partly to the support that it offers to its franchisees:

- **Brand recognition:** The Soya Bean brand is recognised internationally and franchisees are encouraged to get involved in its marketing.
- **Training:** Franchisees attend yearly training 'camps' to ensure they are aware of all new developments and to learn from other franchisees.
- **Open communication:** Franchisees are encouraged to share best practice with each other and their service providers and develop new ideas collaboratively.
- **Supportive decision-making:** The Soya Bean encourages collaboration and tries to induce franchisees in their decision making.
- **Centralised purchasing:** The Soya Bean operates an online ordering system so that the same supplier is used for all food, packaging, equipment and services to franchisees.

Figure 3

Growth in The Soya Bean franchise outlets between 2008 and 2012

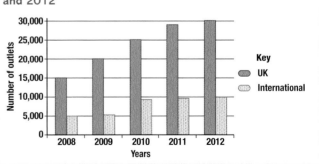

(a) Explain the difference between a franchisor and a franchisee.

(b) Discuss the key benefits to franchisees of taking out a franchise of The Soya Bean.

(c) How does the data in Figure 3 illustrate one of the key advantages to the franchisor of franchising?

Social enterprises

Some businesses operate as **social enterprises**. These organisations trade with the aim of improving human and environmental well-being, rather than making profit for external owners. They are sometimes referred to as not-for-profit organisations. Generally, social enterprises:

- have a clear social and/or environmental mission
- generate most of their income through trade or donations
- reinvest most of their profits
- are not connected to the government
- are majority controlled in the interests of the social mission
- are accountable and transparent.

Social enterprises may take a variety of forms.

Co-operatives: Most modern **co-operatives** operate as consumer or retail co-operatives. They are owned and controlled by their members. Members can purchase shares that entitle them to a vote at annual general meetings (AGMs). The members elect a board of directors to make overall business decisions and appoint managers to run day-to-day business. Co-operatives are run in the interests of their members. Any surplus made by the co-operative is distributed to members as a dividend according to levels of spending.

Worker co-operatives: These are businesses jointly owned by their employees. Examples might be a wine growing co-operative or a co-operative of farmers producing milk. In a worker co-operative, employees are likely to:

- contribute to production and be involved in decision making
- share in the profit (usually on an equal basis)
- provide some capital when buying a share in the business.

Mutual organisations: Most building societies in the UK are **mutual organisations**. They are owned by their customers – or members, as they are known – rather than by shareholders. They offer a wide range of financial services such as mortgages and savings products. Profits are returned to members in the form of better and cheaper products. Friendly societies (also mutual organisations) began in the 18th and 19th centuries to support the working classes. Today, they offer a wide range of affordable financial services. These include savings schemes, insurance plans and protection against the loss of income or death.

Charities: These exist to raise money for various causes and draw attention to the needs of disadvantaged groups in society. For example, Age UK is a charity that raises money on behalf of older people. They also raise awareness of issues that relate to older people, such as the winter fuel payment. Other examples of charities include the British Red Cross, Save the Children Fund and Mencap. Charities rely on donations for their revenue. They may also organise fundraising events such as jumble sales, sponsored activities and raffles. A number of charities also run business ventures such as charity shops.

Lifestyle businesses

A person running a **lifestyle business** aims to make enough money and provide the flexibility needed to sustain a particular lifestyle. The business should be lucrative enough to support the desired lifestyle without having to sacrifice time for the entrepreneur's personal life. Typical examples might include tradespeople such as plumbers and electricians, consultants in a variety of industries, florists, and people who run small retail stores, bed and breakfasts and small lifestyle farms. Many online businesses, such as web design, coaching, advisory or marketing services, also operate as lifestyle businesses. Some features of lifestyle businesses are as follows.

- The business will often be small and is likely to have just one owner.
- The personal interests of the entrepreneur are likely to influence the nature of the business, so that time spent working is enjoyable.
- An owner may undertake a variety of different ventures. For example, a musician may generate income by playing live in a band, teaching people to play an instrument, busking, teaching part-time in a college and writing music for adverts.
- Running the business is likely to be much less stressful than other forms of business.
- The business is likely to be home-based.
- They are likely to have similar advantages and disadvantages to those of sole traders.
- Lifestyle businesses are sometimes considered an alternative to retirement.

Lifestyle businesses are sometimes contrasted with start-up businesses, which are intended to grow and create increasing amounts of profit. Because growth in revenue and profit is not a key objective to lifestyle businesses, owners of lifestyle businesses usually have to provide all the funding themselves. Not many external investors will fund businesses that do not aim to maximise profits. However, there are exceptions. For example, Tim Ferriss runs a large lifestyle business in the US. He is an author, business advisor and angel investor, and in 2014 he was ranked sixth in the Top 20 Angel Investor rankings.

Online businesses

Amazon.com, MoneySuperMarket.com, Confused.com, eBay and Facebook are examples of large and well-known **online businesses**. However, there are many thousands of much smaller examples including retailers, consultants, gaming companies, bloggers, share dealers, teachers, web designers and information providers. Despite being very different companies, they all use the internet to trade and are likely to have the following features in common.

- Customers access the business via the internet. All online businesses have a website which gives information about their products, their prices and general information about the company.
- Online businesses collect payment for goods and services electronically. Credit cards, debit cards and PayPal are the most common methods used.
- There are no formal procedures to follow or legal requirements when starting an online business. However, traders must have secure websites with adequate protection against technical breakdowns and fraud.
- Online businesses have low set-up costs. A trader could build their own website for a few hundred pounds. Alternatively,

for a higher set-up cost, a new online trader could purchase a complete set-up package, including web design, domain name registration and arranging the hosting of the website by an internet service provider. Many online businesses are also run from home, which eliminates the need to find business premises.

- For many online businesses, paid-for or sponsored advertising is their main source of revenue. For example, most people use Facebook's social media services free of charge. However, in 2013, most of the $7.87 billion revenue was generated from advertising on the site.

The majority of businesses have websites that give information about company history, products, services, company aims and contact details. Also, many retailers, such as supermarkets, chain stores and even independent retailers, have an online sales operation.

The internet has fundamentally changed the way products and services are sold. It has also revolutionised the development, design, production and distribution of products and services. Thanks to the internet, even small businesses have access to global markets, international suppliers and foreign employees. Table 6 shows that global internet usage is growing rapidly, from 1,562 million in 2008 to 2,712 million in 2013. It also shows that in the UK, the growth in internet usage is slowing down. This is probably because most people in the UK are now internet users. There is not much scope left for future growth. The value of ecommerce sales rose from £334.6 billion in 2008 to £556.6 billion in 2013. This is still a rapid rate of growth.

Table 6 Growth in global and UK internet users, and total UK ecommerce sales

	2008	2009	2010	2011	2012	2013
Global internet users (million)	1,562	1,752	2,034	2,272	2,511	2,712
UK internet users (million)	48.0	51.6	52.8	54.2	54.6	55.5
UK ecommerce sales (£ billion)*	334.6	375.1	418.9	494.1	479.4	556.6

*Value of total sales derived from ecommerce sales
Sources: adapted from www.ons.gov.uk and www.internetlivestats.com

Maths tip

When analysing data like that shown in Table 6, it may be useful to describe changes over time in percentage terms. For example, total UK ecommerce spending rose from £334.6 billion in 2008 to £556.6 billion in 2013. The percentage increase is calculated as follows:

$$\frac{\text{Difference}}{\text{Original number}} \times 100 =$$

$$\frac{£556.6 \text{ bn} - £334.6 \text{ bn}}{£334.6 \text{ bn}} \times 100 = \frac{£222.0 \text{bn}}{£334.6 \text{ bn}} \times 100 = 66.3\%$$

Therefore, you can say that the value of sales derived from ecommerce sales in the UK rose by 66.3% between 2008 and 2013.

Case study

KHAN ACADEMY

Khan Academy is an example of both a social enterprise and an online business. It is a not-for-profit business that aims to change education for the better by providing a free world-class education for anyone anywhere. In 2014, the organisation employed around 80 people and had around 10 million users each month. All of the site's resources are available to anyone who has an internet connection – there are no subscription fees or other charges. Its services are aimed at students of all ages, teachers and parents.

- The website offers support such as practice exercises and instructional videos. It also provides some teacher aids and is designed to let learners work at their own speed.

- Resources are adjusted to meet individual needs. They offer personalised advice about the order of learning and help to motivate learners.

- Many are from the US but students from countries like India, Brazil, Mexico, South Africa and beyond also use the site. Video lessons have been translated into almost 40 languages to meet the needs of these international students.

- Learning programmes address many subjects such as maths, physics, biology, economics, art history and computer science.

- Most revenue is raised from donations. For example, in November 2011, Khan Academy received a grant of $5 million from the O'Sullivan Foundation.

Source: adapted from www.khanacademy.org.

(a) What is meant by a social enterprise? (2 marks)

(b) Explain one benefit to Khan Academy of operating an online business. (4 marks)

(c) Assess the importance of growth in internet usage on an online business like Khan Academy. (12 marks)

Key terms

Articles of Association – a document that provides details of the internal running of a limited company.

Certificate of Incorporation – a document that declares a business is allowed to trade as a limited company.

Co-operative – a business organisation owned by its members, who have equal voting rights.

Deed of Partnership – a binding legal document that states the formal rights of partners.

Franchise – a business model in which a business (the franchisor) allows another operator (the franchisee) to trade under their name.

Lifestyle business – a business that aims to make enough money and provide the flexibility needed to support a particular lifestyle for the owner.

Limited company – a business organisation that has a separate legal entity from that of its owners.

Limited liability – a legal status which means that a business owner is only liable for the original amount of money invested in the business.

Limited partnership – a partnership where some members contribute capital and enjoy a share of profit, but do not participate in the running of the business. At least one partner must have unlimited liability.

Memorandum of Association – a document that sets out the constitution and states key external details about a limited company.

Mutual organisation – a business owned by its members, who are customers not shareholders.

Online business – a business that uses the global communications infrastructure of the internet as a trading base.

Partnership – a business organisation that is usually owned by between 2–20 people.

Primary sector – production involving the extraction of raw materials from the earth.

Secondary sector – production involving the conversion of raw materials into finished and semi-finished goods.

Sleeping partner – a partner that contributes capital and enjoys a share of the profit but takes no active role in running the business.

Social enterprise – a business that trades with the objective of improving human or environmental well-being – charities and workers' co-operatives, for example.

Sole trader or **sole proprietor** – a business organisation which has a single owner.

Tertiary sector – the production of services in the economy.

Unlimited liability – a legal status which means that the owner of a business is personally liable for all business debts.

Knowledge check

1. State three advantages and three disadvantages of being a sole trader.

2. What is the advantage of a Deed of Partnership?

3. State three advantages and three disadvantages of partnerships.

4. What is meant by a sleeping partner?

5. What is the role of directors in limited companies?

6. What is the difference between the Memorandum of Association and the Articles of Association?

7. State two disadvantages of private limited companies.

8. Give two examples of a social enterprise.

9. State three features of a lifestyle business.

10. State two advantages of online businesses.

23 Forms of business 2

Key points

1. The growth of business to public limited company (plc).
2. Stock market flotation.

Getting started

J D Wetherspoon plc is a British pub chain. Tim Martin set up the business in 1979 when he opened his first pub in London. Since then, the company has expanded into a huge chain. After floating on the stock market in 1992, the company's share price rose by around 1,500 per cent over a 20-year period.

Who now owns J D Wetherspoon plc? Why do you think the company's share price rose by 1,500 per cent? What motivates owners to grow their businesses? How might Tim Martin expand his business further?

The growth of businesses

Most owners want their businesses to grow. This is usually because larger businesses enjoy a higher profile in the market place, larger revenues, lower unit costs due to economies of scale and higher profits. Larger businesses also feel more secure and find it easier to raise money. Many entrepreneurs may dream of owning a huge business that they built from scratch.

Many of the large businesses that dominate markets today started out as small sole traders or partnerships. They may have traded as private limited companies for a period of time in order to raise more capital. Finally they decided to 'go public' and operate as **public limited companies**. For example, Greggs plc is the UK's leading bakery retailer, specialising in sandwiches and baked savouries. John Gregg opened his first bakery in Newcastle upon Tyne in 1951. Since then it has expanded from one shop with a small bakery at the rear into a major UK chain, and in 2015 it had nearly 1,700 shops and 20,000 employees. Its 2013 turnover was £762.4 million.

Public limited companies

A public limited company is owned by shareholders and the name of the company ends in plc. Like a private limited company, it is run by a board of directors under the supervision of a chairperson who is accountable to the shareholders. There are just over one million registered limited companies in the UK, but only around one per cent of them are public limited companies. However, they contribute significantly to national output and employment. The shares of public limited companies can be bought and sold on the **stock market**. This is a market for second-hand shares and is accessible to anyone. It is possible to buy shares in any public limited company by using an online share-dealing site.

Question 1

Sainsbury's was set up in 1869 when John James Sainsbury and his wife Mary Ann formed a partnership and opened a small grocery shop in London. The company was owned wholly by the Sainsbury family until it went public as J Sainsbury plc in 1973. It was the largest ever flotation on the London Stock Exchange at the time. The Sainsbury family retained 85 per cent of the firm's shares. The company's progressive image was strengthened by the excitement of the press reports surrounding the flotation.

In 2014, Sainsbury's generated a turnover of £23.9 billion, up slightly from £23.3 billion in 2013. This represented about 16 per cent of the market. In 2014 it had 1,200 outlets and employed 161,000 people. The Sainsbury family had also sold many of its shares.

Figure 1

J Sainsbury plc share price from 1988 to 2014 (September closing price in pence)

(a) What is meant by a public limited company?

(b) How might a new investor buy shares in J Sainsbury plc?

(c) Explain what might account for the change in the Sainsbury share price between 1988 and 2014.

Stock market flotation

A **stock market flotation** occurs when a company 'goes public'. The process is also called an **initial public offering** (IPO), which means that a company's shares are offered to the public for the first time. The process is time-consuming and expensive. A great deal of administration is necessary and it is common for a specialist such as an investment bank to be awarded the task. One of the first jobs when undertaking an IPO is to publish a prospectus. This is a detailed document that advertises the company to potential investors and invites them to buy shares before the day of the flotation.

The prospectus is likely to contain the following.

- A brief history of the business.
- A list of the directors and other key personnel.
- A description of its operations.
- An outline of how the money raised will be spent.
- The company's future strategy.
- Some financial details such as historic accounts.
- Details of any pending legal action.
- Details of possible risks to investors.
- Clear information about how to buy shares – including key dates for example.
- An application form to buy shares.

'Going public' is expensive. This is because:

- the company needs lawyers to ensure that the prospectus is 'legally' correct
- a large number of 'glossy' publications have to be made available
- the company is likely to pay an investment bank to process share applications
- the share issue has to be underwritten (which means that the company must insure against the possibility of some shares remaining unsold) and a fee is paid to an underwriter who must buy any unsold shares
- the company will have advertising and administrative expenses
- the company must have a minimum of £50,000 share capital.

A public limited company cannot begin trading until it has completed these tasks and has received payment of at least 25 per cent for the value of shares. It will then receive a Trading Certificate and can begin operating, and the shares will be quoted on the stock exchange or the Alternative Investment Market (AIM).

A full stock exchange listing means that the company must comply with the rules and regulations laid down by the stock exchange. Many of these rules are to protect shareholders from fraud. The AIM is designed for companies that want to avoid some of the high costs of a full listing. However, shareholders with shares quoted on the AIM do not have the same protection as those with 'fully' quoted shares.

An example of a successful flotation is the Chinese internet giant Alibaba that was floated on the New York Stock Exchange, as widely reported in September 2014. It controlled 80 per cent of online commerce in China. Shares initially priced at $68 reached a high of $100 at one point before settling back to $93.89 by the end of the day, up 38 per cent. This valued the company at $231 billion.

High-profile flotations attract a lot of media attention. The shares are traded for the first time ever and investors who fail to buy shares initially have the chance to buy them on the open market. If the initial public offering is heavily oversubscribed, the share price can rise very sharply.

Question 2

Sometimes an established business may decide to sell off part of its operations. This may be called a **divestment**. One way to do this is to organise an IPO. In 2014, Lloyds Bank did this when it was ordered by the European Commission to sell TSB, following its £20 billion taxpayer bailout.

At the point of the IPO, TSB provided retail banking services via a network of 631 branches in the UK, employing 8,600 staff. The initial price of TSB shares was 260p. However, at the end of the first day's trading TSB shares rose by 30p to 290p. This meant that some private investors were £231 better off by the end of that first day.

The offer was in high demand, with 60,000 applications from private investors. They ended up with 30 per cent of the shares on offer. Those retaining the shares for 12 months had terms of a free bonus share of one for every 20 shares held. Each member of TSB's 8,600 staff was given £100 worth of free shares as part of the flotation. The idea was to make employees 'TSB Partners' and help with staff motivation.

(a) What is meant by an IPO?

(b) Explain the reasons why a flotation such as an IPO is expensive.

(c) Explain how giving free shares to TSB staff might impact on the company.

Advantages of public limited companies

Some of the advantages of public limited companies are the same as those of private limited companies (see page 132). For example, all members have limited liability, the firm continues to trade if one of the owners dies, and more power is enjoyed due to the larger size of the plc. Other advantages of public limited companies are as follows.

- Huge amounts of money can be raised from the sale of shares to the public. For example, when Alibaba went public in 2014, around $20 billion was raised for the company.
- Production costs may be lower as firms may gain economies of scale. Public limited companies are expected to grow and as they get bigger unit costs are likely to fall. This will improve their competitiveness and help to generate more profit.
- Because of their size, public limited companies can often dominate the market. Most plcs aim to grow and may eventually exercise some control in the market. For example, they may be able to create barriers to entry, preventing competition.

- It becomes easier to raise finance, as financial institutions are more willing to lend to public limited companies. A plc with substantial assets can provide the collateral needed by financial institutions to protect loans. Larger plcs also have a wider range of capital sources to choose from.
- Pressures from the media and financial analysts, as well as the danger that the public limited company might be taken over by another company, encourages executives and managers to perform well and make profits. These pressures do not exist for private limited companies.

Disadvantages of public limited companies

Setting up as a public limited company can also have disadvantages.

- The setting-up costs for public limited companies can be very expensive – running into millions of pounds in some cases. The various costs of 'going public' are listed under 'Stock market flotation' on the previous page.
- As anyone can buy their shares, it is possible for an 'outsider' to exert control on the company. They might even take complete control of a company if they buy enough shares. For example, in 2012 Kraft was able to take over Cadbury for £11.5 billion.
- Members of the public can inspect all of the company's accounts. Competitors may be able to use some of this information to their advantage. Public limited companies have to publish more information than private limited companies.
- Because of their size it is more difficult to deal with customers at a personal level. Some customers do not like dealing with giant 'faceless' corporations. They may prefer the personal service of a much smaller enterprise, perhaps even dealing directly with the owner.
- The way they operate is controlled by various Company Acts, which aim to protect shareholders. Compliance with company legislation will use up company resources. Public limited companies often employ a company secretary to deal solely with compliance issues.
- There may be a divorce of ownership and control. This means that the shareholders may not be able to exert enough pressure on those that end up running the company, such as senior managers. As a result the senior managers might pursue their own objectives, possibly at the expense of shareholders. This may happen if the shares are spread between a very large number of small shareholders. For example, Fred Goodwin, who was CEO of RBS from 2001 to 2009, was criticised for the £350 million spent on a new head office in Gogarburn. It had deep pile carpets and the walls were covered with expensive works of art. Some also criticised the amount of money paid to sponsors such as Jackie Stewart and Jack Nicklaus. Some shareholders may not have been very supportive of such expenditure.
- It is argued that some very large public limited companies are inflexible due to their size.

Some public limited companies are very large indeed. They have millions of shareholders and a wide variety of business interests situated all over the world. They are known as multinationals, which means that they have international markets and production operations in a number of different countries. For example, the UK oil giant BP employs about 84,000 people around the world in over 80 different countries. In 2014, it operated over 17,200 petrol outlets and had 18 operational oil wells. In 2013 its annual profit was $13.4 billion, down from $17.1 in 2012. Multinationals are discussed in Unit 79 and Unit 81.

Question 3

Founded in 2010, Versarien is an advanced materials manufacturer. Its products include a heat transfer material made from porous copper (VersarienCu) for use in cooling systems in computing and power conditioning equipment. It has already gained considerable industry recognition and received a number of awards, including:

- 2013 Racecar Engineering Magazine's Most Innovative Product Award
- 2012 MWP Advanced Manufacturing Award for Research and Development.

In 2013, Versarien floated on the Alternative Investment Market (AIM). It was reported that the company raised £3 million before flotation expenses. Following this, the company acquired Total Carbide, a leading manufacturer of tungsten carbide products, for £2.28 million. This provided extra capacity to meet growing customer demand.

Source adapted from www.versarien.com

(a) What is meant by AIM?

(b) Explain what advantages there are for Versarien of trading as a public limited company.

(c) Explain how the funds raised by the flotation benefited Versarien.

Thinking bigger

Sometimes a business operating as a public limited company is taken back into private ownership. This may be called 'exiting the stock market'. Why does it happen?

- The people responsible for running the business might no longer be willing to tolerate interference from the external shareholders. For example, shareholders such as financial institutions may demand higher dividends when the senior managers would prefer to reinvest profits to generate more growth.

- Sometimes businesses lose favour with the stock market. This may happen when city analysts publish unhelpful or negative reports about companies failing to reach profit targets, for example. Such publicity often has the effect of lowering the share price very sharply.

- One growing trend is for plcs to be bought by **private equity companies**. These are businesses that borrow money from a variety of sources and then use it to buy other businesses. They often aim to increase the value of the business and then sell it about five years later. For example, office2office plc, a major supplier of office supplies, was bought by the private equity firm Endless LLP for around £19 million in 2014.

The above information can be useful if you are asked to evaluate the impact on a company of going public. Although there are numerous advantages, history tells us that some plcs return into private ownership for the reasons given.

Case study

ALEXIS PARKER

In 2014, the luxury shoe brand Alexis Parker floated just over 20 per cent of the business on the stock market. The brand, with over 90 stores, planned to open about 5–10 further stores a year between 2014 and 2016. The brand was popularised after being featured in a Hollywood movie, and its growing popularity in Europe saw it featured on the cover of a leading magazine.

In its prospectus, Alexis Parker promised investors an annual sales growth of more than 7 per cent. The company particularly planned to grow its presence in Europe. The IPO valued Alexis Parker at £272.8 million.

The prospectus also acknowledged that Alexis Parker's success could be negatively affected by downturns in the economy or consumer confidence. The business environment for luxury goods became more challenging in 2014, with flagging demand from shoppers. It was reported that the luxury goods market in 2014 had slowed by an estimated 2 per cent on 2013 figures.

It was reported that Alexis Parker expected to make around £25 million of profit in 2014, on sales of £150 million. It had favourable operating profit margins of around 9 per cent. The flotation raised about £100 million. Alexis Parker's CEO, Andrew Wright, and the company's Creative Director, Carol Anderson, retained small stakes in the company and the flotation enabled them to be rewarded in shares if they improve the company's performance and share price. The share price closed at 162p after the first day's trading, 1p higher than the initial flotation price of 161p.

(a) What is a company prospectus? (2 marks)

(b) Explain one possible motive for the Alexis Parker IPO. (4 marks)

(c) Assess the drawbacks to Alexis Parker of going public. (10 marks)

(d) Assess whether you think the flotation will be successful. (12 marks)

Exam tip

If you are assessing the impact of going public on a particular company, you will need to demonstrate your ability to evaluate. It will be helpful to build your answer around any information given that is specific to the company, to show your skills in application. When you have analysed the advantages and disadvantages of going public you will need to make a judgement. This will depend on the information in the case. However, one approach might be to suggest that some stakeholders will benefit, such as shareholders, and others might lose out, such as customers. Some people argue that this happened in the UK when some of the 'old' nationalised industries went public. For example, the price of shares in privatised water companies has grown well since their initial flotation, which is good for shareholders, but customers have not always seen an equivalent decrease in their water bills.

Key terms

Private equity company – a business usually owned by private individuals backed by financial institutions.
Public limited company – a company owned by shareholders where the shares can be traded openly on the stock market.
Stock market – a market for second-hand shares.
Stock market flotation or **initial public offering (IPO)** – the process of a company 'going public' – making shares available to the public for the first time.

Knowledge check

1. State two possible reasons why owners want their businesses to grow.
2. What are the main legal differences between private and public limited companies?
3. State four financial costs incurred when forming a public limited company.
4. State four pieces of information that are likely to be included in a company prospectus.
5. State three advantages of public limited companies.
6. State three disadvantages of public limited companies.
7. What might happen to the share price of a new public limited company if the share issue is oversubscribed?
8. What is a private equity company?

Key points

1. Opportunity cost.
2. Choices faced by businesses.
3. Potential trade-offs made by businesses.

Getting started

Imagine that your employer has given you an unexpected Christmas bonus of £100. Make a list of all the things you would like to buy with the money. Now arrange that list in order of preference. The item on the top will be the one you decide to spend the money on.

What have you foregone by choosing the preferred item at the top of the list? How often in life are you faced with decisions like this? Why do such decisions arise? Do businesses face similar situations? If so, give some possible examples.

Opportunity cost

Entrepreneurs and other business decision-makers are frequently faced with choices. There are often a number of alternative ways of using resources. As a result businesses have to make a choice about which way to use them. Such choices are common in life and are faced by individuals, businesses and the government.

- Individuals have to choose how to spend their limited budgets. For example, a university student, after all living costs have been met, may have £50 left at the end of the week. This student would like to buy some new books (£20), get the train home for the weekend (£30), go out for a meal with friends (£30) or buy a new pair of designer jeans (£50). Clearly, a choice has to be made because all of these goods together would cost £130.
- Businesses may have to choose between spending £100,000 on an advertising campaign, retraining its workforce, redecorating the reception area or buying new vehicles for sales staff.
- A government may have to decide whether to spend £5 billion on increasing disability benefits, building new hospitals, providing better care for the mentally ill or building a new motorway.

Assume that a business placed its spending desires in the order of preference below.

1 Advertising campaign.
2 Retrain workforce.
3 Redecorate reception area.
4 Buy new vehicles for sales staff.

In this example, the advertising campaign is the preferred choice. Therefore the £100,000 will be allocated to this project. The other three options are foregone or given up. The benefit lost from the next best alternative is called the **opportunity cost** of the choice. In this example, it would be the benefit lost by not retraining the workforce. When making such choices, individuals, businesses and governments can identify and face the opportunity cost once their preferred spending choice has been made.

Question 1

A commercial bank operates 600 branches. The bank is expanding rapidly but is short of funds to meet all of its spending plans. It has £100 million to spend and the bank has drawn up a list of spending options in order of preference. All of the projects will cost around £100 million.

1. Open 50 new branches.
2. Buy an insurance company.
3. Renew all ATMs.
4. Retrain all staff in customer service.

(a) Using this case as an example, explain what is meant by opportunity cost.

Non-monetary opportunity cost

Opportunity costs can quite often be measured in monetary terms. In the above example, the opportunity cost of investing in the advertising campaign is the benefit forgone from retraining the workforce. The business might be able to calculate the value of the extra output generated by the workers after retraining.

However, there may also be some non-monetary or intangible benefits of staff retraining. For example, many workers may feel more confident in their work and as a result they may be happier and more contented. This may improve productivity further. However, such improvements, although real, would be very difficult to measure in monetary terms. Opportunity cost may also be difficult to quantify because such costs are incurred in the future and the future is so difficult to predict.

Opportunity cost can sometimes be personal. For example, an entrepreneur might decide to reinvest profits in the business at the expense of a family holiday. The opportunity cost of this decision might be over-work and disappointed children, which might be felt by the whole family. Clearly, increased happiness and a greater sense of well-being are additional factors that may contribute to opportunity costs.

Thinking bigger

In 2001 Arsenal FC won approval to build a new stadium, increasing capacity from about 38,000 to over 60,000. The club invested about £400 million in the construction of the Emirates Stadium. The Arsenal manager, Arsène Wenger, was reported as describing it as the biggest decision in Arsenal's history since Herbert Chapman was appointed as chairman by the board. The Emirates opened in 2006 and up until 2014, when Arsenal won the FA Cup, the club failed to win a single trophy. For many of the club's supporters, this eight-year period of underachievement on the pitch was an important part of the opportunity cost of the decision to build a new stadium as during this period the club appeared to have only limited resources to invest in new players and improve the quality of the playing staff. However, the true value of the opportunity cost is very difficult to quantify. How can you measure supporters' emotional disappointment at not winning any trophies? Also, if Arsenal had won some trophies their revenue would have been higher, but by how much? This example helps to highlight the difficulties in measuring the precise value of opportunity cost. You could use this example, or ones like it, when discussing the opportunity costs of business decisions.

Business choices and trade-offs

Businesses have to make countless decisions, and decision-makers are frequently faced with **trade-offs**. This means that opting for one choice involves compromising another. For example, a company that prides itself on attention to detail must often sacrifice the speed of production. If a business wants to accumulate stock, it must sacrifice cash. There are many such examples in business.

One very important trade-off is that between risk and reward, as shown in Figure 1. It is often necessary to take bigger risks in order to reap higher rewards. However, with high risk there is the danger of large losses. For example, it was reported in the media that before 2008, banks granted mortgages to high-risk borrowers. The potential returns were high, but unfortunately when the property market collapsed many borrowers could not repay their loans. As a result some banks also collapsed.

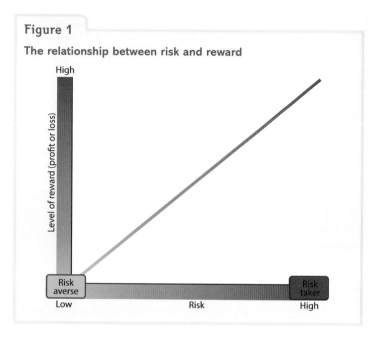

Figure 1

The relationship between risk and reward

Initially, one important decision for an entrepreneur is whether to set up a business in the first place. The benefits of running your own business may include:

- independence, as owners are in complete control and are free to make all decisions
- flexibility, as owners can choose a life balance between work and leisure that suits them
- the chance to make more money than might be earned in employment
- job satisfaction and a sense of achievement in building something from scratch
- the chance of becoming rich – some entrepreneurs become millionaires!

However, there is a trade-off. Many entrepreneurs leave their jobs to set up a business. They give up financial security that a regular salary from employment often affords. Employment may also offer health insurance, employee pensions, holiday pay and sick leave. Running a business is also very challenging, for the following reasons.

- Owners of small businesses are responsible for all day-to-day operations. Unless they have a reliable and trustworthy assistant, they have to be available whenever the business is open.
- The demands of running a business may result in a lack of free time. Also, if working from home the boundaries between work time and personal time may become blurred. Owners may spend too much time in 'work-mode'.
- Business owners need a variety of skills to be successful. Advertising, marketing, interviewing, hiring, management,

stock control and accounting are all part of an entrepreneur's responsibilities. This will be a lot more demanding than working in a specialised area as an employee.

- If owners operate as a sole trader, they have unlimited liability. This means that personal assets are unprotected if the business starts to run up debts.

Potential entrepreneurs would have to give this trade-off serious consideration before taking the risk. Some examples of common trade-offs in business are outlined in Table 1.

Table 1 Examples of common business trade-offs

1. Firms often have to consider the trade-off between holding liquid assets and investing more in productive assets such as machinery. By reducing the amount of liquid assets held, there is a risk of cash-flow problems. However, investing more in productive assets may increase profitability.
2. Directors of public limited companies have to find the right balance when distributing corporate profits. They can re-invest profits and hopefully increase future profitability. However, shareholders may prefer higher current dividend payments and less re-investment.
3. Firms might choose to take a more ethical stance in their operations. However, this is likely to come at a cost, as investment in cleaner technology might be required, for example.
4. A common trade-off is that between higher profit margins or higher turnover. Some businesses can often sell more and raise turnover, but this may come at the expense of lower prices and reduced profit margins.

Question 2

In 2013, a Boeing Dreamliner® caught fire at Boston Airport and all Dreamliners were grounded due to safety concerns. It was widely reported that the aircraft had experienced a variety of incidents up to that point, and that some felt there was an element of risk in Boeing's manufacture and operations decisions. The company chose to have the jet designed and built mostly by other companies. Although Boeing had a record number of orders, the process of designing and manufacturing the jet was problematic.

- The original delivery date of 2008 was significantly delayed, and the first Dreamliner was delivered in 2011.

- Many of the components used in the fuselage failed to conform to Boeing's specifications. This was expensive and caused delays.

- The first Dreamliner to arrive at the company's factory for assembly was missing thousands of parts.

- In January 2013 the entire fleet of 50 Dreamliner planes was grounded after planes had problems with the lithium-ion batteries. One company made the original batteries that were approved but the batteries that were later installed in the Dreamliner were made by another company.

Was Boeing right to outsource the design and production of the Dreamliner? Or did the company save money but at a risk that was too high and a cost that was too great?

Source: adapted frowm the *Financial Times* 11.01.2013. All rights reserved.

(a) What is meant by the trade-off between risk and reward?

(b) Assess the possible costs incurred by Boeing as a result of outsourcing its design and production of the Dreamliner.

Weighing up trade-offs

When businesses are faced with trade-offs similar to the ones shown in Table 1, the following actions might help to find the right balance.

- Obtain information. One approach would be to list the advantages and disadvantages of each choice and try to determine which carries the heaviest weight.
- Balance short term with long term. Try to determine what might be given up in the long run for some important short-term gain – and vice versa.
- Gauge support. When weighing up alternatives, it might be appropriate for the decision-maker to think about which key staff will support a particular idea and who will oppose it. The views of others can be a powerful influence.

Exam tip

When businesses are making decisions in any aspect of their operations, there is likely to be an opportunity cost resulting from that decision. When answering questions, there may be a wide range of situations where you can apply the concept of opportunity cost. For example, in a question about pricing, you could discuss the opportunity costs of a price cut for the business. The use of opportunity cost is likely to provide a counterbalance in an argument and may help you show skills of evaluation.

143

Case study

BENSON FARMS LTD

George and Marion Benson run Benson Farms Ltd, a large arable farm in Suffolk. The farm produces cereal crops, mainly barley for the brewing industry. The business is successful and in 2012 it made a profit of £120,000. However, George and Marion couldn't agree on how to use the profit. Marion was keen to plough it back into the business to increase future profitability. However, in contrast, George wanted to buy a holiday home in Andalucia. This could be rented out to generate an income and provide a second home in one of their favourite holiday destinations. The options in order of preference are listed below.

1. Develop a campsite on the farm.
2. Buy a holiday home in Andalucia.
3. Set up a farm shop.
4. Buy a new tractor.

George and Marion have become increasingly concerned about the use of pesticides and fertilisers in agriculture. They currently use both on their farm but have recently had their attention drawn to a report by the European Environment Agency (EEA) *European waters – assessment of status and pressures*. In this assessment, the agency reports that 48 per cent of streams and lakes in the EU will fail to meet good ecological status by 2015. One problem is the growth of algae that chokes off oxygen to fish and plant life in waterways. However, the fight against pollution clashes head-on with concern about food security. There is growing global pressure for farmers to increase food supplies to help combat rising prices and rising population growth. The trade-off between higher yields (using pesticides and fertilisers) and environmentally friendly farming methods (using less or no fertiliser and pesticides) is well known.

As a result of their concern George and Marion have been considering a switch to organic farming. This method does not use chemical fertilisers or pesticides. It relies upon more natural forms of farming such as biological pest control and crop rotation. Using ladybirds which eat aphids is one example where a natural process replaces a chemical pesticide. However, organic farming is less efficient and so output is more expensive. The demand for organic produce is increasing in the UK but people may return to non-organic produce if incomes fall. George and Marion hope to meet a consultant to consider the switch. Some of the general advantages and disadvantages of organic farming are outlined in Table 2.

Table 2 General advantages and disadvantages of organic farming

Advantages of organic farming	Disadvantages of organic farming
• Natural habitats are protected. • Soil condition is improved because manure is used. • Healthier food is likely to be produced. • Fewer chemicals means more wildlife. • Organic farming is worth over £1 billion a year.	• Yields may be lower due to crop damage by pests. • The crop yield has been reported as around 19 per cent lower on organic farms. • Weed control is very time-consuming and labour intensive. • Some organic pesticides, such as copper, can be harmful. • Some organic farming methods use more water, which can be costly.

(a) Explain what is meant by a trade-off when making a business decision. (2 marks)

(b) Explain the opportunity cost to Benson Farms Ltd of developing the campsite. (4 marks)

(c) Explain one way in which the business might find the 'right balance' when weighing up a trade-off. (4 marks)

(d) Assess the costs to Benson Farms Ltd of switching to organic production. (12 marks)

Key terms

Choices – in business, deciding between alternative uses of resources.
Opportunity cost – when choosing between different alternatives, the opportunity cost is the benefit lost from the next best alternative to the one that has been chosen.
Trade-offs – in business, where a decision-maker faces a compromise between two different alternatives; for example, between paying dividends to shareholders and re-investing profits in the business

Knowledge check

1. What might be the opportunity cost of a business giving workers a six per cent pay increase?

2. Give two possible examples of non-monetary opportunity costs.

3. What might be the consequences of a business investing too heavily in productive assets like machinery?

4. Give two examples of possible trade-offs in business.

5. What might be sacrificed by an entrepreneur starting a new business?

Key points

1. The difficulties in developing from an entrepreneur to a leader.

Getting started

Jennifer Compton is a successful entrepreneur. She owns a large children's retail chain worth £80 million called Under 10s. She first demonstrated her entrepreneurial skills when running a baby-sitting agency whilst studying for her A levels at sixth form college. Then after working in a small store making and selling children's clothes in Preston she started buying very cheap housing in the Preston area. She used the properties to provide student accommodation in Preston. After four years she sold her property business for £2.7 million.

Jenny then saw that the small store that she worked in earlier was for sale. She bought it and began building her chain – Under 10s. The store had been run down and needed a number of key changes to become profitable. She sourced a new and exciting product range from a number of countries in SE Asia to complement her tailor-made clothes. She also employed young and flexible staff who she motivated with her warm and enthusiastic brand of leadership. Jenny worked very hard opening six new shops per year for five years in the north west and then 12 shops a year for 10 years nationally. She is now a respected business person, the CEO of Under 10s and has a reputation for retail development. She has recently started a consultancy business to help young people develop their stores.

Jennifer Compton is both an entrepreneur and a leader. What changes do you think have occurred in her business role over the years? Do you think that entrepreneurs and leaders need different skills? If so, describe them. What particular leadership qualities did Jennifer demonstrate when she developed the Under 10s brand? What difficulties might Jennifer have faced when making the transition to corporate leader?

Moving from entrepreneur to leader

If an entrepreneur sets up a business and it becomes successful, the role of the entrepreneur is likely to change as the business expands. Running a sole trader business with two employees and a turnover of £250,000 is different from the challenge of running a large plc with 59,000 employees and a turnover of £3.6 billion. The change in role stems from the need to deal with growth. For example, there is likely to be a growth in the:

- number of employees
- number and size of financial transactions
- number and size of customers
- amount of regulation
- quantity of resources used
- level and range of communication needed.

The transition from entrepreneur to leader is likely to require a number of changes in the way the business is run. This usually means that entrepreneurs have to adapt and perform different functions.

The need for formality: Small businesses can be run on an informal basis. This means that communication takes place without the need for regular structured meetings, detailed documentation or official communication channels. They employ just a few employees and communication between them can be ongoing as they are likely to be working in close proximity to each other. Decisions can be made swiftly because the entrepreneur is always at hand. However, in a large organisation, where the entrepreneur becomes a leader, there is a need for formality. Communication between thousands of employees requires systems and formal structures. The business is likely to be split up into departments or divisions. There will have to be formal communication channels that are recognised and approved by all staff. There will be a need for a formal organisational structure so that the business can be controlled and employees brought to account. The entrepreneur in a small business may become a chairperson or a senior executive in a large business.

The need for shared ownership: When businesses grow they need capital to fund expansion. To obtain funding it is sometimes necessary to invite new owners to contribute capital. For very large corporations this usually means selling shares and operating as a plc. Entrepreneurs begin their business life as sole owners, but often end up having to share ownership with others. Ownership is likely to be shared with financial institutions, such as pension funds and insurance companies, as well as an army of very small investors.

Greater responsibility to others:
An entrepreneur running a small business is only likely to have responsibility for a small number of employees. However, when a business grows into a corporation the number of people employed could be tens of thousands or more. The livelihoods of these people will often rest on the decisions made by the leader. This is an enormous responsibility. A leader may also have responsibility to other stakeholders, such as shareholders, and a far larger number of suppliers and customers.

The need for motivation and inspiration:
As the size of the business grows there is a need to focus more on the workforce. This is because there are a lot more people to manage. As entrepreneurs develop into leaders, there is a greater need for motivational skills. Some people are self-motivated but most people need encouragement and well-defined goals, which leaders have to provide. Workers are likely to look to the leader for support and inspiration. Leaders also have to develop the talents of others.

The need for strategy and vision:
In a small business the owner is likely to be involved in production and other business functions such as marketing, finance and administration. However, as the business expands, specialists undertake most of these tasks. The leader becomes more concerned with designing business strategies and providing a vision for the future direction of the company. However, there are exceptions to this. For example, TV chef Jamie Oliver is the leader of a sizable catering and restaurant business but is still involved in cooking in various kitchens in his organisation.

Some of the people who have made a success of the transition from entrepreneur to leader include Richard Branson (the Virgin brand), Michelle Mone (founder of Ultimo), Lord Sugar (computers), Deborah Meaden (holiday business), Mike Ashley (Sports Direct and Newcastle Utd FC) and Hilary Devey (logisitics). They all began their careers with modest business start-ups and developed into successful leaders of large corporations.

The difficulties in developing from an entrepreneur to a leader

When dealing with the changes required in the transition from entrepreneur to leader, inevitably there will be difficulties.

Adapting the mindset:
Entrepreneurs usually have a desire for greater control over their life, career and destiny. They want more autonomy and to do things in their own way. However, a different mindset is needed when the business expands. Leaders have to relinquish some control and learn to delegate and focus on different things. They have to believe that specialists will do a better job in certain fields and that they cannot do everything themselves. For some people this is very difficult. They may have doubts, fears and a lack of trust that could create a barrier to development.

Stress:
Running a business is stressful. The livelihood of entrepreneurs and their families are dependent upon the success of the business. There is the constant worry that the business 'won't provide' and what will happen if the business collapses?

One major cause of stress is the worry that debtors will fail to pay what they owe. However, if the business grows it is likely that it is being successful. But with growth comes more stress, as there is more at stake. The business may have borrowed money that must be repaid. There are more staff and more responsibilities, with an increased scope for conflict because more people are involved.

Conflict is a common cause of stress in larger organisations. Some stakeholders have different needs that might cause conflict. For example, workers may want a wage increase but customers want stable or lower prices. The threat of a strike would cause stress in such cases.

Sharing ownership and control:
Some entrepreneurs may struggle with a loss of control when the business expands. Inviting partners, business angels or shareholders to contribute capital means that business ownership is shared. It also means that future profits have to be shared.

Some entrepreneurs may also find it difficult to share control and resent others influencing the shape and direction of a business that they set up from scratch. They may feel that their leadership is being undermined, which may cause conflict.

Trust:
As entrepreneurs develop as leaders, they may have problems trusting people. As the business grows there is a need to delegate and employ specialists. Some leaders find it difficult to delegate and may become suspicious of new senior staff. Where specialists are appointed, the leader may feel that the specialists know more than them. The leader may feel threatened and concerned that they are being kept in the dark or manipulated. If leaders cannot trust the new owners and staff there may be problems because employees may question whether or not the leader trusts them.

Lack of leadership qualities:
As entrepreneurs take on more leadership duties there may be concern that they lack the necessary leadership skills and qualities. These might include management, communication, problem solving, decision making and organisational skills. It is true that entrepreneurs also need these skills to be successful. However, once the business grows, these skills have to be applied on a different scale. The problems are likely to be larger, decisions more important and communication more complex. For example, in communication, entrepreneurs may have to give instructions to employees, discuss specifications with a customer and meet the accountant to finalise a tax return. A high-profile business leader may meet with other leaders and politicians in Germany, speak in more than one language, write reports for shareholders and give presentations to the media. Such demands may cause problems for some entrepreneurs as they develop into leaders.

Overcoming difficulties

The changes required in the transition from entrepreneur to business leader are substantial. It is easy to see why many business owners are happy to remain small traders, maybe preferring a lifestyle business. However, despite the difficulties outlined above, some people do make the transition successfully. They learn to adapt and overcome the difficulties. They might use a number of methods, including those listed below.

Delegation and trust: A successful business leader must be comfortable with delegation. The delegation of tasks to specialists and experts will improve the performance of the business. A good leader will surround themselves with talented, honest and trustworthy people. Leaders can reduce the risk in recruitment if they employ a thorough and effective recruitment process. The ability to delegate and trust will reduce stress.

Earn respect: Many of the difficulties outlined on the previous page can be overcome if a leader can earn respect from all stakeholders. People will be more trustworthy, effective and flexible if they are treated well. This means meeting their needs at work, praising them when they excel, being fair but tough, open and honest. Respect might also be earned if the organisational culture is open, positive and accepted.

Maturity and experience: Some people are born leaders. They find leadership natural and have the charisma and leadership qualities needed to be successful. However, others may develop into good leaders. Through maturity, experience, drive and learning from mistakes, they can overcome any difficulties they may encounter. The transition from entrepreneur to corporate leader may be a lengthy one.

Education: Some of the leadership skills can be learnt by attending specialist courses. There are countless courses designed to help business people improve management, negotiation, communication and decision-making skills. Additional languages can be taught, as can report writing and IT skills.

Reduce stress: Calm leaders are more likely to succeed than stressed leaders. Figure 1 summarises some of the measures that might be used to reduce stress.

Exam tip

You can use your learning from this unit in many ways, because entrepreneurship and leadership are central to business development in an economy. For example, the information might be used when specifically explaining the difficulties in moving from an entrepreneur to a leader. Some of the information might also be used in discussions about the problems with business growth, reasons that account for the performance of a business, the importance of good leaders and risk taking, the characteristics of entrepreneurs and leaders, stakeholder conflict, motivation and business management. This unit links particularly well with Unit 18 on leadership, Unit 19 on the role of an entrepreneur and Unit 20 on entrepreneurial motives and characteristics.

Figure 1

Measures that might help to reduce stress

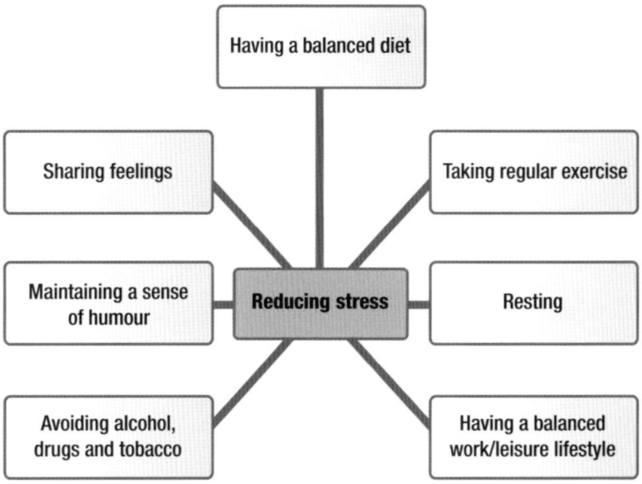

Knowledge check

1. State three ways in which the role of an entrepreneur might change as a business grows.

2. Why is there a need to introduce formality in businesses when they grow?

3. Why might an entrepreneur have difficulty delegating tasks?

4. Why might a leader lack confidence?

5. How might entrepreneurs have to adapt their mindset when developing into a leader?

Case study

BILL GATES

Bill Gates is the founder of the Microsoft® Corporation, a worldwide leader in software, services and solutions that helps people and businesses realise their full potential. Bill Gates formed Microsoft in 1975, dropping out of Harvard University, which might have been considered a risk at the time, to devote his energies to software development. His original vision was reported as 'A computer on every desk and in every home', running Microsoft software. Bill was a visionary person and worked hard to achieve this vision. In 1980, Gates made a deal with IBM to provide the MS-DOS operating system on the new IBM PC for a fee of $50,000. However, he stipulated that he and Microsoft held onto the copyright of the software. When the PC market took off, Microsoft also sold MS-DOS to other PC manufacturers. Not long after, Microsoft operating systems dominated the world.

In 1985, Gates released the Microsoft Windows® operating system, similar to one introduced by Apple® in 1984, taking what some might consider another risk. Originally, some thought that the Apple version was better than Microsoft Windows. However, the Apple operating system only ran on Apple machines, whereas Microsoft Windows could run on a variety of PC-compatible machines. Microsoft won the operating system market and was soon installed on nearly 90 per cent of the world's personal computers. Gates went on to introduce further products such as Windows Office® programs like Word® and Excel®.

In 1986, Microsoft was floated on the stock exchange. The company was valued at $520 million of which Gates owned 45 per cent. As the company grew rapidly, the share price soared. At one point, Gates' share was worth over $100 billion. In 2000, the Bill & Melinda Gates Foundation was set up to support philanthropic initiatives, with Gates devoting a lot of his time to working with, and funding, a wide range of charities.

The story about Bill Gates

Bill Gates was known for his passion for computer programming from a young age and while at college. During his early years at Microsoft, he reportedly oversaw the business detail, yet personally reviewed every line of code and often rewrote parts of it if he felt it was needed. Gates was appointed as president of Microsoft in 1981. He met regularly with senior and program managers, with a management style that some may have found intimidating. He was passionate about the quality and performance of Microsoft products and was reported as rigorous with his employees in ensuring robust business strategies, to protect the company from long-term risk. It was reported that Gates expected his employees to share his drive and dedication, and that he challenged their ideas as part of the creative process, testing out whether they were convincing. His competitive spirit drove Microsoft's success and the company's strength was used to reinforce its dominance in the market place.

Bill Gates stepped down as chairman of Microsoft in 2014 and was the richest person in the world in 2015, with a net worth of $78.3 billion. His philanthropic work, reported as totalling grants from the Foundation of $21.8 billion in 2015, and to involve diplomacy and persuasion, has won many awards. He is known as one of the most influential people of the 20th century.

Source: adapted from the *Financial Times*, 01.11.2013

(a) When Microsoft went public in 1986, Bill Gates owned 45 per cent of the company. Calculate the value of his holding. (4 marks)

(b) Explain how a risk taken by Bill Gates in 1985 might have affected Microsoft. (4 marks)

(c) Explain one way in which the role of an entrepreneur, such as Bill Gates, might change as the business develops. (4 marks)

(d) Assess the difficulties that Bill Gates might have encountered when moving from entrepreneur to the leader of Microsoft. (12 marks)

26 Internal finance

Key points

1. Owner's capital: personal savings.
2. Retained profit.
3. Sale of assets.

Getting started

Ahana Chaudhary started her own business after she was made redundant from her local hospital. She used her £6,000 redundancy money and a further £4,000 from her savings to start a business, providing a home care service for the elderly in Brighton. The business was profitable from the start and five years later she recruited two full-time staff. Eventually, the demand was so great that she decided to operate a care agency, providing staff to deal with the wide-ranging needs of the elderly. She used £25,000 profit from the business to buy an office for the agency.

Why do entrepreneurs need finance to start a business? What sources of finance did Ahana use to start her care business? How did she fund the expansion of the business into an agency? What might be the advantages and disadvantages of using this source of finance?

The need for finance

Firms need money to get started. They might need to buy equipment, raw materials and obtain premises, for example. Once this initial expenditure has been met, the business can get under way. If successful, it will earn money from sales. However, business is a continuous activity and money flowing in may be used to buy more raw materials and settle other trading debts. If the owner wants to expand, extra money may be needed over and above that from sales. Expansion may mean larger premises, more equipment and extra workers. A business will need to find a way of raising this finance.

The items of expenditure above fall into two categories – **capital expenditure** or **revenue expenditure**. Capital expenditure is spending on items that may be used over and over again. A company vehicle, a cutting machine and a new factory all fall into this category. Revenue expenditure refers to payments for goods and services that have either already been consumed or will be very soon. Wages, raw materials and fuel are all examples of this category. Revenue expenditure also includes the maintenance and repair of buildings and machines.

Owner's capital

Capital is the money provided by the owners in a business. It is an example of **internal finance**. Internal finance is money generated by the business or the current owners. In most cases, a business cannot start unless the owners provide capital of their own. Providing capital is part of the risk taken by entrepreneurs when setting up a business.

Owners provide capital from their own personal resources. A common source is personal savings. Some entrepreneurs have deliberately saved up over a period of time so that they can start their own business. Sometimes, people who have lost their jobs may decide to go into business using their redundancy payments. These sources are personal and can be used by sole traders and partnerships. Owners of limited companies also provide their own capital. They have to find money to buy shares. Finally, owners can introduce fresh capital in the future if there is a need. Owner's capital is not just provided at the start-up stage.

Retained profit

Retained profit is profit after tax that is put back into business and not returned to the owners. It is the single most important source of finance for a business. Much of all business funding comes from retained profit. It is the cheapest source of finance, with no financial charges such as interest and administration. However, there is an opportunity cost. If retained profit is used by the business it cannot be returned to the owners. For a small business this might mean that owners and their families have less money to fund their lifestyle. For limited companies it means that shareholders receive lower dividends. In the case of a public limited company this may lead to conflict if the shareholders see that dividend payments have been frozen because the directors have used the profit in the business.

Retained profit is a flexible source of finance. It does not have to be used immediately. It can be accumulated by a business and retained in a bank account where it will earn interest. A business can then use the retained profit at a later date. If a business doesn't make a profit, retained profit is not possible as a source of finance.

Sale of assets

An established business may be able to sell some unwanted assets to raise finance. For example, machinery, obsolete stock, land and buildings that are no longer required could be sold off for cash. Large companies can sell parts of their organisation to raise finance.

Standard Life, the financial services provider, sold its Canadian arm in 2014 for £2.2 billion. The money was used to reward shareholders and allow the business to focus on its UK activities.

Sometimes a business might be pressured into selling assets when quite large amounts of money are needed to overcome a problem. For example, The Co-operative Group sold its farms business to the Wellcome Trust in 2014 for £249 million to help reduce its debt.

Another option is to raise money through a **sale and leaseback** agreement. This involves selling an asset, such as property or machinery that the business still actually needs. The sale is made to a specialist company that leases the asset back to the seller. This is an increasingly popular source of finance. With such agreements instant cash is generated for the seller and the responsibility for the maintenance and upkeep of the asset passes to the new owner.

In 2014 it was reported that the entrepreneur Duncan Bannatyne agreed a sale and leaseback deal with M&G Investments. He sold 39 health clubs for £92 million and then leased them back. The money was used to help clear some business debts.

Advantages and disadvantages of internal finance

There are a number of advantages when using internal finance to fund business activity, though despite the attractive nature of internal finance, there may also be some drawbacks.

Table 1 summarises the advantages and disadvantages of using internal finance.

Table 1 Advantages and disadvantages of internal finance

Advantages
The capital is available immediately — there is no time delay between identifying a need for finance and obtaining it. For instance, retained profit will be in a bank account ready and waiting. Assets can be sold quickly if the price is competitive.
Internal finance is cheap — there are no interest payments, which means that costs will be lower and profit higher. Also, there are no administration costs.
The business will not be subject to credit checks. External finance often requires investigations into credit history of the borrowers.
There is no need to involve third parties.

Disadvantages
Internal finance can be limited — a business may not be sufficiently profitable to use retained profit or may not have unwanted assets to sell. Also, the current owners may not have any personal resources to contribute.
Internal sources of finance are not tax-deductible. If external finance is used, the interest paid on a loan or leasing charges for assets, for example, can be treated as a business cost and offset against tax.
Internal finance can be inflexible compared to external sources of finance. There are a wide variety of funding options for external finance, which can give the business flexibility.
There are no inflationary benefits with internal finance. Inflation can reduce the value of debt if external sources are used.
Opportunity cost of using internal sources of finance can be high. For example, a plc considering the use of retained profits for funding will have to consider the reactions of shareholders if dividends are frozen or cut. Some shareholders may have a very short-term view and demand higher dividends now. This could result in conflict between shareholders and directors.

Question 1

The Priory Group is a leading provider in healthcare and famous for treating various celebrities. It specialises in conditions ranging from addiction to Alzheimer's disease. The Priory Group sold some property in 2014 in a leaseback deal. It was reported that Priory sold six sites for a total of £223 million, in Altrincham, Bristol, Chelmsford, North London, Roehampton and Woking. The deal with M&G Investments, a property development company, involved a lease agreement for 30 years with Priory. Priory planned to use the proceeds, along with other cash reserves, to pay off part of its debt. It was reported that service users and commissioning arrangements at the hospitals were unaffected by this deal.

(a) What is meant by sale and leaseback?

(b) How did The Priory Group plan to use the proceeds from the sale of its properties?

(c) Explain two advantages of the sale and leaseback method of finance for The Priory Group.

Case study

CROMWELL AND JONES

Lisa Jones and Tom Cromwell run their decoration and interior design business as a partnership. They each invested £10,000 into the business start-up in 2008. Although many businesses were facing financial problems in that year, they decided to go ahead anyway. The first few years were difficult, but they worked very well together as a small team. Lisa was a creative interior designer and Tom was a highly skilled painter and decorator. After four years the couple had earned a reputation in the Cheshire area for producing high-quality interior designs and installation. They specialised in bedroom design and started to win some large and lucrative jobs from Premier League footballers living in the Wilmslow area.

In late 2014, they won a £200,000 contract to design and refurbish five bedrooms in a large house. However, they accepted the contract knowing that they would have to outlay £40,000 in equipment and some specialist imported raw materials. They were absolutely committed to raising the finance internally even if it meant selling one of the two vehicles owned by the business. Tom and Lisa did not want the business to go into debt, owing money to people outside the business. They wanted the business to be self-financing.

Figure 1 shows the profit made by the business between 2008 and 2014.

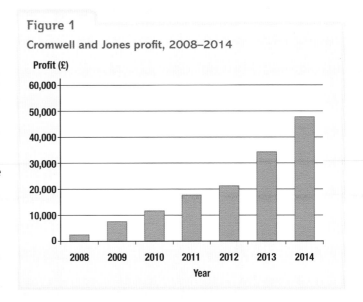

Figure 1

Cromwell and Jones profit, 2008–2014

(a) What is meant by internal finance? (2 marks)

(b) Explain one method of internal finance that Tom and Lisa might have used to raise the initial capital to start the business in 2008. (4 marks)

(c) Explain one opportunity cost to Cromwell and Jones of using retained profit for financing business activity. (4 marks)

(d) Evaluate Tom and Lisa's decision to use internal finance to fund the new contract in this case. (12 marks)

Exam tip

When answering a question on internal sources of finance, remember to consider carefully the financial circumstances of the case in the question. The sources and methods of finance used by a business will depend significantly on the nature of the business and its financial position. For example, smaller businesses may be forced to use internal sources because they present too much of a risk to external providers. In contrast, plcs have a much wider range to choose from because they are more secure and may have large quantities of collateral, which they can use to support a loan. Paying close attention to the business circumstances in the question will help you to show your skills in application.

Key terms

Capital – the money provided by the owners in a business.
Capital expenditure – spending on business resources that can be used repeatedly over a period of time.
Internal finance – money generated by the business or its current owners.
Retained profit – profit after tax that is 'ploughed back' into the business.
Revenue expenditure – spending on business resources that have already been consumed or will be very shortly.
Sale and leaseback – the practice of selling assets, such as property or machinery, and leasing them back from the buyer.

Knowledge check

1. What is the difference between revenue expenditure and capital expenditure?

2. Give three examples of capital expenditure a farmer might undertake.

3. What is meant by capital?

4. State one advantage of using retained profit as a source of finance.

5. State two advantages of using the sale of assets to raise finance.

6. State two disadvantages of using internal finance.

Key points

1. Sources of finance: family and friends, banks and peer-to-peer funding, business angels, crowd funding and other businesses.
2. Methods of finance: loans, share capital and venture capital, overdrafts, leasing, trade credit and grants.

Getting started

Ellerman Construction Ltd is a medium-sized building contractor. It has recently undertaken a lot of sub-contract work for large construction companies involved in the building of Crossrail, the new underground rail link in London. The business carries out concreting work and uses trade credit to buy its raw materials from suppliers. It gets 90 days to pay back the credit. The business has a 25-year mortgage on its premises and owes £5,000 on a two-year bank loan. It owns about half of its plant and machinery, but the other half is leased. Ellerman Construction Ltd is a family-owned business with four members of the family having equal shares.

What is meant by external sources of finance? Suggest the ways in which Ellerman Construction Ltd funds its business. Can you think of any other methods of business finance? How might the business raise £500,000 to buy an expensive machine?

External finance

Few businesses can rely entirely on internal financing (see Unit 26) to fund all business activity. Initially, **external finance**, which is finance from sources outside the business, may not be available. This is because business start-ups have no trading record and present too much risk for many lenders. However, once a business has survived the initial 'uncertain' stages of business development, external sources of finance are likely to become a realistic option.

Sources of finance

There is quite a wide range of external sources that businesses can choose from.

Family and friends: A common source of finance, particularly for small businesses, is family members or close friends. This may be a cheap source because if the money is a loan, interest charges may be low, or possibly zero. In some cases money might be gifted to an entrepreneur. For example, a parent or grandparent might give their child or grandchild a sum of money as a present to help them get started. Another possible advantage of finance from friends or family is that they may not want a stake in the business. Consequently, they will not be able to interfere in the running of the business. However, serious problems could arise if a loan cannot be repaid or the terms of the arrangement lack clarity. This could lead to the loss of friendship or a breakdown in family relations.

Banks: Commercial banks such as Barclays, NatWest, Lloyds and HSBC provide a range of different external funding arrangements for businesses. These include loans, overdrafts and mortgages. Most commercial banks have specialist departments or staff that deal exclusively with businesses. Banks will be involved in a business start-up because businesses need a bank account to facilitate financial transactions with customers and suppliers. Banks might also offer advisory services to businesses. These are often free. A formal application is required to get finance from banks and it will probably be necessary to provide a business plan.

Peer-to-peer lending: Peer-to-peer lending (P2PL) involves people lending money to unrelated individuals or 'peers' and therefore avoiding the use of a bank. Transactions are undertaken online and are organised by specialists such as Zopa, Funding Circle, Lending Works and RateSetter. Although this source of finance can be used by a business, it is not exclusive to businesses. Anyone can apply for a peer-to-peer loan. The key features of peer-to-peer lending include the following.

- All loans are unsecured which means there is no protection for lenders. Therefore, lenders might lose their money if a borrower defaults.
- The whole financial arrangement is conducted for profit.
- All transactions take place online.
- No previous knowledge or relationship between lenders and borrowers is needed.
- Lenders may choose which borrower to lend to.
- Peer-to-peer sites make a charge – typically about one per cent.

The main attraction of P2PL is that interest rates are better for both borrowers and lenders than those offered by a bank. P2PL is also very convenient because it can be completed online fairly quickly. However, the main disadvantage is that the Financial Services Compensation Scheme, which guarantees savings up to the value of £85,000, does not cover participants. Also, if you are a lender, access to cash may not be instant – each operator has different rules, but money might be locked away for months or longer.

Business angels: Business angels are individuals who typically may invest between £10,000 and £100,000+, often in exchange for a stake in a business. An angel might make one or two investments in a three-year period, either individually or together with a small group of friends, relatives or business associates. Most investments are in business start-ups or in early stages of expansion. There are several reasons why people become business angels. Many like the excitement of the risk involved, or being part of a new or developing business. Others are attracted by the tax relief offered by the government. Some are looking for investment opportunities for their unused income.

A problem with this source of finance for businesses is finding a suitable 'angel'. As angels normally take a stake in the business, the angel and the current business owners must have shared interests and a common view about the future direction of the firm. For example, some owners might look for an angel with business experience hoping that they can provide some useful input into the running of the business. In contrast, many owners might want angels to keep their distance and just maintain a financial interest in the business. Also, business angels may be demanding individuals with considerable pressures on their time. They may be overwhelmed by business propositions and spend a lot of time selecting suitable targets for investment.

Business owners must present a compelling business proposition concisely and succinctly. They must highlight the positive aspects of the venture, but with due regard to the risks involved. Business owners also have to be comfortable with sharing profits with the angel for as long as they are involved. One example of a business that used business angels to raise finance is Turbo Drinks, a Leeds-based soft drinks producer. It raised £200,000 in 2011 from three angels who also brought with them a wealth of business experience and financial knowledge.

Question 1

Usman Ahmad Khalid runs Khalid SportsGear Ltd, a sports equipment manufacturing business in Carlisle. After a successful start, Usman saw that the market was expanding and that an opportunity existed for growing the business. However, his current factory was too small and access was poor. Usman had found a new location but £75,000 was needed to complete the move and meet refurbishing costs. He met with a bank manager and it was agreed that a good way forward would be to attract a business angel.

Usman was introduced to Kyle Barton, a wealthy retired businessman. He agreed to put £75,000 in the business for a 20 per cent stake. Kyle advised Usman that he would be looking to 'cash-in' his investment in five years. In 2013, Usman said about the business angel: 'Throughout the last four years Kyle attended monthly meetings, making valuable contributions. With his prudent advice he guided the business through a recession and helped it to double in size. He had a number of useful contacts and was particularly helpful on the marketing side. I will miss him when he moves on next year.'

(a) What is meant by the term 'business angel'?
(b) Explain two possible disadvantages of using business angels as an external source of finance.
(c) Assess the impact Kyle has had on Usman's business.

Crowd funding: **Crowd funding** is similar to peer-to-peer funding in that banks are excluded and individuals can lend money to others without previous knowledge of them. However, the fundraisers tend to be businesses or groups who are involved in a particular venture such as staging a production,

building a school or setting up a community project. The lenders or investors will be large numbers of individuals who collectively represent 'the crowd'. Transactions are conducted online. They are administered by a crowd funding specialist such as Crowdcube, Kickstarter and Crowdfunder. These websites allow those seeking finance to publish details of their business idea or project, including how much cash they need, how they will use it and how investors stand to profit (if at all) in future. Some of the sites carry out checks on the fundraisers but not all of them. In most cases the investors, who can usually subscribe as little as £10 per venture, are offered shares in the business. In 2013, PixelPin, a tech-company which helps customers reduce fraud, raised £150,000 using the crowd funding platform Seedrs.

Thinking bigger

There has been a huge growth in the number of sites offering P2PL and crowd funding since 2008. This is mainly because interest rates have been low for many years, so savers have been desperate to seek alternative ways of using their money to gain a good return. There has also been a 'credit crunch' since 2008, which has resulted in a reduction in the number of loans granted by traditional business lenders such as banks. Further, a string of financial scandals has led to a loss of trust in Britain's banks. In the future, if there is strong growth in these sources of finance, it may become easier for businesses to raise external finance. The market might become more competitive and business funding could get cheaper and more accessible.

You could use this information on sources of external funding in a variety of ways. It will be of use when answering questions on business finance. It might also be useful when discussing changes in technology, competition and business, business and the economy, business efficiency and the causes and effects of change.

Other businesses: Another external source of finance might be provided by other businesses. For example, a business might set up a fully-funded subsidiary. This might occur when a manufacturer sets up a business to supply it with components. Some businesses set up joint ventures, where the businesses share the finance, costs and profits of a specific venture. Some plcs buy shares in other companies. This might be to earn an income, if they have surplus cash for example. Alternatively, plcs might buy shares in other companies to build a controlling stake, perhaps with a view to taking it over in the future.

Methods of finance
Businesses can use a variety of different methods to raise finance.

Loans: A loan is an arrangement where the amount borrowed must be repaid over a clearly stated period of time, in regular instalments. Loans tend to be rigid and interest will be added to the total. There are different sorts of loan capital.
- **Bank loans** are probably the most common type of loan. They may be **unsecured loans**. This means that the lender has no protection if the borrower fails to repay the money owed. They can be used for long-term or short-term purposes depending on the needs of the business. However, the use of unsecured bank loans has probably diminished in recent years due to the high risk they carry for banks.

- **Mortgages** are **secured loans** where the borrower has to provide some assets as collateral to support the loan. This means that if the borrower defaults, the lender is entitled to sell the assets and use the proceeds to repay the outstanding amount. Mortgages are long-term loans and are typically for 25 years or more. They might be used by a business to fund the purchase of premises or a large item of capital equipment. Mortgages are usually cheaper than unsecured loans because there is less risk for the lender.
- **Debentures** are a specialised method of loan finance. The holder of a **debenture** is a creditor (someone to whom the business owes money) of a company, not an owner. Debenture holders are entitled to a fixed rate of return, but have no voting rights. They must also be repaid on a set date – when the debenture matures. Public limited companies use this long-term source of finance.

Maths tip

If a business takes out a four-year bank loan for £50,000 with an interest rate of 10 per cent per annum, what will be the monthly repayments (including interest)?

Total interest = 10% × £50,000 × 4 = £5000 × 4 = £20,000.

$$\text{Monthly repayments} = \frac{£50,000 + £20,000}{4 \times 12} = \frac{£70,000}{48} = £1,458.33 \text{ per month}$$

Question 2

Siobhan Daley runs a haulage company in Bristol. She owns five lorries and has a contract with a supermarket chain. She distributes grocery products from suppliers to a network of supermarkets in the south-west region. In 2013, she needed £60,000 to replace one of the older lorries. Siobhan considered a number of sources but decided to take out a five-year bank loan. The interest rate was 7.5 per cent per annum.

(a) What is meant by a bank loan?
(b) Calculate the total interest charge on the five-year loan.
(c) Calculate the monthly repayments on the loan.

Share capital: For a limited company **share capital** is likely to be the most important source of finance. The sale of shares can raise very large amounts of money. **Issued share capital** is the money raised from the sale of shares. **Authorised share capital** is the maximum amount shareholders want to raise. Share capital is often referred to as **permanent capital**. This is because it is not normally redeemed, i.e. it is not repaid by the business. Once the share has been sold, the buyer is entitled to a share in the profit of the company, i.e. a dividend. Dividends are not always declared. Sometimes a business makes a loss or needs to retain profit to help fund future business activities. A shareholder can make a **capital gain** by selling the share at a higher price than it was originally bought for. Shares are not normally sold back to the business.

The shares of public limited companies are sold in a special share market called the stock market or stock exchange. Shares in private limited companies are transferred privately. Shareholders, because they are part owners of the business, are entitled to a vote. One vote is allowed for each share owned. Voting takes place annually and shareholders vote either to re-elect the existing board of directors or replace them. Different types of shares can be issued.

- **Ordinary shares.** These are also called **equities** and are the most common type of share issued. They are also the riskiest type of share since there is no guaranteed dividend. The size of the dividend depends on how much profit is made and how much the directors decide to retain in the business. All ordinary shareholders have voting rights. When a share is first sold it has a nominal value shown on it – its original value. Share prices will change as they are bought and sold again and again.
- **Preference shares.** The owners of these shares receive a fixed rate of return when a dividend is declared. They carry less risk because shareholders are entitled to their dividend before the holders of ordinary shares. Preference shareholders are not strictly owners of the company. If the company is sold, their rights to dividends and capital repayments are limited to fixed amounts. Some preference shares are cumulative, entitling the holder to dividend arrears from years when dividends were not declared. Some are also redeemable, which means that they can be bought back by the company.
- **Deferred shares.** These are not used often. They are usually held by the founders of the company. Deferred shareholders only receive a dividend after the ordinary shareholders have been paid a minimum amount.

Venture capital: Venture capitalists are specialists in the provision of funds for small and medium-sized businesses. Typically they invest in businesses after the initial start-up and often prefer technology companies with high growth potential. They prefer to take a stake in the company, which means they have some control and are entitled to a share in the profit. Venture capitalists raise their funds from institutional investors such as pension funds, insurance companies and wealthy individuals. They are also likely to exit after about five years. Examples of venture capitalists include MMC Ventures, Index Ventures and AXM Venture Capital. Businesses may turn to venture capitalists for funding when they have been refused by other sources.

Bank overdraft: This is an important source of finance for a large number of businesses. A bank overdraft means that a business can spend more money than it has in its account. In other words they go 'overdrawn'. The bank and the business will agree on an overdraft limit and interest is only charged when the account is overdrawn. The amount by which a business goes overdrawn depends on its needs at the time. This means that bank overdrafts provide a flexible source of funding to businesses. However, a bank has the legal right to call in the money owed at any point in time. This will happen if the bank suspects that the business is struggling and unlikely to repay what is owed.

Leasing: A **lease** is a contract in which a business acquires the use of resources such as property, machinery or equipment, in return for regular payments. In this type of finance, the ownership never passes to the business that is using the resource. With a finance lease, the arrangement is often for three years or longer and, at the end of the period, the business is given the option of then buying the resource.

There are some advantages of leasing.
- No large sums of money are needed to buy the use of equipment.
- Maintenance and repair costs are not the responsibility of the user.
- Hire companies can offer the most up-to-date equipment.
- Leasing is useful when equipment is only required occasionally.
- A leasing agreement is generally easier for a new company to obtain than other forms of loan finance. This is because the assets remain the property of the leasing company.

However:
- over a long period of time leasing is more expensive than the outright purchase of plant and machinery
- loans cannot be secured on assets which are leased.

Trade credit: It is common for businesses to buy raw materials, components and fuel, and pay for them at a later date, usually within 30–90 days. Paying for goods and services using trade credit seems to be an interest-free way of raising finance. It is particularly profitable during periods of inflation. However, many companies encourage early payment by offering discounts. The cost of goods is often higher if the firm does not pay early. Delaying the payment of bills can also result in poor business relations with suppliers.

Grants: Some businesses might qualify for financial support in the form of a grant. Both central and local government back a wide range of schemes. A list of grants available can be accessed using the government's 'business finance support finder' tool. This allows firms to select specific funding options and search for grants by business location, size and type of business activity.

There are also other organisations, such as trusts and industry specialists, which provide funding. For example, the Building Enhancement Programme gives grants to Swansea city-centre businesses to help build new shop fronts or improve their facades. Fuse Fund provides grants for investment projects that will stimulate growth and create jobs in Lancashire, including machinery acquisition and property improvements.

Grants are usually available to small businesses providing they meet certain criteria. Most grants do not have to be repaid, so this is a significant advantage of this type of external finance.

Question 3

Andres Fonseca, co-founder of app company Virtually Free, received a grant of £50,000 from Nominet Trust, the UK's largest 'tech-for-good' funder. The grant enables tech entrepreneurs with a social mission to develop a particular venture. For example, projects that tackle issues such as health (like the Virtually Free app), education, social care and environment.

To get the grant, Virtually Free had to fill in some application forms. There were three forms in total and success at each stage brought on a more detailed form to complete. They had to provide information about different aspects of the business, from financial to technical to academic. The business had to meet a number of conditions to qualify for the grant. They had to have a specific 'social tech' project to spend the money on and demonstrate the social impact of their project.

Virtually Free spent the grant on creating an app to treat agoraphobia. This is a condition that may prevent individuals affected from seeking help as it traps them at home and makes it impossible for them to seek help outside. Virtually Free's digital tool replicates the two parts that make up traditional treatment, namely education and training. Combined with exposure therapy, these techniques are delivered to users via their phones or tablets. One of the benefits of the tool is that it reduces, or even eliminates, the need for support staff or therapists. The grant helped Virtually Free to create what they consider to be their first clinical application.

Source: adapted from: www.smallbusiness.co.uk

(a) Explain one advantage for Virtually Free of getting a grant.

(b) What measures did Virtually Free have to take in order to qualify for its £50,000 grant?

Knowledge check

1. What is meant by external finance?
2. What is the difference between crowd funding and peer-to-peer lending?
3. State two reasons why a business angel would invest in a business.
4. Bank overdrafts are flexible. What does this mean?
5. What is the main advantage of an unsecured bank loan for a business, when raising finance?
6. What is the difference between an ordinary share and a preference share?
7. What is meant by a capital gain?
8. State two advantages of leasing as a method of finance.
9. How might a business use trade credit as a method of finance?
10. What sort of businesses might venture capitalists look to invest in?

Case study

PRINCE HOSPITALITY

Oxford-based Prince Hospitality provides corporate hospitality in the south-east region. They organise trips, visits and events for companies that want to entertain clients. Examples are taking guests to high-profile sporting events such as race meetings and international cricket, football and rugby matches. In the last five years a lot of business has been generated organising hospitality at Premier League football stadiums, particularly for Champions League matches. The market is growing very strongly and Jennifer Prince, the owner of the business, has always been able to get plenty of custom.

The business was started in a warehouse office in Abingdon. However, there is now a need to relocate to more salubrious offices in order to project a more 'up-market' image. There are other investment needs. In total the business requires £200,000 to:

- relocate to a refurbished office in Hinksey
- redesign and upgrade the website
- set up a ticketing agency, 'TicketPrince', to buy and sell tickets for sporting events.

Jennifer is planning to use external funding for the business. Internal funding is not really an option because there are no assets to sell and Jenny has spent most of her profit on developing her home in Woodstock. Figure 1 shows the profit and retained profit for the business between 2008 and 2014. After a meeting with her accountant, the following funding options have been identified.

- A mortgage, using Jennifer's own house as security.
- An unsecured bank loan.
- Set up a private limited company and sell shares to members of the family.
- Attract a business angel to invest in the company.

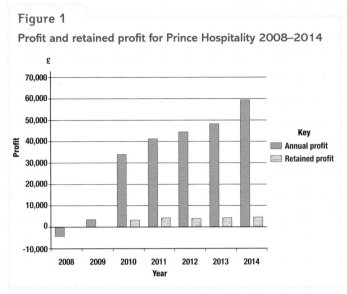

Figure 1

Profit and retained profit for Prince Hospitality 2008–2014

The method of funding preferred by Jennifer is the unsecured bank loan. She does not really want to risk any personal wealth by using her house as security for a mortgage. Also, although her father could easily provide much of the finance in a share issue, she is a little worried that he might try and interfere too much. She thinks the involvement of a business angel might be OK but wonders whether the right sort of investor could be found.

Q

(a) What is meant by an unsecured bank loan? (2 marks)

(b) Explain one disadvantage to Prince Hospitality of issuing share capital. (4 marks)

(c) Explain one possible reason why Jennifer preferred external funding in this case. (4 marks)

(d) Assess which method of finance Prince Hospitality is likely to use in this case. (12 marks)

Key terms

Authorised share capital – the maximum amount that can be legally raised.

Bank overdraft – an agreement between a business and a bank that means a business can spend more money than it has in its account (going 'overdrawn'). The overdraft limit is agreed and interest is only charged when the business goes overdrawn.

Capital gain – the profit made from selling a share for more than it was bought.

Crowd funding – where a large number of individuals (the crowd) invest in a business or project on the internet, avoiding the use of a bank.

Debenture – a long-term loan to a business.

Equities – another name for an ordinary share.

External finance – money raised from outside the business.

Issued share capital – amount of current share capital arising from the sale of shares.

Lease – a contract to acquire the use of resources such as property or equipment.

Peer-to-peer lending (P2PL) – where individuals lend to other individuals without prior knowledge of them, on the internet.

Permanent capital – share capital that is never repaid by the company.

Secured loans – a loan where the lender requires security, such as property, to provide protection in case the borrower defaults.

Share capital – money introduced into the business through the sale of shares.

Unsecured loans – where the lender has no protection if the borrower fails to repay the money owed.

Venture capitalism – providers of funds for small or medium-sized companies that may be considered too risky for other investors.

28 Liability

Key points

1. Implications of limited and unlimited liability.
2. Finance appropriate for unlimited liability businesses.
3. Finance appropriate for limited liability businesses.

Getting started

Collette and Nyran own and run a service station on the A82 in Scotland in partnership. They have **unlimited liability**. Last year the business lost £23,000, mainly because of road closures due to bad weather and ongoing road works. They hope to relaunch the business by opening a café adjacent to the service station. To convert an unused building at the site for this purpose will cost £60,000.

What is meant by the term unlimited liability? How might Collette and Nyran raise the £60,000 needed for the conversion? Under what circumstances might Collette and Nyran be able to obtain a bank loan?

Limited liability and unlimited liability businesses

Whether business owners have limited liability or unlimited liability depends on the legal status of their businesses. This may take one of two different forms.

- **Unlimited liability businesses.** These are businesses where there is no legal difference between the owners and the business. They are sometimes called **unincorporated businesses**. Everything is carried out in the name of the owner or owners. These firms tend to be small, owned either by one person or a few partners. The owners of these businesses will have *unlimited liability*.

- **Limited liability businesses.** A limited liability business has a legal identity separate from its owners. In other word the business (as opposed to the owners) can be sued, taken over or liquidated. These firms are sometimes called **incorporated businesses**. The owners of these businesses will have *limited liability*.

Figure 1 shows the different types of businesses, their legal status, their ownership and the owner's liability.

Implications of unlimited liability

Business owners with unlimited liability are exposed financially to the failure of their businesses. If their business collapses wh owing money to external parties, such as banks, suppliers and the tax authorities, the owners will have to meet these debts from their personal resources. This means that if owners do no have the money to pay off these debts they can be forced to sell private assets to raise the necessary cash. For example, a sole trader can be legally required to sell a house to raise fund to meet a demand from the tax authorities. This is regardless the hardship this might inflict on the owner and their family. Th highlights the risk taken by entrepreneurs when setting up an unincorporated business.

Owners of businesses with unlimited liability are also liable for any unlawful acts committed by the owners or the employees. For example, if an employee wrote something libellous about someone, that person might be able to claim compensation from the business owner. If the business does n

Figure 1

Businesses with unlimited and limited liability

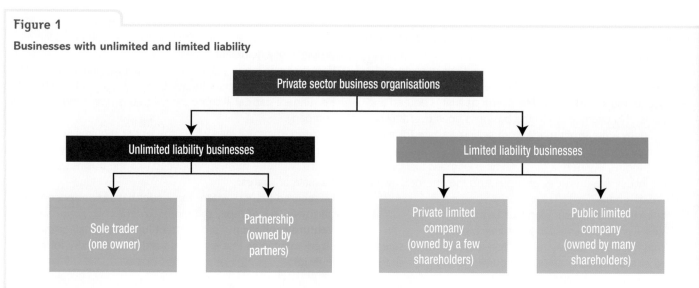

have enough money to pay, the owner would again have to use private funds. The owners may also be financially liable if sued successfully by other stakeholders, such as customers, employees or suppliers. This all arises because *there is no separation of legal identity between the business and the owners.*

Businesses with unlimited liability sometimes find it easier raising finance. This is because lenders will be reimbursed if a business defaults. Unlimited liability businesses are often also seen as more credible. This is because owners are encouraged to be more cautious since their personal assets are at risk.

Question 1

Candy McDougal runs a sandwich bar in Glasgow city centre. She is a sole trader and the business has unlimited liability. The rent she pays on her high street shop is high, but she reckons it is worthwhile because the passing trade is so good. Her rent is £3,000 per month which she pays six months in advance and she has signed a five-year lease.

Unfortunately, three of her customers fell ill as a result of eating contaminated food from her sandwich bar. One customer threatened to take her to court, but eventually settled out of court accepting an £8,000 payout. Candy had to use her own savings to meet this payment because the business bank account only contained £2,300.

(a) What is meant by a business with unlimited liability?

(b) Explain two implications of running a business with unlimited liability.

Implications of limited liability

The owners of businesses with limited liability are shareholders. The main advantage of this is that shareholders' financial liability is limited to the amount of money they invested in the business. It is a fixed sum and equal to the amount of money they paid for their shares. If a limited company collapses, the owners' private assets are fully protected. Shareholders cannot be legally forced to sell personal assets to meet the business's debts.

Shareholders also have protection from legal claims on the business. This is because the owners and the business have separate legal identities. For example, if a customer sues a limited company for damages, there can be no claim on the

private wealth of the business's shareholders if the business cannot pay the compensation. However, there are exceptions to this rule. Courts may decide that individuals are liable if a crime has been committed or if the company has failed to maintain adequate records and accounts, hold annual general meetings or file annual reports. This might be more likely to happen with private limited companies.

Because shareholders' private assets are protected, limited companies may find it easier to raise larger amounts of money from investors. As a result investors are more willing to buy shares in limited companies because they know precisely the extent of their liability – it is limited to the size of their investment. However, in some cases the owners of small limited companies, who are frequently also shareholders, are required to give personal guarantees of the company's debts to those lending to the company. They will then be liable for those debts in the event that the company cannot pay, although the other shareholders will not be.

Choosing appropriate finance

The wide range of sources and methods of finance was discussed in Units 26 and 27. However, not all of these sources can be accessed by all businesses. The method of finance chosen by a business can be influenced by a number of factors.

Whether short-term or long-term finance is needed: If a business needs to borrow money for a lengthy period of time, say ten years or more, certain types of funding are more suitable than others. For example, mortgages can be taken out for 25 years. Unsecured bank loans may be granted for one to five years. Debentures can be issued for up to 30 years. Share capital – money raised from the sale of shares – is permanent capital and never repaid. This is the most **long-term** method of **finance**. A business is not likely to use trade credit, bank overdrafts or leasing for long-term funding. These are more suitable for **short-term borrowing**.

The financial position of the business: The financial situation of businesses is constantly changing. When a business is in a poor financial situation, it finds that lenders are more reluctant to offer finance. At the same time, the cost of borrowing rises. Financial institutions are more willing to lend to secure businesses, which have a large amount of **collateral**.

The type of expenditure for which the money is needed: When a company undertakes heavy capital expenditure, it is usually funded by a long-term source of finance. For example, the building of a new factory might be financed by a share issue or a mortgage. Revenue expenditure tends to be financed by short-term sources. For example, the purchase of raw materials might be funded by trade credit or a bank overdraft.

Cost: Businesses will prefer sources and methods that are less expensive, both in terms of interest payments and administration costs. For example, share issues can carry high administration costs, while the interest payments on bank overdrafts tend to be relatively low.

The legal status of the business: This will depend on whether a business has limited or unlimited liability. This is discussed in more detail below.

Finance appropriate for unlimited liability businesses

Unlimited liability businesses, such as sole traders and partnerships, have fewer sources and methods of finance to choose from. They are most likely to include some of the following.

- **Personal savings.** Most small-business owners with unlimited liability are likely to use their own money to set up a business. It is an important source of finance.
- **Retained profit.** This source can only be used if the business survives and becomes established. As the business develops it must generate enough profit to support both the owner and future business investment. However, for many unlimited liability businesses, the scope for using retained profit is restricted.
- **Mortgage.** It is common for unlimited liability businesses to use the owner's house as collateral for a business loan. This provides a source of long-term finance. However, the owners are at increased risk. If the business goes into heavy debt and fails, the owners can suffer serious financial hardship, such as losing the house.
- **Unsecured bank loans.** On occasion, banks might advance unsecured loans to established and successful businesses. This might depend on the financial climate at the time of request. For example, banks may have tighter criteria for unsecured bank loans if there is a credit crunch. Owners must be prepared to produce detailed business plans to obtain bank loans.
- **Peer-to-peer lending.** Small business owners can raise finance through dedicated websites from people interested in lending money to their enterprise, thus avoiding the need for a bank. However, some peer-to-peer funding is not available to businesses. The owners will have to check with individual P2PL sites to see whether businesses can borrow.
- **Crowd funding.** Crowd funding can provide long-term finance for businesses. Once this new concept has had time to develop and prove to be reliable, it could well become a very popular source for unlimited liability businesses.
- **Bank overdraft.** Most businesses will have access to a bank overdraft. However, the size of the overdraft limit will vary considerably. Established and profitable businesses will have access to much larger overdrafts than those that are not.
- **Grants.** These can provide a 'free' source of finance to unlimited liability businesses. However, businesses have to prove that they qualify for grants and some owners might be put off by the lengthy application process.

All of the finance sources outlined above are appropriate for unlimited businesses because they are accessible to small businesses. Businesses with unlimited liability tend to be small and often struggle to raise finance. Such businesses have access to fewer sources because they have fewer assets that can be used as collateral. Also, they may be new start-ups with no trading record, which can often discourage lenders. However, it must be remembered that there are exceptions to these rules.

For example, the owners of unlimited liability businesses have to meet business debts from their own resources, so lenders might be reimbursed if a business collapses.

Finance appropriate for limited liability businesses

Generally, limited liability businesses, particularly plcs, have a much wider range of funding opportunities. Some methods of finance, such as shares and debentures, for example, are only available to limited companies. The main advantage for limited liability businesses is that they tend to be larger than unlimited liability businesses and have more resources to support loans. Consequently, they are less risky for lenders and other investors. Appropriate sources of finance for limited liability businesses include the following.

- **Share capital.** The sale of shares allows limited companies to raise very large amounts of capital. Share capital is provided by the owners of the business from their own resources. Once shares are purchased, the money raised is not normally repaid to shareholders, so the capital remains in the business for as long as it is trading. Also, a business might raise more money in the future by selling more shares. They may use a **rights issue**, for example. This is where existing shareholders are given the 'right' to buy new shares at a discounted price. This is cheap and simple and creates free publicity. Share allocations are based on current holdings; for example, a one-for-five issue means that shareholders can buy one new share for every five that they currently own. Rights issues are also normally regarded as a cost-effective way of raising fresh capital.
- **Debentures.** Public limited companies can raise large amounts of money by selling debentures. This loan capital can be very long term – up to 30 years. One key advantage of this method to the business is that, unlike shareholders, debenture holders do not have any control over the business.
- **Retained profit.** Around half of all business finance comes from retained profit. Limited liability businesses are no exception. Some very large companies have hundreds of millions of pounds in cash reserves, which have accumulated over the years. Some of this is likely to be used by the business in the future.
- **Venture capitalists.** The majority of finance provided by venture capitalists finds its way into limited companies. One reason is because they usually take a share in the business, thereby having some control over the key decisions. Venture capitalists also like to invest larger amounts of money than business angels – several million pounds sometimes. However, they are also prepared to invest in small and medium-sized enterprises.
- **Business angels.** Business angels may provide funds for both limited and unlimited liability businesses. They will normally take a share in the business, but this does not mean they will avoid sole traders and partnerships. They are also more inclined to invest at an earlier stage than venture capitalists. One problem with business angels is that they are often difficult to find. This sometimes means

that entrepreneurs spend too long searching for suitable angles when their time could be better spent focusing on the development of the business.

- **Other sources.** Businesses with limited liability are all likely to use bank overdrafts, trade credit, leasing, unsecured bank loans, mortgages and grants in some combination or other. Larger limited companies are much less likely to use sources such as crowd funding and P2PL.

All the finance sources outlined above are appropriate for limited liability businesses. One reason for this is due to their legal status. For example, only limited companies can issue shares to raise finance. Other sources, such as business angels and venture capitalists, are likely to be appropriate because they prefer to invest in, or lend to, larger businesses which tend to be limited companies.

Maths tip

It was widely reported that RSA, a large insurance company, planned to raise £748 million in a rights issue. It proposed to offer shareholders three new shares for every eight held at the heavily discounted price of 56p.

If a shareholder owned 240,000 shares, how many new shares would that holder be entitled to buy and how much would they cost them?

Share entitlement = 3/8 x 240,000 = 90,000 shares

Cost of share purchase = 90,000 x 56p = £50,400

Thinking bigger

It has been argued that many businesses in the UK are **undercapitalised**. This means that they did not raise enough capital when setting up. This is particularly true for small and medium-sized businesses.

Most business start ups are funded by personal finance, family, friends and house re-mortgaging. This is often the case when availability of capital for new businesses is very low. Companies at early stages of setting up have low or zero revenues but high expenditure, and are often in need of additional funding to develop.

However, bank loans and overdrafts, historically the only available sources of external finance, are unsuitable for new firms. This is because the cost of servicing the debt comes at a time when cash is short. Also, the lending terms from banks are often demanding and subject to change at any time, which is not good for a new start-up. The advantage of capital finance is that it is permanent. It cannot be withdrawn (although it can be lost) and does not drain cash.

Perhaps the development of crowd funding, where lots of individuals are invited to invest small sums of cash in start-up or early stage companies, will help deal with this problem of undercapitalisation.

Source: adapted from www.support-finance.co.uk

Exam tip

When answering a question on the suitability of different finance sources for a business, it is important to pay close attention to the financial circumstances of the particular business. Theoretically, most sources are available to all businesses (depending on their legal status), but in reality the current financial position of the business will be crucial. Generally, businesses will struggle to raise finance from any source if they are losing money, have cash-flow problems, are encountering trading difficulties, already owe money to other lenders, or have few assets.

Key terms

Collateral – an asset that might be sold to pay a lender when a loan cannot be repaid.
Incorporated business – a business model in which the business and the owner(s) have separate legal identities.
Limited liability – a legal status that means shareholders can only lose the original amount they invested in a business.
Long-term finance – money borrowed for more than one year.
Rights issue – issuing new shares to existing shareholders at a discount.
Short-term borrowing – money borrowed for 12 months or less.
Undercapitalised – a business not raising enough capital when setting up.
Unincorporated businesses – a business model in which there is no legal difference between the owner(s) and the business.
Unlimited liability – a legal status which means that business owners are liable for all business debts

Knowledge check

1. What is the difference between limited and unlimited liability?

2. State two implications of limited liability for a business.

3. Why might a business with unlimited liability sometimes find it easier to raise finance than one with limited liability?

4. How is a limited liability business most likely to raise capital?

5. What is a rights issue?

6. Which sort of business is likely to issue debentures?

7. What is undercapitalisation?

Case study

ILGA SKUJA AND MOTHERCARE PLC

Ilga Skuja

Ilga Skuja, a talented IT expert, arrived in the UK from Latvia in 2006. For two years she worked for a major UK software company. In 2008 she started her own unlimited liability business, investing £10,000 of her savings in an online marketing service. She produced online promotional materials for rock bands and celebrities. The business grew quickly and was profitable for four years. However, in 2013 competitors entered the market and offered better services – making particular use of apps for mobile phones. To maintain her market share, she needed to retrain and invest in new technology. The business also suffered from cash-flow problems as it was owed a total of £7,800 from clients.

The business is now £3,000 overdrawn (it has an overdraft limit of £3,500) and Ilga needs a total of £12,000 to get the business back on its feet. The business has no collateral. Ilga owns a house worth £150,000, but has £110,000 outstanding on the mortgage. The profit made by the business between 2008 and 2014 is shown in Figure 2.

Figure 2

Profit made by Ilga Skuja's business 2008–2014

£

A bar chart showing profit on the vertical axis (from 5,000 to 40,000 in increments of 5,000) against Year on the horizontal axis. Values approximately: 2008 ≈ 11,000; 2009 ≈ 19,500; 2010 ≈ 27,500; 2011 ≈ 38,500; 2012 ≈ 29,000; 2013 ≈ 7,000; 2014* ≈ 5,200.

Year   * Estimated

Mothercare plc

In 2014 Mothercare, the retailer of parent and children's products, raised £100 million in a rights issue. The company offered nine new shares at a price of 125p for every ten shares currently held by shareholders. Mothercare said in a statement that it planned to use the proceeds to modernise and revitalise the group's retail chain and reduce debt. It planned to close 75 stores, improve the company's IT systems and transform the property-heavy business into a digitally led business. Mothercare's share price was 173p on 5 November 2014.

Source: adapted from the *Financial Times* 27.10.14, all rights reserved.

Q

(a) (i) Calculate the cost to a shareholder of taking up the whole entitlement if 2,000,000 shares are currently held. (4 marks)
(ii) Calculate the profit made by the shareholder if 500,000 of the new shares were sold on 5 November 2014. (4 marks)

(b) Explain one implication for Ilga Skuja of unlimited liability. (4 marks)

(c) Explain how raising capital using a rights issue might benefit Mothercare. (4 marks)

(d) Assess the possible funding options available to Ilga Skuja. (12 marks)

29 Planning

Key points

1. The relevance of a business plan in obtaining finance.
2. Interpretation of a simple cash-flow forecast and calculations based on changes in cash-flow variables.
3. The use and limitations of a cash-flow forecast.

Getting started

CoolCo Ltd makes children's clothes. It is a fairly new brand on the market and the manufacturer is beginning to receive interest from high street retailers. However, the board of CoolCo Ltd has agreed that it needs to increase capacity, as it cannot meet large orders from its existing factory. CoolCo Ltd needs to raise £200,000 to upgrade its manufacturing facilities. It would like to attract a business angel or a venture capitalist to invest in the business. The first stage in this process is to draw up a business plan, incorporating a comprehensive **cash-flow forecast**.

Why is it necessary for CoolCo Ltd to draw up a business plan? What information might be contained in a business plan? What is a cash-flow forecast? How might a cash-flow forecast help CoolCo to obtain finance?

The relevance of a business plan

For many people, setting up a business is a life-changing decision and will have far-reaching consequences. It is important, therefore, to carefully plan the whole process. Indeed, research has shown that start-up businesses that have prepared a business plan are more likely to succeed than those that have not. The business plan shows how the business will develop over a period of time.

A business plan is also needed to support applications for finance, both at the start-up stage and in the future. Lenders and other investors are not likely to put money into a business unless the owners can provide a clear, concise vision of future progress and profitability. In particular, investors will want to know how their money is going to be spent and when and how they are going to benefit from their investment. Also, when a company plans to raise money by floating on the stock market, it must publish a prospectus. This is a document that contains important elements of the business plan and other information for investors. This will help potential investors have confidence that the company is going to be a success before they commit to buying shares.

A thorough and well-written business plan is likely to:
- force owners to take an objective, critical and unemotional look at the whole business idea
- provide a 'road map' that shows a clear direction for the development of the business
- provide an action plan that identifies key tasks that must be undertaken and goals that must be met to improve the chances of success
- flag up potential problems in advance so that investors are aware and solutions can be found
- help show lenders and investors that the owner is cautious, responsible, serious and credible.

The contents of a business plan

The outline of a business plan can be obtained from any of the major banks in leaflets they produce on starting up a business. They give a very detailed list of points which must be addressed in the plan. These include the following.
- **An executive summary** – an overview of the business start-up. It describes briefly the business opportunity to be exploited, the marketing and sales strategy, operations and then finance.
- **The business opportunity** – a description of the product or range of products to be made, the quantity to be sold and the estimated price.
- **Buying and production** – where the business will buy its supplies, production methods to be used, the cost of production.
- **Financial forecasts** – a variety of financial forecasts need to be included, such as a sales forecast, a cash-flow forecast, a profit and loss forecast and a break-even analysis.

- **The business and its objectives** – the name of the business, its address, its legal structure and its aims and objectives.
- **The market** – the size of the potential market and a description of the potential customers, the nature of the competition, marketing priorities.
- **Personnel** – who will run the business, how many employees, if any, there will be, the skills, qualifications and experience of those in the business.
- **Premises and equipment** – the premises to be used, equipment which needs to be obtained and financed.
- **Finance** – where the finance to start up and run the business will come from.

Question 1

Cherry Watson is a retired teacher of modern languages. She lives in London and wants to set up a tutoring agency. She thinks there is a demand for private lessons in French and Spanish from students studying modern language GCSEs and A-levels. She also thinks that money could be made setting up short language courses for people wanting to learn English, for instance new arrivals from Eastern Europe.

Cherry has discussed the idea with friends and spoken to some other language teachers who have expressed an interest in using the agency to get work. She has also met with a bank manager to discuss funding for such a business. Cherry calculated that she would need £15,000 to get started. A lot of this money would be used to market the business at the launch stage. However, the bank manager has said that to have any chance of getting funding she will need to write a business plan.

(a) What is meant by a business plan?

(b) Explain how Cherry might benefit from writing a business plan.

Cash-flow forecasts

Without cash a business cannot trade. Experts suggest that about 20 per cent of business failures are due to poor cash flow. Even when trading conditions are good, businesses can fail. A business must ensure that it has enough cash to pay staff wages and bills when they are due. One way for a business to help control its cash flow is to plan ahead by producing accurate cash-flow forecasts. Such forecasts also form an important part of business plans.

Interpreting cash-flow forecasts

A cash-flow forecast lists all the likely receipts (**cash inflows**) and payments (**cash outflows**) over a future period of time. All the entries in the forecast are estimated because they have not occurred yet. The forecast shows the planned cash flow of the business month by month. Table 1 on the next page shows a twelve-month cash-flow forecast statement for Fishan's Ltd, a grocery wholesaler located in Ipswich.

What is predicted to happen to cash flow at Fishan's over the twelve-month period?

January: The company will have an opening cash balance of £11,000 in January. In January receipts are expected to be £451,000 and payments £365,000. This means that an extra £86,000 (£451,000 – £365,000) will be added in this month – a positive **net cash flow**. The closing balance should be £97,000 (£11,000 + £86,000).

February: In February expected payments (£406,000) are greater than expected receipts (£360,000). This means that there will be a negative net cash flow of £46,000 in February. However, the opening balance of £97,000 will cover this and the business will not have a cash-flow problem. It ends the month with a positive closing balance of £51,000 (£97,000 – £46,000).

March: In March payments again will be greater than receipts, giving a negative net cash flow of £92,000. However, this is now greater than the opening balance of £51,000. This means that the business faces a negative closing balance of £41,000 and will have a cash-flow problem. It would have to find some way to finance this, perhaps by borrowing from a bank.

March to May: The business will have cash-flow problems in March and April, when it faces negative closing balances, even though in April receipts are greater than payments (a positive net cash flow). In May, however, the negative opening balance of £26,000 is outweighed by the positive net cash flow of £113,000. The business will have a positive closing balance of £87,000 and no cash-flow problem.

June to December: In June and August, but not July, the business would have cash flow problems. From September onwards, when there will be positive closing balances every month, there appear to be no cash-flow problems. This is because the owners plan to introduce £300,000 into the business in September.

Table 1 Cash-flow forecast for Fishan's Ltd

	Jan	Feb	Mar	Apr	May	Jun	Jul	Aug	Sep	Oct	Nov	(£000s) Dec
Receipts												
Cash sales	451	360	399	410	490	464	452	340	450	390	480	680
Capital introduced									300			
Total receipts	451	360	399	410	490	464	452	340	750	390	480	680
Payments												
Goods for resale	150	180	150	180	150	180	150	180	150	180	220	250
Leasing charges	20	20	20	20	20	20	20	20	20	20	20	20
Motor expenses	40	40	40	40	40	40	40	40	40	40	40	40
Wages	100	100	100	100	100	100	100	105	105	105	125	125
VAT			126			189	187		187			198
Loan repayments	35	35	35	35	35	35	35	35	35	35	35	35
Telephone		11			12			12			14	
Miscellaneous	20	20	20	20	20	20	20	20	20	20	20	20
Total payments	365	406	491	395	377	584	552	412	557	400	474	688
Net cash flow	86	(46)	(92)	15	113	(120)	87	(72)	193	(10)	6	(8)
Opening balance	11	97	51	(41)	(26)	87	(33)	54	(18)	175	165	171
Closing balance	97	51	(41)	(26)	87	(33)	54	(18)	175	165	171	163

Brackets show minus figures.

Question 2

Frank Fullerton owns a bookshop near the University of Hull. He sells educational books to students, but also has a large stock of fiction books. Unfortunately the business has been struggling in recent months. He thinks that students are sharing books and therefore his sales are suffering. Table 2 shows a cash-flow forecast for the bookshop at the beginning of 2014. It is incomplete.

Table 2 Cash-flow forecast for Frank Fullerton's bookshop (£)

	Jan	Feb	Mar
Cash inflows			
Book sales	3,000	3,500	3,100
Fresh capital			2,000
Interest		150	
Total cash inflows	3,000	3,650	5,100
Cash outflows			
Stock	1,700	1,790	1,900
Casual labour	500	500	500
Rent	1,000	1,000	1,000
Other expenses	230	240	230
Total cash outflows	?	?	?
Net cash flow	?	?	?
Opening balance	230	?	?
Closing balance	?	?	?

(a) Using examples from this case, explain the difference between cash inflows and cash outflows.

(b) Complete the cash-flow forecast for Frank Fullerton's bookshop to show:

   (i) the total cash outflows for each month

   (ii) the closing balance for each month

   (iii) the opening balance for February and March.

(c) Assess, using information from the table, whether the business is struggling.

Changes in cash-flow variables

Once a cash-flow forecast has been prepared, it can be adjusted to show the effect on net cash flows of changes in some of the variables.

Table 3 shows a six-month cash-flow forecast for Patel Motors, a small garage and car service business in Bromsgrove. Mr Patel opened a shop inside his garage in May and hopes that this will help to boost his cash flow.

The forecast shows that by the end of the six-month period the cash position of the business is expected to improve. The closing cash balance is forecast to rise from £1,900 in June to £3,550 in November.

However, after a couple of months it became evident that some of the figures in the forecast needed amending.

In August Mr Patel had to buy computer equipment to help in the repair of newer cars. This cost £1,200. He also had to employ more casual labour to help out in the shop. As a result, wages paid to casual labourers rose to £1,100 per month from August onwards. Finally, Mr Patel received a £400 unexpected payment from a customer in September for work carried out two years ago. He had previously written off the debt, that is declared the money lost.

The effects of changes to variables are shown in Table 4. There will be a negative impact on the cash balance of the business at the end of the six months. The closing cash balance is now expected to fall from £1,900 in June to £1,550 in November.

Table 3 Cash-flow forecast for Patel Motors

	June	July	August	September	October	November
Cash inflows						
Petrol and repairs	6,700	6,600	7,200	6,800	7,100	7,600
Shop and other sales	2,250	2,750	2,300	3,300	3,850	4,350
Total cash inflows	8,950	9,350	9,500	10,100	10,950	11,950
Cash outflows						
Casual labour	800	800	800	800	800	800
Petrol and parts	4,250	4,300	4,700	4,500	4,500	5,000
Stock and other expenses	2,450	2,500	4,500	5,000	5,600	5,600
Total cash outflows	7,500	7,600	10,000	10,300	10,900	11,400
Net cash flow	1,450	1,750	(500)	(200)	50	550
Opening balance	450	1,900	3,650	3,150	2,950	3,000
Closing balance	1,900	3,650	3,150	2,950	3,000	3,550

Table 4 Amended cash-flow forecast for Patel Motors

	June	July	August	September	October	November
Cash inflows						
Petrol and repairs	6,700	6,600	7,200	6,800	7,100	7,600
Shop and other sales	2,250	2,750	2,300	3,300	3,850	4,350
Debt repayment				400		
Total cash inflows	8,950	9,350	9,500	10,500	10,950	11,950
Cash outflows						
Casual labour	800	800	1,100	1,100	1,100	1,100
Petrol and parts	4,250	4,300	4,700	4,500	4,500	5,000
Stock and other expenses	2,450	2,500	4,500	5,000	5,600	5,600
Computer equipment			1,200			
Total cash outflows	7500	7600	11500	10600	11200	11700
Net cash flow	1,450	1,750	(2,000)	(100)	(250)	250
Opening balance	450	1,900	3,650	1,650	1,550	1,300
Closing balance	1,900	3,650	1,650	1,550	1,300	1,550

Worked example

The effect of a change in one single variable in a cash-flow forecast has a multiplied effect on the rest of the forecast. The simple cash-flow forecast for a retailer is shown in Table 5. The effect of an increase in stock purchases from £69,000 to £72,000 in June is shown in Table 6. The changes are shown in green. Note that the increase in the value of stock purchases has an impact on five other values – even in this very simple forecast.

Table 5 Simple cash-flow forecast

	JUN	JUL
Cash inflow		
Sales revenue	98,000	107,000
Cash outflow		
Wages	25,000	25,000
Stock	69,000	74,000
Total cash outflow	94,000	99,000
Net cash flow	4,000	8,000
Opening balance	10,000	14,000
Closing balance	14,000	22,000

Table 6 The effect of changes in one variable (shown in light green)

	JUN	JUL
Cash inflow		
Sales revenue	98,000	107,000
Cash outflow		
Wages	25,000	25,000
Stock	72,000	74,000
Total cash outflow	97,000	99,000
Net cash flow	1,000	8,000
Opening balance	10,000	11,000
Closing balance	11,000	19,000

Maths tip

Cash-flow forecasts can be produced on spreadsheets. This means that the effect of changes in some of the variables, such as in the examples above, can be shown very easily. Once the new figures are entered in the spreadsheet, the new totals and balances are calculated automatically.

The use of cash-flow forecasts

Businesses draw up cash-flow forecast statements to help control and monitor cash flow in the business. There are certain advantages in using forecasts to control cash flow.

Identifying the timing of cash shortages and surpluses: A forecast can help to identify in advance when a business might wish to borrow cash. At the bottom of the statement the monthly closing balances are shown clearly. This will help the reader to identify when a bank overdraft will be needed. For example, Table 1 showed that Fishan's would need to borrow money in March, April, June and August. In addition, if a large cash surplus is identified in a particular month, this might provide an opportunity; for example, to buy some new equipment. A business should try to avoid being overdrawn at the bank because interest is charged. If certain payments can be delayed until cash is available, this will avoid unnecessary borrowing.

Cash-flow forecasts are particularly helpful for businesses that have seasonal demand. This is because cash inflows will be irregular, i.e. high during peak season and low at off-peak times. It will be important to delay some payments during periods where cash inflows are expected to be low.

Supporting applications for finance: When trying to raise finance, lenders often insist that businesses support their applications with documents showing business performance, outlook and **solvency**. A cash-flow forecast will help to indicate the future outlook for the business. It is also common practice to produce a cash-flow forecast statement in the planning stages of setting up a business. It is unlikely that any potential investor or lender will finance a business without a thorough business plan supported by a cash-flow forecast.

Enhancing the planning process: Careful planning in business is crucial. It helps to clarify aims and improve performance. Producing a cash flow forecast is a key part of the planning process because it is a document concerned with the future. If business owners try to run a business without any forward planning, mistakes are more likely to be made and it is difficult to identify problems in advance. A lack of planning is likely to result in poor business performance.

Monitoring cash flow: During and at the end of the financial year, a business should make comparisons between the predicted figures in the cash-flow forecast and those that actually occurred. This will help identify where problems have arisen. The business can then try to identify possible reasons for any significant differences between the two sets of figures. For example, it might be that an overpayment was made. Constant monitoring in this way should allow a business to control its cash flow effectively.

The limitations of cash-flow forecasts

Although cash-flow forecasts are extremely useful in helping to manage a business, it is important to recognise their limitations.

- Some of the financial information used in forecasts will be based on estimates. For example, even under normal trading conditions it is very difficult to predict sales revenue for a future time period – it has to be estimated. It is also difficult to estimate future costs – particularly variable costs. These will be dependent on future sales that are uncertain. Fixed costs, such as rent, rates and insurance are more predictable. Consequently, if the figures for cash inflows and cash outflows are not accurate, then the net cash flows and closing balances will be unreliable.

- Business activity is subject to external forces that are beyond the control of owners and managers. Changes in factors such as interest rates, the state of the economy, government legislation, exchange rates, competition and consumer tastes can have an impact on business costs and revenues. As a result, there will be an impact on a cash-flow forecast. For example, the cash-flow forecast for a wheat farm would be affected negatively if poor weather conditions reduced crop yields.

- A business uses resources in preparing a cash-flow forecast. A business owner or employee will spend time gathering the information and assembling the forecast. It will also have to be regularly updated so that the monitoring process is meaningful. There might be a danger, for instance, that an owner spends too much time focusing on the cash-flow forecast at the expense of meeting customer needs.

- A cash-flow forecast only focuses on one important business variable – cash. Other variables are also important, such as profit, profit margins and productivity. The cash-flow forecast is a one-dimensional tool and cannot be used on its own to evaluate the performance of a business.

Exam tip

When answering a question on the usefulness of cash-flow forecasting to a business, remember to analyse both the advantages and the disadvantages. You will need to apply your answer to the case material provided and make a judgement at the end. The judgement might require you to say whether cash-flow forecasting is beneficial overall to the business in your case.

Case study

CHARLTON PLASTICS LTD

Charlton Plastics Ltd manufactures polythene materials for the packaging industry. The family-run business is committed to the use of recycled materials and produces a range of plastic bags, sacks and sheets. In 2011 the business started to export its products and recently overseas sales have grown healthily.

In December 2013, Charlton's financial director produced a cash-flow forecast for the following year. Table 7 shows part of that forecast, from January to April 2014.

Table 7 Cash-flow forecast for Charlton Plastics Ltd

	JAN	FEB	MAR	APR
Cash inflows				
Home sales	124,000	124,000	125,000	128,000
Export sales	62,000	63,000	66,000	72,000
Interest	3,000	3,000	3,000	3,000
Total cash inflows	189,000	190,000	194,000	203,000
Cash outflows				
Wages	55,000	55,000	55,000	55,000
Materials	76,000	78,000	81,000	87,000
Insurance	4,000	4,000	4,000	4,000
Drawings	21,000	21,000	21,000	21,000
Other overheads	24,000	27,000	28,000	30,000
Total cash outflows	180,000	185,000	189,000	197,000
Net cash flow	9,000	5,000	5,000	6,000
Opening balance	12,300	21,300	26,300	31,300
Closing balance	21,300	26,300	31,300	37,300

At the end of January the firm's financial director notified the board that the forecast had to be amended to take into account the following changes.

- Wages would have to rise to £57,000 from February onwards.

- Due to favourable market conditions, material prices would fall to £71,000, £75,000 and £81,000 in February, March and April respectively.

- A payment of £11,500 to the tax authorities would have to be paid in February to compensate for an underpayment in the previous tax year.

Q

(a) Explain one reason why a cash-flow forecast is an important part of a business plan. (4 marks)

(b) Calculate the closing balances in the cash-flow forecast resulting from the changes above. (4 marks)

(c) Assess the impact of the changes in the cash-flow forecast on Charlton Plastics Ltd. (8 marks)

(d) Evaluate the use of cash-flow forecasts by Charlton Plastics Ltd. (20 marks)

Key terms

Business plan – a plan for the development of a business, giving details such as the products to be made, resources needed, and forecasts such as costs, revenues and cash flow.

Cash-flow forecast – the prediction of all expected receipts and expenses of a business over a future time period which shows the expected cash balance at the end of each month.

Cash inflows – the flow of money into a business.

Cash outflows – the flow of money out of a business.

Net cash flow – the difference between the cash flowing in and the cash flowing out of a business in a given time period.

Solvency – the degree to which a business is able to meet its debts when they fall due.

Knowledge check

1. State five pieces of information that are likely to appear in a business plan.

2. Give two examples of cash inflows in a cash-flow forecast.

3. Give two examples of cash outflows in a cash-flow forecast.

4. How is the net cash flow calculated in a cash-flow forecast?

5. How is the closing cash balance calculated in a cash-flow forecast?

6. State three benefits of using a cash-flow forecast.

7. How is a cash-flow forecast used as a planning tool?

8. State three limitations of using a cash-flow forecast.

Key points

1. Purpose of sales forecasts.
2. Factors affecting sales forecasts: consumer trends, economic variables and the actions of competitors.
3. Difficulties of sales forecasting.

Getting started

All business organisations, from the smallest of sole traders to the largest multinational, must try to forecast future sales. Important decisions within the business will be based on these forecasts.

Marco Frederick owns and runs an ice-cream manufacturer that produces high-quality ice cream. Marco was sitting in his office late one evening preparing orders from his suppliers for the following three months. He was deciding how much of his key raw materials he needed to buy. Milk, sugar and ingredients such as vanilla and clotted cream are expensive and are an important cost for his business. But how much of each should he order? If he ordered too much the result would be waste. If he ordered too little he would not be able to meet demand and lose potential profit. He turned to the sales forecasts he had prepared before working out his order.

Why is it important for a business like this to have an idea of what its sales will be next month, next year or in three years? What problems might the business face if Marco did not attempt to forecast future sales? If we accept that this type of prediction is important, how might a business construct its forecasts?

Purpose of sales forecasts

Sales forecasting is one of the most important tasks for a business, and one that will directly affect its efficiency and success. Imagine a business that did not carry out any sales forecasting. How much stock would it buy and hold? What would its staffing levels be? How would it know if it had enough funding? What would its marketing strategy be? Without some

predictions of sales, these questions are impossible to answer. Businesses are keen to know about what might happen in t[he] future. Anything a business can predict accurately will reduc[e] uncertainty and enable it to plan more effectively.

Given the importance of sales forecasting, the next step is to understand how to produce forecasts that will be useful to any business.

Forecasting is a business process, assessing the probable outcome using assumptions about the future. Forecasts may be based on a variety of data, for instance current information provided by managers. Most forecasts are based on data gathered from a variety of market research techniques. The accuracy of forecasts will depend on the reliability of the data.

What might a business like to predict with accuracy? Examples include:

- future sales of products
- the effect of promotion on sales
- possible changes in the size of the market in the future
- the way sales fluctuate at different times of the year.

Time series analysis: A variety of techniques can be use[d] to predict future trends. One of the most popular is **time series** analysis. This involves predicting future levels from pas[t] data. The data used are known as **time series data** – a set of figures arranged in order, based on the time they occurred. Fo[r] example, a business may predict future sales by analysing sale[s] data over the last ten years.

Table 1 Yearly sales of a garden furniture manufacturer

Year	2006	2007	2008	2009	2010	2011	2012	2013	2014	20
Sales (£ 000)	125	130	130	150	140	155	180	190	210	23

The business is assuming that past figures are a useful indica[tor] of what will happen in the future. This is likely to be the case if trading conditions are stable or if the business needs to forecas[t] trends in the short term. Consider Table 1. Based on the trend of sales during preceding years, the business might reasonably forecast that sales will rise in 2016. But precisely what sales mi[ght] the business expect? This forecast is important because it will determine orders of raw materials and component parts, which may need to be placed well in advance. In terms of capacity, if the forecast for 2016 is sales of £250,000, the business will need to consider whether it has the physical capacity to produce this volume, and whether it has the staffing required to produce this. These considerations may require the business to look for additional production capacity, or to recruit more staff. In short, t[he] sales forecast will trigger other decisions within the business.

Time series analysis does not try to explain data, only to describe what is happening to it or predict what will happen to it.

There are likely to be four components that a business wants to identify in time series data.

- **The trend.** 'Raw' data can provide figures for many different things and it may not always be easy to see exactly what is happening from these figures. Consequently businesses often try to identify a **trend**. This shows the pattern that is indicated from the figures. For example, there may be a trend for the sales of a new product to rise sharply in a short period as it becomes very popular. Statistical techniques for calculating trends and using this information are covered in Unit 52.
- **Seasonal fluctuations.** Over a year a business is unlikely to have a constant level of sales. Seasonal variations are very important to certain businesses, such as ice-cream producers or greeting card manufacturers, where there may be large sales at some times but not at others.
- **Cyclical fluctuations.** For many businesses there may be a cycle of 'highs and lows' in their sales figures over a number of years. These can be the result of the recession-boom-recession of the trade cycle in the economy. In a recession, for example, people have less money to spend and so the turnover of a business may fall in that period.
- **Random fluctuations.** At times there will be 'freak' figures that stand out from any trend that is taking place. An example might be the sudden boost in sales of umbrellas in unusually wet summer months, or the impact on consumer spending of a one-off event, such as a summer music festival.

Maths tip

Sales forecasting necessarily involves statistics. It can be useful to show percentage changes in business statistics data.

Example

2012 sales = £400, 000   2013 sales = £450,000

sales have increased by 12.5% between 2012 and 2013.

This is found by: $\dfrac{\text{Change in sales}}{\text{Original}} \times 100\%$

$$\dfrac{£50,000}{£400,000} \times 100\% = 12.5\%$$

Question 1

Drawing on the data in Table 1, Table 2 shows seasonal fluctuations in the sales of garden furniture.

Table 2 Quarterly sales of a garden furniture manufacturer

2013		2014				2015			
Q3	Q4	Q1	Q2	Q3	Q4	Q1	Q2	Q3	Q4
75	30	25	65	80	40	30	65	95	40

(a) Use the data from Table 2 to explain **one** reason why sales for this business are higher in Q3 than in Q1.

(b) Explain why sales forecasting will be useful for this business in terms of: (i) staffing (ii) buying supplies.

The benefits of sales forecasting

Using sales forecasts has some real advantages for businesses. In general it will help the business to plan ahead and avoid surprises. Having a clear idea of what sales will be in the next financial period will:

- inform cash-flow forecasts and give the business a clear idea of what cash inflows will be, so that finances can be managed
- allow the business to plan orders of supplies and components. For some businesses, suppliers will need notice of large orders. Sales forecasts help build relationships with suppliers
- enable the business to ensure it has the correct staffing levels for the projected sales. From Table 1, if the business had a forecast for 2016 of £250,000, this might mean that it needs to recruit more staff to meet these higher sales levels
- enable the business to ensure that it has the capacity to meet the projected orders. If forecasts are for higher sales, the business may need to buy additional equipment or rent/buy premises.

Factors affecting sales forecasting

Sales forecasting is extremely important for a business, but it can be an extremely difficult process to complete. Past data is useful in helping to predict future outcomes, but this is not an exact science. Unexpected things happen and there are other factors that need to be taken into account when trying to forecast future sales. Three crucial factors are consumer trends, economic variables and actions of competitors.

1 Consumer trends

Businesses aim to meet the needs of consumers by providing products and services. In a market economy successful businesses anticipate and meet the needs of consumers by supplying goods and services that are in demand at a point in time. Consumer tastes and preferences can and do change over time. Sometimes these changes can occur quickly. **Consumer trends** are the habits and behaviours of consumers around the products they buy and how they use them.

Today, the most popular use of a smartphone is not the 'phone' at all; it is to access the internet, either through the phone's browser, or through apps. In the late 1980s, when the first mobile phones became widely available, this could not easily be predicted. Consumer behaviour has changed. This affects the decisions and marketing of smartphone producers. This is an example of a long-term trend in consumer spending behaviour. Many changes in consumer behaviour are more short term, and in response to factors such as seasonal variations and fashion.

Seasonal variations. Some products are seasonal in that they are purchased in smaller or greater quantities at different times of the year. Some businesses that are affected by seasonal factors are obvious: coastal hotels and guest houses see a rise in sales during spring and summer months; power companies see a rise in sales of gas and electricity during the winter. Knowledge of the seasonal variation in sales is vital when constructing sales forecasts. This is important for the management of a business, for example when looking at cash-flow. Businesses affected by seasonal factors use sales forecasts to inform cash-flow forecasts and from these forecasts will recognise when lower sales will occur and therefore expect lower cash-flow during certain times of the year. Knowing this is very useful. Businesses can put in place strategies to manage the periods when cash-flow will be less strong.

Time series data is used by businesses to identify seasonal variations. For example, gas companies know that in the winter months they need to have available larger quantities of gas to cope

Table 3 UK gas and electricity consumption (domestic): 2012–14 (Gwh*)

	2012 Qtr 4	2013 Qtr 1	2013 Qtr 2	2013 Qtr 3	2013 Qtr 4	2014 Qtr 1	2014 Qtr 2	2014 Qtr 3	2014 Qtr 4
Gas	121,540	154,453	63,606	25,616	100,827	120,654	45,556	24,381	96,411
Electricity	32,799	34,234	25,521	22,755	30,943	31,438	23,992	22,188	29,572

Source: adapted from www.gov.uk

*Gwh: Gigawatt hour – a measure of a unit of energy. Specifically, the production or consumption of a thousand million watts for one hour.

Question 2

(a) Use the data from Table 3 to explain the meaning of 'seasonal variations'.

(b) Calculate the percentage change in consumption of gas and electricity between:

    (i) 2013 Quarter 1 and Quarter 3

    (ii) 2013 Quarter 4 and 2014 Quarter 4.

(c) Assess **two** possible impacts on energy companies of the seasonal variations shown in Table 3.

with the higher levels of demand from domestic and business consumers.

Energy providers, such as British Gas and npower, are very aware of this type of data. These seasonal variations in consumption of energy – gas and electricity – have important implications for sales and cash flow.

Fashion. Consumer tastes and preferences change and can be highly unpredictable. Fashion – particularly in the area of clothing – changes constantly. This can make accurate sales forecasting very difficult. Any change in fashion will lead to businesses modifying their sales forecasts. Unpredictability is a feature of sales in some industries.

Long-term trends. Whereas fashions can change in the short term, and with little notice, other changes to consumer behaviour are more long term. For example, the trend for consumers today to watch film and TV on demand, and using mobile devices, has led to a growth of media platforms such as Netflix and Amazon Prime, and the demise of operators such as Blockbuster. Long-term changes affect sales forecasts, and business strategic responses based on investment and strategic planning. Consider the motor car market. In recent years it has witnessed a rise in demand for electric cars that do not solely rely on petrol or diesel. There are environmental and cost reasons why consumers may switch their preferences.

The kind of information given in Figure 1 and Figure 2 will be used by car manufacturers when constructing sales forecasts, and also when deciding on corporate strategy. This might influence decisions on what to produce and where. Consumer trends have changed over recent years to favour low-emission cars. This change is due in part to the cost advantage for motorists, and in part to the environmentally friendly aspect. These factors led car-manufacturer Nissan to invest in its Sunderland factory and to produce its European electric car – the Nissan Leaf. This decision was taken due to sales forecast information which showed that customers' preferences were changing. In 2014 the 100,000th Nissan Leaf was produced in Sunderland. Nissan forecast that sales of electric cars would rise.

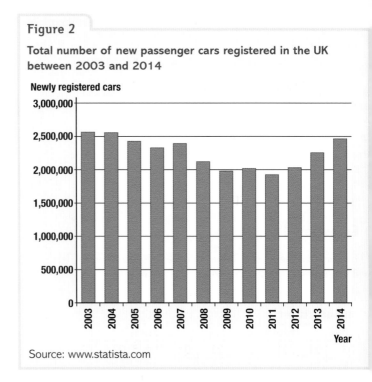

Figure 1

Electric car sales 2010–2014

Key

- ▢ Petrol/electric hybrid
- ▦ Diesel/electric hybrid
- ■ Other electric (plug-in hybrid/range extender)
- ▥ Pure electric

www.smmt.co.uk

Figure 2

Total number of new passenger cars registered in the UK between 2003 and 2014

Source: www.statista.com

2 Economic variables

What happens in the wider economy has some important implications for business sales forecasting. The economy is comprised of consumers (households), businesses and

Question 3

Read the following headlines, Extract A and Extract B, and answer the questions that follow.

Figure 3

Bennet's Lark

Extract A

New model car to be built in Cumbria

The British car industry received a boost on Wednesday when car-maker Bennets annouced that it will build the Lark, its six-seater electric car, in Cumbria.

Extract B

50,000th Bennets Lark to hit the road

The electric revolution has reached a milestone with news that the 50,000th Bennets Lark has hit the roads.

(a) What is meant by consumer trends?

(b) Explain how Bennets might have used the idea of sales forecasting when deciding to build the Lark at its Cumbrian plant.

government. **Economic variables** are measurements of different aspects of an economy that give an indication of how that economy is performing. Economic performance has some important implications for businesses generally, and sales forecasting in particular. Important economic variables are as follows:

- **Economic growth.** Economic growth is judged using Gross Domestic Product (GDP). This is a measure of the total output of an economy. When economic growth is rising, sales for many – but not all – businesses tend to increase. One reason for this is that **consumer incomes** generally increase during periods of economic growth, and this translates into higher spending. In a period of strong economic growth, sales forecasts will often be increased. A slowdown in economic growth leads to lower sales. In this scenario, sales forecasts are often reduced. Many businesses expect to sell less in times of economic downturn. This will affect sales forecasts.
- **Interest rates.** These are charged by banks and other financial institutions for borrowing money. When interest rates are high, the cost of loans increases and the demand for loans falls. Loans are used by consumers and businesses to fund purchases. For example, when a household buys

a new car, the chances are this will be purchased using a bank loan. When interest rates are rising, sales forecasts may be adjusted downwards. Businesses might expect that demand for their product will fall. In contrast, when interest rates fall the cost of loans also falls. This means they are more attractive for consumers. Sales forecasts may be adjusted upwards in response to such a change in interest rates.
- **Inflation.** The general rise in consumer prices over time. When inflation is rising this indicates that prices in the economy are rising also. In such periods consumers and businesses often choose to spend less. Sales forecasts are reduced at these times.
- **Unemployment.** The number of people who are out of work. During a recession, unemployment rises. During the economic crisis that started in 2008, UK unemployment rose to almost 3 million. As a result, spending in the economy fell and this had a huge impact on business sales and orders. At such times, sales forecasts are reduced.
- **Exchange rates.** These reflect the value of one currency in terms of another. An exchange of £1 = US$1.45 means that £1 will buy $1.45. If this exchange rate rises, say to £1 = $1.60, it is cheaper for UK consumers to buy goods and services from the US. As a result, UK businesses might find that sales fall due to the increased price competitiveness of the US. The impact on sales forecasts would be to cause them to fall, as consumers are shifting their spending to US goods and services. In addition, UK goods become more expensive for US consumers; something that used to cost $1.45 now costs $1.60. Demand will tend to fall in such situations.

Table 4 Effect of economic variables

Change in economic variable	Impact on business sales forecasts	
	Higher sales forecast	Lower sales forecast
Strong economic growth	X	
Slower GDP growth		X
Rising inflation		X
Falling inflation/deflation	X	
Rising unemployment		X
Falling unemployment	X	
Rising interest rates		X
Falling interest rates	X	
Higher exchange rate		X
Falling exchange rate	X	

The analysis of economic variables in Table 4 assumes that businesses enjoy 'normal' patterns of demand. When incomes rise consumers tend to buy more of the product. This applies to a large majority of products. For example, the demand for new cars rises when unemployment falls and incomes rise. So does the demand for theatre tickets, books and magazines, fresh food, wine, clothing, and so on. These products are likely to have a positive income elasticity of demand. This means that as incomes rise, demand also rises. For such businesses the impact on sales forecasts will be for them to increase.

However, for some businesses the opposite is true. When incomes rise some businesses expect their sales to fall. Value supermarkets, such as Aldi and Lidl, tend to grow in popularity when incomes are falling, for example during a recession. When incomes start to rise, consumers begin to shift to more expensive providers. The result for such businesses is that sales forecasts actually fall when consumer incomes are rising. However, this is a simplistic interpretation of the current position of supermarkets in the UK. It does not necessarily follow that value supermarkets, such as Aldi and Lidl, will simply accept that customers will shift their allegiance as soon as incomes begin to rise. In fact, these businesses have been very proactive in not only trying to attract customers away from their original supermarket, but also in trying to keep their custom. This is a competitive market and rivals are keen to capture and retain custom. There is some evidence that more affluent customers are now sticking with retailers that would previously have been regarded as perhaps lower in quality.

3 Actions of competitors

The actions of competitors can have a real impact on a business in many ways, from pricing to promotion. Sales forecasting is another area that can be affected by the actions of competitors. Where competitors use a strategy to capture market share from a rival, sales forecasts may need to be adjusted downwards.

The size of the impact on sales forecasts will depend on the type of strategy used by the competing business. A short-term promotion might affect sales for a short period of time only, and not lead to a change to next year's sales forecast. A rival restaurant opening next door to an existing restaurant is likely to have a greater, more long-term effect.

Any significant action by a competitor will affect the reliability of time series data, such as past sales. Effectively, the conditions within the market have been changed.

How the business responds to the actions of competitors is important. If a competing business opened a new branch close to a business, it might realistically be expected that sales at the existing business would fall. Sales forecasts would need to reflect this. However, the dynamic nature of business means that a company does not ignore the actions of competitors. The response will influence sales forecasts. A response that aims to counter the action of the competitors may mean that sales projections remain unchanged.

The effect of the actions of competitors cannot truly be known until some point in the future. Consider the example below.

Table 5 Yearly sales of a coffee shop

	Competitor enters market 2013					
Year	2010	2011	2012	2013 ↓	2014	2015 (forecast)
Sales (£ 000)	78	86	84	79	62	65

The data in Table 5 shows that sales from previous years are fairly stable, and these can be used by the business to forecast sales. The entry into the market of a competitor clearly had some impact on the business. Sales in 2014 fell sharply from the previous year and below the trend. In consequence, the sales forecast for 2015, based on the time series data, reflects the fact that sales are lower due to the entry into the market of a rival.

Question 4

In 2014 German discount supermarket Lidl announced that it planned to spend £20 million on opening 20 new stores in the UK. This was seen as a threat to other supermarkets who were under pressure from Lidl's low price strategy.

In response to Lidl's growth and success, in 2014 Morrisons launched a new loyalty scheme. Its 'Match & More' scheme promised to match the prices charged by other supermarkets, including discount retailers such as Aldi and Lidl. Morrisons planned that this scheme would help to protect sales at a time when competition was increasing.

(a) Explain one impact on Morrisons' sales forecast in response to Lidl's expansion plan.

(b) Why might time series data from Morrisons – details of sales in previous years – be less reliable following the announcement from Lidl?

Thinking bigger

Sales forecasting is extremely important for businesses. Whether they do it formally, using statistical trend analysis and modelling, or less formally, using estimates based loosely on sales from previous series or informed by 'gut instinct', all businesses aim to forecast what sales will be in the next period.

There are lots of opportunities for questions requiring analysis and evaluation in this topic. The statistical element of sales data means that analytical considerations can be made.

A key thing to consider in this topic is the difficulty of forecasting in different industries. Whereas time series data may be useful for businesses in some sectors, such as energy or greeting cards, this is less useful for others. For example, industries where many new competitors enter the market, such as new technology businesses, may struggle.

Another consideration when analysing business cash flow is the nature of the business. Rising incomes in the economy would ordinarily lead a business to expect higher sales and to therefore reflect this expectation in their sales forecast. However, for businesses that sell at the lower end of quality goods, the opposite may be true. This is an important consideration when analysing business sales forecasting due to changing economic variables.

The difficulties of sales forecasting

Predicting the future is not easy. This uncertainty applies in all spheres of life. What will the weather be like next week? How will my football team perform next season? Will the value of my house rise or fall over the next 12 months? This affects many aspects of life, but especially business.

In this Unit we have explored how businesses can use techniques to help minimise this uncertainty, by using statistical methods and time series analysis to help predict with more certainty what might happen to sales in the future. These quantitative methods will be explained more fully in Unit 52. In fact, some of the factors we have explored in this unit give rise to the very difficulties involved in sales forecasting.

Volatile consumer tastes and preferences: We have seen how a business can use past sales data to identify future sales. This is called **extrapolation**. This is often a good starting point and a reasonable basis on which to base forecasts. However, extrapolation is not a perfect method to base future predictions. If Chelsea wins the Premiership for two consecutive years, does this mean they will win a third time? Possibly, but this is not guaranteed. Crocs produce rubber shoes that were once very fashionable. Inaccurate sales forecasts from 2008 onwards nearly caused the collapse of the business. Sales from 2004–2007 were increasing steeply and it was therefore reasonable, based on extrapolation of this data, to forecast strong growth in subsequent years. Capacity and production were increased. Unfortunately, these decisions by the business coincided with changing consumer tastes. The perception of Crocs changed from trendy 'must have' to very off trend.

Range of data: There is a lot of data available to consumers, business and government. Which data is most important for a business to use? In addition to its own sales data, what about wider economic data, such as unemployment, average income growth, commodity prices, exchange rates and so on? This extensive range of data can be difficult enough for a large multinational business to make sense of, let alone a small business. A real difficulty of accurate sales forecasting lies in the sheer amount of data that exists which might inform the forecast.

Subjective expert opinion: However statistical and quantitative time series data might be, the final decisions around sales forecasts are often left to business experts, such as sales analysts. Experts will base their judgements in part on their own opinion and knowledge of the market and wider economic variables. These opinions are necessarily subjective and can be wrong. Crocs almost collapsed because of the well-intentioned but ultimately inaccurate sales forecasts of its marketing team

Exam tip

Think about the type of business in any exam question. Context is important. When questions refer to particular businesses or industries, it is important that your answers are in the correct context. Apply your knowledge to the specific business and avoid 'general' answers that could apply to any business.

You will be asked questions with the command word 'assess', for example, 'Assess the importance of X to a business'. In this type of question, it is possible to introduce the idea of sales forecasting as a balancing item (evaluation). For example, if the question asked you to assess the importance of budgeting for the success of a business, it would clearly be appropriate to consider that other factors, such as sales forecasting, were even more important. When concluding questions such as this, the 'it depends' rule can be used. This involves consideration of the type of industry involved.

Knowledge check

1. Why might a business want to predict future sales?

2. State three advantages to a business of using sales forecasts.

3. What is time series data?

4. What is meant by 'trend'?

5. State three economic variables that might affect the sales forecasts of a business.

6. Give three reasons why consumer trends might change.

7. State three difficulties in accurately forecasting sales.

ROLLS-ROYCE

Rolls-Royce is a British aeroplane engine manufacturer producing jet engines for major aeroplane producers, such as Boeing and Airbus. Rolls-Royce received an order in 2015 to supply 50 Emirates airline A380 'superjumbo' planes with their engines.

In 2015 Emirates, based in Dubai, was the seventh largest airline company in the world. It had experienced strong growth in previous years and was looking to expand its fleet of aircraft. The order of 50 new A380 planes was in response to growing demand in the Middle East. The airline believed that strengthening economic growth and rising incomes in the region would lead to greater demand for air travel.

The order for Rolls-Royce was worth £6.1 billion and was a new order for the company. Engines for the A380 were previously supplied by Rolls-Royce's main competitor – Engine Alliance.

The deal has secured the jobs of Rolls-Royce workers for some years. Its sales forecasts for future years will include the Emirates order.

(a) What is meant by sales forecast? (2 marks)

(b) Explain how the order might affect future sales forecasts for Rolls-Royce. (4 marks)

(c) Assess the extent to which consumer trends are affecting sales forecasting at Rolls-Royce. (10 marks)

Key terms

Consumer income – the amount of income remaining after taxes and expenses have been deducted from wages.
Consumer trends – the habits or behaviours of consumers that determine the goods and services they buy.
Economic growth – the rise in output of an economy as measured by the growth in Gross Domestic Product (GDP), usually as a percentage.
Economic variables – measures within the economy which have effects on business and consumers. Examples include unemployment, inflation and exchange rates.
Extrapolation – forecasting future trends based on past data.
Forecasting – a business process, assessing the probable outcome using assumptions about the future.
Sales forecast – projection of future sales revenue, often based on previous sales data.
Time series data – a method that allows a business to predict future levels from past figures.

31 Sales, revenue and costs

Key points

1. Calculating sales volume and sales revenue.
2. Calculating fixed and variable costs.

Getting started

OzzyTrek organises specialised adventure holidays in Australia where customers can enjoy a range of outdoor pursuits, such as canoeing, hiking, camping and kangaroo watching. The target market is young adults in the UK. In 2011, OzzyTrek lowered the price of its trips by 20 per cent to try to boost sales. Figures 1 and 2 show **sales volume** and **sales revenue** for the business between 2005 and 2014.

Figure 1

Sales volume for OzzyTrek 2005 to 2014

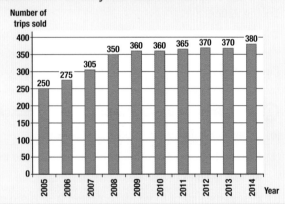

Figure 2

Sales revenue for OzzyTrek 2005 to 2014

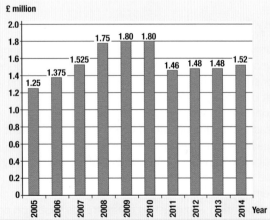

What is the difference between sales revenue and sales volume? What price was charged between 2005 and 2010? What price was charged after 2010? What impact did the price change in 2011 have on sales volume and sales revenue? What types of business costs might be incurred by OzzyTrek?

Sales volume

The output produced by businesses is eventually sold. Businesses measure and monitor sales levels. One approach is to measure the sales volume. This is the number of units sold by a business. However, depending on the nature of the business, sales volume can be measured in different ways. Some examples are illustrated in Table 1.

Table 1 Measuring sales volume

Type of business	How sales volume is measured
Cereal farmer	Tonnes of wheat sold
Car manufacturer	Number of cars sold
Airline	Number of passengers carried
Oil company	Barrels of oil sold
Haulage business	Number of miles travelled
Hotel	Number of rooms let
Driving instructor	Number of hourly lessons given
Insurance company	Number of policies sold
Music tutor	Number of hourly lessons given
Dairy farmer	Litres of milk sold
Power generator	Megawatt hours sold

When a business sells clearly identifiable units of output, such as the examples shown in Table 1, measuring or calculating sales volume is straightforward. However, in some cases it is difficult to identify single units of output. For example, how might you measure the sales volume of a supermarket that sells thousands of different products each day? Or how would you measure the annual sales volume of a construction company that builds 25 semi-detached houses, 5 apartment blocks, 2 warehouses, 2 office blocks, 2 tunnels, 5 different-sized factories and a bridge? In these cases the units sold are different – they are not standard. To overcome this problem it may be easier, and more meaningful, to calculate the sales revenue.

Sales revenue

Sales revenue is the *value* of output sold by a business. It may be calculated for a specific time period, such as a day, week, month or year. It can also be calculated for individual products when a business has a wide product range. Sales revenue, which is often called **total revenue**, is calculated using the following formula:

Sales revenue = Price × Quantity of output

Worked example

In 2014, Gartex Mining Ltd sold 1,433,400 tonnes of limestone to customers. The price per tonne was £12.60. What is the sales revenue for 2014?

Sales revenue = £12.60 × 1,433,400 = £18,060,840

All businesses have to calculate the value of their sales revenue each year. Sales revenue can be used as a measure of business performance. Most businesses would want to see their sales revenue grow each year.

Question 1

Manchester United is one of the richest football clubs in the world. In the 2012/13 season the total revenue generated by the club, as reported in the media, was £350-360 million. Figure 3 shows the key sources of this revenue. However, the pie chart does not reflect accurately the wide range of revenue sources enjoyed by the football club. For example, on a match day revenues are likely to be generated from the sale of match tickets, match programmes, food and beverages, hospitality boxes, special functions and concessions (revenue from vendors given the right to trade in or around the stadium). Sources of commercial revenues are also diverse. Examples might be the sale of merchandising, such as replica shirts, clothes and virtually anything using the MUFC logo; sponsorship; advertising; travel packages to overseas fixtures; weddings; business meetings and other functions held at the stadium; stadium tours and revenue from providing hospitality for Old Trafford International cricket matches.

Figure 3

Manchester United revenue by source 2012/13 (€)

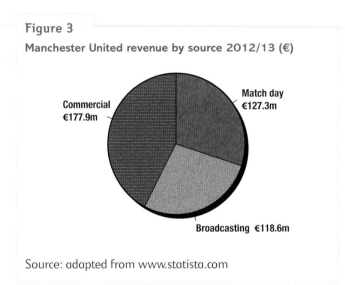

Source: adapted from www.statista.com

(a) Why might Manchester United find it difficult to calculate sales volume?

(b) If Manchester United play 19 Premier League fixtures at home in a season, calculate the total revenue from programme sales if an average of 26,200 programmes are sold at each match for £3.

Business costs

A business needs accurate and reliable cost information to make decisions. For example, a firm that is aiming to expand production or deliver more services to meet rising demand must know how much that extra production or services delivery will cost. In the same way that you are familiar with your own personal costs – these are the regular expenses you have, such as travel to school or college – so businesses will know what their expenses are. These might include wages, raw materials, insurance and rent.

It is important to understand how the costs of a business change in the **short run** and the **long run**.

- The short run is the period of time when at least one factor of production is **fixed**. For example, in the short run, a firm might want to expand production in its factory. It can acquire more labour and buy more raw materials, but it has a fixed amount of space in the factory and a limited number of machines.
- In the long run, all factors can vary. The firm can buy another factory and add to the number of machines. This will increase **capacity** (the maximum amount that can be produced) and begin another short-run period. In the service industry, an airline, for example, can buy or lease another plane in the long run to increase capacity. In the short run it may be able to fly more passengers by using its fleet of planes more frequently.

Fixed costs

Costs which stay the same at all levels of output in the short run are called **fixed costs**. Examples might be rent, insurance, heating bills, depreciation and business rates, as well as capital costs such as factories and machinery. These costs remain the same whether a business produces nothing or is working at full capacity. For example, rent must still be paid even if a factory is shut for a two-week holiday when nothing is produced. Importantly, 'fixed' here means costs do not change as a result of a change in output in the short run. But they may increase due to, say, inflation. Figure 4 shows what happens to fixed costs as a firm increases production. The line on the graph is horizontal which shows that fixed costs are £400,000 no matter how much is produced. The firm is a doll manufacturer.

What happens over a longer period? Figure 5 on the next page illustrates 'stepped' fixed costs. If a firm is at full capacity, but needs to raise production, it might decide to invest in more equipment. The new machines raise overall fixed costs as well as capacity. The rise in fixed costs is shown by a 'step' in the graph. This illustrates how fixed costs can change in the long run.

Figure 4

Fixed costs of a doll manufacturer

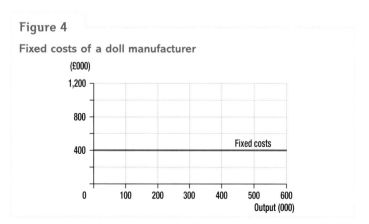

Figure 5

Stepped fixed costs of a doll manufacturer

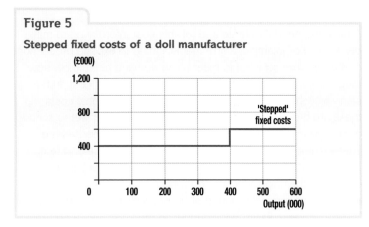

Variable costs

Costs of production which increase directly as output rises are called **variable costs**. For example, a baker will require more flour if more loaves are to be produced. Raw materials are just one example of variable costs. Others might include fuel, packaging and wages. If the firm does not produce anything then variable costs will be zero.

Figure 6 shows the variable costs of the doll manufacturer mentioned above. Variable costs are £2 per doll. If the firm produces 100,000 dolls it will have variable costs of £200,000 (£2 × 100,000).

Producing 600,000 dolls will incur variable costs of £1,200,000 (£2 × 600,000). Joining these points together shows the firm's variable costs at any level of output. As output increases, so do variable costs. Notice that the graph is linear. This means that it is a straight line.

Figure 6

Variable costs of a doll manufacturer

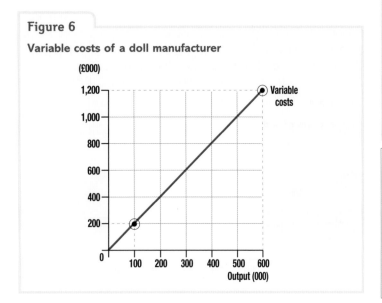

Thinking bigger

Some production costs do not fit neatly into our definitions of fixed and variable costs. This is because they are not entirely fixed or variable costs. Labour is a good example. If a firm employs a member of staff on a permanent basis, no matter what level of output, then this is a fixed cost. If this member of staff is asked to work overtime at nights and weekends to cope with extra production levels, then the extra cost is variable. Such labour costs are said to be **semi-variable costs**. Another example could be the cost of telephone charges. This often consists of a fixed or 'standing charge' plus an extra rate which varies according to the number of calls made.

Total cost

If fixed and variable costs are added together they show the **total cost** of a business. The total cost of production is the cost of producing any given level of output. As output increases total costs will rise. This is shown in Figure 7, which again shows the production of dolls. We can say:

Total cost (TC) = Fixed cost (FC) + Variable cost (VC)

The business has fixed costs of £400,000 and variable costs of £2 per doll. When output is 0, total costs are £400,000. When output has risen to 300,000 dolls, total costs are £1,000,000, made up of fixed costs of £400,000 and variable costs of £600,000 (£2 × 300,000). When output is 600,000, total costs are £1,600,000, made up of fixed costs of £400,000 and variable costs of £1,200,000 (£2 × 600,000). Figure 7 shows the way that total costs increase as output increases. Notice that as output increases fixed costs become a smaller proportion of total costs.

Figure 7

Total cost of a doll manufacturer

Thinking bigger

Costs can also be divided into direct and indirect costs. Direct costs are costs which can be identified with a particular product or process. Examples of direct costs are raw materials, packaging and direct labour. Indirect costs or overheads result from the whole business. It is not possible to associate these costs directly with particular products or processes. Examples are rent, insurance, the salaries of office staff and audit fees. Indirect costs are usually fixed costs and direct costs variable costs, although in theory both direct and indirect costs can be fixed or variable.

Average cost or unit cost

The average cost is the cost per unit of production, also known as the unit cost. To calculate average cost, the total cost of production should be divided by the number of units produced, or output.

$$\text{Average cost} = \frac{\text{Total cost}}{\text{Output}}$$

Worked example

Take the example of the doll manufacturer with fixed costs of £400,000 and variable costs of £2 per unit. If output was 100,000 units:

$$\text{Average cost} = \frac{£400,000 + (£2 \times 100,000)}{100,000}$$

$$= \frac{£600,000}{100,000} = £6$$

The importance of average cost is discussed in more detail in Unit 37.

Profit and loss

One of the main reasons why firms calculate their costs and revenue is to enable them to work out their profit or loss. Profit is the difference between revenue and costs.

Profit = total revenue − total costs

For example, if the doll manufacturer produces and sells 300,000 dolls, they sell for £5, fixed costs are £400,000 and variable costs are £2 per unit, then:

Profit = £5 × 300,000 − (£400,000 + [£2 x 300,000])
= £1,500,000 − (£400,000 + [£600,000])
= £1,500,000 − £1,000,000
= £500,000

It is possible to calculate the profit for a business at any level of output using this method.

If the variable costs were £4 per unit, the business would make a loss.

Loss = £5 x 300,000 − (£400,000 + [£4 × 300,000])
= £1,500,000 − (£400,000 + £1,200,000)
= £1,500,000 − £1,600,000
= − £100,000

Knowledge check

1. What is the difference between sales volume and sales revenue?

2. How is sales revenue calculated?

3. What is the difference between the short run and the long run in business?

4. Give two examples of fixed costs for a taxi driver.

5. Give two examples of variable costs for an online retailer.

6. What is meant by a semi-variable cost?

7. How is profit calculated?

Key terms

Average cost or **unit cost** – the cost of producing one unit, calculated by dividing the total cost by the output.

Fixed cost – a cost that does not change as a result of a change in output in the short run.

Long run – the time period where all factors of production are variable.

Profit – the difference between total costs and total revenue. It can be negative.

Sales revenue – the value of output sold in a particular time period. It is calculated by price × quantity of output.

Sales volume – the quantity of output sold in a particular time period.

Semi-variable cost – a cost that consists of both fixed and variable elements.

Short run – the time period where at least one factor of production is fixed.

Total cost – the entire cost of producing a given level of output.

Total revenue – the amount of money the business receives from selling output.

Variable cost – a cost that rises as output rises.

Case study

RAZIA MALIK

Razia Malik operates as a sole trader. She offers one-day courses in business start-ups for Urdu-speaking people in the Midlands. The courses cover all aspects of business start-ups, such as writing a business plan, market research, financial management, negotiation skills and legal issues. Most of her work comes from local authorities.

The business charges £600 for a one-day course and can enrol up to 20 entrepreneurs. Razia rents function rooms in small hotels for £150 per day to run the courses. The course fee also includes refreshments.

In 2013 the business provided a total of 200 courses and made a reasonable profit. However, Razia felt that she could improve the sales revenue of the business by marketing the business more aggressively in the Birmingham area. Her aim was to raise profit by 10 per cent. She thought that she could charge more and also reduce the amount of time travelling around the region. She spent £3,000 advertising on specialist Urdu websites and raised the price of the courses to £800. As a result, the number of courses sold fell to 150 in 2014. Details of the costs incurred by Razia's business are shown in Table 2.

Table 2 Financial information for Razia Malik's business training courses (£)

	2013	2014
Car lease per annum	5,000	5,000
Insurance per annum	1,000	1,200
Other fixed costs per annum	2,000	2,800
Special promotion	0	3,000
Room hire fees per course	150	200
Refreshment costs per course	150	180
Training materials per course	50	50
Other variable costs per course	50	70
Price per course	600	800

(a) What is meant by fixed costs? (2 marks)

(b) What is meant by sales volume? (2 marks)

(c) (i)   Calculate the sales revenue in 2013. (4 marks)
   (ii) Calculate the variable costs in 2013. (4 marks)
   (iii) Calculate the total costs in 2013. (4 marks)
   (iv) Calculate the profit made in 2013. (4 marks)

(d) Assess the extent to which Razia achieved her objective by raising the price of the courses from £600 to £800. (12 marks)

Key points

1. Calculating contribution (selling price − variable cost per unit).
2. Break-even point (total fixed costs + total variable costs = total revenue).
3. Using contribution to calculate break-even point.
4. Margin of safety.
5. Interpretation of break-even charts.
6. Limitations of break-even analysis.

Getting started

Anna Powell runs a company that provides a 24-hour taxi service from Huddersfield to Manchester Airport. Fixed costs each month are usually £3,000 and variable costs are £10 per trip. Anna charges £40 per trip. In the summer months (June to September) the business can make 250 trips a month.

Calculate the total cost of 250 trips to the airport in June (total cost = fixed costs + variable costs). Calculate the total revenue from 250 trips to the airport. How much profit is made from 250 trips? How many trips would be needed in a month for the business to break-even?

Contribution

Craig Eckert sells second-hand cars. His last sale was £990 for a Golf GTI. He bought the Golf at a car auction for £890. The difference between what he paid for the car and the price he sold it for is £100 (£990 − £890). This difference is called the **contribution**. It is not profit because Craig has fixed costs to pay such as rent, insurance and administration expenses. Contribution is the difference between selling price and variable costs. In this case the selling price was £990 and the variable cost was £890. The £100 will **contribute** to the **total fixed costs** of the business and the profit.

Contribution per unit and total contribution

A business might calculate the contribution on the sale of a single unit, or the sale of a larger quantity, such as a whole year's output.

Unit contribution: In the above example the unit contribution was calculated. It was the contribution on the sale of one unit, a single car. The formula for calculating the unit contribution is:

$$\text{Contribution per unit} = \text{Selling price} - \text{Variable cost}$$
$$= £990 - £890$$
$$= £100$$

Total contribution: When more than one unit is sold the total contribution can be calculated. For example, a textile company receives an order for 1,000 pairs of trousers. The variable costs are £7.50 a pair and they will be sold for £9.00 a pair. The total contribution made by the order is:

$$\text{Total contribution} = \text{Total revenue} - \text{Total variable cost}$$
$$= (£9.00 \times 1,000) - (£7.50 \times 1,000)$$
$$= £9,000 - £7,500$$
$$= £1,500$$

The £1,500 in this example will contribute to the textile company's fixed costs and profit. The total contribution can also be calculated by multiplying the unit contribution by the number of units sold.

$$\text{Total contribution} = \text{Unit contribution} \times \text{Number of units sold}$$
$$= (£9.00 - £7.50) \times 1,000$$
$$= £1.50 \times 1,000$$
$$= £1,500$$

Exam tip

Contribution can be used to calculate the profit made by a business. The formula needed is:

Profit = Total contribution − Fixed costs

Question 1

Westwood Holdings is a manufacturer of camping trailers. The factory is located near Dover and nearly 70 per cent of the company's output is exported to France, Italy and Spain. The fixed costs are £200,000 per annum and the variable costs are £500 per trailer. The trailers are sold for £800.

(a) What is meant by the term contribution?

(b) Calculate the contribution made by each trailer.

(c) Calculate the profit made by Westwood Holdings if 2,000 trailers are made and sold in a year.

(d) Due to a new entrant in the market, Westwood Holdings is forced to lower its price to £650 in the coming year. Calculate the impact the price cut will have on annual profit.

Break-even point

Businesses, particularly those that are just starting up, often like to know how much they need to produce and sell to break-even. If a business has information about fixed costs and variable costs and knows what price it is going to charge, it can calculate how many units it needs to sell to cover all of its costs. The point where total costs (fixed costs + variable costs) are exactly the same as total revenue is called the **break-even point**. The level of output a business needs to produce so that total costs are exactly the same as total revenue is called the **break-even output**. It makes neither a profit nor a loss. For many businesses the break-even point is a sort of 'performance milestone'. It shows the level of output where all costs have been covered and that all future sales will generate a profit for the business.

Worked example

A business produces 1,000 units and sells them for £50 each. Total fixed costs are £10,000. Variable costs are £40 per unit. So total variable costs are £40 × 1,000 = £40,000.

Therefore:

Total costs = £10,000 + £40,000   = **£50,000**
Total revenue = £50 × 1,000   = **£50,000**

Total revenue and total costs are exactly the same at £50,000. Therefore the business will break even at this level of output. So the break-even output is 1,000 units.

Calculating break-even using contribution

It is possible to calculate the break-even output if a firm knows the value of its fixed costs, variable costs and the price it will charge. The simplest way to calculate the break-even output is to use contribution. The following formula can be used.

$$\text{Break-even output} = \frac{\text{Fixed costs}}{\text{Contribution}}$$

Worked example

Jack Cadwallader makes wrought-iron park benches. His fixed costs (FC) are £60,000 and variable costs (VC) £40 per bench. He sells the benches to local authorities across the country for £100 each. Therefore contribution is given by:

Contribution = Selling price – Variable cost
Contribution = £100 – £40
Contribution = £60

Once the contribution has been calculated, the number of benches Jack needs to sell to break-even can then be determined.

$$\text{Break-even output} = \frac{\text{Fixed costs}}{\text{Contribution}}$$

$$= \frac{£60,000}{£60}$$

$$= 1,000 \text{ benches}$$

Jack Cadwallader's business will break even when 1,000 park benches are sold.

Question 2

Karen Ficenec assembles presentational gift packs that she sells online. She operates from a small warehouse in Swindon that she rents for £400 per month. She incurs other fixed costs of £100 per month and sells the gift packs for £10 each (including postage and packaging). She employs two part-time staff and variable costs are £8 per gift pack.

(a) Calculate the monthly break-even output for Karen Ficenec's business.

(b) Calculate the total cost and total revenue at the break-even level of output.

(c) Calculate the profit made by the business if 2,000 gift packs are sold in a month.

Break-even chart

The use of graphs is often helpful in break-even analysis. It is possible to identify the break-even point and break-even output by plotting the total cost and total revenue equations on a graph. This graph is called a **break-even chart**. Figure 1 on the next page shows the break-even chart for Jack Cadwallader's business.

Output is measured on the horizontal axis and revenue, costs and profit are measured on the vertical axis. What does the break-even chart show?

- **The value of total cost over a range of output.** For example, when Jack produces 1,500 benches total costs are £120,000.
- **The value of total revenue over a range of output.** For example, when Jack produces 1,500 benches total revenue is £150,000.
- **Break-even charts can show the level of fixed costs over a range of output.** For example, the fixed costs for Jack's business are £60,000.
- **The level of output needed to break-even.** The break-even point is where total costs equal total revenue of £100,000. This is when 1,000 benches are produced. So the break-even output is 1,000 benches.
- **The profit at a particular level of output.** If Jack produces 1,500 benches, profit is shown by the vertical gap between the total cost and total revenue equations. It is £30,000.
- **At levels of output below the break-even output, losses are made.** This is because total costs exceed total revenue. At an output of 500, a £30,000 loss is made.
- **At levels of output above the break-even output, a profit is made.** This profit gets larger as output rises. At an output of 1,500 a profit of £30,000 is made.
- **The relationship between fixed costs and variable costs as output rises.** At low levels of output, fixed costs represent a large proportion of total costs. As output rises, fixed costs become a smaller proportion of total costs.

Figure 1

Break-even chart for Jack Cadwallader

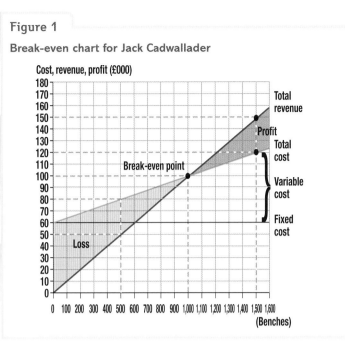

Using break-even analysis

Break-even analysis is used in business as a tool to make decisions about the future. It helps answer 'what if' questions. For instance:

- if the price went up, what would happen to the break-even point?
- if the business introduced a new product line, how many would the new product have to sell to at least break-even?
- if the business is just starting up, what has to be the level of output to prevent a loss being incurred?
- what will happen to the break-even point if costs are forecast to rise?
- would the break-even point be lower if components were bought in from outside suppliers rather than being made in-house?

Break-even analysis is also found in business plans. Banks often ask for business plans when deciding whether or not to give a loan. So break-even analysis can be vital in gaining finance, especially when starting up a business.

Margin of safety

What if a business is producing more than the break-even output? It might be useful to know by how much sales could fall before a loss is made. This is called the **margin of safety**. It refers to the range of output over which a profit can be made. The margin of safety can be identified on the break-even chart by measuring the distance between the break-even level of output and the current (profitable) level of output. For example, Figure 2 shows the break-even chart for Jack Cadwallader. If Jack produces 1,200 benches the margin of safety is 200 benches. This means that output can fall by 200 before a loss is made. If Jack sells 1,200 benches the chart shows that total revenue is £120,000, total cost is £108,000 and profit is £12,000.

Businesses prefer to operate with a large margin of safety. This means that if sales drop they still might make some profit. With a small margin of safety there is a risk that the business is more likely to make losses if sales fall.

Limitations of break-even analysis

Break-even analysis does have some limitations. It is often regarded as too simplistic and some of its assumptions are unrealistic.

Output and stocks: It assumes that all output is sold, so that output equals sales, and no stocks are held. Many businesses hold stocks of finished goods to cope with changes in demand. There are also times when firms cannot sell what they produce and choose to stockpile their output to avoid laying off staff.

Unchanging conditions: The break-even chart is drawn for a given set of conditions. It cannot cope with a sudden increase in wages and prices or changes in technology.

Accuracy of data: The effectiveness of break-even analysis depends on the quality and accuracy of the data used to construct cost and revenue functions. If the data is poor and inaccurate, the conclusions drawn on the basis of the data are flawed. For example, if fixed costs are underestimated, the level of output required to break-even will be higher than suggested by the break-even chart.

Non-linear relationships: It is assumed that the total revenue and total cost lines are linear or straight. This may not always be the case. For example, a business may have to offer discounts on large orders, so total revenues fall at high outputs. In this case the total revenue line would rise and then fall, and be curved. A business can lower costs by buying in bulk. So costs may fall at high outputs and the costs function will be curved.

Multi-product businesses: Many businesses produce more than one single product. It is likely that each product will have different variable costs and different prices. The problem is how to allocate the fixed costs of the multi-product business to each individual product. There are a number of ways, but none is perfect. Therefore, if the fixed costs incurred by each product are inaccurate, break-even analysis is less useful.

Figure 2

Break-even chart showing the margin of safety for Jack Cadwallader's business

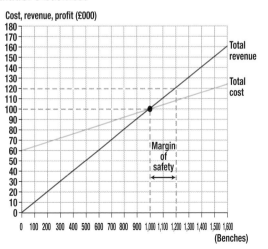

Stepped fixed costs: Some fixed costs are stepped. For example, in order to increase output a manufacturer may need to acquire more capacity. This may result in rent increases and thus fixed costs will rise sharply. Under these circumstances it is difficult to use break-even analysis.

Maths tip

A break-even chart can be used to work out the price charged and the variable cost per unit. To calculate the price charged, look at the total revenue at the break-even level of output and divide this by the break-even output. To calculate the variable cost you need to look at the total cost at the break-even level of output, subtract fixed costs and then divide the answer by the break-even level of output.

Case study

GOWDA CHANDA LTD

Gowda Chanda runs a plastics recycling plant. The business incurs quite high monthly fixed costs, which include leasing charges for premises and machinery. He also employs five staff. Figure 3 shows a monthly break-even chart for the business in November. The planned output of pellets for the month is 1,000 tonnes and the margin of safety is also shown on the chart.

Unfortunately there was a machinery breakdown on 12 November and the monthly output was only 700 tonnes. Essential repairs had to be carried out which stopped production for several days.

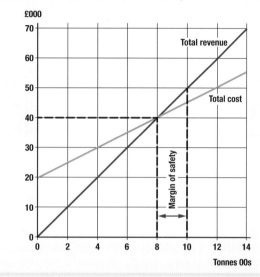

Figure 3

Break-even chart for Gowda Chanda Ltd

Q

(a) What is meant by the margin of safety? (2 marks)

(b) Calculate the price charged for pellets per tonne. (4 marks)

(c) Calculate the variable cost per tonne of pellets. (4 marks)

(d) Explain the impact on Gowda Chanda Ltd of the machinery breakdown. (4 marks)

(e) Assess the usefulness of break-even analysis to Gowda Chanda Ltd. (12 marks)

Key terms

Break-even – when a business generates just enough revenue to cover its total costs

Break-even chart – a graph containing the total cost and total revenue lines, illustrating the break-even output.

Break-even output – the output a business needs to produce so that its total revenue and total costs are the same.

Break-even point – the point at which total revenue and total costs are the same.

Contribution – the amount of money left over after variable costs have been subtracted from revenue. The money contributes towards fixed costs and profit.

Margin of safety – the range of output between the break-even level and the current level of output, over which a profit is made.

Knowledge check

1. A product sells for £10 and the variable costs are £8.50. What is the contribution per unit?

2. A clothes retailer buys 240 jumpers for £27 each. The jumpers are sold for £39 each. What is the total contribution made by the jumpers?

3. If total contribution is £120,000 and fixed costs are £96,000, what is the profit?

4. If total variable costs are £450,000 and contribution is £225,000, what is the total revenue?

5. How can the contribution be used to calculate the break-even level of output?

6. How can the break-even level of output calculation be checked?

7. What effect will a price increase have on the margin of safety?

8. What effect will a fall in fixed costs have on the margin of safety?

9. State three uses of break-even analysis.

10. State three limitations of break-even analysis.

33 Budgets

Key points

1. Purpose of budgets.
2. Types of budget – historical figures and zero-based budgets.
3. Variance analysis.
4. Difficulties of budgeting.

Getting started

Lizzy Bennett runs a hair salon. She likes to keep control of business costs and uses budgets to help her. Table 1 shows the cost budget for a six-month period.

Table 1 A cost budget for Lizzy Bennett's hair salon

	JUL	AUG	SEP	OCT	NOV	DEC	Total
Wages	4,200	4,200	4,200	4,200	4,400	5,000	26,200
Rent	1,400	1,400	1,400	1,400	1,400	1,400	8,400
Materials	450	450	460	460	470	520	2810
Electricity	100	100	110	130	180	200	820
Advertising	500	500	500	500	500	500	3000
Other overheads	300	300	300	310	310	330	1850
Total	6,950	6,950	6,970	7,000	7,260	7,950	43,080

What is the total expected cost of running the business for the six-month period? What is happening to planned costs over the time period? Why might costs be so high in December? How might this cost budget help Lizzy?

Purpose of budgets

A **budget** is a financial plan that is agreed in advance. It must be a plan and not a forecast – a forecast is a prediction of what might happen in the future, whereas a budget is a planned outcome that the firm hopes to achieve. A budget will show the money needed for spending and how this might be financed. Budgets are based on the objectives of businesses. They force managers to think ahead and improve co-ordination. Most budgets are set for twelve months to coincide with the accounting period, but there are exceptions.

Budgets are likely to be used by both large and small businesses. Small business owners often underestimate the importance of financial control when running their businesses and budgeting is a method of control that could easily be employed. This might help avoid problems in the future.

Budgets fulfil the following specific purposes.

Control and monitoring: Budgeting allows management to control the business. It does this by setting objectives and targets. These are then translated into budgets for a particular period; say, the coming year. How successful the business has been in achieving those targets can be found by comparing the actual results with the budget. Any reasons for failing to achieve the budget can then be analysed and appropriate action taken. For more effective control it is helpful to monitor budgets continually. Some businesses produce weekly budgets to allow for swift intervention.

Planning: Budgeting forces management to think ahead. Without budgeting, managers might work on a day-by-day basis, only dealing with opportunities and problems as they arise. Budgeting, however, plans for the future. It anticipates problems and their solutions.

Co-ordination: Larger businesses are often complex organisations. There may be many departments and different operating sites – for instance for production and administration. A multinational company will have sites and workers spread across the world. Budgeting is one way in which managers can co-ordinate and control activities of the many areas of business.

Communication: Planning allows the objectives of the business to be communicated to the workforce. By keeping to a budget, managers and workers have a clear framework within which to operate. So budgeting removes an element of uncertainty within decision-making throughout the business. Budgeting also shows the priorities of the business and highlights costs that need to be kept under control.

Efficiency: In a business with many workers, it becomes important for management to empower staff by delegating decision-making. In a medium to large business, senior management cannot efficiently make every decision on behalf of every employee, department or site. Budgeting gives financial control to lower levels of management who are best able to make decisions at their point within the organisation.

Motivation: Budgeting should act as a motivator to the workforce. It provides workers with targets and standards. Improving on the budget position is an indication of success for a department or group of workers. Fear of failing to reach budgeted targets can be an incentive to the workforce.

Types of budget

Businesses might use a wide range of different budget types. However, some budgets are more frequently used than others. Two key types are the **sales budget** and the **production cost budget**. Budgets are often prepared using **historical figures**. This means that the data used to prepare the budgets is based on data that the business has gathered in the past. Obviously adjustments will be made to take into account future known events, such as planned changes in production or changes in costs or prices. Examples of budgets that make use of historical figures are shown in Table 2.

Table 2 Types of budgets – some examples

Budget	Description
Sales volume	A key budget – shows planned sales levels
Sales revenue	Uses sales volume budget and prices to show planned revenue
Production cost	Based on sales volume budget and shows all planned production costs
Overheads	Shows all planned indirect costs, such as insurance, rent and office wages
Total cost	Shows all planned business costs
Marketing	Shows planned spending on, for example, research, advertising, promotion and sales
R & D	Shows planned expenditure in research and development
Profit	Shows planned revenue, costs and profit
Cash	Shows planned cash inflows and outflows and cash balances
Master	Shows a summary of all budgets – including cost, revenue and profit

Worked examples

Sales volume budget

Table 3 shows a sales volume budget for Emerald Artwork. The company produces four products: AD23, AD24, AE12 and AE13.

Table 3 Sales volume budget for Emerald Artwork

	Feb	Mar	Apr	May
AD23	100	100	100	100
AD24	50	80	80	100
AE12	40	50	40	50
AE13	30	30	50	50

Sales revenue budget

The sales revenue budget for Emerald Artwork is shown in Table 4. The planned sales revenue for each month is calculated by multiplying the planned sales volume by the prices of each product. The prices for AD23, AD24, AE12 and AE13 are £12, £20, £25 and £30 respectively.

Table 4 Sales revenue budget for Emerald Artwork

	Feb	Mar	Apr	May (£)
AD23	1,200 (12 × 100)	1,200 (12 × 100)	1,200 (12 × 100)	1,200 (12 × 100)
AD24	1,000 (20 × 50)	1,600 (20 × 80)	1,600 (20 × 80)	2,000 (20 × 100)
AE12	1,000 (25 × 40)	1,250 (25 × 50)	1,000 (25 × 40)	1,250 (25 × 50)
AE13	900 (30 × 30)	900 (30 × 30)	1,500 (30 × 50)	1,500 (30 × 50)
Total	4,100	4,950	5,300	5,950

Production budget

Emerald Artwork's production costs include materials, direct labour, indirect labour and overheads. Table 5 shows the production cost budget for Emerald Artwork. The budget shows that total production costs are planned to rise over the time period.

Table 5 Production cost budget for Emerald Artwork

	FEB	MAR	APR	MAY (£)
Cost of materials (£3 per unit)	660 (3 × 220)	780 (3 × 260)	810 (3 × 270)	900 (3 × 300)
Direct labour costs (£4 per unit)	880 (4 × 220)	1,040 (4 × 260)	1,080 (4 × 270)	1,200 (4 × 300)
Indirect labour costs (£2 per unit)	440 (2 × 220)	520 (2 × 260)	540 (2 × 270)	600 (2 × 300)
Production overheads (10% of direct & indirect costs)	1,320 × 10% = 132	1,560 × 10% = 156	1,620 × 10% = 162	1,800 × 10% = 180
Total	2,112	2,496	2,592	2,880

Question 1

FibreCraft Ltd produces three types of canoe for the UK market – the Kayak, the Explorer and the Twin-seater. The products sell for £200, £220 and £280 respectively. The financial director produces six-monthly budgets to help control the business. Table 6 shows the sales volume budget for January to June 2014.

Table 6 Sales volume budget for FibreCraft Ltd January–June 2014

	JAN	FEB	MAR	APR	MAY	JUN
Kayak	210	210	210	230	250	300
Explorer	100	100	110	110	120	130
Twin-seater	30	35	35	40	40	50

(a) Prepare the sales revenue budget for FibreCraft Ltd.

(b) Use the sales volume budget to calculate total revenue for each month and for the whole six-month budget period.

(c) What does the budget show over the time period?

Zero-based budget: The financial information used in most budgets is based on historical data. For example, the cost of materials in this year's production budget may be based on last year's figure, with perhaps an allowance for inflation. Production and manufacturing costs, such as labour, raw materials and overheads, are relatively easy to value and tend to be controlled using methods such as standard costing.

However, in some areas of business it is not so easy to quantify costs. Examples might be certain marketing, administration or computer services costs. Where costs cannot be justified then no money is allocated in the budget for those costs. This is known as zero-based budgeting (ZBB) or zero budgeting. A manager must show that a particular item of spending generates an adequate amount of benefit in relation to the general objectives of the business in order for money to be allocated in a budget.

This approach is different to the common practice of extrapolating from past costs. It encourages the regular evaluation of costs and helps to minimise unnecessary purchases. The concept of opportunity cost is linked to ZBB. Opportunity cost is the cost of the next best alternative. When choices are made, businesses try to minimise the opportunity cost. ZBB also involves a cautious approach to spending, so that costs are minimised. Both approaches include an element of 'value for money'.

The main advantages of ZBB are that:
- the allocation of resources should be improved
- a questioning attitude is developed which will help to reduce unnecessary costs and eliminate inefficient practices
- staff motivation might improve because evaluation skills are practised and a greater knowledge of the firm's operations might develop
- it encourages managers to look for alternatives.

ZBB also has some disadvantages.
- It is time-consuming because the budgeting process involves the collection and analysis of quite detailed information so that spending decisions can be made.
- Skilful decision-making is required. Such skills may not be available in the organisation. In addition, decisions may be influenced by subjective opinions.
- It threatens the status quo. This might adversely affect motivation.
- Managers may not be prepared to justify spending on certain costs. Money, therefore, may not be allocated to spending which could benefit the business.

To deal with these possible problems, a business might give each department a 'base' budget of, say, 50 per cent. Departments could then be invited to bid for increased expenditure on a ZBB basis.

Using budgets

Budgetary control or budgeting involves a business using budgets to look into the future, stating what it wants to happen, and then deciding how to achieve these aims. The control process is shown in Figure 1 and explained below.

Preparation of plans: All businesses have objectives. If the sales department increases sales by 10 per cent, how does it know whether or not this is satisfactory? Targets are usually set which allow a business to determine whether its objectives have been met. The results it achieves can then be compared with the targets it sets.

Comparisons of plans with actual results: Control will be effective if information is available as quickly as possible. Managers need budgetary data as soon as it is available. Recent developments in information technology have helped to speed up the supply of data. For budgeting purposes the financial year

has been divided up into smaller control periods – usually four weeks or one calendar month. It is common to prepare a budget for each control period. At the end of the period the actual results can then be compared with targets set in the budget.

Analysis of variances: This is the most important stage in the control process. **Variance analysis** involves trying to find reasons for the differences between actual and expected financial outcomes. Variances are explained in the next section. A variance might be the result of some external factor influencing the business. In this case the business may need to change its business plans and adjust the next budget.

Figure 1

Stages in budgetary control

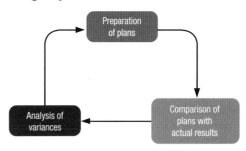

Variances

A **variance** in budgeting is the difference between the figure that the business has budgeted for and the actual figure. Variances are usually calculated at the end of the budget period, as that is when the actual figure will be known.

Variances can be **favourable** (F) or **adverse** (A). Favourable variances occur when the actual figures are 'better' than the budgeted figures.
- If the sales revenue for a month was budgeted at £25,000, but turned out to be £29,000, there would be a £4,000 favourable variance (£29,000 – £25,000) as sales revenue was higher than planned.
- If costs were planned to be £20,000 and turned out to be £18,000, this would also be a favourable variance of £2,000, as actual costs were lower than planned.

Adverse variances are when the actual figures are worse than the budgeted figures. Actual sales revenues may be lower than planned, or actual costs may be higher than planned. Managers will examine variances and try to identify reasons why they have occurred. By doing this they might be able to improve the performance of the business in the future.

Types of variance

Variances can be calculated for a wide range of financial outcomes. Most budgets are set for expenditure (costs) and income (sales revenue). Consequently, variances will also focus on a firm's expenditure and income. This suggests that variance analysis provides a very good way of monitoring business costs. Examples of variances could be wages, materials, overheads and sales revenue. Variances can also be calculated for volumes. For example, it is possible to calculate a sales variance or a labour hours variance. One of the most important variances of all is the profit variance. The profit variance is influenced by all other variances. A change in any variance will affect profit. This is because all variances relate to either the costs or the revenue of a business, both of which affect profit levels. The number of possible variances is equal to the number of factors which can influence business costs and revenue.

Worked example

Table 7 calculates the income variances for Wishart Ltd, a bamboo and wicker furniture manufacturer. Most of the variances are favourable (F) and might be the result of:

- the ability to charge higher prices
- an increase in demand due to a marketing campaign
- improvements in the quality of the product
- an increase in consumer incomes
- a change in consumers' tastes in favour of bamboo and wicker furniture.

Table 7 Income budget, actual income and income variances for Wishart Ltd

	Jan	Feb	Mar	Apr	May	Jun	Total
Budgeted income	16,500	17,000	17,500	18,000	19,000	20,000	108,000
Actual income	16,600	17,400	17,900	17,700	18,500	20,800	108,900
Variance	100F	400F	400F	300A	500A	800F	900F

(£)

Worked example

Table 8 calculates the expenditure or cost variances for Wishart Ltd. Most of these variances are adverse (A) – possibly because:

- costs might be higher due to production being higher
- suppliers may have raised prices
- there may be some inefficiencies in production
- wages may have been higher due to wage demands by workers.

Table 8 Budgeted expenditure, actual expenditure and expenditure variances for Wishart Ltd

	Jan	Feb	Mar	Apr	May	Jun	Total
Budgeted expenditure	11,400	11,900	12,500	13,000	14,000	15,000	77,800
Actual expenditure	11,500	11,600	12,700	13,500	14,200	15,600	79,100
Expenditure variances	100A	300F	200A	500A	200A	600A	1,300A

(£)

Worked example

Table 9 calculates the profit variances for Wishart Ltd. Over the six-month period the variance is adverse – mainly because costs have been higher than planned.

Table 9 Budgeted profit, actual profit and profit variances for Wishart Ltd

	Jan	Feb	Mar	Apr	May	Jun	Total
Budgeted profit	5,100	5,100	5,000	5,000	5,000	5,000	30,200
Actual profit	5,100	5,800	5,200	4,200	4,300	5,200	29,800
Profit variances	0	700F	200F	800A	700A	200F	400A

(£)

Question 2

Gerrard & Co repairs, maintains and services agricultural machinery for farmers in the Norfolk area. The business has a workshop in Swaffham but also does 'call-out' work to fix tractors, combine harvesters and other farm machinery on location. Table 10 shows the income (sales revenue) budget and actual income for the business between January and June 2014.

Table 10 Income budget and actual income for Gerrard & Co January–June 2014

	JAN	FEB	MAR	APR	MAY	JUN
Budgeted income (£)	100,000	110,000	120,000	125,000	140,000	175,000
Actual income (£)	90,000	110,000	128,000	129,000	152,000	197,000

(a) Calculate the sales revenue variances for each month and the total sales revenue variance for the whole budget period.

(b) Explain the variance in February.

(c) Explain two possible reasons for the pattern of variances over the six-month time period.

Using variances for decision making

The final stage in budgetary control is the analysis of variances. It is important to identify the reasons why variances have occurred. If variances are adverse it will be necessary to take action to ensure that adverse variances are avoided in future. If variances are favourable the business can learn from understanding the reasons why this has occurred and can introduce strategies and systems to help sustain performance improvements in the future.

When making decisions about how the business should be run, information about the causes of variances will be very helpful. For example, if a business has an adverse cost variance, it might discover that the cause was higher prices charged by suppliers. The business might then decide to look for new suppliers. A favourable sales revenue variance might be the result of an effective advertising campaign. The business might decide to make more use of the same or similar campaigns in the future. Variance analysis can help business decision-makers because of the information it provides about financial outcomes and their causes.

Difficulties of budgeting

Businesses may encounter problems when setting budgets and using them as tools for financial management.

Setting budgets:

- Problems may arise because figures in budgets are not actual figures. The figures are plans based on historical data, forecasts or human judgement. A business might simply take historical data and add an arbitrary percentage to arrive at the budgeted value.
- The most important data in the preparation of nearly all budgets is sales data. If sales data are inaccurate, many of the firm's budgets will be inexact.
- The setting of budgets may lead to conflict between departments or staff. A business may only have limited funds and departments compete against each other for those funds. For instance, the marketing department may want to promote a product, but new machinery may be needed in the R&D department.
- The time spent setting budgets could have been spent on other tasks. For example, sales managers could be securing new customers and increasing revenue for the business instead of drawing up this year's budget.

Sometimes businesses set over-ambitious objectives. When this happens, the budgeting process is pointless because budgets are being drawn up for targets that are unachievable. The budget then ceases to become a benchmark with which to compare the outcome.

Motivation: In some businesses, workers are left out of the planning process. If workers are not consulted about the budget, it could be difficult to use that budget to motivate them. Budgets that are unrealistic can also fail to motivate staff.

Manipulation: Budgets can be manipulated by managers. For example, a departmental manager might have great influence over those co-ordinating and setting budgets. The manager may be able to set a budget that is easy to achieve and consequently makes the department look successful, but ultimately that budget might not help the business achieve its objectives.

Rigidity: Budgets can sometimes constrain business activities. For instance, departments within a business may have different views about when to replace delivery vehicles. The more often vehicles are replaced, the higher the cost. However, the newer the vehicle, the lower the maintenance cost and the less likely it will be off the road for repairs. The budget may be set so that older vehicles have to be kept rather than replaced. But this may lead to customer dissatisfaction and lost orders because deliveries are unreliable.

Short-termism: Some managers might be too focused on the current budget. They might take actions that undermine the future performance of the business just to meet current budget targets. For example, to keep labour costs down in the current budget period, the manager of a supermarket might reduce staffing on customer service. This may well save costs now, but it could lead to customers drifting away due to poor service. Consequently the long-term performance of the business would suffer.

Key terms

Budget – a quantitative economic plan prepared and agreed in advance.
Budgetary control – a business system that involves making future plans, comparing the actual results with the planned results and then investigating the causes of any differences.
Historical figures – quantitative information based on past trading records.
Production cost budget – a firm's planned production costs for a future period of time.
Sales budget – a firm's planned sales for a future period of time – can be measured in terms of volume or revenue.
Variance – the difference between actual financial outcomes and those budgeted.
Variance analysis – the process of calculating variances and attempting to identify their causes.
Zero-based budgeting or **zero budgeting** – a system of budgeting where no money is allocated for costs or spending unless they can be justified by the fund holder (they are given a zero value).

Case study

BUYAMOTORJON.COM

The website buyamotorjon.com is an online business that brings together buyers and sellers of second-hand cars. The business charges car owners a fixed price to list their cars for sale on the site for two weeks. Anyone searching to buy a car can use the site free of charge. The business also earns a growing stream of income from selling advertising space on the site.

In 2012 the directors took a decision to incorporate and develop a comparison site for second-hand cars. However, the decision was not unanimous because two of the directors thought that the level of expenditure needed to develop and launch the site was too high. They also thought that competition would be tough. Table 11 shows the budgeted expenditure, revenue and profit for 2012–2016 and the actual figures for 2012–2014.

Table 11 Budgeted expenditure, costs and profit, and actual figures 2012–2014 (£ million)

	2012	2013	2014	2015	2016
Budgeted income	2.14	2.2	2.6	3	3.8
Actual income	**2.13**	**2.14**	**2.22**		
Budgeted expenditure	1.99	2.11	2.01	2.01	2.1
Actual expenditure	**2.01**	**2.21**	**2.3**		
Budgeted profit	0.15	0.09	0.59	0.99	1.7
Actual profit	**0.12**	**−0.07**	**−0.08**		

(a) What is meant by a variance? (2 marks)

(b) Calculate the income, expenditure and profit variances for 2012, 2013 and 2014 for buyamotorjon.com. (6 marks)

(c) Explain the possible impact of the new comparison site on buyamotorjon.com. (8 marks)

(d) Assess the usefulness to buyamotorjon.com of using variance analysis. (12 marks)

Knowledge check

1. How might a budget improve managerial accountability?
2. Why is the sales budget such an important budget?
3. How might budgets motivate staff?
4. Give examples of three types of budget.
5. Why might a business use zero-based budgeting?
6. Describe the three steps in budgetary control.
7. How is a variance calculated?
8. What is meant by an adverse variance?
9. State two possible causes of a favourable sales revenue variance.
10. State two possible causes of an adverse cost variance.
11. State four benefits of using budgets.

34 Profit

Key points

1. Calculation of gross profit, operating profit and profit for the year (net profit).
2. Statement of comprehensive income (profit and loss account).
3. Measuring profitability – calculation of gross profit margin, operating profit margin and profit for the year (net profit) margin.
4. Ways to improve profitability.
5. Distinction between profit and cash.

Getting started

Halfords is the UK's leading retailer of automotive and cycling products. It is also the main operator in garage servicing and auto repair in the UK. In 2014 it was reported that the business made a profit after tax of £55.5 million on a turnover/revenue of £939.7 million. This was an increase on 2013 when turnover was £871.3 million and profit after tax was £52.7 million. The sales of cycles did particularly well during the year, rising by 21 per cent.

Source: adapted from www.halfordscompany.com

Calculate the percentage change in turnover between 2013 and 2014. Calculate the percentage change in profit between 2013 and 2014. What might account for the differences in these percentages? What measures might Halfords take to improve its profitability in the future?

Exam tip

The accounting ratios in the Edexcel specification use the term 'profit for the year (net profit)'. In business, you might see the terms 'profit for the year (net profit)' or 'net profit' used interchangeably. The accounting ratios in the Edexcel specification use the term 'revenue'. In business, you might see the terms 'revenue' or 'turnover' used interchangeably.

Profit

As explained in Unit 31, if total costs are subtracted from total revenue you arrive at a business's profit. This is the money left over after all costs have been met, and belongs to the owners of the business. Accountants calculate and define profit in a number of ways.

Gross profit: Gross profit is the difference between revenue/turnover and cost of sales.

- Turnover, also called revenue or sales revenue, can be calculated as price × quantity of sales.
- Cost of sales are the direct costs of a business.
- Gross profit is the profit made by a business after direct costs have been met.

For a retailer or wholesaler the cost of sales is the cost of buying in stock to re-sell. For a manufacturer the cost of sales is any costs associated directly with production, such as raw materials, factory wages and other direct costs. For a supplier of services it is any direct costs, such as direct labour.

Gross profit is calculated by:

Gross profit = Revenue − Cost of sales

Operating profit: Operating profit is the difference between gross profit and business overheads. Overheads are indirect costs, such as selling and administrative expenses. Operating profit is calculated by:

Operating profit = Gross profit − Operating expenses

Profit for the year (net profit): Net profit or profit for the year is the profit made by the business for the year. It is the difference between operating profit and interest and any other exceptional costs. Net profit may be calculated before or after the subtraction of taxation. It is calculated by:

Profit for the year (net profit) = Operating profit − Interest (and exceptional costs)

Sometimes net interest is shown in the statement of comprehensive income. This is the difference between any interest paid by a business (on loans and overdrafts, for example) and any interest received by the business (from money placed in deposit accounts, for example).

Worked example

HLD plc is a large paper manufacturer. In 2014 its turnover was £46 million. Its cost of sales was £23.5 million, operating expenses £12.4 million and interest paid £2.1 million. What was the gross profit, operating profit and net profit?

Gross profit   = Revenue/turnover − Cost of sales
     = £46 million − £23.5 million
     = £22.5 million

Operating profit   = Gross profit − Operating expenses
     = £22.5 million − £12.4 million
     = £10.1 million

Profit for the year = Operating profit − Interest (and any
(net profit)   exceptional items)
     = £10.1 million − £2.1 million
     = £8 million

Question 1

Weston Manor Hotel is an established and successful four-star hotel in Somerset. It has 43 rooms, employs 42 staff and its restaurant has a reputation for fine dining. Some financial information for the hotel for 2014 and 2013 is shown in Table 1.

Table 1 Financial information for Weston Manor Hotel

	2014	2013
Revenue/turnover	£2,341,700	£2,600,700
Cost of sales	£1,090,000	£980,500
Administration expenses	£399,100	£388,900
Interest	£21,000	£19,300

(a) Calculate: (i) gross profit, (ii) operating profit, (iii) profit for the year (net profit) for 2014 and 2013.

(b) Calculate the percentage change in net profit between 2013 and 2014.

Statement of comprehensive income (profit and loss account)

At the end of the trading year, businesses produce documents that show key information relating to the financial performance of the business. One of these documents is the **statement of comprehensive income**. This shows the income and expenses of a business during the financial year. It is used to calculate gross profit, operating profit and profit for the year (net profit). The layout of the statement is important. The financial information must be presented in a standard way. An example from a statement for Forest Way Autotraders Ltd, a second-hand car dealership, is shown in Table 2.

Table 2 Selected information from the statement of comprehensive income for Forest Way Autotraders Ltd for the year ending 31.1.14

	2014 (£)	2013 (£)
Revenue/turnover	561,000	498,200
Cost of sales	331,000	322,100
Gross profit	230,000	176,100
Selling expenses	45,300	38,200
Admin expenses	122,500	102,800
Operating profit	62,200	35,100
Interest	22,100	21,000
Profit for the year (net profit)	40,100	14,100
Taxation	8,000	2,800
Profit for the year (net profit) after tax	32,100	11,300

The statement always shows the figures for the current trading year and the previous year. This allows a comparison to be made. In this case, the statement shows that net profit before tax has increased from £14,100 to £40,100. This is a significant increase, probably because turnover has increased quite sharply. The statement in Table 2 also shows the taxation paid by the business and the net profit after tax. Statements of comprehensive income are discussed in more detail in Unit 60.

Question 2

AppGame Ltd is a new, but growing, company. It designs children's game apps on mobile phones. During 2014 the company had some staff shortages and invested in an expensive recruitment campaign. Selected information from the statement of comprehensive income for AppGame Ltd is shown in Table 3 (three figures are missing).

Table 3 Selected information from the statement of comprehensive income for AppGame Ltd, year ending 31.12.14

	2014 (£m)	2013 (£m)
Revenue/turnover	6.444	5.871
Cost of sales	4.191	3.713
Gross profit	?	2.158
Selling expenses	1.223	1.112
Admin expenses	?	0.211
Operating profit	0.796	0.835
Interest	?	0.216
Profit for the year (net profit)	0.595	0.619
Taxation	0.120	0.121
Profit for the year (net profit) after taxation	0.475	0.498

(a) What is meant by a statement of comprehensive income?

(b) Calculate the missing figures in the statement for AppGame Ltd.

(c) Assess the possible impact on AppGame Ltd of the staff shortages in 2014.

Measuring profitability

The information contained in the statement of comprehensive income can show how well a business is performing. As mentioned earlier, in Table 2 the statement for Forest Way Autotraders Ltd shows that net profit for the year has increased from £14,100 to £40,100. This is a significant increase. However, it is possible to measure the profitability of a business in a more meaningful way. This can be done by calculating profit margins, which measure the size of profit in relation to revenue/turnover. Three profit margins can be calculated.

Gross profit margin: The **gross profit margin** shows the gross profit made on sales turnover/revenue. It is calculated using the formula:

$$\text{Gross profit margin} = \frac{\text{Gross profit}}{\text{Revenue}} \times 100\%$$

Higher gross margins are usually preferable to lower ones because it means that more gross profit is being made per £1 of sales. The gross profit margin:

- may be increased by raising revenue/turnover relative to the cost of sales, by increasing price
- may be increased by cutting the cost of sales; this might be achieved by finding cheaper suppliers of key materials
- will vary between different industries. As a rule, the quicker the turnover of inventory, the lower the gross margin that is needed. So, for example, a supermarket with a fast stock turnover is likely to have a lower gross margin than a car retailer with a

much slower stock (inventory) turnover. Some supermarkets are therefore very successful with relatively low gross profit margins because of the regular and fast turnover of inventory.

Operating profit margin: The operating profit margin shows the operating profit made on sales revenue/turnover. Operating margin is used to measure a company's pricing strategy and operating efficiency. It gives an idea of how much a company makes (before interest and taxes) on each pound of sales. It is calculated using the formula:

$$\text{Operating profit margin} = \frac{\text{Operating profit}}{\text{Revenue}} \times 100\%$$

A high or increasing operating margin is preferred. This is because more money is made on each £1 of sales. If the operating margin is increasing, the company is earning more per pound of sales. Operating margin shows the profitability of sales resulting from regular business. Operating income results from ordinary business operations and excludes other revenue or losses, exceptional items, interest and income taxes.

Profit for the year (net profit) margin: The net profit margin takes into account all business costs, including interest, other non-operating costs and exceptional items. It is usually calculated before tax has been deducted.

The profit for the year (net profit) margin can be calculated by:

$$\text{Profit for the year (net profit) margin} = \frac{\text{Net profit before tax}}{\text{Revenue}} \times 100\%$$

Worked example

On the previous page, Table 2 shows the income statement for Forest Way Autotraders Ltd. The profit margins for 2014 can be calculated as follows.

$$\text{Gross profit margin} = \frac{\text{Gross Profit} \times 100\%}{\text{Revenue}} = \frac{£230,000 \times 100\%}{£561,000} = \textbf{41\%}$$

$$\text{Operating profit margin} = \frac{\text{Operating profit} \times 100\%}{\text{Revenue}} = \frac{£62,200}{£561,000} = \textbf{11.1\%}$$

$$\text{Profit for the year (net profit) margin} = \frac{\text{Net profit (before tax)} \times 100\%}{\text{Revenue}} = \frac{£40,100}{£561,000} = \textbf{7.1\%}$$

Table 4 provides a summary of the profit margins for both 2014 and 2013. Over the two years there is a clear improvement in all of the profit margins. This suggests that the business has performed well – improving efficiency and possibly raising prices.

Table 4 Profit margins for Forest Way Autotraders Ltd 2014 and 2013

	2014	2013
Gross profit margin	41%	35.3%
Operating profit margin	11.1%	7%
Profit for the year (net profit) margin	7.1%	2.8%

Again, higher margins are usually better than lower ones. The profit for the year (net profit) margin focuses on the profit left after all deductions have been made.

Question 3

Chapperton Ltd develops wearable technology. UK shoppers spent around £105 million on wearable tech devices during the Christmas shopping period in 2014, a massive increase of 182 per cent compared to the previous year. Fitness and activity trackers are the most popular wearable devices, accounting for over £29 million, followed by smart watches at £25 million, healthcare wearable devices at £22 million, and the remainder on other wearable devices. Table 5 shows the company's statement of comprehensive income at 31 March 2014.

Table 5 Selected information from the statement of comprehensive income for Chapperton Ltd 31.03.14

	2014 £000s	2013 £000s
Revenue/turnover	7,800	5,700
Cost of sales	3,780	2,100
Gross profit	4,020	3,600
Admin expenses	1,560	1,800
Operating profit	2,460	1,800
Interest	70	45
Profit for the year (net profit)	2,390	1,755
Taxation	580	450
Profit for the year (net profit) after tax	1,810	1,305

(a) Explain the difference between the gross profit margin and the profit for the year (net profit) margin.

(b) Calculate the gross, operating and profit for the year (net profit) margins for 2013 and 2014. Present the information in a table.

(c) Assess the financial performance of Chapperton Ltd in 2014.

Ways to improve profitability

All businesses will want to improve their performance. An improved performance is likely to benefit all stakeholders. The returns on capital can be increased by making more profit with the same level of investment. This might be achieved by growth funded externally. This means the business increases sales using fresh capital.

Increasing profit margins will also improve performance. If profit margins can be raised, the business will make more profit at the existing level of sales. The profit margins can be improved in two ways.

Raising prices: If a business raises its price it will get more revenue for every unit sold. If costs remain the same then profitability should improve. However, raising price might have an impact on the level of sales. Generally, when price is raised demand will fall. However, if demand is not too responsive to changes in price, the increase in price will generate more revenue even though fewer units are sold. Raising price is always risky because it is never certain how competitors will react.

Lowering costs: A business can also raise profit margins by lowering its costs. It can do this by buying cheaper resources or using the existing resources more effectively.

- **Buying cheaper resources.** It might be possible to buy raw materials and components from new suppliers that offer better prices. It may also be possible to find new providers of essential services such as telecommunications, electricity, insurance and IT support. For example, there has been increased competition recently in the supply of gas, electricity and telecommunications. Another option might be to find ways of using cheaper labour. For example, some businesses have moved overseas to take advantage of cheap labour in places like China and eastern Europe. However, these measures may have drawbacks. When taking on new suppliers the possibility that they are cheaper because they are not as good should be considered. The quality of raw materials might be inferior, they may be unreliable and supply might not be guaranteed. For example, a number of new, and cheaper, broadband providers have not been able to

guarantee supply. Moving abroad to take advantage of cheap labour may be disruptive. It may also damage the image of the company if it lays off large numbers of staff in the UK. Consequently, when looking to acquire cheaper resources, a business must be cautious and understand the pitfalls.

- **Using existing resources more efficiently.** Making better use of current resources will improve efficiency and lower costs. A business might do this by introducing new working practices or training staff. This would help to raise labour productivity. It could upgrade its machinery by acquiring newer, more efficient models. This would raise capital productivity. A business might be able to reduce waste by recycling materials, for example. Some of these measures might also have drawbacks. For example, the workers might resist new working practices and new technology often has teething problems. This could disrupt the business.

Distinction between cash and profit

It is important for businesses to recognise the difference between cash and profit. At the end of a trading year it is unlikely that the value of profit will be the same as the cash balance. Differences between cash and profit can arise for a number of reasons.

- During the trading year a business might sell £200,000 worth of goods with total costs of £160,000. Its profit would be £40,000. However, if some goods had been sold on credit, payment by certain customers may not yet have been received. If £12,000 was still owing, the amount of cash the business had would be £28,000 (£40,000 − £12,000). Thus, profit is greater than cash.
- A business may receive cash at the beginning of the trading year from sales made in the previous year. This would increase the cash balance, but would not affect profit. In addition, the business may buy resources from suppliers and not pay for them until the next trading year. As a result its trading costs will not be the same as cash paid out.
- Sometimes the owners might introduce more cash into the business. This will increase the cash balance, but will have no effect on the profit made. This is because the introduction of capital is not treated as business revenue in the profit and loss account. The effect will be the same if a business borrows money from a bank.
- Purchases of fixed assets will reduce cash balances, but will have no effect on the profit a company makes. This is because the purchase of assets is not treated as a business cost in the profit and loss account.
- Sales of fixed assets will increase cash balances but will have no effect on profit unless a profit or loss is made on disposal of the asset. This is because the cash from the sale of a fixed asset is not included in business turnover.
- The amount of cash at the end of the year will be different from profit because at the beginning of the year the cash balance is unlikely to be zero. If, at the beginning of the year, the cash balance for a business is £23,000, then the amount of cash a business has at the end of the year will exceed profit by £23,000.

Case study

SALWELL

Leeds-based Salwell plc is a world leader in reinforced polymer technology. It employs over 5,000 people and serves markets all over the world. Since 2007 the company has grown its revenue by around 57 per cent. However, in 2014 revenue actually fell a little. This may have been due to slower than expected economic growth in emerging markets, such as China and India.

In 2015, Salwell plc experienced a further reduction in turnover and profits. This was due mainly to a slowdown in demand for one of the components that they produce that is normally one of their biggest sellers. As a result, factory staff were put on a shorter working week for much of the year. In 2015, Salwell's chief executive officer suggested that the weakness in the mining market, caused by political and economic uncertainties, might undermine the strength and resilience of their businesses. Table 6 shows an extract from the statement of comprehensive income for Salwell plc.

Table 6 Salwell plc – extract from statement of comprehensive income for 2014

	2014 (£m)	2013 (£m)
Revenue/turnover	650.3	670.7
Cost of sales	443.1	442.8
Gross profit	**207.2**	**227.9**
Distribution costs	51.0	51.3
Admin expenses	89.2	79.7
Operating profit*	**67.0**	**96.9**
Net interest**	13.9	15.1
Profit for the year (net profit)	**53.1**	**81.8**
Taxation	14.8	20.8
Profit for the year (net profit) after taxation	**38.3**	**61.0**

Operating profit* – after amortisation of costs resulting from acquisitions

Net interest** = Interest paid – Interest received

Q

(a) Calculate the gross profit margin for Salwell plc in 2014 and 2013. (4 marks)

(b) Calculate the profit for the year (net profit) margin for Salwell plc in 2014 and 2013. (4 marks)

(c) Assess the impact on Salwell plc of difficult global trading conditions. (8 marks)

(d) Assess the measures a company like Salwell plc might take to improve profitability. (12 marks)

Key terms

Amortisation – the writing off of an intangible asset.
Cost of sales – the direct costs of a business.
Exceptional costs – a one-off cost, such as a large bad debt.
Gross profit – the difference between revenue/turnover and cost of sales.
Gross profit margin – gross profit expressed as a percentage of revenue/turnover.
Operating profit – the difference between gross profit and business overheads, such as selling and administrative expenses.
Operating profit margin – operating profit expressed as a percentage of revenue/turnover.
Profit for the year (net profit) or net profit – the difference between operating profit and interest and exceptional items.
Profit for the year (net profit) margin or net profit margin – net profit before tax, expressed as a percentage of revenue/turnover.
Statement of comprehensive income – a financial document showing a company's income and expenditure over a particular time period, usually one year.
Revenue or turnover – the total income of a business resulting from sales of goods or services.

Knowledge check

1. How is gross profit calculated?

2. If operating profit is £32 million and interest is £670,000, what is the profit for the year (net profit)?

3. What is meant by the 'bottom line'?

4. What does a statement of comprehensive income show?

5. What does the operating profit margin measure?

6. What is the profit for the year (net profit) margin if revenue is £128,000 and profit for the year (net profit) is £18,000?

7. State two ways a business might increase its gross profit margin.

8. State two ways a business might lower its costs.

9. Describe briefly the difference between cash and profit.

10. State two reasons why profit may be higher than cash.

Key points

1. Statement of financial position (balance sheet):
   - measuring liquidity – calculating current ratio and acid test ratio
   - ways to improve liquidity.
2. Working capital and its management: the importance of cash.

Getting started

To run a business effectively it must have enough money to pay its day-to-day bills, such as wages, raw materials, fuel and overheads. This money is called working capital. In 2014 a shortage of working capital resulted in the closure of Tyneside Autobuy Ltd with the loss of 48 jobs. According to media sources, the Creditors Report stated that the shortage of working capital was caused by poor cost controls and excessive overheads. The Gosforth-based used-car supermarket was also reported by administrators to have been making losses since 2010, despite turnover/revenue of nearly £23 million in 2014. Prior to its closure in July, the company had struggled to make payments to a supplier. In June, corporate finance specialists were brought in to prepare a short-term cash-flow forecast for the business and found that a substantial working capital investment was needed to continue. Unable to raise this, the firm was put up for sale. However, prospective buyers failed to make a deal with the landlords of Autobuy's premises, Autoparc, and the business went into administration.

Source: adapted from www.chroniclelive.co.uk

Why do businesses need working capital? What might be the consequences of not having enough working capital? Why did Tyneside Autobuy Ltd have insufficient working capital? What measures might have avoided the closure of Tyneside Autobuy Ltd?

Statement of financial position (balance sheet)

Many businesses produce a **statement of financial position** at the end of the financial year. This document can also be called a **balance sheet**. It is like a photograph of the financial position of a business at a particular point in time. It provides a summary of its **assets**, **liabilities** and **capital**.

- **Assets.** The resources owned by a business. Examples include buildings, machinery, equipment, vehicles, stock and cash. Businesses use assets to make products or provide services.
- **Liabilities.** The debts of the business, in other words what it owes to others. Liabilities are a source of funds for a business. They might be short term, such as an overdraft, or long term, such as a mortgage.
- **Capital.** The money put into the business by the owners. Along with other sources of finance it is used to buy assets.

In a statement of financial position, the value of assets (what a business uses or owns) will equal the value of liabilities and capital (what the business owes). This is because all resources purchased by a business have to be financed from either capital or liabilities. Therefore:

Assets = Capital + Liabilities

So, if a business has capital of £5 million and liabilities of £2.6 million, the value of assets must be £7.6 million (£5 million + £2.6 million).

Question 1

Britvic is the second largest soft drinks producer in the United Kingdom. Although most of its operations are concentrated in the UK and Ireland, the company's international arm is expanding and it now exports to over 50 countries. In 2013 the value of its assets was £1,062.8 million and its total liabilities were £1,021.9 million.

(a) Give two examples of assets that Britvic might own.

(b) Explain the difference between liabilities and capital.

(c) Calculate the value of capital for Britvic in 2013.

The presentation of the statement of financial position (balance sheet)

The presentation of these statements varies between different businesses. For example, the statement of financial position for a limited company is likely to be slightly different from that of a sole trader. Table 1 shows a statement of financial position for Kingham plc, a chain store selling clothes and fashion accessories. The structure of this statement is fairly typical. Information is presented in a vertical fashion, with assets at the top and liabilities and equity at the bottom.

Non-current assets: Non-current assets are long-term resources that will be used repeatedly by the business over a period of time. They may be called fixed assets. Common examples include land, property, plant, equipment, tools, vehicles, and fixtures and fittings. Intangible assets are also included in this category. These are non-physical assets, such as customer lists, franchising agreements and brand names. These are discussed in more detail in Unit 60.

Current assets: Current assets are assets that will be changed into cash within 12 months. They are liquid assets. The liquidity of an asset is how easily it can be converted into cash. Common examples include:

- inventories, such as stocks of raw materials, components and finished goods
- trade and other receivables, which relate to money that is owed to the business. Examples might be debtors (the money owed by customers) and prepayments (where a business has paid in advance for a resource, such as an insurance premium)
- cash or cash equivalents, which usually refers to cash on the business premises and money held in bank accounts.

Current liabilities: Any money owed by a business that must be repaid within one year is called a current liability. Examples include:

- loans and other borrowings, which include short-term bank loans and bank overdrafts
- trade and other payables, which refer to money owed by the business to suppliers of raw materials, components, business services and utilities. These are sometimes called trade creditors
- current tax liabilities. A business is likely to owe money to the tax authorities. This might include employees' income tax, VAT and corporation tax. Tax must be paid within one year.

Non-current liabilities: Non-current liabilities relate to long-term loans and any other money owed by the business that does not have to be repaid for at least one year. Long-term bank loans, mortgages and company pension funds are examples.

Net assets: net assets are calculated by subtracting the value of total liabilities from total assets. This will be equal to shareholders' equity at the bottom of the balance sheet.

Table 1 Statement of financial position for Kingham plc 2014

	2014 (£m)	2013 (£m)
Non-current assets		
Property and equipment	176.5	189.3
Intangible assets	45.2	41.6
	221.7	230.9
Current assets		
Inventories	32.1	28.3
Trade and other receivables	7.3	6.8
Cash and cash equivalents	3.1	6.2
	42.5	41.3
Total assets	**264.2**	**272.2**
Current liabilities		
Trade and other payables	25.6	24.9
Current tax liabilities	11.1	10.5
	36.7	35.4
Non-current liabilities		
Loans	24.5	26.1
Pensions	7.8	6.7
	32.3	32.8
Total liabilities	**69.0**	**68.2**
Net assets	**195.2**	**204.0**
Shareholders' equity		
Share capital	25.0	25.0
Retained earnings	170.2	179.0
Total equity	**195.2**	**204.0**

Shareholders' equity: The final section of the balance sheet is the shareholders' equity. This provides a summary of what is owed to the owners of the business. Share capital and retained earnings (retained profit) are common examples.

The statement of financial position can be used in a number of ways, which is discussed in more detail in Unit 60.

Maths tip

In some financial statements figures may be shown in brackets. This just means that they are negative or should be subtracted.

Measuring liquidity

Information contained in the balance sheet can be used to measure the liquidity of a business. It is important that a business is able to meet its short-term debts. This means a business must have enough liquid resources to pay its immediate bills. Failure to do so could result in the financial collapse of the business. Two financial ratios can be used to measure liquidity.

Current ratio: The current ratio is a liquidity ratio and focuses on the current assets and current liabilities of a business. It can be calculated using the formula:

$$\text{Current ratio} = \frac{\text{Current assets}}{\text{Current liabilities}}$$

A business is generally regarded as having sufficient liquid resources if the current ratio is between 1.5:1 and 2:1. If the current ratio is below 1.5 it could be argued that the business does not have enough working capital. This might mean that a business is over-borrowing or overtrading. However, some businesses, such as retailers, often have very low current ratios, perhaps 1:1 or below. This is because they hold fast-selling stocks and generate cash from sales. In contrast, operating above a ratio of 2:1 may suggest that too much money is tied up unproductively. Money tied up in stocks, for example, does not earn any return.

Acid test ratio: The **acid test ratio** is a more severe test of liquidity. This is because inventories (stocks) are not treated as liquid resources. There is no guarantee that stocks can be sold and they may become obsolete or deteriorate. They are therefore excluded from current assets when calculating the ratio. The acid test ratio can be calculated using the formula:

$$\text{Acid test ratio} = \frac{\text{Current assets} - \text{Inventories}}{\text{Current liabilities}}$$

If a business has an acid test ratio of less than 1:1 it means that its current assets minus stocks do not cover its current liabilities. This could indicate a potential problem. However, as with the current ratio, there is considerable variation between the typical acid test ratios of businesses in different industries. Again, retailers with strong cash flows may operate comfortably with an acid test ratio of less than 1.

Worked example

Current and acid test ratios can be used to measure the liquidity of Kingham plc. The information needed is contained in the balance sheet in Table 1 for 2014.

$$\text{Current ratio} = \frac{\text{Current assets}}{\text{Current liabilities}} = \frac{\pounds42.5\,\text{m}}{\pounds36.7\,\text{m}} = 1.16$$

$$\text{Acid test ratio} = \frac{\text{Current assets} - \text{Inventories}}{\text{Current liabilities}}$$

$$= \frac{\pounds42.5\,\text{m} - \pounds32.1\,\text{m}}{36.7\,\text{m}} = \frac{\pounds10.4\,\text{m}}{\pounds36.7\,\text{m}} = 0.28$$

Table 2 provides a summary of the liquidity ratios for Kingham plc. It could be argued that in 2014 both ratios are on the low side. The current ratio is below 1.5 and the acid test ratio is well below 1. This could mean that the business is short of liquid resources. The position has also worsened over the two years. The acid test ratio in particular has fallen significantly. However, Kingham plc is a chain store selling clothes. Most of its sales will be for cash so it may well be able to operate with much lower liquidity ratios.

Table 2 Liquidity ratios for Kingham plc 2013 and 2014

	2014	2013
Current ratio	1.16	1.17
Acid test ratio	0.28	0.37

Question 2

Simpsons Ltd is a family business based in Coventry. It produces components for the car industry. It has been struggling to control inventories. Simpsons' customers insist that they supply products just-in-time (at very short notice) and as a result the burden of storage lies with Simpsons. Some financial information for Simpsons Ltd is shown in Table 3.

Table 3 Financial information for Simpsons Ltd

	2014 (£m)	2013 (£m)	2012 (£m)
Inventories	34.2	28.3	27.8
Trade and other receivables	12.4	11.2	13.8
Cash and cash equivalents	5.7	3.1	4.9
Loans and other borrowings	14.2	16.2	13.1
Trade and other payables	11.9	13.1	10.7
Current tax liabilities	4.1	5.2	4.2

(a) Calculate the current ratios and acid test ratios for Simpsons Ltd between 2012 and 2014.

(b) Assess whether Simpsons Ltd has enough liquid assets.

What is working capital?

Working capital, sometimes called circulating capital, is the amount of money needed to pay for the day-to-day trading of a business. A business needs working capital to pay expenses such as wages, electricity and gas charges, and to buy components to make products. The working capital of a business is the amount left over after all current debts have been paid. It is:

- the relatively liquid assets of a business that can easily be turned into cash (cash itself, inventories, the money owing from debtors who have bought goods or services); *minus*
- the money owed by a business which needs to be paid in the short term (to the bank, to creditors who have supplied goods or services, to government in the form of tax or shareholders' dividends payable within the year).

In the balance sheet of a company, working capital is calculated by subtracting current liabilities from current assets:

Working capital = Current assets − Current liabilities

The amount of working capital a business has is an important issue. It can reflect how well a business is performing. For example, a business that is struggling and threatened with closure is likely to have low levels of working capital. Consequently, if a balance sheet shows a low level of working capital, this should act as a signal that the business may be in trouble.

Managing working capital
Different businesses have different working capital needs.

Size of business. Sales typically generate a need for stocks, trade credit and cash. Hence the larger the business, the larger the amount of working capital there is likely to be. Equally, expanding businesses are likely to need growing amounts of working capital.

Stock levels. Businesses in different industries have different needs for stocks. A window cleaning business is unlikely to carry much stock. A retailer is likely to carry considerable amounts of stock. Businesses which are able to adopt just-in-time techniques will carry lower stocks than other businesses. The more stocks a business needs, the higher will be its working capital, all other things being equal.

Debtors and creditors. The time between buying stock financed by trade credit and selling finished products can influence levels of working capital. For example, a builder may need high levels of working capital because the time between starting a project and receiving payment from the client may be long.

At the other extreme, large supermarket chains can often operate with negative working capital (i.e. the current assets are less than their current liabilities). This happens because they buy in stock from suppliers and do not pay them for at least 30 days. The stock though is sold quickly on supermarket shelves, often within days of delivery from suppliers. Customers pay cash. So large supermarket chains can operate safely owing suppliers large amounts, but having very few debtors. The result is negative working capital.

Few businesses are fortunate enough to be able to operate with negative working capital. The textbook rule is that the typical business needs around twice the amount of current assets as current liabilities to operate safely. This means that its current ratio is between 1.5:1 and 2:1. This is how we can measure whether the business is performing effectively with regard to working capital.

Maintaining adequate levels of working capital:
Businesses need to keep adequate levels of working capital. If they keep too little (i.e. current assets are too low and current liabilities are too high) they will start to encounter trading problems.
- If a business does not carry enough stocks of raw materials, it could find that production is halted when items run out of stock. If it does not carry enough finished stock, it might be unable to fulfil orders on time.
- If there is not enough cash in the business, it might not be able to pay its bills on time.
- If it has borrowed too much through trade credit, so it owes too much to creditors, it might be unable to pay invoices when they are due.

On the other hand, a business does not want too much working capital (i.e current assets are too high and current liabilities are too low).
- Stocks are costly to keep. The more stock, the higher the cost of physically storing and handling it. The stock will need to be insured while it may be liable to shrinkage (a business term for theft, usually by employees). Stock is also financially

expensive because money tied up in stock could be used to reduce borrowing and so save interest for the business.
- Too much cash is also a problem because the cash is unlikely to be earning very high rates of interest. It could be used, perhaps, to pay back debts or to invest in higher interest long-term investments.

The importance of cash
Cash is the most liquid of all business assets. A business's cash is the notes and coins it keeps on the premises and any money it has in the bank, for example. Cash is part of, but not the same as, working capital. Working capital includes other current assets, such as debtors; however this cannot be used to pay bills.

Cash is vital to a business. Without cash, the business would cease to exist. There are a number of reasons why firms fail, but according to a Confederation of British Industry (CBI) survey, 21 per cent of business failures are due to poor cash flow or a lack of working capital. Even when trading conditions are good, businesses can fail. Many of these businesses may offer good products for which there is some demand. They have the potential to be profitable and yet still collapse. Probably the most likely cause of this is that they run out of cash. Business failure is discussed in more detail in Unit 36.

Ways to improve liquidity
Liquidity problems can be prevented by keeping a tight control on financial resources. The use of budgets and cash-flow forecasts will improve the financial management of the business. Inevitably, though, there will be occasions when firms run short of cash. When this does happen the firm's main aim will be survival rather than profit. If a business is experiencing liquidity problems it must raise current assets or reduce current liabilities, or both. The following measures might be used to either generate cash or save it.

Use of overdraft facilities: Most businesses have an overdraft facility with their banks. A business can increase its cash by borrowing more money on its overdraft. For example, it might have an overdraft limit of £5,000. If it is currently borrowing £3,000 it could borrow up to £2,000 extra. However, there may be a problem if it is already up to its overdraft limit. Then it has to negotiate with its bank to increase its overdraft limit. There is no guarantee that the bank will do this. A business experiencing cash-flow problems could well be a business in difficulties. The bank will not want to increase lending to a business that could cease trading in the immediate future.

Negotiate additional short-term or long-term loans:
A business may be able to obtain a short-term loan from a bank to inject some extra cash. If a business feels that extra money will be needed for a longer period of time, a long-term loan might be considered. A business could pay back smaller instalments over a longer period of time to help cash flow. However, once it is known that a business is short of cash, banks and other moneylenders may be reluctant to provide cash for fear of the business collapsing.

Encourage cash sales and sell off stocks:

Many businesses, retailers for example, can generate cash by offering large discounts for customers who pay in cash. Sometimes it may be possible to sell stocks of raw materials, components or semi-finished goods for cash. To generate cash quickly they can be sold cheaply in a sale or below cost if necessary. A business might simply reduce the amount of stocks it holds. Stocks cost money to hold. So fewer stocks can increase cash in the business. The danger is that stocks will not be available to make products that are required for sale.

Sale and leaseback:

Assets including property and machinery can be sold to specialists in the market such as Arnold Clark. The assets are then leased back to the seller. This means that cash can be raised and the business can continue to use the assets. However, it may take a while to set up such agreements and can be an expensive way to fund assets in the long term. If assets are no longer needed it may be possible to sell them for cash.

Only make essential purchases:

It obviously makes sense during a cash crisis to postpone or cancel all unnecessary spending. A business should only buy resources for cash when it absolutely has to. Also, a business may simply delay payments. It then keeps this cash in the business for a longer period of time. It will only make payments when it is put under pressure to do so by creditors.

Extend credit with selected suppliers:

A business can save cash if it delays paying suppliers for goods and services that have already been bought. It may be able to extend its credit payment period from 30 to 60 days, for example. However, delaying for too long could mean that suppliers withdraw their credit facilities or refuse to deliver goods in the future.

Reduce personal drawings from the business:

Owners that regularly take cash from the business for their own personal use could attempt to take less. Obviously some cash might be needed for living expenses, but a reduction in drawings is a quick way to stop cash leaving the business.

Introduce fresh capital:

Owners may be able to provide some new capital to improve cash flow. For example, small businesses may be able to use savings or take out loans using personal possessions as security. A small business may be able to persuade friends or relatives to invest in the firm – new partners might be taken on for example. Larger companies may be able to sell shares to raise fresh capital. However, attracting fresh capital might be very difficult if the business is struggling. It is likely to be down to the current owners to provide more capital.

Question 3

In 2014, it was widely reported that Euro Disney, operating company of Disneyland Paris, Europe's largest tourist attraction by visitor numbers, needed an injection of finance to pay off debts and provide extra cash. A plan was announced that The Walt Disney Company, the theme park's main shareholder, would back a €420 million rights issue and convert a further €600 million of loans into equity.

One of Euro Disney's main problems since it opened has been the servicing of its debt. This was about €1.75 billion before the recapitalisation of the business. It had always been a financial pressure on the company. It was reported that the planned injection of fresh capital would help to boost cash flow by around €800 million for a period of ten years

Source: adapted from the *Financial Times* 11.10.2014, all rights reserved

(a) Explain the main cause of Euro Disney's liquidity problems.

(b) Explain how Euro Disney might benefit from its plans to improve liquidity.

Thinking bigger

Some people might incorrectly assume that working capital problems are the same as cash-flow problems. Although cash flow and working capital are interlinked, and many working capital problems are cash-flow problems as well, they are not the same. For example, one way of dealing with a cash-flow problem is to get an overdraft or a short-term bank loan. Borrowing more in the short term will lead to an increase in cash, a current asset. So it could solve a cash-flow problem. But it will not increase working capital. This is because such borrowing also increases current liabilities. The money borrowed is, in theory, repayable within 12 months. Another way in which a business can solve a cash-flow problem is to run down its stocks. Not reordering stock means that cash is preserved. But improving cash flow in this way leaves the amount of working capital the same. On the balance sheet the value of stocks falls whilst the value of cash rises. Equally, one way of dealing with a cash-flow problem is to delay paying bills. This increases the amount of cash in the business, but it also increases the amount of creditors. There is no change in overall working capital. However, a business with persistent cash-flow problems is likely to have a shortage of working capital. The most likely solution to both problems is to increase the equity in the business or to borrow more in the long term. You may need to think about this when answering questions such as (d) and (e) in the case study.

Case study

FALCON TOYS PLC

Falcon Toys plc manufactures a range of toys for the UK market. Most of its products are plastic-based and targeted at the 4–6 age group. Examples include dolls, planes, trains, cars, creative games, discovery toys, farms and animals. Like many toy manufacturers Falcon attends toy fairs at the beginning of the year to display new designs and take orders from large buyers for the Christmas period. However, one of the problems that Falcon has is the amount of trade credit they have to offer buyers to secure sales. Most buyers want at least 120 days credit. This has increased from 60 days in 2011.

Another problem Falcon Toys encounters is in the build up to Christmas. Production levels are higher during the late summer and autumn months as they accumulate stocks ready for the very busy buying period. This puts an even greater strain on liquid resources. Working capital is actually high during this period but a large proportion is held in stocks. This does not show up in the statement of financial position because the accounts are produced at the end of the tax year (April) when most of the stocks have been sold. This seasonal demand creates quite a challenge for the financial manager of Falcon. Table 4 shows some information from Falcon Toys plc's statement of financial position 2011–2014.

Table 4 Extracts from Falcon Toys plc's statement of financial position 2011–2014

	2014 (£m)	2013 (£m)	2012 (£m)	2011 (£m)
Non-current assets	131.6	126.5	118.2	104.2
Current assets	34.2	30.9	28.3	23.4
Current liabilities	28.1	23.1	16.5	11.6
Non-current liabilities	44.8	41.6	38.5	37.7
Share capital	50	50	50	50
Retained earnings	42.9	42.7	41.5	28.3

Q

(a) What is meant by working capital? (2 marks)

(b) Calculate the value of working capital for Falcon Toys plc between 2011 and 2014. (4 marks)

(c) Calculate the current ratio for Falcon Toys plc between 2011 and 2014. (4 marks)

(d) Explain how reducing debtors may not lead to an increase in the value of working capital for Falcon Toys plc. (4 marks)

(e) Assess the measures that Falcon Toys plc might use to deal with its problems. (12 marks)

Key terms

Acid test ratio – similar to the current ratio but excludes stocks from current assets. A more severe test of liquidity.
Assets – resources that belong to a business.
Capital – money put into the business by the owners.
Current assets – liquid assets, i.e. those assets that will be converted into cash within one year.
Current liabilities – money owed by the business that must be repaid within one year.
Current ratio – assesses whether or not a business has enough resources to meet any debts that arise in the next 12 months. It is found by dividing current liabilities into current assets.
Intangible assets – non-physical assets, such as brand names, patents and customer lists.
Inventories – stocks, such as raw materials and finished goods held by a business.
Liabilities – money owed by the business to banks and suppliers, for example.
Liquidity – the ease with which assets can be converted into cash.
Net assets – total assets – total liabilities.
Non-current assets – long-term resources that will be used by the business repeatedly over a period of time.
Non-current liabilities – money owed by the business for more than one year, sometimes called long-term liabilities.
Shareholders' equity – the amount of money owed by the business to the shareholders.
Statement of financial position (balance sheet) – a summary at a particular point in time of the value of a firm's assets, liabilities and capital.
Trade and other payables – money owed by the business to suppliers and utilities, for example. Sometimes called trade creditors.
Trade and other receivables – money owed to the business by customers and any prepayments made by the business.
Working capital – the funds left over to meet day-to-day expenses after current debts have been paid. It is calculated by subtracting current liabilities from current assets.

Knowledge check

1. What does a statement of financial position (balance sheet) show?

2. What is the difference between current assets and current liabilities?

3. Where will retained earnings appear in a balance sheet?

4. Give two examples of non-current assets.

5. How is the value of working capital calculated?

6. What is the difference between the current ratio and the acid test ratio?

7. What might be the 'ideal' value for the acid test ratio?

8. What sort of businesses may operate with a relatively low current ratio?

9. State four measures a business can take to improve liquidity.

10. Can a business have too much working capital? Explain.

Key points

1. Internal causes of business failure.
2. External causes of business failure.
3. Failure due to financial factors.
4. Failure due to non-financial factors.

Getting started

In 2014 Albemarle & Bond, one of the largest pawnbrokers in the UK, went into **administration**. The economic downturn after 2011 meant that pawnbrokers became more popular. This encouraged some companies, including Albermarle & Bond, to expand rapidly. But the fall in gold prices in 2013 and the reported overexpansion produced cash-flow problems, turning profit into loss for the company. The company attempted to restructure, to merge with another company – Better Capital, and sought further bank loans, but it came to nothing. The only option was to file a notice of administration, after its main creditors (banks) withdrew their support.

In April, Promethean Investments bought 128 of the 187 outlets. Out of a workforce of 800, this saved 628 jobs.

Source: adapted from www.retailresearch.org

What caused Albemarle & Bond to collapse? Which factors that caused the collapse were outside the business (**external factors**)? How can overexpansion cause a business to fail?

Business failure in the UK

Every year thousands of new businesses are set up in the UK, but at the same time, unfortunately, thousands of existing businesses collapse. Between 2003 and the end of 2007 failures were below 20,000 per annum. However, after they peaked in 2009 at around 26,000, the annual rate of failure was around 24,000 and predicted to remain roughly at that level until 2016. In 2013 there were 4.9 million businesses in the UK. If around 23,000 fail in a given year it is not a large proportion; however, most business start-ups, possibly in excess of 90 per cent, cease to trade after five years. What is the cause of business failure?

Internal causes of business failure

Businesses fail for a wide variety of reasons. In some cases the cause of failure comes from within the business, for example through ineffective management. Some of the common **internal factors** that cause business failure are outlined below.

Lack of planning: The failure of new businesses in particular may be caused by a lack of planning. At the start-up stage entrepreneurs can be prone to overlook the importance of planning. A thorough business plan is needed to provide a clear vision for the future so that owners can take an objective and critical look at the whole business idea. A plan will provide a roadmap that shows a clear direction for the development of the business and help to identify potential problems in advance so that the business is better prepared to deal with them.

Financial planning is crucial. Entrepreneurs need to ensure that the business is sufficiently funded to cope with weak cash flow in the initial stages. Business plans clarify the relationships between operating expenses, prices and profits – all essential information for an entrepreneur. Small businesses may fail because owners do not put enough time and research into a comprehensive business plan.

Part of the planning process should involve seeking advice from relevant business people, potential investors and specialists. A range of courses are also available to help entrepreneurs in the setting up of a business. Attending such courses will help entrepreneurs to appreciate the importance of planning and hopefully reduce the risk of failure.

Cash-flow problems: Many businesses fail because they run out of cash. In some cases entrepreneurs focus too much on profit and neglect the importance of cash. There are a number of reasons why a business might run short of cash.

- **Overtrading.** Young and rapidly growing businesses are particularly prone to **overtrading**. This occurs when a business is attempting to fund a large volume of production with inadequate cash. Established companies trying to expand can also face this problem.
- **Investing too much in fixed assets.** In the initial stages of a business, funds are limited. Spending large amounts at the outset on equipment, vehicles and other capital items drains resources. It may be better to lease some of these fixed assets, leaving sufficient cash funds.
- **Allowing too much credit.** A great deal of business is done on credit. One of the dangers is that businesses allow their customers too long for payment. This means that they are waiting for money and may actually be forced to borrow during this period. Failure to control debtors may also lead to bad debts.
- **Over-borrowing.** Businesses may borrow to finance growth. As more loans are taken out interest costs rise. Over-borrowing not only threatens a firm's cash position, but also the overall control of the business. It is important to fund growth in a balanced way, perhaps by raising some capital from share issues.
- **Seasonal factors.** Sometimes trade fluctuates for seasonal reasons. In agriculture, for instance, cereal farmers have a large cash inflow when their harvest is sold, but for much of the year they have to pay expenses without any cash flowing in. This situation requires careful management, although it is possible to predict these fluctuations.
- **Unforeseen expenditure.** Businesses need to be prepared for any unforeseen expenditure. Equipment breakdowns, tax demands, strikes and bad debts are common examples of this type of emergency expense. In the early stages of business development, owners are often hit by unforeseen expenditure. This can be because they lack experience or have not undertaken sufficient planning.
- **External factors.** Sometimes events that are outside the control of the business cause cash-flow problems. Examples include changes in consumer tastes, changes in legislation or a downturn in the economy. These are discussed in more detail later in this unit.
- **Poor financial management.** Inexperience in managing cash or a poor understanding of the way cash flows into and out of a business may lead to cash-flow problems. For example, if a business plans to spend heavily just before it receives large amounts of cash from customers that have bought on credit, it is likely to face problems. It is not prudent

to spend cash when it is not definitely there. The control of cash flow will be improved if owners and managers produce regular cash-flow forecasts, keep up-to-date financial records and operate an efficient credit control system.

The *Northern Echo* reported in 2014 that Apex Electrical Solutions, an electrical wholesaler in Gateshead, collapsed due to severe cash-flow problems. The cash shortage apparently resulted from the collapse of a big customer and a subsequent bad debt of £100,000. The company recorded £190,000 losses in its last yearly results, owed over £580,000 to RBS Invoice Finance and was also £11,000 in arrears on staff wages.

Exam tip

It is important to remember that it is possible for a profitable business to collapse if it runs out of cash. One likely scenario is that a business is overtrading. If a business grows too quickly it uses up liquid resources to fund the growth. Profitable businesses can also fail if they get a large bad debt, if they are faced with a large and unexpected payment or if they offer trade credit that is too generous. You can use this information to answer questions such as (b) in Question I.

Question 1

In 2014 Astec, a specialist in the design, supply and installation of external building envelopes, collapsed owing money to more than 300 suppliers and subcontractors. It was reported that up to 2012, the business had grown to £30 million sales and was trading profitably. The directors decided to grow the business further after several contract opportunities arose, and during 2013 recorded sales of £45 million. One reason for its difficulties could have been that the company was growing too quickly and resources had become strained — it was unable to fund the additional working capital requirements of the enlarged business. This resulted in catastrophic cash-flow problems. The failure of the business resulted in the redundancy of 85 staff and debts of around £12 million.

(a) What is meant by overtrading?

(b) Explain how it is possible for a profitable business, like Astec, to fail.

Lack of funds: Some businesses fail because they cannot attract funding. A lack of funding can affect both established businesses and new businesses. Established businesses may fail to attract funding because their track record is not as good as it needs to be. As a result they present too much of a risk for investors and other lenders. New businesses often struggle to attract funding because they do not have a trading history, and again, they are too risky for investors. Some business owners think they can survive with limited amounts of capital by being cautious. However, if a business is undercapitalised it is likely to fail. A lot of businesses failed during the 'credit crunch' just after the global financial crisis in 2008. Lenders became extremely cautious and businesses were starved of essential funding.

Relying on a narrow customer base: Some businesses fail because their customer base is too narrow. This means they rely too heavily on a small number of large customers. Obviously if they lose these large customers, sales will fall dramatically and survival becomes difficult. In recent years many farmers have gone out of business because they relied too heavily on contracts with large supermarkets. When terms for new contracts could not be agreed, farmers were left with an inadequate customer base.

Marketing problems: A range of marketing problems could be the cause of business failure. Businesses that launch new products that fail to meet customer needs are likely to stumble. The use of inappropriate pricing strategies could mean that prices are too high or too low. A business may invest too heavily in extravagant or inappropriate promotional campaigns.

Correct positioning in the market is also vital. For example, Jane Norman, the women's fashion chain, went into administration in 2014. It was reported as being neither cheap nor upmarket, so strategically 'stuck in the middle'. In a tough retail environment, the 24-store chain in Britain and Ireland had been making losses. Eventually its owner, Edinburgh Woollen Mill, was unable to continue to fund the losses and put the chain into administration. It was also reported that the positioning of the brand might move forward online.

Failure to innovate: In some cases businesses have failed because they have resisted the need to innovate and not changed with the times. One common reason is that they may have been reluctant to adopt new technology. For example, the main reason for camera company Kodak's demise was its failure to recognise the importance of digital photography. It was said that Kodak's top management never fully grasped how the world around them was changing. Kodak was reported as thinking that people would prefer hard-copy prints because they valued film-based photos for their high quality. In the end, digital cameras came to dominate because people no longer felt the need to have high quality prints.

Lack of business skills: Inevitably some small businesses fail because their owners may not be fully competent in the required skills. Running a business is challenging and requires a multitude of skills. Entrepreneurs have to be creative, numerate, motivational and good decision-makers. They also need skills in communication, IT, marketing, negotiating, financial management and more. It is perhaps not surprising that entrepreneurs may sometimes lack the skills required to be successful in a business context.

In 2014, Variety Shopping Ltd, a store owned by Lewis's Southport Ltd, failed after just a few months of trading. The local press reported that the owner said he had limited retail experience at the beginning of the development and that the venture had not been a very nice experience. He said that it was something that he wouldn't do again, adding that he had lost a lot of money.

Poor leadership: Senior managers and business leaders may bring down companies almost singlehandedly. Such failures are often reported as the result of poor decision-making and not making urgent changes. Kodak, the camera business, Blockbuster, the DVD retailer and Nokia, the mobile phone maker are all examples where senior managers have been criticised for failing to implement crucial strategies needed to protect their business from changes in the market place and save the companies from collapse. Some leaders have come unstuck when merging or taking over other businesses. For example, some have blamed the near collapse of the Co-operative Bank on its takeover of the Britannia Building Society, and the failure of RBS was attributed to poor leadership from Fred Goodwin and his decision to take over ABN Amro.

External causes of business failure

Failed business owners may often try to cite external factors for their demise, as this deflects blame away from themselves. However, some commentators argue that only about 20 per cent of business failure is due to external forces. The most likely external factors to cause business failure are outlined below.

Competition: The strength and success of business rivals can push others out of business. Competitors might bring out superior products or read market conditions more effectively. They may charge lower prices because their costs are lower. They may be a larger, more powerful company and use destroyer pricing to drive smaller rivals out of the market. In recent years many manufacturers in the West have been outcompeted by low-cost producers from China and other emerging nations.

Changes in legislation: Sometimes changes in government legislation can lead to business failure. For example, a number of failing pubs and bars blamed the legislation that banned smoking from public places for their demise. In 2014 a number of lenders withdrew from the market after the government passed legislation to control the supply of so-called 'payday loans'. In April 2014 the West Cornwall Pasty Company, a supplier and retailer of pasties and snacks, went into administration citing the government's so-called 'pasty tax' (tax on items sold hot) as one reason. The company ran 45 retail outlets plus facilities in 20 railway stations and employed 350 people. However, the company was taken over shortly afterwards and survived.

Changes in consumer tastes: Consumer tastes are not constant. They are likely to change over time and businesses that cannot adapt to such changes are more likely to fail. For example, in 2014 two Northern Ireland fashion chains, NV and All Gino Casuals (womenswear and menswear respectively), closed 15 stores after the parent company went into liquidation. A retail analyst was reported as saying that they had fallen victim to the changing patterns and trends in consumer behaviour in the fashion industry, and that others in a similar position needed to learn lessons from this failure.

Economic conditions: The general state of the economy, both domestic and global, can have an impact on the success of businesses. It was widely reported that the level of business failures rose after the financial crisis in 2008. After this crisis many countries in the world went into recession and thousands of businesses in the UK collapsed as a result. A government's economic policies can also contribute to business failure. For example, in the last five years there have been cuts in the public sector, which have resulted in job losses, wages in the public sector have been frozen and some taxes have increased. This has led to a drop in disposable income for many people in the UK, which results in lower demand, particularly for non-essential products and services. Businesses that produce these are likely to feel the effects of an economic downturn more severely.

Other important economic variables include interest rates and exchange rates. Interest rates dropped after 2008, making borrowing cheaper. However, a sharp increase in interest rates could cause difficulties for some businesses. Those with large debts would be at risk, as would businesses that depend on consumers using credit to fund their purchasing. Businesses that import and export are also affected by changes in the exchange rate. For example, a business that relies heavily on the export market will suffer if the exchange rate rises sharply. Higher exchange rates mean that overseas customers have to pay more for UK goods and services. This can reduce demand and force marginal firms into administration.

Changes in market prices: Some businesses have very little control over the prices they charge. In certain industries firms are 'price takers'. For example, oil producers have to sell their output at the global market price. Consequently, when these prices fall, marginal producers will leave the market. For example, in late 2014 the price of oil fell from around $103 a barrel in June to around $74 in November. This is shown in Figure 1. For some oil producers $73 per barrel is the break-even price. If the price were to fall below this for a long period of time these producers might not survive. Many farmers in the UK are also 'price takers'. In 2014 the livelihoods of many dairy farmers were threatened because the price of milk dropped in the market to about 27p per litre. It was reported that this was below the break-even price of around 30p per litre for many farmers.

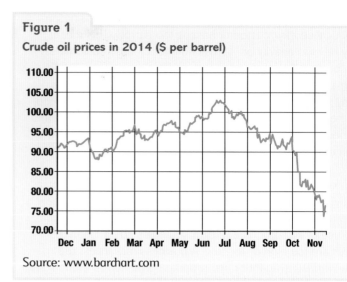

Figure 1

Crude oil prices in 2014 ($ per barrel)

Source: www.barchart.com

Question 2

In April 2014 Paul Simon, the Barking-based furniture, curtains and carpets retailer, went into administration. This resulted in the closure of some of their 51 stores, based mainly in retail parks in the south east of England, and the loss of jobs. Poor trading conditions caused by the uncertain economic environment and online competitors adversely affected the business. Also, bad weather and floods in 2013/2014 restricted customers' access to stores and led to a further decline in sales.

Source: adapted from www.retailresearch.org

(a) Explain two external factors that have resulted in the collapse of Paul Simon.

(b) Assess whether it is possible for a business like Paul Simon to protect itself from the effect of external factors.

Financial and non-financial causes of business failure

The reasons for business failure can be classified as financial or non-financial.

Financial factors: Many businesses fail for financial reasons. They either become bankrupt (where they are taken to court by creditors) or they become insolvent (where they cease trading of their own accord). The most common reason for this failure is the shortage of cash – the inability to pay immediate debts. A number of things can cause cash shortages, as outlined earlier in this unit. The importance of effective cash-flow management in business cannot be overemphasised.

Non-financial factors: In some cases business failure results from factors such as a lack of planning, a lack of business skills, inability to compete effectively, failure to meet customer needs, reluctance to change and adverse economic conditions. These may be classified as non-financial factors as they are not linked directly to money issues. However, even these factors are likely to result in financial failure if they are not addressed by a business.

Case study

JACKSONS OF READING

Some consumers value tradition and authenticity highly. Jacksons was a traditional department store in Reading town centre. Its fittings included glass counters set before wooden shelves. It used a system of pneumatic tubes to transport money from customers to a central cash office and its receipts were hand-written. The Jacksons shopping experience reminded people of the 1970s TV series *Are You Being Served?*, a sitcom that mocked traditional retailing. However, on Christmas Eve 2013 the store closed and its 60 employees were laid off.

It was reported that competition and failure to innovate may have been a reason for the closure. The Oracle, a shopping mall that opened in Reading in 1999, gradually attracted trade away from the Jacksons end of the shopping district. However, Jacksons battled on, relying heavily on being a supplier of school uniforms. It also opened a bowls department to help it compete with online retailers. Thomas Macey, the company archivist, was reported as saying that if Jacksons changed with the times, it would lose its appeal. Despite this confidence, its appeal did fade away.

Other problems encountered by Jacksons included care of its old multi-level labyrinthine building, which was hard to manage, along with its old-fashioned labour-intensive approach to customer service. The final straw for Jacksons was probably the news that the shop roof was rotting and needed to be replaced at a cost of £60,000.

In general, stand-alone department stores have declined since the 1970s. Customers have been attracted by shopping malls with their specialist and stylish shops. However, some are surviving. For example, Jarrold in Norwich attract customers through events, including Gok Wan, the celebrity fashion stylist, who signed cookery books and prepared a dish in the store's demonstration kitchen. In Trowbridge, the traditional department store H J Knee, established in 1879, teamed up with Euronics to sell electronics. These shops have combined their traditional pedigrees and local roots with ways of adapting to meet changing patterns in demand.

Source: adapted from www.retailresearch.org

(a) What is meant by the non-financial causes of business failure? (2 marks)

(b) Evaluate the extent to which internal factors contributed to the failure of Jacksons. (20 marks)

Key terms

Administration – a failing business appoints a specialist to rescue the business or wind it up.
External factors – factors beyond the control of businesses cause it to collapse.
Internal factors – factors that businesses are able to control cause it to collapse.
Overtrading – the situation where a business does not have enough cash to support its production and sales, usually because it is growing too fast.

Knowledge check

1. Explain the internal and external factors that cause business failure.

2. Why has the business failure rate in the UK risen since 2008?

3. What happens when a business goes into administration?

4. Explain why the management of cash is so important to the survival of a business.

5. Give four possible causes of cash-flow problems for a business.

6. State two ways that poor marketing could result in business failure.

7. How can business failure be caused by poor leadership?

8. State two ways in which competitors might cause business failure.

9. How might a change in interest rates result in business failure?

10. State two non-financial reasons why businesses fail.

37 Production, productivity and efficiency

Key points

1. Methods of production – job, batch, flow and cell.
2. Productivity – output per unit of input per time period.
3. Factors influencing productivity.
4. The link between productivity and competitiveness.
5. Efficiency – production at minimum average cost.
6. Factors influencing efficiency.
7. Distinction between labour intensive production and capital intensive production.

Getting started

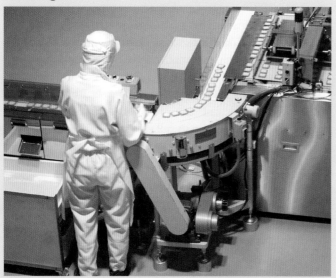

Describe the two different methods of production used above. Why are different methods necessary? Which do you think is the most efficient method of production? What might be the advantages of each method of production?

What is production?

Production takes place when resources, such as raw materials or components, are changed into 'products'. Land, labour, capital and enterprise, the factors of production, are used in the production process. The use of land and a tractor to grow cabbages is an example of production in **primary industry**. An example of **secondary industry** would be the use of wood, plastic, glue, screws, labour, drilling and cutting equipment to manufacture furniture.

Today production is often referred to more generally as those activities that 'bring a product into being'. Activities whic are part of **tertiary industry**, such as services, would be included in this definition. A bank might talk about providing a 'product' in the same way as a carpet manufacturer. Examples of products in a bank's product portfolio might include mortgages, current accounts, house insurance and foreign currency. Direct services from the producer to the consumer, such as car repairs or decorating, can also be regarded as production in this sense.

Job production

Job production involves the production of a single product at a time. It is used when orders for products are small, such as 'one-offs'. Production is organised so that one 'job' is completed at a time. There are a wide variety of goods and services which are produced or provided using this method of production. Small-scale examples include the baking of a child' birthday cake, a dentist's treatment session or the construction of an extension to a house. On a large scale, examples could include the building of a ship, the construction of the Crossrail link in London or the manufacture of specialised machinery. Job production is found in both manufacturing and the service industries. Because the numbers of units produced is small, the production process tends to be labour intensive. The workforce is usually made up of skilled workers or specialists and the possibility of using labour-saving machinery is limited. Many businesses adopt this method of production when they are 'starting up'. The advantages and disadvantages of job production are shown in Table 1 on the next page.

Table 1 The advantages and disadvantages of job production

Advantages	Disadvantages
Quality is high because workers are skilled	High labour costs due to skilled workers
Workers are well motivated because work is varied	Production may be slow – long lead times
Products can be custom made	A wide range of specialist tools may be needed
Production is easy to organise	Generally an expensive method of production

Question 1

Harrods Christmas displays have become a traditional spot to visit in London during the holiday season. The window displays are a real attraction for both children and adults. In 2014, each window display for 'the land of magic', including Christmas mice and Father Christmas, had an element of mechanism, with the most amount of movement ever.

Millington Associates was involved in the production of the window displays. Millington Associates is an internationally established business offering design, prototyping, project management, build, logistics and installation. It has a proven track record of delivering outstanding work for retail windows, interiors, travel retail, exhibitions and events.

Source: adapted from *All about London*

(a) What is meant by job production?

(b) Explain one advantage of job production for a company like Millington Associates.

(c) Explain one reason why job production might motivate employees at Millington Associates.

Batch production

Batch production may be used when demand for a firm's product or service is regular rather than a 'one-off'. An example might be a furniture factory, where a batch of armchairs is made to a particular design. Production is divided into a number of operations. A particular operation is carried out on all products in a batch. The batch then moves to the next operation. A baker uses batch production when baking bread. The operations in the baking process are broken down in Table 2.

These operations would be performed on every batch of bread. There is some standardisation because each loaf in the batch will be the same. However, it may be possible to vary each batch. The ingredients could be changed to produce brown bread or the style of baking tin could be changed for different-shaped loaves.

A great number of products are produced using this method, particularly in manufacturing, such as the production of components and food processing. For example, in a canning plant, a firm may can several different batches of soup, each batch being a different recipe. Products can be produced in very large or very small batches, depending on the level of demand.

Larger production runs tend to lower the **unit** or **average cost** of production. New technology is increasingly being introduced to make batch production more efficient. The advantages and disadvantages of batch production are shown in Table 3.

Table 2 Operations involved in the production of a batch of bread

1.	Blend ingredients in a mixing container until a dough is formed.
2.	Knead the dough for a period of time.
3.	Leave the dough to rise for a period of time.
4.	Divide the dough into suitable units (loaves) for baking.
5.	Bake the loaves.
6.	Allow loaves to cool.

Table 3 The advantages and disadvantages of batch production

Advantages	Disadvantages
Workers are likely to specialise in one process	More complex machinery may be needed
Unit costs are lower because output is higher	Careful planning and co-ordination is needed
Production is flexible since different orders can be met	Less motivation because workers specialise
More use of machinery is made	If batches are small, costs will still be high
	Money may be tied up in work-in-progress

Question 2

Radford Textiles Ltd makes workwear, leisurewear and promotional clothing for UK customers. In 2013, the company moved to a new factory in Rochdale. The company has an excellent reputation in the industry. This is because it:

- provides a wide choice of quality clothing at low prices
- provides excellent customer service
- is flexible and can meet orders quickly.

Like most companies in the clothes industry, Radford Textiles Ltd uses batch production. The company can meet a wide range of different orders due to the flexibility of their machinery and multi-skilled workforce.

(a) What is meant by batch production?

(b) Explain why batch production is common in the clothes industry.

(c) Explain one way in which Radford Textiles Ltd might have overcome some of the typical problems associated with batch production.

Flow production

Most people will have some idea of flow production from pictures of motor car factories. Production is organised so that different operations can be carried out, one after the other, in a continuous sequence. Vehicles move from one operation to the next, often on a conveyer belt.

The main features of flow production are:

- the production of large quantities
- a simplified or standardised product
- a semi-skilled workforce, specialising in one operation only
- large amounts of machinery and equipment
- large stocks of raw materials and components.

Flow production is used in the manufacture of products as varied as newspapers, food and cement. It is sometimes called **mass production**, as it tends to be used for the production of large numbers of standard products, such as cars or breakfast cereals. Certain types of flow production are known as **continual flow production**, because products such as clothing material pass continually through a series of processes. **Repetitive flow production** is the manufacture of large numbers of the same product, such as plastic toy parts or metal cans.

The advantages and disadvantages of flow production are shown in Table 4. In the 1990s flow production processes were changed in an attempt to solve some of the problems. Japanese manufacturers setting up businesses in the UK introduced methods to improve efficiency. Just-in-time manufacturing, for example, helped to reduce the cost of holding stocks. Some vehicle manufacturers attempted to introduce an element of job production into flow processes by **customising** products for clients. For example, a range of different cars was produced on the same production line. Cars in the same model range differed in colour, engine size, trim and interior design.

Table 4 The advantages and disadvantages of flow production

Advantages	Disadvantages
Very low unit costs due to economies of scale	Products may be too standardised
Output can be produced very quickly	Huge set-up costs before production can begin
Modern plant and machines can allow some flexibility	Worker motivation can be very low – repetitive tasks
Production speed can vary according to demand	Breaks in production can be very expensive

Cell production

Flow production involves mass producing a standard product on a production line. The product undergoes a series of operations in sequence on a continuous basis until a finished product rolls off the 'end of the line'.

Cellular manufacturing or **cell production** adopts a different approach and involves dividing the workplace into 'cells'. Each cell occupies an area on the factory floor and focuses on the production of a 'product family'. A 'product family' is a group of products which requires a sequence of similar operations. For example, the metal body part of a machine might require the operations cut, punch, fold, spot weld, dispatch. This could all be carried out in one cell. Inside a cell, machines are grouped together and a team of workers sees the production of a good from start to finish.

Take the example of a furniture manufacturer making parts for a kitchen range in a cell. The raw material, such as wood, would be brought into the cell. Tasks such as turning on a lathe

or shaping by routing would be carried out at workstations. The part would then be assembled and passed on to stock. The cell may also be responsible for tasks such as designing, schedule planning, maintenance and problem solving, as well as the manufacturing tasks which are shared by the team.

Here are some advantages of cellular manufacturing.

- Floor space is released because cells use less space than a linear production line.
- Product flexibility is improved.
- Lead times are cut.
- Movement of resources and handling time is reduced.
- There is less work-in-progress.
- Teamworking is encouraged.
- There may be a safer working environment and more efficient maintenance.

Productivity

Output can be increased if **productivity** is raised. Productivity is the amount of output that can be produced with a given input of resources. It is common to measure the productivity of specific resources in a period of time. A business may measure **labour productivity** – this is output per worker per period of time. For example, a factory producing standard mobile homes employed 40 workers in 2014. During the year a total of 1,200 mobile homes were produced. Therefore labour productivity was 30 homes per worker (1,200/40).

This ratio is a useful measure of labour productivity, but there are some problems that need to be recognised. For example, which workers should be counted? Should maintenance crew, management and clerical staff be counted, or should the ratio concentrate on direct labour only, i.e. shop floor workers? How should part-time workers and the long-term sick be treated? How can the ratio accommodate a multi-product plant, where the efforts of an employee might contribute to the production of more than one product?

A business may be interested in the productivity of its capital. This is becoming increasingly the case as more firms become capital intensive. A **capital productivity** ratio can be calculated by dividing output by the amount of capital employed in a given period. For example, if a factory used 10 sewing machines and a total of 900 garments were sewn in a day, the productivity of capital would be 90 garments per machine each day.

> **Exam tip**
> You need to be careful not to confuse production with productivity. Remember that production involves transforming resources into useful goods and services that meet customer needs – it refers to the **level** of output produced. Productivity is the **rate** of production. It is the amount of output that can be produced with a given quantity of resources in a period of time. Productivity will increase if more output can be made with the same amount of resources.

Factors influencing productivity

Over time a business wants to improve productivity if possible. This is because costs will be lower and profit will be higher. Some of the key factors that can be used to influence productivity are outlined below.

Specialisation and the division of labour: One feature of modern business is specialisation. This is the production of a limited range of goods by an individual, business, region or nation. For example, Coca-Cola specialises in soft drinks, Toyota makes cars and Emirates provides air travel. Specialisation inside a business is also common. Departments specialise in different activities, such as marketing, production, finance, personnel and purchasing. Workers will also specialise in certain tasks and skills. This is called the division of labour. It allows people to concentrate on a limited range of tasks. For example, in construction an architect will draw up plans, a bricklayer will build walls, a roofer will lay the roof, and so on.

Education and training: The government can help improve the quality of labour by investing in education. This might involve providing more equipment for schools or improving the quality of teaching. Firms can also improve the productivity of their workers by providing their own training.

Motivation of workers: If people are motivated at work they will be more productive. Firms might use financial incentives, such as piece rates. Workers who are not motivated by money may respond to other incentives. For example, job rotation might be introduced. This involves an employee changing jobs from time to time. If people are trained to do different jobs, their time at work may be more interesting because there is more variety.

Working practices: The way labour is organised and managed can affect productivity. Working practices are the methods and systems that employees adopt when working. For example, productivity might be increased by changing the factory layout – repositioning workstations or reorganising the flow of production. Such changes may improve productivity because workers do not have to move around as much, for example.

Labour flexibility: Labour can be more flexible if workers are trained to do different jobs and can switch from one to the other at short notice. For example, some supermarkets train most of their staff to operate checkouts. Then, during a busy period, workers can be switched from other jobs to operate checkouts to prevent long queues from forming. Some businesses use flexitime where workers can choose their own hours of work (within limits). For example, a call centre can be kept open from 7.00 a.m. to 8.00 p.m. if individual workers choose to work at different times of the day. Shift work can be used to keep factories running for 24 hours a day. For example, many factories operate three daily shifts – 08.00 to 16.00, 16.00 to 00.00 and 00.00 to 08.00.

Capital productivity: Productivity usually increases when new technology is introduced. This is because new technology is more efficient. Productivity is also likely to increase if production becomes more capital intensive. The benefits of more capital intensive production are summarised in Table 5 at the end of this unit.

Productivity and competitiveness

If businesses can raise productivity they will be able to produce more output with the same level of resources. This will mean that costs will be lower and they can charge lower prices than

rivals. This makes businesses more competitive in the market place. As a result they are likely to win more customers, increase market share and possibly threaten the survival of their rivals.

If UK businesses can be more productive then they may become more competitive in overseas markets. This will help to boost the nation's exports and improve the performance of the UK economy. This could help increase the standard of living in the UK. However, improving productivity may not be enough to outcompete overseas rivals. Other factors have to be taken into account. For example, the price of exports is influenced by exchange rates. If the exchange rate improves for the UK the price of exports will rise. This will reduce the competitiveness of UK goods sold abroad.

Efficiency

Efficiency is about making the best possible use of all a business's resources. A business will want to use its materials, labour and capital as effectively as possible. Businesses often use costs as an indicator of efficiency. Production is said to be efficient if average costs are minimised. Figure 1 shows the average cost curve for a business. The diagram shows that average costs fall at first, reach a minimum and then rise again. In this example the business will minimise its average cost when output is 500 units. At this level of output average cost is £20 per unit and efficiency cannot be improved. All resources are being used as effectively as possible. If the business was producing just 200 units of output, efficiency is not being maximised because average cost is higher at £30.

Figure 1

The average cost curve for a business

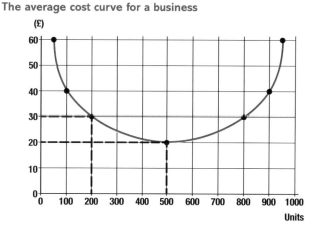

Factors influencing efficiency

The efficiency of businesses can be influenced by a very wide range of factors. If a business can reduce average costs, efficiency will improve. Some of the measures that a business might use to reduce costs are outlined below.

Introducing standardisation: Standardisation involves using uniform resources and activities or producing a uniform product. It can be applied to tools, components, equipment, procedures and documents. For example, a construction company building an apartment block would benefit if all the flats were fitted with the same kitchen and bathroom units. Bulk purchases can be made, the same tools and procedures could be used for fitting, and training time could be reduced. In general, efficiency will improve if there are standard components, such as nuts, screws, bolts, pipes and wire, and standard measurements terminology, procedures and equipment. However, standardisation is somewhat inflexible because it makes customisation more difficult and design more challenging.

Outsourcing: It may be possible to improve efficiency by **outsourcing** specific business activities. This means that work currently done by a business is given to specialists outside the business that can do the same work at a lower cost or more flexibly. For example, a call centre might outsource its staff catering facilities to a specialist catering company that can operate more effectively and at a cheaper rate.

Relocating: Moving the entire business to a new site is a drastic measure, but can result in much lower costs. By relocating, businesses might enjoy lower rents, lower wages and better transport links. Many businesses have relocated their operations overseas to countries such as China, Thailand and India, where labour costs in particular are substantially lower.

Downsizing: **Downsizing** involves reducing capacity, i.e. laying off workers and closing unprofitable divisions. The advantages of this for businesses can include:
- cost savings and increased profit
- a leaner, more competitive operation
- removal of unprofitable or inefficient parts of a business
- profitable businesses no longer subsidising unprofitable ones.

However, downsizing can have drawbacks. For example, laying off workers means that businesses lose skills, experience and knowledge. In some cases businesses have been forced to hire back redundant staff as expensive consultants. Downsizing might also have an adverse effect on the morale of workers.

Delayering: Delayering also involves reducing staff. Cuts are directed at particular levels of a business, such as managerial posts. Many traditional organisational charts are hierarchical, with several layers of management. Delayering involves removing some of these layers to give a flatter structure. In the late 1980s, the average number of layers in a typical organisational structure was 7, although some were as high as 14. By 2000 this had been reduced to less than five. The main advantage of delayering is the savings made from laying off expensive managers. It may also lead to better communication and better-motivated staff if they are **empowered** and allowed to make their own decisions.

Investing in new technology: New technology can often improve efficiency. New machinery may be quicker, more accurate, be capable of more tasks, and carry out work in more extreme conditions than older equipment or labour. Many machines are controlled by computers and can undertake very complex tasks. The use of information and communications technology has helped most businesses improve efficiency.

Lean production: **Lean production** is an approach developed by Toyota, the Japanese car manufacturer. Its aim is to use fewer resources in production. Lean producers use less of everything. This includes factory space, materials, stocks, suppliers, labour, capital and time. As a result, lean production:
- raises productivity
- reduces costs and cuts lead times
- reduces the number of defective products
- improves reliability and speeds up product design.

Lean production involves using a range of practices designed to reduce waste and improve productivity and quality. Examples include **Kaizen**, just-in-time production, cell production, empowerment and teamworking.

Kaizen: There is a strong link between Kaizen and lean production. Kaizen is a Japanese word that means *continuous improvement*. There is a belief in Japan that everything can be improved. This means that workers are always coming up with ideas to improve quality, reduce waste or increase efficiency. The improvements may be very small, but over a long period of time they can have a huge impact.

Just-in-time production (JIT): This involves minimising or eliminating the amount of stock held by a business. It reduces all of the costs associated with stock holding.

Question 3

For several years, it was widely reported that HSBC, one of the world's leading banks, was downsizing its operations. In 2013 it planned to lay off up to 14,000 staff globally in a cost-cutting move, planning to include redundancies among the bank's back-office IT employees. HSBC outlined the plan in its three-year strategy. The bank said it aimed to save $2-3 billion in annual costs, on top of the $4 billion it had already saved. The move planned to reduce the total headcount to 240,000 by 2016, bringing the total number of redundancies to 55,000 since 2010. These losses formed part of a plan to streamline HSBC's global operations: providing more control to their London head office and to try to avoid overlaps in job roles and to remove inefficiencies in processes. They were also looking to move away from their traditional in-house software development. Though still aiming to remain an international bank HSBC planned to focus on 22 countries, despite their presence in 80 countries around the world.

Source: adapted from the *Financial Times*, 17.3.13, 23.4.13, 15.5.13. All rights reserved

(a) What is meant by downsizing?

(b) Explain (i) one benefit and (ii) one drawback to HSBC of downsizing.

Distinction between labour and capital intensive production

One of the most important production decisions which operations managers have to make is what combination of capital and labour to use. **Labour intensive** production techniques involve using a larger proportion of labour than capital. **Capital intensive** production techniques involve employing more machinery relative to labour. For example, chemical production is capital intensive, with only a relatively small workforce to oversee the process. The postal service is labour intensive, with a considerable amount of sorting and delivery done by hand.

The optimal resource mix between labour and capital depends on a number of factors.

- **The nature of the product.** Everyday products with high demand, like newspapers, are mass produced in huge plants using large quantities of machinery. However, in modern economies like the UK an increasing number of the products supplied by businesses are services. Generally, the provision of services is labour intensive.

- **The relative prices of the two factors.** If labour costs are rising then it may be worth the company employing more capital instead. In countries like China and India where labour is relatively cheap, labour intensive production methods are preferred. However, in most developed economies like the UK, labour is more expensive and a great deal of manufacturing is capital intensive.

- **The size of the firm.** As a firm grows and the scale of production increases, it tends to employ more capital relative to labour. For example, in the UK, Morgan cars, a small sports car manufacturer, uses a labour intensive approach to production. In contrast, Honda, which has a huge car factory in Derby, uses capital intensive production.

Table 5 The benefits and drawbacks of capital and labour intensive strategies

Capital intensive strategies
Benefits
• Generally more cost-effective if large quantities are produced
• Machinery is often more precise and consistent
• Machinery can operate 24/7
• Machinery is easier to manage than people
Drawbacks
• Huge set-up costs
• Huge delays and costs if machinery breaks down
• Can be inflexible – much machinery is highly specialised
• Often poses a threat to the workforce and could reduce morale
Labour intensive strategies
Benefits
• Generally more flexible than capital – can be retrained for example
• Cheaper for small-scale production
• Cheaper for large-scale production in countries like China and India
• People are creative and can therefore solve problems and make improvements
Drawbacks
• People are more difficult to manage than machines. They have feelings and react
• People can be unreliable. They may be sick or leave suddenly
• People cannot work without breaks and holidays
• People sometimes need to be motivated to improve performance

Knowledge check

1. State two disadvantages of job production.

2. Explain why batch production is a flexible method of production.

3. Give two examples of industries where process production is likely to be used.

4. What is the difference between production and productivity?

5. State two ways in which labour productivity might be improved.

6. What is the difference between downsizing and delayering?

7. How will specialisation improve efficiency?

8. Give two advantages of outsourcing.

9. What is meant by cell production?

10. What is the aim of Kaizen?

11. Explain why the provision of services is often labour intensive.

12. Give two examples of businesses that are likely to be capital intensive.

Case study

JAGUAR LAND ROVER

In 2012 it was reported that Jaguar Land Rover (JLR), the luxury car maker owned by Tata, had invested £370 million to increase productivity and upgrade its UK manufacturing facilities. This was to help prepare for the launch of the new Range Rover in 170 countries. JLR installed a new aluminium body shop at the company's Solihull plant as part of the investment package. It upgraded paint-applications technologies, trim assembly, warehousing and JLR's first customer handover centre. The company also invested heavily in all-aluminium production processes at Land Rover's Solihull plant, where more than 6,800 workers were employed.

A spokesman for Jaguar said that news of the investment was good for the thousands of JLR workers, the UK automotive industry and the wider economy. He commented that the wave of investments from global automotive companies demonstrated the growing strength and competitiveness of the manufacturing sector. It showed what could happen when industry and government worked together to build a better business environment. As part of its expansion, Jaguar Land Rover:

- created 1,100 new jobs at Jaguar's Castle Bromwich plant
- began work on a £355 million engine factory near Wolverhampton
- moved to 24-hour production at Halewood on Merseyside to meet demand for the Range Rover Evoque
- opened a new state-of-the-art manufacturing facility at Solihull.

To create a lean production strategy, Jaguar also streamlined its production methods, operations and processes. This enabled it to compete globally and retain quality, yet drive down costs. For example, 'just in time' was introduced to improve efficiency, reshaping workshops where many parts had been in stock. Workers could then call for additional spares when needed, rather than having parts on hand if required. To assist with the change to just-in-time ordering and ensure that lean production ideas were implemented smoothly with suppliers and cut costs, the firm introduced dedicated Customer Relationship Management (CRM) software.

Sources: adapted from www.smmt.co.uk

(a) What is meant by flow production? (2 marks)

(b) Assess the benefits to Jaguar of using flow production. (8 marks)

(c) Evaluate the importance to Jaguar of continual investment in new technology. (20 marks)

Key terms

Batch production – a method that involves completing one operation at a time on all units before performing the next.
Capital intensive – production methods that make more use of machinery relative to labour.
Capital productivity – the amount of output each unit of capital (e.g. one machine) produces.
Cell production – involves producing a family of products in a small self-contained unit (a cell) within a factory.
Division of labour – specialisation in specific tasks or skills by an individual.
Downsizing – the process of reducing capacity, usually by laying off staff.
Efficiency – producing a level of output where average cost is minimised.
Flow production – large-scale production of a standard product, where each operation on a unit is performed continuously one after the other, usually on a production line.

Job production – a method of production that involves employing all factors to complete one unit of output at a time.
Kaizen – a Japanese term that means continuous improvement.
Labour intensive – production methods that make more use of labour relative to machinery.
Labour productivity – the amount of output each unit of labour (e.g. one worker) produces.
Lean production – an approach to operations that focuses on the reduction of resource use.
Outsourcing – giving work to sub-contractors to reduce costs.
Production – the transformation of resources into goods or services.
Productivity – the output per unit of input per time period.
Specialisation – in business, the production of a limited range of goods.
Standardisation – using uniform resources and activities or producing a uniform product.

Capacity utilisation

Key points

1. Calculating capacity utilisation: current output (divided by) maximum possible output (×100)
2. Implications of under-utilisation and over-utilisation of capacity.
3. Ways of improving capacity utilisation.

Getting started

Ruta and Gatis Dukurs run the Mansion Hotel in Bournemouth. The hotel has 30 rooms and the average occupancy per night each month for 2014 is shown in Figure 1. The business only made a very small profit in 2014 and the owners are keen to raise occupancy rates during the next year.

Figure 1

Mansion Hotel occupancy for 2014

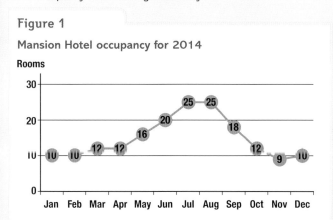

How well is the business using its resources in this case? What problems are encountered when a business does not operate at full capacity? What measures might the hotel take to improve room occupancy?

The formula for capacity utilisation is:

$$\text{Capacity utilisation} = \frac{\text{Current output}}{\text{Maximum possible output}} \times 100$$

Worked example

A printing operation is capable of printing 10,000 leaflets in a particular time period but only prints 9,000. Capacity utilisation would be:

$$\text{Capacity utilisation} = \frac{9,000}{10,000} \times 100 = 90 \text{ per cent}$$

Here the printing operation has 10 per cent unused capacity.

Worked example

Alternatively, consider a printing operation that is able to operate for ten hours, six days a week, using shifts. If last week it only had sufficient work to operate for 48 hours, the capacity utilisation would be:

$$\text{Capacity utilisation} = \frac{48}{(10 \times 6)} \times 100 = 80 \text{ per cent}$$

In this case the operation has spare capacity of 20 per cent.

Capacity utilisation

Capacity utilisation is about the use that a business makes of its resources. If a business is not able to increase output, it is said to be running at **full capacity**. Its capacity utilisation is 100 per cent. If a London to Edinburgh coach with 52 seats had only 30 passengers it would be operating at less than full capacity and would have spare, **excess, surplus** or unused **capacity**.

Businesses do not always operate at full capacity. It may not be possible to keep all resources and machinery fully employed all the time. However, most businesses would wish to be operating at close to full capacity, say 90 per cent. In some cases businesses choose to operate at less than full capacity to be flexible. For example, they might want to have spare capacity to cope with increased orders from regular customers. Without this, a business might let down its customers and risk losing them.

Measuring capacity utilisation

Capacity utilisation can be measured by comparing actual or current output with the potential output at full capacity.

Implications of under-utilisation

A business might be **under-utilising** capacity if it has experienced a drop in demand, due for example to increased competition in the market. Some businesses have to deal with seasonal demand where at certain times of the year demand is expected to be low. For example, toy manufacturers expect most of their sales to fall in the run-up to Christmas. Just after Christmas such manufacturers are likely to operate below capacity.

Drawbacks: If a business is working with under-utilised capacity it will not be making the most of its resources. It may be operating inefficiently because its unit costs are not minimised. Table 1 shows capacity utilisation, output, variable cost, fixed cost, total cost and average cost (unit cost) for a component manufacturer. When capacity utilisation is raised from 60 per cent to 80 per cent, for example, unit cost falls from £2.42 to £2.31. This is because the fixed costs of £50,000 are spread over more units of output. This explains why firms will always be keen to raise capacity utilisation.

Table 1 Capacity utilisation, output, variable cost, fixed cost, total cost and unit cost for a component manufacturer

Actual output (units)	120,000	160,000
Maximum possible output (units)	200,000	200,000
Capacity utilisation	60%	80%
Variable costs (£2 per unit)	£240,000	£320,000
Fixed costs	£50,000	£50,000
Total cost	£290,000	£370,000
Unit cost	£2.42	£2.31

Operating with too much spare capacity may also affect the morale of workers. They may feel that the business is struggling to generate orders. This might mean that workers feel insecure in their jobs. Also, if workers become accustomed to a 'light' workload, they may resent working harder if the business suddenly gets more orders.

Benefits: It could be argued that operating at below capacity does have some benefits. For example, a business would be able to cope more easily with sudden increases in demand. A business that is not able to meet immediate customer needs may lose out in the long term. Customers might go to rivals that are able to deal with demand fluctuations. Also, when working below full capacity there is likely to be less work-related stress. Both workers and managers will be more relaxed and comfortable with their workloads. This can reduce sickness and absenteeism.

Implications of over-utilisation

Many businesses would prefer to operate at close to full capacity because average costs are lower. However, if a business is running at full capacity it might be **over-utilising** its resources. This means that resources will be stretched uncomfortably. For example, over-utilisation might occur if people are being asked to work long periods of overtime without a reasonable break for rest. There are both drawbacks and benefits of over-utilisation.

Drawbacks: The pressure of constantly working at full capacity can put a strain on some of the resources. As well as causing stress and tiredness to the workforce, possibly increasing the risk of accidents or absence, machines may also be overworked to breaking point. If a business is using flow production techniques, breakdowns on a production line can be hugely expensive – especially if production is stopped completely for a period of time. Another problem is that a business may not be able to respond to an increase in demand. For example, the business might lose lucrative orders from new customers. Finally, there may be insufficient time for staff training and important maintenance work. This might save money in the short term, but in the long term staff may be lacking in vital skills and machinery may break down.

Benefits: Average costs will be lower because fixed costs will be spread across more units of output. This will help to improve competitiveness and raise profits. Also, staff motivation might be good if workers feel secure in their jobs. People in the organisation may also be happier if there is lots of work

with opportunities to increase their earnings by doing overtime. Finally, a busy operation can improve the company's image. As a result customers might be more confident when placing orders.

Question 1

Hardwick Ltd is a bottling company and has contracts with a number of independent brewers in the UK. It has benefited from a growth in the home consumption of bottled beer. Table 2 shows the capacity and actual output of Hardwick Ltd for 2013 and 2014.

Table 2 Capacity and actual production for Hardwick Ltd 2013 and 2014

	2013	2014
Production capacity (bottles)	42m	42m
Actual output (bottles)	34m	40m

(a) Calculate capacity utilisation in 2013 and 2014.

(b) Explain one reason that could account for the change in capacity utilisation between 2013 and 2014.

(c) Explain one benefit of operating close to full capacity for a business like Hardwick Ltd.

Ways of improving capacity utilisation

Reduce capacity: A business might decide to cut capacity, for instance by **rationalising**. This involves reducing excess capacity by getting rid of resources that the business can do without. A business could take a number of measures.

- Reduce staff by making people redundant, employing more part-time and temporary staff, and offering early retirement.
- Sell off unused fixed assets, such as machinery, vehicles, office space, warehouses and factory space.
- Review leasing capacity. For example, Debenhams has leased unused floor space in its stores to other retailers. Parts of a factory could also be leased to another manufacturer. The advantage of this is that the space may be reclaimed if demand picks up again.
- Move to smaller premises where costs are lower.
- **Mothball** some resources. This means that fixed assets, such as machinery, are left unused, but maintained, so that they can be brought back into use if necessary.

Increase sales: If a business sells more of its output, it will have to produce more. Therefore capacity utilisation will rise. A business might need to spend on promotion to increase sales, for example. However, if these costs are not covered by the extra revenue generated, raising capacity utilisation in this way may not be viable.

Increase usage: A problem that many businesses face is dealing with peak demand. Train operators can find that capacity utilisation is close to 100 per cent during the 'rush hour', but perhaps as low as 10 per cent late at night. Such businesses would like to increase capacity utilisation during off-peak hours.

incentives might include discounts for off-peak travel. For example, many rail companies offer some of their customers railcards to travel cheaply on off-peak trains.

Outsourcing: Capacity utilisation can vary considerably within a business. Where capital equipment has low utilisation rates, it might be more efficient for the business to sub-contract or outsource the work. This means hiring or contracting another business to do work which was previously done in-house. For example, a business might run a small fleet of delivery vans, which on average are on the road for four hours per day. It is likely that it would be cheaper for the business to sell the vans and employ a company to make the deliveries. The delivery company will be more efficient because it will be running its vans for much longer during the day. There may also be cost savings in terms of staff. If the business employed full-time drivers for the vans, they would have been under-utilised for four hours per day.

Outsourcing can also lead to other cost advantages. The delivery business will be a specialist business. It should operate its delivery service more efficiently than a business with a few vans and little knowledge of the industry. If nothing else, it should have greater buying power. It might be able, for instance, to negotiate lower prices for its vans because it is buying several at a time. If it is a very small business, its hourly wages may be less than, say, a union negotiated rate at a larger business.

An alternative outsourcing strategy is to take on outsourcing contracts for other businesses. For example, a major manufacturer of soap could accept contracts from rival soap manufacturers to improve its capacity utilisation. Outsourcing then becomes a strategy for increasing demand for the business.

Redeployment: If a business has too many resources in one part of the business, it may be possible to deploy them in another part. For example, a bank may ask some of its employees to work in another branch for a short period.

Key terms

Capacity utilisation – the use that a business makes of its resources.

Excess or **surplus capacity** – when a business has too many resources, such as labour and capital, to produce its desired level of output.

Full capacity – the point where a business cannot produce any more output.

Mothballing – leaving machines, equipment or building space unused, but maintained, so they could be brought back into use if necessary.

Over-utilisation – the position where a business is running at full capacity and 'straining' resources.

Rationalisation – reducing the number of resources, particularly labour and capital, put into the production process, usually undertaken because a business has excess capacity.

Under-utilisation – the position where a business is producing at less than full capacity.

Knowledge check

1. What is meant by spare capacity?

2. If a train carries an average of 340 passengers between London and Glasgow, what is capacity utilisation if the train's capacity is 500?

3. State two drawbacks of operating well below full capacity.

4. State two drawbacks of operating at full capacity.

5. How might a large retailer use outsourcing to improve capacity utilisation?

6. How will rationalisation improve capacity utilisation?

7. What sort of resources can be effectively mothballed?

Exam tip

When answering a question on capacity utilisation where a business has under-utilised capacity or is over-utilising capacity, you need to assess whether a business has long-term or short-term problems. For example, a business with seasonal demand, where under-utilisation is not permanent, will address problems slightly differently. Drawing distinctions between the long term and the short term in business will help show your skills for evaluation.

Maths tip

If you know both the capacity of a business and the capacity utilisation, it is possible to calculate the current output of a business. For example, if the capacity of a manufacturer is 120,000 units per month and capacity utilisation is at 91 per cent, current output is 109,200 units (120,000 × 91/100).

Case study

ENFIELD SHIPPING LTD

Enfield Shipping Ltd is a small shipping company and owns just a single container ship. The capacity of the ship is 16,000 containers. The company ships containers between the UK and the Middle East. It offers a full range of shipping services that includes:

- competitive deep sea rates to ports throughout the Middle East
- customs clearance services
- a choice of receiving shipping containers delivered on to the ground in the UK for safer, more convenient loading
- project loads
- full import and export services.

Due to the political difficulties in the Middle East a number of Enfield's regular customers have stopped exporting to the region. Consequently, the average number of containers carried per trip has fallen since 2011. The managing director of the company says, 'The situation is worsening almost by the month. I get far more phone calls from customers who say they've decided to quit than those that are interested in exporting to the Middle East.

We need to carry 9,000 containers per trip to break-even. We're close to collapse unless we do something to improve capacity utilisation.' Table 3 shows the average number of containers shipped by Enfield Shipping Ltd per trip between 2011 and 2014.

Table 3 The average number of containers shipped by Enfield Shipping Ltd per trip 2011 to 2014

	2011	2012	2013	2014
Average number of containers per trip	14,500	13,600	12,000	9,500

(a) What is meant by capacity utilisation? (2 marks)

(b) Calculate the capacity utilisation for Enfield Shipping Ltd between 2011 and 2014. (4 marks)

(c) Assess the importance to Enfield Shipping Ltd of increasing capacity utilisation. (8 marks)

(d) Assess the measures that Enfield Shipping Ltd might take to increase capacity utilisation. (12 marks)

39 Stock control

Key points

1. Interpretation of stock control diagram.
2. Buffer stocks.
3. Implications of poor stock control.
4. Just-in-time (JIT) management of stock.
5. Waste minimisation.
6. Competitive advantage from lean production.

Getting started

Why do you think the business in the photograph holds such large amounts of stock? What might be the opportunity cost of holding stock? What other costs might be incurred when storing stock like this?

What is stock?

Businesses purchase raw materials, semi-finished goods and components. A washing machine manufacturer, for example, may buy electric motors, circuit boards, rubber drive belts, nuts, bolts, sheet metal, and a variety of metal and plastic components. These stocks, also called inventories, are used to make products, which are then sold to customers. Some businesses also hold stocks of their finished goods before they are delivered to customers. In practice a variety of stocks are held, for different reasons.

- **Raw materials and components.** These are purchased from suppliers before production. They are stored by firms to cope with changes in production levels. Delays in production can be avoided if materials and components can be supplied from stores rather than waiting for a new delivery to arrive. Also, if a company is let down by suppliers it can use stocks to carry on production.
- **Work-in-progress.** These are partly finished goods. In a TV assembly plant, work-in-progress would be TVs on the assembly line which are only partly built.
- **Finished goods.** The main reason for keeping finished goods is to cope with changes in demand. If there is a sudden rise in demand, a firm can meet urgent orders by supplying customers from stock holdings. This avoids the need to step up production rates quickly.

Stock control

One of the most important tasks in stock control is to maintain the right level of stocks. This involves keeping stock levels as low as possible, so that the costs of holding them are minimised. At the same time stocks must not be allowed to run out, which can result in production being halted and customers being let down. A number of factors influence stock levels.

- **Demand.** Sufficient stocks need to be kept to satisfy normal demand. Firms must also carry enough stock to cover growth in sales and unexpected demand. The term buffer stock is used to describe stock held to cover unforeseen rises in demand or breaks in supply. This is discussed later in this unit.
- **Stockpile goods.** Toy manufacturers, for example, build up stocks in the few months up to December ready for the Christmas period. Coal-fired power stations build up stocks of fuel in the summer when demand for electricity is low so less coal is needed and the price of coal is lower. This means they have stocks ready for higher demand in the winter, and they have made savings on the cost.
- **The costs of stock holding.** If stock is expensive to hold then only a small quantity will be kept. Furniture retailers may keep low stock levels because the cost is high and sales levels are uncertain.
- **The amount of working capital available.** A business that is short of working capital may not be able to purchase more stock, even if it is needed.
- **The type of stock.** Businesses can only hold small stocks of perishable products. The stock levels of food items and fresh ingredients will be very small. Almost the entire stock of finished goods is often sold in one day. The 'life' of stock, however, does not solely depend on its perishability. Stocks can become out of date when they are replaced by new models, for example.
- **Lead time.** This is the amount of time it takes for a stock purchase to be ordered, received, inspected and made ready for use. The longer the lead time, the higher the minimum level of stock needed.
- **External factors.** Fear of future shortages may prompt firms to hold higher levels of raw materials in stock as a precaution.

Interpretation of a stock control diagram

The flow of stocks in a business can be illustrated using a stock control diagram like the one shown in Figure 1. The diagram focuses on the **re-order quantity** (the amount of stock ordered when a new order is placed) and the **re-order level** (the level of stock currently held when an order is placed).

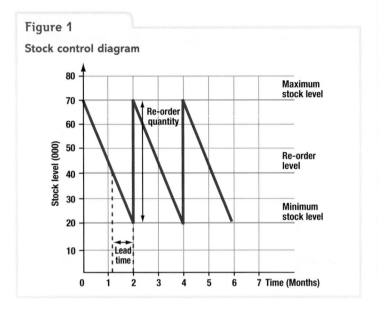

Figure 1

Stock control diagram

The stock control diagram shown in Figure 1 assumes that:

- 50,000 units are used every two months (25,000 each month)
- the maximum stock level, above which stocks never rise, is 70,000 units
- the minimum stock level, below which stocks should never fall, is 20,000 units, so there is a buffer against delays in delivery
- stock is re-ordered when it reaches a level of 40,000 units (the re-order level)
- the re-order quantity is 50,000 units – the same quantity is used up every two months
- the lead time is just under one month. This is the time between the order being placed and the date it arrives in stock.

This is a hypothetical model, which would be the ideal for a business. In practice deliveries are sometimes late, so there is a delay in stocks arriving. Firms may need to use their buffer stocks in this case. It is likely that re-order quantities will need to be reviewed from time to time. Suppliers might offer discounts for ordering larger quantities. The quantities of stocks used in each time period are unlikely to be constant, for instance because production levels fluctuate according to demand.

Buffer stocks

Some businesses keep buffer stocks. This is an emergency stock held in case there is a stock shortage. A business might hold buffer stocks of finished goods in case there is a sudden increase in demand. If a business is not able to meet a surge

Question 1

MelCo Electronics assembles control panels for computer games. The company imports a number of components from around the world – mainly China. One supplier in Shanghai ships a particular circuit board to the company. This is a new supplier and was given the contract to supply circuit boards because they were 19 per cent cheaper than the original supplier. The change in supplier occurred 12 months ago. Figure 2 shows stock movements of this component over an eight-month period.

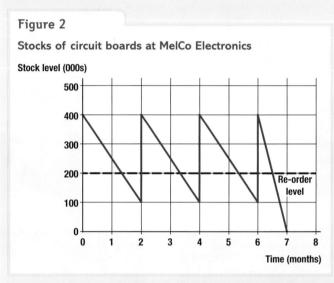

Figure 2

Stocks of circuit boards at MelCo Electronics

(a) Calculate the (i) minimum stock level, (ii) re-order level, (iii) re-order quantity, (iv) lead time for the circuit boards.

(b) Explain one reason for the change in stock level after the sixth month.

(c) Discuss the possible consequences of the change in stock level after the sixth month for MelCo Electronics.

in demand it will miss out on sales opportunities. There is also the fear of losing regular customers, which is a serious long-term problem. Businesses that need to hold buffer stocks of finished goods are those that experience sharp fluctuations in demand.

Some businesses need to hold buffer stocks of important raw materials or components. This is to protect themselves from a break in supply, which can lead to a halt in production. With some production processes this could be catastrophic. For example, if there was a break in the supply of soda ash for sheet glass production, this could involve halting an enormous plant with hundreds of millions of pounds worth of labour and capital resources being made idle. Some coal-powered electricity generators keep large buffer stocks of coal so that they can deal with surges in demand for electricity – if there is a 'cold snap' in the winter, for example. Finally, some businesses may keep buffer stocks to give them a competitive edge – if they can respond to customer orders quickly, they may get more custom.

Implications of poor stock control

Businesses need to hold the 'right' amount of stock. Holding too much stock or too little stock can both have a negative impact on the business.

Holding too much stock: If too much stock is held a business will incur unnecessary costs.

- **Storage.** Stocks of raw materials, components and finished goods occupy space in buildings. A firm may also have to pay heating, lighting and labour costs if, for example, a security guard is employed to safeguard stores when the business is closed. Some products require very special storage conditions. Food items may need expensive refrigerated storage facilities. A firm may have to insure against fire, theft and other damages.
- **Opportunity cost.** Capital tied up in stocks earns no rewards. The money used to purchase stocks could have been put to other uses, such as new machinery. This might have earned the business money.
- **Spoilage costs.** The quality of some stock may deteriorate over time, for example perishable goods. In addition, if some finished goods are held too long they may become outdated and difficult to sell.
- **Administrative and financial costs.** These include the cost of placing and processing orders, handling costs and the costs of failing to anticipate price increases.
- **Unsold stock.** If there is an unexpected reduction in demand, the firm may be left with stocks that it cannot sell.
- **Shrinkage.** Very large stocks might result in an increase in theft by employees. They may feel the business would not miss a small amount of stock relative to the total stock.

Too little stock: To reduce the costs of holding too much stock a business may fall into the trap of holding too little. There are several problems with holding too little stock.

- The business may not be able to cope with unexpected increases in demand. This might result in lost customers if they are let down too often.
- If stock deliveries are delayed, the firm may run out of stock and have to halt production. This can lead to idle labour and machinery while the firm waits for delivery.
- The firm is less able to cope with unexpected shortages of materials. Again, this could result in lost production.
- A firm which holds very low stocks may have to place more orders. This will raise total ordering costs. It might also miss out on discounts from bulk buying.

Just-in-time (JIT) management of stock

Just-in-time (JIT) manufacturing is an important part of lean production and the Kaizen approach. It was developed in the Japanese shipbuilding industry in the 1950s and 1960s. The industry recognised that a great deal of money was tied up in stocks. Traditionally, one month's supply of steel was held by a shipyard. However, as the industry became more competitive, shipbuilders insisted that steel suppliers deliver orders 'just in time', i.e. a few hours or less before the steel was

needed. This reduced the need for high levels of working capital and improved the financial performance of the business. JIT was extended to every stage of production. For example, raw materials were delivered JIT to be made into parts, parts were delivered JIT to be made into goods and goods were produced and delivered JIT to be sold.

JIT was introduced in other Japanese industries, such as the car industry, and then spread to other parts of the world, such as the USA and Europe. JCB has used JIT in its Rochester plant. When JCB excavators are manufactured, every machine on the production line has already been sold. Supplies of components, such as engines from Perkins, and raw materials, such as steel plate, arrive on the day they are needed. JIT manufacturing requires high levels of organisational skills and reliable suppliers.

Table 1 shows the advantages and disadvantages of JIT manufacturing.

Table 1 Advantages and disadvantages of JIT

Advantages	Disadvantages
- It improves cash flow since money is not tied up in stocks	- A lot of faith is placed in the reliability and flexibility of suppliers
- The system reduces waste, obsolete and damaged stock	- Increased ordering and administration costs
- More factory space is made available for productive use	- Advantages of bulk buying may be lost
- The costs of stockholding are reduced significantly	- Vulnerable to a break in supply and machinery breakdowns
- Links with and the control of suppliers are improved	- Difficult to cope with sharp increases in demand
- The supplier base is reduced significantly	- Possible loss of reputation if customers are let down by late deliveries
- More scope for integration within the factory's computer system	
- The motivation of workers is improved. They are given more responsibility and encouraged to work in teams	

Thinking bigger

Many firms using JIT stock control make use of **Kanban** systems. Kanban is a Japanese term that means signboards or cards. The kanban system is a method used to control the transfer of materials between different stages of production. The kanban might be a solid plastic marker or coloured ping-pong ball used to, for instance:

- inform employees in the previous stage of production that a particular part must be taken from stocks and sent to a specific destination (conveyance kanbans)
- tell employees involved in a particular operation that they can begin production and add their output to stock (production kanbans)
- instruct external suppliers to send parts to a destination (vendor kanbans).

Kanbans are used to trigger the movement or production of resources. Used properly, they will be the only means of authorising movement. Kanbans are an important part of JIT manufacturing as they prevent the build-up of stock or parts in a factory.

Question 2

Like many construction companies, Balfour Beatty is making increased use of off-site modularisation. This is where the individual modules of a building are constructed in a factory and then transported to the site on specially designed trailers. Once on site, the modules are fixed together.

In 2013, Balfour Beatty won a contract from the developer Ballymore Group to build its 43-storey Providence Tower residential skyscraper in London Docklands, the tallest building constructed by Balfour Beatty in the UK to date. Balfour Beatty won the job with its plan to use modularised mechanical and electrical services. These would be constructed off site and delivered just in time, to reduce vehicle movements to and from the site, and reduce timescales for site construction.

Source: adapted from www.balfourbeattycsuk.com

(a) What stocks might a company like Balfour Beatty hold on a construction site?

(b) Assess the costs and benefits to Balfour Beatty of using a just-in-time approach to construction.

Waste minimisation

A failure to control stock adequately can result in wasted stock. This is most likely to happen if stocks are perishable. Perishable stocks or goods are those which physically deteriorate after a certain amount of time and therefore cannot be used. Consequently they have to be thrown away. Examples include fresh produce, such as fruit, vegetables, meat, cakes and flowers, ready-mix concrete, airline meals and some medical products, like stored blood, vaccines and biological medicines.

Stock can also be wasted if it has a limited life span and becomes obsolete after a certain amount of time. Examples might include newspapers and magazines, seasonal goods, such as Valentine's Day cards, and merchandising produced for specific events like a concert or sports fixture. It is important for businesses that produce these types of goods to control stock levels very carefully indeed. They may adopt some of the methods outlined below to minimise waste.

- If goods are perishable they must be stored in refrigerated units. Refrigeration can prolong the life of perishable goods – particularly in warm weather.
- Businesses have to be diligent when forecasting demand patterns for perishable goods. If they overestimate demand they could be left with a lot of unsold stock. Some businesses use complex quantitative techniques to predict the demand of perishable goods. Such techniques use historic data relating to demand, the shelf life of products, lead times and storage costs.
- A suitable **stock rotation** method should be adopted. With perishable goods the FIFO method (first in first out) is used. This means that the stocks that were delivered first must be issued first. Using this method ensures that older stock is used up first.
- Many businesses use computers to manage stock control. Computerised systems are programmed to automatically order stock when the re-order level is reached. In supermarkets, computerised checkout systems record every item of stock purchased by customers and automatically subtract items from total stock levels. Most very large businesses use computerised stock control.
- Some businesses might be able to use adjustable pricing strategies to help minimise waste. For example, if stocks remain high as the 'sell-by date' approaches, prices might be reduced to encourage purchases.
- Perishable goods need to be transported rapidly. If transportation can be speeded up then goods will reach the market place more quickly and be available for sale in the best condition. Some perishable goods, such as food and flowers, are flown to customers to increase the speed of delivery.
- To minimise waste, a business might find creative methods in the disposal of goods that have passed their sell-by date. For example, food products might be given to charities or sold as animal feed. Newspapers and magazines are likely to be recycled.

Competitive advantage from lean production

The use of just-in-time stock control is often an important element if a business is adopting lean production. Lean production aims to use fewer resources in production. A range of production techniques, such as Kaizen, cell production, flexible manufacturing, teamworking, empowerment and multi-skilling, are used to minimise waste. Lean producers use less time, less stock, fewer materials, less labour, less space and fewer suppliers. Lean producers are likely to have a competitive advantage because the reduction in waste and resource use will lower production costs. Specifically, competitiveness will be improved because lean production:

- raises productivity
- reduces costs and cuts lead times
- lowers the number of defective products
- improves reliability and speeds up design time.

With these improvements businesses will be able to charge lower prices, offer better quality and reliability, and fight off rivals in the global market place.

Key terms

Buffer stocks – stocks held as a precaution to cope with unforeseen demand.
Kanban – a card or an object that acts as a signal to move or provide resources in a factory.
Lead time – the time between placing the order and the delivery of goods.
Re-order level – the level of current stock when new orders are placed.
Re-order quantity – the amount of stock ordered when an order is placed.
Stock rotation – the flow of stock into and out of storage.
Work-in-progress – partly finished goods.

Thinking bigger

Stock control has been improved by the use of computers. Many businesses hold details of their entire stock on computer databases. All additions to and issues from stocks are recorded and up-to-date stock levels can be found instantly. Actual levels of stock should be the same as shown in the computer printout. A prudent firm will carry out regular stock checks to identify differences. Some systems are programmed to automatically order stock when the re-order level is reached. Access to stock levels is useful when manufacturers are dealing with large orders. The firm might need to find out whether there are enough materials in stock to complete an order. If this information is available, then the firm can give a more accurate delivery date.

Knowledge check

1. Why do businesses prefer to minimise stock holdings?
2. What is meant by work-in-progress?
3. State four costs of holding stocks.
4. Why are buffer stocks held by firms?
5. State two drawbacks of holding too little stock.
6. State two possible disadvantages of just-in-time stock management.
7. What types of stocks are most likely to be wasted?
8. What method of stock rotation is most suitable for perishable goods?
9. State two ways of minimising waste stock.
10. How might lean production improve competitiveness?

Case study

TOYOTA

Toyota, the Japanese car manufacturer, has developed a production system that aims to completely eliminate waste. The Toyota Production System (TPS) is based on just-in-time production, but also uses other lean production methods, such as Kaizen, in an attempt to completely eliminate seven sources of waste:

1. over production (largest waste)
2. time on hand (waiting)
3. transportation
4. processing itself
5. stock at hand
6. movement
7. making defective products.

Building on the just-in-time method of production, Toyota has produced an efficient system that reduces waste and demands on the production line, meaning that the vehicle can be built in the shortest period of time possible. The following principles help Toyota to achieve its aims.

1. When a vehicle order is received, a production instruction must be issued to the beginning of the vehicle production line.
2. The assembly line must be stocked with the required number of all needed parts so that any type of ordered vehicle can be assembled.

3. The assembly line must replace the parts used by retrieving the same number of parts from the parts-producing process (the preceding process).
4. The preceding process must be stocked with small numbers of all types of parts. Also, they should only produce what was taken by an operator from the next process.

TPS has helped Toyota to keep improving the way it manufactures vehicles. It has also developed a corporate culture where employees have to constantly grapple with challenges and problems, and must come up with fresh ideas. TPS has been so successful over the years that Toyota has gained a competitive advantage in the car industry. Indeed, many other manufacturers have adopted TPS or adapted it to meet their own needs.

Reproduced with permission from Toyota (GB) PLC.

(a) What is meant by just-in-time stock management? (2 marks)

(b) Explain one reason why Toyota does not hold buffer stocks. (4 marks)

(c) Assess the importance to Toyota of minimising waste. (8 marks)

(d) Assess the extent to which lean production has helped Toyota to gain a competitive edge. (12 marks)

Key points

1. Quality control, quality assurance and quality circles.
2. Total quality management (TQM).
3. Continuous improvement (Kaizen).
4. Competitive advantage from quality management.

Getting started

Michelin stars are awarded to restaurants for the excellence of their food and service. In the UK only four restaurants have been awarded three Michelin stars (the highest award). One of these is The Fat Duck, Bray, owned by the well-known chef, Heston Blumenthal. In 2015, a meal for two at The Fat Duck could cost up to £440 (without wine).

What is meant by quality to a customer in this business? Why would the award of a Michelin star be coveted by a chef or restaurant owner? What are the advantages of selling quality products? Why might quality be increasingly important to businesses?

What is quality?

Consumers, faced with many goods or services at similar prices, are likely to consider quality when making choices. Quality could be described as those features of a product or service that allow it to satisfy customers' wants. Take an example of a family buying a television. They may consider:

- physical appearance – they may want a certain style
- reliability and durability – will it last for 10 years?
- special features – does it have stereo sound?
- suitability – they may want a portable television
- parts – are spare parts available?
- repairs – does the shop carry out maintenance?
- after-sales service – how prompt is delivery?

They may also consider features which they perceive as important, such as:

- image – is the manufacturer's name widely recognised?
- reputation – what do other consumers think of the business or product?

The importance of quality has grown in recent years. Consumers are more aware. They get information through magazines such as *Which?* that contain reports on the quality of certain products. They also have more disposable income and higher expectations than ever before. Legislation and competition have also forced firms to improve the quality of their products.

Businesses, faced with competition, are also concerned about the quality of their:

- design – the ideas and plans for the product or service
- production processes – the methods used to manufacture the goods or provide the services.

Poor designs may lead to problems with the materials and the functions of the finished good or service. It costs time and money to redesign poor products. Clients are unlikely to use businesses with poor designs again. Problems also occur with poor-quality production processes. Faulty products are costly for a business. Machinery that breaks down or constantly needs to be repaired will also be expensive. Late delivery and ineffective productivity that results in poor quality can harm a business's reputation.

Quality control

Traditionally, in manufacturing, production departments have been responsible for ensuring quality.

Their objectives might have been to make sure that products:

- satisfied consumers' needs
- worked under conditions they were likely to face
- operated in the way they should
- could be produced cost-effectively
- could be repaired easily
- conformed to safety standards set down by legislation and independent bodies.

At Kellogg's, for example, samples of breakfast cereal have, in the past, been taken from the production line every half hour and tested. The testing took place in a food review room twice a day and was undertaken by a small group of staff. Each sample, about 50 in total, was compared with a 'perfect' Kellogg's sample and given a grade between 1 and 10. 10 was perfect but between 9.8 and 7, although noticeable to the trained eye, was acceptable to the customer. Below 7 the consumer would notice the reduction in quality. The cereals were tested for appearance, texture, colour, taste, etc. More sophisticated tests were carried out in a laboratory where the nutritional value of a sample, for example, was measured.

Quality control in UK organisations, in the past, often meant **quality controllers** or **quality inspectors** checking other people's work and the product itself after production had taken place. By today's standards this is not quality control, but a method of finding a poor-quality product (or a problem) before it is sold to the consumer.

Quality assurance

Today businesses are less concerned about 'Has the job been done properly?' than 'Are we able to do the job properly?' In other words inspection is carried out during the production process. This means that problems and poor-quality products can be prevented before final production.

Such a preventative approach has been used by Japanese businesses and is known as total quality management (TQM). It is now being adopted by many companies in the UK. It involves all employees in a business contributing to and being responsible for ensuring quality at all stages in the production process. **Quality assurance** is a commitment by a business to maintain quality throughout the organisation. The aim is to stop problems before they occur rather than finding them after they occur.

Quality assurance also takes into account customers' views when planning the production process. For example, customers may be consulted about their views through market research before a product is manufactured or a service provided. They may also be part of a consultation group involved at the design and manufacturing stage.

Exam tip

You need to avoid confusion between quality assurance and quality control. Remember that quality assurance aims to prevent defects with a focus on the **processes** used to make the product. It is a **proactive** quality task. Quality control aims to identify (and correct) defects in the finished **product**. Quality control, therefore, is a **reactive** task.

Question 1

The Quality Assurance Agency (QAA) is an independent body entrusted with monitoring and advising on standards and quality in UK higher education. The agency is responsible for ensuring that the UK's three million higher education students get the experience they are entitled to expect. The QAA is independent of both the government and of the higher education providers. It acts in the public interest, for the benefit of students. Its work involves matters such as:

- publishing and maintaining the UK Quality Code for Higher Education
- conducting external reviews of higher education providers and publishing their reports
- investigating concerns about academic quality and standards
- conducting research and sharing information about good practice to improve quality
- providing training and events to help higher education providers develop and improve their own quality assurance processes.

(a) Explain one example in higher education where quality would be of concern to students.

(b) Explain one way in which the QAA might gather information relating to the quality of higher education.

Quality circles

Quality control circles or **quality circles** are small groups of workers (about 5–20) in the same area of production who meet regularly to study and solve production problems. In addition, such groups are intended to motivate and involve workers on the shopfloor. They allow the workforce directly to improve the nature of the work they are doing.

Quality control circles started in America, where it was felt workers could be motivated by being involved in decision making. The idea gained in popularity in Japan and was taken up by Western businesses. Examples of their use can be found in Japanese companies setting up plants in the UK in the 1990s. For example, Honda at Swindon had 52 teams of six people looking at improvements that could be made in areas allocated to the groups, such as, safety.

Quality control circles are only likely to work if they have the support of both management and employees. Businesses have to want worker participation and involvement in decision making, and set up a structure that supports this. Workers and their representatives also need to support the scheme. Employees must feel that their views within the circle are valued and must make a contribution to decisions.

Question 2

Winnebago is a well-known producer of recreational vehicles (RVs). It has a reputation among motorhome enthusiasts for high quality and innovation, dating back to its founding in 1958. Every Winnebago motorhome integrates superior construction, design and comfort. In its effort to maintain very high quality standards, Winnebago has used quality circles for many years. Indeed, the company has won the Recreational Vehicle Dealers Association's prestigious Quality Circle Award every year since its inception in 1996.

Winnebago designs and manufactures components to high specifications. It has been able to deliver high quality at competitive prices. Higher quality is also the result of ongoing testing. Winnebago has a state-of-the-art, 40,000-square-foot testing facility. The computerised road simulator (nicknamed 'The Shaker') and the half-mile test track can simulate the effects of years of normal driving in just a few days. Components are checked under hot, cold, wet and dry conditions, and every Winnebago RV goes through a high-pressure water tunnel and is checked for leaks before shipping.

(a) What is meant by quality circles?

(b) Assess the importance of quality circles to Winnebago.

Total quality management (TQM)

Errors are costly for business. It is estimated that about one-third of all the effort of British businesses is wasted in correcting errors. There are benefits if something is done right the first time. Total quality management (TQM) is a method designed to prevent errors, such as the creation of poor-quality products, from happening. The business is organised so that the manufacturing process is investigated at every stage. It is argued that the success of Japanese companies is based on their superior organisation. Every department, activity and individual is organised to take into account quality at all times. What are the features of TQM?

Quality chains: Great stress is placed on the operation of quality chains. In any business a series of suppliers and customers exists. For example, a secretary is a supplier to a manager, who is the customer. The secretarial duties must be carried out to the satisfaction of the manager. The chain also includes customers and suppliers outside the business. The chain remains intact if the supplier satisfies the customer. It is broken if a person or item of equipment does not satisfy the needs of the customer. Failure to meet the requirements in any part of the quality chain creates problems, such as delays in the next stage of production.

Company policy, accountability and empowerment: There will only be improvements in quality if there is a company-wide quality policy. TQM must start from the top with the most senior executive and spread throughout the business to every employee. People must be totally committed and take a 'pride in the job'. This might be considered as an example of job enrichment. Lack of commitment, particularly at the top, causes problems. For example, if the managing director lacks commitment, employees lower down are unlikely to commit themselves. TQM stresses the role of the individual and aims to make everyone accountable for their own performance. For example, a machine operator may be accountable to a workshop supervisor for their work. They may also be empowered to make decisions.

Control: Consumers' needs will only be satisfied if the business has control of the factors that affect a product's quality. These may be human, administrative or technical factors, shown in Figure 1 on the next page. The process is only under control if materials, equipment and tasks are used in the same way every time. Take an example of a firm making biscuits. Only by cooking in the same way can the quality be consistent every time.

These methods can be documented and used to assess operations. Regular audits must be carried out by the firm to check quality. Information is then fed back from the customer to the 'operator' or producer, and from the operator to the supplier of inputs, such as raw materials. For example, a retailer may return a batch of vehicles to the manufacturer because the gears were faulty. The manufacturer might then identify the person responsible for fitting the gears. An investigation might reveal that the faulty gears were the responsibility of a component supplier. The supplier can then be contacted and the problem resolved. Quality audits and reviews may lead to suggestions for improvements – a different material, perhaps, or a new piece of equipment.

Monitoring the process: TQM relies on monitoring the business process to find possible improvements. Methods have been developed to help achieve this. **Statistical process control (SPC)** involves collecting data relating to the performance of a process. Data is presented in diagrams, charts and graphs. The information is then passed to all those concerned.

SPC can be used to reduce variability, which is the cause of most quality problems. Variations in products, delivery times, methods, materials, people's attitudes and staff performance often occur. For example, statistical data may show that worker attitudes may have led to variations in output late on Friday afternoon. Discussion might result in a change in the 'clocking on' and 'clocking off' times to solve the problem.

Teamwork: TQM stresses that teamwork is the most effective way of solving problems. The main advantages are:

- a greater range of skills, knowledge and experience can be used to solve the problem
- employee morale is often improved
- problems across departments are better dealt with
- a greater variety of problems can be tackled
- team 'ideas' are more likely to be used than individual ones.

TQM strongly favours teamwork throughout the business. It builds trust and morale, improves communications and co-operation, and develops interdependence. Many UK firms in the past have suffered due to lack of sharing of information and ideas. Such approaches have often led to division between sections of the workforce.

Consumer views: Firms using TQM must be committed to their customers. They must be responsive to changes in people's needs and expectations. To do this, information must be gathered on a regular basis and there must be clear communication channels for customers to express their views. Consumers are often influential in setting quality standards. For example, holiday companies issue questionnaires to their customers on the way back from a package holiday. The information can be used to identify the strengths and weaknesses of their operations. Such information can be used to monitor and upgrade quality standards.

Zero defects: Many business quality systems have a zero defect policy. This aims to ensure that every product that is manufactured is free from defects. A business that is able to guarantee zero defects in customers' orders is likely to gain a good reputation. This could lead to new clients and improved sales.

Quality circles: TQM stresses the importance of teamwork in a business. Many businesses have introduced quality circles into their operations. In order for quality circles to be successful certain conditions must exist.

- A steering committee should be set up to oversee the whole quality circle programme.
- A senior manager should ideally chair the committee. Managers must show commitment to the principle of quality circles.
- At least one person on the committee should be accountable for the programme.
- Team leaders should be properly trained.

Using TQM: TQM helps companies to:

- focus clearly on the needs of customers and relationships between suppliers and customers
- achieve quality in all aspects of business, not just product or service quality
- critically analyse all processes to remove waste and inefficiencies
- find improvements and develop measures of performance
- develop a team approach to problem solving
- develop effective procedures for communication and acknowledgement of work
- continually review the processes to develop a strategy of constant improvement.

There are, however, some problems.

- There will be training and development costs of the new system.
- TQM will only work if there is commitment from the entire business.
- There will be a great deal of bureaucracy and documents, and regular audits will be needed. This may be a problem for small firms.
- Stress is placed on the process and not the product.

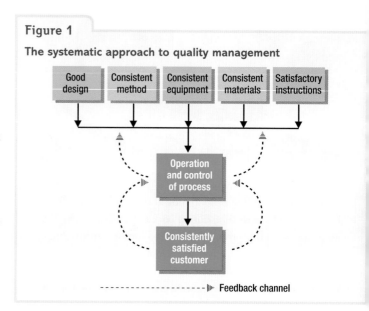

Figure 1

The systematic approach to quality management

Feedback channel

Kaizen

Kaizen is perhaps the most important concept in Japanese management. It means continuous improvement. Every aspect of life, including social life, working life and home life, is constantly improved. Everyone in the business is involved. Kaizen is said to be an 'umbrella concept'. A wide range of different production techniques and working practices must be carried out for it to be effective. Figure 2 on the next page shows examples of the techniques, principles and practices. They should result in ongoing improvements. This approach argues that a day should not pass without some kind of improvement being made somewhere in the business.

There are a number of features of Kaizen which affect a business.

Continuous improvement: Kaizen has been the main difference between the Japanese and the Western approaches to management in the past. The attempts of Western businesses to improve efficiency and quality have tended to be 'one-offs'. In Figure 3 on the next page the solid line illustrates the Western approach. Productivity remains the same for long periods of time, then suddenly rises. The increase is followed by another period of stability, before another rise. Increases in productivity may result from new working practices or new technology. The dotted line shows the Japanese approach. Improvements are continuous. They result from changes in production techniques which are introduced gradually.

Eliminating waste: The elimination of waste (called muda in Japan) in business practices is an important part of Kaizen. Waste is any activity which raises costs without adding value to a product. Examples may be:

- time wasted while staff wait around before starting tasks, such as waiting for materials to arrive
- time wasted when workers move unnecessarily in the workplace, such as walking to a central point in the factory to get tools
- the irregular use of a machine, such as a machine which is only used once a month for a special order
- excessive demands upon machines or workers, such as staff working overtime seven days a week which causes them to be tired and work poorly.

Firms that adopt the Kaizen approach train and reward workers to continually search for waste and to suggest how it might be eliminated.

Implementing continuous improvement: It is often difficult for workers in a business to look for continuous improvement all the time. Japanese businesses tried to solve this problem by introducing the PDCA (Plan, Do, Check, Action) cycle. It is a series of activities that lead to improvement.

- **Plan.** Businesses must identify where improvement is needed. Data must be gathered and used to develop a plan which will result in improvement.
- **Do.** Once the plan has been finalised it must be carried out. The plan is likely to be implemented by workers, on the production line perhaps.
- **Check.** The next stage in the cycle is to check whether or not there has been an improvement. This task may be carried out by inspectors.
- **Action.** If the plan has been successful, it must be introduced in all parts of the business.

Figure 2

The Kaizen umbrella

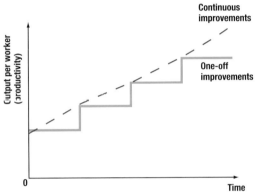

Customer orientation	Just in time
Total Quality Management (TQM)	Zero defects
Quality control circles	Cooperative staff–management relations
Suggestion system	Kanban
Robotics Automation	Quality improvement
Discipline in the workplace	Productivity improvement
TPM (Total Productive Maintenance)	Small group activities
	New product development

Figure 3

The Western and Japanese approaches to improvement

Output per worker (productivity) / Time

Continuous improvements

One-off improvements

Question 3

Sylvie Bennet, based in Yorkshire, produces high-quality children's clothing and the family-owned company has been trading for over 100 years. Their total commitment to quality and innovative design has seen the company produce products that are often featured in magazines and even sometimes purchased by celebrities for their children to wear.

As a company that is always looking to improve processes, the managing director, Julia Humphrey, decided to introduce Kaizen. She'd read about how the car industry used Kaizen to improve their productivity and felt that their product could be treated the same in many respects as each product was made from the same basic body shape. She also wanted to look at how the company could gain profit at each step. In the year after introducing Kaizen productivity rose 5 per cent, which helped them increase their profit by 10 per cent as well.

To make Kaizen work for their business Humphrey looked at each point of the production chain and identified ways it could be improved. This included additional staff training so staff members could take on different tasks, to better purchasing negotiations with their material suppliers. They even looked at the way the product was sold. They identified that users on their website were not completing their purchases and investigated reasons why. They realised that their 'checkout' button was not very clear and resolved the issue, pushing online sales up 10 per cent.

Humphrey thinks that their productivity will continue to grow and estimates that they can increase it by at least another 5 per cent. By increasing the number of garments made at each stage, they will make the company more profitable as the costs per item of manufacture will decrease.

(a) Explain one way in which Kaizen can help a business improve productivity.

(b) Explain one way in which Sylvie Bennet has benefited from the introduction of Kaizen.

Competitive advantage from quality management

Supplying high-quality goods and services can have a huge positive impact on businesses. The main one is that product quality should be improved, which should help to increase sales. Also, business costs may be cut if faults in products are identified before the product reaches the market. The costs of failure once the product has reached the market are likely to be much higher than those during manufacture.

Some businesses use quality as a means of developing a USP. If a business can differentiate its product on grounds of quality and persuade the customer that their product is superior to its rivals, it may enjoy some benefits, particularly the ability to charge a higher price. This gives a business more flexibility in pricing.

Inevitably a business that can deliver quality will develop a competitive advantage. This will allow firms to win customers from rivals, increase market share, raise revenue and improve profitability. A number of British firms have been successful in overseas markets due to the competitive edge they have gained as a result of marketing quality products. Examples include Rolls-Royce, Burberry, Jaguar Land Rover (owned by Tata), British Airways and Jimmy Choo.

Key terms

Quality – features of a product that allow it to satisfy customers' needs. It may refer to some standard of excellence.
Quality assurance – a method of working for businesses that takes into account customers' wants when standardising quality. It often involves guaranteeing that quality standards are met.
Quality chains – when employees form a series of links between customers and suppliers in business, both internally and externally.
Quality circles – groups of workers meeting regularly to solve problems and discuss work issues.
Quality control – making sure that the quality of a product meets specified quality performance criteria.
Statistical process control – the collection of data about the performance of a particular process in a business.
Total quality management (TQM) – a managerial approach that focuses on quality and aims to improve the effectiveness, flexibility and competitiveness of the business.

Thinking bigger

Despite the benefits from improving quality, it is important to recognise the costs.

- **Designing and setting up a quality control system.** This might include the time used to 'think through' a system and the training of staff to use it.
- **Lost production.** When a business introduces a major new system there can be some serious disruption while the new system is bedded-in. This could lead to a loss of output and damage to customer relations if orders are not met.
- **Improving the actual quality.** This may be the cost of better materials, superior methods, new machinery or training staff in new working practices. If the whole quality system fails, there may be costs in setting it up again. Time may be needed to rethink or adjust the system. Retraining might also be necessary.
- **Training.** Quality initiatives will only be successful if the people involved in their implementation are properly trained. This can prove very costly. For example, if TQM is introduced the entire workforce will have to be trained. This may involve sending all staff on specialist training courses or outsourcing training to an expert in TQM.

It has been suggested that 10–20 per cent of the revenue of a business is accounted for by quality-related costs. The vast majority of these costs are related to appraisal and failure, which add very little to the quality of the product. Eliminating such failure would help to reduce these costs, saving UK businesses billions of pounds.

Knowledge check

1. What is meant by the quality of a product?
2. Explain the difference between actual and perceived quality.
3. Explain the difference between quality control and quality assurance.
4. What is the main purpose of using quality circles?
5. State five implications of TQM for a business.
6. Why is teamwork so important in TQM?
7. What is meant by the Kaizen umbrella?
8. Explain the purpose of the PDCA cycle.
9. What are the costs and benefits of ensuring quality?

Case study

THE POWARTH GROUP

The Powarth Group owns a small chain of 23 hotels in Europe. Up until 2010 the group's performance had been lacklustre with flat sales for five consecutive years. However, in 2010 the group signed a deal with an online booking company in the hope that sales would soar, raising occupancy rates above the current 52 per cent. This turned out to be a disaster. The booking site also has a customer review system where people can give feedback about their experience. The review below is typical of the many posted on the site relating to Powarth Group hotels.

The Globe – Milan

This is one of the worst hotels my husband and I have ever stayed in. The main problem was the staff – they were totally disinterested and as guests we felt that we were an inconvenience. When we arrived there was a queue to check in and only one youngster on duty who could not speak English. The whole process took 55 minutes and the receptionist tried to charge us again even though we had paid in advance. There was quite a heated dispute and communication was difficult – the hotel manager, who could speak English, was on a break and could not be contacted.

Things did not get better. Our room was dark, musty and in a very poor decorative state. There were no coat-hangers, the towels did not look clean, the furniture was old and the television did not work. I could go on but the next day my husband and I checked out even though we had paid for two nights in advance.

Mrs T. Ellington

After several emergency board meetings the directors decided that some drastic action was necessary. They decided to invest in total quality management (TQM) to try and improve the quality of the hotel service. In 2013, they took the following measures to introduce TQM at a total cost of €5.6 million.

- Organised an outside agency to train all staff in TQM.

- Employed another agency to train staff in customer service.

- Set up a suggestions box to encourage staff ideas. €1,000 was given to a member of staff if their idea was implemented by management.

- Organised the staff into teams.

- Kept records of all guest complaints and followed every single one up with a personal letter from the manager.

The group also invested €4.3 million in the refurbishment of half of the hotels – pledging another €5 million in investment in three years' time for refurbishing the remainder. The group also upgraded their website, changed the mission statement to emphasise the quality of their service and purchased a smart new hotel uniform. All staff were consulted on the uniform design and the wording of the mission statement.

At the end of 2014 profits rose from €120,000 to €1.67 million, guest complaints fell by 82 per cent, staff morale improved and hotel occupancy rates had increased to 74 per cent.

(a) What is meant by total quality management? (2 marks)

(b) Explain how the use of teamworking might improve the quality of service at the Powarth Group hotels. (4 marks)

(c) Assess the possible benefits to the Powarth Group of total quality management. (8 marks)

(d) Assess the extent to which the introduction of total quality management at the Powarth Group was a success. (12 marks)

Key points

The effect on businesses of changes in economic influences:

1. Inflation (the rate of inflation and consumer price index).
2. Exchange rates (appreciation and depreciation).
3. Interest rates.
4. Taxation and government spending.
5. The business cycle.
6. The effect of economic uncertainty on the business environment.

Getting started

Dunelm is a well-known homewares retailer. It has over 120 stores and sells household goods, such as bedding, blinds, curtains, cushions, décor, lights, mirrors, some electrical goods and kitchenware. The company has performed well, increasing revenue from £423.8 million in 2009 to £677.2 million in 2013.

Give four examples of economic influences that might affect the performance of Dunelm. How might a cut in income tax affect Dunelm? How might Dunelm react to people having less to spend or other businesses closing down? Would Dunelm benefit from higher interest rates?

External influences

Business activity is influenced by a number of external influences. These are factors beyond the control of businesses. In some cases they constrain a business's decisions and may prevent its growth and development. Examples of these external influences are summarised in Figure 1.

Economic influences, such as inflation, exchange rates, interest rates, taxation, government expenditure and the business cycle can have many effects on a business. The government is responsible for the management of the economy. The aim of many governments is to keep prices stable, keep unemployment down, keep borrowing down and help the economy grow. The measures a government might use to achieve these aims can have an impact on businesses.

Inflation

A government will want to keep prices stable in the country's economy. This means that **inflation** must be kept under control. Inflation is when the general price level is rising. For example, if a basket of goods cost £100 on 1.1.2013, and the same basket cost £103 on 1.1.2014, prices have gone up by three per cent. This means that the inflation rate is three per cent. If inflation is too high it can harm the economy. Figure 2 shows inflation rates in the UK between 2004 and 2014. The graph shows that the rate of inflation has been quite low, fluctuating between one and five per cent. Inflation rates at these levels are not really troublesome. However, in the 1970s, inflation reached levels of 25 per cent, which was a serious threat to businesses and the economy.

Figure 1

External influences on businesses

- Government
- Legislation and regulation
- World events
- Environmental factors
- **External influences**
- Consumer tastes
- Social factors
- Economic climate
- Changes in population
- Pressure groups

Figure 2

UK inflation rates between 2004 and 2014

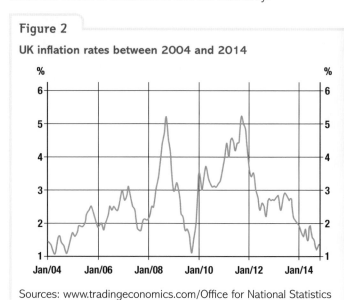

Sources: www.tradingeconomics.com/Office for National Statistics

How is inflation measured?

A common approach to measuring inflation is to calculate changes in the **consumer price index (CPI)**. This involves gathering information about the prices of goods and services in the economy. Each month the government records price changes of about 600 goods and services. From these records an average price change is calculated and converted into an index number. The month's figures can then be compared with the previous month's, or that of 12 months ago, to calculate the percentage change in prices (i.e. the inflation rate) over the time period. The inflation rates shown in Figure 2 use the CPI.

Maths tip

The use of index numbers is common in business and economics. An index number is an indication of change in a series of figures where one figure is given a value of 100 and others are adjusted in proportion to it. It is often used as an average of a number of figures like when measuring the CPI.

How does inflation affect businesses?

Inflation rates between one and five per cent, like those in the UK between 2004 and 2014 in Figure 2, are not likely to have a big impact on businesses. However, once the CPI gets into double figures and beyond, inflation can have some damaging effects on businesses.

High and particularly fluctuating inflation is likely to be damaging to businesses for a number of reasons.

Increased costs: High or fluctuating inflation imposes a variety of costs on businesses.

- With suppliers' prices rising all the time, but at different rates, time must be spent researching the market for the best deals. Equally, more time has to be spent tracking the prices of competitors to decide when and by how much to increase your own prices. These costs are called **shoe leather costs**, because before the age of the telephone and the internet, businesses would have to send their employees round on foot to gather this information.
- Raising prices costs money. Customers have to be informed of the new prices. Brochures might have to be reprinted and sent out. Websites might have to be updated. The sales force has to be made familiar with new prices. These costs are called **menu costs** because, for a restaurant, increasing prices means that it has to reprint its menus.
- Management is likely to have to spend more time dealing with workers' pay claims. Instead of being able to sign a two- or three-year deal, annual pay negotiations are likely to be the norm. If there is **hyperinflation**, where inflation is running into 100 per cent per annum or over, pay negotiations may have to take place each month. There is also a much larger risk of strikes because workers and managers will probably have different views of future inflation rates. Workers will be worried that any deal they make will leave them worse off after inflation. So they might be more willing to take industrial action to get high pay settlements.

Uncertainty: With high and fluctuating inflation, businesses don't know what prices will be in three or six months' time, let alone in one or five years. But decisions have to be made now which will affect the business in the long term. For example, businesses need to invest to survive. But how much should they invest? The price of a new machine, a shop or a new computer system will probably be higher in six months than today. But are they worth buying if interest rates are at very high levels? What if the new machine is bought, financed by very high cost borrowing and there is a **recession**, where demand for goods and services falls?

Another problem with uncertainty is linked to entering long-term contracts. A customer might approach a business wanting to buy products on a regular monthly basis for the next two years. How can the supplier put a price on this contract if it doesn't know what the inflation rate will be over the next 24 months?

Borrowing and lending: Borrowing and lending becomes an opportunity and a problem for businesses. On the one hand, the real value of debts incurred in the past can become quickly eroded by inflation. If inflation is 100 per cent per annum, the real value of money borrowed a year ago is halved in one year. Inflation initially benefits borrowers and harms lenders.

But in an inflationary environment, interest rates rise to match inflation. If there is prolonged inflation, interest rates are likely to become **index linked** – linked to the index of prices. So interest might be charged at the rate of inflation plus 5 per cent or plus 10 per cent.

Consumer reactions: Consumers react to inflation as well as businesses. Prolonged inflation tends to lead to more saving. Inflation unsettles consumers. They become less willing to borrow money, not knowing what will happen in the future. The value of savings tends to fall as inflation erodes their real value. So people react by saving more to make up savings to their previous real value. Increased saving means less spending and so businesses will sell less.

If inflation is very high, consumers will adopt different spending patterns which may affect businesses. For example, if there is hyperinflation, prices will be changing by the day. Consumers will then tend to spend wages or interest as soon as they receive them. On 'pay day' there can be huge activity in shops. Supermarkets have to be geared up to selling most of the weekly or monthly turnover in just a few hours. Suppliers of fresh produce to supermarkets have to be geared to delivering most of their goods on one day a week.

International competitiveness: High inflation can have an impact on businesses that import or export goods and services. For example, if the UK has higher inflation rates than its trading partners, UK businesses will become uncompetitive. As a result, they are likely to lose sales and shares in overseas markets. Also, UK businesses facing competition from overseas will lose out because imports become relatively cheaper. For example, consumers in the UK may buy foreign goods instead of UK goods because their prices are rising less quickly than those in the UK. The impact of changes in the price of imports and exports are discussed in more detail later in this unit.

Deflation

Some countries in the world have experienced **deflation**. This is where the general price level starts to fall and can also be a problem for businesses. This is mainly because deflation is usually associated with a fall in demand. When prices are falling consumers may delay spending because they think they can make purchases in the future at lower prices. As a result businesses postpone investment and may lay off workers due to the need to cut production. Businesses may also have to lower their prices, which can reduce their profits. In 2014, there were some deflationary pressures in the EU when the oil price fell sharply, inflation was very low and a number of countries were in recession. However, if deflation is the result of falling import prices or falls in the prices of commodities, such as oil, the effects could be positive. For example, a fall in UK import prices could be the result of a strong pound. This means that imported goods will be cheaper and will put downward pressure on the CPI. This may not have a negative impact on the UK economy. Also, if commodity prices (such as oil) fall, this might reduce the cost of inputs for many businesses. As a result they may respond by actually increasing production.

Exchange rates

Different countries in the world have their own currencies. For example, the USA uses the dollar, Japan uses the yen, many EU countries use the euro and the UK has the pound. When countries use different currencies transactions between people and businesses are affected. For example, an Indian visitor to the UK cannot use rupees, they would have to buy some British pounds. How many pounds would the Indian visitor get for 150,000 rupees? This depends on the **exchange rate** between the pound and the rupee. If it were £1 = ₹100 the visitor would get £1,500 (₹150,000 ÷ ₹100). The exchange rate shows the price of pounds in terms of rupees. When businesses buy goods and services from other countries, payments are usually made in the supplier's currency. Some examples are given below.

Worked example

1. How much will it cost a French business to buy goods from a British business which cost £400,000 if £1 = €1.25? The cost to the French business in euros is:

    £400,000 × 1.25 = €500,000

2. How many US dollars will it cost a British business buying £55,000 of goods from an American business if £1 = US$1.50? The cost to the British business in US dollars is:

    £55,000 × 1.50 = $82,500

3. How much will it cost a British business in pounds to buy $300,000 of goods from a US business if £1 = US$1.50? The cost in pounds is:

    $300,000 ÷ 1.50 = £200,000

4. How many pounds can a Japanese business person buy with ¥100,000 when visiting London if £1 = ¥190? The quantity of pounds that can be bought is:

    ¥100,000 ÷ 190 = £526.32

The impact of an appreciation in the exchange rate on imports and exports

The exchange rate is the price of one currency in terms of another. Like all prices the exchange rate can change. This is because prices are determined by market forces, and supply and demand conditions can change at any time. For example, if the demand for UK exports rises, there will be an increase in the demand for pounds. This is because foreigners need pounds to pay for exports. The increase in demand for pounds will raise the exchange rate (i.e. raise the value of the currency, the pound, against that of another currency). When it rises, the exchange rate has **appreciated**.

Changes in the exchange rate can have an impact on the demand for exports and imports. This is because, when the exchange rate changes, the prices of exports and imports also change.

Worked example

What happens when the exchange rate rises (i.e. the value of the pound rises) from, say, £1 = US$1.50 to £1 = US$2?

Impact on exports: If a UK business **sells** goods worth £2 million to a US customer, the dollar price at the original exchange rate is $3 million (£2 million × 1.50). When the exchange rate rises the dollar price of the goods also rises to $4 million (£2 million × 2). This means that demand for UK exports is likely to fall because they are now dearer.

Impact on imports: If another UK firm **buys** goods worth $600,000 from a US supplier, the price in pounds at the original exchange rate is £400,000 ($600,000 ÷ 1.50). When the exchange rate rises the sterling price to the importer falls to £300,000 ($600,000 ÷ 2). This means that demand for imports is likely to rise, because they are cheaper.

The impact of a depreciation in the exchange rate on imports and exports

When the exchange rate falls it has **depreciated**. The impact on the demand for imports and exports is the opposite.

Worked example

What happens when the exchange rate falls (i.e. the value of the pound falls) from, say, £1 = US$1.50 to £1 = US$1.20?

Impact on exports: If a UK business **sells** goods worth £2 million to a US customer, the dollar price at the original exchange rate is $3 million (£2 million × 1.50). When the exchange falls the dollar price of the goods also falls to $2.4 million (£2 million × 1.20). This means that demand for UK exports is likely to rise because they are now cheaper.

Impact on imports: If another UK business **buys** goods worth $600,000 from a US supplier, the price in pounds at the original exchange rate is £400,000 ($600,000 ÷ 1.50). When the exchange rate falls the sterling price to the importer rises to £500,000 ($600,000 ÷ 1.20). This means that demand for imports is likely to fall because they are dearer.

The effects of changes in the exchange rate on the demand for exports and imports are summarised in Table 1.

Table 1 Summary of the effects of changing exchange rates

Exchange rate	Price of exports	Demand for exports	Price of imports	Demand for imports
Falls	Falls	Rises	Rises	Falls
Rises	Rises	Falls	Falls	Rises

How are businesses affected by exchange rates?

The examples on the previous page show what happens to the prices of imports and exports when exchange rates appreciate and depreciate. Sometimes these changes will benefit a business, other times they will not. For example, if the value of the rupee falls, Indian exporters will benefit because the price of exports falls and demand should increase. However, Indian importers will lose out because their purchases will be more expensive.

Fluctuating exchange rates cause uncertainty. Businesses do not know what is going to happen to exchange rates in the future. This means that it is difficult to predict demand for exports and the cost of imports. This makes planning and budgeting more difficult. Another problem is that it costs money to switch from one currency to another. There is usually a commission charge of around two per cent. This represents a cost to importers and therefore reduces profit.

Question 1

Burberry Group plc is a British luxury fashion house, distributing clothing, fashion accessories, fragrances, sunglasses and cosmetics. Burberry is most famous for its trench coat with its distinctive tartan pattern, which was designed by founder Thomas Burberry. The company has branded stores and franchises around the world, and also sells through concessions in third-party stores. Burberry has several shops in Japan including five in Tokyo.

(a) Explain why exchange rates are necessary.

(b) One of Burberry's products is the Sandringham Short Heritage Trench Coat. If this sells for £995 in the UK, calculate how much it would cost a Japanese shopper in Tokyo if £1 = ¥190.

(c) Assess the possible impact on Burberry if the exchange rate changed to £1 = ¥150.

Interest rates

If a business or an individual borrows money, they usually have to pay **interest** on the loan. Equally, if they put their savings into a bank or building society, they expect to receive interest.

The interest rate is the price of borrowing or saving money. For example, if a small business borrows £10,000 from a bank for one year, and the interest rate is 7 per cent, it has to pay £700 in interest. Equally, if a business has £1 million in the bank for a year which it uses as working capital, and the rate of interest the bank offers is 3 per cent, it will earn £30,000 in interest.

The impact of low interest rates on businesses has been generally helpful. Figure 3 shows the level of interest rates in the UK between 1984 and 2014. Since 2008 the **base rate** has been 0.5 per cent. However, previously to this in the late 1980s, rates were much higher, reaching a peak of 15 per cent. Rates this high can have damaging effects on businesses, as outlined below.

Finally, the use of interest rates to help control the economy is called **monetary policy**. For example, a government might raise interest rates to dampen demand in the economy if they thought that inflation was being caused by demand rising too quickly.

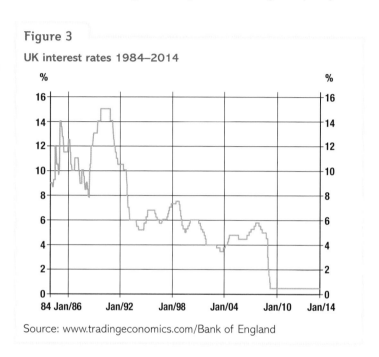

Figure 3

UK interest rates 1984–2014

Source: www.tradingeconomics.com/Bank of England

Effect of interest rates on costs

Changes in interest rates are likely to affect the overheads of a business. Interest charges are part of overhead costs. If interest rates rise, businesses are likely to have to pay higher interest payments on their borrowing. For example, a business might borrow £10,000 on overdraft. The annual payments on this would rise from £600 to £700 if the rate of interest rose from 6 to 7 per cent a year.

Not all borrowing is at variable rates of interest. Variable rates mean that banks or other lenders are free to change the rate of interest on any money borrowed. Many loans to businesses are at fixed rates of interest. This is where the bank cannot change the rate of interest over the agreed term (the time over which the loan will be paid off) of the loan. A rise in interest rates in the economy won't affect the overheads of a business with only fixed term loans. But, if a business wanted to take out new loans, it would have to pay the higher rates of interest the bank or other lender was now charging. So overhead costs would rise.

Effect of interest rates on investment

Changes in the rate of interest affect the amount that businesses invest, for example in new buildings, plant and machinery. There are four main reasons for this.

The cost of loans: Investment projects are often financed through loans. A rise in interest rates increases the cost of borrowing money. So projects financed this way will find that the total costs have risen, reducing profitability. This might be enough to persuade some businesses to shelve their investment plans. Total investment in the economy will then fall.

Attractiveness of saving: Businesses have the alternative of putting their funds into savings schemes rather than investing in machinery or buildings, for example. A rise in interest rates makes putting money into financial assets relatively more attractive. For example, if interest rates rise from 5 to 8 per cent, a business might decide to shelve an investment project and save the funds instead.

Paying off existing loans: A rise in interest rates will increase the cost of existing variable rate borrowing. A business could choose to pay off existing loans rather than increase its investment. This will reduce its costs. It also reduces the risk associated with borrowing.

A fall in demand: A rise in interest rates is likely to reduce total spending in the economy, as explained below. This might affect the profitability of many investment projects. For example, a business might forecast that an investment project would be profitable with 20,000 sales a year. But if sales were projected to be only 15,000 a year because of a downturn in demand, then the investment project could be unprofitable and might not go ahead.

Effect of interest rates on demand

The level of interest rates affects aggregate demand (i.e. total demand) for goods and services in the economy. A rise in interest rates will tend to push down aggregate demand. A fall in interest rates will tend to increase demand.

Businesses are directly affected by changes in demand. When demand falls, their sales go down because less is being bought. If demand rises, businesses receive more orders and more sales.

There are many different ways in which changes in interest rates lead to changes in the sales of businesses.

Domestic consumption: Consumers will be hit by a rise in interest rates. The cost of loans will rise. This will deter consumers from buying goods bought on credit, such as cars, furniture and electrical equipment. These goods are known as consumer durables because they are 'used up' over a long period.

In the UK, people who have a mortgage (a loan to buy a house) are also likely to see their monthly repayments rise because many mortgages are variable rate loans. Existing mortgage holders will then have less to spend on other goods and services. Some potential new home buyers will be put off because they can't afford the repayments, directly hitting the new housing market. If unemployment begins to rise because of less spending, consumer confidence will fall. This will make consumers even less willing to take out loans and spend.

Domestic investment: As explained above, businesses are likely to cut back plans for new investment if interest rates rise. Investment goods, like new buildings or machines, are made by businesses. So these businesses will see a fall in their demand.

Stocks: Businesses keep stocks of raw materials and finished goods. Stocks cost money to keep, because a fall in stock levels could be used to finance a fall in borrowing and interest payments. So a rise in interest rates will increase the cost of keeping stock. This will encourage businesses to destock, i.e. reduce their stock levels. This will be especially true if the rise in interest rates has hit demand in the economy. With fewer sales, less needs to be produced. So less stock needs to be kept. But cutting stock reduces orders for businesses further up the chain of production. For example, a retailer cutting stocks affects demand from its suppliers. Destocking due to higher interest rates will therefore cause a fall in demand throughout much of industry.

Exports and imports: A rise in interest rates tends to lead to a rise in the value of one currency against others. A rise in the pound, for example, will make it harder for UK businesses to export profitably. At the same time, foreign firms will find it easier to gain sales in the UK domestic market because they will be able to reduce their prices. The result is likely to be a fall in exports and a loss of sales to importers in the domestic market. Both will reduce demand and hit UK businesses.

Question 2

In 1990, restaurateur Ernie Carter was declared bankrupt. His restaurant business went into liquidation when he failed to pay interest owing on a mortgage. The interest payments on his £155,000 mortgage were £2,400 a month. The mortgage, taken out on his private residence, had been used to help fund the restaurant. However, the restaurant struggled and was not generating enough revenue to meet the high mortgage payments. Ernie lost everything. He borrowed £2,000 from his father and went to New Zealand. Fifteen years later, after working as a chef in various hotels in Wellington and Queenstown, he returned to England with £30,000 of savings.

Ernie invested £20,000 setting up a new catering venture specialising in the provision of food for weddings, business functions and parties. The business went very well and even grew during the recession in the UK between 2008 and 2012. In 2013, Ernie decided to expand his business and invest some retained profit in an outdoor catering operation. His idea was to provide 'instant party facilities'. This included a marquee, music system, bar, spit-roasting and full buffet service. The idea worked very well indeed. He took on four more employees and since interest rates were at 'rock bottom' decided to borrow £10,000 to double the size of his outdoor catering operation.

(a) Explain one effect that high interest rates can have on businesses.

(b) Explain why a business like Ernie's is likely to invest more when interest rates are low.

Taxation

Governments can affect business decision-making using fiscal policy. This involves changing **taxation** and **government expenditure** to influence the economy. Taxes vary from country to country but are paid by both businesses and individuals. The main taxes levied in the UK are shown in Table 2.

Table 2 The main taxes levied in the UK

Direct taxes (taxes on income)	
Income tax	Paid on personal income and that from paid and self-employment
National Insurance contributions	Paid by businesses and individuals on employee's earnings
Corporation tax	Paid by companies based on how much profit they make
Capital gains tax	Paid on the capital gain (profit) made when selling an asset
Inheritance tax	Paid on money transferred to another individual, usually after death
Indirect taxes (taxes on spending)	
Value Added Tax (VAT)	Paid mainly when buying goods and services (except food)
Excise duties	Paid when buying certain goods such as petrol and tobacco
Customs duties	Paid when buying certain goods from abroad
Council tax	Paid by residents to the council to help fund local services
Business rates	Paid by businesses to the council to help fund local services

The effect on businesses of changes in taxation

How might changes in taxation affect businesses in the UK?

Consumer spending: Changes in certain types of taxation are likely to increase the income consumers have left after tax. These include reductions in income tax rates, increases in personal allowances and an increase in the limits on which inheritance tax is paid or a reduction in the rate of inheritance tax. If consumers have more income left they might increase spending on the products of businesses. Increases in income tax, National Insurance contributions and council taxes are all likely to leave consumers with less income and could reduce spending on products.

Prices: An increase in VAT or excise duty will raise the costs of a business. Businesses often pass this on to customers by raising the price of goods. An increase in customs duty will increase the price of goods being imported into a country.

Business costs, revenue and profits: Increases in some taxes might raise the costs of business. For example, VAT will raise costs. A business might try to raise prices to cover this and maintain profit. However, higher prices can reduce sales and so profit could still be affected if revenue falls. Rises in corporation tax, business rates, employers' National Insurance contributions and landfill tax will all tend to reduce business profits. Reductions in taxes are likely to increase the profits of a business.

Business spending and investment: Increases in costs and reduced profits mean that businesses have less retained profit. This can affect the ability of the business to pay its debts, buy stocks and meet other expenses. It can also affect whether it invests in new factories or machinery.

Shares: Changes in capital gains tax and stamp duty might affect shareholding. For example, an increase in capital gains tax might deter shareholders or delay sales of shares.

Importing and exporting: Increases in customs duties can affect businesses. For example, if the UK raised customs duties on imported products a UK business might benefit because imports against which it competed would then have a higher price. However, UK businesses buying imported supplies would have to pay higher prices.

Business operations and employees: Increases in National Insurance contributions of employers might deter employers from recruiting extra workers. Changes in taxation on company cars or mileage allowances might also change how a business offers these benefits to employees.

Other effects: Certain types of business might be affected by changes in tax. For example, an increase in landfill tax might encourage businesses to recycle. A rise in passenger duty could discourage holiday makers and reduce the demand for holidays.

Tax avoidance and evasion: Increases in taxation often lead businesses to try to avoid paying the tax. For example, they might not hire workers to avoid higher National Insurance contributions or switch from buying imports to avoid customs duties. In some cases they might even try to evade the law, for example dumping waste in the countryside to avoid landfill taxes, which is illegal.

Government expenditure

The government is responsible for spending in the public sector. It provides a range of services, such as education, defence, welfare benefits, transport and healthcare. In 2014, the UK government spent £732 billion. Figure 4 shows the categories of planned expenditure for 2014 in the UK.

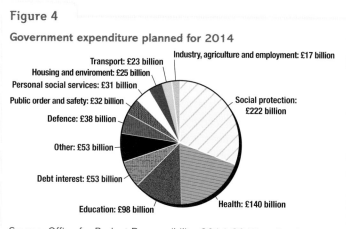

Figure 4

Government expenditure planned for 2014

Transport: £23 billion
Housing and enviroment: £25 billion
Personal social services: £31 billion
Public order and safety: £32 billion
Defence: £38 billion
Other: £53 billion
Debt interest: £53 billion
Education: £98 billion
Industry, agriculture and employment: £17 billion
Social protection: £222 billion
Health: £140 billion

Source: Office for Budget Responsibility, 2014-2015, estimate. Allocations to function are based on HM Treasury analysis

The effect of changes in government expenditure on businesses

Levels of government expenditure can influence business activity. If the government increases spending to more than it raises in taxes, total spending in the economy will rise. The exact impact of such a measure is complex. Although many businesses may benefit from higher spending levels in the economy, too much spending can lead to other problems, such as inflation and higher interest rates.

In recent years the UK government has tried to cut spending in some departments to reduce government borrowing. The pie chart in Figure 4 on the previous page shows that the amount of debt interest paid by the government in 2014 is planned to be £53 billion. This is a huge amount of money and could be used for other departments, such as healthcare or education, if government debt was eliminated. The government has tried to reduce the annual deficit (the difference between spending and government income) for nearly five years, but it is proving to be a difficult objective. However, the government has made cuts in expenditure. For example, it has frozen most public sector pay since 2010. This, along with other government measures, has led to a drop in disposable income for many, which has affected some businesses adversely. For example, quite a few retailers have experienced a drop in demand and some have collapsed. However, the impact on businesses of changes in government spending depends upon the industry in which they operate.

Question 3

Carillion is a British multinational facilities management and construction services company with headquarters in Wolverhampton. It undertakes a range of construction projects including roads and hospitals. Most of its business is in the United Kingdom, but it also operates in several other regions, such as Canada, the Middle East and the Caribbean. In 2014 it was reported to have been awarded the contract to redevelop Anfield, Liverpool FC's stadium.

Despite efforts by the government since 2009 to cut its expenditure, at the end of 2014 it was announced that it would be spending £15 billion on more than 80 new road schemes. This included a long-awaited plan to tunnel under Stonehenge. The £15 billion initiative, which covers investment lasting up to 2021, was set out in the government's first road investment strategy, which also included improvements to junctions on the M25, to the A27 in Sussex, to approaches to Liverpool, and to the A1 in the north-east of England. It comes as a report from the RAC Foundation predicts there could be an additional 7 million road users in England and Wales – taking the total to 43 million – by 2034.

(a) Explain one way in which businesses are likely to be affected by cuts in government expenditure.

(b) Assess the extent to which a company like Carillion will benefit from the government's announcement to spend £15 billion on road improvements.

The business cycle

Over a period of time gross domestic product (GDP) (output in the economy) is expected to grow. However, the rate of growth is rarely smooth; there are likely to be some fluctuations. It is also possible for GDP to fall. These fluctuations are often referred to as the economic, trade or business cycle. Figure 5 shows these fluctuations and identifies four different phases in the cycle.

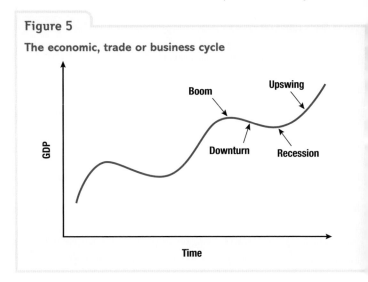

Figure 5

The economic, trade or business cycle

Boom: The peak of the cycle is called a boom. During a boom GDP is growing fast because the economy is performing well. Existing firms will be expanding and new firms will be entering the market. Demand will be rising, jobs will be created, wages will be rising and the profits made by firms will be rising. However, prices may also be rising. For example, in the UK, the price of houses rose sharply when GDP was growing rapidly in the 1990s and 2000s.

Downturn: A boom will be followed by a downturn. The economy is still growing, but at a slower rate. Demand for goods and services will flatten out or begin to fall, unemployment will start to rise and wage increases will slow down. Many firms will stop expanding, profits may fall and some firms will leave the market. Prices will rise more slowly.

Recession or depression: At the bottom of the business cycle GDP may be flat. If GDP starts to fall, the bottom of the cycle may be referred to as a slump or depression. Such a period is often associated with hardship. Demand will start to fall for many goods and services – particularly non-essentials. Unemployment rises sharply, business confidence is very low, bankruptcies rise and prices become flat. The prices of some things may even fall. A less severe version of a depression is a recession.

Recovery or upswing: When GDP starts to rise again there is a recovery or an upswing in the economy. Businesses and consumers regain their confidence and economic activity is on the increase. Demand starts to rise, unemployment begins to fall and prices start to rise again.

The impact of the business cycle on business

The uneven pattern of growth, shown by the business cycle, can have an impact on businesses. However, the size of the impact will depend on the financial position of the business and what it produces.

- **Output.** During a boom, businesses increase output to meet rising demand. Some will increase capacity. Businesses providing non-essential products and luxury items will benefit more than those that produce necessities. Businesses operating in the holiday, restaurant, air transport, jewellery and fashion industries are likely to benefit most. In contrast, during a recession or a depression output will fall. Businesses respond by reducing output and cutting capacity. Businesses that trade in essential items, such as supermarkets, will avoid the worst of the downturn.
- **Profit.** During a boom business profits are likely to rise. This is because demand is rising and it is easier to raise prices. However, when national income starts to decline, it is harder to make a profit. Businesses may cut their costs to maintain profit levels. Many will have to tolerate lower profits and some will make losses.
- **Business confidence and investment.** During an economic recovery and into a boom, business confidence is high. Business owners are optimistic about the future and are prepared to take more risks. For example, they are more inclined to launch new products, enter new markets and expand. In contrast, during a recession business confidence is low and business owners are pessimistic, cautious and anxious about the future. Consequently, they are not likely to take risks and are more inclined to contract their businesses. Investment is likely to fall. For example, instead of replacing outdated machinery they will make do with what they have.
- **Employment.** During a boom unemployment falls because businesses are taking on more workers to cope with rising demand. Sometimes firms might struggle to recruit the quantity and quality of staff that they need as there are fewer people seeking work. However, during a recession the opposite happens. Businesses lay off workers and unemployment rises.
- **Business start-ups and closures.** In a boom more people are prepared to set up a new business. This is because demand is rising and it is easier to make a profit. Business confidence will be high so new entrepreneurs will be more enthusiastic. However, a recession is not a good time to start a new business. Business closures will be rising and inefficient businesses, those with cash-flow problems and those producing non-essential products, are most at risk.

The effect of economic uncertainty on the business environment

One big problem for businesses in relation to economic influences is the uncertainty which results from their behaviour. The pattern of economic variables such as inflation, exchange rates, interest rates, taxation, government expenditure and the business cycle cannot be predicted with any accuracy. For example, few people would have predicted that interest rates in the UK would have been so low for so long. In 2015 they had been stuck at 0.5 per cent for six years. Uncertainty makes decision-making more difficult, reduces business confidence and presents businesses with some unexpected events which they have to deal with.

Decision making: The uncertainty which results from the unpredictable behaviour of economic variables can have an impact on some of the strategic decisions made by a business. For example, when evaluating an investment project which is expected to yield a 20-year return, a business would have to consider the possible effects of higher or lower inflation, higher or lower interest rates, stronger or weaker exchange rates, changes in the levels and pattern of government expenditure, and what might happen to economic growth. This is very difficult indeed. The level of uncertainty will increase some of the risks that businesses take when making long-term decisions. Consequently, marginal investment projects, for example, are not likely to be undertaken.

Unexpected events: The behaviour of some economic variables can be volatile. This means that they can fluctuate, sometimes alarmingly. For example, in 1992, on a day which became 'Black Wednesday', the Chancellor of the Exchequer increased interest rates from 10 per cent to 15 per cent. This means that a business with a £50 million loan would see its annual interest charges rise from £5 million to £7.5 million. The effect of such volatility can have a very unsettling effect on business. More recently, the financial crisis in 2008, which plunged many Western economies into recession, happened very suddenly and unexpectedly. Even in 2015, the UK, and the Eurozone in particular, were struggling to recover from its effects.

Business confidence: The economist John Maynard Keynes suggested that business confidence can affect investment decisions. His suggestion was that if business people were optimistic about the future, they are far more likely to take the risk and invest in new projects. In contrast, those with a pessimistic outlook would be less inclined to invest. This is important because there is probably a link between uncertainty and business confidence. If levels of uncertainty are high, business decision-makers are more likely to be pessimistic and lack the confidence to invest. This means that high levels of economic uncertainty will result in low levels of investment and business development.

All businesses are faced with the problem of economic uncertainty. Business owners and senior managers would hope that the government's economic policies are as business-friendly as the current economic climate permits. Ideally, a business would want stable prices, low interest rates, stable exchange rates, and steady and sustainable economic growth.

Finally, a business might use methods such as PESTLE analysis, SWOT analysis, risk assessment and scenario planning to help reduce uncertainty, prepare for unexpected economic events and improve the quality of decision-making.

Exam tip

When answering questions about the impact of events on a business, it may be useful to distinguish between whether they are internal or external. Credit may be given to answers which distinguish clearly between influences that a business can control and those that it cannot. For example, if a business is performing well it might be because it is being well managed. However, it might also be because a key rival has left the market. Evaluation marks may be awarded for answers that recognise this distinction.

Knowledge check

1. What is meant by an external influence on business?

2. How is inflation measured?

3. State three drawbacks of inflation for businesses.

4. How might deflation affect a business?

5. Why does the government impose taxes on individuals and businesses?

6. What is the difference between direct and indirect taxes?

7. State four examples of direct taxes.

8. What might be the impact on businesses of a fall in corporation tax?

9. Explain the link between business investment and the interest rate.

10. How will a business be affected by a depreciating exchange rate if it exports 80 per cent of its output?

11. If £1 = AU$1.85, how much will a British tourist pay in pounds for a meal in a Sydney restaurant that cost AU$245.00?

12. What is meant by a boom in the economy?

Key terms

Appreciation of a currency – a rise in the value of a currency.

Base rate – the rate of interest around which a bank structures other interest rates. If the Bank of England raises the base rate, all other borrowing and savings rates are likely to move in the same direction and vice versa.

Boom – the peak of the economic cycle where GDP is growing at its fastest.

Consumer price index (CPI) – a common measure of price changes used in the EU.

Deflation – a fall in the general price level. Also used to describe a situation where economic growth is falling or negative when inflation is falling.

Depreciation (of a currency) – a fall in the value of a currency.

Downturn – a period in the economic cycle where GDP grows, but more slowly.

Economic, trade or **business cycle** – regular fluctuations in the level of output in the economy.

Exchange rate – the price of one currency in terms of another.

Fiscal policy – using changes in taxation and government expenditure to manage the economy.

Government expenditure – the amount spent by the government in its provision of public services.

Gross domestic product (GDP) – a common measure of national income, output or employment.

Index linked – the linking of certain payments, such as benefits, to the rate of inflation.

Inflation – a general rise in prices.

Monetary policy – using changes in the interest rate and money supply to manage the economy.

Recession – a less severe form of depression.

Recover or **upswing** – a period where economic growth begins to increase again after a recession.

Slump or **depression** – the bottom of the economic cycle where GDP starts to fall with significant increases in unemployment.

Taxation – the charges made by government on the activities, earnings and income of businesses and individuals.

Case study

UpFLY

UpFLY, a budget airline with bases in leading airports, is the largest airline in the UK by the number of passengers carried. In 2015 it had 500 routes, 160 aircraft, 20 bases and carried 50.7 million passengers. The airline serves over 35 countries.

Like other low-cost airlines in the European market, UpFly performs better than long-haul operators because it keeps its planes in the air for as long as possible every day. It also charges passengers for add-ons, such as baggage check-in, food and hotel hire. Costs are kept low by buying fuel-efficient aircraft in bulk with aggressive discounts, reducing baggage-handling costs by charging passengers for check-in luggage and operating a younger, more efficient fleet of aircraft. Similar airlines in the US have fleets with an average age of around 12 years. The average age of an UpFly plane is just over five years. Finally, UpFly has a good record for their flights being on time and they have easy-to-use web and mobile sites, which attract over a million visits each day. Some operating information is shown in Figures 6, 7 and 8. Figure 9 shows some economic data.

(a) What is meant by a slump? (2 marks)

(b) Explain one reason why a business like UpFLY might be affected by a cut in income tax. (4 marks)

(c) Explain whether UpFly was affected by the UK slump. (8 marks)

(d) Assess the possible impact on UpFly of an appreciation in the exchange rate. (12 marks)

Figure 7

UpFLY profit 2009–2013

£ million

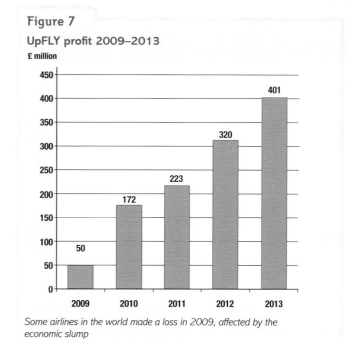

Some airlines in the world made a loss in 2009, affected by the economic slump

Figure 8

UpFLY passengers by country (2014)

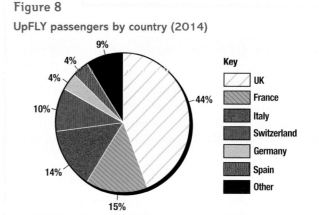

Key
- UK
- France
- Italy
- Switzerland
- Germany
- Spain
- Other

Figure 9

Growth in GDP 2006–2014

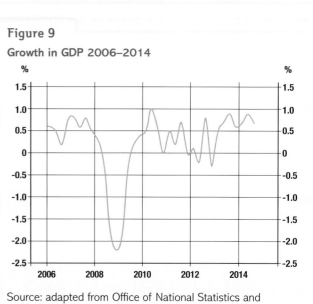

Source: adapted from Office of National Statistics and www.tradingeconomics.com

Figure 6

UpFLY number of passengers carried 2009–2013

Millions

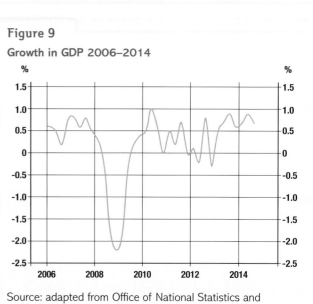

42 Legislation

Key points

1. The effects on businesses of: consumer protection, employee protection, environmental protection, competition policy, and health and safety.

Getting started

In 2014, two Northamptonshire firms were fined after a safety inspection unearthed serious asbestos-related breaches. Lifting Systems Ltd (fined £14,000 plus £523 in costs) had contracted Durasteel Services Ltd (fined £10,000 plus £523 in costs) to refurbish an asbestos cement roof at one of its sites. When inspectors carried out a check, they found asbestos insulation board had been removed and stored on the premises. They also found that debris had been placed in waste skips around the site. As a result the Health and Safety Exective (HSE) served a Prohibition Notice to stop work immediately. The two companies were in breach of health and safety regulations since neither had a licence to remove asbestos.

Source: adapted from www.press.hse.gov.uk

How have the businesses in this case been affected by government legislation? What is the purpose of legislation in this case? State two other areas where these businesses might be affected by government legislation. How might complying with government legislation benefit these businesses?

Figure 1

Consumer issues affected by legislation

Product quality · Product safety · Prices and payment methods · Consumer rights · Promotion and advertising · Trading and age restrictions · **Consumer issues influenced by legislation**

The need for legislation in business

Without legislation it is possible that some businesses could neglect the needs of certain stakeholders. For example, workers might be paid low wages or forced to work in an uncomfortable or even dangerous environment. One of the roles of the government is to provide a legal framework in which businesses can operate and ensure that vulnerable groups are protected.

It is important for the government to find the 'right balance'. Too much legislation will discourage enterprise and deter foreign investment in the UK. This might stifle growth in national income, reduce job creation, decrease tax revenues and reduce consumer choice. Too little, and some stakeholders' best interests might be neglected.

Consumer protection

Consumers want to buy good-quality products at fair prices and receive good customer service. They also want clear and accurate information about products. They do not want to buy goods that may be dangerous, overpriced or sold to them on false grounds. Without government legislation some firms would exploit consumers. Some of the consumer issues affected by government legislation are summarised in Figure 1. Some examples of legislation introduced by the government to protect consumers is summarised in Table 2 at the end of the unit.

How does consumer legislation affect businesses?

The UK has lot of consumer legislation compared with some other countries. There is also a body of EU legislation that affects UK businesses. Businesses have to ensure that their products, marketing and other activities comply with this legislation.

The increase in the number of consumer laws and the concern about protecting consumers has a number of possible implications for firms.

- **Increases in costs.** Improving the safety of a good or ensuring that measuring equipment is more accurate can increase the costs of a firm. For example, an electrical firm producing table lamps may find that its product contravened legislation. The firm would have to change or improve the components used to make the lamps or re-design the lamp itself. Such changes would be likely to raise the firm's costs.
- **Quality control.** Many firms have needed to improve their quality control procedures as a result of legislation. For example, firms involved in bagging or packaging goods must ensure that the correct quantities are weighed out. Failure to do so could result in prosecution. In addition, businesses must be careful not to sell substandard or damaged products.

- **Dealing with customer complaints.** Many businesses now have a customer service or customer complaints department to deal with customers. These allow firms to deal with problems quickly and efficiently, and to 'nip problems in the bud' – dealing with any problems before the customer turns to the legal system.
- **Changes in business practice.** Attempts to ensure that customers are treated fairly by a business may place pressure on it to become more market-orientated. The firm would attempt to ensure that it is actually meeting the needs of those people it is attempting to serve. Such a change, for example, may lead to greater use of market research.

Employee protection

Employers have a responsibility towards their employees, but legislation is necessary to ensure that minimum standards are applied. Without legislative protection some businesses could exploit their workers. For example, they might pay low wages, make them work long hours, deny them employment rights, discriminate against certain groups and dismiss them unfairly. Businesses have a number of legal obligations when employing people.

Employment contract: Workers are entitled to a contract of employment. This is a legally binding agreement between the employer and the employee. It is likely to contain details including the start date, term of employment, job title and duties, place and hours of work, pay and holiday entitlement, pension and sickness absence, termination conditions and details relating to disciplinary, dismissal and grievance procedures.

Discrimination: Businesses have to make a choice when recruiting staff or selecting employees for promotion or training. Businesses will evaluate candidates in order to choose which one to employ or promote. It usual to choose the person that is most experienced or better qualified; this is **legal discrimination**. However, it is illegal in most countries to discriminate on grounds of gender, race, disability, sexual orientation or age. This is **unfair discrimination**. When employing and promoting people, employers must base their decisions on the ability of candidates, and not for example, whether they are male or female. There have been a number of acts addressing discrimination in the UK. One example is the Equality Act 2010 – which replaced the Sex Discrimination Act 1975 – the original legislation that made it unlawful to discriminate either directly or indirectly against someone on the grounds of their gender or marital status.

Unfair dismissal: The Employment Relations Act, 1999, states that employees who have worked for an employer for a year have the right not to be unfairly dismissed. Employees may have grounds to claim unfair dismissal if they were dismissed because they:

- were trying to join a trade union
- became pregnant
- refused to work on a Sunday
- were made redundant without a proper procedure.

Employees can be dismissed fairly if they are incapable of doing their job, found guilty of misconduct, become ineligible to work

(drivers losing their driving licence, for example), are made redundant or for any other substantial reason, such as giving false details on an application form. However, if employees feel that they have been unfairly dismissed they can take their case to an employment tribunal. If the tribunal finds in favour of the employee, it has the power to reinstate that worker. Some examples of legislation designed to protect people at work are summarised in Table 2 at the end of the unit.

Equal pay: Historically, in many professions and occupations women have not received the same pay as men. To address this issue the government introduced the Equal Pay Act 1970. This stated that an employee (whatever their gender) doing the same or 'broadly similar' work as a member of staff of the opposite sex is entitled to equal rates of pay and conditions. The Act aimed to eliminate discrimination in wages and other conditions of work, such as holidays, overtime, hours and duties. The Act was updated in 1983 to allow female workers to claim for work of 'equal value' to that done by a man.

How does employment legislation affect businesses?

Businesses often complain about the burden of employment legislation. Many say that the legislation discourages them from taking on staff. Some of the negative effects of employment legislation are outlined below.

Compliance costs: The expenses incurred by a business in meeting the requirements of employment and related legislation can be significant.

- When taking on a new employee a business must check that the person is entitled to work in the UK. This involves checking a passport, or any other means of identification, which shows that a person is a national of an EU country. If the person was born in the UK then documents, such as their birth certificate, and tax forms, such as a P60 and a P45, must be inspected and their National Insurance number provided. A business must also check that the documents belong to the applicant. If a business only checks the documents of people whom they suspect might not be entitled to work in the UK, they may face a claim for discrimination. Copies of the documents must also be made.
- Employers are responsible for the well-being of employees at work. They must take out the necessary insurance policies and guard against discrimination or harassment. They may also have to deal with matters such as health and safety, discipline and grievances, discrimination in the workplace, bullying, annual leave and redundancy.
- Businesses must also deal with the tax authorities. For example, they must tell Her Majesty's Revenue and Customs (HMRC) whenever someone is employed, deduct tax and National Insurance contributions (NICs) from earnings, provide employees with a P60 tax form every year and a P45 if they leave the business's employment. They also have to provide HMRC with an annual return for every employee.

These are just a few of the legal requirements when employing someone. These tasks and responsibilities take time and money to manage. Large businesses have specialists employed in this field to deal with compliance and the necessary administration. Costs will also be incurred if a business gets involved in a dispute with an employee. For example, a business might need to employ a legal team for representation.

Higher labour costs: Some employment legislation has resulted in certain businesses having to meet higher labour costs. For example, the **national minimum wage** was introduced in the UK in 1999 to boost the pay of very low-paid workers – taking some people out of poverty. The legal minimum wage is reviewed and updated each year. This usually means that it goes up. As a result, businesses paying the minimum wage rate to employees have to meet this increase by law.

Changing working practices: As a business employs more people it will have to introduce systems to deal with compliance and human resource management. It will also have to ensure that job advertisements do not discriminate on the basis of gender or marital status. For example, job titles should be gender neutral, as in 'cashier' or 'salesperson'. There will be a greater need for job descriptions and person specifications. For example, generally speaking, a person specification must not restrict the job to men or women, although there are exceptions. It is possible to offer a job to someone of a particular sex if the work is exempt from gender discrimination legislation. This could include teaching in single-sex schools, jobs in welfare services, e.g. the right to employ a female in a women's refuge, and acting roles. Interviews must be carried out in a structured way to help limit any prejudice that an interviewer might have. Selection procedures must not discriminate against certain groups. For example, a test style must not be used if it is alien to a particular ethnic culture.

Loss of flexibility: Some businesses argue that sections of the legislation make it more difficult to run a business because the laws are too rigid. For example, employees can ask for flexible working arrangements that suit them if they have worked continuously for 26 weeks or if they have a child under the age of six (or a disabled child under the age of 18). Reasons for refusing an employee flexible working must be set out in writing and be legally justified.

Penalties: If businesses fail to comply with the laws outlined above there may be penalties. For example, fines can be imposed and the image or reputation of a business might be damaged. Businesses might also be forced to backdate claims from employees where 'wrongdoing' is proven. This can be very expensive.

Employment legislation can also have a positive effect on businesses. For example, legislation creates a 'level playing field' when employing people. This means that unscrupulous businesses that want to exploit workers to lower costs so that they can gain a competitive edge in the market are prevented from doing so. Complying with employment legislation is also likely to improve

worker motivation and employee welfare, which will help raise productivity, reduce absenteeism and cut staff turnover. It might also help to foster a more positive and friendly culture within organisations. This can improve the image of businesses and make it easier to recruit and retain high-quality staff.

Question 1

A ruling by the employment appeal tribunal in 2014 stated that employees' holiday pay should reflect the pay levels that employees actually receive while working. This meant that overtime and other supplementary payments would be included in holiday pay. According to the European Court of Justice (ECJ) the change was necessary so that workers would not be discouraged from taking holiday (for health and safety reasons). This ruling was not welcomed by businesses. For example, John Cridland, Director-General of the CBI, suggested that it would be hard for UK businesses, who faced the prospect of costs potentially running into billions of pounds, and might result in business closures and significant job losses. Cridland suggested that the uncertainty created by the cases would impact on investment and resourcing decisions.

As a result of the new rulings, businesses faced higher labour costs, with an increase in wages and National Insurance costs. It was suggested that the impact was greatest on smaller businesses because they often paid lower basic salaries, but used commission and performance-based pay to 'top-up' staff wages. It was also reckoned that about a third of small businesses paid their workers overtime and the extra costs were a negative impact on small businesses. Also, the impact on costs from the time managers spent reviewing their employment contracts and working practices would be an extra burden for small businesses without a specialist human resources department.

(a) Explain one reason for the ruling relating to holiday pay.

(b) Explain one possible impact on a small business of the ruling.

Environmental protection

Without regulation, business activity can have an adverse effect on the environment. For example, governments are becoming concerned about global warming and consequent changes in weather patterns and climates. Some of the greenhouse gases that contribute to global warming come from businesses, such as power generators. As business activity increases there is more gas emission. Also, economic development means that car ownership and air travel increases. The emissions from cars and aircraft also add to global warming. Some specific problems include the following.

- **Pollution.** There are different types of pollution. Water pollution may be caused by businesses dumping waste into rivers, streams, canals, lakes and the sea. An example would be warm water or chemicals being leaked into rivers. Air pollution may be caused by businesses discharging particulate waste or gases into the air. Noise pollution can also be a problem. Noise from factory machinery, loud music from pubs and night clubs, and low flying aircraft by airports are examples.

- **Destruction of wildlife habitats.** Some business development destroys wildlife habitats and spoils the natural environment. For example, around half of the forests that once covered the planet are now gone. Forests are vital for the ecological balance of the planet. It is also reckoned that more than half of the world's primates will become extinct due to habitat destruction. Many other species are under threat from human activity, such as tigers, pandas, and myriad plant and insect species.
- **Traffic congestion.** Extra traffic caused by commercial vehicles or workers travelling to and from work can cause congestion resulting in delays and accidents. Traffic in London got so bad that a congestion charge was introduced in 2003 to discourage vehicles from entering the centre of London during the week.
- **Resource depletion.** Non-renewable resources, such as oil, coal, gas and minerals, cannot be replaced. Therefore, as business development gathers pace these resources are depleted. Once they have run out, future generations will have to do without. Fertile soil, which is needed to grow food, is also being lost. Around 40 per cent of the world's agricultural land is seriously degraded. This is due to poor farming practices, overgrazing, urban sprawl and land pollution. Also, some businesses waste resources. For example, many argue that some of the packaging used by businesses is unnecessary and that not enough use is made of recycled materials.

One approach used by many governments to minimise the damage done by businesses to the environment is to pass new laws. Much of the pressure for environmental legislation has emerged due to the growing concerns about global warming. If businesses fail to comply with environmental laws they may be fined or forced to close until the problem is resolved. Examples of environmental legislation are shown in Table 2 at the end of the unit.

How does environmental legislation affect businesses?

Environmental issues offer both threats and opportunities to businesses. Businesses which stand to gain the most from growing environmental regulation are those selling pro-environmental and anti-pollution products. These businesses range from engineering companies selling equipment designed to reduce emissions, to service companies which advise other businesses on how they can comply with regulations, to businesses selling environmentally friendly products, such as managed wood.

Those which stand to lose the most are companies which are high polluters and who face competition from other businesses which don't face similar problems. For example, a specialist chemicals company may cease trading because there are many good substitutes to its products which have only a fraction of the environmental impact in production. Or a heavily regulated UK company may face competition from a Third World producer whose government places little restriction on its activity.

Marketing: Environmental issues can be a highly effective marketing tool for some businesses. Some companies, such as IKEA, which uses sustainable forestry techniques when sourcing wood for its products, and Johnson & Johnson, which uses mainly solar energy in its production processes, have made a particular point of pursuing environmentally friendly policies, and feature these on their websites. Many businesses claim on their packaging to be environmentally friendly in some way. However, some businesses have found that environmental issues pose a marketing threat. Oil companies, for example, are frequently accused by pressure groups, such as Greenpeace, of harming the environment. Shell has been heavily criticised for its oil exploration projects in the Arctic and it was widely reported that partly as a result of pressure from Greenpeace, Lego ended its co-promotion with Shell after a 50 years' association. Such examples show that businesses must take quick and positive action when an environmental issue suddenly arises. It also shows that some businesses have to work constantly to protect and improve their environmental image.

Finance: In some cases, responding to environmental concerns or new laws and regulations can have a positive financial impact on a business. Energy-saving measures, for example, can lead to a business having lower costs than before because of previous inefficiencies. In most cases, though, taking environmental action is likely to lead to higher costs. If all businesses in the industry also face these higher costs, prices are likely to rise to reflect the higher costs. Profits would then be largely unaffected. But if higher costs fall more heavily on one business than another, then some will gain a competitive advantage and others lose it. This in turn will have different impacts on profitability. Installing expensive new equipment will also have a negative impact on cash flow. In the nuclear power industry and the car industry, businesses must also make investment decisions knowing that there will be heavy costs at the end of a product's life. In the case of the nuclear power industry, this is in terms of decommissioning plant. For motor manufacturers, they have to take back old cars for recycling. This will affect the outcomes of appraisal methods like the payback method and discounted cash flow.

Operations management: Pollution controls and other environmental measures could have an impact on how a product is made. This could range from changes in the type of materials used, to production methods, to storage and after-sales service. For example, asbestos was widely used in industry years ago but its use today is severely restricted. Industries such as electricity generation and chemicals have had to introduce much cleaner production methods to reduce emissions. The landfill tax encourages businesses to reduce the amount of waste they produce.

Human resources: Environmental concerns and policies have human resource implications. Staff will need to be recruited and trained to deal with ever increasing government regulations concerning the environment. Some businesses may choose to outsource the guidance they need. Larger businesses are likely to put environmental policies in place. This could include an environmental audit where key measures relating to the impact of the business on the environment are audited each year and the results are made public. Implementing policies means that staff throughout the organisation are aware of the policies and what they must do to comply with the policies. As with any policy, unless there are good procedures and training in place to ensure compliance, staff will tend to interpret the policies as they see fit. Effective communication up and down the hierarchy is therefore essential. The very small minority of businesses which make environmental concerns an important business objective can use this as a way of motivating staff. Over time, it will tend to attract employees who are interested in this aspect of business. However, a tension between meeting financial targets such as profit targets and meeting environmental targets is likely to arise. For a business to survive, it must at least break-even. In this sense, financial targets tend to be more important than environmental targets. This tension between targets could demotivate staff who want to see environmental targets as the most important for the business.

Question 2

CMI Demolition Ltd is a waste management business based in Glasgow. In 2014 the company was reported as being in breach of the Environmental Protection Act 1990 and fined £16,000 (reduced from an original £24,000 fine because of the company's acceptance of responsibility and subsequent co-operation). According to the report, CMI Demolition Ltd used an unlicensed company to transport and dispose of waste materials from its transfer station. This occurred between March and June 2011. According to the Act, waste management companies must ensure that any carriers of waste are licensed by the Scottish Environment Protection Agency (SEPA). The Act also states that companies must produce Waste Transfer Notes to show what waste is being transported, when and where it is going, and who is carrying it. This is to discourage the illegal dumping of waste materials.

A SEPA officer said, 'It's critically important that waste management companies ensure their contractors are fully licensed and credible operators to transport their waste materials. Providing business to unlicensed groups or individuals is not only illegal, it undercuts legitimate waste carriers and impacts on the wider industry as a whole.'

Source: adapted from www.media.sepa.org.uk

(a) Explain one way in which CMI Demolition is affected by environmental legislation.

(b) Give one reason why such legislation is required.

Competition policy

There is a need to monitor the activities of monopolies and markets that are dominated by a small number of large businesses. Without government regulation some businesses would exploit consumers by using **anti-competitive practices** or **restrictive practices** to reduce competition in the market. Such practices might include the following.

- **Increasing prices.** Raising prices to levels above what they would be in a competitive market. For example, some manufacturers supply goods to retailers and insist that they are retailed at a fixed price.
- **Restricting consumer choice.** A manufacturer might refuse to supply a retailer if that retailer stocks rival products. This will reduce choice for the consumer.
- **Raise barriers to entry.** By spending huge amounts of money on advertising, for example, a dominant firm can squeeze others out of the market. It might also lower its price for a temporary period. This would make it difficult for a new business to get established in the market. Once the new business disappears the price would go up again.
- **Market sharing.** This might occur if there is **collusion**. When a market is shared out between the dominant firms, choice is restricted and prices rise.

In the UK, the Competition and Markets Authority (CMA) is responsible for serving the interests of consumers and protecting them from restrictive practices. This body was formed in 2014 and replaced the Office of Fair Trading (OFT) and the Competition Commission. Its responsibilities are summarised in Table 1.

Table 1 Responsibilities of the Competition and Markets Authority for protecting consumers from restrictive practices

• Investigating mergers which could restrict competition
• Conducting market studies and investigations in markets where there may be competition and consumer problems
• Investigating where there may be breaches of UK or EU prohibitions against anti-competitive agreements and abuses of dominant positions
• Bringing criminal proceedings against individuals who commit the cartel offence
• Enforcing consumer protection legislation to tackle practices and market conditions that make it difficult for consumers to exercise choice
• Co-operating with sector regulators and encouraging them to use their competition powers
• Considering regulatory references and appeals

Source: www.gov.uk

How does competition policy affect businesses?

It might be argued that competition policy will have both a positive and a negative impact on businesses.

Positive: Businesses might get frustrated if their restrictive practices are deemed illegal and are forced to comply with the law. This is because such practices are often very lucrative. However, since competition policy is designed to promote competition, many firms will actually benefit from it. For example, if dominant firms erect barriers to entry, this will make it very difficult for smaller firms to break into the market. Thus, if such barriers are outlawed then it is easier for new firms to break into the market. This will give opportunities to more businesses.

A more competitive business environment will benefit the economy. Competition will encourage innovation and improve efficiency as businesses try to survive in the market. As a result, UK businesses are more likely to develop new products, reduce costs and make progress in overseas markets. This will help businesses to generate more revenue and profit from exports. It will also raise income and employment in the UK.

Negative: Some businesses might argue that competition policy acts as a constraint on their activities. For example, if a proposed merger or takeover is investigated by the CMA, this might slow down the whole process. This could cause delays and cost the businesses involved a lot of money. In 2014, a proposed merger between soft drinks companies, Britvic and AG Barr, was investigated by the authorities. The decision was delayed for about four months.

Sometimes, after an investigation, a merger or takeover might be permitted, but with provisos. For example, in 2014 a merger between two large cement producers, Lafarge and Holcim, was approved by the European Union. However, the EU directed Lafarge to sell all of its German and Romanian business activities, and instructed Holcim to unload all of its Slovak business and most of its activities in France.

Health and safety

Figure 2 shows that work can be a dangerous environment. Because of the danger to employees, governments aim to protect workers by passing legislation that forces businesses to provide a safe and healthy workplace. This might involve:

- providing and maintaining adequate safety equipment and protective clothing, such as fire extinguishers, protective overalls, hard hats, ear plugs and safety goggles
- ensuring workers have enough space to do their jobs
- guaranteeing a hygienic environment with adequate toilet and washing facilities
- maintaining workplace temperatures and reasonable noise levels
- providing protection from hazardous substances
- providing protection from violence, bullying, threats and stress in the workplace
- providing adequate breaks for rest.

In the UK, laws to protect employees have existed for over 100 years. There are also many regulations concerning health and safety at work that are regularly updated. In addition, businesses may follow codes of practice designed to protect workers. Finally, UK regulations are influenced by EU directives relating to health and safety at work. Some examples of health and safety legislation are given in Table 2 on the next page.

Figure 2

Standardised incidence rates (per 100,000 workers) of fatal injuries at work in GB/UK

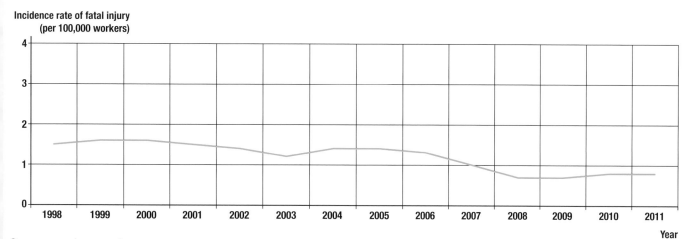

Source: www.hse.gov.uk

Table 2 Examples of legislation directed at businesses

Legislation	Date	Brief description and example
Sale of Goods Act (Consumer legislation)	1979	Products must be of a merchantable quality and fit for purpose Example: a garment sold as 'waterproof' must not let in the rain
Food Safety Act (Consumer legislation)	1990	Food should be fit for human consumption and comply with safety standards Example: food should not be sold if decaying or contaminated
Equal Pay Act (Employment legislation)	1970	Pay and conditions must be the same for all people doing the same or 'broadly similar' work Example: male and female bus drivers must be paid the same rates
National Minimum Wage Act (Employment legislation)	1998	It is unlawful to pay a worker a wage rate below the set minimum wage rate Example: in 2014 a wage of £6.00 per hr would be illegal (£6.50 was the minimum wage)
Environment Act (Environmental legislation)	1995	Set up the Environment Agency to monitor and control pollution Example: it is unlawful to discharge emissions into the air (above certain levels)
Environmental Protection Act (Environmental legislation)	1990	Controls pollution caused by the disposal of waste into land, water and air Example: an unlicensed carrier of waste can be fined
Competition Act (Competition policy)	1998	Prohibits agreements, cartels or practices that restrict or prevent competition Example: it is illegal for a group of businesses to charge an agreed price
Enterprise Act (Competition policy)	2002	Established the Office of Fair Trading (OFT)* as an independent body Example: the OFT can refer investigations to the Competition Commission**
Health and Safety at Work Act (Health and safety)	1974	Aimed to raise the standard of health and safety at work Example: employers must provide a written statement of policy on health and safety
Working Time Regulations Act (Health and safety)	1998	Clarifies hours of work and break entitlements for workers Example: 48 hours is the maximum working week

* The Office of Fair Trading was replaced by the Competition and Market Authority in 2014

** The Competition Commission was replaced by the Competition and Market Authority in 2014

How does health and safety legislation affect businesses?

Costs: The Health and Safety at Work Act 1974 requires businesses to prepare a written statement of their general policy on health and safety. Businesses also have to give training, information, instruction and supervision to ensure the health and safety of workers. Many businesses also follow codes of practice to meet health and safety standards at work. Meeting these requirements will raise business costs. Many large businesses, for example, employ a health and safety officer whose sole responsibility is ensuring that health and safety issues are addressed in accordance with the law. Smaller firms are likely to attach health and safety duties to the job description of a senior member of staff, to ensure compliance. Finally, health and safety inspectors have the right to enter business premises to ensure that health and safety measures are being carried out by businesses.

Penalties: Failure to comply with the law can be serious. At worst, employees' safety might be compromised, which could lead to accidents – in some cases fatal. Businesses can also be fined if they fail to comply with legislation. For example, in 2014, Lincolnshire-based BW Biddle, a well-established metal recycling business, was fined £70,000 and ordered to pay £18,000 in costs for breaching Section 2(1) of the Health and Safety at Work Act 1974. An employee was carrying out maintenance

on a conveyor belt when the main power was switched on. As a result the whole line, including the belt, reactivated and the worker fell, breaking ribs on both sides of his body. An investigation by the Health and Safety Executive (HSE) found the electricity source for the conveyor belt had not been isolated.

Benefits: Although complying with health and safety legislation imposes costs on businesses, there are some considerable benefits that result from it. For example, a good health and safety record will help to improve the image of a business. This will make it easier to attract and retain high-quality staff – especially in industries with 'hostile' working conditions where health and safety issues are of the utmost importance. Also, if businesses are genuinely committed to maintaining high standards of health and safety, workers will feel protected and more secure. As a result they may be better motivated and more loyal. This will benefit the business as workers will be more productive. Absence through injuries at work will be reduced, as might staff turnover.

Exam tip
It is not necessary to learn all the legislative Acts that relate to the protection of consumers, employees and the environment. However, it might be useful if you can remember, generally, the issues that are addressed by the Acts. You do need to be fully aware of the impact that the legislation has on businesses. Also, remember that the legislation can have both positive and negative effects on business.

Case study

PADWELL ELECTRONICS PLC

Padwell Electronics manufacture diodes, resistors, capacitors and transistors to standard sizes and standard electrical specifications. The Walsall-based company employs 4,800 people in a large factory on an industrial estate. Most of the components are sold to the manufacturers of mobile phones. Padwell Electronics has a reputation in the industry for being one of the cheapest producers. However, its image in the local area is not very positive. Although it is a large employer, people often see jobs at Padwell Electronics as a 'last resort'. This is mainly because the pay is low, the work is very boring and working conditions are harsh. The factory is said to be noisy, cold and poorly lit. Staff turnover is 39 per cent.

In October 2014, the national legal minimum wage rate in the UK was increased by 3 per cent from £6.31 to £6.50. At Padwell Electronics, 90 per cent of employees are paid the national minimum wage for a standard 36-hour week (four shifts of nine hours). After the increase, Business Secretary Vince Cable said, 'The National Minimum Wage provides a vital safety net for the lowest paid, ensuring they get a fair wage whilst not costing jobs. This year's rise will mean that they will enjoy the biggest cash increase in their take-home pay since the banking crisis, benefiting over one million people in total.' However, Sally Castle, the CEO at Padwell Electronics, had this to say when talking to the local press:

'This pay increase is very bad for us. We try to be efficient here at Padwell, we keep our costs low, we aim to be the cheapest in the industry – it's what keeps us going. The government is always creating new demands. Just last month we had to spend £100,000 on a new toilet block for staff. There was nothing wrong with the old block until the HSE [Health and Safety Executive] got involved.'

Sally also mentioned the proposed merger with Deptford Electricals as an example of government intervention that's 'gone too far'. When the merger was proposed the authorities said that an investigation may be necessary because the two businesses together would dominate the market. The two companies were still waiting for an official announcement from the authorities seven months after the initial proposal.

Sources: adapted from www.gov.uk and www.hse.gov.uk

(a) Calculate the increase in the weekly wage bill as a result of the increase in the minimum wage. (4 marks)

(b) Explain the main impact of the national minimum wage on Padwell Electronics. (4 marks)

(c) Explain one way in which the proposed merger with Deptford Electricals might be affected by competition policy. (4 marks)

(d) Assess the extent to which the costs of complying with legislation outweigh the benefits to a business like Padwell Electronics plc. (12 marks)

Key terms

Anti-competitive or **restrictive practices** – attempts by firms to prevent or restrict competition.
Barriers to entry – obstacles that make it difficult for new firms to enter a market.
Collusion – two (or more) businesses agreeing to a restrictive practice, such as price fixing.
Contract of employment – a written agreement between an employer and an employee in which each has certain obligations.
Discrimination – favouring one person over another. For example, in the EU it is unlawful to discriminate on grounds of race, gender, age and disability.
Employment tribunal – a court that deals with cases involving disputes between employers and employees.
National minimum wage – a wage rate set by the government below which it is illegal to pay people at work.
Unfair dismissal – the illegal dismissal of a worker by a business.

Knowledge check

1. State four consumer issues covered by consumer legislation.

2. How might a food producer be affected by consumer legislation?

3. How might business adverts be affected by consumer legislation?

4. What is the main purpose of the Sale of Goods Act?

5. What is a contract of employment?

6. How might an employee claim unfair dismissal?

7. State two restrictive practices that a business might try to engage in.

8. State three responsibilities of the CMA.

9. Why do businesses often regard legislation as a burden?

10. State two benefits to a business of complying with health and safety legislation.

Key points

1. Competition and market size.

Getting started

During 2013 the price of motor insurance in the UK fell. According to commentators this was the result of fierce competition. However, despite the intense competition, esure, the insurance company behind the Sheilas' Wheels brand, saw its pre-tax profits rise by 2.5 per cent to £118.4 million. It also reported a 4 per cent increase in gross insurance premiums (total revenue).

Source: adapted from www.esuregroup.com

What is meant by a 'fiercely competitive market'? Suggest how esure was able to increase both profit and revenue in such a competitive market. How might a business reduce competition in a market?

The competitive environment

One of the most important external influences faced by a business is the threat posed by competitors. This was mentioned first in Unit 1. The majority of markets are competitive and some are extremely competitive. For example, the UK market for clothes, which was worth about £26 billion in 2014, is highly competitive. There are many thousands of businesses competing to sell a wide range of clothes to the UK population. These include:

- *specialist clothes chains*, such as Next, River Island, Dorothy Perkins, Warehouse, Jaeger, Miss Selfridge, Monsoon, Topshop, Prada, Gucci and Wallis

- *department or variety stores*, such as Marks & Spencer, Matalan, Primark, TK Maxx, Debenhams and John Lewis, which sell clothes along with other items, such as make-up, leisure goods, fashion accessories, sportswear, groceries, soft furnishings, household goods and bedding
- *independents*, which are often quite specialised, and cater for particular market niches; for example, an independent store might specialise in clothes for toddlers or wealthy shoppers looking for exclusivity
- *supermarkets*, such as Tesco and Asda, which have branched out into non-food goods including clothes
- *online retailers*, the numbers of which have grown very quickly since the introduction of the internet. Many online suppliers belong to the stores mentioned above. However, there are a growing number of online retailers that sell solely from a website. Examples of these are the two global giants Amazon and Alibaba.

In a minority of markets there is very little competition. For example, in the UK the supply of water is organised on a regional basis. In each region there is usually only one supplier, such as Wessex Water, the sole supplier for Dorset, Somerset, Bristol, most of Wiltshire, and parts of Gloucestershire and Hampshire. The company, which is owned by the Malaysian company YTL Power International, serves a total of 2.7 million customers. People in this region cannot obtain a domestic water supply from any other provider, so Wessex Water operates as a monopoly. This arrangement is typical for the supply of water in the UK.

Determinants of competitiveness

Not all markets are the same. Different markets have different features and characteristics. The features and characteristics of markets are known as **market structures**. It is these market structures that largely determine how competitive a market is.

The number and relative size of businesses in the market: In some markets, such as farming, a large number of businesses compete with each other. None of these businesses are particularly large compared to other businesses in the market. So the market share of any single business is small.

In other markets, a few businesses dominate the market, even though there might be a large number of other small firms. In some markets, there is only one business, a monopolist. For example, on some railway routes in the UK, there is only one train company operating a service.

The extent of barriers to entry: In some markets, it is easy for a new business to set up. Many people each year set up small shops selling everything from groceries to clothes to toys. This is because the **barriers to entry** are low. It doesn't cost much to open a shop. The amount of knowledge of the industry required is fairly little. In most cases, there are no special licences or other legal obstacles in the way. In certain markets, barriers to entry are high. In the rail transport industry or mobile telephone industry, the government gives licences to a limited number of businesses to operate. In the drug industry, newer drugs are protected by patent. This prevents other businesses from copying them.

In other markets, the costs of starting up a business are large. Car manufacturing, aeroplane production or oil refining are examples. In the perfume industry, the main companies devote a large proportion of their costs to marketing. Any new entrant then has to be able to afford to spend millions of pounds launching its new product.

Where barriers to entry are high, competition tends to be lower. One consequence of this is that businesses often compete on issues other than price. This means that they tend to emphasise the non-price elements of the marketing mix, such as promotion and place.

The extent to which products can be differentiated: In some markets, products are homogeneous. This means that they are the same whichever business produces them. Typically, there are standards to which products conform. So nine carat gold is the same quality whatever business produces it. Homogeneous, products are often found in raw materials markets and in basic manufacturing, such as steel. Where products are homogenous, competition tends to be largely based upon price with this element of the marketing mix emphasised.

In other markets, products differ according to which business makes them. A McDonald's meal is different from a Burger King meal. Ford cars differ from Volkswagen cars. Heineken lager is different from Budweiser lager. Individual products or product ranges can then be branded. The stronger the perceived difference, the stronger the brand. Where product differentiation is strong the non-price elements of the marketing mix such as promotion tend to be emphasised by businesses.

The knowledge that buyers and sellers possess: In some markets, buyers and sellers have access to all the information they need to make rational decisions. Buyers, for instance, would be able to find out the best price in the market. Sellers would have open access to the most efficient methods of production. This is known as having perfect knowledge. Where knowledge is perfect, price is strongly emphasised in the marketing mix.

In other markets, knowledge is not available to all. One business might not be able to find out how much a rival business is charging for its products. A consumer might not know which of 20 cars will be most environmentally friendly. If there is imperfect information in the market, this can give a competitive advantage to some businesses over others. Where knowledge is imperfect, businesses will tend to place a great deal of importance upon non-price elements of the marketing mix such as the product and promotion.

Degree of interrelationship: In some markets, the actions of one business have no effect on another business. Businesses are independent of one another. In farming, the decision by one farmer to plant a field with carrots has no impact on a nearby farm in terms of the price it will receive or how much it produces.

In other markets, such as car production, increased sales by one business will mean reduced sales by another business if the size of the market remains the same. Businesses are then interdependent.

Legal factors: Competition between businesses is generally seen as being in the best interests of customers. They can shop around between businesses offering the same or similar products for the best deal. This means that businesses have to offer what the customer wants or face closing down through lack of customers.

In contrast, monopoly is usually argued to be bad for customers. They are forced to buy from one supplier whatever the quality of the product and whatever the prices. The monopolist has enormous power over customers and acts to maximise the benefits to itself.

Monopolies, therefore, tend to be controlled by governments. In the USA, they are illegal. In the UK and the rest of the European Union they are **regulated**. A monopolist exists where there is only one firm in a market. However, firms in a market can act as if they were a monopoly by **colluding**. This means they get together, usually to fix prices and output in a market. They then have formed a **cartel**. For example, a group of firms making vitamins may fix a high price between themselves at which they will sell vitamins to customers. Then they have to restrict output between themselves to sustain those high prices.

Impact on businesses of a competitive environment

Operating in a competitive market is likely to have a number of implications for a business. Businesses will be challenged and forced to monitor the activities of rivals in order to minimise the threat they pose. Some specific implications are outlined below.

Price: In a highly competitive market, businesses have less control over the prices they charge. Prices are likely to be forced down. A business that charges a price that is significantly higher than those of rivals risks losing sales because consumers can switch easily from one supplier to another. If a business can effectively differentiate its product there may be some scope for price increases. For example, in the fashion industry, businesses such as Burberry, Prada and Gucci can charge higher prices than rivals because the quality of their products is perceived to be superior.

Profit: The profit available in a highly competitive market has to be shared between a greater number of players. Profit margins are likely to be squeezed because prices will be forced down. However, businesses that can operate more efficiently and reduce their costs may be able to enjoy higher profits than rivals that operate with a higher cost base.

Communication with customers: Businesses will be under pressure to meet customer needs. Those businesses that meet customer needs effectively are more likely to survive in the market. This competitive pressure may mean that businesses make more of an effort to communicate with their customers. They may carry out more market research, for example. They may also use social media to keep in touch with consumer sentiment.

For example, comments relating to what people think about products can be picked up on Twitter accounts. On Twitter, O2 used social media to address customer complaints with a friendly, personal approach. This helped O2 to win back their customers.

An important part of good customer service is effective communication with customers. It is reckoned by some commentators that customer engagement is set to overtake productivity as a key driver of profitable growth.

Innovation: In highly competitive markets, innovation will be encouraged. This is because if a business can design new products, they may be of more interest to consumers and allow a business to gain a competitive edge in the market. The development of a USP can go a long way towards aiding survival in a competitive market. Many people prefer to buy products that are differentiated from those of rivals.

For example, Durham-based Orsto Ltd produces a smartwatch called the Orsto X3. The wearable technology market is in its infancy, but it is likely to be dominated by huge companies like Apple, Google, IBM and Samsung. However, the Orsto X3 has a USP. It is British designed and offers a suite of specifications that are unique. For example, it does not rely on a smartphone connection for functionality.

Product range: The range of products sold by a business is likely to be strongly influenced by competitors. If a business extends its range with a new product, this usually puts pressure on rivals to do the same.

For example, following the success of Magners cider in the early 2000s, other beverage producers, such as Carling (owned by Molson Coors) and Stella Artois (owned by Inbev), launched their own brands of cider – Carling British Cider and Stella Artois Cidre respectively. The failure to match a rival's extensive product range might result in lost customers.

Marketing: In highly competitive markets the quality of marketing, and the amount of money invested in marketing strategies, is very important. Businesses will be heavily influenced by the marketing methods used by rivals. If a business enjoys a fruitful advertising campaign, rivals are put under pressure to match that success. It is quite common for businesses to imitate or replicate the campaigns of rivals.

For example, a wide range of businesses in many different markets are all trying to exploit social media in their marketing strategies. One growing trend is the use of viral marketing. This is where a short video clip relating to a product, or a story about a product, is sent globally across the internet by people who have seen and enjoyed the clip.

There are many examples where the adverts of businesses in the same industry have similar features. For example, many TV adverts for perfumes feature celebrities or models wearing expensive clothes and jewellery in glamorous surroundings. Many TV adverts for cars show them being driven in stunning scenic locations. One of the reasons for the similarity of marketing campaigns in certain industries is the fear that a business will get left behind if it fails to match the campaigns of rivals.

Competition and market size

The size of a market refers to the number of customers and businesses that buy and sell a particular product or product group. Market size may be measured in terms of value, and can vary considerably.

Global markets: These are obviously the largest markets in which a business can compete. Due to the process of globalisation an increasing number of worldwide markets have opened up for businesses. Even small businesses can now access global markets because they can market their products online. One example of a rapidly growing global market is for cars. In 2010 the market was worth $728.3 billion, with predictions of growth to $904 billion by 2015.

National markets: These are markets confined to national borders. In 2012 the value of the new car market in the UK was about £32 billion. The new car market is highly competitive in the UK because manufacturers from all over the world compete in the market.

Regional markets: Some businesses serve regional markets. For example, Merseyrail provides train services in the Merseyside region. It operates trains between Liverpool and Southport, Liverpool and Chester, and Liverpool and Ormskirk. Merseyrail has the monopoly on rail transport in the region.

Local markets: By their very nature, local markets are much smaller. Businesses in these markets serve limited areas such as villages, small towns and specific residential areas. In some cases there may only be one business serving a local market. For example, many rural villages are served by just one shop or one pub. However, this does not mean that they do not face any competition. Most people in rural areas have cars and can travel to other shops and pubs.

The size of a market in which a business competes can influence the way it operates. For example, businesses operating in small markets are not likely to undertake large-scale production in an effort to exploit economies of scale. Also, large markets are likely to be more competitive than small ones. For instance, a grocery shop in a Scottish Highland village is not likely to face the same competition as a branch of Sainsbury's in a large town.

Operating in large markets

National and global markets are likely to be more challenging for businesses. Even in large markets that are dominated by just a few producers, competition can be still be severe. For example, the UK grocery industry is dominated by a small number of very large operators. These comprise mainly large supermarket chains, such as Asda, Morrisons, Sainsbury's, Tesco, Aldi, Lidl and Waitrose. Since 2009, competition has intensified, with the low-cost operators, including Aldi and Lidl, gaining market share at the expense of the other large chains. This intense pressure has caused some operators, such as Tesco, to review their operations. For example, in 2014 Tesco responded to the competition by implementing a loyalty scheme shake-up, improving its online delivery service and refreshing some of its stores.

In large competitive markets it is vital for businesses to monitor the activities of rivals. A business needs to be aware of the pricing strategies that rivals use, changes in their product ranges, the promotional and production methods used, and any other information that might have an impact in the market. Close monitoring often results in businesses copying their rivals. They might copy product designs, packaging, pricing strategies and promotions. Copying rivals is common practice in many industries.

Operating in small markets

One of the main problems when operating in small markets is whether the volume of sales will be sufficient to generate the desired rate of return. Small markets might be attractive because they may lack competition. However, if the market is too small then trying to serve it might be a mistake. In 2015, the US aircraft manufacturer Boeing said that it would not make any more Boeing 757s as the market was not large enough.

In South Australia, the market for kangaroo meat reduced and some businesses left the industry or extended their product range to include some value added meat products.

Another problem operating in a small market is the fear that a larger, stronger rival will enter the market and take away all the custom. Small independents often find it difficult to compete with a large corporation if they decide to compete directly. A large corporation has much greater resources. For example, they can afford to spend more on advertising and other forms of promotion. Also, their costs are likely to be lower because larger firms canexploit economies of scale. This means they can charge lower prices.

Key terms

Barriers to entry – factors which make it difficult or impossible for businesses to enter a market and compete with existing producers.

Cartel – a group of businesses (or countries) which join together to agree on pricing and output in a market in an attempt to gain higher profits at the expense of customers.

Colluding – in business, where several businesses (or countries) make agreements among themselves which benefit them at the expense of either rival businesses or customers.

Market structures – the characteristics of a market, such as the size of the barriers to entry to the market, the number of businesses in the market or whether they produce identical products, which determine the behaviour of businesses within the market.

Knowledge check

1. Give two examples of highly competitive markets.
2. Give two examples of markets that might lack competition.
3. How might consumers benefit from competition in a market?
4. Describe two determinants of competition in a market.
5. Explain why global markets are likely to be highly competitive.
6. Outline two implications of operating in a relatively small market.

Exam tip

Remember that in a minority of large markets there may be a lack of competition. For example, the energy markets in the UK are huge. However, there is a lack of proper competition and it has been alleged that many of the operators in the industry are exploiting consumers.

Case study

MOBILE GAMING MARKET

The global mobile gaming industry is not only large, but also growing. In early 2014 Newzoo, a games research agency, predicted that the market would grow by about 8 per cent a year for at least three years, this growth being driven by the rising popularity of mobile gaming and increasing incomes in Asia. The firm increased this forecast slightly in the course of 2014. Figure 1 shows the total and mobile global gaming market between 2012 and 2017.

Game designers have responded to this rapid growth. A survey by the Game Developers Conference showed that 52 per cent of developers design games specifically for mobile devices, such as tablets and smartphones. However, according to a report by New Relic Mobile, developers need to be aware of the possible pitfalls in this highly competitive market. This is because designs for mobile games apps often include features that slow down performance. For example, they integrate media-rich and animation-heavy content. Also, users can easily delete games and download other ones from the enormous choice available. The report offered three pieces of advice to game developers.

- **Monitor current industry trends.** In this industry it is vital that new games do not lag behind those of rivals. However, it is also bad practice to replicate a game that already exists (although many designers do blatantly copy those of rivals). Some of the key trends in 2014 included big-screen functionality, free-to-play models, 3D gaming and growing interest from emerging markets.

- **Focus sharply on game design.** As freemium games become the norm, the quality of new games will have to be extremely high to enjoy any sort of success. Freemium pricing is where a basic version of a game is provided free to all users. However, any special features or superior levels come with a fee. Designers will need to be inventive to retain customers. They will also have to meet the high performance expectations of users. For example, since gaming enthusiasts are using a wider range of devices to play games, simpler games, such as *Flappy Bird*, are likely to perform better.

- **Invest in a mobile APM tool.** To make apps competitive it is important to keep up to date with technology. An application performance monitoring (APM) tool will help to improve the performance of games, particularly those that are media and animation heavy.

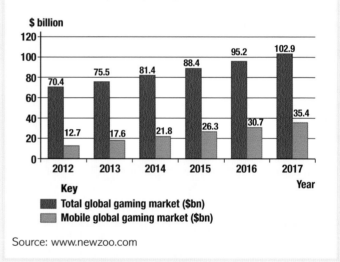

Figure 1

Total and mobile global gaming market ($ billion)

Source: www.newzoo.com

Source: adapted from www.newzoo.com

Q

(a) Calculate the percentage growth in the mobile global, and the total global gaming markets, between 2012 and 2017, to determine which is the fastest growing. (4 marks)

(b) Evaluate the implications for businesses of operating in a large and highly competitive market, like the mobile gaming market. (20 marks)

Preparing for your AS Level Paper 1 exam

Advance planning

1. Draw up a timetable for your revision and try to keep to it. Spread your timetable over a number of weeks, and aim to cover a chosen number of topics each week.
2. Spend longer on topics that you have found difficult, and revise them several times.
3. Do not try to limit your revision by attempting to 'question spot'. Revise so that you are confident about all aspects of your work.

Paper 1 overview

AS Paper 1: Marketing and people: 1 hour 30 minutes	
Section A, Theme 1 , Question 1	2×2 mark questions
	2×4 mark questions
	1×8 mark question
	1×10 mark question
Total marks for Section A	***30 marks***
Section B, Theme 1, Question 2	2×2 mark questions
	2×4 mark questions
	1×8 mark question
	1×10 mark question
Total marks for Section B	***30 marks***
Section C, Theme 1 and Theme 2, Question 3	1×20 mark question
Total marks for Section C	***20 marks***
	Total marks = 80 marks

Paper 1 will assess your knowledge and understanding of **Theme 1 – Marketing and people**. It is a written examination and the paper is divided into three sections. The duration of Paper 1 will be 1 hour and 30 minutes. You have to answer **ALL** questions. There is no choice. However, this can be an advantage because it means you do not have to waste time deciding which questions to answer.

Section A questions

In Section A you will be given Extract A as a stimulus (probably some information about a business) and you will need to answer Question 1, a–f. The parts of Question 1 require a range of depths in your responses.

Section B questions

In Section B you will be given Extract B as a stimulus and you will need to answer Question 2, a–f. The parts of Question 2 require a range of depths in your responses.

Section C questions

In Section C you will be given Extract C as a stimulus. You will need to answer Question 3, which is not broken down into parts. You will be expected to give an extended answer. This means that you will need to write more.

You should familiarise yourself with the layout of the paper by looking at the examples published by Edexcel. The questions within each section are followed by lined spaces where you should write your answer. Use the mark allocation as a guide to how much time to spend on each question.

Skills required when answering questions

If you are entered for the AS Level qualification you will be required to sit two examinations. You should be aware of the skills that you need to demonstrate when answering questions.

You will need to demonstrate four different skills referred to as assessment objectives (AOs).

AO1 – Knowledge: this means you have to show that you:

- recognise and understand business terms, concepts and theories
- understand how individuals and organisations are affected by and respond to business issues.

All questions will test knowledge to some extent. A minority of questions will test knowledge alone. These can be recognised by the mark allocation. They will tend to carry just two or four marks.

AO2 – Application: this means that you have to apply knowledge and understanding to various contexts to show how individuals and organisations are affected by and respond to issues. This might involve:

- using a business formula in appropriate circumstances, for example calculating the price elasticity of demand for a product
- using a theory to show why a business has chosen a particular course of action
- using a theory to show the impact on a business of choosing a particular course of action.

Most questions in the examination will require you to demonstrate application. This means that you have to ensure that your answers relate directly to the context given in the question. You must discuss the implications of issues to the particular business or industry in the context you are given.

AO3 – Analysis: this means you have to show that you can break down information and understand the implications of the information presented in the question. You will need to show an understanding of the impact on individuals and organisations of external and internal influences. This might involve:

- explaining causes and effects and interrelationships, for example by recognising from a graph that sales are falling and could be the result of new competition in the market
- breaking down information to identify specific causes or problems, for example by realising that a business is suffering from inefficiency because staff motivation has fallen as a result of a pay cut
- using appropriate techniques to analyse data, for example by calculating the net profit ratio.

You will often be required to construct an argument, for example by explaining the possible reasons for events or discussing the advantages or disadvantages of particular courses of action.

Questions that carry more than four marks will require analysis in the answer. Some questions that carry four marks may also require you to demonstrate some analytical skills.

AO4 – Evaluation: evaluation involves making a judgement. You will need to evaluate both qualitative and quantitative evidence to make informed judgements and propose evidence-based solutions to business issues. This might involve:

- showing judgement when weighing up the relative importance of different points or sides of an argument in order to reach a conclusion
- drawing conclusions from the evidence that you present
- assessing the relative importance of particular issues to a business
- suggesting a course of action for a business, supported by plausible motives or evidence.

When evaluating, it is often possible to draw a number of different conclusions. Very often in business studies there is no 'right' answer, so examiners are likely to be more interested in whether your judgement is plausible and in the quality of your argument in support of that judgement. Questions that carry eight marks or more are likely to test evaluation.

Preparing for your AS exams

Sample answer with comments

Paper 1: Marketing and people

These questions will help you prepare for your AS Business Paper 1 examination. Some sample answers and comments are provided for you to review and you will have the opportunity to answer some questions yourself.

Section A, Question 1

In Section A, Question 1, you will need to read Extract A before answering Question 1 a–f (no example is provided in this section).

Section B, Question 2

Read Extract B before answering Question 2.

Extract B

Brainwave

In 2014, Richard Baister launched Brainwave, a world-first soft drink designed to keep the mind healthy. It may reduce the risk of Alzheimer's and other forms of cognitive decline. Brainwave does not contain any added sugar, preservatives or colourings and uses only natural fruit flavourings. It was developed with the help of Newcastle Science City. Brainwave delivers the key ingredients the body needs to help maintain brain health and cognitive performance.

There is likely to be increasing demand for a product that can reduce the risk of Alzheimer's and dementia as people live longer and the proportion of older people in the global population gets larger. However, although the drink is targeted at 'everyone with a brain', Baister said that early adopting young professionals greatly interest Brainwave, as they ask a lot of their brains every day. The total market size for soft drinks in the UK was about £15.6 billion in 2013.

At launch in 2014, a pack of 8 × 330 ml of Brainwave was available online for £16. That retail price of around £2.00 per pack was planned to be reflected as the brand rolled out to more stockists. The business donates 10 per cent of profits to funding research into Alzheimer's and dementia.

Source: adapted from www.brainwavedrinks.com

2 (a) What is meant by market size? (2 marks)

Question 2 (a), student answer

The total size of a market can be estimated or calculated by the total sales of all businesses in the market. Market size can be measured by volume, which is the number of units sold in the market, or by value, which is the amount spent by consumers in the market. In this case the size of the UK soft drinks market is measured by value. It is worth about £15.6 billion.

Comment, Question 2 (a)

Questions like this require you to demonstrate knowledge. One mark might be awarded for defining market size and another for showing that you recognise that it can be calculated in two ways. It is always helpful to give an example if there is one available – in this case you are told that the size of the soft drinks market is £15.6 billion.

2 (b) Explain one advantage of online retailing to Brainwave. (4 marks)

Question 2 (b), student answer

One of the biggest changes to occur in the marketing of products in recent years has been the development of online retailing. This is a popular branch of e-commerce that has emerged along with the development of the internet. It involves shoppers ordering goods online and taking delivery at home. In this case, Brainwave is sold online. For example, an 8-pack of Brainwave can be purchased online for £16.

There are a number of advantages of selling products online. One of the main ones is that costs will be lower. Brainwave will avoid selling costs such as sales staff, display units, rent, rates, lighting and heating, and other store overheads. The savings might be enormous and allow Brainwave to charge lower prices. This might help Brainwave to break into the soft drinks market.

Comment, Question 2 (b)

Questions like this require you to demonstrate knowledge, application and possibly analysis. One or two marks might be awarded for showing that you understand what online retailing means. Another one or two marks might be awarded for identifying one advantage. Finally, credit may be given for analysis. In this case, explaining that lower costs will allow Brainwave to charge lower prices and break into the market is an example of analysis. Note that the answer is always about Brainwave. This shows application, for which marks will be awarded.

---

2 (c) What is meant by supply? (2 marks)

No sample answer has been provided for question 2 (c) so that you can answer it yourself, for exam practice.

2 (d) Explain one reason why Richard Baister may have set up his business. (4 marks)

No sample answer has been provided for question 2 (d) so that you can answer it yourself, for exam practice.

2 (e) Assess two possible impacts on Brainwave of employing more staff if the business starts to expand rapidly. (8 marks)

No sample answer has been provided for question 2 (e) so that you can answer it yourself, for exam practice.

2 (f) Assess the factors that might influence the demand for Brainwave in the future. (10 marks)

Question 2 (f), student answer

One of the reasons why Brainwave was developed was to help combat Alzheimer's and other cognitive diseases. Brainwave delivers key ingredients the body needs to help maintain brain health and cognitive performance. Older members of the population are more prone to such diseases so Brainwave may be an appealing product for this target group. In the future the size of this market is likely to grow because globally the population is aging. Consequently demand for Brainwave is also likely to grow.

Brainwave is priced at £16.00 a pack for 8 drinks. That is £2.00 per drink, and price has a big influence on the demand for a product. Brainwave must ensure that the price is 'right'. Brainwave may have carried out some research to determine what customers are prepared to pay for the product. In the future Brainwave must keep in touch with consumer sentiment and be prepared to change the price if market conditions change. If the price is too high, then demand may fall in the future.

Future demand might also depend on the incomes of potential customers. If the incomes of the target group rise, then demand for Brainwave might also rise. However, many elderly people have to live on fixed incomes and price may be a consideration for purchase. Over time, incomes in the UK would be expected to rise so the drink might become more affordable. However, since 2009 real incomes for many people have stayed pretty much the same, or even declined, due to the recession and the austerity measures of the government.

Finally, the effectiveness of Brainwave's marketing strategy could have a big impact on future demand. If the business invests in clever marketing strategies and builds a strong brand, then demand is likely to rise in the future. However, if the Brainwave brand does become successful, rivals might bring out their own versions of the product. If a company like Coca-Cola were to launch such a brand, Brainwave might find it difficult to compete. To conclude, it is difficult to predict what might happen to demand for Brainwave in the future. If its health benefits are proven, then it could become 'big'. I think future demand will depend largely on whether rivals enter the market, and if they do, whether Brainwave can deal with the increased competition.

Comment, Question 2 (f)

Questions like this require you to demonstrate knowledge, application, analysis and evaluation. Two marks might be awarded for demonstrating knowledge, such as identifying two factors that might affect future demand, for instance aging population, price, incomes or the effectiveness of marketing. Two marks might be awarded for application. The whole of this answer is embedded in the soft drinks industry, Brainwave's product and closely related issues. Three marks might be awarded for analysis. An example of analysis in this answer is the explanation of how future demand for Brainwave is dependent upon the growth of the aging population and the product's link with the target market, i.e. the health-related benefits to the elderly. Three marks might be awarded for evaluation. An example of evaluation in this answer is the attempt to determine what might happen to future demand for Brainwave. This is difficult to predict because there are so many variables to consider. However, by acknowledging this, and exploring, for example, what could happen if a strong rival enters the market, a plausible conclusion is drawn. In this answer, counterbalance arguments are raised more than once. For example, the effects on demand of rising incomes in the future and the recent decline in incomes have both been recognised. Evaluation marks are likely to be awarded for this inclusion.

Section C, Question 3

Read Extract C before answering Question 3.

Extract C

Working in social media

ChitChat is an online social networking service. It allows users to communicate with each other by sending short messages. ChitChat, which is based in Manchester, employs about 2000 people globally.

Many employees think that ChitChat is a good place to work. They get free meals at onsite cafés; they have access to a gym that offers group exercise and yoga classes, personal fitness instructors and massage therapists; they have games rooms and very flexible working hours; and they have access to company-subsidised childcare.

Staff work together in small teams, but they are regularly allowed to work on projects of their choice. If they come up with good ideas they are given awards. There is also evidence to suggest that staff feel empowered by this workplace environment. For example, in a recent survey, over 80 per cent of workers agreed that they felt like they had a high level of responsibility, while about 75 per cent agreed that they could complete their work without interference from the senior leadership team.

3 Evaluate the importance of non-financial methods of employee motivation to a business such as ChitChat. (20 marks)

Question 3, student answer

Businesses will gain a lot if their workforce is motivated. Generally, people will be happier, easier to manage, more productive, more co-operative and less resistant to change. One notable advantage is a low staff turnover. If workers are well-motivated they are less likely to leave the company. Having a low staff turnover can save a business with large numbers of employees, such as ChitChat, a lot of money in recruitment, selection and training costs. It will also provide a more stable environment for workers.

One non-financial method that can be used to motivate staff is empowerment. This involves giving employees control to make decisions, giving them more self-confidence and recognising their achievements. There is evidence to suggest that staff at ChitChat are empowered. For example, over 80 per cent of workers claim that they carry a lot of responsibility in the business. Also, around 75 per cent say that they are allowed to carry out their responsibilities without management interference. The main benefit to a business like ChitChat of empowering its workforce is that workers will be better motivated. They will feel trusted and that the business recognises their talents. Workers will also have a greater control over their working day and this could reduce illness and absenteeism. Employees might develop new skills that will help their personal development. Empowerment will also help to generate more ideas and different ways of solving problems. At ChitChat, staff are allowed to work regularly on any project of their choice. If they come up with good ideas they are given awards.

However, empowerment is sometimes criticised as simply a means of cutting costs and removing layers of management from the business. Employees may also resent being given more responsibility if they are not paid more. Sometimes managers resent giving power away because it undermines their importance. In the case of ChitChat though, empowerment seems to have worked well – there is no evidence of resentment.

ChitChat seems to have created a good working environment, offering staff a number of 'perks' so their time at work will be more tolerable – perhaps even enjoyable. For example, employees get free meals at onsite cafés; they have access to a gym that offers group exercise and yoga classes, personal fitness instructors and massage therapists; they have games rooms and very flexible working hours. According to Herzberg these non-financial benefits should help to remove dissatisfaction amongst workers. Although such benefits may not be motivators, they will help to develop a satisfied workforce.

According to Maslow, workers have needs and employers can meet some of these needs at work. For example, one level that Maslow identified in his hierarchy of needs was love and belonging. ChitChat seems to understand this notion and organises its workers into small teams. If employees are allowed to work in groups they will have the opportunity to foster relationships with their work colleagues. This will help them to develop a sense of belonging. ChitChat might also enjoy other benefits from teamwork. For example, productivity might be higher because of pooled talents, more ideas might be created, problems are often more easily solved by teams and responsibility can be shared around. ChitChat also allows flexible working. However, team working may have some drawbacks. For example, there may be conflict between team members, which might result in wasted resources as time is spent on resolving differences of opinion.

To conclude, many businesses favour the use of non-financial methods when motivating staff. In industries where it is difficult to measure the output of workers, the use of financial methods of motivation, such as piece rates or commission, are not really suitable. In the case of ChitChat, where many employees are involved in research and project work, and most employees are highly skilled professionals, the use of non-financial methods of motivation are likely to be very important. ChitChat's approach seems to be working because it is regarded by many as a good place to work.

Comment, Question 3

Questions like this require you to demonstrate knowledge, application, analysis and evaluation. Four marks might be awarded for demonstrating knowledge, such as understanding the meaning of non-financial motivational factors and defining terms like 'empowerment' in this case, and identifying its benefits. Four marks might be awarded for application. The whole of this answer focuses on non-financial motivational factors, ChitChat's use of such methods and closely related issues. Two motivational theories (Herzberg and Maslow) are also applied to the case.

Six marks might be awarded for analysis. An example of analysis in the first part of this answer is the explanation of how non-motivational factors can benefit businesses such as ChitChat. Six marks might be awarded for evaluation. An example of evaluation in this answer is how the importance of non-financial awards is shown to be important to businesses like ChitChat.

A judgement is made and supported with an argument. For example, one of the reasons why non-financial methods are important is because financial methods of motivation in this case may not be appropriate. They are not suited to industries where it is difficult to measure a worker's output. The answer also considers potential counterbalances, the drawbacks of empowerment and team working, for example.

Practice question – AS Level, Paper I: Marketing and people

The more you practise for your examination, the more confident you will feel. The following question provides practice for Section B, Question 2.

Section B, Question 2

Read Extract B before answering Question 2.

Extract B

Fit Britches

Fit Britches supplies a range of garments designed to help slimmers lose inches, reduce signs of cellulite and aid skin elasticity in just 30 days. It was founded by entrepreneur Farnaz Khan. She developed the products after she struggled to lose weight after childbirth. Farnaz found a link between weight-loss and heat after experimenting with enormous underpants and clingfilm. Eventually, Farnaz developed a special shapewear garment made from using a combination of advanced knitting technology, intelligent fibres and compression which can help stimulate blood circulation. By bringing the blood flow back into the areas it causes the matabolism rates to rise through release of the body's own nitric oxide. This in turn improves blood flow and oxygen supply at the skin level, causing the fat layers that make up cellulite to be melted down, leaving the wearer with smoother and firmer skin.

A study was carried out independently following scientific protocols in a double blind, paired and controlled experiments using a total of 90 subjects. They wore the pants for 6 hours a day over 30 days. The study found that participants agreed improvements of smoother skin, improvement in the appearance of cellulite and agreed their blood flow had improved in the area covered by the fabric in less than 4 weeks.

Farnaz launched her business in 2013. The main products, which are manufactured in Italy and can be bought online, are called Skinny Knickers, Skinny Top, Skinny Shorts and Skinny Leggings. Fit Britches uses psychological pricing. For example, a Skinny Top is priced at £49.99. By 2014 the business was doing very well and planned to launch into the US market.

Source: adapted from www.fitbritches.com

2 (a) What is meant by psychological pricing? (2 marks)

   (b) What is meant by an entrepreneur? (2 marks)

   (c) Calculate the percentage mark-up if a Skinny Top cost £30 to make. (4 marks)

   (d) Explain one aspect of the design mix that might be important to Fit Britches. (4 marks)

   (e) Assess two possible reasons why Farnaz set up Fit Britches. (8 marks)

   (f) Assess the possible business objectives of Fit Britches. (10 marks)

Preparing for your AS Level Paper 2 exam

Advance planning

1. Draw up a timetable for your revision and try to keep to it. Spread your timetable over a number of weeks, and aim to cover a chosen number of topics each week.
2. Spend longer on topics that you have found difficult, and revise them several times.
3. Do not try to limit your revision by attempting to 'question spot'. Revise so that you are confident about all aspects of your work.

Paper 2 overview

AS Paper 2: Managing business activities: 1 hour 30 minutes	
Section A, Theme 2, Question 1	2×2 mark questions
	2×4 mark questions
	1×8 mark question
	1×10 mark question
Total marks for Section A	***30 marks***
Section B, Theme 2, Question 2	2×2 mark questions
	2×4 mark questions
	1×8 mark question
	1×10 mark question
Total marks for Section B	***30 marks***
Section C, Theme 1 and Theme 2, Question 3	1×20 mark question
Total marks for Section C	***20 marks***
	Total marks = 80 marks

Paper 2 will assess your knowledge and understanding of **Theme 2 – Managing business activities**. It is a written examination and the paper is divided into three sections. The duration of Paper 1 will be 1 hour and 30 minutes. You have to answer **ALL** questions. There is no choice. However, this can be an advantage because it means you do not have to waste time deciding which questions to answer.

Section A questions

In Section A you will be given Extracts A–C as a stimulus and you will need to answer Question 1, a–f. The parts of Question 1 require a range of depths in your responses.

Section B questions

In Section B you will be given Extract D as a stimulus and you will need to answer Question 2, a–f. The parts of Question 2 require a range of depths in your responses.

Section C questions

In Section C you will be given Extract E as a stimulus. You will need to answer Question 3, which is not broken down into parts. You will be expected to give an extended answer. This means that you will need to write more.

You should familiarise yourself with the layout of the paper by looking at the examples published by Edexcel. The questions within each section are followed by lined spaces where you should write your answer. Use the mark allocation as a guide to how much time to spend on each question.

Skills required when answering questions

If you are entered for the AS Level qualification you will be required to sit two examinations. You should be aware of the skills that you need to demonstrate when answering questions.

You will need to demonstrate four different skills referred to as assessment objectives (AOs).

AO1 – Knowledge: this means you have to show that you:

- recognise and understand business terms, concepts and theories
- understand how individuals and organisations are affected by and respond to business issues.

All questions will test knowledge to some extent. A minority of questions will test knowledge alone. These can be recognised by the mark allocation. They will tend to carry just two or four marks.

AO2 – Application: this means that you have to apply knowledge and understanding to various contexts to show how individuals and organisations are affected by and respond to issues. This might involve:

- using a business formula in appropriate circumstances, for example calculating the break-even point for a product
- using a theory to show why a business has chosen a particular course of action
- using a theory to show the impact on a business of choosing a particular course of action.

Most questions in the examination will require you to demonstrate application. This means that you have to ensure that your answers relate directly to the context given in the question. You must discuss the implications of issues to the particular business or industry in the context you are given.

AO3 – Analysis: this means you have to show that you can break down information and understand the implications of the information presented in the question. You will need to show an understanding of the impact on individuals and organisations of external and internal influences. This might involve:

- explaining causes and effects and interrelationships, for example by recognising from a graph that sales are falling and could be the result of new competition in the market
- breaking down information to identify specific causes or problems, for example by realising that quality has improved as a result of introducing continuous improvement
- using appropriate techniques to analyse data, for example by calculating the return on capital employed (ROCE).

You will often be required to construct an argument, for example by explaining the possible reasons for events or discussing the advantages or disadvantages of particular courses of action. Questions that carry more than four marks will require analysis in the answer. Some questions that carry four marks may also require you to demonstrate some analytical skills.

AO4 – Evaluation: evaluation involves making a judgement. You will need to evaluate both qualitative and quantitative evidence to make informed judgements and propose evidence-based solutions to business issues. This might involve:

- showing judgement when weighing up the relative importance of different points or sides of an argument in order to reach a conclusion
- drawing conclusions from the evidence that you present
- assessing the relative importance of particular issues to a business
- suggesting a course of action for a business, supported by plausible motives or evidence.

When evaluating, it is often possible to draw a number of different conclusions. Very often in business studies there is no 'right' answer, so examiners are likely to be more interested in whether your judgement is plausible and in the quality of your argument in support of that judgement. Questions that carry eight marks or more are likely to test evaluation.

Preparing for your AS exams

Sample answer with comments

Paper 2: Managing business activities

These questions will help you prepare for your AS Business Paper 2 examination. Some sample answers and comments are provided for you to review and you will have the opportunity to answer some questions yourself.

Section A, Question 1

Read the following extracts (A–C) before answering Question 1.

Extract A

JLR balance sheet

An extract from the statement of financial position (balance sheet) for Jaguar Land Rover 2013/14

	2014 £ million
Non-current assets	8,359
Current assets	7,230
Non-current liabilities	3,591
Current liabilities	6,134

Source: www.jaguarlandrover.com

Extract B

Production at JLR

Jaguar Land Rover (JLR) uses state-of-the-art technology and modern production methods in its factories. It also uses methods such as continuous improvement and lean production. At its plant in Halewood, JLR has its Lean Learning Academy training centre. It provides a range of courses for its own employees, but also attracts learners from a broader range of manufacturers.

In 2013 Jaguar Land Rover recorded sales in over 170 countries. It exports around 80 per cent of production from its UK factories. In 2014 pre-tax profits were £2.5 billion as it sold 434,311 vehicles bringing in £19.4 billion. With the introduction of the fourth generation Range Rover, which is being produced in Solihull, it is on course to improve its financial performance.

Source: adapted from www.jaguarlandrover.com

Extract C

A strengthening pound

The pound has strengthened against a number of global currencies since the beginning of 2013. For example, in March 2013 £1 = €1.17 but in March 2015 £1 = €1.41. The pound has also strengthened against the Australian dollar. In March 2013 £1 = AUS$1.40 but by March 2015 £1 = AUS$1.95.

1 (a) What is meant by lean production? (2 marks)

Question 1 (a), student answer

Lean production aims to use fewer resources in production. A range of production techniques, such as continuous improvement, flexible manufacturing, team working, empowerment and multi-skilling, are used to minimise waste.

Lean producers, such as Jaguar Land Rover, use less time, less stock, fewer materials, less labour, less space and fewer suppliers. Lean producers are likely to have a competitive advantage because the reduction in waste and resource use will lower production costs.

Comment, Question 1 (a)

Questions with a small mark allocation require you to demonstrate knowledge. One mark might be awarded for defining lean production and another for showing that you understand that it involves using a range of different production techniques, such as continuous improvement.

1 (b) What is meant by continuous improvement? (2 marks)

No sample answer has been provided for question 1 (b) so that you can answer it yourself, for exam practice.

1 (c) Using Extract A, calculate the current ratio for Jaguar Land Rover in 2014. (4 marks)

Question 1 (c), student answer

The current ratio is a liquidity ratio and is given by:

$$\text{Current ratio} = \frac{\text{Current assets}}{\text{Current liabilities}} = \frac{£7,230m}{£6,134m} = 1.18$$

Comment, Question 1 (c)

There is always likely to be a question requiring a calculation in Paper 1, or Paper 2, or both. For this question you will need to remember the formula for calculating the current ratio. It is important to write down the formula and show all of your working out. Even if you make a mistake in the calculation you might pick up some marks for using the correct formula and identifying some appropriate financial information in your working out.

1 (d) Explain one way a business like JLR might improve its liquidity. (4 marks)

No sample answer has been provided for question 1 (d) so that you can answer it yourself, for exam practice.

1 (e) Assess two implications for JLR of using modern production techniques in its operations. (8 marks)

No sample answer has been provided for question 1 (e) so that you can answer it yourself, for exam practice.

1 (f) Assess the possible impact of the stronger pound on Jaguar Land Rover. (10 marks)

Question 1 (f), student answer

Jaguar Land Rover exports a significant amount of its output. For example, in 2013 around 80 per cent of the vehicles produced in its UK factories were sold overseas. Consequently, movements in the exchange rate could have an impact on the prices of JLR's vehicles when sold overseas. When the domestic exchange rate appreciates, exports become dearer. Information in Extract C shows that the value of the pound against the euro has increased from £1 = €1.17 in 2013 to £1 = €1.41 in 2015. This is an increase of around 21 per cent. This means that the price of JLR vehicles will be 21 per cent more expensive for European customers. This could lead to a fall in demand in the European market because a 21 per cent increase in price is significant. If JLR sells cars to Australia from its UK factories there may be a similar problem for Australian customers. The pound has also appreciated against the Australian dollar – by almost 40 per cent. This is an even bigger price increase.

However, although JLR's products will be dearer to buy for some overseas customers, it does not necessarily mean that demand will fall. To some extent it will depend on the price elasticity of demand for JLR's products in these markets. If demand is price inelastic, the fall in demand will be proportionately less than the increase in price. JLR has a good reputation overseas for high-quality products and its brand is strong. Consequently current demand levels might be sustained even if prices rise.

JLR might compensate for the appreciation in the exchange rate by lowering prices slightly to remain competitive. However, this is likely to lower revenues and have a negative impact on profits. Alternatively, JLR might invest some more money in marketing to try and drive overseas sales up.

Finally, JLR may actually derive some direct benefit from the strong pound. This is because when the exchange rate appreciates the price of imports will fall. Therefore, if JLR imports any raw materials or components, they will be cheaper. This will help to lower production costs and have a positive effect on profits. However, there is no information in the extracts about the source of JLR's inputs.

To conclude, it is difficult to predict the impact of a stronger pound on JLR because more information is needed. However,

trading results are favourable. In 2014 pre-tax profits were £2.5 billion as it sold 434,311 vehicles that pushed revenues to £19.4 billion. With the introduction of the fourth generation Range Rover, which is being produced in Solihull, it is on course to improve its financial performance. Also, although the pound was quite strong at the time of writing the extracts, future movements in the exchange rate could be in the opposite direction. Exchange rates are quite volatile and JLR may have taken some protection against their fluctuation. At the moment, the impact of the strong pound does not seem to be overwhelming.

Comment, Question 1 (f)

This is another question that requires you to demonstrate knowledge, application, analysis and evaluation. Two marks might be awarded for demonstrating knowledge, for instance identifying two possible effects of a strong pound on JLR, such as higher export prices and lower import prices. Two marks might be awarded for application. All of this answer is directed at the effect of changes in the exchange rate on JLR. Some of the financial information in the extracts (actual exchange rates and profit figures for JLR) is also used to support arguments.

Three marks might be awarded for analysis. An example of analysis in this answer is the explanation of exactly how stronger exchange rates might reduce demand for exports, and as a result, reduce the profit made by JLR. Three marks might be awarded for evaluation. In this answer, evidence of evaluation is the way the different impacts of a strong pound on JLR are weighed up. There are both positive and negative effects. The conclusion suggests that the final impact of a strong pound may not be too dramatic.

Section B, Question 2

In Section B, Question 2, you will need to read stimulus Extract D before answering Question 2 a–f (no example is provided in this section).

Section C, Question 3

Read Extract E before answering Question 3.

Extract E

AutoTrader

In 2015, private equity company Apax Partners planned to sell off between 35 and 50 per cent of its used-car sales website, AutoTrader. The company, valued at around £2.5 billion, was being floated on the London Stock Exchange. The shares were expected to be priced between 200p and 250p each.

3 Evaluate the possible benefits to AutoTrader of operating as a plc. (20 marks)

Question 3, student answer

A public limited company is owned by shareholders and the name of the company ends in plc. Like a private limited company it is run by a board of directors under the supervision of a chairperson who is accountable to the shareholders. However, shares in a public limited company can be purchased by anyone on the open market. In this case, AutoTrader was set to become a plc in 2015. Prior to flotation on the London stock market it was owned by Apax Partners, a private equity company.

Operating as a plc, AutoTrader might enjoy some possible benefits. For example, the owners or shareholders have limited liability. This means that if the business collapses investors can only lose the money that they used to purchase the shares. Investors cannot be forced to contribute more money if the company is seriously in debt. As a result, plcs like AutoTrader are able to raise large amounts of capital from issuing more shares. People are happier to invest when they know exactly the extent of their possible losses if things go wrong. Also, in the future AutoTrader may find it easier to raise finance as financial institutions are more willing to lend to plcs. A plc with substantial assets can provide the collateral needed by financial institutions to protect loans. Larger plcs also have a wider range of financial sources from which to choose.

Another benefit is that plcs tend to be large companies. Therefore, AutoTrader's operating costs may be lower as it may benefit from economies of scale. Plcs are expected to grow and as they get bigger unit costs are likely to fall. This will improve their competitiveness and hopefully generate more profit.

Because of their size, plcs can often dominate the market. Most plcs aim to grow and may eventually exercise some control in the market. For example, they may be able to create barriers to entry preventing competition. In this case, AutoTrader may be able to invest large amounts of money in advertising to strengthen its brand. Finally, pressures from the media and financial analysts, as well as the danger that the plc might be taken over by another company, encourages executives and managers to perform well and make profits. These pressures do not exist for private limited companies.

However, despite these advantages there may be some drawbacks when operating as a plc. The setting up costs can be high. The various costs of 'going public' include lawyers' fees to ensure that the prospectus is 'legally' correct, the printing and distribution of prospectuses to potential investors, and the fees paid to an investment bank to process all the share applications. Also, the share issue has to be underwritten (which means that the company

must insure against the possibility of some shares remaining unsold) and a fee is paid to an underwriter who must buy any unsold shares.

Another potential problem is that anyone can buy AutoTrader's shares. It is therefore possible, at least in theory, for an outsider to buy sufficient shares to be able to exert control over the company, or worse take control of the company. Also, AutoTrader's accounts can be inspected by members of the public. Competitors may be able to use some of this information to their advantage. AutoTrader will also be influenced by various Company Acts, which aim to protect shareholders. Compliance with company legislation will use up company resources. For example, plcs often employ a company secretary to deal solely with compliance issues.

There may also be operational problems. For example, because of the company's size it is more difficult to deal with customers at a personal level. Some customers do not like dealing with giant 'faceless' corporations. They may prefer the personal service of a much smaller enterprise – dealing directly with the owner perhaps.

In this case, AutoTrader may avoid some of the possible drawbacks. For example, only between 35 and 50 per cent of the company is being sold. Consequently, it will be difficult for an outsider to exert much control. AutoTrader may also avoid the operational problems because it is an online business and does not really interact with its customers. To conclude, AutoTrader may flourish as a plc. The benefits are likely to outweigh the drawbacks. For example, it will have easier access to greater funding, expand and enjoy economies of scale, strengthen its brand and enjoy greater profitability.

Comment, Question 3

This question requires an extended answer and you need to demonstrate knowledge, application, analysis and evaluation. Four marks might be awarded for demonstrating knowledge such as understanding the implications of operating as a plc and identifying some benefits and possible drawbacks. Four marks might be awarded for application. This answer recognises that the sale of AutoTrader is only a partial sale and that it is an online business. Specific references to AutoTrader's unique circumstances are referred to throughout.

Six marks might be awarded for analysis. Examples of analysis in this answer are the explanation of how the benefits and

drawbacks of operating as a plc in each case will impact on AutoTrader and its performance. Six marks might be awarded for evaluation. In this case, there is a need to weigh up the benefits and possible drawbacks and make a final judgement as to whether the flotation is the right thing for AutoTrader.

Another approach could have been to rank the benefits and decide which was the most important to AutoTrader. There are often a number of ways in which judgements can be made in answers. Examiners do not expect all students to make exactly the same judgements.

Practice question – AS Level, Paper 2: Managing business activities

The more you practise for your examination, the more confident you will feel. The following question provides practice for Section C, Question 3.

Section C, Question 3

Read Extract E before answering Question 3.

Extract E

The oil industry

As a result of the falling oil price in 2014/15, BP announced that it would cut investment from around $24 billion to $20 billion by reducing exploration expenditure and postponing or cancelling marginal projects.

In his 2015 budget, George Osborne, the Chancellor of the Exchequer, announced that the oil industry would receive tax cuts of £1.3 billion.

Source: adapted from the *Financial Times* 3.2.2015, 8.4.2015. All rights reserved.

3 Evaluate the possible impact on companies like BP of the cut in taxes in the oil industry announced by the Chancellor of the Exchequer. (20 marks)

Key points

1. Development of corporate objectives from mission statement/corporate aims.
2. Critical appraisal of mission statements/corporate aims.

Getting started

An objective is something that a business intends to achieve. The nature and purpose of business objectives is explored in Unit 21. This unit explores the role of corporate aims and corporate objectives in shaping the strategy that a business follows.

Look at the following two statements.

R&F Fitness Centre corporate aim

To encourage targeted activity to improve levels of fitness.

A&L Entertainment Group corporate objective (one of several)

To establish two new attractions every new season.

The first is an aim and the second an objective. What is the difference between an aim and an objective? How do the two work together?

Business aims

All businesses have **aims**, the things the business intends to do in the long term — its purpose or reason for being. Ultimately its aims are what the business is striving to achieve. The aim of a business will be less specific than its objectives and could be expressed as a vision. A business will often communicate its aim through a mission statement.

Mission statements

A **mission statement** declares the business's overriding purpose, but may also reflect its goals and values. It describes in general terms what it considers to be the company's core activities and may also reference such information as the markets in which it operates, what its key commercial objectives are, in what way it values its stakeholders, or what its ethics involve. A good mission statement should help guide the decision making of the firm. Running a business can be extremely complicated and it is very easy to get lost in the finer details of business decision-making. When all else fails a good mission statement can clarify the direction a business should take by reminding the owners and directors of the reason why the business exists. Many people would argue that the sole purpose of a business is to generate a profit for its owners. However, most people would like to believe that they go to work to achieve something more than this – a mission statement makes this point.

There are two reasons why a business may form and share a mission statement. The first is to make a commitment to its customers. A mission statement forms a promise to customers on what they can expect the business to strive for. Secondly, a mission statement can be used to bring a company's workforce together with a shared purpose. Many successful businesses have a mission statement that their employees believe in. This is why a mission statement is important in forming a strong corporate culture (see Unit 57).

Some mission statements are short and succinct, while others are lengthy and relatively detailed.

- R&F Fitness Centre: 'We improve levels of fitness by providing individual plans for people of all ages and helping them to achieve their aims'.
- R&B furniture maker: 'To help create practical and beautiful homes for our customers.'
- 18EC, energy company: To achieve sustainable energy that delivers shareholder value by:
  - researching and innovating new products and services that meets the needs of our customers
  - maintaining a safe end efficient working environment
  - achieving technical and operational excellence
  - creating a team of flexible and adaptive individuals who strive for sustainable energy solutions and continually offer value to customers.
- Amnesty International, NGO: 'To undertake research and action focused on preventing and ending grave abuses of human rights.'
- DHC coffee shop: 'To offer a comfortable environment and excellent range of coffee to refresh our customers in body, mind and spirit.'

Question 1

Choose one of the industries listed below and devise a mission statement for a business in that sector. Use some of the examples above for inspiration, but try to link your mission statement to the context of the industry. Present your mission statement and explain your thinking behind it. How does it convey the vision and aims of the business you have chosen?

1. Airline industry
2. Soft drinks industry
3. Container shipping industry

Development of corporate objectives

Corporate objectives are objectives set by senior managers and directors for a company. They should be specific to the company, its particular history and vision of the future, and sit well with its mission statement. They should focus mainly on desired performance and results of the business over time, and may include such goals as market share, profit levels, creation of new products or processes, resource usage and scale economies, management of people and ethical behaviours.

To be of any real use to a business in achieving its aims, corporate objectives must be Specific, Measurable, Agreed, Realistic and Time specific. These criteria are known as SMART criteria.

- **Specific** means that the objective sets out clearly what the business is aiming to achieve and should refer to a particular aspect or function of the business.
- **Measurable** involves evidence to demonstrate whether or not the objectives have actually been achieved. For this reason most corporate objectives will have a financial or quantifiable element because this makes it easier to measure the success of that objective.
- **Agreed** implies that everyone responsible for achieving the objective has agreed with the objective and understands what it means for them. Without an objective being agreed by all those involved there will be no motivation or commitment to achieve it.
- **Realistic** ensures that the objective can be met within the resources available and the prevailing market conditions. If an objective is unrealistic people will soon ignore it, and failing to achieve the objective is likely to have a negative impact on the business.
- **Time specific** gives the stated time frame within which the objectives are to be achieved. All objectives must have an end point to ensure urgency and a point at which the objective can be assessed.

Departmental and functional objectives

From general objectives that flow from the mission statement come more specific corporate objectives that detail specifically what the firm does. Following this hierarchy come the even more specific **departmental and functional objectives**, which set the day-to-day goals and may include human resources, finance, operations, logistics and marketing. These all refer back up the hierarchy to the corporate objectives and mission statement, so that the goals and activities of the business are consistent. In this way, functional objectives will directly support the corporate objectives. As all business functions are guided by the corporate objectives they should all be aligned with one another. For example, if the operations department sets a departmental objective to reduce waste by 25 per cent within the next year, it is likely that this will have to feed into the objectives set by the human resources (HR) department. For instance, HR will need to ensure all production workers complete a specific training programme focusing on quality management (see Unit 40).

The objectives hierarchy

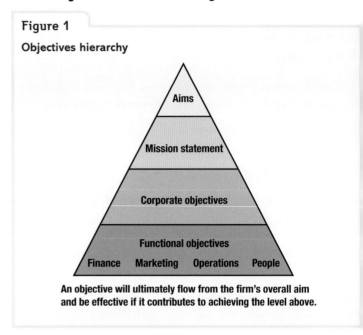

Figure 1

Objectives hierarchy

An objective will ultimately flow from the firm's overall aim and be effective if it contributes to achieving the level above.

The difference between small and large firms

Unit 1 explored the possible objectives that may drive a business. Usually, a business aims to make a profit. However, businesses may have other goals as well, such as maximising sales, sales revenue or market share; achieving efficiencies in cost; looking after its employees or ensuring its customers are satisfied. It may even aim to achieve a social purpose. An objective is a desired outcome that allows a business to achieve its stated aims. While some objectives are general, others can be very specific, including the quantification or precise statement of a particular goal for a department or functional area.

Small businesses may have a wide variety of objectives, such as the following.

- To ensure that the company breaks even at the end of the tax year (see Unit 32).
- To improve the firm's liquidity in the next six months (see Unit 35).
- To increase sales by 10 per cent over the next three years (see Unit 30).
- To increase pre-tax profits by 5 per cent over the next 12 months (see Unit 34).
- To hire five new staff with skills in sales and marketing, and build a strong marketing department over the next year.
- To reduce energy consumption by 2 per cent and cut use of non-recyclable packaging over the next three years.

By contrast, the objectives of large firms and multinationals tend to be mostly financial. This is because they have many stakeholders to satisfy, the foremost being the shareholders. Financial objectives are more objective and quantifiable, and therefore easier to communicate to a wide variety of interested parties. For example, a supermarket chain such as Lidl might state an objective that covers its entire operation: 'To increase market share by 5 per cent over the next two years.'

Question 2

Tesco states that its core purpose and values is a clear and simple statement of what it does and what it stands for: 'Serving Britain's shoppers a little better every day'. It explains that:

'Our Core Purpose needs to reflect how much society has changed in recent years — more scepticism about corporations, more desire to see business demonstrate it has a purpose beyond profit, a sense that large companies should be contributing more to tackling some of the big challenges. The world has changed from a culture of "more is better" to "making what matters better".

That's why we've changed our Core Purpose — this profound shift in society must be reflected in the way we think and behave as a business. Today, our brand must be about more than simply function. It's about the way we work, the values we live by, the legacy we leave. '

As part of this, Tesco has a commitment to the local communities in which it operates and has clear policies to maintain a socially responsible ethos. One of Tesco's corporate objectives is to: 'support the well-being of the community and to protect the environment'.

Source: www.tescoplc.com

(a) Explain how the functional objectives of Tesco's marketing department could support this corporate objective.

(b) Explain how the functional objectives of Tesco's operations department could support this corporate objective.

Critical appraisal of mission statements and corporate aims

Mission statements must be constantly assessed to ensure they have continued relevance for the business. Sometimes they are not appropriate. For example, a company with a mission statement that includes respect and integrity would not align if fraud were to be reported. Many organisations may put in place a mission statement that is appealing to its customers, but if it is not believed and followed by employees then the customers may soon lose faith in the business. On any corporate website you will find objectives relating to corporate social responsibility, ethical practices and sustainable business growth. However, businesses may need to consider the balance of the appeal of some of these objectives to their customers if the organisation is not achieving a profit for shareholders.

A critical re-assessment should involve an appraisal of the following.

- What is the purpose of the mission statement?
- Who is its intended audience?
- How does the strategy followed by the business fit with its stated mission?
- Are the aims and objectives realistic and achievable?

Question 3

1. RWDC, technology company: RWDC innovates and creates cutting edge mobile technology and software. It is a leader in games and music technology and its focus is on increasing shared experiences and customer fun.

2. PM Camping, active guides company: 'PM Camping unites a community of campers, suppliers and advertisers online, in-print and on-site, sharing experiences in a spirit of trust and co-operation.'

3. Thomas Therapeutics and Pharmacy: 'To research, develop, monitor and deliver complementary therapy that eases patients' symptoms and helps to overcome cancer'.

(a) What is the purpose of each of the statements?
(b) Who are the intended audiences?

Key terms

Corporate objectives — the objectives of a medium to large-sized business as a whole.
Departmental and functional objectives — the objectives of a department within a business.
Mission statement — a brief statement, written by the business, describing its purpose and objectives, designed to encapsulate its present operations.
Objective (or goal) — a target of or outcome for a business that allows it to achieve its aims.
SMART — acronym for the attributes of a good objective: Specific, Measurable, Agreed, Realistic and Time specific.

Knowledge check

1. Explain the difference between a functional objective and a corporate objective.

2. Why should objectives be SMART?

3. Why might corporate objectives mainly be expressed as financial objectives?

4. What is the purpose of a mission statement?

5. State three areas of business activity that corporate objectives might refer to.

Thinking bigger

Most large businesses identify various corporate objectives that cover a range of issues and facets of the business. These range from objectives centred on profitability to ones that guide corporate social responsibility. For example, see the list of corporate objectives below for LPW Car Rental company.

Customer loyalty

We conduct business in an honorable and transparent way that develops customer loyalty and respect.

Growth

We target new opportunities and ideas to encourage and extend high performance.

Profit

We deliver high returns for our shareholders through achieving our objectives.

Market leadership

We provide excellent service and trusted products, continually innovating to lead provision for changing customer needs.

Commitment to employees

We are committed to open and supportive teamwork, providing honest feedback and rewarding employer achievement.

Leadership capability

We encourage leadership qualities at all levels, developing career opportunities for those who achieve business results and enhancing individual potential to lead to growth and profitability.

Sustainability

We research, adopt and promote best working practices that help protect the environment and to contribute to local and global environmental sustainability as part of our charitable giving.

Most large businesses state their corporate objectives on their websites. How SMART would you say the above objectives are? Why might objectives, as shown on a company website, be more general than those discussed around the boardroom table?

It is common for a business to have a number of objectives that cover a number of areas. As a result, these objectives may sometimes conflict with each other. In other words, the achievement of one objective can hinder a business achieving another. For example, it could be theorised that providing rewards for staff performance could detract from financial profit. The same could be said for environmental objectives. Although it's attractive to promote a company as an ethical business, the development of technologies and strategies to ensure environmental compliance could lead to the company not achieving its financial objectives.

Exam tip

When analysing a case study, always try to identify the business's objectives. If a business achieves its objectives then it is a successful business. Remember that not all objectives are as important as one another. Therefore by prioritising an objective with a clear justification you can provide the basis for a recommendation when answering a question. For example, if you can justify that the objective to 'develop leaders at all levels' is the most important, then this helps you justify, for instance, a decision to invest in a new employee training programme.

Evaluation is about picking out the key issues facing a business. Therefore, if you can argue that a certain course of action will support a business in achieving its objectives then you have a strong point of evaluation.

Case study

LEGO® CORPORATE OBJECTIVES

LEGO® is the world's largest toy manufacturer and a highly popular toy with children. LEGO®'s mission is 'to inspire and develop the builders of tomorrow'. In Danish the word LEGO® is an abbreviation meaning 'play well', and this unique value is at the core of what the company does to change the way people understand learning and the huge value play has in helping children learn essential skills for life in the twenty-first century.

In 2013 LEGO® assessed the needs and attitudes of its stakeholders through an online survey of more than 1,500 respondents. They interviewed almost 1,500 additional participants from their most significant stakeholder groups and industry associates. LEGO® found that the following three issues were the most important:

• the safety and quality of their products

• supporting children's right to develop

• communication with children.

In 2014 a letter to the company employees from the Chief Executive Officer, Jørgen Vig Knudstorp, said that LEGO® should continue to strive to be the best, and that while 2014 was a good year there was also room for improvement.' As part of the LEGO® Group Responsibility Report 2014, the company analysed its performance against a set of corporate objectives that were defined in 2009. These were:

1. Zero product recalls – always.
2. To be ranked in the Top 10 companies for employee safety by 2015.
3. To support learning for 101 million children by 2015.
4. To use 100 per cent renewable energy by 2020.
5. Adopt a zero-waste mindset.

The LEGO® Group believes in transparency and always tries to provide a very honest assessment of its performance against specific targets. The 2014 report highlighted a number of targets related to its corporate objectives.

Table 1 LEGO® Group targets linked to corporate objectives

Objective	Target	Actual
1	Zero product recalls	0
2	Score of +10 for employee satisfaction and motivation	+14
3	101 million children educated	95.4 million
4	+10 per cent improvement in energy efficiency by 2016	+9%
5	90 per cent waste recycled	91%

LEGO® now plans to expand overseas with the opening of offices in Malaysia and China. LEGO® still has a relatively small market share of the toy market in Asia compared to Europe and North America, but as these countries become wealthier so will consumers' willingness and ability to purchase LEGO® products.

Source: adapted from www.lego.com

All information in this case study is collected and interpreted by its authors and does not represent the opinion of the LEGO® Group.

(a) What is meant by corporate objective? (2 marks)

(b) Explain why LEGO® might set an objective to achieve 100 per cent renewable energy by 2020. (4 marks)

(c) Explain why LEGO® has a mission statement. (4 marks)

(d) Assess which of the LEGO® Group's corporate objectives is the most important for the long-term success of the business. (12 marks)

45 Theories of corporate strategy

Key points

1. Development of corporate strategy:
   - Ansoff's Matrix
   - Porter's Strategic Matrix.
2. Aim of portfolio analysis.
3. Achieving competitive advantage through distinctive capabilities.
4. Effect of strategic and tactical decisions on human, physical and financial resources.

Getting started

The Restaurant Group (TRG) operates over 400 restaurants and pubs, including Frankie & Benny's, Chiquito, Garfunkel's and Coast to Coast. TRG's competitive advantage comes from their choice of locations, differentiation and culture. Rather than try to compete on the high street – and pay the high rents for space, TRG locates on leisure parks and in airports, and two thirds of their Frankie & Benny's restaurants are near cinemas. Its customers do not have to contend with parking issues and can come out of the cinema or bowling alley and walk next door into one of its eateries. The restaurants are differentiated to attract different customers and their tastes. For instance, Frankie & Benny's caters to families while Coast to Coast targets adults on a night out. In the future, TRG plans to continue to grow organically, rather than acquire new brands or take over competing firms.

Source: adapted from www.ft.com

What is TRG's competitive advantage and how does it inform its strategy? Do you think that its strategy will change in the future?

Business strategy

Businesses have aims that they hope to achieve through their stated objectives. However, this requires a considerable amount of planning. Such planning to achieve corporate objectives is known as strategy. The first part of the process involves using analytical tools to understand where the business currently sits in the market and then evaluating where it wants to be. A firm might begin this analytical process with a SWOT analysis (see Unit 46), followed by a Five Forces Analysis (see Unit 47). The corporate strategy derived from this process is the long-term plan to achieve the aims of the entire business. A successful strategy will give the firm an advantage in the competitive market place and fulfil stakeholder expectations.

Development of corporate strategy

Developing an effective corporate strategy requires a significant amount of time and research. The process of strategic planning involves key members of management looking critically at what the business has done before and what it may need to do in the future in order to achieve its corporate objectives. This is a very big task but there are numerous tools to help managers during the planning process, including value chain analysis, Ansoff's Matrix, Porter's Strategic Matrix and portfolio analysis.

Ansoff's Matrix

Igor Ansoff was an applied mathematician and influential business strategist. He developed Ansoff's Matrix as a strategic tool to help a business achieve growth. Figure 1 illustrates both existing and new products within existing and new markets. Ansoff's Matrix is a useful decision-making tool because it allows the owners of a business to consider a number of factors that will determine its corporate strategy:

- the level of investment in existing and new products
- the exploitation of different markets
- the growth strategy for the business
- the level of risk the business is willing to accept.

Ansoff's Matrix reveals four possible strategies that a business might adopt. The key issue is that risk becomes greater the further a firm strays from its core of existing products and consumers, i.e. the further it gets from the top left-hand corner of the matrix.

Figure 1
Ansoff's Matrix

		PRODUCT	
		Existing	**New**
MARKET	**Existing**	Market penetration	Product development
	New	Market development	Diversification

Market penetration: As suggested by Ansoff's Matrix, the purpose of **market penetration** is to achieve growth in existing markets with existing products. There are several ways a business can achieve this.

- Increase the brand loyalty of customers so that they use substitute brands less frequently, for instance by adopting a loyalty scheme such as Costa Coffee's reward card.
- Encourage consumers to use the product more regularly. An example might be encouraging people to eat breakfast cereal as a night-time snack.
- Encourage consumers to use more of the product. An example might be a crisps manufacturer producing maxi-sized crisp packets rather than standard-sized crisp packets.

If it has a successful product and believes that it can generate more revenue from it, a business might adopt a market penetration strategy. This is the strategy with the lowest risk because it involves the lowest level of investment. In addition the business will have a good understanding of the product and how the market might respond.

Product development: Product development is concerned with marketing new or modified products in existing markets. This might be an appropriate strategy to adopt where the product life cycle is traditionally short, or where trends or technology change quickly. This strategy is associated with product innovation and continuous development. The confectionery market is famous for product development. Take for example Cadbury's Dairy Milk. The brand has been around for over 100 years, but new extensions of the product are continuously launched, for example Dairy Milk Marvellous Creations, with Oreos and with jelly, popping candy and candy shells. Some businesses have gained a reputation for continuous product development and used this strategy to stay ahead of the competition. Apple has achieved this through the iPhone, iPad and Apple Watch. A strategy of product development requires significant investment in research and development, and there may be a high level of risk in developing new products – it may be that only one in five product launches succeed. For those that succeed, heavy investment in promotion may be required.

Market development: Market development involves the marketing of existing products in new markets. The most basic form of the strategy is entering geographically new markets. This is not always simple as customers from different regions of the same country, let alone a different country, may have different tastes and preferences. Although Tesco is an extremely successful company in the UK, the success was not matched when it opened stores in France in the 1990s. A market development strategy relies heavily on understanding local habits, tastes and needs. Enterprise Rent-A-Car is one example of a business that has adopted a very successful strategy of market development. The car leasing company's model was very successful, but the business achieved exponential growth when it started to locate its branches at airport locations. This move opened the company up to an entirely different profile of customer and by 2005 Enterprise had over 200 airport branches worldwide.

Even where market development is appropriate and successful, it is often necessary to make slight modifications to suit the new market, even if this is simply changing the name to be more acceptable or accessible in a different language, or labelling the product differently to meet international laws.

Diversification: Diversification occurs when new products are developed for new markets. It enables a business to move away from reliance upon existing markets and products, thus allowing the company to spread risk and increase safety. If one product faces difficulties or fails, a successful product in another market may prevent the business overall facing problems. However, diversification will take a business outside its area of expertise, and for this reason it is the strategy with the highest risk. This might mean that its performance in new markets is relatively poor compared with more experienced operators.

The move by Mercedes Benz into the market for small, high-volume cars, and the diversification by Virgin into financial services and the air passenger business, are examples of this marketing strategy. Diversification is generally adopted by large corporations and conglomerates that have extensive business networks, considerable capital and strong corporate brands. Virgin is one such business where the brand has allowed it to diversify into a range of industries. A consideration with diversification is that there may be significant barriers to entering a new industry (see Porter's Five Forces in Unit 47).

Question 1

Tough Mudder is an extreme events company founded in the USA by Will Dean. It is the UK market leader for endurance events. The company runs extreme obstacle events across the country where participants pay up to £125 to take part. Teams of competitors face obstacles, such as 'Arctic Enema' (swimming through a skip full of ice), 'Everest' (climbing a quarter pike slicked with mud) and 'Electroshock Therapy' (running through a field of hanging electric wires). In 2013 there were 35 Tough Mudder events across the globe; this number grew to over 50 events in 2015. Tough Mudder also uses a number of tactics to encourage customers to return to their events in the future, including different-coloured headbands representing the number of times a competitor has completed the course and exclusive obstacles for returning 'mudders'.

(a) With reference to Ansoff's Matrix, assess the strategies Tough Mudder uses to fuel growth.

Porter's Strategic Matrix

Porter's Strategic Matrix was developed by Michael Porter, a professor at Harvard Business School, to identify the sources of competitive advantage that a business might achieve in a market. Porter stated that any business that does not adopt one of these generic strategies is 'stuck in the middle' and unlikely to succeed.

Figure 2

Porter's Strategic Matrix

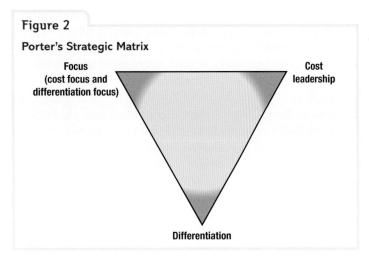

Cost leadership: This involves striving to be the lowest-cost provider in the market. This does not necessarily mean that the business will offer the lowest price, although this may be an option. Generally speaking, the firm that is able to operate as the lowest-cost provider in a market will compete in two ways.
1. Increase profits, while still charging market level prices.
2. Increase market share, while charging lower prices (still making a profit since costs are reduced).

Cost leadership is generally held by one business in the market as it requires having a significant market share in order to achieve the lowest costs. A firm will achieve the lowest costs by operating on a large scale and therefore leveraging economies of scale. The business will also have a clear focus on reducing costs through negotiation with suppliers, efficiency and streamlining operations. A cost leader will also offer a 'no-frills' product in order to minimise costs and limit the options for adding value. The level of service and variation in the product will be minimal and the scale associated with mass production.

Differentiation: This involves a business operating in a mass market but adopting a unique position instead of the lowest-cost position. Unlike cost leadership, a differentiation strategy may be adopted by any business providing it can deliver a defensible way of differentiating itself from the competition. A business adopting differentiation will do so through adding value to their products in a unique way. This might include quality, design, brand identity or customer service. The advantage of operating under a differentiation strategy is that the business may be able to charge a premium price if customers value their unique selling point. However, it is difficult to guarantee that the rewards of differentiation will justify the additional costs. For example, differentiation will require good research and development as well as effective marketing to highlight the uniqueness to the customer. Comparatively, differentiation is much easier to copy than cost leadership unless the differentiation is sustainable and defensible. For example, a business may be able to acquire a patent on a design or register a logo as a trademark so that competitors cannot copy it.

Focus: This strategy involves targeting a narrow range of customers in one of two ways. A focus strategy is closely aligned

to niche marketing (Unit 77). It tends to be used by small or very specialist firms. As a business is focusing on a very narrow segment of the market, it is able to gain an advantage by understanding its customers very well and delivering products and services that are very specific to their needs. As a result, this can create a high level of customer satisfaction and loyalty. Furthermore, by definition a focus strategy will result in less competition and higher profit margins. On the other hand, as the market is very small, a firm adopting this strategy tends to have low bargaining power with suppliers. A focus strategy can take one of two forms.
- **Cost focus** – emphasising cost-minimisation within a focused or niche market. Aldi is a good example of this strategy. Although it does not operate as the cost leader in the market, it is able to offer a focused range of products at very low prices.
- **Differentiation focus** – pursuing different strategies within a focused market. Ferrari is an example of this strategy as its high performance cars are targeted at a very small percentage of the population.

Question 2

The BBC iPlayer service has been in operation since 2007. Since then, there has been a significant change in the competitive landscape of online programme and film providers. Many other UK channels have also launched online sites. Netflix joined the UK market in 2012, reaching one million users in July of that year. Amazon also launched an online programming system with their Amazon Prime subscription. All of these providers can be viewed as competition to BBC iPlayer.

(a) Explain how the BBC might adapt its strategy to compete with other online programme providers.

Achieving competitive advantage through distinctive capabilities

Unit 3 looked at how a business is likely to be more successful if it can gain a competitive advantage in the market place. Competitive advantage is a set of unique features of a company and its products that are perceived by customers as significant and superior to the competition. These features will allow a business to perform better than its competitors in the market.

A business can develop a competitive advantage in many ways, such as through superior quality or design, by using creative advertising to promote the product, or by offering very good after-sales care and service. It could also achieve scale economies and thereby be able to charge a lower price, provide greater flexibility in delivery times or product attributes. A business might also be able to create an advantage through its reputation or ethical stance.

A **distinctive capability** is a form of competitive advantage that is difficult for competitors to understand, let alone imitate. The importance of a distinctive capability is that, because it cannot be easily reproduced, it can be the source of a sustainable competitive advantage.

In his bestseller *The Foundations of Corporate Success* (1995), John Kay argues that the source of competitive advantage is the exploitation of distinctive capabilities. Kay identified three types of distinctive capability.

1. **Architecture** – refers to the contracts and relationships within and around an organisation. These include the relationships between the business and its employees, and the collaborative relationships it has with partners, suppliers and customers. Some firms build and manage relationships extremely well. These effective relationships allow a business to add value by being more efficient through easy and open transfer of knowledge and information. The value of this architecture is often intangible and is closely linked to the culture within an organisation.

2. **Reputation** – closely linked to brand image and takes time for a business to build. Reputation refers to the positive associations a business builds around issues such as quality, reliability, service, prestige and honesty. The organisational characteristics cannot be built overnight, and any negative publicity or deterioration of the brand can have a lasting impact on a firm's reputation.

3. **Innovation** – often a sustainable competitive advantage will arise when a business is able to innovate by developing a new product or process in the production of a product. For successful innovation to take place, considerable investment in research and development, and in no small part the presence of luck, is often required. Sometimes innovation will not only give a business a distinctive capability, but on occasion it might also create a whole new market or industry.

Aim of portfolio analysis

Portfolio analysis is a method of categorising all of the products and services of a firm (its 'portfolio') so as to decide where each fits within the strategic plans. The products are then evaluated according to their competitive position and potential growth rates. This involves a two-step process.

- Step 1: Give a full and detailed overview of all of the products and services in the current business portfolio.
- Step 2: Look at the performance of each of these products and services by examining:
  o current and projected sales
  o current and projected costs
  o competitor activity and future competition
  o risks that may affect performance.

The Boston Consulting Group (BCG) has created an advanced tool for portfolio analysis. First, a business gathers market-share and growth-rate data on all of its products. Next, the Boston Consulting Group Matrix (or 'Boston Matrix' / Growth Share Matrix) categorises these products into one of four different areas based upon their current and potential market share or market growth.

1. **Stars** are high-growth products that are strong compared to those of competitors. Stars require investment, but the hope is that they will become cash cows.

2. **Cash cows** are low-growth products with high market shares. They generate more cash than they consume, and so can provide a return for investors and can fund investment in other areas.

3. **Question marks** are products with low market shares in high-growth markets. They consume a lot of cash, but give little return. However, they have the potential to turn into stars. Keeping these lines requires a belief that there is a potential for growth.

4. **Dogs** are products with low market share in low-growth markets. They may break-even, but nevertheless take up time and effort with little prospect of future growth. They should be sold or divested.

Figure 3

The Boston Matrix

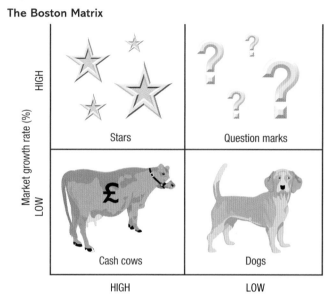

Source: adapted from The BCG Portfolio Matrix from the Product Portfolio Matrix, © 1970, The Boston Consulting Group (BCG)

The Boston Matrix may be used to assist a business in identifying which strategy to adopt. For example, if a firm believes that it has a 'Star' it may decide to adopt a market penetration strategy to increase sales revenue and maximise market share while the product is competitive. Similarly, a firm may choose to move a product out of a low-growth market and target a market with high-growth prospects. On the other hand, the matrix could be used to identify those 'Dogs' that need to be discontinued in order to cut costs and follow its strategy of cost leadership.

Question 3

De Vere is a British car manufacturer owned by a Chinese company called MXJ. Since MXJ bought De Vere in 2009 it has invested heavily in product development, building on De Vere's reputation for luxury sport and executive saloon cars. Since 2009, De Vere has launched four new models across these vehicle categories.

Table 1 De Vere product range and sales figures

Models	Sales – Feb 2012	Sales – Feb 2013	Year on year change (%)
P4	2,033	2,784	36.94
P6	473	337	−28.75
P7	–	79	–
P901	943	1,201	27.36

(a) Using the information in Table 1 and the BCG Matrix, analyse De Vere's product portfolio.

Strategies and tactics

Strategies set out the long-term direction that a firm will take to achieve its objectives. In contrast, tactics are short-term responses to an opportunity or threat in the market. Most day-to-day decisions in business are tactical and involve decision making responding to the current business conditions. For example, a business might put on an impromptu sale in order to disrupt a competitor who has similar plans. A tactical decision might be to buy an exceptionally large order of stock because the opportunity arises to buy it at a low price, even if the stock is not necessarily needed. Although tactics should ideally support the corporate strategy, tactical decisions are often made in isolation of the 'bigger picture' and are more responsive in nature. While strategy is often based on a set of principles or guidelines set down by the CEO and board of directors, tactical decisions happen at managerial or even supervisory level.

By nature, tactical decisions have to be made quickly and without significant research or planning. For this reason tactical decisions can backfire if they are made poorly. For example, a business might exaggerate the benefits of a product through an advert, which then comes under scrutiny from a social media campaign against the company. Although this decision was made to try and boost sales, it might have been against the corporate social responsibility policy outlined by the board and may have a lasting impact on the firm's reputation.

Thinking bigger

There are a range of concepts and theories surrounding the development of corporate strategies and this can sometimes make the concept a confusing one. The reality is that corporate strategy and what actually makes one business successful while another might miserably fail is not straightforward. There are just too many variables and external factors for anyone to be able to write a definitive formula for success. Nevertheless, theoretical models help businesses simplify reality in order to understand it better. It is perhaps useful to consider how the three main models within this unit fit together and see more clearly how they are each separate but still related to one another.

For example, Ansoff's Matrix is a useful tool for a business to identify its current position and choose an appropriate direction for the company – the 'what and where tool'. Whereas Porter's Strategic Matrix presents three strategies that a business might use to compete in its market – the 'how tool'. Finally, Kay's theory of distinctive capabilities will help a business decide whether its strategy is sustainable, defensible and has longevity.

Similarly, using the BCG Matrix can help you categorise a firm's products and make informed recommendations on how it should use them for future growth. Business models are not just useful tools for business, they are also useful tools to help guide your analysis and evaluation in examinations.

Case study

BUSINESS TACTICS:
TIES.COM, ZARA, JCB AND IKEA

Ties.com

Ties.com was founded in 1998 as an online company specialising in men's neckties, bow ties, cufflinks and a range of related men's accessories. The company carries popular brands, such as Tommy Hilfiger and Jerry Garcia, but a highly talented team at its head office in California designs most of their products. The company prides itself on having the widest range of neckties anywhere and guarantees 100 per cent customer satisfaction. Ties.com believes in the personal touch and tries to build relationships with its customers. For example, Ties.com has the tactic of only using real people to answer their phone lines, no automated menus, and makes sure that every package sent to the customer includes a personalised note inside. The company also runs a blog entitled *TheGentleManual*, where customers and experts discuss all matter of men's fashion and grooming.

Zara

Zara is an international clothing company and part of the Inditex Group. Zara is a recognised high street name in the UK with branches in most towns and cities. It has also penetrated many international markets, including China where it has opened over 200 very successful stores. The Inditex Group also owns a range of highly automated factories and a huge team of fashion designers. This vertical integration of the business has allowed Zara and Inditex's other brands to deliver exceptionally fast lead times on all of their products. Zara realised that women wanted clothes that reflected current trends and Zara's ability to design and deliver new clothing lines to their stores in a few weeks allows it to meet this demand. Zara's ability to respond quickly to emerging trends can help it to stay one step ahead of its competitors.

JCB

JCB is a British manufacturing company that specialises in construction machinery and vehicles, with a 12 per cent share of the global market. JCB dominates in a number of international markets, including Britain, India and Brazil. JCB's leading product is a digger known as a backhoe loader, which is a staple feature of most construction sites around the world. JCB has focused on producing smaller vehicles rather than some other segments of the market, such as large-scale construction vehicles used for mining and drilling, which is dominated by US firm and market leader, Caterpillar. JCB is renowned for innovation and exceptional quality. JCB realised that their customers valued speed and efficiency, as a digger is at the centre of most construction sites and any breakdown will inevitably result in the build grinding to a halt.

IKEA

The Swedish furniture retailer IKEA revolutionised the furniture industry by offering affordable but stylish furniture. The company is known for its modern architectural designs for various types of appliances and furniture, and its interior design is often associated with an eco-friendly simplicity. IKEA maintains its competitive prices by careful sourcing of products to selected countries and offering a service that is consistent with affordability. IKEA does not assemble or deliver furniture; customers must collect the furniture in the warehouse and assemble it at home themselves. During a ten-year period of global expansion, IKEA has been able to further reduce its prices on average by two to three per cent.

Q

(a) What is meant by business tactic? (2 marks)

(b) Explain one reason why Ties.com is a successful business. (4 marks)

(c) Discuss how IKEA's corporate strategy compares to that of JCB. (8 marks)

(d) Assess the competitive advantages of each business and which might be most sustainable. (12 marks)

Key terms

Corporate strategy – the plans and policies developed to meet a company's objectives. It is concerned with what range of activities the business needs to undertake in order to achieve its goals. It is also concerned with whether the size of the business organisation makes it capable of achieving the objectives set.

Distinctive capability – a form of competitive advantage that is sustainable because it cannot easily be replicated by a competitor.

Diversification – developing new products in new markets.

Market development – the marketing of existing products in new markets.

Penetration – using tactics such as the marketing mix to increase the growth of existing products in an existing market.

Portfolio analysis – a method of categorising all the products and services of a firm (its portfolio) to decide where each fits within the strategic plans.

Product development – marketing new or modified products in existing markets.

Knowledge check

1. Explain the connection between corporate strategy and business aims.

2. Why is a long-term decision to move into a new market an example of corporate strategy?

3. What are the four strategies outlined by Ansoff's Matrix?

4. Which of Porter's strategies is focused on achieving the lowest costs of production?

5. What is a distinctive capability?

6. Explain what is meant by a sustainable competitive advantage.

7. How might a business use the BCG Matrix to make strategic decisions?

8. What is the difference between a long-term strategy and a tactic?

Exam tip

In your examination it is important to understand a range of theoretical models that explain corporate strategy and the issues surrounding each distinguishable strategy. By understanding theories of corporate strategy you can categorise any business that features in the case study and they can help you trigger points of analysis in your answers. For example, being able to identify a firm as adopting a market penetration strategy will allow you to discuss the following issues and relate them to the firm.

- It is a comparatively low-risk strategy.
- It might require heavy investment in marketing.
- Success relies on building loyal relationships with customers.
- There is a danger of falling behind competitors who innovate.

Key points

1. SWOT analysis:
   - internal considerations: strengths and weaknesses
   - external considerations: opportunities and threats.

Getting started

Glympton Enterprises Ltd operates three businesses. One is a roofing specialist, another is a household maintenance business and the third is a solar heating provider. The solar heating business is fairly new and has encountered one or two problems since its inception. It has been a drain on cash resources and has forced the group to borrow a lot of money. However, sales are growing fast and the future looks bright, although the CEO is worried about overtrading.

The roofing business is established and has an excellent reputation for reliability in the local area. It has high profit margins and currently generates 75 per cent of the group's profits. The housing maintenance business struggled a little during the recession, but is starting to recover as homeowners increase spending on home improvements. The business offers a 24-hour call-out service, which none of its competitors can match. However, it has had difficulties attracting staff, and existing workers are pushing hard for a seven per cent pay increase, which will hit margins if granted.

Identify the strengths of Glympton Enterprises. Identify the weaknesses of Glympton Enterprises. Why might it be important for Glympton Enterprises to understand the strengths and weaknesses of its operations? Suggest some possible external factors that might threaten the performance of the business in the future.

Gathering information to help develop a strategy

When making plans or developing a business strategy it is important to gather appropriate information. A business can use a variety of methods to do this.

The internal audit: An internal audit is an analysis of the business itself and how it operates. It attempts to identify the strengths and weaknesses of its operations. It might cover areas such as:
- products and their costs, quality and development
- finance, including profit, assets and cash flow
- production, including capacity, quality, efficiency and stock management
- internal organisation, including divisional and departmental structures
- human resources, including skills, training and recruitment.

In a large business, the internal audit might be conducted by outside management consultants. This could help to produce a more independent-minded analysis of the business's situation.

The external audit: An external audit is an analysis of the environment in which the business operates and over which it has little or no control. This audit may address three key areas: the market; competition; and the political, economic, social, technological, legal and environmental issues relevant to the business.

The audit should analyse the market or markets in which the business operates. For example, it should analyse:
- the size and growth potential of the market
- the characteristics of the customers in the market
- the products on offer
- the pricing structure
- how products are distributed
- how products are promoted
- industry practices, such as whether there is a **trade association** or government regulation.

The audit should also analyse the competition in the market. The nature and strength of competitors will be an important influence on the development of a strategy. For example, it should analyse:
- the structure of the industry, including the number and size of competitors, their production capacity and marketing methods, the likelihood of new entrants to the market or businesses leaving the industry
- finance, including profits of competitors, their investment programmes, costs, revenues, cash and assets.

PESTLE analysis is an analysis of the political (P), economic (E), social (S), technological (T), legal (L) and environmental (E) issues relevant to the business. It is discussed in more detail in Unit 47.

What is SWOT analysis?

It is helpful if the information gathered can then be summarised and presented in a meaningful way. One approach is to use **SWOT analysis**. This involves looking at the **internal** strengths (S) and weaknesses (W) of a business and the **external** opportunities (O) and threats (T) that it faces.

Strengths: These are the positive aspects of a business that may be identified from the internal audit. Strengths are what the business is good at – they are what help make the business a success. Examples might include:

- a respected, intelligent, inspirational and visionary leader
- a highly motivated and loyal workforce
- a product with a unique selling point
- 'state of the art' production facilities
- a loyal customer base
- an innovative marketing department.

Weaknesses: These are the negative aspects of a business that may be identified from the internal audit. Weaknesses are what the business lacks or does poorly, for example in relation to its competitors. They are the characteristics that undermine the performance of a business – perhaps even preventing it from growing. They are also areas for improvement. Examples might include:

- a poorly motivated workforce with a high staff turnover
- an organisational structure that has too many layers of management
- a product range that is getting out of date
- poor cash flow and growing debt
- outdated tools and machinery
- a poorly presented and out-of-date website.

Opportunities: The external audit should show up what opportunities are available to the business. These are the options or openings that the business might be able to exploit – resulting in improvements, such as higher revenues or lower costs. Examples might include:

- a new overseas market opening up following a political change
- a fall in the cost of an essential raw material, such as oil
- low interest rates, which provide cheap finance for investment
- a fall in the exchange rate, which will make exports cheaper
- the abolition of some burdensome regulations
- the collapse of a major rival in the market.

Threats: The external audit should show up what threats face the business. Threats are the possible hazards or perils that have the potential to damage the performance of the business. Examples might include:

- a new entrant in the market
- a rival appointing a new and highly successful CEO
- a looming recession
- new legislation aimed at improving the rights of employees
- mounting pressure from environmentalists
- a change in social attitudes towards the business's key product.

SWOT analysis is often carried out in mind-mapping or 'blue skies thinking' sessions before being documented. It can be a powerful way of summarising and building upon the results of internal and external audits. Clearly, it will be a useful tool when developing a corporate strategy, but it may have other uses. For example, it might be used to:

- make a decision about which new product to launch
- help design a new marketing strategy
- help decide whether to outsource a specific business task or activity, such as IT
- prepare for a completely new business venture
- help prepare for a restructuring of the business.

Finally, by identifying clearly the strengths, weaknesses, opportunities and threats, it may be possible to improve the performance of a business. However, this will depend on the action it takes after carrying out the analysis. For example, only if a business takes measures to eliminate weaknesses will performance improve.

An example of a SWOT analysis

Thorntons is a well-established and well-known confectionery business. It has been trading for over 100 years and now has around 250 shops located in prominent positions around the UK. In 2014 the business made a pre-tax profit of £7.5 million, but a profits warning in December 2014 suggested that this might be difficult to match. In the years running up to 2014 the business had focused on improving profitability. It had closed down marginal stores and tried to increase sales using other outlets. Figure 1 shows a SWOT analysis for Thorntons.

Figure 1

SWOT analysis for Thorntons

STRENGTHS
- Progress is being made developing wholesale and third-party sales
- Market research suggests that the business is increasing its market share
- Online sales have increased significantly – albeit from a low base
- The historic brand is widely recognised

WEAKNESSES
- Profits declining
- Still too much reliance on high street shops (250 in 2014)
- Falling sales, partly caused by operational difficulties at a depot in Derbyshire

SWOT ANALYSIS

OPPORTUNITIES
- Overseas markets offer considerable potential for growth only 3 per cent of sales are currently from exports
- The business is working hard to get its products on the shelves of other retailers
- A number of new products could help lift sales, revenue and market share

THREATS
- Profit margins could suffer as a result of supermarket price wars
- Emerging competition from gift-selling rivals, such as Hotel Chocolat and Moonpig
- The cost of raw materials, such as sugar and cocoa, is subject to volatility

Source: adapted from www.thorntons.co.uk

Case study

BHP BILLITON

The company and its products

BHP Billiton is a large Anglo-Australian mining company. In 2014 it employed over 120,000 people and had operations in 130 locations in 21 different countries. The company's revenue was US$67.2 billion. This was generated from the sale of minerals and petroleum products including iron ore, coal, copper, oil and gas.

BHP Billiton's portfolio of assets, operations and interests are separated into just four business units, which creates a simple organisation for a company of its scale. This helps to keep costs down. The company holds a dominant position in some of the world's richest resource basins.

BHP Billiton is the largest exporter of seaborne metallurgical coal, a global top three producer of iron ore, a global top four producer of copper and the largest overseas investor in onshore US shale oil and gas. It is also the developer of the world's best undeveloped potash resource – in Saskatchewan, Canada. However, in the 2014 financial year about half of its earnings was generated from iron ore.

In the 2014 financial year, the company delivered a strong financial performance. It had a strong balance sheet and maintained a solid 'A' credit rating. BHP Billiton reported a profit of US$13.8 billion and a net operating cash flow of US$25.4 billion.

Iron-ore prices

Iron-ore prices have come under considerable pressure since 2012. Figure 2 shows that the price fell by nearly 50 per cent from $135 to $69 between December 2013 and December 2014. Also, the combination of a further increase in global iron ore supply in 2014 and only subdued demand growth suggested that prices would continue to drift lower.

Competition

BHP Billiton does have some sizable rivals in the market. Glencore and Rio Tinto were two of its closest competitors in

2014 and there were rumours of a possible merger between them. Mergers of competitor companies could have a negative impact on BHP. Also, reports from Australia suggested that the mining boom in the country was under threat from increased international competition. One report showed that the minerals sector was losing out to increased competition from other minerals-exporting regions, such as Brazil and West Africa.

Markets

China has been the driving force behind the mining industry since the 1990s. This has been due to its insatiable demand for commodities needed for the development of its infrastructure. However, economic growth in China has slowed down. Also, some of the Chinese steel plants have purchased their own mining operations, which is likely to impact on BHP. Economic recovery in the US, Japan and the UK should help to compensate a little for the fall in demand from China. However, the European market was weak in 2014.

Costs

In 2014, BHP Billiton and Rio Tinto reported their average production cost in Pilbara, where most of Australia's iron-ore production is located, was around $25 a tonne. So even at low prices ($60 per tonne), these producers were still profitable. Smaller mining companies might struggle to survive if prices continue to fall. However, rising wages in Australia could also erode profit margins. BHP is striving to reduce costs and improve efficiency. New production records were set at a number of BHP operations. Investment in up-to-date technology and improved working practices ensured that BHP was ahead of rivals in cutting costs.

The decline in the Australian dollar could have an impact on BHP. For example, it was suggested that the company would find it difficult to cut capital expenditure costs. Between 2012 and 2015 the Australian dollar fell around 26 per cent, from 70.4p/AUS$1 to 52.0p/AUS$1.

Source: adapted from www.bhpbilliton.com

(a) Explain how an internal audit might play a role in SWOT analysis. (4 marks)

(b) Explain how an external audit might play a role in SWOT analysis. (4 marks)

(c) Assess the position of BHP Billiton by carrying out a SWOT analysis. (12 marks)

Figure 2

The price of iron ore in US dollars (per dry metric tonne)

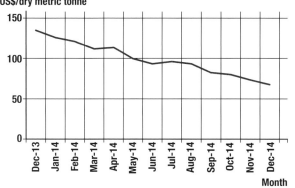

US$/dry metric tonne

Links 🔗

A business may use SWOT analysis to help make decisions. Therefore, you could link information in this unit to any answer where decision making is being discussed. For example, a business might be deciding whether or not to penetrate an overseas market, which is discussed in Unit 72. You could explain that a business might carry out a SWOT analysis to help decide whether such a move would be desirable given the company's current situation. Other examples of units to which SWOT analysis might be linked include Market positioning (Unit 3), Pricing strategies (Unit 11), Marketing strategy (Unit 13), Business choices (Unit 24), Corporate objectives (Unit 45), Mergers and takeovers (Unit 49), Investment appraisal (Unit 53) and Key factors in change (Unit 64).

Exam tip

You need to remember that strengths and weaknesses are internal factors and opportunities and threats are external factors. It is important not to get them mixed up.

Key terms

External audit – an audit of the external environment in which a business finds itself, such as the market within which it operates or government restrictions on its operations.

Internal audit – an analysis of the business itself and how it operates.

SWOT analysis – an analysis of the internal strengths and weaknesses of the business and the opportunities and threats presented by its external environment.

Trade association – an organisation whose members are all involved in the same industry or trade. The organisation pursues the interests of these businesses.

Knowledge check

1. Give three examples of information that an internal audit might find.

2. Give three examples of information that an external audit might find.

3. Why might SWOT analysis help a business to make decisions?

4. Give three possible examples of uses for SWOT analysis.

5. How might SWOT analysis help to improve the performance of a business?

Impact of external influences

Key points

1. PESTLE (political, economic, social, technological, legal and environmental).
2. The changing competitive environment.
3. Porter's Five Forces.

Getting started

In 2014, it was widely reported that the daily newspaper market was falling at a rate of 8 per cent a year. The Sunday newspaper market was said to be falling at an even faster rate of 9 per cent. Some newspapers were struggling more than others. For example, one of the national newspapers saw its sales drop by around 13 per cent.

In 2013, the main newspaper companies included the Telegraph Media Group, News Corporation, Daily Mail and General Trust, and Johnston Press. The top four businesses in the UK newspaper market were reported to account for around 50% of industry revenue in 2012–2013, with a medium level of market share concentration. The future potential for the newspaper industry could be seen as uncertain, and affected by many factors.

Identify possible external factors that might account for the decline in the newspaper industry. Do you think that there is a lot of competition in the newspaper industry? Explain whether you think that new newspaper businesses are likely to enter the market for newspapers in the near future.

PESTLE analysis

The impact of external influences on business can be enormous and can be both positive and negative. For example, if interest rates fall, the costs of repayment of loans for a business will fall and profits could rise. Businesses may also be encouraged to invest more. In contrast, if interest rates rise, interest charges will rise and profits will fall. Also, demand for

goods, such as cars and houses, which are often funded by borrowing, will fall.

Consequently, it will be helpful to businesses if they can monitor and analyse the likely impact of external influences in some way. One approach is to use **PESTLE analysis**. This involves identifying the political (P), economic (E), social (S), technological (T), legal (L) and environmental (E) factors that might influence business activity and performance.

Political: Some parts of the world are politically volatile and special attention has to be paid if businesses venture into politically unstable countries. However, political factors can also influence businesses in stable, democratic countries. The activities of pressure groups can play a role in influencing business activity. Some examples of political factors include the following.

- Members joining or leaving the EU. This could disrupt financial markets and create a great deal of uncertainty in the Eurozone. For example, in 2015, some felt that Greece might leave the EU.
- The issue of national security has become a priority for many governments. If measures designed to improve national security restrict the movement of goods, people and capital, this could have a negative impact on businesses.
- Pressure groups, such as ASH (Action on Smoking and Health), which aims to eliminate the harm done by smoking, can affect businesses. For example, ASH might persuade government to increase the tax on tobacco, which would clearly affect the tobacco industry.
- Changes in government. For example, a new government might be elected which is very pro-business.

Economic: The general state of the economy can have a huge impact on business activity. Since the financial crisis in 2008, a number of countries have suffered a recession, which has made trading conditions very difficult for many businesses. However, some specific examples include the following.

- Falling unemployment might help to increase demand for many businesses.
- Stable prices would create more certainty, which should encourage businesses to invest for the future.
- A strengthening exchange rate could make exporting more difficult. However, in contrast, imports become cheaper.
- Lower interest rates would make borrowing cheaper and encourage more investment.
- Some businesses may suffer badly during a recession. Those which produce goods and services that are income

elastic will tend to have the most problems. For example, car producers, housebuilders, holiday companies, computer games and 'white goods' such as freezers, cookers and washing machines, are likely to get hit the hardest. This is because people can postpone purchases of these items until incomes pick up again.

Social: Over time there are likely to be changes in the way society operates. Although social and cultural changes tend to be gradual, they can still have an impact.

- In the UK, greater numbers of people are going to university. This could increase the quality of human resources, which would benefit businesses.
- The population in many countries is ageing. This could affect demand patterns and create new opportunities for some businesses.
- Increasing migration might increase the size of the potential workforce, making recruitment easier. It might also provide a boost to demand.
- People appear to be becoming more health conscious. This might create opportunities for certain businesses, such as those selling healthy foods or running fitness centres.

Technological: The rate of technological change seems to gather pace all the time. Businesses usually welcome technological developments because they often provide new product opportunities or help to improve efficiency.

- Changes in technology can shorten product life cycles. This is because new products are quickly developed to replace ones that use older technology.
- Developments in technology often mean that businesses can replace labour with capital. This is welcomed because human resources are often said to be the most expensive and difficult to manage. New technology also lowers unit costs.
- The development of social media has helped to improve communications between businesses and customers. This allows businesses to keep abreast of changing consumer needs.

Legal: The government provides the legal framework in which businesses operate. However, it also directs legislation at businesses to protect vulnerable groups that might otherwise get exploited. UK businesses are also affected by EU regulations.

- EU legislation can affect tax laws. In 2015, for example, rules changed so that EU VAT would be charged in the country where products were bought as opposed to the country where they were sold. The legislation only applied to digital products, such as e-books, online courses or downloads.
- There have been calls to ban the advertising of alcohol on television. If introduced, such legislation might have a negative impact on the beverages industry.
- Businesses in the food industry are currently under pressure to reduce the amount of sugar and salt they add to products.
- The government in the UK often states that it wants to reduce the amount of 'red tape' in business. This might benefit a wide range of businesses.

Environmental: People are increasingly protective of the environment, for instance because of the threats posed by global warming. People are also concerned about the threats to wildlife and natural habitats that businesses sometimes pose.

- People are more inclined to buy 'green' goods. This provides opportunities for businesses that specialise in such products.
- New ways of generating power using renewable sources rather than by burning hydrocarbons are providing new opportunities.
- The trend towards recycling is gathering pace in the UK. By using recycled resources, businesses can cut their costs.

Question 1

Royal Mail provides a universal postal service in the UK. It delivers mail to anywhere in the country using a 'one-price-goes-anywhere' capability. After a turbulent period of trading, the business was privatised (sold to shareholders by the state) in 2013. It then started to transform its business in response to the continuing decline in letter volumes caused by the increased use of email and the rise in demand for parcel delivery as a result of more online shopping.

One of the reasons why Royal Mail was privatised was so that it could attract private sector investment – investment that the public sector could no longer afford. The money was needed for a strategy to transform the business and maintain efficient operations. With the 'pick-up' in the economy, low interest rates and higher future growth predictions, Royal Mail could see its performance improve.

(a) Explain the purpose of PESTLE analysis.

(b) Assess the political, economic and technological factors that have affected Royal Mail in this case.

The structure of markets

Competition is the rivalry that exists between firms when trying to sell goods in a particular market. In some markets there is a lot of competition. For example, the restaurant market in London is very competitive, with more than 5,500 restaurants competing for customers. However, in other markets there is very little competition. Thames Water, for example, is the sole supplier of tap water in London. No other firm competes with Thames Water.

Competitive markets: In a competitive market there is likely to be a large number of buyers and sellers, and the products sold by each business are close substitutes for each other. Barriers to entry in competitive markets will be low and businesses have very little control over the price charged. For example, if a firm tries to charge more than its rivals it is likely to lose nearly all of its business. Finally, there will be a free flow of information about the nature of products, availability at different outlets, prices, methods of production and the cost and availability of production factors.

Uncompetitive markets: Some markets are dominated by a single producer or just a few large businesses. In a small number of markets such as rail travel and water supply, a **monopoly** exists. This means that just one business supplies the entire market. For example, if you want to get a train from Glasgow to Edinburgh there is only one operator – ScotRail. A monopoly might also exist in a local market where a village shop, for example, serves the whole community without any competition. Monopolies may attempt to exploit consumers by charging higher prices and preventing competition – by erecting barriers to entry, for example. As a consequence the government is obliged to monitor the activities of monopolies closely.

A market that is dominated by a few very large producers is called an **oligopoly**. For example, there might be 2,000 businesses in a market, but if three of those businesses share 70 per cent of the market between them, an oligopoly is said to exist. One of the key features of an oligopolistic market is interdependence. This means the actions of one business will affect other businesses. For example, if one business gains an extra 4 per cent of the market, others must have lost 4 per cent between them. There are usually high barriers to entry in oligopolistic markets and the larger firms can exploit economies of scale. Also, because of interdependence, prices tend to remain stable for long periods of time. This is because all firms in the market are afraid of a price war. In an oligopoly businesses are more likely to engage in non-price competition, such as advertising and promotion. The car industry, confectionery industry and the potato crisp industry are good examples of oligopolies in the UK.

The changing competitive environment

Over time, the structure of markets is likely to change. In some markets competition intensifies as new businesses enter the market. A new entrant might be a business with a novel product. Alternatively, the newcomer might be an established business that wants to diversify into a different business area. Since 1980, UK governments have tried to make markets more competitive by reducing the amount of regulation. For example, at one time only local councils were permitted to operate bus services. However, today anyone can obtain a licence and provide bus services on any route they choose. In contrast, in some markets there has been some consolidation. This means that there are now fewer businesses in the market. This might result from takeover or merger activity when two or more firms join together. Some examples of changes in the competitive environment are outlined below.

- The supermarket industry has become more competitive since 2010. For example, in the last four months of 2014, Tesco, Sainsbury's, Asda and Morrisons all lost market share to Aldi, Lidl and Waitrose.
- Retailing in general has become more competitive due to the increasing use made by consumers of online shopping facilities. For example, people can buy products from all over the world when shopping online.

- There has been a significant consolidation in the global airline industry. For example, in 2005 there were 11 US airlines sharing 96 per cent of the domestic market. In 2014 this had fallen to just 6 airlines sharing 94 per cent of the market. In Europe, there were mergers between national airlines. BA and Iberian Airlines merged to become IAG, now one of the biggest carriers in the world. Air France and KLM have also merged, as have Swiss Air and Lufthansa.
- The number of businesses in the mobile telephone industry is falling. For example, in 2015 Hutchison Whampoa bought O_2 for £10.25 billion. This reduced the number of operators in the UK from four to three.

The impact on businesses of a changing competitive environment

Many markets are dynamic and businesses need to be aware of the changes that are taking place. They may have to react to certain changes when they occur.

New entrants: When competition gets stronger, as a result of new entrants in the market, existing businesses have to consider their position. For example, the growth in online shopping has forced many retailers to offer their own online shopping services. In some cases, failure to compete online has resulted in the collapse of retailers. In the first half of 2014, 16 shops a day in the UK were closing down, although this was a slight fall from the first half of 2013 when it was 18 per day. Some of the casualties include building societies, video rental shops, pawnbrokers, mobile phone shops and fashion retailers. Not all of these closures are due to online shopping, but retailers that fail to offer an online service in the future may find it difficult to survive.

New products: When a new product appears in the market, businesses may be forced to make changes of their own. They might adapt their own products, lower the price of existing products or invest in an aggressive marketing campaign. In the banking industry a number of new entrants have appeared offering peer-to-peer (P2P) lending. This has obviously been noticed by the traditional banks and some have started to make a move. The majority have looked to joining with portals that are already up and running, but the Royal Bank of Scotland plans to pilot a new P2P platform of its own.

Consolidation: When consolidation occurs in markets the number of businesses in the market falls, but some of the existing businesses get bigger. These bigger organisations are likely to pose more of a threat to the others. They may be able to lower their costs and they will have a larger market share. Other businesses in the market might respond by organising mergers or takeovers of their own. Alternatively they may look to develop their products, diversify, or cut their costs in some way. As a last resort they may continue to operate in much the same way, but accept lower profit margins.

Failure to respond effectively to the changing competitive environment could adversely affect the performance of a business. At worst, certain changes may threaten the business's survival.

Question 2

Many consumers have complained about rising energy prices in the UK. Between 2003 and 2015, gas prices, for example, increased by nearly 200 per cent. As a result, a household with a gas bill of £300 in 2003 would be paying around £900 in 2015. One possible reason for these significant price increases is the lack of competition in energy markets. At the end of the 1990s there were 14 regional monopolies supplying the UK. In 2015 there were just six big companies: British Gas, npower, SSE, E.ON UK, EDF Energy and Scottish Power.

However, since the market consolidated, a number of new, smaller firms started to emerge. The competitive landscape could change in the future and prices might start to fall. Some of the entrants to the market, such as GnERGY, FlowEnergy, First Utility, extraenergy, ecotricity and green energy, are keen, agile and offer innovative services. For example, many provide smart meters, new technology, a commitment to energy efficiency and green energy, and a range of different contracts. Some also claim that their pricing strategies are much easier to understand.

When people complain about energy price increases the government often responds by saying that consumers have the freedom to switch suppliers. Many of the new suppliers offer lower prices, but only between 15 and 17 per cent of customers per year have switched. In 2015, these entrants had only captured between 2 and 3 per cent of the total market. However, with more awareness and possibly more government intervention, the energy market might become more competitive in the future.

Sources: adapted from the Office for National Statistics and www.ofgem.gov.uk

(a) Assess the possible impact on the existing energy providers of the growing number of new entrants.

Porter's Five Forces

Another way of looking at the competitive environment is to consider a model put forward by Michael Porter in his book, *Competitive advantage: creating and sustaining superior performance* (1985). In the book, he outlines five forces or factors which determine the profitability of an industry. He argues that the ultimate aim of competitive strategy is to cope with and ideally change those rules in favour of the business. Where the collective strength of those five forces is favourable, a business will be able to earn above-average rates of return on capital. Where they are unfavourable, a business will be locked into low returns or wildly fluctuating returns. The five forces, shown in Figure 1 on the next page, are as follows.

The bargaining power of suppliers: Suppliers, like any business, want to maximise the profit they make from their customers. The more power a supplier has over its customers, the higher the prices it can charge and the more it can re-allocate profit from the customer to itself. Limiting the power of its supplier, therefore, will improve the competitive position of a business. It has a variety of strategies it can

adopt to achieve this. It can grow vertically (backward vertical integration, see Unit 49), either acquiring a supplier or setting up its own business by growing organically upwards. It can seek out new suppliers to create more competition amongst suppliers. It might be able to engage in technical research to find substitutes for a particular input to broaden the supply base. It may also minimise the information provided to suppliers in order to prevent the supplier realising its power over the customer.

Bargaining power of buyers: Just as suppliers want to charge maximum prices to customers, so buyers want to obtain supplies for the lowest price. If buyers or customers have considerable market power, they will be able to beat down prices offered by suppliers. For example, the major car manufacturers have succeeded in forcing down the price of components from component suppliers because of their enormous buying power and the relatively few number of major car manufacturers in the world. One way a business can improve its competitive position viz-a-viz buyers is to extend into the buyers' market through forward vertical integration. A car manufacturer might set up its own dealership, for example. It could encourage other businesses to set up in its customers' market to reduce the power of existing customers. It could also try to make it expensive for customers to switch to another supplier. For example, one way in which games console manufacturers keep up the price of computer games for their machines on which they receive a royalty is by making them technically incompatible with other machines.

Threat of new entrants: If businesses can easily come into an industry and leave it again if profits are low, it becomes difficult for existing businesses in the industry to charge high prices and make high profits. Existing businesses are constantly under threat that if their profits rise too much, this will attract new suppliers into the market who will undercut their prices. Businesses can counter this by erecting barriers to entry to the industry. For example, a business may apply for patents and copyright to protect its intellectual property and prevent other businesses using it. It can attempt to create strong brands which will attract customer loyalty and make customers less price sensitive. Large amounts of advertising can be a deterrent because it represents a large cost to a new entrant which might have to match the spending to grow some market share. Large sunk costs, costs which have to paid at the start but are difficult to recoup if the business leaves the industry, can deter new entrants.

Substitutes: The more substitutes there are for a particular product, the fiercer the competitive pressure on a business making the product. Equally, a business making a product with few or no substitutes is likely to be able to charge high prices and make high profits. A business can reduce the number of potential substitutes through research and development, and then patenting the substitutes itself. Sometimes, a business will buy the patent for a new invention from a third party and do nothing with it simply to prevent the product coming to market. Businesses can also use marketing tactics to stop the spread of substitute products. A local newspaper, for example, might use predatory pricing if a new competitor comes into its market to drive it out again.

Rivalry among existing firms: The degree of rivalry among existing firms in an industry will also determine prices and profits for any single firm. If rivalry is fierce, businesses can reduce that rivalry by forming cartels or engaging in a broad range of anti-competitive practices. In UK and EU law this is illegal but it is not uncommon. Businesses can also reduce competition by buying up their rivals (horizontal integration, see Unit 49). Again, competition law may intervene to prevent this happening but most horizontal mergers are allowed to proceed. In industries where there are relatively few businesses, often businesses don't compete on price. This allows them to maintain high profitability. Instead they tend to compete by bringing out new products and through advertising, thus creating strong brands. As a result their costs are higher than they might otherwise be, but they can also charge higher prices than in a more competitive market, creating high profits.

Figure 1

The five competitive forces that determine industry profitability

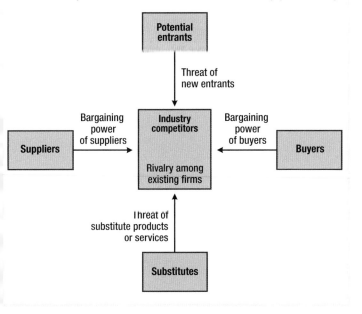

Exam tip
When answering a question about factors that might influence business performance or any of its activities, it is good practice to distinguish between internal and external factors. This may provide a useful opportunity to demonstrate your evaluation skills.

Key terms

Monopoly – a market dominated by a single business.

Oligopoly – a market dominated by a few large businesses.

PESTLE analysis – analysis of the external political, economic, social, technological, legal and environmental factors affecting a business.

Links

External influences can have an impact on a wide range of business activities. It is a topic area that allows you to demonstrate your synoptic skills. For example, you might need to answer a question explaining the impact on a particular business of economic growth. Or you might need to explain the impact of higher interest rates on a business that is planning to increase investment. Examples of other units that could be linked to external influences include: Marketing strategy (Unit 13), Business failure (Unit 36), Theories of corporate strategy (Unit 45), Marketing (Unit 76), Cultural/social factors (Unit 78), Global competitiveness (Unit 75), Ethics (Unit 80) and Controlling MNCs (Unit 81). There are many others.

Knowledge check

1. Give two examples of political factors that might affect the food industry.

2. Give two examples of economic factors that might affect the holiday industry.

3. Give two examples of technological factors that might affect the motor industry.

4. Give two examples of environmental factors that might affect the chemical-processing industry.

5. How does PESTLE analysis help a business?

6. What is meant by an oligopoly?

7. State two possible effects on a business of a strong new entrant in a market.

8. How might the degree of rivalry in a market affect prices and profits?

9. What action might businesses take to deal with the threat of potential entrants?

Case study

THE HOUSING MARKET

In 2007, construction companies Taylor Woodrow and George Wimpey, joined together in a merger to form Taylor Wimpey to become the largest housebuilder in the UK. This was an example of the consolidation that has been taking place in the housebuilding market since the 1980s. In 1988 the 25 largest housebuilders shared about 37 per cent of the market. By 1999 this had risen to about 55 per cent. In 2015 the top 10 companies had about 60 per cent of the market and Persimmon, Barratt and Taylor Wimpey dominated about 25 per cent. Just after the Taylor Wimpey merger the Office of Fair Trading carried out an investigation into the industry but found 'little evidence' of anti-competitive behaviour by housebuilders and 'no evidence' of monopolies. However, Rob Perrins, managing director of upmarket builder Berkeley, says of the big companies: 'They're too powerful… They haven't wanted to be that dominant, but small builders are just not there at the moment.' In contrast to the strengthening of big housebuilders, the number of small and medium-sized developers has dwindled. In 1988 two-thirds of all new homes were built by developers with an annual output of fewer than 500 units. By 2012 that was down to less than a third.

There is currently a housing shortage in the UK. This is reflected in the price increases shown in Figure 2. However, the graph shows that the price increases are not evenly distributed around the country. Demand for housing outstrips supply. There are several reasons for the rise in demand.

- The UK population is growing – it is around 64 million at the moment, but is forecast to grow to around 70 million by 2030. Some of the population growth is due to migration from parts of Eastern Europe as more countries join the EU.

- A significant number of houses are being bought up by property dealers in the 'buy-to-let' market. This means there are fewer properties left for other buyers.

- People are delaying marriage, which means that there are more single people looking for property.

- The population is aging so more properties are needed because people are living for longer and people are living in their houses for longer.

- Foreign investors have stepped up their demand for property – particularly at the high end of the market, and especially in London.

On the supply side, fewer houses are being built as shown in Figure 3 on the next page. Possible reasons for this are as follows:

- Smaller builders have been hit hard by the recession and a lack of bank finance, meaning they have found it difficult to buy land and deal with the often costly and time-consuming planning system.

- Resources in the construction industry are being stretched. Other projects, such as roads, schools, hospitals and railways, are competing for resources. Some construction companies have found it difficult to recruit skilled workers, for example.

- Some of the big housebuilders are being very cautious, following the financial crisis and the recession in the UK. They are planning a more measured growth strategy and are returning money to shareholders.

The housing shortage has prompted a small measure of action from the government. A 'Help to buy' equity loan scheme was introduced, with the first phase starting in April 2013 in England. This saw the government offering a 20 per cent equity loan to buyers of newly built properties. These buyers must offer a 5 per cent deposit. The government also sought to help smaller developers by launching the £500 million Builders' Finance Fund, which provides loans to small housebuilders.

In 2015, interest rates in the UK economy were still at an historic low and there were signs that the government would continue to encourage more house building. For example, it announced the development of a new eco-town in Bicester, Oxfordshire, which would provide around 6,000 sustainable new houses. The first phase of this development would see the construction of energy-efficient, zero-carbon homes, creating the UK's first true zero-carbon community. The plan is to keep the environment at the core of the project, adopting cutting-edge technology and ensuring that the provision of green space in the community is key.

Builders in the construction industry have also seen signs of recovery with reports in indicating that builders in the FTSE 350 saw their highest revenues for five years in 2014. However, it still faced difficulties. The industry is the biggest producer of waste in the economy and is closely regulated. In 2013 there were 42 fatal injuries in construction and around 5,000 injuries, which showed that the health and safety issues were still a concern. Suitable land was difficult to obtain and there was increasing regulation relating to the UK's commitment to build zero-carbon homes.

Source: adapted from the *Financial Times* 28.07.14, 27.01.15. All rights reserved.

(a) Explain what is meant by the changing competitive environment in the housebuilding market. (4 marks)

(b) Assess how Porter's Five Forces analysis might be used by one of the major suppliers in the housebuilding market. (8 marks)

(c) Assess the possible political, economic, social, technological, legal and environmental factors affecting the housing market. (12 marks)

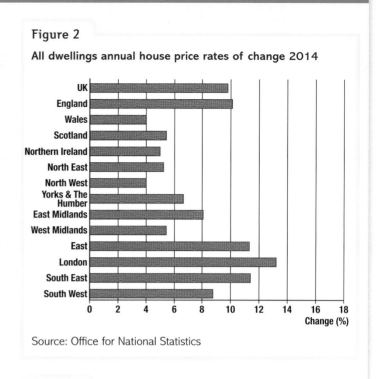

Figure 2

All dwellings annual house price rates of change 2014

Source: Office for National Statistics

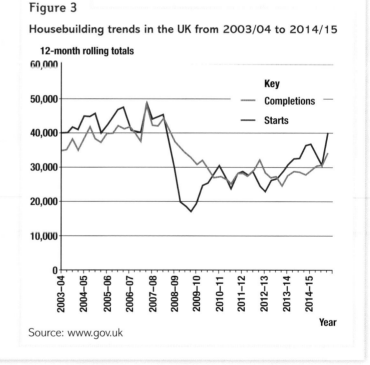

Figure 3

Housebuilding trends in the UK from 2003/04 to 2014/15

12-month rolling totals

Source: www.gov.uk

48 Growth

Key points

1. Objectives of growth:
   - to achieve economies of scale (internal and external)
   - increased market power over customers and suppliers
   - increased market share and brand recognition
   - increased profitability.
2. Problems arising from growth:
   - diseconomies of scale
   - internal communication
   - overtrading.

Getting started

The Cambridge Satchel Company was founded in 2008 by Julie Deane, OBE, and her mother Freda Thomas. Investing just £600 to get the idea off the ground, the company is now a Made-in-Britain worldwide phenomenon, employing more than 140 people and selling to over 120 countries across the globe. Turning over £15,000 in the first year, the company made £10 million turnover in 2014 following an appearance in a Google Chrome ad and collaborations with the likes of Vivienne Westwood and Comme des Garcons.

In 2014 it was the seventh fastest growing company in the UK according to the Sunday Times Fast Track 100. The brand sells from its global website as well as the flagship store in London's Covent Garden, a store in Cambridge, a 'Pop Up' store in Glasgow and a dedicated Men's Store in London's Seven Dials.

Source: adapted from www.cambridgesatchel.com

Calculate the percentage growth in the turnover between the first year and 2014. State the possible benefits to the Cambridge Satchel Company of growing the business. Explain possible problems arising from the growth of the business. Do you think this business will continue to grow? Explain reasons for your answer.

Growth

Most businesses start small and then grow. For example, Salford-based online retailer Missguided was set up in 2009 by Nitin Passi. The fashion retailer offers catwalk looks and celebrity-inspired fashion to women aged between 16 and 35. Two years after the company was founded sales were £2.1 million. However, since 2011 the annual growth rate was 191 per cent and in 2014 sales were £51 million. Businesses like to grow because the benefits can be very attractive. For example, revenues will be higher, unit costs are likely to be low and the business will have a higher profile with a larger market share. The specific objectives that a business might have when growing, such as economies of scale and increased market power, are outlined below.

Economies of scale

The size of a business has a major impact on average costs of production. Typically, there is a range of output over which average costs fall as output rises. Over this range, larger businesses have a competitive advantage over smaller businesses. They enjoy **economies of scale**. In the long run, a business can build another factory or purchase more machine. This can cause the average cost of production to fall.

In Figure 1 a firm is currently producing in a small plant an its short-run costs are SRAC$_1$. When it produces an output equ to Q$_1$ its average cost will be AC$_1$. If it raises production to Q$_2$, average costs will rise to AC$_2$. This is the result of the **law of diminishing returns**.

If the firm expands the scale of its operations (which it can do in the long run) the same level of output can be produced more efficiently. With a bigger plant, represented by SRAC$_2$, Q$_2$ can be produced at an average cost of just AC$_3$. Long-run average costs fall due to economies of scale and will continue to do so until the firm has built a plant which minimises long-r average costs. In the diagram this occurs when a plant shown SRAC$_3$ is built. This is sometimes called the **minimum efficient scale** of plant. When output reaches Q* in this plant, long-run average costs cannot be reduced any further through expansion. The business is said to be **productively efficient** at this point.

At any output level higher or lower than Q*, the business is productively inefficient because average costs could be lower. For example, if the firm continues to grow it will experience rising average costs due to **diseconomies of scale**, as in $SRAC_4$ in Figure 1. This is dealt with later in the unit.

Figure 1

The long-run average cost curve and the effect of economies of scale

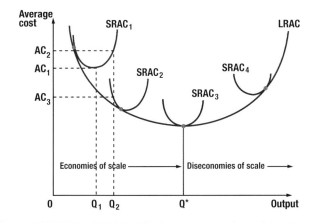

Internal economies of scale

What are the different economies of scale a firm can gain? Internal **economies of sale** are the benefits of growth that arise within the firm. They occur for a number of reasons.

Purchasing and marketing economies: Large firms are likely to get better rates when buying raw materials and components in bulk. In addition, the administration costs involved do not rise in proportion to the size of the order. The cost of processing an order for 10,000 tonnes of coal does not treble when 30,000 tonnes are ordered.

A number of marketing economies exist. A large company may find it cost-effective to acquire its own fleet of vans and lorries, for example. The cost to the sales force of selling 30 product lines is not double that of selling 15 lines. Again, the administration costs of selling do not rise in proportion to the size of the sale.

Technical economies: Technical economies arise because larger plants are often more efficient. The capital costs and the running costs of plants do not rise in proportion to their size. For example, the capital cost of a double decker bus will not be twice that of a single decker bus. This is because the main cost (engine and chassis) does not double when the capacity of the bus doubles. Increased size may mean a doubling of output but not cost. The average cost will therefore fall. This is sometimes called the **principle of increased dimensions**. In addition, the cost of the crew and fuel will not increase in proportion to its size.

Another technical economy is that of **indivisibility**. Many firms need a particular item of equipment or machinery, but fail to make full use of it. A small business may pay £400 for a laptop computer. The cost will be the same whether it is used twice a week by a part-time clerical worker or every day. As the business expands, more use will be made of it and so the **average cost** of the machine will fall.

As the scale of operations expands the firm may switch to mass production techniques. Flow production, which involves breaking down the production process into a very large number of small operations, allows greater use of highly specialised machinery. This results in large improvements in efficiency as labour is replaced by capital.

Businesses often employ a variety of machines which have different capacities. A slow machine may increase production time. As the firm expands and produces more output, it can employ more of the slower machines in order to match the capacity of the faster machines. This is called the **law of multiples**. It involves firms finding a balanced team of machines so that when they operate together they are all running at full capacity.

Specialisation and managerial economies: As the firm grows it can afford to employ specialist managers. In a small business one general manager may be responsible for finance, marketing, production and human resources. The manager may find her role demanding. If a business employs specialists in these fields, efficiency may improve and average costs fall. If specialists were employed in a small firm they would be an indivisibility.

Financial economies: Large firms have advantages when they try to raise finance. They will have a wider variety of sources from which to choose. For example, sole traders cannot sell more shares to raise extra funds but large public limited companies can. Very large firms will often find it easier to persuade institutions to lend them money since they will have large assets to offer as security. Finally, large firms borrowing very large amounts of money can often gain better interest rates. In the past the government has recognised the problems facing small firms. A number of schemes have been designed to help small firms raise funds.

Risk-bearing economies: As a firm grows it may well diversify to reduce risk. For example, breweries have diversified into the provision of food and other forms of entertainment in their public houses. Large businesses can also reduce risk by carrying out research and development. The development of new products can help firms gain a competitive edge over smaller rivals.

External economies of scale

External **economies of sale** are the reductions in cost which any business in an industry might enjoy as the industry grows. External economies are more likely to arise if the industry is concentrated in a particular region.

Labour: The concentration of firms may lead to the build-up of a labour force equipped with the skills required by the industry. Training costs may be reduced if workers have gained skills at another firm in the same industry. Local schools and colleges, or even local government, may offer training courses which are aimed at the needs of the local industry.

Ancillary and commercial services: An established industry, particularly if it is growing, tends to attract smaller firms trying to serve its needs. A wide range of commercial and support services can be offered. Specialist banking, insurance, marketing, waste disposal, maintenance, cleaning, components and distribution services are just some examples.

Co-operation: Firms in the same industry are more likely to co-operate if they are concentrated in the same region. They might join forces to fund a research and development centre for the industry. An industry journal might be published, so that information can be shared.

Disintegration: Disintegration occurs when production is broken up so that more specialisation can take place. When an industry is concentrated in an area, firms might specialise in the production of one component and then transport it to a main assembly car plant. In the West Midlands a few large car assembly plants exist, while there are many supporting firms.

> **Exam tip**
>
> *You need to remember that economies of scale are a long-run phenomenon. This means that average costs will fall when a business increases the scale of its operations. This involves changing fixed factors of production, such as machinery or premises.*

Increased market power

As businesses get bigger they become more dominant. As a result rivals are left with a smaller market share and some weaker businesses may be forced to close down. If a business is large enough it may be able to dominate two particular stakeholders.

- **Customers.** A dominant business may be able to charge higher prices if competition in the market is limited. In the absence of choice, customers are forced to pay higher prices. Also, if there is a lack of competitive pressure in the market there is less need to develop new products. This means that a dominant firm will not have to meet the costs of expensive and risky innovation. As a result, product choice may remain limited for consumers.
- **Suppliers.** Sometimes a business can dominate its suppliers. For example, it may be able to force the costs of materials and commercial services down if it buys large quantities from relatively small suppliers. Dominant businesses will be in a particularly good position if their suppliers rely heavily upon them for their custom. For example, if a small supplier sells all of its output to just one large business, it is in a vulnerable position and may have to accept the prices that the customer is prepared to pay.

However, if a business becomes too dominant it might attract the attention of the authorities. If it is felt that the dominant business is exploiting consumers or suppliers there may be an investigation into the industry. In 2014, energy companies were criticised for charging high prices and some supermarkets were accused of 'bullying suppliers'.

Question 1

There is some evidence in the dairy industry that larger herds result in higher yields and lower costs. For example, Table 1 shows that when the herd size rises from 85 cows to 339 cows, the average milk yield per cow rises from 6,247 litres per year to 8,135 litres per year. Figure 2 shows the impact of larger herds on revenue, costs and profit margins.

Table 1 The impact of larger herds on milk production and yields

Summary of milk production quartiles	Quartile 1 (small)	Quartile 2 (small/ medium)	Quartile 3 (medium/ large)	Quartile 4 (large)
Average annual milk production (litres)	531,000	1,033,000	1,535,000	2,758,000
Herd size (number cows)	85	157	205	339
Average yield (1/cow/year)	6,247	6,580	7,488	8,135

Figure 2 shows that costs ppl (pence per litre) fall as herd size gets bigger. There are at least two reasons for this. A farmer with a larger herd will need larger quantities of inputs – cattle feed, for example. Suppliers might offer farmers discounts for buying larger amounts. It is also possible that farmers can make better use of technology with larger herds. For example, automatic milking units are likely to become cost-effective with larger herds.

There is evidence of different farms at any herd size on the scale achieving positive margins. However, it is notable that the lowest herd margins are all among the smaller sized sized herds.

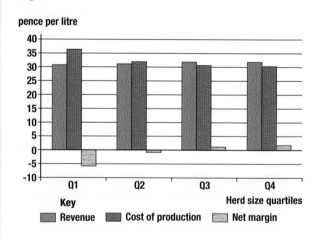

Figure 2

The impact of larger herds on costs, revenue and profit margins

Source: adapted from www.dairy.ahdb.org.uk

(a) Explain what is meant by economies of scale in the case of the dairy industry.

(b) Explain one internal economy that might account for lower unit costs when larger herds are used in the dairy industry.

Increased market share and brand recognition

As businesses grow, their share of the market is also likely to grow. This will give them more power and they may be able to enjoy the benefits outlined above. However, they will also benefit from having a greater brand recognition. As a business gets a larger and larger share of the market, customers become more aware of the brand name because they see the brand advertised and for sale in stores or online. As the brand becomes stronger, a business may be able to:

- charge higher prices
- differentiate the product from those of rivals
- create customer loyalty
- enhance product recognition
- develop an image
- launch new products more easily.

A business with a larger market share is also more likely to attract media attention, which helps to promote the company.

Increased profitability

One of the main objectives of growth is to make more profit. Larger businesses tend to make bigger profits than smaller ones. As profits grow, returns to the owners will also grow. For example, Whitbread, which owns brands including Premier Inn, Costa Coffee, Beefeater Grill and Brewers Fayre, grew its revenue from £1,599.6 million in 2010–11 to £2,294.3 million in 2013–14 – a 43.4 per cent increase. During the same time period profit before tax grew by 44 per cent from £287.1 million to £411.8 million. The benefit to shareholders of this growth was significant. Whitbread increased its dividend payment to shareholders from 44.5p in 2010–11 to 68.8p in 2013–14. In addition to this, when a company grows, shareholders are likely to see the price of their shares rise. The Whitbread share price rose by around 300 per cent in five years to just over £53 in April 2015.

If a business grows and increases its profitability, it will have more profit for investment and innovation. This will allow the business to develop and launch new products and make acquisitions. If these investments are successful the business is likely to grow even further.

Problems arising from growth

A business that aims to grow must ensure that the growth is sustainable. It is possible for a business to encounter problems if it grows too big or too fast.

Diseconomies of scale

If a business expands the scale of its operations beyond the minimum efficient scale, diseconomies of scale may result. This is where average costs rise as output rises. There are a variety of sources of diseconomies of scale. As shown in Figure 1, long-run average costs start to rise once the output of a business passes Q* on the diagram.

Question 2

RTR Ltd was originally set up as a satellite TV company in 1991. Originally most famous for its sports channels it has since branched out into a range of different services, including broadband and telephony.

In 2008 RTR's revenue was £5,200 million. By 2013 it had grown to £7,691 million.

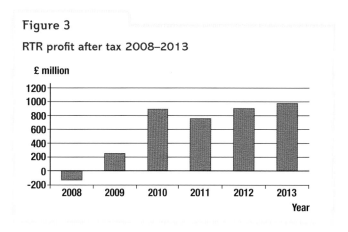

Figure 3

RTR profit after tax 2008–2013

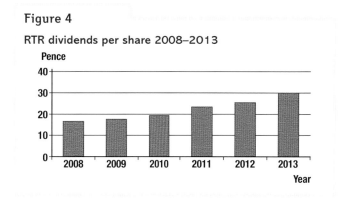

Figure 4

RTR dividends per share 2008–2013

(a) Calculate the percentage increase in dividend payments between 2008 and 2013.

(b) Explain one benefit of growth to the shareholders of RTR.

Internal diseconomies of scale: Most internal diseconomies are caused by the problem of managing large businesses.

- Communication becomes more complicated and co-ordination more difficult because a large firm is divided into departments.
- The control and **co-ordination** of large businesses is also demanding. Thousands of employees, billions of pounds and dozens of plants all mean added responsibility and more supervision.
- Motivation may suffer as individual workers become a minor part of the total workforce. This can cause poor relations between management and the workforce.

- Technical diseconomies also arise. In the chemical industry, construction problems often mean that two smaller plants are more cost-effective than one very large one. Also, if a business employs one huge plant and a breakdown occurs, production will stop. With two smaller plants, production can continue even if one breaks down.

External diseconomies of scale: These may occur from overcrowding in industrial areas. The price of land, labour, services and materials might rise as firms compete for a limited amount. Congestion might lead to inefficiency, as travelling workers and deliveries are delayed.

Internal communication

Internal communication is the exchange of messages and the flow of information inside a business – between individual workers or between departments, for example. If a business grows too big there could be a problem with internal communication. The number of layers in the management structure is likely to grow and as a result channels of communication get longer and the scope for error in the transmission of messages increases. Distortions to information may occur is it is passed through the managerial hierarchy. At worst this could lead to misunderstandings and disputes between workers and managers. Such disputes are a drain on resources and any cost resulting from a misunderstanding or dispute will reduce productivity.

With the rapid development in information and communication technology (ICT) some of these problems may have been reduced. For example, any number of people can be copied into an email so that important messages can be transmitted instantly to 10,000s of people all over the world. The use of video conferencing might also help internal communication, where members of staff in different geographical locations can communicate face to face. However, it might also be argued that IT has also brought a whole new set of communication problems. For example, communications can be seriously hampered when IT systems fail.

Sometimes resources might be wasted due to a lack of effective communication. One problem that might occur is the duplication of resources. This is where two or more identical activities or projects are being pursued in the same organisation at the same time. For example, the division of a company in the UK may be writing a new grievance procedure policy. If another division, say the Australian division, is doing exactly the same, resources will be wasted. Better communication would ensure that only one new grievance procedure policy is produced.

If communication is poor between different departments, competition between them may have negative effects. As different departments compete for company resources they may adopt a 'silo mentality'. This is where individual departments become reluctant to share information with others in the organisation. Such behaviour could result in conflict between departments, stifle development and result in missed opportunities and higher costs.

Question 3

In 2014, the large mining company, BHP Billiton, announced that it would sell off about £15 billion of non-core assets. This was the company's response to its dwindling productivity. For many years prior to this announcement the whole mining industry had been increasing the scale of its operations in the belief that 'bigger was better', i.e. that costs would continue to fall as individual mines grew.

However, Andrew Mackenzie, chief executive at BHP Billiton, said that he was worried about diseconomies of scale at the company. Also, according to a report by consultant EY, individual mining operations were sometimes getting too large to manage effectively, thereby resulting in lower productivity. 'The industry thought that bigger was always going to be better and it hasn't always worked out that way.' Paul Mitchell, global mining and metals advisory leader at EY, observed, 'It is bad enough [managing a mine] with 100 people on site – with 1,000 it becomes much more complex.'

The rapid growth in the size of mines has resulted in several problems. The cost of resources, such as labour and materials, has risen sharply increasing average costs. The EY report identified the increased complexity of running larger mines. It said that very high staff turnover in the industry meant that mines were being run by inexperienced managers who were not being given the resources needed to deal with the increased complexity. Executives in the industry said that communication across departments was poor and that a 'silo mentality' had developed in some quarters.

Source: adapted from the *Financial Times* 20.10.14, all rights reserved

(a) Explain what is meant by diseconomies of scale and, using the example of BHP Billiton, explain why they occur.

(b) Explain one way in which BHP Billiton has dealt with the problem of diseconomies of scale.

Overtrading

If a business grows too fast there is a danger that it might suffer from overtrading. This is more likely to happen to young, rapidly growing businesses. Overtrading occurs when a business tries to fund a large volume of new business without sufficient resources. As a result it runs out of cash, and at worst, it can collapse. Overtrading is most likely to occur if a business:

- does not have enough capital. It is not uncommon for a new business to be undercapitalised. This means that it has started trading with insufficient capital. It does not have enough cash to buy the resources needed to meet the growing orders
- offers too much trade credit to customers. It may be tempting for a new business to allow its customers 90 or 120 days trade credit. However, this means that the business has to wait that length of time, or more, to be paid. During this time it will be short of cash to buy the resources needed to meet new orders
- is operating with slim profit margins. In order to make an impact in the market, a new business may offer its products a lower prices. However, with lower prices and subsequent low

profit margins, it may not generate enough profit to fund the growing volume of business.

Whatever the cause, if a business is overtrading it can run out of cash and this threatens its survival. Therefore, growth has to be managed carefully.

Links 🔗

You can demonstrate synoptic skills by linking information on business growth to a number of other areas in the specification. For example, you could link business growth to the effects it might have on the environment or human resources. It is often said that very large businesses can have a negative impact on the environment. Business growth also has important links to the development of multinational companies (Unit 79), corporate strategies (Unit 45), business objectives (Unit 21), decision making (Unit 54), business ethics (Unit 59), human resources (Unit 62), causes and effects of change (Unit 63), and international trade and business growth (Unit 67).

Case study

ANESCO

In 2010, Adrian Pike and Tim Payne founded Anesco, an energy and efficiencies solutions company. Anesco advises homeowners, businesses – including Whitbread, and local authorities on renewable energy and energy efficiency products and services. The company provides equipment and financing as well as offering operation and maintenance.

By growing at a rate of 374.3 per cent over three years, Anesco saw its revenue rise from £1 million in 2011 to £106.7 million in 2014. It was the fastest growing company in the UK, according to the *Sunday Times* Fast Track 100 league table. Anesco's revenue comes from a range of business streams covering energy efficiency measures including biomass, LED lighting, insulation, battery storage solutions and domestic and commercial solar installations. The business was responsible for the installation and maintenance of one of Britain's largest solar farms. In 2014 this plant generated enough electricity to power 2,000 homes. Investors in such schemes can get tax breaks and subsidies from the government.

Anesco was the first UK business in the energy efficiency sector to combine different technologies to help meet customers' needs. The company understood the government's incentive schemes, utility obligations and the importance of tackling climate change.

Some of the funding for the business came from venture capitalists. One such company is CBPE Capital. It is a leading private equity firm with eight funds raised over 30 years. CBPE likes to invest in companies seeking growth or development capital, with an enterprise value of up to £150 million. Ian Moore, partner at CBPE Capital, said 'Anesco's management team has built a fantastic business and have an unrivalled knowledge of the sector, as well as a genuine passion for delivering energy-efficient solutions to their customers. We are very excited to be working with them to facilitate Anesco's growth plans over the coming years.'

Anesco plans further growth in the future. It expects much of this growth to come from developing new markets and products that will benefit the UK.

Sources: adapted from www.anesco.co.uk

(a) Explain one way in which Anesco might benefit from exploiting financial economies of scale. (4 marks)

(b) Explain one danger that a rapidly growing company like Anesco might need to be aware of. (4 marks)

(c) Evaluate the possible growth objectives of Anesco. (20 marks)

Key terms

Diseconomies of scale – rising long-run average costs as a business expands beyond its minimum efficient scale.
Economies of scale – the reductions in average costs enjoyed by a business as output increases.
External economies of scale – the cost reductions available to all businesses as the industry grows.
Internal economies of scale – the cost reductions enjoyed by a single business as it grows.
Minimum efficient scale – the output that minimises long-run average costs.

Knowledge check

1. What is the difference between internal and external economies of scale?
2. Explain what is meant by technical economies of scale.
3. Explain how a supermarket chain would benefit from purchasing economies.
4. What is meant by risk-bearing economies?
5. Give two possible examples of external economies of scale.
6. What is meant by the minimum efficient scale of plant?
7. Give one reason why average costs might start to rise when output is pushed beyond the minimum efficient scale.
8. How can a business enjoy market power over its suppliers?
9. How might internal communication be affected if a business grows too quickly?
10. What is meant by overtrading?

49 Mergers and takeovers

Key points

1. Reasons for mergers and takeovers.
2. Distinction between mergers and takeovers.
3. Horizontal and vertical integration.
4. Financial risks and rewards.
5. Problems of rapid growth.

Getting started

In 2014, Swedish-based Spotify, the on-demand music streaming service, bought The Echo Nest, a Massachusetts-based music data firm. Spotify bought The Echo Nest for its technology. The Echo Nest's core product is a database that stores the characteristics of millions of songs. The data held by The Echo Nest can be used to do things such as recognise and name songs by listening to them, make music recommendations and generate playlists. Spotify hoped to use this technology to drive its music discovery features and help its partners to build new music experiences. The purchase was widely reported, with Daniel Ek, founder of Spotify, commenting that they had been fans of The Echo Nest for a long time and were honoured to have their talented team joining Spotify.

Source: adapted from the *Financial Times* 06.03.2014. All rights reserved.

What do you think is meant by a takeover? Why has Spotify bought The Echo Nest? Are there any alternatives to taking over another business in order to grow? What problems might businesses encounter when taking over another company?

Reasons for mergers and takeovers

Mergers and takeovers take place when firms join together and operate as one organisation. Why do some businesses act in this way?

- One of the main motives for integration is to exploit the **synergies** that might exist following a merger or takeover. This means that two businesses joined together form an organisation that is more powerful and efficient than the two companies operating on their own. Synergy occurs when the 'the whole is greater than the sum of the parts', for example when 2 + 2 = 5. Synergies may arise from economies of scale, the potential for asset stripping, the reduction of risk through diversification or the potential for gains by management.
- It is a quick and easy way to expand the business. For example, if a supermarket chain wanted to open another twenty stores in the UK, it could find sites and build new premises. A quicker way could be to buy a company that already owns some stores and convert them.

- Buying a business is often cheaper than growing internally. A business may calculate that the cost of internal growth is £80 million. However, it might be possible to buy another company for £55 million on the stock market. The process of buying the company might inflate its price, but it could st work out much cheaper.
- Some businesses have cash available which they want to u Buying another business is one way of doing this.
- Mergers take place for defensive reasons. A business migh buy another to consolidate its position in the market. Also, firm can increase its size through merging, it may avoid bei the victim of a takeover itself.
- Businesses respond to economic changes. For example, some businesses may have merged before the introduction the euro in 1999 in certain European countries or before th expansion of the EU in 2004.
- Merging with a business in a different country is one way in which a business can gain entry into foreign markets. It may also avoid restrictions that prevent it from locating in a country or avoid paying tariffs on goods sold in that countr
- The globalisation of markets has encouraged mergers between foreign businesses. This could allow a company to operate and sell worldwide, rather than in particular countri or regions.
- A business may want to gain economies of scale. Firms car often lower their costs by joining with another firm.
- Some firms are asset strippers. They buy a company, sell off profitable parts, close down unprofitable sections and perhaps integrate other activities into the existing business. Some private equity companies have been accused of asse stripping in recent years.
- Management may want to increase the size of the company This is because the growth of the business is their main objective.

Distinction between mergers and takeovers

Both mergers and takeovers are corporate strategies that aim to improve the performance of a business. However, there is a clear distinction between the two.

Merger: A merger is where two (or more) businesses join together and operate as one. Mergers are usually conducted with the agreement of both businesses. They are generally 'friendly' in nature. The name of the new business is often formed out of the names of the two original businesses. For example, one of the biggest mergers that was approved in 2014 was between Swiss-based cement producer Holcim Ltd and French cement company Lafarge SA, forming LafargeHolcim. It was widely reported that the new company would be the world's largest cement producer with annual sales over $40 billion. The main reason for this merger was to help cut costs and cope better with overcapacity and weak demand.

Takeover: A takeover, sometimes called an acquisition, occurs when one business buys another. Takeovers among public limited companies can occur because their shares are traded openly and anyone can buy them. One business can acquire another by buying 51 per cent of the shares. Some of these can be bought on the stock market and others might be bought directly from existing shareholders. When a takeover is complete, the company that has been 'bought' loses its identity and becomes part of the **predator** company. Private limited companies, however, cannot be taken over unless the majority shareholders 'invite' others to buy their shares.

In practice, a firm can take control of another company by buying less than 51 per cent of the shares. This may happen when share ownership is widely spread and little communication takes place between shareholders. In some cases a predator can take control of a company by purchasing as little as 15 per cent of the total share issue. Once a company has bought 3 per cent of another company it must make a declaration to the stock market. This is a legal requirement designed to ensure that the existing shareholders are aware of the situation.

Takeovers of public limited companies often result in a sudden increase in their share price. This is due to the volume of buying by the predator and also speculation by investors.

Once it is known that a takeover is likely, investors scramble to buy shares, anticipating a quick price rise. Sometimes more than one firm might attempt to take over a company. This can result in very sharp increases in the share price as the two buyers bid up the price.

An example of a takeover in the UK in 2015 was the purchase of mobile operator O_2 by another mobile operator, Three. It was reported that the cost of the takeover would be £10.5 billion. The deal would make Three the biggest mobile operator in the UK with around 32 million customers.

Figure 1 shows the number and value of mergers and acquisitions in the UK from 1988 to 2013. For example, since 2003 the value of mergers and acquisitions rose sharply up until 2007 and then fell sharply just after. The financial crisis followed by the recession was probably responsible for the rapid decline.

Thinking bigger

Takeovers can be **hostile** or **friendly**. A hostile takeover means that the victim tries to resist the bid. Resistance is usually co-ordinated by the board of directors. They attempt to persuade the shareholders that their interests would be best protected if the company remains under the control of the existing board of directors. Shareholders then have to weigh up the advantages and disadvantages of a new 'owner'. It was reported in 2014 that a hostile takeover bid was made by the pharmaceuticals company Pfizer for its UK rival AstraZeneca. The bid, reported to be worth around £70 billion, was eventually rejected by AstraZeneca. The board felt that AstraZeneca could get better returns for the shareholders by remaining an independent company.

A takeover may be invited. A firm might be struggling because it has cash-flow problems, for example. It might want the current business activity to continue, but under the control of another, stronger company. The new company would inject some cash in exchange for control. Such a company is sometimes referred to as a 'white knight'.

Source: adapted from www.ft.com/indepth

Figure 1

Announced mergers and acquisitions in the UK 1988–2013

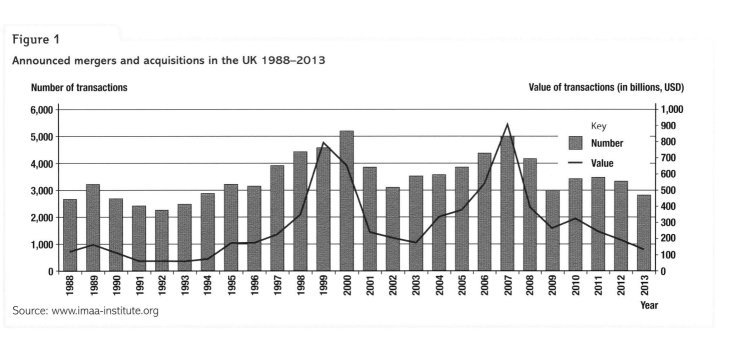

Source: www.imaa-institute.org

Question 1

In 2015 a communications giant was formed when telecoms group BT confirmed that it would buy mobile operator EE for £12.5 billion. This takeover would create a company offering a range of telecommunications services, such as broadband, fixed telephony and pay-TV services. BT planned to sell these services to those EE customers who did not currently subscribe to BT. It also hoped to speed up the sale of other services to its existing customers. The takeover was subject to approval by BT shareholders and scrutiny from the Competition and Markets Authority, and was planned to finalise in up to a year.

The takeover was to result in estimated savings to BT of about £360 million a year in operating and capital costs after four years. Combining the two businesses could also result in the generation of an extra £1.6 billion a year. However, BT would have to raise about £1 billion by selling some fresh shares. BT chief executive Gavin Patterson said, 'This is a major milestone for BT as it will allow us to accelerate our mobility plans and increase our investment in them.'

Source: adapted from the *Financial Times* 05.02.2015. All rights reserved.

(a) Explain what is meant by a takeover, using the communications industry as an example.

(b) Explain one reason why BT has taken over EE.

Horizontal and vertical integration

Integration is when businesses join together to form one. It can be classified in a number of ways, although not all mergers and acquisitions fit neatly into these categories.

Horizontal integration occurs when two firms that are in exactly the same line of business and the same stage of production join together. The merger described above between the two cement producers, Lafarge SA and Holcim Ltd, is an example of a horizontal merger. The benefits of mergers between such firms include:

- a common knowledge of the markets in which they operate
- less likelihood of failure than merging two different areas of business
- similar skills of employees
- less disruption.

Vertical integration occurs when firms in different stages of production join together. **Forward vertical integration** is where a business joins with another that is in the next stage of production whereas **backward vertical integration** is where a business joins with another in the previous stage of production.

Consider a business that manufactures and assembles mountain bikes. If it bought a supplier of tyres for the bikes, this would be an example of backward vertical integration. The two firms are at different stages of production. The main motives for such a merger would be to guarantee and control the supply of components and raw materials, and to remove the profit margin the supplier would demand. Forward vertical integration involves merging with a firm that is in the next stage of production rather than the previous stage. For example, the mountain bike manufacturer might merge with a retail outlet selling bikes. Again this eliminates the profit margin expected by the firm in the next stage of production. It also gives manufacturers guaranteed outlets for their output.

Question 2

In contrast to some other supermarket chains in the industry, Morrisons employs a different approach to its supply chain. It has a history of owning suppliers of fresh produce dating back to 1970, but recently, through a series of acquisitions, Morrisons has expanded its supply operation. In 2010, it announced that it would invest £200 million over three years to grow its supply chain. In 2011 it bought Derby-based horticulture supplier Flower World – which had sales of £34 million in 2010. This was followed by the acquisition of Vion UK's meat-processing plant in Cheshire. Just after that Morrisons bought an empty seafood-processing factory in Grimsby. The store also planned several other acquisitions in the fresh produce industry.

A spokesperson explained that owning suppliers gave Morrisons more control over quality and cost. Morrisons was trying to get a competitive edge over its rivals by having the freshest produce available. The approach also helped to reduce waste in the supply chain. It was possible that Morrisons would adopt this approach in non-food products. For example, Morrisons' clothing director, Tim Bettley, said that the retailer may consider acquiring a clothing manufacturer to support its new Nutmeg brand.

The key advantages of Morrisons' approach are summarised below.

- Higher profit margins by owning the product from source to customer.
- Greater control over price and product quality.
- Less waste.
- Faster lead-time.
- New opportunities for product development.
- Improves its image in its support for British farmers.

However, some of the possible drawbacks of the policy might be as follows.

- High capital outlays for acquisitions and research.
- More difficult to manage businesses that are in different stages of production.
- Loss of flexibility, for example Morrisons cannot switch suppliers if needed like rivals can.
- Increased pressure on company resources as Morrisons is also committed to developing online business and opening convenience stores.

Source: adapted from www.retailtimes.co.uk

(a) Explain what is meant by vertical integration, using the supermarket industry as an example.

(b) Explain one advantage to Morrisons of vertical integration in this case.

(c) Explain one possible drawback to Morrisons of vertical integration in this case.

Financial risks and rewards

Mergers and takeovers are common corporate strategies. They allow businesses to grow quickly and may create benefits for a range of stakeholders. However, they can sometimes go wrong and may have a negative long-term impact on a business. Some of the key financial risks are outlined below.

Regulatory intervention: Mergers and takeovers in the UK may attract the attention of the Competition and Markets Authority (CMA). If they think that a merger or takeover acts against the interests of the consumer, they have the power to order an investigation. This takes time and may cause delays. After the investigation, the CMA has the power to recommend that the merger be blocked. Alternatively, they may allow a merger or takeover to go ahead, but with certain conditions. The Lafarge Holcim merger was only permitted after the companies agreed to sell off assets around the world. The EU directed Lafarge to sell all of its German and Romanian business activities and instructed Holcim to unload all of its Slovak business and most of its activities in France. Delays in proceedings and undertakings, such as the sale of assets, take time and cost money.

Resistance from employees: In some cases, mergers and takeovers result in job losses. This is because when two companies join together certain resources are likely to be duplicated. For example, after a merger the single company will probably not require two head offices. Therefore one can be closed down, which will result in job losses. If job losses are on a large scale, employees are likely to react. They might disrupt proceedings, for example by going on strike.

Integration costs: After a merger or takeover has been agreed, the next step is to physically integrate the two organisations. This can be a very complex, expensive and time-consuming process, the effects of which may be felt for many years. Some of the costs incurred result from the organisational and personnel changes, severance pay for dismissed workers, technical changes, systems changes, training and many others. It is not uncommon for businesses to underestimate these costs and encounter problems when carrying out the consolidation process. For example, merging two different cultures can be particularly problematic.

Bidding wars: In a minority of cases it is possible that one business attracts more than one potential buyer. If this happens the price of the acquisition will start to rise, as it would do in an auction. This makes the takeover more expensive. One example of this in 2014 was the takeover of the American food company Hillshire Brands Co. by Tyson Foods Inc. Earlier, another company, poultry producer Pilgrim's Pride, had made an offer of $6.4 billion for Hillshire. However, within 48 hours Tyson offered $6.8 billion. Pilgrim then raised its bid to $7.7 billion, but this was outstripped by Tyson's further bid of $8.55 billion, which was finally accepted by Hillshire. This case helps to show how the cost of a takeover can escalate when more than one business is interested in a target. The overall price rose from $6.4 billion to $8.55 billion, an increase of 33.6 per cent.

Despite these financial risks, companies are happy to pursue takeovers and mergers if the conditions are deemed right. This is probably because the rewards are potentially high.

Speedy growth: Businesses can grow far more quickly through mergers and takeovers than growing internally. This means that the benefits of growth, such as larger market share, lower costs resulting from economies of scale, more market power and higher profitability, can be enjoyed more immediately. This might benefit a range of stakeholders.

Higher remuneration for senior staff: After a merger or a takeover it is likely that executives' salaries will rise because they are now responsible for running a much bigger business. There may also be bonus- or performance-related payments if part of the remuneration package is linked to growth rates.

Rewards to previous owners: Quite often the owners of the business that is taken over get significant financial rewards when the business is sold. For example, in 2014 Synergy Health, a British outsourcing company, was taken over by US company, Steris Corporation. Just before a bid was made, shares in Synergy Health were trading at £14. Steris said they would pay £19.50 per share to take over the company. Consequently, shareholders make an immediate 39 per cent gain on completion of the takeover.

Increased profitability: If a merger or takeover is successful, future revenues will be higher because market share will be higher. In addition, costs will be lower if economies of scale can be exploited. As a result, in the long-term profits should rise. If the merger or takeover results in a significantly larger business, it may be able to dominate the market and generate even bigger profits.

Problems of rapid growth

Businesses that use external growth strategies are usually trying to grow rapidly. Unfortunately, there is risk associated with this and some mergers and takeovers actually fail. In this case failure probably means that outcomes did not match expectations. However, occasionally failures can be quite spectacular. For example, some have argued that the merger of the Britannia Building Society and the Co-operative Bank in 2009 should never have happened, given that it almost led to the collapse of the Co-op Bank. A report by Sir Christopher Kelly said that both the Co-op Bank and Britannia had problems at the time of the merger.

Companies that pursue growth through mergers and takeovers have to be cautious. In some cases, if growth is too rapid serious problems might be encountered. Some examples are outlined below.

Drain on resources: Mergers and takeovers can cost a lot of money. For example, Three spent £10.5 billion buying O_2 in 2015. In the US in 2012 Google paid $12.5 billion for Motorola and in 2014/15, Actavis, the Ireland-based drug-maker, bought Allergan, the maker of botox, for a huge $66 billion. These are clearly very large amounts of money and companies that spend such sums on mergers and takeovers have to be very well resourced. If a company grows too rapidly by embarking on an aggressive acquisition trail, it may stretch financial resources and impair other aspects of the business.

Coping with change: When businesses merge, the integration process can be challenging because lots of changes have to be made. One of the main difficulties is merging two different cultures. It can be very difficult to impose a new culture on a business and there may be resistance. If changes are forced through too quickly, without proper consultation for example, this resistance is likely to be stronger. Such problems are likely to be more intense if growth is too rapid and firms are combining two different cultures too quickly.

The alienation of customers: Companies that are growing too fast might lose touch with their customers. Too much attention and resources get focused on the process of growth. As a consequence the needs of customers can be overlooked. For example, after a takeover or merger the name of a business may change; some consumers may be confused by this, wondering what the new name stands for and what values might be attached to it. Ultimately this could damage the image of the company and result in the loss of customers.

Loss of control: If growth is too rapid the company might get too big too fast. This can result in a loss of control by the senior executives. With a bigger organisation come extra layers of management. This may lengthen communication channels and impact negatively on the chain of command. As a result costs may start to rise as diseconomies of scale set in.

Shortages of resources: A rapidly growing business will be thirsty for resources. As a result demand for these resources may drive up prices. This may happen when there is a shortage of skilled labour and wages are driven up, for example.

> **Exam tip**
> When answering questions on mergers and takeovers it is important not to get too carried away with the potential benefits. You must provide a balanced answer and remember that there are some significant problems with this strategy. Try to remember that according to the KPMG report in 2013, 90 per cent of mergers and takeovers actually fail. What failure means may be open to debate, but it is an important issue.

> **Links** 🔗
> Many businesses pursue growth through mergers and takeovers. To demonstrate your synoptic skills you could link answers on this topic to a range of other areas covered by the specification. For example, when discussing multinational businesses you might add to your discussion the role played by mergers and takeovers in becoming a multinational. You may connect this unit with others in the book such as Marketing strategy (Unit 13), Business failure (Unit 36), Production, productivity and efficiency (Unit 37), Legislation (Unit 42), Corporate objectives (Unit 44), Theories of corporate strategy (Unit 45), Growth (Unit 48), Business ethics (Unit 59) and Reasons for global mergers or joint ventures (Unit 74).

Key terms

Backward vertical integration – joining with a business in the previous stage of production.
Forward vertical integration – joining with a business in the next stage of production.
Horizontal integration – the joining of businesses that are in exactly the same line of business.
Integration – the joining together of two businesses as a result of a merger or takeover.
Merger – occurs when two (or more) businesses join together and operate as one.
Synergy – the combining of two or more activities or businesses creating a better outcome than the sum of the individual parts.
Takeover – the process of one business buying another.
Vertical integration – the joining of two businesses at different stages of production.

Knowledge check

1. Give three reasons why two businesses might choose to join together.

2. Give two examples of horizontal integration.

3. Give an example of forward vertical integration in the car industry.

4. Give an example of backward vertical integration in the airline industry.

5. Briefly explain how an acquisition is carried out.

6. Give an example of a problem that a business might encounter when integrating two organisations.

7. Explain one financial reward of a merger or takeover.

8. Why might job losses result from a takeover or merger?

9. Explain one financial risk of a merger or takeover.

10. Outline two problems of rapid growth.

Case study

DIXONS CARPHONE

In 2014, it was reported that Dixons Retail, owner of Currys and PC World, would merge with the mobile phone retailer, Carphone Warehouse. The new company would be called Dixons Carphone and the £3.8 billion deal would be shared equally between the two sets of shareholders. The combined group would own around 1,300 stores in the UK and almost 3,000 worldwide with potential annual revenues of over £10 billion.

The newly formed company planned to branch out into domestic heating, lighting and security services – all controlled by mobile phone. It was also felt that the combined force would benefit from greater buying power and a wider range of growth options. For example, it hoped to sell the combined broadband, pay TV and phone services offered by operators such as BT and Virgin. It also planned

to take commissions from supermarkets or music services for pre-installing their apps on smartphones. Dixons Carphone wanted to develop an end-to-end service, from sales to set-up advice, service, insurance, repairs and recycling.

The deal was also put together as a means of competing with rapidly growing online rivals, such as Amazon and AO.com. Electrical retailers are in danger of following the declining sales of physical book and music stores. Comet was recently pushed into receivership, while Carphone's short-lived attempt to sell electrical products with Best Buy ended in failure.

It was reported that the merger would generate annual savings of around £80 million after three years. The effect on jobs was reported to be positive with an increase overall. Dixons Carphone said it would cut about 800 of its combined workforce in a rationalisation process to reduce costs. However, it said it would add 1,600 jobs to exploit growth opportunities.

Some saw the merger as one step closer to a connected world, while others felt there were still too many stores in the UK trying to sell phones and fridges. David Alexander, consultant at Conlumino, said: 'Although there are plenty of reasons to view the merger in a positive light, the history of mergers and acquisitions is littered with the corpses of failed unions . . . Carphone Warehouse itself is no stranger to this, having seen its partnership with US electronics giant Best Buy in 2008 peter out three years later in the face of intense competition from Dixons.' Another analyst, Louise Cooper, said there would be 'much scepticism' about the idea that the merger would produce better growth.

Shares in both companies fell after the announcement. Dixons' share price closed down 10.3 per cent after the news and Carphone Warehouse's dropped 8 per cent.

Source: adapted from the *Financial Times*, 15.05.2014. All rights reserved.

(a) Explain one reason for the merger between Dixons Retail and Carphone Warehouse. (4 marks)

(b) Evaluate the possible financial risks and rewards of the Dixons Carphone merger. (20 marks)

50 Organic growth

Key points

1. Distinction between inorganic and organic growth.
2. Methods of growing organically.
3. Advantages and disadvantages of organic growth.

Getting started

Co-wheels is a national car club that operates as a social enterprise. It provides a network of community car clubs across the UK. Members can access cars on a 'pay by the hour' basis without any of the costs or inconveniences of owning a car. After joining the club members are issued with a smartcard that allows them to book cars online or by phone.

Co-wheels has grown organically (without mergers or takeovers) and in 2015 had over 350 vehicles and a turnover of £2 million. 2014 saw a big expansion both in service provision and in staff, bringing car clubs to new locations and increasing the fleet size. Co-wheels plans to develop the club further across more areas. It has already developed an electric bike hire operation and offers wheelchair accessible vehicles for the social care sector. It also plans to launch the world's first fully hydrogen powered car club vehicles in Aberdeen.

Source: adapted from Co-wheels car club Community Interest Company, www.co-wheels.org.uk

What might be two possible advantages to a business like Co-wheels of growing without mergers and takeovers? What might be the disadvantages of this approach to growth?

Distinction between inorganic and organic growth

Unit 49 looked at how businesses can grow using mergers and takeovers. This type of growth is called external growth or **inorganic growth**. It involves businesses joining together so that theoretically they might double in size overnight. For example, when the Finsbury Food Group took over Fletchers Group, the fresh and frozen bakery supplier, for £56 million in 2014, it was expected to nearly double sales from £175 million to £300 million.

In contrast, internal growth or **organic growth** occurs when a business grows naturally by selling more of its output using its own resources. For example, Fog Creek Software is a US company owned by its employees. It develops project management tools and has been growing organically since it was set up in 2000. It has built itself gradually by gaining more customers and consultancy work. In 2014 it employed over 40 people and generated a substantial income.

One of the key differences between the two growth strategies is speed. Inorganic growth is much faster. As the example above shows, it is possible to instantly double in size as a result of joining with another business. Organic growth

is normally much slower. It takes time to develop and grow a business using its own resources.

Another difference is the potential risk involved in the two different strategies. It could be argued that organic growth is a safer strategy because owners expand their businesses by developing their current expertise. They may be growing by 'doing more of the same'. There is not much risk involved in th strategy. In contrast, growing through mergers or acquisitions has risk attached because when two organisations are brough together the integration process can create problems. For example, there may be a clash of cultures, which could result conflict, delays and instability.

In the early stages of business development, after the initial launch and 'settling down' period, most owners pursue organic growth strategies. Entrepreneurs are likely to be cautious and grow their businesses gradually, perhaps by selling more products to existing customers or by trying to attract new customers. However, once business owners have built up their confidence and generated some cash, they may be tempted to speed up growth by making acquisitions.

Methods of growing organically

Organic growth usually involves a business growing by buildin on its strengths to increase sales. However, there are several different approaches to growing organically.

New customers: Perhaps the easiest approach is to rely on driving sales from existing activities. For example, a food processing company supplying local shops may gradually step up production to supply more and more customers. If the factory reaches full capacity, the business can carry on growing organically by building an extension or moving to larger premises. It may be possible to find new customers by exploiting new distribution channels. For example, the food processor above may start selling to supermarkets. This approach to growth may need investment in marketing to increase the customer base.

New products: Some businesses grow by developing new products. They may be very innovative and committed to research and development. For example, a business that desig software for computer games can grow by designing new games. Alternatively, a business might identify customers with slightly different needs. This could require adapting or modifyi existing products to meet these needs. A business might need to invest some of its profit into product development.

New markets: Some businesses grow organically by finding new markets for their products. For example, a hairdresser could open another salon in a different location. The assets, systems and working practices used in the original salon can be replicated in another location. New premises can be adapted and refurbished in the style that has already been successful. Some businesses may look to overseas markets to grow. However, this approach carries more risk because of the unfamiliarity of markets abroad. Growing by selling in new areas is sometimes called geographic expansion. For example, it was reported that in 2014 the UK fashion retailer, New Look, planned to expand to China. Opening with two stores intially, it then hoped to have between 15 and 20 stores in Beijing and Shanghai.

New business model: It is possible to grow organically by using a new business model. Developments in technology or social change may give rise to such a step. For example, a retailer selling children's toys may start an online operation. This approach could see the business grow very quickly because the size of the potential market opened up could be considerable – possibly global.

Franchising: To speed up organic growth a business might set up a franchising operation. This approach allows other entrepreneurs to trade under the name of the original business. The fast-food outlet SUBWAY is an example of a business that has used this method to grow. Franchising is discussed in detail in Unit 22.

Advantages of organic growth

The benefits of organic growth are numerous. Entrepreneurs should know their business 'inside out' and grow their company by exploiting its own strengths and expertise. They can move quickly, for example by adapting to changes in the market. Entrepreneurs can experience the satisfaction of seeing their business develop and flourish. They can also choose the pace of growth – a rate that is comfortable for their own personal needs. Eventually, owners may choose to sell the business and cash in on their investment and hard work. Some specific advantages are outlined below.

- Organic growth might be less risky than other growth strategies. Growth can be achieved by extending practices that are well known and understood. This can prevent errors, as the culture, norms and practices of the business are already established and effective. Organic growth can also avoid the complications that might arise when integrating with another organisation.

- Growing organically might be relatively cheaper than using other methods. Organic growth can be financed from retained profit, which is likely to be the cheapest of all sources of finance. There will be an opportunity cost, but the financial cost can be zero. Businesses that grow inorganically often have to borrow money or raise fresh capital. This will add to the costs of growth. Organic growth also avoids the premium prices that can be paid when buying other businesses.

Question 1

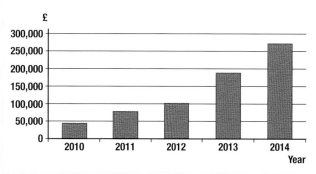

Figure 1

Sales revenue for APPicon 2010–2014

Rufus Storm owns a business called APPicon, which designs icons for apps. He set up APPicon after graduating from art school in 2010. He worked alone at home for two years, but after early successes he opened up an office in Cambridge. Since then he has taken on four staff. He has designed 25,000 icons that might be used for apps. However, now that the business is established he is getting enquiries from app developers that want tailor-made designs for their icons. This work is more lucrative and is helping to increase revenue. In the future Rufus wants to carry on growing the business organically. The success of the business is reflected by the sales data shown in Figure 1.

(a) Explain what is meant by organic growth, using APPicon as an example.

(b) Explain two ways in which Rufus might continue to grow his business organically in the future.

- A business will retain more control when growing organically. Owners, or the senior management team, will have complete control of the growth process because there are no outsiders with any controlling interest. For example, if a retail chain is growing by opening a new store in a new location every six months, the business is likely to have a team of employees who are experienced at opening new stores. They can go in, recruit and train new staff, and ensure that the store is run in the way that has proved a success in the past, then move on to the next. This approach means that the business has full control and is much easier to organise. If growth were achieved by joining with another business, some control would be lost because the other organisation will probably want to retain some control of its own.

- The financial position of a business might be better protected with organic growth. Since growth is gradual, there is less strain on financial resources. As a result, cash flow is stronger and the business will retain more liquidity. Inorganic growth often requires huge outlays of money. For example, the purchase of O_2 by Three was reported to have cost £10.5 billion. Such high expenditure can put financial pressure on the business.

- A business that grows organically is less likely to encounter diseconomies of scale. Sharp increases in unit costs are not likely to occur if growth is steady and measured. It may be easier for a business growing organically to spot in advance possible difficulties resulting from scale increases. This will help to keep costs under control.

Disadvantages of organic growth

Although there are advantages of organic growth, there is the argument that it prevents a business from reaching its full potential. It may miss out on lucrative opportunities and get left behind in the market. Some specific disadvantages are outlined below.

- The pace of organic growth may be too slow for some stakeholders. For example, shareholders in a plc may want the business to provide quicker returns on their investments than organic growth can deliver. If shareholders are unhappy with the current pace of growth they may sell their shares. As a result the share price can fall, possibly making the company vulnerable to a takeover.

- Organic growth may prevent the business from 'tapping into' the resources owned by other businesses. As a result it might miss out on some profitable developments. For example, a construction firm might want to develop expertise in energy-saving technology so it can build more houses with solar panels. It could do both of these by gradually developing its own expertise. However, it might be better for it to buy a company that already has a proven track record in these fields rather than trying to acquire this expertise from scratch. Such companies will be specialists and can provide the knowledge and experience required by the housebuilder.

- Growing slowly may mean that a business gets left behind in the market. If competitors are growing through mergers and acquisitions, the business may end up feeling small in comparison. As a result it may lose its ability to compete effectively. For example, it may not be able to match the advertising budgets of its larger rivals.

- As a business grows it may be able to exploit economies of scale. However, if a business is growing organically it may take some time before such economies are fully exploited. This could mean that a business is having to operate with higher costs for longer periods of time. This could lower profit margins and make it less competitive. Also, some lines of business, such as shipbuilding, require investment in large-scale production before trading can begin. Businesses that grow organically may be prevented from entering such industries.

- If a particular market is growing rapidly, organic growth may not be appropriate. For example, when mobile telephones were first introduced, the market expanded very quickly. Businesses making the best progress were those that were growing through mergers or acquisitions. The three firms now remaining in the UK market are all the result of multiple takeovers and mergers.

Exam tip
You need to remember that companies may use organic and inorganic growth strategies together to increase the size of their businesses. It does not have to be a straight choice between one or the other. For example, a supermarket chain may grow organically by opening brand new stores in new locations, and inorganically at the same time by acquiring another chain.

Links
Organic growth is an example of a growth strategy. The information in this unit could be used when discussing issues in exam questions such as Business objectives (Unit 21), Corporate objectives (Unit 44), Theories of corporate strategy (Unit 45), Growth (Unit 48), Causes and effects of change (Unit 63), Key factors in change (Unit 64) and International trade and business growth (Unit 67). For example, in a question on choosing an appropriate corporate strategy for a business, organic growth might be one of the options. Or, in a question on key factors in change, a decision to grow organically might be a reason why changes are necessary. In a question on business objectives, organic growth might feature as a possible option.

Key terms
Inorganic growth – a business growth strategy that involves two (or more) businesses joining together to form one much larger one.
Organic growth – a business growth strategy that involves a business growing gradually using its own resources.

Knowledge check
1. What is the difference between organic and inorganic growth?
2. Why are businesses likely to grow organically in their early stages of development?
3. Outline two methods of growing organically.
4. Why is organic growth likely to be slower than inorganic growth?
5. Why is organic growth less risky than inorganic growth?
6. Why might a business growing inorganically experience higher costs than some of its rivals in the market?
7. How might shareholders in a plc feel about organic growth?

Case study

THE CAR FINANCE COMPANY

According to the *Sunday Times* Fast Track 100, The Car Finance Company was the second fastest growing company in the UK in 2013. Founded in 2007, The Car Finance Company has grown to become Europe's leading alternative lender by serving a sector of the community ordinarily excluded from mainstream financing.

What makes The Car Finance Company the preferred choice in the market is their approach to customers, treating them fairly and putting their needs first. The Car Finance Company considers every application, no matter what the customer's credit history, and accept more than 50% of all applicants. This unique approach allows partners to sell more cars.

The Car Finance Company has provided loans to over 30,000 customers who have been denied access to mainstream credit. They finance nearly 2,000 customers every month which is set to rise to 3,000 by December 2015. The business also helped customers rebuild their credit rating and get back on track after financial difficulties.

Customers are referred to The Car Finance Company by partners such as car dealers and finance brokers or customers apply directly via the company website www.thecarfinancecompany.co.uk.

Their continual growth and commitment has been supported by industry recognition and multiple awards, including the Consumer Credit Team of the Year at the ICM British Credit Awards. Also, as a testament to its commitment to customer care, it has one of the highest customer renewal rates in the industry.

A combination of being attractive to consumers, technology deployment and leading underwriting and customer services allow The Car Finance Company to have the highest approval to deal conversion rates. The Car Finance Company has become the preferred partner by providing consistent, predictable and fast credit decisions along with tailored and flexible funding options which enable access to the large sector of the population ordinarily excluded from mainstream financing.

In 2015, the company planned to explore further opportunities within the market, with a view to continuing to grow its market share.

Source: adapted from www.thecarfinancecompany.co.uk

(a) Explain the main method used by The Car Finance Company to grow. (4 marks)

(b) Evaluate the advantages to The Car Finance Company if it continued to grow organically. (20 marks)

Key points

1. Small business survival in competitive markets:
   - product differentiation and USPs
   - flexibility in responding to customer needs
   - customer services
   - e-commerce.

Getting started

The brewing industry in the UK is dominated by a few very large producers. 170 new breweries started up in the UK in 2013/14. There were 1,285 breweries operating in Britain in 2014. One of these small brewers is Smith's Brewery, a family-run business, which brews traditional, handcrafted quality beers and supplies local pubs and retail outlets. The brewery also supplies individuals. It is possible to ring the brewery and place an order with the owner. The brewery will deliver it to a customer's home or venue. Upon arrival the deliverer will set up the barrel, give advice on storage and dispensing, and answer any questions. When the barrel is finished the brewery will collect it.

Explain how a small brewer like Smith's Brewery can survive alongside a multinational company like Heineken. How does Smith's Brewery offer a personal service? Do you think this small brewery will survive in the future? Give reasons for your answer.

Reasons for staying small

Despite the advantages of large-scale production, many firms choose to remain small. Also, small firms sometimes have advantages over larger ones.

- **Personal service.** As a firm expands it becomes increasing difficult to deal with individuals, rather than departments or automated systems. Many people prefer to do business with the owner of the company directly and are prepared to pay higher prices for the privilege. For example, people may prefer to deal directly with one of the partners in an accountancy practice. This is discussed in more detail later. Many businesses serve niche markets. It is usually easier for business to deliver a personal service in such circumstance. For example, Rolls-Royce cars are sold to a select number of exclusive buyers. It was widely reported that in 2014 they sold 4,063 cars worldwide (this was the highest number in its 111-year history). In addition to the high quality of their vehicles, Rolls-Royce emphasises the quality of their person service. A record number of customers spent personal one-on-one time with Rolls-Royce bespoke design consultants in 2014, commissioning their personalised vehicles.
- **Owner's preference.** Some entrepreneurs may be content with the current level of profits, for instance remaining below the VAT threshold to avoid the administrative burden of increased correspondence with HMRC. Some will want to avoid the added responsibilities that growth brings.
- **Flexibility and efficiency.** Small firms are more often flexible and innovative. They may be able to react more quickly to changes in market conditions or technology. Management can make decisions quickly, without following lengthy procedures. This is discussed in more detail later.
- **Lower costs.** In some cases, small firms might have lower costs than larger producers in the same market. For example large firms often have to pay their employees nationally agreed wage rates. A small firm may be able to pay lower wages to non-union workers.
- **Low barriers to entry.** In some types of business activity, such as grocery, gardening services, window cleaning and many online businesses, the set-up costs are relatively low. There is little to stop competitors setting up in business.
- **Small firms can be monopolists.** Many small firms survive because they supply a service to members of the local community that no other business does. People often use their local shop, for instance, because it provides a convenient nearby service, saving them the trouble of travelling.

Product differentiation and USPs

Even in competitive markets that might be dominated by large businesses, it is still possible to flourish operating as a small business. One way to survive in this situation is to differentiate the product or develop a USP. If a small business can offer customers something that their larger rivals do not, survival is possible. People often prefer to buy products that are different from the majority of others on the market – products that 'stand out from the crowd'. Some examples from 2015 are outlined below.

- The banking industry in the UK is dominated by a few very large banks, including HSBC, NatWest, Lloyds, RBS and Barclays. However, a number of small businesses have entered the market by offering peer-to-peer lending. These small businesses allow individuals to lend money to other individuals using an online site. Lenders get higher interest rates than banks offer and borrowers can often get loans when they have been refused by banks.

- In the confectionery industry, which is dominated by some huge companies, such as Cadbury, Mars and Nestlé, small firms co-exist by developing a USP. Starting in the US, a business called Mast Brothers flourishes by selling hand-crafted chocolate. They make every bar themselves including the packaging. Rick and Michael Mast also travel to source their own cacao, and then ship the beans back. This may seem an unusual approach but the story of their commitment to craft is a USP.

- In retailing, small specialists may be able to offer more product choice than larger rivals. For example, a small toy shop specialising in the sale of working model aircraft, helicopters, cars, trains and boats could offer a huge range of different makes and models. It may also offer a wide range of related accessories, such as engines, spare parts, lubricants, batteries and chargers. A large toy chain store is not likely to offer such a wide choice in this product range, so the specialist has an advantage.

Flexibility in responding to customer needs

Small firms can survive alongside larger ones by offering customers flexibility. Small and nimble businesses are often quick in identifying new opportunities and meeting the changing needs of customers. Large corporations are often hampered by a complex organisational structure where approval for a business decision can take days, or even longer. Smaller firms are not constrained in this way – in this case their size can be their strength.

- Smaller businesses can often make changes to customer orders even though a start has been made on production. For example, a small housebuilder may be able to change the design and specifications on a new house as it is being built. The customer may decide that triple-glazed windows are preferred to double-glazed and that a swimming pool is now required in the back garden. A large housebuilding corporation committed to building, say, 50 houses on a particular site may not be able to accommodate such changes.

- A small business can often respond to changes in external factors, such as shifts in customer needs, exchange rates or legislation, more quickly than larger rivals. For example, a small firm may be able to bring a new product to the market more quickly because there will be fewer people involved in its creation. A larger company will involve many people, departments and processes in product development. This slows down the process. A large corporation may have to gather, analyse and evaluate information, consider multiple options and gain multiple approvals before the process is complete. By which time the advantage of 'first mover' may be lost. This can be important in a world where the pace of change seems to accelerate all of the time.

- Sometimes a customer may have a special request. Small businesses are often able to cater for such requests because they do not have rigid systems. For example, a large car dealership may have a rigid car finance agreement that requires customers to repay what they owe in fixed monthly instalments over a fixed period of time. A small dealer may accept variable payments or allow customers to pay off what is owed before the agreed time period is up.

Customer service

Offering high-quality customer service is a way of adding value to products. It can also give firms a competitive edge in a market and allow smaller firms to survive in markets dominated by large corporations.

- It is a lot easier for a small business than for a giant corporation to offer customers a personal service. This can sometimes give a small business a competitive edge. Because customers attach value to dealing directly with the owner of a business, the business can charge a premium for this. A simple, friendly greeting with a handshake from the owner of an independent restaurant upon arrival is something that a large restaurant chain can rarely match.

- Small retailers may have a geographical advantage over their larger rivals. For example, a local grocer offers convenience for customers – they do not have to travel far for their shopping. Local businesses also get to know their customers. They may carry stock lines to cater for individual needs or help carry shopping to the customer's car. An out-of-town superstore is not likely to offer this level of customer service.

- Communications in smaller organisations may be more effective than those in giant corporations. For example, customers trying to contact someone in a position of authority in a large corporation will often be met with an automated answering machine. Such systems often lack flexibility and have a habit of directing customers into a labyrinth of recorded messages where it is seemingly impossible to get access to someone who has the expertise and authority to deal with a specific problem. In a small business it might be possible to get straight through to the owner of the business, where an issue can be addressed and resolved immediately.

- It is often said that customer care is about building relationships with customers. It is a lot easier for small businesses to do this because they are usually closer to their customers. Also, with the use of social media, businesses can get instant customer feedback. What is more important, though, is responding positively to that feedback. Small businesses may be able to do this more effectively because they are closer to their customers.

Question 1

Helen and David Watson run their own nursery business in Banbury, Oxfordshire. The couple met when they were at college fifteen years ago. Since then they have both worked with children in the NHS and have got married and had three children of their own. The nursery is profitable and both Helen and David enjoy looking after people's children while they are at work. The business serves the local area and employs three other staff. The Watsons have no ambition to expand their business at the moment. They earn enough money to support their lifestyle. They can also spend more time with their own children and do not want the extra work and responsibility that expanding a business would bring.

Last year a leading national provider of nursery care opened up a centre just 500 yards from their business. However, the impact was virtually zero. Helen and David are well known and trusted in the area. They do not advertise and their business is generated through 'word of mouth'. They offer a very personal service. For example, they will collect children and return them if parents occasionally have transport difficulties, they are on first name terms with all their customers and will sometimes look after children at weekends.

(a) Explain one reason why this business is likely to remain small.

(b) Explain one reason why Helen and David's business was not affected when a larger rival set up close by.

E-commerce

Developments in technology mean that it is not difficult to set up an online business. It could be argued that e-commerce helps smaller firms to compete more easily with larger firms. If a website is attractive and professionally presented, it may not be possible to distinguish whether the trader is large or small. Barriers to entry are small, with it being possible to set up a site for little cost. Many online businesses are initially run from home, which eliminates the need to find business premises. For around £2,000 new online traders can buy a package that includes web design, domain name registration and arranging hosting of the website by an internet service provider.

- **Online shops.** In this simple model, small online retailers can compete alongside larger businesses quite effectively. For example, Naked Wines is an online wine retailer. It was founded in 2008 and has been able to compete effectively with the retail giants. It is reckoned that 38 per cent of people in the UK buy their online wine from just three stores – Tesco, Sainsbury's and Asda.

- **Social media consultants.** There are a growing number of these businesses delivering online services. Large companies can often afford to employ their own staff to operate their Facebook and Twitter accounts. However, smaller businesses might need the help of a specialist, such as Carvill Creative. This business helps those starting out with social media who might need support with set-up and social network creation. There are even websites that can help set up a business as a social media consultant, such as Shawn Christenson's 'More Than a Webmaster' site. Social media is now very important to businesses. The Pew Internet Social Networking study found that in January of 2014, 76 percent of women and 72 per cent of men who use the internet also use social media.

- **Information and advice sites.** Some small online businesses make money by providing information and advice or bringing people together who have common interests. Some people run businesses by setting up blogging sites. To generate revenue from sites like these it is necessary to build up high volumes of traffic. Once this is achieved money can be earned from selling banner advertising, using AdSense, affiliating to large sites such as Amazon or eBay, and offering premium services that people are willing to pay for.

- **Tutoring, training or mentoring.** These types of businesses could teach a foreign language, offer marketing training, help to improve writing skills or help deliver academic courses. One approach is to offer a free service now and build a 'freemium' model (offer free accounts with limited features, then charge for upgrades) for the future, in order to generate cash.

Thinking bigger

Since the 1990s there has been a growth in the number of small businesses in the UK. This growth has accelerated since 2000 and self-employment in particular has grown rapidly. In 2014 there were 4.6 million self-employed people in the UK. Most of these people did not employ other workers in their business activities. Figure 1 shows that the number of single-person businesses in the UK rose by 68 per cent from 2.355 million in 2000 to 3.965 million in 2014. What factors led to these trends?

- High unemployment between 2007 and 2014 had an important impact. The number of jobs being created by existing businesses fell during this time. As a result many people saw self-employment as the only means of support. Also, some people had the capital to set up a business from their redundancy pay-outs.

- Government and local authorities introduced a number of measures to encourage the development of small businesses. Business start-up schemes provided funds for small businesses for an initial period. Government helpline Business Link (replaced in 2012 by Gov.UK) gave advice on running businesses and obtaining finance. European initiatives included loans from the European Investment Fund and finance for training from the European Social Fund.

- Increasing numbers of people over the age of 65 have gone into self-employment. Between 2008 and 2014 this number doubled. One reason for this may be the desire to keep economically active after retirement.

- More women have opted for self-employment. Between 2008 and 2011 women accounted for an unprecedented 80 per cent of the newly self-employed (Labour Force Survey, Office of National Statistics 2013). In 2014 there were almost 1.5 million self-employed women, an increase of around 300,000 since the start of the economic downturn.

- Changes in the structure of the economy. The expansion of the tertiary sector has contributed to the growth in small businesses. Many services can be undertaken more effectively on a small scale.

- The development of e-commerce has also had a large impact. By using the internet, a wide range of business opportunities have opened up. For example, some types of business activity, such as online tutoring, can be delivered from anywhere in the world by using an online business model.

Sources: adapted from www.gov.uk, www.ons.gov.uk, Labour Force Survey, Office of National Statistics 2013

Figure 1

The growth in the number of single-person businesses in the UK 2000 to 2014

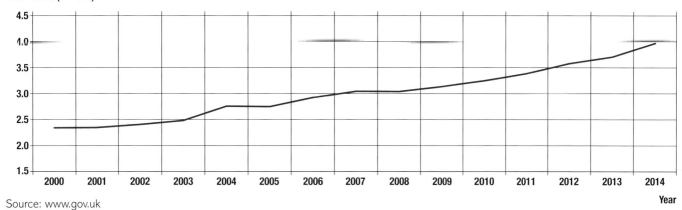

Source: www.gov.uk

Exam tip

When answering exam questions in general it is important to remember that small businesses play a big role in the economy. When giving examples to support your arguments it is easy to remember the names of big companies. However, do not neglect the importance of small businesses. Remember that at the beginning of 2014, 99.4 per cent of the 5.2 million businesses in the UK were classified as small, according to government statistics.

Links 🔗

One way of demonstrating synoptic skills here is to link the role played by small firms in niche marketing, which is discussed in Units 1 and 13. There are many examples of small businesses that have learnt how to co-exist with large corporations by carving out a niche for themselves. Also, when answering a question on flexibility in business you could link this to how small businesses can offer flexibility as discussed in this unit. The survival of small firms in competitive markets can also be linked to the development of online businesses in Unit 22, and the use of USPs and product differentiation in Units 10 and 13. There are also links between this unit on small businesses and units relating to entrepreneurs, such as Units 19, 20 and 22. As stated in the exam tip, there will be many opportunities where the role of small businesses will be relevant.

Case study

ENCLOTHED

Enclothed is an online retailer founded by Levi Young and Dana Zingher in 2013. The business focuses specifically on the needs of fashion-conscious, time-starved men, or men who simply lack the motivation to shop on the high street. The service provided by Enclothed is hassle-free and very customer-orientated. Men can sign up for the service online. They give information about their size, style and any price or clothing preferences they may have. This information is processed by clever software which produces a profile of the customer. Stylists, or personal shoppers employed by Enclothed, then handpick a collection of clothing and outfits that match the customer's profile. The items are packed into attractive boxes and despatched. Clients can then try on the outfits in the comfort of their own homes, decide which items to buy and return those that are unwanted. The client doesn't even have to bother with the hassle of repackaging and posting the unwanted items as the Enclothed service includes collection.

Both of the founders have experience in business. Levi was head of sales at a branding and marketing firm, and is now in charge of the sales and marketing team at Enclothed. Dana began her career with a first degree in fashion and masters in Business and Management, followed by work in the City as a technology consultant. She is now in charge of the styling and technology department. In February 2015, the pair presented their business to the *Dragon's Den* team on BBC television. They impressed and succeeded in raising £70,000 from Dragon investors Kelly Hoppen and Piers Linny.

Sources: adapted from www.startups.co.uk and www.enclothed.co.uk

(a) Explain one way in which Enclothed differentiates its product from those of larger online clothes retailers. (4 marks)

(b) Evaluate the possible methods a small business like Enclothed might use to survive in competitive markets. (20 marks)

Knowledge check

1. State two reasons why the owners of a successful small business might choose not to grow.

2. Give an example of how a small newsagent might offer some flexibility to its customers.

3. How might a small publisher differentiate its product?

4. State two ways a business can offer a more personal service than a much larger rival.

5. Explain one reason why online businesses are popular with small enterprises.

6. State three reasons why the popularity of small businesses has grown.

52 Quantitative sales forecasting

Key points

1. Calculation of time-series analysis:
   - moving averages (three period/four quarter).
2. Interpretation of scatter graphs and line of best fit – extrapolation of past data to future.
3. Limitations of quantitative sales forecasting techniques.

Getting started

Unit 30 showed how sales forecasting is vitally important to business and that this process informs key decisions of business. In Theme 3 the aim is to explore and develop an understanding of some of the key statistical tools that are used to make this forecasting as accurate and robust as possible.

Marco, in deciding on his sales forecasts for the coming months and years, has produced a range of time series data that records previous sales and includes a trend analysis. A breakdown of sales, and predictions for coming months, is shown in Table 1.

Table 1 Sales breakdown and predictions by quarter

	2014 Q1	2014 Q2	2014 Q3	2014 Q4	Total 2014	2015 Q1	2015 Q2	2015 Q3	2015 Q4	Total 2015
Sales (thousands)	17	19	34	16	86	18	21	33	16	88

What will Marco's sales forecast be for the first three months of 2016? What is the trend of his sales? Is there any evidence that sales are generally increasing? To what extent is the business affected by seasonal factors?

Calculating time series data

The four main components that a business wants to identify in time series data are:

- trend
- seasonal fluctuations
- cyclical fluctuations
- random fluctuations.

This unit is concerned with identifying the trend.

Identifying the trend

An analysis of figures will tell a business whether there is an upward, downward or constant trend. Identifying the trend allows the business to predict what is likely to happen in future. The first step is to smooth out the raw data. Take the example of the garden furniture manufacturer from Unit 30, whose yearly sales over ten years are shown in Table 2 on the next page.

Table 2 Yearly sales of a garden furniture manufacturer

Year	2006	2007	2008	2009	2010	2011	2012	2013	2014	2015
Sales (£ 000)	125	130	130	150	140	155	180	190	210	230

It is possible to calculate a trend by using a **moving average**. The average can be taken for any period the business wants, such as a year, a month or a quarter. For now we will assume the garden furniture manufacturer uses a three-year average. The average of sales in the first three years was:

$$\frac{125 + 130 + 130}{3} = \frac{385}{3} = 128.3$$

To calculate the moving average, the first year's sales drop out and the next year's sales (2009) are added. The average for the next three years was:

$$\frac{130 + 130 + 150}{3} = \frac{410}{3} = 136.7$$

If the business continues to do this, the results will be as shown in Table 3. Notice that the moving average is placed at the centre of the three years (i.e. the average for 2006–2008 is plotted next to 2007).

Table 3 Three-year moving average for sales of a garden furniture manufacturer

Year	2006	2007	2008	2009	2010	2011	2012	2013	2014	2015
Sales (£000)	125	130	130	150	140	155	180	190	210	230
		128.3	136.7	140	148.3	158.3	175	193.3	210	

What if the firm had used a four-year period instead of three years? No one year is the centre point and simply placing the figure in between two years may result in misleading predictions in future. The solution is to use **centring**. This uses a four- and eight-year moving total to find a mid-point, as shown in Table 4.

Table 4 Centring

Year	2006	2007	2008	2009	2010
Sales (£ 000)	125	130	130	150	140

535 + 550 = 1085
(Four-year moving totals) (Eight-year moving total)

Here, the mid-point is 2008. The **trend** or **four-period centred moving average** can be found by dividing the eight-year moving total by 8, the number of years, as shown in Table 5.

Plotting the four-period centred moving average figures onto a graph (as shown in Figure 1) shows the trend in the figures. It is clear to see that sales appear to be rising over the period. The trend line is 'smoother' than the line showing the actual sales figures. It eliminates any fluctuations in sales each year and gives a more obvious picture of the trend that has been taking place.

Table 5 Calculating a four-year moving average for a garden furniture manufacturer

Year	Sales	Four-year moving total	Eight-year moving total	Trend (Four-year centred moving average = Eight-year moving total / 8)
2006	125			
2007	130			
2008	130	535	1,085	135.63
2009	150		1,125	140.63
2010	140	550	1,200	150
2011	155	575	1,290	161.25
2012	180	625	1,400	175
2013	190	665	1,535	193.13
2014	210	735		
2015	230	810		

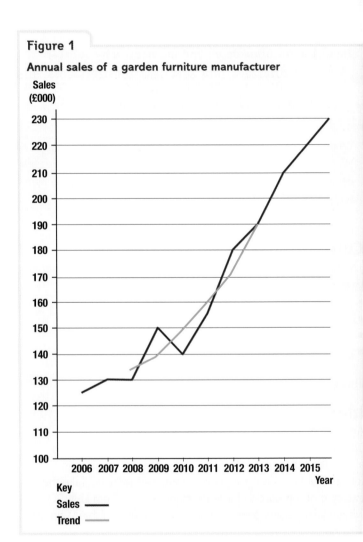

Figure 1

Annual sales of a garden furniture manufacturer

Key
Sales ——
Trend ——

Question 1

A business has recently gathered data on its sales revenue as shown in Table 6, and wants to calculate a three- and four-period moving average.

Table 6 Sales revenue

										(£000)
Period	1	2	3	4	5	6	7	8	9	10
Sales revenue	100	130	160	175	180	190	190	180	220	250
3-period moving average		130	155							
4-period moving average		151.3								

(a) Calculate the three- and four-period moving averages for as many years as you can to complete the table.

(b) Plot the sales figures and both trend lines onto a graph on graph paper and explain the relationship between the trend and the actual sales revenue figures.

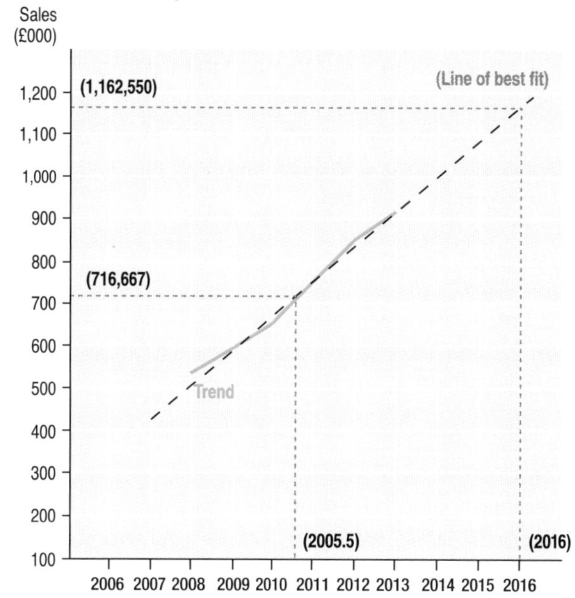

Predicting the line of best fit from the trend

Having identified a trend that is taking place, it is possible for a business to now predict what may happen in future. Consider the business represented in Table 7.

Table 7 Four-year moving average and trend for a toy manufacturer

Year	Sales	Four-year moving total	Eight-year moving total	Trend (Four-year centred moving average = Eight-year-moving total / 8)
2006	300			
2007	500			
2008	600	1,950	4,200	525.00
2009	550	2,250	4,750	593.75
2010	600	2,500	5,250	656.25
2011	750	2,750	6,050	756.25
2012	850	3,300	6,800	850
2013	1,100	3,500	7,350	918.75
2014	800	3,850		
2015	1,100			

Consider the sales of this business during the period 2006–2015. These data have been used to calculate four-year moving averages and this information used to calculate the trend. Extrapolation involves the use of past sales data to forecast future sales. Figure 2 shows that sales of the toy manufacturer's goods may reach about £1,160,000.

The business has made certain assumptions when predicting this figure. Firstly, no other factors were likely to have changed to affect the trend. If other factors changed, resulting in different sales figures, then the prediction is likely to be inaccurate.

Figure 2

Annual sales of a toy manufacturer

Secondly, the sales figures are predicted by drawing a line through the trend figures and extending it to the year 2016. The broken line through the trend in Figure 2 is called the **line of best fit**. It is the best line that can be drawn that matches the general slope of all points in the trend. The line is an average, where points in the trend on one side of the line are balanced with those on the other. In other words, it is a line that 'best fits' all points in the trend.

It is possible to draw the line of best fit by plotting the trend figures on graph paper accurately and then adding the line of best fit 'by eye', so that points fit equally either side of the line. Extending the line carefully should give a reasonable prediction.

To help draw the line, it should pass through the coordinates (X,Y) where X is the average of the years and Y is the average sales. These coordinates can be calculated using the figures in Table 7.

$$\bar{X} = \frac{\Sigma X \text{ (the total years)}}{N \text{ (the number of years)}} = \frac{2006+2007+2008+2009+2010+2011}{6} = \frac{12,051}{6} = 2008.5$$

$$\bar{Y} = \frac{\Sigma Y \text{ (the total sales in the trend)}}{N \text{ (the number of years)}}$$

$$= \frac{£525,000 + £593,750 + £656,250 + £756,250 + £850,000 + £918,750}{6} = \frac{£4,300,000}{6}$$

$$= £716,667$$

This point is shown on Figure 2. The actual predicted figure for the year 2016 is £1,162,550. This can be found by a method known as 'the sum of least squares'. Computer software can be used by businesses to calculate the line of best fit and to predict from the trend.

Variations from the trend

How accurate is the prediction of around £1,160,000 sales of toys by the year 2016? Even allowing for the assumptions on the previous page, the prediction may not be accurate because it is taken from the trend, and the trend 'smoothed out' variations in sales figures. To make an accurate prediction, the business will have to find the average variation over the period and take this into account. We can find how much variation there is from the trend by calculating:

Actual sales – trend

So, for example, the cyclical variation in Table 7 would be as shown in Table 8. The average of the variations over the period 2006–2015 is (in £000):

$$\frac{+75 -43.75 -56.25 -6.25 +/-0 +181.25}{6} = \frac{+150}{6} = +25 \text{ (or } +£25,000)$$

If the predicted value based on the trend was £1,160,000, then adding £25,000 may give a more accurate predicted figure of £1,185,000.

Table 8 Cyclical variations

Year	Sales	Trend (four-year centred moving average)	Variation in each year (£000)
2006	300		
2007	500		
2008	600	525.00	+75.00
2009	550	593.75	−43.75
2010	600	656.25	−56.25
2011	750	756.25	−6.25
2012	850	850.00	+/− 0
2013	1,100	918.75	+181.25
2014	800		
2015	1,100		

Seasonal variations

It is possible to predict from a trend and use seasonal variations to make a more accurate prediction. Table 9 shows sales of a different business over a three-year period, including sales in each quarter. A four-quarter moving average has been calculated and also the variation in each quarter.

Carrying on the trend to predict the sales for the fourth quarter of the year 2015 might give a figure of £470,000. (It would be possible to find this by drawing and extending a line of best fit through the trend.) As we know, this is a 'smoothed out' figure. A more accurate prediction might be to calculate the average seasonal variation in the fourth quarter, for example (in £000):

$$\frac{-97.125 -117.5}{2} = \frac{-214.625}{2} = -107.313$$

By subtracting £107,313 from the total of £470,000, this gives a more accurate prediction of £362,687.

Table 9 Seasonal variations

Year	Quarter	Sales	Four-quarter moving average	Variation (£000)
2012	3	460		
	4	218		
2013	1	205	328.5	−123.5
	2	388	346.0	+42.0
	3	546	358.25	−187.75
	4	272	369.125	−97.125
2014	1	249	383.625	−134.625
	2	431	396.625	+34.375
	3	619	404.0	+215.0
	4	303	420.5	−117.5
2015	1	277		
	2	535		

Question 2

Table 10 shows the yearly sales figures of a furniture manufacturer over a period of ten years.

Table 10

Period	1	2	3	4	5	6	7	8	9	10 (£000)
Sales	5,000	5,200	5,800	6,000	5,800	7,000	8,200	7,400	7,600	8,400

(a) Calculate a four-yearly moving average from the figures to show the trend taking place.

(b) Plot the trend onto a graph on graph paper and predict the likely output in year 11.

(c) Calculate:

  (i) the cyclical variation for each year

  (ii) the average cyclical variation over the period.

The limitations of quantitative sales forecasts

Quantitative sales forecasts are powerful tools for businesses and are used to inform key decisions. The fact that they are often produced using advanced computer models and algorithms, and managed by expert sales analysts, does not mean such methods are infallible – what has gone before is not always the best predictor of what is to come.

Sales forecasts are likely to be more reliable when:

- the forecast is for a short period of time in the future, such as six months, rather than a long time, such as five years
- they are revised frequently to take account of new data and other information
- the market is slow changing
- market research data, including test marketing data, is available
- those preparing the forecast have a good understanding of how to use data to produce a forecast
- those preparing the forecast have a good 'feel' for the market and can adjust the forecast to take account of their hunches and guesses about the future.

No forecaster is accurate all the time. Even in slow-moving markets, sales can change by a few per cent for no apparent reason. One way to take this into account is to produce a forecast range. Forecasters might, for example, prepare three sets of figures – an optimistic forecast, a pessimistic forecast and a central forecast. The two outlying forecasts would have low probabilities of occurring, but would indicate a best and worst case scenarios. The central forecast would be the forecast that had the highest probability of occurring. Supplying these forecasts to other departments, such as production, would give them an indication of the possible variations they might have to face. They could then prepare their own plans for these eventualities. In a very sophisticated forecast there would be a whole range of possible outcomes, each with a probability attached to its occurring.

Even though forecasts are rarely 100 per cent accurate, they do provide an indication of likely future trends. As such, they are important tools for any planning or budgeting.

Causal modelling and line of best fit

Time series analysis only describes what is happening to information. Causal modelling tries to explain data, usually by finding a link between one set of data and another. For example, a business may want to find whether there is a link between the amount that it spends on advertising and its sales.

Table 11 shows data that have been collected about advertising and sales by a business at different times. The data in the table are plotted onto a scatter graph in Figure 3.

Advertising (the independent variable) is shown on the horizontal (X) axis. Sales (the dependent variable) are shown on the vertical (Y) axis. The figure shows, for example, that in one period (E) the business had advertising spending of £1,500 and sales of 1,800 units. In another period (G) the business had advertising spending of £3,500 and sales of 5,800 units.

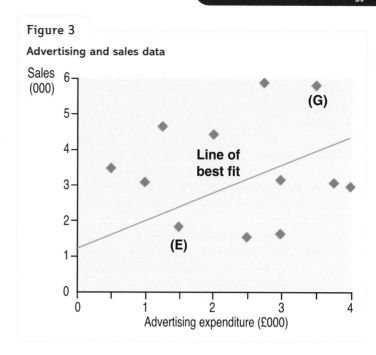

Figure 3

Advertising and sales data

Looking at the graph, there appears to be a positive **correlation** between the two variables. The more that is spent on advertising, the higher the level of sales. The line of best fit is drawn through the data to show this relationship better. It is also possible to calculate the extent of the relationship by means of a **correlation coefficient**, using the formula:

$$r = \frac{\Sigma XY}{\sqrt{(\Sigma X^2)\ (\Sigma Y^2)}}$$

Using the data in Table 11, the correlation coefficient for advertising and sales can be calculated as follows.

$$r = \frac{£102.28m}{\sqrt{£81.93m \times 173.18m}}$$

$$r = \frac{£102.28m}{£119.117m}$$

$$r = +0.86$$

- A correlation coefficient of +1 means that there is an absolute positive relationship between the two variables. All points in the scatter graph fall on the line of best fit and the line slopes upwards from left to right. As the values of the independent variable increase, so do the dependent variable values.
- A correlation coefficient of 0 means that there is no relationship between the variables.
- A correlation coefficient of –1 means that there is an absolute negative relationship between the two variables. All points in the scatter graph fall on the line of best fit and the line slopes downwards from left to right. As the values of the independent variable increase, the values of the dependent variable fall.

Table 11 Advertising and sales data

Period	Advertising expenditure (£000)	Sales (000)	(£million)	(million)	(£million)
	X	Y	X²	Y²	XY
A	1.0	3.2	1.0	10.24	3.2
B	2.0	4.5	4.0	20.25	9.0
C	3.0	1.8	9.0	3.24	5.4
D	4.0	3.0	16	9.0	12.0
E	1.5	1.8	2.25	3.24	2.7
F	2.5	1.6	6.25	2.56	4.0
G	3.5	5.8	12.25	33.64	20.3
H	1.2	4.7	1.44	22.09	5.64
I	2.7	5.9	7.29	34.81	15.93
J	3.0	3.5	9.0	12.25	10.5
K	3.6	3.1	12.96	9.61	11.16
L	7.0	3.5	0.49	12.25	2.45
			ΣX² =81.93	ΣY²=173.18	ΣXY=102.28

The formula itself does not show positive and negative values. However, it is easy to see whether the relationship is positive or negative from the graph. A positive coefficient of 0.86 suggests a strong correlation between the spending on advertising and the level of sales. As advertising increases, so do sales. This information could help a business in future when making decisions about its marketing. It is suggested that if the figure falls below 0.7 it becomes difficult to see any correlation from the scatter graph. An example of a negative correlation might be the relationship between prices and customer demand. As prices rise, demand falls. Examples of different correlations are shown in Figure 4.

Businesses must be careful when basing decisions on such calculations.

- A large quantity of sales in any period may be due to factors other than advertising, such as other forms of promotion.
- There are sometimes examples of 'nonsense correlations'. These are correlation coefficients that appear to show a strong relationship between two variables, when in fact the relationship between the figures is pure coincidence.

Qualitative forecasting

Qualitative forecasting uses people's opinions or judgements rather than numerical data. A business could base its predictions on the views of so-called experts, or on the opinions of experienced managers in the marketing or production department. Such methods are usually used by businesses:

- where there is insufficient numerical data
- where figures date quickly because the market is changing rapidly.

Question 3

Denten Limited is a manufacturer of bins and other storage equipment. It exports a large amount of its products abroad. It makes use of direct sales to customers and also employs some overseas agents. The managing director has asked the marketing department to examine the relationship between the number of agents it employs and sales of three of its most popular products, and make recommendations. The research found the following information.

Product 1 ΣY^2 = 5,360 ΣXY = 2,720
Product 2 ΣY^2 = 17,360 ΣXY = 3,200
Product 3 ΣY^2 = 25,080 ΣXY = 3,240
Agents ΣX^2 = 1,400

(a) Calculate the correlation coefficients to show the relationship between spending on overseas agents and products 1, 2 and 3.

(b) Explain the relationship between the variables in each case.

(c) Evaluate the performance of the overseas agents in terms of the sales of the three products.

Figure 4

A weak positive correlation, a strong negative correlation and little or no correlation

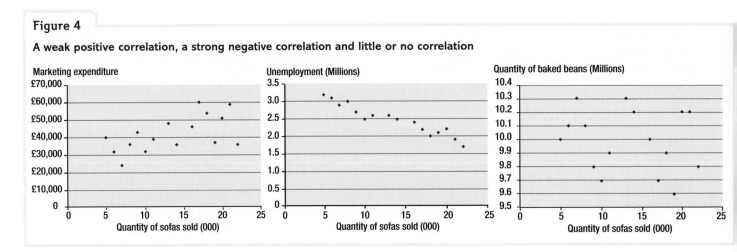

Exam tip

There are lots of opportunities for exam questions requiring analysis and evaluation in this topic. The statistical element of quantitative sales data means that analytical considerations can be made. Imagine data being presented from which a question is asked regarding the likely sales in the next period where sales in previous years have been shown to be growing.

Table 12 Sales

	2014	2015
Sales (£ '000)	50	60

It might appear reasonable to suggest that sales in the following year will increase. However, it is important to take account of other

information before jumping to this conclusion. Considerations might include the following.

- What were sales before 2014? Is 2015 a blip?
- What market does the business operate within? Might there be some reason why sales in 2015 were so high?
- Are sales of this business cyclical?
- What is the seasonal breakdown throughout the year?

The 'it depends' rule is a useful tool when faced with exam questions. Sales might increase further in 2016; the evidence available – and there is not much of it – points to this conclusion. However, it depends on other factors. This is an important consideration and can be used to help prompt further questions.

Case study

PROSPER-i

In 2011 Prosper-i, a global electronics company and developer of toys and games, launched the latest version of its popular robot toy. Called the i-do, the new robot offered new features such as the ability to be controlled by a smart phone app, and programmed to play music and video. The new features were designed to appeal to new market segments including adults. It was also designed to compete with two main competitors – ChiBot and Pal-i.

i-do was initially well-received by consumers and by reviewers. In the US the entire stock of over 40,000 units was sold in the first three months of release. Over 300,000 units were sold in 2011. Table 13 summarises sales in 2012.

Table 13 i-do sales 2012

	2012 Q1	2012 Q2	2012 Q3	2012 Q4
Sales (thousands)	39	16	30	1.95

From March to June 2012, i-do sold approximately 16,000 units, which was down 51 per cent on the previous three months. Some retailers were considering whether to continue to stock i-do.

The sales performance led Prosper-i to lower its 2013 sales forecast by 70 per cent from 900,000 units to 280,000. The reported actual sales for 2013 are shown below.

Table 14 i-do sales 2013

	2013 Q1	2013 Q2	2013 Q3	2013 Q4
Sales (thousands)	31	51	61	1.91

In 2014, Prosper-i reported that sales of i-do were running ahead of its sales forecast.

(a) What is meant by a sales forecast? (2 marks)

(b) Using the information in the case study, explain the extent to which sales of i-do could be described as being influenced by seasonal factors. (4 marks)

(c) Assess the extent to which quantitative sales forecasting is useful to Prosper-i. (10 marks)

Key terms

Centring – a method used in the calculation of a moving average where the average is plotted or calculated in relation to the central figure.

Correlation – the relationship between two sets of variables.

Correlation coefficient – a measure of the extent of the relationship between two sets of variables.

Moving average – a succession of averages derived from successive segments (typically of constant size and overlapping) of a series of values.

Scatter graph – a graph showing the performance of one variable against another independent variable on a variety of occasions. It is used to show whether a correlation exists between the variables.

Time series analysis – a method that allows a business to predict future levels from past figures.

Knowledge check

1. Why might a business want to predict the future?

2. What are the four components of time series data that a business will take into account?

3. What does a trend show?

4. How might a business use the calculation of a trend?

5. What does a scatter graph show?

6. What is meant by causal modelling?

7. State two difficulties with quantitative sales forecasting.

8. How would a line of best fit be useful for a business when looking to forecast sales?

Thinking bigger

Quantitative sales forecasting is an important technique for businesses, but it is not without contention. Even with the most powerful statistical models and forecasts, at some point the judgement needs to be made by someone within a business about what the forecast will be. From this forecast decisions will be made concerning staffing, ordering of materials, marketing, and so on. Importantly, ultimate decisions are subjective in the sense that they are judgements made by individuals or departments. Individuals may be driven by competing motives. The sales manager may be motivated to have forecasts that paint a positive picture.

This lack of certainty is a good opportunity for the development of balanced arguments in any written response to a question. The statistically produced trend may well point to a particular level of sales. However, wider economic factors might make this forecast unlikely. A rise in average incomes in an economy, combined with a weakening exchange rate, for instance, may mean that the forecast is an under-prediction. The topic lends itself to an evaluative approach. In essence, avoid basing forecasts on a very small range of factors. Time series analysis is a useful tool for business, but it is risky to rely heavily on what has gone before.

53 Investment appraisal

Key points

1. Simple payback.
2. Average (accounting) rate of return.
3. Discounted cash flow (net present value only).
4. Calculations and interpretations of figures generated by these techniques.
5. Limitations of these techniques.

Getting started

Clifton recycling is a recycling plant owned by the Anderson family in Essex. In 2014 the business invested £1.2 million in a new plant designed to convert plastic bottles into plastic flakes and pellets. Table 1 shows the net cash flow the business hoped to receive over the life of the investment (expected to be 10 years). Once the plant was constructed in 2015 at a cost of £50 million, revenue flows were due to begin in 2016. James Anderson, the managing director, commented that the growth in the recycling of plastic bottles was around 45 per cent and looked to grow in the future and, if so, it would be a profitable investment.

The investment would create 20 new jobs at the plant. However, some local residents were worried about the noise the new plant might make and were meeting with the local council about their concerns.

Calculate the expected cash flow from the investment over the time period. Investment is often said to be risky. Can you account for this view using this investment as an example? What non-financial factors might Clifton recycling have taken into account when deciding whether to build the new plant?

Table 1 Expected net cash flow from the new plant

	2015	2016	2017	2018	2019	2020	2021	2022	2023	2024	2025
Net cash flow (£000s)	-50	10	110	180	230	300	340	370	400	390	370

Investment appraisal

Investment refers to the purchase of capital goods. Capital goods are used in the production of other goods. For example, a building contractor who buys a cement mixer, some scaffolding, a lorry, a computer, some office furniture and five shovels has invested. These goods will be used repeatedly by the business over a period of time.

Investment might also refer to expenditure by a business that is likely to yield a return in the future. For example, a business might spend £20 million on research and development into a new product or invest £10 million in a promotion campaign. In each case, money is being spent on projects now in the hope that a greater amount of money will be generated in the future as a result of that expenditure.

Investment appraisal describes how a business might objectively evaluate an investment project to determine whether or not it is likely to be profitable. It also allows businesses to make comparisons between different investment projects. There are several quantitative methods that a business might use when evaluating projects. However, they all involve comparing the capital cost of the project with the net cash flow.

- The capital cost is the amount of money spent when setting up a new venture.
- Net cash flow is cash inflows minus cash outflows.

Simple payback

The payback period refers to the amount of time it takes for a project to recover or pay back the initial outlay. For example, an engineer may invest £500,000 in new cutting machinery and estimate that it will lead to a net cash flow over the next five years, as in the Table 2 on the next page. Here the payback period is four years. If we add together the net cash flows from the project in the first four years it amounts to £500,000 (i.e. £100,000 + £125,000 + £125,000 + £150,000).

The payback period can also be found by calculating the **cumulative net cash flow**. This is the net cash flow each year taking into account the initial cost of the machine. When the machine is first bought, in year 0, there is negative cash flow of minus £500,000, the cost of the machine. Next year the net cash flow minus operating costs is £100,000. So the cumulative net cash flow is –£500,000 + £100,000 = –£400,000. In year 4 it is zero, so all costs have been covered.

Table 2 Expected net cash flow from some new cutting machinery

	Yr 0	Yr 1	Yr 2	Yr 3	Yr 4	Yr 5
						£000
Net cash flow	(500)	100	125	125	150	150
Cumulative net cash flow	(500)	(400)	(275)	(150)	0	150

Worked example

When using the payback method to choose between projects, you are looking for the project with the shortest payback period. Assume a business is appraising three investment projects, all of which cost £70,000. The net cash flow expected from each project is shown in Table 3.

Table 3 Expected net cash flow from three projects

	Yr 0	Yr 1	Yr 2	Yr 3	Yr 4	Yr 5	Yr 6	Total net cash flow	Payback period
									£000
A Net cash flow	(70)	10	10	20	20	30	40	60	4 yrs 4 mths
A Cumulative cash flow	(70)	(60)	(50)	(30)	(10)	20	60		
B Net cash flow	(70)	20	20	20	20	20	20	50	3 yrs 6 mths
B Cumulative cash flow	(70)	(50)	(30)	(10)	10	30	50		
C Net cash flow	(70)	30	30	20	10	10	10	40	2 yrs 6 mths
C Cumulative cash flow	(70)	(40)	(10)	10	20	30	40		

In this example Project C would be chosen because it has the shortest payback time: 2 years and 6 months. How is this calculated? In years 1 and 2 the net cash flow is £30,000 + £30,000 = £60,000. To pay for an investment of £70,000 the remaining £10,000 (£70,000 − £60,000) comes from year 3's net cash flow. This is £20,000, which is more. So the number of months in year 3 it takes to pay the £10,000 can be calculated as:

$$\frac{\text{Amount required}}{\text{Net cash flow in year}} \times 12 = \frac{£10,000}{£20,000} \times 12 = 6 \text{ months}$$

Project A's payback is 4 years 4 months and Project B's is 3 years and 6 months. Note that total cash flow is not taken into account in this method. In fact Project C has the lowest total return over the six years.

Advantages of the payback method

There are certain advantages to a business of the use of the payback method to appraise the potential success of an investment.

- This method is useful when technology changes rapidly, as it is important to recover the cost of investment before a new model or equipment is designed. This is true of the agriculture industry where new farm machinery is designed and introduced into the market regularly.
- It is simple to use.
- Firms might adopt this method if they have cash-flow problems. This is because the project chosen will 'payback' the investment more quickly than others.

Question 1

Delrose Associates is a full service digital marketing agency. The company offers a blend of consultancy and creativity, resulting in fully managed, highly successful online marketing campaigns. Delrose has clients in a variety of sectors including consumer, corporate, commercial, retail and not-for-profit. Their main work is developing targeted campaigns to drive quality traffic to websites using highly cost-effective methods.

In 2015 the managing director of the company recognised the need for a new computer system. She carried out some research into three new systems and put together the financial information shown in Table 4.

(a) Explain what is meant by 'expected net cash flow'.

(b) Calculate the payback period for each system and state which system Delrose Associates should select.

(c) Explain one reason why Delrose used the payback method of investment appraisal in this case.

Table 4 Capital costs and expected net cash flows from three new computer systems

Computer system	Capital cost	2015	2016	2017	2018	2019	2020	Total
System A	24,000	6,000	6,000	6,000	6,000	6,000	6,000	36,000
System B	37,000	8,000	8,000	9,000	9,000	6,000	6,000	46,000
System C	12,000	4,000	4,000	4,000	2,000	1,000	1,000	16,000

Average (Accounting) Rate of Return (ARR)

The average rate of return or the accounting rate of return method measures the net return each year as a percentage of the capital cost of the investment.

$$\text{Average Rate of Return (ARR) (\%)} = \frac{\text{Net return (profit) per annum}}{\text{Capital outlay (cost)}} \times 100$$

Worked example

The capital cost and expected net cash flow from three investment projects is shown in Table 5.

Table 5 The capital cost and net cash flow from three investment projects

	Project X	Project Y	Project Z
Capital cost	£50,000	£40,000	£90,000
Return Yr 1	£10,000	£10,000	£20,000
Yr 2	£10,000	£10,000	£20,000
Yr 3	£15,000	£10,000	£30,000
Yr 4	£15,000	£15,000	£30,000
Yr 5	£20,000	£15,000	£30,000
Total net cash flows	£70,000	£60,000	£130,000

A business would first calculate the net cash flow from each project by subtracting its capital cost from the total net cash flow of the project, i.e. £70,000 - £50,000 = £20,000 for Project X. The next step is to calculate the profit per annum by dividing the profit by the number of years the project runs for, i.e. £20,000 ÷ 5 = £4,000 for X. Finally, the ARR is calculated by using the above formula, i.e.:

$$\text{ARR (Project X)} = \frac{£4,000}{£50,000} \times 100 = \textbf{8\%}$$

The results for all three projects are shown in Table 6. Project Y would be chosen because it gives a higher ARR (10 per cent) than the other two.

Table 6 The ARR calculated for three investment projects

	Project X	Project Y	Project Z
Capital cost	£50,000	£40,000	£90,000
Total net profit (net cash flow – capital cost)	£20,000	£20,000	£40,000
Net profit p.a. (profit ÷ 5)	£4,000	£4,000	£8,000
ARR	8%	10%	8.9%

Advantages of the ARR method

The advantage of this method is that it shows clearly the profitability of an investment project. Not only does it allow a range of projects to be compared, the overall rate of return can be compared to other uses for investment funds. In the example in Table 6, if a company can gain 12 per cent by placing its funds in a bank account, it might choose to postpone the investment project until interest rates fall. It is also easier to identify the opportunity cost of investment.

Question 2

Hastings Group focuses on the development, production, installation and support of electrical, electronic and mechanical components for aircraft, helicopters, missiles and targeting systems. The company has a leading position in the field of aircraft and helicopter services, customisation and modification. Hastings' employees are engineers and skilled workers. In 2015 the directors identified three investment projects that would benefit the company:

· research and development (R & D)
· marketing campaign
· some new CNC machinery.

Discounted cash flow (net present value or NPV)

When making an investment decision a business might take into account what cash flow or profit earned in the future is worth at the present value. Look at Table 8. This shows that £100 invested today at a compound interest rate of 10 per cent would be worth £161 in five years' time.

- In one year's time, the investment would be worth £110. Of this, £10 would be the interest and £100 would be the initial investment.
- In two years' time, it would be worth £121. With compound interest, the interest is based not on the initial investment but on the investment at the end of the first year. So interest is 10 per cent of £110, making £11. Then this has to be added to the £110 value at the end of the first year to make a total of £121 for the second year.

This carries on until the value after five years is £161.

Table 8 Value of £100 invested over five years at 10 per cent per annum compound interest

Year	1	2	3	4	5
Value of £100	£110	£121	£133	£146	£161

If £100 today is worth £161 in five years' time, it must be true that £161 in five years' time is worth just £100 today. This is an example of an important insight of discounted cash-flow techniques. Money in the future is worth less than the same amount now (the **present value**). This is because money available today could be invested and it could earn interest.

Note that this is a completely different idea to the fact that money in the future can also become devalued due to the effects of inflation. Inflation does indeed affect future values of money. So there are two effects on the value of future money. Discounted cash-flow techniques just deal with one of these, the effect of interest rates.

The capital cost and expected cash flows for the investment projects are shown in Table 7.

(a) (i) Calculate the average rate of return for each project.

(ii) Explain which project should be selected.

(b) Explain the advantages to Hastings Group of using this method of appraisal.

Table 7 Capital cost and net cash flow for three investment projects

								£000
Investment project	Capital cost	2015	2016	2017	2018	2019	2020	Total
R & D	9,600	0	0	2,500	4,600	5,000	5,500	17,600
Marketing campaign	9,000	5,000	4,000	3,000	2,000	1,000	1,000	16,000
New CNC machinery	7,800	2,000	2,000	2,000	2,000	2,000	2,000	12,000

Discount tables can be used to show by how much a future value must be multiplied to calculate its present value. Table 9 shows a discount table with five different rates of interest. If an investment project was predicted to give a net cash flow of £10,000 in three years' time, and the discount rate was 10 per cent, then reading off the table, the £10,000 would need to be multiplied by 0.75. To arrive at its present value the calculation would be:

£10,000 × 0.75 = £7,500

Cash flow or profit of £15,000 from a project received in five years' time, at a discount rate of 20 per cent, would be worth £6,000 in the present (£15,000 × 0.40).

The discount table shown in Table 9 also shows two features of discounting.

- The higher the rate of discount, the less the present value of cash flow in future. This is the reverse of saying that the higher the rate of interest, the greater will be the value of an investment in the future.
- The further into the future the cash flow or earnings from an investment project, the less is their present value. So £1,000 earned in five years' time is worth less than £1,000 earned in one year's time. Again this is simply the opposite way of saying that £1,000 invested today at a fixed rate of interest will be worth more in five years' time than in one year's time.

Table 9 Discount table

Year	5%	10%	15%	20%	25%
				Rate of discount	
0	1.00	1.00	1.00	1.00	1.00
1	0.95	0.91	0.87	0.83	0.80
2	0.91	0.83	0.76	0.69	0.64
3	0.86	0.75	0.66	0.58	0.51
4	0.82	0.68	0.57	0.48	0.41
5	0.78	0.62	0.50	0.40	0.33
6	0.75	0.56	0.43	0.33	0.26
7	0.71	0.51	0.38	0.28	0.21
8	0.68	0.47	0.33	0.23	0.17
9	0.64	0.42	0.28	0.19	0.13
10	0.61	0.39	0.25	0.16	0.11

Calculating NPV: The **net present value** method makes use of discounted cash flow. It calculates the rate of return on an investment project taking into account the effects of interest rates and time. Using discount tables, it is possible to calculate the net present value of an investment project.

Worked example

Table 10 shows three investment projects. The initial cost of each investment project is £50,000, shown in the Year 0 row. In years 1 to 10, each produces a stream of net cash flow. When added up, these exceed the initial £50,000. So it might appear that each investment project is profitable. However, if the net cash flow is discounted using a discount rate of 20 per cent, the picture is very different.

Table 10 Net present value of three investment projects discounted at 20 per cent

Year	Project A		Project B		Project C		
	Net cash flow £	Present value £	Net cash flow £	Present value £	Net cash flow £	Present value £	Discount table Rate of discount at 20%
0	(50,000)	(50,000)	(50,000)	(50,000)	(50,000)	(50,000)	1.00
1	10,000	8,300	5,000	4,150	20,000	16,600	0.83
2	10,000	6,900	8,000	5,520	16,000	11,040	0.69
3	10,000	5,800	10,000	5,800	14,000	8,120	0.58
4	10,000	4,800	12,000	5,760	12,000	5,760	0.48
5	10,000	4,000	12,000	4,800	12,000	4,800	0.40
6	10,000	3,300	12,000	3,960	12,000	3,960	0.33
7	10,000	2,800	12,000	3,360	12,000	3,360	0.28
8	10,000	2,300	14,000	3,220	10,000	2,300	0.23
9	10,000	1,900	16,000	3,040	8,000	1,520	0.19
10	10,000	1,600	20,000	3,200	5,000	800	0.16
Total net cash flow before discounting	50,000		71,000		71,000		
Present values years 1–10		41,700		42,810		£58.260	
Net present value (NPV)		(8,300)		(7,190)		+8,260	

- **Project A.** The sum of the present values in years 1–10 for Project A is just £41,700. The net cash flow each year is constant at £10,000, but the present value of each of those £10,000 falls the further away it is received. By year 10, the present value of £10,000 discounted at 20 per cent is just £1,600. The net present value can be calculated simply by totalling the present value figures in years 0–10, including subtracting the initial cost. Or it can be calculated using the formula:

  Net present value = present values − initial cost = £41,700 − £50,000 = −£8,300

  So Project A is unprofitable according to discounted cash-flow techniques.

- **Project B.** The total net cash flow before discounting is higher than for Project A: £71,000 compared to £50,000. But once discounted, there is little difference in the sum of the present values. This is because net cash flow in Project B is weighted towards later years. The net present value of this project is £42,810 − £50,000 = −£7,190. Again, Project B is unprofitable according to discounted cash-flow techniques.

- **Project C.** The total net cash flow before discounting is the same as with Project B. Indeed, the pattern of net cash flow is an exact reverse of those of Project B. Here, the higher net cash-flow figures are concentrated at the start and fall off towards the end. This means that the total present value is much higher than with Project B. The net present value of Project C is £58,260 − £50,000 = £8,260. This is the discounted profit that the business will make on this project.

The net present value method would suggest that a business should go ahead with any investment projects that have a positive net present value. If a business has to make a choice between investment projects for whatever reason, it should go for those with the highest net present value. So in this case it would choose Project C.

Advantages of the discounted cash-flow method

- The discounted cash-flow method, unlike the payback method and the average rate of return, correctly accounts for the value of future earnings by calculating present values.
- The discount rate used can be changed as risk and conditions in financial markets change. For example, in the 1990s, the cost of bank borrowing for many businesses fell from over 15 per cent to 7–8 per cent. Investment projects therefore did not need to make such a high rate of return to be profitable and so the rate of discount could be lowered. Since 2008 rates have been even lower.

Exam tip

Remember that discounted cash flow is used to take into account the effect that interest rates have on investment decisions. It **does not** take into account the effects of inflation. This is a common error made by students.

Limitations of these techniques

Each of the three methods of investment appraisal outlined above has some limitations. These are summarised in Table 11.

Table 11 Limitations of the methods of investment

Appraisal method	Limitations
Simple payback	Cash earned after the payback period is ignored
	The profitability of the method is overlooked
Average rate of return	The effects of time on the value of money are ignored
Discounted cash flow	The calculation is more complex than the other methods
	The rate of discount is critical – if it is high, fewer projects will be profitable

Question 3

Gethings is a garment manufacturer in London. It is considering making an investment in one of two machines, A and B. The projected net cash flows for each machine are shown in Table 12.

Table 12 Expected net cash flow from two investment projects

							£000
Year	0	1	2	3	4	5	6
	Initial cost						
Machine A							
Net cash flow	(600)	100	150	200	300	200	100
Discounted cash flow							
Machine B							
Net cash flow	(600)	200	300	200	150	100	100
Discounted cash flow							

(a) Calculate the discounted cash flow for each machine and each year using a discount rate of 15 per cent from the discount table on the previous page, Table 9.

(b) Calculate the net present value for each machine.

(c) Explain why Gethings might buy Machine B if it uses the net present value method of decision making.

Thinking bigger

A number of qualitative factors should also be taken into account when appraising investment opportunities. These are non-financial considerations.

Human relations: Some investment projects can have a huge impact on the staff in an organisation. For example, investment in plant automation might lead to mass redundancies. A business might decide to postpone plans to automate their plant if it thought the damage to human relations in the organisation would be too severe.

Ethical considerations: Along with many other business decisions, managers are taking more of an ethical stance when choosing courses of action. For example, a chemicals producer might decide to build a new plant in a location that does not minimise financial costs, but does reduce environmental damage. Such a decision might help to enhance the image of a company. Companies are increasingly keen to be seen as 'good corporate citizens'.

Risk: The financial position in which a business finds itself is one factor in assessing the risk of an investment project. Others include the state of the economy and the markets into which a business sells. Investment projects that have long payback periods are also riskier than ones with shorter payback periods.

Availability of funds: Some investment projects fail to get started because businesses are unable to raise the money needed to fund the project. A significant proportion of these will be small businesses that have difficulty in persuading investors and lenders to provide finance.

Business confidence: Entrepreneurs, managers and businesses tend to have different attitudes and cultures from each other. One aspect of this is confidence or optimism. Some decision makers tend to be very cautious, seeing all the problems that might arise if things go wrong. Others are confident and optimistic. They see the future as much better and brighter than the average. This has a crucial impact on investment. The cautious, unconfident entrepreneur or manager may delay or abandon possible investment projects. In the same circumstances with the same investment projects, confident and optimistic managers will tend to go ahead and authorise the expenditure. So the deeply held attitudes of decision makers have an important influence on investment decision-making.

Links 🔗

One way you can demonstrate synoptic skills here is to link investment appraisal with a possible decision to locate a production operation abroad. For example, a business might face a choice between several different overseas locations. It might use one of the investment appraisal techniques discussed in this unit to help decide which location might generate the best returns. Choosing an overseas location is discussed in Unit 73. In general, investment appraisal might be used to help make decisions when the costs and expected net cash flows from different options can be clearly identified or estimated – when choosing between different corporate strategies, for example.

Key terms

Average rate of return or **accounting rate of return (ARR)** – a method of investment appraisal that measures the net return per annum as a percentage of the initial spending.

Capital cost – the amount of money spent when setting up a new venture.

Discounted cash flow (DCF) – a method of investment appraisal that takes interest rates into account by calculating the present value of future income.

Investment – the purchase of capital goods.

Investment appraisal – the evaluation of an investment project to determine whether or not it is likely to be worthwhile.

Net cash flow – cash inflows minus cash outflows.

Net present value (NPV) – the present value of future income from an investment project, minus the cost.

Payback period – the amount of time it takes to recover the cost of an investment project.

Present value – the value today of a sum of money available in the future.

Knowledge check

1. What is meant by the term 'investment in business'?

2. Explain briefly how a business would appraise investment using the payback period.

3. What are the advantages of the payback method of investment appraisal?

4. What is the formula for calculating ARR?

5. What does the average or accounting rate of return method of investment appraisal aim to measure?

6. Give one advantage of the ARR method of investment appraisal.

7. What is the formula for calculating NPV?

8. Why is the discounted cash flow/NPV method of appraisal used in business?

9. Give one limitation of the payback method of investment appraisal.

10. Suggest how environmental considerations may affect an investment decision.

11. Give two other qualitative factors that might influence an investment decision.

Case study

FLORIpori LTD

The management team of FLORIpori Ltd, a large but poorly performing flower grower, has recently bought the company for £100,000. The company employs 112 staff and operates from a farm in Devon. It grows a range of cut flowers, pot plants, herbs and shrubs.

The new management team believes it can transform the business into a profit-making concern. In the previous year the company lost £260,000 on sales of £1,256,000. The team believes that the old management were not prepared to take risks. Consequently they have failed to invest in new technology and working methods, and fallen behind their competitors.

Dave Williams, the new managing director, has already earmarked £5 million for investment. Initially four investment projects were identified, but two were eliminated at a preliminary stage using the payback method of appraisal. The two remaining projects are now being appraised. One of these projects involves constructing some giant 'state-of-the-art' greenhouses to extend the growing season by up to 25 per cent. The other involves introducing total quality management (TQM) right across the organisation. The capital cost of the two projects and the expected cash flows are shown in Table 13. The present value of £1 receivable at the end of 5 years at 5 per cent is shown in Table 14.

The new owners of the company are very optimistic about its future direction. However, the workforce does not share their enthusiasm. Many of them are worried about the proposed investment plans. The age profile of the workforce is high. More than 50 per cent of the workers are over 55 and have never worked anywhere else. Many of them joined the company when they left school and undertook horticulture apprenticeships. If FLORIpori select the greenhouse project about 40 staff may lose their jobs because of the improved efficiency of the new system. Also, an employee representative said, 'The introduction of TQM will create pressure and stress for many of the folk here . . . Some of them just aren't up to it.'

Table 13 Capital cost and expected cash flows for FLORIpori Ltd investment projects

Investment project	Cost	Year 1	Year 2	Year 3	Year 4	Year 5	Total
Greenhouses (£m)	5	2.3	2.6	2.8	3.3	3.2	14.2
Introduce TQM (£m)	4.4	2.1	2.1	2.3	2.4	2.5	11.4

Table 14 The present value of £1 receivable at the end of five years at 5 per cent

After	0 yr	1 yr	2 yrs	3 yrs	4 yrs	5 yrs
Present value of £1	£1.00	£0.95	£0.90	£0.86	£0.82	£0.78

(a) Calculate the average rate of return of each investment project. (4 marks)

(b) Calculate the net present value of each investment project. (4 marks)

(c) Explain one advantage of the net present value method of investment appraisal to FLORIpori Ltd. (4 marks)

(d) Assess which investment project FLORIpori should select. (12 marks)

Key points

1. Construct and interpret simple decision tree diagrams.
2. Calculations and interpretations of figures generated by these techniques.
3. Limitations of using decision trees.

Getting started

When making a business decision it is helpful to use a quantitative decision-making technique, if possible. This involves the application of numerical values, which can be compared easily. For example, Latika Naidu runs a successful import business, Gujurat Craftwork, based in Coventry, buying craft products from India. The company sells the items to a network of retailers in the UK. Latika wants to expand the business and has identified two clear options.

1. Begin importing products from the Middle East to expand the product range.

2. Set up an online operation to sell more widely.

Latika paid a business consultant £500 to help make the decision. This was quite helpful. The consultant said the probability of success for the first option was 0.5, or 50 per cent. In contrast, the probability of success for the second option was 0.72, or 72 per cent. The cost of both options is very similar, but Latika will only choose one option.

Which option do you think Latika should choose? Explain your answer. Why might using a quantitative decision-making approach improve the quality of decision making? What might be the drawbacks of using such an approach?

Making decisions

Every day, businesses make decisions. Most, if not all, involve some risk. This could be because the business has limited information on which to base the decision. Furthermore, the outcome of the decision may be uncertain. Launching a new product in a market abroad can be risky because a firm may not have experience of selling in that market. It may also be unsure about how consumers will react.

When faced with a number of different decisions a business will want to choose the course of action which gives the most return. What if a printing company had to decide whether to invest £750,000 in a new printing press now or wait a few years? If it bought now and a more efficient machine became available next year then it might have been more profitable to wait. Alternatively, if it waits it may find the old machine has problems and costs increase.

When the outcome is uncertain, decision trees can be used to help a business reach a decision which could minimise risk and gain the greatest return.

What are decision trees?

A **decision tree** is a method of tracing the alternative outcome of any decision. The likely results can then be compared so that the business can find the most profitable alternative. For example, a business may be faced with two alternatives – to launch a new product in Europe or in the USA. A decision tree may show that launching a new product in Europe is likely to be more successful than launching a new product in the USA.

It is argued by some that decision making is more effective if a **quantitative approach** is taken. This is where information on which decisions are based, and the outcomes of decisions, are expressed as numbers. In a decision tree, numerical values are given to such information. The decision tree also provides a pictorial approach to decision making because a diagram is used which resembles the branches of a tree. The diagram maps out different courses of action, possible outcomes of decisions and points where decisions have to be made. Calculations based on the decision tree can be used to determine the 'best' likely outcome for the business and hence the most suitable decision.

Features of decision trees

Decision trees have a number of features. These can be seen in Figure 1 which shows the decision tree for a business that has to decide whether to launch a new advertising campaign or retain an old one.

Figure 1

A simple decision tree based on a decision whether to retain an existing advertising campaign or begin a new one

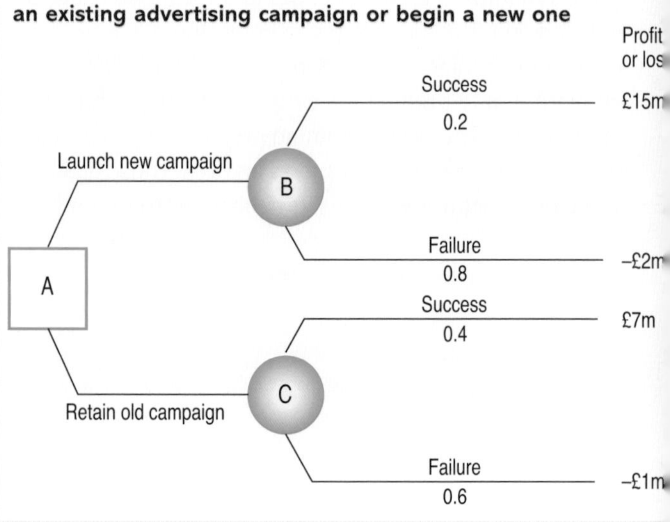

Decision points: Points where decisions have to be made in a decision tree are represented by squares and are called decision points. The decision maker has to choose between certain courses of action. In this example, the decision is whether to launch a new campaign or retain the old one.

Outcomes: Points where there are different possible outcomes in a decision tree are represented by circles and are called **chance nodes**. At these chance nodes it can be shown that a particular course of action might result in a number of outcomes. In this example, at 'B' there is a chance of failure or success of the new campaign.

Probability or chance: The **likelihood** of possible outcomes happening is represented by probabilities in decision trees. The chance of a particular outcome occurring is given a value. If the outcome is certain then the probability is 1. Alternatively, if there is no chance at all of a particular outcome occurring, the probability will be 0. In practice the value will lie between 0 and 1. In Figure 1, at 'B' the chance of success for the new campaign is 0.2 and the chance of failure is 0.8.

It is possible to estimate the probability of events occurring provided information about these events can be found. There are two sources of information which can be used to help estimate probabilities. One source is **backdata**. For example, if a business has opened 10 new stores in recent years, and 9 of them have been successful, it might be reasonable to assume that the chances of another new store being successful are 9/10 or 0.9. Another source is research data. For example, a business might carry out market research to find out how customers would react to a new product design. 80 per cent of people surveyed may like the product and 20 per cent may dislike it.

Expected monetary values: This is the financial outcome of a decision. It is based on the predicted profit or loss of an outcome and the probability of that outcome occurring. The profit or loss of any decision is shown on the right-hand side of Figure 1. For example, if the launch of a new campaign is a success, a £15 million profit is expected. If it fails a loss of £2 million is expected

Calculating expected monetary values (EMV)

What should the firm decide? It has to work out the expected values of each decision, taking into account the expected profit or loss and the probabilities. So, for example, the expected value of a new campaign is:

$$\begin{array}{cc} \text{Success} & \text{Failure} \\ \text{Expected value} = 0.2 \times £15m & + 0.8 \times (-£2m) \\ \text{(probability) (expected profit)} & \text{(probability) (expected loss)} \\ = £3m & - £1.6m \\ = 1.4m \end{array}$$

The expected value of retaining the current campaign is:

$$\begin{array}{cc} \text{Success} & \text{Failure} \\ \text{Expected value} = 0.4 \times £7m & + 0.6 \times (-£1m) \\ = £2.8m & - £0.6m \\ = 2.2m \end{array}$$

From these figures the firm should continue with the existing campaign because the expected value is higher.

Numerous outcomes

It is possible to have more than two outcomes at a chance node. For example, at point 'B' in Figure 1 there might have been three outcomes.

- The probability of great success may be 0.2 with a profit of £15 million.
- The probability of average success may be 0.4 with a profit of £6 million.
- The probability of failure may be 0.4 with a loss of −£2 million.

The expected value is now:

$$\begin{aligned} &= (0.2 \times £15m) + (0.4 \times £6m) + (0.4 \times -£2m) \\ &= £3m + £2.4m - £0.8m \\ &= £4.6m \end{aligned}$$

Question 1

BGS Holdings owns a chain of 32 pubs and bars in the north of England. Due to intense competition, revenue has fallen in the last couple of years. As a means of boosting revenue it has been suggested that the chain, in line with many other competitors, should use 'happy hours' to attract more customers. Traditionally a 'happy hour' is a period of time (not always an hour) where drinks are sold at reduced prices. The problem though is choosing the right 'hour' when prices should be reduced. It is thought not to be a good idea to choose a period of time which is already popular. This is because sales of drinks would already be very high and to cut prices during this time would reduce margins significantly. In order to help make the decision an investigation was carried out in a sample of four pubs. The data gathered during the investigation is shown in Table 1.

Table 1 Happy hour data gathered by BGS Holdings

Happy hour period	Probability of success	Estimated effect on profit	Probability of failure	Estimated effect on profit	Expected monetary value
3–4pm	0.5	+£1,300	?	−£200	?
4–5pm	0.5	+£1,700	?	−£400	?
5–6pm	0.7	+£400	?	−£1,200	?
6–7pm	0.6	+£1,000	?	−£800	?
7–8pm	0.6	+£1,100	?	−£400	?

(a) Complete Table 1.

(b) On financial grounds, when should the 'happy hour' be arranged?

Decisions, outcomes and costs

In practice businesses face many alternative decisions and possible outcomes. Take a farmer who has inherited some land, but does not wish to use it with his existing farming business. There are three possible decisions that the farmer could make.

- Sell the land. The market is depressed and this will earn £0.6 million.
- Wait for one year and hope that the market price improves. A land agent has told the farmer that the chance of an upturn in the market is 0.3, while the probabilities of it staying the same or worsening are 0.5 and 0.2 respectively. The likely proceeds from a sale in each of the circumstances are £1 million, £0.6 million and £0.5 million.
- Seek planning permission to develop the land. The legal and administration fees would be £0.5 million and the probability of being refused permission would be 0.8, which means the likelihood of obtaining permission is 0.2. If refused, the farmer would be left with the same set of circumstances described in the second option.

If planning permission is granted the farmer has to make a decision (at node E). If the farmer decides to sell, the probability of getting a good price, i.e. £10 million, is estimated

to be 0.4, while the probability of getting a low price, i.e. £6 million, is 0.6. The farmer could also develop the land himself at a cost of £5 million. The probability of selling the developed land at a good price, i.e. £25 million, is estimated to be 0.3 while the likelihood of getting a low price, i.e. £10 million, is 0.7. The information about probability and earnings is shown in Figure 2.

Figure 2

The decisions faced by a farmer in the disposal of land

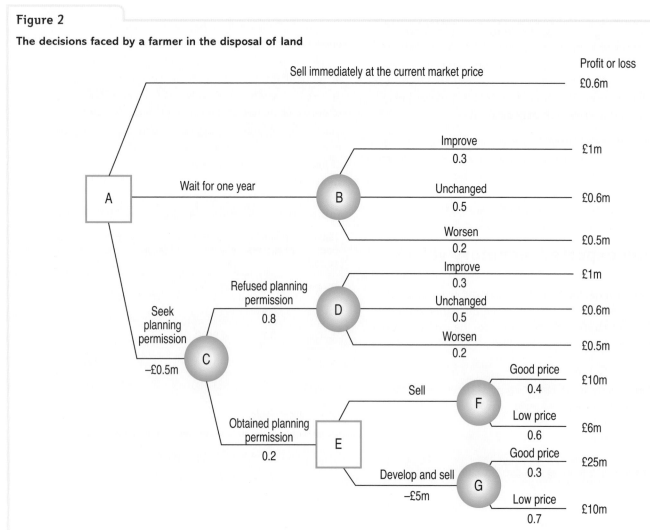

What decision should the farmer make? The sale of the land immediately will earn £0.6 million.

The expected monetary value of the second option, waiting a year, is:

Expected monetary value
= 0.3 × £1m + 0.5 × £0.6m + 0.2 × £0.5m
= £0.3m + £0.3m + £0.1m
= £0.7m

Since this earns more than the first option, it would be a better choice. We could show this in Figure 4 (on the next page) by crossing the 'selling immediately' path with a //, indicating that the first option will not be taken up. The expected value of the second option (£0.7 million) is shown in the diagram at node B.

A **rollback technique** can then be used to work out the expected value of the third option, seeking planning permission. This means working from right to left, calculating the expected values at each node in the diagram. The expected value at node D is:

Expected value = 0.3 × £1m + 0.5 × £0.6m + 0.2 × £0.5m
= £0.7m

The expected monetary value at node F is:

Expected value = 0.4 × £10m + 0.6 × £6m
= £4m + £3.6m
= £7.6m

The expected value at node G is:

Expected monetary value = 0.3 × £25m + 0.7 x £10m
= £7.5m + £7m
= £14.5m

At node E, a decision node, the farmer would choose to develop the land before selling it. This would yield an expected return of £9.5 million (£14.5 million – £5 million) which is higher than £7.6 million, i.e. the expected return from selling the land undeveloped. Thus, in Figure 4 the path representing this option can be crossed. The expected value at node C is now:

Expected monetary value = 0.2 × £9.5m + 0.8 × £0.7m
= £1.9m + £0.56m
= £2.46m

Finally, by subtracting the extra cost of seeking planning permission (£0.5 million), the expected value of the final option can be found. It is £1.96 million. Since this is the highest value, this would be the best option for the farmer. This means a // can be placed on the line to node B as £0.7 million is lower than £1.96 million. All of the expected values are shown in Figure 4 on the next page.

Figure 4 shows profit or loss (taking into account costs) and then the **extra** costs of planning permission are subtracted in the calculation. However, a decision tree may show revenue on

Question 2

Colin Andrews is the owner of Slade Farm near Spalding. He specialises in vegetable crops and allocates about 400 acres of land each year to the production of potatoes and swedes. He decides what crops to plant in October each year.

If Colin plants potatoes he estimates that the probability of a good crop is 0.3, which will generate £50,000 profit. The probability of an average crop is 0.3, which would result in £30,000 profit. The probability of a poor crop is 0.4, which would result in only £10,000 profit.

If swedes are planted, either a good crop or a bad crop will result. He estimates that the probability in each case is 0.5. A good crop will generate a profit of £40,000 and a poor crop only £10,000. Figure 3 is a decision tree which shows this information.

Figure 3
The alternative courses of action faced by Colin Andrews

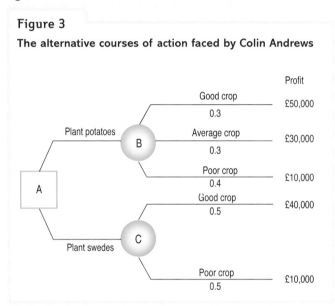

(a) What is happening at points B and C in the decision tree?
(b) Calculate the expected values of each course of action and decide, on financial grounds, which course Colin should take.

Maths tip

Probability can be expressed as a decimal, a fraction or a percentage. For example, the probability of an event might be 0.8, $\frac{4}{5}$ or 80 per cent. They all mean the same. However, when using decision trees it is common to use decimals to represent probability.

Exam tip

It is important to recognise that once a particular course of action has been chosen, the profit or revenue generated by that choice **is not** the same as the expected value. In the first example shown by the decision tree in Figure I, the expected value of the best option (retain the old campaign) was £4.6 million. However, the profit resulting from the decision will be either £7 million, or a loss of £1 million – it depends on the success of the campaign. But it is not £4.6 million, which is the expected value. Expected values are used to make the choice but they do not represent the actual amount of money made.

Figure 4

The final solution
to the farmer's decision problem (all expected values and unused routes are shown)

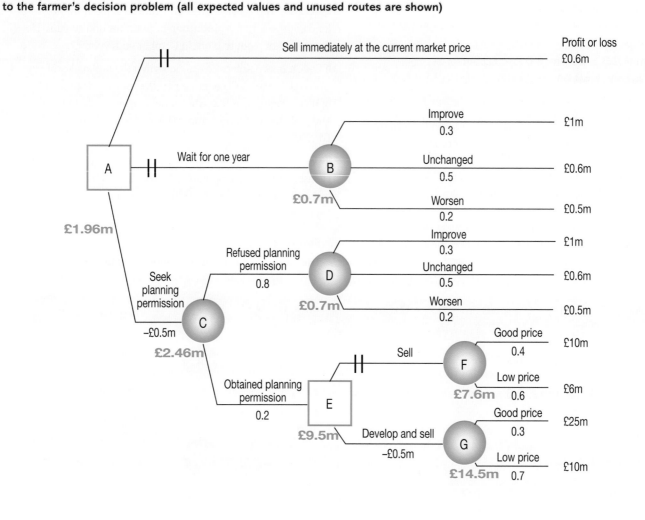

Advantages of decision trees

Decision trees can be applied to much more complicated problems. They have some major advantages.

- Constructing the tree diagram may show possible courses of action not previously considered.
- They involve placing numerical values on decisions. This tends to improve results.
- They force management to take account of the risks involved in decisions and help to separate important from unimportant risks.

Limitations of decision trees

The technique also has some limitations.

- The information which the technique 'throws out' is not exact. Much of it is based on probabilities which are often estimated.
- Decisions are not always concerned with quantities and the right side instead of profit, and all costs indicated on the diagram must be subtracted. Whichever is shown, the method of calculation is the same.

probabilities. They often involve people and are influenced by legal constraints or people's opinions, for example. These factors cannot always be shown by numerical values. Qualitatitive data may also be important.

- Time lags often occur in decision making. By the time a decision is finally made, some of the numerical information may be out of date.
- The process can be quite time-consuming, using up valuable business resources. However, computerised decision-making models can be used to analyse decision trees which can save some time.
- It is argued that decision makers, in an attempt to encourage a particular course of action, may manipulate the data. For example, a manager might be 'biased' when attaching probabilities to certain outcomes. This will distort the final results.
- Decision trees are not able to take into account the dynamic nature of business. For example, a sudden change in the economic climate might render a decision based on a decision tree obsolete.

Question 3

Trumed plc is a medical company that carries out research into new treatments for colds and influenza. It has won a contract from a large pharmaceuticals corporation to carry out research into new treatments. Trumed has identified three distinct research programmes to develop a vaccination to combat the strain. The code names for each programme are VAC1, VAC2 and VAC3. The cost of the programmes, the expected returns and the probabilities of success and failure are illustrated in the decision tree in Figure 5.

Figure 5

The costs, revenues and probabilities of success and failure of each research programme for Trumed plc

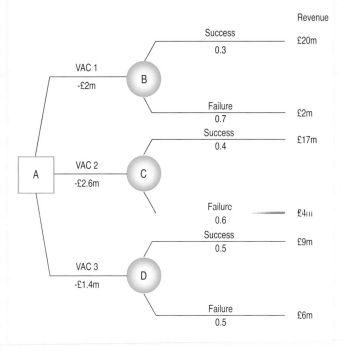

(a) Calculate the expected values of each research programme and advise Trumed which is the best option.

Links 🔗

Decision trees are quite a versatile decision-making technique. They can be used in a variety of circumstances. Consequently, it will be easier to demonstrate synoptic skills when discussing decision trees. For example, a business might use decision trees to help determine which course of action to take when deciding upon a price change, or which marketing strategy to select. Links can be made to a range of different areas in the specification – wherever a business might need to make a decision. Some examples of links between this unit and others include Pricing strategies (Unit 11), Marketing strategy (Unit 13), Business choices (Unit 24), Internal finance (Unit 26), External finance (Unit 27), Theories of corporate strategy (Unit 45), Investment appraisal (Unit 53) and Assessment of a country as a production location (Unit 73).

Key terms

Decision tree – a technique which shows all possible outcomes of a decision. The name comes from the similarity of the diagrams to the branches of trees.

Knowledge check

1. Why are decision trees useful when a business has to make important decisions?

2. What is meant by a quantitative approach to decision making?

3. What is meant by probability in a decision tree?

4. What is the difference between chance nodes and decision nodes?

5. How is the expected value of a course of action calculated?

6. What are the advantages and disadvantages of using decision trees?

7. State three possible situations where a business might make use of a decision tree.

Case study

OPAL MEDIA

Opal Media publishes a number of consumer magazines in the UK. It specialises in magazines for people involved in sports such as canoeing, snow boarding, surfing, paragliding, bowling, archery, skydiving and water-skiing. Opal Media currently owns 18 publications. In 2014, the company was concerned that one of its magazines, *Squash Monthly*, was not performing well enough. Its circulation figures had dwindled slowly but consistently over the last ten years. Pat

McMahon, head of marketing, believed that the fall in sales was due mainly to the decline in the popularity of the sport. Twenty years ago, *Squash Monthly*, was one of the company's 'stars'. It was now regarded as a 'dog' by many in the department and was barely breaking even.

The board at Opal Media asked Pat to look into the situation and make a recommendation. Pat identified a number of options open to the company. These are outlined on the next page.

Withdraw *Squash Monthly* from the market and replace it with a new magazine

The marketing department believes there might be a gap in the market for a magazine devoted entirely to the World Cup 2018. Obviously this would have a short life cycle because once the event is over sales would fall to zero. However, the amount of publicity that the event would get suggests that the potential for high sales levels for a short period of time could be enormous. It was also felt that competitors would not be interested in a magazine with such a short life cycle.

- With a thorough development programme the new magazine, called *World Cup '18*, could be launched in September 2016. The cost of thorough product development would be £400,000 and once launched net revenue of £3.5 million would be generated if the magazine was a complete success. The chances of this were estimated to be 0.5. If the magazine flopped, sales would only be £900,000. The chances of this were thought to be 0.2. If the magazine enjoyed moderate success (0.3 chance) sales of £1.8 million would be generated.

- If the product was launched with a rapid development programme it could come out in December 2015. This would cost £100,000. However, with a short development programme the quality would not be as good and as a result advertising revenue would be lower. If the launch was a complete success (0.6 chance) sales revenue of £2.8 million would be generated. If the magazine flopped (0.2 chance) revenue would be £500,000. With moderate success (0.2 chance) revenue would be £1.2 million.

Retain *Squash Monthly* in its existing form and invest £500,000 in an above-the-line promotion

This strategy would generate £3.9 million if successful and the chances of success are 0.4. If the investment fails to be a success only £700,000 will be generated.

Retain *Squash Monthly* and develop some extension strategies

Two alternative extension strategies were identified by the marketing department.

- Relaunch the magazine with new features, articles and some below-the-line promotion. The cost of this strategy would be £300,000 and if successful would generate revenue of £3 million. The probability of this was estimated at 0.5. If the strategy was unsuccessful only £600,000 would be generated.

- Launch *Squash Monthly* in Canada and America. This would be risky and more expensive but the rewards potentially higher at £8 million if completely successful. The costs would be £600,000 and the chance of complete success is estimated to be 0.3. If the magazine flopped in the new markets the revenue would only amount to £800,000.

The costs, revenues and probabilities of success and failure of Opal Media's options are shown in Figure 6.

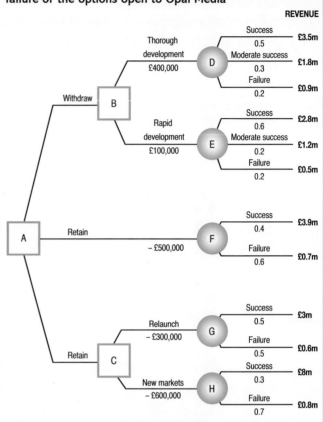

Figure 6

The costs, revenues and probabilities of success and failure of the options open to Opal Media

(Q)

(a) Calculate the expected values for each option and determine on financial grounds which option Opal Media should select. (10 marks)

(b) Just before the final decision was made by Opal, it was brought to the attention of the marketing department that future exchange rate forecasts would have an impact on the revenues earned in Canada and the USA. It was estimated that the pound would rise against the dollar over the next few years and the revenues earned could fall to £6.5m and £0.6m (depending on the success of the launch). How might this affect the decision? (4 marks)

(c) Evaluate the limitations to Opal Media of using decision trees to make a decision about the future of *Squash Monthly*. (20 marks)

Key points

1. Nature and purpose of critical path analysis.
2. Complete and interpret simple networks to identify the critical path.
3. Calculate: earliest start time, latest finish time and total float.
4. Limitations of using critical path analysis.

Getting started

Sometimes business activity involves project management. A project could be planning a product launch, refurbishing some premises, installing some new machinery, moving to a new location or constructing a factory. These projects are 'big jobs'. They involve lots of different tasks and might use a wide range of business resources. It is important to calculate how much time it will take to complete such a project and whether or not the completion time will be extended if a particular task is held up. Look at the example below.

Scotnect+ provides a connection service for the supply of electricity. It currently has a job connecting a new hotel to the national grid in a remote part of Scotland. The tasks required in the connection, and the order in which they should be completed, are as follows.

- Task A   Clear land   (3 days)
- Task B   Erect ten pylons   (6 days)
- Task C   Fit cabling   (4 days)
- Task D   Fit fuse box, junction and meter   (2 days)
- Task E   Safety testing   (1 day)

In this project Task C and Task D can be done at the same time.

What is meant by project management? How many days will it take Scotnect+ to complete the project? If Task D were delayed by 1 day what impact would this have on the completion time? Why is it important to know how long a project will take to complete before starting?

Nature and purposes of critical path analysis

In business there is a well-known saying that 'time is money'. What exactly does this mean? One interpretation is that if tasks are completed more quickly, the business will benefit financially. For example, if a company completes an order in five weeks instead of six weeks there will be some real benefits. Once the order is completed resources are available for other tasks, the customer will get the order more quickly and the business can ask for payment earlier. Completing tasks more quickly will improve efficiency and profitability. One established method used to improve the management of time and other resources is critical path analysis (CPA). The technique, which makes use of network diagrams, can be used to calculate the minimum

time needed to complete a project. It can also identify possible delays, which could have a crucial effect on its completion date. CPA has a number of uses and can be used in a range of industries. It is a helpful tool when managing large projects that may take many days, weeks, months or even years to complete. If such projects have hundreds or thousands of tasks, CPA can aid planning, organisation and resource management. It is used commonly in the construction industry, engineering, product development, software design, plant maintenance, aerospace and defence industries.

Efficiency: Producing a network diagram can help a business to operate efficiently. For example, a network shows those tasks that can be carried out at the same time. This can help save production or installation time and the use of resources. Highlighting exactly which delays are crucial to the timing of the project can help a business to meet deadlines. Inability to meet a deadline can be costly for a business. Orders may be lost if goods are not produced on time. In the construction industry, clients sometimes have penalty clauses in contracts. These are costs payable by the building company if it does not meet its deadlines. Sometimes building firms earn bonuses for coming in 'on time' or beating deadlines.

Decision making: The use of business models, such as network analysis, is argued to be a more scientific and objective method of making decisions. It is suggested that estimating the length of time a project will take based on past information and an analysis of the tasks involved should lead to deadlines being met more effectively, as the implications of delays can be assessed, identified and prevented.

Time-based management: Some businesses operate time-based management systems. These are techniques to minimise the length of time spent in business processes. Identifying tasks that have to be done in order, tasks that can be done together and tasks that may delay the whole project if not completed on time will all help to ensure that the least time is taken to complete an operation.

Working capital control: Identifying when resources will be required in projects can help a business to manage its working capital cycle. Network diagrams allow a business to identify exactly when materials and equipment will be used in a project. For instance, materials can be purchased when required, rather

Maths tip

The arithmetic needed for critical path analysis is very basic – just adding and subtracting. However, to avoid mistakes it is important that your network diagram is big enough to contain all the information needed and is also clearly labelled. Try to draw all arrows with straight lines. It might also be helpful to use more than one colour.

than holding costly stocks. This is especially important if a business operates a 'just-in-time' system of stock control. If a business has to borrow to purchase materials then charges or interest costs may be reduced if materials are only bought when required. If delays are identified and taken into account then resources can be allocated to other operations until they are needed.

Networks

Many of the operations carried out by businesses are made up of a number of tasks. The operation is only complete when all of the tasks have taken place. For example, the tasks involved in changing a set of strings on a guitar for an instrument repairer might include:

- slackening the strings
- removing the strings
- cleaning the fretboard
- attaching new strings
- retuning the strings.

These tasks must be carried out in order for the operation to take place. Each task will take a certain amount of time. The operation is shown in Figure 1 on a network diagram. The operation takes 20 minutes to carry out (1 minute + 1 minute + 5 minutes + 10 minutes + 3 minutes).

Some operations are less simple, with many tasks involved. Figure 2 shows a network diagram for an operation carried out by a cake manufacturer to make cakes for a wedding reception. In this operation some of the tasks can be carried out at the same time. So, for example, some of the ingredients can be prepared at the same time. Ingredient A takes 10 minutes to

Figure 1

A simple network

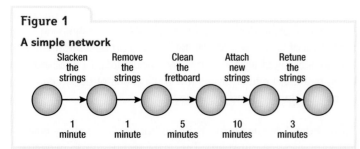

Figure 2

A more complex network

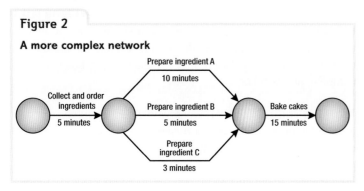

Question 1

An airline company is considering improvements to its turnaround time for planes from the moment a plane arrives at the airport terminal to the time it leaves. Figure 3 shows a network diagram for the turnaround.

Figure 3

Turnaround time for a passenger aircraft

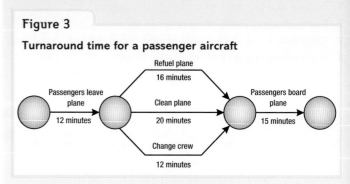

(a) What is the minimum amount of time it takes for the turnaround of the aeroplane?

(b) If the company could cut the time it takes to clean a plane from 20 minutes to 14 minutes, would that affect the time change?

prepare, which is longer than any of the other ingredients. So the whole operation must take 30 minutes (5 minutes + 10 minutes + 15 minutes). This assumes tasks A, B and C can be carried out at the same time.

Network analysis

Businesses often have to complete large projects, which involve a series of complicated tasks or activities which must be carried out in a certain order. The use of networks helps a business to manage these projects effectively.

It is vital that a business knows the minimum length of time a project will take to complete. It is also important to know whether a delay in completing individual tasks in an operation will delay the whole project. Network analysis allows a business to find the sequence or 'path' of tasks which are critical to the project and which, if delayed, will cause delays in the entire operation. In practice, businesses may use computers to manage large projects, such as the construction of a road system or hospital, or the manufacture of a large urgent overseas order for new machinery.

Before any project starts, it is important that networks are planned. This involves identifying the tasks that are to take place, how long each will take and the order in which they will take place. This information may be based on previous experience of projects or from research carried out by the business.

Figure 4 on the next page shows a network for a construction company which is renovating a cottage. There are certain features to note about the network.

- Arrows and lines show the tasks or activities to be carried out to complete the project. For example, Task B involves removing and replacing brickwork and flooring in the cottage.
- Some tasks can be carried out together, at the same time. For example, Tasks B and C can take place together but only after Task A has been completed.
- Arrows and lines cannot cross.

- Each task takes a certain amount of time. For example, the business plans to take four days to complete Task B, removing and replacing the brickwork and flooring in the cottage.
- Tasks must be completed in a certain order. Certain tasks are dependent on others being completed. For example, Task D, fitting new windows, and Task E, rewiring, cannot begin until Task B, removing and replacing brickwork and flooring, has taken place.
- Circles on the diagram, called **nodes**, show the start and finish of a task or activity. For example, Task A, preparing and organising materials, starts at Node 1 and ends at Node 2.
- There is always a node at the start and end of the project.
- Nodes contain information about the timing involved in the project.

Figure 4

Network for a cottage renovation

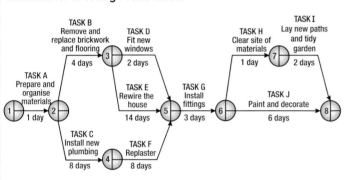

Calculating the earliest start times

The first stage in determining the critical path in the network is to calculate the earliest time at which each of the tasks or activities can start, called the **earliest start time** (EST). These are shown in the top right of the nodes. Figure 5 shows the earliest start times for all tasks in the renovation of the cottage.

Node 1: Task A can begin immediately. So 0 is placed in the EST in Node 1.

Node 2: Task A takes 1 day to complete. Tasks B and C, which can be carried out at the same time, can only begin after Task A is completed. So they can only begin after 1 day. This is placed in the EST in Node 2.

Node 3: Task B takes 4 days to complete. Together with the 1 day to complete Task A, this means that Tasks D and E can't

Figure 5

Network showing the earliest start times for the cottage renovation

- Earliest start time

start until after 5 days (4 days + 1 day). This is placed in the EST in Node 3.

Node 4: Task C takes 8 days to complete. Together with the 1 day to complete Task A, this means that Task F can't start until after 9 days (8 days + 1 day). This is placed in the EST in Node 4.

Node 5: What will be the earliest start time for Task G which begins at Node 5?

- Tasks A, B and D take 7 days to complete (1 day + 4 days + 2 days)
- Tasks A, C and F take 17 days to complete (1 day + 8 days + 8 days)
- Tasks A, B and E take 19 days to complete (1 day + 4 days + 14 days).

Task G can only begin when all preceding tasks are completed. It is dependent on earlier tasks. The longest time to complete these tasks is 19 days. So the EST in Node 5 is 19 days and Task G can't start until after 19 days. This highlights an important rule when calculating earliest start times. Always choose the longest amount of time when placing the ESTs in nodes.

Node 8: Another example of this can be found when calculating the final node, Node 8. Tasks up to Node 6 have taken 22 days to complete. So Tasks H and J can only begin after 22 days. The time taken to complete Task J is 6 days. This is longer than the time taken to complete Tasks H and I, which is 3 days (2 days + 1 day). So the EST placed in Node 8 is 22 days + 6 days = 28 days.

As Node 8 is the final node, then 28 days is the time taken to complete the entire project.

Question 2

An advertising agency is working on a campaign for a large client for the launch of a new product. It has constructed a network showing the earliest start times for the different phases of the campaign.

Figure 6

Network for an advertising campaign

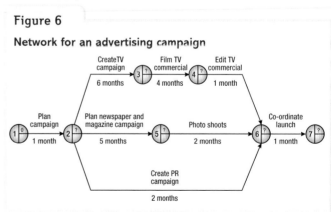

(a) Copy out the network in Figure 6 and fill in the earliest start times marked by '?'.

(b) What is the minimum amount of time the campaign will take to complete?

(c) In the one month taken to plan the campaign at the start, the advertising agency revises its estimate of the time taken to plan the newspaper and magazine campaign to 10 months. How will this affect (i) the earliest starting times and (ii) the overall time taken to complete the campaign?

337

Calculating the latest finish times

The next step involves calculating the latest times that each task can finish without causing the project to be delayed. The latest finish times (LFTs) of the project to renovate a cottage are shown in Figure 7. They appear at the bottom right of the nodes.

Calculating the latest finish times begins at the final node, Node 8. It has already been calculated that the project will take 28 days. This is placed in the LFT of Node 8. To calculate the LFTs of earlier nodes, use the formula:

LFT at node – time taken to complete previous task

So the LFT at Node 7, for Task H, is 28 days – 2 days = 26 days.

To calculate the LFT for Task G, to be placed in Node 6, again use the tasks which take the longest amount of time. Task J takes 6 days and Tasks H and I only 3 days (2 days + 1 day). So the LFT at Node 6 is 28 – 6 days = 22 days.

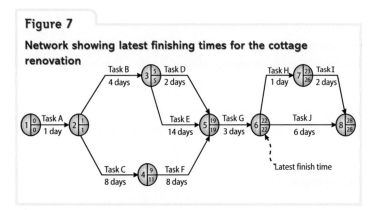

Figure 7

Network showing latest finishing times for the cottage renovation

Identifying the critical path

It is now possible to identify the critical path through the network. This shows the tasks which, if delayed, will lead to a delay in the project. The critical path on any network is where the earliest start times and the latest finish times in the nodes are the same. But it must also be the route through the nodes which takes the longest time.

Figure 8 shows the critical path and the tasks which can't be delayed if the renovation of the cottage is to be completed on time. These are tasks A, B, E, G and J. The critical path can be indicated by a broken line or crossed lines, or by some other method, such as highlighting the line in colour, by pen or on computer. Other tasks in the network do not lie on the critical path.

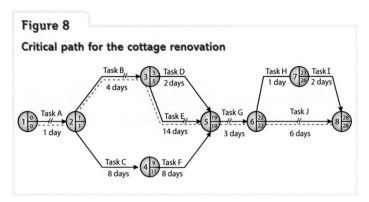

Figure 8

Critical path for the cottage renovation

Calculating the float

A business can use the information in the network to calculate the float time in the project. This is the amount of time by which a task can be delayed without causing the project to be delayed. For example, Task I takes 2 days to complete. However, as it does not lie on the critical path, it is possible that some delay can take place in this task without delaying the whole project. A delay of 1 day, for instance, would not lead to the project taking longer than 28 days.

How much delay can there be in tasks which do not lie on the critical path?

Total float: The total float is the amount of time by which a task can be delayed without affecting the project. It can be calculated as:

LFT of activity – EST of activity – duration

So for Task B in Figure 8, for example, it would be:

5 days – 1 day – 4 days = 0 days

Activities which lie on the critical path will always have a zero total float value.

For Task C, which does not lie on the critical path, the total float is:

11 days – 1 day – 8 days = 2 days

Table 1 shows the total float for all tasks.

Free float: The free float is the amount of time by which a task can be delayed without affecting the following task. It can be calculated by:

EST start of next task – EST start of this task – duration

So for Task C it would be:

9 – 1 – 8 = 0 days

Table 1 Float

									(days)
Task/activity	LFT	EST	Duration	Total float	EST next	EST this	Duration	Free float
A	1	0	1	0	1	0	1	0
B	5	1	4	0	5	1	4	0
C	11	1	8	2	9	1	8	0
D	19	5	2	12	19	5	2	12
E	19	5	14	0	19	5	14	0
F	19	9	8	2	19	9	8	2
G	22	19	3	0	22	19	3	0
H	26	22	1	3	23	22	1	0
I	28	23	2	3	28	23	2	3
J	28	22	6	0	28	22	6	0

Question 3

Hurford's is a specialist zinc galvanising business, coating steel components with zinc to prevent them from rusting. A network for one of its processes is shown in Figure 9.

Figure 9

Network for a zinc galvanising business

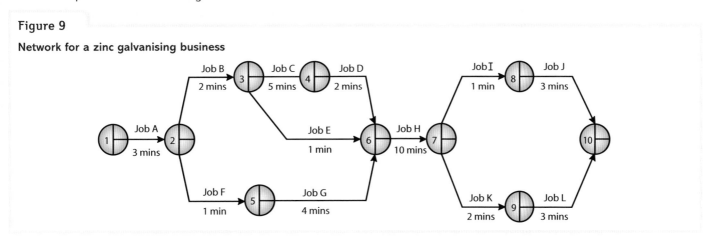

(a) Copy out Figure 9 and fill in the earliest start times for each job on your diagram.

(b) Fill in the latest finishing times on the diagram.

(c) Show the critical path on the diagram.

Limitations of critical path analysis

Although critical path analysis is clearly of value, a business must not assume that simply because it produces a network its project will be completed without delay. There are some limitations that businesses need to be aware of when using this technique.

- Information used to estimate times in the network may be incorrect. For example, management might have estimated times based on past performance, but a new project could have special requirements that take longer.
- Changes sometimes occur during the life of the project. For example, construction companies may need contingency plans to deal with unforeseen events, such as bad weather delaying operations. These need to be taken into account when producing a network.
- Although critical path analysis identifies times when resources might be used somewhere else in the business, these resources may be inflexible. For example, a giant crane may be identified as being available for a few days. However, if it takes several days to dismantle the crane, move it and reassemble it, it may not be feasible to use it at another location.
- With very large projects, such as building a skyscraper, network analysis can become complex with hundreds of thousands of tasks to take into account. However, the use of a computer may simplify the whole approach.

Exam tip

Drawing network diagrams, calculating ESTs, LFTs and floats may be challenging. However, with practice it becomes a lot easier. It is also important not to neglect your understanding of the nature, purpose and limitations of critical path analysis. It is possible for exam questions to focus on this and/or calculations.

Links 🔗

To demonstrate your synoptic skills when discussing critical path analysis in an exam you could make relevant links to a number of areas in the specification. For example, critical path analysis is used to improve efficiency and reduce waste in a business. Therefore it could be linked to Production, productivity and efficiency (Unit 37), Capacity utilisation (Unit 38) and lean production in Stock control (Unit 39). Remember also that critical path analysis can be used to manage a wide range of projects in business, such as planning marketing strategy, planning a product launch or relocating premises, for example.

Key terms

Earliest start time – how soon a task in a project can begin. It is influenced by the length of time taken by tasks which must be completed before it can begin.

Critical path – the tasks involved in a project which, if delayed, could delay the project.

Critical path analysis (CPA)/network analysis – a method of calculating the minimum time required to complete a project, identifying delays which could be critical to its completion.

Free float – the time by which a task can be delayed without affecting the following task.

Latest finish time – the latest time that a task in a project can finish.

Network diagram – a chart showing the order of the tasks involved in completing a project, containing information about the times taken to complete the tasks.

Nodes – positions in a network diagram which indicate the start and finish times of a task.

Total float – the time by which a task can be delayed without affecting the project.

Case study

NEWPORT HOLDINGS

Newport Holdings manufactures electronic components for domestic appliances. The company has received some large orders recently after a successful sales drive. However, to increase capacity and improve productivity it must replace the entire assembly line with up-to-date technology. The directors are keen to go ahead with the investment, but are worried about the disruption that will be caused. During the construction of the new assembly line production will be zero. The company can hold up to 30 days of stocks so the new line must be up and running within one month. If the new line isn't ready, Newport Holdings will lose approximately £200,000 per day. This will be unacceptable to the directors.

Figure 10 shows the network diagram for the installation of the new technology and Table 2 shows the tasks, task order and task times required to construct the new assembly line.

Figure 10

Network diagram for the installation of new technology at Newport Holdings

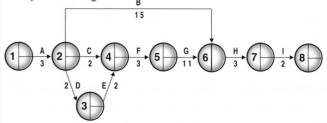

(a) For the activities required to install the new technology, calculate the earliest start times (ESTs). (4 marks)

(b) For the activities required to install the new technology, calculate the latest finish times (LFTs). (4 marks)

(c) Identify the critical path on the network diagram and hence, state the minimum amount of time in which the project can be completed. (4 marks)

(d) How will the construction time be affected if Task B is delayed by 4 days? (4 marks)

Table 2 The tasks, task order and task times required to construct the new assembly line

Task	Description	Order/dependency	Duration
A	Dismantle old line	Must be done first	3 days
B	Retrain staff	Must follow A	15 days
C	Position lifting gear	Must follow A	2 days
D	Remove roof panels	Must follow A	2 days
E	Lower in new plant	Must follow D	2 days
F	Replace roof panels	Must follow C and E	3 days
G	Install new plant	Must follow F	11 days
H	Test run	Must follow B and G	3 days
I	Safety checks	Must follow H	2 days

(e) Assess the advantages and disadvantages to Newport Holdings of using critical path analysis. (12 marks)

Knowledge check

1. Why is network analysis also known as 'critical path analysis'?
2. What is shown by a node on a network diagram?
3. Explain the difference between (a) the earliest start time and the latest finish time; (b) the total float and the free float.
4. Why can network analysis help improve the efficiency of a business?
5. What are the implications of network analysis for working capital control?

Key points

1. Corporate timescales: short-termism versus long-termism.
2. Evidence-based versus subjective decision making.

Getting started

Vincenzo Cicotti is the well-liked but 'maverick' leader of LiftWithPower, a manufacturer of forklift trucks. In 2014, a fierce rival made an offer for LiftWithPower that looked quite generous to shareholders. However, Vincenzo, who makes all the key decisions at the company, turned it down flat. He said: 'They'll change the name of the company. It's been in the family for years and I want to keep it the same.' However, at least one angry shareholder said that Vincenzo should have made a more informed decision. 'Why not get all the facts together, analyse them and then get back to them', was a view held by several others. Since Vincenzo had a history of making good business decisions the bid was soon forgotten. Also, Vincenzo wanted to build a business for the future and believed that his workforce of 3,200 would deliver results for the owners.

In the above case, Vincenzo made a subjective decision. What do you think this means? What approach to decision making did some of the shareholders recommend? Does Vincenzo take a short-term or long-term view when running LiftWithPower? Explain your answer.

Influences on business decisions

One of the main functions of the senior management team in a corporation is to make **strategic decisions**. These are important, far-reaching decisions that can have a **long-term** impact on a business. For example, if a business decides to build a new factory in an overseas location, this is not a decision that can be easily reversed. As a result the impact of the decision on the finances of the business, employees and operations will be felt for a long time. For large corporations, important business decisions are likely to be influenced by a number of key factors.

Corporate influences: Most businesses have a set strategy which has long-term objectives and **short-term** goals. Sometimes, in an attempt to boost profits they might make short-term decisions which do not fit into the long-term strategy. As a result they may decide, for example, to limit wage increases to just 1 per cent for three years. This might help to boost profits in the short term, but could adversely affect the long-term performance of the business if worker motivation declines.

Another corporate influence is whether business decisions are based on evidence or the subjective views of key decision makers. Subjective decision making is likely to carry more risk.

These corporate influences are discussed in more detail below.

Corporate culture: The culture of an organisation can influence decision making. For example, if the culture is open, creative, flexible and innovative, a business is more likely to make decisions that involve change. If a culture is more resistant to change, decisions are likely to be more cautious and involve less risk. This might result in less innovation and a loss of competitive edge. The effect of corporate culture on decision making is discussed in Unit 57.

Stakeholder perspective: Some corporations take a 'shareholder approach' when making business decisions. This means that the views of shareholders influence decision making, while those of other stakeholders are marginalised. For example, large shareholders, such as institutional investors like pension funds, may have an impact on the amount of risk taken by a company. In contrast, some corporations take a 'stakeholder approach'. This means that the views and needs of a wider range of stakeholders, such as customers, employees, suppliers and the environment, are considered when making strategic decisions. This is discussed in Unit 58.

Business ethics: Corporations with a strong ethical stance are likely to make different decisions from those that have little regard for ethics. For example, businesses with a strong sense of corporate social responsibility are not likely to choose a course of action that may threaten the environment, damage relations with local communities or upset the workforce. In contrast, a corporation that is not concerned with ethical issues may decide to invest cash reserves in, for example, a weapons manufacturer. However, even those who do not have a strong ethical stance or who would not make ethical decisions out of choice will still be influenced by these issues or potential bad publicity. The effect of ethical issues on decision making is discussed in Unit 59.

Corporate timescales

The outcome of decisions can have both a short-term and a long-term impact on a company. The long-term decisions are those that affect the vision, mission and objectives of the company. They could have an impact on the business in five or even ten years' time, for example. Short-term decisions are more operational in nature and are designed to achieve goals in, say, 12 months' time. Companies recognise this and therefore have to decide which is most important to them.

Short-termism

Some companies appear to be more short-termist than others. If this is the case they are likely to choose certain courses of action when making a decision. For example, they are more likely to do the following.

- **Maximise short-term profits.** Most companies that pursue short-term objectives aim to increase shareholder value. They are likely to do this by trying to maximise short-term profits. There are several ways they can do this. For example, they might try to maximise revenue by charging higher prices or investing heavily in persuasive advertising. They may also try to cut costs by investing less in research and development, which is discussed below, using cheaper resources (perhaps at the expense of quality) and switching suppliers on a regular basis.

- **Invest less money in research and development (R&D).** This is because research and development can be a big drain on cash reserves. A company will prefer to use this to help fund short-term objectives. Investment in R&D is also risky. Returns could be negative if R&D projects are fruitless. Even if R&D is successful, the financial returns can take many years to reap.

- **Invest less in training.** Training staff is also expensive and the returns are not immediate. The returns from training are likely to be positive because workers will be better motivated, better equipped to do their job and staff turnover will be lower. However, it will take time for the benefits to materialise.

- **Return cash to shareholders.** A business with large cash reserves may pay special dividends to shareholders instead of investing for the long term. For example, in 2014 Rexam, the beverage can-maker, returned £450 million to shareholders by paying them 57p per share. This was after the sale of the bulk of its healthcare business for £490 million.

- **Engage in asset stripping.** Asset stripping is where a business buys another business, often in financial difficulty, and breaks it up. The profitable parts are sold for cash and the loss-making sections are closed down. This practice is often considered unethical because there is no regard for the future of the company and its stakeholders. However, in the short term it can generate a quick cash return for shareholders of the predator.

- **Arrange more short-term contracts.** Companies with short-term objectives may rely more heavily on short-term contracts, for example with suppliers. They may also employ more agency and temporary staff, and favour short-term leases for machinery and other essential assets. Entering short-term contracts obviously does not really commit a business to any long-term objectives.

- **Pursue external growth rather than organic growth.** Organic growth may be considered too slow for companies with a short-termist approach. Growth through mergers and acquisitions is much faster and may generate swifter returns, if successful.

Drawbacks of short-termism: Here are some of the specific drawbacks of short-termism.

- The long-term profitability of a business might be threatened by focusing too much on the short term. It is possible that some very lucrative long-term opportunities might be overlooked. For example, a failure to invest in R&D might mean that the chance to discover a potentially lucrative innovation is lost forever.

- Companies may lose their competitive edge in overseas markets. The ability to compete internationally may be hampered if the long-term performance of business is ignored. If businesses fail to invest in the future by developing new products and new technology to reduce costs, they will eventually lose their market shares. As a result, there will be less job and wealth creation, and the economy will suffer.

- One of the features of short-termism is the need for companies to make quarterly financial reports. It is argued that these are required in order to force companies to be disciplined. However, others say that it is a dangerous waste of time. For example, if two quarterly reports were eliminated, an extra two weeks of time would be created for CEOs and other key staff in a corporation. This extra time could be used productively. There is also the risk that senior managers are likely to make the wrong long-term decisions if they are wholly focused on reaching short-term quarterly forecasts.

- Over-reliance on short-term contracts may be inappropriate. In some cases the cost of resources when acquired on a temporary basis can be higher than when sourced for longer time periods. For example, the wages paid to agency staff are often higher than the equivalent full-time rate for a permanently employed worker. A commitment to short-term contracts is likely to send out the 'wrong message'. For example, it may be difficult to recruit high-quality staff and find good-quality and reliable suppliers.

Long-termism

Long-termism is clearly the opposite of short-termism. Therefore, businesses with a long-term outlook would not suffer the drawbacks that are associated with short-termism. For example, businesses are less likely to overlook lucrative opportunities that yield long-term profits. They are more likely to invest in R&D, new-product development and other innovations. This will help them gain a competitive edge. They will attach much less importance to quarterly reports and emphasise the importance of the long-term outlook. They will be more interested in recruiting high-quality staff, training them, building loyalty and retaining them. Finally, they are likely to be more interested in long-term contracts with suppliers and other agents, in order to develop meaningful and profitable relationships.

Thinking bigger

It has been suggested that many companies are too short-termist in their approach to business. This corporate focus on short-term objectives might be the result of the way senior managers are remunerated. For example, the performance of senior managers in corporations is focused on short-term share prices rather than long-term value creation. Also, there is a lot of pressure from institutional investors who want to make a quick return for the investment funds they manage, and who have little concern for a company's long-term prosperity. It is suggested that the average holding period for shares bought on the New York Stock Exchange has fallen from six years to just six months.

In a report written for the Labour Party in 2013 by the former Institute of Directors boss, Sir George Cox, it was suggested that short-termism was becoming an entrenched feature in British business. Sir George suggested that short-termism curtailed ambition, inhibited long-term thinking and provided a disincentive to invest in research, new capabilities, products, training, recruitment and skills.

Source: adapted from *Overcoming short-termism*, Labour Party, 2013

Evidence-based versus subjective decision making

When making important strategic decisions, businesses are likely to gather a range of information before choosing a course of action. This information will be used to make an evidence-based decision.

- **Evidence-based decision making** requires a systematic and rational approach to researching and analysing all the available information before a conclusion is reached.
- **Subjective decision making** is where the personal opinions of the key decision maker strongly influence the course of action chosen.

Evidence-based decision making

Many would argue that the best way to make an informed decision is to use an evidence-based approach. For complex and strategic decisions there is likely to be more data available; consequently there needs to be a scientific approach to making a decision. One such approach is summarised in Figure 1. It is based on a number of stages.

Identifying objectives: The first stage in the process is to identify the objective a business wants to achieve. The objective might be a corporate objective, such as growth or survival in a poor trading period. These decisions are likely to be complex and might be taken by the board of directors.

For lower-level objectives, such as filling a part-time vacancy, decisions may be taken by junior managers. A business's objectives might be different at different stages in its growth. Business activities controlled by local government may have different objectives from public limited companies. The business also needs to develop criteria to measure whether it has achieved its objectives. Quite often the objective is to solve a problem. This might be planning for an uncertain future or dealing with a low level of profitability.

Figure 1

An evidence-based approach to decision making

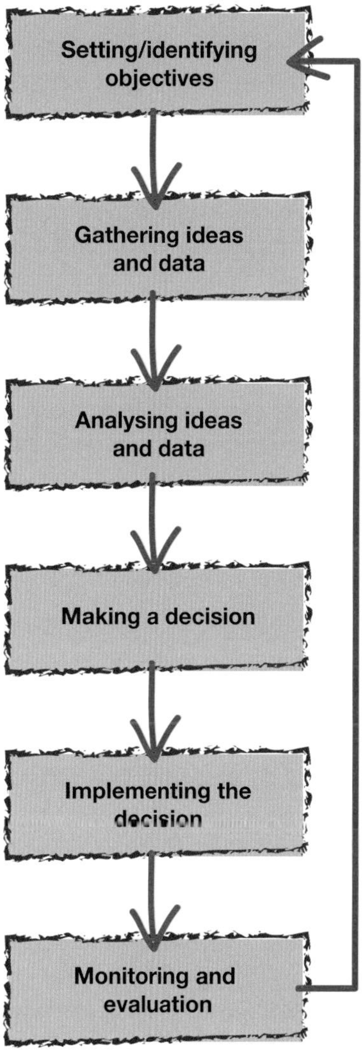

Collecting information and ideas: People need information and ideas to make decisions. The amount and nature of the information needed will depend on the decision. For example, the decision whether or not to launch a new product might require some information about possible sales levels and consumer reactions, costs of production and reactions of competitors. It could take several months to collect all this information. Other decisions could perhaps be made from information which the business already has. A decision whether or not to dismiss an employee might be made on the basis of information from the human resources department.

Where does the business get its ideas? It might set up a working party to collect information and ideas from within the firm. The working party would then produce a report or make a presentation to the decision makers. Alternatively, individuals or departments might submit ideas and information. Another way of obtaining information and ideas is to hold discussions amongst staff in the firm.

Analysing information and ideas: The next stage in the process is to analyse information to look for alternative courses of action. Possible courses of action may be based on previous ideas or completely new ideas. The aim is to identify which course of action will best achieve the business's objective or solve the problem. It may be possible to test the alternatives before the one that is chosen is carried out.

Making a decision: Next the decision has to be made. This is the most important stage in the process. Decision makers have to commit themselves to one course of action. It is difficult to change the decision, so getting it right is vital. For example, once production begins following the decision to launch a new product, it is difficult for the firm to change its mind. If the product does not sell, this can lead to a loss of money. Some decisions can be reversed. For example, if the owner of a shop decides to close on Tuesday afternoons, but then finds the loss of sales is intolerable, the owner can easily reopen again. Sometimes the decision makers feel that they cannot reach a decision. They may have to obtain more information and complete the previous two stages in the process again.

Communication: Once a decision has been made, personnel are informed and the decision is carried out. Quite often the people making the decisions are not those that carry them out. Instructions may be passed by the decision makers to someone else, probably a manager, explaining what action should be taken. For example, if the directors decide to begin selling their products in a new country, instructions must be sent to the marketing manager. In smaller firms, decision makers are more likely to carry out their own decisions.

Outcome: Once a decision has been carried out it will take time before the results are known. Sometimes this can be quite a long time. For example, the companies which decided to build the Channel Tunnel will not know for several decades whether or not it will be a commercial success.

Evaluate the results: Finally, decision makers need to evaluate the outcome of their decisions. This is often presented as a report. It may be necessary to modify the course of action on the basis of the report. For example, it might be necessary to revise the objectives or collect some more information, as shown in Figure 1 on the previous page.

There may be problems in following such an approach. Objectives may be difficult to identify or unrealistic. Information may be limited, incorrect or misleading. People making decisions in the process may have different views and this may lead to differences of opinion about what is the best course of action, for example.

Thinking bigger

The use of models or simulations is widespread in business. Models are replicas or copies of problem areas in business. They are theories, laws or equations, stating things about a problem and helping in our understanding of it. There are a number of common features to models.

- They reflect the key characteristics or behaviour of an area of concern.
- They tend to be simplified versions of areas of concern.
- They simulate the actions and processes that operate in the problem area.
- They provide an aid to problem solving or decision making.
- Models often make use of formulae to express concepts.

Some models can be carried out using computer software. This allows decisions to be made quickly and many variables affecting decisions can be included.

Management science and operations research are areas which often make use of decision-making models. For example, linear programming provides a model which allows decision makers to determine optimal solutions to a wide range of business problems. It has been used to make decisions such as:

- how to minimise waste in production
- how to allocate resources between two competing tasks
- how to find the least cost mix of ingredients for a product.

Another example in the area of marketing is the use of Ansoff's Matrix. This model is used to help consider the relationship between the strategic direction of the business and its marketing strategy.

A simulation involves trying to mimic what might happen in reality. It allows a business to test ideas and make decisions without bearing the consequences of 'real action' if things go wrong. Imagine a business has a problem. A simulation can be carried out several times, quickly and cheaply, in order to test alternative decisions. There is no risk and resources are not used up. Simulations are often used to deal with problems such as queues in business.

Subjective decision making

Making a subjective decision involves choosing a course of action that you 'feel' is right. For example, it might be necessary to make such a decision when driving to an unfamiliar destination. If you come to a fork in the road and there is no signpost, which way do you go? The route you take is the one you 'feel' is right. This is not an evidence-based decision. Some might argue that subjective decision making is too risky when making strategic decisions. This is because subjective decisions may be based purely on the opinions and emotions of perhaps just one person. However, there are times when such an approach might be appropriate.

- If there is a lack of current, accurate and meaningful information relating to a decision, decision makers may be forced to take a subjective approach. For example, a business may be contemplating selling £5 million of goods to a large, but new customer. If the customer does not have a trading history but promises to pay in 90 days, place regular large orders and meet a range of other contractual obligations, in the absence of 'hard information' the decision to sell to the new customer might be subjective.

- Some corporations are dominated by a powerful and persuasive leader. There may be occasions where such a leader makes strategic decisions singled-handedly, without consultation and perhaps with only a limited range of information. This can be acceptable, particularly if the leader is experienced, has a good track record with decisions and there is a culture of trust in the organisation.

- In some industries subjective decision making may be quite normal. For example, in the fashion industry people may have to make decisions, for instance, about which collection of designs to purchase, based purely on what they feel. People in businesses that make subjective decisions like this are often successful because they have good instincts for what will be a hit.

- There are times when some decisions have to be made very quickly indeed. There may not be enough time to follow the scientific approach outlined earlier. Consequently, such decisions are more likely to be subjective. Where speed is of the essence it may be preferable to make a quick decision based on 'gut feeling' rather than wait to gather and analyse information. Opportunities can often be lost if a quick decision is not made.

The level of reliance on subjective decision making might be surprising. In 2014 a study on business decision making was carried out by the global creative agency gyro and the Fortune Knowledge Group. The study resulted in findings that showed that factors such as emotion played a big role in business decision making. The report, called *Only Human: The Emotional Logic of Business Decisions,* gathered feedback from 720 US senior executives. It found that many executives believed that subjective factors, such as corporate culture and corporate values, had an impact on decision making. It also found that factors such as trust, reputation and 'gut instinct' were influential.

The success of subjective decisions is variable as they can involve more risk. For example, some put forward that the decision made by Kodak not to exploit digital cameras – a technology that Kodak actually developed, may have been subjective, when they placed confidence in the long-term future of film.

Links 🔗

When evaluating in answers to exam questions it is often helpful to distinguish between the short term and the long term. Consequently you may get an opportunity to demonstrate your synoptic skills by linking your answer to issues on corporate timescales discussed in this unit. Corporate influences on decision making might also be linked to other units on decision making such as Decision trees (Unit 54), SWOT analysis (Unit 46) and Shareholders versus stakeholders (Unit 58).

Key terms

Asset stripping – the practice of buying businesses and breaking them up. The profitable parts are sold for cash and the rest are closed down.

Evidence-based decision making – an approach to decision making that involves gathering information and using a systematic and rational approach to reach a conclusion.

Long term – the time period where decisions have an impact on the vision, mission and objectives of a business – typically longer than five years.

Short term – the time period where decisions only have an impact on the operational activities of a business – typically less than five years.

Strategic decisions – decisions concerning policy that can have a long-term impact on a business. Can be risky.

Subjective decision making – an approach to decision making where the personal opinions of the key decision maker strongly influence the course of action chosen.

Knowledge check

1. State two possible influences on corporate decision making.

2. Explain the importance of strategic decisions.

3. State three activities that a company with a short-term outlook might engage in.

4. State three possible drawbacks of short-termism.

5. What is meant by evidence-based decision making?

6. Outline the different stages that might be used in an evidence-based decision making process.

7. Give two examples of circumstances where subjective decision making might be appropriate.

8. Explain why subjective decision making might be more risky than evidence-based decision making.

Case study

ROLLS-ROYCE

Rolls-Royce (RR) is a well-known global brand. The company provides products for the aerospace, power systems, marine energy and defence industries. It is well established, has a reputation for quality and aims to deliver 'better power for a changing world'. In 2014, its revenue was £14.588 billion and its profit was £1.617 billion. The value of Rolls-Royce's order book rose from £71.6 billion in 2013 to £73.7 billion in 2014.

It could be argued that RR has benefited from its commitment to the long term. Some of its key staff have been with the company for many years. For example, until his resignation in 2014, Mark Morris, the Chief Finance Officer (CFO), had been with RR for 27 years. In 2014 Colin Smith, Director of Engineering and Technology, had been with the company for 40 years and James M. Guyette, President and CEO of US operations, 17 years. These employees have a wealth of experience and demonstrate that RR has a long-term view.

Further evidence of its commitment to the long term was provided by an announcement in 2015 that it would be modernising its facilities in Derby by replacing some

buildings that were built in the 1940s. RR wants to invest in its Civil Aerospace division at Sinfin and eventually create an aerospace campus similar to those it owns in Bristol, the US and Singapore. A spokesman for RR said: 'We need to modernise our facilities to help us continue to be competitive and continue to meet the needs of our customers . . . This is a long-term programme. Our wider plans for a campus are at an early stage in their development and, as they evolve, we'll share more details.'

In 2014, RR spent £819 million on research and development (R&D). According to the chairman, R&D and innovation are crucial to the development of the company. He said: 'A key characteristic of RR is that it is a long-term business with technologies that take years to develop. This creates the necessity of a long-term view and for long-term investment, together with a commensurate attitude and mind-set for risk.' One example of this commitment to R&D is provided by the development of the Trent XWB engine, which is now the most efficient large civil aero engine in the world. Development on this new product started back in 2006. Another product that has taken a lot of time and money to develop is the liquefied natural gas (LNG) power system. This system allows ships to reduce their carbon dioxide emissions by 40 per cent and has almost wiped out emissions of sulphur and nitrogen oxides.

However, the chairman emphasised in his 2013 report that RR is committed to both the short-term performance and long-term health of the business. He said: 'It is a matter of "both-and", not "either-or". In my experience the most successful, most enduring organisations invest equivalent resource and imagination in the long-term health of their business as they do in their short- to medium-term performance.'

Evidence of RR's short-term commitment came in 2014 when it announced a £1 billion share buyback programme. (This benefits shareholders because the share price rises quickly.) This came after the company sold one of its businesses to Siemens.

Sources: adapted from www.rolls-royce.com, www.derbytelegraph.co.uk and the *Financial Times* 19.06.2014, all rights reserved

(a) Explain one reason why a business like Rolls-Royce might use evidence-based decision making. (4 marks)

(b) Evaluate the importance of timescale to Rolls-Royce in its approach to decision making. (20 marks)

57 Corporate culture

Key points

1. Strong and weak cultures.
2. Classification of company cultures: power, role, task, person.
3. How corporate culture is formed.
4. Difficulties in changing an established culture.

Getting started

In 2015, investor Warren Buffett, aged 84, was displaying few signs of slowing down. Buffett is the CEO and chairman of Berkshire Hathaway, a multinational conglomerate that has stakes in many famous brands, such as Heinz, American Express and Coca-Cola, since 1970. In 2015, he was personally worth $58.5 billion. A known philanthropist, Buffet devotes a large portion of this vast fortune to good deeds. In July 2013 he bestowed $2 billion of his company's stock on the Bill and Melinda Gates Foundation.

Source: adapted from www.berkshirehathaway.com

Having held the position of CEO for over 40 years, what long-term influence will Warren Buffett have on his company?

Strong and weak corporate cultures

Every place of work has a slightly different atmosphere. Some are busy, some are friendly, some are disorganised and some are challenging. This reflects the **organisational culture** (sometimes also called the **organisation, corporate** or **business culture**) of a business. The organisational culture is the values, attitudes, beliefs, meanings and norms that are shared by people and groups within an organisation.

Advantages of a strong corporate culture

A **strong culture** is one that is deeply embedded into the ways a business or organisation does things. It is argued that there are certain advantages to a business of establishing a strong corporate culture.

- It provides a sense of identity for employees. They feel part of the business. This may lead workers to be flexible when the company needs to change or is having difficulties.
- Workers identify with other employees. This may help with aspects of the business such as teamwork.
- It increases the commitment of employees to the company. This may prevent problems such as high labour turnover or industrial relations problems.
- It motivates workers in their jobs. This may lead to increased productivity.
- It helps employees understand what is going on around them. This can prevent misunderstanding in operations or instructions passed to them.
- It helps to reinforce the values of the organisation and senior management.

- It acts as a control device for management. This can help when setting company strategy.

In comparison to a strong culture, a weak culture exists where it is difficult to identify the factors that form the culture or where a wide range of sub-cultures exists, making the culture difficult to define.

There are certain factors that are likely to determine whether a business has a strong or weak culture.

Surface manifestations: These include:
- artefacts, such as furniture, clothes or tools – wearing a uniform would be an example
- ceremonials, such as award-giving ceremonies or the singing of the company song at the start of work
- courses, such as induction courses, or ongoing training courses for workers used to instil the organisational culture
- heroes of the business, living or dead, such as Bill Gates, Richard Branson or Walt Disney, whose way of working provides a role model within the business
- language used in a business-specific way, such as referring to workers as 'colleagues' or calling workers 'crew members'
- mottoes, which are short statements that never change, expressing the values of an organisation
- stories, which tell of some important event that exemplifies the values of the business, such as the history and role of the founders
- myths, which are frequently told stories within a business about itself, but are not necessarily literally true
- norms, which are the ways in which most workers behave, such as worrying if you turn up for work late, always being prepared to cover for workers who are off sick, or not using the company's telephone to make personal calls
- physical layout of premises, such as open plan offices, 'hot desking', or allocating the size of an office according to a manager's place in the hierarchy
- rituals, which are regular events that reinforce the culture of an organisation, such as always supporting Red Nose Day (we are a caring organisation), having a weekly 'dress down day' (we are a relaxed organisation), or holding an annual Christmas party (we are a sociable organisation).

Core organisational values: Core values are located below the surface manifestations of organisational culture. They are consciously thought-out and expressed in words and policies. The values expressed in a mission statement would be an example. Often these are the values that have come from the top of an organisation. They may have come from the original founder of the business, or the current senior management, which has attempted to impose a culture on the business. Core organisational values can reflect the actual culture of a business, but, equally, they might not. Workers at the bottom of the hierarchy might have very different values from the ones that senior management want them to possess. For example, workers who face a very difficult environment where customers often complain might not share the views of the CEO that the customer is always right and at the heart of the business.

Basic assumptions: Basic assumptions are the unsaid beliefs and ways of working; they form the general attitude of the workforce and represent the totality of individuals' beliefs and how they then behave. They are 'invisible' and below the surface, and therefore often difficult to see, understand and change.

In practice, there may be discrepancies between the three levels of surface manifestations, core organisational values and basic assumptions. For example, a company might organise regular social events for employees (a surface manifestation). It might say in documents that it is a 'friendly and caring employer' (its organisational values). Yet, throughout the organisation there might be a culture of competitiveness that tends to make people 'look out for themselves' and distrustful of everyone else. In this situation, the actual organisational culture is different from the surface manifestation and the organisational values. In contrast, another organisation might call its employees 'partners' (the surface manifestation). Its mission statement may say that it is committed to 'rewarding employees as well as shareholders' (its organisational values). It may then, year after year, pay employees above the average for the industry and give regular annual bonuses based upon how much profit the business has made during the year (the organisational culture). Here the underlying organisational culture fits with the stated values and the surface manifestation. There is a culture of rewarding employees because they are stakeholders, for instance the John Lewis Partnership.

Classification of company cultures

There are many ways of classifying organisational culture. One attempt was made by Charles Handy in *Understanding Organisations* (1993). He argued that there were four main types of organisational culture.

Power culture: A power culture is one where there is a central source of power responsible for decision making. There are few rules and procedures within the business and these are overridden by the individuals who hold power when it suits them. There is a competitive atmosphere amongst employees. Among other things, they compete to gain power because this allows them to achieve their own objectives. This creates a political atmosphere within the business. Relatively young, small- to medium-sized businesses, where a single owner founded the firm and is

still very much in control, could typically have power cultures.

Role culture: In a role culture, decisions are made through well-established rules and procedures. Power is associated with a role, such as marketing director or supervisor, rather than with individuals. In contrast to a power culture, influence and control lies with the roles that individuals play rather than with the individuals themselves. An organisation with a role culture will have a tall – or flat – hierarchy with a long chain of command. Role cultures could be described as bureaucratic cultures. The Civil Service is an example of a role culture.

Task culture: In a task culture, power is given to those who can accomplish tasks. Power therefore lies with those with expertise rather than a particular role, as in a role culture. In a task culture, teamworking is common, with teams made up of the experts needed to get a job done. Teams are created and then dissolved as the work changes. Adaptability and dynamism are important in this culture.

Person culture: A person culture is one where there are a number of individuals in the business who have expertise, but who don't necessarily work together particularly closely. The purpose of the organisation is to support those individuals. The business will be full of people with a similar background, skills set and training. Examples of person cultures could be firms of accountants, lawyers, doctors or architects.

Question 1

Each year *The Sunday Times* conducts a survey to establish which are the best UK businesses to work for. Companies sign up to enter the survey and in 2015 more than 1,000 businesses registered to take part. All of the data is based on employee opinions through a questionnaire. The questionnaire is updated each year to reflect current workplace concerns. Below is the top ten of the '25 Best Big Companies' to work for from the 2015 list:

1. TGI Friday's
2. Sytner Group
3. American Express
4. Marriott Hotels International
5. Admiral Group
6. Nationwide Building Society
7. Bourne Leisure
8. Inchcape UK
9. McDonald's Restaurants
10. Iceland Foods

Source: adapted from www.features.thesundaytimes.co.uk

(a) Discuss the cultural factors that may have led to these companies being voted into the top ten '25 Best Big Companies' to work for. You could pick two companies and carry out your own research.

Effects of organisational culture

Organisational culture affects a business in a wide variety of ways. Three of these ways are motivation, organisational structures and change (for example, new management and mergers and takeovers).

Motivation: Organisational culture affects the motivation of staff. It can have a direct effect because the way in which staff treat each other impacts on motivation. For example, motivation is likely to be greater if the culture of the organisation respects individual workers and their achievements. A highly competitive culture might motivate some workers and demotivate others. Organisational culture can also indirectly affect motivation. An organisational culture which leads to a successful business is likely in itself to motivate staff because they feel part of the successful business.

Organisational structures: Organisational culture can affect the organisational structure of a business. In a person culture, for example, the hierarchy is likely to be fairly flat. So in a doctors' practice, for instance, there are unlikely to be many layers of management. This is because a number of key workers share the senior management roles. In contrast there are likely to be more layers of management in a large multinational business that might require regional and divisional managers and multiple product teams. The larger the business, the more layers in the hierarchy there are likely to be as specialist roles are assigned.

New management: One way for a business to change is for new management to be appointed. The greater the change needed, the more likely it is that the new management will have to confront the existing organisational culture. The organisational culture is likely to be part of the problem that needs addressing if the business is to be turned around.

Mergers and takeovers: When two businesses merge or one takes over another, each business is likely to have a different organisational culture. The process of creating a single business out of the two organisations will therefore involve changing organisational culture. In a takeover, one simple way of making that change quickly is for the senior management in the company being taken over to be made

Thinking bigger

In the 1970s and 1980s, Dutch psychologist Professor Geert Hofstede conducted one of the most thorough pieces of research into how culture differs between organisations across international barriers. (Geert Hofstede, *Comparing Values, Behaviors, Insititions and Organizations Across Nations*, Second Edition, 2003) He examined these cultural dimensions by studying work-related values and identified five key variables, or dimensions, that vary across businesses in different countries. These variables impact organisational culture and how the business may react in certain circumstances.

Power distance

This is the distance between managers and subordinates. A high power distance suggests that managers will have significantly more power and privileges than their subordinates. They probably will not socialise and communication is generally top down. A lower power distance culture has greater collaboration and discussion between employees of different rank. Chinese companies tend to have a very high power distance, while Scandinavian countries have a low power distance.

Individualism

This is how people see themselves within their organisation. Where individualism is high, people tend to focus on their own success above that of the organisation or their team. The level of individualism versus collectivism within a culture can determine organisational structure, motivation and internal competition.

Masculinity

The management style in a masculine organisation is competitive and assertive. A more feminine approach is considered to be caring and co-operative. This may determine how people respond to targets and goals, and relate to one another in the business.

Uncertainty avoidance

This is the level at which an organisation will accept risk. A high level of uncertainty avoidance suggests a business will want evidence, security and proof before acting. By contrast a business with a low uncertainty avoidance might take 'a long shot' if it believes the rewards are worthwhile. Organisations with low uncertainty avoidance are more entrepreneurial and agile in their decision making.

Long-term versus short-term orientation

This addresses a culture's 'time horizon' and the basis on which decisions are made. A high score indicates business decisions are made to achieve success in the long term. A low score suggests an organisation makes decisions to achieve short-term rewards and immediate gratification in terms of shareholder value. UK businesses have been criticised in the past for their short-termism.

Hofstede's cultural dimensions go beyond simply identifying behavioural differences – they present a useful framework for understanding the cultural setting of a business. This is particularly useful when analysing businesses across borders and interpreting how international businesses might react and interact in different circumstances, such as international trade, partnerships, mergers and takeovers.

Question 2

In March 2015, Chinese company Fosun International bought a 5 per cent stake in Thomas Cook, the British tour operator. It paid almost £92 million for the stake, which formed part of a larger expansion into the European travel and tourism sector. It also expressed its intention to raise its stake in the future, to about 10 per cent.

The chief executive of Thomas Cook said Fosun's portfolio of travel investments would allow his company to exploit new opportunities for growth abroad.

Thomas Cook and Fosun will work together to capitalise on the Chinese domestic and international tourism market, which is expanding rapidly as the middle classes in the world's second-largest economy swell. The two companies also plan to jointly develop a hotel portfolio designed for Chinese travellers.

Source: adapted from the *Financial Times* 06.03.2015. All rights reserved.

(a) Assess the factors that Thomas Cook and Fosun may have to consider to ensure their cultural differences impact in a successful way on their partnership.

redundant. Without powerful advocates at the top of the organisation, those lower down will find it difficult to resist the change that will be imposed upon them. However, motivation and morale is often low in a company that has been taken over for the first year or so because they are being forced to change.

In the same way that you might identify a patent on an invention or an established brand as an asset, culture too can be a distinctive and sustainable competitive advantage. Unit 45 discussed distinctive capabilities as a route to achieving competitive advantage for a business. John Kay (1993) referred to 'architecture' as one of the types of distinctive capability that could lead to competitive advantage. Architecture refers to the relationships and networks within an organisation and those that it develops with its external stakeholders – corporate culture would fall into this category. Whenever discussing corporate culture, it is worth considering it in terms of an asset that can be used to add value and compete in the market. However, it is also worth remembering that culture is very difficult to manipulate and shape in order to meet the changing needs of the business.

How corporate culture is formed

Many factors contribute to the formation of organisational culture. These include the role of the founding members of the organisation, their personalities and beliefs. Often a strong leader's attitudes will permeate the organisation. For example, Jan Koum, the CEO of WhatsApp, has refused to let advertisers buy space on the WhatsApp application. His belief has influenced the strategy and values of the company.

Other factors that are likely to have a significant impact on the formation of a firm's culture are the environmental factors that the business was born into. For example, the history or heritage of a business may determine certain values and norms because they form part of what employees 'buy into'. However, such a factor may not play a part in a new company such as Pinterest, which was set up in 2010. Similarly, the success of a company will play a big part in setting the values and expectations of staff. Pinterest was the most rapidly growing social network site in 2012 and 2013, and was named one of the most innovative companies, all of which will contribute to the motivation and belief of its workforce.

The type of product is another factor in creating culture. For example, the technological complexity of a product may determine the skill and expertise of the workforce (perhaps contributing to a role culture) and the pace of change or need for innovation.

Figure 1 shows the overlapping factors that form the culture of an organisation. These factors play a part in forming the culture in every business. However, each business is unique and the factors will have varying levels of influence and connection. As you can see, the leader in Business A has a big influence on the formation of the overall culture. However, in Business B it is the well-established values that play a significant role in shaping the culture.

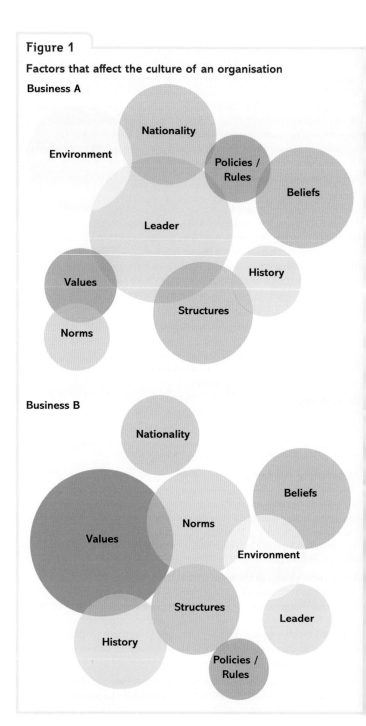

Figure 1

Factors that affect the culture of an organisation

Difficulties in changing an established culture

Unit 63 explores the causes and effects of change on a business. From time to time it might be desirable for a business to change its culture to one that is stronger and more productive. A firm's culture can provide it with a competitive advantage over its rivals. The problem with organisational culture is that although it may be easy to describe, identifying the factors that contribute towards that culture and their significance is very difficult. Even changing one of these factors may not have a significant influence on shifting the culture. Furthermore, most organisations have sub-cultures within specific teams or functions. Some aspects of organisational culture might also be easier to change than others. For example, it might be easy o change the policies, rules and working practices within a firm – these are tangible factors. However, it is much harder to manipulate people's attitudes and beliefs.

Overall, culture can be changed if the right factors are influenced and the leaders within the organisation are strong, but changing culture is not easy and can be a long process. Many factors contribute to the formation of corporate culture. It is important for the directors of a company to understand these factors and the role they play before they can hope to manage cultural change.

Case study

MOSAIC

Since 1995, Mosaic has grown from two to over 25,000 employees. Mosaic Ltd has an organisational culture that encourages employees to be creative and loyal. It encourages innovation, and as a result has created some leading products, including an advanced Mosaic search engine, a leading smartphone and a music-streaming service.

The founders of Mosaic, Dominic Moore and Rita Singh, brought flexible and hard-working approaches to Mosaic, and these qualities have survived as the business has grown. There has been a purposeful emphasis within the company on developing a corporate culture that is open and creative.

At Mosaic's head office, known as 'Mosaic Towers', employees are encouraged to keep fit and healthy through heavily subsidised membership of the next-door gym. A free healthy breakfast is also provided for all employees, and on-site childcare facilities are part of a supportive package for parents. These benefits are designed to build a happy and healthy company where employees can focus on productivity and innovation.

Dominic Moore places an emphasis on ability and creativity when the company appoints new employees, not only on experience. All new employees are invited

to become a member of the 'Mosicians' – a company social and sports club that builds a sense of belonging and networking within the organisation.

Mosaic is continually flexible with its corporate culture. Each week, alongside working on allocated projects, half a day is devoted to new ideas on existing products, and research and development of new projects, reflecting individual interests. Dominic Moore suggests that this creates key opportunities for innovation and is also motivating for employees. Every other month there is a meeting between employees and the executive team, where new ideas and concepts can be put forward and discussed.

Mosaic has an informal motto created by a young employee – 'Live to give'. Alongside the business decisions that are focused on strong revenue growth, the company philosophy is to work creatively to build success and to develop products that enhance people's lives.

Q

(a) Explain one reason why Mosaic's corporate culture could be referred to as a 'strong culture'. (4 marks)

(b) Assess the benefits for Mosaic of fostering a creative culture. (10 marks)

(c) Evaluate the extent to which a strong corporate culture is important to the long-term success of Mosaic. (20 marks)

Key terms

Cultural dimensions – a set of characteristics that form the international context of business culture.
Organisational, organisation, corporate or **business culture** – the values, attitudes, beliefs, meanings and norms that are shared by people and groups within an organisation.
Strong culture – a culture where the values, beliefs and ways of working are deeply embedded within the business and its employees.

Knowledge check

1. Explain the difference between surface manifestations, organisational values and basic assumptions of corporate culture.

2. Explain the differences between power culture, role culture, task culture and person culture.

3. How can an organisational culture give a business a competitive advantage?

4. How might Hofstede's cultural dimensions influence the culture of international businesses?

5. Outline the possible impact of organisational culture on (a) staff motivation and (b) the organisational structure of a business.

6. State five advantages of a strong organisational culture.

7. Can an organisation's culture be changed?

58 Shareholders versus stakeholders

Key points

1. Internal and external stakeholders.
2. Stakeholder objectives.
3. Stakeholder influences: that the business considers all of its stakeholders in its business decisions/objectives.
4. Shareholder influences: that the business should focus purely on shareholder returns (increasing share price and dividends) in its business decisions/objectives.
5. The potential for conflict between profit-based (shareholder) and wider (stakeholder) objectives.

Getting started

Identify the two groups of people in the photograph who have an interest in this business. Identify another group that might have an interest in this business. What might be the objectives of the groups that you have identified? Do you think these groups have all the same objectives? If they differ, why? To what extent might each of these groups influence decision making in the business?

Internal and external stakeholders

A stakeholder is a person, group or organisation who can affect or be affected by the organisation's actions, objectives and policies. Stakeholders can be directors, employees, owners, suppliers, unions and customers. The interest each stakeholder has will vary according to the nature of their stake; for example, whether they are inside or outside the business.

Internal stakeholders

Some groups of people inside the business have a direct interest in its survival and well-being. These may be referred to as internal stakeholders.

Business owners: A business is the property of the owners. Owners are stakeholders because they stand to gain, or lose, financially from the performance of the business. If the business does well they will enjoy a share of the profit. They will also benefit if the value of business increases. However, if the business fails owners may lose the money they invested in the business. With larger companies, such as large plcs, the shareholders may be internal and external. Most are likely to be external since the majority of large plcs are owned by financial institutions, such as pension funds,

investment banks and insurance companies. Their interests are discussed later. However, in most large plcs some of the senior managers and members of the board are likely to own shares. One reason for this is because part of their remuneration often consists of shares. Finally, in some companies employees may own a small number of shares. For example, about one third of all BT workers are signed up to a 'saveshare' scheme. They make a contribution to the scheme from their monthly salary and get the right to buy shares at a discount when the scheme matures. It was widely reported that in August 2014, around 23,000 BT workers received an average of £42,000 when one of the schemes matured. If employees own shares in the company they work for, then they are also part-owners of that company.

Employees: Employees are internal stakeholders because they work for businesses. Employees depend on businesses for their livelihood. Most employees have no other sources of income and rely on wages to live on. Some employees are represented at work by trade unions. If this is the case, then trade unions also become stakeholders. The needs of employees are often in conflict with those of other stakeholders, such as owners and managers. This is discussed later in the unit.

Managers and directors: In small businesses managerial tasks, such as organising, decision making, planning and control, are undertaken by the entrepreneur themselves. However, in large businesses, the key decisions relating to company policy and strategy are made by the board of directors. It is then the responsibility of managers to ensure that the policies and strategies are implemented. Large businesses employ specialists in managerial positions. For example, managers are often employed to run the different departments in businesses, such as marketing, production, finance and human resources. They are responsible for the work carried out in their departments and for the people employed to do the work.

Managers have to show leadership, solve problems, make decisions, settle disputes and motivate workers. Managers are likely to help plan the direction of the business with owners. They also have to control resources, such as finance, equipment, time and people. Managers are also accountable. This means they are responsible for their actions and the actions of their subordinates. Managers are accountable to senior managers in the managerial hierarchy. The board of directors is accountable to the shareholders.

External stakeholders

A range of groups outside a business may have an interest in its activities. Such groups are called **external stakeholders**.

Shareholders: Most shareholders in large companies are not involved in the day-to-day running of the business. They are investors and have a purely financial interest. External shareholders, who might be individuals, or more likely, large financial institutions, invest their money to get a financial return. Shareholders are also entitled to a vote at the AGM of a plc. They can vote to re-elect or dismiss the current board of directors. However, many external shareholders do not take up this entitlement. If they are not happy with the way the company is being run, or the return they get is inadequate, external shareholders can sell their shares and invest their money elsewhere.

Customers: Customers buy the goods and services that businesses sell. Through their purchases they provide the revenue and profit that businesses need to survive. However, customers need businesses because they provide the goods and services they require and want. Most customers are consumers (individuals and families) who use or 'consume' products. However, some may be other businesses. For example, JCB manufactures a range of construction machinery that it sells to other businesses.

Creditors: Creditors lend money to a business. They may be banks, but could also be individuals, such as family members, or private investors, such as venture capitalists. Clearly these stakeholders have a financial interest in a business and will be keen for it to do well. Creditors will expect their interest

payments to be met and their money returned at the end of the loan period. They will also want clear communication links with the business.

Suppliers: Businesses that provide raw materials, components, commercial services and utilities to other businesses are called suppliers. Relations between businesses and their suppliers need to be good because they rely on each other. Businesses want good-quality resources at reasonable prices. They also want prompt delivery, trade credit (buy now pay later) and flexibility. In return, suppliers require prompt payment and regular orders. As with customers and businesses, there is a mutual dependence between suppliers and businesses.

The local community: Most businesses are likely to have an impact on the local community.
- **Positive impact.** A business may employ people locally and if the business does well the community may prosper. There may be more jobs, more overtime and possibly higher pay. This will have a knock-on effect in the community. For example, shops, restaurants and cinemas may benefit from extra spending.
- **Negative impact.** A business may be criticised by the local community. For example, if a factory is noisy, polluting or works at night there may be complaints from local residents. If a business that employed a lot of local people closes down, the impact on the community can be devastating. In the 1980s when many coal mines were closed in the UK, the mining communities suffered badly due to very high unemployment.

The government: The government has an interest in all businesses. Generally the government will want businesses to be successful. They provide employment, generate wealth and pay taxes. Taxes from businesses and their employees are used to fund government expenditure. It helps to pay for benefits, the NHS, schools and other services. If businesses fail, the government loses tax revenue and has to pay benefits to the unemployed. However, the government will also require businesses to comply with the law. A significant amount of legislation exists to protect those who might be exploited by businesses if they were too powerful.

The environment: Business activity can have an impact on the environment. For example, if a business releases toxic waste into the waterway system, wildlife and its habitats could be destroyed. Thus, representatives of the environment have an interest in business activity. These representatives may be individuals or environmental groups, such as Friends of the Earth and Greenpeace. An increasing number of people are concerned about environmental issues; consequently environmental groups are becoming more influential in business decision making.

Question 1

In 2015 it was announced that data centre providers, TelecityGroup and Interxion, were going to merge. The new group would give Telecity shareholders 55 per cent of the shares and Interxion shareholders 45 per cent. The boards of directors of both companies felt that customers would be better served by the combined group. It would be stronger and able to supply customers with a greater range of products. The company hoped to expand into markets in Africa, Asia and Eastern Europe. John Hughes, chairman of the merged group, suggested that the combination of TelecityGroup and Interxion would represent an extremely compelling combination for all stakeholders in both groups.

Source: adapted from the *Financial Times* 11.02.2015, all rights reserved

(a) What is the difference between internal and external stakeholders? Use examples from this case.

(b) Explain how the two groups of stakeholders might benefit from this merger.

Stakeholder objectives

Many stakeholders have common objectives. For example, most stakeholders will want a business to survive and be successful. However, each group of stakeholders is likely to have some of their own specific objectives.

Shareholders: The majority of shareholders will want the business to maximise shareholder value. This is a measure of company performance that takes into account the size of dividends (share in profits) and the share price. Over time shareholders want this to grow. If the growth in shareholder value is not to the satisfaction of external investors they may sell their shares. This could result in a fall in the share price, which might make the company vulnerable to a takeover.

Employee objectives: Employees want the business that they work for to prosper. If a business is growing and profitable, employees are likely to get higher wages, more perks and perhaps a bonus. They will also feel more secure in their jobs. It could be argued that, according to Herzberg, employees *expect* good pay and comfortable working conditions. However, they will also *want* responsibility, interaction with colleagues, to be

valued, personal development, fair and honest treatment, and opportunities for promotion. Safety at work is also important, as are issues to do with equal opportunities. Generally, employees will want to maximise their financial rewards and welfare.

Managerial objectives: Managers and directors are likely to have similar needs to those of employees. Many managers (and employees) have part of their remuneration linked to the performance of the business and will therefore want the business to perform well. Managers may also press for other benefits, for instance bonus payments if they perform well, expense allowances when travelling on company business, and benefits such as a company car, free health insurance and more flexibility. Some senior executives may see power as an objective; they like 'empire building'. As a result, the shareholders may lose the ability to influence key decisions in the organisation.

Customer objectives: Customers want good-quality products at a fair price. They also want clear and accurate information about products and high-quality customer service. They may also want choice, innovative products and flexibility. For some products, such as machinery, electrical goods and children's products, safety is an important issue. If these needs are not met, customers will spend their money elsewhere. Customers have a powerful influence on businesses. They are also more aware today about the range of products available and about their rights as consumers. In competitive markets only those businesses that meet customer needs are likely to survive.

Supplier objectives: Suppliers want to be treated fairly by businesses. They would prefer to have long-term contracts and regular orders. They will also want a fair price for their goods or services and to be paid in reasonable time. In 2013/14 it was suggested in the media that some businesses might 'bully' suppliers. For example, some stores might put pressure on suppliers and demand price cuts because of falls in commodity prices. They might threaten to withdraw products if suppliers refuse to comply. In cases such as these, an investigation might take place by the Groceries Code Adjudicator, for example.

Government objectives: The government will want businesses to grow and make more profit. They will also want them to comply with legislation and not exploit vulnerable groups.

Environmental objectives: Environmental groups will want businesses to avoid having any negative impact on the environment. For example, they will demand that business activity does not damage wildlife and its habitats, pollute the atmosphere or waste resources.

Local community objectives: Local communities will want businesses to contribute to the prosperity of the community and be good corporate citizens. Communities would probably want businesses to create employment and, depending on their size, nature of business and capabilities, build links with schools and charities, maintain open communications, and avoid or minimise congestion and pollution in the area.

Stakeholder influences – stakeholder approach

Some corporations take into account the objectives of a wider group of stakeholders in addition to shareholders when making business decisions. According to the Clarkson Principles (www.cauxroundtable.org), this means that corporations should:

- recognise the interests of other stakeholders and take their views into account when running the business and making decisions
- maintain open communication channels with other stakeholders and consult with them before making radical changes
- recognise the interdependence that exists between different stakeholders, ensuring that the benefits of enterprise are distributed fairly after taking into account the level of effort and risk each group contributes
- minimise or eliminate the adverse effects of business activity. If such effects cannot be avoided then those affected should be adequately compensated.

Some businesses might claim to have adopted this stakeholder approach. Part of the reason for this is that corporations are coming under increasing pressure from stakeholders, the media and the wider public to be more socially responsible. It might be argued that some businesses like to give the impression that they consider the needs of a wider range of stakeholders, but in reality they are still more focused on shareholder needs. For example, a business might claim to adopt an ethical stance purely to increase sales, revenue and profit. Corporate social responsibility is discussed in Unit 59.

Stakeholder influences – shareholder approach

Traditionally, many corporations have focused on growth or profit when making important business decisions. The objectives of shareholders have had more influence on decision making than those of other stakeholders. This approach was based on the idea that directors and managers are employed by shareholders and should therefore serve their interests. This meant that they should make as much money as possible for the owners of the business provided they comply with the law. Some businesses still adopt this approach and their main objective is to maximise shareholder returns by raising both dividends paid to shareholders and the share price.

The potential for conflict between shareholders and other stakeholders

Problems are likely to arise between shareholders and other stakeholders when their objectives are in direct conflict. Some examples of this conflict are outlined below.

Shareholders and employees: Meeting the objectives of employees in terms of higher wages, better conditions, more perks and bonuses, providing training and improving

Thinking bigger

In the UK, adopting a 'stakeholder approach' means giving less importance to the interests of owners and more importance to other stakeholders than the typical business. The costs and benefits to businesses of adopting such an approach tend to be measured in terms of their impact on profits, sales, revenues and accounting costs. The advantages include the following.

- Having good employment policies will tend to attract better applicants for posts, and help motivate and retain existing staff. Improved motivation and retention should lead to increased profits.
- Effective customer care policies should lead to higher sales and hence higher profits.
- Working well with suppliers should enable the purchaser to get value for money. It should be much easier to sort out problems of late deliveries or defective work with suppliers with whom there is a good relationship.
- Putting something into the community, such as giving to local charities, taking on workers or backing training projects should give the business good public relations. This might help sell products or attract good applicants for jobs.
- Being environmentally friendly could lead to lower overall costs. For example, recycling heat in a boiler might cost money for new equipment but quickly save money because of the lower fuel inputs needed. Being seen as environmentally friendly may help sales of products and thus increase profit.
- For some high-profile companies, becoming more socially responsible can deflect the criticisms of pressure groups. For example, Foxconn, an electronics company that reportedly used child labour in some of its factories, said it would take action against any of its plants if violations are discovered. Foxconn carries out work for companies such as Apple and Samsung, and considers attention to social responsibility an important part of its business context..

The main disadvantage of the stakeholder approach is that, in practice, it tends to add to costs and thus lower profits for most businesses. If this weren't the case, every employer would increase the benefits given to workers, or give money to local charities, or devote resources to pursuing environmentally friendly policies. Only some businesses benefit from a 'stakeholder approach'.

employee welfare comes at a cost. If the needs of employees are met in full there is likely to be a negative impact on profit and dividends. Conflict will arise if shareholders insist that the rewards to employees should not come at the expense of dividends. Employees may try to put pressure on the business to ensure their objectives are met by threatening industrial action. However, if this action is too disruptive it may jeopardise the survival of the business. Employees have to be careful not to push their claims too far. In 2014, workers at Jaguar Land Rover (JLR) in the Midlands were given an 'inflation-busting' pay rise after threatening strike action. Staff had turned down an earlier offer saying it failed to reflect the contribution made by workers to the company's turnaround. The Unite trade union recommended that workers should accept JLR's new offer of 4.5% and a £825 lump sum in the first year of a two-year deal, followed by RPI inflation plus 0.5% in the second year or 3%, whichever is higher.

Shareholders and customers: Conflict between shareholders and customers is most likely to arise if a business charges prices that are too high. Higher prices will help to boost shareholder returns but reduce the purchasing power of customers. In 2014, many customers complained about the rising prices of gas and electricity. For example, gas bills rose 3.5 per cent between April and June 2014. At the same time the cost of gas paid by suppliers fell by 21 per cent. Many customers were annoyed by this. Customers might also come into conflict with businesses if levels of customer service are poor or if businesses fail to invest in research and development and bring out new products. However, if businesses can cut back on research and development expenditure they can pay shareholders higher dividends.

Shareholders and directors and managers: Senior managers and directors are employed to further the interests of shareholders. However, conflict might arise if they start to prioritise their own objectives, such as maximising remuneration, expenses, perks and other benefits. If these are too high, profit and dividends may suffer. This is most likely to happen if shareholders lose some of their control over the business. There may be a 'divorce of ownership and control'. This can happen if shares are held by a very large number of different shareholders where no single shareholder has any significant control. A common conflict between shareholders and directors is the balance between paying dividends and retaining profit for investment. Shareholders may prefer to have higher dividends while the directors may prefer to retain more profit for investment.

Shareholders and the environment: In an effort to maximise profit, a business might neglect its responsibilities towards the environment. For example, in 2011 it was widely reported that some of the UK's water companies were accused of draining rivers that were at risk of completely drying up. As a result some wildlife was destroyed and there was a build-up of chemicals, which threatened some fragile ecosystems. The report suggested that companies were extracting water from these sources because they were the cheapest. Activities such as these may attract the attention of the media and environmental groups, resulting in conflict between the company and environmentalists.

Shareholders and the government: Conflict between shareholders and the government is likely if businesses break the law. However, the judicial system should resolve such conflicts. In 2013 and 2014 there was evidence of uneasiness between the government and large corporations. It came to light that some big corporations were avoiding the payment of tax in the UK. For example, it was widely reported that Amazon only paid £4.2 million of tax in 2013 on sales in the UK of £4.3 billion. If corporations can reduce the amount of tax they pay then the shareholders will enjoy bigger profits. However, if businesses are able to avoid paying taxes the government is likely to be criticised. In the future, governments might have to pursue such businesses for the payment of taxes or risk losing their political support.

Question 2

In 2014 the number of customer complaints about energy providers in the UK doubled during the first half of the year. It was reported that the largest number of complaints were about npower, which received 1.48 million complaints in 2014. This represented 28 per cent of all npower's customers and an increase from 25.1 per cent in 2013. In fact, npower had been the subject of complaints for several years. In 2011, it was fined £2 million by Ofgem (the industry regulator) for failing to deal with customer complaints adequately. In December 2013 npower acknowledged that it had problems with its billing system (the source of many complaints) and agreed a recovery plan with the regulator. The company had installed a new computer system and as a result around 300,000 bills were sent out late. In recognition of this the company made a public apology and gave a £1 million donation to charity. It also agreed to pay $3.5 million in compensation to customers that had been mis-sold some energy services.

In October 2013, npower increased its dual-fuel prices by 10.4 per cent (much in line with other providers). Table 1 shows the price increases required of customers by npower between 2011 and 2013. In 2013, npower made a profit of £390 million. This was an increase of 25 per cent on the previous year. This attitude to making profit was criticised by Labour MP John Robertson, who sits on the Commons energy select committee.

Table 1 Increases in the price of gas and electricity to npower customers

	Jan-11	Oct-11	Feb-12	Nov-12	Dec-13
Gas	5.1%	15.7%	−5%	8.8%	7.7%
Electricity	5.1%	7.2%	0	9.1%	9.3%

Source: adapted from the *Financial Times* 20.06.2014. All rights reserved.

(a) What are likely to be the main objectives for customers as stakeholders in the market for energy?
(b) Discuss the conflict between stakeholders that has occurred in this case.

Links 🔗

The experiences of stakeholders could be linked to most topics in the specification. This is because stakeholders are at the heart of business activity. Any decision made by a business is likely to have an impact on at least one stakeholder. For example, pricing decisions affect customers and shareholders. Location decisions affect communities and employees. Marketing decisions will affect customers and employees. Wage negotiations will have an impact on employees, shareholders and managers. It is not difficult to identify links. And do not forget, decisions are also made by stakeholders.

Case study

HALFORDS

Redditch-based Halfords is a leading retailer in leisure and car products. It is also the UK's top seller of bicycles with sales of around one million a year. The business operates over 460 stores and employs more than 11,000 people. It is a customer-orientated business and prides itself on the help that staff give to customers. For example, Halfords offers free summer and winter checks to customers at its stores. Halfords grew revenues from £809.5 million to £871.3 million between 2009 and 2013. Figure 1 shows the dividend payments to shareholders in that period.

In 2015, Halfords was ranked 18th in the *Sunday Times* 25 Best Big Companies to Work For, having been ranked 25th in 2014. Employees say that they enjoy working in teams at Halfords, they are happy to help each other out, that it is fun working with each other and that there is a strong sense of family in the organisation. Managers at Halfords listen to their staff. Regular meetings are held to find out how employees feel about working for the company and what ideas they might have. For example, as a result of some meetings with trainees, a new induction programme was introduced. Some 78 per cent of staff say that managers are open and honest, while 73 per cent of employees say that managers are happy to share important information.

During the school holidays Halfords organises Kids' Clubs. Up to 2015 these have attracted over 24,000 children. Staff give advice on bike maintenance and demonstrate how to mend a puncture. The retailer also offers free bike workshops aimed at women and GEAR UP! which teaches school children the basics of bike maintenance.

Halfords is committed to local communities and the environment. It recognises that there are gains to be made from acting responsibly and meeting the needs of a wider range of stakeholders. For example, it has taken measures to reduce carbon emissions by using larger trailers to distribute stock around the country so that fewer miles are travelled. It also uses 'smart meters' to control water consumption and tries to increase the amount of recycling from its autocentres.

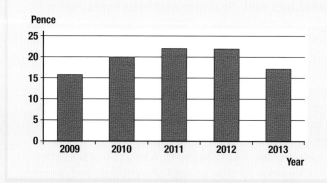

Figure 1

Dividend payments to shareholders 2009–2013

Source: adapted from www.halfords.com

Q

(a) Assess the possible benefits to a business like Halfords of adopting a stakeholder approach to decision making. (10 marks)

(b) Evaluate the extent to which Halfords has adopted a stakeholder approach to business. (20 marks)

Knowledge check

1. Give two examples of internal stakeholders in a business.

2. Give two examples of external stakeholders in a business.

3. Explain how employees might also be shareholders.

4. What are the objectives of suppliers as stakeholders?

5. What are the objectives of the government as a stakeholder?

6. Explain the difference between the 'shareholder approach' and the 'stakeholder approach' when running a company.

7. How might the objectives of shareholders and employees come into conflict?

8. How might the objectives of shareholders and the local community come into conflict?

Exam tip

Do not confuse stakeholders with shareholders. When you write the word shareholders, make sure that you mean shareholders, that is the owners of the business who hold shares in it.

Key points

1. Ethics of strategic decisions:
   - trade-offs between profit and ethics..
2. Pay and rewards.
3. Corporate Social Responsibility (CSR).

Getting started

In August 2013 it was widely reported that Tesco would close its distribution centre at Harlow in Essex. The depot employed 800 workers. Tesco offered many of these workers positions in Dagenham, its next closest depot.

Many people objected to the closure, and were concerned about the changes in pay and terms and conditions. A local MP commented on the impact on some workers of reduced pay and increased travel costs. The MP also commented that the Dagenham depot employed agency workers on lower wages.

In response, Tesco commented that it had one of the best pay and benefits packages in the industry, and paid the same rate whether the colleagues are British or from the EU.

What is most important for a business — looking after its stakeholders or looking after its shareholders? Do you think a business has done anything wrong if it relocates, with an impact on some of its workers? To what extent should a business take into account the views of local stakeholders when making strategic decisions?

Ethics

Ethics, in the context of business ethics, considers the moral 'rights and wrongs' of a decision, focusing more on a strategic level, rather than the decisions made by, tor example, individual employees. All businesses have to make many ethical decisions. Some are affected by the law. For example, it is illegal for businesses to dump waste by the roadside or send their drivers out on the road in unroadworthy vehicles. However, many ethical decisions have to be made without the help of the law. For example, should an employer allow a worker to take a day off work to look after a sick child and still be paid? Should a company stop buying goods from a factory in the Far East where it knows that work conditions are poor and wages are very low?

Every business should have a stated code of conduct within which employees operate in respect of ethical business decisions, although at a senior level and on a personal level some employees might have differences of opinion. For example, some individuals may argue that it is wrong for businesses to manufacture toy guns to sell to children. Others may suggest that they do no real harm. Some restaurant owners might face a dilemma about whether to sell alcoholic drink because of religious beliefs about alcohol. Other restaurant owners might not face such an ethical dilemma. Despite these differences, in many situations most people often take the same ethical stance and are anyway required to operate within the business code of conduct and mission statements. For example, most would agree that a company should not use employees' money in a pension fund to bail it out if it is making a loss.

Ethics of strategic decisions

Strategic decisions are those that affect how a business operates in the long term. All businesses have to make ethical decisions as part of their corporate strategy and these are usually the responsibility of senior management. These decisions then affect the direction of the business, with medium-term tactical decisions usually the responsibility of middle managers. Should a finance manager delay payments if the business has cash-flow difficulties? Should a self-employed plumber charge a senior citizen extra when a job takes longer than estimated? Over the past 20 years, a number of issues have arisen for large corporations that require strategic decisions based on ethics.

The environment: In countries such as the UK or the USA, the law limits the amount of pollution or environmental damage a business can do. However, businesses must decide whether to adopt even more stringent measures to protect the environment. For example, should a business recycle materials, especially if this will lower profits? Multinational businesses often face lower environmental standards in developing countries. Should they lower their own environmental standards in such locations to take advantage of this?

Animal rights: Some companies, such as pharmaceutical companies or cosmetics manufacturers, might use animals to test products. Animal rights groups argue this is unethical. Other companies, particularly food manufacturers or oil businesses, can destroy habitats and endanger animals. Wildlife conservation groups argue against farming activities that destroy forests or other habitats and oil installations that can pollute the environment, leading to the destruction of animal and plant life.

Workers in developing countries: A number of companies have been criticised for exploiting workers in developing countries. Companies manufacture in countries with emerging economies because production costs are much lower. However, there is an ethical question about the extent to which low costs should be at the expense of workers.

Corruption: In some industries bribes might be used to persuade customers to sign contracts. It has been suggested that this takes place in certain emerging economies, where civil servants or government ministers want money from big business deals, for instance arms deals. The ethical question is whether it is right to use bribes even if a business knows that its competitors do, and whether such involvement in arms with unstable political areas is ethical.

New technologies: Most new products, such as mobile phones or a new chocolate bar, do not cause ethical problems. But some technological developments seem always to be controversial. Nuclear power generation, for instance, has been an issue since the 1950s. More recently, genetically modified (GM) crops have hit the headlines. In the future, other biological processes, such as cloning, could arouse strong ethical reactions.

Product availability: If a person cannot afford an expensive car or some other luxury goods, most would not see this as an ethical issue. But if someone is HIV positive in South Africa and cannot afford drugs for treatment because pharmaceutical businesses charge such a high price, many would argue that it is an ethical issue. The direction of research is also important. Companies might research new drugs for complaints suffered by only a few in the industrialised world. Or they might research illnesses such as malaria, which kill millions each year in many developing counties. The choice that businesses make is an ethical issue.

Trading issues: Some countries have been condemned internationally for the policies pursued by their governments. They may even have had **sanctions** or **trade embargoes** placed upon them. Companies must decide whether to trade with or invest in these countries.

Codes of practice

In recent years, some large businesses have adopted **ethical codes of practice**. These lay down how employees in the business should respond in situations where ethical issues arise. Ethical codes will differ from one business and one industry to another. However, they may contain statements about:

- environmental responsibility
- dealing with customers and suppliers in a fair and honest manner
- competing fairly and not engaging in practices such as collusion or destroyer pricing
- the workforce and responding fairly to their needs.

Ethical objectives

Ethical codes of practice may develop from ethical objectives of businesses. Ethical objectives may be explicit. For example, a large business may have as its stated objectives that:

- it will not test its products on animals
- it will deal with suppliers fairly
- it will not accept bribes from customers.

Question 1

Chiquita is an American producer and distributor of bananas and other fruit. Its distinctive blue brand logo is a familiar adornment to bananas found in UK supermarkets.

In the past, Chiquita faced criticism for its ethical decisions having been reportedly accused of having a poor record in terms of its environmental responsibility and with workers' rights. In response to this criticism, Chiquita has attempted to improve its record by having a large push to promote Corporate Social Responsibility (CSR).

- After a campaign by the pressure group ForestEthics, the business agreed to stop using fuel produced from Canada's tar sands. This fuel is extremely polluting and is a large producer of carbon dioxide.

- In 2012 Chiquita signed an agreement with local and international trade unions that committed the business to paying fair rates of pay and promised to promote more women within the organisation.

- Chiquita formed working relationships with environmental groups, such as Rainforest Alliance, and gained certification from this group, which served to improve its environmental performance.

However, not everyone was happy with Chiquita's strategy. The decision to stop using tar sands oil was unpopular in Canada, which relies on its oil exports.

Time will tell how Chiquita benefits from this stance. As of early 2015, the business had not out-performed such rivals as Dole and Fresh Del Monte.

Source: adapted from the *Financial Times* 15.11.2011.
All rights reserved.

(a) Explain what is meant by an 'ethical stance'.

(b) How might a pressure group encourage a business to become more ethical? Use examples from the text to support your answer.

Explicit objectives will have been carefully thought out. Partly this is because the business could get bad publicity if t went against its stated ethical objectives.

However, most businesses have implicit ethical objectives. Most businesses aim to deal fairly with customers, for example. However, implicit ethical objectives are not written down. Instead, they form part of the corporate culture of the organisation. They are part of the unwritten rules about how the business deals with its stakeholders, such as customers, suppliers and workers.

Corporate Social Responsibility (CSR)

Some large businesses have responded to concerns about Corporate Social Responsibility, their responsibility not just to their shareholders, but to all stakeholders, by auditing relevant activities. These audits may then be made available to the public in a Corporate Responsibility Report, in the same way that the financial accounts of the company are published. Auditing involves inspecting evidence against established standards. Auditors can then say that the evidence presented by the business is 'true and fair'.

In accounting, standards for accounting audits are set by accounting bodies, such as the Accounting Standards Board. In contrast, social and environmental auditing is voluntary and there is no body that draws up rules about how audits should take place. At present, companies are free to choose what standards they should be measured against and who the auditors will be. Indeed, the vast majority of businesses do not undertake any social or environmental accounting.

Businesses that do compile social and environmental audits use a wide range of measures, which differ from business to business. An oil company, for example, may measure the number of oil spills for which it is responsible. This would not be appropriate for a drinks company, which might use other indicators such as levels of air pollution created by its breweries and distilleries. Social and environmental audits might include some of the following.

Employment indicators: How well does the business treat its staff? This might include indicators about pensions, healthcare benefits, union representation, training and education, number of accidents involving staff, payment of minimum wages, equal opportunities and the level of women in higher management or director positions.

Human rights indicators: How well does the company perform on human rights issues? For example, does it encourage its workers to join trade unions and give those trade unions negotiating rights with the company? Does it have works councils? Does it or its suppliers use child labour? Does the company operate in, buy supplies from or sell products to countries that have a poor human rights record? Does it discriminate on grounds of race, gender or age when recruiting or promoting staff?

The communities in which the business operates: What impact does the business have on the life of the communities in which it operates? For example, how much does it give to charities? How much is spent on local schools, hospitals and housing?

Business integrity and ethics: How ethical is the business in its activities? For example, has the company been involved in any cases of trading that break legislation? Did the company make political contributions and to whom? Was the company involved in cases associated with unfair competition?

Product responsibility: What was the social impact of the products sold by the business? For example, were there health and safety issues? Was after-sales service adequate? Was advertising true and fair? Did the company manage its information on customers and suppliers in such a way as to preserve their privacy?

The environment: These indicators can form a separate environmental audit. Some businesses may only compile an environmental audit and not include any of the other social indicators described above. Indicators might include the amount of energy or other raw materials, such as water or pesticides, used by the business; how much waste or effluent was produced; the levels of greenhouse gases or ozone-depleting emissions; what percentage of materials used were recycled; the company's impact on bio-diversity; what impact it had on protected and sensitive areas; how many times it was fined during the period for failure to comply with environmental regulations and the total level of fines.

Some of these measures are financial, i.e. they are measured in monetary terms. Many, however, are non-financial. For this reason, it is difficult to get a quick and easy overall measure of how well a business is doing from its social and environmental audit. In contrast to a financial audit, like a set of financial accounts, where it is possible to look at the profit and loss account and say that the business has performed better or worse in terms of revenues, costs and profit, the data from social audits are more difficult to assess and compare from year to year.

Pay and rewards

An important issue in the area of business ethics relates to pay and rewards. **Remuneration** is the reward from work, in the form of pay, wages or salary. Businesses use pay and rewards for different purposes.

- To attract employees with the right skills, experience and knowledge. Where jobs are less skilled the available number of workers is very high, which means pay can be relatively low. Where skills are extremely rare, for example with top Premier League footballers, pay rates need to be very high to attract the best.

Question 2

Lucent Technologies was a US manufacturer of telecommunications equipment. It was created by a demerger with AT&T, a large US telecommunications company, in 1996. In 2006, Lucent merged with Alcatel, the French telecommunications equipment company.

Whilst still an independent company, Lucent was pursuing a strategy of selling into the Chinese telecommunications market. As part of its marketing effort, it invited Chinese officials to the USA. The US Department of Justice in an investigation found that the company spent more than $10 million (£5 million) on about 315 trips for 1,000 Chinese government officials and telecoms executives. The problem was that they 'spent little or no time' touring Lucent's production facilities. Instead, they enjoyed sightseeing in Hawaii, Las Vegas, the Grand Canyon, Niagara Falls, Disneyland and Universal Studies. Despite paying for travel, hotels and meals, Lucent also gave some Chinese officials a daily cash allowance of $500 to $1,000. As for relatives or associates of the invited Chinese officials, they were offered 'educational opportunities' both in the USA and back in China. The total cost of these 'educational opportunities' to Lucent was over $100,000.

Lucent was fined $2.5 million by the US Department of Justice under the Foreign Corrupt Practices Act for attempting to bribe Chinese officials to place orders with the company.

Source: adapted from The *Financial Times* 06.03.2008. All rights reserved.

(a) Explain why Lucent was fined $2.5 million.

(b) Assess whether European and US businesses should be allowed by their governments to use bribery to win contracts in emerging markets such as China and India.

- To reward and motivate existing staff. The ultimate aim of businesses is to make profit. Rather than pay the lowest possible rates of pay, to keep costs down and profit margins high, businesses need to ensure that their pay rates ensure that staff are motivated to work to the best of their ability.
- Maximise productivity levels. Pay is an important motivator and highly motivated staff are more productive.

In 2015 a widely publicised report by the pressure group Citizens UK found that some UK employers, including supermarkets and other companies, pay their workers at a low rate, resulting in the government spending around £11 billion per year topping up their pay through benefits such as Tax Credits. Some businesses such as supermarkets often take on a number of apprenticeships, which is a positive thing, although it can involve significant public subsidy. Businesses are organisations that need to make a profit if they are to survive. Although higher profits can be achieved by reducing the pay of employees within legal limits, is this ethical?

Generally it is the role of individual businesses to decide on rates of pay. An exception to this relates to low pay. In the UK there exists a **National Minimum Wage**. Details are shown in Table 1.

Table 1 UK National Minimum Wage – from October 2015

Adult rate (21+)	£6.70 per hour
18–20 year olds	£5.30 per hour
16–17 year olds	£3.87 per hour
Apprentice rate	£3.30 per hour

Source: www.gov.uk

This type of government-imposed regulation effectively forces businesses to pay their workers a fair rate of pay. It is a legal lim on what can be paid and means that businesses cannot pay very low wages.

Some argue the National Minimum Wage is not high enough to provide an adequate standard of living. As in the example of supermarkets above, workers on low pay often qualify for Tax Credits, paid by the government to workers who earn below a certain amount of money. Effectively, the government is making up the difference between the wages paid by a business and the amount needed for a person to live on. The Living Wage Foundatio is an independent organisation that campaigns for fair pay. The Foundation has developed the idea of a **living wage**, which is set higher than the National Minimum Wage and covers the basic cost of living. The 2015 rate is £7.85 per hour (£9.15 in London), compared to that for the adult National Minimum Wage of £6.70.

Remuneration is extremely important for a business. The extent to which decisions on pay are an ethical matter depends on which perspective this is being viewed from. Free market proponents would argue that decisions on pay should be left to businesses to decide. The aim of business is to maximise profits and returns for owners/shareholders. If, to achieve this, a business needs to pay millions to attract the most highly skilled staff, then this is their decision. In 2014 Wayne Rooney, striker for Manchester United, earned a reported £14.4 million. Is it 'right' that one person can earn so much money, while others have to make do with the minimum wage? From a business point of view it makes sense to pay the highest salaries to the most highly skilled people. If Manchester United did not buy the best players, it would not be able to compete for league titles and other trophies.

Question 3

Ocado is an online UK supermarket that has grown over time. In 2015 it was widely reported that the business would not commit to paying all of its workers the living wage. At an Annual Shareholder Meeting, it was widely reported that the Chairman put forward that a majority of Ocado employees were already paid above the living wage. He also put forward that it was necessary to balance off what can be afforded and what is right to do.

He stated that the vast majority of businesses want to do the right thing on employee pay, but have a responsibility to shareholders to only do what they can afford to do.

(a) Explain what is meant by the 'living wage'.

(b) Assess the case for paying the living wage from the point of view of:
   (i) Ocado shareholders
   (ii) Ocado employees.

Trade-offs between profit and ethics

As with social responsibility, there can exist a conflict between ethical objectives and profitability. A trade-off exists when the selection of one choice results in the loss of another. This applies at all levels, from individuals through to the largest corporation and even governments. If I choose to buy a new car the trade-off might be that I cannot have a holiday. The trade-off of a government decision to increase the income tax personal allowance might be that it cannot afford to spend more money on a high-speed rail upgrade. Similarly for businesses, trade-offs exist with any decision. Investing in a new production facility may mean that a new fleet of vans cannot be purchased. The idea of such trade-offs is particularly apparent when considering ethics. Is the cost of acting ethically an acceptance of lower profit?

For businesses, acting ethically when not required to do so by the law can have a negative impact on profit in a number of ways. The result can be a trade-off.

- *It can raise costs.* For example, paying higher wages than is necessary to overseas workers increases costs. Having to find other ways than animal experiments to test a new drug might add to costs. Adopting an ethical code of practice can raise costs. Staff have to be made aware of the code and trained to implement it. It takes management time to prepare a code of practice. Paying workers more than a legal minimum directly increases costs.
- *It can reduce revenues.* A business might lose a contract if it refuses to give a bribe. Selling medicines to emerging economies at low prices might increase sales, but total revenue is likely to be lower. Refusing to develop GM crops might mean a competitor getting into the market first and becoming the market leader. Acting ethically might even mean the destruction of the company. For example, a cigarette manufacturer that took full account of the costs it causes to customers would probably decide to cease trading.

However, adopting an ethical stance can produce benefits.

- Some companies have used their ethical stance for marketing purposes. In the UK, for example, the Co-operative Bank and The Body Shop have both increased sales by having a strong ethical stance and drawing in customers who are attracted by this. But adopting an ethical stance is no guarantee of success. In Question 1, Chiquita's more ethical approach has not yet appeared to result in higher sales or profits. Many high street coffee shops stress their ethical credentials. Starbucks stated in 2015 that 99 per cent of its coffee was ethically sourced through a partnership with Conservation International. Costa, in its Corporate Responsibility Report, states that it only uses Forest Stewardship Council (FSC) certified wood for furniture in its stores. However, Harris + Hoole, an artisan coffee shop brand launched in 2012 which emphasised its ethical credentials, closed a number of its London stores in 2014.
- For most companies that have taken Corporate Social Responsibility seriously, informed by ethics, it can also act as the equivalent of an insurance policy. Businesses don't want to be seen to be behaving unethically and face serious penalties for breaking the law, or see sales fall as customers protest against this behaviour. In 2002, two major companies paid the price for reported unethical behaviour. Enron, a large US energy trading company, collapsed. It was found to have manipulated its accounts to inflate its profits. Senior management was reported as acting unethically by hiding this from shareholders and government. This also led to the collapse of one of the world's top five accounting firms, Arthur Andersen. It had audited Enron's accounts and was accused of hiding the irregularities. As a result, it began to lose its major customers and decided to close down.

Large companies need to take seriously the consequences of their behaviour and decision making. Customers and society have become less tolerant of businesses that behave in a way they regard as unethical. However, most companies tend to follow trends and adopt ethical policies that will prevent them from coming to harm in the market place or by law. A few have adopted an aggressive ethical stance, which sometimes has led to them gaining more customers. Often, small to medium-sized businesses do not have management time or resources to draw up an ethical code of practice. Their ethical stance and behaviour is more organic, and influenced by the society in which they operate.

Exam tip

Exam questions on this topic offer opportunities for analysis and evaluation. When asked to consider the extent to which a business decision is the right one, it is possible to consider this from different angles. For a typical question in this area there will not be a right or a wrong answer, and marks will be based on the strength of your arguments.

In short, when asked if a business decision is an ethical one, the answer will almost certainly be, 'it depends'. It depends on the type of business, the market it operates in, economic conditions, staff recruitment and retention, and so on. Using this 'it depends' approach is useful when tackling questions around ethics. Having this in mind when considering an exam scenario will help you to focus on the need for evaluation and give some structure to a response.

Thinking bigger

The question of business ethics is loaded with contention and controversy. What factors does a business need to consider when weighing up being 'good' and being profitable as part of its decision-making processes? Is this a zero sum game, or can one improve the other? What considerations influence decision making? For example, is the priority to drive down costs or to encourage professional development to upskill a workforce?

It is worth actually thinking through your own beliefs in this area. These views can be used in constructing arguments one way or the other. On the one hand, being ethical can increase the costs of a business. This might have implications for prices and thus competitiveness. It may mean that a business loses market position due to its ethical stance. Conversely, being ethical can have positive implications for a business. Lush is a soap and cosmetics manufacturer that refuses to test on animals. It supports various campaign organisations, such as the Hunt Saboteurs Association and Plane Stupid, which campaigns against the expansion of the airline industry. It tries to use only natural ingredients and most things are made in the UK. In 2014 the business saw a large increase in sales and profits, part of which it attributed to its ethical stance.

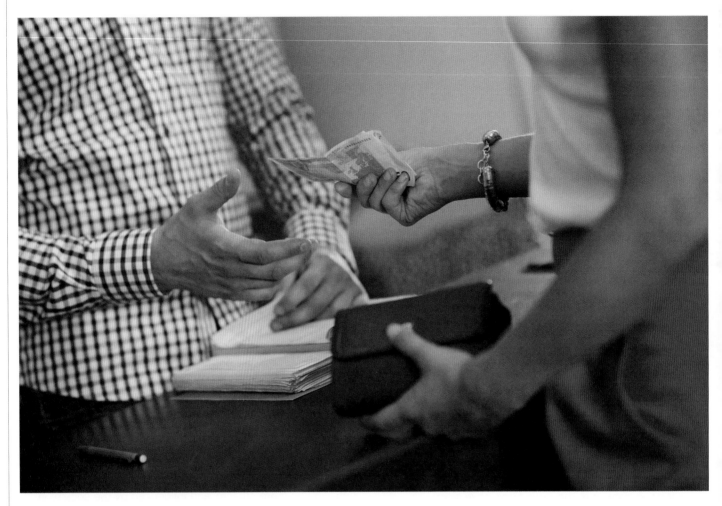

Table 2 Factors that businesses may consider in the context of decision-making processes, weighing up being 'good' and being profitable

Good	Profitable
• Businesses have responsibilities to a wide range of stakeholders, not only shareholders. While profits may satisfy shareholders, employees may be less happy if they are paid low wages.	• Unprofitable businesses do not survive. An ethical stance is a luxury that can be indulged when a business is established and successful.
• A business that treats its workers well, be it with pay or opportunities in the workplace, is more likely to retain its employees. This is extremely important for businesses as recruiting and training new staff is very costly.	• A trade-off can exist between being ethical and being profitable. For example, paying the living wage will increase the costs of a business that would otherwise have paid the minimum wage. If the market is competitive these higher costs may lead to uncompetitive prices.
• Being good actually increases the chance of being profitable. An ethical stance can bring reputational benefits. Many consumers today are conscious about ethical matters and are increasingly prepared to spend money on products that are more ethically based.	• Profitable businesses are more able to invest and innovate products that improve society. Pharmaceutical companies make vast profits. These are used, in part, to develop new drugs, such as those designed to treat cancer. Car manufacturers use profits to develop technologies such as fuel cell power units that reduce reliance on fossil fuels. These developments and advancements would not happen without profits.

Case study

DIRECTORS' PAY

In 2014, the High Pay Centre, a UK non-party think tank, reported that the directors of the top 100 listed UK companies now earned 130 times the average sum earned by their employees. This difference between directors and employees is growing. In 1998 the difference was 47 times. It is estimated that pay received by the average FTSE top 100 CEO increased from £4.1 million to £4.7 million in 2013, roughly 174 times that of the average UK worker.

Table 3 shows the pay ratios of some of the top directors of UK companies compared to employees.

The highest paid director earned 780 times more than the average employee of the business.

Some directors may put forward that the pay system is fair as the main increases are in the performance-related area of pay. Basic salaries, although high compared to most employees, have not increased greatly. But bonuses and share awards, both based on how the company performs, have increased when the businesses have performed well.

Source: adapted from www.highpaycentre.org

(a) Calculate the CEO/average employee pay multiple for:
  i)   Next (2 marks)
  ii) Unilever (2 marks)

(b) Explain one reason why directors' pay is significantly higher than that of employees. (4 marks)

(c) Assess the extent to which the difference in pay between top directors and employees might be considered an ethical issue. (12 marks)

Table 3 The 10 highest pay ratios at FTSE 100 companies

Company name	CEO	CEO Pay/£*	Average employee pay/£	CEO/average employee pay multiple
WPP	Martin Sorrell	29.8m	38265	780
Next	Lord Simon Wolfson	4.6m**	10125	?
Compass	Richard Cousins	5.5m	13248	418
Whitbread	Andy Harrison	6.4m	15362	415
TUI Travel	Peter Long	10.1m	26874	377
SAB Miller	Alan Clark	6.5m	17698	365
Associated British Foods	George Weston	5.3m	14558	361
Unilever	Paul Polman	6.4m	23920	?
G4S	Ashley Almanza	2m	7415	266
Anglo-American	Mark Cutifani/Cynthia Carroll	6.8m***	27346	247

The disclosure of the historic data used to calculate these ratios is inconsistent and therefore figures are estimated.

*CEO pay figures rounded to 1dp

**Wolfson donated annual bonus element of his pay package to staff

***Cumulative total paid for CEO role

Key terms

Corporate Social Responsibility (CSR) – a business assessing and taking responsibility for its effects on the environment and its impact on social welfare. It involves the idea that businesses bear a responsibility that stretches beyond their shareholders.

Ethical codes of practice – statements about how employees in a business should behave in particular circumstances where ethical issues arise.

Ethics – in the context of business ethics, consideration of the moral 'rights and wrongs' of a decision at an often strategic level, in accordance with the law, and a business's code of conduct in relationship to Corporate Social Responsibility.

Living wage – an hourly rate of pay based on the basic cost of living, set independently of government and updated annually.

National Minimum Wage – the minimum pay per hour all workers are entitled to by law.

Remuneration – the reward for work in the form of pay, salary or wages, including allowances and benefits, such as company cars, health insurance, pension, bonuses and non-cash incentives.

Sanctions or Trade embargoes – sanctions are restrictions imposed on trade or investment with the aim of influencing a policy change in another country. Trade embargoes can be included in sanctions, where commercial shipments are banned in and out of a particular country, or where an embargo is placed on a particular product.

Knowledge check

1. Give two examples of ethical decisions an oil production company might have to make.

2. What is meant by a trade-off?

3. Explain which types of companies might be particularly affected by ethical issues relating to: (a) the environment; (b) animal rights issues; (c) workers in developing countries; (d) bribery; (e) new technologies; (f) access to products; (g) trading with politically unstable countries.

4. What might be contained in an ethical code of practice?

5. How are the National Minimum Wage and the 'living wage' different?

6. To what extent can businesses increase profits by becoming more ethical?

7. 'Businesses should not be expected to act ethically.' Explain the two sides to this argument.

8. To whom might a business have social responsibilities?

Key points

1. Statement of comprehensive income (profit and loss account): key information and stakeholder interest.
2. Statement of financial position (balance sheet): key information and stakeholder interest.

Getting started

Marks & Spencer (M&S) is an established retailer with nearly 800 stores in the UK. It has around 34 million customers and is the market leader in womenswear, lingerie and menswear. However, in 2014 around 55 per cent of its turnover was generated by food sales. Tables 1 and 2 show some financial information for M&S.

Table 1 Extracts from M&S statement of comprehensive income 2014

	2014 (£m)	2013 (£m)
Revenue	10,309.70	10,026.80
Cost of sales	6,439.00	6,230.30
Gross profit	3,870.70	3,796.50
Selling and admin expenses	3,224.30	3,110.00
Operating profit	694.50	753.00
Profit before tax	622.90	648.10

Table 2 Extracts from M&S statement of financial position 2014

	2014 (£m)	2013 (£m)
Non-current assets	6,534.50	6,342.80
Current assets	1,368.50	1,267.90
Current liabilities	2,349.30	2,238.30
Non-current liabilities	2,847.00	2,852.90
Share capital	408.10	403.40
Retained earnings	6,325.10	6,150.30

Source: adapted from Companies House, www.gov.uk

What is the key information in the above extracts? Comment on the performance of the business between 2013 and 2014. Why might shareholders be interested in this information?

Financial statements

Companies are required by law to produce financial statements at the end of the financial year – although many plcs produce them on a quarterly basis. According to the International Accounting Standards Board, the body responsible for developing and approving International Financial Reporting Standards since 1 January 2015, the following statements are required.

1. **Statement of financial position** (balance sheet), which shows the assets, liabilities and capital of the business.
2. **Statement of comprehensive income** (profit and loss account), which starts with the profit or loss for the year and

then shows other items of comprehensive income, such as gains made on currency transactions.

Sole traders and partnerships also produce financial statements. They tend to be less complex than those of companies and may be presented in a slightly different style. However, the majority of small businesses produce a balance sheet and a profit and loss account (or an income and expenditure account). In this unit the focus is on the statement of financial position (balance sheet) and the income statement (profit and loss account).

The statement of comprehensive income

For most plcs the statement of comprehensive income is used to show the income and expenditure of the business for a period of time (usually one year) and calculate the profit made by the business. The financial information has to be presented in a standard way. An example for a limited company, WellFed Ltd, is shown in Table 3 on the next page. WellFed Ltd supplies cattle and sheep feed to farmers in the UK.

Key information

The statement of comprehensive income contains the following information.

- **Revenue.** This is the money the business receives from selling goods and services. It is sometimes called turnover. Revenue must not include VAT. This is because VAT does not belong to the business. The revenue for WellFed Ltd in 2014 was £25.4 million.
- **Cost of sales.** This refers to the production costs of a business. More specifically it relates to direct costs, such as raw materials and labour. In the case of WellFed Ltd the cost of sales would be the cost of grain, nutrients, electricity, wages to factory workers and any sales taxes paid such as VAT. For a retailer it will be the cost of buying in stock to re-sell and direct labour. For a service provider it will include the direct costs of providing a service, such as labour. In 2014 the cost of sales for WellFed was £12.3 million.
- **Gross profit.** This is the cost of sales subtracted from the revenue. It is the profit made before the deduction of general overheads. The gross profit made by WellFed in 2014 was £13.1 million (£25.4 million – £12.3 million).
- **Selling expenses.** A business is likely to incur a range of expenses that are directly related to the selling of its products. Examples might include sales commissions, advertising, distribution and promotional costs. In 2014 WellFed Ltd spent £3.2 million on selling expenses.

Table 3 Extract from the statement of comprehensive income for WellFed Ltd, year ending 31.12.14

	2014 (£m)	2013 (£m)
Revenue	25.4	21.2
Cost of sales	12.3	11.7
Gross profit	**13.1**	**9.5**
Selling expenses	3.2	2.3
Admin expenses	6.4	5.2
Operating profit	**3.5**	**2.0**
Finance costs	0.4	0.4
Profit for the year (net profit)	**3.1**	**1.6**
Taxation	0.6	0.3
Profit for the year (net profit) after taxation	**2.5**	**1.3**

- **Administrative expenses.** These are the general overheads or indirect costs of the business. Examples might include office salaries, expenses claimed by senior staff, stationery supplies, IT expenses, accountancy fees and telephone bills. WellFed Ltd incurred £6.4 million of administrative expenses in 2014.
- **Operating profit.** If the selling and administrative costs are subtracted from gross profit we get the operating profit. The operating profit is the profit generated from the firm's core activities. It does not include any income from financial investments made by the business. WellFed Ltd made an operating profit of £3.5 million in 2014.
- **Finance costs.** If a business borrows money it will have to pay interest to the lender. The amount paid will be entered in the statement of comprehensive income as a **finance cost**. However, a business may also receive interest if it has money in deposit accounts. This will appear as **finance income** in the accounts. In 2014 WellFed Ltd paid £400,000 in interest.
- **Profit for the year (net profit).** If the cost of finance is subtracted from the operating profit the net profit for the year is determined. This is the profit before taxation. WellFed Ltd made a profit for the year (net profit) of £3.1 million in 2014.
- **Profit for the year (net profit) after tax.** This is the amount of money that is left over after all expenses, including taxation, have been deducted from revenue. It is often referred to as the 'bottom line'. The money belongs to the owners of the business. In the case of a limited company it belongs to the shareholders. However, it may not necessarily be distributed to the shareholders. Some of it may be retained. This is discussed later in the unit. WellFed Ltd made a profit for the year (net profit) after tax of £2.5 million in 2014.

The extract from the statement of comprehensive income for WellFed Ltd in Table 3 shows figures for both 2014 and the previous year. This is standard practice and helps to make comparisons over time. For example, the performance of WellFed Ltd has improved over the two years. Its profit for the year (net profit) after tax (the 'bottom line') has nearly doubled from £1.3 million in 2013 to £2.5 million in 2014.

Stakeholder interest

The statement of comprehensive income can be used to help evaluate the performance of a business. Consequently, it is likely to be of interest to a range of stakeholders.

Shareholders: Naturally the owners of a business will be interested in its performance. Shareholders are likely to be interested in the profit made by the business – particularly the profit for the year (net profit) after tax. This is an effective guide to the performance of a business, but by no means the only guide. Rising profits are an indication of improving performance. It is possible for shareholders, or their representatives, to calculate profit for the year (net profit) and gross profit margins using information from the statement of comprehensive income to assess performance more rigorously. This is discussed in Unit 34.

It is also possible to gauge the growth of the business by looking at the statement of comprehensive income. If the revenue is rising this suggests that the business is growing. In the WellFed Ltd statement, revenue rises from £21.2 million in 2013 to £25.4 million in 2014. This is an increase of 19.8 per cent and indicates a growth rate of nearly one fifth.

Managers and directors: Since managers and directors are responsible for running the business, they are likely to use key information in the statement of comprehensive income to monitor progress. For example, they might be setting annual targets for growth in revenue or profit for the year (net profit). Changes in the revenue, for example, will show how fast a company has grown and whether targets have been met.

Employees: If employees, or their representatives, are seeking a wage increase, it may be helpful to have access to some of the information in the statement of comprehensive income when presenting a claim. For example, if WellFed Ltd employees wanted a 5 per cent wage increase, they might point to the 92 per cent increase in profit for the year (net profit) (from £1.3 million in 2013 to £2.5 million in 2014) as an argument that the company could afford it.

Suppliers: Before a supplier accepts an order from a new customer on trade credit, it is prudent to carry out a check on their creditworthiness. One way to do this is to look at the trading history of the customer. If the customer can provide several years of authenticated accounts, this might help to show whether the customer is able to pay what is owed at the end of the credit period. If the statement of comprehensive income show that a customer is consistently profitable, this might be enough proof for the supplier.

The government: Companies have to produce a statement of comprehensive income by law. It is needed by the tax authorities to help assess how much tax a business has to pay. HMRC collects taxes on behalf of the government and requires all business owners to provide documentary evidence of the profits or losses made by the business every year. Also, the ONS (Office for National Statistics), a government agency, may have an interest in business accounts because it collects economic data, which is collated and presented for public consumption.

Question 1

Moosewear Ltd is an online shopping site. It sells mainly winter clothing imported from Alaska and Canada. The majority of its products are made from fake fur. In 2013 it launched a range of furry 'onesies', which sold very well. An extract from the statement of comprehensive income for Moosewear Ltd is shown in Table 4.

Table 4 Extract from the statement of comprehensive income for Moosewear Ltd, 31.12.14

	2014 (£000)	2013 (£000)
Revenue	3,450	2,980
Cost of sales	1,210	990
Gross profit	2,240	1,990
Selling expenses	760	560
Admin expenses	780	870
Operating profit	700	560
Finance costs	80	70
Profit for the year (net profit)	620	490
Taxation	120	110
Profit for the year (net profit) after taxation	500	380

(a) What is meant by cost of sales? Use examples from this case to illustrate your answer.

(b) Calculate the percentage increase in (i) revenue and (ii) profit for the year (net profit) after tax for Moosewear Ltd from 2013 to 2014.

(c) Discuss whether shareholders are likely to be happy with the performance of Moosewear Ltd in 2014.

Statement of financial position

The statement of financial position (balance sheet) provides a summary of a firm's assets, liabilities and capital. It is like a photograph of the financial position of a business at a particular point in time.

- **Assets.** Assets are the resources that a business owns and uses. Assets are usually divided into current assets and non-current assets. Current assets are used up in production, such as stocks of raw materials. They can also be money owed to the business by debtors. Non-current assets, such as machinery, are used again and again over a period of time.

- **Liabilities.** Liabilities are the debts of the business, that is, what it owes to other businesses, individuals and institutions. Liabilities are a source of funds for a business. They might be short term, such as an overdraft, or long term, such as a mortgage. In the balance sheet liabilities are divided into current liabilities and non-current liabilities.

- **Capital.** This is the money introduced by the owners of the business, for example when they buy shares. It is another source of funds and can be used to purchase assets.

In all balance sheets the value of assets (what a business uses or owns) will equal the value of liabilities and capital (what the business owes). This is because any increase in total assets must be funded by an equal increase in capital or liabilities. A business wanting to buy extra machinery (an asset) may need to obtain a bank loan (a liability), for example. Alternatively, a reduction in credit from suppliers (a liability) may mean a reduction in stocks that can be bought (an asset). So:

$$\text{Assets} = \text{capital} + \text{liabilities}$$

Worked example

A business has assets of £437.6 million, its capital is £250.1 million, therefore its liabilities must be £187.5 million (£437.6 − £250.1).

If this business took out a £15 million mortgage to pay for a new building, liabilities would rise by £15 million and the value of assets would also rise by £15 million. As a result the business's assets would be £452.6 million and its liabilities would be £202.5 million. Capital and liabilities added together would be £452.6 million, that is, exactly the same as total assets.

Key information

The key information that is likely to be listed in a statement of financial position is shown in Table 5 on the next page. It shows the assets, liabilities and capital of WellFed Ltd, the cattle feed producer mentioned earlier.

Table 5 Statement of financial position for WellFed Ltd, as at 31.12.14

	2014 (£m)	2013 (£m)
Non-current assets		
Goodwill	30.5	27.8
Other intangible assets	15.2	11.6
Property, plant & equipment	97.7	94.1
	143.4	133.5
Current assets		
Inventories	8.6	6.7
Trade and other receivables	3.4	3.1
Cash and cash equivalents	3.1	2.7
	15.1	12.5
Total assets	**158.5**	**146.0**
Current liabilities		
Trade and other payables	5.5	5.1
Dividends payable	1.2	0.8
Current tax liabilities	6.7	5.7
	13.4	11.6
Non-current liabilities		
Borrowings	24.5	26.1
Provisions	4.1	3.4
Pensions	7.8	6.7
	36.4	36.2
Total liabilities	**49.8**	**47.8**
Net assets	**108.7**	**98.2**
Shareholders' equity		
Share capital	30.0	30.0
Other reserves	17.7	9.7
Retained earnings	61.0	58.5
Total equity	**108.7**	**98.2**

Non-current assets: Non-current assets are any assets that are not expected to be sold within 12 months. They are the long-term resources of the business. A number of entries are likely to be found in this section of the balance sheet.

- **Goodwill.** This is an example of an intangible asset. This is a non-physical asset of a business (i.e. it is not a visible asset). It is the amount the business is worth above the value of net assets. Goodwill exists if a company has built up a good reputation and its customers are likely to return. The goodwill for WellFed Ltd in 2014 was valued at £30.5 million.
- **Other intangible assets.** These may appear in some plc balance sheets. Examples include brand names, copyrights, trademarks and patents. The value of other intangible assets for WellFed Ltd in 2014 was £15.2 million.
- **Property, plant and equipment.** These are the tangible assets that the business owns. Tangible assets are the physical assets of a business (i.e. they are visible). Examples for WellFed Ltd might be a factory, and the machines and equipment used to process cattle feed from raw materials. In 2014, WellFed Ltd had £97.7 million of tangible assets. The total for non-current assets is also shown in the balance sheet – it was £143.4 million.

- **Investments.** These are the financial assets owned by the company. An example might be shares held in other companies. If investments are listed under non-current assets it means that they are not expected to be sold for at least 12 months. If investments are likely to be sold within 12 months they should be listed under current assets. According to the balance sheet in Table 5, WellFed Ltd does not own any investments.

Current assets: Current assets are the liquid assets that belong to the business. These assets are either cash, or are expected to be converted into cash within 12 months.
- **Inventories.** This refers to stocks of raw materials and components, stocks of finished goods and work in progress. For WellFed Ltd examples might be grain, such as barley and wheat, nutrients and packaging. The value of WellFed's inventories in 2014 was £8.6 m.
- **Trade and other receivables.** These are trade debtors, prepayments and any other amounts owed to the business that are likely to be repaid within 12 months. If WellFed Ltd gives its customers trade credit, the money owed by customers would be an example. In 2014 WellFed Ltd was owed a total of £3.4 million by debtors.
- **Cash at bank and in hand.** This is the money held by a business on the premises or in bank accounts. WellFed Ltd had £3.1 million of cash or cash equivalents in 2014. Also, WellFed's current assets totaled £15.1 million and the value of total assets for the business was £158.5 million.

Current liabilities: Any money owed by the business that is expected to be repaid within 12 months is called a current liability. Some examples are outlined below.
- **Borrowings.** Any short-term loans or bank overdrafts taken out by the business. In this case WellFed does not have any short-term loans.
- **Trade and other payables.** Trade creditors and other amounts owed by the business to suppliers of goods, services and utilities, for example. Table 5 shows that WellFed owed £5.5 million to its suppliers in 2014.
- **Dividends payable.** When the balance sheet is prepared (at the end of the financial year perhaps) it is possible that the company has decided how much it will pay to the shareholders in dividends. However, the money has not yet been paid so it appears in the balance sheet as dividends payable. WellFed Ltd owed £1.2 million dividends to shareholders on 31.12.14.
- **Current tax liabilities.** Corporation tax, employees' income tax and any other tax owed by the business that must be repaid within 12 months. WellFed Ltd owed £6.7 million to the tax authorities on 31.12.14. The total value of WellFed's current liabilities in 2014 was £13.4 million.

Non-current liabilities: These are the long-term liabilities of a business. Any amount of money owed for more than one year will appear in this section of the balance sheet.
- **Other loans and borrowings.** Money owed by the company that does not have to be repaid for at least 12 months. Examples would be long-term bank loans and mortgages. Table 5 shows that WellFed Ltd owed £24.5 million in 2014.

- **Retirement pension obligations.** Companies need to show any money owed to past employees in the form of pension obligations. In 2014 WellFed Ltd had £7.8 million of pension commitments.
- **Provisions.** Provisions have to be made if a company is likely to incur expenditure in the future. Such expenditure might arise as a result of agreements in contracts or warranties. An example for WellFed Ltd might be a possible bad debt that it may incur. If these provisions are short term they will appear under current liabilities. In 2014 WellFed Ltd had £4.1 million of provisions. The total value of its non-current liabilities was £36.4 million. Its total liabilities were £49.8 million.

Net assets: Net assets is simply the value of all assets minus the value of all liabilities. It will be the same value as shareholders' equity at the bottom of the balance sheet. The value of WellFed's net assets in 2014 was £108.7 million. The net assets provide a guide to the value of a business.

Equity: The bottom section of the balance sheet shows the amounts of money owed to the shareholders. It will contain details of share capital and reserves.

- **Share capital.** The amount of money paid by shareholders for their shares when they were originally issued. It does not represent the current value of those shares on the stock market. Share capital is not usually repaid to the shareholders in the lifetime of a company. The value of WellFed's issued share capital in 2014 was £30 million.
- **Share premium account.** This shows the difference between the value of new shares issued by the company and their nominal value. For example, the nominal value of a share may have been £1. The company may decide to issue 2 million new shares. If the company sold them for £3, each new share is now worth £2 more than the nominal price. In total this would be £4 million (£2 x 2 million). This £4 million would be entered on the share premium account in the balance sheet. WellFed Ltd does not have any share premium.
- **Other reserves.** Refers to any amounts owing to the shareholders not covered by the other entries under equity. WellFed Ltd had £17.7 million of other reserves in 2014.
- **Retained earnings.** The same as retained profit. It is the amount of profit retained by the business to be used in the future, for example to fund investment projects. WellFed Ltd had £61 million of retained profit in 2014.

The total value of shareholders' equity, £108.7 million in the case of WellFed Ltd, is the same as net assets. This will always be the case and explains why the statement of financial position is sometimes called the balance sheet. Company law requires companies to show both this year's and last year's figures in published accounts. This allows comparisons to be made.

Exam tip

Remember that retained profit in the balance sheet is not cash. It is the amount owed to shareholders that has accumulated over the years of trading. The amount of cash a business has is shown in current assets. Some of the retained profit may have been used to buy more assets. Only if the company was liquidated would retained profit be returned to shareholders.

Question 2

Steepwell Ltd makes cakes and biscuits for supermarkets and large retailers. Table 6 shows the statement of financial position for the company as at 31.12.14.

Table 6 Statement of financial position for Steepwell Ltd, as at 31.12.14

	2014 (£000)	2013 (£000)
Non-current assets		
Intangible assets	8,667	8,009
Property and equipment	11,987	12,134
	20,654	20,143
Current assets		
Inventories	4,501	4,511
Trade and other receivables	3,444	4,100
Cash and cash equivalents	1,200	1,300
	9,145	9,911
Total assets	29,799	30,054
Current liabilities		
Trade and other payables	4,888	4,976
Current tax liabilities	?????	2,009
	6,009	6,985
Non-current liabilities		
Borrowings	4,222	4,777
Pensions	1,233	1,341
	5,455	6,118
Total liabilities	11,464	13,103
Net assets	??????	16,951
Shareholders' equity		
Share capital	10,000	10,000
Retained earnings	8,335	6,951
Total equity	18,335	16,951

(a) Complete the balance sheet by calculating the missing values for (i) net assets and (ii) current tax liabilities.

(b) Give two possible examples of trade and other payables for Steepwell Ltd.

(c) Explain the difference between current liabilities and non-current liabilities.

(d) What has happened to the value of Steepwell Ltd between 2013 and 2014?

Stakeholder interest

The statement of financial position can also be used to help evaluate the performance of a business. It shows different information from that of the statement of comprehensive income, and stakeholders are likely to be interested in both statements together.

Shareholders: Shareholders might use the balance sheet to analyse the asset structure of the business. This shows how the funds raised by the business have been put to use. For example, shareholders in WellFed Ltd in Table 5 can see that more than 60 per cent of the assets (£97.7 million) are tied up in property, plant and equipment. The balance sheet also shows the capital structure of the business, i.e. the different sources of funds used by the business. For WellFed Ltd nearly 67 per cent of the firm's funding comes from the shareholders.

The balance sheet can also be used to assess the solvency of the business. A business is solvent if it has enough liquid assets to pay its bills. The value of working capital will help to assess solvency. The working capital of a business can be calculated by subtracting current liabilities from current assets. For WellFed the value of working capital is £1.7 million (£15.1 million – £13.4 million). This might be regarded as inadequate because the value of current liabilities is only just covered by current assets.

Worked example

Gallagher & Sons Ltd is a manufacturer of sweets and desserts. It supplies supermarkets and other large retailers. Table 7 shows some financial information taken from the statement of financial position.

Table 7 Extract from Gallagher & Sons Ltd, statement of financial position, 2014

	2014 £ million
Current assets	
Inventories	34.9
Trade and receivables	28.6
Cash and equivalents	31.8
Current liabilities	
Trade and other payables	25.1
Borrowings	32.1
Other tax liabilities	11.9

The working capital for Gallagher & Sons Ltd is given by:

Working capital = current assets – current liabilities

$$= £95,300,000 – £69,100,000$$
$$= £26,200,000$$

In this example, Gallagher & Sons Ltd has £26,200,000 of working capital. This may be an adequate amount of working capital for the business because current assets exceed current liabilities by about 1.5 times. Working capital is discussed in more detail in Unit 35.

The value of a business is roughly equivalent to the value of net assets in the business. This means that shareholders can use the balance sheet to see if their investment is growing. Between 2013 and 2014 the value of WellFed Ltd grew from £98.2 million to £108.7 million.

Managers and directors: The balance sheet might be used by the management of a business. For example, it is important for senior managers to be aware of the firm's financial position at any given point in time. It will need to monitor working capital levels to ensure that the business does not overspend. Also, if the business is considering raising some more finance, it will have to consider the current capital structure before choosing a suitable source. For example, it might want to avoid borrowing more money if the business is already in debt. Raising fresh capital might be a better option.

Suppliers and creditors: Suppliers will be most interested in the solvency of the business. Suppliers are not likely to offer trade credit to a business that only has a limited amount of working capital. WellFed Ltd only has a small amount of working capital; as a result it might struggle to get generous trade credit terms. However, this will also depend on WellFed's trading history and it past credit record. Banks and other lenders will be interested in the balance sheet for the same reasons.

Others: It is possible that employees might use the balance sheet to assess whether a business can afford a pay rise or whether their jobs are secure. The Office for National Statistics might also extract information from the balance sheet to compile national statistics.

Links 🔗

Information in this unit could be used in a range of answers. For example, if you are discussing sources of finance for a business you could explain how the capital structure of the business might influence the decision. Businesses that already have a large quantity of borrowings might be better to raise fresh capital, for example. This unit could also be linked with Internal finance (Unit 26), External finance (Unit 27), Planning (Unit 29), Break-even (Unit 32), Profit (Unit 34), Liquidity (Unit 35), SWOT analysis (Unit 46), Decision trees (Unit 54), Ratio analysis (Unit 61) and Global competitiveness (Unit 75).

Knowledge check

1. How is gross profit calculated in a statement of comprehensive income?
2. How is operating profit calculated in a statement of comprehensive income?
3. Give three examples of selling expenses for a business.
4. What is meant by finance costs in a statement of comprehensive income?
5. What is the difference between non-current assets and current assets?
6. Give two examples of intangible assets.
7. What information is needed from the balance sheet to calculate working capital?
8. Give two examples of non-current liabilities.
9. What is meant by 'retained earnings'?
10. Give two reasons why shareholders might be interested in company accounts.
11. Why might the government be interested in company accounts?

Case study

SWANPOOL MARINE PARK

Swanpool Marine Park, Cornwall, has experienced difficult trading conditions since 2011. The business has also come under fire from pressure groups representing animal rights. Although the marine park has a good reputation for the care of its dolphins, seals, sharks and other sea creatures, negative publicity relating to the captive environment in which the animals are kept has hit the park's popularity. However, in 2014 the good weather in the UK saw a return to profit for the park as visitor numbers rose sharply. The marine park hopes to improve its image in the future by emphasising the work it does protecting the environment and saving rare marine species. An extract from the statement of comprehensive income and statement of financial position for the business are shown in Tables 8 and 9 respectively.

Table 8 Extract from statement of comprehensive income for Swanpool Marine Park, year ending 31.12.14

	2014 (£000)	2013 (£000)
Revenue	6,110	4,180
Cost of sales	4,210	2,990
Gross profit	**1,900**	**1,190**
Selling expenses	460	470
Admin expenses	380	480
Operating profit	**1,060**	**240**
Finance costs	500	600
Profit/loss for the year (net profit/loss)	**560**	**(360)**
Taxation	110	0
Profit for the year (net profit) after tax	**450**	**(360)**

Table 9 Statement of financial position for Swanpool Marine Park as at 31.12.14

	2014 (£000)	2013 (£000)
Non-current assets		
Intangible assets	1,100	900
Property and equipment	8,556	7,986
	9,656	8,886
Current assets		
Inventories	1,200	1,170
Trade and other receivables	780	750
Cash and cash equivalents	600	200
	2,580	2,120
Total assets	**12,236**	**11,006**
Current liabilities		
Trade and other payables	1,091	1,136
Borrowings	1,400	1,750
Current tax liabilities	60	76
	2,551	2,962
Non-current liabilities		
Borrowings	2,050	2,160
Pensions	833	841
	2,883	3,001
Total liabilities	**5,434**	**5,963**
Net assets	**6,802**	**5,043**
Shareholders' equity		
Share capital	3,000	3,000
Other reserves	2,348	1,039
Retained earnings	1,454	1,004
Total equity	**6,802**	**5,043**

(a) Explain one reason why suppliers might want access to the statement of financial position for Swanpool Marine Park. (4 marks)

(b) Explain one reason why managers and directors might want access to the statement of comprehensive income for Swanpool Marine Park. (4 marks)

(c) Evaluate the performance of Swanpool Marine Park between 2013 and 2014. (20 marks)

Key terms

Finance cost – interest paid by a business on any borrowed money.
Finance income – interest received by a business on any money held in deposit accounts.

61 Ratio analysis

Key points

1. Calculate gearing ratio and return on capital employed (ROCE).
2. Interpret ratios to make business decisions.
3. The limitations of ratio analysis.

Getting started

Businesses need to know what returns they are getting on the money invested in the business and whether the business is on a strong financial footing. They also like to make comparisons with their rivals. For example, Jones Ltd, a small property developer, made a profit of £340,500 while a much larger rival, Acorn Properties, made £78.5 million. But which of these companies has performed the best? Clearly one has made more profit than the other, but it does not necessarily mean it has performed the best.

What other information might be needed to determine the best performing company in the above example? Explain your answer. If Jones Ltd has borrowed 25 per cent of its finance while Acorn Properties borrowed a much larger 86 per cent, to which business is a bank most likely to lend more money? Explain your answer.

Financial ratios

It is possible to extract key information from the income statement and the statement of financial position to help assess the performance of a business. This approach was used in Unit 60. However, a more rigorous approach is to use **ratio analysis**. Financial ratios can be calculated and used to analyse the performance of businesses more precisely. A financial ratio is one number divided by another or one number expressed as a percentage of another. There are different types of ratio, which address different aspects of financial performance.

Gearing ratios

Gearing ratios show the long-term financial position of the business. They can be used to show the relationship between loans on which interest is paid, and shareholders' equity on which dividends might be paid. There are several different versions of the gearing ratio. One relates the non-current liabilities (total long-term loans) to the capital employed. If not stated clearly, the capital employed can be determined by subtracting current liabilities from total assets. The formula is:

$$\text{Gearing ratio} = \frac{\text{Non-current liabilities}}{\text{Capital employed}} \times 100\%$$

Worked example

Table 1 Selective financial information for Washytree Holdings 2013–2014

	2014 (£000)	2013 (£000)
Operating profit	6,570	5,430
Non-current assets	21,900	20,100
Current assets	5,430	4,300
Current liabilities	3,333	3,100
Non-current liabilities	6,900	5,490

Washytree Holdings is a farm machinery repair and maintenance company based in Northumberland. Using the information in Table 1, the gearing ratio for the business is given by

$$\text{Gearing ratio} = \frac{\text{Non-current liabilities}}{\text{Capital employed}} \times 100\%$$

For 2014
$$= \frac{£6,900,000}{(£21,900,000 + £5,430,000) - £3,333,000} \times 100\%$$

$$= \frac{£6,900,000}{£27,330,000 - £3,333,000} \times 100\%$$

$$= \frac{£6,900,000}{£23,997,000} \times 100\%$$

$$= 28.8\%$$

For 2013
$$= \frac{£5,490,000}{(£20,100,000 + £4,300,000) - £3,100,000} \times 100\%$$

$$= \frac{£5,490,000}{£24,400,000 - £3,100,000} \times 100\%$$

$$= \frac{£5,490,000}{£21,300,000} \times 100\%$$

$$= 25.8\%$$

Interpret the gearing ratio

Creditors are likely to be concerned about a firm's gearing. Loans, for example, have interest charges that must be paid. Dividends do not have to be paid to ordinary shareholders. As a business becomes more highly geared (loans are high relative to share capital) it is considered more risky by creditors. The owners of a business might prefer to raise extra funds by borrowing. They might not want to issue more shares and share control of the business.

Gearing ratios can be used to analyse the capital structure of a business. They compare the amount of capital raised from ordinary shareholders with that raised in loans. This is important because the interest on loans is a fixed commitment, whereas the dividends for ordinary shareholders are not. Gearing ratios can assess whether or not a business is burdened by its loans. This is because highly geared companies must still pay their interest even when trading becomes difficult.

Maths tip

You need to be careful when calculating ratios to ensure that the correct units are used. For example, financial information might be measured in 100s, 1000s, 100,000s, millions or billions. You need to make sure that decimal points are in the right place, otherwise you might end up with miscalculations. As a result you might draw some inaccurate conclusions from your calculations, which might have an adverse impact on your answer.

The gearing ratio for Washytree Holdings has risen slightly from 25.8 per cent in 2013 to 28.8 per cent in 2014. Most would regard this as a relatively low gearing ratio. It is not until the gearing ratio reaches 50 per cent that concerns are raised. A gearing ratio of around 25 per cent means that the business is not overburdened with long-term debt. Higher gearing ratios mean that a much larger proportion of business finance is borrowed. With low-geared companies more finance is provided by shareholders (the owners).

Profitability ratios

Profitability or performance ratios help to show how well a business is doing. They tend to focus on profit, capital employed and revenue. The profit figure alone is not a useful performance indicator. It is necessary to look at the value of profit in relation to the value of revenue or the amount of money that has been invested in the business.

Return on capital employed (ROCE)

One of the most important ratios used to measure the profitability of a business is the return on capital employed (ROCE). This is sometimes referred to as the primary ratio. It compares the profit, i.e. return, made by the business with the amount of money invested, i.e. its capital. The advantage of this ratio is that it relates profit to the size of the business. When calculating ROCE, it is standard practice to define profit as operating profit (net profit before tax and interest). This is sometimes described as earnings before interest and tax (EBIT). Tax is ignored because it is determined by the government and is therefore outside the control of the company. Interest is excluded because it does not relate to the business's ordinary trading activities. The capital employed, if not stated clearly, can be determined by subtracting current liabilities from total assets. ROCE can be calculated using the formula:

$$ROCE = \frac{Operating\ profit}{Capital\ employed} \times 100\%$$

Question 1

Edinburgh-based Cairn Energy is an oil exploration company. It owns oil wells in a range of locations including the Atlantic margin, Asia, the Mediterranean, the UK and Norway. In 2011 it sold a 40 per cent shareholding in Cairn India to Vedanta Resources, a global mining company, for $5.5 billion.

Table 2 Selective financial information for Cairn Energy 2012–2013

	2013 ($m)	2012 ($m)
Non-current assets	2,054	2,602
Current assets	1,551	1,726
Current liabilities	268	153
Non-current liabilities	150	533

Source: adapted from www.ft.com

(a) Calculate the gearing ratio for Cairn Energy in 2013 and 2012.

(b) Assess the extent to which Cairn Energy is low geared.

Worked example

For Washytree Holdings the return on capital employed is given by:

For 2014 $= \dfrac{£6,570,000}{(£21,900,000 + £5,430,000) - £3,333,000} \times 100\%$

$= \dfrac{£6,570,000}{£27,330,000 - £3,333,000} \times 100\%$

$= \dfrac{£6,570,000}{£23,997,000} \times 100\%$

$= \mathbf{27.4\%}$

For 2013 $= \dfrac{£5,430,000}{(£20,100,000 + £4,300,000) - £3,100,000} \times 100\%$

$= \dfrac{£5,430,000}{£24,400,000 - £3,100,000} \times 100\%$

$= \dfrac{£5,430,000}{£21,300,000} \times 100\%$

$= \mathbf{25.5\%}$

Interpret ROCE

The return on capital employed will vary between industries. However, the higher the ratio the better. Over the two years Washytree Holdings has seen its ROCE increase from 25.5 per cent to 27.4 per cent. This appears to be an impressive performance. However, to decide whether Washytree Holdings has performed well, this would have to be compared with another business in the same industry. An investor might also compare the ROCE with the possible return if the capital was invested elsewhere. For example, if £23,977,000 was placed in a bank account in 2014 it might have earned a 3 per cent return. So the 27.4 per cent ROCE in 2014 seems very impressive. However, an investor in the company will also want to be rewarded for the risk involved. The £23,977,000 invested by shareholders in Washytree Holdings is at risk if the business fails. So, for the investment to be worthwhile, the ROCE must be far greater than the return that could be earned in a 'safe' investment.

Limitations to ratio analysis

Unfortunately, ratio analysis is not without its problems, so it must be used with caution. Some of the key limitations are outlined here.

The basis for comparison: A great deal of care must be taken when making comparisons using ratios. It is very important to compare 'like with like'.

- **Comparisons over time.** Care must be taken when comparing ratios from the same company over time. Many companies remain broadly in the same industrial sector over time, but others can diversify and change very rapidly.

Question 2

Debenhams is a multinational retailer. In 2014 it had around 240 department stores in 27 different countries. It also runs an online operation, which delivers to 66 different countries. Debenhams has a top-four market share in womenswear and menswear, and leads the market in premium health and beauty. It employs nearly 29,000 people and sells clothes, fashion accessories, household items and furniture.

Table 3 Selective financial information for Debenhams 2013–2014

	2014 (£m)	2013 (£m)
Revenue	2,313	2,282
Operating profit	106	139
Non-current assets	1,662	1,662
Current assets	486	471
Current liabilities	758	742
Non-current liabilities	623	646

Source: adapted from www.ft.com

(a) Calculate the return on capital employed (ROCE) for Debenhams for 2014 and 2013.

(b) Discuss the performance of Debenhams between 2013 and 2014.

Equally, some companies remain the same size over time. Others grow rapidly or shrink quickly. Such factors can affect the way in which ratios can be used as a measure of performance. For example, the measures of performance of a small company that starts off in the defence sector and grows rapidly to become a leading telecommunications equipment manufacturer, will change over time. The value of a particular ratio that is appropriate for the company will therefore change. This must be taken into account when comparing ratios.

- **Inter-firm comparisons.** Caution must also be used when comparing ratios between companies at a point in time. Comparing the ratios of two companies that make broadly the same products is likely to say something about their relative performance. But comparing the ratios of a supermarket chain with those of a cement manufacturer is unlikely to be helpful. For example, the two companies will have different working capital needs and different profit margins. Even companies operating in the same industry can have subtle differences. For example, Tesco and Waitrose are both supermarket chains. However, Tesco is selling more and more non-food products, such as electrical goods, clothing and kitchen equipment. This makes a direct comparison less meaningful because, for instance, the profit margins on non-food items might be different from those on groceries.

- **Other differences.** Even when companies are well matched in their activities and operating circumstances, there may be other differences between them that must be observed. For example, two similar companies may use different accounting techniques, different methods to calculate depreciation or different stock valuation methods. If the same accounting conventions have not been used, comparisons may be misleading. Companies can also have different year ends. For example, if one company ended its financial year on 31 December and the other on 31 July, although their accounts would nominally be for the same year they would actually be presenting financial information about two quite different time periods. In this case only six months of the year would be truly comparable.

The quality of final accounts: Ratios are based on financial accounts, such as balance sheets and income statements. Consequently ratio analysis is only useful if the accounts are accurate. One factor that can affect the quality of accounting information is the change in monetary values caused by inflation. Rising prices can distort comparisons made between different time periods. For example, in times of high inflation, asset values and revenue might rise rapidly in monetary terms. However, when the figures are adjusted for inflation, there might be no increase in real terms. There is also the possibility that the accounts have been **window dressed**. This is discussed in more detail below.

Limitations of the balance sheet: Because the balance sheet is a 'snapshot' of the business at the end of the financial year, it might not be representative of the business's circumstances throughout the whole of the year. If, for example, a business experiences its peak trading activity in the summer, and it has its year end in January when trade is slow, figures for stock and debtors will be unrepresentative.

Qualitative information is ignored: Ratios only use quantitative information. However, some important qualitative factors may affect the performance of a business that are ignored by ratio analysis. For example, in the service industry the quality of customer service may be an important performance indicator. However, ratio analysis cannot isolate the impact that good customer service might have on sales. Sales might be higher as a result of good customer service but there might be other factors that have helped to increase sales, such as advertising.

Window dressing: Accounts must represent a 'true and fair record' of the financial affairs of a business. Legislation and financial reporting standards place limits on the different ways in which a business can present financial information. These limits are designed to prevent fraud and misrepresentation in the compilation and presentation of accounts. However, businesses can manipulate their accounts legally to present different financial pictures. This is known as window dressing. Businesses may want to window dress their accounts for a variety of reasons.

- Managers of companies might want to put as good a financial picture forward as possible for shareholders and potential shareholders. Good financial results will attract praise and perhaps rewards. They might also prevent criticism from shareholders and the financial press.
- If a business wants to raise new capital from investors, then it will want its financial accounts to look as good as possible.
- Where a business has experienced severe difficulties during the accounting period, it may decide to take action that will make the financial position look even worse now, but which will improve figures in the future.
- Making the financial picture look worse may be a way of lowering the amount of tax that is paid.
- If the owners of a business want to sell it, the better the financial position shown on the accounts, the higher the price they are likely to get.

There are several ways of window dressing accounts. For example, a business may manipulate its sales by increasing the level of revenue recorded in the income statement. This will increase profit in that accounting period. It may be able to suppress costs by changing its accounting policies or choosing when to 'write off' unprofitable activities. It can also 'write off' bad debts, revalue property, boost liquidity through the sale and leaseback of assets, and manipulate current assets and current liabilities. The methods required to conduct these transactions are beyond the scope of this book, but you should be aware such methods exist.

Exam tip

When using ratio analysis you must understand the importance of interpreting your results. The calculation of financial ratios is relatively straightforward and quite often more marks are awarded for understanding the implications of your results. For example, you need to understand that if ROCE is 2.3 per cent, this is not a very good return on capital. You might get more than this from a bank deposit.

Links 🔗

In addition to assessing the performance of a business, ratio analysis might also be used when making decisions. Consequently, you can demonstrate synoptic skills by linking ratio analysis to answers that involve making business decisions, such as whether to start exporting, investing in growth or launching a new product. Ratio analysis might be linked to Internal finance (Unit 26), External finance (Unit 27), Planning (Unit 29), Break-even (Unit 32), Profit (Unit 34), Liquidity (Unit 35), Theories of corporate strategy (Unit 45), SWOT analysis (Unit 46), Decision trees (Unit 54) and Global competitiveness (Unit 75).

Case study

JD SPORTS

JD Sports was set up in 1981 as a single sports shop in Bury. It is now a major retailer of branded and own-brand sportswear, fashionwear, outdoor clothing, footwear and equipment in the UK. It operates over 800 stores across Europe under fascia such as JD, Size?, Blacks, Millets, Scotts, Chausport, Sprinter, Tessuti and Bank, as well as JD Sports. It also has a large online operation.

During 2014 the business made some operational changes to the Blacks and Millets Outdoor business, with the relocation of some offices and a warehouse to the group's main facilities. This resulted in some disruption, but with the aim of providing scope for future efficiency gains. Table 4 shows some selective information for JD Sports taken from the income statement and statement of financial position.

Table 4 Selective financial information for JD Sports 2013–2014

	2014 (£000)	2013 (£000)
Revenue	1,330,578	1,258,892
Operating profit	57,850	55,117
Non-current assets	269,706	245,693
Current assets	329,879	256,814
Current liabilities	285,651	212,749
Non-current liabilities	41,094	38,001

Source: adapted from www.jdplc.com

(a) Calculate the gearing ratios for 2013 and 2014. (4 marks)

(b) Calculate the return on capital employed for 2013 and 2014. (4 marks)

(c) Assess the performance of JD Sports over the two years. (10 marks)

(d) Evaluate the usefulness of ratio analysis to a company like JD Sports. (20 marks)

Key terms

Gearing ratios – exploration of the capital structure of the business by comparing the proportions of capital raised by debt and equity.

Profitability or performance ratios – illustration of the relative profitability of a business.

Ratio analysis – a numerical approach to investigating accounts by comparing two related figures.

Return on capital employed (ROCE) – the profit of a business as a percentage of the total amount of money used to generate it.

Window dressing – the legal manipulation of accounts by a business to present a financial picture that is to its benefit.

Knowledge check

1. What is the difference between liquidity ratios and gearing ratios?

2. How can capital employed be calculated using information from the balance sheet?

3. What is meant by a highly geared company?

4. A business has a gearing ratio of 76 per cent. Comment on this.

5. What is the formula for calculating return on capital employed?

6. Why is the return on capital employed an important ratio?

7. When using ratios it is important to compare 'like with like'. What does this mean?

8. Why does ratio analysis ignore qualitative information?

9. What is meant by window dressing accounts?

10. Outline three reasons why a business would choose to window dress its accounts.

Key points

1. Calculate and interpret the following to help make business decisions:
   - labour productivity
   - labour turnover and retention
   - absenteeism.
2. Human resources strategies to increase productivity and retention, and to reduce turnover and absenteeism:
   - financial rewards
   - employee share ownership
   - consultation strategies
   - empowerment strategies.

Getting started

Nissan, the Japanese car producer, has a large production plant in Sunderland. It was widely reported that productivity at the plant fell by 1.7 per cent in 2013. However, this was thought to be a temporary downturn caused by the introduction of new models. One of these new models, the Nissan Qashqai, is built on Line One, which has been operating for 24 hours a day since 2010. The production of the new model means more jobs for local people and the total number employed by Nissan in its Wearside plant was reported to have topped 7,000 in 2014. Nissan produces around 500,000 cars a year in Sunderland.

Source: adapted from the *Financial Times* 09.01.2014. All rights reserved.

How might productivity be measured at the Nissan factory? How might productivity be improved using financial methods? Give an example of a non-financial method to improve productivity. How might a business reduce absenteeism in its organisation?

Labour productivity

Labour productivity is defined as output per worker. As a formula:

$$\text{Labour productivity} = \frac{\text{Total output (per period of time)}}{\text{Average number of employees (per period of time)}}$$

Labour productivity is an important measure of the efficiency of a workforce. For example, if there are two teams of workers in a factory, each with identical equipment and the same number of workers, then the team with the highest productivity could be identified as the most effective team.

Figures for labour productivity need to be used with caution. For example, differences in labour productivity between factories or plants may be accounted for by differences in equipment used rather than the efficiency of the workforce. A plant with newer equipment is likely to have higher labour productivity than one with old equipment. Equally, productivity differs widely between processes within a business and between businesses in different industries. A highly automated section of a factory is likely to have much higher labour productivity than a labour-intensive packing section in the same factory using little capital equipment. The manufacturing industry may have a higher average labour productivity than service industries simply because more capital is used per employee in manufacturing.

Increasing labour productivity is generally assumed to increase the competitiveness of a business. Higher labour productivity should drive down costs, allowing a business either to lower its prices and so gain higher sales, or to keep its prices the same but increase its profit margins.

However, businesses sometimes find that they become less competitive despite increasing their labour productivity. This may occur for a number of reasons.

- Rival businesses may increase their productivity at an even faster rate.
- New rival businesses may set up which pay considerably lower wages. Many UK manufacturing businesses have become less competitive over the past ten years due to the emergence of competition from low-wage, low-cost businesses in the Far East and eastern Europe.
- Other factors apart from cost may change adversely for a business. For example, a rival business may bring out a far better new product. However productive the workforce and however low the cost, customers may prefer to buy the new product rather than a cheaper old product.

Worked example

Massamore Ltd operates a call centre in Glasgow where customer service is provided for a large energy company. One week in October 2014, a total of 157,500 calls were handled by the centre's 140 staff. Labour productivity at the call centre is given by:

$$\text{Labour productivity} = \frac{\text{Total output}}{\text{Average number of employees}}$$

$$= \frac{157,500}{140}$$

$$= 1,125 \text{ calls per employee}$$

This means that during that week in October each employee took 1,125 calls (on average).

Question 1

Jengril Ltd manufactures and distributes household appliances. In one of its Asian factories it has a production line making kettles. Table 1 shows the total output of kettles, and staffing levels on the production line, between 2010 and 2014.

Table 1 Total output and staffing levels on the kettle production line

	2010	2011	2012	2013	2014
Total output (number of kettles)	23,200	24,800	24,700	25,300	24,900
Average number of employees	11	12	13	14	14

(a) Calculate the labour productivity on the kettle line at Jengril Ltd for each year between 2010 and 2014.

(b) Explain one possible reason for the pattern of labour productivity on the kettle production line between 2010 and 2014.

Labour turnover

Labour or staff turnover is another measure of personnel effectiveness. **Labour turnover** is the proportion of staff leaving a business over a period of time. It is measured by the formula:

$$\text{Labour turnover} = \frac{\text{Number of staff leaving over time period}}{\text{Average number of staff in post during the period}} \times 100\%$$

As with other measures of personnel performance, labour turnover differs from department to department within a business, from business to business within an industry and from industry to industry within an economy. Relatively high labour turnover is caused by a number of factors.

- Relatively low pay leads to higher labour turnover as workers leave to get better paid jobs.
- Relatively few training and promotion opportunities will encourage workers to leave their current jobs.
- Poor working conditions, low job satisfaction, bullying and harassment in the workplace are other factors.
- Some businesses are relatively poor at selecting and recruiting the right candidates for posts. Where workers are ill-suited to their jobs, there is more chance that they will leave relatively quickly.
- In a recession, labour turnover tends to fall as the number of vacancies falls and workers become worried that if they leave their job without having another one to go to, they will become part of the long-term unemployed. In a boom, when there might be labour shortages, there are far more vacancies and so labour turnover tends to rise.

Relatively high labour turnover is usually seen as a problem for businesses for a number of reasons.

- Recruiting new staff can be costly.
- It takes time for new staff to become familiar with their roles and the way in which the business operates. High labour turnover is likely to reduce the human process advantage of a business.
- Larger companies may put on induction programmes which further adds to costs.
- If the post is filled internally, there may be training needs for the worker who gets the job.

However, some labour turnover is usually beneficial to a business.

- New staff can bring in fresh ideas and experience from their work with other businesses.
- Some workers may be ineffective and need to be encouraged to leave. Getting rid of ineffective staff leads to labour turnover.
- If a business is shrinking in size, reducing the size of the workforce will lead to higher labour turnover.
- Where a business pays low wages, or where conditions of work are poor, it may be more profitable to have a constant turnover of staff rather than raise wages or improve conditions of work.

Worked example

During 2014, 60 staff left Massamore Ltd, the business in the above example. Therefore, labour turnover is given by:

$$\text{Labour turnover} = \frac{\text{Number of staff leaving (over a time period)}}{\text{Average number of staff in post (in the time period)}} \times 100\%$$

$$= \frac{60 \times 100}{140}$$

$$= \textbf{42.9\%}$$

This means that during the year, 42.9 per cent of staff left Massamore Ltd.

Labour retention

Labour retention and labour turnover are related. This is because labour turnover looks at the rate at which employees leave a business, while labour retention looks at the rate at which they stay with the business. Therefore, labour retention is the opposite of labour turnover. It can be calculated using the following formula:

$$\text{Labour retention} = \frac{\text{Number of staff staying (over a time period)}}{\text{Average number of staff in post (in the time period)}} \times 100\%$$

The benefits to a business of a high retention rate are the same as the advantages of a low staff turnover rate, such as lower recruitment and selection costs, more continuity and a stable workforce.

Worked example

During 2014, the number of staff that left Massamore Ltd, was 60. This means that 80 (140 − 60) staff remained. Therefore, the retention rate is given by:

$$\text{Retention rate} = \frac{\text{Number of staff staying (over a time period)}}{\text{Average number of staff in post (in the time period)}} \times 100\%$$

$$= \frac{80 \times 100\%}{140}$$

$$= \textbf{57.1\%}$$

This means that during the year, 57.1 per cent of staff stayed with Massamore Ltd.

Absenteeism

Absenteeism is a problem for all businesses for a number of reasons.

- Staff who are absent often claim to be ill. The business then, in most cases, has to pay sick pay.
- If temporary staff are brought in to cover for absent staff, this leads to increased costs. Equally, costs will increase if

permanent staff have to work overtime and are paid at higher rates than their basic rate of pay.
- Output may suffer if workers are expected to cover for sick colleagues or if temporary staff are not as productive as the absent workers.
- Prolonged absences can lead to major disruption if the worker is key to a particular area of work or a new project.
- If production is delayed or there are problems with quality, customers can be lost.
- Absenteeism can demotivate staff left to cope with problems.
- The higher the rate of absenteeism, the more likely it is that workers will report ill. This is because a culture of absenteeism will develop where it becomes acceptable for workers to take extra days holiday by reporting in sick.

The **rate of absenteeism**, or absenteeism rate, or absentee rate can be calculated by dividing the number of staff absent by the total number of staff employed. The rate is expressed as a percentage. It can be calculated as a daily rate using the formula:

$$\frac{\text{Number of staff absent on a day}}{\text{Total number of staff employed}} \times 100\%$$

Worked example

On 24 October 2014, eight staff were absent from work at Massamore Ltd, the business in the above examples. Therefore, the rate of absenteeism is given by:

$$\text{Absenteeism rate} = \frac{\text{Number of staff absent on a day}}{\text{Total number of staff employed}} \times 100\%$$

$$= \frac{8}{140} \times 100\%$$

$$= \textbf{5.7\%}$$

This means that on 24 October 2014, 5.7 per cent of Massamore staff were absent from work.

Worked example

During 2014 a total of 1,000 staff days were lost through staff absence at Massamore Ltd. Each of the 140 staff should have worked 240 days during the year. So the total number of staff days that should have been worked was 33,600 (140 x 240). Therefore the rate of absenteeism for the year is given by:

$$\text{Annual absenteeism rate} = \frac{\text{Total number of staff absence days over the year}}{\text{Total number of staff days that should have been worked}} \times 100\%$$

$$= \frac{1,000}{33,600} \times 100\%$$

$$= \textbf{3\%}$$

This means that the absenteeism rate throughout 2014 was 3 per cent. Note that this annual rate for Massamore Ltd is lower than the absenteeism rate on 24 October 2014, when it was 5.7 per cent.

Rates of absenteeism can be calculated for a business as a whole and compared to industry averages or national averages. They can also be compared between one part of a business and another, or compared over time. Differences in rates of absenteeism occur for a number of reasons.

- Small businesses tend to have lower rates of absenteeism than larger businesses. Arguably this is because there is much more commitment and feeling of teamwork in a small business than in a large business. Workers in large businesses can feel that no one will suffer if they take a day off work and so absenteeism is acceptable.
- Health and safety is a factor. Businesses which have good health and safety procedures will tend to suffer less illness-related absenteeism than those with poor procedures. Equally, some jobs are inherently more dangerous to health than others and so absenteeism is more likely.
- The nature of the tasks given to workers is another factor. Tasks which are fragmented and repetitive lead to low job satisfaction and demotivation. This encourages workers to report sick. Workers in jobs which are interesting and rewarding tend to have lower absentee rates.
- The culture of a workplace can cause absenteeism. Where workers are overworked, where there is a climate of intimidation and bullying by superiors of subordinates, and where the needs of workers are ignored, work-related stress becomes much more common. Workers who are off through stress are a particular problem because they often take months off work at a time.
- Stress-related illness is also more common where workers are oversupervised and feel that they are not trusted by their superiors to accomplish tasks.
- Workers who feel that they are grossly underpaid are more likely to take time off work. They see it as compensation for the lack of monetary reward they receive. Low pay is also a demotivator and so contributes to absenteeism.

Strategies to increase productivity and retention, and to reduce turnover and absenteeism

If businesses can raise productivity and retention rates, and reduce staff turnover and absenteeism, the benefits will be significant. Here are a couple of reasons why.

- If productivity rises, output per employee will be higher so there is more output to sell. This will raise revenue and profit.
- If staff turnover can be reduced, money will be saved on recruitment, selection and training. This will help to cut costs and again increase profit.

A number of human resources strategies might be used to help achieve these aims.

Question 2

Hunter & Co runs an online gift business. It has a warehouse in Staffordshire where orders are packed and dispatched. In 2012, a new warehouse manager was employed who introduced some new working practices. However, there was a three-month consultation process before the new arrangements were introduced. This gave all staff the opportunity to express their views and preferences about the proposed arrangements. Table 2 shows the average number of staff employed at the warehouse, the number of staff leaving each year, and the total number of days missed through absence between 2010 and 2014.

Table 2 Staffing information for Hunter & Co's warehouse 2010–2014

	2010	2011	2012	2013	2014
Average number of staff employed	1,590	1,610	1,620	1,670	1,710
Average number of staff leaving	410	440	500	410	310
Total number of staff absences (in days)	5,760	5,890	6,180	5,200	4,200

NB According to a survey, the average staff turnover rate for the UK in 2011 was 15.6 per cent. Also, according to the Office for National Statistics (ONS), staff absence in the UK in 2011 was 1.8 per cent.

Source: www.ons.gov.uk

(a) Calculate the annual staff turnover at Hunter & Co's warehouse between 2010 and 2014.

(b) Calculate the annual absenteeism rate at Hunter & Co's warehouse between 2010 and 2014 (assume that each employee can work 240 days per year).

(c) Assess whether the decision to change working practices in 2012 was a good one for Hunter & Co.

Financial rewards

According to some theories of motivation, if financial rewards are increased, employees will work harder and produce more. For example, American engineer and pioneer business consultant, F. W. Taylor, in his theory of scientific management, suggested that once the best way to carry out a task had been identified, workers should be paid according to what they produce. He suggested that people should be paid a fair day's pay for a fair day's work. He argued that people are motivated mainly by money and would work harder to earn more. Therefore, employees should be paid piece rates if it is possible. The main benefit of piece rates for businesses is that it rewards productive workers. Workers who are lazy or slow will not earn as much as those who are conscientious and productive. This system helps to motivate workers, and businesses are likely to get more out of their employees.

Other ways of improving the performance of workers using financial rewards might be to adopt performance-related pay, bonus systems, profit-related pay or commission systems. All of these methods reward employees for their effort – both in terms of results and attendance. Also, if financial rewards are lucrative, it is unlikely that staff will want to leave a business so staff turnover will be lower. For example, bonuses can be paid in addition to the basic wage or salary. Operatives may be paid a bonus if they reach a weekly production target. The main advantage to businesses of bonus payments is that they are only paid if targets are met. This means that money is only paid if it has been earned. Some businesses pay their staff loyalty bonuses. These are usually paid annually, often at Christmas. Such bonuses are not necessarily linked to productivity. They are designed to reward workers for their loyalty and to help to reduce staff turnover.

Finally, some businesses use financial rewards to reduce absenteeism rates. In 2013 in the UK, the cost to organisations of sickness absence was widely reported to be nearly £29 billion. Therefore it is perhaps not surprising that some businesses try to reduce absenteeism by offering money if attendance targets are met. A system might involve paying an employee with a 100 per cent attendance record a bonus of £1,000 in, say, a six-month period, or a £200 bonus for a 98 per cent attendance record. However, attendance systems should not penalise employees who take time off to which they are entitled.

Employee share ownership

Some businesses reward employees by giving them company shares. Such schemes are particularly common when remunerating senior managers and executives in plcs. The idea is that key employees will be paid a 'tranche' of shares (probably in addition to cash bonuses) if the business reaches important performance targets, such as growth in turnover, profit or share price.

Some businesses offer shares to a wider range of employees. A common method of share distribution is to use a sharesave scheme, sometimes called a Savings Related Share Option Scheme. These involve employees putting aside part of their monthly pay for a fixed number of years. At the end of the period employees get the chance to use the money saved to buy shares at a price that was fixed at the outset, often at a discount. If the share price has increased over the time period, employees can often make a capital gain. However, if the share price has fallen to below the price that was fixed at the outset, employees get their cash back, perhaps with a small cash bonus. Such schemes are considered to be a 'safe bet' and are therefore very popular with employees. UK government statistics suggest that, in 2012–13, over 1,000 companies offered such sharesave schemes. Examples include BT, Ocado, Asda, Tesco and Whitbread.

The benefit to employers is that workers are likely to be better motivated and more loyal to the company if they own shares. They may work harder, take less time off sick and are less likely to leave. For example, once staff have signed up for a five-year sharesave scheme, they may be reluctant to leave half way through the term and miss out on possible gains.

Consultation strategies

Employees are likely to be better motivated and more productive if they are involved in decision making. Staff often complain when changes are made and they are not consulted. For example, if a business introduced new working practices to improve the level of customer service without consulting staff, they may feel resentful. If staff are consulted by employers when changes are proposed they are more likely to see their views as being valued. Three different types of consultation can be identified.

Pseudo-consultation: Pseudo-consultation is where management makes a decision and informs employees of that decision through their representatives. Employees have no power to influence these decisions. Some have suggested that it would be more accurately described as information giving.

Classical consultation: Classical consultation is a way of involving employees, through their representatives, in discussions on matters which affect them. This allows employees to have an influence on management decisions. Unions may be involved, for example, in restructuring

Integrative consultation: Pseudo- and classical consultation do not directly involve employees in decisions which affect them. Integrative consultation is a more democratic method of decision making. Arguably it is neither consultation nor negotiation. Management and unions discuss and explore matters which are of common concern, such as ways of increasing productivity or methods of changing work practices. The two groups come to a joint decision having used, in many cases, problem-solving techniques. An example of an integrative approach to consultation might be the use of quality circles in a number of UK businesses and in foreign firms setting up in the UK.

In addition to improving motivation and worker productivity, consultation has other advantages. Changes are less likely to be resisted if staff have been consulted and it is also possible that employees have ideas of their own which might benefit a business. Such ideas can only be expressed if there is a proper consultation process. However, some might argue that consultation takes too long and slows down the process of change. Also, some see consultation as a 'cosmetic' process where the views of workers are heard, but then ignored.

Empowerment strategies

Empowerment involves making better use of the knowledge, experience and creative talents of employees. It is achieved by granting employees more authority in the workplace. Empowering staff may be a way of creating a positive working environment where employees are happy, motivated and productive, and therefore engaged. The following strategies might be used to help empower employees.

- **Training.** It is not really possible to empower staff effectively without first equipping them with the skills needed to take on more advanced tasks. A business needs to identify any 'skills gap'. This is the difference between an employee's current skills and those required to undertake new tasks. This gap can be bridged by training.

- **Provide the necessary resources.** There is little point empowering staff if they are not given the resources and information needed to undertake more complex tasks. For example, if an employee is tasked with leading a small team to solve a problem, such as improving the response time to customer complaints, they will need a range of information and enough resources to make the improvements.

- **Hand over authority.** Once employees have been empowered they must be confident that they have complete authority to make decisions. The methods they choose and approaches they take must not be questioned. If employees are challenged or asked to explain themselves each time they make a decision, empowerment is not likely to work.

- **Inspire confidence.** If employees are being empowered it is important that they feel confident about their new role. A lack of confidence can lead to anxiety, hesitancy and mistakes. Senior managers can help to inspire confidence by emphasising the strengths that an individual has, showing trust, and by recognising and praising achievements.

- **Provide feedback.** At an appropriate time it will be necessary to provide positive feedback to empowered workers. Workers need to know how they have performed in their new roles. Feedback will help to guide them in the future and build more confidence.

Giving people more control over their own work role should help to improve their motivation and productivity. They will feel valued, more loyal and less likely to leave an organisation. It may also help to reduce absenteeism because empowered staff may have a greater sense of responsibility.

Links 🔗

To demonstrate your synoptic skills you could link information in this unit to answers relating to global competitiveness, for example. UK businesses trying to compete globally may try to improve productivity and staff retention to gain a competitive edge. Information in this unit might also be linked with issues covered in Motivation in theory and practice (Unit 17), Business objectives (Unit 21), Production, productivity and efficiency (Unit 37) and Corporate culture (Unit 57).

Key terms

Labour productivity – output per worker in a given time period.
Labour retention – the number of employees that remain in a business over a period of time.
Labour turnover – the rate at which staff leave a business.
Rate of absenteeism – the number of staff who are absent as a percentage of the total workforce. It can be calculated for different periods of time, e.g. daily or annually.

Knowledge check

1. The factory output for a manufacturer in 2014 was 2.4 million units. The business employed 1,200 people in the factory. Calculate the labour productivity.

2. How is labour turnover calculated?

3. Give three reasons why staff might be absent from work.

4. How is the daily absenteeism rate calculated?

5. Explain one way a business might reduce absenteeism.

6. What is meant by retention?

7. Explain one advantage of having a high retention rate.

8. Give two financial methods that a business might use to raise productivity.

9. Explain one advantage of giving employees shares.

10. Explain how empowerment might help improve productivity.

Case study

LINDUM GROUP

Lindum Group is a construction company that provides a wide range of construction services such as design, building, roofing, security and waste recycling. Between 55 and 60 per cent of its business is private sector work and its clients include Morrisons, Perkins, Bombardier, Siemens and Premier Foods. It also does public sector work for clients in Lincolnshire, the East Midlands, East Anglia and the Yorkshire/Humberside area.

Lindum Group has a reputation for caring for its 480 staff. It believes that if the company looks after its staff, then the staff will look after its customers. In 2014 the labour turnover was 12 per cent, which is below the national average of around 15 per cent. In a survey by the *Sunday Times*, it was found that more than half of the firm's staff have worked for Lindum for more than five years. Also, 81 per cent of workers said they would not leave Lindum if they were offered alternative employment elsewhere.

Financial rewards are used to help motivate staff and encourage loyalty. For example, every year the company shares 10 per cent of the profits equally between all members of staff. The company also gives free shares to its employees. The company believes that by giving shares to employees they will have an interest in the company performing well and will therefore take more care to ensure that customer needs are met.

Lindum managers have very good relations with staff. The views of workers are valued and people are encouraged to share information and come up with ideas. For example, one member of staff suggested that the waste oil from company vehicles could be utilised. The company responded by using the oil to fuel heaters. Everyone in the organisation is on first-name terms, and managers and directors operate an 'open door policy' where staff are welcome at any time to express their concerns and views.

Between 2012 and 2013 group revenue rose from £83 million to £93.7 million. However, its profit after tax dipped slightly from £1.8 million to £1.7 million. The company's success comes a lot from its reputation as a customer-focused organisation. According to the chairman, David Chambers, 'Our approach is to understand and forge a good working relationship with our customers.'

Source: adapted from www.lindumgroup.com

Q

(a) Calculate the number of people who left the Lindum Group during the year. (4 marks)

(b) Explain one advantage of a low staff turnover to the Lindum Group. (4 marks)

(c) Explain one method used by the Lindum Group to help improve productivity and retention. (4 marks)

(d) Assess the extent to which Lindum's human resources policies may have improved the competitiveness of the business. (12 marks)

Key points

1. Causes of change:
   - changes in organisational size
   - poor business performance
   - new ownership
   - transformational leadership
   - the market and other external factors (PESTLE).
2. Possible effects on:
   - competitiveness
   - productivity
   - financial performance
   - stakeholders.

Getting started

In 2014, an American car manufacturer called Local Motors used 3D printing to manufacture a drivable car. The car took 44 hours to print. In 2015, a company took an ultrasound image of an unborn baby and printed a 3D model of the little boy so that his blind mother could touch and feel her child for the first time. These are just some of the applications of the technology commonly known as 3D printing. Thanks to the advancements in the technology it is becoming cheaper to print out physical models and objects for a wide range of uses.

How might businesses change as technologies like 3D printing advance?

The causes of change in business

Businesses today have to operate in rapidly changing markets and conditions. They can no longer rely on a constant stream of customers, the same production process or selling the same product over a long period of time. They must constantly be aware of, and be prepared to respond to, **organisational change** in a number of areas.

Changes in organisational size

The size of an organisation will naturally change as it seeks to grow. Growth is a key corporate objective as it allows a firm to satisfy shareholders and create security for its stakeholders. One of the most significant drivers of change as a business grows is the need to restructure and adopt policies and processes to manage expansion.

Sometimes a business will look to grow externally by merging or taking over another business. This can bring very sudden change to all aspects of the business. How an organisation manages growth can be the difference between success and failure. Most businesses are unable to operate as they once did when they were a small business. There are particular advantages to being a small business, which can be lost as companies grow.

Effects of changes in organisational size

- **Competitiveness.** There are significant advantages to growth in the form of economies of scale, brand recognition and financial security. Many of these benefits were explored in Theme 2. Overall, a business will grow to achieve these benefits.
- **Productivity.** Firms are certainly more productive as they grow in size. However, in order to capitalise on size a business will have to alter the scale and methods of production. For some organisations this may require investment in automated production facilities and the loss of a highly skilled small workforce.
- **Financial performance.** With growth comes the need to invest. This investment could come from the reinvestment of profits, but more often than not, a firm will need to finance growth through borrowing. A highly geared business is a risky business. Nevertheless, growth will often bring with it increased profit in real terms and this is likely to please shareholders.
- **Stakeholders.** Fortunately, growth brings with it new opportunities for employees through bonuses and promotion prospects. It may also be necessary to recruit new employees and this is another important change to manage. Individual workers might be concerned that they will no longer work with 'friends', or may be moved to a job that they dislike. As a firm grows there is the danger of losing connections with its customer base. Larger organisations sometimes find it more difficult to offer a personal service. Trying to maintain a personal service has been the focus of many high street banks. For example, NatWest has looked at extending branch opening hours and, historically, HSBC's strapline focused on being the world's local bank. The expansion of business can also create pressures for local communities. For example, the increased traffic caused by a growing factory can cause negative externalities in the form of noise pollution, damage to roads and congestion.

Poor business performance

The poor performance of an organisation will invariably bring with it a period of change as the company strives to regain customers, sales, profit or reputation. Often the change after a period of poor performance will happen quickly as the business leaders try to 'turn the tide' and improve the fortunes of the company before failure and possibly closure. For this reason, change will often be very quick and may focus on the corporate objectives (Unit 44) or change in corporate strategy (Unit 45).

Sometimes when a large business has a period of poor performance, a change of higher management or the Chief Executive Officer (CEO) is made. New leadership usually brings significant change as the new boss attempts to assert themselves and strike a new course for the business. In 2015 Deutsche Bank, the world's largest lender, appointed John Cryan as their new CEO following years of reported scandals. His appointment had an immediate impact of raising share prices by 8 per cent before he made any decisions.

Effects of change on business performance

- **Competitiveness.** Poor performance will often go hand in hand with a loss of competitiveness.
- **Productivity.** With poor performance comes a fall in sales, productivity and profitability. A fall in production will leave the business with a low rate of capacity utilisation (Unit 38). The key question is how will the firm manage its excess capacity and the threat of rising unit costs? Businesses must take account of changes in their human resource planning. This could mean employing a more flexible workforce that could be changed quickly to meet the needs of the business, for example employing part-time workers, or introducing job sharing. It might also mean employing workers in low-cost countries, such as in call centres abroad.
- **Financial performance.** A firm going through a period of poor performance is likely to be subject to liquidity problems. A reduction in sales will result in a reduction in cash flow and this might lead to cost cutting. In times of financial difficulty it is important for a business to find ways of being leaner and more efficient.
- **Stakeholders.** Poor performance brings uncertainty and this can have a negative impact on motivation within the workforce. A firm can find itself managing low morale and giving reassurances. Nevertheless, poor performance sometimes signals redundancies and this can be an extremely difficult process to manage. In 2015 UK retailer Boots announced the decision to cut 700 jobs at its Head Office as part of its cost-cutting plans over the next few years, following a slump in profits. All corporations are answerable to their shareholders and a poor performing company is likely to lose value on the stock market. Following the announcement of redundancies at Boots, the share price fell by 35%.

Question 1

KDDR Steel's financial performance slowed in 2014–15, with the Chinese company announcing a $473 million annual net loss in May 2015. The price of shares in the steelmaker fell throughout the year 2014-15, and KDDR Steel's European bases faced a threat of strikes in May 2015.

The weak commodity price of steel along with some operational problems in a key plant in China led to this lowering in KDDR Steel's profitability throughout 2014–15. The fall in profitability was also linked to a lower demand for steel and a change in some export and import patterns for steel.

In 2014, KDDR Steel's operations in China accounted for 26 per cent of its overall global revenue.

(a) Explain the impact that KDDR Steel's performance may have on stakeholders.

(b) Assess the impact on KDDR Steel of a lower demand for steel.

Change to the market and other external factors (PESTLE)

Unit 47 explores external influences on a business. These include political, economic, social, technological, legal and environmental – PESTLE). Companies will often be required to adapt and change in line with these external influences, as shown in the examples below.

- **Technological.** The introduction of new technology can affect a business in many ways. Advances in ever more powerful computer components, telecommunications and the power of handheld devices change not only how businesses communicate with their customers and suppliers, but also the pace of innovation and business processes.
- **Social.** Businesses must be prepared for changes in the tastes of consumers. Examples include the increasing demand for environmentally friendly products, the desire for greater knowledge about products or the need for more convenient methods of shopping, such as purchasing via the internet. Population changes will also affect the age and make-up of the workforce. The ageing of the population in the UK in the early part of the twenty-first century is likely to result in changing recruitment policies for businesses. A falling population is also likely to change how a business plans its human resources.
- **Legal.** Government legislation can force changes in business activity. Taxation of pollution, for instance, would affect the production methods of many firms. Safety standards, such as EU regulations, the minimum wage or the governance of zero hour contracts are likely to determine how businesses operate.
- **Economic.** It is argued that economies go through periods of boom and slump, recession and recovery. This is known as the business cycle. Income, spending, saving, investment and economic variables, such as unemployment and inflation, are all likely to be different at different stages in the cycle. Businesses have to deal with these economic factors. For example, through the financial crisis of 2008 many firms had to find ways of becoming leaner and more efficient in order to survive.

Effects of change to the market and other external factors (PESTLE)

- **Competitiveness.** The impact on competitiveness of PESTLE factors is very much determined by how quickly a business is able to respond to these changing forces. For example, if a business is the first to innovate or adopt a new technology, responds fastest to consumer needs or embeds policies that adhere to new legislation, it might be able to gain an advantage over its competitors.
- **Productivity.** New technology can feed into the production processes of a business. Whether that be a manufacturer or service provider, new technology brings with it the opportunity to increase scale, productivity and efficiency. As the economy goes through periods of boom and slump, businesses will be required to adapt to changing demands for their products and services. As productivity rises and falls a business must change to cope with different levels of capacity utilisation. These can require fast expansion or the need to rationalise.
- **Financial performance.** In most instances any change in these external forces means an increase in costs for a business. From simply having to adapt its packaging to meet new consumer legislation or the complete revamp of its product line to introduce new technology, these changes are not going to be cheap. However, it is likely that the costs will have to be absorbed by the whole industry and not just one firm.
- **Stakeholders.** The impact of change as a result of a business having to respond to external influences is likely to be felt by all stakeholders. Any impact of rising costs through legal implications is likely to be passed on to consumers. New technology may require retraining or, in a worse case scenario, could lead to parts of the workforce becoming redundant.

Changes in ownership

The change in ownership of a business may come from internal growth, the transition from a private limited company to a public limited company and flotation of a firm's shares on the stock market. With the flotation of a business on the stock market comes the opportunity to raise fresh capital for further investment and expansion, again fuelling more change ahead. A change in ownership may also become necessary as a business goes through the process of a merger or acquisition (Unit 74), which can bring very sudden change to a company.

Effects of changes in ownership

- **Competitiveness.** The impact on competitiveness will very much be determined by how the companies integrate and complement one another. However, significant economies of scale may come from two firms merging.
- **Productivity.** Productivity may eventually rise as a result of a merger, but in the short term it is likely that business operations will be disrupted as the two firms work out how to get along and integrate all aspects of the business.
- **Financial performance.** Acquisitions can be very expensive, and should the venture fail it can lead to huge losses being incurred by the buyer. However, acquisitions

are good for share prices and the announcement of an acquisition or merger can increase demand for the company's stocks.

- **Stakeholders.** With a merger or acquisition comes the danger of a clash between two corporate cultures. One of the most famous merger failures occurred in 1998 when Daimler and Chrysler attempted to merge. The merger was quoted as being like 'trying to mix oil and water'. The occurrence of a merger will always lead to restructuring of the two companies (or at least one of them) and may also lead to redundancies.

Question 2

Property website Zoopla bought the price comparison site uSwitch in a deal worth up to £190m, bringing together two well-known UK consumer brands. Shares in Zoopla jumped 16 per cent to 215p on news of the deal, but remained below the flotation price of 220p.

Zoopla, which gets an average of 44m visits a month from consumers searching for properties, said bringing together the brands was a good fit, creating a single portal where consumers can find their home and manage it once they have moved in. uSwitch is devoted to helping consumers to compare deals for energy, TV, broadband, phone and other services. In 2014, it achieved revenues of £63m and adjusted profits of £16m.

Source: adapted from the *Financial Times*, 30.04.2015. All rights reserved.

(a) Explain why Zoopla believes buying uSwitch was a good fit for its business.
(b) Assess the potential impact on Zoopla of the acquisition of uSwitch.

Change and effects of transformational leadership

Occasionally change occurs as a result of a change in management or leadership. When a new CEO takes the helm of a business it is often because the previous CEO has retired, stepped down or has been replaced due to poor performance. In these circumstances the new CEO will bring in their own ideas and changes to the company. This **transformational leadership** might be in the form of a new vision or strategic direction for the business. If the new CEO has been brought in following a challenging period of performance, they might have been chosen as a catalyst for change to bring in new and fresh ideas. For example, at the start of 2015 McDonald's replaced its CEO, Don Thompson, with Steve Easterbrook, who was formerly the president of McDonald's Europe. Macdonald's sales had dropped by just over 1 per cent at the end of 2014. This was attributed to a range of reasons such as the McDonald's brand image, the company's market positioning in emerging markets, and its menu choices. They hoped that the introduction of a new CEO with new ideas would stimulate change and increase sales.

Thinking bigger

Change is a topic that encapsulates all other issues in business and is not a standalone issue. Any change will naturally affect all other functions of a business. It is difficult to separate the topic of change from others, such as leadership (Unit 18), Corporate culture (Unit 57) and Corporate strategy (Unit 45).

Not only will change affect issues such as competitiveness and stakeholders, the functions within a business, for instance marketing,

finance, operations and human resources, will all be affected. You should consider change in one of two ways. Firstly, does it pose a threat to the business? (The answer is often yes.) If so, what can the business do to manage the threat and negate the impact? Secondly, change may bring opportunities that the business can capitalise on. If so, how can the business lever these opportunities to create a competitive advantage?

Case study

AIRBUS GROUP

In 2013 the European Aeronautic Defence and Space Company (EADS) officially changed its name to Airbus Group, the group's most famous brand used on its commercial aircraft.

The name change came with a restructuring of the company into three distinctive divisions:

1 Airbus, maker of passenger jets

2 Airbus Defence and Space, created by combining existing defence and space businesses

3 Airbus Helicopters, manufacturer of civil and military helicopters.

The restructuring of the company allowed the various subsidiaries of the business to come together under the strong Airbus brand with the purpose of moving forward to capture the global aviation market.

It is anticipated that the global market for aviation will go through considerable growth in the future, driven by developments in emerging markets. Airbus Group revenue by region in 2013 is shown in Figure 1. Overall, air traffic is expected to double in the next 15 years. Emerging economies, such as China, India and Latin America, have a joint population of 6.2 billion people with anticipated air travel growth of 6 per cent by 2033. Comparatively, developed countries in Western Europe and North America, whose citizens are currently the most frequent flyers, equate to 1 billion people, with a growth forecast of 4.2 per cent. These statistics are a significant indication of where much of Airbus's revenue growth is likely to occur in the future.

Over the past nine years, Airbus has captured a significant proportion of new aircraft contracts. For example, orders in the category of passenger widebody planes, such as the Airbus A350, have totalled 1,761.

Figure 1

Airbus Group revenue by region in 2013

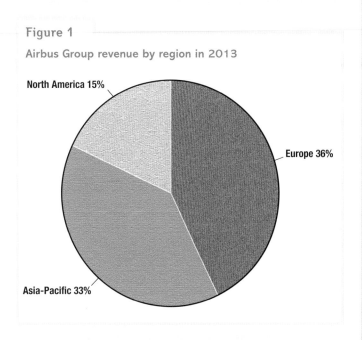

North America 15%

Europe 36%

Asia-Pacific 33%

Figure 2

Market forecast 2014–2033

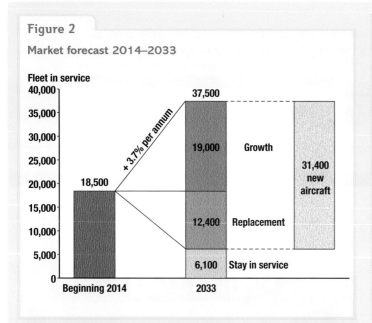

Figure 3

Forecast of Brent crude oil to 2030

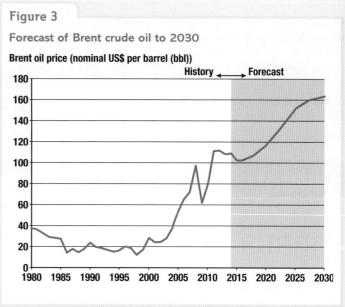

Source: adapted from www.airbus.com

With over 31,000 new aircraft required globally by 2033 there are significant opportunities for Airbus to grow, as shown in Figure 2. It may be challenging to keep up with the numbers required. There are also considerable pressures on the industry to produce ever more environmentally efficient planes. This is driven by consumer expectations and the long-term projection of fuel prices, as shown in Figure 3.

Q

(a) Explain one factor that may have driven the decision for Airbus Group to change its organisation structure. (4 marks)

(b) Assess the impact of changing market conditions on the stakeholders of Airbus Group. (12 marks)

(c) Evaluate the factors that may lead to change within the Airbus Group over the next two decades. (20 marks)

Key terms

Organisational change – a process in which a large company or organisation changes its working methods or aims, for example in order to develop and deal with new situations or markets.

Transformational leadership – where new leadership such as a new CEO brings about change with the purpose of improving business performance.

Knowledge check

1. State four factors that may cause change in a business.
2. How might change affect:
   a) motivation of employees?
   b) financial performance of a business?
3. What changes might a business go through when merging with another company?
4. What changes might a business face as it moves from being a private limited company (Ltd) to a public limited company (plc)?
5. Why might a business replace its CEO?
6. How might poor performance affect a business?

64 Key factors in change

Key points

1. The key factors in managing change:
- organisational culture
- size of organisation
- time/speed of change
- managing resistance to change.

Getting started

'The only thing that is constant is change.'

The above quotation, associated with Heraclitus, an ancient Greek philosopher who lived about 100 years before Plato, suggests that change is a fundamental aspect of our lives.

How might this quotation relate to the management of business?

Managing change

Change management is the process of organising and introducing new methods of working in a business. These changes can be driven from within the business or as a result of responding to the external environment (as seen in Unit 63). The **management of change** in business is becoming increasingly important. Under pressure from competitors, higher costs and tougher economic conditions, many firms in the UK have developed company-wide change programmes. Some firms have made only minor changes to their business operations and remained successful.

The Morgan Motor Company, for instance, still retains many of the original production methods and design features that have been part of its operation since the 1930s. It argues that it is exactly these 'original' features that attract consumers. However, many businesses need to change to stay successful in business. Unit 63 explored some of the factors that cause change and the impact of this change. This unit will look at some of the key issues in managing successful business change.

Organisational culture

Organisational culture in its simplest form can be described as 'the way things are done around here'. This is a simplistic view of extremely powerful phenomena that play a significant role in the success of a business. Resistance to change may often be found in the culture of an organisation. Customs and practices are embedded in systems that reflect the norms, values and beliefs of the organisation. While this may give stability, it presents problems of rigidity when a business needs to change. Unit 57 describes how corporate culture is formed by a multitude of factors that can be significantly different from business to business. For example, an organisation's culture may be personified by a strong leader, such as the company's founder, or by a particular operational principle, such as the John Lewis Partnership. Although a strong culture may give a company a competitive advantage, it can also be its downfall. For example, Kodak pioneered digital technology. Yet the changes in the digital market moved quickly and some competitors had an organisational culture that was reported to respond at a faster pace than Kodak to meet market demand. Despite its previous dominance in the market place, the changes resulted in Kodak filing for bankruptcy in 2012.

One of the most significant drivers for organisational change is external growth as a result of a merger or acquisition. In such cases two organisational cultures will come together and their compatibility will often be the key factor that leads to success or failure.

Size of the organisation

Growth is a key objective for most businesses and organisational change may come about as a result of mergers and acquisitions, change in organisational structure, strategic direction or a change in ownership. However, the size of a business may significantly affect its ability to manage successful change.

It is a fair generalisation that the larger the organisation the less adaptable and flexible it becomes. This might simply be because there is more change to manage and on a larger scale, but also because decision making takes longer in firms with a longer chain of command and subdivisions. This might be due to the number of people it is necessary to be involved in the decision-making process, or the number of people necessary to communicate with or train during the changes. In contrast, smaller businesses are far more flexible because decisions can be taken quickly and implemented without the involvement of a large number of stakeholders.

As companies expand it is also necessary for them to change the way decisions are made. Multinational, or even regional, businesses may be required to adapt their approach to suit the local context. For example, Starbucks is one company that has adopted a 'glocalised' (coined with the phrase 'think global, act local') approach with a number of its franchise stores. Instead of having a standardised format, it has adapted some of its franchises to meet local contexts to capture the feel of a local coffee shop, which would otherwise be threatened by the existence of Starbucks in its vicinity. The decisions in

Question 1

In 2010 Kraft, the US food giant, made a successful takeover bid of Cadbury, the UK chocolate manufacturer. An article in the *Financial Times*, published in 2011, explored some of the issues surrounding the changes that took place in both companies.

> At the height of the battle over the £11.7bn takeover – which was agreed a year ago next week – there were fears that jobs and taxes would divert to Zurich, and that chocolate would taste like plastic and the family culture fostered by the Quaker-founded company would become a distant memory.
>
> But the real loser, according to some analysts, is Kraft. 'Cadbury had a cutting edge understanding of the shopper and its retail customers,' says one former Cadbury employee. 'We spent years building that at Cadbury, and that's been lost.'
>
> Kraft disagrees. Trevor Bond, who ran Cadbury in the UK and now has an expanded Europe-wide portfolio at Kraft, says that Cadbury sales have gone 'incredibly well' in the UK, and promises many product launches under the Cadbury name. 'There have been a lot [of product launches] under Kraft, for example the Spots v Stripes Challenge Bar as part of the

Olympic campaign,' he says. The 5 to 10 launches under the Cadbury brand last year will be repeated this year.

'The culture of the two organisations is so similar it's been easy to get Kraft and Cadbury to mingle and get together,' says Mike Clarke, Kraft's head of Europe.

But insiders retort that Kraft's propensity for lengthy meetings, and a desire to include top-level executives on every decision, made the new jobs less compelling in any case.

'Put simply, Gorilla would never have got done under Kraft,' says one, referring to the ground-breaking TV ads (which featured a gorilla playing the drums to the Phil Collins hit, 'In The Air Tonight').

Another says there is much grumbling about 'the number of layers and amount of people that have to be involved to make things happen ... Forget the brand manager having a voice in anything.'

Source: adapted from the *Financial Times* 14.01.2011, 12.08.2013, 22.07.2014. All rights reserved.

(a) Explain the problems that Cadbury and Kraft have faced as a result of the Kraft takeover in 2010.

these areas are then decentralised to local store and regional managers. Where it is necessary for a business to move from a centralised decision-making approach (or 'top down' structure) to a decentralised strategy, change management may be more difficult to implement.

Culture is a key factor in any change process. However, it is also true that in large organisations it is easier for sub-cultures to develop. Multiple cultures are more difficult to manage through any change than simply one.

Question 2

Jon Clemence opened his first restaurant on Edinburgh's Royal Mile in 2004. His business was called 'Relish' and specialised in selling traditional hamburgers to tourists. In its first two years the company was extremely successful and began to make a profit.

In 2006 Jon Clemence decided to open his second restaurant in Edinburgh city centre, but changed the name of his two outlets to 'Wannaburger'. He wanted to add more fun to his brand and develop a system that allowed his restaurants to offer burgers in a faster, slicker way, with a more enjoyable experience. Along with the opening of the new store came a wider product range and a focus on simplified packaging.

(a) Discuss the benefits of managing change in a small business like Wannaburger.

Speed of change

Size is just one factor that can determine the pace of change in a business. Other factors also play their part. For example, in some contexts change can take its time and happen organically. This might be the case where a business is successful and perhaps leading the market. The development of new products, technology and processes can then evolve in the knowledge that the business is in a safe position. Over the past 10 years Apple has been at the forefront of innovation in the personal computing market through continual change at a steady, but regular pace.

By contrast, other organisations have to go through change very rapidly. Fashion is one example of an industry that is forever involved in product development and innovation. Similarly, crisis can also lead to very fast change. For example, the financial crisis of 2008 led to many organisations having to change very quickly to rationalise and improve efficiency in order to survive. Finnish company Nokia is a classic example of this. In 1980 Nokia was a television manufacturer, but because of a recession in Finland in the 1990s, it streamlined its business to focus on its most profitable products – mobile phones.

Managing resistance to change

Businesses are likely to face a certain amount of resistance to change from parts of the workforce for a number of reasons.
- Fear of the unknown. People often feel safe with familiar work practices, conditions and relationships.
- Employees and managers may fear that they will be unable to carry out new tasks, may be made redundant or may face a fall in earnings.

- Individual workers might be concerned that they will no longer work with their preferred colleagues or may be moved to a job that they dislike.

If change is to be carried out effectively, the business must make certain that these fears are taken into account. Only if employees feel they can cope with change will the business be able to operate to its optimum potential.

Owners: Owners of businesses may also be resistant to change for similar reasons. They might fear operating in unknown markets and conditions. They might not want the cost of any changes. They may also fear that they might not be able to adjust to new situations and be forced out of business.

Customers and suppliers: These too may resist change. They may be unwilling to change their own practices when the business they are dealing with changes. For example, a company may reorganise its sales force and decide that it will no longer visit clients that give it less than £5,000 worth of orders per year. Instead, it will develop a website and telesales operation to deal with small customers. Inevitably, the company will lose some customers who are not prepared to place orders in this new way.

Generally speaking therefore, stakeholders in a business may resist change for any of the following reasons.
- Disagreement with the reasons for or necessity to change.
- Fear of the impact.
- Lack of understanding.
- Disagreement with the process involved in delivering the change.
- Lack of involvement.
- General inertia – satisfaction with the current situation / way of working.

Harvard Business School professor John Kotter proposed in Leading Change (1996) that are eight steps necessary to manage successful change in a business. The first step is to create a sense of urgency – getting people to actually see and feel the need for change. Stakeholders must understand the need for change through effective communication if anger and fear are to be overcome and the management of change has any chance of succeeding.

Exam tip

Change management needs to be approached with care in any examination because it can incorporate all aspects and functions of a business. It is therefore worth examining change and the management of change in a systematic way.

- *What are the driving forces behind the change? Are these internal or external?*
- *What is the likely impact of the change?*
- *What factors might determine its success? Think about the issues covered in this unit.*
- *What are the key steps the business must take to ensure the change is successful? This will often come from the context of the business you are analysing.*

Case study

ERNST & YOUNG

Ernst & Young Global Ltd (EY) is a global financial audit firm with its headquarters in London. EY provides financial services, such as auditing, tax and advice for companies.

In 2013 EY adopted a comprehensive flexible working arrangement across the company. EY already supported both informal and formal (reduced hours) flexible working arrangements. But in 2013 the company aimed to make it 'business as usual' rather than the exception by giving its people more opportunity to choose when, where and how they worked – while ensuring clients still took priority.

EY set out its vision 'to be the leaders in flexible working in professional services. We trust our people to create a sustainable, high performing environment for our clients, our people and our firm through being empowered to choose how, when and where they work.'

Robin Tye, Chief Executive Officer for the UK and Ireland, said:

'Flexibility isn't about working less or working more, but about having greater control over how to get your work done more effectively. Our aim, therefore, is to support teams in "making it real", so that flexibility is a part of our working culture, enabled by the right policies, technology tools and effective use of space across all of our offices. This is a really important issue for our business because having a mobile and flexible workforce means that we can operate more effectively across time zones and respond more quickly to client needs. And as individuals, it means that you have autonomy to perform in the most effective way that suits you best, whilst meeting the needs of your teams and your clients.'

In order to implement these flexible working practices, EY introduced a range of measures.

- A central team of change managers supported by the leadership team, who are responsible for implementing and monitoring flexible working practices.

- Workforce training, which identifies the desired behaviours required to be an effective flexible worker. This training has also become an integral part of recruitment, induction and appraisal.

- A dedicated intranet site with information and advice on how to achieve flexible working and a HR helpline.

- Investment in workspaces and in new technology to support remote working, including new video conferencing facilities, global messaging and collaboration tools.

The feedback EY have received from their employees since the introduction of flexible working shows that having the ability to choose how their work is delivered makes employees feel more engaged.

Already, flexible working has had an impact on the amount of time workers spend travelling, reducing costs by £0.5 million in 2014, in turn reducing EY's carbon footprint. Furthermore, empowered flexible workers are more productive, happy and healthy employees.

Source: adapted from www.ey.com

 Q

(a) Explain how the changes introduced at EY will impact clients. (4 marks)

(b) Assess the factors that are driving changes in working practices at EY. (10 marks)

(c) Evaluate the key factors that the managing partners of EY will need to consider in order to ensure the flexible working practices are successful. (20 marks)

Thinking bigger

This unit has examined some of the factors that can determine the success of change. However, does the level of success of a business influence the likely success of change? Can a very successful business be complacent, and thus its satisfaction with the way things are result in inertia, making change difficult? Can failure be a good thing? Businesses that have made mistakes build a certain resilience that makes them more prepared for the next round of change. For example, Firestone tyres had a product recall in 2000. The company revised its approach with its 'Making it right' campaign and regained the trust of consumers.

It is also worth considering the nature of the industry when discussing change. Are some industries simply more adaptable because of their context and the nature of their product? Fashion and information technology are two industries that are in a continuous state of change. Change management must be an integral characteristic of any business that operates within industries like these. Nevertheless, there is much to be said for the status quo. Change can bring about new opportunities, but long periods of stability and consistency can help a business build efficiencies and get good at what it does.

Key terms

Management of change – the process of organising and introducing new methods of working within a business.

Knowledge check

1. State four factors that may have an impact on the success of organisational change.

2. Explain why a large firm may find change more difficult to manage than a small business.

3. How are culture and change management linked?

4. Why do people resist change?

5. How might a business implement effective change management?

Key points

1. Identifying key risks through risk assessment:
   - natural disasters
   - IT systems failure
   - loss of key staff.
2. Planning for risk mitigation:
   - business continuity
   - succession planning.

Getting started

In October 2014 it was widely reported that Christophe de Margerie, the CEO of Total, Europe's third largest oil company, was killed in an air crash. The corporate jet in which he was travelling collided with a snowplough on a runway at Moscow airport. This was a sad loss to the company. The French Prime Minister commented that France had lost an extraordinary business leader who had turned Total into a world giant.

In December 2013 it was widely reported that NatWest bank was subject to a cyberattack. The bank's online service was interrupted after it was deliberately bombarded with heavy internet traffic. It was reported that customers could not access their accounts to transfer money and pay bills. Another systems failure at NatWest in June 2013 saw payments go missing. Some customers did not get their wages, and home purchases and holidays were interrupted for several weeks. This cost NatWest £175 million in compensation.

Describe the possible impacts of these events on each of the businesses. Could these events have been predicted? What possible measures might businesses take to prepare for such events?

What is scenario planning?

Businesses may be subject to unforeseen events, which could hamper their activities. Examples might be a fire that destroys premises, a breakdown in the internal back-up system that stores business information, or the sudden retirement of a CEO.

Many businesses undertake **scenario planning** in an effort to deal with these events. Scenario planning is not about trying to predict future events. It is a strategic planning method designed to explore uncertainties, work out how to protect the business from their worst consequences and prepare how to exploit any opportunities that might present themselves. It is a disciplined approach to dealing with uncertainty in the future.

Scenario planning helps to:
- clarify some of the future uncertainties in business, identify risks and opportunities, and prepare for their eventuality

- teach managers how events may transpire, develop and affect the business
- understand the causes and effects of change in business and how to manage it.

There may be different approaches to scenario planning, but there are a number of important steps in the process.

1. **Identify possible trends and issues.** This involves scanning the internal and external environment in an effort to 'spot' any emerging threats that might impact on the business. PESTLE analysis might be used to help this process.
2. **Build possible scenarios.** Businesses need to imagine a range of possible scenarios that might affect their operations. The background for these scenarios will be provided by the information gathered in the previous stage. These scenarios will vary between different businesses because different businesses are likely to be presented with different threats. For example, a supermarket chain is not likely to develop a scenario for people trapped in an aircraft taken over by terrorists.
3. **Plan response.** This involves identifying as precisely as possible the impact scenarios will have on the business and developing plans to deal with them. This is a lengthy process because such impacts might be numerous and complex.
4. **Identify the most likely scenarios.** A business may identify a wide range of scenarios that could affect a business. However, the likelihood of different events occurring will have different probabilities. A business is not likely to have enough resources to plan responses to every single scenario. Therefore, it will be necessary to prioritise, say, the five most likely and the business can plan thorough responses to each.
5. **Capitalise on scenarios.** This involves implementing the planned responses when scenarios appear a likely reality. Not all scenarios have negative outcomes. For example, if the global economy goes into recession some firms can flourish by catering for new needs. Those that are prepared for such a scenario may prosper.

Risk assessment

When a business attempts to identify the possible scenarios it might face in the future, it might use **risk assessment**. This involves examining what might cause harm to people and identifying the precautions that might be taken to protect them from harm. One of the main purposes of risk assessment is to help comply with health and safety legislation. Workers have a legal right to protection in the workplace. However, the use of risk assessment might be extended to assess risks to the business in general. Therefore, it has a role to play in scenario planning. It can be used to help identify hazards, decide who might be harmed and estimate the probability of events occurring. This will help in the first stage of scenario planning where the possible trends and issues are identified.

Possible scenarios

The range of possible scenarios facing a business is huge. However, some are more likely than others. Three of the most likely scenarios are discussed below.

Natural disasters: The Earth is susceptible to natural disasters. These are catastrophic events that usually occur suddenly and are caused by environmental factors. Examples include floods, hurricanes, volcanic eruptions, tsunamis, earthquakes, forest fires, snowstorms and epidemics. Such events can have devastating effects and may result in high levels of damage, death and disruption. Some UK firms are multinationals with operations all over the world where some of these events are perhaps more likely to occur. Thus, multinationals are likely to be more exposed to the risk of natural disasters.

One common example of a natural disaster that causes difficulties for UK businesses is flooding. It is estimated that around £1 billion is spent every year repairing flood damage. It has also been suggested that this could rise to £27 billion a year by 2080. In 2014 some serious floods caused severe damage and disruption to the southwest. A storm, followed by several weeks of heavy rain, destroyed the only rail link to the southwest. This cut off the region for several months until the line was repaired. West Country leaders said that the local economy had been devastated by the floods. Tourism in particular had suffered badly. Farmers in low-lying areas in Somerset, many of whom were just recovering from devastation caused by floods in 2012, were hit again. Farmers had spent tens of thousands or even hundreds of thousands of pounds on repairing their farms after the 2012 floods. In 2013, some then had to cope with almost all of their land being flooded again.

Although there are no volcanoes in the UK, some disruption was caused in the spring of 2010 when a volcano erupted in Iceland. Eyjafjallajökull erupted sending millions of cubic feet of ash billowing over Europe, including the UK. This posed a threat to aircraft so many airports in Europe were closed for a period of time. Estimates suggested that the cost of grounded flights to the global airline industry was over £1 billion. However, some businesses actually benefited from the closure of European airspace. Airport hotels were full of stranded travellers; trains, buses and coaches were extremely busy; Eurostar trains between London and Paris or Brussels were sold out.

IT systems failure: Most businesses employ IT systems in their organisation. However, the extent to which businesses depend on such systems will vary. Generally, the larger the business, the more investment it will have in IT. Consequently, an IT systems failure, or worse still, a cyberattack, could be a serious disaster. Many small businesses may have only modest investments in IT systems. Perhaps computers are used for data storage, email communication, research and website display. However, even smaller businesses are increasing their reliance on IT. For example, many conduct transactions online. This makes them more vulnerable to breakdowns.

In December 2014, it was widely reported that Nats, an air traffic control company, experienced a serious systems failure. The failure meant that air traffic controllers were not able to access all of the available data to the flight paths of individual aircraft. As a result the controllers had to find ways of reducing the traffic. This led to the cancellation of many flights. Nats reassured people that the controllers had a clear radar picture and that all communication channels with aircraft were open during the incident. It said that passengers travelling on aircraft were never in any danger. However, the incident raised questions about what could happen in the future. Airports around the UK had to cancel many flights and a number of planes were diverted, meaning that passengers ended up in destinations that they were not expecting.

Businesses, and the public at large, are becoming increasingly concerned about the threat of cyberattacks. A cyberattack is where computer hackers break into computer systems and steal data. For many, the consequence of such attacks is largely a mystery. However, as the number of attacks increase, awareness of their effects is gradually being raised. In 2014 it was widely reported that hackers breached security at eBay, the online auction site. Hackers stole the names, emails, postal addresses, phone numbers and dates of birth of its 233 million users. eBay was criticised for not notifying its customers what had happened. So far the consequences of such attacks have been manageable. But in the future more serious consequences might materialise.

Loss of key staff: People leave businesses all of the time. This may not be a problem because, as the saying goes, 'no one is indispensable'. However, losing key members of staff can cause difficulties – especially if preparations for this eventuality have not been fully considered. It can also be a very serious problem in small businesses, which are often dominated by a single person. It was reported in 2013 by Scottish Widows that around 55 per cent of businesses would cease trading if they lost one or more key people from the business. Unexpected losses through illness, long-term incapacity or death are the most likely causes of such an event. In a small business, where perhaps the owner employs only a few other people, the loss of the owner could result in the closure of the business. This is because the other employees may not have the resources or the desire to take ownership of the company. Finding an outside agent to take over the business might also be difficult.

In 2012, it was widely reported that Intel, the microchip manufacturer, lost its CEO Paul Otellini when he announced his retirement. The company did not have a successor lined up. Intel is widely regarded as a well-run and methodical company and changes of leadership are unusual. In its 44-year history only five CEOs had ever been employed and Mr Otellini had been an Intel employee for 40 of those years – he was an experienced and valuable employee.

Thinking bigger

Although scenario planning has some obvious benefits, since it forces decision makers to consider the future and plan for possible changes, it does have some drawbacks. It is time-consuming and expensive. As a result there is a risk that a business may not devote sufficient resources to it and therefore fail to carry out the process effectively. Also, some people might argue that preparing for events that may never happen is a waste of money. Another problem might be finding people in the business who have a deep enough understanding of possible scenarios. Therefore, it might be necessary to invite external agents to participate, which will add to the cost. Finally, only large corporations are likely to have the resources to undertake full-scale scenario planning. Most small businesses have much less to lose and would probably see the opportunity cost of scenario planning as too high.

Exam tip

You need to remember that scenario planning can be used to prepare for uncertain events that provide a business with opportunities. It is not just about planning for disasters. For example, a surge in demand as the global population booms (it is expected to double by 2050) can provide many opportunities for businesses around the world.

Planning for risk mitigation

Risk mitigation plans identify, assess and prioritise risks. They also plan responses to deal with the impact of these risks to the operation of the business. In general a business can use a number of mitigation strategies to reduce the damage caused by serious disruptive events. For example, it can:

- set up in a location that is not vulnerable to flooding, earthquakes, bush fires and other potential natural hazards
- ensure that premises are constructed according to building codes that are designed for safety and protection
- take out adequate insurance policies to cover losses resulting from disasters; for example, it may be possible to take out 'business interruption cover'
- ensure that data stored on computers is as secure as possible and that back-up systems are adequate
- organise back-up power, such as a generator, to ensure that vital machinery and other equipment can still be used in the event of a power interruption
- ensure that valuable assets, such as expensive machinery and tools, are protected as much as possible
- ensure that there is access to emergency funding
- ensure that adequate communication channels are set up to deal with crises
- produce a business continuity plan to deal with crises. This is discussed next.

Business continuity: When an incident occurs, a business will want to minimise disruption. After safeguarding human life, one of the most important priorities is to get the business 'up and running' again. Some firms produce business continuity plans. These show how a business will operate after a serious incident and how it expects to return to normal in the quickest time possible. There may be four stages in such a plan.

1. **Carry out a business impact analysis.** This will identify those functions and processes that are essential to the running of the business. This involves gathering information so that appropriate recovery strategies can be designed. The process also involves identifying the financial consequences of such incidents, like loss of revenue, customer defection, increased costs, penalties and disruption to business plans. This information may be gathered by using questionnaires and workshop sessions with appropriate employees. Once the information has been gathered it must be analysed, reviewed and if necessary updated to reflect changing circumstances.

2. **Formulate recovery strategies.** These are the actions taken to restore the business to a minimum acceptable level after an incident. This will involve identifying the resources needed, such as people, facilities, equipment, utilities, IT and materials to aid recovery. Examples of recovery strategies that might be used include:
   - setting up agreements with another business to share resources and support each other should either party encounter serious disruption
   - planning to convert resources for new usages; for example, a canteen might be used as office space
   - contracting out work to third parties
   - prioritising production – perhaps according to customer value
   - maintaining higher stock levels
   - placing restrictions on orders
   - shifting production from one plant to another.

3. **Plan development.** This involves developing a detailed plan to ensure that the recovery strategies are carried out in an organised way. A business is likely to appoint recovery teams, develop relocation plans, and document recovery strategies and procedures so that key staff are aware of what is expected of them.

4. **Testing and training.** Once the recovery plan has gained approval it is necessary to design testing exercises and train staff in their roles during the execution of the recovery plan. The recovery teams will be the main focus of such training. After testing and training it may be necessary to update the business continuity plan to take into account any discoveries made during this process. Finally, it may be necessary to review and update the plan on a regular basis to take into account any changes that have occurred in the business, such as key personnel, vital equipment or premises.

Succession planning: Part of risk mitigation involves identifying and developing current employees who have the potential to occupy key roles in the future. This is called succession planning. This is an important process because it will help a business deal with the problem of losing key staff. However, succession planning will also help to develop the staff needed to fill posts as the business expands. Without succession planning a business might end up promoting a person who is not equipped to do the job or recruiting an unknown outsider at a far greater risk and expense. Some research suggests that CEOs appointed from internal sources tend to outperform those from outside. Some key steps involved in a succession planning process are outlined below.

- **Identify the characteristics a successor should possess.** This task can be undertaken by looking at the job description and developing a person specification giving the characteristics of the person who currently occupies the key role and identifying any new skills and traits that may be required.
- **Decide how the successor will be found.** This might involve scrutinising the credentials of every prospective internal candidate. Alternatively, an outside agency might be employed to 'headhunt' possible candidates from outside. To 'widen the net' some businesses might use both approaches.
- **Undertake a rigorous selection process.** Examine the strengths and weaknesses of all the candidates. It is important to involve several key personnel, and perhaps other specialists, in this process in order to gain a broad view of the candidates.
- **Make the decision.** The people tasked with this duty need to analyse and evaluate the performance of each candidate. It is important to reach a conclusion and make an appointment. Failure to do this might demoralise and undermine internal candidates. They may think that they are not valued by the business.
- **Communicate the decision.** It is important for everyone affected by the decision to be informed about the appointment.
- **Implement a training and preparation plan.** The person appointed will need to be trained and prepared for the final transition into the post when needed. This may involve 'shadowing' the person who currently occupies the position for a period of time. It might also involve going on specialist courses to enhance the skills and knowledge needed.

In 2014, it was reported that the UK regulators were not happy with some of the succession planning undertaken by corporations. The criticism came after Tesco reportedly left the post of financial director vacant for several months, and at one stage had only one board member with retail experience. Succession planning should play a very important role in business.

Links 🔗

There may only be limited opportunities to demonstrate synoptic skills using information about scenario planning and risk mitigation. This is because it is quite a specialised topic. However, chances might arise when you are writing answers about Demand (Unit 4), Business failure (Unit 36), Economic influences (Unit 41) and SWOT analysis (Unit 46). There may be a particularly strong link with Unit 47, which is about the impact of external influences on a business.

Key terms

Business continuity plan – shows how a business will operate after a serious incident and how it expects to return to normal in the quickest time possible.

Risk assessment – identifying and evaluating the potential risks that may be involved in an activity that a business proposes to undertake, ensuring compliance with health and safety legislation.

Risk mitigation plans – identify, assess and prioritise risks, and plan responses to deal with the impact of these risks on the operation of the business.

Scenario planning – a strategic planning method designed to explore uncertainties, learn how to protect the business from their worst consequences and prepare how to exploit any opportunities that might present themselves.

Succession planning – identifying and developing people who have the potential to occupy key roles in a business in the future.

Knowledge check

1. Outline the important steps in a scenario plan.

2. Give three specific benefits of scenario planning.

3. Give three examples of natural disasters that could impact on a business.

4. What role might risk assessment play in scenario planning?

5. How might the loss of key staff impact a business?

6. Give three examples of problems that a breakdown in IT systems might cause a business.

7. What is meant by risk mitigation planning?

8. Outline the four stages in a business continuity plan.

9. Give four examples of recovery strategies that a business might employ.

Case study

ROYAL DUTCH SHELL

Royal Dutch Shell is a large energy and petrochemicals multinational. It employs around 92,000 people in over 70 countries. It has more than 30 refineries and chemical plants, and in 2013 its revenue was $452.1 billion. It made a profit of $16 billion and invested $44 billion in capital expenditure.

Royal Dutch Shell is a business that is exposed to a wide range of global uncertainties. Consequently, it is no surprise that Shell has been using scenario planning for over 40 years. It helps the company to understand how external influences might affect the business and the petrochemicals industry as a whole. It could be argued that scenario planning originally helped Shell to develop as the market leader during the global gas shortage in 1973. Since then scenario planning has helped Shell to anticipate and prepare for:

- the world energy crisis in 1979
- the collapse of the energy market in 1986
- the break-up of the Soviet Union
- rising terrorism in the Middle East
- global pressure for greater environmental and social responsibility.

In 2013, Shell published a report outlining two possible scenarios looking as far ahead as 2100, taking into account the fact that by 2060 the global population will be around 9 billion, meaning that demand for energy will rise by about 80 per cent. Shell's scenarios look at what might happen to the global economy, energy provision and political situations up until 2100. Entitled 'Oceans' and 'Mountains' the main points of the scenarios are outlined briefly below.

Mountains – describes a more stable political environment

- Governments hold the balance of power and are able to introduce firm and far-reaching policies.
- A switch from fossil fuels is anticipated and governments design compact cities and overhaul transport systems. For example, in Japan it is expected that 10 per cent of car travel will be electric powered.
- By 2030 there is serious investment in carbon capture and storage. Gas is the primary energy source.

- By 2060 electricity will become carbon neutral.
- By 2100 global social mobility will be thwarted as a result of interference in the free market.

Oceans – describes a more prosperous and volatile world

- Power is devolved, competing interests accommodated.
- Economic reforms improve productivity, but there is less social cohesion and more political instability. This results in government policies being too slow-moving and decision making being driven by market forces.
- Chinese GDP will reach $20,000 per capita by 2025 and there will be a surge in the global demand for energy. This will bring strong social and political tensions.
- Emerging economies will boom. The number of cars in India will reach 500 million and air travel will increase five-fold. But the effects of carbon dioxide emissions will be neglected.
- Fossil fuels will be important to the energy mix but renewables will grow, until in 2070 solar will be the largest energy source.

Source: adapted from Shell International B.V.

(a) Assess the importance to a business such as Shell of succession planning. (10 marks)

(b) Evaluate the usefulness of these scenario plans to Shell. (20 marks)

Key points

1. Growth rate of the UK economy compared to emerging economies.
2. Growing economic power of countries within Asia, Africa and other parts of the world.
3. Implications of economic growth for individuals and businesses:
   - trade opportunities for businesses
   - employment patterns.
4. Indicators of growth:
   - Gross Domestic Product (GDP) per capita
   - literacy
   - health
   - Human Development Index (HDI).

Getting started

James Martin runs a furniture-making business. It has been operating for ten years and grown from just a few people to a workforce of over five hundred. James started selling his products in France and Spain in the Euro Area in 2012, opening small offices in both countries to deal with the distribution. James wants to build the long-term plan for his business and plans to expand internationally.

Looking at Figure 1, which countries would you advise James to consider expanding into, bearing in mind the highest growth rates? How do you think expanding into these countries might affect his business? What other details about each country do you think James will need to consider?

Figure 1

The emerging economies of the MINT countries (Mexico, Indonesia, Nigeria and Turkey)

Country name	2012	2013e	2014e	2015f	2016f	2017f
	(percent change from previous year, except interest rates)					
US	2.3	2.2	2.4	2.7	2.8	2.4
Japan	1.7	1.6	0.0	1.1	1.7	1.2
Euro Area	−0.7	−0.4	0.9	1.5	1.8	1.6
United Kingdom	0.7	1.7	2.8	2.6	2.6	2.2
Brazil	1.8	2.7	0.1	−1.3	1.1	2.0
Russia	3.4	1.3	0.6	−2.7	0.7	2.5
India	6.0	5.6	5.0	4.7	5.5	5.5
China	7.7	7.7	7.4	7.1	7.0	6.9
South Africa	2.5	1.9	1.5	2.0	2.1	2.4
Mexico	4.0	1.4	2.1	2.6	3.2	3.5
Indonesia	6.0	5.6	5.0	4.7	5.5	5.5
Nigeria	4.3	5.4	6.2	4.5	5.0	5.5
Turkey	2.1	4.2	2.9	3.0	3.9	3.7

Notes:
1 The table shows selected entries from the global outlook summary in *Global Economic Prospects, The Global Economy in Transition, A World Bank Group Flagship Report*, June 2015.
2 PPP = purchasing power parity; e = estimate; f = forecast.
3 Aggregate growth rates calculated using constant 2010 US dollars GDP weights.
4 Based on real GDP and the percent change from previous year, except interest rates.
5 World Bank forecasts are frequently updated based on new information and changing (global) circumstances. Consequently, projections may differ from those contained in other documents.

Key: MINT countries are shown in red

Source: World Bank

Growth rate of the UK economy compared to emerging economies

Around 150 years ago, Britain was an industrial powerhouse, producing manufactured goods that were exported all over the world. In the modern era of emerging economies and increased competition, the Office for National Statistics (ONS) figures published in 2014 showed that UK manufacturing output made recent improvements, with an average of 2.8 per cent growth. UK products were reported as more competitive than at any time in the modern era. Alongside this, however, the UK has a strong and growing service sector, and the world's **emerging economies** produce most of the manufactured goods that are globally consumed.

Emerging economies and markets: An emerging market may be thought of as one where there is rapid growth, but also a lot of risk. Investors like emerging markets since they are likely to grow more quickly than more mature markets. Therefore a business should be able to increase profits and dividends. Economists sometimes group emerging economies together, e.g. BRICS: Brazil, Russia, India, China and South Africa, and MINT: Mexico, Indonesia, Nigeria and Turkey.

Where an emerging market is experiencing an increase in average incomes, it is likely that the middle classes are expanding. Increasing income allows consumers to spend more, on both imports and domestically produced goods and services. Buying more domestic goods encourages the growth of domestic firms, giving them increased market power and allowing them to compete internationally. Consumers may also buy more imported goods and services from businesses in more developed economies, thereby increasing their profitability and making the emerging market more attractive to new entrants. Consequently, many economists assume that the growth rates of emerging market economies will exceed those of the more developed economies, including the UK. It is worth remembering however, that this is a trend and not a certainty. Emerging markets will continue to encounter many risks that might seriously affect overall economic performance. Moreover, countries differ in how vulnerable they are to certain risks and how well they will be able to cope should such risks become reality.

Economic growth, the increase in a country's productive capacity, is usually measured using Gross Domestic Product (GDP). GDP for the UK is available from the ONS. Figure 2 illustrates the growth rates of the UK economy compared with a selection of countries from emerging markets.

Growing economic power of Asian, African and other countries

Most of the BRICS and MINT countries have experienced strong growth over the past few years. This growth is increasing the overall economic power of many of the countries in Asia, Africa and other parts of the world. China, according to some measures, had the largest economy in the world in 2015. If so, it overtook the US, which has been the global leader since the late 1800s. It frequently comes at or near the top of the rankings as an exporter and as a destination for foreign investment. Its growing economic power means that it is also one of the world's biggest investors in other countries.

In 1990, China produced less than three per cent of global manufacturing output by value, but by early 2015 this had risen to nearly a quarter. China's industrial might impacts all across South East Asia, through supply chains and outsourcing. In fact, China drives what has come to be known as 'Factory Asia' for its dominance of global manufacturing. The strength of this regional trading bloc (known as the ASEAN, see Unit 70) looks set to continue in the near future. First, China has very efficient clusters of suppliers and excellent infrastructure, allowing for further cost-effective growth. Second, it has access to lower-cost labour throughout South East Asia, including Myanmar (Burma) and the Philippines. Finally, Chinese and other Asian consumers are spending more each year, driving increases in demand and reinforcing local production and distribution.

Other emerging markets, such as Central and South America and Africa, are creating big international companies that increasingly are challenging the dominance of firms from the developed regions. However, because of China's dominance in manufacturing, these other regions may be less likely to follow this route to development. They may have to find new ways to grow and develop in the future.

According to the World Bank, the largest economies in the world include US, Japan, Germany and the UK. However, the order of leading economies may change many times in the future. Regardless, roughly 70 per cent of world GDP growth is likely to come from emerging market economies, with China and India accounting for between 40–50 per cent of this figure. It follows then that 20–30 per cent of future global growth may come from the rest.

Figure 2

The 12 largest economies in nominal GDP terms ($ trillion, 1997, 2007 and 2012)

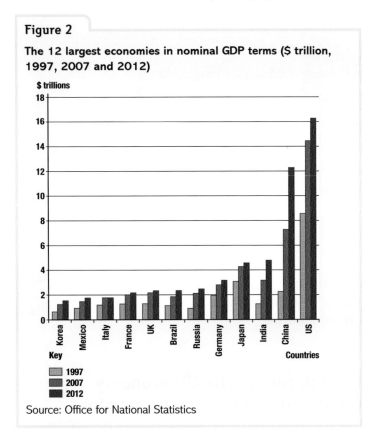

Key
- 1997
- 2007
- 2012

Source: Office for National Statistics

Question 1

Through its offices in the Netherlands, Japan and the US, Mark Lyndon Paper Enterprises makes money exporting paper and cardboard to be recycled, in a circular trade that demonstrates many of the benefits of global markets. The business works as follows: a factory in China produces a good that is boxed, put into a container and shipped to the US and Europe, where a customer buys the product. Mark Lyndon Paper recovers the box and sends it back to China – probably in a similar shipping container to the one that transported the original product. There the packaging is pulped and made into a new cardboard box, whereupon the cycle begins again.

The value of the UK trade in goods in 2014 was around £24.6 billion, with exports including cars and jewellery, for example, and a trend for growth. Yet Mark Lyndon Paper illustrates some profound changes in the UK economy since the turn of the 21st century. It is owned by a Chinese firm, and owes its success to the fact that the UK, amongst others, imports many goods made elsewhere and sends back empty cardboard boxes.

(a) What is meant by circular trade?

(b) Explain how Mark Lyndon Paper reflects the changing economic relationship between the emerging economy of China and the developed one in the UK.

Question 2

Figure 3 indicates that the Gross Domestic Product (GDP) in China was worth US$9240.27 billion in 2014. The GDP value of China represents 14.90 per cent of the world economy. GDP in China averaged US$1252.79 billion from 1960 until 2014, reaching an all-time high of US$9240.27 billion in 2014 and a record low of US$46.50 billion in 1962.

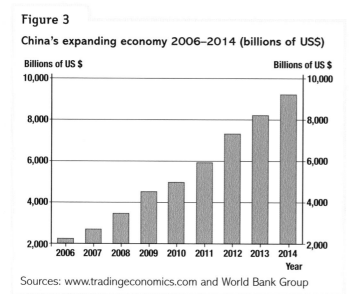

Figure 3

China's expanding economy 2006–2014 (billions of US$)

Sources: www.tradingeconomics.com and World Bank Group

(a) What are the key factors that are likely to have led to growth in GDP in China?

(b) Discuss the advantages and disadvantages of high growth rates for China.

Implications of economic growth for individuals and businesses

As noted earlier, consumers in emerging markets may be buying more goods and services, both from domestic companies and from those from more developed economies. This may make the emerging markets even more attractive to new entrants, create trade opportunities and alter existing employment patterns.

Trade opportunities: Where an economy is growing, consumption may also be growing, and this is good news for firms looking to invest or sell their products and services. Thus with growth, it is likely that disposable income is also rising. Individuals may therefore have more money in their pockets to spend, increasing the overall demand for goods and services. Demand is likely to become income elastic, providing greater opportunities for increased revenues and profit. These goods and services can be produced domestically or imported from abroad. This creates many opportunities for trade.

Employment patterns: In addition to looking at growth rates, a business might want to assess the employment patterns across an economy. Employment is one of the most important indicators of the health of an economy. A firm might want information on unemployment rates and trends, labour costs and productivity, as well as the educational qualifications of potential employees.

The employment rate gives a snapshot of the numbers of jobs that are being gained or lost across an economy. The level of unemployment can reveal a lot about an economy, but not all of it straightforward. As noted above, the amount of money that consumers have in their pockets (disposable income) indicates whether or not they may be able to buy goods in the future. When people are out of work, they do not have much money to spend or save. Consequently, if there is a high level of unemployment in a country, it may not be a good time to consider exporting there. On the other hand, unemployed individuals may be looking for jobs and so a firm could find a pool of labour to make goods that it could then export elsewhere. In this case, directly investing in a country by building a factory, for instance, might be a good idea to consider.

The unemployment rate in the UK in 2014 was 5.8 per cent according to the Office for National Statistics, a big improvement on 2009, when unemployment hit 8 per cent. The International Labour Organization (ILO) supplies figures for other countries. The European Union has had persistent unemployment, and as of 2014 the number of people out of work showed no signs of decreasing. In 2014 Greece and Spain had unemployment rates at or above 25 per cent, which indicates weakness in their economies. By contrast, according to the ILO China's unemployment rate has remained around 3 per cent (2.9 per cent in 2012).

Future employment trends are also important. For example, new technology may mean that fewer workers are required to manufacture goods. As a consequence, having cheap labour may no longer be as significant a comparative advantage for an emerging economy as it once was.

Question 3

In March 2015 unemployment in Ireland was at the lowest rate since 2009, when the country began its bailout programme after the 2008 financial crisis.

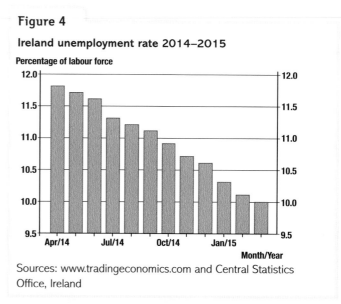

Figure 4

Ireland unemployment rate 2014–2015

Sources: www.tradingeconomics.com and Central Statistics Office, Ireland

(a) What are the main influences on employment patterns within an economy?

(b) Explain why a declining rate of unemployment may indicate that the Irish economy is improving and may be more attractive for businesses looking to invest.

Indicators of growth

In order to spot opportunities to trade or evaluate markets for potential investment, a business needs to be able to recognise where an economy is likely to grow. There are numerous indicators of economic growth, including GDP per capita and the Human Development Index (HDI).

Gross Domestic Product (GDP) per capita: This is a measure of economic activity, including all of the goods and services produced in a year, divided by the number of people in the country. What a business looking to invest in a particular country may be most interested in, however, is the trend or direction in GDP per capita. For instance, China reported a very high growth rate of 7.4 per cent in 2014, but this was actually down from the figure of 7.7 reported in 2013.

Finding and evaluating data on GDP:

Figures for the UK are compiled by the ONS and are rigorously assessed and adjusted for errors. GDP for other countries is obtained from other sources, such as the World Bank, International Monetary Fund or some other non-governmental organisation. It is important to understand that data is only as good as the source it comes from and the methods used to collect it. Thus, data may not always be consistent, comparable or easy to verify. You should always give your sources and be cautious about using data from different sources.

Sources of data need to be used with care and it is important to understand what the figures imply. GDP figures do indicate the value of economic activity, but care must be taken as there are a variety of GDP statistics. GDP can be calculated to show the value of all of the goods as either produced or sold or purchased in an economy. They may take account of price changes over time (**real GDP**, which adjusts GDP figures for inflation, verses **nominal GDP**, which does not). They may also be reported for the economy as a whole or for each resident (**per capita GDP**), as explained above.

Moreover, the figures, even where they show the same thing, may be hard to compare across countries, owing to the statistics being reported in different currencies. GDP figures usually use **market exchange rates**, which are derived in the foreign exchange markets. We know that foreign exchange markets by their nature are constantly changing, and so GDP figures derived using market rates may also change rapidly over time. It is necessary to use figures over a period of time to draw any reliable conclusions. Also, goods and services tend to be more expensive in high-income countries, and as a result GDP figures for those countries may overstate what people can actually buy there.

For these reasons, statisticians prefer to use **purchasing power parity (PPP)** exchange rates. PPP is the price of purchasing a standardized basket of goods and services and allows you to compare prices across economies. The **PPP exchange rate** is the rate at which one country's currency must be exchanged for that of another country in order to buy the same basket of goods and services there. Using PPP estimates of GDP, an investor has a good idea of what buyers in different countries can afford, and what their overall welfare might be in real terms.

GDP figures may not mean the same thing, and may have very different implications for investment decisions. The difference is often greatest for lower income or developing countries, as can be seen from data available from the IMF's World Economic Outlook or if the CIA World Factbook is reviewed. According to the ONS and CIA Factbook the GDP of the UK in 2014 was around $2.9 trillion based upon market exchange rates. However, GDP was only around $2.4 trillion where based upon PPP. For India, the Ministry of Statistics reports its GDP in market exchange rates as just over $2 trillion, yet this rises above $7 trillion in PPP terms.

Literacy: Just as important for a business as the level of employment is the quality of those employees, both as workers and as potential consumers. A company looking to invest in a country will need to hire a workforce. They will want the most productive employees they can find at the lowest possible cost. Equally, a firm looking to export to a country will want to consider the consumers to which it will sell. It will want to understand its potential customers and how to market its goods or services to them.

Literacy is one of the key indicators that firms will assess when making strategic decisions. The **literacy rate** is the percentage of adults that can read and write. The UN provides data on the literacy rate of most countries, and Table 1 gives an example of the literacy attainment of a few countries. For assessing literacy, someone above the age of 15 is considered to be an adult.

Table 1 Literacy rates compared for different countries – 2010

Country (in 2010)	Literacy rate (per cent)	Country (in 2010)	Literacy rate (per cent)
China	94	Russia	100
South Korea	100	South Africa	89
Malaysia	93	Sierra Leone	42
Mexico	93	Brazil	90
Nigeria	61		

Health: As with educational attainment, the state of a country's health is important for investors to consider. It is another key indicator of the level of development of an economy. An assessment of the health of a population may include:

- life expectancy at birth
- infant and maternal mortality
- pollution exposure
- access to clean water.

The World Health Organization collects and evaluates statistics relating to a broad range of indicators that can be used to assess population health. These include the following.

1. Life expectancy and mortality (see Table 2).
2. Causes of death including communicable and non-communicable causes and injury.
3. Infectious diseases.
4. Risk factors, such as sanitation, access to clean water, rates of breast-feeding.
5. Health infrastructure and access to essential medicines.
6. Other factors, such as overall health expenditure, immunisation rates, access to contraception and socio-economic factors.

Table 2 Life expectancy at birth and infant mortality statistics of a few select countries

Country	Life expectancy at birth (years)		Infant mortality (probability of dying before age 5 per 1,000 live births)	
	1990	2009	1990	2010
Best*	79	83	6	2
UK	76	80	9	5
China	68	74	48	18
India	58	65	115	63
Mexico	71	76	49	17
South Africa	63	55	60	57

* 'Best' describes either the longest average life span or the lowest probability of dying before age five.

Source: www.who.int

Human Development Index:

The Human Development Index (HDI) combines statistics on life expectancy, education and income for any particular country into a single rankable value. Published by the United Nations Development Programme (www.hdr.undp.org), the index attempts to assess a country's people and their skills, rather than simply the economic conditions.

- **Life expectancy** is how many years a person can, on average, expect to live. It is an important indicator of the health of a nation as well as the quality of its health care and social systems. Countries with the longest life expectancy in 2014 include Japan (83.6 years), followed by Hong Kong (83.4), Switzerland (82.4) and Italy (82.4). At the other end, Sierra Leone had the lowest at only 45.6 years, followed by Swaziland (49 years) and Lesotho (49.4 years).

- **Mean years of schooling** help to assess the average amount of education a 25-year-old person might have had, though it does not consider the nature or quality of that education. Countries with the highest average number of years of study include the US and Germany (12.9 years), followed by Australia (12.8 years), New Zealand/Israel (12.5 years) and Lithuania (12.4 years). The lowest include Burkina Faso (1.3 years), Niger (1.4 years) and Chad (1.5 years).

- **Gross National Income per capita (GNI)** illustrates the relative wealth of the population (as measured in PPP$). Countries with a wealthy population include: Qatar (119,029); Kuwait (85, 820); Liechtenstein (87,000) and Singapore (72,300). At the other end, the poorest populations include: the Democratic Republic of the Congo (444); Central African Republic (588); Malawi (715) and Burundi (749).

A business looking to expand might want to use the Human Development Index to investigate a potential market or location for investment. For example, a company that makes and sells products for the elderly would need to evaluate the life expectancy in a target country, to assess how many people might want to buy their products in the future. Were this same business to sell products that came with a high price, it would also want to try and match countries that have the longest life expectancy to those that have high levels of GNI, so as to ensure that their potential customers could actually afford their products. The company may also be looking to hire technicians and scientists to research and develop its new products. By searching the tables for mean years of schooling, it can highlight places where potential employees could be found and so target its recruitment there.

Thinking bigger

The success of the UK TV and film industry between 2004–2014 was impressive. One of the attractions for Hollywood investing in the UK was tax credits but the attraction was more than that. The UK has a talented TV and film workforce. The National Film and Television School continually dominates global industry awards. The UK has led the way in innovation such as CGI and some of the biggest box-office winners have been filmed in the UK. The HBO series *Games of Thrones* made Northern Ireland its production home and big budget movies including *Star Wars* are filmed in the UK. A UK Television Exports Survey in 2014 (www.pact.co.uk) reported that the film sector contributes £4.6 billion to GDP and supports 117,000 jobs. Annual revenues for television exceed £3 billion, with TV exports alone worth more than £1.28 billion.

You could use this information in a variety of ways. Obviously, it can be used when answering questions on UK exports. But it might also be useful when discussing influences on inward investment, and the impact of a skilled workforce on business and within an economy.

Links

The growth rates of certain countries, in areas such as Africa and Asia, for example, can affect other parts of the world. They may contribute to the growth of globalisation (Unit 68). They are also an important factor in influencing the assessment of a country as a market (Unit 72) and as a location for production (Unit 73). Further rapid growth may be a contribution to the growth of international trade (Unit 67) and an influence on possible mergers and joint ventures (Unit 74).

Key terms

Economic growth – an increase in a country's productive capacity.

Emerging economies – the economies of developing countries where there is rapid growth, but also significant risk.

Human Development Index (HDI) – a collection of statistics that are combined into an index, ranking countries according to their human development.

Literacy rate – the percentage of adults (over 15) that can read and write.

Purchasing Power Parity (PPP) – a measure of real growth that uses the price of purchasing a standardised basket of goods and services in order to compare prices across economies.

Knowledge check

1. List the countries associated with the acronyms BRICS and MINT.

2. Explain why employment patterns are one of the most important indicators of the health of an economy.

3. Why have many Asian economies experienced high levels of growth?

4. Explain why a business may prefer PPP to GDP as a measure of growth.

5. What are the key factors that affect external investment in an economy?

6. What does the Human Development Index (HDI) indicate about an economy?

Case study

ASSESSING FUTURE UK GROWTH

The UK was one of the world's largest economies in 2015, by most measures of real GDP. The UK exported more manufacturing than ever before in 2014, with manufacturing growth outpacing other elements of the UK economy. The nature of its trade, however, has changed from predominantly exporting manufactured goods to also providing competitive services. As the pound began to slide following the 2008 financial crisis, it looked as though the UK might as a result experience a boom in the export of manufactured goods. However, while it continued to attract foreign investment, an export boom in manufactured goods never occurred. This can be explained by several factors.

- The weakness of the global economy, and especially of the UK's major trading partners, Europe and America. Europe and the US remained in recession, and as a consequence their consumers had less money to spend on British exports.

- The recession, coupled with the decline in energy sector productivity, resulted in the UK exporting less oil and gas.

- The relative strength of the services sector, which continued to attract more money and talented staff than manufacturing.

Although the make-up of the British economy continues to change, it is nevertheless still growing. In fact, in 2014, Britain grew faster than any other European economy. However, what this means for growth in the future is not straightforward. For instance, Britain is a good source of low-cost workers, but these workers are not very productive, as Table 3 shows. The hourly wages of workers in the UK is now sufficiently low compared to competing countries, to make British workers more attractive to domestic businesses as well as international firms looking to invest.

So where might growth come from in the future? It may come from existing areas where Britain has been consistently strong. For instance:

- luxury cars, such as Jaguar Land Rover and Rolls Royce

- jewellery

- high-value chemicals and medicines, such as those produced by the pharmaceutical firm GlaxoSmithKline

- media and entertainment, such as newspapers, television programmes, music and films

- services, especially financial services, which for many years have accounted for a larger share of Britain's net exports than all of the other services combined.

However, there are many threats to this future growth. Britain has a low level of investment in infrastructure, such as transport, housing, broadband and energy. An aging and over-stretched infrastructure is likely to constrain future growth over the medium to long term. Also, the fastest-growing companies are very often small, yet they need to be able to attract employees with the right skills. This is proving increasingly difficult, and limits on immigration may make it harder still. Another threat might be if Britain were to exit from Europe. An increase in trade barriers might follow, making Britain less attractive as an investment destination.

Source: www.economist.com

Table 3 Productivity of British workers in comparison to competitors, as measured in GDP per hour worked.

Country	Britain	Germany	USA	France	Italy	Japan
GDP per hour worked in 2013	100	125	130	124	110	85

Source: Office for National Statistics (ONS)

(a) Assess where UK growth might come from in the future. (10 marks)

(b) Evaluate the various threats facing the UK economy and how they might affect future growth. (20 marks)

67 International trade and business growth

Key points

1. Exports and imports.
2. The link between business specialisation and competitive advantage.
3. Foreign direct investment (FDI) and link to business growth.

Getting started

Cheese Cellar, a business owned by the fine foods company Harvey & Brockless, has been in business since 1970. The company has used its knowledge of the cheese market to export its products abroad and has seen sales grow by 30–35 per cent. It recognised a demand for high-end British food abroad and capitalised on this.

By tailoring its products to different markets, Cheese Cellar has been very successful in its chosen export countries of Sri Lanka, France and the Caribbean. It used its existing relationships with top-end hotels to reach the same market overseas and used its knowledge of airlines to expand into that market.

Why do you think Cheese Cellar decided to start exporting? How do you think it chose which countries to export to? What was the advantage to Cheese Cellar of using its existing relationships with top-end hotels?

Exports and imports

Businesses that trade internationally export and import goods and services. Exports and imports generate revenue for businesses in different countries and contribute to business growth.

Exports: Exporting is the most common route for a firm into the international market as it is the easiest mode of entry. A firm continues to produce in its home market but exports some of what it makes to a foreign market. Exporting has become easier owing to trade liberalisation (see Unit 69), which has reduced tariffs and quotas that may otherwise have limited the imports into a country.

Exporting often involves physical goods, but may also include services or so-called 'invisible' exports. These include anything other than manufacturing, mining and agriculture. For example, the UK is very competitive in financial services, particularly banking and insurance. Other types of services that are frequently exported include tourism, transport, education, entertainment, information and professional services from accountants and lawyers.

Imports: Imports are the goods and services that are brought into one country from another. For example, a Brazilian firm exports its cars and South Africa imports them. To do so, Brazil imports the transportation services of a Liberian shipping firm to collect the cars and deliver them to South Africa.

Many countries try to limit the importation of goods by placing trade barriers in the way. These barriers often involve **tariffs**, which are taxes that are imposed on imports. Trade liberalisation, through hundreds of treaties as well as through monitoring by the World Trade Organization, has reduced the use of tariffs or limited the levels of tariffs that can be levied. However, non-tariff barriers (NTBs), are proving harder to manage. These include practices such as giving subsidies to local firms, putting numerical limits (quotas) on imports and creating rules about how much of a product must be made in the country or in what way.

A firm can export or import directly, whereby it distributes and sells its own products, usually by hiring someone to be its local agent. However, it can also operate indirectly, getting another person or firm to prepare the documents and take on all of the responsibility for selling and distributing the products or services for them. Exporting is not only the easiest way for a firm to internationalise, it is also the least risky. A firm can limit the amount of money it spends, and 'test the water' to see if there is a good level of demand for its products.

This does not mean, however, that exporting and importing are totally risk-free. For instance, if exchange rates move the wrong way between the currency of the exporter and that of the importer, the consequences can be financially very serious. Also, governments can impose barriers to imports that limit a firm's access to the market. There may be conflicts with agents or distributors that are difficult to resolve from outside the country.

International trade consists of exporting (selling abroad) and importing (buying from abroad). Firms trade within and between countries because they benefit from doing so, even where it is sometimes difficult for them. Moreover, countries generally benefit from trade and see it as a good thing, though these benefits are sometimes indirect, complex or controversial, as shall be touched upon in the units that follow.

Question 1

The Herdy Company Ltd makes a wide range of products based around the Herdwick, a sheep breed from the English Lake District, Cumbria. The company sells its products online and in a few retail outlets. Its range is popular with tourists visiting the area, many of whom are Japanese and adore the characters and books of Beatrix Potter. Noting this, and thinking that Japanese consumers might also like their own lovable sheep creations, the owners, Spencer and Diane Hannah, decided to look at selling their products in Japan. The first thing they did was contact UK Trade & Investment (UKTI) and accessed the Passport to Export Programme. This programme gives advice and training for firms looking to export, and even provides some matching funding to help exporters find partners in their target markets. However, countries such as Japan may not be an easy market in which to do business and so the Hannahs needed local assistance in order to grow. The company now has a representative in Japan, who helps distribute their products as well as manage publicity and promotion.

(a) Using examples from this case, explain what is meant by exports.

(b) Explain why countries such as Japan may not be an easy market in which to do business.

The link between business specialisation and competitive advantage

At the core of the modern exchange economy, and thus of international trade, is the concept of the **division of labour** whereby workers specialise in a productive activity. Economist Adam Smith (1776) famously used a well-known example involving the making of pins: 'One man draws out the wire, another straightens it, a third cuts it, a fourth points it, a fifth grinds it at the top for receiving the head: to make

the head requires two or three distinct operations.' By each worker focusing on a particular operation, output could be increased and many, many more pins be produced than if each worker made the entire pin. **Specialisation** increases the speed and skill with which a task can be done, and also saves time, thereby improving efficiency. As the market becomes larger, the opportunities for specialisation become greater and narrower.

Comparative advantages: From a country's perspective, it is beneficial to specialise and engage in trade according to each country's **comparative advantages**. David Ricardo illustrated this in 1817 when he showed, using the example of wool (cloth manufacture) and wine, that England and Portugal will always benefit from trade if they specialise and produce according to what each does best. At the start, Portugal requires fewer days than England to make both wine and cloth. It has an absolute advantage in both products. However, Ricardo showed that there would be a net gain to both countries if Portugal switched all of its production to wine and England switched all of its wine workers to cloth, and then the two countries traded. Total output of both products goes up and consumers in both countries are better off.

This theory of comparative advantage has many limitations, not least of which is that it assumes that the world does not change. Yet our modern, globalised world changes rapidly, and often unpredictably. Nevertheless, the theory provides a good base for understanding why two countries, and their consumers, can benefit from specialisation and trade.

Competitive advantages: Michael Porter (*Competitive Advantage*, 1990) extended the comparative advantage theory to show that countries may gain a **competitive advantage** in international trade, and that this also holds true to a large extent for businesses engaged in international trade. Put simply, a business should specialise in what it does well and adds value, and this competitive advantage can help it to make a profit abroad. Competitive advantages can take many forms for a business when engaging in trading.

- A business may have particular resources that it can use wherever it goes, such as a business model, highly trained and specialised staff, or intellectual property.
- It may have acquired access to local markets, local resources and materials.
- It may be able to better organise and replace separate, cross-border trading enterprises (exporting and importing) with one firm that does it all: organises, manages and controls all trading activities.

Specialisation in production, whereby a business focuses on a limited scope of products or services, results in greater efficiency, allowing for goods and services to be produced at a lower cost per unit. This in turn allows for businesses to reduce prices or to increase profit margins, both of which can lead to business growth.

Firms may expand abroad in stages, beginning with exporting and gradually increasing their involvement in foreign markets as they gain knowledge and experience. However, exporting has its limitations and many companies need to find other ways to expand. For example, producing abroad can be less expensive, making moving of manufacturing to a lower-cost country attractive. Or it may be that transporting the goods or services is too expensive and so the firm needs to locate closer to where it sells or hopes to sell in the future. Moreover, governments may limit the importation of products and services, making exporting unviable, so the firm may have to find other avenues to get its products to markets in other countries. Increasingly firms are skipping these stages and taking quicker routes to the international market. For instance, firms can enter a market by buying or merging with a firm that is already operating there. Some firms, especially those trading through the internet, may even be 'born global'.

Foreign direct investment (FDI) and link to business growth

Many businesses outgrow their home markets and in order to grow need to expand into other markets. Others become aware of opportunities for growth in new markets (see Unit 65). When the potential competitive advantages listed above (ownership of resources, locations and internal organisation) combine, a firm can benefit from becoming a multinational company (MNC) and investing directly in other countries. Firms may choose to invest directly because the business:

- has a high potential for making a profit if it invests in a new location
- needs to maintain control over its subsidiaries in the new market
- is trying to acquire direct knowledge of the local market
- is attempting to avoid barriers to the market.

What is FDI?: Foreign direct investment (FDI) is the most complicated and expensive form of involvement in a country; it is also the most risky. Nevertheless, according to *The Economist*, 'The point about FDI is that it is far more than mere "capital": it is a uniquely potent bundle of capital, contacts, and managerial and technical knowledge. It is the cutting edge of globalisation.'

Simply defined, foreign direct investment is investing by setting up operations or buying assets in businesses in another country. The United Nations considers FDI to occur where a firm takes an equity stake of more than 10 per cent in a foreign enterprise. It is not the same as a foreign portfolio investment, which refers to holding stocks or bonds but not tangible assets such as buildings or machinery. The main identifying aspect of FDI, however, is control. Thus, a firm might prefer FDI over exporting or licensing for many reasons, including the following.

- Managers want to keep tight control over operations in the other country or countries. The businesses may need to share a common culture or communications systems, or they may want to ensure that agreements are enforced.
- A firm wants to protect its intellectual property (such as patents, copyrights, trademarks and management know-how).
- It needs to be close to its customers.
- Its products incur high transportation and logistics costs.
- It faces trade barriers or political opposition.

Horizontal and vertical FDI: FDI can be horizontal or vertical. Horizontal refers to producing the same products or services as is done at home. For example, the takeover of the British bank TSB by the Spanish bank Sabadell in April 2015 was a horizontal merger of two firms in the same industry.

Vertical FDI is where one firm is seeking to acquire materials or support for its own products or services. Put another way, the firm is moving into another part of the value chain, such as when a firm opens a call centre in another country to deliver customer or staffing support. This should help lower its costs, allowing growth in revenue or profit.

Different forms of FDI: FDI can take many forms, which involve either buying, building or collaborating.

- A joint venture is a collaborative agreement between two parties to invest in a business and share ownership and control. (See Unit 73.)
- Strategic alliances are collaborations created when firms contract to share resources (often intellectual property in the form of patents or copyrights) or certain skills (such as cultural understanding or managerial expertise). For example, Star Alliance – the largest airline alliance in the world – operates by codeshare, whereby its member airlines' operations and bookings are all done through a central hub based in Frankfurt.
- Buying through cross-border mergers and acquisitions (M&A) is the main way that businesses undertake FDI. Most M&A are actually acquisitions, with over 90 per cent of cross-border ventures involving the purchase of the entire target business. There are many reasons for buying other firms, several of which are explored in Unit 73.

- A firm may build 'greenfield' facilities if they are unable to collaborate or to find another firm to buy, or where it is too expensive for one reason or another. Also, many local governments may prevent certain acquisitions in order to protect competition. For example, the Chinese firm Haier is now one of the world's largest appliance makers. It began testing the international markets by exporting small refrigerators, which filled a neglected niche in the international market. It then began building manufacturing facilities abroad, including India, Indonesia and Iran. In 2000, it built a factory in South Carolina, USA, in order to be closer to American consumers and reduce the costs of transporting

its appliances from elsewhere. However, there was another, less obvious reason for the investment. At the time, China was getting poor press for 'stealing American jobs', but by building its appliances in South Carolina it could put a 'Made in the USA' sticker on these products.

Firms engaged in FDI used to come mainly from developed countries, but the number and size of multinational corporations coming from emerging market countries, such as China, Brazil, Mexico and South Africa, is increasing.

Question 2

Founded in 1886, Coca-Cola creates, manufactures, distributes and markets soft drinks, and has a very long history as an international firm. It began exporting in 1897, and engaged in direct investment for the first time in 1906. While Coca-Cola has one of the world's best-known brands, much of its global success is down to its very flexible international operations.

Although it retains absolute control over the formula for Coke, the company has created a variety of joint ventures or flexible ownership structures to support its business. Thus, many of its bottlers operate under franchise agreements. The franchises bottle, sell, deliver and help to market all of Coca-Cola's soft drinks in a given area. However, in China, it has joint ventures with a variety of bottling plants. In some countries, the firm has opted to take full control, especially where it is just starting to trade or the local bottlers need financial help.

The company will also acquire firms that have complementary product lines or form joint ventures with them, such as those established with Nestlé for tea and Danone for water.

Sources: adapted from: the *Financial Times* 18.02.2005, 16.04.2013. All rights reserved.

(a) Using Coca-Cola as an example, explain what is meant by foreign direct investment.

(b) Explain how the use of foreign direct investment has allowed the business to grow.

Exam tip

You should recognise that a country can export and import both goods and services. A useful tip to help you identify whether there has been an export or import is to think about the way the money moves when it is paid. This is particularly useful in identifying exports and imports of services.

Let's look at the UK.

- Exports – goods or services are sold abroad and money comes into the UK.
- Imports – goods or services are bought from abroad and money leaves the UK.

Some examples help to illustrate this.

- **Exports of goods** – a UK manufacturer of racing cycles sells its cycles to Italy. This is an **export** of **goods** from the UK and money **comes into** the country. The UK business sells its products to Italian customers or businesses.
- **Exports of services** – a German company uses the financial services of a UK bank. This is the **export** of a **service** to a German business and money **comes into** the UK. The German business pays the UK bank.
- **Imports of goods** – a UK manufacturer of toys buys parts for its toys from the USA. This is an **import** of **goods** to the UK and money **leaves** the UK. The UK business pays the USA business for the parts.
- **Imports of services** – UK tourists visit Australia for a holiday and book with an Australian travel agent. This is the **import** of a **service** to the UK and money **leaves** the UK. UK tourists are spending their money abroad.

Links 🔗

One factor influencing the exports and imports of goods and services is the rate of exchange between countries. The exchange rate between two currencies is explained in Unit 72. The role that FDI plays in business growth can be discussed when considering growing economies (Unit 66). Further, any question considering the role that MNCs play in world trade and generating FDI (Unit 79) can be supported by information in this unit.

Key terms

Comparative advantage – the theory that a country should specialise in products and services that it can produce more efficiently than other countries.

Competitive advantage – the idea that a business should specialise in any area (products, services, management, research, etc.) where it can perform better than its competitors.

Division of labour – different workers specialising in different productive activities.

Exports – goods or services that a firm produces in its home market, but sells in a foreign market.

Foreign direct investment – investing by setting up operations or buying assets in businesses in another country.

Imports – goods and services that are bought into one country from another.

International trade – exporting (selling abroad) and importing (buying from abroad).

Specialisation – a production strategy where a business focuses on a limited scope of products or services. This results in greater efficiency, allowing for goods and services to be produced at a lower cost per unit.

Tariffs – taxes that are imposed on imports.

Knowledge check

1. Why do some countries try to limit imports?

2. What are the risks of being involved in exporting and importing?

3. What is meant by comparative advantage?

4. How does specialisation lead to greater efficiency?

5. Explain what is meant by foreign direct investment.

6. What are the different forms of foreign direct investment?

Case study

ANGELBERRY

Many firms try their hand at exporting only when they are established. They want to find new markets for their product range. This is not always the case, however, as shown by Ryan Pasco and James Taylor of Bristol when they founded AngelBerry in September 2011.

They came up with the idea of frozen yogurt from a Californian road trip in July 2011, when Ryan noticed the popularity of self-service frozen yogurt stores. As a frozen yogurt retailer, they established just two UK stores in Bristol. They then concentrated on establishing themselves in hot climates and established six international stores across the UAE, Mauritius and South Africa.

The franchising model has helped the business expand into warmer climates where frozen products sell well all year round. The company now has deals in place for 80 stores across the Gulf States by 2018, following second stores in both UAE and in Johannesburg, South Africa in 2014, and a deal with a cinema chain to roll out a kiosk version. There are a number of potential deals in the pipeline, with further expansion into Europe and Asia planned in 2015.

AngelBerry also went to a trade show in Dubai where they pitched to potential franchisees and secured a major deal with TriStar Corporation, planning to open 80 franchises across the region. That led to the decision to expand production and after perfecting their recipe they did a deal with an Italian producer that could make enough frozen yogurt to order to meet their ambitions.

Their tips for those who want to export are simple. They think it is essential to carry out thorough research before starting exporting. This will prevent costly mistakes and boost chances of choosing the right market. They used the services of their local Chamber of Commerce, and James was full of praise for the help the company has had from UK Trade & Investment, which he said had helped with market research and making contacts.

Sources: adapted from www.exportbritain.org.uk

Q

(a) Assess the benefits of the services provided by the Chamber of Commerce to a small business seeking to export. (10 marks)

(b) Evaluate the reasons why AngelBerry has been a success. (20 marks)

Thinking bigger

The case study on AngelBerry highlights the help received from a variety of sources. How should firms approach exporting? There are a number of 'to dos', especially for smaller firms. There is a need to build a research checklist assessing the potential markets in each territory. When identifying possible markets, a firm must define where it may be able to sell its products or services. It also needs to decide which markets should be considered. Competitor markets overseas need to be assessed and this is where UK Trade & Investment can help in providing contacts. Firms should visit each territory and get advice on local customs and culture, as well as planning how to sell. On visits, firms should check with the UK Embassy, which is geared up to provide advice. In the UK, firms should check with the local trade association, which will provide data on exporting within the sector. Firms might consider using an agency and it might be useful to commission research. In the end it is a judgement call as to whether there is a gap in the market for products and services.

You could use this information in a variety of ways. Obviously, it can be used when answering questions on how firms can successfully export but it might also be useful when discussing influences on foreign direct investment.

68 Factors contributing to increased globalisation

Key points

1. Reduction of international trade barriers/trade liberalisation.
2. Political change.
3. Reduced cost of transport and communication.
4. Increased significance of global (transnational) companies.
5. Increased investment flows (FDI).
6. Migration (within and between economies).
7. Growth of the global labour force.
8. Structural change.

Getting started

In 1991 Estonia broke its ties with the Soviet Union and became independent. Since then it has developed strong political and economic links with the West. Estonia is located in the Baltic Sea region, with a population in 2015 of 1.3 million. Since independence Estonia has embraced the market mechanism in its economic policies. For example, it has privatised state industries, deregulated a number of markets, and encouraged free trade by opening up its economy to foreign businesses. Estonia has also emphasised the importance of technology and aims to be a world leader in the industry. For example, it is creating one of the world's fastest broadband networks, offering free wireless internet, encouraging technology start-ups and putting government services online. Estonia has attracted substantial investment from overseas businesses. Figure 1 shows the origin of this investment.

Figure 1

Foreign direct investment stock by countries 2012

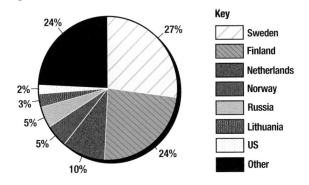

Key	
	Sweden
	Finland
	Netherlands
	Norway
	Russia
	Lithuania
	US
	Other

Source: adapted from www.estonianexport.ee

How has political change influenced the development of business in Estonia? Why are an increasing number of companies trying to develop business in foreign countries? From which countries do most business investments in Estonia originate? What reasons might there be for this? What contributions has new technology made to the spread of international business?

What is globalisation?

Many markets today are global. This means that some firms expect to sell their products anywhere in the world. A firm could have a head office in London, borrow money from a bank in Japan, manufacture products in China, deal with customers from a call centre in India and sell goods to countries all over the world. Firms and people are behaving as though there is just one market or one economy in the whole world. This development is called **globalisation**. It is often defined as the growing integration of the world's economies.

Some of the key features of globalisation are outlined below.

- Goods and services are traded throughout the world. This means that firms like GlaxoSmithKline, the UK pharmaceuticals company, can sell their products as easily, say, in Australia as in England.
- Many people are able to live and work in a country of their choice. This has resulted in more multicultural societies where people from many different nations live and work together, for example in the same city.
- There is a high level of interdependence between countries. This means that events in one economy are likely to affect other economies. For example, the financial crisis in the US in 2008 had an impact on many economies all over the world.
- Capital flows freely between different countries. This means, for instance, that a business or consumer in Australia can put their savings in a bank in the UK. This also means that investors can buy shares in foreign companies and businesses can buy companies that operate in other countries. For example, in 2014, a Chinese insurance company bought New York's glamorous Waldorf Astoria Hotel for $2 billion.
- There is an interchange of technology and intellectual property across borders. Increasingly, for instance, patents granted in the US are recognised in other countries.

It should be noted that the process of globalisation is not complete. This is because restrictions still exist. Many countries, such as Australia and the US, restrict the number of immigrants entering the country. There are also some trade barriers, such as **tariffs** and **quotas**, which make it more difficult to sell goods in certain countries. Trade barriers are discussed in Unit 69.

413

Factors contributing to globalisation

Countries and businesses have been trading with each other for centuries, and the world economy has been interdependent for some time. However, modern globalisation probably started in the 1980s and since then the pace of globalisation has accelerated. There are a number of reasons for this trend.

Reduction of international trade barriers/trade liberalisation

An increasing number of countries around the world have opened up their economies. This means that they have allowed trade to flow without any barriers. One reason for this is the influence of the **World Trade Organization (WTO)**. The role played by the WTO in the liberalisation of trade is discussed in Unit 70. Here are some examples of trade agreements.

- In 2012, Australia and Malaysia agreed to remove the majority of tariffs on each other's exports. It was hoped that the new agreement would increase trade between the two countries significantly from its current level of £8 billion.
- The EU and Singapore signed a free trade agreement in 2012. This was expected to help the export of cars and financial services from the EU. The EU is already Singapore's second largest trading partner. In 2011, the EU had a trade surplus of €8 billion.

Free trade agreements help to encourage trade between nations. As a result the volume of international trade increases and businesses can sell goods and services in new foreign markets without penalties. This increase in international trade helps to maintain the process of globalisation. However, despite the numerous trade agreements that have already been established, there is still a long way to go before the entire world embraces complete free trade.

Question 1

In 2014 China and Australia had almost finalised a free trade agreement (FTA). Negotiations relating to the agreement first started in 2005. The terms of the agreement mean that Australia will reduce the tariffs on all Chinese goods to zero. In return, China will reduce the tariffs on most Australian goods to zero. In the services sector a number of opening promises were made to liberalise trade. In the investment field, both sides agreed to grant each other 'most favoured nation' status once the FTA takes effect. Favourable agreements were also reached relating to the flow of investment between the two nations.

Before this new agreement, Australia had seven other free trade agreements in place with New Zealand, Singapore, Thailand, USA, Chile, the Association of Southeast Asian Nations (ASEAN) and Malaysia.

The benefits of free trade agreements, such as eliminating tariffs, stimulating economic growth and enabling countries to specialise in what they do best, generally outweigh the drawbacks, such as exposure to foreign imports. Free trade agreements mean that consumers today have far greater access to products manufactured all over the world than ever before. Free trade and globalisation means that consumers can buy goods from a huge range of suppliers in global markets.

Source: adapted from the *Financial Times* 17.11.2014.

(a) What is meant by a free trade agreement?

(b) Explain how free trade agreements, like the one between China and Australia, contribute to globalisation.

Political change

Some radical changes in the political regimes of certain nations have helped to increase globalisation. Some examples of these are outlined below.

- In 1991 communist rule ended in the Soviet Union and the dissolution of the old soviet bloc was complete. After years of economic decline and the relative rise of prosperity in the West, it was clear that the Soviet Union had to make some changes. Mikhail Gorbachev was responsible for introducing the two key policies of Glasnost and Perestroika in the 1980s. Glasnost was the vehicle of political reform, and Perestroika was responsible for restructuring the economy. Old soviet bloc countries, such as Latvia, Georgia, Lithuania, Belarus, Estonia and Moldova, were given independence. As a result these countries began to open up their economies and develop trading ties with the rest of the world. Some of them joined the EU and Russia also began to permit a greater movement of goods, services and capital. In the whole region the introduction of market forces helped to liberalise trade.
- In addition to the break-up of the Soviet Union, a number of other countries in eastern Europe sought political and economic reform as their ties with the old soviet bloc were severed. For example, the Berlin wall was removed

which brought together West Germany and East Germany as a single nation. In Romania, communist leader Nicolae Ceausescu was removed from power in 1989 and executed. Czechoslovakia was divided peacefully into the Czech Republic and Slovakia. Other eastern European countries, such as Poland, Hungary and Bulgaria, also enjoyed more democracy. This helped initiate economic reform, which again encouraged the operation of market economies.

- Economic changes in China first began in the 1970s following the death of Chairman Mao in 1976. The strong communist grip on the nation was loosened and economic reforms began with changes in agriculture, where efficiency was improved by handing over plots of land to farmers. They were allowed to keep the output after paying a share to the state. Then, between the mid-1990s and 2005, a large-scale privatisation programme was organised by the government. Trade was gradually opened up and China became a member of the WTO. China is now a booming economy with a well-established manufacturing sector, heavy state expenditure on infrastructure and rising prosperity among the Chinese 'middle-classes' who have a thirst for Western goods. However, China is seen as an economy that is at a stage of newly advanced economic development, not yet completely 'open for business'.

Reduced cost of transport and communication

International transport networks have improved considerably in recent years. In particular, the cost of flying has fallen and the number of flights and destinations has increased. This means that people can travel to business meetings more easily and goods can be transported more cheaply. For example, a number of low-cost airlines have entered the market and brought air travel to the masses. In the UK, easyJet, Ryanair and Flybe offer flights to a wide range of European destinations, which are affordable to the majority of the population. India has also begun to enjoy low-cost air travel. Airlines such as SpiceJet, GoAir and Jet Airways offer cheap internal flights and some provide international services.

Modern technology allows firms to transfer complex data instantly to any part of the world. It also means that more people can work at home, or any other location that they choose. Many people do not have to be office-based to do their jobs. This makes it easier for firms to have operations all over the world. The internet also allows consumers to gather information and buy goods online from businesses located in different parts of the world. Further, businesses, both large and small, can reach out to global markets by promoting their activities and products using the internet.

Containerisation has also made a significant contribution to globalisation. Containers are uniform metal boxes that can be loaded and unloaded easily from ships, lorries and trains. They provide a flexible means of transporting goods. But most importantly their use has reduced the cost of transportation significantly.

- Before the use of containers it cost $5.83 per tonne to load a ship manually. The use of containers has reduced this to just $0.16 per tonne.
- There has been a 50 per cent reduction in the amount of capital tied up in a tonne of stock in a journey from Hamburg to Sydney.
- The loss to theft has tumbled because containers are locked. This has in turn reduced insurance costs.
- The speed of loading has increased drastically, cutting costs. Before containerisation labour could only load 1.7 tonnes per hour onto a ship. This has risen to 30 tonnes per hour with containers. As a result ships have got bigger and spend less time in ports.

Containerisation revolutionised the transportation of goods and since it was so easy to distribute goods by lorry due to the flexibility of containers, the number of loading ports used in Europe has fallen from 11 to just 3.

Question 2

Carol and Martin McDonald have run The Scourie Bay Guest House in Scotland for 30 years. However, in 2008 they expanded by purchasing the property next door and increasing the number of rooms to let from 6 to 14. This decision was taken after they advertised the guest house on their own website and started to attract visitors from Europe, Japan and Australia. The expansion cost a total of £300,000 and initially they were worried that they might struggle to fill the rooms during the quiet winter period. However, due to the global exposure of their business via their website, the clever use of social media, and the growing popularity of low-cost flights, business has boomed. In 2014 the business made a record profit of £105,000. More than 55 per cent of guests during 2014 were from overseas.

(a) Discuss the factors in this case that have contributed to globalisation.

Increased significance of global (transnational) companies

One of the reasons why globalisation has flourished in recent years is because a growing number of large firms have developed significant business interests overseas. Some of these firms are very powerful. They sell goods and services into global markets and have production plants and other operating facilities all over the world. They are called **transnational** or **multinational companies** (MNCs). Multinational companies play a large and growing role in the world economy. They make significant contributions to world GDP and represent about two thirds of global exports. They also make huge global investments in research and development. Figure 2 on the next page shows a list of the biggest MNCs in the world.

Figure 2

Biggest MNCs – 2011

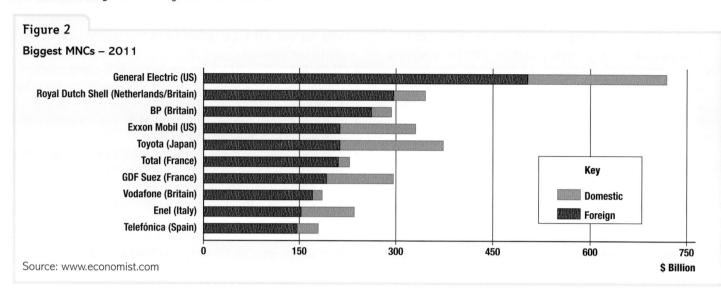

Source: www.economist.com

The contribution made by MNCs to globalisation is likely to continue growing. This is because these corporations are under pressure to increase returns to their owners. Consequently they will expand their current activities and search for new business opportunities anywhere in the world wherever it is cost-effective. The role played by MNCs is discussed in more detail in Unit 79.

Exam tip

You need to remember that it is not just large MNCs that contribute to and benefit from globalisation. Small businesses also play their role. The Scottish guest house in Question 2 is one example. Also, many small businesses play a role as suppliers to the multinationals.

Increased investment flows

Foreign direct investment (FDI) occurs when a company makes an investment in a foreign country. This may involve, for example, the construction of a factory, distribution centre or store, or the development of a mine or tea plantation. Another part of FDI is the purchase of shares in a foreign business (10 per cent or more). Most FDI is undertaken by multinational companies. The UK has attracted more FDI than any other country in the world, except the US. Figure 3 shows the stock of inward investment for a selection of countries in 2013. The overwhelming majority of this investment comes from Europe and the Americas.

Some specific examples of FDI in the UK are outlined below.

- In 2013 a Malaysian consortium paid £400 million for Battersea Power Station. The buyers plan a 15-year development consisting of homes and offices. The investment was expected to create around 13,000 jobs.
- In the UK car industry, BMW invested £500 million in its Oxford plant where Minis are produced. Nissan, the Japanese car manufacturer, has decided to make Infiniti, its premium brand car, at its plant in Sunderland. Jaguar Land Rover, owned by Indian company Tata, has expanded production of the Range Rover in its West Midlands plant, creating a further 1,500 jobs.

The examples above show foreign investment flowing into the UK. However, UK businesses also invest in projects overseas. For example, in 2015 Marks & Spencer (M&S) announced plans to open 250 stores overseas, including 20 new food outlets in Paris. M&S already had a substantial number of overseas stores,

Figure 3

Stock of inward investment – 2013

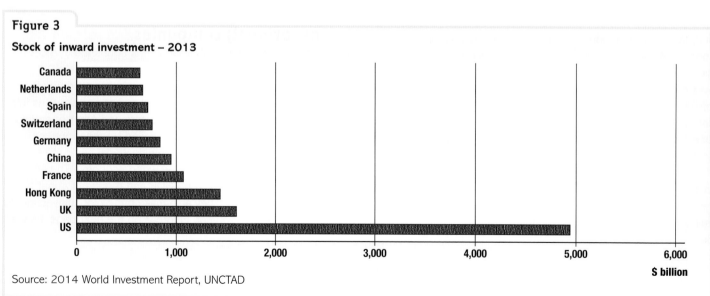

Source: 2014 World Investment Report, UNCTAD

out saw expansion abroad as a means of raising the financial performance of the business.

FDI is often helpful in contributing to the development of emerging nations. For example, in 2015 M&S also announced plans to build 100 sites in India, creating jobs and helping to boost local economic activity. China has made significant investments in Africa. For example, in 2014 there were over 500 Chinese companies with operations in Zambia.

FDI spreads business activity, job creation and wealth all over the globe. It makes a huge contribution to globalisation. FDI also allows businesses to penetrate markets where trade barriers exist. Countries are more likely to welcome a foreign business building a factory than one that just wants to sell products.

Migration

Migration is the movement of people who aim to set up permanent or temporary residence in a new location. It is commonly associated with the movement of people between different countries. In 2013/14 a total of 624,000 people moved to live in the UK. However, at the same time 327,000 people left the UK to go and live in another country. Therefore, net migration into the UK was 297,000. It is argued that 3 per cent of the world's population live outside their country of birth. However, in some countries, such as Australia and Switzerland, migrants make up around 23 per cent of the population. How does migration contribute to globalisation?

- Migrants often import their cultures into their new environment. Along with this often comes the importation of goods from their home countries. For example, in the UK there are many specialist shops that cater for Polish immigrants. Much of the produce sold in these stores is imported from Poland.
- Migrants often provide a supply of low-cost labour to a nation. As a result businesses can lower their costs and gain a competitive edge in overseas markets. This helps them to sell more overseas.
- A significant proportion of the money earned by migrants is sent back to their place of birth. This money is usually spent by families and helps to generate demand in these countries. Transnationals are likely to benefit from this increase in demand so economic activity is spread around the globe by the migrants.
- Some migrants, such as lawyers, doctors, teachers, musicians, writers, academics and Premier League footballers, are highly skilled people. They can help to fill 'skills gaps' and therefore make big contributions to businesses and national income.

Migration can also take place within a country, where people move from one region to another. This has happened on a large scale in China. During the past thirty years workers have moved from inland regions to coastal cities within China. These people have moved in search of jobs and new opportunities that are not available in rural areas. Domestic Chinese migrants now account for approximately one third of all domestic migrants worldwide. This movement of people in China has been the result of international investment and the development of the manufacturing sector. A lot of overseas businesses have invested in these manufacturing 'hotspots' because land and labour are cheap. As a result globalisation has been given a boost.

Although migration is helping to boost global wealth, some countries are worried that migration might lead to social instability. Sectors of the population might blame immigration for a range of domestic problems, such as overcrowding and unemployment. As a result, governments are under pressure to reduce flows of migrants into the country. In the UK, the UK Independence Party has won some support by making the reduction of immigration their main priority.

Growth of the global labour force

The global labour force has grown substantially. In 1980 the total number of people employed in the world was 1.7 billion. By 2010 this had grown to 2.9 billion. A significant proportion of these extra workers are Chinese and Indian. Growth in the global labour market might also be accounted for by an increase in global population from 4.45 billion in 1980 to 6.85 billion in 2010, an increasing number of women entering the market, and people living longer and working longer, as well as the effects of migration.

This growth in the size of the global labour market has contributed to globalisation for the following reasons.

- A bigger global labour market helps to drive global demand. This is because people in employment earn money which can be spent on goods and services. Some of this extra demand will be directed at imports sold by MNCs and other exporters. In countries like China and India, where much larger numbers of people have moved into employment, millions of people have been lifted out of poverty and are making significant contributions to global demand
- The rising numbers of people making themselves available for work has acted as a drag on labour costs, especially in developed countries. This is because the rising supply of labour forces wages down. This has helped to keep costs down and encouraged businesses to expand their activities more widely.
- Some of the people moving into the labour market will set up their own businesses once they have gained work experience. This will boost the number of businesses globally, some of which might grow and develop their activities around the world adding another lift to globalisation.

Structural change

Over time the structure of economies is likely to change. For example, in most Western economies the contribution made to national income by the primary and secondary sectors has fallen. In these economies it is the huge growth in services (the tertiary sector) that has provided most of the income, employment and wealth. It could also be argued that it is the movement away from these once traditional sectors and into services that allows businesses and economies to flourish. This is because the returns on capital invested in many service industries are often higher. It is the development of knowledge-based industries, such as biotechnology, information technology, research and development, education, software development, pharmaceuticals, care, finance, aerospace and security, that has helped countries to improve the standard of living for their citizens.

These structural changes have contributed to globalisation because most of the industries mentioned above are export-orientated. As a result, in addition to selling these services abroad, these industries are likely to set up operations in a range of countries, recruit high-quality staff from anywhere in the world and try to foster a global presence. It might also be argued that the internet and social media have helped to deliver services to global markets. Both large and small businesses can use the internet and social media to raise their profiles, communicate with potential customers and sell products.

Finally, many industries in the tertiary sector can locate anywhere, provided there is a market. They are not tied to specific geographical locations or influenced by other locational factors. For example, a chain store like M&S can locate anywhere in the world, provided there are people within close proximity who want to go shopping.

Links 🔗

Globalisation is an important business development. You may get the opportunity to make links to the topic of globalisation in a wide variety of answers. For example, when discussing the importance of exporting, importing, exchange rates, overseas marketing or outsourcing to a business, globalisation is clearly a related issue. Globalisation may be linked to many units but some obvious examples include Impact of external influences (Unit 47), Causes and effects of change (Unit 63), Scenario planning (Unit 65), Trading blocs (Unit 70), Assessment of a country as a market (Unit 72), The impact of MNCs (Unit 79) and other units in Theme 4.

Knowledge check

1. State three features of globalisation.
2. Describe briefly the role played by the WTO in globalisation.
3. What is meant by a free trade agreement?
4. How do free trade agreements help to foster globalisation?
5. How might political change contribute to globalisation?
6. Describe briefly the role played by lower transport costs in the spread of globalisation.
7. How has containerisation had an impact on globalisation?
8. Outline one way in which transnational companies contribute to globalisation.
9. What impact can FDI have on globalisation?
10. How has migration had an impact on globalisation?
11. How has the growth in the global labour force contributed to globalisation?

Key terms

Foreign direct investment (FDI) – business investment undertaken by a firm in another country; building a factory for example.
Globalisation – the growing integration of the world's economies.
Transnational or multinational companies – companies that own or control production or service facilities outside the country in which they are based.
World Trade Organization (WTO) – an international organisation that promotes free trade by persuading countries to abolish tariffs and other barriers. It polices free trade agreements, settles trade disputes between governments and organises trade negotiations.

Case study

NESTLÉ

Nestlé is a large MNC based in Switzerland. It is the world leader in nutrition, health and wellness products. In 2014 its revenue was CHF91.6 billion and net profit CHF14.5 billion (approximately £63.9 billion and £10.1 billion respectively). Some of its globally recognised brands include KitKat, Nescafé, Perrier, Carnation, Nesquik and Purina.

The company has more than 400 operations, including factories, distribution centres, offices and laboratories in nearly 200 countries around the world. It directly employs around 339,000 people. It also has connections with a huge army of suppliers. For example, the company relies on around five million farmers around the world to supply agricultural goods to make its high-quality food and beverage products.

For many decades Nestlé has invested heavily in operations around the world. In some cases it has built brand new facilities, in others it has bought foreign businesses. For example, in 2011 Nestlé Health Science S.A. acquired Prometheus Laboratories Inc., a US-based company that specialises in diagnostics, and treatments in gastroenterology and oncology. It also acquired a minority stake in Vital Foods, a New Zealand-based company that specialises in the development of solutions for gastrointestinal conditions using kiwi fruit. In 2013 it opened an extension to its milk production factory in the Dominican Republic. It also announced the building of a new factory in Poland to make Purina pet food, at a cost of CHF93 million (£65 million). This investment was planned to create 200 jobs.

The company also enjoys a number of business partnerships with foreign companies. For example, in 2011 it set up some joint ventures with Chinese partners, including food company Yinlu, which makes ready-to-drink peanut milk and canned rice porridge, and Hsu Fu Chi, a confectionery and snacks producer.

In 2015, Nestlé launched the *Nestlé Global Youth Initiative* to help young people around the world develop the skills needed for employment. It aims to develop young talent for the company and help create work and training opportunities for youngsters in an effort to reduce global youth unemployment. In 2013, Nestlé had organised a similar initiative in Europe that aimed to create 20,000 jobs for European young people over three years.

Sources: adapted from www.nestle.com and www.statista.com

(a) Explain the role played by foreign direct investment (FDI) in globalisation. (4 marks)

(b) Evaluate the extent to which companies like Nestlé contribute to increased globalisation. (20 marks)

Key points

1. Tariffs.
2. Import quotas.
3. Other trade barriers:
   - government legislation
   - domestic subsidies.

Getting started

Australia produces some of the cheapest sugar in the world. However, Australian sugar producers face difficulties when it comes to selling to many other countries because of trade barriers. For example, sugar farmers are heavily subsidised in the US and there are also quotas and tariffs (import controls) imposed on imports. Farmers in Europe are also heavily supported and trade with the EU is challenging. Australian Greg Beashel, chairman of the Global Sugar Alliance, suggested that Australia is one of the lowest cost producers of sugar in the world, but could not make the money it should because of corruption in the global market.

Why is it hard for Australian sugar producers to sell in overseas markets? Why do you think countries erect trade barriers like those in the case above? What might be the benefits of lifting all trade barriers?

Protectionism

Most economists would argue that free trade will benefit the global economy. However, sometimes countries believe that it is in their interests to restrict trade. For example, governments may think it is necessary to protect their domestic producers from overseas competition. Or they may give financial help to exporters. This approach is called **protectionism**. Unit 67 outlined the benefits of free trade. However, there are reasons why governments feel that the use of trade barriers is sometimes justified.

- **Protect jobs.** They may be used if domestic industries need protection from overseas competitors to save jobs. Unemployment is undesirable and a government may be criticised if jobs are being lost because of cheap imports.
- **Protect infant industries.** It is often argued that **infant industries** need protecting from strong overseas rivals until they can grow, become established and exploit economies of scale. However, it is also argued that this approach may not be successful because governments have a poor record in identifying these new industries with potential.
- **Prevent dumping.** A government may use trade barriers if it feels that an overseas business is **dumping** goods. Dumping is where foreign producers sell goods below cost in a

domestic market. This is considered to be unfair competition for domestic producers.
- **Raise revenue.** A government can raise revenue if it imposes tariffs on imports. This money can be spent on government services to improve living standards.
- **Prevent the entry of harmful or undesirable goods.** A government might be justified in protectionism if it is felt that overseas producers are trying to sell goods that are harmful or undesirable.
- **Improve the balance of payments.** A country might need to use trade barriers because it has a very large balance of payments deficit (where the spending on imports exceeds income on exports). A country has to pay its way in the world and if the balance of payments deficit gets out of control, action may be needed. A government might try to reduce imports and increase exports at the same time to reduce the deficit.

Tariffs

Governments can use a number of **trade barriers** to restrict trade. One approach is to make imports more expensive. This will reduce demand for imports and increase demand for goods produced at home. Imports can be made more expensive if the government imposes a special tax on them. For example, if a government adds £50 to the price of an imported camera, demand should switch from foreign cameras to home-produced cameras. Taxes on imports are called **tariffs** or **customs duties**. In addition to reducing imports, tariffs also raise revenue for the government. However, the imposition of a tariff may only have limited impact if demand for the import is price inelastic. This is because demand will not fall in proportion to the price increase. The fall in demand will be proportionately less.

Even though the pace of globalisation is accelerating and an increasing number of countries are opening up their economies to foreign businesses, there are countless examples of countries imposing tariffs on imports. Here is a selection.

- In 2015 Ecuador imposed tariffs of 21 per cent and 7 per cent on imports from Columbia and Peru respectively. The main purpose of these tariffs was to offset the effects of a strong US dollar. Columbian and Peruvian officials claimed that the tariffs were a protectionist move and that their imposition contravened the principles of the Andean Community (CAN, a customs union formed by Bolivia, Ecuador, Columbia and Peru.

In 2014, the US imposed tariffs on solar products coming in from China and Taiwan. The anti-dumping duties on Chinese solar goods were 165 per cent, compared to 27 per cent on Taiwanese solar panels. A Chinese official suggested that the tariff abused trade remedy measures, damaging the legitimate rights of Chinese companies and violating the United States' duty to respect World Trade Organization rules. In 2015 the US lowered some of these tariffs.

In 2014, some African countries imposed higher tariffs on imported goods. Some staple goods such as beans, rice, flour, palm oil and sugar were exempt, but not fruit and vegetables from Europe and neighbouring countries. The duties were up to 50 per cent on many items. The trade barriers were designed to encourage domestic production.

Question 1

The falling price of coal has prompted some protectionism from a number of countries. In 2014, it was widely reported that China imposed tariffs of 6 per cent and 3 per cent on Australian thermal coal and coking coal respectively. The Australian coal industry said that the effects would be felt more harshly by Australia because Indonesian coal producers, who also export to China, would not be affected by the tariffs. This is because China and Indonesia have a bilateral free trade agreement. The Minerals Council of Australia argued that the tariffs would raise the price of energy in China and jeopardise ongoing trade talks between China and Australia.

China's decision to impose the tariffs was designed to protect the domestic industry in the face of falling global prices. The price of coal fell from $136 in 2011 to $65 in 2015. China estimated that 70 per cent of its coal mines were making a loss. However, some analysts suggested that too much coal is being produced in relation to demand. China's growth has slowed and it is making some effort to use cleaner fuels.

Source: adapted from the *Financial Times* 10.10.2014. All rights reserved.

(a) What is meant by a tariff?
(b) Explain why China has imposed tariffs on Australian coal.

Import quotas

Another way of reducing imports is to place a physical limit on the amount allowed into the country. This is called an **import quota**. By restricting the quantity of imports, domestic producers face less of a threat. They will have more of the market for themselves. However, quotas will raise prices because fewer of the cheaper imports are available. An extreme form of quota is an **embargo**. This is where imports are completely banned from a country. Most embargos are imposed for political reasons. For example, in 2015 an arms embargo was imposed on Libya to prevent military goods being exported to the country. A number of embargos exist between Russia and the EU as a result of Russia's involvement in the war between the Ukraine and Russian-speaking rebels.

Placing physical limits on the flow of imports means that some demand for those goods will be met by domestic producers. This will help to protect or increase domestic employment. At the same time, quotas help to prevent domestic or imported goods from overpowering the market. This improves consumer choice. Some examples of countries using import quotas are given below.

In 2014 Indonesia imposed a quota on wheat flour imports, in an effort to protect the financial interests of local producers. The total allowance of wheat flour imports between May and the end of the year was limited to 441,141 tons, with the three main importers of Turkey, Sri Lanka and Ukraine all being given fixed quotas. The remainder of the quota was given to other trading partners.

In 2011 China announced that it would retain its quota of foreign films being imported. In 2012 the quota was set at a maximum of 34 foreign films per year coming into the country. China's film industry is the second largest in the world after the US, and was worth £2.1 billion in 2013. Film imports are restricted because China fears that an open market would damage the domestic industry.

Problems with trade barriers

Although there are several motives for restricting trade, some barriers may not be effective. One problem is that countries may retaliate when barriers are imposed. For example, if one country imposes a tariff on another country's goods, that country may well impose tariffs of its own to block goods coming in. This 'tit-for-tat' behaviour could escalate into a trade war where trade between countries eventually stops.

Tariffs might also be ineffective if demand for imports is inelastic. For example, if tariffs increase the price of an import by 20 per cent, demand will only fall by 2 per cent if price elasticity of demand is −0.1. Therefore, the imposition of the tariff will only have a very limited impact.

Thinking bigger

When considering trade barriers, countries seem to favour the use of tariffs rather than import quotas. Typically, the tariff is seen as a more efficient way to place limits on the inflow of international goods without placing undue hardship on producers who import goods. For many, tariffs represent the best approach to supporting the domestic economy, providing consumers with a wider choice, and promoting genuine competition between businesses.

Government legislation

Some countries avoid the use of tariffs and quotas, but still manage to reduce the amount of imports coming in. They do this by insisting that imported goods meet strict regulations and specifications. In some cases legislation can be passed to prevent entry. For example, a shipment of toys might be returned if they fail to meet strict safety regulations that are imposed by legislation.

Goods that fail to reach cultural or environmental standards may also face **administrative barriers**. Some products cannot be imported into the EU. For some other products there are restrictions, or the Food Standards Agency has issued advice saying that particular food products should not be eaten. The most common examples of legal import bans aim to protect consumers from dangerous goods. For example, in 2011 a ban was imposed on feed and food coming in from Japan because there were fears of it being contaminated by radioactivity resulting from earthquake and tsunami damage to Japanese nuclear power stations.

Subsidies

Quotas and tariffs aim to reduce imports. Another approach to protectionism is to give a **subsidy** to domestic producers. This involves giving financial support, such as grants, interest-free loans or tax breaks, to exporters or domestic producers that face fierce competition from imports. If subsidies are given to domestic producers, this will lower prices for consumers because subsidies reduce production costs and increase supply. This forces equilibrium prices down. If subsidies are given to exporters it makes it easier for home businesses to break into foreign markets.

Although government subsidies to either domestic producers or exporters may contravene free trade agreements, there are many examples of governments using subsidies to influence the flow of exports and imports. A small sample is given below.

- In 2012 the Indian government announced that it would re-introduce subsidies to help boost exports of textiles and engineering goods. The Indian government proposed to hand over around $375 million of subsidies to producers. The purpose of the subsidies was to revive India's flagging export industry and to help reduce the widening trade deficit.

- To reduce the nation's reliance on rare-earth imports from China, the Japanese government promised $65 million subsidies in 2012 to domestic businesses, the funds to be directed to businesses that support projects to reduce consumption of rare earths.

- In the UK a number of businesses received subsidies from the government to support the development of fossil-fuel projects overseas. For example, businesses involved in oil exploration projects with Petrobras in Brazil were handed £528 million, while Rolls-Royce was loaned £330 million to work with Russia's Gazprom on gas power initiatives.

Exam tip

If considering the possible effects of protectionism, it might be helpful to distinguish between the short-term and the long-term effects. For example, in the short term protectionism might reduce imports and help domestic industries. However, in the long term it might stifle competition, protect ailing and inefficient industries, provoke retaliation and possibly lead to a trade war. Making a distinction like this is a way of demonstrating evaluation skills.

Links 🔗

You can demonstrate your synoptic skills by linking this topic to answers relating to global competitiveness, assessing overseas markets and assessing a country as a suitable production location. For example, businesses often choose a particular international location for a factory to avoid trade barriers. This is because if an overseas business produces goods in another country, the output is not classified as an import for that country. Links might be made to other units, such as SWOT analysis (Unit 46), Impact of external influences (Unit 47), International trade and business growth (Unit 67) and Trading blocs (Unit 70).

Key terms

Administrative barriers – rules and regulations (such as trading standards and strict specifications) that make it difficult for importers to penetrate an overseas market.
Dumping – where an overseas firm sells large quantities of a product below cost in the domestic market.
Embargo – a complete ban on international trade – usually for political reasons.
Import quota – a physical limit on the quantity of imports allowed into a country.
Infant industries – new industries that have yet to establish themselves.
Protectionism – an approach used by a government to protect domestic producers.
Subsidy – financial support given to a domestic producer to help compete with overseas firms.
Tariffs or **customs duties** – a tax on imports to make them more expensive.
Trade barriers – measures designed to restrict trade.

Knowledge check

1. State three reasons why a country might impose trade barriers.

2. Explain the impact of tariffs on domestic producers.

3. What is the aim of dumping by businesses?

4. How do import quotas reduce imports?

5. Which type of trade restriction will help to raise revenue for a government?

6. What is meant by administrative barriers to trade?

7. How might subsidies be used as a form of protectionism?

Case study

US TARIFFS ON FOREIGN STEEL PRODUCERS

In 2014 the US government announced that it would impose tariffs worth several hundred millions of dollars on imports of steel. The US Commerce Department imposed tariffs of up to 16 per cent on imports from South Korea of steel pipe and tubes used for oil drilling. The department claimed that these products were being dumped in US markets – being sold at unfair prices.

It was hoped that the tariffs would help the US steel industry by raising prices and protecting hundreds of jobs that had been threatened by cheap imports. Steel workers in the US had been holding rallies around the country to urge the government to do something about cheap imports. However, some industry analysts said that the tariffs would only have a short-term impact. This was because of the worldwide glut of steel products resulting from the slowdown in the Chinese economy and the 'softening' of the US shale gas boom.

Just after the announcement by the US, South Korea said it would take action against the US in order to protect its exports of steel products to the country. South Korean officials claimed that US steel producers charged higher than market prices for their products. The South Korean trade ministry suggested it would come up with appropriate

counter measures based on legal reviews and discussions with the local industry, when commenting on the measures introduced by the US. Officials also added that steel is a tariff-free item in US–South Korean trade under the WTO multilateral regime. Options that South Korea could consider included making a request to the WTO to adjudicate on the matter or press charges in a US court.

One of the dangers of imposing trade barriers is that an all-out trade war can break out between countries, where one country retaliates to the imposition of trade barriers by imposing some of its own. This can lead to an escalation where more counter-actions are taken and trade between nations eventually comes to a standstill. This would obviously be detrimental to both parties. In this case, the dispute came just a couple of years after the US and South Korea signed a bilateral trade agreement in 2012.

(a) Explain how the dumping of steel products from overseas might impact on US steel producers. (4 marks)

(b) Evaluate the possible effects of the US imposing tariffs on steel imports. (20 marks)

70 Trading blocs

Key points

1. Expansion of trading blocs:
   - EU and the single market
   - ASEAN
   - NAFTA.
2. Impact on businesses of trading blocs.

Getting started

Ludvik Andel owns a large motor-parts firm in the Czech Republic that produces very specialised items. His business has been in operation for twenty years. He has always exported his goods internationally and works quite closely with automobile companies based in Germany.

Between 2004 and 2014, 13 countries joined the European Union (EU), including the Czech Republic, Estonia, Poland and Croatia. By joining the EU these countries were able to participate in the EU's single market. This meant they could enjoy the lack of tariff barriers and customs procedures between member countries. By co-ordinating product regulations, trade between countries is easier. Additionally, because of the EU having a strong presence globally, trade to other countries outside the EU is also easier.

What do you think the Czech Republic joining the EU meant for Ludvik's company? What do you think the benefits are for him now of doing business with companies in Germany? Do you think there are any benefits for the companies in Germany as well?

The expansion of trading blocs

Just as people generally prefer to shop close to where they live, countries also prefer to trade within their geographical region. It is cheaper to transport goods shorter distances, so logistics costs will generally be lower. Moreover, cultural ties and familiarity with nearby markets reinforce regional trading preferences. So even though the General Agreement on Tariffs and Trade (GATT) and later the World Trade Organization have promoted a multilateral approach to encouraging the growth of global trade, regional agreements nevertheless remain attractive. In fact, whereas big international trade agreements have foundered, **regional trade agreements (RTAs)** have grown in number and scope. There are now over 300 RTAs, involving countries all over the world.

RTAs are made between two or more countries within a geographical region, and are designed to facilitate trade by bringing down barriers. These arrangements include several varieties of agreement as the level of integration increases. RTAs create **trading blocs**. A trading bloc is a group of countries that have signed a regional trade agreement to reduce or eliminate tariffs, quotas and other protectionist barriers between themselves. These countries play a very big role in shaping patterns of business expansion. Trading blocs can take a number of different forms.

Preferential trading areas: Preferential trading areas (PTA) allow certain types of products from participating countries to receive a reduced tariff rate. This is the beginning of the process of economic integration and a PTA may become a free trade area over time. In fact, this increasing integration is one of the goals of GATT. The Association of Southeast Asian Nations (ASEAN) has a PTA with China, for example.

Free trade areas: A free trade area (FTA) exists where member states remove all trade barriers, such as tariffs and import quotas, between themselves, but each member state keeps different barriers against non-member states. However, within FTAs, taxes and excise duties may be different. The North American Free Trade Agreement (NAFTA) is an example of an FTA. It is essentially a PTA, but with much greater depth and scope in its tariff reductions.

In order to protect the region, countries may use a system of allocating certificates, known as **rules of origin**, whereby a defined amount of a product or service must be certified as being created within that region. Consequently, when a product enters Canada from the US, it must come with a customs invoice that certifies where the product came from. Free trade agreements may also impose additional qualifying rules for members, such as minimum content or value requirements.

Customs unions: A customs union is similar to a free trade area, except that the members adopt a common set of barriers against non-members. This means that when a product is shipped from outside the union to any of the member states, only one set of rules regarding customs duties and rules of origin will apply. Moreover, the product can then be moved freely throughout the countries within the union.

An example of a customs union is CARICOM, or the 'Caribbean Community', which includes 15 nations and dependencies (colonies). It was created to co-ordinate economic policies and promote integration to encourage development, and is trying to mirror the stages through which the EU developed.

Common markets: A common market is much more integrated than free trade arrangements or customs unions since goods, labour and capital can move freely across the member states. Tariffs are generally removed and non-tariff barriers eliminated, or at least reduced. Workers can relocate from one country to another without restriction. All of this integration means that the members of a common market must work together on economic and political policies that affect the market. Examples of common markets include ASEAN and the Southern Common Market (Mercosur) in South America.

Single market: A common market is considered to be the starting point for the creation of a **single market**, whereby almost all trade barriers between members have been removed and common laws or policies work to make the movement of goods and services, labour and capital between countries as easy as the movement within each country. Borders, standards and taxes are harmonised as much as possible, so as not to interfere with the commerce between members. The EU is a single market, but it is also an economic and monetary union (see below).

Economic unions: An **economic union** is a type of trade bloc involving both a customs union and a common market. Its aim is normally closer economic, political and cultural ties between member states. Where an economic union involves a common currency it is called an **economic and monetary union**. The EU is one of the few fully operating economic and monetary unions, but there are ongoing attempts to create others, such as Mercosur and the Economic Community of West African States (ECOWAS).

Table 1 distinguishes between the various forms of integration involved in the formation of trade blocs.

Table 1 Integration and trading blocs

Integration	Common external tariff	No internal trade barriers	Free movement of goods, labour and capital	Common currency
Preferential trading area		(lower tariffs on certain products)		
Free trade area		x		
Customs union	x	x		
Common or single market	x	x	x	
Economic and monetary union	x	x	x	x

This unit focuses on the impact on businesses of three main trading blocs – the EU, ASEAN and NAFTA. Some information on each of these is shown in Table 2 and Figure 1.

Table 2 Trading bloc data for the EU, ASEAN and NAFTA–2015

Region	Group	Member countries	Date of formation	Type of agreement
Europe	EU	Austria, Belgium, Bulgaria, Croatia, Denmark, France, Finland, Germany, Greece, Ireland, Italy, Luxembourg, Netherlands, Portugal, Spain, Sweden, the UK, the Czech Republic, Poland, Romania, Hungary, Slovenia, Slovakia, Estonia, Lithuania, Latvia, Cyprus, Malta	1993	Economic union
Southeast Asia	ASEAN	Indonesia, Malaysia, Philippines, Singapore, Thailand, Brunei, Cambodia, Laos, Myanmar, Vietnam	1967	Free trade area
North and Central America	NAFTA	Canada, Mexico, US	1994	Free trade area

Figure 1

A map showing the EU, NAFTA and ASEAN trade blocs

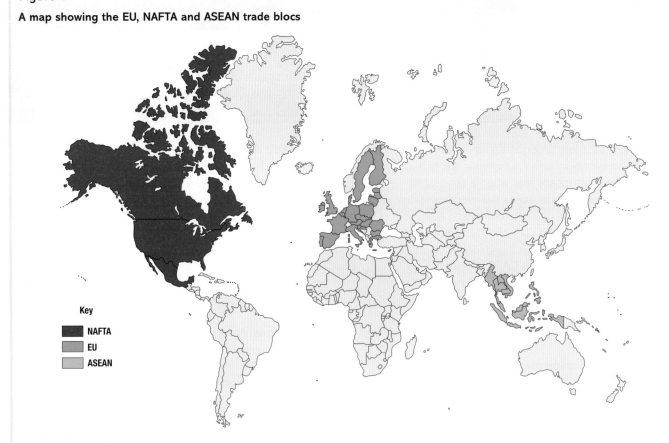

Key
- NAFTA
- EU
- ASEAN

Question 1

Mercosur, or the Southern Common Market, is a customs union and trading bloc comprising Argentina, Brazil, Paraguay, Uruguay and Venezuela, with Bolivia, Chile, Columbia, Ecuador and Peru as associate members, and Mexico and New Zealand as observers. Although Mercosur originated in 1991, its creation and operation has not been straightforward, because of the political difficulties of many of its member countries. For instance, Paraguay was suspended in 2012 after the ousting of its elected president and Venezuela's political and economic problems have raised concerns over its membership.

However, the trading bloc has contributed to a substantial increase in trade between most of the members, with Brazil and Argentina accounting for just under half of the total. The Southern Common Market allows for free movement of goods, services and factors of production among member states, sets a common external tariff and trade policy for non-member states, co-ordinates policies affecting competition between the member states (for example, taxes, trade, monetary systems, customs, transport, etc.) and a commitment to continuing integration.

Source: adapted from the *Financial Times*, 1.4.2014. All rights reserved.

(a) Explain what is meant by a trading bloc, using Mercosur as an example.

(b) Explain one reason why a business operating in Brazil might want to recruit workers from Argentina rather than the UK.

The European Union and the single market

The European Union is the most powerful trading bloc in the world. Its first foundations date from 1993, and the trading bloc has expanded from the six founding members to 28 countries today. The Single European Act of 1987 supported internal liberalisation, but barriers to cross-border trade continued to exist, and deeply rooted national cultures slowed the process. After gradual integration and consolidation, the European Union emerged with the Maastricht Treaty in 1992, although with it has come a great deal of controversy.

The EU developed a single market. The single market guarantees the free movement of people, goods, services and capital throughout the member states, as well as harmonising laws, policies and regulations in key areas. A monetary union was completed in 2002, further integrating most of the European economies. Consequently, businesses operating in most European countries are able to move and compete equally in all other countries, operating to similar standards and processes, and paying in a common currency, the euro. Once goods enter anywhere at an EU border, they cannot be subject to customs duties, taxes or import quotas as they are transported throughout the bloc. The same general principle applies to the movement of people and the purchasing of property (including shares in companies).

However, this process has not been straightforward and is not yet fully complete. As at 2015, not all European countries belong to the union, including Iceland, Norway, Liechtenstein and Switzerland (see Figure 1). Nor did all sign up to a single currency: the UK, Denmark and Sweden decided not to join the euro and have kept their own separate currencies. Moreover, most European countries remain culturally distinct, having separate languages, customs and religions, and integration into the EU does not appear to be changing this over time.

ASEAN free trade agreement

South East Asia is a very diverse region: economically, politically and culturally. According to its charter, the Association of Southeast Asian Nations (ASEAN) was established in 1967 to promote growth, social progress and socio-cultural evolution among its members. It also aims to promote regional peace and stability. The associated free trade area covers a population in excess of 500 million and continues to expand in a piecemeal fashion: it has also completed free trade agreements with China, Korea, Japan, Australia, India and New Zealand.

ASEAN has an agreement covering trade in goods as well as one relating to customs, which are part of a drive to create a common market to be known as the ASEAN Economic Community (AEC). As a common market, it will promote the free flow of goods and services, investment, labour and capital. Areas of co-operation include:

- macro-economic and financial policy
- labour policies, including education and professional qualifications
- infrastructure and communications
- e-commerce
- regional sourcing.

The AEC is a very ambitious plan. In early 2015 some countries appeared ready to move to a fully integrated system, including Singapore, Thailand, the Philippines, Malaysia, Indonesia and Brunei, while others, such as Cambodia, Vietnam, Laos and Myanmar (Burma), lagged a little behind in eliminating tariffs.

NAFTA

The North American Free Trade Agreement (NAFTA) – see Figure 1 – dates back to 1994 and pulls together Canada, Mexico and the United States in a free trade zone. The agreement covers trade and investment, labour, financial dealings and intellectual property as well as common environmental issues. Members agree to eliminate tariffs on most manufactured goods and to treat investors from the other two countries as if they were domestic investors.

However, as is normal with a free trade agreement, the members do not share a common external trade policy, nor do they have any provision for co-ordinating exchange rates. Thus the US, Mexico and Canada still negotiate independently with non-NAFTA countries, organisations and trading blocs over the rules that govern their trading relationships.

As a free trade area, NAFTA does not aspire to the level of integration of the EU. Nevertheless, its operation elicits concerns over sovereignty. The United States, with a GDP ten times the other members, is clearly the dominant power, raising issues of dependency for Canada and Mexico. In an effort to address this, the members signed up to a dispute resolution system designed to balance out the rights and obligations of each member. Nevertheless, this system has been criticised for being weakly enforced.

NAFTA has been beneficial to US and Canadian consumers through the lowering of prices for agricultural products. Sellers in each country have benefited from the larger and more diverse markets on offer, and producers from the lower-cost locations closer to home.

However, some believe that the agreement has been bad for Mexico, and especially its farmers. Since joining NAFTA, overall economic growth has not increased significantly, real wages have declined and unemployment has increased. Although this economic weakness may be due to many factors beyond NAFTA's influence, the flood of heavily subsidised corn from the US clearly caused problems for Mexican farmers. When the lower priced corn first entered the market, it was a boon to Mexico's consumers, who could buy cheaper flour for their staple food, tortillas. However, the competition drove many poor, small farms out of business. The US government then began to encourage the manufacturing of ethanol, a 'green' fuel, and corn was diverted to this new use. The supplies of corn to Mexico dried up and yet the farms that used to grow it no longer existed and so there was nothing to fill the resulting shortage. Consequently, the price of corn rocketed and the Mexican consumer suffered.

Factors to consider in trading blocs

There are four key factors to consider in trading blocs.

- **Where to produce.** A company may be able to locate in a neighbouring country where the costs of land, labour or capital are most favourable to it, and then ship goods and services to other members.
- **Where to sell.** Companies may view a trading bloc as one big market for their goods and services. This can present opportunities, but also threats. For example, with the creation of NAFTA, many Mexican retailers were driven out of business by big American and Canadian firms, including Walmart.
- **How to enter a market.** The market entry strategy may be adapted according to the opportunities presented by the free trade areas or common market, and can range from new investments through to joint ventures and mergers.
- **Business strategy.** A business may not have been able to export to a neighbouring country because of the existence of trade barriers. Once these barriers are negotiated away as part of a trade agreement, they may be able to do so. For instance, once fully operating, the AEC should encourage firms from Vietnam to increase trade with Malaysia.

Impacts on businesses of trading blocs

Trading blocs are likely to create both opportunities and drawbacks for businesses.

Opportunities for business: Businesses may be able to benefit in a number of ways and there might be certain opportunities that result from operating within a trading bloc.

- Freeing regional trade may allow individual members to specialise in line with their country's comparative advantages.
- The market for firms' goods and services should increase. Since trading blocs often do more than reduce tariffs – they also often improve capital flows, streamline regulations and improve competition – they may actually improve the market for non-members as well, even if not by as much as for members.
- As the volume of trade increases within the region, producers are able to benefit from economies of scale; this leads to lower costs for them and usually lower prices for consumers.
- Resources may be easier to source and labour easier to recruit, while production and transport costs may continue to fall.
- As trade increases, it may result in greater competition and thereby more efficiency in the market.
- Trading blocs may also provide a counter-balance against globalisation, protecting industries in an area against predatory competitors from more economically powerful regions. Moreover, being part of an RTA may give regions the power to negotiate for better deals in the global market. Thus for large, well-placed firms, trade blocs offer new potential markets as well as the prospect of higher efficiency and productivity through larger factories, lower overheads, and faster and possibly less costly logistics. For example,

from a firm's perspective, NAFTA allows it to conduct business in the US, Mexico and Canada, so long as it meets certain rules relating to content, labour standards, safety requirements and environmental regulation. Prior to NAFTA's formation, many US and Canadian producers looked to South East Asia or China for lower-cost production sites for building a new factory. With the free trade agreement, Mexico's lower-cost labour force and proximity made it a viable alternative. Firms such as IBM and Gap moved their production to Mexico, where manufacturing costs were competitive and delivery faster.

Drawbacks for business: On the other hand, existing businesses within a trading bloc, or those seeking to locate in a country within the trading bloc, could face drawbacks and problems.

- Trade blocs may actually harm overall trade because countries outside the region may be better placed to specialise or develop a competitive advantage in a product or service, and yet they are closed out of the market. Thus, blocs may lead to trade diversion rather than trade creation. For example, Indonesia may produce a crop more cheaply than countries in the EU, but the EU's agricultural subsidies and abolition of tariffs may make the price of the Europe-produced crop artificially low.
- Inefficient producers may be protected from competition, thereby diverting trade away from more efficient producers and potentially harming consumers. For example, less efficient producers within regions may lobby for protection, so that they do not have to reform and compete.
- The overall benefits may turn out to be small if an agreement limits the goods/services that are traded.
- Locally, some of the benefits may be distributed unequally, causing political and social tensions within the region.
- Globally, the benefits accrued inside the bloc may lead to tensions with other regions, leading to possible retaliation, further harming global trade.
- Members of RTAs, especially those in free trade agreements, may have differing levels of economic power, causing long-term economic and political imbalance, and potential conflict.
- For smaller organisations, opening up competition and the large market may result in more competitors. This can put pressure on their pricing strategies, since larger producers may be able to produce at a lower cost in a better location. Small firms often fear the consolidation of a trading bloc and the competitive changes in the market place that it brings.

Exam tip

Although you should be aware of the three main trading blocs (the EU, ASEAN and NAFTA), a detailed in-depth knowledge of each is not required. However, you could be asked to explain and assess the opportunities and problems for (a) a business located within a trading bloc member country or (b) a business that aims to sell into a trading bloc from a country that is not a member. The Eurasian Economic Union, in 'Thinking bigger' at the end of the unit, suggests certain benefits (free movement, co-ordinated policy and improved ties and relations), but also possible drawbacks (trade diversion from other countries) for businesses operating in the bloc.

Question 2

BWD Entertainment is a UK-based media company. Originally a magazine company, it has diversified into radio and trade newspapers, and also runs a book publishing business. In the 2000s, it acquired stakes in magazine publishing companies in Spain, the Netherlands and Italy, and owns radio companies in both Germany and France.

The directors of the company recently completed a strategic review and decided to target Croatia as an entrant to the EU in 2013. The directors felt the Croatian economy was likely to grow at a faster rate than the EU average over the next 10–20 years and this should give scope for increasing sales over time.

One strategy would be to buy an established Croatian magazine company and use its editorial expertise and distribution system to push a number of new magazines based on ones which have proved popular in the UK, Spain and Italy. A different strategy would be to buy a Croatian magazine company which already had strong market share. By giving new finance, BWD would allow the existing Croatian management greater opportunities to launch new magazines aimed at the local market. A third possible strategy would be to set up a company from scratch, recruiting editors and other workers from established Croatian magazine companies, but also putting in staff from existing BWD operations in other European countries. This would probably be the highest-risk strategy.

(a) Explain why there might be greater scope for marketing magazines in Croatia than in, say, the UK or Italy over the next ten years.

(b) By considering the possible advantages and disadvantages of each of the three strategic options, discuss which is likely to be the most successful for BWD. In your answer, identify what other information would be needed to make an informed choice.

Links 🔗

Trading blocs can have a great effect on the selling and trade patterns or businesses that sell within countries that are members, and also on businesses selling from a country that is not a member. You could use this to consider why businesses have chosen to relocate operations globally (Unit 73) or enter into mergers (Unit 74) and the effect on globalisation (Unit 68). You could also consider how selling into countries that are part of a trading bloc could affect a business's view of that country as a market (Unit 72).

Key terms

Common market – a market where goods, labour and capital can move freely across the member states; tariffs are generally removed and non-tariff barriers eliminated, or at least reduced.

Customs union – a union where member states remove all trade barriers between themselves and members adopt a common set of barriers against non-members.

Economic and monetary union – an economic union that uses a common currency.

Economic union – a type of trade bloc involving both a customs union and a common market.

Free trade area (FTA) – a region where member states remove all trade barriers between themselves, but each member state nevertheless keeps different barriers against non-member states.

Preferential trading area (PTA) – a type of trading bloc where certain types of products from participating countries receive a reduced tariff rate.

Regional trade agreement (RTA) – agreement made between two or more countries within a geographical region, which is designed to facilitate trade by bringing down barriers.

Rules of origin – a system of allocating certificates whereby a defined amount of a product or service must be certified as being created within that region.

Single market – a market where almost all trade barriers between members have been removed and common laws or policies aim to make the movement of goods and services, labour and capital between countries as easy as the movement within each country.

Trading bloc – a group of countries that has signed a regional trade agreement to reduce or eliminate tariffs, quotas and other protectionist barriers between themselves.

Knowledge check

1. Name four trading blocs.

2. Briefly explain why there has been an expansion in trading blocs.

3. How important are preferential trading areas?

4. What impact do trading blocs have on business?

5. What are the drawbacks of trading blocs on business?

6. What impact might EU enlargement have had on a) a farmer in Norfolk and b) a shoe manufacturer in Northampton?

7. Explain how a UK manufacturer might be at a competitive disadvantage because the UK does not use the single currency.

Case study

TOYOTA'S EUROPEAN EXPANSION

Toyota began selling cars in Europe in 1963, but through very limited distribution agreements. After the Second World War, the Japanese government and the European Community (EC, the EU's predecessor) negotiated an annual quota as to how many cars could be shipped to the EC market. This protectionist arrangement was in place to help support European car makers after the war and then during the transition to a full economic union. It meant that Japanese cars were relatively rare in the European market, and expensive to market or to accurately price. Moreover, the difficulties in obtaining parts and servicing meant that the cars were less attractive than they might otherwise have been to the average consumer. However, in 1999 the EU lifted the import quota and opened up the market to allow Japanese auto companies to expand distribution, invest in design and manufacturing facilities, and spend more on marketing to specific European tastes.

By 2002, while its competitors were struggling with restructuring or consolidation, Toyota had become extremely competitive in the European market, and had even more ambitious expansion plans for the future. In order to take advantage of economies of scale and to limit external currency risks, Toyota decided to move towards local procurement and production. Given the downturn in the European economy, some saw Toyota's strategy as over ambitious, but Toyota's planning was for the long term, so as to be ready when the economic upturn came.

In terms of strategy, rather than taking a limited export approach, it established full design and manufacturing facilities throughout Europe. This expansion strategy was designed for the EU as a whole, rather than for individual European countries. Thus, once Toyota decided to produce in the EU, it could locate its operations in the lowest-cost area. So rather than go to Germany, where labour cost $40 per hour, it chose to go to Poland and the Czech Republic, where the wages were much lower. Moreover, it could continue its expansion through joint ventures with European firms, so as to take advantage of existing supply and logistics networks.

The best-selling Yaris, Corolla and Avensis models were all designed and built in Europe, at facilities located to take advantage of lower-cost wages or other efficiencies, and the Avensis was even exported to Japan. The Prius, an innovative and environmentally friendly hybrid, was European 'Car of the Year' in 2005. By 2006, with a net worldwide income of around $14 billion, Toyota had become the second largest producer of cars in the world, as well as the most profitable. Although there was a need for a global recall in 2010, Toyota's presence in the European market has continued to grow, as have its profit margins. Toyota has staked much of its future growth on hybrid models, with sales growing by 20 per cent in 2014.

Reproduced with permission from Toyota (GB) PLC.

(a) Explain how the change in the EU trading arrangements affected Toyota. (4 marks)

(b) Explain one reason why production costs may have fallen. (4 marks)

(c) Assess whether, without the changes in the system surrounding import quotas, Toyota could have successfully expanded into the European market. (12 marks)

Thinking bigger

On 1 January 2015 a new trading bloc 'opened its doors'. Russia, Belarus and Kazakhstan signed a treaty in 2014 formally creating the Eurasian Economic Union. Armenia and Kyrgyzstan followed, officially becoming part of the bloc in early 2015. Whether this will stand the test of time is a key question, especially as a trade war seemed to emerge in April 2015 between Russia and Kazakhstan. Political observers have stated that the signing of the treaty, years in the making, was part of a continuing effort by Mr Putin to create an independent economic force led by Russia.

The creation of the bloc, which has a combined $2.7 trillion economy and vast energy resources, deepens ties among the three countries that began with the creation of a customs union in 2010. It guarantees the free transit of goods, services, capital and workforce, and will result in a co-ordinated policy for key economic sectors.

The trading bloc was devised as the cornerstone of what will become the Eurasian Union and include more former Soviet states. Mr Putin hopes the bigger bloc will one day stand on equal economic footing with the US, the EU and China, and serve as a counterweight to what Russia sees as the West's growing influence in former Soviet states.

Russia's efforts to form the union have included pressure on its neighbours to shun seeking economic integration with the EU instead, most notably Ukraine. Kiev had been in talks for years to join the Eurasian Union, then opted for a trade pact with the EU instead.

Source: adapted from the *Financial Times* 08.01.2015. All rights reserved.

Conditions that prompt trade

Key points

1. Push factors:
   - saturated markets
   - competition.
2. Pull factors:
   - economies of scale
   - risk spreading.
3. Possibility of off-shoring and outsourcing.
4. Extending the product life cycle by selling in multiple markets.

Getting started

The rock crystals of pure, unadulterated salt, which formed in a saucepan 19 years ago in a family home near Anglesey, led to the creation of a staple condiment in the kitchens of most upmarket restaurants, and on the shelves of high-end stores and supermarkets such as Harvey Nichols, Waitrose, Fortnum & Mason and Marks & Spencer, and not just in the UK – it is exported to more than 20 countries across the globe. It is claimed that US President Barack Obama is a fan. Halen Môn also seems to have the endorsement of many celebrity chefs in the country: from the Two Fat Ladies (the late Clarissa Dickson Wright and the late Jennifer Patterson) in the late 1990s, to Delia Smith and Heston Blumenthal today.

David and Alison Lea-Wilson started their business in 1996. They make hand-harvested sea salt using water from the Menai Straits. They dry the salt, season it and pack it. Forty per cent of all the salt they produce is exported. With the help of a Welsh Government grant they attended a trade fair in Ireland where a US firm was impressed by the product. They now sell to most of Europe and as far as Australia. One of the key factors has been the popularity of their salt with chefs. Halen Môn has also joined the ranks of champagne, parma ham and Melton Mowbray pork pies by being awarded protected food name status by the European Commission. The owners feel that Halen Môn's success is due to the purity of the product and the simplicity in which it is refined. They don't boil up the seawater on the cooker any more and there has been significant investment in carbon filters and heaters, but is still hand-harvested and each packet has the harvester's initial on.

The above example shows how it is possible to build a business from a kitchen to trading successfully around the world. Why do you think David and Alison were successful? To ensure future long-term growth, what do the Lee-Wilsons need to consider? Explain your answer.

Conditions that prompt trade

International trade has been vital for the UK economy since pre-historic times. As an island, the UK must import supplies of raw materials to use in making many products. But the UK has also exported them. For instance, thousands of years ago, Bronze Age miners were excavating copper from Great Orme in Wales and objects made from the ore have been found at archaeological sites throughout the Mediterranean. The Anglo Saxons were heavily involved in international trade. In the 8th century, glass was imported from Gaul, and iron as well as cheese was exported to Flanders. However, the industrial revolution acted as a catalyst, prompting an explosion in international trade that has continued to this day.

Innovation and the entrepreneurial spirit provided the impetus to trade that led to the UK dominating the world economy throughout the 19th century. Britain exported pumps, steamships, railway locomotives and textile equipment. It influenced the development of railway systems throughout the world, as well as the building of dams and canals. As a consequence, the UK also became a leader in international and domestic banking. It is no surprise that successive UK governments after 1840 preached free trade and advocated no tariffs or quotas. In 2013, the UK was the fifth largest national economy and second largest in Europe as measured by nominal GDP. In recent years the UK has been the fourth largest exporter in the world with exports of £334 billion, and remains one of the world's most globalised economies. The financial services sector is particularly important, with London being the world's largest financial centre. The pharmaceutical industry is another major exporter. Alongside this, the UK was also the fifth largest importer in 2013.

There are many conditions that promote trade. On one level there are economic factors such as the impact of being a member of the European Union, but there are also the creative and entrepreneurial drives to seek new markets that dominate the push for trade. These are facilitated by a skilled workforce that contributes by providing high-quality goods and services that are in demand.

Although the politics and economics of free trade will never be straightforward, trade has continued to expand and many consider that we have a 'global consumer culture' stretching around the planet. Regardless, businesses see expanding into international markets as an opportunity to find new resources and markets for their goods, as well as producing their goods and services at a lower cost, thereby making them more money or extending the life of their products or services.

Firms may be motivated to go abroad for many reasons. One way this can be categorised is to divide them into 'push' factors, where firms are seeking opportunities, or 'pull' factors, where a market overseas holds a particular attraction.

Push factors

Push factors are adverse factors in the existing market that encourage an organisation to seek international opportunities. They force a business to seek overseas markets in which to sell their products. A firm may be attempting to overcome weaknesses in its existing markets or looking to lower its costs. Push factors include saturated markets and competition. Competition may drive prices down due to lowered costs, or there may be declining demand for a product, due to changes in tastes, availability of substitutes or superseding technologies.

Saturated markets: A saturated market is one where most of the customers who would buy a particular product already have it, or there is limited remaining opportunity for growth in sales. For example, a cycle manufacturer may have limited opportunities to sell in countries where cycling is very popular. However, it may be able to find a new market in a country where the sport is just taking off. For example, most people in the UK own mobile phones, all of which have the same basic functions. In order to increase sales, the firms in this saturated market need to either differentiate their products within the home market, or sell their product in a market where there is still a demand for it.

Competition: A rise in competitors or a high level of competition in the domestic market may force a business to sell abroad. Competitors could be selling similar products at a lower price or a higher quality, which may make selling the original product difficult or unprofitable. Taking the same example as above, the market for mobile phones is highly competitive: Apple, Samsung, Nokia, HTC, Blackberry and Sony are just a few of the many providers. Where all of the brands are able to compete in a market, the businesses will be forced to differentiate their products or to move to a market where the competition is less fierce for reasons of price, quality or novelty.

Faced with competition in its domestic market, a business may be forced to look at markets abroad. This may involve changing the product to meet the tastes of those consumers. For example, many people enjoy popcorn when at the cinema. It is often sold as sweet or salted in cinemas in the UK. It is also sold in supermarkets. However, in 2010 UK manufacturer Joe &

Seph's Gourmet Popcorn looked for a different market abroad. It experimented with 30 classic British flavours and its own secret production process. It found that flavours such as strawberries and cream, and cheddar cheese were popular with foreign consumers. In 2015 it sold in over 1,000 retailers in countries including Australia, Qatar, Saudi Arabia and Switzerland.

Question 1

James Dyson designed and produced his first vacuum cleaner in 1983. His appliances were double the price of existing brands, but of innovative design and very high quality, and they sold well. All production was done domestically, and Dyson established a research and development centre in England in 1993. Nevertheless, the Dyson company did not make enough money. The reasons were many. UK employment costs were high relative to Dyson's competitors; the pound was strong, making exporting expensive; logistical costs were high and the factory was not large enough to optimise economies of scale. So when the company was refused planning permission to expand the factory, Dyson decided he had no choice but to move production abroad.

Dyson chose Malaysia as a location for a giant new factory, near to where the majority of his suppliers were located, as well as many of the new markets for Dyson's products. Malaysia's overall costs of production were also far lower than those of the UK, meaning the firm could lower costs and improve profit margins. By 2015, these profits had allowed Dyson to begin expanding the research and development centre back in the UK, invest £12m at Imperial College London for a school of engineering, and create new and innovative products.

Sources: adapted from the *Financial Times*, 22.03.2015, 10.04.2015. All rights reserved.

(a) Explain one push factor that affected Dyson's decision to move his production abroad.

(b) Assess Dyson's decision to keep his research and development centre in the UK.

Pull factors

Pull factors entice firms into new markets. They are the opportunities that businesses can take advantage of when selling into overseas markets. There are many pull factors, and those that are the most important to a firm depend upon the nature of the business and the current state of its home market. However, the following lists many common attractions.

- New or bigger markets.
- Lower-cost or secure resources, such as minerals, land or labour.
- Lower cost of transportation.
- Technological expertise, including research facilities.
- Managerial or financial expertise.
- Organisational skills.
- Assets, such as brands, patents or other intellectual property.

A firm may be enticed by these factors since they may help it to achieve economies of scale or to spread its risks.

Economies of scale: Economies of scale occur where increasing the scale of production leads to a lower cost per unit of output. Put simply, increasing size or speed increases efficiency and lowers costs. Unit 67 described Adam Smith's pin production and how division of labour can lead to more units being produced in a shorter period of time. Likewise, if a factory were to increase its size, many of its fixed costs would decline relative to output. The firm could buy supplies in bulk, usually at a discount. It could apply relatively expensive technology to automate its processes and train its workers in ever more specialist tasks. However, bigger is not always better. Beyond a certain size, unit costs can rise and resources can be spread too thinly.

As seen in Question 1, a push factor for Dyson's decision to go abroad was the fact that the company was refused planning permission to expand its production facility in England. This meant that it could not achieve the scale efficiencies needed to compete against the increasing number of lower-cost foreign competitors that it was facing in the UK. So a push factor was that it needed to find a place to build a big, new and highly efficient factory. Malaysia offered such a location and its many attractions were a pull factor for Dyson.

Risk spreading: Risk and how to mitigate it were addressed in Unit 65 in the context of scenario planning. One way of defining risk is the probability of a (bad) event happening multiplied by its (negative) impact. This can range across financial, strategic, operational and hazard-related risks. Where they can be recognised and quantified, risks can usually be insured against. Where they cannot, they pose a threat to a firm's strategy and need to be addressed.

By expanding into other countries and markets, a firm may be able to limit the various risks that it faces. For instance, over-dependence upon one market may leave a firm vulnerable in the short term if that market faces an economic challenge, such as a recession, where growth slows and perhaps people lose their jobs. Or, for example, in the long term, a region characterised by a rapidly aging population may not be a viable place for a business that sells mainly to the under-30s. Expanding abroad may help a firm to minimise the impact of such risks upon its overall profitability.

Possibility of off-shoring and outsourcing

Put simply, **off-shoring** is shifting jobs to other countries, while **outsourcing** is shifting jobs to other organisations.

Off-shoring: Off-shoring involves moving manufacturing or service industries to a location with lower costs. A classic example is the relocation in the 1980s of many call centres from the UK to India, where well-educated workers speaking good English were employed on a lower wage and for longer hours than British workers. It follows, therefore, that a firm may off-shore in order to:
- reduce costs
- hire workers with particular skills.

Moving jobs to other countries can be controversial, especially where a lot of jobs are lost in the home country. This could potentially damage a firm's reputation. Other risks may also emerge, such as complications caused by language or cultural differences, as well as any political, economic, technological or intellectual property risks associated with the host country. Some firms, focused on reducing costs, don't realise that off-shoring can actually fail. The process may increase management costs, reduce efficiency or quality, expose firms to corruption and loss of intellectual property – and even end up as too expensive to continue.

Outsourcing: Outsourcing involves moving an entire business function or project to a specialist external provider. For instance, many large firms have outsourced their information technology and payroll functions, while others have shifted human resources, accounting, supply and logistics, and transportation. In general, a firm might outsource for similar reasons to off-shoring, to:
- reduce costs
- specialise areas of the business
  - to focus on the core competences of the business rather than the support functions
  - in order to improve speed, flexibility or quality
- comply with rules or regulations.

Shifting jobs to other organisations does have risks, but is often less controversial than off-shoring. Reliance on third parties can leave a firm vulnerable through loss of expertise or knowledge. In addition, the parties' interests may not remain aligned, so that the efficiencies sought by shifting the jobs are not as great as expected. Poor communication issues can be disruptive and indirectly expensive to the business.

Labour productivity: Firms often cite 'cheaper' labour as a pull factor, but this is not a good way to describe the quest for lower labour costs. For a business, it is not simply that a worker can be paid a lower wage, but rather that each worker costs less per unit of output that they produce. This is known as **labour productivity**. This is defined as the amount of goods and services produced by one hour of labour. Many factors may affect the productivity of a worker. These include skills and qualifications, working conditions and technological support, as well as rules and regulations.

Question 2

In 2013, the US Federal Aviation Administration grounded all of Boeing's brand new 787 Dreamliners because of the possibility that their lithium-ion batteries would overheat and catch fire. This was one of many problems plaguing the new plane and critics attributed this to the fact that 30 per cent of its construction had been outsourced, as opposed to 5 per cent of previous models. The suspect lithium-ion batteries were made in Japan, and it was not until after changes were made to the batteries to contain the fire risk that the planes were again allowed to fly. However, the problems were more complex than just faulty parts. Because there were so many components coming from different countries, it was difficult to monitor all of them for quality or to correct flaws during the assembly process. Although outsourcing may or may not be to blame for the problems Boeing experienced, it did make the process of quality assurance much more complex.

Source: the *Financial Times*, 11.1.2013.

(a) Explain the difference between outsourcing and off-shoring.

(b) Assess whether outsourcing is always in the interest of consumers and manufacturers.

Extending the product life cycle by selling in multiple markets

The concept of the product life cycle was developed in the 1960s to describe the stages in the life of a product, as explained in Unit 13.

These stages again in brief are as follows:

- **Development.** The product is researched and designed, and a decision made about whether to launch the product.
- **Introduction.** From the development of an original idea to the launch of the product on the market.
- **Growth.** When the product takes off and sales increase.
- **Maturity.** When sales are near their highest but are slowing down.
- **Decline.** When sales begin to fall.

When a product has reached the decline stage, with falling sales, market saturation and a decline in profits, a firm has to decide whether to get out of the market for that product altogether, or to attempt to extend the product life cycle in some way. The firm could choose to move production to new markets in order to reduce costs, allowing the firm to increase margins. Or it could explore selling to new markets. A product that is in a mature stage in one market may be at an introductory stage elsewhere, and so a firm can sell a product in the new market and extend its life cycle.

For example, the Apple iPod was launched in 2001 and went through many changes to remain competitive with new technologies, music streaming, fashion and changing tastes. By 2009 sales had begun to decline. By outsourcing production, adding new uses and variations, Apple extended the life cycle of the iPod, though in 2013 it ceased introducing new models.

When extending the product life cycle into international markets, a firm has to make a decision as to whether to modify or adapt the product for the new markets, or whether to standardise the product for global use. Also, it is worth noting that the life cycles of products can vary considerably. For example, fashion items or highly innovative technologies may have very short life cycles, while luxury goods and precision watches may have very long ones.

Thinking bigger

The product life cycle has been used by firms as an instrument of competitive power and it remains as the hub of the marketing strategy of many firms as they maximise product lines along the bell-shaped curves. Why then do some products 'defeat' the curve? Business writers talk about repositioning products so that they are 'rescued'. They add new attributes, sell in multiple markets and can convince customers that a new offering is different.

It is useful to reflect on why a brand such as Kit Kat, introduced by Rowntree's in York in 1911 and relaunched in 1935, is still the number one selling chocolate bar in many countries, including Japan. Reflect also on *The Simpsons*, the animated show conceived by Matt Groening as a brand that in TV history is unique. The 27th season has started production. *The Simpsons'* positioning has had an important impact on its progress along the life cycle. Most live-action sitcoms have a compressed life cycle, in part because actors age. *Friends* exited after a 10-year run when its stars, originally cast as 20-somethings, started approaching 40. But cartoon characters are ageless (Bart Simpson has been ten years old for a decade and a half). Just as Bugs Bunny exploited the cartoon medium to stay fresh for 65 years, *The Simpsons'* breakaway status has allowed the series to pause seemingly indefinitely on the life cycle curve at a point at which live-action sitcoms usually head into decline. *The Simpsons* is just as much a brand as Kit Kat. The UK has some of the oldest iconic brands such as Twinings Tea (1706) and Lyle's Golden Syrup (1883). Why do they last?

You could use this information in a variety of ways. Obviously, it can be used if answering questions on product life cycle and selling in multiple markets. It is also useful to think through why some products do last the test of time and whether others can adopt their techniques.

Knowledge check

1. Outline the factors that can prompt trade.
2. What are push factors?
3. Explain how a market becomes saturated.
4. What impact might competition in domestic markets have on business strategy?
5. How do pull factors entice firms into the market?
6. Describe the impact of economies of scale.
7. Outline how exporting could limit risks.
8. Describe how the product life cycle can be extended by selling in multiple markets.

Case study

ZARA

Founded in La Coruña in north-west Spain with its first store in 1975, Zara has become one of the largest clothing retailers in the world. Zara is the successful brand of the multinational clothing company, Inditex. Founder Amancio Ortega, one of the wealthiest men in the world, has established over 6000 stores since 1988 and profits exceed €2 billion a year. It is unique in that it is a fashion house as well as producer of most of the clothes sold in its shops. Between 1975 and 1988, Zara concentrated on developing its home market. By 1988, facing a saturated market and limited growth in Spain, Zara decided that it had to expand internationally if it was to continue to grow.

Spain joined the European Union (EU) in 1986, and thus gained barrier-free access to the huge European consumer market. Moreover, the 1980s were also a time of rapid globalisation and converging fashion tastes. So Zara saw many market opportunities, as well as a chance to gain economies of scale and spread its risks.

Zara's first foray was into the similar cultural environment of Portugal. Between 1989 and 1996, Zara opened stores in several European countries and Mexico, as well as the key fashion centre of New York in 1989. The New York expansion held risk, but also provided insight into competitor business models, such as Gap. After 1997, Zara began a rapid phase of international expansion that has made it into a globally recognised brand. Inditex, Zara's parent company, saw growth and then share prices soar (see Figure 1) partly as a result of these strategies. In recent years it has also moved into online trading as a new route to growth – opening e-commerce operations in Russia and Canada, for example.

(a) Evaluate the importance of push and pull factors in Zara's decision to expand in the EU. (20 marks)

(b) Evaluate the success of Zara's expansion strategies. (20 marks)

Figure 1

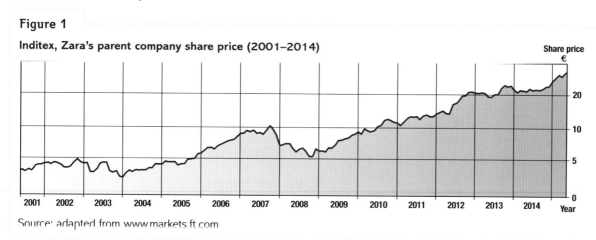

Inditex, Zara's parent company share price (2001–2014)

Source: adapted from www.markets.ft.com

Key terms

Economies of scale – increasing the scale of production leads to a lower cost per unit of output. Increasing size or speed increases efficiency and lowers costs.

Labour productivity – the amount of goods and services produced by one hour of labour.

Off-shoring – shifting jobs to other countries.

Outsourcing – shifting jobs to other organisations.

Product life cycle – the stages that many products go through: development; introduction; growth; maturity; decline.

Pull factors – factors that entice firms into new markets and are the opportunities that businesses can take advantage of when selling into overseas markets.

Push factors – factors in the existing market that encourage an organisation to seek international opportunities.

Risk – the probability of a (bad) event happening multiplied by its (negative) impact.

Saturation – the point when most of the customers who want to buy a product already have it, or there is limited remaining opportunity for growth in sales.

Links

As we have touched on in this unit, extending the product life cycle of a business can be one factor that prompts a business to trade. Unit 13 explains the stages of a product life cycle for products, and information there can be used to help answer questions relating to this as an appropriate reason for trade. Other factors that might be important are push factors such as competition (Unit 75) and pull factors such as economies of scale (Unit 48).

72 Assessment of a country as a market

Key points

Factors to consider:
1. Levels and growth of disposable income.
2. Ease of doing business.
3. Infrastructure.
4. Political stability.
5. Exchange rate.

Getting started

Like China, its populous neighbour, India has long looked like an attractive market for business. With 1.2 billion people and growth in GDP (as shown in Table 1), this South East Asian economy presents many opportunities for businesses wishing to invest.

Table 1 India: growth in GDP as an annual percentage

	2011	2012	2013
India	6.6	5.1	6.9

Source: adapted from World Bank

However, unlike China, India has yet to fully convince international investors that its considerable attractions can be offset against some aspects, still in development, that are required for a good environment when carrying out business. When Narendra Modi became India's prime minister in 2014 he promised that his government would improve the environment for doing business. India had just been ranked 142 in the world under the World Bank's 'Ease of doing business' rankings and this was attributed to a high level of corruption, red tape and regulation that stifled investment. This was two places lower than the previous year.

India's 2015/2016 Union Budget reforms were designed to make India's business environment more attractive to entrepreneurs and investors. The reforms included simplifying regulations, streamlining infrastructure, speeding up procedures for the resolution of disputes, and instituting a single national goods and services tax, to raise more revenue and help create an internal market for India. Companies wishing to start a new business should be able to acquire land for development more easily and obtain all the permits for that development through a single portal covering all of the government departments.

Source: adapted from www.doingbusiness.org

Do you think these reforms and their impact might make the market more attractive to businesses looking to invest or sell goods or services in India? What benefits to India do you think there would be of more businesses moving into their market?

Factors to consider

Assessing a country as a market is never easy. To even begin to make a decision as to whether a place is good for investment requires a huge amount of research, as well as a full understand of the company's competitive advantages and whether the investment, if successful, will enhance these. Even then, many companies make a wrong decision. There are however, some ke factors for initial consideration, and these are covered in this un

Levels and growth of disposable incom

There may be many reasons a business might look to sell its go and services in other countries, as explored in Unit 71. Howeve an enterprise wants to sell to a customer, the customer must ha the money with which to buy that good or service. It is therefor important for a business to evaluate whether the consumers in a particular country currently have – and will have in the future sufficient **disposable income**.

Disposable income: Disposable income, as briefly introduce in Unit 4, is essentially the amount of money that a person has over after they have paid their taxes, national insurance and oth deductions. This remaining or 'disposable' income can then be used for consumption or for saving.

When thinking about international trade, it is important to understand the average level of household disposable income comparison to other countries. A business can find out about th level of disposable income in the UK from the Office for Nation Statistics (ONS). Data for other countries may be found throug sources such as the OECD, Euromonitor, the World Bank or the

A falling level of disposable income may mean that people with low incomes are struggling to pay for what they consider a minimum standard of living, and those on higher incomes are reducing expenditure on luxuries or unnecessary items. As a result, people will be consuming less, total expenditure in markets may be falling and there is likely to be reduced savir For example, from Table 2, we can see how the Greek consum has suffered significant falls in disposable income every year between 2011 and 2014, due to Greece's poor financial situati The Greek consumer now has less money to buy new cars and Table 2 shows, is spending less money on food.

Table 2 Greece's disposable income and food expenditure 2011–2014*

	2011	2012	2013	2014
Annual disposable income	206,783	173,804	173,247	171,669
Consumer expenditure on food	31,982	27,824	28,002	27,632

*Figures in US dollars (millions)

Source: Euromonitor

By contrast, Table 3 shows the same data for the UK. The disposable income of UK consumers, already significantly higher than that of Greek consumers in 2011, rose throughout the same time period. This meant that many British consumers had more money to buy goods and services or to add to their savings.

Table 3 Britain's disposable income and food expenditure 2011–2014*

	2011	2012	2013	2014
Annual disposable income	1,690,166	1,754,166	1,784,101	1,856,096
Consumer expenditure on food	124,962	131,803	139,497	138,701

*Figures in US dollars (millions)

Source: Euromonitor

A business looking to expand into a market wants to ensure not only that consumers have sufficient disposable income to purchase its goods and services, but also that the country's level of disposable income is at least steady and preferably growing over time. If disposable income is steady or rising, and has been so for several years, it may mean that the consumers will be able to buy a business's products or services both now and in the future, and may therefore make the market an attractive one to expand into.

For example, because of the rising disposable incomes of the growing young professional class, India's luxury goods market has been on the increase. This is not only for reasons of fashion, because items such as jewellery and watches are also purchased as investments. According to Euromonitor, up to 2030 the number of Indian households with a disposable income of between $10,000 and $25,000 will continue to increase significantly, making India a growth market for the makers of many products and services.

Ease of doing business

The ease with which a company can do business is an important factor to consider when evaluating a country as a potential market. If a business faces problems with its goods entering a country, setting up premises or dealing with everyday trading activities in a particular country, it is likely to look at alternative locations or markets. Such problems with the ease of doing business are likely to cause delays in sales, increasing costs and potentially affect other parts of the business in the distribution chain.

Every year, the World Bank Group publishes a report summarising its research into the regulatory burden that each country places on its business. The higher the ranking, the easier it is to start and operate a business in a country.

Table 4 shows that Singapore and New Zealand are consistently at the top of the rankings, indicating that they are good locations for a company to consider with respect to the ease of doing business. On the other hand, Eritrea, South Sudan and Afghanistan are consistently near the bottom, making these locations unattractive for creating and running businesses. As noted in the 'Getting started' activity, India fell two places in the World Bank's Ease of doing business rankings for 2014, from 140 to 142.

Table 4 Ease of doing business rankings 2014*

Country	Rank	Starting a business	Dealing with construction permits
Singapore	1	6	2
United States	7	46	41
United Kingdom	8	45	17
Australia	10	7	19
Germany	14	114	8
Malaysia	18	13	28
Mexico	39	67	108
Greece	61	52	88
Russian Federation	62	34	156
China	90	128	179
India	142	158	184
Afghanistan	183	24	167
South Sudan	186	178	189
Eritrea	189	183	189

*Countries are ranked from 1 to 189.

Sources: adapted from World Bank and www.doingbusiness.org

There are ten indicators produced by the World Bank that track the life cycle of the business from its creation to its possible end. At each stage the potential problems that might exist are indicated.

1. Starting a business (number of procedures, time it takes, cost and minimal capital requirements).

2. Dealing with construction permits (number of procedures, time it takes, days and cost).

3. Getting electricity (number of procedures, time it takes, days and cost).

4. Registering property (number of procedures, time it takes, days and cost).

5. Getting credit (strength of legal rights, information required).

6. Protecting minority investors.

7. Paying taxes (payments per year, time, percentage of profit).

8. Trading across borders (documents required, time to export/import, cost to export/import).

9. Enforcing contracts (number of procedures, time, cost as percentage of claim).

10. Resolving insolvency.

Question 1

In May 2014, two years after Argentina's government seized its assets, Spanish energy firm Repsol left the Argentine market. It was reported that Repsol agreed to a settlement that was worth only half of its original investment, but would nevertheless allow it to end years of lawsuits and further uncertainty. Repsol once owned 50 per cent of YPF, an Argentine oil and gas business, but was reportedly accused of under-investing in oil production and draining the local business's resources. YPF was originally state-owned, but was privatised in 1993, allowing Repsol to acquire a majority stake. In 2011, oil and gas production had fallen below the level of domestic demand, with the business and the government disagreeing as to the reasons why. Repsol, and most market analysts, blamed government controls and red tape, as well as price controls on domestic oil and gas that made such investments unprofitable. By contrast, the government reportedly accused Repsol of using the money it had made in Argentina to finance expansion elsewhere in the world. Argentina re-nationalised YPF in 2012.

Source: adapted from the *Financial Times* 07.05.2014. All rights reserved.

(a) Explain one reason why Repsol left the Argentinian market.

(b) Discuss how, when buying assets in a country, a PESTLE analysis could be used to identify threats to their investment.

Infrastructure

The quality of a country's **infrastructure** is an important factor in any decision to move into a new market. Customers may have sufficient disposable income to purchase a business's goods and services. However, those goods and services must still be made and delivered to the buyer, and this requires a certain level of communication and adequate transportation links, for example. Many developing countries have underdeveloped and unreliable transportation infrastructure, and this can add significantly to a company's production and operating costs. For instance, there may be awkward or inefficient entry points (airports, sea ports), few or unreliable trains or shipping lanes, incomplete road networks or limited warehousing facilities. A delay or failure to deliver due to poor infrastructure can lead to lost sales and increased costs, which can make a market less attractive to a business.

Communication infrastructure is equally important. Many companies want to co-ordinate production, sales and distribution, and this is best done electronically. However, electricity shortages and limited internet coverage may mean that such efficiencies are not practicable.

With huge oil reserves and a good location, Dubai has used the proceeds from the sale of its oil to further develop its infrastructure, including the following.

- An artificial harbour for ships.
- The Jebel Ali Free Trade Zone.
- An information technology hub, called Dubai Internet City, where businesses such as IBM pay no tax, have few currency restrictions and limited regulation.
- The 'Dubai Ideas Oasis' to encourage venture capital and new business start-ups.
- The 'Dubai Knowledge Village' to improve educational opportunities.
- Many hotels and residential complexes to make Dubai an attractive destination for visitors.

This infrastructure investment appears to be getting results. Dubai is one of the seven monarchies of the United Arab Emirates, so it is difficult to separate out its growth rate from the others using the World Bank statistics. Nevertheless, according to Dubai government statistics, foreign direct investment has significantly risen year on year since 2012.

Political stability

Political decisions and events can have a significant effect on a country's business environment and can cost investors some or all of the value of their investment. A country with a calm political climate can minimise uncertainty, which might make that country attractive as a potential market to businesses.

It is therefore important to evaluate the political climate of a country before investing and to critically assess the potential risks. There are a few obvious issues to check for the target market.

- The nature of the government and its relationship with business.
- The nature of the government and its relationship with major international institutions, such as the United Nations, the World Trade Organization, the International Monetary Fund and the World Bank.

- The government's legal orientation and approach to regulation and taxation.
- The possible political risks that may emerge in the near future, such as elections, political vacuums, coups, terrorism, human rights issues, or protests.

There are also numerous risks that a business might need to be aware of.

- Instability during an election.
- The emergence of political vacuums.
- Increasing authoritarianism.
- Factions in government, such as when political parties split.
- Increasing levels of corruption.
- Threats from terrorism.
- External threats (border conflicts, trade disputes, invasion) that may cause internal power changes.

It is often difficult for a business to gauge the level of corruption that it might face when entering a market. Transparency International is a non-governmental organisation established to combat corruption. Every year, it publishes the global Corruption Perceptions Index, which measures the perceived levels of public sector corruption in countries and territories around the world. It is a useful starting point for understanding whether a country is perceived by others to be corrupt. Some examples of countries are shown in Table 5.

Table 5 Selected ranks from Transparency International's Corruption Perceptions Index, 2014

Country	Rank (1=least corrupt)
Denmark	1
Norway	5
Singapore	7
United Kingdom	14
Japan	15
United States	17
Chile	21
South Korea	43
Malaysia	50
Saudi Arabia	55
South Africa	67
Brazil, Italy, Greece, Swaziland, Romania	69
India	85
China	100
Argentina, Indonesia, Djibouti	107
Russia, Nigeria, Lebanon, Kyrgyzstan, Iran, Cameroon	136

Source: www.transparency.org

Exchange rate

The **exchange rate** is the price of one currency against another. A currency can rise in value – or appreciate – against other currencies. For instance, when the pound rises, or appreciates, against the euro, one pound will buy more euros. Likewise,

a currency can fall in value – or depreciate – against other currencies. In this case, if the pound was to depreciate against the euro, it would be able to buy fewer euros. Appreciation and depreciation of currencies is explored further in Unit 74.

Changes in exchange rates can have a very large impact on a business that is operating internationally. For instance, if a small business from the UK was planning to export its goods to Japan, it would want those goods to be purchased in pounds. However, if the pound was to appreciate against the yen, this would make the business's goods more expensive to Japanese consumers and might reduce its sales and profits. Or, if a large UK business was considering buying a Japanese business, it would want to buy yen to pay the Japanese shareholders for their shares. A strong pound would lower the price that the UK business had to pay because it would take fewer pounds to buy the required amount of yen. Consequently, a business looking to expand abroad would want

Worked example

Assume that a car made in Sunderland costs £10,000 to produce and sells for £12,000 in the British market.

The exact same car, exported and sold in a European country, would be much more expensive in 2015 than it was in 2014 (assuming no change in production costs).

- 2014: €12,000 × 1.2 = €14,400
- 2015: €12,000 × 1.4 = €16,800

This may lead to a decrease in demand for the car and lower profit margins for the car maker. However, this will also depend on other factors, including the price elasticity of demand for the model and the level of growth in the various markets where the car is sold. Moreover, it is very unlikely (as assumed above) that production costs would remain the same. This is because some of the components for the car are likely to come from countries that use the euro (e.g. many car engines are made in Germany and interior fixtures and fittings in Spain). The exchange rate will therefore affect the cost of these components and thus the overall cost of making the car.

In this case, it could lower production costs – and the car company could possibly afford to lower the price of the car as a result.

to think about the relationship between its home currency and the currency of the country or countries with which it is trading. Furthermore, it would want to consider this relationship over time, since currencies can fluctuate in the short run. That is, if the pound was appreciating one week yet falling the next, the business may not be very concerned unless the overall trend was for the pound to get stronger.

However, there is another side to this relationship. Suppose that rather than export, a business wants to buy or build a factory in another country. If the pound is tending to appreciate, then the overall cost of the purchase or construction may actually be lower over time and vice versa.

To illustrate this, suppose that a UK business signs a contract with a Malaysian builder to erect a vacuum factory in Malaysia. It will take two years to complete the build, but the business will not pay for the factory until it is up and ready to start making the appliances. The contract for the build states that the UK business will pay the builder £10 million, converted to the Malaysian currency at the 2014 average exchange rate. Table 6 shows that, in 2014, it took on average 5.39 ringgits to buy one pound. If the cost of building the factory is £10 million, the business will have to pay the Malaysian business 53.9 million ringgits at the end of two years. However, suppose the exchange rate moves against the UK business, and the ringgit strengthens to 5 ringgits per pound. The contract says £10 million, but £10 million will now only buy 50 million ringgits, so the UK business needs to pay 3.9 million ringgits more.

Table 6 Average exchange rates of a range of currencies against £ sterling (January 2014 to January 2015)

Country or region	Currency	Average of currency units needed to buy one £ (January 2014 to January 2015)
European Union	Euro	1.2
Australia	Dollar	1.82
Brazil	Real	3.86
India	Rupee	100.64
Malaysia	Ringgit	5.39
Nigeria	Naira	271.102
Russia	Rouble	62.44
South Korea	Won	1733.92
USA	Dollar	1.65

Sources: markets.ft.com and www.gov.uk

A business might want to protect itself from adverse movements in the price of currencies. It can do this in many ways, including:
- taking out insurance to protect it from financial loss
- using financial instruments, such as hedging, to try and hedge against the financial risks.

Exam tip

The title of this unit is 'Assessment of a country as a market'. The command word 'assess' in an exam requires you to make a judgement of some form. To assess you could weigh up different arguments and then come to a conclusion or judgement, backed up by evidence. So, for example, you could consider a variety of factors that might influence a business to market its products to a particular country and then judge which of these is likely to be the most important. Alternatively, you might consider a variety of factors and their benefits and drawbacks, and then judge whether the country is worth exporting to or setting up a business in.

Links 🔗

Several factors can be taken into account when assessing a country as a potential market. You can demonstrate your synoptic skills by drawing on other areas of the specification to support the arguments that you put forward in answers.

This could include information in, for example, Unit 4 (Demand), Unit 66 (Growing economies), Unit 69 (Protectionism), Unit 70 (Trading blocs), Unit 75 (Global competitiveness) and Unit 80 (Ethics).

Question 2

During 2014, the pound appreciated against the euro meaning that every pound bought more euros in 2014 than in 2013. While this was good news for tourists heading for Spain's or Greece's beaches, it was not good news for British manufacturers who export to Madrid or Athens.

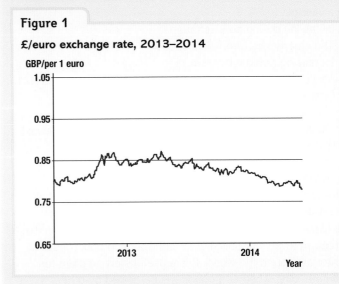

Figure 1

£/euro exchange rate, 2013–2014

(a) Explain why a British manufacturer might not want the pound to appreciate, while a British holidaymaker might.

Thinking bigger

The Walt Disney Company plans for massive success with its Shanghai, China resort in 2016. Over $5 billion dollars have been spent in constructing the largest theme park in the world. Disney expects 25 million visitors in its first full year, drawn in by state-of-the-art technology, new attractions, as well as a Toy Story themed hotel. Shanghai is no stranger to large crowds as the World Expo held in 2010 attracted 73 million people. This indicates that disposable income in China is sufficient to lead to this significant investment. It also shows that Shanghai is becoming a tourist destination with all the infrastructure that is needed in place.

You could use this information in a variety of ways. Obviously, it can be used if answering questions on assessment of a country as a market. It is also useful in evaluating how that market might develop in the future.

Source: adapted from the *Financial Times* 22.05.2015. All rights reserved.

Case study

BRAZIL

In a world of near-zero interest rates in early 2015, how about this? In spring 2015 Brazil's central bank increased its main interest rate to 13.25 per cent. The 50 basis-point rise was part of Brazil's efforts to put its house in order. The Brazilian economy was expected to shrink by 1 per cent in 2015, the deepest recession in 25 years; unemployment had been rising; while inflation had been running at over 8 per cent – almost twice the official target, hence the rate rise. After years of fast growth and easy credit, in 2015 Brazil was on its back.

In 2015, Latin America's biggest economy was also reported as reeling from a corruption scandal at Petrobas. Release of the state-controlled energy company's long-delayed results in spring 2015 reportedly estimated losses, due to corruption, of more than $2bn – much of them due to political kickbacks. Dozens of politicians, senior business figures and middle-men were arrested. They were reportedly accused of running an elaborate scheme that benefited individuals, and also the governing Workers' Party, to the tune of hundreds of millions of dollars. Across Brazil tens of thousands of jobs were reportedly lost as Petrobras and other big firms caught up in the scandal laid off workers and delayed investments. Petrobras is not just a huge oil company. It is emblematic of Brazil, and a source of great national pride. The scandal shocked the country and shook the government. Partnering with Petrobras is reported as near essential and somewhat unavoidable if you are to make good on any attempt to tap hydrocarbons in Brazil. So investors were shocked to be confronted by the sight of the company reportedly mired in corruption allegations on an industrial scale. The company's crisis has had a negative impact on the economy, delaying investments in infrastructure and the oil and gas sector.

There were three main reasons reported for Brazil's gloom. China's slowing economy had punctured the commodity price boom, forcing Brazil, and other commodity countries in the region, to tighten their belts. The prospect of higher US interest rates had threatened to suck international liquidity out of the country. Most of all, Brazil was paying the cost of Ms Rousseff's reportedly mistaken faith during her first term in so-called 'developmentalism'.

This belief in state intervention included artificially low interest rates, fiscal expansionism, limited returns for private investment in much-needed infrastructure, and petrol and electricity prices fixed below cost. Such measures were supposed to boost growth. Instead they resulted in the collapse of business investment. In March 2015, industry confidence fell to its lowest level since 1998.

Despite all these issues, there is one aspect that could help Brazil grow in 2015: the exchange rate. If taking July 2011 as a comparison base, the exchange rate of the Brazilian real versus the US dollar has increased 105 per cent, but the accumulated inflation in the country during this same period has only been 26 per cent.

Source: adapted from the *Financial Times* 04.05.2015.

(a) Explain why raising interest rates would be part of Brazil's efforts to put its house in order. (4 marks)

(b) Explain why corruption might influence investment in Brazil. (4 marks)

(c) Explain how changes in exchange rate could help the Brazilian economy to grow. (4 marks)

(d) Assess why developmentalism could lead to collapse in business investment. (12 marks)

Key terms

Disposable income – the amount of money that a person has left over after they have paid their taxes, national insurance and other deductions.
Exchange rate – the price of one currency against another.
Infrastructure – the basic systems, facilities, services and capital equipment required for a country's economy to function, which might include its roads, communication systems and power services.

Knowledge check

1. What is disposable income?

2. Why is disposable income important when a business considers investment?

3. Explain how ease of doing business affects investment.

4. Show how a country's infrastructure is an important factor in investment.

5. How might political stability affect investment?

6. What impact might exchange rate fluctuation have on investment decisions?

73

Assessment of a country as a production location

Key points

Factors to consider:
1. Costs of production.
2. Skills and availability of labour force.
3. Infrastructure.
4. Location in a trade bloc.
5. Government incentives.
6. Ease of doing business.
7. Political stability.
8. Natural resources.
9. Likely return on investment.

Getting started

In 2014, Jaguar Land Rover (JLR) opened its first factory in China. The factory, based in Jiangsu, was built in partnership with the Chinese company, Chery Automobile. It was expected to produce 130,000 cars a year. Between 2000 and 2014, JLR had seen sales of its vehicles rise rapidly in the Chinese market. By 2014, China accounted for almost a quarter of JLR's sales. Building cars in China will give JLR a number of advantages. The main benefit is that cars produced in the Jiangsu factory will not be subject to Chinese import duties. JLR has invested over £1 billion in the plant.

Source: adapted from the *Financial Times* 21.10.2014

Give reasons why JLR has located a production plant in China. Do you think that other UK businesses will do the same as JLR?

Locating production

A new business organisation, or an existing business that is expanding its operations, will need to consider in which country it wishes to locate production. French car manufacturer Renault, for example, has factories in Morocco, Slovenia, Turkey, Russia, Romania and Argentina. Only about 25 per cent of Renault's cars are now produced in France, its original production location. There are several factors that have to be taken into account when choosing a suitable location. These are discussed in this unit.

According to a 2014 report by global real estate firm Cushman & Wakefield, the most popular location for manufacturing is Malaysia. The report took into account a wide range of location factors when compiling the list shown in Table However, these factors were placed into three key areas and given different weights.

- **Costs (40%)** such as labour, land and energy.
- **Risks (20%)** such as natural disasters, energy and econom
- **Conditions (40%)** such as labour quality, sustainability an access to markets.

Table 1 shows that Asia is the preferred region for locating production facilities, with the top five positions being occupie by Asian countries. Canada achieved its high ranking of sixth due to it being a relatively 'risk-free' country. Malaysia was to because of its low costs and relatively low risks. The UK was ranked 18th.

Table 1 The top ten best countries for a production location, 2

Ranking	Country
1	Malaysia
2	Taiwan
3	South Korea
4	Thailand
5	China
6	Canada
7	Russia
8	Indonesia
9	United States
10	Mexico

Source: adapted from www.cushmanwakefield.co.uk

Costs of production

Many businesses locate factories in countries that have low production costs. By keeping these low, a business may gain a competitive edge in the market. Some of the main production costs, such as labour, energy, raw materials and land, are a lot lower in Asia than in many other parts of the world, hence the high position of five Asian countries in Table 1.

Low wage costs are often an important factor in attracting businesses, particularly for businesses that employ a large labour force. For example, Dyson moved production of their bagless vacuum cleaners from the UK to Malaysia in 2003 where production costs were 30 per cent lower. Dyson said that wages in Malaysia were £3 per hour compared with £9 per hour in the UK. As a result profits more than doubled from £18 million in 2002 to £40 million in 2003.

Labour costs in some countries that were traditionally low, such as China, have started to rise and look set to continue their upward trend. In 2015, the lowest wages were to be found in Burma, Bangladesh and Cambodia, but such locations have a developing infrastructure and political instability. The rising cost of energy and land is having an increasing impact on the location plans of some businesses. For example, energy prices in Europe were rising fast in 2013 and this was beginning to impact on business location decisions.

Skills and availability of labour

When a business is considering locations for its production facilities it is not just the cost of labour that is important, it is also the quality of human capital. A business is not likely to locate a factory in another country only for cheaper labour. A business has to consider whether the labour force in a country has the skills required to maintain quality standards. Businesses cannot afford the consequences of poor-quality work. In some countries where labour is cheaper, workers might be unskilled and poorly educated. Consequently, a business locating production in that country may have to invest substantial sums of money in training, unless all the work on offer is unskilled.

Between 2012 and 2015, a number of businesses moved production back from the Far East to the West in a process called **reshoring**, often because of poor quality control in Far Eastern factories. Figure 2 shows that the main reason for bringing manufacturing back to the UK is to improve the quality of work.

Question 1

In 2014, German company BASF, the world's largest chemical producer, announced that it would be expanding overseas, rather than at home. The reason for this decision was the rising cost of energy in Germany. BASF has production facilities in the US where plunging gas prices made production there very attractive relative to its more expensive European plants. In 2015 natural gas prices in the US were around one quarter of those in Europe, mainly because of contributions made by the growing shale gas industry in the US. Between 2009 and 2014, BASF invested around $5.7 billion in the US and in 2015 was building a formic acid plant in Louisiana. An increasing number of energy-intensive businesses, such as steel and chemical producers, are looking at the US as a possible location for their production. Figure 1 shows the natural gas prices in Japan, Europe and the USA between 2000 and 2014.

Figure 1

Natural gas prices

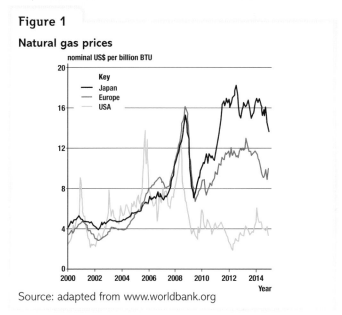

Source: adapted from www.worldbank.org

Source: adapted from the *Financial Times* 21.10.2014, 22.10.2014.

(a) Assess the extent to which production costs have influenced the decision by BASF to expand its production facilities in the USA rather than in Germany.

Figure 2

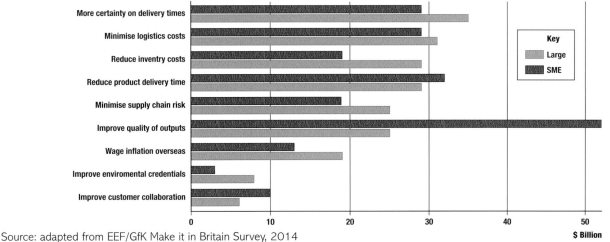

Source: adapted from EEF/GfK Make it in Britain Survey, 2014

Any business that locates production in a particular country will have to ensure that there are enough workers near to the chosen site. The business will also have to consider whether there would be enough workers in the future if the facilities needed to expand. In 2014 it was widely reported that some businesses were beginning to find recruitment difficult in China. For example, Jenlo Apparel Manufacturing, a Canadian-owned clothing company, opened a factory in southern China in 2008 but had recruitment problems because China's 30-year one-child policy means there is now a shortage of workers. In addition, economic commentators noted that increasingly workers did not want to work in factories, nor did they want to work for exporters because the quality standards are more challenging than those for goods produced for the domestic market.

Infrastructure

When considering a suitable country for a location, the quality of infrastructure is important. In some countries the infrastructure might be poor. In some developing countries, for example, where labour might be cheap, the quality of infrastructure might be inadequate to support a large production facility. Any of the following factors might be encountered.

- Roads might be poorly constructed and inadequately maintained. In some countries they may be unsealed. This slows down the transportation of finished goods to customers, and raw materials and components to the site from suppliers. Some areas might be prone to natural disasters, such as flooding, which may cause a break in the supply of vital components, for example.
- Increasingly, access to good broadband networks is of vital importance to businesses when considering locations for production. Some countries may still be developing their broadband networks, while other networks might be slow and unreliable.
- Some countries may not have modern airports and ports. This might make it difficult for business personnel to travel to and from production facilities and to ship goods out of the country.
- Railway networks may be undeveloped or non-existent. This might be a problem if bulky or heavy goods need to be transported in large quantities.
- There may be a lack of investment in education, which can affect the quality of human capital and may discourage managers and other senior staff from locating near to the site. Families moving to the location would desire good-quality schools for their children.
- There may be a difference in the quality of hospitals. Again this may discourage senior employees from moving away from their home country. The quality of health care generally might also impact on the quality of human capital.
- A lack of commercial services and suppliers may discourage a business from locating in some countries. Businesses may need access to printers, IT support, bankers, insurance providers, advertising agencies, cleaners, maintenance companies and manufacturers of components. Some countries cannot guarantee such facilities.

Generally, before locating a factory overseas, a business will need to identify its infrastructure needs and determine whether a particular country is able to meet them.

Location in a trade bloc

Some businesses locate production facilities in certain countries to avoid trade barriers, such as tariffs and quotas. This can be achieved by siting a plant inside a **trade bloc**. Trading blocs are discussed in detail in Unit 70. The output of a business located inside a trade bloc will be free from trade barriers when sold to any member of that bloc. For example, one of the reasons why Japanese car manufacturers, such as Nissan, Honda and Toyota, have located car factories in the UK is to avoid EU trade barriers. Cars made in the UK, even though the business owners are Japanese, can be sold in France, Germany, Italy and all other EU member countries without attracting tariffs. This makes the cars cheaper when sold in these countries.

Government incentives

Governments may be able to influence the location of business. They are usually keen to attract foreign direct investment (FDI) because of the benefits it brings, such as income and employment. They can do this by providing incentives to businesses to locate their production facilities in their country. Generally, governments may offer financial incentives, such as tax breaks, lower rates of company tax, interest-free loans, cheap land and preferential rates on business premises. The UK, which has the highest level of FDI in Europe, offers foreign businesses a wide range of guidance and support services. UK Trade & Investment (UKTI), a government department responsible for helping UK businesses to establish links abroad, is also tasked with attracting FDI. It offers a range of specialist advisory services to businesses that are considering the UK as a possible location. For example, UKTI provides quite detailed industry-based information to foreign investors. Publications are available for industries, such as aerospace, communications, financial services, nuclear power, food and drink, railways, creative industries, and electronics and IT hardware. In addition to the printed information foreign businesses can get specialist advice direct from industry experts.

Tax regimes are very important to businesses when considering location. The UK government recognised this and in April 2015 lowered the rate of corporation tax to just 20 per cent. This is the lowest rate in the whole of the G20 (the 20 most advanced economies in the world).

Financial incentives may also be offered to businesses locating in developing countries. For example, governments in Kenya, Tanzania, Uganda and Rwanda in East Africa have offered a wide range of tax incentives. Examples include corporation tax holidays and reductions in standard taxes, such as VAT and customs duties.

Ease of doing business

When choosing a suitable location the commercial environment is a very important consideration. This is often referred to as the 'ease of doing business'. It is a lot easier to do business in some countries than others. It is important to choose a location where it is relatively easy to do business because trading restrictions and additional costs can be both frustrating and expensive for businesses. The 'ease of doing business' may depend on factors like the following.

- The ease with which businesses can be started and closed down.
- The efficiency with which contracts are enforced.
- The amount of bureaucracy, e.g. the ease with which permits can be obtained for construction projects.
- The availability of trade credit.
- The efficiency of tax collection.
- The ease of resolving insolvency.

Table 2 shows the top ten easiest places in the world to do business in 2015. Singapore is ranked number one while the UK is ranked number eight. The UK scores particularly well when it comes to protecting minority investors in business. These rankings are likely to provide a very useful guide to businesses looking for a suitable overseas location. They will also provide some incentive to governments to introduce measures that might improve their ranking – that is if the government is concerned about flows of FDI into the country.

Political stability

Some countries are politically unstable. This might mean that it is too dangerous to do business in such countries. Alternatively, the exposure to possible financial loss might be far too high due to political tensions. Examples of 'hotspots' that might be avoided by foreign businesses looking for an overseas location include, for example, Libya, Yemen, Ukraine, Syria, Pakistan, Iraq, Afghanistan, Somalia and parts of Latin America, to name but a few.

One of the problems in some of these countries is the risk of kidnapping. It is widely reported that Western business people are common targets for kidnappers aiming to extract ransoms from employers and relatives. Latin America is reported as one of the most dangerous places for kidnapping, with Mexico reported as the most dangerous of all. Statistics on kidnapping are not reliable, but reports estimate them to be between 5,000 and 10,000 per year.

In some countries political systems are corrupt and bribery is commonly reported as an accepted feature of 'doing business'. Most Western businesses are likely to avoid countries where this is the case. However, some may try to overcome these obstacles.

Finally, businesses may avoid locating operations in some countries due to their human rights records. One of the main reasons for this is to avoid consumer boycotts or shareholder disapproval.

Natural resources

Some types of business activity require large quantities of natural resources. The obvious example is mining. Mines can only be sunk in locations where there are proven mineral deposits. Consequently, mining companies can only choose locations where these deposits exist. Up until 2014, when commodity prices were booming, Africa attracted a number of mining companies. For example, Rio Tinto acquired a coal mining project in Mozambique for $2.7 billion in 2011. However, following a fall in commodity prices even Africa suffered a drop in foreign business interests.

Businesses that use substantial natural resources in their production processes are also likely to set up in proximity to their sources. For example, steel producers may locate production plants near iron ore mines or coal mines. ArcelorMittal, the Luxembourg-based multinational steel producer, has operations in more than 60 countries around the world. It is the largest steel company operating in South Africa, where it has several mines and steel works producing long and flat steel for a range of different industries. Steel producers are keen to locate close to mines as the transportation of iron ore and coke can be very expensive because these materials are bulky and heavy.

Question 2

Singapore claims to have an excellent infrastructure, transparent laws, a sound economy and convenient online portals. In 2015 it was ranked the 'easiest place in the world to do business' by a World Bank survey.

(a) Businesses prefer to locate operations where it is 'easy to do business'. Explain what this might mean.

(b) Assess the possible attractions of Singapore to a business looking for a suitable overseas location.

Table 2 Ease of doing business – top ten world rankings, 2015 (from 189 countries)

	Singapore	New Zealand	Hong Kong	Denmark	Korea	Norway	US	UK	Finland	Australia
Ranking	1	2	3	4	5	6	7	8	9	10
Starting a business	6	1	8	25	17	22	46	45	27	7
Dealing with construction permits	2	13	1	5	12	27	41	17	33	19
Getting electricity	11	48	13	14	1	25	61	70	33	55
Registering property	24	2	96	8	79	5	29	68	38	53
Getting credit	17	1	23	23	36	61	2	17	36	4
Protecting minority investors	3	1	2	17	21	12	25	4	76	71
Paying taxes	5	22	4	12	25	15	47	16	21	39
Trading across borders	1	27	2	7	3	24	16	15	14	49
Enforcing contracts	1	9	6	34	4	8	41	36	17	12
Resolving insolvency	19	28	25	9	5	8	4	13	1	14

Source: www.doingbusiness.org, World Bank Group

Likely return on investment

Businesses looking for locations are likely to consider a number of different options before making their final decision. Many of the factors above are likely to be taken into account, depending on the nature of the industry in which a business operates. During the decision-making process SWOT analysis and PESTLE analysis can help to assess the suitability of different locations. Also, quantitative techniques might be used to help make the final location decision. Quantitative techniques can aid evaluation of the financial costs and benefits of investing in particular locations.

Quantitative methods

Table 3 shows two possible sites for a business which is considering relocating its premises. It gives the initial cost of the move and then the cost savings to be made in each year compared with the existing site. Three investment appraisal methods can be used to show which, if any, site should be chosen. It is assumed that at the end of five years, the business will be relocating again. So no cost savings will be taken into account after the end of five years.

Payback method: With the payback method, the business calculates how long it will take to recoup the initial investment. In location A, the initial cost is £12 million and with annual savings (the equivalent of increased cash flows) of £3 million, the investment will be recouped in 4 years. With location B, the initial cost is higher at £15 million, but the cost savings are £5 million per year. The result is that the investment will be recouped in 3 years. So on the payback method, location B is the preferred location.

Average rate of return (ARR): With the average annual rate of return method, the net return is divided by the initial investment and expressed as a percentage. With location A, there will be a total cost saving (i.e. increased cash flow) over 5 years of £15 million. With an initial cost of £12 million, this gives a return of £3 million (£15 million − £12 million). So the ARR is [(£3 million ÷ £15 million) ÷ 5 years] × 100 per cent, which is 4 per cent. With location B, the cost saving is £25 million over 5 years with an initial cost of £15 million. So the ARR is [(£10 million ÷ £25 million) ÷ 5 years] × 100 per cent, which is 8 per cent. On the average rate of return method, location B is also the preferred location.

Discounted cash flow: With discounted cash flow, the value of future cash flows must be discounted back to the present. The important point about discounted cash flow is that, just as money invested today will grow in value because of compound interest, so the reverse is true: the value of cash available in the future is worth less today. In Table 4, the cost savings (or net cash flows) have been discounted back assuming a discount rate of 15 per cent. The net present

value of the cost savings falls the further into the future it occurs. When it is totalled up, the net present value of the cost savings at location A don't cover the initial investment needed. So moving to location A is unprofitable at this rate of discount. On the other hand, moving to location B shows a positive net cash flow. The cost savings outweigh the initial cost of the investment by £1.9 million. So this would suggest that the company should move to location B. Whatever the rate of discount used, location B would always be preferred over location A. However, if the rate of discount were much higher than 15 per cent, the discounted cash-flow technique would suggest that even location B would give overall negative cash flows and therefore moving would not be profitable.

Table 3 Initial costs and cost savings of two new locations

	£ million	
	Location A	Location B
Initial cost	12	15
Annual cost savings/increased cash flow		
Year 1	3	5
Year 2	3	5
Year 3	3	5
Year 4	3	5
Year 5	3	5

Table 4 Initial costs and cost savings of two new locations discounted at 15 per cent

	£ million				
	Location A £ millions	Location B £ millions	Discount table 15%	Location A £ millions	Location B £ millions
Initial cost	12	15	1.00	12.0	15.0
Annual cost savings/ increased cash flow					
Year 1	3	5	0.87	2.6	4.4
Year 2	3	5	0.76	2.3	3.8
Year 3	3	5	0.66	2.0	3.3
Year 4	3	5	0.57	1.7	2.9
Year 5	3	5	0.50	1.5	2.5
Total cost savings	15	25		10.1	16.9
Net cash flow	3	10		−1.9	1.9

Exam tip

When answering questions on assessing countries as business or production locations, you need to remember that you are not discussing assessment of a country as a market in the context of exporting, for example. This is dealt with in Unit 72. There is quite a difference between selling in different countries and setting up factories in different countries. A huge financial commitment is necessary when setting up production plants in different countries. There can be far more at stake.

Case study

NEW WING FOOTWEAR

Frank Leung owns New Wing Footwear, a manufacturer of women's footwear. In 2011, he began a search for a new manufacturing base. It was reported that production at his factory in Dongguan in South China was becoming too expensive. Wages were rising every year and profit margins were being squeezed. The value of the yuan renminbi (the Chinese currency) had also been rising, which was making his shoes more expensive for buyers overseas. As a result of these factors he had been forced to reduce his workforce from 8,000 to 3,000 in just three years.

During his search Mr Leung looked at Bangladesh. Here labour was much cheaper – about 20 to 30 per cent the cost of Chinese labour. Also, the normal working week in Bangladesh was 48 hours compared to 40 hours in China. The Bangladeshi government was also offering a ten-year tax holiday to businesses locating in the country. However, Mr Leung was concerned by the congestion in the city of Dhaka and was also worried about the intermittent power supply. He said that most factories had to buy their own power generators.

Mr Leung also travelled to Addis Ababa. Here wages were even lower than in Bangladesh. However, he was concerned about the location in relationship to the lack of infrastructure. Although there was much less congestion in the country, there was a lack of support for his industry. For

example, there were no suitable suppliers of shoe soles and cardboard. A trip to India also ended in frustration for Mr Leung. He visited Chennai but was upset by the poverty in the area.

Other business people have looked to move their factories away from China. For example, David Lui, the owner of a handbag manufacturer, was reported as visiting Vietnam, but the supplier networks and rates of productivity were better in China. Mr Lui has also experienced a squeeze in profit margins, although some of the rising costs of manufacturing in China were reported to have been passed on to his European customers.

The increase in wages in China is likely to continue because the government wants to double workers' wages over a ten-year period by raising the national minimum wage. However, despite this, many Chinese business owners are reported as remaining in China for the time being. China has a huge workforce with higher productivity and far superior ports and highways compared with many other developing countries.

Source: adapted from the *Financial Times* 08.11.2011. All rights reserved.

(a) Explain one way in which governments can influence business location overseas. (4 marks)

(b) Evaluate the factors that businesses like New Wing Footwear take into account when assessing a country as a production location. (20 marks)

Links 🔗

The information in this unit may be of use when demonstrating your synoptic skills when answering questions on global competitiveness. For example, you could explain how government incentives to locate in a particular country could lower costs and give a business a competitive edge. Other units that link effectively to this unit include Production, productivity and efficiency (Unit 37), Economic influences (Unit 41), SWOT analysis (Unit 46), Impact of external influences (Unit 47), Investment appraisal (Unit 53), Business ethics (Unit 59), Protectionism (Unit 69), Trading blocs (Unit 70) and The impact of MNCs (Unit 79).

Key terms

Reshoring – bringing production back home after using foreign production facilities for a period of time.
Trade bloc – a group of countries situated in the same region that join together and enjoy trade free of tariffs, quotas and other forms of trade barrier.

Knowledge check

1. Why are labour costs in China starting to rise?
2. For which industries are energy costs likely to be important when looking for an overseas location?
3. Explain why the quality of human capital in a potential location might be important to a business looking for a new site.
4. How might the quality of a nation's infrastructure be an important factor in factory location?
5. What sort of incentives might a government offer to encourage a business to locate a site in its country?
6. What is meant by the 'ease of doing business' when looking for a suitable country to locate production?
7. Why is political stability an important issue when locating plants overseas?
8. For which types of industry is the availability of natural resources an important location factor?
9. State three quantitative methods that might be used when choosing production locations abroad.
10. What is the main advantage of using quantitative methods when making a location decision?

74

Reasons for global mergers or joint ventures

Key points

1. Spreading risk over different countries/regions.
2. Entering new markets/trade blocs.
3. Acquiring national/international brand names/patents.
4. Securing resources/supplies.
5. Maintaining/increasing global competitiveness.

Getting started

The Brazilian aircraft manufacturer, Embraer, has pursued a strategy of growth through acquisitions. It began as a maker of military aircraft and then moved into the small private and commercial plane sector. It was privatised in 1994, and entered into a series of strategic alliances in order to gain access to technology, resources and brand recognition. Next, it began to base production facilities in other countries, including China, France, the USA and Portugal. By 2012, 90 per cent of its global sales were outside of Brazil.

Source: adapted from the *Financial Times* 22.10.2013

Why do you think acquiring or allying with other firms was important to Embraer? What benefits do you think they gained from becoming an international company? What risks do you think were involved?

Reasons why businesses join together

As discussed in Unit 66 (see also Units 14 and 63), there are many reasons why a firm might wish to make a direct equity investment in another country. Exporting may not make sense if, for instance, other countries can produce the product or service more cheaply. Arrangements such as **licensing** or **franchising** may not make commercial sense either.

Licensing: A firm enters into a licensing contract with another firm to use its brand, intellectual property or to produce its product or service in return for a fee. For example, Disney licenses its brand name for merchandise and inventors license their patents to manufacturers.

Franchising: Franchising involves a long-term co-operative relationship whereby one party, the franchisor, contracts with another, the franchisee, to run its business. McDonald's is a well-known example of a franchise.

Rather than licensing or franchising, firms may opt for joint ventures or cross-border mergers and acquisitions. In fact, these two forms of investment are the main foreign investment routes for most international companies.

Table 1 shows the number of cross-border sales and purchases of companies in 2014. There are many reasons why cross-border deals are completed, and some of these are explained below. However, it is important to remember that every investment decision is specific to the firms involved and the particular circumstances that each firm faces. Moreover, in the decision-making process, the personal role that senior managers play also needs to be considered, taking into account factors of confidence or uncertainty.

Table 1 Numbers of cross-border mergers and acquisitions by country in 2014

Country (2014)	As seller	As purchaser
Australia	355	244
Brazil	219	28
Canada	512	573
China	337	331
France	422	481
Germany	616	423
Hong Kong	145	222
India	225	130
Indonesia	68	18
Ireland (Republic)	96	92
Italy	240	118
Japan	179	440
Malaysia	91	98
Mexico	82	48
The Netherlands	219	236
Nigeria	20	10
Poland	156	63
Russia	302	135
Singapore	135	233
South Africa	71	71
South Korea	119	76
Turkey	95	17
UK	879	859
US	1545	2061

Source: adapted from www.unctad.org

With this in mind, the rest of the unit looks at some of the reasons why acquiring another firm or arranging a joint venture might be a sensible move. Often these reasons overlap, for instance the need to spread risks will be connected to a desire to enter a new market or trade bloc. Further, what is often referred to as a merger is actually a takeover or acquisition, though sometimes this is not obvious until well after an agreement is completed.

Spreading risk over different countries or regions

During economic downturns, even companies with strong balance sheets can face serious difficulties, as outlined in Unit 36. Thus it makes sense to try and insulate the firm from the consequences of a downturn or crisis by locating in markets where these risks are less likely to occur – or at least less likely to occur at the same time as they occur in the home market.

For example, Pingo Doce, founded in 1980, but with its origins going back two hundred years, is a Portuguese no-frills supermarket chain. It began its expansion in the 1990s in order to diversify away from the Portuguese market. Though its first venture in Brazil failed, its second one in Poland succeeded. Instead of building huge stores like Tesco and Carrefour, it chose to focus on small, local shops, and bought the discount chain Biedronka, which is now Poland's biggest food retailer. In 2012, Pingo Doce began trying to diversify away from the struggling European market and into the growth markets of Latin America.

Entering new markets and trade blocs

Instead of growing organically, businesses can take a shorter route to international growth through mergers and acquisitions. For example, Tata Motors purchased Jaguar Land Rover from the Ford Motor Company. This route appears increasingly popular. From Figure 1, we can see how investment has been increasingly flowing from developing and transition economies. China, Thailand, Mexico and India are leading this trend.

Equally, firms in maturing industries may find that the only way that they can grow is through merging with or acquiring firms in other markets. For example, the international market for beer is quite mature, with slow growth in the most developed markets. Consequently, in a quest for new markets and for economies of scale, there have been many cross-border mergers in the last decade. As a result, four big brewers (AB-InBev; SABMiller; Heineken and Carlsberg) now have over 50 per cent of the global market by volume.

Firms may want to tap into markets that are growing, but they do not always find it easy to gain access. For example, the Chinese auto firm Shanghai Automotive Industry Corporation (SAIC) operates factories with Volkswagen (VW) and General Motors (GM). This long-running joint venture began solely because of limits that the Chinese government placed upon foreign firms entering the Chinese market. In order to gain access to the billions of Chinese consumers, VW and GM had to work with SAIC through a joint-venture arrangement. VW and GM count the agreement as a success and much of SAIC's profits come from the joint venture. Some commentators feel that SAIC would benefit from developing further their own technology and capabilities.

Acquiring national and international brand names or patents

A business may want to become a global player in the international market. However, it may lack brand recognition or a patent that prevents other businesses from copying its product or producing similar products. By purchasing a business or a product with a strong brand name, it could obtain both quickly.

Question 1

In 2004, Lenovo, a Chinese firm listed in Hong Kong, had 27 per cent of its home market and dreamt of being a big player on the global market. It decided on two possible routes: either creating a foreign subsidiary or buying an existing global player. Since it had little experience of foreign markets itself, and didn't have any distribution channels or a well-recognised brand, it chose to acquire another firm.

In 2005, it bought the personal computer business of IBM, the iconic American computer giant, for £1.75 billion. With the purchase, the company gained instant presence outside of China, access to IBM's markets and sales channels, to its technology, and its well-known 'ThinkPad' and 'ThinkCentre' brands. It also found cost savings through economies of scale and many experienced researchers, technicians and managers. Lenovo overnight became one of the largest computer makers in the world. The deal was also good for IBM as its PC division had been losing money for some time. Some experts believe that Lenovo brought a fresh outlook as well as a young, ambitious workforce to inject new thinking into the established computer firm.

Sources: adapted from the *Financial Times* 02.11.2007.

(a) Explain the factors that Lenovo would have taken into account in their decision to create a foreign subsidiary or buy an existing global player.

(b) Why do you think Lenovo succeeded where IBM had seemed to struggle?

Using mergers, acquisitions and joint ventures is quite an effective way to gain a reputational foothold or to get access to intellectual property. It can have a number of benefits for a business.

- There is likely to be strong brand recognition.
- There will be brand loyalty.
- It limits competition for the product.
- A business will not face the high risk, cost and uncertainty of launching a new product.

It is important to realise how easily a brand can be destroyed if care is not taken post-merger to ensure that employee morale and customer satisfaction are looked after. It may be that the strongest brand is adopted over the weakest one, or some sort of portfolio of brands can be created as part of a differentiation strategy.

Gaining access to intellectual property

Developing intellectual property internally, through in-house research and development, can take a very long time and involve a lot of financial risk. Intellectual property involves a creation of the mind, such as an invention, literary work or artwork, that the law protects from unauthorised use by others. This protection occurs through such legal mechanisms as:

- patents for inventions
- copyrights for literary works or computer programs
- trademarks for brand names or designs.

Since establishing intellectual property can be expensive, it is often easier to gain access to intellectual property by buying it in an acquisition or through a joint-venture agreement. Table 2 shows some examples of acquisitions in agriculture and biotechnology, all of which were completed in order to acquire scale in intellectual property.

Table 2 Mergers and acquisitions in agriculture and biotechnology

Year	Companies	Merged company
1996	Ciba and Sandoz	Novartis
1997, 1999	Zeneca, Astra and Mogen	Zeneca Agrochemicals
2000	Novartis Agri and Zeneca Agro	Syngenta

Securing resources or supplies

Firms may often choose to merge with another firm to secure resources or supplies further back in the supply chain. This is known as backward vertical integration (see Unit 49). A firm may want, or even need, to merge with another firm because:

- the resources used in the creation of its product or service are scarce or hard to acquire, and it needs to ensure reliable sourcing
- it needs to ensure that the inputs are of a suitable quality or price.

For example, Starbucks' rapid international expansion, coupled with several disease threats to coffee plants, has meant that it faces intense competition for supplies of high-quality coffee beans. In order to help secure a reliable supply of the best coffee beans, it bought its own coffee farm in Costa Rica.

Maintaining or increasing global competitiveness

Merging or joining another firm can provide bigger markets, scale and scope economies and cost savings. This in turn could make the firm much more competitive in terms of its pricing power over customers and suppliers. Where there is a lot of competition in the market, or where a firm is hoping to become a dominant player on a global scale, merging or acquiring another firm can be part of a successful strategy.

For example, a proposed merger between Applied Materials and Tokyo Electron came down to a need for scale. There is an increasing demand for computer chips, but the machines that make the chips are extremely expensive. This merger gives the two firms a quarter of the market and strengthens their hand against their customers (Intel, Samsung, Taiwan Semiconductor). In summary, the objective of the merger was to acquire scale and cut costs, thereby reducing downward pressure on prices. In turn this would allow for long-term planning (research and development is hugely expensive).

Alternatively, two firms can cross-sell product ranges or services, thereby increasing overall sales and perhaps lowering internal costs. For example, mergers of banks or financial services firms have occurred in order to provide one contact point for customers to a range of financial services products.

Likewise, engaging in a geographically diverse collaboration can improve a firm's tax position. For instance, a firm may select a merger partner that is located in a country where the overall tax take is lower. The merged firm can then relocate its headquarters to the lower tax venue in order to save money. Such moves are a source of considerable political controversy, but there is little question that a firm, where it can do so legally and ethically, will want to minimise its overall taxation. The money saved from lower tax bills can be used to invest and to further improve the firm's competitive position.

In 2014, Facebook spent $22 billion on buying WhatsApp, a mobile messaging service. WhatsApp had made $10.2 million the year before, and was reported as loss-making. So why would Facebook want to buy the firm and pay that much for it? Partly it may have been to eliminate a competitor in the market, but equally important was that WhatsApp is a resource, with a superior form of messaging. However, another important reason for such a takeover might be defensive: if Facebook hadn't bought it, one of its competitors might have. Time will tell how Facebook's purchase of WhatsApp develops commercially or whether it may have also been more of a defensive purchase.

Nevertheless, there is an old saying: 'Two dogs do not make a tiger'. Put another way, a purchase might turn out to be mistaken and waste money, but at its worst it might severely impact on a firm's competitiveness.

Exam tip

You may be asked to 'assess' or 'evaluate' in an exam question about global mergers and joint ventures. Both of these require you to consider a variety of factors and then make a judgement. For example, you may be asked to evaluate the success of a global merger or joint venture. In this case you could make a judgement about whether the merger has been a success or failure based on data provided about the businesses involved. You might evaluate whether another form of merger or joint venture might have been more successful, if appropriate data is provided. Alternatively, you may be asked to assess the reasons for a merger or joint venture. In this case you could consider the main influences from data provided and then make a judgement about the most important influence or influences, or those that have had the greatest effect. You might also be asked to assess the costs and benefits of a particular type of merger or joint venture. In this case you could consider the main costs and benefits to the firm or firms involved, make a judgement on which have had the most effect and then indicate whether the costs would outweigh the benefits.

Thinking bigger

When German Daimler (the makers of Mercedes-Benz) merged with American company Chrysler in the late 1990s, it was called a 'merger of equals'. Daimler was reported as paying $37 billion for Chrysler. A few years later it was reported as a merger that struggled. The company cultures were different and it was reported that the two divisions started to battle with each other.

Differences between the companies included their level of formality, philosophy on issues such as expenses, and operating styles. The German culture became dominant. Employee satisfaction at Chrysler dropped and by 2000 major losses were projected and layoffs began. In 2007, it was reported that Daimler sold Chrysler for $6 billion – $31 billion less than they had paid out. This 'failed' merger demonstrates that mergers need to do more than make business sense. A range of dynamics will influence success.

You could use this information in a variety of ways. Obviously, it can be used when answering questions on mergers. But it might also be useful when discussing motivation, business efficiency, and the causes and effects of change.

Source: www.economist.com

Question 2

In April 2015 it was announced that Royal Dutch Shell had agreed to buy the British oil and gas exploration firm BG Group in a deal that valued the business at £47 billion. The deal could be one of the biggest of 2015, and could produce a company with a value of over £200 billion. In 2015, BG was the UK's third largest energy company and in spring 2015 employed 5,200 people. It was created in 1997 when British Gas was demerged into two separate companies: BG and Centrica.

Investors received a 50 per cent premium on BG April 2015 share prices. Shell said the deal would add 25 per cent to its proven oil and gas reserves and 20 per cent to production capacity, particularly in Australia's liquid natural gas market and deep water exploration off the Brazilian coast. Commentators have pointed out that there is great uncertainty for the industry as oil prices fell by 50 per cent in late 2014 to spring 2015. BG warned in early 2015 that they had written down the value of their assests by £6 billion and Shell by £10 billion.

The industry had been expecting such a tie-up but this defensive merger may to lead to job cuts. In 2015, it was reported that Shell took on more debt to finance the deal which will put pressure on dividends. BG made a loss in 2014 and reportedly struggled in some of its markets. Some say that Shell has estimated that buying access to new reserves is quicker than finding them itself. In 2015, BG was reported as one of the biggest suppliers of natural gas to China, which Shell has found attractive. Some believe that there will be further mergers and that BP could be a target from a predator.

Source: adapted from the *Financial Times*, 08.04.2015, 30.04.2015. All rights reserved.

(a) In what ways do you think that this defensive merger makes sense for Royal Dutch Shell?

(b) Why might commentators think that there might be further mergers in the industry?

Links

There are a variety of reasons for mergers and joint ventures. To demonstrate your synoptic skills, you could use information from other units to support your arguments about the main reasons for mergers and takeovers in a global context. This could include using information about the reasons why businesses want to invest in other countries (Unit 68), how mergers can change and improve channels of distribution (Unit 12), how entering new markets through mergers can help a business overcome trading blocs (Unit 70), how mergers might improve marketing globally (Unit 76), global competitiveness (Unit 75) or the effect on economies of scale (Unit 48). The effect that mergers and joint ventures might have on globalisation could be considered when answering questions in Unit 68 or when considering types of business growth (Unit 49).

Key terms

Franchising – establishing a long-term co-operative relationship whereby one party, the franchisor, contracts with another, the franchisee, to run its business. McDonald's is a well-known example of a franchise.

Intellectual property – a product that is a creation of the mind, such as an invention, literary work or artwork, that the law protects from unauthorised use by others. Types include patents, copyrights and trademarks.

Licensing – a contract with another firm to use its intellectual property or to produce its product or service in return for a fee.

Knowledge check

1. Why might firms choose to join together?
2. What benefits are there to a business of merging?
3. Briefly explain how an acquisition is carried out.
4. What is the difference between a joint venture and a merger?
5. Explain why it often makes more sense for businesses to acquire intellectual property rather than developing it themselves.
6. Explain how mergers can lead to increasing competiveness.

Case study

CEMENT AND CEMEX

The cement industry has been relatively mature for some time, so one of the few ways of staying competitive is to ensure that costs are kept low. However, inefficient plants and transport costs are particular problems for firms making cement. Consequently, cement firms must continuously look for scale economies in their path to growth. Another issue for such firms is that demand for their products tends to be cyclical. That is, demand for cement goes up and down in line with GDP and other economic factors. Thus, in order to remain competitive, the industry needs to consolidate in order to gain economies of scale and limit the risks from an economic downturn in key markets.

By 2000, global cement production involved just seven big firms, but the consolidation was continuing. Firms merged or acquired other firms in order to achieve scale, expand cash flow, enter new markets or spread their risks. During this period, the Mexican firm CEMEX, through a strategy of growth through acquisitions, became one of the main global cement companies. Rather than export or build its own

factories in new markets, it bought cement firms in the US, Spain, Venezuela, Columbia and throughout Latin America. Later, it expanded into South East Asia.

CEMEX's expansion strategy allowed it to lower its dependence upon the Mexican market while growing internationally. However, this strategy was not without risk, and CEMEX has faced many issues in its various markets. As a result of the 2008 downturn, many countries built less property and roads, and therefore required less cement. Consequently, CEMEX experienced a stagnation in sales, alongside debt from its acquisitions.

Source: adapted from the *Financial Times* 22.10.2012.

Q

(a) Explain one reason why mature industries such as cement need to worry about their costs. (4 marks)

(b) Assess the potential costs and benefits of CEMEX's strategy of 'growth through acquisitions'. (10 marks)

75 Global competitiveness

Key points

1. The impact of movements in exchange rates.
2. Competitive advantage through:
   - cost competitiveness
   - differentiation.
3. Skill shortages and their impact on international competitiveness.

Getting started

The Gherkin is one of the world's most instantly recognisable buildings and is a symbol of the global dominance of London's financial district. In April 2014, it was put up for sale by receivers Deloitte after they were called in by its creditors, a consortium of German banks. This was no ordinary victim of the credit crunch. The Gherkin was in good shape and fully let with its original tenant, Swiss Re, the global insurance group, still in occupation and a further 17 years on its lease. Experts say that it is a good building with a bad finance deal.

As the global financial crisis took hold in 2007–2008, investors around the world sought safety in the Swiss franc, sending its value soaring. The sudden currency appreciation caught the Gherkin's new owner unawares as they had borrowed in Swiss francs. They could have survived a 10–15 per cent fluctuation, but nobody expected a 60 per cent appreciation. Critics suggested that they may have struggled from trying to beat the market by taking on foreign exchange risk. The losses amounted to £240 million and falling property prices meant that the value of the Gherkin fell to £480 million. The owners had paid £600 million, and defaulted on their loans.

Source: adapted from the *Financial Times* 01.08.2014.
All rights reserved.

Describe the impact of these events. Could they have been predicted? What possible measures might businesses take to prepare for such events?

Achieving global competitiveness

Being multinational can help an enterprise to develop competitive advantages that are not open to single-nation companies. Multinational corporations (MNCs) often benefit from the following.

- Global operations can bring much bigger economies of scale.
- Global sourcing can give firms more scope to find the best-quality sources at the right prices.
- Global operations allow companies to get closer to their international customers, both before and after sales.
- MNCs can tap into a much bigger range of knowledge and scope for innovation.
- MNCs can diversify risk.

However, global competitiveness is not just something that firms seek strategically. As examined below, the competitiveness of a firm is also affected through the global market in which it operates.

Effect of exchange rate fluctuations on business

The exchange rate between currencies is important for businesses that export and import goods and services. A depreciation in the exchange rate will make exports cheaper and so exporters could benefit. An appreciation will make exports more expensive and will have an impact on the competitiveness of exporting firms.

Table 1 Exchange rate of GBP to Yen

Year	GDP to Yen exchange rate
4/1/2011	128
2/1/2012	119
2/1/2013	141
3/1/2014	172
3/1/2015	184

Imagine a British firm that makes car parts for the automotive industry. Suppose a particular car part costs £90 to make in its factory in Sunderland and it then sells for £100 in the UK.

In 2011, this component, if exported and bought by a Japanese automaker, would cost 12,800 Yen. However, every year thereafter more yen are needed to obtain one pound, so that by 2015, this same car part would cost 18,400 Yen to buy. The Japanese manufacturers now find the British product much more expensive, and may need to buy from elsewhere in order to control their costs. The British firm must therefore decide how to keep its product competitive so that its customers in Japan continue to buy it. It could keep its price the same and ensure that its quality remains an advantage, even though the high price may cost it sales. Or it could lower the price for the Japanese market, and make a smaller profit margin.

The appreciation in the pound may have advantages for the manufacturer, however. The rising buying power of the pound might allow it to pay a lower price for the raw materials to make its products. This could help it to lower its costs from £90 thereby giving it room to lower prices. It may then be able to maintain its profit margin. Of course, where the pound depreciates, the outcomes above are reversed: the demand for the manufacturer's products may increase, but so might also the costs of making them. It is therefore essential that a business considers all of the potential implications of changing exchange rates upon its current and future competitiveness.

The significance of changes in the exchange rate on business

Elasticity of demand: If there is a depreciation in the value of the pound the effect it will have on a business and its products depends on price elasticity of demand. If UK businesses sell goods where demand is price inelastic, then the fall in price would have only a relatively small increase in demand. If demand for exports is price elastic, then there will be a bigger percentage increase in demand. The evidence is that the demand for British exports tends to be price inelastic, which is good news for exporters if there is appreciation, but bad news if there is depreciation.

Economic growth in other countries: In 2009/10 the pound depreciated in value, but the EU economy in particular was in recession and so the demand for UK exports was weak.

Significance of the cause of the fluctuation in exchange rate: If there is an appreciation in the pound because there have been improvements in efficiency and productivity, then businesses will be able to absorb the stronger pound more easily. However, if the pound rises due to speculation or due to weaknesses in other countries, then businesses could be uncompetitive because the rise in the pound is not related to either improved competiveness or productivity.

Fixed contracts

Many businesses use fixed contracts to counter fluctuations in the exchange rate. This means that temporary changes in the exchange rate will have a smaller impact. The price of buying raw materials is often set 12 to 18 months in the future. Exporters may also use future options to hedge against dramatic changes in the exchange rate. It is these fixed contracts that help to lessen the uncertainty around exchange rate fluctuations. It also means that there are time lags between changes in exchange rates and the impact on business.

Economic risk

As covered in Unit 72, firms trading internationally are almost always exposed to movements in exchange rates. Risks associated with this come in several forms. The most serious is the long-term risk that a strategy of locating in a low-cost production area is undermined by the appreciation of the target country's currency. For example, in the 1990s many firms built factories in China where the costs of production were low and cost savings could therefore be made. These savings depended, at least in part, on the Chinese government's policy of pegging its currency to the US dollar. Over time, for a variety of political reasons, this peg has relaxed and the yuan has steadily appreciated. This has eroded these low-cost advantages.

The risk described above is known as **economic risk**, which is defined as a risk that future cash flows will change due to unexpected exchange rate fluctuations. This is one of the gravest financial risks facing an international firm because future cash flows form the basis of a business's overall value. Consequently, managing economic risk requires careful analysis of the political, regulatory and cultural environments affecting the currency over time.

For example, the US dollar is the most important international currency. Besides having one of the largest economies in the world, the dollar has a role in almost every international transaction, either directly or indirectly. As a consequence, any movement in the dollar will have an impact on international trade

At the start of 2015, with the US economy recovering and interest rates likely to rise, the dollar looked set to appreciate against most other currencies. The areas that are most likely to feel the impact of any rise in the dollar are the emerging market economies. This is because many companies from the developing world take out loans in dollars.

For example, Petrobras, the Brazilian state-owned oil company, issued billions in bonds that were denominated in dollars. With falling energy prices, Petrobras is reportedly not making as much income as it expected when it took on the debt and is now finding it hard to repay it. It will find it harder still if the dollar continues to appreciate against its home currency, the real

---

Question 1

Walkmill Industries is based in Wales and makes specialist monitors used in intensive care facilities in hospitals. One of its major clients is based in South Africa and one of its most successful products sells in the UK for £5,000.

In 2013 the exchange rate was 13.50 rands to the pound.

In 2015 the exchange rate was 18.50 rands to the pound.

(a) Has the pound appreciated or depreciated in value against the South African rand?

(b) Calculate the price the monitor would sell for in South Africa in 2013 and in 2015, assuming the UK price remains the same.

(c) If price elasticity of demand for Walkmill products is 0.8, what likely impact would the change in exchange rate have on Walkmill's revenue?

Competitive advantage

As covered in Units 65 and 66, a firm can be said to have a **competitive advantage** when it has some sort of distinctive strength that its competitors do not, such as cost advantages, size, technical or managerial expertise, or an ability to innovate. Having a competitive advantage is key to entering and succeeding in an overseas market. MNCs will want somewhere to operate where they can find the resources and capabilities to maximize their competitive advantages.

The two types of competitive advantage that play a role in many international firms' success are **cost competitiveness** and **differentiation**.

Cost competitiveness: This is where an international firm is able to achieve scale and scope economies, which may give it a cost advantage over its competitors. Cost competitiveness allows the firm to deliver the same product or service as its competitors, but at a lower cost, which allows it to make more profits.

For example, through acquiring ever-increasing economies of scale, a company may attempt to create the cheapest product on the market. This **cost leadership** strategy can be a competitive advantage provided that the firm meets the minimum quality standards of the industry. A good illustration of this comes from the discount supermarkets Aldi and Lidl. Another example comes from the budget airline easyJet, which pared its costs down to the bone by, for instance, eliminating tickets, check-ins, and even in-flight meals and cutting turn-around times at airports.

Differentiation: Differentiation is where, rather than focusing on costs, the firm selects certain attributes of its products or services and then tries to match this with specific customers. The firm may then try to command a higher price for creating this differentiated product.

For example, many of the big beer breweries (ABInBEV, Carlsberg, SAB Miller) formed as part of a wave of mergers designed to gain scale economies and compete on cost. However, facing increasing competition in key markets from small-scale 'craft brewers' and makers of cask-conditioned ale, most have differentiated their brand portfolios, buying the small firms, but allowing them to retain their brand names and independence. They can, therefore, satisfy the tastes of more local markets that may be very loyal to particular brands as well as offer choice to their more traditional consumers.

In order to sustain differentiation over the long term, a firm must fully understand its own strategy and its customers, as well as keep one step ahead of its competitors, who may be following similar strategies themselves. This is where **barriers to entry** are important: a large firm would have advantages over a new entrant to the industry who face barriers to entry because they don't have brand recognition for example. The firm needs to either have brand recognition, intellectual property, or protected supply and distribution chains if it is to use differentiation to remain competitive.

Question 2

Product differentiation is a critical strategic marketing process. It is key to building competitive advantage. Firms need continually to differentiate their products from their competitors'. It is an obvious thing to state, but if there were no differentiation why would a customer buy one product compared to a competitor's product?

Starbucks was formed in 1971 by three entrepreneurs and initially sold coffee beans. In the 1990s it expanded and there was rapid growth, with the first store outside the US opening in Japan in 1996. Starbucks is a common sight on the UK high street, but there are also more than 700 stores across six countries in South East Asia, including Indonesia, Malaysia, the Philippines, Singapore, Thailand and Vietnam. Starbucks has managed to take one of the world's oldest products and turn it into a differentiated, lasting and value-added brand.

What might the sources of differentiation be? It could be high quality, extraordinary service, innovative design, technological capability or a strong brand image. The key to competitive advantage is that Starbucks set itself apart from its competitors to justify a price premium that exceeds the cost of differentiating. There are 21,536 stores worldwide and revenue in 2013 was $15 billion.

(a) What is meant by product differentiation?

(b) Explain how Starbucks used the idea of product differentiation to grow its brand.

(c) What might businesses such as Starbucks need to do to maintain their competitive advantage?

Skill shortages and their impact on international competitiveness

Many industries require highly trained engineers, scientists, technicians or professionals, to compete. Companies that have long-term access to skilled and low-cost labour have an advantage over their competitors who do not. Where a firm owns these advantages in its home market, it may be able to produce and export more effectively than its competitors. Where it wishes to expand production and chooses to locate abroad, it will hope to enhance these competitive advantages, or at least ensure that they are not eroded.

For example, Castle Precision Engineering began making parts for sewing machines in 1951, and then expanded into car parts, medical equipment and aerospace engineering. It relies on a skilled workforce for its success. It has made the wheels for the 'Bloodhound' car, which aims to hit 1,000 mph in 55 seconds and hopefully set a new land speed record. Even though Castle exports at least one third of what it produces, it may remain a small to medium-sized firm for the foreseeable future as there are similar firms elsewhere in Britain. One big reason for this is that there has been a persistent shortage of skilled workers and engineers. In fact, Castle became involved in the 'Bloodhound' project in order to attract talent to its apprenticeship scheme.

Castle is facing strong competition in Britain, as well as abroad, for a limited pool of highly trained engineers. Were Castle Precision Engineering to expand by locating some of its production abroad, it could perhaps tap into a larger pool. For instance, in 2013 the USA, India and China produced the most engineers in the world, so perhaps they would be good locations if Castle decided to locate offshore.

Governments and businesses define **skills shortages** slightly differently. From the perspective of national comparative advantage, a government will be concerned that the relative education and skills of other countries make them more competitive. However, employers are most concerned when they cannot fill specific vacancies, or cannot do so at the right skill level.

In 2015 a major new survey by specialist recruitment agency JAM revealed widespread concerns that a skills shortage could lead to the UK lagging behind international rivals in food and drink manufacturing. It highlighted that the shortage of talented candidates was threatening future competiveness. The US was singled out as the main rival. UK firms were struggling to recruit shift managers and product development specialists. Experts felt that the sector was failing to recruit new talent.

The Border Agency produces a shortage occupation list that is used to guide the granting of work visas into the UK. Guidance on salary is given for each skills shortage. Table 2 shows the range of occupations suffering from a skills shortage in 2014.

Table 2 UK border shortage occupation list 2014

Occupation	Experienced worker salary
Production managers in mining and energy	£37,900
Biological scientists and biochemists	£27,000
Physical scientists	£27,000
Natural and social science professionals	£27,000
Civil engineers	£28,700
Mechanical engineers	£31,200
Electrical engineers	£32,300
Design and development engineers	£29,900
Business analysts	£31,200
Software development professionals	£29,600
Medical practitioners	£75,000
Neonatal nurses	£39,200
Ballet dancers	£17,000
Maths and science teachers	£34,000

Source: www.gov.uk

Thinking bigger

Muhammad Hazim left Malaysia to come to the UK and pursue an accountancy career in Coventry, but now his home nation wants him back. The fastest growing South East Asian country is looking for thousands like him to return to address a 'brain drain'. Malaysia has gone to great lengths to counter the high percentage of skilled workers who leave the country. The same is true in India where the cost of Indians studying abroad is as much as $17 billion a year in lost revenue. The African brain drain is also acute, but the same phenomenon is also affecting European countries. Some 23,000 German scientists have left the country and in 2015 Chancellor Angela Merkel devised programmes to attract them back. In 2015 over 1.3 million UK university graduates worked overseas. The US also faces a shortage of IT specialists.

The Malaysian government has run careers fairs in the UK bringing together UK-based Malaysian students with Malaysian employers. Over 4,000 Malaysians attended one fair in London. Their sell is that 'you can have an international career in Malaysia'. The government also offers tax breaks for five years if they return.

Skills shortage is therefore a global problem and one solution is for countries to encourage their own skilled workers to return.

You could use this information in a variety of ways. Obviously, it can be used when answering questions on skills shortages. It might also be useful when discussing influences on competitive advantage and the impact of a skilled workforce on business.

Links 🔗

Businesses operating internationally usually began as successful businesses operating in one domestic environment. As such, they understood their market (Units 1–13) and how to operate successfully within it (Units 14–18). They managed their business activities well (Units 26–40) and knew how to assess their competitive environment (Units 41-43). As they grew, they adapted their strategy to suit the evolving business (Units 46–50) and planned for where they wanted to be in the future (Units 63–65). Making the decision to expand internationally involves understanding the competitive advantages held by the firm, and evaluating whether these advantages will apply in the international market (Units 65 and 66). Retaining or adapting those advantages requires that a business thoroughly understands the markets in which it is competing (Units 66, 70, 72, 73 and 78).

Case study

THE GLOBAL GROCERY MARKET

As they have grown, many of the biggest names in food retailing have decided to take their brand abroad, only to find that they could not compete successfully in their target markets. Tesco (UK), for instance, failed in the US, Walmart (US) failed in Germany and South Korea, and Carrefour (France) has left almost 20 of the markets it tried to break into. Not all grocery stores have failed in the global marketplace, however. Aldi and Lidl, for instance, two German 'deep discounters' have been successful in the global market, especially in Britain. In 2014, Aldi grew by 22.6 per cent and Lidl by 15.1 per cent, at a time when almost all other grocery stores in the UK were contracting.

How did they succeed where others were failing? First, they were patient and only chose markets where they knew they had a competitive advantage to exploit. For instance, Aldi invested in countries where there was some concentration in the market and the returns of food sales were higher than the global average. Neither firm invested anywhere they might face corruption or other damage to their reputations.

Second, they put an emphasis on quality and low price. In one UK TV advertisement, a group of friends in a country house near London tuck into a sumptuous Christmas dinner. When the host says that all the food was from the German discount store Lidl the guests cannot contain their surprise. The growth of Aldi and Lidl has astonished the industry. The two are colonising the market with their no-frills approach to food retailing, taking sales from some of the biggest global grocers.

Perhaps the UK is the most extreme example with Aldi and Lidl doubling their market share. Aldi has increased its sales density from £10 per square foot to £25. This is what a successful player might normally expect to achieve in 20 years. Aldi has also set up in Australia and has quietly amassed 1,350 stores in the US, though it is bracing itself for the arrival of Lidl in the American market. Lidl will focus on brands Americans like.

The hallmarks of both retailers are limited ranges and selling predominantly own-label goods. They rely on buying power, but adapt to buy locally sourced products and they identify stores where customer profiles indicate a demand for more fresh products, which has helped to appeal to a new set of customers. Lidl UK now sources 60 per cent of it products nationally. There has been a cultural tipping point where both discounters feel that their brands are now acceptable to high-income shoppers. This has reportedly left other UK grocers floundering. Lidl has stated that its competitors dropping their prices will not work. They believe their growth is unrelated to competitor activity and that their brand is now ingrained in customers' psyches.

Sources: *The Economist*, 14.3.15 and the *Financial Times* 10.12.2014. All rights reserved.

(a) Assess the competitive advantages that Aldi and Lidl have over other grocery retailers. (10 marks)

(b) Evaluate the extent to which competitors can respond to Aldi and Lidl to win back customers. (20 marks)

Key terms

Barriers to entry – factors that make it difficult for a company to enter an industry or type of business and compete effectively. These can include incumbents' high capital investment and strong economies of scale, restrictive government policies, and labour unions.

Competitive advantage – the advantage one company has over another, or several others, in the provision of a particular product or service. For instance, a carmaker may have a competitive advantage because its cars break down less often – in other words are of a higher quality – even though they may be more expensive.

Cost competitiveness – through acquiring ever-increasing economies of scale, a company creates the cheapest product on the market.

Cost leadership – a concept developed by economist and Harvard professor, Michael Porter, used in business strategy. It describes a way to establish the competitive advantage and essentially means the lowest cost of operation in the industry.

Differentiation – rather than focusing on costs, differentiation is when a firm selects certain attributes of its products or services and tries to match these with specific customers. The business may then try to command a higher price for creating this differentiated product.

Economic risk – risk that future cash flows will change due to unexpected exchange rate changes.

Global competitiveness – the extent to which a business or a geographical area such as a country, can compete successfully against rivals.

Skills shortages – where potential employees do not have the skills demanded by employers.

Knowledge check

1. What is meant by appreciation of a currency?
2. What is meant by depreciation of a currency?
3. Explain the significance of changes in the exchange rates for business.
4. What impact does price elasticity of demand have on businesses facing changes in exchange rates?
5. How can firms reduce the risks of fluctuating exchange rates?
6. What is meant by competitive advantage?
7. How can a business in a global market improve its competitiveness?
8. What impact do skills shortages have on international competitiveness?

Exam tip

When considering a question involving global competitiveness, it is useful to reflect on all the basic definitions and concepts that apply to a small, domestic business. They are often the same for a large multinational firm – it is just that the context is different and the application more complex.

Some students wrongly assume that different rules apply to MNCs and so they need to be evaluated differently. This is rarely the case.

For example, the problems (and opportunities) that MNCs face in trading in different currencies mostly come down to familiar concepts: supply and demand, pricing strategies, cash flow and managing risk.

The competitive advantages that they hope to rely upon for growth are perhaps more complicated, but they may be derived from the same sources as those of domestic firms. The same is often true for the threats that they face: for instance, all businesses need suitable employees if their businesses are to succeed and grow.

76 Marketing

Key points

1. Global marketing strategy and global localisation (glocalisation).
2. Different marketing approaches:
   - domestic/ethnocentric
   - mixed/geocentric
   - international/polycentric
3. Application and adaptation of the marketing mix (4Ps) and Ansoff's Matrix to global markets.

Getting started

Pret á Manger (also known as Pret) is a UK sandwich shop that focuses on fresh ingredients and prompt service. The name of the business means 'ready to eat' in French, which fits neatly with its emphasis on serving quality food and prompt, friendly service.

Pret opened its first shop in 1986. By 2014, it had 289 shops in the UK. In addition to its UK growth, the business developed a global marketing strategy, which involved opening branches in other countries. In 2015, Pret had 350 shops worldwide. It announced that it would almost double the number of its shops in France and increase the number in the USA.

Although the service and approach in its shops is similar around the world, some products differ to cater for local tastes. For example, in the UK, the most popular sandwich is crayfish with rocket. In Hong Kong, however, locals prefer hot food, so Pret shops in Hong Kong prepare and sell more hot wraps and soups.

Why has Pret grown so much since opening its first shop? What is meant by a global marketing strategy? Why might Pret have wanted to expand into countries such as France, China and the USA? Why does Pret sell different types of products in different countries?

Global marketing strategy

Unit 13 explored a marketing strategy as a set of plans that aim to achieve a specific marketing objective. When some businesses operate outside their country of origin, they operate a common global marketing strategy in order to sell their products beyond their national borders. Global marketing involves the planning, producing, placing and promoting of a business's products in a worldwide market. This process can involve a business having offices in different countries, but the process is also facilitated by the growth of the internet.

Global localisation (glocalisation)

The global localisation approach differs from having a common strategy for all countries. Instead, it involves adapting

to local expectations in order for a business to succeed in an international market. The phrase, 'think global, act local' is a good summary of what is meant by **glocalisation**. The phrase suggests that businesses should aim to reach potential customers around the world, but that, to be successful with those potential customers, businesses need to take account of local tastes, customs and traditions. Global businesses should be sensitive to the specific preferences of the different markets in which they want to operate and succeed.

Different marketing approaches

When considering entering international markets, businesses use a range of different marketing approaches for their products.

Ethnocentric (domestic) approach: Overseas markets are seen as identical or similar to domestic markets, and the approach assumes that what is good for the domestic market will be good for global markets. Businesses using this approach make little or no attempt to adapt their product for different markets. For example, Sony's PlayStation 4 is a very popular console worldwide. The console is sold in most countries but it is the same in every market. Compare this approach with the approach of Pret á Manger, where different types of products are sold to reflect the different tastes of different markets.

Many businesses use an ethnocentric approach, including:

- PizzaExpress, which expanded into China to meet the growing taste for western food by Chinese customers
- Apple, with products such as the iPhone®, iPad® and MacBook®
- Swatch watches
- Rolls Royce cars.

Using an ethnocentric marketing approach has its advantages, such as **economies of scale**. Because a product is standardised across markets, the scale of production is much larger and so savings can be made on raw materials. In addition, there are no development costs involved in adapting products for different markets. In the case of Pret, market research and product development had to be carried out to identify and develop products that served local demand. This type of research is costly and leads to further costs in product development. Where this type of marketing activity is not required, average costs can be reduced and this can lead to lower prices and increased competitiveness.

However, this approach may also have disadvantages, as a product may not sell well if it is not adapted to the local market. Where a marketing mix is not geared to a local market, a business may be taking a risk about the appeal to a new market.

Question 1

Cath Kidston is a UK-owned chain of home furnishing retail stores. Despite the fact that the business produces and sells products that are quintessentially British, it has expanded successfully into overseas markets.

In 2014, the business announced a plan to open 100 new stores in China. This followed a year of growth abroad, in European markets such as Spain and also in Asia. The new stores planned to sell largely the same product range for which Cath Kidston is famous in the UK. The offering from the business seems to have a global appeal, successfully attracting international consumers with its colourful retro patterns.

Source: adapted from the *Financial Times* 12.8.2013, 22.07.2014. All rights reserved.

(a) Explain two reasons why Cath Kidston has a strategy of global expansion.

(b) Explain one advantage and one disadvantage to Cath Kidston of adopting an ethnocentric strategy when opening stores in different countries.

Polycentric (international) approach: Businesses adapt their product to the local markets in which they plan to sell the product. This involves developing and marketing different products for the demands of local customers in different markets. For example, car manufacturers will adapt cars and model names to meet the expectations of their local markets.

One advantage of this approach is that the product should sell well. By tailoring products to specific customer needs, the product can be targeted precisely within the particular market.

A disadvantage of this approach lies in the cost involved. Developing bespoke products is expensive, and these costs can be so high that the project itself can be jeopardised. For example, in 2007 Tesco launched a new, UK-style supermarket, Fresh & Easy, into the US, that was tailored to meet American consumers' demands. The stores focused heavily on fresh ready meals, for example, to cater for the convenience that American customers expected. They also chose not to use the Tesco name in the American market. However, the project was not as successful as the approach in the UK market and Tesco sold its Fresh & Easy stores. The project reportedly cost Tesco billions of pounds.

Geocentric (mixed) approach: Businesses use a combination of the ethnocentric and polycentric marketing approaches. This 'glocalisation' approach is used by many multinational corporations, and is summed up by the phrase, 'think global, act local'. The business's strategy is to maintain and promote the global brand name, but to tailor its products to local markets. For example, McDonald's makes sure that its Big Mac® burger tastes the same in every country in which it is sold. This approach is used by various fast food chains. Some examples of the type of foods they might use to replace what you're used to are shown in Table 1.

Table 1 Types of foods that could be used in 'glocal' meals

Country: Egypt	Country: Japan
Food might include kofta meat, fava beans and different types of bread, like baladi bread.	Food might include teriyaki sauce, noodles or even sushi. Desserts might be different with sweets called wagashi.
Country: Greece	Country: India
Food might include tzatziki sauce, fried cheese (saganaki) or cheese pie (tyropita). Desserts might be more honey-based, like baklava.	Food might include breads like roti or naans and more rice dishes. Drinks might include lassi or masala tea.

Table 2 provides a summary of the advantages and disadvantages of the different market approaches.

Table 2 Advantages and disadvantages of different marketing approaches

	Advantages	Disadvantages
Ethnocentric	Lower cost of development and production Economies of scale	Product may not sell well Does not take account of national/cultural differences
Polycentric	Targeted products for different markets – higher sales	Higher cost of development Difficult to compete with established local brands
Geocentric	Tailoring product to local tastes and needs – higher sales	Higher cost of product development

Adapting and applying the marketing mix and Ansoff's Matrix to global markets

The marketing mix (the 4Ps)

As mentioned earlier in the unit, a marketing strategy is the set of plans that a business uses to achieve specific marketing objectives. For example, a local takeaway may aim to become the market leader in the town in which it operates. To achieve this objective, the strategy might be:

- offering locally sourced, organic ingredients (**p**roduct)
- lowering off-peak prices (**p**rice)
- establishing a delivery service (**p**lace)
- a loyalty scheme which offers discounts to regular customers (**p**romotion).

But what about a business that operates on a global scale? What strategies might a business use when operating in mass markets? The marketing mix is used in global markets, and must be considered as part of a global marketing strategy.

- **Price.** Decisions around price need to take into account local factors such as incomes, taxes, rents and other costs. It is unlikely that a business will charge the same price in all markets. An Apple iPhone® might cost less in the US than in Russia, for example. Price will also reflect different local factors, such as wage rates and taxes.
- **Product.** To what extent should a business modify or adapt its product for global markets? The section above looked at the different approaches that businesses can take with

their products when moving into international markets (ethnocentric, polycentric and geocentric).
- **Promotion.** When promoting products in global markets, businesses need to be conscious of language differences.
- **Place.** Businesses need to take account of how local consumers typically buy their products. For example, the Tesco Fresh & Easy stores may not have appealed to how some US consumers shop, using larger supermarkets.

Table 3 provides a summary of some questions to ask when considering the 4Ps.

Table 3 The marketing mix in global markets: a summary

Product	Price
Should the product be adapted for different markets, or can it stay as it is?	What price should be charged in the global markets? What prices are charged by local competitors?
Promotion	Place
What are the most effective promotion methods in different countries?	How do consumers buy their products in local markets?

Ansoff's Matrix

Ansoff's Matrix was discussed in Unit 45. It is a strategic tool to help a business achieve growth, which can be applied to global markets and can help to inform decisions around marketing strategy. It is possible to apply this model to a globalisation strategy, as used by multinational brands such as Starbucks, Ford and McDonald's.

Figure 1

Ansoff's Matrix

As discussed in Unit 45, Ansoff's Matrix shows four possible strategies that a business might adopt. Risk can become greater the further a firm extends from its core of existing products and consumers, i.e. the further it extends from the top left-hand corner of the matrix. This can become particularly pronounced when businesses extend into international markets, where expertise of local conditions and tastes might be less secure. When considering global marketing, the focus is on businesses introducing new or existing products into new markets that may have national and cultural differences.

- **Market penetration:** exists where a business adapts products for markets in which it already operates. For example, McDonald's already operates in Japan. By developing and launching the Teriyaki McBurger® into this (existing) market, the strategy is clearly one of market penetration.

- **Market development:** involves the marketing of existing products in new markets. This is not always straightforward as customers from different regions of the same country, let alone a different country, may have different tastes and preferences. Unit 45 showed how a market development strategy relies heavily on understanding local habits, tastes and needs. Even where market development is appropriate and successful, it is often necessary to make slight modifications to suit the new market, for instance in terms of language or labelling. Pret á Manger adapted its products slightly to meet local palates, in France and the US, although retained its model of customer service and prompt delivery. This refining of an existing product, to fit into a new – in this case, overseas – market is an example of a market development strategy. This is also an example of glocalisation, where products are modified for local tastes.
- **Diversification:** occurs when new products are developed for new markets, as explored in Unit 45.

Key terms

Economies of scale – savings facilitated by an increased level of production.
Globalisation – the process of businesses starting to operate internationally and develop international influence.
Global marketing strategy – the process of adjusting a company's marketing strategies to reflect conditions, consumer tastes and demand in other countries.
Glocalisation – a combination of the words 'globalisation' and 'localisation'. It involves the development and sale of products to customers around the world which reflect specific local customs, tastes and traditions.
Localisation – strategies that adjust products to fit with target customers.

Exam tip

If answering a question on this topic, you should feel prepared enough to use a wide range of knowledge and concepts from the whole course. Any discussion of a business wanting to expand should make you think about economies of scale. One benefit that any business hopes to achieve by expansion – at home or abroad – is the reduction in unit costs that can be achieved by operating on a larger scale. This might be achieved by being able to purchase components or raw materials on a larger scale, or by having one head office serving different markets.

Any discussion of this topic in an exam question should not end at the 4Ps or Ansoff's Matrix. There are many other concepts to consider when analysing global marketing strategy, including:

- markets – supply and demand in local markets
- price and income elasticity of demand – pricing decisions need to take account of demand factors in local markets
- recruitment – the presence or lack of skilled staff in the new market
- ethical considerations
- legislation
- the importance of the internet in marketing.

Thinking bigger

What is the best marketing approach for a business planning to expand into international markets? We live in a global economy, full of global brands, and this has largely been facilitated by the spread of the internet. To what extent is this **globalisation** a desirable development for businesses? The ability to exploit new markets is an obvious advantage. Some of the regions with the highest rates of economic growth – such as China and India – are also the most populous, and consumers in these regions should benefit from having access to a wider range of goods and services. The internet is also directly impacting on global marketing, effectively reducing the costs involved in operating on a global scale. These regions offer exciting opportunities for western business, but there are also risks for businesses embarking on international expansion. These require careful strategic consideration.

Knowledge check

1. What is meant by the term glocalisation?
2. Give three reasons why a business may want to expand into global markets.
3. What is meant by an ethnocentric marketing strategy?
4. What are the advantages to a business of adopting a geocentric marketing approach?
5. State the four strategies outlined by Ansoff's Matrix.

Case study

THE GLOBAL MARKET

In 2009, the American toy maker, Mattel, opened a new flagship store called House of Barbie in Shanghai, China. The store was intended to celebrate and promote the iconic doll, Barbie, which had recently been launched in China. Mattel was keen to expand into international markets.

China was regarded as an ideal market for Mattel to enter in order to establish Barbie as a successful product. China's economy was growing strongly and there was a growing middle class with a taste for western culture. Shanghai in particular was regarded as an innovative, cosmopolitan city with an aspirational population, and it represented a significant proportion of China's GDP. Mattel's market research also indicated that Barbie was popular with local girls.

Mattel invested millions of dollars in launching House of Barbie, which was located in Shanghai's luxury shopping area. The store included a restaurant and spa as well as its extensive ranges of Barbie dolls and accessories. Although the Barbie dolls sold in Shanghai were essentially the same as those sold throughout the world, some changes were made. For example, one model had black hair and wore Chinese clothes.

In 2011, Mattel closed House of Barbie, in consideration of the sales figures. Some analysts suggested that this was partly because Chinese girls and parents preferred dolls to be cute rather than fashionable. Others pointed out that, in the USA, the Barbie brand was established enough to be a cultural icon, but in China Barbie may have been considered as just another doll. There were also questions around the prices of products and accessories in House of Barbie. Some felt that they were too expensive for local consumers who may not have recognised the Barbie brand or know what it stood for.

(a) What is meant by 'international market'? (2 marks)

(b) Using Ansoff's Matrix model, explain which strategy Mattel used when opening House of Barbie in Shanghai. (4 marks)

(c) Explain which marketing approach – ethnocentric, polycentric or geocentric – Mattel used when launching House of Barbie. (4 marks)

(d) Assess the marketing strategy Mattel used with House of Barbie in Shanghai. (10 marks)

Key points

1. Cultural diversity: recognition that groups of people across the globe have different interests and values.
2. Features of global niche markets.
3. Application and adaptation of the marketing mix (4Ps) to suit global niches.

Getting started

Ties.com is an internet-based retail company that focuses exclusively on neckties and related products. The business claims to have the most comprehensive selection of neckwear anywhere in the world and stresses the quality of its operation on its website:

> We're not some fly-by-night company. In fact, we've been a leader in the industry for more than 15 wonderful (and crazy) years. We've got real humans answering phones, we gingerly pack our boxes by hand and we take absolute pride in everything we do.

> From neckties and skinny ties, to bow ties, socks, tie racks and more — nearly everything you'll find at Ties.com is designed by our talented team in sunny Southern California. That's a level of intimacy and attention to detail that few can match.

> Besides the best selection of premium neckwear on the internet, you can expect a fast & secure checkout, a no-hassle return policy and a 100% satisfaction guarantee. That's how confident we are that you're going to find something you love.

Source: www.ties.com

Why do some businesses choose to produce or sell a small range of products? To what extent does Ties.com operate in a niche market? Why might Ties.com not be a popular business in every country? Describe how the internet has enabled businesses like Ties.com to expand into different countries.

Global niche markets

Global niche markets are similar to the niche markets covered in Unit 13 in the sense that they target a very specific range of people, often referred to as subcultures. These are groups of customers with common interests or hobbies. In global niche markets, the customers live in more than one country and have particular needs that are not met fully by the global mass market. For example, the toy market has millions of different products aimed at all age groups. But the market for interlocking toy bricks is much smaller. The case study in this unit considers how Lego® operates in this global niche market.

Features of global niche markets

The opposite of niche markets are mass markets. As discussed in Unit 1, mass markets are huge, often global and have millions of customers. Customers in niche markets have very particular needs that are sometimes not catered for by local businesses.

Higher prices can be charged for products in niche market than can be charged in mass markets, and this is a very desirable position for a business. The reason for this is that the products cater for very particular needs. The features of businesses that operate in global market niches are:

- a clear understanding of the needs and wants of the market segment
- an emphasis on quality
- excellent customer service
- expertise in the product area
- prioritising profit rather than market share
- innovation.

Question 1

Virgin Atlantic is an airline that operates to destinations in North America, the Caribbean, Africa and Asia. It also operates domestic flights in the UK. The airline operates within the broad market for air travel, and competes with other airlines to fly passengers to holiday destinations.

Virgin Atlantic also caters for a niche market in passengers who are prepared to pay more for a much more luxurious experience The Virgin Upper Class offer includes:

· chauffeur driven pick-up for the airport and transfers from airport to destination

· a private security channel at the airport to avoid queues

· exclusive clubhouses at airports with free restaurants and bars

· leather seats and luxury beds in-flight

· extensive entertainment services in-flight.

The price of such luxury is several times higher than competitors This is aimed at business travellers, whose businesses may be paying for the flight, or at individuals for whom a ticket price may not be such a significant expenditure.

(a) Describe three different market segments that Virgin Atlantic targets.

(b) Explain why Virgin Atlantic offers different types of ticket for different customers.

(c) Explain how Virgin Atlantic demonstrates that it has a clear understanding of the needs of its customers.

Virgin Atlantic does not only offer flights to customers in its home country – the UK. It has identified a global niche, where customers in different countries are prepared to pay for the luxury flight experience. This is the key to global market niches. It does not matter whether the customer who is prepared to pay a higher price is in the home country or abroad.

Why, though, are customers prepared to pay higher prices for these global brands, rather than local equivalents? The answer partly lies in the global nature of the world economy. Aspirational, niche brands in the UK are likely to be similarly aspirational in other countries. This transmission of desirability is the function of a range of factors.

- **The internet and e-commerce** – these have proved an important marketing tool and an opportunity to spread information. With the advent of e-commerce, businesses have been able to spread into foreign markets, and create and meet local demands that would otherwise have been impossible.
- **Social media** – the rise of platforms such as Facebook, Twitter and YouTube has given birth to a new brand of commentators known as 'vloggers'. These are people who use video to comment on a range of current topics, issues and – crucially – products. Vloggers are a growing group who promote niche brands to subscribers.
- **Ease of travel** – facilitated by low-cost airlines. The world, in a real sense, has become a smaller place. Visitors to foreign countries are exposed to well-known global brands, in places far away from their home country.

Cultural diversity

One difference, which in the past may have caused problems for British businesses, is that English was not the main or even the second language in many countries. In Eastern Europe, for example, German and Russian may have been more widely spoken than English. The expansion of the EU has led to English being spoken in more countries, helping to solve this problem to some extent.

Other cultural differences may influence the way a product is marketed. For example, a product name suitable in one country may have a totally different meaning in another – the French lemonade Pschitt would require a new name were it to be sold in the UK. The example of Ties.com at the start of this unit suggests how a brand can grow into different countries, but would neckties be successful in all countries? Some cultures and traditions do not wear ties at all, and so expanding into these markets is less likely to be successful.

Colours have different meanings throughout the world. In the Far East, white rather than black is associated with mourning. In India, fashion models of the sort used to promote products in the West might be considered too thin. In some countries, what may be regarded as a possible 'bribe' in the UK might be common business practice. Payments to government or industry officials may be required to get things done, from electricity connection to securing contracts.

Question 2

Mercedes-Benz is a German car manufacturer and focuses on luxury cars, coaches and trucks. Although it is a German company, Mercedes-Benz manufactures its vehicles in over 30 countries, from Argentina to Russia to Vietnam.

Mercedes-Benz cars meet the needs of global customers who value the luxury of the product and who have a strong sense of brand loyalty to the business. The business works hard to ensure that its brand is distinguished from other car manufacturers. This stems from a strong emphasis on quality drawn from expertise in the area of luxury car-making.

Mercedes-Benz cars can be more expensive than other cars in the same sector. Customers in this global niche are prepared to pay for the brand name and the luxury this brings. Demand for such luxury products is often price inelastic. This is a real advantage for businesses that serve such niche markets.

(a) Explain what is meant by 'global niche'.
(b) Why is the demand for Mercedes-Benz cars price inelastic?
(c) Explain one advantage to Mercedes-Benz of demand for its cars being price inelastic.

Application and adaptation of the marketing mix to suit global niches

Businesses that operate in global niche markets need to distinguish themselves from the mainstream (or mass) market. This can be done through adaptations to the marketing mix (4Ps).

Product: Global niche products often place an emphasis on quality. Examples include luxury cars, watches and perfumes. For example, Montblanc produces and sells exclusive pens, watches and luggage products that are sold around the world and are marketed as exclusive, desirable products. For Virgin Atlantic, the key is to differentiate its standard product into something that demonstrates it is meeting the needs of niche customers.

Price: The point of niche marketing is to charge higher prices by providing a product not intended for mass market. The point behind such markets is the ability to charge premium prices. Virgin Atlantic has the ability – through its Upper Class package – to charge prices much higher than for its standard flight ticket.

Promotion: Strategies to promote products to global niches are often based around the brand name and reinforcing the exclusivity of the brand, and need to be more targeted than in mass market promotion. Consideration has to be given to the language differences that might exist between countries. For example, Dublin-based drinks distributor, C&C Group, marketed a brand of golden whiskey liqueur called Irish Mist to Germany. However, in Germany the word mist is translated into a form of manure! The product needed to be rebranded. Car companies

465

often give different names to the same cars in different countries. One problem with this need to be sensitive to national and cultural differences is that promotion costs will be higher, and this may impact on price and ultimately competitiveness.

Place: Businesses serving niche markets are often more careful when selecting distribution channels for their product. This is particularly important where exclusive brands are involved. Networks of exclusive dealers are a common method of selling products to global customers. Mercedes-Benz has exclusive dealerships around the world. Montblanc sells its products through an exclusive network of authorised retailers, jewellers and over 360 Montblanc Boutiques worldwide.

With the 4Ps in mind, Table 1 summarises the advantages and disadvantages of niche marketing.

Table 1 Advantages and disadvantages of niche marketing

Advantages	Disadvantages
Prices are higher than in mass markets – demand is more price inelastic.	Products sell in relatively low volumes (compared with mass markets), so profits need to be high enough to make it worthwhile.
The product is distributed through specialist retailers or directly to the consumer. This has advantages in terms of image. For example, the Billabong surfer image might be compromised if sold widely in supermarkets.	The niche market must be large enough to support the business and specialist distribution. The small size may prevent economies of scale that compete with larger competitors.

Global niches exist where the local market for a product is too small to be profitable but at a global level the market is very viable. These trends may be present due to international perceptions about certain goods being the same (for example, agreement that Mercedes is a good car). Firms large and small may exploit these niches as part of a global marketing strategy. Niches are particularly present in high-end goods or high-tech medical or computing goods.

Thinking bigger

Wider business ideas can be applied to the topic of global market niches. To what extent should a business seek to extend a niche product into global markets? The fact that a niche product is successful in one country is no guarantee of success with consumers globally. Indeed, one of the reasons for the success at home may well be due to the fact that the business has identified a particular need of domestic consumers and meets this need with a bespoke product. This can be the case with restaurants. A strong reputation for quality using local food may work in a regional setting, but can this be translated to another country? The nature of the restaurant business, with quality being overseen by an owner, may be changed through expansion and seeking out global niche markets. Gordon Ramsay, a well-known UK chef, successfully opened Maze restaurant in New York after the success of the UK equivalent by the same name in London. Careful marketing, operations and leadership are needed to translate a local niche market into a global niche market.

Exam tip

When considering global niche markets as an extension of domestic niche markets, you need to consider why a business might want to extend its reach beyond its own national borders. A key benefit of targeting a niche market, rather than a mass market, is the opportunity to charge higher prices than an equivalent, mass-market product. Why, though, are customers in different countries prepared to pay higher prices for such products? Concepts such as price elasticity of demand can be used to explain this appeal. If a product is desirable and has few close substitutes due to its quality or features, then consumers are likely to be less price sensitive, so the demand is likely to be price inelastic. With the latest iPhone, for example, it does not matter whether the consumer is in New York, London or Tokyo. The product has such niche appeal that relatively high prices do not deter demand. For a business, having a product with low price elasticity of demand is a very appealing position. But how can this be achieved? One way is by identifying and filling global niches.

If answering a question on global niche markets, it is crucial to take account of the appropriate **context**. You must apply your answer to the case study and the product being considered. Using the mobile phone example, you could contextualise your response by comparing to competitors (Samsung, HTC), or referring to alternative methods of communication (telephone, email).

Key terms

Global niche market – customers who live in more than one country and have particular needs that are not met fully by the global mass market.

Knowledge check

1. What is meant by a niche market?

2. Distinguish between a niche market and a mass market.

3. What is a global niche market?

4. Give three examples of products that are targeted at global niche markets.

5. Describe how social media can encourage the growth of a global brand.

6. How does cultural diversity affect global niche markets?

7. How do businesses responsible for luxury products ensure their brand is maintained in different global markets?

Case study

GLOBAL NICHES

"Scandinavian countries [Denmark, Sweden and Finland] have an impressive number of globally competitive companies. Denmark is a world leader in hearing aids (Oticon), shipping (Maersk), toys (Lego®), drink (Carlsberg) and wind power (with more than 200 companies that account for a third of the world's wind-turbine market). Novo Nordisk is at the centre of a biotech cluster, dubbed Medicon Valley, that stretches from Copenhagen to Malmö in neighbouring Sweden and has an annual turnover of €13.4 billion.

"Sweden boasts some world-class manufacturing companies, particularly in mining equipment and machine tools (Sandvik and Atlas Copco), as well as retail stars such as IKEA and H&M. Finland's Kone is one of the world's leading lift and escalator companies. Nokia's problems are being offset by the rise of electronic-games makers such as Rovio, the creator of Angry Birds. Norway is a world leader in oil services and fish farming."

These globally competitive companies thrive in well-defined global niches. Here are some examples.

- "Lego® dominates the market for interlocking bricks." It began producing them in 1949 and has since grown to be one of the world's most successful companies. By 2015 Lego® had replaced Ferrari as 'the world's most powerful brand'. This is a niche market as there are not many different types of such bricks. The global niche for Lego® can be defined as a brick-based construction toy within a larger toy market.

- "Volvo Trucks produces the world's best high-quality lorries."

- "Sandvik is a machine-tool superpower."

"Nichification protects high-cost companies from emerging-market competitors. Nobody wants the cheapest machine tool when a defective one can cause millions of pounds worth of damage."

There are four qualities that explain the success of these companies in exploiting these global niches.

1. Relentless innovation of products.
2. Taking long-term growth into consideration.
3. Consensus-based approaches to management, where flat organisational structures and democratic systems of corporate leadership promote trust and co-operation.
4. A passion for replacing labour with machines to increase productivity.

"To see these forces in action, consider two companies in different industries. Sandvik started making steel in the late

19th century in the small town of Sandviken, two hours north of Stockholm. It is now a global giant that produces everything from machine tools to steel rods for nuclear reactors. Sandvik's small-town roots have not prevented it from becoming a global leader in its core businesses. 'Expanding abroad is how we save jobs at home' is a common refrain.

Sandvik is obsessed by promoting productivity – both its own and its customers'. A giant factory that produces steel rods looks as if it is run by ghosts: four people monitor computer screens in a command centre and a few others patrol the floor. A productivity centre is devoted to pushing forward the frontiers of technology – making the world's fastest drills, for example – and training employees to help customers. The company's mantra is 'we sell productivity not products'.

Haldor Topsøe founded the company that bears his name back in 1940 [and as at 2015] … he remains chairman. His company, meanwhile, has grown into a global giant…

Mr Topsøe ascribes its success to two things. He found a perfect niche in catalysis. Catalysts accelerate lots of chemical processes that are vital to a modern economy. They are also extremely hard to copy. So demand is growing and barriers to entry are high. He believes that his company benefits from being a family affair, which allows it both to invest for the long term and to take advantage of the global market."

Source: www.economist.com

 Q

(a) Explain one advantage to a business of identifying a global market niche. (4 marks)

(b) Explain one example of how 'replacing labour with machines' might increase productivity for a business such as Lego®. (4 marks)

(c) Assess the importance of the global market to Lego®, making reference to the niche in which it operates. (12 marks)

Key points

Considerations for businesses:
1. Cultural differences.
2. Language.
3. Unintended meanings.
4. Inappropriate/inaccurate translations.
5. Differing tastes.
6. Inappropriate branding and promotion.

Getting started

According to the US Commerce Department, doing business in Russia mixes formality with a personal touch. Business people are expected to dress formally and conservatively. In the initial meeting, it is recommended that Western business people lean more towards formality. Russian business people also consider written material important. They may expect slides, brochures and samples. According to the Australian Trade Commission such written materials, as well as websites and business cards, should look to be high-quality. Russian business people expect agreements and deals to be written and signed.

Having said this, the Russian approach can be to chat and get to know potential business partners on a personal level before any discussion of hard details. It is noted that once a Russian partner becomes more familiar with western business people, they may show more emotion such as a positive pat on the shoulder, or show emotions of displeasure more openly.

Russian business people are reported to expect western counterparts to be on time for appointments. However, the International Business Centre advises that the Russian themselves may be late in order to test the patience of their partner. Russian business people also expect a prompt and comprehensive follow-up of the meeting from the western negotiators in order to keep the business deal positively moving forward.

Source: adapted from www.ibtimes.com

What might people from other countries think of your own cultural and social factors? Why might being aware of cultural factors help or hinder business?

Cultural and social factors affecting global marketing

Doing business across cultures can be challenging. Without an understanding of national and corporate cultures and languages, the potential to offend is very real. These cultural and social factors and how they affect global marketing are examined in this unit.

In order to market effectively in other countries, businesses must overcome **ethnocentrism**. This is the tendency of people to view their own cultures, ethics and norms as superior. For example, people tend to accept the values of the culture around them as absolute values. Since each culture has its own set of values, often quite divergent from those values held in other cultures, the concepts of proper and improper, foolish and wise, and even right and wrong become blurred. In international business, questions arise regarding what is proper by which culture's values, what is wise by which culture's view of the world, and what is right by whose standards.

Question 1

Cordex, a British shoe making firm, decided to expand internationally by acquiring a Vietnamese firm, Vetex. In planning the takeover, Cordex's senior managers had not given enough thought to the process of integrating Vetex after the merger. Once the deal was complete, Cordex selected staff from its London headquarters to relocate in Hanoi and began the process of moulding Vetex into Cordex's way of doing business, a process that was hugely expensive. After six months, it was clear that the process of integration had not been handled well. One member of staff returned home as her family did not like living in Vietnam. The remaining members of staff were finding it difficult to understand the business culture and did not speak Vietnamese or French and so were having trouble communicating effectively. Two key Vetex staff members quit and many of the remaining managers found the situation so challenging they were also considering leaving. The CFO of Cordex was deeply concerned at the escalating costs, and the CEO was worried that Cordex's international expansion strategy might fail.

(a) Explain how Cordex was ethnocentric in its approach to the process of integrating the two firms.

(b) Explain the approach that Cordex could have taken.

Cultural differences

Unit 57 explained how corporate culture can affect how a business operates. However, working across differing national cultures can add levels of complexity. Each step in conducting business needs to be carefully prepared for and considered, to take account of cultural differences and build trust. To understand how, companies need to think about each level of the business relationship: the introductions, the negotiations and communicating on a day-to-day level.

Meeting someone from a different culture is often awkward, but in a business setting there can be elaborate formal and informal procedures that have developed over time and, if not followed, can cause much offence. For example, in Asian cultures, such as Vietnam, a person is expected to shake hands when first entering a room. Participants are expected to shake using both hands, upon meeting and when saying goodbye and need to nod the head slightly while doing so as a sign of respect. The two parties must then exchange business cards. The etiquette surrounding these is also extremely important. Business cards are thoughtfully crafted, giving an individual's name and contact details, and always kept in a special case to ensure they are in perfect condition when handed out. The card must be given and received with both hands.

The recipient should pause upon taking the card, study it thoroughly and then place in their special case. All of this is done with great formality. Failure to treat a business card with respect can cause grave offence.

Every country in every region will have its own norms governing introductions, so it is important to conduct thorough research before the first meeting.

Language

Although much of international business is conducted in the English language, understanding other languages makes communication much easier and helps to cement relationships. Over-reliance on one language is also risky, in that it may lead to miscommunication and less sensitivity towards other cultures. Communication is much more than simply language, however. For instance, there are differences in the nature of communication between **high-context** and **low-context** cultures. Low-context cultures, such as those of North America and much of Europe, tend to say what they mean. That is, in discussions, what is said can usually be taken at face value. Firms 'get down to business' and view socialising as being for after the deal is done. Agendas, letters, contracts and other formal documentation are essential and relied upon during negotiations as well as after they are completed.

However, in high-context cultures, 'yes' often does not mean 'yes'. In Saudi Arabia, for example, 'Yes, I agree' might mean, 'I hear you' rather than 'I agree with you'. Much of Arab and Asian communication is high-context, and this has big implications for conducting business. For instance, after making a pitch for business in Japan the Japanese negotiator might close the long meeting saying, 'We are going to study your proposal and get back to you.' Far from expecting to hear from them in a few days or weeks with a positive response, as might be the norm in a low-context culture, in Japan – a high-context culture – such language may mean 'no'. However, the Japanese never use that word in negotiations. Initial meetings are there to build trust, and socialising is used to create relationships for the next stage of negotiations. This is very different from what might take place between, for instance, a British firm negotiating with a Danish one.

Question 2

L12, a Chinese business, purchased Mobi-Nev, a North American mobile communications business in 2001. The deal involved a developing understanding of cultural contexts. For example, L12 was based in Shanghai and Mobi-Nev in Phoenix, Arizona, where no-one in the company spoke Chinese. However, the company carried out a **cultural audit** of its employees and this highlighted some cultural considerations, most of which concerned communication.

An illustration of this came in 2003, when the Human Resources Officer (HRO) was taking forward her role in the Phoenix office. The process of updating a diversity policy seemed to be running smoothly, yet it became apparent that there were some cultural differences and some Chinese colleagues felt she was being disrespectful when organising meetings. This was due to the Mandarin translation of the word 'request', which implied that she was asking to meet someone below her in status and caused offence to some Chinese colleagues. To develop understanding and establish trust and a common culture for the future, the company HRO worked for a period in the Shanghai office. This gave her the opportunity to to learn first hand the subtleties of Chinese language and culture..

(a) Explain what problems could have emerged if the HRO hadn't decided to go and work at the Chinese headquarters.

(b) Assess the importance of understanding the language and culture of countries when taking over a business in another territory.

Unintended meanings

Verbal communication has many pitfalls, but so does physical communication. Gestures common in one region, may have differing meanings in other regions and cultures.

Table 1 Some examples of gestures common in Britain that can cause offence in cross-cultural business settings

Gesture	Examples of countries or regions where gesture might be considered offensive
Thumbs-up gesture, meaning 'well done'	Australia, Greece, Middle East
The OK sign made with forefinger and thumb	Brazil, Uruguay, Germany, Russia
Pointing with the index finger	China, Japan, Indonesia, Latin America, Africa, parts of Europe
Beckoning by curling the index finger with the palm facing up, to indicate 'come here'	Greece, Pakistan, parts of Africa and Asia
Use of left hand	Never shake hands with left hand in a Muslim country and try to avoid using it if at all possible
Snapping fingers	Latin America

Differing tastes

Depending on the product and the country, there may be the need for more or fewer adaptations. For example, UK products for the Australian market may require fewer adaptations than those for the Chinese market since the cultural and social differences between Australia and the UK are relatively small.

Some differences in taste are due to local variants – for example, Coca-Cola has the same base concentrate in every country, but due because it is mixed with the water in local countries it has a slight variation in taste depending on location. This sort of adaptation is not something that a business can control and not something that they would implement themselves.

Other differences can be based on religious beliefs. The use of halal meat is common in fast-food restaurants in Middle Eastern countries. In India, many international fast food restaurants will not sell pork or beef due to the prevailing religious beliefs of that country. By respecting these beliefs and catering to their market in these countries, businesses ensure that they adapt sufficiently to gain a market share from local businesses who may be better suited to understand the regional specifications.

Some adaptations to products are based upon legal requirements. For instance there are many food products used in the US that are banned for use within the European Union. Brands that want to transfer their products from, for example, the US to the UK will have to adapt them to meet the necessary legal requirements. For example, brands such as Pringles and Starburst have had additives removed from their US ingredients list to be able to be sold in the UK.

Table 2 Product adaptations for different cultures

Product	Adaptation
Cadbury chocolate	In the US, Cadbury chocolate tastes markedly different from its UK counterpart. The same is true of the version found in Australia. This can be put down to the difference in taste of the milk used to make the chocolate.
McDonald's	There are significant variations in what is sold in different parts of the world. These are often due to religious beliefs but there are variants based on the tastes of different countries as well – Japanese branches offer a Chicken Katsu burger and in Finland you can have your burger served on a rye bun. In France you can have doughnuts for breakfast, whereas in Hong Kong you can have pasta soup for breakfast.
Samsung	Samsung have created products that meet specific local demands. For example, in China the number 8 and the colour red are considered lucky, so some products have been fitted with red covers and TV stands have been shaped into the figure eight. In Korea, a specialised refrigerator has been built to be perfect for kimchi, a local delicacy; and the demand for sparkling water in the US has been met by installing a dispenser in certain refrigerator models.

Inappropriate branding and promotion

There are many accounts of mistakes involving language, mistranslations and unintended meanings when businesses operate abroad.

Sometimes this can be due to laziness and poor efforts to check with native speakers of a language that a translation is correct. Here are two well-known examples that caused embarrassment:

- the beer maker Coors translated its slogan 'Turn it loose' into Spanish, where it meant 'Drink Coors and get diarrhoea'
- General Motors sold its branded 'Nova' car in Latin America, where its name in Spanish means 'No go'. Not a very good name for a car!

However, mistakes can also be due to one language not having any direct translation for particular words in another. Transferring brand names even just across from the UK to the US or vice versa can still cause issues – cultural, dialectal and grammatical differences can all be a barrier to the brand name being accepted and not becoming a joke. One example of transferring a brand without considering the new market was when Gerber, a Nestlé-owned baby food company, replicated the packaging on their products in Africa, displaying an image of a smiling baby. However, most African products include an image of what is found inside the product due to high levels of illiteracy in the country.

Promotions must also be versioned across different international markets. Many brands want to create a global image and become an internationally recognised brand – this does not mean that the same marketing campaign that worked so successfully in the US will work as successfully in an entirely different market.

Audience is key when crafting marketing campaigns, and if you do not consider the cultural norms of your audience then your expansion into that region will not be successful. For example, a Proctor and Gamble television advert was originally made for the American market. It featured a husband and wife in a bathroom and intended to show how soap could make the woman more attractive. However, it was considered inappropriate when transferred to the Japanese market where

some found it sexist. During the 1994 World Cup, bottles of Heineken beer displayed flags of all the participating countries, including those of Muslim countries where alcohol is forbidden. This prompted numerous complaints.

Not considering your new market will be costly to businesses – not only is there outlay on any advertising campaigns or packaging costs, but also there can be a greater cost to the business if sales of the product are adversely affected in that country for its entire life cycle.

Table 3 Examples of inappropriate brand naming

Product	Issue
Irish Mist, a whiskey liqueur	An Irish product that exports internationally – in German, 'mist' means 'manure'.
Nokia Lumia, a mobile phone	This brand name could not be used in Spain as the direct translation for 'Lumia' is 'prostitute'.
Pee cola, a soft drink	A popular soft drink in Ghana, this product would not be suitable for sale in the UK.
Barf, a detergent powder	An Iranian product where its name means 'snow'. It has less pleasant connotations in English.

Thinking bigger

It has been a mantra in business that international companies must 'think global, act local'. This suggests that operating as they do in a global marketplace they should respect local norms, values and expectations or face the consequences. The same has applied to the management practices of top employers. International branches might have the same logo above the door, but what happens behind it, from pay and benefits to leadership styles and attitude toward diversity, can vary widely from country to country. However, organisations such as international bank Santander are rejecting such localised approaches and instead are unifying their global operations under one banner of 'the way we do things'. In 2014, Santander had banking operations in more than 40 countries with 182,000 employees, primarily in Europe and North and South America. They were moving towards having more corporate policies and ensuring that the same experience is felt in all places.

Javier Bugallo, its head of corporate policies said: 'Some of the really recognisable values, such as the focus on the client, compliance and ethics – all these have to be truly the same and cannot be changed. It is important that the employee experience, the employee value proposition is similar… and harmonised.'

While some scope remains for local differences, the idea is that a Santander manager can step into a branch in Argentina and feel a culture similar to that of the US or Portuguese offices.

Source: adapted from the *Financial Times* 25.03.2014. All rights reserved.

Links 🔗

Unit 57 explores how corporate culture affects business operations, while the focus of Unit 78 is making sense of culture in the context of international businesses. This builds on your understanding of how culture affects marketing and people (Theme 1) and impacts directly upon business decisions and strategy (Theme 3). You will need a thorough grasp of the relevant cultural and social factors when you focus on global business (Theme 4) as this will inform your understanding of a market or location (Units 72, 73, 76 and 77), helping you to assess the impact of MNCs and how to control them (Unit 79 and 81) and to evaluate the ethical issues that may be involved (Unit 80).

Case study

BRIDGING THE CULTURAL GAP

On the 24th floor of a building on New York's Avenue of the Americas a group of British entrepreneurs are attending a master class in how to do business in the US. A more mature start-up scene and access to a large English-speaking market are two factors tempting UK start-ups in the US. UK digital companies have opened US offices while a number of British executives are relocating to head US businesses. As the UK and the US share the same language there is an assumption that the countries make obvious partners. But this assumption may come unstuck when trying to do business. For instance, there are different approaches to hiring staff – US executives can be more self confident than their UK counterparts. A consideration is to evaluate between candidates where some may have been trained from a young age to put forward that they are the best. UK firms may be more used to evaluating candidates who are culturally more measured in putting forward their achievements. The advice for Britons working in the US is to be confident and self-assured.

Alex Kelleher, founder of internet marketing provider Cognitive Match, relocated the business from London to New York. He says that as soon as he arrived he found attitudes different. When pitching ideas to an investor Americans welcome simplicity rather than multi-slide presentations that are ineffective for a US audience. The advice when doing business in the US is to keep the proposition simple and to the point. Cut to the chase in presentations or you will lose the audience. This is even more vital when pitching to customers rather than co-workers.

While some of these differences may not be deal breakers and the English accent can be a welcome part of the culture, it is important for executives to make adjustments to their business style each time they pass border control.

At the New York master class Londoner Nikhil Shah, the founder of a music-sharing website, has been doing business in the US for several years. His assessment of the cultural divide is that 'in the States they are louder, more upfront and more direct. We tend to be more reserved, more tentative and certainly more modest. However you'll find there's a lot more hot air out here and it requires careful filtering'.

Source: adapted from the *Financial Times* 16.05.2015.

(a) Assess the reasons for master classes for those thinking of doing business in the US. (10 marks)

(b) Evaluate the importance of being aware of cultural differences in the success of a company or brand. (20 marks)

Key terms

Cultural audit – study and examination of an organisation's cultural characteristics (such as its assumptions, norms, philosophy, and values) to determine whether they hinder or support its vision and mission.

Ethnocentrism – the tendency of people to view their own cultures, ethics and norms as superior. The evaluation of other cultures according to preconceptions originating in the standards and customs of one's own culture.

High-context cultures – cultures, including much of the Middle East, Asia, Africa, and South America, that are relational, collectivist, intuitive, and contemplative. This means that people in these cultures emphasise interpersonal relationships. Developing trust is an important first step to any business transaction.

Low-context cultures – cultures such as those of North America and much of Europe, that tend to say what they mean. A communication style that relies heavily on explicit and direct language.

Knowledge check

1. Give two examples of ethnocentrism.

2. Explain how cultural differences can impact on business.

3. Why is over-reliance on one language risky?

4. What are the pitfalls of verbal communication?

5. How do differing tastes impact on marketing

6. Why must care be taken in transferring brand names?

Exam tip

Working across differing national cultures adds a new dimension to any assessment or evaluation. You must be able to define what you mean by culture in particular contexts, and you also need a balanced understanding of how a variety of cultures and societies might differ from your own. Independent reading and reflection will help you to provide evidence in support of your judgements.

79 The impact of MNCs

Key points

1. Impact of multinational companies (MNCs) on the local economy:
   - local labour, wages, working conditions and job creation
   - local businesses
   - the local community and environment.
2. Impact of MNCs on the national economy:
   - FDI flows
   - balance of payments
   - technology and skills transfer
   - consumers
   - business culture
   - tax revenues and transfer pricing.

Getting started

In 2012, a Japanese company, Arata Dairy Ltd, opened a factory on the South Island of New Zealand. Arata Dairy is owned by a large multinational company (MNC). The plant, which produces infant formula and other processed milk products, cost NZ$206 million to build and at its opening the company promised to invest another NZ$300 million over the following five years. The factory employs 60 people and processes 150 million litres of milk per season, which is supplied by about 40 local farms. A further 125 jobs were expected to be created in the future.

What are the possible benefits to the community of the new factory? How might the New Zealand national economy benefit from the development? What might be the drawbacks to the new development?

Impact of MNCs on the local economy

The arrival of MNCs in local communities is generally welcomed. This is because a new factory is likely to create employment, provide work for businesses in the supply chain, give a boost to the local economy and provide an opportunity for people to learn new skills.

Local labour and job creation: One of the main impacts of MNCs on local economies is the creation of jobs. For many people the opportunity to work for a large MNC is welcomed and valued. Full-time jobs with the possibility of training, a regular income, financial security and the opportunity to build a career, is very appealing. For example, in 2014 Tenneco-Walker, part of Tenneco Inc., a global US headquartered company, opened a new factory in Merthyr Tydfil, South Wales. The new plant, which makes exhausts for a range of car manufacturers, including Jaguar Land Rover, was expected to create 220 local jobs, providing a boost for the area where unemployment has tended to be high. For example, in 2014 it was reported as 8.3 per cent, which was above the then national average of around 6 per cent.

Wages and working conditions: When a large new business is opened, wages in the locality may rise. This is because the demand for workers in the local economy is likely to drive up rates. If unemployment is relatively low, and if other employment opportunities already exist in the area, wages are much more likely to go up. It is also possible that the jobs created will have favourable working conditions because MNCs often have a modern approach to business development. Their facilities are likely to be new and up to date, adopting the latest technologies, and their working practices are likely to be modern and efficient. Most MNCs are also likely to adopt internationally recognised standards of health and safety, and employee welfare.

Local businesses: MNCs can have a positive impact on local businesses when they arrive. Initially, local businesses may be involved in the construction of the new plant. There may be jobs for builders, carpenters, plumbers, electricians and welders, for example. Once a new facility is 'up and running' there may be a need for local businesses to supply materials, components, commercial services and utilities. As a result businesses in the area may benefit from an increase in trade, higher revenues and more profit. They may also need to recruit more workers of their own to meet demand. There will be other benefits to local businesses. People who take up jobs created by the MNC will have income to spend. This spending will provide more demand for local businesses in general. For example, retailers, restaurants, service providers and the entertainments industry in the area are likely to enjoy a boost in trade.

However, when MNCs develop operations overseas, there may also be a negative effect on local businesses. This is most likely to happen if MNCs lure workers away from other businesses by offering better conditions or higher wages, or supply products that compete directly with those produced by local businesses. For example, in 2015 Marks & Spencer announced plans to open 250 new stores in locations including Russia, China, India, the Middle East and France. Although these new developments were likely to create employment in those locations, they would also take trade away from local rivals, who may struggle to compete and be forced out of business. This means that some people will lose their jobs. However, the competition from MNCs might put pressure on local businesses to make improvements. This might provide some longer-term benefits, such as more efficient and more innovative local enterprises.

The local community and environment: Residents in local communities are likely to welcome the location of MNCs in their area, provided the benefits outweigh the drawbacks. In addition to employment opportunities and a boost to the local economy, MNCs might also provide the following benefits.

- **Improvements in infrastructure.** MNCs might invest some of their own money to help develop roads, electricity, water and gas supplies, schools, hospitals and other public amenities. They might do this to help build trust with the community, but also because a better infrastructure is likely to improve the quality of human capital in the area. Better roads and improved transport links would also benefit MNCs.

- **Contributions to local government taxes.** In the UK businesses have to pay rates to local authorities. Similar payments are likely to be paid by MNCs when they operate in other countries. This money can be used by local government to help fund spending in the area.

- **Help in local communities.** Some MNCs make an effort to build strong links with the local community. They might participate in local cultural or sporting events. They may give money to local charities, organise fundraising events or give locals access to the company's facilities. For example, Scotiabank, the Canada-based global financial services provider, has a 175-year history of making contributions to local communities around the world. One of its initiatives, called the Scotiabank Bright Future program, involves supporting children and children's causes. In 2013, as part of the Bright Future program, Scotiabank presented 81 grants to primary schools in Belize to help pay for tuition fees and books.

Some MNCs may have a negative impact when operating overseas. As a result of environmental damage, communities may

Question 1

The MNC Panasonic is one of Japan's largest producers of electronic goods. In 2014 it opened a new factory in Binh Duong province, Vietnam, making wiring devices and circuit breakers. It said it expected the initial operating output to double after four years.

The factory is large, occupying nearly 9,000 square metres and employing 670 people. It has an environmentally friendly design, adopting Panasonic's energy-saving and energy-creating products including solar power generation systems, LED lighting products, and motion sensor lighting control systems. It also uses fast and flexible Japanese processes and technologies. Panasonic planned to use the factory as a showroom to allow visitors to experience high-quality manufacturing. Panasonic is committed to the principle of using local production for local consumption, with products from this factory helping to meet the increasing demand for electrical construction materials and equipment in Vietnam.

(a) Assess the impact on the local community of the new Panasonic factory in Binh Duong province, Vietnam.

be left struggling to survive in areas where farming and other subsistence activities are almost impossible. Mining industries in particular can have an impact if there are oil spills that lead to environmental harm from oil pollution. This can have a significant impact on the health and activities of local people, especially farming and fishing.

Impact of MNCs on the national economy

The overwhelming majority of governments around the world are in favour of MNCs setting up operations in their countries. This is because they are likely to generate income, employment, wealth and prosperity.

FDI flows: When an overseas business locates a new facility in a foreign country, the amount of money spent on establishing that facility is classified as foreign direct investment (FDI). For example, it was widely reported that in 2014 Honda, the Japanese vehicle producer, opened a factory in Guanajuato, Mexico, costing Honda around £489 million. The factory employed 3,200 workers and produced around 200,000 cars per annum. This inflow of money from an overseas business into a country, such as from Honda to Mexico in the above example, is likely to be welcomed by the host country. This is because the national economy will benefit. Examples of specific benefits to the economy include the following.

- **Increase in income.** Generally, flows of FDI should result in higher levels of GDP (the total level of income for a country) for the host nation. The extra output and employment resulting from new FDI will increase economic growth and should help to raise the living standards for people in the host country.
- **Increase in tax revenue.** The profits made by MNCs are taxed by the host nation. This increases tax revenue for the government. This money can be spent on improving government services, such as healthcare, education, housing and transport networks.
- **Increase in employment.** The flow of FDI creates new jobs in the host nation. For example, the single investment by Honda in Mexico created 3,200 jobs in the Guanajuato region. This helps to reduce unemployment and save money that would otherwise be paid out in benefits to the unemployed. Businesses in the host country may also get a boost when an MNC invests in a project because a range of local suppliers will be needed. For example, the Honda factory in the above example is likely to need supplies of raw materials, car components, utilities, telephone services, commercial services, distribution services, maintenance crews and cleaning contractors. Such demands will help to sustain and expand businesses in Mexico and therefore create even more jobs in the national economy.
- **Reduce national debt.** Some of the money received by the government from FDI might be used to reduce national debt. This has a positive impact on a country's finances. If a country can reduce its debt it sends out a message to the rest of the world that it is more financially stable. As a result interest payments might be reduced and the country should find it easier to borrow in the future.

Balance of payments: Investment by MNCs will have a positive impact on the host nation's balance of payments. There will be a double impact. Initially, the flow of FDI when a project is being established will improve the balance of payments because money will flow into the host nation's account. For example, the £489 million spent by Honda when building the new car plant in Guanajuato will improve the balance of payments for Mexico.

Once a facility is 'up and running' there may be a further boost to the balance of payments. This is because if any of the output from a new factory is sold abroad, there will be a further flow of money into the balance of payments account of the host nation. For example, if some of the cars produced in Guanajuato are sold to the US, the value of those sales represents a flow of money into Mexico's account (even though the company has a Japanese owner). This boost in the balance of payments will help a host nation to 'pay its way' when trading internationally. In the UK, car sales to the rest of the EU from Japanese-owned producers, such as Nissan, Honda and Toyota, help to improve the UK's balance of payments.

For some less developed countries the impact on the balance of payments from MNC investment may be even more significant. This is because they often find it difficult to get established in global markets and FDI allows them to boost sales of goods overseas.

If MNCs buy resources from overseas, such as machinery, tools and equipment, this will have a negative effect on the balance of payments of the host country. This is because there will be a flow of money out of the country. There will also be a negative impact if profits are repatriated to the MNC's base. Repatriated profits represent a **flow of money** away from the host country.

Technology and skills transfer: MNC investment in foreign countries often means that new technologies and modern working practices are introduced into the host nation. This might result in the transfer of technologies and knowledge to local businesses. This transfer may be horizontal or vertical.

- Horizontal transfers are when knowledge is transferred across the same industry. For example, new technologies and working practices used by Japanese car manufacturers, such as Nissan and Toyota, when these companies established production in the UK, were copied by other car producers in the UK.
- Vertical transfers may be forward or backward. For example, MNCs often provide technical assistance, training and other information to their suppliers located in the host country. Many MNCs also assist local suppliers in purchasing resources and in modernising production facilities. These are examples of backward vertical transfers.
- Forward vertical transfers are likely to occur when businesses in the host nation purchase goods and services from the MNCs. For example, a domestic business assembling

washing machines using components made by a multinational may adopt and adapt technologies, working practices and managerial methods used by the MNC.

The transfer of technology and skills from an MNC to businesses in the host nation will help to improve efficiency and productivity. This will help to make domestic producers more competitive and generate sales both at home and abroad if the improvements are significant. In some cases, the copying of technologies, products and working practices can lead to domestic producers posing a real threat to MNCs in their markets. Through a process called **reverse engineering** some businesses analyse a rival's product very closely by taking it apart to see how it has been produced. They then identify those features of the product that they think are worth copying. For example, it was reported that China built its first stealth bomber using technology based on a US fighter plane that was shot down over Serbia years previously. Military officials were reported as saying it was likely that the Chinese developed the stealth technology used in the Chengdu J-20 from parts of an American F-117 Nighthawk.

Question 2

Jones Construction is a leading manufacturer of construction machinery and equipment. In 2012 it opened a new factory in Malaysia to add to the one it already operated in the country. The new plant cost £25 million to construct.

The investment by Jones Construction is expected to generate around 500 new jobs and the company's chairman commented that he could never have imagined that our family business would employ 2,000 people in Malaysia making our products, with thousands more employed elsewhere in the supply chain. The new factories mean our contribution to the Malaysian economy will grow and I am grateful to the Pengang Government for their support in helping Jones Construction make our investment ambitions a reality.'

(a) Explain the benefits to Malaysia of FDI like the investment made by Jones Construction.

(b) Explain the possible impact on the Malaysian balance of payments of the investment by Jones Construction.

Consumers: Consumers are likely to benefit from the arrival of MNCs in their countries. This is because they will be free to buy some of the goods that they produce. Specific benefits to consumers include the following.

- **More choice.** The products supplied by MNCs will add to the choice already available in the host country. For example, MNCs like Coca-Cola, Starbucks and McDonald's set up in many countries around the world to sell their products. However, not all MNCs produce consumer goods. Some make components or provide services for other businesses.
- **Lower prices.** The arrival of MNCs is likely to increase competition in the host country. The products made by MNCs

may be cheaper because they use modern and efficient production techniques. Since their costs will be lower, they can offer products at lower prices. This competitive pressure may also force domestic producers to lower their prices.

- **Improved quality.** If MNCs use 'state-of-the-art' technologies, modern materials and more efficient working practices, such as total quality management, the quality of products might also be improved. For example, they may be better designed, more durable, more efficient and more aesthetically pleasing.
- **Better living standards.** In general, it is possible that many people in the host nation will enjoy better living standards when MNCs set up operations. Initially, they may benefit from employment opportunities and enjoy higher incomes. They will have more choice and enjoy access to cheaper and better quality products. If products are generally cheaper then they will have more income left over to fund other expenditure.

Some MNCs are very powerful. In some cases the annual revenue of a multinational can be greater than the GDP of an entire country. This can give them a formidable presence. If too many domestic producers leave the market due to intense competition, this could result in less choice for consumers in the long term. Also, if MNCs are left with little or no competition, they may come to dominate the market and exploit consumers.

Business culture: There is some evidence to suggest that the proliferation of MNCs can have an impact on the business culture in the countries where they set up operations. In some cases, people who are employed by MNCs may eventually leave their jobs and start their own businesses. This might happen because

- individuals may have saved some money from employment, which can be used for start-up capital
- workers may have developed skills that they think could be put to better use working for themselves
- multinationals may encourage workers to set up businesses and become suppliers. If quality standards can be maintained, MNCs might welcome this development because it can provide them with more flexibility.

As more MNCs develop enterprises around the world, and the pace of globalisation accelerates, it will become more culturally acceptable for people in a wide range of countries to set up their own businesses. MNCs may help to foster a culture of enterprise and encourage entrepreneurs to set up new businesses.

It is also possible that business cultures in the host country will be influenced by the cultures in MNCs. For example, when Japanese MNCs started to build factories in the UK they used modern production methods and developed different corporate cultures to those in UK businesses. As a result, over a period of time, many UK businesses reflected the production techniques and working practices of the Japanese. This eventually led to a change in corporate cultures. In many UK organisations the culture became more open and less confrontational. Arguably, managers began to recognise the wider talents of their employees, which also had an impact on the workplace culture.

Tax revenues and transfer pricing: Multinationals pay taxes to national economies. This can then pay for government spending in areas such as health and education. Multinationals are often accused of paying as little tax as possible and seeking out locations where taxes are low. A common technique to avoid tax on profits is **transfer pricing**. Assume a multinational company has to make a product in country A, a country which charges high taxes on profits. The company will therefore want to make as little profit as possible in country A. The company also has operations in country B, a country which charges low taxes on profits. By selling the product made in country A at an artificially low price to its operations in country B, it can minimise its profits in country A. It then sells the product from country B at the market price, perhaps even back to customers in country A. But then it makes high profits in country B because it has bought the good at an artifically low price from country A. It still has to pay taxes on profits in country B, but its overall tax liability in countries A and B is much lower because of transfer pricing. Inevitably, because multinationals are profit-seeking companies, they will seek to minimise their tax liabilities. If Slovakia offers lower taxes than the UK, this will be one factor which a US multinational will take into account when deciding where to put a new plant in the EU. Governments therefore need to weigh up the benefits of attracting investment by offering low taxes against loss of tax revenues. They also need to be robust in their dealings with multinationals to ensure that they pay their fair share of taxes.

Exam tip
The impact of MNCs is often very positive for a country. However, it is important to remember when discussing the impact of MNCs that they can have negative effects. For example, some MNCs might damage the environment, exploit local workers and have a detrimental impact on local businesses, causing them to fold.

Links 🔗
There may be a number of opportunities for you to demonstrate your synoptic skills when discussing MNCs. For example, there is a very strong link between the impact of MNCs and their control (Unit 81). Information in this unit might also be linked with Distribution (Unit 12), Legislation (Unit 42), Theories of corporate strategy (Unit 45), Growth (Unit 48), Corporate culture (Unit 57), Business ethics (Unit 59), Scenario planning (Unit 65) and many of the units in Theme 4.

Key terms

Reverse engineering – a method of analysing a product's design by taking it apart.
Transfer pricing – a system operated by MNCs. It is an attempt to avoid relatively high tax rates through the prices which one subsidiary charges another for components and finished goods.

Knowledge check

1. What might be the main advantage to a local economy when an MNC arrives?

2. How might wage rates rise as a result of MNC operations in a local economy?

3. How might local businesses benefit from the arrival of an MNC?

4. How might local businesses be adversely affected by the arrival of an MNC?

5. State two impacts an MNC might have on the local community.

6. How might the arrival of an MNC impact on the local environment?

7. How does an MNC influence the flow of FDI into a country?

8. How might the location of an MNC improve the balance of payments for a nation?

9. How might consumers be affected by the arrival of an MNC?

10. Explain how technologies and skills might be transferred from an MNC to a country.

Case study

GlaxoSmithKline (GSK)

GSK, a UK-based MNC, is a science-led healthcare company. It employs around 100,000 people in over 115 countries. It produces vaccines, medicines and consumer healthcare products. In 2014 the company's turnover was £23 billion. It made a total operating profit of £3.6 billion.

In 2014 GSK announced plans to invest around £130 million in its operations in Africa, £100 million of which was earmarked to expand existing manufacturing facilities in Nigeria and Kenya and to construct five new factories in places such as Rwanda, Ethiopia and Ghana. The investment was expected to create hundreds of jobs. The plan was for the new factories to produce antibiotics, respiratory and HIV medicines. At the same time the technology, skills and knowledge would be transferred to help local manufacturers make more complex products in the future.

GSK announced that the move would create at least 500 jobs in Africa and help to build upon the skills of the African workforce across the continent. He also suggested that it was time for businesses to contribute more to the development of Africa by investing in infrastructure, developing skills and creating employment.

Some of the £130 million investment was to create the first R&D lab for non-communicable diseases (NCDs) in Africa that would also support the training and education of African researchers, and help to develop a new generation of African NCD experts. GSK also announced that it would create up to 25 academic Chairs in African universities in subjects such as pharmaceuticals, logistics, public health and engineering. GSK said that it hoped that these academic roles would 'facilitate the development of new courses as well as internships and student exchanges, and will be pivotal to ensuring manufacturing capability is locked into the continent to help attract further manufacturing investment.'

In addition, GSK announced plans to set up regional supply hubs so that products, such as medicines, could be distributed to more isolated communities across Africa. The company said that it hoped that working in partnership with local people would help to reduce shortages and improve the security of Africa's medical supplies. It would also lower production costs, cut prices and reduce Africa's reliance on imports.

Finally, GSK said it would remain committed to the training of healthcare workers in Africa. It aimed to develop partnerships with charities and local organisations to train around 10,000 community healthcare workers in countries such as Kenya, Ghana and Nigeria. GSK said: 'The investment will be targeted at supporting the most remote and marginalised communities to help address healthcare inequalities that exist even in fast-growing countries.'

Sources: adapted from www.gsk.com

(a) Explain how MNCs like GSK can help to foster a business culture in the countries where they locate operations. (4 marks)

(b) Evaluate the impact that GSK might have on the national economies of some African states. (20 marks)

Key points

1. Stakeholder conflicts.
2. Pay and working conditions.
3. Environmental considerations:
   - emissions
   - waste disposal.
4. Supply chain considerations:
   - exploitation of labour
   - child labour.
5. Marketing considerations:
   - misleading product labelling
   - inappropriate promotional activities.

Getting started

A firm makes parts for oil wells and exports them overseas. A customs official in a capital city says there is a big delay in clearing their shipment through customs, but if they pay him an 'expediting fee', the shipment will be moved further up the queue.

Is this situation a question of law or of ethics? What should the company do?

Ethics

Ethics refers to the principles and norms that govern behaviour. Business ethics at the company level was introduced in Unit 58, which looked at the trade-off between profit and ethics and how ethics might affect pay and rewards, as well what is meant by corporate social responsibility. At the international level, ethics may or may not be reflected in a country's laws and regulations. If a firm establishes in a country, it will have to work within the institutional framework of both the home and the host country. Consequently, a firm may be acting within the law of its home country and nevertheless be deemed to be acting unethically in the other. Equally, although a business may be matching the ethical norms abroad, its activities could breach the ethics of its domestic base.

Generally, ethics involves respecting human rights and local traditions, but avoiding corruption. Corruption is using public power for personal benefit. Bribery is the most common example of a corrupt practice, but what constitutes a bribe is often not easy to figure out. For instance, gift-giving between business colleagues is very common in most Asian and some Arab cultures, but considered wrong or even illegal in North America and Europe. In fact, if you work for a British firm, you could face prosecution for offering or accepting a bribe. Consequently, many international businesses have written codes of conduct that set out policies to guide employees' decision making.

Stakeholder conflicts

Many people have a stake in the decisions that firms make. That is, they have an interest in it or a right associated with it.

As explored in Unit 58, a **stakeholder** in a firm is an individual or a group that is affected by – and in turn can affect – an organisation. The types of stakeholders in an international firm are listed in Figure 1.

Figure 1

Types of stakeholders in an international firm

Stakeholder issues can arise in any area of a business, including the following.

Consumers:

- Conflicts of interest, such as where an energy firm manipulates the markets, resulting in consumers paying more than they otherwise would have. This is done by using a different measure to report on their profit margins to the public, which can mean that an increase in household bills could be made to seem justifiable.
- Product safety, such as involving tainted meat that reaches consumers in the supply chain.
- Misleading advertising.

Employees:

- Employee safety, ensuring healthy and safe conditions, avoiding failings that might lead to injury or death, for example at refineries and oil rigs, including the Deep Water Horizon oil spill in the Gulf of Mexico in 2010.
- Employee redundancies. A company may need to reduce staff numbers to regain profitability or they may choose to outsource some work for cheaper returns.
- Pay and conditions.

Shareholders:

- Conflicts of interest between the management and the shareholders.
- Short-term versus long-term returns on shares. Shareholders invest for a variety of reasons, but one of the major factors is seeking a return on their investment through dividends. The business will make a decision on how much profit it will retain each year for investment and how much to return in dividends to the owners – the shareholders. The business will take a long-term view in that it needs to invest in new equipment or expand its branches. Reinvesting profit can finance future growth. Using retained profits is the cheapest way to reinvest and it needs to persuade shareholders that investing to earn profits in the future is in their long-term interests, rather than paying out more in dividends in the short term.

Countries or communities:

- Safety, where people's well-being is compromised, such as the reported pesticide chemical leak at the Union Carbide plant in Bhopal, India, that poisoned over 300,000 people and caused 5,200 deaths.
- Environmental concerns, where the activities of the business pollute or damage the environment. For example, the mining of tar sands impacts on the local wildlife and air and water quality.

Question 1

Ten people are sitting around a table giving feedback to Vodafone, one of the world's biggest mobile operators by revenue, on its UK corporate responsibility report. Discussion ranges across the company's handling of controversial issues, such as the siting of masts and the protection of children from adult content on their phones. The debate is polite but lively and Vodafone's representative quietly takes notes. Seeking the views of stakeholders has become accepted practice among larger companies, especially multinationals. They are concerned to understand external expectations of their business and to manage their impact on society and the environment. So what does a company do when stakeholder interests collide, either with each other or with the interests of the business? Vodafone believes that an effective stakeholder programme is essential. It has many meetings with stakeholders and it commissions in-depth opinion surveys and holds detailed discussions with specific interest groups.

Marks & Spencer agrees with this approach. Its engagement with stakeholders charts the shifts in consumer attitudes. Through this engagement it has realised that the vast majority of customers have quite strong expectations of issues such as fair trade and animal welfare. Marks & Spencer believes that talking to stakeholders is vital to help it define bad and good practice.

Some critics, however, feel that there is a danger of allowing pressure groups too much power.

Source: adapted from the *Financial Times* 28.11.2005. All rights reserved.

(a) Describe the types of conflict that could emerge between Vodafone stakeholders.

(b) Why do Vodafone and Marks & Spencer establish stakeholder programmes?

- Resource depletion, where a company's extraction objectives conflict with the best possible future for that country. For instance if resources are depleted before they are able to be replenished or are exploited to the detriment of the country's environment. An example of this is the pollution associated with the extraction of rare earths, such as yttrium and lanthanum. There is a high demand for these elements for electrical components and other hi-tech applications, but they are only found in certain countries.

Pay and working conditions

A major problem for business ethics involves the complexities of global supply chains and the working conditions of employees in other countries. UK law covers pay and working conditions of local suppliers, employees and managers. Thus, all employees have certain defined rights at work governing their pay, conditions, holiday entitlement, sickness and time off work, health and safety, discrimination and bullying, and there are detailed procedures and protections for dismissing an employee. However, such clear guidance does not always exist in many countries. As a result of globalisation, many MNCs have their manufacturing operations in other countries. The business rationale for this is often the availability of cheap labour in less economically developed countries (LEDCs). Because some of these countries do not have the same level of legislation to protect employees as countries such as the UK, the standard of working conditions is low. Work is primarily done by women, who are not necessarily paid a living wage as there is no legal requirement to do so.

These factories are sometimes referred to as sweatshops and can be hazardous with poor ventilation, little space and, in some cases, exposure to dangerous chemicals. The buildings themselves can also be poorly built, as evidenced by the collapse of a factory in Dhaka, Bangladesh in 2013 that killed over 1,000 people. These working conditions could not occur in the UK due to tight controls on the environment in which people work.

As MNCs can locate anywhere in the world, the market for their business is very competitive – this is why the practice of offering below the living wage can continue. The lower the wage, the less money the MNC needs to invest in that manufacturing area and so it can increase its revenues. This practice has become less prevalent in recent years due to international outcry over whether it is ethical to pay workers in LEDCs a lower wage than their equivalent in, say, the UK. For example, clothing manufacturers may outsource the manufacturing of their products to overseas factories in order to increase their profits. However, if the factories in developing countries do not pay a decent wage, this may provoke criticism. Some companies try to reduce the negative attention by annually publishing list of the factories that they use and an audit of these factories' ethical practices. This is an example of conflicting interests, not only between the larger business and their employees, but also between the business and its customers, due to consumers being unhappy with its practices.

There are a number of initiatives and organisations that are working to ensure fair working practices for all. The Ethical Trading Initiative is a British NGO concerned with the employment practices of multinationals, and is supported by Marks & Spencer,

The Body Shop and Inditex. It is concerned with the following.

- Employment is freely chosen.
- Freedom of association and collective bargaining is freely chosen.
- Working conditions are safe and hygienic.
- Child labour is not used.
- Living wages are paid.
- Working hours are not excessive.
- No discrimination is practised.
- Regular employment is provided.
- No harsh or inhumane treatment is allowed.

Pay can also be an issue between different structural levels within companies. Managers are responsible for trying to balance the interests of stakeholders (in this instance, their employees), yet they are themselves stakeholders, and this can lead to numerous conflicts. Where a manager is in a position of power, the balance between interests is an important consideration, especially in relationship to, for example, executive pay.

Question 2

Starbucks, an American coffee retailer, emphasises the role of ethics in its operations. It has a Corporate Social Responsibility Department and works with NGOs to ensure its coffee is sourced fairly. However, in 2000, an NGO named Global Exchange suggested that it was not providing a living wage for its coffee producers. Global Exchange put forward that Starbucks should pay the 'living wage' of US$1.26 per pound (the market price at the time of 64 cents per pound). They planned a protest at Starbucks' stores if the firm did not agree. Starbucks was already paying $1.20 per pound so the wage increase was not substantial and the impact to the quality assurance of the business could be significant. Its customers expect only the best coffee from Starbucks and any changing perceptions of the quality of how the business operates might have affected its brand.

This example illustrates the difficulties of ensuring that the expectations of stakeholders are met. Starbucks' stakeholders include its suppliers, especially the people who grow its coffee, but also social organisations, such as Global Exchange, who have an impact not only upon the treatment of the supplier-stakeholders, but also upon operations and future strategy.

Managers must try and balance the interests of stakeholders, and obviously this is difficult and can lead to balancing different viewpoints. For instance, with Starbucks, many of its suppliers and the NGOs supporting them, wanted higher payments for coffee beans. This was a different perspective than some of its consumers who wanted to pay less while also ensuring the consistent quality of their brew. Consequently, the managers must prioritise to ensure that, whatever the conflict, the firm continues to survive and grow. Starbucks addressed the issue by increasing its purchases of Fair Trade Coffee, which meets an international standard for pay and conditions of suppliers. It also created guidelines for the purchase of the most ethically sourced coffee that it could and made this process fully transparent in its annual Corporate Social Responsibility Report.

Source: adapted from the *Financial Times* 27.08.2014, all rights reserved.

(a) Is the quality assurance of how a business operates to provide a quality brew more important for a quality coffee retailer than paying more for coffee beans?

(b) 'You can never keep all stakeholders happy.' Discuss this statement.

Environmental considerations

Companies today are concerned about the environment for many reasons, including the effect on all of their stakeholders, the ramifications of increasing government regulation and how to reduce operating costs. Consequently, businesses will evaluate the level of concern of host governments and of consumers, as well as how environmental issues will affect the firm's operations in the short, medium and long term.

HSBC is active in a Climate Partnership with the World Wildlife Fund and belongs to various forest stewardship schemes. Yet it's reported that HSBC also funds unsustainable logging in Malaysia that has denuded more than 90 per cent of the old growth forests on the island of Sarawak. NGS Global Witness suggests that over three decades, loans and financial services to logging interests have generated close to $120 million in revenue for the bank.

Emissions: Climate change is an important international issue. Since emissions cross borders, it involves many institutions and stakeholders. The US Department of Energy's Carbon Dioxide Information and Analysis Centre puts global industrial emissions at 1,450 gigatonnes since 1751. Research has suggested that two-thirds of greenhouse-gas emissions have been caused by just 90 companies, based in countries around the world.

There is strict legislation in the UK governing the environmental output of a business, including legislation that requires all UK quoted companies to report on their greenhouse gas emissions. This strict legislation is a result of requirements made in the Climate Change Act 2008. This sort of legislation does not always exist in LEDCs where many MNCs base their manufacturing industry. As they are creating employment within the LEDC, environmental protection may not be a key concern.

The highly urbanised areas that develop around industry in LEDCs can suffer from bad air pollution and issues with waste disposal. This was the case, for example, with the Bhopal chemical leak in India, mentioned earlier. A lot of those affected were living in slum towns surrounding the plant.

Waste disposal: As with the guidance surrounding air emissions, the UK government enforces legislation regarding how companies dispose of waste. This sort of legislation is also often missing or not enforced in LEDCs. There are many barriers to effective waste disposal in LEDCs, such as the lack of a proper infrastructure to allow for efficient waste removal – poor roads can mean that lorries are not able to remove waste effectively. There are huge environmental considerations when looking at the ways companies dispose of waste – the UN's Step Initiative estimated that by 2017 there will be enough 'e-waste' (discarded electrical products) to fill a 24,000 kilometre line of 40 tonne lorries. This waste contains toxic elements that deteriorate over time and are being dumped illegally in LEDCs, causing a huge environmental concern.

For example, Trafigura, a Swiss commodities-trading firm was reportedly fined one million euros by a Dutch court in 2010 for dumping toxic waste on waste tips in the Ivory Coast. The waste was supposed to have been processed in the Netherlands, but after a Dutch firm demanded a higher price, the unprocessed waste was taken to the Ivory Coast, risking the health of local people.

Supply chain considerations

Global businesses have global supply chains. Numerous ethical issues come with the increasing complexity involved in global sourcing and logistics. For instance, if you have a mobile phone, it is very likely that at least some of the components within it have been sourced from conflict zones. Many of the world's rarest and most valuable minerals are sourced from The Democratic Republic of the Congo (DRC). It is reported that in some of the DRC mines, illegal armed gangs enslave workforces (including very young children) and commit human rights abuses. Yet many of the firms buying these minerals may be reluctant to look more closely at their supply chains because of the costs of doing so. To try and address the issue, the Organisation for Economic Co-operation and Development (OECD) has drawn up guidelines designed to minimise the use of so-called conflict minerals.

Exploitation of labour: From the number of cases that appear in national courts and are documented by the International Labour Organisation, it appears that exploitation of labour is common throughout the world. The ILO, part of the United Nations, estimated that in 2014 there were around 21 million people being exploited by their employers.

A life as a 'modern slave' often begins when an individual in a LEDC seeking work contacts a recruiter. The recruiter charges the employee fees to find them a job, then once a position is found the employing firm will repay the recruiter, but insist that the new employee pay them back. This is called 'bonded labour' and it binds the worker to the employer until the hefty debt, plus interest, is repaid.

For example, in 2014 NGO Verite found that around 30 per cent of workers in Malaysia's electronics industry were forced to work. In Thailand, according to Freedom Fund, another NGO, most of the workers in the seafood industry are bonded labourers. Newspapers in the UK have highlighted concerns about the treatment of migrant workers employed in Qatar on World Cup construction.

Businesses are taking steps to keep products free from exploited labour. The British Retail Consortium has guidelines for its members' supply chains that ban bonded labour and set minimum working conditions.

Child labour: Many businesses who outsource production overseas rely on local suppliers who follow local traditions and norms, some of which are not acceptable practice in developed economies. Nowhere is the ethical dilemma more difficult than with child labour. In most cases, child labour has nothing to do with MNCs, but rather may be commonplace in local area businesses and on farms, where very young children are put to work as soon as they are able.

While child labour is unacceptable in Britain, it has not been – until very recently – in Bangladesh. But there can be undesirable consequences to clamping down on child labour without further protection for the young workers. For instance, when Bangladesh was forced to stop employing children in some of its factories or face trade sanctions, the reported result was that up to 7,000 young girls went from being factory workers to becoming prostitutes.

The issue of child labour in the supply chain is not as clear-cut as it may first appear. From a western-centric point of view child labour is clearly not ethical and in 1973, Convention 138, ratified by 135 countries, banned all forms of child labour. However, in 1999, Convention 182 changed this to cover only the worst examples of labour. Some suggest that stopping child labour in developing countries can, in fact, be damaging to families: where the child's earnings are a key source of income for the family, the loss of that income can be devastating. Additionally, there may not be a formal education system that the child can join and, as in the case of Bangladesh, it may force children into worse situations.

However, MNCs do not have to passively accept child labour as normal. They can choose to locate elsewhere, in places where child labour is not acceptable. Alternatively, they can take the approach of IKEA, and help the families to support their children by providing working mothers with a good wage and their children with an education while they work.

Question 3

Boehm Clothing is a clothing manufacturer. It uses factories in Bangladesh where child labour has been common, and businesses including Boehm, have been the subject of campaigns against the use of child labour. However, Boehm has collaborated with international organisations to provide training for unskilled child labourers in Bangladesh who became unemployed due to international pressure to eradicate child labour. Boehm has established training centres in Bangladesh to teach young people the skills required by sewing machinists and to help combat child labour. On completing their vocational training courses, as long as they are old enough, young people can then take work in Boehm's suppliers' factories. In most cases, as a result of the skills gained from their training, they have secured better positions and salaries. These child labourers can be their families' sole breadwinners, and so simply making it illegal for them to work might push them into taking more dangerous employment.

(a) Why do you think Boehm Clothing has invested in the training centres?

(b) How do you think families in Bangladesh might view measures to combat child labour?

Marketing considerations

There are a number of issues that companies must consider when they are looking to market their products. These will be dependent upon the type of business and their type of product as well as the specific market. Often elements will need to be altered to be suitable for the market. Cultural and social factors that could affect this are considered in Unit 78.

Misleading labelling: Businesses should ensure that the labels on their products are not misleading, so that consumers can make a fully informed choice as to whether to purchase their products and how to use them once bought. In the UK,

this is enshrined in the Trade Descriptions Act and enforced by the Trading Standards Authority. Labels must be accurate, and so cannot contain false information on price, quantity or size, materials the product is made of, what it can do, or who might have endorsed it. They must also explain if there is any aspect of the product that could be hazardous.

However, the Trade Descriptions act does not apply outside the UK, so businesses have to be aware of local legislation and ensure that they comply with the laws that apply. What does a firm do when there is no law governing labelling? This is an ethical question. Should it abide by the highest standards of all of the countries that it operates in, the minimum ones, or none at all?

The United Nations Economic and Social Council has published guidance on this, at least with respect to food labelling. False labelling is not permitted, but it may be difficult for a consumer to distinguish between labels that are 'truthful and non-misleading' or 'truthful but misleading'. Moreover, one culture may find a label to be misleading while another might not.

An example of a misleading statement might be: 'Contains only 1 gram of sodium'. This seems to imply that the product is low in salt (sodium chloride), when it is actually very high in salt.

Inappropriate promotional activities: Product and business promotion can cover a broad range of different activities, such as advertising, publicity and direct marketing. These can be considered inappropriate if they are actually illegal or are offensive. In 2013, the Chinese government suggested that GlaxoSmithKlein (GSK), a British pharmaceutical firm, was involved in 'illegal marketing activities' in order to increase drug sales. These activities supposedly included generous entertainment, including all expenses paid conferences for doctors, gift-giving and case payments.

Promotional activities in China can follow the Chinese cultural tradition of guanxi, involving the use of personal connections in business activity that can include gift-giving, doing favours and socialising. In England, for example, practices such as these might be deemed unethical and may be illegal. However, many businesses acknowledge that these cultural aspects are part of their business context when operating in a global environment with China and many other countries.

Unit 71 explores factors to consider, including aspects such as corruption, when assessing whether a country is an attractive place for investment.

Exam tip

When you see the command word 'Assess', you know that you must give a balanced answer, often employing competing arguments. Therefore, when looking at ethics in the context of international business, you should be aware of the differing corporate and national cultures that may affect business and employee behaviour. Reading widely about different countries and their cultures will help you to draw on examples in support of your points.

Links 🔗

Ethical considerations run through almost every aspect of international business, including: what motivates people (Unit 17); what areas governments choose to legislate (Units 42 and 81); how corporate and national cultures impact upon operations (Units 57, 78 and 81); and what might drive change or choices of markets (Units 63, 72 and 73).

Thinking bigger

The corporate world has many examples of where ethics within business are key considerations. For example, when two children tragically died from carbon monoxide poisoning from a faulty boiler at a hotel on a Thomas Cook holiday, the travel company could have been more sympathetic. The group was not directly responsible for the deaths but the media reported their somewhat corporate manner as heartless and the way that it handled the case didn't put it in a good light. It was reported that the management stuck narrowly to a legal brief and executives were silent at the children's long delayed inquest. It took 10 years to offer an apology and Thomas Cook reportedly received £3m in compensation, nearly ten times the amount received by the parents of the children who died. The group was criticised for the approach taken. Yet some reports also said that by the standards of most modern corporations, Thomas Cook did little out of the ordinary. The board was reported as acting in a way to protect its investors' interests. However, the shareholders' near-term interest was in direct conflict with the company's wider commercial one. It was reported that management had not appreciated how the company's behaviour would be viewed, and that it should have shown compassion and not only paid attention to its lawyers, as consumers have their own logic and it is in the eyes of the paying public not the law, that it will ultimately be judged. In this way it would also have balanced the needs of all its stakeholders.

You could use this information in a variety of ways. Obviously, it can be used when answering questions on business ethics but it might also be useful when discussing corporate governance and the influence of stakeholders.

Source: adapted from the *Financial Times* 18.05.2015. All rights reserved.

Case study

TIPTREE TEXTILES

Tiptree Textiles is an American company that produces clothing for customers around the world. It is well-known for its unusual print designs and styles. About five years ago, Tiptree became a focus for considerations around ethical treatment of workers in their overseas factories.

Tiptree had outsourced its production to factories in developing countries, in order to reduce manufacturing costs and gain economies of scale. However, it was alleged by some that Tiptree would manufacture in a particular country until local workers demanded higher wages and safer working practices, and then Tiptree would move production out of that country and into another location where their costs would be lower.

Tiptree responded that it couldn't be held responsible for the treatment of the workers at the factories that it used. It said that, as it had outsourced the work to a third party, it had no control over the working conditions in the factories. However, the issue was taken up by a number of British and American news outlets and non-governmental organisations, who campaigned to influence Tiptree's attitude towards working practices.

News coverage of Tiptree at this time was almost entirely negative. Journalists focused on the issue and conducted undercover investigations of conditions in the factories run by Tiptree's suppliers. Some of these reports showed that child labour was used in some of the factories run by Tiptree's suppliers. As popular opinion turned against Tiptree, people also took to social media to make their opinion heard. Pressure groups used social media to spread the word and to encourage people to boycott the company's products.

Tiptree could not deny that their suppliers were treating their workers very badly. There was a lot of evidence to show that workers were not paid fairly or compensated for doing overtime; that factories were using child labour and, in some cases, forced labour; that workers were not permitted to join trades unions; and that the health and safety standards in the factories were shockingly low. Tiptree responded that other clothing companies used similar factories with similar working conditions.

In response to the issues arising, Tiptree drew up a code of standards for its suppliers. The company will not work with suppliers who refuse to sign up to and implement the standards. Tiptree also started to report annually on ethical issues in its supply chain, and appointed independent factory inspectors to audit working standards with no warning.

In the last nine months, Tiptree also announced that it intends to set up a training programme for young people in the countries where their suppliers' factories are located. This programme will train them how to become skilled sewing machinists and therefore ensure that they will earn a higher wage in the future.

Q

(a) Assess the impact of the publicity surrounding child labour on Tiptree. (10 marks)

(b) Evaluate the influence of pressure groups on changing the behaviours of a business. (20 marks)

Key terms

Ethics – moral rules or principles of behaviour that should guide members of a profession or organisation and make them deal honestly and fairly with each other and with their stakeholders.

Institutional framework – the system of formal laws, regulations and procedures, and informal conventions customs and norms that shape activity and behaviour.

Code of conduct – a set of rules outlining the proper practices of an organisation that contributes to the welfare of key stakeholders and respects the rights of all affected by its operations.

Stakeholders – groups or individuals who can affect or be affected by the actions of a business.

Knowledge check

1. How might a business be operating within the law, but be acting unethically?

2. How might stakeholder conflicts arise?

3. How might conflict be avoided?

4. Why are MNCs criticised for their activities in developing countries?

5. What incentives exist to ensure fair working practices for all?

6. Why does the existence of global supply chains create ethical issues?

81 Controlling MNCs

Key points

Factors to consider:
1. Political influence.
2. Legal control.
3. Pressure groups.
4. Social media.

Getting started

The English East India Company (EIC) was founded in 1600 when Queen Elizabeth I granted merchants a monopoly on trade in many basic commodities, including cotton, salt, silk and tea. At first the company docked its ships wherever it could, then it began establishing trading posts along the Indian coast, and eventually started building factories and establishing commercial and political relationships with the Mughal rulers. The EIC was a huge money-making machine for the English economy well into the 19th century, at one point controlling nearly half of all global trade.

The EIC is considered to be the first modern company as it was the first to be granted limited liability. Before limited liability, an investor could lose everything that they owned if something went wrong on a trading voyage. With limited liability, their losses were limited to the amount they had actually invested. The EIC was given a monopoly over trade, since, even with limited liability, the voyages were risky and consequently the returns needed to be high to encourage people to invest. Having a monopoly meant that the firm did not have to compete on price, at least not against English firms.

However, like some big firms today, the EIC was also supported by the state, with the result that the company served two masters: its investors and the political rulers. This was to create many problems over time. The instructions for those running the company appeared to be strict, with prospective employees having to post a large bond guaranteeing the quality of their service before they left England. However, once an employee arrived in India, he could choose to fulfil these instructions in pretty much any way that earned the company money. Although at first managers avoided politics and respected the local culture, their reportedly unchecked and increasing power, coupled with individual greed, eventually led to conflict. The autonomy of the managers and the great distances involved meant that the headquarters and politicians back in England did not realise that the EIC was creating the toehold of an empire. And once they did, it was too late to regain control.

What do you think were the political and legal controls that had to be imposed on the East India Company? Considering how the EIC's activities developed in India, do you think these were effective? Do you think any of these controls are still relevant when looking at MNCs today?

Control of MNCs

Controlling companies that operate across borders has been an issue since the 17th century and the founding of the East India Company (EIC). However today, with interconnected international markets and globalised businesses, controlling multinational companies (MNCs) is much more complex. Queen Elizabeth I, and the monarchs and governments who followed her, could possibly have exerted some control over the EIC had they understood the risks of allowing it autonomy. Today, however, many modern global companies have huge economic power and can relocate their headquarters with relative ease, giving national governments less direct control over their behaviour. These 'footloose' MNCs can simply threaten to relocate out of a country – and take their FDI, tax revenues and employment with them.

This raises very big questions about who is in control over the actions of a company. The shareholders? The managers? The home or host governments? And furthermore, how is control enforced?

Unit 79 explained how, when a firm establishes in a country, it has to work within the institutional frameworks of both the home and the host country. An MNC will have to abide by all of the applicable laws and regulations established by these institutions.

Table 1 illustrates just a few of the many institutions that might exert political and regulatory control over a business based in the UK, but operating internationally.

Table 1 A selection of institutional controls on British businesses that cross international borders

Area of jurisdiction	National – UK	International
Financial	Bank of England Treasury Financial Conduct Authority	International Monetary Fund World Bank European Banking Authority
Commercial	Competition and Markets Authority Trading Standards Institute Department for Business, Innovation & Skills UK Trade & Investment UK Export Finance HM Revenue & Customs	World Trade Organization European Commission Regional trade blocs
Employment	Department for Business, Innovation & Skills Department for Education Department for Work and Pensions	International Labour Organization European Commission
Environmental	Department of Energy and Climate Change Department for Environment, Food & Rural Affairs Department for International Development	United Nations Environment Programme European Commission
Legal	Ministry of Justice Attorney General's Office Crown Prosecution Service Serious Fraud Office	International Criminal Court European Court of Justice European Court of Human Rights

Political influence

Queen Elizabeth I sanctioned the creation of the EIC, and today many countries have similar policies encouraging the creation and protection of state owned enterprises (SOEs). For example, in China, over 120 companies are owned or controlled directly by the state, involving almost all sectors, including manufacturing, banks, telecommunications, transport, agriculture and basic commodities. State ownership is a very effective method of control, as political power can be exercised to create, manage and end a business. Political influence over these organisations is therefore extensive, and this can lead to numerous commercial and ethical issues.

State ownership or control is not very efficient, however, and so the drawbacks often outweigh the benefits.

- Corruption can be a problem as SOEs might be favoured by powerful politicians. For example, in spring 2015 the state oil company of Brazil, Petrobras, was reportedly mired in a scandal that threatened the entire political establishment. A former president, the speakers of both Chambers of Congress

and 54 others were accused of taking illicit payments from the company in return for facilitating outcomes that were favourable to the company. Petrobras has lost much of its market value since the allegation became public.

- State owned operations may soak up the capital that other firms might better employ. This is because politicians or regulators, rather than the market, decide where funding should go. Consequently, inefficient businesses may be given more money than they need while also not being subjected to competitive forces that would otherwise drive down price and improve efficiency.

- Shareholders' and other investors' rights may be reduced or ignored because they are not the true beneficiaries of the business. The actual beneficiaries, as may be the case with Petrobras, may be the politicians themselves. However, some state enterprises benefit the population as a whole. For example, the international oil company Statoil, mostly owned by the Norwegian government, puts a percentage of proceeds into its government pension fund, known as the 'Oil Fund'. The remainder of the shares in Statoil are publicly traded.

- Investment expenditure, especially on research and development, may be ignored. With state ownership, there is likely to be less competitive pressure from other firms. Consequently, there will be less incentive to undertake expensive research to create new or better products or services.

Even where a firm is not owned or controlled by the state, political influence may nevertheless still be important. There could be national strategic priorities, such as energy independence or the development and preservation of key industries. Governments may want to boost employment or regulate financial institutions.

Privately owned businesses can be controlled using a number of political initiatives.

- Tariffs, quotas, regulations and local content requirements can be used to protect domestic businesses from international competitors. For instance, Nigeria has a law stipulating the 'minimum amount' (by value) of 'Nigerian content' that must exist in equipment used for the extraction of oil and gas in the country.

- Many countries even place direct or indirect ownership restrictions on businesses that they consider to be key. Thus, political opposition prevented the Chinese state oil company, CNOOC, from taking over Unocal, a private US firm.

- Countries can also support domestic industries through subsidies or tax breaks. Subsidies can be designed to:
  - help create factories to produce and distribute goods
  - help consumers to buy products
  - assist domestic firms in exporting their goods and services.

There are many other forms of political influence that can serve to direct the behaviour of businesses, including the following.

Lobbying by politicians to influence the decisions of businesses. For example, a politician may wish to prevent the foreign direct investment of a competitor that might threaten jobs in his or her constituency.

Politicians 'retiring' to seats on the boards of plcs. It is not clear whether having former politicians on a board adds value because of the extent of their knowledge or because of their influence or connections, but many businesses hire politicians as soon as they leave office.

Some benefits and drawbacks of using political influence to control MNCs are shown in Table 2.

Table 2 Benefits and drawbacks of using political influence to control MNCs

Benefits	Drawbacks
Can create, manage and end a business	Facilitates corruption
Helps elected officials to challenge the power of private business and to address issues of concern, such as ethics and the environment	Entrenches inefficiencies, such as the misallocation of capital and lack of research and development

Question 1

'Global network banks' do everything that a multinational might need from a bank: they lend money, move money around the world, provide advice and trade in bonds and currencies. These big MNCs, such as HSBC (UK), Santander (Spain), Citigroup (US) and Deutsche Bank (Germany), all grow through a series of acquisitions mainly since the turn of the 21st century, but they are now facing threats to their global competitiveness.

As the firms grew, they found it increasingly difficult to create common management cultures, or develop workable IT platforms and consistent business practices. They also faced more competition. With the financial crisis of 2008, smaller firms that were being squeezed at home began to expand internationally in a search for new markets. Also, big regional banks, often backed by the state, began to emerge. Finally, the big banks faced much tighter regulation in all aspects of their business. Thus, they have had to update their operating systems to ensure they meet capital requirements for operating as a bank, and they have to police their customers to ensure that they are not supporting money laundering, tax evasion or unsustainable debt. For instance, HSBC had to pay huge fines for breaking new rules imposed by the US and UK regulators.

(a) Explain how the activities of the 'global network banks' can be controlled, using the above information.

(b) Assess the effectiveness of using tighter regulation on the control of banks.

Legal control

One of the best mechanisms for controlling large international businesses is through regulation, competition laws and taxation policies.

Competition policy: Competition policy exists to promote competition and ensure that markets operate as efficiently as is possible. In the UK, the Office of Fair Trading and the Competition and Markets Authority protect producers and consumers from unfair or anti-competitive practices. The EU Competition Commission takes on this role across Europe. These institutions ensure that firms do not abuse their market power, do not attempt to fix prices or use pricing strategies to drive out competition, and do not collude against other producers or the consumer.

For example, over the years, Microsoft has faced many legal challenges asserting that it has abused its market position through the global operation of its Windows operating system. One particular issue arose over the way the operating system prevented interoperability with other firms' systems and applications. The EU Treaty prevents the abuse by a firm of a 'dominant market position', and in March 2004 the EU Competition Commissioner ruled against Microsoft, ordering it to offer information to rivals so that their systems could work with Windows software. Microsoft eventually gave up its appeals and agreed to allow access to open-source software developers. However, in this case, as elsewhere, tension can exist between national laws. The US disagreed with the ruling, putting forward that the EU ruling would not encourage competition and would actually discourage innovation.

Similar issues arose in 2015 with EU regulatory challenges to internet giant Google in response to issues surrounding tax avoidance. Britain and the EU were unhappy with Google's complex structures for avoiding tax, and took steps to ensure that Google could not avoid paying tax in the European countries in which it operates. The US objected, countering that Google was a victim of commercially driven protectionism on the part of the EU.

Tension may also exist between the various national and international laws. Nowhere is this more obvious than in the case of taxation policy.

Taxation policy

Governments use taxation policies to raise the revenue to run their countries. However, these policies can also be employed to help control the activities of MNCs. For example, Ireland maintains a policy of low corporate taxation in order to attract huge amounts of foreign direct investment. This policy can upset politicians in other countries who see it as an unfair practice that allows businesses to avoid paying their fair share of tax. Thus, Ireland's corporation tax in 2013 was 12.5 per cent compared to the US's 35 per cent.

Related to this are concerns that many big companies can use countries' differing systems to avoid tax. **Tax avoidance** involves using legal methods to reduce the amount of tax that a company pays. This differs from **tax evasion**, which is the illegal avoidance of tax. Tax avoidance is an issue of ethics that can bring bad publicity, as was the case with Google. In 2011 it was revealed that it had paid £6 million in tax on a turnover of £395 million. (See the case study at the end of this unit.)

Table 3 Benefits and drawbacks of using laws to control MNCs

Benefits	Drawbacks
Can be used to improve competition in the domestic market	It is difficult to achieve consistent legal practice between countries, so businesses have an incentive to find the most friendly legal environment, where the laws and tax policies are the best for them
Helps to check corporate power	It is relatively easy for big footloose international firms to move to friendly environments and avoid treatment that they consider to be unfavourable to their business
Facilitates consumer protection	Even where there is agreement over laws, policies and standards, they are often not easy to enforce

Question 2

In 2014, a tobacco industry funded lobby group attempted to derail a World Health Organization (WHO) summit aimed at agreeing increased taxes on smoking, according to leaked documents seen by the Financial Times. The International Tax and Investment Center (ITIC), sponsored by all of the major tobacco groups, met on the eve of the WHO's global summit on tobacco policy in a bid to head off unwanted duty increases. The ITIC meeting occurred in spite of rules aimed at banning tobacco companies from interfering with anti-tobacco policies. The WHO sent a letter to delegates warning them about the activities of the ITIC and their obligations not to let the tobacco industry influence policy.

The four largest tobacco multinationals sponsor the ITIC, whose meeting was closed to the media. Anti-smoking advocates argued that increased excise duty is the most effective way of reducing cigarette consumption. The ITIC argued that it provides independent advice to governments on tax policy. In April 2015, British American Tobacco raised cigarette prices to offset decline in smoking. Sales in Russia had fallen by 11 per cent, in Brazil by 6 per cent and in Vietnam by 5 per cent. They threatened legal action in the UK if plain packaging went ahead.

Source: adapted from the *Financial Times*, 6.10.2014. All rights reserved

(a) Explain why the tobacco companies might want to head off unwanted duty increases.

(b) Assess the effectiveness of using tighter regulation on multinational tobacco companies.

Pressure groups

Companies' behaviours may violate what many people consider to be acceptable standards, but nevertheless those behaviours may not break any laws. **Pressure groups** act as another control on MNCs in that they can publicise undesirable behaviour and thereby threaten to damage the image of the firm. Pressure groups are generally voluntary organisations that operate at all levels of society, including international levels, and aim to change either political or commercial decision-making. For example, organisations like Corporate Watch investigate such areas of concern as tax avoidance and payday lending, and attempt to provide information on the unethical practices of corporations. However, pressure groups can also act to support business interests. For example, the Confederation of British Industry (CBI) is Britain's biggest business lobbying group, with over 190,000 business members. Its role is to promote businesses' interests, and it does so by lobbying and advising the government on issues of importance to its members. Pressure groups have several methods that they can use to control MNCs.

- **Naming and shaming.** Business ethics can be promoted through publicity and **naming and shaming**, which involves publicising behaviour that is considered to be unethical as widely as possible and thereby threatening the business's reputation. For example, in 1977 the Swiss food company Nestlé was 'named and shamed' for aggressively marketing its baby milk formula in lesser-developed countries. Pressure groups highlighted research that indicated that breast milk is not only better for babies, but it is also safer given sanitation issues associated with making the formula. Moreover, breast milk is free. A variety of pressure groups started a boycott of Nestlé's products, and continue to monitor the company's international sales of baby milk formula.

  Starbucks, Google and Amazon have also been 'named and shamed' in the British media for what some have seen as their complex tax avoidance schemes, in which they paid less than some considered to be their 'fair share' of taxes. In the past, the mining firm DeBeers was 'named and shamed' in film and print media for contributing to the problem of 'conflict diamonds', which were being used to finance civil wars and helping to increase bloodshed in parts of Africa. Perhaps even better known historically was the policy of naming and shaming firms that continued to trade in South Africa when the official 'Apartheid' policy was still in place. Apartheid was a government-supported system of racial segregation that existed between 1948 and 1994. The system provoked many worldwide protest movements against firms, such as Coca-Cola, that continued to trade with or in South Africa.

- **Direct action.** **Direct action** is the use of demonstrations, protests, strikes or even sabotage to achieve a political or social goal. Environmental protection can receive a boost from pressure groups such as Greenpeace, which uses direct action. Interventions have included using its ships to interfere with whaling or to disrupt drilling in the Arctic. Direct action can be controversial, as is the case with Greenpeace's active opposition to so-called 'golden rice', strains that have been genetically modified or enhanced to contain additional nutrients. Greenpeace opposes any genetically modified food entering the food chain, while on the other hand many non-governmental organisations and health organisations believe that golden rice could help save millions of undernourished children in the developing world.

- **Lobbying.** This is the taking of issues directly to government in an effort to influence change. Organisations such as Amnesty International and the World Development Movement frequently lobby governments on human rights and development issues in addition to publishing their own research. They also make detailed suggestions for addressing the issues of concern, actively lobbying for change. As noted above, businesses also engage in lobbying. In addition to the CBI, many large firms lobby politicians on issues of importance to them.

Table 4 Benefits and drawbacks of using pressure groups and social media to control MNCs

Benefits	Drawbacks
Enlists committed people, including volunteers	Campaigns may be ill-informed or misguided
Particularly where social media is involved, activists can be enlisted incredibly quickly to engage in information gathering or protest	When information goes 'viral', it may be impossible for a pressure group to influence the message that is ultimately communicated
Raises issues that may otherwise not become public knowledge	Direct action can lead to violence or miscarriages of justice
Alerts politicians and authorities to issues of concern to the public	

Social media

Social media can be defined as an interaction between electronic and mobile devices, applications and people, that allows users to create content. Such media include online magazines, weblogs, social blogs (Twitter), podcasts and wikis (YouTube, Wikipedia), and social networking (Facebook, Instagram).

As well as being a tool for the promotion of a business's objectives, social media also can act as a means of controlling its behaviour by:

- making the collection of information from a variety of sources easier
- increasing social awareness through communication
- ensuring greater transparency
- bringing together people in order to create a kind of social authority to challenge the power of large companies.

For example, Greenpeace has used social media extensively in its 'Save the Arctic' campaign, which included efforts to thwart Lego's partnership with the oil company Shell. The campaign began with an animated film using Lego and showing the Arctic being flooded with oil. Though the film has been watched by millions of viewers, the campaign

has so far not achieved its aims. However, Greenpeace met with greater success in its campaign to stop Nestlé's use of palm oil from producers linked to deforestation. Nestlé vowed to remove all potentially offending companies from its supply chain.

As noted in Table 4, the benefits and drawbacks of using social media to control MNCs are similar to those for pressure groups, but the speed with which something can now go 'viral' means that it is increasingly hard to control the message that the pressure group may want to convey.

Thinking bigger

Who won the 2014 World Cup? For footballers the answer is a matter of record; Germany beat Argentina in the final. For the companies involved in the World Cup, the success of brands is not so clear-cut. Adidas, the German brand, has been a long-time sponsor of the World Cup. Nike, the US-based sportswear brand, was not a sponsor, yet sponsored ten of the World Cup teams. However, local brands in South America – who also were not sponsors – are fighting back against multinational brands. One example is Peru's Inca Kola, which has now overtaken Coca-Cola with a 30 per cent market share against 20 per cent for the American giant. It now exports to Asia. Falabella, the Chilean retailer, is now expanding across the continent and South American brands are now selling widely in Europe. Brahma beer, based in Brazil, is now the fifth largest brewery in the world and their brand can be bought at Asda, Sainsbury's and Tesco in the UK.

South Americans are switching away from multinational brands to local cheaper ones as South American companies consolidate their brand access across the region. More local icons will appear in the top 50 South American brands. If so, that will spell good news for local brand enthusiasts but tougher times for the multinationals. Perhaps encouraging local brand buying is the best control of multinational behaviour.

Source: adapted from the *Financial Times*, 23.9.2014. All rights reserved

You could use this information in a variety of ways. Obviously, it can be used when answering questions on the influence of multinationals but it might also be useful when discussing factors influencing globalisation and global competitiveness, and the impact of multinationals.

Case study

CONTROLLING TAX AVOIDANCE

Senior managers may feel that they have a duty to minimise the taxes that their company pays to a host government, so that they can maximise their revenues and returns to shareholders. It has been widely reported that Google has taken this approach in the UK, paying only £6 million in tax on £395 million of revenue in 2011, while in the same year Amazon made £3.35 billion and had a tax bill of £1.8 million.

None of this was illegal, but some consider it to be unfair. The firms avoided the taxes through all sorts of ways, but chiefly by locating parts of their businesses in low-tax jurisdictions, and then moving money around so that profits were declared there and not in higher tax places.

The issue was raised after several newspapers revealed the practice. This galvanised several pressure groups, including UKUncut, and War on Want, and protests followed.

Arriving at the depth of a very bad recession, this was an issue that the public cared about, and social media began to reflect some of the public's condemnation for the tax-avoiding firms. The issue soon posed a threat to the companies' reputations as well as their business, since tax avoidance quickly became a political issue.

Sources: adapted from the *Financial Times* 02.05.2013, all rights reserved

(a) Assess the role that social media and pressure groups played in bringing the issue of corporate tax avoidance to the attention of the public. (10 marks)

(b) Evaluate the arguments for and against the government changing tax policy so that businesses are not able to avoid paying their 'fair share' of UK tax in future. (20 marks)

Exam tip

When evaluating the method used to control MNCs, you could consider the extent and impact of control from different areas. For example, is political and legal control or consumer pressure coming from the country of origin of the MNC, which may be a Western developed country, or from other countries in which the MNC is operating? Are these controls consistent or are there conflicting objectives? Further, you could consider the effect that the controls can have on both the country of origin/country in which the MNC has its headquarters, and other countries in which it operates. Again, consider to what extent these effects may differ and whether there is any conflict.

Key terms

Competition policy – government policy that exists to promote competition and ensure that firms don't abuse their market power, do not attempt to fix prices or use pricing strategies to drive out competition, and do not collude against other producers or the consumer.
Direct action – the use of demonstrations, protests, strikes or even sabotage to achieve a political or social goal.
Naming and shaming – publicising behaviour that is considered to be unethical as widely as possible and thereby threatening a business's reputation.
Pressure groups – generally voluntary organisations that operate at all levels of society, including international levels, and aim to change either political or commercial decision-making.
Tax avoidance – using legal methods to reduce the amount of tax that a company pays.
Tax evasion – using illegal means to avoid paying taxes that are owed.

Links 🔗

To demonstrate your synoptic skills, you could use information from other units to help support your answers. For example, you might use the information about the impact that tariffs and quotas, protectionism and trading blocs (Units 69 and 70) can have on the countries in which MNCs operate to assess the types and extent of control. Further, you might consider to what extent MNCs take into account ethical practices and how these might affect controls of MNCs (Unit 59 and Unit 80). Unit 79, which focuses on the impact of MNCs, could also be used to support arguments for controlling their activities.

Knowledge check

1. Why are there legal controls on the activities of multinationals?

2. What are the benefits of multinationals in the global market place?

3. How are multinationals' global activities controlled?

4. What political influences do multinationals possess?

5. How can taxation policies influence the activities of multinationals?

6. What role can social media have on controlling multinationals' behaviour?

Preparing for your A Level Paper 1 exam

Advance planning

1. Draw up a timetable for your revision and try to keep to it. Spread your timetable over a number of weeks, and aim to cover a chosen number of topics each week.
2. Spend longer on topics that you have found difficult, and revise them several times.
3. Do not try to limit your revision by attempting to 'question spot'. Revise so that you are confident about all aspects of your work.

Paper 1 overview:

A Level Paper 1: Marketing, people and global business: 2 hours (Themes 1 and 4)	
Section A, Question 1	2×4 mark questions
	1×10 mark question
	1×12 mark question
	1×20 mark question
Total marks for Section A	**50 marks**
Section B, Question 2	2×4 mark questions
	1×10 mark question
	1×12 mark question
	1×20 mark question
Total marks for Section B	**50 marks**
	Total marks = 100 marks

Paper 1, **Marketing, people and global business**, will assess your knowledge and understanding of **Themes 1 and 4**, marketing, people and global business. It is a written examination and the paper is divided into two sections. The duration of Paper 1 will be 2 hours. You have to answer **ALL** questions. There is no choice. However, this can be an advantage because it means you do not have to waste time deciding which questions to answer.

Section A questions

In Section A you will be given Extracts A–C as a stimulus and you will need to answer Question 1, a–e. The parts of Question 1 require a range of depths in your responses, depending on the mark allocation. Question 1e is an extended question.

Section B questions

In Section B you will be given Extracts D–F as stimulus and you will need to answer Question 2, a–e. The parts of Question 2 require a range of depths in your responses, depending on the mark allocation. Question 2e is an extended question.

- You should familiarise yourself with the layout of the paper by looking at the examples published by Edexcel. The questions within each section are followed by lined spaces where you should write your answer. Use the mark allocation as a guide to how much time to spend on each question.

Skills required when answering questions

If you are entered for the A Level qualification you will be required to sit three examinations. You should be aware of the skills that you need to demonstrate when answering questions.

You will need to demonstrate four different skills referred to as assessment objectives (AOs):

AO1 – Knowledge: this means you have to show that you:

- recognise and understand business terms, concepts and theories
- understand how individuals and organisations are affected by and respond to business issues.

All questions will test knowledge to some extent. A minority of questions will test knowledge alone. These can be recognised by the mark allocation. They will tend to carry just four marks.

AO2 – Application: this means that you have to apply knowledge and understanding to various contexts to show how individuals and organisations are affected by and respond to issues. This might involve:

- using a business formula in appropriate circumstances, for example, calculating the price elasticity of demand for a product
- using a theory to show why a business has chosen a particular course of action
- using a theory to show the impact on a business of choosing a particular course of action.

Most questions in the examination will require you to demonstrate application. This means that you have to ensure that your answers relate directly to the context given in the question. You must discuss the implications of issues to the particular business or industry in the context you are given.

AO3 – Analysis: this means you have to show that you can break down information and understand the implications of the information presented in the question. You will need to show an understanding of the impact on individuals and organisations of external and internal influences. This might involve:

- explaining causes and effects and interrelationships, for example by recognising from a graph that sales are falling and could be the result of new competition in the market

- breaking down information to identify specific causes or problems, for example by realising that a business is suffering from inefficiency because staff motivation has fallen as a result of a pay cut
- using appropriate techniques to analyse data, for example using the net profit ratio to assess the performance of a business.

You will often be required to construct an argument, for example by explaining the possible reasons for events or discussing the advantages or disadvantages of particular courses of action. Those questions that carry more than four marks will require analysis in the answer. Some questions that carry four marks may also require you to demonstrate some analytical skills.

AO4 – Evaluation: evaluation involves making a judgement. You will need to evaluate both qualitative and quantitative evidence to make informed judgements and propose evidence-based solutions to business issues. This might involve:

- showing judgement when weighing up the relative importance of different points or sides of an argument in order to reach a conclusion
- drawing conclusions from the evidence that you present
- assessing the relative importance of particular issues to a business
- suggesting a course of action for a business, supported by plausible motives or evidence.

When evaluating, it is often possible to draw a number of different conclusions. Very often in business studies there is no 'right' answer, so examiners are likely to be more interested in whether your judgement is plausible and in the quality of your argument in support of that judgement. Questions that carry eight marks or more are likely to test evaluation.

Quantitative skills

In all three A level examination papers you will need to demonstrate your numeracy and quantitative skills. The specific tasks you might be asked to complete are shown below. Note that QS 6, calculate investment appraisal outcomes and interpret results, does not form part of the GCE AS level core content.

Quantitative skills that you need to demonstrate	
QS 1	Calculate, use and understand ratios, averages and fractions
QS 2	Calculate, use and understand percentages and percentage changes
QS 3	Construct and interpret a range of standard graphical forms
QS 4	Interpret index numbers
QS 5	Calculate cost, revenue and break even
QS 7	Interpret values of price and income elasticity of demand
QS 8	Use and interpret quantitative and non-quantitative information in order to make decisions
QS 9	Interpret, apply and analyse information in written graphical and numerical form

Preparing for your A Level exams

Sample answer with comments

Paper I: Marketing, people and global business

These questions will help you prepare for your A Level Business Paper 1 examination. Some sample answers and comments are provided for you to review and you will have the opportunity to answer some questions yourself.

Section A, Question 1

Read the following extracts (A to C) before answering Question 1.

Extract A

Global confectionery market

The global confectionery market is worth hundreds of millions of dollars, and the size of the market is growing. One important part of the total confectionery market is chocolate. It was reported in 2014 that rural India had become a target market for many chocolate producers. It was felt that improved infrastructure and rising incomes would help to boost demand for chocolate in rural India where it is reckoned that 68 per cent of India's 1.2 billion population live.

Cadbury, the UK confectionery company owned by the Chinese multinational Mondelez, was one of the first entrants into the market. Intense competition in urban India pushed Cadbury towards rural customers. Cadbury was quick to realise an important feature in the market. The regular 42g size Cadbury chocolate bar, priced at 45 rupees, was too expensive for the market. As a result the company launched a 15g bar priced at 5 rupees to make the product more accessible.

The pie chart shows the market shares for chocolate in India.

Sources: adapted from www.confectionerynews.com

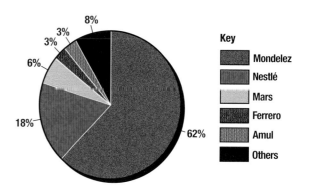

India chocolate market shares (%)

Source: Chocolate Industry in India 2014-19, www.valuenotes.biz

Extract B

Rising cocoa prices

In 2014 it was reported that chocolate prices were expected to rise. This was due to problems with the supply of cocoa. Poor weather conditions in the Ivory Coast, where 40 per cent of the world's cocoa is produced, was said to be a key factor. In 2013 the price of cocoa beans was about $2,447 per tonne. This was expected to rise to about $3,000 in 2014.

Some producers said that they would reduce the size of their chocolate bars rather than raise the price, an approach used by Mars in the UK with its Mars and Snickers brands.

Source: adapted from www.confectionerynews.com

Extract C

Booja-Booja

Norwich-based Booja-Booja is a relatively small independent UK chocolate maker that produces a range of organic chocolate truffles and ice cream alternatives. Suitable for vegetarians and vegans, Booja-Booja's range is organic. It is also dairy, gluten, wheat and soya-free, and free of genetically modifed organsims.

Booja-Booja distributes its products through a range of channels. They are stocked in independent health food stores, farm shops and delis nationwide, along with Waitrose, Holland & Barrett and Ocado. The company also uses select online distributors that have a commitment to vegetarian, fairly traded, organic and natural products. Examples include Planet Organic, Wholefoods Market, Earthfare, EcoLife Global, Animal Aid, Ethical Treats and Greenlife.

Source: adapted from www.boojabooja.com

1 (a) Using a supply and demand diagram, illustrate the impact on the global market for chocolate of the rising cost of cocoa.
(4 marks)

Question 1 (a), student answer

The global market for chocolate

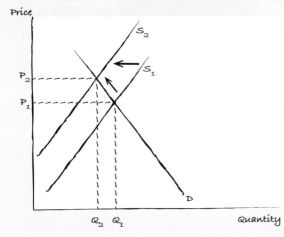

Comment, Question 1 (a)

It is not unusual to be asked to draw a supply and demand diagram in the examination. You may be awarded 1 mark for correctly showing the supply and demand curves. You may get another mark for labelling the axis correctly and another mark for shifting the supply curve to the left. This shows that producers reduce the supply of chocolate because costs have increased (more expensive cocoa). Another mark might be given for showing the new equilibrium price and quantity. Price has risen from P_1 to P_2 and the quantity traded in the market has fallen from Q_1 to Q_2. Note that the impact on price and quantity depends on how elastic/inelastic demand is. If demand is relatively elastic then the impact on price would be less.

1 (b) Explain one possible disadvantage to Booja-Booja of operating in a niche market. (4 marks)

No sample answer has been provided for question 1 (b) so that you can answer it yourself, for exam practice.

1 (c) Assess the importance to a business like Cadbury of carrying out primary market research. (10 marks)

Question 1 (c), student answer

Market research involves gathering, presenting and analysing information about the marketing and consumption of goods and services. Businesses spend money on market research because it helps to reduce the risk of failure. Products that are well researched are more likely to be successful. Market research data can help to quantify the likely demand for a product and provide an insight into consumer behaviour. Primary research involves collecting primary data. This is information that did not exist before. This has to be collected by a researcher either by the business itself or an agent.

Primary research is arguably more useful than desk research because the information gathered can be tailored to the precise needs of the business. In this case, Cadbury may have carried out some research before entering the rural market for chocolate in India. For example, Cadbury discovered an important feature in the market. The regular 42g size Cadbury chocolate bar, priced at 45 rupees, was too expensive for the market. As a result the company launched a 15g bar priced at 5 rupees to make the product more accessible. This information may have been gathered using primary research. This valuable information meant that Cadbury could adapt its product to suit the needs of a specific market. This would help to reduce the risk of venturing into a completely new market. According to the information in the pie chart Cadbury, which is owned by Mondelez, is currently the market leader in India with 62 per cent of

the market. This position of strength may have been aided by gauging the needs of potential customers by carrying out primary market research.

However, there are limitations to market research, which companies like Cadbury need to be aware of. Businesses need to be sure that the data they collect is reliable. For example, that they have chosen a representative sample from which to gather information. If there is a sampling discrepancy, any predictions based on the information in the sample would be flawed. The greater the sampling discrepancy, the less reliable will be the data obtained. Companies must also appreciate that respondents' answers may not match their behaviour. This is because human behaviour is unpredictable and there may be a difference between what people say they will do and what they actually do. Consequently the information gathered may again be unreliable.

However, companies like Cadbury, or their agencies, will be experienced in conducting market research and should therefore be aware of such pitfalls. It is likely that the benefits of carrying out primary research outweigh any potential drawbacks. Cadbury's position as market leader in India might help to support this view. Primary market research is likely to be very important to companies like Cadbury operating in highly competitive markets. It might help them to get a competitive edge. Therefore, it can be concluded that primary market research is very important to a company like Cadbury.

Comment, Question 1 (c)

Questions like this require you to demonstrate knowledge, application, analysis and evaluation. Two marks might be awarded for demonstrating knowledge, such as defining primary market research and identifying one benefit of carrying out primary research. Two marks might be awarded for application. This answer is focused on the use of primary market research by Cadbury in the market for chocolate in rural India. An example is used of how Cadbury identified a particular customer need in this rural market (the need for smaller and cheaper chocolate bars).

Three marks might be awarded for analysis. Examples of analysis in this answer are the explanation of how primary research can benefit a business and the explanation of two key

limitations of primary market research. Three marks might be awarded for evaluation. An example of evaluation in this answer is the judgement made weighing up the importance of primary market research to a company like Cadbury. This argument is clear and well supported with evidence from the case and business theory. In this answer counterbalance arguments are also raised. For example, although there are clear benefits of conducting primary research, there are also some limitations. These are identified, analysed and then explained away. The final judgement is that the benefits of primary research to an experienced company like Cadbury exceed the limitations.

---

1 (d) Assess the possible factors that might be taken into account by a company like Cadbury before selling into a new overseas market. (12 marks)

No sample answer has been provided for question 1 (d) so that you can answer it yourself, for exam practice.

1 (e) Evaluate how changes in social trends might affect the choice of distribution channels used by businesses like Booja-Booja. (20 marks)

Question I (e), student answer

Booja-Booja is a small operator in the global market for confectionery. It is an independent company that produces organic chocolate truffles. All of Booja-Booja's products are organic; free of dairy, wheat, soya and gluten. Booja-Booja distributes its products using a range of channels. They are stocked in independent health food stores, farm shops and delis nationwide, along with Waitrose, Holland & Barrett and Ocado. The company also uses select online distributors that have a commitment to vegetarian, fairly traded, organic and natural products. Examples include Earthfare, EcoLife Global, Animal Aid, Ethical Treats and Greenlife.

In recent years there have been a number of changes in the way goods and services are sold. Some of these methods reflect changes in social trends. For example, large US-style shopping malls have been built, such as the Trafford Centre, many sellers use call centres to sell products, such as financial services, many supermarkets have extended their product ranges and opening hours and for many people shopping has become more of a leisure activity. However, from Booja-Booja's point of view, one recent social change is important. There has been a huge growth in online shopping and online distribution. It is often called e-commerce because it involves the use of electronic systems to sell goods and services. Booja-Booja uses select online distributors, such as Planet Organic, Wholefoods Market, Animal Aid, Ethical Treats and Greenlife to help ensure that it can get its products to those customers who like to shop online.

There are a number of benefits to businesses of selling online. For example, e-tailers may not have to meet the costs of operating stores, such as rent, fixtures and fittings, customer service staff and other store overheads. They also have lower costs when processing transactions – many systems are automated and less paper is needed for documents, such as invoices and receipts. Businesses selling online can offer goods to a much wider market – e.g. global. Businesses can serve their customers 24/7 and collect payments online using credit cards or PayPal, for example. However, despite these advantages of online distribution, there are some drawbacks. Businesses will face increasing competition since selling online is a relatively cheaper method of distribution and can be organised from any location in the world. Consequently, businesses will face more competition from overseas. There may also be technical problems online. For example, websites may crash, viruses may be contracted and internet connections can get lost. Also, there is the problem of making yourself known. How do people find out about you among a large number of other online sellers? One way is through social media, another is through using online distributors, as Booja-Booja has done.

Although it is important to reflect social trends when selecting distribution channels, companies like Booja-Booja are also likely to consider other factors. For example, different types of products may require different distribution channels. Fast moving consumer goods such as breakfast cereals, confectionery, crisps and toilet paper cannot be sold directly by manufacturers to consumers. Wholesalers and retailers are needed because they break bulk. Booja-Booja is a small chocolate manufacturer and could not easily distribute its products without the help of retailers. Businesses producing high quality 'exclusive' products such as perfume and designer clothes will choose their outlets very carefully. The image of their products is important, so they are not likely to use supermarkets, for example. Information in the case suggests that Booja-Booja has selected its online partners carefully. The company uses distributors that have a commitment to vegetarian, fairly traded, organic and natural products, such as Earthfare, EcoLife Global and Animal Aid.

Businesses will also choose the cheapest distribution channels, and prefer direct channels. This is because if intermediaries are used they will take a share of the profit. Large supermarkets will try to buy direct from manufacturers. This is because they can bulk buy and get lower prices. Independents are more likely to buy from wholesalers. They have to charge higher prices as a result. Many producers now sell direct to consumers from their websites. This helps to keep costs down. However, producers selling to mass markets are likely to use intermediaries. In contrast, businesses targeting smaller markets are more likely to target customers directly. For example, a building contractor in a small town will deal directly with customers. Producers selling in overseas markets are likely to use agents because they know the market better. Businesses selling goods to other businesses are likely to use more direct channels. Booja-Booja uses a range of retailers and online distributors because it would not be cost effective to sell directly to their target market.

To conclude, there is a range of factors that will influence the choice of distribution channels. It could be argued that Booja-Booja has responded to social changes in the distribution of its products by making its products available online. However, since Booja-Booja is a small chocolate maker with a limited product range its choice of channels is limited. It does not have enough products to sell directly or operate retail outlets. It is likely that these factors have influenced the choice of distribution channels rather than changes in social trends. Nevertheless, Booja-Booja is exploiting one important social trend.

Comment, Question 1 (e)

This question requires an extended answer and you need to demonstrate knowledge, application, analysis and evaluation. Four marks might be awarded for demonstrating knowledge, such as understanding the meaning of social trends in business, distribution channels and the factors that influence the choice of distribution channel. Four marks might be awarded for application. This answer focuses throughout on the distribution channels used by Booja-Booja and draws on a range of relevant examples, such as the distribution channels that are available to a small chocolate maker in the confectionery industry.

Six marks might be awarded for analysis. Examples of analysis in this answer are explanations of how online selling will benefit small businesses like Booja-Booja and the different methods of distribution that might be used. Six marks might be awarded for evaluation. In this case, one approach is to weigh up the extent to which social trends have influenced the choice of distribution channel used by Booja-Booja. The judgement made is that social trends may be influential but not as much as other factors, such as cost and the nature of the product. As a small business, Booja-Booja's choice of channel is a little restricted. There is also an attempt here to discuss both the advantages and the disadvantages of online selling. This provides an argument with a counterbalance.

Section B, Question 2

Read the following extracts (D to F) before answering Question 2.

Extract D

The global hotel market

Following a dip in 2009, possibly the result of a global downturn in demand, revenue in the global hotel market has shown consistent growth. It was expected to generate around $550 billion in 2016.

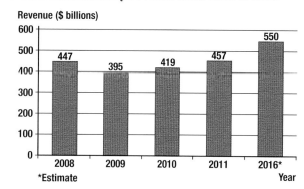

Global hotel industry revenue from 2008 to 2016

Source: adapted from www.statista.com

Extract E

InterContinental Hotels Group

In 2014, InterContinental Hotels Group (IHG®) a giant multinational, operated around 4,800 hotels worldwide and employed over 350,000 people across its ten brands, which included InterContinental®, Holiday Inn®, Holiday Inn Express®, Crowne Plaza®, Candlewood Suites® and Hotel Indigo®. The company's head office is located in Buckinghamshire, UK.

IHG opened a new Holiday Inn in Jaipur, India, in 2014. The 172-room hotel is located in the city centre, close to the main shopping centre, railway station, multinational companies and cultural venues. It also has access to tourist attractions, such as Amber Fort, Hawa Mahal and Birla Temple. Each room is equipped with a 37-inch LED TV, iPod docking station and a media hub, with hi-speed complimentary internet access across the hotel. The hotel also provides a gym and roof-top pool.

For an initial period rooms could be booked at a discount when it first opened. In 2014, IHG operated 19 hotels across 10 cities in India. It also expected to open another 45 hotels across India over the next three to five years.

Sources: taken from IHG's Annual Report 2014, IHG news release 2014 and www.ihg.com

Extract F

Red Carnation Hotels

Red Carnation Hotels (RCH) was founded by Stanley and Beatrice Tollman. The small chain of 17 five- and four-star boutique luxury hotels has a reputation for taste and excellence in dining, accommodation and service. The business has won a number of prestigious industry awards and also operates a gastro-pub and a South African inspired London restaurant. Beatrice Tollman believes that much of their success has come from listening to guests. She reads every guest comment from every source because that is where she can learn how to improve. Beatrice says: 'Our guests teach us our business.'

Beatrice also believes that if you look after employees they, in turn, will look after the guests. In her opinion, caring for the workforce is simply good business practice. In a 2015 survey by the *Sunday Times,* RCH was ranked second in the 100 best companies to work for. Staff gave her an 87 per cent positive score for being an inspiring leader. About 53 per cent of the workforce has been with RCH for five years or longer and more than 90 per cent of the managers have been promoted from within the company. This is a testimony to the company's commitment to employees.

Sources: adapted from www.redcarnationhotels.com and www.belleabouttown.com

2 (a) Explain how social media could be used by a business like Red Carnation Hotels to help meet customer needs. (4 marks)

No sample answer has been provided for question 2 (a) so that you can answer it yourself, for exam practice.

2 (b) Explain one possible reason for the pattern of consumer spending on hotel accommodation shown in Extract D. (4 marks)

Question 2 (b), Student answer

Since 2008 revenue in the global hotel industry has grown significantly. By 2016 it is expected to have grown by 23 per cent from $447 billion to $550 billion. One possible reason for this pattern of spending on hotel accommodation could be the growth in global incomes. There is usually a strong link between consumer incomes and the demand for products. In recent years the BRIC countries of Brazil, Russia, India and China, have enjoyed relatively high levels of economic growth. This has resulted in people earning more money and having extra to spend on non-essentials, such as hotel accommodation. The expansion in India planned by InterContinental Hotels (IHG) supports this view. IHG currently operates 19 hotels across 10 cities in India. It also expects to open another 45 hotels in the country over the next few years. The company is likely to be responding to rising demand for hotel accommodation in India resulting from growth in incomes. The hotels are likely to serve both Indians and overseas tourists visiting the country.

Comment, Question 2 (b)

Questions like this require you to demonstrate knowledge, application and possibly analysis. One or two marks might be awarded for identifying one factor that might have led to more spending on hotel accommodation over the time period, i.e. growing incomes. Up to two application marks might be awarded for keeping the answer in context. This answer focuses on the hotel industry. Finally, credit may be given for analysis. In this case, explaining how economic growth in developing nations has resulted in higher spending on hotel accommodation.

2 (c) Assess the impact good leadership might have on a business such as Red Carnation Hotels. (10 marks)

No sample answer has been provided for question 2 (c) so that you can answer it yourself, for exam practice.

2 (d) Assess the benefits to a company like Red Carnation Hotels of treating staff like assets. (12 marks)

Question 2 (d), Student answer

Different businesses have different approaches to their staff. Some businesses view their staff as assets, while others view them as costs. These approaches are very different and might have implications for their levels of productivity. Evidence in this case suggests that the Red Carnation Hotel is an employer that treats its staff as assets. Employers who view their staff as assets will value their employees and have concern for their welfare. Staff will be valued because employers recognise that their efforts will help the business to perform more effectively. Such employers will therefore try to meet the needs of employees. This might involve providing adequate remuneration, reasonable holidays, sick leave, maternity leave, pensions and a safe and comfortable working environment. Employers taking this approach will also be prepared to invest in training so that staff can develop skills and carry out work tasks competently and safely. They will also provide job security and opportunities to interact with colleagues, recognition and professional relationships and opportunities to solve problems. Staff might be encouraged to work in teams and be creative and they might be clearly and effectively led. The Red Carnation Hotel group is run by Beatrice Tollman. She is perceived to be a good leader by employees. Indeed, in a survey carried out by the 'Sunday Times', staff gave Beatrice an 87 per cent positive score for being an inspiring leader

Beatrice also believes that If you look after employees they, in turn, will look after the guests. In her opinion, caring for the workforce is simply good business practice. This is clear evidence that she treats staff as assets.

If employers treat staff as assets, they will also make an effort to retain them. They know employees want to be challenged, acknowledged and rewarded. These employers know that while money may not be the motivator for many employees, it is still important and they are likely to provide above average wages. This approach is likely to help recruit, retain and motivate high-quality staff. About 53 per cent of the workforce has been with RCH for five years or longer and more than 90 per cent of the managers have been promoted from within the company. This is a testament to RCH's commitment to employees.

In contrast, some employers view their staff as a cost and their focus is completely different. Like any other cost, they will try to minimise it wherever possible. This might involve paying the minimum legal wage, using zero hours contracts, neglecting investment in training, providing the minimum legal 'employee rights' in relation to sick leave, holiday pay and working conditions and using cheap and inferior recruitment methods. This approach might lower employment costs but it may also be a 'false economy'. This is because productivity might be lower due to poor motivation. Staff turnover and absenteeism may also be higher and there may be more conflict between staff and management. Treating staff as a cost may leave workers feeling exploited, neglected, stressed and unhappy in their work. At RCH it is clear that Beatrice Tollman recognises the talents of staff and values them. Using this approach the business has flourished and has a reputation for taste and excellence in dining, accommodation and service. The business has also won a number of prestigious industry awards.

Comment, Question 2 (d)

Questions like this require you to demonstrate knowledge, application, analysis and evaluation. Two marks might be awarded for demonstrating knowledge, such as explaining what is meant by treating staff as assets or identifying the benefits of such an approach like lower staff turnover and higher labour productivity. Two marks might be awarded for application. This answer focuses on the two possible approaches to staff in the hotel industry and in particular by Red Carnation Hotels. In this case it is the leader, Beatrice Tollman, who is responsible for the positive approach to staff management.

Four marks might be awarded for analysis. Examples of analysis in this answer are the detailed explanations of how staff might be treated as assets and the nature of the benefits to the hotel group of adopting this positive approach. The answer also considers a contrasting approach whereby staff are treated as a cost, which is explained in detail.

Four marks might be awarded for evaluation. An example of evaluation in this answer is the judgement made weighing up the benefits of treating staff as assets. Although a contrasting approach might result in lower costs for a business, this answer clearly shows that the Red Carnation Hotel Group has definitely benefited from treating staff as assets. The final judgement in the answer uses the examples of the hotel's reputation for taste and excellence and its prestigious awards to support the argument.

---

2 (e) Evaluate the possible impact on India's national economy of multinational developments, such as that planned by InterContinental Hotels (IHG®). (20 marks)

Question 2 (e), Student answer

Most governments around the world are in favour of multinational companies (MNCs) setting up operations in their countries. This is because they are likely to generate income, employment, wealth and prosperity. In this case, InterContinental Hotels Group has recently opened a new Holiday Inn in Jaipur, India. It also plans the development of another 45 hotels in the next few years.

When an overseas business like IHG locates a new facility in a foreign country, the amount of money spent on establishing that facility is classified as foreign direct investment (FDI). So the money spent by IHG opening the Holiday Inn in Jaipur represents an inflow of money from IHG to India. This is likely to be welcomed by the Indian government because the national economy will benefit. For example, the FDI should result in higher levels of GDP for India. The revenue resulting from the new hotel will increase economic growth and help to raise the living standards for people in the host country. Also, the profit made by IHG is likely to be taxed, unless the company has negotiated tax breaks with the government. This increases tax revenue for the Indian government, which can be spent improving public services, such as health care, education, housing, and transport networks. The IHG investment in Jaipur will also create local jobs. This will help to reduce unemployment, poverty and hardship in the area. Businesses in India may also get a boost when a multinational invests in a project. This is because a range of suppliers will be needed. For example, the hotel in Jaipur is likely to need supplies of furniture, fittings, raw materials, utilities, telephone services, commercial services, gardeners and cleaning contractors. Such demands will help to sustain and expand businesses in India and therefore create even more jobs in the national economy. There may also be a boost in tourism, which will help boost GDP.

Investment by MNCs will have a positive impact on the host nation's balance of payments. There will be a double impact. Initially, the flow of FDI when a project is being established will be classified as an export. For example, the money used to construct and furnish the hotel. Once the hotel is 'up and running' there may be a further boost to the balance of payments. This is because India's exports will rise if the hotel is used by overseas tourists. This boost in the balance of payments will help India to 'pay its way' when trading internationally.

MNC investment in foreign countries often means that new technologies and modern working practices are introduced into the host nation. This might result in the transfer of technologies and knowledge to local businesses. For example, new working practices in IHG's hotels may be copied by domestically owned hotels in India. IHG may also provide technical assistance, training and other information to their suppliers located in India. Many multinationals also assist local suppliers in purchasing resources and in modernising production facilities. The transfer of technology and skills from an MNC like IHG to businesses in India will help to improve efficiency and productivity.

Consumers are likely to benefit from the arrival of MNCs in their countries. This is because they will be free to buy some of the goods and services that they provide. In this case, they will be free to use the facilities provided by the Holiday Inn and any other hotels built by IHG. This will extend the choice of hotels in India. The arrival of MNCs is likely to increase competition in the host country. The products made by MNCs may be cheaper because they use modern and efficient production techniques. Since their costs will be lower, they can offer products at lower prices. This competitive pressure may also force domestic producers to lower their prices. For example, when IHG opened the Holiday Inn in Jaipur, for an initial period rooms could be booked at a discount. Other hotels may have been forced to lower their prices as a result. If MNCs use 'state-of-the-art' technologies, modern materials and more efficient working practices, such as total quality management, the quality of products might also be improved. For example, they may be better designed, more durable, more efficient and more aesthetically pleasing. In this case, the hotels being opened by IHG are modern with good facilities. For example, the Jaipur hotel had access to tourist attractions such as Amber Fort, Hawa Mahal and Birla Temple. Each room was equipped with a 37-inch LED TV, iPod docking station and a media hub, with hi-speed complimentary internet access across the hotel. The hotel also provides a gym and a roof-top pool. In general, it is possible that many people in the host nation will enjoy better living standards when MNCs set up operations. Initially, they may benefit from employment opportunities and enjoy higher incomes. They will have more choice and enjoy access to cheaper and better quality products.

In contrast, some MNCs are very powerful. In some cases the annual revenue of a MNC can be greater than the GDP of an entire country. This can give them a formidable presence. If too many domestic producers leave the market due to intense competition, this could result in less choice for consumers in the long term. Also, if MNCs are left with little or no competition, they may come to dominate the market and exploit consumers. There is also the possibility that profits will be repatriated to the MNC's home country and therefore the benefits to the host will be reduced. The impact of MNCs, when they first arrive, is often very positive for a country. However, it is important to remember that the impact of MNCs can have negative effects. For example, they may damage the environment, exploit local workers and force local businesses to fold. In this case there is no evidence to suggest that IHG has had a negative impact as a result of their investments in India. IHG already owns many hotels in the country and plans a further 45 in the next few years. These investments are likely to benefit India and its economy significantly.

Comment, Question 2 (e)

This question requires an extended answer and you need to demonstrate knowledge, application, analysis and evaluation. Four marks might be awarded for demonstrating knowledge, such as understanding the meaning of a multinational company and identifying some of the possible effects an MNC might have when it sets up operations in a new country.

Four marks might be awarded for application. This answer focuses throughout on the impact that IHG might have on the Indian national economy when it opens new hotels in the country. For example, it explains that new jobs will be created when the new Holiday Inn opens in Jaipur.

Six marks might be awarded for analysis. An example of analysis in this answer is the detailed explanation of the benefits to the Indian national economy of MNCs establishing themselves. These include more employment, more tax revenues, more exports, and the transfer of skills. These will all help to raise living standards in India. There will also be more consumer choice, which will also improve the quality of life for Indians. Six marks might be awarded for evaluation. In this case, one approach is to weigh up the benefits and the drawbacks of an MNC arriving in a country. This approach is taken here. The final judgement clearly suggests that the benefits outweigh the drawbacks. Indeed, in this case there is no evidence that the arrival of IHG has had a negative impact on the Indian national economy. Another approach that could have been used would be to rank in order of importance the benefits to the Indian economy of MNC activity.

Practice question – A Level, Paper I: Marketing, people and global business

Paper 1 – Marketing, people and global business

The more you practise for your examination, the more confident you will feel. The following question provides practice for Section A, Question 1.

Section A, Question I

Read the following extracts (A–C) before answering Question 1.

Extract A

Success at iOutlet

Entrepreneurs Liam James and Matthew Green set up iOutlet in 2012. The business sells second-hand refurbished iPhones and carries out repairs to smartphones. The pair recognised that although the global demand for iPhones was rising, not everyone could afford to pay for a brand new handset. The business uses eBay to sell its products, which helps to keep costs low and gives the brand access to the wider global market.

Since its inception, iOutlet has enjoyed astounding financial success. It managed to grow revenue to £2.4 million in its second year – a 400 per cent increase on year one. The business now has 16,000 clients in over 40 countries across six continents. The owners believe that good customer service has helped the business to succeed. Liam James said, 'We don't have any negative reviews with both accounts we sell from having 100 per cent positive feedback, something which proves our hard work before and after the sale is working and also something we are immensely proud of.'

Source: adapted from www.startups.co.uk

Extract B

Working conditions at Chess Telecom

Chess Telecom, based in Alderley Edge, Cheshire, provides services including line rental, broadband, mobile and telephone systems to UK businesses. It has a reputation as a very good employer. For example, the company has created a special team, selected because of their commitment to the company's vision and culture, who help new recruits to settle in to their new work environment. According to a survey 89 per cent of staff say they go out of their way to help each other and that events such as the summer conference, the Chesstival family fun day and sports clubs help to bond employees. Some 90 per cent of employees said that people within the company care a lot about each other.

There is also evidence that the owner consults staff on important issues. For example, a share-option scheme was introduced in response to staff suggestions. According to 80 per cent of employees Chess Telecom is run on strong principles by its boss. He takes part in fundraising challenges for the Prince's Trust and has climbed Kilimanjaro and Mont Blanc for charity.

Source: www.b.co.uk

Extract C

The globalisation of mobile phones

In 2014, it was thought that there were around 3 billion users of mobile phones worldwide. More than half of those users were located in developing countries.

In many developing countries, where average incomes are considerably lower than those in the developed world, mobile phone rates are also lower. Telecoms companies have adapted to this market environment and managed to maintain their profitability. As a result, a sizable number of people on very low incomes now have access to mobile telecommunications and the telecoms market.

Source: adapted from www.pewglobal.org

Percentage of people who own a mobile phone or smartphone in a selection of developing countries

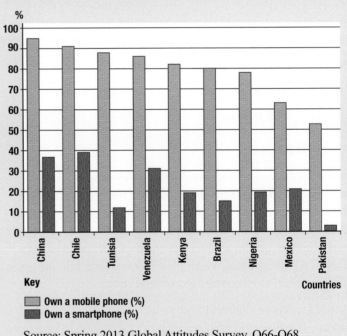

Source: Spring 2013 Global Attitudes Survey. Q66-Q68. Pew Research Center.

---

1 (a) Explain one method used by iOutlet to add value to their service. (4 marks)

   (b) Use the information in Extract A to calculate iOutlet's revenue in year 1. (4 marks)

   (c) Assess the characteristics and skills needed by entrepreneurs, such as Liam James and Matthew Green, to help run a successful business. (10 marks)

   (d) Assess the importance of team working to a company like Chess Telecom. (12 marks)

   (e) Evaluate the impact increasing globalisation might have on companies in the telecommunications industry. (20 marks)

Preparing for your A Level Paper 2 exam

Advance planning

1. Draw up a timetable for your revision and try to keep to it. Spread your timetable over a number of weeks, and aim to cover a chosen number of topics each week.
2. Spend longer on topics that you have found difficult, and revise them several times.
3. Do not try to limit your revision by attempting to 'question spot'. Revise so that you are confident about all aspects of your work.

Paper 2 overview:

A Level Paper 2: Business activities, decisions and strategy: 2 hours (Themes 2 and 3)	
Section A, Question 1	2×4 mark questions
	1×10 mark question
	1×12 mark question
	1×20 mark question
Total marks for Section A	*50 marks*
Section B, Question 2	2×4 mark questions
	1×10 mark question
	1×12 mark question
	1×20 mark question
Total marks for Section B	*50 marks*
	Total marks = 100 marks

Paper 2, **Business activities, decisions and strategy**, will assess your knowledge and understanding of **Themes 2** and **3**. It will assess business finance and operations, business decisions and strategy. You will need to make connections between Themes 2 and 3 when appropriate. For example, when discussing growth strategies (Theme 3) you could mention the possible need to raise further finance (Theme 2) to help fund growth. It is a written examination and the paper is divided into two sections. The duration of Paper 2 will be 2 hours. You have to answer **ALL** questions. There is no choice. However, this can be an advantage because it means you do not have to waste time deciding which questions to answer.

Section A questions

In Section A you will be given Extracts A–D as a stimulus and you will need to answer Question 1, a–e. The parts of Question 1 require a range of depths in your responses, depending on the mark allocation. Question 1e is an extended question.

Section B questions

In Section B you will be given Extracts E–H as stimulus and you will need to answer Question 2, a–e. The parts of Question 2 require a range of depths in your responses, depending on the mark allocation. Question 2e is an extended question.

You should familiarise yourself with the layout of the paper by looking at the examples published by Edexcel. The questions within each section are followed by lined spaces where you should write your answer. Use the mark allocation as a guide to how much time to spend on each question.

Skills required when answering questions

If you are entered for the A Level qualification you will be required to sit three examinations. You should be aware of the skills that you need to demonstrate when answering questions.

You will need to demonstrate four different skills referred to as assessment objectives (AOs).

AO1 – Knowledge: this means you have to show that you:

- recognise and understand business terms, concepts and theories
- understand how individuals and organisations are affected by and respond to business issues.

All questions will test knowledge to some extent. A minority of questions will test knowledge alone. These can be recognised by the mark allocation. They will tend to carry just two or four marks.

AO2 – Application: this means that you have to apply knowledge and understanding to various contexts to show how individuals and organisations are affected by and respond to issues. This might involve:

- using a business formula in appropriate circumstances, for example calculating the break-even point for a product
- using a theory to show why a business has chosen a particular course of action
- using a theory to show the impact on a business of choosing a particular course of action.

Most questions in the examination will require you to demonstrate application. This means that you have to ensure that your answers relate directly to the context given in the question. You must discuss the implications of issues to the particular business or industry in the context you are given.

AO3 – Analysis: this means you have to show that you can break down information and understand the implications of the information presented in the question. You will need to show an understanding of the impact on individuals and organisations of external and internal influences. This might involve:

- explaining causes and effects and interrelationships, for example by recognising from a graph that sales are falling and could be the result of new competition in the market
- breaking down information to identify specific causes or problems, for example by realising that quality has improved as a result of introducing continuous improvement
- using appropriate techniques to analyse data, for example by calculating the return on capital employed (ROCE).

You will often be required to construct an argument, for example by explaining the possible reasons for events or discussing the advantages or disadvantages of particular courses of action. Questions that carry more than four marks will require analysis in the answer. Some questions that carry four marks may also require you to demonstrate some analytical skills.

AO4 – Evaluation: evaluation involves making a judgement. You will need to evaluate both qualitative and quantitative evidence to make informed judgements and propose evidence-based solutions to business issues. This might involve:

- showing judgement when weighing up the relative importance of different points or sides of an argument in order to reach a conclusion
- drawing conclusions from the evidence that you present
- assessing the relative importance of particular issues to a business
- suggesting a course of action for a business, supported by plausible motives or evidence.

When evaluating, it is often possible to draw a number of different conclusions. Very often in business studies there is no 'right' answer, so examiners are likely to be more interested in whether your judgement is plausible and in the quality of your argument in support of that judgement. Questions that carry eight marks or more are likely to test evaluation.

Preparing for your A Level exams

Sample answer with comments

Paper 2: Business activities, decisions and strategy

These questions will help you prepare for your A Level Business Paper 2 examination. Some sample answers and comments are provided for you to review and you will have the opportunity to answer some questions yourself.

Section A, Question I

Read the following extracts (A–D) before answering Question 1.

Extract A

The popularity of fish and chips

Fish and chips is still one of the UK's favourite takeaway meals. In 2014, there were around 10,500 fish and chip shops in the country compared with about 1,200 McDonald's outlets. It is estimated that £1.2 billion is spent on fish and chips every year, with 80 per cent of the UK population visiting a specialist fish and chip shop at least once a year. About 22 per cent of the UK population visit a shop at least once a week.

One possible reason for the popularity of fish and chips is the nutritional value of the food. Fish and chips are said to be a source of vitamins, iron, fibre and protein. It is also reckoned that a portion of fish and chips contains less saturated fat, just 2.8 per cent, than a pork pie, which contains 10.8 per cent. An average portion also has less than 1,000 calories.

The National Fish & Chip Awards' number one fish and chip shop in the UK in 2015 was Frankie's, a shop and restaurant located in the Shetland Isles. The price of a fish and chip supper (muckle haddock with chips) in the shop was £6.70.

Source: adapted from www.federationoffishfriers.co.uk

Extract B

Takeaway expenditure in the UK

The amount of money UK consumers spent on takeaway food in 2014 was around £29.4 billion, according to research by vouchercodes.co.uk. The study identified laziness as an important determinant when selecting fast food options. Around 25 per cent of British people say that laziness is the main reason for their expenditure on takeaway food.

Source: adapted from www.vouchercodes.co.uk

Extract C

GDP growth forecasts

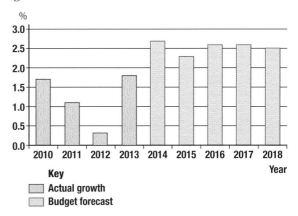

Source: ONS, Office for Budget Responsibility

Extract D

Business closure

In 2014, Wallace & Co, a restaurant run by Gregg Wallace, the MasterChef host, closed down after trading for four years. Based in Putney, southwest London, the restaurant closed owing its suppliers thousands of pounds. Wallace was not personally responsible for paying back the money because the debts were in the business's name, not his. After the business was liquidated and the assets sold off, creditors received less than half the amount they were owed. Companies House records show that Wallace was once a director of nine firms. As of July 2015, seven had been dissolved.

It was thought that one of the reasons for the closure of Wallace & Co was a lack of customers. The restaurant also suffered poor restaurant reviews in national newspapers.

Source: adapted from www.gov.uk

1 (a) Use Extract A and Extract B to calculate the percentage of the takeaway food market that is served by fish and chip shops. (4 marks)

Question 1 (a), student answer

The total market for fast food in 2014 was £29.4 billion.

The amount spent on fish and chips in 2014 was £1.2 billion.

The proportion of the market served by fish and chips is given by:

$$\frac{£1.2 \text{ billion}}{£29.4 \text{ billion}} \times 100\% = \textbf{4.08\%}$$

Comment, Question 1 (a)

There will always be calculation questions on Paper 2. This one involves calculating the share held by fish and chips in the fast food market. Your answer should be expressed as a percentage so you must show the % sign. You must also show the working out in case you make a simple calculation error using your calculator.

1 (b) Explain the advantage of limited liability to an entrepreneur like Gregg Wallace. (4 marks)

No sample answer has been provided for question 1 (b) so that you can answer it yourself, for exam practice.

1 (c) Assess the possible internal factors that might have been responsible for the closure of Wallace & Co. (10 marks)

Question 1 (c), student answer

Businesses fail for a wide variety of reasons. In some cases the cause of failure comes from within. One common internal cause of business failure, especially for new businesses, is a lack of planning. A plan will provide a roadmap that shows a clear direction for the development of the business and helps to identify potential problems in advance so that solutions can be found. In this case, it might be argued that insufficient planning went into marketing. One of the reasons why Wallace & Co failed was due to lack of customers. It is possible that potential customers were not aware of the business.

Also, Wallace & Co may not have spent enough money promoting the restaurant.

It seems from information provided that the quality of the product was also at fault. This is clearly an internal factor. The restaurant received poor reviews in national newspapers, which would have affected its reputation and made it difficult for the enterprise to survive. If businesses serve poor-quality products, customers will go elsewhere. The restaurant industry is very competitive and it is easy for customers to find substitutes nearby.

There may have been other internal reasons for the failure of Wallace & Co. For example, financial management may have been inadequate, there may have been a lack of funding or leadership may have been poor – it is possible that the person in charge lacked the necessary skills to run a business successfully. Inevitably many small businesses fail because their owners do not have all the competencies required. Running a business is challenging and requires a multitude of skills. Entrepreneurs have to be creative, numerate, motivational and good decision makers. They also need

skills in communication, IT, marketing, negotiating, financial management and probably much more. It is perhaps not surprising that willing entrepreneurs are sometimes lacking in the skills required to be successful. In the case of Wallace & Co, some of the skills required to be successful in the restaurant industry may have needed enhancing. To conclude, the failure of Wallace & Co was almost entirely the result of internal factors – ineffective marketing and a poor-quality product in an industry where competition is ruthless.

Comment, Question 1 (c)

Questions like this require you to demonstrate knowledge, application, analysis and evaluation. Two marks might be awarded for demonstrating knowledge, such as identifying two internal factors that might result in business failure, in this case poor-quality products and ineffective marketing. Two marks might be awarded for application. The whole of this answer is focused on the restaurant industry, and in particular the failure of Wallace & Co. The reasons for business failure are linked entirely to the failure of Wallace & Co. Three marks might be awarded for analysis. One example of analysis in this answer is

the explanation of how a business might fail if the owner lacks the expertise needed to run a business successfully. Three marks might be awarded for evaluation. An example of evaluation in this answer is the judgement made relating to the reasons for failure in this extract. It states in the answer that failure is clearly to do with internal factors. This argument is clear and well supported with evidence from the extract and business theory. In this answer counterbalance arguments are also raised. For example, other internal causes of failure are identified but ruled out. In this case, the cause of failure is fairly clear.

---

1 (d) Evaluate the benefits of using SWOT analysis for a business considering entry into the restaurant industry. (12 marks)

No sample answer has been provided for question 1 (d) so that you can answer it yourself, for exam practice.

1 (e) Evaluate the possible impact of economic influences, such as economic growth, on businesses like Frankie's in the next five years. (20 marks)

Question 1 (e), student answer

Business activity is influenced by a number of external influences. These are factors beyond the control of businesses. In some cases they constrain a business's decisions and may prevent its growth and development. Economic influences, such as inflation, exchange rates, interest rates, taxation, government expenditure and the business cycle, can have many effects on a business. The government is responsible for the management of the economy. The aim of many governments is to keep prices stable, reduce unemployment, keep borrowing down and help the economy grow. The measures a government might use to achieve these aims can have an impact on businesses.

The current state of the economy can have a big impact on many businesses. In this case, the restaurant industry in general is likely to be affected by levels of national income and economic growth. Extract C shows that the UK's economy is expected to grow up to 2018. According to the budget statement, growth rates are predicted to be around 2.5 per cent per annum. This is steady and sustainable growth. It means that national income is expected to carry on rising and as a result people's incomes should also rise. This is likely to have an impact on the restaurant industry in the next few years. When people have a higher income and consequently more money to spend, they are likely

to buy more non-essential products. Spending money in restaurants is regarded by most as non-essential, therefore demand for the services provided by restaurants is likely to rise. However, in this case, the impact on Frankie's fish and chip shop may not be clear cut. Fish and chips is regarded by many as an affordable takeaway option – something that people will still buy even when incomes are squeezed. However, when incomes rise, some people may spend less on fish and chips and more on 'up-market' takeaway food. If fish and chips are income elastic and considered to be an inferior good, then demand may fall. Consequently Frankie's may suffer a loss in trade.

Another possible economic influence on businesses like Frankie's in the next few years is taxation. If governments promise to reduce the amount they borrow each year, this is likely to mean cuts in government expenditure, rises in taxation, or a combination of both. Cuts in government expenditure are not likely to have a direct impact on the restaurant industry, but there may be an indirect impact if cuts in government expenditure mean that people have to spend more of their income on services that were once funded or subsidised by the state. For example, if people have to pay more for rail transport or dental treatment, they might have less to spend on leisure and entertainment, in which case the restaurant industry might be adversely affected.

If the government increases taxes, the restaurant industry could be adversely affected. For example, if income tax is increased then disposable incomes will be reduced. This could result in a fall in demand for restaurant services. Frankie's might be affected by such a measure (depending on the income elasticity of fish and chips). Restaurants will also be affected if the government decides to raise VAT. This will increase costs for restaurants and marginal operators will be squeezed. Some may go out of business. However, Frankie's is the number one fish and chip shop in the UK, so it could probably cope with higher VAT. Finally, government might increase business taxes, such as corporation tax. This would have a negative impact on restaurants that trade as limited companies or plcs.

To conclude, the overall impact of economic influences on businesses like Frankie's depends on a range of factors. If the influence of economic factors is favourable, such as higher economic growth, the restaurant industry is likely to benefit. However, cuts in government expenditure and higher taxes will have a negative effect. The overall impact is very difficult to assess because it is impossible to predict with any accuracy how economic influences will develop. The effect on Frankie's might also depend on the income elasticity of demand for fish and chips. But, since Frankie's is the number one fish and chip shop in the UK, it is probably strong enough to survive a range of negative influences, and would probably do very well in a strengthening economy.

Comment, Question 1 (e)

This question requires an extended answer and you need to demonstrate knowledge, application, analysis and evaluation. Four marks might be awarded for demonstrating knowledge, such as understanding the meaning of economic influences like economic growth and identifying other possible economic influences, such as taxation and government expenditure. Four marks might be awarded for application. This answer focuses throughout on the impact of economic influences on the restaurant industry and Frankie's fish and chip shop in particular. Income elasticity is also applied to the demand for fish and chips.

Six marks might be awarded for analysis. Examples of analysis in this answer are the explanation of how economic growth, cuts in government expenditure and higher taxes are likely to impact on the restaurant industry and Frankie's in particular. Six marks might be awarded for evaluation. In this case, one approach is to weigh up the possible economic influences and decide which is most likely to have an impact on businesses like Frankie's. It is an impossible task to draw a definitive conclusion because the possible economic influences cannot be predicted – some might be positive (economic growth) and some negative (cuts in government expenditure and higher taxes). However, this is clearly stated and there is still an attempt to make a judgement. It is recognised that Frankie's is in a good position because it is the UK's number one fish and chip shop. However, overall, the impact might depend on the income elasticity of demand for fish and chips.

Section B, Question 2

Read the following extracts (E–H) before answering Question 2.

Extract E

Rapid growth at Concrete Canvas Ltd

Concrete Canvas Ltd produce a concrete impregnated fabric that was developed by Peter Brewin and Will Crawford when they were at the Royal College of Art together. In 2014, according to a survey by the *Sunday Times*, Concrete Canvas Ltd was ranked the 16th fastest-growing company in the UK. Between 2010 and 2013 sales grew at an average annual rate of 118 per cent. In 2013 it employed 26 people and enjoyed sales of £5.1 million.

Concrete Canvas is a concrete impregnated fabric that hardens when sprayed with water, creating a waterproof and fire resistant concrete layer. It was first developed as a material from which concrete shelters could be made. The idea was to design shelters that could be dropped into disaster zones or areas of military conflict and swiftly assembled. However, the pair discovered that the material technology itself was the marketable product.

The material is sold in small (batched) and large (bulk) rolls, which can be manipulated to shape, unrolled onto the ground, on slopes and on existing concrete. It is used in mining, civil infrastructure and the petrochemicals industry.

Source: adapted from www.concretecanvas.com

Extract F

Raising finance at John Laing

In 2015, infrastructure investment group John Laing announced that it would raise around £130 million by selling some new shares on the stock market. It was explained that the money would be used to help finance international investment. John Laing was already involved in a range of construction projects around the world such as the building of a 60,000-seat stadium in Perth, Australia, roads in the US, wind farms across Europe, prisons in New Zealand and the construction of the second Severn Crossing, which links England and Wales.

Source: adapted from the *Financial Times* 29.01.2015. All rights reserved.

Extract G

Barratt Homes' financial position

Barratt Homes' is an established housebuilder. It has been building homes since 1958. Like other builders it struggled during the financial crisis and recession between 2008 and 2013. However, in 2014 the company increased its revenue and made a profit of £305.4 million.

Selected information from Barratt Homes' statement of financial position 2014

	2014 £ million
Revenue	3,157.0
Gross profit	529.4
Operating profit	305.4
Non-current assets	1,248.4
Current assets	3,895.9
Current liabilities	1,160.1
Non-current liabilities	630.2

Source: www.barrattdevelopments.co.uk

Extract H

Wates takeover?

In March 2015, it was reported that Wates, one of the UK's largest family-owned construction businesses, was involved in preliminary talks to take over one of its rivals, Shepherd Construction. Shepherd has suffered some disruption due to disappointing results. Peter Lewis, who was described as an inspirational leader, left Shepherd Construction at the beginning of 2015.

Financial and other information for Wates and Shepherd 2013

	Wates	Shepherd
Revenue	£931 million	£686 million
Profit	£22 million	£11 million
Staff	2,074	3,235
Established	1897	1890

Source: www.wates.co.uk

2 (a) Calculate the return on capital employed for Barratt Homes in 2014. (4 marks)

Question 2 (a), student answer

The return on capital employed for Barratt Homes is given by:

Net profit is £305.4 million

Capital employed = total assets − current liabilities
= (£1,248.4m + £3,895.9m) − £1,160.1m
= £5,114.3m − £1,160.1m = £3,984.2m

ROCE = $\frac{\text{Operating profit}}{\text{Capital employed}}$ x 100% = $\frac{£305.4m}{£3,984.2}$ x 100% = **7.7 %**

Comment, Question 2 (a)

You need to remember the formula for calculating return on capital employed (ROCE) in this question. You also need to remember how to identify capital employed. You should write down the formula and show all your working out. Even if you get the wrong answer you may still be awarded some marks for stating the correct formula and identifying some relevant information.

2 (b) Explain one reason why Wates might want to take over Shepherd. (4 marks)

Question 2 (b), student answer

A takeover occurs when one business buys another from its current owners. Once the business has been bought, its resources are absorbed by the buyer and the name usually disappears. There are several motives for takeovers. In this case, Wates may take over a close rival in the construction industry, Shepherd Construction. If the takeover is agreed, Wates will have a bigger market share since it will have absorbed one of its competitors. This means that it will increase its revenue by over 70 per cent and have less competition in the construction market. This will make Wates stronger and more resourceful. It might be able to win bigger contracts, raise prices or be more selective when bidding for contracts, i.e. choosing those that are most lucrative. This should help the business improve its financial performance in the long term.

Comment, Question 2 (b)

Questions like this require you to demonstrate knowledge, application and possibly analysis. One or two marks might be awarded for showing that you understand the nature of a takeover and identifying one reason why Wates may want to take over Shepherd Construction. Up to two application marks might be awarded for keeping the answer in context. This answer focuses on the construction industry. Finally, credit may be given for analysis. In this case, explaining how the financial performance of Wates might be improved as a result of the takeover is an example of analysis.

2 (c) Assess two possible growth objectives for Concrete Canvas. (10 marks)

Question 2 (c), student answer

Most businesses start small and then grow. In this case, Concrete Canvas grew very quickly in the three years between 2010 and 2013. Indeed, the annual growth rate was 118 per cent. Generally, businesses like to grow because the benefits can be very attractive. For example, revenues will be higher, unit costs are likely to be lower and the business will have a higher profile with a larger market share.

One specific growth objective is the ability to enjoy economies of scale. As Concrete Canvas gets larger it will be able to secure lower unit costs. Costs might fall for a number of reasons. For example, there may be purchasing economies. This means that Concrete Canvas will probably get discounts for buying larger quantities of inputs such as fabric, cement and other raw materials. The company may also experience managerial economies. This means that it will be cost-effective to employ specialist managers, such as accountants, marketing managers and production managers. These people will be experts in their fields and will help to raise productivity and therefore reduce average costs.

Another growth objective might be to increase market share. Concrete Canvas is a relatively new company so its market share would be low to begin with. A higher market share will eventually give Concrete Canvas more power, which means it might be able to raise price. However, it will also benefit from having a greater brand recognition. This might be because customers are more likely to see the brand advertised or on business websites. As the brand becomes stronger, Concrete Canvas may be able to charge higher prices, differentiate the product from those of other producers of concrete products, create customer loyalty in the construction industry, develop an image and launch new products more easily. A business with a larger market share is also more likely to attract media attention. In this case, because the product is a fairly new innovation, the business might attract quite a lot of media attention – particularly if the product is considered unique and used throughout the whole of the construction industry.

It might be argued that the main growth objective for Concrete Canvas would be to increase market share. This is because the company is new and needs to establish itself in the industry. Other growth objectives, such as economies of scale, might become more important once Concrete Canvas has established a solid market share. Evidence suggests that Concrete Canvas is already making very good progress in this respect. Its average annual growth rate in the last three years has been a huge 118 per cent.

Comment, Question 2 (c)

You will need to demonstrate knowledge, application, analysis and evaluation. Two marks might be awarded for demonstrating knowledge, such as identifying two specific growth objectives – economies of scale and increased market share. Two marks might be awarded for application. The whole of this answer is focused on the growth objectives of Concrete Canvas and the construction industry. For example, there is the suggestion that the media might be interested in Concrete Canvas because its product is innovative. Three marks might be awarded for analysis.

One example of analysis in this answer is the explanation of how Concrete Canvas might benefit from specific economies of scale, such as purchasing economies and managerial economies. Three marks might be awarded for evaluation. An example of evaluation in this answer is the judgement suggesting which growth objective might be most important to Concrete Canvas. It is suggested that building market share is most important because the business is relatively new in the market. The judgement here is clearly supported with an argument.

---

2 (d) Assess the usefulness to companies like Wates and John Laing of using quantitative investment appraisal techniques before investing their money in new projects. (12 marks)

No sample answer has been provided for question 2 (d) so that you can answer it yourself, for exam practice.

2 (e) Evaluate the importance of external sources of funding, such as issuing shares, to a company like John Laing. (20 marks)

Question 2 (e), student answer

Few businesses can rely entirely on internal financing to fund all business activity. Initially, external finance, which is finance from sources outside the business, may not be available. This is because business start-ups have no trading record and present too much risk for many lenders. However, once a business has survived the initial 'uncertain' stages of business development, external sources of finance are likely to become a realistic option. In this case, John Laing is an established business. It plans to raise £130 million by selling some shares.

Issuing shares is a common external source of finance for companies. Issuing shares can raise huge amounts of money. In this case, £130 million is being raised to help finance new overseas construction projects. Share capital is permanent capital, which means that it is never repaid by the business. Once John Laing has sold the shares and raised the £130 million, the money will never be repaid. If shareholders want their money back from buying the shares they must sell them on the stock market. This is one of the main advantages of raising money by issuing shares – there is no debt burden. However, shareholders will expect a return and John Laing will be obliged to pay dividends to shareholders when the company makes sufficient profit. Shareholders would also hope that the share price increases in the future. This means they can make a capital gain if they sell them. The share price is likely to rise if John Laing grows and performs well.

One drawback of selling shares is the initial cost of the share issue. A number of costs will be incurred, such as fees to an investment bank to process share applications. The share issue has to be underwritten (which means that the company must insure against the possibility of some shares remaining unsold) and a fee is paid to an underwriter who must buy any unsold shares. Finally, the company will also have to meet advertising and administrative costs. However, once these costs have been met, there are no further charges on the finance, except for dividends.

John Laing could have used other external sources of finance, such as bank loans, debentures, venture capital or a mortgage. However, these sources may have been considered unsuitable by John Laing. This might be because they incur costs. For example, if bank loans and mortgages are taken out, interest has to be paid. Interest charges will reduce profits. Also, any money borrowed will eventually have to be repaid. This places a financial burden on the company. The advantage of share capital is that it does not have to be paid.

Another option that may have been open to John Laing is internal finance. This usually comes from retained profit or the sale of assets. The main advantage of using internal sources is that there is no financial cost – there is no interest to pay because the money used belongs to the business. However, there is an opportunity cost when using internal sources. For example, if John Laing used retained profit to fund the development of its overseas construction projects, it would have less money to return to the shareholders. Reducing dividend payments may attract a negative reaction from the shareholders. There is also the likelihood that John Laing did not have £130 million available to invest. Neither was the company inclined to sell off any assets to raise the cash.

To conclude, external sources of finance are very important to companies like John Laing. These sources are needed to help grow businesses and generate higher profits in the future. When raising very large amounts of money, such as £130 million in this case, external sources are crucial. The sale of shares to raise money keeps the gearing of the business lower, avoids interest payments and ensures that the business is not undercapitalised. Consequently, the benefits of using external sources of finance are likely to outweigh the drawbacks for companies like John Laing.

Comment, Question 2 (e)

This question requires an extended answer and you need to demonstrate knowledge, application, analysis and evaluation. Four marks might be awarded for demonstrating knowledge, such as understanding the meaning of external sources of finance and share capital. Marks might also be awarded for identifying other sources of external finance, such as bank loans and debentures, and showing that you understand the advantages and disadvantages of raising money by issuing shares. Four marks might be awarded for application. This answer focuses throughout on John Laing and its legal status as a plc. Only companies can raise money by issuing shares.

Six marks might be awarded for analysis. One example of analysis in this answer is the explanation of how John Laing will benefit from selling shares, i.e. by raising permanent capital and avoiding interest charges. Analysis is also demonstrated when explaining the drawbacks of issuing shares, i.e. the initial cost and the company's permanent commitment to dividend payments. Six marks might be awarded for evaluation. In this case, evaluation can be demonstrated by weighing up the benefits and drawbacks of using share capital as external finance to raise £130 million. The implications of using external sources as opposed to internal sources is also debated, and so are the implications of using share capital as opposed to other sources of external finance. A clear conclusion is drawn and it is supported with coherent argument.

Practice question – A Level, Paper 2: Business activities, decisions and strategy

The more you practise for your examination, the more confident you will feel. The following question provides practice for Section A, Question 1.

Section A, Question 1

Read the following extracts (A–D) before answering Question 1.

Extract A

Working at Foxconn

Foxconn is a multinational electronics manufacturer that carries out contract work for high-profile customers. Microsoft's Xbox, Nintendo's Wii U and the Sony's PlayStation are examples of the products made by Foxconn. The Taiwanese company is owned by Hon Hai Precision Industry Company Ltd and has factories in many countries, employing over a million people.

In 2012, the *Financial Times* reported that workers at a Chinese Foxconn factory 'threatened collective suicide in a pay dispute gone wrong'. Workers who took part tried to 'force the company to agree a wage raise by threatening to jump off a building'. They said they 'took the drastic step because the company denied them a pay raise it had promised earlier when transferring them to Wuhan from another plant.'

Foxconn had made a lot of changes over time. It 'set up a range of counselling systems' and 'raised wages especially for those willing to stay longer in order to lower turnover rates'.

In 2013, the *Financial Times* reported that, 'an inspection by the Fair Labour association, a monitoring group brought in by Apple to help the company improve working conditions, said in its final verification that "Foxconn, also known as Hon Hai Precisions Industries, is adhering to earlier agreed upon plans to improve working conditions. Although overtime remains a problem, the company made progress reducing working hours and improved factory facilities". The report also found that 'workers still do more overtime than permitted by Chinese labour law'. In a statement, 'Apple said the average workweek at Foxconn … was… below the limit in the brand's code of conduct'. The *Financial Times* also noted that 'limiting overtime is a particularly challenging issue in Chinese factories as many workers…. prefer to do overtime as a way to improve their often low base pay'.

Source: adapted from the *Financial Times* 12.01.2012, 12.12.2013.

Extract B

Nintendo cuts sales forecast

In 2015 Nintendo, the computer games company, was forced to cut its annual sales forecast in half. Despite strong Christmas sales in 2014, the company lowered its annual sales forecast to £112 million, half of the original forecast. Despite Nintendo's problems, its reported software sales were more promising, where Super Smash Bros generated sales of 6.19 million copies in the third quarter of 2014.

Extract C

GameGirl new product development

GameGirl Ltd is a computer games designer. It is owned by the Charles family and based in Cambridge. Sally Charles is the 'brains' behind the business. She and her small team of software designers produce software for video games and apps.

In 2013, a new game called Harbour was developed. The fixed costs of development were £190,000. The variable costs per unit were 100p. Harbour, which can be downloaded online, was sold for £20 per unit.

Extract D

Computer hackers

On Christmas Day in 2014, computer hackers claimed to have taken the personal details of around 13,000 users of PlayStation, Xbox and online stores, including Amazon. Details, such as passwords and credit card data, were leaked according to the hackers, who claimed to be linked to the anarchist group Anonymous. As a result of the security breach, thousands of people, including children, were unable to play with their new games online. The hackers, a group called Lizard Squad, said it carried out the hack for amusement and to expose poor online security.

Source: adapted from the *Financial Times*, 26.12.2014.

1 (a) Use the information in Extract C to calculate the number of units Harbour must sell to break-even. (4 marks)

(b) Explain how businesses such as Amazon and Microsoft might use risk assessment to help deal with the threat of computer hackers. (4 marks)

(c) Assess the factors that might affect the sales forecasts made by Nintendo. (10 marks)

(d) Assess the possible stakeholder conflict that might exist at Foxconn. (12 marks)

(e) Evaluate the possible impact of tighter employment legislation on businesses like Foxconn. (20 marks)

Preparing for your A Level Paper 3 exam

Advance planning

This paper is a little different from Papers 1 and 2 because you will be given some pre-released information in advance of the examination to help you prepare. The information will suggest areas for closer scrutiny and research in your revision. Their purpose is to provide a context in which questions will be asked. The context will be broad, such as an industry or market in which businesses operate. You cannot take any records of your research into the examination with you.

Paper 3 overview

A Level Paper 3: Investigating business in a competitive environment (pre-release): 2 hours (Themes 1–4)	
Section A, Question 1	1×8 mark question
	1×10 mark question
	1×12 mark question
	1×20 mark question
Total marks for Section A	*50 marks*
Section B, Question 2	1×8 mark question
	1×10 mark question
	1×12 mark question
	1×20 mark question
Total marks for Section B	*50 marks*
Total marks = 100 marks	

Pre-release

Paper 3 will assess your knowledge and understanding of **all four themes** and is called **Investigating business in a competitive environment**. You will be given some pre-released information in advance of the examination to help you prepare, which provides a context in which questions will be asked. The context will be broad, such as industry or market in which businesses operate. You will be given areas for closer scrutiny and research in your revision.

This is a written examination and is divided into two sections. The duration of Paper 3 will be 2 hours. You have to answer **ALL** questions. There is no choice. However, this can be an advantage because it means you do not have to waste time deciding which questions to answer. You cannot take any records of your research into the examination with you.

Synoptic skills

You will also be required to demonstrate synoptic skills.

This means that you need to work across different parts of the specification and show your accumulated knowledge and understanding of a topic or subject area. You will need to demonstrate your ability to combine skills, knowledge and understanding with breadth and depth of the subject. You will also need to identify and discuss links between the different topic areas on the specification. For example, if you are answering a question on the impact that economic growth might have on a business, you could discuss the possible effects on the:

* marketing strategies used by the business (Theme 1)
* aims and objectives of the business (Theme 1)
* sales and the financial performance of the business (Themes 2 and 3)
* production department in the business (Theme 2)
* growth and investment strategies of the business (Theme 3)
* global outlook of the business (Theme 4).

Section A and Section B questions

In both Section A and Section B you will be given a range of unseen stimulus material (several pieces of information about business and industry) and you will need to answer a number of questions. The questions will require a range of depths in your response, depending on the mark allocation. One of these will be an extended question.

Section A questions

In Section A you will be given Extracts A–D as a stimulus and you will need to answer Question 1, a–d. The parts of Question 1 will focus on the broad context of the materials provided.

Section B questions

In Section B you will be given Extracts E–H as a stimulus and you will need to answer Question 2, a–d. The parts of Question 2 will focus on at least one strand within the context provided, such as a particular business.

You should familiarise yourself with the layout of the paper by looking at the examples published by Edexcel. The questions within each section are followed by lined spaces where you should write your answer. Use the mark allocation as a guide to how much time to spend on each question.

Skills required when answering questions

If you are entered for the A Level qualification you will be required to sit three examinations. You should be aware of the skills that you need to demonstrate when answering questions.

You will need to demonstrate four different skills referred to as assessment objectives (AOs).

AO1 – Knowledge: this means you have to show that you:

- recognise and understand business terms, concepts and theories
- understand how individuals and organisations are affected by and respond to business issues.

All questions will test knowledge to some extent. A minority of questions will test knowledge alone. These can be recognised by the mark allocation. They will tend to carry just two or four marks.

AO2 – Application: this means that you have to apply knowledge and understanding to various contexts to show how individuals and organisations are affected by and respond to issues. This might involve:

- using a business formula in appropriate circumstances, for example calculating the price elasticity of demand for a product
- using a theory to show why a business has chosen a particular course of action
- using a theory to show the impact on a business of choosing a particular course of action.

Most questions in the examination will require you to demonstrate application. This means that you have to ensure that your answers relate directly to the context given in the question. You must discuss the implications of issues to the particular business or industry in the context you are given.

AO3 – Analysis: this means you have to show that you can break down information and understand the implications of the information presented in the question. You will need to show an understanding of the impact on individuals and organisations of external and internal influences. This might involve:

- explaining causes and effects and interrelationships, for example by recognising from a graph that sales are falling and could be the result of new competition in the market

- breaking down information to identify specific causes or problems, for example by realising that a business is suffering from inefficiency because staff motivation has fallen as a result of a pay cut
- using appropriate techniques to analyse data, for example by calculating the net profit ratio.

You will often be required to construct an argument, for example by explaining the possible reasons for events or discussing the advantages or disadvantages of particular courses of action. Questions that carry more than four marks will require analysis in the answer. Some questions that carry four marks may also require you to demonstrate some analytical skills.

AO4 – Evaluation: evaluation involves making a judgement. You will need to evaluate both qualitative and quantitative evidence to make informed judgements and propose evidence-based solutions to business issues. This might involve:

- showing judgement when weighing up the relative importance of different points or sides of an argument in order to reach a conclusion
- drawing conclusions from the evidence that you present
- assessing the relative importance of particular issues to a business
- suggesting a course of action for a business, supported by plausible motives or evidence.

When evaluating, it is often possible to draw a number of different conclusions. Very often in business studies there is no 'right' answer, so examiners are likely to be more interested in whether your judgement is plausible and in the quality of your argument in support of that judgement. Questions that carry eight marks or more are likely to test evaluation.

Preparing for your A Level exams

Paper 3: Investigating business in a competitive environment (pre-release)

These questions will help you prepare for your A Level Business Paper 3 examination. Some sample answers and comments are provided for you to review and you will have the opportunity to answer some questions yourself.

Pre-released information

Context

This year the context is the market for fashion accessories and the businesses operating in this market in the UK.

Research

To prepare for this context you should research:

- trends in the market for fashion accessories
- influences on the market for fashion accessories, such as marketing and income
- major businesses and niche operators in the fashion accessories market
- the competitive environment facing fashion accessory businesses.

You **cannot** take any of your research or investigation data carried out as part of the pre-release into the examination. Answer all questions.

Section A, Question 1

Read the following extracts (A–D) before answering Question 1.

Extract A

Market research in the fashion accessories industry

Market research agency Mintel reckoned that UK consumers spent about £2.5 billion on fashion accessories in 2013. Around £1.2 billion of this expenditure went on handbags – an increase of 11 per cent on the previous year. Research showed that more than 13.5 million women bought at least one new handbag in 2013. However, sales of handbags to men also rose and in 2013 one in ten men bought a 'manbag'.

The market for handbags is highly competitive with companies like Chanel, Gucci, Louis Vuitton, Hèrmes, Burberry and Michael Kors operating at both global and regional levels. It seems that sales and special offers help to generate sales of fashion accessories, with nearly 60 per cent of women responding positively to discounts. Impulse buying is common in the fashion accessories market, with the over 55s being the most likely group to buy on impulse. Finally, about 50 per cent of the people who bought fashion accessories in 2013 used online shopping methods, with 25 per cent buying from internet specialists.

Source: adapted from www.mintel.com

Extract B

Men's fashion accessories

The men's accessories market is dynamic and fast growing. In the 12 months ending May 2014, global sales of men's accessories grew 9 per cent, reaching $13.6 billion according to market research. This trend is unlikely to be reversed any time soon and the fashion industry is clamouring to cash in on the rapid expansion in the market. For example, designers such as Michael Kors are recruiting new menswear executives and investing highly in this growing market, thought to be worth billions of dollars.

Shifting social attitudes is one reason for the market growth. In the 1990s the only males that would regularly wear jewellery, for example, were rock stars and celebrities. The emergence of metrosexuals and the influence of role models, such as David Beckham, have helped to drive demand.

Source: adapted from www.businessoffashion.com

Extract C

Final consumption expenditure (% of GDP) in BRIC countries, 2005–2013

Country Name	2005	2006	2007	2008	2009	2010	2011	2012	2013
Brazil	79.17	79.25	78.65	78.39	81.45	79.24	78.96	81.01	81.65
Russian Federation	66.23	66.10	67.21	65.26	73.63	69.31	66.48	68.17	71.30
India	68.47	67.29	65.98	69.54	69.08	67.84	67.54	70.40	70.44
China	53.61	50.76	51.02	49.74	48.54	49.64	50.75	49.95	49.58

Source: www.data.worldbank.org

Extract D

Smartwatches

A smartwatch is a wrist-worn device that shows the time and has a wireless internet connection. In 2013 the market was worth $700 million. By 2020 the market is expected to be worth around $33 billion. In 2014, Samsung dominated the market with 34 per cent share. However, in 2015 Apple launched its version of a smartwatch and expected to generate sales of around 19 million – 56 per cent of the global market. The development of wearable technology, such as smartwatches, may become a threat to traditional watchmakers.

Growth in wearable technology 2012 to 2020

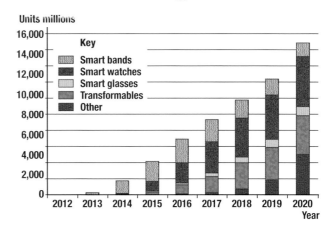

Source: www.analysysmason.com

1 (a) Assess the importance of the design mix to products in the fashion accessories industry. (8 marks)

No sample answer has been provided for question 1 (a) so that you can answer it yourself, for exam practice.

1 (b) Assess the implications of using sales and special offers in the market for fashion accessories. (10 marks)

Question 1 (b), student answer

An important element in the marketing mix is promotion. This involves businesses drawing attention to their products, services or companies. Generally, businesses use promotion to obtain and retain customers. In this case, promotions, such as sales and special offers, are used to drive up sales of fashion accessories. They are both examples of below-the-line promotion, which refers to any form of promotion that does not involve advertising. In the fashion accessories market, sales often coincide with the end of buying seasons for clothes. For example, just before the end of summer, many retailers have sales to sell off unsold stocks of summer clothes to clear the way for the autumn season's stock. Businesses selling fashion accessories are likely to do exactly the same. There are also one or two special sales periods in the UK. One is the 'January sales', which start on Boxing Day, and more recently 'Black Friday Sales', an idea imported from the US. Since the early 2000s, sales in the US have begun on the day after Thanksgiving Day (the fourth Thursday of November). This has been regarded as the beginning of the Christmas shopping season in the US, and most major retailers open very early and offer promotional sales. During sales, products are often heavily discounted and can generate large volumes of business.

The use of sales and discounts can have a number of implications for a business. One is that profit margins will be squeezed if prices are cut sharply to generate sales. For example, if the price of a handbag is cut from £199 to £49, this suggests that a huge amount of profit is being conceded by the seller. However, it is very likely that the margins on many fashion accessories are so high to begin with that businesses are able to tolerate dramatic price cuts. Such drastic price cuts are also what drives sales because consumers think they are getting a real bargain.

Businesses that sell larger volumes during sales have to ensure that stocks at the point of sale are adequate to meet the sharp increase in demand. This might mean that manufacturers have to step up production in the run up to sales. Alternatively they may just accumulate stocks for a period of time in preparation. It is important to provide effective co-ordination between suppliers and the retail outlet. Customers are likely to get very frustrated if they cannot buy a product in the sale because they have sold out. This could damage customer loyalty.

In some cases, up-market producers of fashion accessories, such as Gucci, may be very reluctant to use sales and special offers as a means of promotion. This is because their goods are often very high in quality and targeted at the 'top end' of the market. As a result sharp discounting could suggest a fall in quality and adversely affect their image.

Finally, companies that rely heavily on sales for their business might have to pay special attention to financial management. In particular, they will have to manage their cash flow carefully. This is because cash flow is likely to be irregular. For example, during sales periods cash inflows will be very high but at other times they will be much lower and could cause cash shortages.

To conclude, businesses in the fashion accessories market are probably very experienced at dealing with some of the issues discussed above. The sale of such products has always been linked to specific buying seasons and individual businesses have probably learned to live with these problems. However, they will still need to be vigilant and monitor any changes that occur in the market.

Comment, Question 1 (b)

You will need to demonstrate knowledge, application, analysis and evaluation. You also need to remember that information from all four themes can be used. Answers that make links between the different themes are likely to be better. Two marks might be awarded for demonstrating knowledge, such as defining below-the-line promotion and identifying implications of using sales and special offers to generate business. Two marks might be awarded for application. The whole of this answer is focused on the use of sales and special offers in the fashion accessories market and the implications of their use. For example, sales and discounting are used by the fashion industry in general at the end of buying seasons and during traditional sales like the January sales.

Three marks might be awarded for analysis. Examples of analysis in this answer include the explanation of how the use of sales and discounts will squeeze profit margins, cause cash-flow problems or tarnish the image of the business. Three marks might be awarded for evaluation. An example of evaluation in this answer is the judgement suggesting that businesses in the fashion accessories market are probably used to the problems discussed throughout the answer. However, they still need to be vigilant in case there are sudden changes in market conditions. Finally, notice that information from a range of topics in the specification are being linked here – sales promotions, profit margins, financial management, production and business image, for example, are all mentioned.

1 (c) Assess the possible impact of globalisation on the operations of businesses in the fashion accessories market. (12 marks)

No sample answer has been provided for question 1 (c) so that you can answer it yourself, for exam practice.

1 (d) Evaluate the impact on businesses in the fashion accessories industry of operating in a dynamic market. (20 marks)

Question 1 (d), student answer

Most markets do not remain the same over time. Markets tend to be dynamic, which means they are likely to change. They may grow, shrink, fragment and emerge, or completely disappear. For example, there is no longer a market in the UK for cassettes. Most people buy DVDs or download material from the internet if they want to listen to music. The market for fashion accessories is very dynamic. The extracts in this case provide some evidence. For example, the size of the market is growing. Market research agency, Mintel, reckoned that UK consumers spent about £2.5 billion on fashion accessories in 2013. Around £1.2 billion of this expenditure went on handbags – an increase of 11 per cent on the previous year.

New markets are always developing in the fashion accessories industry. One big source of new markets is from the development of the so-called 'emerging markets'. These include the BRIC countries (Brazil, Russia, India and China) countries. In this case, the information in Extract C shows that consumption has risen in three of four of these countries, indicating that there will be new opportunities for firms operating in the fashion accessories industry.

Also in this case, the market for men's fashion accessories looks set to boom. In the 12 months ending May 2014, global sales of men's accessories grew 9 per cent, reaching $13.6 billion according to market research. This trend is unlikely to be reversed and the fashion industry is clamouring to cash in on the rapid expansion in the market. Shifting social attitudes is one reason for the market growth. In the 1990s the only males that would regularly wear jewellery, for example, were rock stars and celebrities. The emergence of metrosexuals and the influence of celebrities, such as David Beckham, have helped to drive demand.

New markets also appear when completely new products are launched. In this case, the introduction of the smartwatch is likely to have an impact in the market. In 2013 the market was worth $700 million. However, by 2020 it is predicted that the global smartwatch market will grow to around $33 billion. The development of wearable technology, such as smartwatches, may become a threat to traditional watchmakers very soon.

Dynamic markets can have a huge impact on businesses. If businesses do not adapt to market changes, they are likely to lose market share. At worst they could collapse.

What might help businesses adapt to market changes? One way is to develop a culture of flexibility in an organisation. A business will need flexible working practices, flexible machinery, flexible pricing and flexible staff. This might mean that staff have to be trained in a variety of skills and be prepared to change the tasks they undertake in the workplace. This might help businesses to serve customers more effectively when changes occur. If businesses have flexible operations it will be a lot easier for them to adapt to market changes.

Businesses must keep in touch with developments in the market. One way to do this is to undertake regular market research. Research might be aimed at current customers or potential customers in the fashion accessories market. Firms need to be aware of any changes in customer needs or tastes. Communication with customers and potential customers should be an ongoing process if firms want to keep completely up to date. For example, it was reported that designers such as Michael Kors are recruiting new menswear executives and investing highly in this growing market, thought to be worth billions of dollars.

Those businesses that invest in new product development are likely to survive for longer in the market. Although expenditure on research and development is expensive, a failure to innovate could be costly. A unique new version of a product or a brand-new model could rejuvenate sales and help win a larger share of the market. In this case, the next 'big move' could be the introduction of wearable technology. This is a very new development and already the smartwatch market is dominated by Samsung, with around a third of the market. If people divert their expenditure away from traditional fashion accessories to wearable technology, many firms could lose out.

To conclude, operating in a dynamic market puts pressure on businesses. Some of the information in the extracts suggests that the market is 'throwing up' some interesting opportunities. The growth in demand for men's fashion accessories and the rising consumption of emerging economies means that all firms could enjoy rising sales. However, there is threat from wearable technology. If firms do not look at this new development effectively they could lose market share to technology companies that diversify into fashion accessories.

Comment, Question I (d)

This question requires an extended answer and you need to demonstrate knowledge, application, analysis and evaluation. Again, you need to remember that information from all four themes can be used. Answers that make links between the different themes are likely to be better. Four marks might be awarded for demonstrating knowledge, such as understanding the meaning of a dynamic market. Marks might also be awarded for identifying ways in which a business might deal with a dynamic market, such as improving flexibility, carrying out market research and investing in product development. Four marks might be awarded for application. This answer focuses throughout on the dynamic market for fashion accessories and developments in that market, such as increasing demand for men's accessories and the smartwatch.

Six marks might be awarded for analysis. An example of analysis in this answer is the explanation of the measures a business might adopt to cope with existence in a dynamic market, such as carrying out regular market research and investment in new product development. Six marks might be awarded for evaluation. In this case, evaluation can be demonstrated by weighing up the approaches businesses might use to cope with a dynamic market and suggesting which might be the best in the given context. In this case, the final judgement is that firms in the fashion accessories industry must be wary of developments in wearable technology. The main reason for this is because such products are likely to come from another industry, which clearly poses a threat.

Section B, Question 2

Read the following extracts (E–H) before answering Question 2.

Extract E

Production at Émile

Émile is a French luxury fashion house. It produces a range of ready-to-wear fashion accessories, such as handbags, shoes, luggage, wallets and sunglasses. It employs over 10,000 people and has about 150 stores in 60 countries.

Émile charges extremely high prices for some of its products. For example, many of its handbags for sale online cost more than £1,000. These high prices reflect the quality of Émile's products. The company is committed to producing high quality goods and uses the very best materials in its manufacturing processes. Its designs are exclusive and made to very detailed specifications. Since Émile can guarantee very large orders it receives priority attention from the world's best fabric makers, furriers and tanners. Products are made in state-of-the-art facilities by highly skilled craft workers, and most of Émile's core production workers have an average of 15 years' experience.

Extract F

Business ethics

Many of Émile's products are made from animal skins. As a result it has been criticised by animal rights groups. For example, in 2014 animal rights activists protested outside Émile's Paris headquarters. Protestors also picketed stores across Europe that stocked Émile's products. These protests were part of a global campaign against the apparent resurgence of fur in fashion.

Extract G

Government intervention

Émile saw its sales in Asia fall in 2014. One of the reasons for this was the clampdown by the Chinese government on conspicuous consumption (where consumers buy expensive products to overtly demonstrate their wealth). The clampdown was part of an overall policy to reduce corruption in China. It involved scaling back lavish ceremonies, celebrations and extravagant gift-giving among Chinese officials and other elite members of society. Ms Rose Martel, Émile CEO, said that Émile Éclat was considering whether to slow down its expansion plans in Asia. It was also exploring ways of reducing costs to protect profit margins.

Extract H

Selected information from Émile's Annual Reports and Accounts – 2014

	2014 (€ billion)	2012 (€ billion)
Revenue	3,228.50	2,300.00
Gross profit	2,383.74	1,645.20
Operating profit	845.28	566.01
Profit for the year (net profit)	565.00	388.71

2 (a) Assess the possible disadvantages to a business like Émile of using animal skins in the manufacturing of its products.
(8 marks)

Question 2 (a), student answer

The use of animal skins in the manufacturing of consumer products is likely to be controversial. A significant number of consumers would not purchase such products for ethical reasons. Ethics is about morality and doing 'what is right' and not 'what is wrong'. Many people would argue that killing an animal to make fashion accessories such as a handbag is wrong.

Businesses that use animal skins in production have been targeted by animal rights groups in the past. For example, in 2014 animal rights activists protested outside Émile's Paris headquarters, as well as outside stores that stocked Émile's products. These protests formed part of a global campaign against the use of fur in fashion. This type of action usually attracts media attention and can sometimes do damage to the image of companies. If the image is badly tarnished this might result in customers boycotting stores that sell products made from animal skins. As a result revenues and profits could fall.

Another disadvantage of using animal skins in production is their high cost. There are lots of synthetic substitutes that could be used in production instead of animal skins. These man-made fabrics are usually much cheaper than leathers and furs, which would help to reduce costs. Consequently, by using animal skins firms such as Émile have higher costs and have to charge higher prices.

However, despite these disadvantages, Émile chooses to use animal skins in production and appears to make a success of it. In the market for fashion accessories there is a significant market segment that contains enough consumers who seem not to care about the ethical issues surrounding the use of certain animal skins. They are even prepared to pay the very high prices that are often charged to cover the higher production costs. At the moment, the bad publicity and higher production costs resulting from the use of animal skins does not seem to outweigh the commercial benefits in terms of higher prices, higher revenues and higher profits for businesses like Émile.

Comment, Question 2 (a)

You will need to demonstrate knowledge, application, analysis and evaluation. You also need to remember that information from all four themes can be used. Answers that make links between the different themes are likely to be better. Two marks might be awarded for demonstrating knowledge, such as defining ethics in business and identifying two commercial disadvantages of using animal skins in production. Two marks might be awarded for application. This answer is focused on the use of animal skins in the fashion accessories industry. For example, it mentions the impact of what many would consider to be unethical behaviour by businesses in the fashion accessories industry.

Two marks might be awarded for analysis. An example of analysis in this answer is the explanation of how the use of animal skins in production will impact on the image, sales, costs, revenues and profits of companies in the fashion accessories industry. Two marks might be awarded for evaluation. An example of evaluation in this answer is the judgement suggesting that businesses in the fashion accessories market seem to have overcome the problems associated with the use of animal skins. Despite the clear disadvantages, the counterbalance is that enough people do not care and are prepared to pay very high prices for such products at the moment. Notice that topics from different themes are used in this answer, such as ethics from Theme 3, costs, revenues and profits from Theme 2, and market segments from Theme 1.

2 (b) Assess the importance of Émile's commitment to quality. (10 marks)

No sample answer has been provided for question 2 (b) so that you can answer it yourself, for exam practice.

2 (c) Use ratio analysis to assess the profitability of Émile between 2012 and 2014. (12 marks)

Question 2 (c), student answer

Three ratios could be used in this case to assess Émile's profitability: the gross profit margin, operating profit margin and the Profit for the year (net profit) margin.

For 2014

Gross profit margin $= \dfrac{\text{Gross profit}}{\text{Revenue}} \times 100\% = \dfrac{€2,383.74 \text{ bn}}{€3,228.50 \text{ bn}} \times 100\% = \textbf{73.8\%}$

Operating profit margin $= \dfrac{\text{Operating profit}}{\text{Revenue}} \times 100\% = \dfrac{€845.28 \text{ bn}}{€3,228.50 \text{ bn}} \times 100\% = \textbf{26.2\%}$

Profit for the year (net profit) margin $= \dfrac{\text{Profit for the year (net profit)}}{\text{Revenue}} \times 100\% = \dfrac{€565.00 \text{ bn}}{€3,228.50 \text{ bn}} \times 100\% = \textbf{17.5\%}$

For 2012

Gross profit margin $= \dfrac{\text{Gross profit}}{\text{Revenue}} \times 100\% = \dfrac{€1,645.20 \text{ bn}}{€2,300.00 \text{ bn}} \times 100\% = \textbf{71.5\%}$

Operating profit margin $= \dfrac{\text{Operating profit}}{\text{Revenue}} \times 100\% = \dfrac{€566.01 \text{ bn}}{€2,300.00 \text{ bn}} \times 100\% = \textbf{24.6\%}$

Profit for the year (net profit) margin $= \dfrac{\text{Profit for the year (net profit)}}{\text{Revenue}} \times 100\% = \dfrac{€388.71 \text{ bn}}{€2,300.00 \text{ bn}} \times 100\% = \textbf{16.9\%}$

The calculations above show that the profit margins for Émile have all increased between 2012 and 2014. The gross profit margin, which measures the gross profit made on revenue/turnover, has risen from 71.5 per cent to 73.8 per cent. Higher gross margins are usually preferable to lower ones. It may be possible to increase the gross profit margin by raising revenue relative to cost of sales, for example by increasing price. In this case, Émile charges very high prices for most of its products. This might help to explain why its gross margins are so good. Gross profit margins will tend to vary in different industries. As a rule, the quicker the turnover of stock, the lower the gross margin that is needed. In this example, gross margins are often high in the fashion industry – particularly for businesses like Émile, which focus on quality products.

The operating profit margins for Émile, which show the operating profit made on sales revenue, have also increased over the two years from 24.6 per cent to 26.2 per cent. Operating margin is used to measure a company's pricing strategy and operating efficiency. It gives an idea of how much a company makes (before interest and taxes) on each euro of sales. A high or increasing operating margin is preferred. If the operating margin is increasing, the company is earning more per euro of sales.

Operating margin shows the profitability of sales resulting from regular business. The improvement between 2012 and 2014 is likely to be welcomed by Émile.

The profit for the year (net profit) margin takes into account all business costs, including interest, other non-operating costs and exceptional items. It is also usually calculated after tax has been deducted. Between 2012 and 2014 the profit for the year (net profit) margins have increased slightly from 16.9 per cent to 17.5 per cent. Again, higher margins are better than lower ones. The profit for the year (net profit) margin focuses on the so-called 'bottom line' in business. The 'bottom line' refers to the very last line in the income statement, which shows the profit left after all deductions have been made. It is the final amount of profit left over for the shareholders.

Émile stakeholders are likely to be pleased with the slight improvement in all profit margins. Compared with other industries the margins are probably very favourable. For example, the profit for the year (net profit) margins for supermarket chains are usually in low single figures. However, supermarket chains may have much higher turnovers so lower profit margins are acceptable. Finally, even though the improvements in margins are quite small, if they are continuous over a long period of time, they will add up and result in quite significant improvements in profitability for Émile.

Comment, Question 2 (c)

You will need to demonstrate knowledge, application, analysis and evaluation. You also need to remember that information from all four themes can be used. Answers that make links between the different themes are likely to be better.

Around five marks can be awarded for the quantitative elements in this question. You will need to know the formulae for the ratios and carry out the calculations correctly. Remember to write down the formulae and show all your working out.

You also need to demonstrate that you understand what you have calculated and draw some conclusions about your findings. In this case, you need to understand that Émile's profit margins have improved slightly over the two years and that if such improvements were continuous over a long period of time, the impact of Émile's profitability would be significant. Another approach taken here is to compare the margins with those of another industry. This helps to reinforce the argument you make. In this case it is argued that the margins are good compared with the supermarket industry. A counterbalance, though, is that revenues in the supermarket industry are likely to be much higher and therefore lower margins can be tolerated. Overall, Émile is likely to be very pleased with its performance. You could also say that a more rigorous analysis of performance could have been made if you'd had access to information about Émile's capital employed. This would have allowed you to calculate ROCE.

2 (d) Evaluate the possible impact of political, economic, social, technological, legal and environmental (PESTLE) influences on a business like Émile. (20 marks)

No sample answer has been provided for question 2 (d) so that you can answer it yourself, for exam practice.

Index

Acknowledgements

The publisher would like to thank the following individuals and organisations for their approval and permission to reproduce their materials:

p.1 Extract taken from adage.com. Used with permission; **pages 389, 390** Extract from Airbus Group. Used with permission; **p.209** Extract from "All About London.com". Used with permission; **p.269** www.amnesty.org.uk; **p.517** Analysys Mason (global specialists on telecoms, media and technology) http://www.analysysmason.com/About-Us/News/Insight/smart-wearables-forecast-Sep2014/ ; **p. 297** www.anesco.co.uk; **p. 445** ArcelorMittal; **pages 78, 102, 107, 502** www.b.co.uk; **p.222** www.balfourbeattycsuk.com; **p.2** Extract from Bananaguard.com. Used with permission **p.233** Bank of England; **p.206** Extract from www.barchart.com. Used with permission; **p.26** www.barchester. com; **p.102** Extract from Bardpharmaceuticals. Used with permission; **p.509** Extract from Barratt Developments. Used with permission; **p.498** Extract from "Belle About Town". Used with permission; **pages 111, 347** Extract from Berkshirehathaway.com. This material is copyrighted and used with permission of the author; **p.7** Extract from blueandgreentomorrow.com. Used with permission; **p.277** Adapted from The BCG Portfolio Matrix from the Product Portfolio Matrix, © 1970, The Boston Consulting Group (BCG). Used with permission; **p.283** www.bhpbilliton.com; **p.494** www.boojabooja. com; **p.257** www.brainwavedrinks.com; **p.48** Extract from Branz © BRANZ, REBRI, case study, Stanley Modular Flatpack Homes and Classrooms – Construction. Used with permission; **p.517** Extract from Business of Fashion, 'www.businessoffashion.com/2014/10/attitudes-shift-mens-jewellery-grows. html' by Robin Mellery-Pratt, 2014. Used with permission. **p.292** www.cambridgesatchel.com; **p.307** www.thecarfinancecompany.co.uk; **p.26** Extract from Carehomes.co.uk. Used by permission; **p.403** Central Statistics Office, Ireland; **pages 203, 205, 206, 207** Extract from 'the Centre for Retail Research' (http://www.retailresearch.org/whosegonebust.php). Used with permission; **p.196** www. chroniclelive.co.uk; **p.1** www.cim.co.uk; **p.54** *The CMO Survey – Highlights and Insights Report*, Figure 5.1, February 2015; **p.508** www.concretecanvas.com; **p.493** Extract from Confectionery News "http:// www.confectionerynews.com/Markets/Rural-India-chocolate-market-set-for-growth" by Oliver Nieburg. Used with permission; **p.304** Extract from 'Co-wheels car club Community Interest Company" www.co-wheels.org.uk. Used with permission; **p.129** Extract from "Country Life". Used with permission; **p.294** Extract from dairy.ahdb.org.uk. Used with permission; **p.346** Extract from the *Derby Telegraph*. Used with permission; **pages 406, 409, 415, 416, 442, 443, 451, 454, 455, 456, 457, 467** www. economist.com; **p. 443** Extract from EEF, the manufacturers' organisation/GfK 'Make it Britain' survey, 2014. Used with permission; **p.3** Extract from Lisa Byfield-Green, senior retail analyst, online and digital at IGD © copyright 2014, writing for Essentialretail.com. Used with permission; **p.413** Extract from "Catalogue-Estonian Export Directory 2014". Used with permission; **p.250** www.esuregroup.com; **p. 437** Euromonitor; **p.144** Extract from a report by the European Environment Agency (EEA); **p.412** www.exportbritain.org.uk; **p.394** www.ey.com; **p.505** www.federationoffishfriers.co.uk; **pages 19, 28, 78, 79, 81, 95, 98, 143, 148, 150, 161, 162, 175, 200, 212, 266, 268, 276, 290, 291, 296, 298, 299, 300, 301, 302, 303, 346, 349, 355, 356, 360, 362, 375, 376, 379, 387, 388, 392, 402, 410, 414, 420, 421, 426, 430, 432, 434, 435, 438, 440, 441, 442, 443, 445, 447, 448, 449, 452, 453, 456, 457, 471, 472, 480, 481, 482, 483, 486, 487, 488, 489, 490, 509, 512, 513** adapted from the *Financial Times*, all rights reserved; **p.261** www. fitbritches.com; **p. 478** Extract from GlaxoSmithKline. Used with permission; **p.78** www.gore.com; **pages 29, 78, 172, 246, 249, 291, 295, 311, 367, 422, 432, 440, 456, 506 www.gov. uk; p.29** www.theguardian.com; **p.358** www.halfords.com; **p.191** www.halfordscompany.com; **p.129** Extract from Hawkshead Relish Company. Used with permission; **p.405** www.hdr.undp.org; **p.365** www.highpaycentre.org; **p.130** House of Commons Library Standard Note SN/EP/6152, updated 28th November 2014; **p.87** Extract from HRreview.co.uk. Used with permission; **pages 242, 247, 248, 249** www.hse.gov.uk; **p.195** Extract from The Hull Daily Mail. Used with permission; **p.64** IGD copyright 2014; **p.497** taken from IHG's Annual Report 2014, IHG news release 2014 and www.ihg. com; **p.7** www.infomine.com; **p.299** Extract from the Institute of Mergers, Acquisitions and Alliances (IMAA). Used with permission; **p.468** International Business Times; **p.135** Extract from International Telecommunication Union (ITU). Used with permission; **p.135** Extract from Internet Live Stats "http://www.internetlivestats.com/internet-users/". Used with permission; **p.129** Extract from Invest in South Lakeland. Used with permission; **p.264** www.jaguarlandrover.com; **p.378** www.jdplc.com; **p.5** Extract from Robert Angart, "Surviving in Stagnant or Declining Industries," The Journal of Corporate Renewal, Vol. 15, No. 2, February 2002. Used with permission; **p.2** www.johnlewis.com; **p.2** www.kantarworldpanel.com; **p.135** www.khanacademy.org; **p353** Labour Party, *Overcoming shorter-termism*, 2013; **p.273** www.lego.com. All information in this case study is collected and interpreted by its authors and does not represent the opinion of the LEGO® Group; **p.385** www.lindumgroup.com; **p.55** Extract from Lithium Technologies, Inc. Copyright © 2013 Lithium Technologies, Inc. All Rights Reserved. Used with permission; Lithium social software helps the world's most iconic brands to build brand nations—vibrant online communities of passionate social customers. Lithium helps top brands such as AT&T, Sephora, Univision, and PayPal build active online communities that turn customer passion into social media marketing ROI. For more information on how to create lasting competitive advantage with the social customer experience, visit lithium.com, or connect with us on Twitter, Facebook and the Lithosphere; **p.21** www.lloydsbank.com; **p.18** Extract from M&M'S®, is a registered trademarks of Mars, Incorporated and its affiliates. The M&M'S® trademark and associated slogan is used with permission. Mars, Incorporated is not associated with Edexcel; **pages 17, 156** www.mintel.com; **p.419** www.nestle.com; **p. 254** www.newzoo.com; **p.65** www.nibusinessinfo.co.uk; **p.237** Office for Budget Responsibility, 2014-2015, estimate. Allocations to function are based on HM Treasury analysis; **p.288** www.ofgem.gov.uk; **pages 26, 79, 80, 232, 241, 288, 291, 311, 382, 402, 406, 417, 505** www.ons.gov.uk; **p.34** Parliament briefing papers: *The construction industry: statistics and policy, House of Commons;* **p.107** Extract from Peninsula group limited.com. Used with permission; **p.24** Extract from Petrolprices.com. Used with permission; **p.502** www.pewglobal.org; **p.310** www.pewinternet.org; **p.125** www.picaloulou.com; **pages 301, 302** www.publications.parliament.uk; **p.498** www.redcarnationhotels.com; **p.300** www.retailtimes.co.uk; **p.117** www.rightformula.com; **p.346** Extract from Rolls-Royce.com. Used with permission; **p.246** Extract "Contains SEPA data © Scottish Environment Protection Agency and database right. All rights reserved." Used with permission; p.**400** Shell International B.V. **p.30** Extract data taken from Shelter.org.uk. Used with permission; **p.34** Extract from "singletrackworld.com". Used with permission; **p.156** www.smallbusiness.co.uk; **pages 7, 172, 214** Extract from The Society of Motor Manufacturers and Traders Ltd. Used with permission; **p.205** www.southportvisiter.co.uk; **pages 22, 501** Extract from "Startups.co.uk". Used with permission; **p.312** Extract from "Startups.co.uk", "Enclothed". Used with permission; **pages 9, 51, 53, 67, 172, 177, 419, 497** www.statista.com; **p.348** www.features.thesundaytimes.co.uk; **p.161** Extract from www.support-finance.co.uk. Used with permission; **p.24** Extract from Sustrans.org.uk. Used with permission; **p.58, 122** www.telegraph.co.uk; **p.271** www.tescoplc.com; **p.282** All information extracted/adapted with permission of Thorntons PLC; **p. 279** Ties.com and Inditex, 9.6.2015; **p. 464** www.ties.com; **pages 224, 430** Extract from Toyota (GB) PLC. Reproduced with permission from Toyota (GB) PLC; **pages 12, 232, 233, 241, 403** www.tradingeconomics.com; **p. 439** Extract from Transparency International "© Transparency International. All Rights Reserved. For more information, visit http://www.transparency.org" Used with permission; **p.80** Extract from "TUC report findings on zero hour working" https://www.tuc.org.uk/sites/default/files/DecentJobsDeficitReport.pdf. Used with permission from the Trades Union Congress; **p.416** 2014 World Investment Report, UNCTAD; **p. 448** United Nations Conference on Trade and Development (UNCTAD); **p. 481** United Nations StEP Initiative; **p.60** Extract from uSwitch.com. Used with permission; **p.493** Extract from "Chocolate Industry in India 2014-19,ValueNotes, www.valuenotes.biz". Used with permission; **p.139** Extract from Versarien.com. Used with permission; **p.71** www.volkswagen.co.uk; **p.505** www.vouchercodes.co.uk; **p.509** www.wates.co.uk; **p.405** www.who.int; **p.106** From Anderton and Bevan (2014) Constrained Work? Job enrichment & employee engagement in low wage, low skill jobs. London: The Work Foundation based on R. Suff (2005); www.theworkfoundation.com; **p.401, 403, 436, 437, 443, 445** World Bank Group; **p517** World Bank Datasets, http://databank.worldbank.org/data/reports.aspx?source=Global-Economic-Monitor-(GEM)-Commodities; http://data.worldbank.org/indicator/NE.CON.TETC.ZS; **p.106** Extract from xperthr. Used with permission; **p.46** Extract from Yube Cube. Used with permission; **p.49** www.zenithoptimedia.com.

Every effort has been made to trace the copyright holders and we apologise in advance for any unintentional omissions. We would be pleased to insert the appropriate acknowledgement in any subsequent edition of this publication.

Photograph acknowledgements

The publisher would like to thank the following for their kind permission to reproduce their photographs:

(Key: b-bottom; c-centre; l-left; r-right; t-top)

123RF.com: 30, 116, 120, 163, 266, 279, 281, 327, 341, 346, 378, 452, 455, 473, 506, 30, 116, 120, 163, 266, 279, 281, 327, 341, 346, 378, 452, 455, 473, 506, 30, 116, 120, 163, 266, 279, 281, 327, 341, 346, 378, 452, 455, 473, 506, 30, 116, 120, 163, 266, 279, 281, 327, 341, 346, 378, 452, 455, 473, 506, 30, 116, 120, 163, 266, 279, 281, 327, 341, 346, 378, 452, 455, 473, 506, andrej_sv 65, Darren Bradley 283, Dotschock 165, Ernest Prim 31, Jens Brüggemann 43, 159, odessa4 190, Pakete 285, Andriy Popov 97; **Alamy Images**: A Room With Views 509, 421, ableimages 369, Asia 432, Lee Beel 408, Ira Berger 517, Cernan Elias 6, Thomas Cockrem 456, Construction Photography 290, David R. Frazier Photolibrary, Inc. 240, Kathy deWitt 40l, David J. Green 207, Matthew Richardson 18b, Andrew Michael 222, Peter Phipp / Travelshots.com 91, Radharc Images 48, Simon Turner 47, Kumar Sriskandan 180, Travel Pictures 150; **Corbis**: ALY SONG / Reuters 406, LY SONG / Reuters 442, Reuters 213; **Fotolia.com**: Antonioguillem 501, artfood 98, Darren Baker 113, diego cervo 364, diversphoto89 307, doble.d 208b, emde71 67b, EvrenKalinbacak 424, Sergii Figurnyi 467, HappyAlex 412, imtmphoto 284, Michael Jung 94, Kadmy 162, 261, 468, Kurhan 489, Kzenon 478, len44ik 56, Tsung-Lin Wu 122, 147, 193, midosemsem 200, MNStudio 273, Monkey Business 303, oneinchpunch 254, Picture-Factory 128, Science Photo 474, Sean Pavone Photo 512, Maksim Shebeko 460, Robert Wilson 389, 434, xy 103, yolfran 40r; **Getty Images**: 29, Andresr 353, David M Benett 292, Bloomberg 17, Danny Birrell Photograph 379, David Joel 223, Emmanuel Dunand 148, Amy Eckert 313b, Mike Harrington 414, iStock / 360 23, 227, kali9 440, William King 257, Maridav 250, Ben Stansall 225, Stockbyte 410r, Mary Turner 82; **Hawkshead Relish**: 129; **Imagestate Media**: BananaStock 310t, John Foxx Collection 385; **Jupiterimages**: Photos.com 375; **Pearson Education Ltd**: Sian Bradfield. Pearson Education Australia Pty Ltd 360; **PhotoDisc**: Brofsky Studio Inc 141, 217, 477, L. Hobbs. Photolink. 494; **Picaloulou.com; picaloulou.com; Picaloulou**: 125; **Rex Features**: Albanpix Ltd 3, 118, Nicholas Bailey 142; **RSPCA Marketing**: 50; **Shutterstock.com**: 06photo 409, Andy Dean Photography 498, Marilyn Barbone 34, Bartosz Zakrzewski 179, beboy 449, bikeriderlondon 394, CandyBox Images 75, Lynne Carpenter 138, Stephen Coburn 391, 410l, Stephen Coburn. 302, zhu difeng 483, dotshock 355, Dragon Images 272, Elena Efimova 137, Julio Embun 340, Alfio Ferlito 330, Natali Glado 373, Goodluz 136, Kheng Guan Toh 505, imtmphoto 112, iofoto 90, Artur Janichev 39t, Stuart Jenner 135, jordache 371, Jurand 425, Dmitry Kalinovsky 83, Levent Konuk 423, Lasse Kristensen 268, l i g h t p o e t 457, Lucky Business 54, Izf 466, Arek Malang 319, Mark Bennetts 152, michaeljung 169, Milkovasa 189, Monkey Business Images 107, 149, 469, Maks Narodenko 2, Andrey Popov 230, Tatiana Popova 380, Poznyakov 310, Pressmaster 253, Pressmaster. 418, QQ7 453, racorn 145, Rainer Plendl 214, Rafael Ramirez Lee 411, Alexander Raths 151, Rawpixel 106, 384, RedTC 208t, Kendall Rittenour 400, ronfromyork 62, SasinT 219, Adrin Shamsudin. 170, 313t, Sozaijiten 459, ssguy 463, Stanimir G.Stoev 203, Alex Staroseltsev 369b, James Steidl 218, Syda Productions 305, tandemich 419, Ingvar Tjostheim 438, tratong 196, Tumarkin Igor - ITPS 59, Valentyn Volkov 308, wavebreakmedia 143, 164, 312, Zurijeta 201; **Specialized.com**: 44; **Volkswagen Group**: 18t

Cover images: *Front:* Plainpicture Ltd: Fancy Images (George Hammerstein)

All other images © Pearson Education

Every effort has been made to trace the copyright holders and we apologise in advance for any unintentional omissions. We would be pleased to insert the appropriate acknowledgement in any subsequent edition of this publication